Election Law and Litigation

EDITORIAL ADVISORS

Aspen Casebook Series

Election Law and Litigation
The Judicial Regulation of Politics

Edward B. Foley
Chief Justice Thomas J. Moyer Professor for the Administration of Justice and the Rule of Law
The Ohio State University, Moritz College of Law

Michael J. Pitts
Professor of Law and Dean's Fellow
Indiana University Robert H. McKinney School of Law

Joshua A. Douglas
Assistant Professor of Law
University of Kentucky College of Law

Published by Wolters Kluwer Law & Business in New York.

Wolters Kluwer Law & Business serves customers worldwide with CCH, Aspen Publishers, and Kluwer Law International products. (www.wolterskluwerlb.com)

To contact Customer Service, e-mail customer.service@wolterskluwer.com,
call 1-800-234-1660, fax 1-800-901-9075, or mail correspondence to:

Wolters Kluwer Law & Business
Attn: Order Department
PO Box 990
Frederick, MD 21705

Printed in the United States of America.

1 2 3 4 5 6 7 8 9 0

ISBN 978-0-7355-6999-7 (Casebound)

ISBN 978-1-4548-4822-6 (Loose-leaf)

Library of Congress Cataloging-in-Publication Data

Foley, Edward B., author.

Election law and litigation : the judicial regulation of politics / Edward B. Foley, Chief Justice Thomas J. Moyer Professor for the Administration of Justice and the Rule of Law, The Ohio State University; Michael J. Pitts, Professor of Law, Indiana University School of Law; Joshua A. Douglas, Assistant Professor of Law, University of Kentucky College of Law.

pages cm. — (Aspen casebook series)
Includes bibliographical references and index.
ISBN 978-0-7355-6999-7 (alk. paper)
1. Election law — United States. I. Pitts, Michael J., author. II. Douglas, Joshua A., author. III. Title.
KF4886.F65 2014
342.73′07 — dc23

2014000119

Certified Sourcing
www.sfiprogram.org
SFI-01234

SFI label applies to the text stock

About Wolters Kluwer Law & Business

Wolters Kluwer Law & Business is a leading global provider of intelligent information and digital solutions for legal and business professionals in key specialty areas, and respected educational resources for professors and law students. Wolters Kluwer Law & Business connects legal and business professionals as well as those in the education market with timely, specialized authoritative content and information-enabled solutions to support success through productivity, accuracy and mobility.

Serving customers worldwide, Wolters Kluwer Law & Business products include those under the Aspen Publishers, CCH, Kluwer Law International, Loislaw, ftwilliam.com and MediRegs family of products.

CCH products have been a trusted resource since 1913, and are highly regarded resources for legal, securities, antitrust and trade regulation, government contracting, banking, pension, payroll, employment and labor, and healthcare reimbursement and compliance professionals.

Aspen Publishers products provide essential information to attorneys, business professionals and law students. Written by preeminent authorities, the product line offers analytical and practical information in a range of specialty practice areas from securities law and intellectual property to mergers and acquisitions and pension/benefits. Aspen's trusted legal education resources provide professors and students with high-quality, up-to-date and effective resources for successful instruction and study in all areas of the law.

Kluwer Law International products provide the global business community with reliable international legal information in English. Legal practitioners, corporate counsel and business executives around the world rely on Kluwer Law journals, looseleafs, books, and electronic products for comprehensive information in many areas of international legal practice.

Loislaw is a comprehensive online legal research product providing legal content to law firm practitioners of various specializations. Loislaw provides attorneys with the ability to quickly and efficiently find the necessary legal information they need, when and where they need it, by facilitating access to primary law as well as state-specific law, records, forms and treatises.

ftwilliam.com offers employee benefits professionals the highest quality plan documents (retirement, welfare and non-qualified) and government forms (5500/PBGC, 1099 and IRS) software at highly competitive prices.

MediRegs products provide integrated health care compliance content and software solutions for professionals in healthcare, higher education and life sciences, including professionals in accounting, law and consulting.

Wolters Kluwer Law & Business, a division of Wolters Kluwer, is headquartered in New York. Wolters Kluwer is a market-leading global information services company focused on professionals.

To Miranda, Max, and Robbie, who have been enthusiastic supporters of this project ever since its origins.

—Ned

To Jenny, William, and Jonathan, who are the best family one could ever hope for.

—Mike

To my wife Bari and daughter Caitlyn, who gave me the vote of confidence to take on this project.

—Josh

To our wonderful students, whose feedback on earlier drafts helped make this book as student-friendly as possible.

—Ned, Mike, and Josh

Summary of Contents

Contents

Introduction

This book covers the law that governs the operation of elections as well as the campaigns leading up to those elections. Implicit in this very first sentence is the fact that this field can be subdivided between "election" law on the one hand and "campaign" law on the other. Further subdivisions of election law are useful. There is the law that governs the nomination of candidates, sometimes called "ballot access" law and which includes the distinctive rules concerning primary elections, to be distinguished from the law that governs the casting and counting of votes for the nominated candidates. This latter area, regulating the voting process itself, is sometimes called "election administration," although that term is confusing since the distinctive rules for nominating candidates could be considered an aspect of election administration. Consequently, we prefer to call this latter area simply "voting" law.

Another distinctive component of election law is the law that governs the drawing of boundary lines for legislative districts, to define the specific constituency that will elect each member of the legislature. Obviously, this "districting" law is inapplicable to the election of candidates for statewide offices, such as Governor or U.S. Senator. Thus, districting law might be considered as belonging to a subfield of election law that concerns the special rules for different types of election offices. The distinctive rules for the operation of the Electoral College, which uniquely govern the election of the U.S. President, would be considered another component of this office-specific set of election laws. (The same holds true for the distinctive rules concerning referenda, initiatives, and other ballot propositions, even though they involve voting on issues rather than candidates.)

Nonetheless, the U.S. Supreme Court cases in the particular area of districting law loom sufficiently large over the entire field of election law that not only do they deserve separate consideration, but they also provide the best place to start one's study of this field. In the 1960s, as the Warren Court was reaching the apex of its activism, the Court ushered in what has been called the "reapportionment revolution," whereby the Court interpreted the Equal Protection Clause of the U.S. Constitution to require both houses of every state legislature to comply with a requirement of equally populated districts (or at least approximately so—more on that later). Not only did this revolution newly subject the districting of state legislatures to federal judicial oversight, but the interpretive principle upon which this revolution relied—that the Equal Protection Clause guarantees each citizen equal voting rights and, even more broadly, equal rights with respect to participating in the electoral process in various ways—has had profound ramifications in other areas of election law besides districting.

As we shall see, soon after the reapportionment revolution, the Warren Court extended this Equal Protection principle to the nomination of candidates, to assure that each citizen had an equal opportunity to run for office. Most significantly, and much more recently, the Supreme Court invoked this same Equal Protection principle in *Bush v. Gore*, 513 U.S. 98 (2000), to rule that a state's procedures for recounting ballots must contain standards of sufficient specificity to avoid disparate treatment of similar ballots depending upon the particular recounting panel that happens to review them. Thus, one of the major unsettled questions of U.S. election law is whether, or the extent to which, the Court will continue to apply this same Equal Protection principle to other aspects of the vote casting-and-counting process: for example, the administration of voter identification requirements or the verification of so-called "provisional" ballots.

If one had studied election law in 1950, before the reapportionment revolution occurred, the subject would have seemed entirely different than it does today. Consisting mostly of state-court cases interpreting state statutes and some state constitutional provisions, a book like this one would have contained hardly any federal law—and almost none of it federal constitutional law. Now, we have major federal statutes regulating various aspects of the subject: the Voting Rights Act of 1965, the Federal Election Campaign Act of 1974 (when its most important provisions were adopted), and the Help America Vote Act of 2002, among the most significant. Although many students today are surprised when they first learn how much state law, rather than federal law, still controls even elections to federal office (Congress and the President), the degree of federal-law control over U.S. elections, including those for state and local offices, is vastly greater than it was a half-century ago. And a considerable portion of this new federal-law control results from judicial interpretation of the U.S. Constitution, starting with the reapportionment revolution of the 1960s.

While it is conceivable that judicial oversight of elections as an exercise of interpreting the U.S. Constitution may recede somewhat in the future, it is also possible that it might not, and perhaps might even increase. In any event, one objective of this book is to convey an appropriate balance between the roles that federal and state law play in resolving election-related disputes. Although we start with federal constitutional law, because it is the "supreme law of the land" and thus necessarily frames the consideration of any election-related issue to which it might conceivably apply, we end by devoting considerable attention to the vote-counting questions that remain largely governed by state law notwithstanding *Bush v. Gore.* Even if the domain of *Bush v. Gore* increases significantly over the next several decades, as the Equal Protection principle is extended to other issues that arise in the vote-counting process, the basic decision of whether to overturn the outcome of an election because of a defect that emerges in the counting process—the issue at the heart of the dispute over the presidential election in 2000 and the issue that with increasing frequency is the focus of election-related disputes—will be determined largely by state law. Nonetheless, whatever the balance of federal and state law proves to be applicable to this particular area of election law, the law of the vote-counting process is undoubtedly an important topic. In this respect, one might say that this book has saved the best for last.

In another sense, however, we end with the same fundamental question with which we begin: to what extent, if at all, should the judiciary attempt to resolve election disputes, being as they are often contests between the two major political parties in our democracy and it is important that judges be seen as independent of partisan politics? Before the Warren Court could undertake its reapportionment revolution, it first had to consider whether it should consider challenges to legislative districting as being off-limits to the judiciary, according to the so-called "political question" doctrine. The Court said no, but the same basic question remains whenever the judiciary purports to settle an election-related dispute. As we shall see, the applicability of this same "political question" doctrine was raised in *Bush v. Gore*, and state law also must wrestle with whether it wishes to give its judges the authority to invalidate elections on the ground of vote-counting improprieties. Consequently, from beginning to end, as you consider each judicial ruling you read, you should be asking yourself whether judges should be deciding the dispute at all in the first place.

The four-part division of this book is designed to reflect what might be considered the natural lifecycle of the process that governs any particular election. First, it is necessary to define the office to which the election applies. Thus, we start with the law of districting, which defines each seat in the legislative body. Then, it is necessary for candidates to appear on the ballot, and so we turn in Part II to the law of candidate nominations. Once the candidates are on the ballot, the campaigning to win the election officially can begin. Consequently, we next consider, in Part III, the various regulations of campaign practices, including campaign finance. Finally, the election itself consists of casting and counting votes, and thus the Law of Voting in Part IV addresses not only the basic question of who is eligible to vote, but also the subsidiary questions of how to implement the voting process—including registration laws, voter identification rules, the times and places for casting ballots, and the procedures for resolving any disputes that may arise over the counting of ballots. This order roughly tracks the chronological cycle of an election, although there are certainly overlaps. The goal of presenting the material in this manner is to help you place the doctrine within the setting of how an election actually proceeds.

Before we move on, a note about how we edited the judicial opinions that appear in this casebook. We view a casebook as a tool for teaching students fundamental principles and as a launching off point for discussing the intricacies of election law rather than as a reference resource. For this reason, we have tried to edit the opinions in a streamlined manner so that instructors can construct assignments of reasonable length for students while still having the capability of covering the entire casebook within the confines of a three-credit law school course. We have also tried to edit the opinions to make them relatively easy to read. Many of the opinions in the area of election law are quite lengthy and in some instances we have substantially trimmed the opinions. The omissions in the opinions are not indicated with ellipses; however, we have endeavored to indicate when we have edited out an entire part (e.g., Part I) of an opinion. We also adopted the editing philosophy of limiting citations to precedent and quotations from precedent, and limiting the citations themselves to the case names, years (where necessary), and court (when it is not the U.S. Supreme Court). We did this to make the opinions easier for students to read, and on the theory that when an opinion quotes directly from a prior opinion, it is adopting that language verbatim. While we recognize there is no perfect way to edit an opinion, we hope that our editing assists students in understanding the basics of this admittedly complex area of the law. Finally, we strongly encourage you to read the notes after the cases. We believe that they are unlike the notes you may typically have encountered in other case books, which often present many "case notes" describing detailed permutations of the law or citations to law review articles. We have chosen a different path that we hope is more helpful to students: the notes are designed to present the exact kinds of questions your professor might ask in class. In this way, the notes are intended to focus your reading and help you prepare for each day's class. We hope that this book, with its focus on being as accessible to students as possible, will serve as a valued introduction to the exciting field of election law.

Edward B. Foley
Michael J. Pitts
Joshua A. Douglas

March 2014

PART I

THE LAW OF LEGISLATIVE DISTRICTING

Districting law, generally speaking, involves four distinct concepts, each with its own line of cases.

- The first is the constitutional principle of one person, one vote.
- The second is the prohibition against racial vote dilution under the U.S. Constitution and Section 2 of the Federal Voting Rights Act.
- The third is the constitutional constraint against race-based districting (i.e., "racial gerrymandering").
- The fourth is the constitutional treatment of "political gerrymanders"—that is, the distortion of district boundaries to secure partisan advantage.

Although each of these areas has developed its own separate set of rules, it is also true that these areas are interrelated, and cases in each often refer to cases, principles, and doctrines developed in the others. This book presents the four lines of cases in the order listed, from first to fourth, because that way they become least entangled with one another. Even so, it will be necessary—especially as one reviews all four—to consider how they have affected each other's developments.

In addition to the four lines of cases, there is a fifth area that merits discussion—Section 5 of the Voting Rights Act. As you will learn, Section 5 was essentially neutralized by the Supreme Court's 2013 decision in *Shelby County v. Holder*. Yet even though Section 5, in essence, has been stripped of much, if not all, of its vitality, it is still worth studying because of its importance to the development of voting rights for racial and ethnic minorities, the recency of the Supreme Court's decision in *Shelby County*, and because discussion of Section 5 and some of its basic principles will likely remain salient for the foreseeable future. For these reasons, this book discusses Section 5 between the discussion of racial vote dilution and the constitutional constraints on race-based districting.

Before considering any of these various topics in districting law, however, it is first necessary to address whether the judiciary should review the legality of legislative districting at all, a question that implicates the so-called "political question" doctrine.

A. The Political Question Doctrine

The most fundamental question to be addressed in the law of legislative redistricting (at least as it relates to constitutional, rather than statutory, law) is whether there should be a "law" of legislative redistricting at all. By "law" in this context, what is connoted is whether the judiciary should pass judgment upon the merits of claims that legislative redistricting plans violate some provision of the U.S. Constitution. The case you are about to read, *Baker v. Carr*, lays the groundwork for judicial intervention in the realm of legislative redistricting, and in many respects the *Baker* decision is the foundation for the entirety of the federal constitutional cases that appear in this casebook.

Before reading *Baker*, it is useful to have some background on a case that was decided about 16 years earlier—*Colegrove v. Green*, 328 U.S. 549 (1946). *Colegrove* was a case that presented a similar federal constitutional question as the one you are about to encounter in *Baker v. Carr*: whether legislative malapportionment (i.e., legislative districts with different numbers of people) violates the federal Constitution. In *Colegrove*, the Illinois legislature had failed to change the congressional district lines since 1901, with the result that population disparities developed between the districts. In *Colegrove*, the most populated congressional district had 914,000 persons while the least populated congressional district had 112,116. Residents of the most populated districts sued, alleging a violation of the federal Constitution.

Only seven justices participated in *Colegrove*, and they split 4-3 on the result without a majority opinion for the Court. A three-justice plurality opinion written by Justice Frankfurter invoked the political question doctrine and refused to consider the merits of any federal constitutional challenge to the alleged malapportionment of Illinois's congressional districts. Justice Frankfurter wrote these words, which have become oft-quoted in the area of election law:

> Courts ought not enter this political thicket. . . . The Constitution has many commands that are not enforceable by courts because they clearly fall outside the conditions and purposes that circumscribe judicial action.

Justice Rutledge, who provided the necessary fourth vote for the Court's ruling, wrote a cryptic concurrence saying that even if the federal judiciary had the power to order a redrawing of the state's congressional districts, it should decline to do so. Because the issuance of an injunction is always a matter of discretion, Justice Rutledge thought that the public interest weighed in favor of withholding injunctive relief, in part because of the timing of the litigation in relation to the next upcoming election.

Justices Black, Douglas, and Murphy dissented and would have found a violation of the Equal Protection Clause. Justice Jackson did not participate in *Colegrove*, and Chief Justice Stone had recently died without his successor yet in place.

As you are reading this case, consider the best arguments for why the judiciary should or should not become involved in reviewing the process of drawing district lines. Is line drawing a purely legislative judgment? Do judges have the necessary tools to determine when redistricting has become unfair? Note that the Court creates six categories of cases that are nonjusticiable under the political question doctrine. Ultimately, did the Supreme Court adequately justify its decision to make redistricting questions "justiciable"? What are the consequences of saying that those unhappy with legislative districts may challenge them in court? Will the Court's entanglement in "political cases" erode the public's confidence in the Court, as the dissent suggests?

BAKER v. CARR

369 U.S. 186 (1962)

Mr. Justice BRENNAN delivered the opinion of the Court.

[Plaintiffs claim that they have been denied "equal protection of the Laws" within the meaning of the Fourteenth Amendment to the U.S. Constitution as a result of an apportionment of the Tennessee General Assembly pursuant to a 1901 state statute. The district court dismissed the complaint, holding] that it lacked jurisdiction of the subject matter and also that no claim was stated upon which relief could be granted. We noted probable jurisdiction of the appeal. We hold that the dismissal was error, and remand the cause to the District Court for trial and further proceedings consistent with this opinion.

The General Assembly of Tennessee consists of the Senate with 33 members and the House of Representatives with 99 members. [The facts indicate that 33 percent of the voters of Tennessee can elect 20 of the 33 Senators while 40 percent of the voters can elect 63 of the 99 members of the House. The facts also indicate that there is a wide disparity of voting strength between the large and small counties. Some examples are: Moore County has a total representation of two with a population (2,340) of only one-eleventh of Rutherford County (25,316) with the same representation; Decatur County (5,563) has the same representation as Carter (23,303) though the latter has four times the population; Loudon County (13,264), Houston County (3,084), and Anderson County (33,990) have the same representation.]

Tennessee's constitutional standard for allocating legislative representation among her counties is the total number of qualified voters resident in the respective counties, subject only to minor qualifications. Decennial reapportionment in compliance with the constitutional scheme was effected by the General Assembly each decade from 1871 to 1901. In the more than 60 years since [enactment of the 1901 statute], all proposals in both Houses of the General Assembly for reapportionment have failed to pass.

Between 1901 and 1961, Tennessee has experienced substantial growth and redistribution of her population. In 1901 the population was 2,020,616, of whom 487,380 were eligible to vote. The 1960 Federal Census reports the State's population at 3,567,089, of whom 2,092,891 are eligible to vote. The relative standings of the counties in terms of qualified voters have changed significantly. It is primarily the continued application of the 1901 Apportionment Act to this shifted and enlarged voting population which gives rise to the present controversy.

Indeed, the complaint alleges that the 1901 statute, even as of the time of its passage, "made no apportionment of Representatives and Senators in accordance with the constitutional formula . . . , but instead arbitrarily and capriciously apportioned representatives in the Senate and House without reference . . . to any logical or reasonable formula whatever." It is further alleged that "because of the population changes since 1900, and the failure of the Legislature to reapportion itself since 1901, the 1901 statute became unconstitutional and obsolete." Appellants also argue that, because of the composition of the legislature effected by the 1901 Apportionment Act, redress in the form of a state constitutional amendment to change the entire mechanism for reapportioning, or any other change short of that, is difficult or impossible.[14] The complaint concludes that "these plaintiffs and others similarly situated are denied the equal protection of the laws accorded them by the Fourteenth Amendment to the Constitution of the United States by virtue of the debasement of their votes." They seek a declaration that the 1901 statute is unconstitutional and an injunction restraining the appellees from acting to conduct any further elections under it. They also pray that unless and until the General Assembly enacts a valid reapportionment, the District Court should either decree a reapportionment by mathematical application of the Tennessee constitutional formulae to the most recent Federal Census figures, or direct the appellees to conduct legislative elections, primary and general, at large. They also pray for such other and further relief as may be appropriate.

JUSTICIABILITY

In holding that the subject matter of this suit was not justiciable, the District Court relied on *Colegrove v. Green* (1946) (plurality)]. We understand the District Court to have read [*Colegrove*] as compelling the conclusion that since the appellants sought to have a legislative apportionment held unconstitutional, their suit presented a "political question" and was therefore nonjusticiable. We hold that this challenge to an apportionment presents no nonjusticiable "political question."

[T]he mere fact that the suit seeks protection of a political right does not mean it presents a political question. Such an objection "is little more than a play upon words." *Nixon v. Herndon*. Rather, it is argued that apportionment cases, whatever the actual wording of the complaint, can involve no federal constitutional right except one resting

14. The appellants claim that no General Assembly constituted according to the 1901 Act will submit reapportionment proposals either to the people or to a Constitutional Convention. There is no provision for popular initiative in Tennessee.

on the guaranty of a republican form of government[30] and that complaints based on that clause have been held to present political questions which are nonjusticiable.

We hold that the claim pleaded here neither rests upon nor implicates the Guaranty Clause and that its justiciability is therefore not foreclosed by our decisions of cases involving that clause. The District Court misinterpreted *Colegrove v. Green*. Appellants' claim that they are being denied equal protection is justiciable.

[I]t is the relationship between the judiciary and the coordinate branches of the Federal Government, and not the federal judiciary's relationship to the States, which gives rise to the "political question."

The nonjusticiability of a political question is primarily a function of the separation of powers. Much confusion results from the capacity of the "political question" label to obscure the need for case-by-case inquiry. Deciding whether a matter has in any measure been committed by the Constitution to another branch of government, or whether the action of that branch exceeds whatever authority has been committed, is itself a delicate exercise in constitutional interpretation, and is a responsibility of this Court as ultimate interpreter of the Constitution.

Prominent on the surface of any case held to involve a political question is found a textually demonstrable constitutional commitment of the issue to a coordinate political department; or a lack of judicially discoverable and manageable standards for resolving it; or the impossibility of deciding without an initial policy determination of a kind clearly for nonjudicial discretion; or the impossibility of a court's undertaking independent resolution without expressing lack of the respect due coordinate branches of government; or an unusual need for unquestioning adherence to a political decision already made; or the potentiality of embarrassment from multifarious pronouncements by various departments on one question.

Unless one of these formulations is inextricable from the case at bar, there should be no dismissal for nonjusticiability on the ground of a political question's presence. The doctrine of which we treat is one of "political questions," not one of "political cases." The courts cannot reject as "no law suit" a bona fide controversy as to whether some action denominated "political" exceeds constitutional authority.

We come to the ultimate inquiry whether our precedents as to what constitutes a nonjusticiable "political question" bring the case before us under the umbrella of that doctrine. A natural beginning is to note whether any of the common characteristics which we have been able to identify and label descriptively are present. We find none: The question here is the consistency of state action with the Federal Constitution. We

30. "The United States shall guarantee to every State in this Union a Republican Form of Government, and shall protect each of them against Invasion; and on Application of the Legislature, or of the Executive (when the Legislature cannot be convened) against domestic Violence." U.S. Const. Art IV, § 4.

have no question decided, or to be decided, by a political branch of government coequal with this Court. Nor do we risk embarrassment of our government abroad, or grave disturbance at home if we take issue with Tennessee as to the constitutionality of her action here challenged. Nor need the appellants, in order to succeed in this action, ask the Court to enter upon policy determinations for which judicially manageable standards are lacking. Judicial standards under the Equal Protection Clause are well developed and familiar, and it has been open to courts since the enactment of the Fourteenth Amendment to determine, if on the particular facts they must, that a discrimination reflects no policy, but simply arbitrary and capricious action.

This case does, in one sense, involve the allocation of political power within a State, and the appellants might conceivably have added a claim under the Guaranty Clause. Of course any reliance on that clause would be futile. But because any reliance on the Guaranty Clause could not have succeeded it does not follow that appellants may not be heard on the equal protection claim which in fact they tender. True, it must be clear that the Fourteenth Amendment claim is not so enmeshed with those political question elements which render Guaranty Clause claims nonjusticiable as actually to present a political question itself. But we have found that not to be the case here.

We conclude then that the nonjusticiability of claims resting on the Guaranty Clause which arises from their embodiment of questions that were thought "political," can have no bearing upon the justiciability of the equal protection claim presented in this case. Finally, we emphasize that it is the involvement in Guaranty Clause claims of the elements thought to define "political questions," and no other feature, which could render them nonjusticiable. Specifically, we have said that such claims are not held nonjusticiable because they touch matters of state governmental organization.

We have already noted that the District Court's holding that the subject matter of this complaint was nonjusticiable relied upon *Colegrove v. Green*. In *Colegrove*, Mr. Justice Rutledge joined in the conclusion that the case was justiciable, although he held that the dismissal of the complaint should be affirmed.

No constitutional questions, including the question whether voters have a judicially enforceable constitutional right to vote at elections of congressmen from districts of equal population, were decided in *Colegrove*. Six of the participating Justices reached the questions but divided three to three on their merits. Mr. Justice Rutledge believed that it was not necessary to decide them.

Article I, §§ 2, 4, and 5, and Amendment XIV, § 2, relate only to congressional elections and obviously do not govern apportionment of state legislatures. However, our decisions in favor of justiciability even in light of those provisions plainly afford no support for the District Court's conclusion that the subject matter of this controversy presents a political question. Indeed, the refusal to award relief in *Colegrove* resulted only from the controlling view of a want of equity.

We conclude that the complaint's allegations of a denial of equal protection present a justiciable constitutional cause of action upon which appellants are entitled to a trial and a decision. The right asserted is within the reach of judicial protection under the Fourteenth Amendment.

The judgment of the District Court is reversed and the cause is remanded for further proceedings consistent with this opinion.

Reversed and remanded.

Mr. Justice WHITTAKER did not participate in the decision of this case.

Mr. Justice DOUGLAS, concurring.

[Omitted]

Mr. Justice CLARK, concurring.

[Omitted]

Mr. Justice STEWART, concurring.

The separate writings of my dissenting and concurring Brothers stray so far from the subject of today's decision as to convey, I think, a distressingly inaccurate impression of what the Court decides. For that reason, I think it appropriate, in joining the opinion of the Court, to emphasize in a few words what the opinion does and does not say.

The Court today decides three things and no more: "(a) that the court possessed jurisdiction of the subject matter; (b) that a justiciable cause of action is stated upon which appellants would be entitled to appropriate relief; and (c) . . . that the appellants have standing to challenge the Tennessee apportionment statutes."

The complaint in this case asserts that Tennessee's system of apportionment is utterly arbitrary—without any possible justification in rationality. The District Court did not reach the merits of that claim, and this Court quite properly expresses no view on the subject. Contrary to the suggestion of my Brother Harlan, the Court does not say or imply that "state legislatures must be so structured as to reflect with approximate equality the voice of every voter." The Court does not say or imply that there is anything in the Federal Constitution "to prevent a State, acting not irrationally, from choosing any electoral legislative structure it thinks best suited to the interests, temper, and customs of its people." And contrary to the suggestion of my Brother Douglas, the Court most assuredly does not decide the question, "may a State weight the vote of one county or one district more heavily than it weights the vote in another?"

My Brother Clark has made a convincing prima facie showing that Tennessee's system of apportionment is in fact utterly arbitrary—without any possible justification in rationality. My Brother Harlan has, with imagination and ingenuity, hypothesized possibly rational bases for Tennessee's system. But the merits of this case are not before us now. The defendants have not yet had an opportunity to be heard in defense of the State's system of apportionment; indeed, they have not yet even filed an answer to the complaint. As in other cases, the proper place for the trial is in the trial court, not here.

Mr. Justice FRANKFURTER, whom Mr. Justice HARLAN joins, dissenting.

The Court today reverses a uniform course of decision established by a dozen cases, including one by which the very claim now sustained was unanimously rejected only five years ago. The impressive body of rulings thus cast aside reflected the equally uniform course of our political history regarding the relationship between population and legislative representation—a wholly different matter from denial of the franchise to individuals because of race, color, religion or sex. Such a massive repudiation of the experience of our whole past in asserting destructively novel judicial power demands a detailed analysis of the role of this Court in our constitutional scheme. Disregard of inherent limits in the effective exercise of the Court's "judicial Power" not only presages the futility of judicial intervention in the essentially political conflict of forces by which the relation between population and representation has time out of mind been and now is determined. It may well impair the Court's position as the ultimate organ of "the supreme Law of the Land" in that vast range of legal problems, often strongly entangled in popular feeling, on which this Court must pronounce. The Court's authority—possessed of neither the purse nor the sword—ultimately rests on sustained public confidence in its moral sanction. Such feeling must be nourished by the Court's complete detachment, in fact and in appearance, from political entanglements and by abstention from injecting itself into the clash of political forces in political settlements.

Even assuming the indispensable intellectual disinterestedness on the part of judges in such matters, they do not have accepted legal standards or criteria or even reliable analogies to draw upon for making judicial judgments. To charge courts with the task of accommodating the incommensurable factors of policy that underlie these mathematical puzzles is to attribute, however flatteringly, omnicompetence to judges. The Framers of the Constitution persistently rejected a proposal that embodied this assumption.

Recent legislation, creating a district appropriately described as "an atrocity of ingenuity," is not unique. Considering the gross inequality among legislative electoral units within almost every State, the Court naturally shrinks from asserting that in districting at least substantial equality is a constitutional requirement enforceable by courts. Room continues to be allowed for weighting. This of course implies that geography, economics, urban-rural conflict, and all the other non-legal factors which have throughout our history entered into political districting are to some extent not to be ruled out in the undefined vista now opened up by review in the federal courts of state reapportionments. To some extent—aye, there's the rub. In effect, today's decision empowers the courts of the country to devise what should constitute the proper composition of the legislatures of the fifty States. If state courts should for one reason or another find themselves unable to discharge this task, the duty of doing so is put on the federal courts or on this Court, if State views do not satisfy this Court's notion of what is proper districting.

We were soothingly told at the bar of this Court that we need not worry about the kind of remedy a court could effectively fashion once the abstract constitutional right to have courts pass on a state-wide system of electoral districting is recognized as a matter of judicial rhetoric, because legislatures would heed the Court's admonition. This is not only a euphoric hope. It implies a sorry confession of judicial impotence in place of a frank acknowledgment that there is not under our Constitution a judicial remedy for every political mischief, for every undesirable exercise of legislative power. The Framers carefully and with deliberate forethought refused so to enthrone the judiciary. In this situation, as in others of like nature, appeal for relief does not belong here. Appeal must be to an informed, civically militant electorate. In a democratic society like ours, relief must come through an aroused popular conscience that sears the conscience of the people's representatives. In any event there is nothing judicially more unseemly nor more self-defeating than for this Court to make *in terrorem* pronouncements, to indulge in merely empty rhetoric, sounding a word of promise to the ear, sure to be disappointing to the hope.

Colegrove held that a federal court should not entertain an action for declaratory and injunctive relief to adjudicate the constitutionality, under the Equal Protection Clause and other federal constitutional and statutory provisions, of a state statute establishing the respective districts for the State's election of Representatives to the Congress. Two opinions were written by the four Justices who composed the majority of the seven sitting members of the Court. Both opinions joining in the result in *Colegrove v. Green* agreed that considerations were controlling which dictated denial of jurisdiction though not in the strict sense of want of power. While the two opinions show a divergence of view regarding some of these considerations, there are important points of concurrence. Both opinions demonstrate a predominant concern, first, with avoiding federal judicial involvement in matters traditionally left to legislative policy making; second, with respect to the difficulty—in view of the nature of the problems of apportionment and its history in this country—of drawing on or devising judicial standards for judgment, as opposed to legislative determinations, of the part which mere numerical equality among voters should play as a criterion for the allocation of political power; and, third, with problems of finding appropriate modes of relief—particularly, the problem of resolving the essentially political issue of the relative merits of at large elections and elections held in districts of unequal population.

The *Colegrove* doctrine, in the form in which repeated decisions have settled it, was not an innovation. It represents long judicial thought and experience. From its earliest opinions this Court has consistently recognized a class of controversies which do not lend themselves to judicial standards and judicial remedies. To classify the various instances as "political questions" is rather a form of stating this conclusion than revealing of analysis. Some of the cases so labeled have no relevance here. But from others emerge unifying considerations that are compelling.

The cases involving Negro disfranchisement are no exception to the principle of avoiding federal judicial intervention into matters of state government in the absence of an explicit and clear constitutional imperative. For here the controlling command of Supreme Law is plain and unequivocal. An end of discrimination against the Negro was the compelling motive of the Civil War Amendments. The Fifteenth expresses this in terms, and it is no less true of the Equal Protection Clause of the Fourteenth. Thus the Court, in cases involving discrimination against the Negro's right to vote, has recognized not only the action at law for damages, but, in appropriate circumstances, the extraordinary remedy of declaratory or injunctive relief. Injunctions in these cases, it should be noted, would not have restrained statewide general elections.

The influence of these converging considerations—the caution not to undertake decision where standards meet for judicial judgment are lacking, the reluctance to interfere with matters of state government in the absence of an unquestionable and effectively enforceable mandate, the unwillingness to make courts arbiters of the broad issues of political organization historically committed to other institutions and for whose adjustment the judicial process is ill adapted—has been decisive of the settled line of cases, reaching back more than a century, which holds that Art. IV, § 4, of the Constitution, guaranteeing to the States "a Republican Form of Government," is not enforceable through the courts.

The present case involves all of the elements that have made the Guarantee Clause cases nonjusticiable. It is, in effect, a Guarantee Clause claim masquerading under a different label. But it cannot make the case more fit for judicial action that appellants invoke the Fourteenth Amendment rather than Art. IV, § 4, where, in fact, the gist of their complaint is the same—unless it can be found that the Fourteenth Amendment speaks with greater particularity to their situation. Art. IV, § 4, is not committed by express constitutional terms to Congress. It is the nature of the controversies arising under it, nothing else, which has made it judicially unenforceable. But where judicial competence is wanting, it cannot be created by invoking one clause of the Constitution rather than another.

Here appellants assert that "a minority now rules in Tennessee," that the apportionment statute results in a "distortion of the constitutional system," that the General Assembly is no longer "a body representative of the people of the State of Tennessee," all "contrary to the basic principle of representative government. . . ." Such a claim would be nonjusticiable not merely under Art. IV, § 4, but under any clause of the Constitution, by virtue of the very fact that a federal court is not a forum for political debate.

But appellants, of course, do not rest on this claim *simpliciter*. In invoking the Equal Protection Clause, they assert that the distortion of representative government complained of is produced by systematic discrimination against them, by way of "a debasement of their votes. . . ." Does this characterization, with due regard for the facts from which it is derived, add anything to appellants' case?

At first blush, this charge of discrimination based on legislative underrepresentation is given the appearance of a more private, less impersonal claim, than the assertion that the frame of government is askew. Appellants appear as representatives of a class that is prejudiced as a class, in contradistinction to the polity in its entirety. However, the discrimination relied on is the deprivation of what appellants conceive to be their proportionate share of political influence. This, of course, is the practical effect of any allocation of power within the institutions of government. Hardly any distribution of political authority that could be assailed as rendering government non-republican would fail similarly to operate to the prejudice of some groups, and to the advantage of others, within the body politic. It would be ingenuous not to see, or consciously blind to deny, that the real battle over the initiative and referendum, or over a delegation of power to local rather than state-wide authority, is the battle between forces whose influence is disparate among the various organs of government to whom power may be given. No shift of power but works a corresponding shift in political influence among the groups composing a society.

What, then, is this question of legislative apportionment? Appellants invoke the right to vote and to have their votes counted. But they are permitted to vote and their votes are counted. They go to the polls, they cast their ballots, they send their representatives to the state councils. Their complaint is simply that the representatives are not sufficiently numerous or powerful—in short, that Tennessee has adopted a basis of representation with which they are dissatisfied. Talk of "debasement" or "dilution" is circular talk. One cannot speak of "debasement" or "dilution" of the value of a vote until there is first defined a standard of reference as to what a vote should be worth. What is actually asked of the Court in this case is to choose among competing bases of representation—ultimately, really, among competing theories of political philosophy—in order to establish an appropriate frame of government for the State of Tennessee and thereby for all the States of the Union.

In such a matter, abstract analogies which ignore the facts of history deal in unrealities; they betray reason. This is not a case in which a State has, through a device however oblique and sophisticated, denied Negroes or Jews or redheaded persons a vote, or given them only a third or a sixth of a vote. What Tennessee illustrates is an old and still widespread method of representation—representation by local geographical division, only in part respective of population—in preference to others, others, forsooth, more appealing. Appellants contest this choice and seek to make this Court the arbiter of the disagreement. They would make the Equal Protection Clause the charter of adjudication, asserting that the equality which it guarantees comports, if not the assurance of equal weight to every voter's vote, at least the basic conception that representation ought to be proportionate to population, a standard by reference to which the reasonableness of apportionment plans may be judged.

To find such a political conception legally enforceable in the broad and unspecific guarantee of equal protection is to rewrite the Constitution. Certainly, "equal protection" is no more secure a foundation for judicial judgment of the permissibility of varying forms of representative government than is "Republican Form." Indeed since "equal protection of the laws" can only mean an equality of persons standing in the same relation to whatever governmental action is challenged, the determination whether treatment is equal presupposes a determination concerning the nature of the relationship. This, with respect to apportionment, means an inquiry into the theoretic base of representation in an acceptably republican state. For a court could not determine the equal-protection issue without in fact first determining the Republican-Form issue, simply because what is reasonable for equal-protection purposes will depend upon what frame of government, basically, is allowed. To divorce "equal protection" from "Republican Form" is to talk about half a question.

The notion that representation proportioned to the geographic spread of population is so universally accepted as a necessary element of equality between man and man that it must be taken to be the standard of a political equality preserved by the Fourteenth Amendment—that it is, in appellants' words "the basic principle of representative government"—is, to put it bluntly, not true. However desirable and however desired by some among the great political thinkers and framers of our government, it has never been generally practiced, today or in the past. It was not the English system, it was not the colonial system, it was not the system chosen for the national government by the Constitution, it was not the system exclusively or even predominantly practiced by the States at the time of adoption of the Fourteenth Amendment, it is not predominantly practiced by the States today. Unless judges, the judges of this Court, are to make their private views of political wisdom the measure of the Constitution—views which in all honesty cannot but give the appearance, if not reflect the reality, of involvement with the business of partisan politics so inescapably a part of apportionment controversies—the Fourteenth Amendment, "itself a historical product," provides no guide for judicial oversight of the representation problem.

The stark fact is that if among the numerous widely varying principles and practices that control state legislative apportionment today there is any generally prevailing feature, that feature is geographic inequality in relation to the population standard. Examples could be endlessly multiplied. In New Jersey, counties of thirty-five thousand and of more than nine hundred and five thousand inhabitants respectively each have a single senator. Representative districts in Minnesota range from 7,290 inhabitants to 107,246 inhabitants. Ratios of senatorial representation in California vary as much as two hundred and ninety-seven to one. In Oklahoma, the range is ten to one for House constituencies and roughly sixteen to one for Senate constituencies. Colebrook, Connecticut—population 592—elects two House representatives; Hartford—population 177,397—also elects two. The first, third and fifth of these examples are the products of constitutional provisions which subordinate population to regional considerations in apportionment; the second is the result of legislative inaction; the fourth derives from both constitutional and legislative sources. A survey made in 1955, in sum, reveals that less than thirty percent of the population inhabit districts sufficient to elect a House majority in thirteen States and a

Senate majority in nineteen States. These figures show more than individual variations from a generally accepted standard of electoral equality. They show that there is not—as there has never been—a standard by which the place of equality as a factor in apportionment can be measured.

Manifestly, the Equal Protection Clause supplies no clearer guide for judicial examination of apportionment methods than would the Guarantee Clause itself. Apportionment, by its character, is a subject of extraordinary complexity, involving—even after the fundamental theoretical issues concerning what is to be represented in a representative legislature have been fought out or compromised—considerations of geography, demography, electoral convenience, economic and social cohesions or divergencies among particular local groups, communications, the practical effects of political institutions like the lobby and the city machine, ancient traditions and ties of settled usage, respect for proven incumbents of long experience and senior status, mathematical mechanics, censuses compiling relevant data, and a host of others. Legislative responses throughout the country to the reapportionment demands of the 1960 Census have glaringly confirmed that these are not factors that lend themselves to evaluations of a nature that are the staple of judicial determinations or for which judges are equipped to adjudicate by legal training or experience or native wit. And this is the more so true because in every strand of this complicated, intricate web of values meet the contending forces of partisan politics. The practical significance of apportionment is that the next election results may differ because of it. Apportionment battles are overwhelmingly party or intra-party contests. It will add a virulent source of friction and tension in federal-state relations to embroil the federal judiciary in them.

Dissenting opinion of Mr. Justice HARLAN, whom Mr. Justice FRANKFURTER joins.

[Justice Harlan noted that Tennessee might have retained the current legislative districts to "protect the State's agricultural interests from the sheer weight of numbers of those residing in its cities."]

NOTES ON *BAKER v. CARR* AND THE POLITICAL QUESTION DOCTRINE

1. As mentioned in the introduction to this case, *Colegrove v. Green* raised the exact same basic question as *Baker* yet, as you have now learned, the Court's approach in *Baker* was much different than the Court's approach in *Colegrove*. One factual difference was that *Colegrove* concerned a state's *congressional* delegation, whereas *Baker* concerned a state's own legislature. Should that factual distinction make a difference under the Equal Protection Clause?
2. Even if *Baker* did not technically overrule *Colegrove*, the two cases are very much inconsistent, as Justice Frankfurter observes in his *Baker* dissent. Why did the Court adopt a very different approach only 16 years after *Colegrove* itself? Was the Court justified in departing from the *Colegrove* approach? If so,

why? Does the majority opinion in *Baker* even attempt to justify taking a different approach from *Colegrove* (as opposed to trying to cast aside *Colegrove* as irrelevant)?

3. In both *Baker* and *Colegrove*, there was a discussion of the so-called Guaranty Clause of the U.S. Constitution, which says that the federal government will guarantee the states a "Republican Form of Government." Early in the Court's history, in a fascinating case called *Luther v. Borden*, 48 U.S. 1 (1849), the Court refused to entertain any judicial claim based on this clause. Rather, the Court held, it is up to Congress to enforce this constitutional guarantee. The context was attempted political revolution in Rhode Island, where the existing state constitution limited the suffrage to property owners, and opponents of this restriction held a constitutional convention for the state, submitted a new constitution to the citizenry for ratification, and attempted to elect a new government under the new constitution. Defenders of the old state constitution, however, refused to acquiesce, and they declared martial law and arrested supporters of the new state constitution. After their arrest, these supporters of the new state constitution filed suit in state court, claiming protection under the Guaranty Clause. The U.S. Supreme Court ruled that the federal courts were not entitled to intervene in this political dispute, thus invoking what has come to be known as the political question doctrine.
4. The significance of *Baker* is that it reinterprets the political question doctrine so that the "nonjusticiability" of Guaranty Clause claims is clause-specific, meaning that the obstacle to judicial involvement is reliance on that particular clause, not the nature of the controversy itself. *Colegrove*, by contrast, had taken the approach that the problem was the subject matter of the litigation: It would not matter which particular clause of the U.S. Constitution was invoked to challenge disparities of population among legislative districts; according to *Colegrove*, courts cannot become involved in that subject matter. *Baker* says the opposite: The federal judiciary is entitled to entertain an Equal Protection claim with respect to districting because that involves a different clause than the Guaranty Clause.

B. One Person, One Vote

Baker v. Carr declared that federal courts would entertain Equal Protection challenges to state legislative districts that were malapportioned. However, as Justice Stewart notes in his concurrence in *Baker*, the *Baker* Court did not deliniate the full scope of the constitutional right or remedy in this area. The next two cases illustrate both the nature of the remedy and the breadth of the right. As you are reading, consider the source of the right the Court identifies. What authority does the Court rely upon to craft the "one person, one vote" right and the corresponding remedy for a violation of that right?

REYNOLDS v. SIMS

377 U.S. 533 (1964)

[This case was one of six decided the same day concerning the make-up of state legislatures. Alabama's legislature had not been redistricted for over 60 years. As a result, neither house of Alabama's legislature had representation based even remotely on population. In the Senate, the ratio between the most populated and least populated district was 41:1; in the House, the ratio between the most populated and least populated district was 16:1. Accordingly, a group of Alabama citizens sued various state officials in federal court, claiming that the make-up of Alabama's legislature violated the Equal Protection Clause. The District Court ruled in plaintiffs' favor, and the case was appealed directly to the Supreme Court.]

Mr. Chief Justice WARREN delivered the opinion of the Court.

The right to vote freely for the candidate of one's choice is of the essence of a democratic society, and any restrictions on that right strike at the heart of representative government. And the right of suffrage can be denied by a debasement or dilution of the weight of a citizen's vote just as effectively as by wholly prohibiting the free exercise of the franchise.

A predominant consideration in determining whether a State's legislative apportionment scheme constitutes an invidious discrimination violative of rights asserted under the Equal Protection Clause is that the rights allegedly impaired are individual and personal in nature. Undoubtedly, the right of suffrage is a fundamental matter in a free and democratic society. Especially since the right to exercise the franchise in a free and unimpaired manner is preservative of other basic civil and political rights, any alleged infringement of the right of citizens to vote must be carefully and meticulously scrutinized.

Legislators represent people, not trees or acres. Legislators are elected by voters, not farms or cities or economic interests. As long as ours is a representative form of government, and our legislatures are those instruments of government elected directly by and directly representative of the people, the right to elect legislators in a free and unimpaired fashion is a bedrock of our political system. It could hardly be gainsaid that a constitutional claim had been asserted by an allegation that certain otherwise qualified voters had been entirely prohibited from voting for members of their state legislature. And, if a State should provide that the votes of citizens in one part of the State should be given two times, or five times, or 10 times the weight of votes of citizens in another part of the State, it could hardly be contended that the right to vote of those residing in the disfavored areas had not been effectively diluted. It would appear extraordinary to suggest that a State could be constitutionally permitted to enact a law providing that certain of the State's voters could vote two, five, or 10 times for their legislative representatives, while voters living elsewhere could vote only once. And it is inconceivable that a state law to the effect that, in counting votes for legislators, the votes of citizens in one part of the State would be multiplied by two, five, or 10, while the votes of persons in another area would be counted only at face value, could be constitutionally sustainable. Of course, the effect of state legislative districting schemes which give the same number of representatives to unequal numbers of constituents is identical. Overweighting and overvaluation of the votes of those living here has the certain effect of dilution and undervaluation of the votes of those living there. The resulting discrimination against those individual voters living in disfavored areas is easily demonstrable mathematically. Their right to vote is simply not the same right to vote as that of those living in a favored part of the State. Two, five, or 10 of them must vote before the effect of their voting is equivalent to that of their favored neighbor. Weighting the votes of citizens differently, by any method or means, merely because of where they happen to reside, hardly seems justifiable.

State legislatures are, historically, the fountainhead of representative government in this country. A number of them have their roots in colonial times, and substantially antedate the creation of our Nation and our Federal Government. In fact, the first formal stirrings of American political independence are to be found, in large part, in the views and actions of several of the colonial legislative bodies. With the birth of our National Government, and the adoption and ratification of the Federal Constitution, state legislatures retained a most important place in our Nation's governmental structure. But representative government is in essence self-government through the medium of elected representatives of the people, and each and every citizen has an inalienable right to full and effective participation in the political processes of his State's legislative bodies. Most citizens can achieve this participation only as qualified voters through the election of legislators to represent them. Full and effective participation by all citizens in state government requires, therefore, that each citizen have an equally effective voice in the election of members of his state legislature. Modern and viable state government needs, and the Constitution demands, no less.

Logically, in a society ostensibly grounded on representative government, it would seem reasonable that a majority of the people of a State could elect a majority of that State's legislators. To conclude differently, and to sanction minority control of state legislative bodies, would appear to deny majority rights in a way that far surpasses any possible denial of minority rights that might otherwise be thought to result. Since legislatures are responsible for enacting laws by which all citizens are to be governed, they should be bodies which are collectively responsive to the popular will. And the concept of equal protection has been traditionally viewed as requiring the uniform treatment of persons standing in the same relation to the governmental action questioned or challenged. With respect to the allocation of legislative representation, all voters, as citizens of a State, stand in the same relation regardless of where they live. Any suggested criteria for the differentiation of citizens are insufficient to justify any discrimination, as to the weight of their votes, unless relevant to the permissible purposes of legislative apportionment. Since the achieving of fair and effective representation for all citizens is concededly the basic aim of legislative apportionment, we conclude that the Equal Protection Clause guarantees the opportunity for equal participation by all voters in the election of state legislators. Our constitutional system amply provides for the protection of minorities by means other than giving them majority control of state legislatures. And the democratic ideals of equality and majority rule, which have served this Nation so well in the past, are hardly of any less significance for the present and the future.

We are told that the matter of apportioning representation in a state legislature is a complex and many-faceted one. We are advised that States can rationally consider factors other than population in apportioning legislative representation. We are admonished not to restrict the power of the States to impose differing views as to political philosophy on their citizens. We are cautioned about the dangers of entering into political thickets and mathematical quagmires. Our answer is this: a denial of constitutionally protected rights demands judicial protection; our oath and our office require no less of us.

To the extent that a citizen's right to vote is debased, he is that much less a citizen. The fact that an individual lives here or there is not a legitimate reason for overweighting or diluting the efficacy of his vote. The complexions of societies and civilizations change, often with amazing rapidity. A nation once primarily rural in character becomes predominantly urban. Representation schemes once fair and equitable become archaic and outdated. But the basic principle of representative government remains, and must remain, unchanged—the weight of a citizen's vote cannot be made to depend on where he lives. Population is, of necessity, the starting point for consideration and the controlling criterion for judgment in legislative apportionment controversies. A citizen, a qualified voter, is no more nor no less so because he lives in the city or on the farm. This is the clear and strong command of our Constitution's Equal Protection Clause. This is an essential part of the concept of a government of laws and not men. This is at the heart of Lincoln's vision of "government of the people, by the people, (and) for the people." The Equal Protection Clause demands no less than substantially equal state legislative representation for all citizens, of all places as well as of all races.

We hold that, as a basic constitutional standard, the Equal Protection Clause requires that the seats in both houses of a bicameral state legislature must be apportioned on a population basis. Simply stated, an individual's right to vote for state legislators is unconstitutionally impaired when its weight is in a substantial fashion diluted when compared with votes of citizens living on other parts of the State.

Much has been written since our decision in *Baker v. Carr* about the applicability of the so-called federal analogy to state legislative apportionment arrangements. We find the federal analogy inapposite and irrelevant to state legislative districting schemes. Attempted reliance on the federal analogy appears often to be little more than an after-the-fact rationalization offered in defense of maladjusted state apportionment arrangements. The original constitutions of 36 of our States provided that representation in both houses of the state legislatures would be based completely, or predominantly, on population. And the Founding Fathers clearly had no intention of establishing a pattern or model for the apportionment of seats in state legislatures when the system of representation in the Federal Congress was adopted.

The system of representation in the two Houses of the Federal Congress is one ingrained in our Constitution, as part of the law of the land. It is one conceived out of compromise and concession indispensable to the establishment of our federal republic. Arising from unique historical circumstances, it is based on the consideration that in establishing our type of federalism a group of formerly independent States bound themselves together under one national government. Admittedly, the original 13 States surrendered some of their sovereignty in agreeing to join together "to form a more perfect Union." But at the heart of our constitutional system remains the concept of separate and distinct governmental entities which have delegated some, but not all, of their formerly held powers to the single national government. The fact that almost three-fourths of our present States were never in fact independently sovereign does not detract from our view that the so-called federal analogy is inapplicable as a sustaining precedent for state legislative apportionments. The developing history and growth of our republic cannot cloud the fact that, at the time of the inception of the system of representation in the Federal Congress, a compromise between the larger and smaller States on this matter averted a deadlock in the Constitutional Convention which had threatened to abort the birth of our Nation.

Political subdivisions of States—counties, cities, or whatever—never were and never have been considered as sovereign entities. Rather, they have been traditionally regarded as subordinate governmental instrumentalities created by the State to assist in the carrying out of state governmental functions. These governmental units are "created as convenient agencies for exercising such of the governmental powers of the state as may be entrusted to them," and the "number, nature, and duration of the powers conferred upon (them) . . . and the territory over which they shall be exercised rests in the absolute discretion of the state." The relationship of the States to the Federal Government could hardly be less analogous.

Since we find the so-called federal analogy inapposite to a consideration of the constitutional validity of state legislative apportionment schemes, we necessarily hold that the Equal Protection Clause requires both houses of a state legislature to be apportioned on a population basis. The right of a citizen to equal representation and to have his vote weighted equally with those of all other citizens in the election of members of one house of a bicameral state legislature would amount to little if States could effectively submerge the equal-population principle in the apportionment of seats in the other house. If such a scheme were permissible, an individual citizen's ability to exercise an effective voice in the only instrument of state government directly representative of the people might be almost as effectively thwarted as if neither house were apportioned on a population basis. Deadlock between the two bodies might result in compromise and concession on some issues. But in all too many cases the more probable result would be frustration of the majority will through minority veto in the house not apportioned on a population basis, stemming directly from the failure to accord adequate overall legislative representation to all of the State's citizens on a nondiscriminatory basis. In summary, we can perceive no constitutional difference, with respect to the geographical distribution of state legislative representation, between the two houses of a bicameral state legislature.

By holding that as a federal constitutional requisite both houses of a state legislature must be apportioned on a population basis, we mean that the Equal Protection Clause requires that a State make an honest and good faith effort to construct districts, in both houses of its legislature, as nearly of equal population as is practicable. We realize that it is a practical impossibility to arrange legislative districts so that each one has an identical number of residents, or citizens, or voters. Mathematical exactness or precision is hardly a workable constitutional requirement.

For the present, we deem it expedient not to attempt to spell out any precise constitutional tests. What is marginally permissible in one State may be unsatisfactory in another, depending on the particular circumstances of the case. Developing a body of doctrine on a case-by-case basis appears to us to provide the most satisfactory means of arriving at detailed constitutional requirements in the area of state legislative apportionment. Thus, we proceed to state here only a few rather general considerations which appear to us to be relevant.

A State may legitimately desire to maintain the integrity of various political subdivisions, insofar as possible, and provide for compact districts of contiguous territory in designing a legislative apportionment scheme. Valid considerations may underlie such aims. Indiscriminate districting, without any regard for political subdivision or natural or historical boundary lines, may be little more than an open invitation to partisan gerrymandering. Single-member districts may be the rule in one State, while another State might desire to achieve some flexibility by creating multimember or floterial districts. Whatever the means of accomplishment, the overriding objective must be substantial equality of population among the various districts, so that the vote of any citizen is approximately equal in weight to that of any other citizen in the State.

History indicates, however, that many States have deviated, to a greater or lesser degree, from the equal-population principle in the apportionment of seats in at least one house of their legislatures. So long as the divergences from a strict population standard are based on legitimate considerations incident to the effectuation of a rational state policy, some deviations from the equal-population principle are constitutionally permissible with respect to the apportionment of seats in either or both of the two houses of a bicameral state legislature. But neither history alone, nor economic or other sorts of group interests, are permissible factors in attempting to justify disparities from population-based representation. Citizens, not history or economic interests, cast votes. Considerations of area alone provide an insufficient justification for deviations from the equal-population principle. Again, people, not land or trees or pastures, vote. Modern developments and improvements in transportation and communications make rather hollow, in the mid-1960's, most claims that deviations from population-based representation can validly be based solely on geographical considerations. Arguments for allowing such deviations in order to insure effective representation for sparsely settled areas and to prevent legislative districts from becoming so large that the availability of access of citizens to their representatives is impaired are today, for the most part, unconvincing.

A consideration that appears to be of more substance in justifying some deviations from population-based representation in state legislatures is that of insuring some voice to political subdivisions, as political subdivisions. Several factors make more than insubstantial claims that a State can rationally consider according political subdivisions some independent representation in at least one body of the state legislature, as long as the basic standard of equality of population among districts is maintained. Local governmental entities are frequently charged with various responsibilities incident to the operation of state government. In many States much of the legislature's activity involves the enactment of so-called local legislation, directed only to the concerns of particular political subdivisions. And a State may legitimately desire to construct districts along political subdivision lines to deter the possibilities of gerrymandering. However, permitting deviations from population-based representation does not mean that each local governmental unit or political subdivision can be given separate representation, regardless of population. Carried too far, a scheme of giving at least one seat in one house to each political subdivision (for example, to each county) could easily result, in many States, in a total subversion of the equal-population principle in that legislative body. This would be especially true in a State where the number of counties is large and many of them are sparsely populated, and the number of seats in the legislative body being apportioned does not significantly exceed the number of counties. Such a result, we conclude, would be constitutionally impermissible. And careful judicial scrutiny must of course be given, in evaluating state apportionment schemes, to the character as well as the degree of deviations from a strict population basis. But if, even as a result of a clearly rational state policy of according some legislative representation to political subdivisions, population is submerged as the controlling consideration in the apportionment of seats in the particular legislative body, then the right of all of the State's citizens to cast an effective and adequately weighted vote would be unconstitutionally impaired.

That the Equal Protection Clause requires that both houses of a state legislature be apportioned on a population basis does not mean that States cannot adopt some reasonable plan for periodic revision of their apportionment schemes. Decennial reapportionment appears to be a rational approach to readjustment of legislative representation in order to take into account population shifts and growth. Reallocation of legislative seats every 10 years coincides with the prescribed practice in 41 of the States, often honored more in the breach than the observance, however. Illustratively, the Alabama Constitution requires decennial reapportionment, yet the last reapportionment of the Alabama Legislature, when this suit was brought, was in 1901. Limitations on the frequency of reapportionment are justified by the need for stability and continuity in the organization of the legislative system, although undoubtedly reapportioning no more frequently than every 10 years leads to some imbalance in the population of districts toward the end of the decennial period and also to the development of resistance to change on the part of some incumbent legislators. In substance, we do not regard the Equal Protection Clause as requiring daily, monthly, annual or biennial reapportionment, so long as a State has a reasonably conceived plan for periodic readjustment of legislative representation. While we do not intend to indicate that decennial reapportionment is a constitutional requisite, compliance with such an approach would clearly meet the minimal requirements for maintaining a reasonably current scheme of legislative representation. And we do not mean to intimate that more frequent reapportionment would not be constitutionally permissible or practicably desirable. But if reapportionment were accomplished with less frequency, it would assuredly be constitutionally suspect.

We do not consider here the difficult question of the proper remedial devices which federal courts should utilize in state legislative apportionment cases. Remedial techniques in this new and developing area of the law will probably often differ with the circumstances of the challenged apportionment and a variety of local conditions. It is enough to say now that, once a State's legislative apportionment scheme has been found to be unconstitutional, it would be the unusual case in which a court would be justified in not taking appropriate action to insure that no further elections are conducted under the invalid plan. However, under certain circumstances, such as where an impending election is imminent and a State's election machinery is already in progress, equitable considerations might justify a court in withholding the granting of immediately effective relief in a legislative apportionment case, even though the existing apportionment scheme was found invalid. In awarding or withholding immediate relief, a court is entitled to and should consider the proximity of a forthcoming election and the mechanics and complexities of state election laws, and should act and rely upon general equitable principles. With respect to the timing of relief, a court can reasonably endeavor to avoid a disruption of the election process which might result from requiring precipitate changes that could make unreasonable or embarrassing demands on a State in adjusting to the requirements of the court's decree.

Affirmed and remanded.

Mr. Justice CLARK, concurring in the affirmance.

[Omitted]

Mr. Justice STEWART.

[Omitted]

Mr. Justice HARLAN, dissenting.

[Omitted]

LUCAS v. 44th GENERAL ASSEMBLY OF COLORADO

377 U.S. 713 (1964)

[This case was a companion to *Reynolds v. Sims*. It concerned the structure of Colorado's General Assembly. As the Court noted, however, the facts of *Lucas* differed significantly from the facts of *Reynolds*. In Colorado, unlike in Alabama, the issue of the state legislature's makeup had been put directly to the electorate in a referendum held in 1962. In this referendum, which complied with the principle of one person, one vote, the Colorado voters had been asked to choose between two alternative plans.

One plan, which we shall call "Plan A," would have apportioned Colorado's House of Representatives strictly according to population, but would have apportioned the Senate based partly on population and also partly on the desire to protect the interests of those citizens who lived in sparsely populated, geographically distinctive regions within the state. The result of Plan A would be that the ratio of persons in the most populated Senate district to the least populated Senate district would have been 3:1. The other plan on the ballot, which we shall call "Plan B," would have apportioned both the House and the Senate strictly according to population.

The voters adopted Plan A and rejected Plan B by more than a three-to-two margin. Moreover, a majority of voters in every county in Colorado, *including those counties within the highly populous urban region of the state*, approved of Plan A in preference to Plan B.

Shortly thereafter, a group of Colorado voters sued the state legislature in federal district court, claiming that Plan A violated the Equal Protection Clause of the Fourteenth Amendment. The district court rejected the plaintiffs' claim, and this appeal followed.]

Chief Justice WARREN delivered the opinion of the Court.

In *Reynolds v. Sims*, we held that the Equal Protection Clause requires that both houses of a bicameral state legislature must be apportioned substantially on a population basis.

An individual's constitutionally protected right to cast an equally weighted vote cannot be denied even by a vote of a majority of a State's electorate, if the apportionment scheme adopted by the voters fails to measure up to the requirements of the Equal Protection Clause. Manifestly, the fact that an apportionment plan is adopted in a popular referendum is insufficient to sustain its constitutionality or to induce a court of equity to refuse to act. As stated by this Court in *West Virginia State Bd. of Educ. v. Barnette* "One's right to life, liberty, and property . . . and other fundamental rights may not be submitted to vote; they depend on the outcome of no elections." A citizen's constitutional rights can hardly be infringed simply because a majority of the people choose that it be. We hold that the fact that a challenged legislative apportionment plan was approved by the electorate is without federal constitutional significance, if the scheme adopted fails to satisfy the basic requirements of the Equal Protection Clause, as delineated in our opinion in *Reynolds v. Sims*.

Appellees' argument, accepted by the court below, that the apportionment of the Colorado Senate [under Plan A] is rational because it takes into account a variety of geographical, historical, topographic and economic considerations fails to provide an adequate justification for the substantial disparities from population-based representation in the allocation of Senate seats to the disfavored populous areas.

Reversed and remanded.

Mr. Justice CLARK, dissenting.

While I join my Brother Stewart's opinion, I have some additional observations with reference to this case.

I would refuse to interfere with this apportionment for several reasons. First, Colorado enjoys the initiative and referendum system which it often utilizes and which, indeed, produced the present apportionment. As a result of the action of the Legislature and the use of initiative and referendum, the State Assembly has been reapportioned eight times since 1881. This indicates the complete awareness of the people of Colorado to apportionment problems and their continuing efforts to solve them. The courts should not interfere in such a situation. Next, as my Brother Stewart has pointed out, there are rational and most persuasive reasons for some deviations in the representation in the Colorado Assembly. The State has mountainous areas which divide it into four regions, some parts of which are almost impenetrable. There are also some depressed areas, diversified industry and varied climate, as well as enormous recreational regions and difficulties in transportation. These factors give rise to problems indigenous to Colorado, which only its people can intelligently solve. This they have done in the present apportionment.

Finally, I cannot agree to the arbitrary application of the "one man, one vote" principle for both houses of a State Legislature. In my view, if one house is fairly apportioned by population (as is admitted here) then the people should have some latitude in providing, on a rational basis, for representation in the other house. The Court seems to approve the federal arrangement of two Senators from each State on the ground that it was a compromise reached by the framers of our Constitution and is a part of the fabric of our national charter. But what the Court overlooks is that Colorado, by an overwhelming vote, has likewise written the organization of its legislative body into its Constitution, and our dual federalism requires that we give it recognition. After all, the Equal Protection Clause is not an algebraic formula. Equal protection does not rest on whether the practice assailed "results in some inequality" but rather on whether "any state of facts reasonably can be conceived that would sustain it"; and one who attacks it must show "that it does not rest upon any reasonable basis, but is essentially arbitrary." Certainly Colorado's arrangement is not arbitrary. On the contrary, it rests on reasonable grounds which, as I have pointed out, are peculiar to that State. It is argued that the Colorado apportionment would lead only to a legislative stalemate between the two houses, but the experience of the Congress completely refutes this argument. Now in its 176th year, the federal plan has worked well.

It is further said that in any event Colorado's apportionment would substitute compromise for the legislative process. But most legislation is the product of compromise between the various forces acting for and against its enactment.

In striking down Colorado's plan of apportionment, the Court, I believe, is exceeding its powers under the Equal Protection Clause; it is invading the valid functioning of the procedures of the States, and thereby is committing a grievous error which will do irreparable damage to our federal-state relationship. I dissent.

Mr. Justice STEWART, whom Mr. Justice CLARK joins, dissenting.

I find it impossible to understand how or why a voter in California, for instance, either feels or is less a citizen than a voter in Nevada, simply because, despite their population disparities, each of these States is represented by two United States Senators.

The Court's draconian pronouncement, which makes unconstitutional the legislatures of most of the 50 States, finds no support in the words of the Constitution, in any prior decision of this Court, or in the 175-year political history of our Federal Union. With all respect, I am convinced these decisions mark a long step backward into that unhappy era when a majority of the members of this Court were thought by many to have convinced themselves and each other that the demands of the Constitution were to be measured not by what it says, but by their own notions of wise political theory. The rule announced today is at odds with long-established principles of constitutional adjudication under the Equal Protection Clause, and it stifles values of local individuality and initiative vital to the character of the Federal Union which it was the genius of our Constitution to create.

I

What the Court has done is to convert a particular political philosophy into a constitutional rule, binding upon each of the 50 States, from Maine to Hawaii, from Alaska to Texas, without regard and without respect for the many individualized and differentiated characteristics of each State, characteristics stemming from each State's distinct history, distinct geography, distinct distribution of population, and distinct political heritage. My own understanding of the various theories of representative government is that no one theory has ever commanded unanimous assent among political scientists, historians, or others who have considered the problem. But even if it were thought that the rule announced today by the Court is, as a matter of political theory, the most desirable general rule which can be devised as a basis for the make-up of the representative assembly of a typical State, I could not join in the fabrication of a constitutional mandate which imports and forever freezes one theory of political thought into our Constitution, and forever denies to every State any opportunity for enlightened and progressive innovation in the design of its democratic institutions, so as to accommodate within a system of representative government the interests and aspirations of diverse groups of people, without subjecting any group or class to absolute domination by a geographically concentrated or highly organized majority.

Representative government is a process of accommodating group interests through democratic institutional arrangements. Its function is to channel the numerous opinions, interests, and abilities of the people of a State into the making of the State's public policy. Appropriate legislative apportionment, therefore, should ideally be designed to insure effective representation in the State's legislature, in cooperation with other organs of political power, of the various groups and interests making up the electorate. In practice, of course, this ideal is approximated in the particular apportionment system of any State by a realistic accommodation of the diverse and often conflicting political forces operating within the State.

I do not pretend to any specialized knowledge of the myriad of individual characteristics of the several States, beyond the records in the cases before us today. But I do know enough to be aware that a system of legislative apportionment which might be best for South Dakota might be unwise for Hawaii with its many islands, or Michigan with its Northern Peninsula. I do know enough to realize that Montana with its vast distances is not Rhode Island with its heavy concentrations of people. I do know enough to be aware of the great variations among the several States in their historic manner of distributing legislative power—of the Governors' Councils in New England, of the broad powers of initiative and referendum retained in some States by the people, of the legislative power which some States give to their Governors, by the right of veto or otherwise of the widely autonomous home rule which many States give to their cities. The Court today declines to give any recognition to these considerations and countless others, tangible and intangible, in holding unconstitutional the particular systems of legislative apportionment which these States have chosen. Instead, the Court says that the requirements of the Equal Protection Clause can be met in any State only by the uncritical, simplistic, and heavy-handed application of sixth-grade arithmetic.

But legislators do not represent faceless numbers. They represent people, or, more accurately, a majority of the voters in their districts—people with identifiable needs and interests which require legislative representation, and which can often be related to the geographical areas in which these people live. The very fact of geographic districting, the constitutional validity of which the Court does not question, carries with it an acceptance of the idea of legislative representation of regional needs and interests. Yet if geographical residence is irrelevant, as the Court suggests, and the goal is solely that of equally "weighted" votes, I do not understand why the Court's constitutional rule does not require the abolition of districts and the holding of all elections at large.[12]

12. Even with legislative districts of exactly equal voter population, 26% of the electorate (a bare majority of the voters in a bare majority of the districts) can, as a matter of the kind of theoretical mathematics embraced by the Court, elect a majority of the legislature under our simple majority electoral system. Thus, the Court's constitutional rule permits minority rule. Students of the mechanics of voting systems tell us that if all that matters is that votes count equally, the best vote-counting electoral system is proportional representation in state-wide elections. It is just because electoral systems are intended to serve functions other than satisfying mathematical theories, however, that the system of proportional representation has not been widely adopted.

The fact is, of course, that population factors must often to some degree be subordinated in devising a legislative apportionment plan which is to achieve the important goal of ensuring a fair, effective, and balanced representation of the regional, social, and economic interests within a State. And the further fact is that throughout our history the apportionments of State Legislatures have reflected the strongly felt American tradition that the public interest is composed of many diverse interests, and that in the long run it can better be expressed by a medley of component voices than by the majority's monolithic command. What constitutes a rational plan reasonably designed to achieve this objective will vary from State to State, since each State is unique, in terms of topography, geography, demography, history, heterogeneity and concentration of population, variety of social and economic interests, and in the operation and interrelation of its political institutions. But so long as a State's apportionment plan reasonably achieves, in the light of the State's own characteristics, effective and balanced representation of all substantial interests, without sacrificing the principle of effective majority rule, that plan cannot be considered irrational.

II

This brings me to what I consider to be the proper constitutional standards to be applied in these cases. Quite simply, I think the cases should be decided by application of accepted principles of constitutional adjudication under the Equal Protection Clause. A recent expression by the Court of these principles will serve as a generalized compendium:

> [T]he Fourteenth Amendment permits the States a wide scope of discretion in enacting laws which affect some groups of citizens differently than others. The constitutional safeguard is offended only if the classification rests on grounds wholly irrelevant to the achievement of the State's objective. State legislatures are presumed to have acted within their constitutional power despite the fact that, in practice, their laws result in some inequality. A statutory discrimination will not be set aside if any state of facts reasonably may be conceived to justify it. *McGowan v. Maryland.*

These principles reflect an understanding respect for the unique values inherent in the Federal Union of States established by our Constitution. They reflect, too, a wise perception of this Court's role in that constitutional system. The point was never better made than by Mr. Justice Brandeis, dissenting in *New State Ice Co. v. Liebmann.* The final paragraph of that classic dissent is worth repeating here:

> To stay experimentation in things social and economic is a grave responsibility. Denial of the right to experiment may be fraught with serious consequences to the nation. It is one of the happy incidents of the federal system that a single courageous state may, if its citizens choose, serve as a laboratory; and try novel social and economic experiments without risk to the rest of the country. This Court has the power to prevent an

experiment. We may strike down the statute which embodies it on the ground that, in our opinion, the measure is arbitrary, capricious or unreasonable. . . . But, in the exercise of this high power, we must be ever on our guard, lest we erect our prejudices into legal principles. If we would guide by the light of reason we must let our minds be bold.

Moving from the general to the specific, I think that the Equal Protection Clause demands but two basic attributes of any plan of state legislative apportionment. First, it demands that, in the light of the State's own characteristics and needs, the plan must be a rational one. Secondly, it demands that the plan must be such as not to permit the systematic frustration of the will of a majority of the electorate of the State. I think it is apparent that any plan of legislative apportionment which could be shown to reflect no policy, but simply arbitrary and capricious action or inaction, and that any plan which could be shown systematically to prevent ultimate effective majority rule, would be invalid under accepted Equal Protection Clause standards. But, beyond this, I think there is nothing in the Federal Constitution to prevent a State from choosing any electoral legislative structure it thinks best suited to the interests, temper, and customs of its people.

III

The Colorado plan creates a General Assembly composed of a Senate of 39 members and a House of 65 members. The State is divided into 65 equal population representative districts, with one representative to be elected from each district, and 39 senatorial districts, 14 of which include more than one county. In the Colorado House, the majority unquestionably rules supreme, with the population factor untempered by other considerations. In the Senate rural minorities do not have effective control, and therefore do not have even a veto power over the will of the urban majorities. It is true that, as a matter of theoretical arithmetic, a minority of 36% of the voters could elect a majority of the Senate, but this percentage has no real meaning in terms of the legislative process. Under the Colorado plan, no possible combination of Colorado senators from rural districts, even assuming arguendo that they would vote as a bloc, could control the Senate. To arrive at the 36% figure, one must include with the rural districts a substantial number of urban districts, districts with substantially dissimilar interests. There is absolutely no reason to assume that this theoretical majority would ever vote together on any issue so as to thwart the wishes of the majority of the voters of Colorado. Indeed, when we eschew the world of numbers, and look to the real world of effective representation, the simple fact of the matter is that Colorado's three metropolitan areas, Denver, Pueblo, and Colorado Springs, elect a majority of the Senate.[14]

14. The theoretical figure is arrived at by placing the legislative districts for each house in rank order of population, and by counting down the smallest population end of the list a sufficient distance to accumulate the minimum population which could elect a majority of the house in question. It is a meaningless abstraction as applied to a multimembered body because the factors of political party alignment and interest representation make such theoretical bloc voting a practical impossibility. For example, 31,000,000 people in the 26 least populous States representing only 17% of United States population have 52% of the Senators in the United States Senate. But no one contends that this bloc controls the Senate's legislative process.

[Justice Stewart then explains why Plan A is reasonable given Colorado's unique geography and issues.]

The present apportionment, adopted overwhelmingly by the people in a 1962 popular referendum as a state constitutional amendment, is entirely rational, and the amendment by its terms provides for keeping the apportionment current. Thus the majority has consciously chosen to protect the minority's interests, and under the liberal initiative provisions of the Colorado Constitution, it retains the power to reverse its decision to do so. Therefore, there can be no question of frustration of the basic principle of majority rule.

NOTES ON *REYNOLDS* AND *LUCAS*

1. *Reynolds* is the famous case, but *Lucas* is the more important one because it shows the full reach of the one person, one vote principle adopted in those cases.
2. Where does the one person, one vote principle, and the corresponding constitutional "right to vote," come from? The text of the Fourteenth Amendment? Political philosophy? (Is political philosophy able to identify objectively "true" or "correct" principles of democracy?) The personal political beliefs of Chief Justice Warren and other members of the Court majority? (If so, is *Reynolds* a valid decision?)
3. Were you persuaded by the majority's rejection of the so-called "federal analogy"? In other words, if it is okay for each state to have equal representation in the U.S. Senate (should it be okay?), then why isn't it okay for each county to have equal representation in a state senate?
4. Based on *Reynolds* itself, do you understand how much deviation from strict compliance with one person, one vote is permissible? In other words, would it be okay for one district to have 110,000 persons, while another district has 90,000? Does the permissibility of such deviation from strict equality depend upon the state's reason for the deviation as well as its (mathematical) extent?
5. Aside from how much deviation from strict equality of population between districts is allowed is a separate question of which *population* statistic should be used in making that assessment. Total population? Voting-age (over 18-years old) population? Citizen voting-age population? Voting-eligible population (i.e., excluding noncitizens, those under 18-years old, and disfranchised felons)? Registered voters? The vast majority of plans drawn to comply with one person, one vote use total population as the baseline for comparison. However, at least in the context of state (as opposed to congressional) legislative districts, it would appear that states have the flexibility to use something other than total population. In *Burns v. Richardson*, 384 U.S. 73, 90-97 (1966), the Supreme Court declined to invalidate Hawaii's legislative plan that used registered voters as a basis for measuring equality amongst legislative districts.

Reynolds and *Lucas* leave the requirement for equal population among districts relatively open-ended. The Court's more recent pronouncements in the one person, one vote area demonstrate how the Court has put a bit more definition into the standards and how the Court's doctrine seems to differentiate between legislative and congressional districts. As the next three cases will demonstrate, the Court has generally allowed for higher deviations in population in state legislative districts than in congressional districts. The next three cases (and the notes that follow) also demonstrate that in both the legislative and congressional districting context, the Court—despite the opportunity to do so—has avoided adopting clear mathematical rules to separate those districting plans that violate one person, one vote from those districting plans that do not.

BROWN v. THOMSON

462 U.S. 835 (1983)

Justice POWELL delivered the opinion of the Court.

[The Wyoming constitution provided that each county should have at least one member of its House of Representatives. The 1980 Census placed Wyoming's total population at 469,557. The plan adopted in 1981 provided for 64 representatives, meaning the ideal population would be 7,377 persons per representative. The maximum deviation for the plan was 89 percent.

Plaintiffs challenged the allocation of one representative to Niobrara, the State's least populous county. Niobrara County had a population of 2,924. In providing Niobrara County with a representative, the state legislature found that "the opportunity for oppression of the people of this state or of any of them is greater if any county is denied representation in the legislature than if each is guaranteed at least (1) representative."]

The issue is whether the State of Wyoming violated the Equal Protection Clause by allocating one of the 64 seats in its House of Representatives to a county the population of which is considerably lower than the average population per state representative.

II

A

In *Reynolds v. Sims,* the Court held that "the Equal Protection Clause requires that the seats in both houses of a bicameral state legislature must be apportioned on a population basis." This holding requires only "that a State make an honest and good faith effort to construct districts ... as nearly of equal population as is practicable," for "it is a practical impossibility to arrange legislative districts so that each one has an identical number of residents, or citizens, or voters." *Id.*

We have recognized that some deviations from population equality may be necessary to permit the States to pursue other legitimate objectives such as "maintain[ing] the integrity of various political subdivisions" and "provid[ing] for compact districts of contiguous territory." *Reynolds.*

In view of these considerations, we have held that minor deviations from mathematical equality among state legislative districts are insufficient to make out a prima facie case of invidious discrimination under the Fourteenth Amendment so as to require justification by the State. Our decisions have established, as a general matter, that an apportionment plan with a maximum population deviation under 10% falls within this category of minor deviations. A plan with larger disparities in population, however, creates a prima facie case of discrimination and therefore must be justified by the State. *See Swann v. Adams* ("*De minimis* deviations are unavoidable, but variations of 30% among senate districts and 40% among house districts can hardly be deemed *de minimis* and none of our cases suggests that differences of this magnitude will be accepted, without a satisfactory explanation grounded on acceptable state policy.") The ultimate inquiry, therefore, is whether the legislature's plan "may reasonably be said to advance [a] rational state policy" and, if so, "whether the population disparities among the districts that have resulted from the pursuit of this plan exceed constitutional limits." *Mahan v. Howell.*

B

In this case there is no question that Niobrara County's deviation from population equality—60% below the mean—is more than minor. There also can be no question that Wyoming's constitutional policy—followed since statehood—of using counties as representative districts and ensuring that each county has one representative is supported by substantial and legitimate state concerns. In *Abate v. Mundt,* the Court held that "a desire to preserve the integrity of political subdivisions may justify an apportionment plan which departs from numerical equality." Indeed, the Court in *Reynolds v. Sims* singled out preservation of political subdivisions as a clearly legitimate policy.

Moreover, it is undisputed that Wyoming has applied this factor in a manner free from any taint of arbitrariness or discrimination. The State's policy of preserving county boundaries is based on the state Constitution, has been followed for decades, and has been applied consistently throughout the State. As the District Court found, this policy has particular force given the peculiar size and population of the State and the nature of its governmental structure. In addition, population equality is the sole other criterion used, and the State's apportionment formula ensures that population deviations are no greater than necessary to preserve counties as representative districts. *See Mahan v. Howell* (evidence is clear that the plan "produces the minimum deviation above and below the norm, keeping intact political boundaries"). Finally, there is no evidence of "a built-in bias tending to favor particular political interests or geographic areas." *Abate v. Mundt.* As Judge Doyle stated below, "there is not the slightest sign of any group of people being discriminated against here. There is no indication that the larger cities or towns are being discriminated against; on the contrary, Cheyenne, Laramie, Casper, Sheridan, are not shown to have suffered in the slightest degree. There has been no preference for the cattle-raising or agricultural areas as such."

In short, this case presents an unusually strong example of an apportionment plan the population variations of which are entirely the result of the consistent and nondiscriminatory application of a legitimate state policy. This does not mean that population deviations of any magnitude necessarily are acceptable. Even a neutral and consistently applied criterion such as use of counties as representative districts can frustrate *Reynolds'* mandate of fair and effective representation if the population disparities are excessively high. "[A] State's policy urged in justification of disparity in district population, however rational, cannot constitutionally be permitted to emasculate the goal of substantial equality." *Mahan v. Howell.* It remains true, however, as the Court in *Reynolds* noted, that consideration must be given "to the character as well as the degree of deviations from a strict population basis." The consistency of application and the neutrality of effect of the nonpopulation criteria must be considered along with the size of the population disparities in determining whether a state legislative apportionment plan contravenes the Equal Protection Clause.

C

Here we are not required to decide whether Wyoming's nondiscriminatory adherence to county boundaries justifies the population deviations that exist throughout Wyoming's representative districts. Appellants deliberately have limited their challenge to the alleged dilution of their voting power resulting from the one representative given to Niobrara County. The issue therefore is not whether a 16% average deviation and an 89% maximum deviation, considering the state apportionment plan as a whole, are constitutionally permissible. Rather, the issue is whether Wyoming's policy of preserving county boundaries justifies the additional deviations from population equality resulting from the provision of representation to Niobrara County.

It scarcely can be denied that in terms of actual effect on appellants' voting power, it matters little whether the 63-member or 64-member House is used. The District Court noted, for example, that the seven counties in which appellants reside will elect 28 representatives under either plan. The only difference, therefore, is whether they elect 43.75% of the legislature (28 of 64 members) or 44.44% of the legislature (28 of 63 members).[10] The District Court aptly described this difference as "de minimis."

We do not suggest that a State is free to create and allocate an additional representative seat in any way it chooses simply because that additional seat will have little or no effect on the remainder of the State's voters. The allocation of a representative to a particular political subdivision still may violate the Equal Protection Clause if it greatly

10. Similarly, appellees note that under the 64-member plan, 46.65% of the State's voters theoretically could elect 51.56% of the representatives. Under the 63-member plan, 46.65% of the population could elect 50.79% of the representatives.

exceeds the population variations existing in the rest of the State and if the State provides no legitimate justifications for the creation of that seat. Here, however, considerable population variations will remain even if Niobrara County's representative is eliminated. Under the 63-member plan, the average deviation per representative would be 13% and the maximum deviation would be 66%. These statistics make clear that the grant of a representative to Niobrara County is not a significant cause of the population deviations that exist in Wyoming.

Moreover, we believe that the differences between the two plans are justified on the basis of Wyoming's longstanding and legitimate policy of preserving county boundaries. Particularly where there is no taint of arbitrariness or discrimination, substantial deference is to be accorded the political decisions of the people of a State acting through their elected representatives. Here it is noteworthy that by enacting the 64-member plan the State ensured that its policy of preserving county boundaries applies nondiscriminatorily. The effect of the 63-member plan would be to deprive the voters of Niobrara County of their own representative, even though the remainder of the House of Representatives would be constituted so as to facilitate representation of the interests of each county. In these circumstances, we are not persuaded that Wyoming has violated the Fourteenth Amendment by permitting Niobrara County to have its own representative.

The judgment of the District Court is *Affirmed.*

Justice O'CONNOR, with whom Justice STEVENS joins, concurring.

By its decisions today in this case and in *Karcher v. Daggett,* the Court upholds, in the former, the allocation of one representative to a county in a state legislative plan with an 89% maximum deviation from population equality and strikes down, in the latter, a congressional reapportionment plan for the State of New Jersey where the maximum deviation is 0.6984%. As a member of the majority in both cases, I feel compelled to explain the reasons for my joinder in these apparently divergent decisions.

In my view, the "one-person, one-vote" principle is the guiding ideal in evaluating both congressional and legislative redistricting schemes. In both situations, however, ensuring equal representation is not simply a matter of numbers. There must be flexibility in assessing the size of the deviation against the importance, consistency, and neutrality of the state policies alleged to require the population disparities.

Both opinions recognize this need for flexibility in examining the asserted state policies. In *Karcher,* New Jersey has not demonstrated that the population variances in congressional districts were necessary to preserve minority voting strength—the only justification offered by the State. Here, by contrast, there can be no doubt that the population deviation resulting from the provision of one representative to Niobrara County is the product of the consistent and nondiscriminatory application of Wyoming's longstanding policy of preserving county boundaries.

In addition, as the Court emphasizes, in this case we are not required to decide whether, and do not suggest that, Wyoming's nondiscriminatory adherence to county boundaries justifies the population deviations that exist throughout Wyoming's representative districts. Thus, the relevant percentage in this case is not the 89% maximum deviation when the State of Wyoming is viewed as a whole, but the additional deviation from equality produced by the allocation of one representative to Niobrara County.

In this regard, I would emphasize a point acknowledged by the majority. Although the maximum deviation figure is not the controlling element in an apportionment challenge, even the consistent and nondiscriminatory application of a legitimate state policy cannot justify substantial population deviations throughout the State where the effect would be to eviscerate the one-person, one-vote principle. In short, as the Court observes, there is clearly some outer limit to the magnitude of the deviation that is constitutionally permissible even in the face of the strongest justifications.

In the past, this Court has recognized that a state legislative apportionment scheme with a maximum population deviation exceeding 10% creates a prima facie case of discrimination. Moreover, in *Mahan v. Howell,* we suggested that a 16.4% maximum deviation "may well approach tolerable limits."[2] I have the gravest doubts that a statewide legislative plan with an 89% maximum deviation could survive constitutional scrutiny despite the presence of the State's strong interest in preserving county boundaries. I join the Court's opinion on the understanding that nothing in it suggests that this Court would uphold such a scheme.

Justice BRENNAN, with whom Justice WHITE, Justice MARSHALL, and Justice BLACKMUN join, dissenting.

[Omitted]

KARCHER v. DAGGETT

462 U.S. 725 (1983)

Justice BRENNAN delivered the opinion of the Court.

The question presented by this appeal is whether an apportionment plan for congressional districts satisfies Art. I, § 2* without need for further justification if the population of the largest district is less than one percent greater than the population of the smallest district. A three-judge District Court declared New Jersey's 1982

2. The Court has recognized that States enjoy a somewhat greater degree of latitude as to population disparities in a state legislative apportionment scheme, which is tested under Equal Protection Clause standards, than in a congressional redistricting scheme, for which the Court has held that Art. I, § 2 of the Constitution provides the governing standard. *White v. Regester* (1973).

* [Art. I § 2 provides, in relevant part, "Representatives . . . shall be apportioned among the several States which may be included within this Union, according to their respective Numbers . . . The actual Enumeration shall be made within three Years after the first Meeting of the Congress of the United States, and within every subsequent Term of ten Years, in such Manner as they shall by Law direct." [—Eds.]

reapportionment plan unconstitutional because the population deviations among districts, although small, were not the result of a good-faith effort to achieve population equality. We affirm.

I

[Following the 1980 Census, the New Jersey legislature passed what was known as the Feldman Plan.] The Feldman Plan contained 14 districts with an average population per district (as determined by the 1980 census) of 526,059. Each district did not have the same population. On the average, each district differed from the "ideal" figure by 0.1384%, or about 726 people. The largest district, the Fourth District, which includes Trenton, had a population of 527,472, and the smallest, the Sixth District, embracing most of Middlesex County, a population of 523,798. The difference between them was 3,674 people, or 0.6984% of the average district.

The Legislature had before it other plans with appreciably smaller population deviations between the largest and smallest districts . . . [One of those plans] had a maximum population difference of 2,375, or 0.4514% of the average figure.

II

Article I, § 2 establishes a "high standard of justice and common sense" for the apportionment of congressional districts: "equal representation for equal numbers of people." *Wesberry v. Sanders* (1964). Precise mathematical equality, however, may be impossible to achieve in an imperfect world; therefore the "equal representation" standard is enforced only to the extent of requiring that districts be apportioned to achieve population equality "as nearly as is practicable." As we explained further in *Kirkpatrick v. Preisler*:

> "[T]he 'as nearly as practicable' standard requires that the State make a good-faith effort to achieve precise mathematical equality. Unless population variances among congressional districts are shown to have resulted despite such effort, the State must justify each variance, no matter how small."

Article I, § 2, therefore, "permits only the limited population variances which are unavoidable despite a good-faith effort to achieve absolute equality, or for which justification is shown." *Id.*

Thus two basic questions shape litigation over population deviations in state legislation apportioning congressional districts. First, the court must consider whether the population differences among districts could have been reduced or eliminated altogether by a good-faith effort to draw districts of equal population. Parties challenging apportionment legislation must bear the burden of proof on this issue, and if they fail to show that the differences could have been avoided the apportionment scheme must be upheld. If, however, the plaintiffs can establish that the population differences were not the result of a good-faith effort to achieve equality, the State must bear the burden of proving that each significant variance between districts was necessary to achieve some legitimate goal.

III

Appellants' principal argument in this case is addressed to the first question described above. They contend that the Feldman Plan should be regarded *per se* as the product of a good-faith effort to achieve population equality because the maximum population deviation among districts is smaller than the predictable undercount in available census data.

A

Kirkpatrick squarely rejected a nearly identical argument. "The whole thrust of the 'as nearly as practicable' approach is inconsistent with adoption of fixed numerical standards which excuse population variances without regard to the circumstances of each particular case." Adopting any standard other than population equality, using the best census data available, would subtly erode the Constitution's ideal of equal representation. If state legislators knew that a certain *de minimis* level of population differences were acceptable, they would doubtless strive to achieve that level rather than equality. Furthermore, choosing a different standard would import a high degree of arbitrariness into the process of reviewing apportionment plans. In this case, appellants argue that a maximum deviation of approximately 0.7% should be considered *de minimis*. If we accept that argument, how are we to regard deviations of 0.8%, 0.95%, 1%, or 1.1%?

Any standard, including absolute equality, involves a certain artificiality. As appellants point out, even the census data are not perfect, and the well-known restlessness of the American people means that population counts for particular localities are outdated long before they are completed. Yet problems with the data at hand apply equally to any population-based standard we could choose. As between two standards—equality or something-less-than equality—only the former reflects the aspirations of Art. I, § 2.

To accept the legitimacy of unjustified, though small population deviations in this case would mean to reject the basic premise of *Kirkpatrick* and *Wesberry*. We decline appellants' invitation to go that far. The unusual rigor of their standard has been noted several times. Because of that rigor, we have required that absolute population equality be the paramount objective of apportionment only in the case of congressional districts, for which the command of Art. I, § 2 as regards the national legislature outweighs the local interests that a State may deem relevant in apportioning districts for representatives to state and local legislatures, but we have not questioned the population equality standard for congressional districts. The principle of population equality for congressional districts has not proved unjust or socially or economically harmful in experience. If anything, this standard should cause less difficulty now for state legislatures than it did when we adopted it in *Wesberry*. The rapid advances in computer technology and education during the last two decades make it relatively simple to draw contiguous districts of equal population and at the same time to further whatever secondary goals the State has. Finally, to abandon unnecessarily a clear and oft-confirmed constitutional interpretation would impair our authority in other cases, would implicitly open the door to a plethora of requests that we reexamine other rules that some may consider burdensome, and would prejudice those who have relied upon the rule of law in seeking an equipopulous congressional apportionment in New Jersey. We thus reaffirm that there are no *de minimis* population variations, which could practicably be avoided, but which nonetheless meet the standard of Art. I, § 2 without justification.[6]

C

Given that the census-based population deviations in the Feldman Plan reflect real differences among the districts, it is clear that they could have been avoided or significantly reduced with a good-faith effort to achieve population equality.

The District Court found that several other plans introduced in the 200th Legislature had smaller maximum deviations than the Feldman Plan. Appellants object that the alternative plans considered by the District Court were not comparable to the Feldman Plan because their political characters differed profoundly. We have never denied that apportionment is a political process, or that state legislatures could pursue legitimate secondary objectives as long as those objectives were consistent with a good-faith effort to achieve population equality at the same time. Nevertheless, the claim that political considerations require population differences among congressional districts belongs more properly to the second level of judicial inquiry in these cases, in which the State bears the burden of justifying the differences with particularity.

In any event, it was unnecessary for the District Court to rest its finding on the existence of alternative plans with radically different political effects. As in *Kirkpatrick,* "resort to the simple device of transferring entire political subdivisions of known population between contiguous districts would have produced districts much closer to numerical equality." Starting with the Feldman Plan itself and the census data available to the Legislature at the time it was enacted, one can reduce the maximum population deviation of the plan merely by shifting a handful of municipalities from one district to another. Thus the District Court did not err in finding that appellees had met their burden of showing that the Feldman Plan did not come as nearly as practicable to population equality.

IV

By itself, the foregoing discussion does not establish that the Feldman Plan is unconstitutional. Rather, appellees' success in proving that the Feldman Plan was not the product

6. Justice White objects that "the rule of absolute equality is perfectly compatible with [gerrymandering] of the worst sort." That may certainly be true to some extent: beyond requiring States to justify population deviations with explicit, precise reasons, which might be expected to have some inhibitory effect, *Kirkpatrick* does little to prevent what is known as gerrymandering.

of a good-faith effort to achieve population equality means only that the burden shifted to the State to prove that the population deviations in its plan were necessary to achieve some legitimate state objective. [W]e are willing to defer to state legislative policies, so long as they are consistent with constitutional norms, even if they require small differences in the population of congressional districts. Any number of consistently applied legislative policies might justify some variance, including, for instance, making districts compact, respecting municipal boundaries, preserving the cores of prior districts, and avoiding contests between incumbent Representatives. As long as the criteria are nondiscriminatory, these are all legitimate objectives that on a proper showing could justify minor population deviations. The State must, however, show with some specificity that a particular objective required the specific deviations in its plan, rather than simply relying on general assertions. The showing required to justify population deviations is flexible, depending on the size of the deviations, the importance of the State's interests, the consistency with which the plan as a whole reflects those interests, and the availability of alternatives that might substantially vindicate those interests yet approximate population equality more closely. By necessity, whether deviations are justified requires case-by-case attention to these factors.

The District Court properly found that appellants did not justify the population deviations in this case. At argument before the District Court and on appeal in this Court, appellants emphasized only one justification for the Feldman Plan's population deviations—preserving the voting strength of racial minority groups. They submitted affidavits from mayors Kenneth Gibson of Newark and Thomas Cooke of East Orange, discussing the importance of having a large majority of black voters in Newark's Tenth District, as well as an affidavit from S. Howard Woodson, Jr., a candidate for mayor of Trenton, [discussing] the Feldman Plan's treatment of black voters in the Trenton and Camden areas. The District Court found, however:

> "[Appellants] have not attempted to demonstrate, nor can they demonstrate, any causal relationship between the goal of preserving minority voting strength in the Tenth District and the population variances in the other districts. . . . We find that the goal of preserving minority voting strength in the Tenth District is not related in any way to the population deviations in the Fourth and Sixth Districts."

Under the Feldman Plan, the largest districts are the Fourth and Ninth Districts, and the smallest are the Third and Sixth. None of these districts borders on the Tenth, and only one—the Fourth—is even mentioned in appellants' discussions of preserving minority voting strength. Nowhere do appellants suggest that the large population of the Fourth District was necessary to preserve minority voting strength; in fact, the deviation between the Fourth District and other districts has the effect of diluting the votes of all residents of that district, including members of racial minorities, as compared with other districts with fewer minority voters. The record is completely silent on the relationship between preserving minority voting strength and the small populations of the Third and Sixth Districts. Therefore, the District Court's findings easily pass the "clearly erroneous" test.

Affirmed.

Justice STEVENS concurring.

[Omitted]

Justice WHITE, with whom THE CHIEF JUSTICE, Justice POWELL, and Justice REHNQUIST join, dissenting.

I respectfully dissent from the Court's unreasonable insistence on an unattainable perfection in the equalizing of congressional districts.

I

One must suspend credulity to believe that the Court's draconian response to a trifling 0.6984% maximum deviation promotes "fair and effective representation" for the people of New Jersey. The requirement that "as nearly as is practicable one man's vote in a congressional election is to be worth as much as another's," *Wesberry v. Sanders* (1964), must be understood in light of the malapportionment in the states at the time *Wesberry* was decided. The plaintiffs in *Wesberry* were voters in a congressional district (pop. 823,680) encompassing Atlanta that was three times larger than Georgia's smallest district (272,154) and more than double the size of an average district. Because the state had not reapportioned for 30 years, the Atlanta District possessing one-fifth of Georgia's population had only one-tenth of the Congressmen. Georgia was not atypical; congressional districts throughout the country had not been redrawn for decades and deviations of over 50% were the rule. These substantial differences in district size diminished, in a real sense, the representativeness of congressional elections. The Court's invalidation of these profoundly unequal districts should not be read as a demand for precise mathematical equality between the districts.

The states responded to *Wesberry* by eliminating gross disparities between congressional districts. Nevertheless, redistricting plans with far smaller variations were struck by the Court five years later in *Kirkpatrick v. Preisler,* and its companion, *Wells v. Rockefeller.* The redistricting statutes before the Court contained total percentage deviations of 5.97% and 13.1%, respectively. But *Wesberry's* "as nearly as practicable" standard was read to require "a good faith effort to achieve precise numerical equality." [*Kirkpatrick*]. Over the objections of four Justices, *Kirkpatrick* rejected the argument that there is a fixed numerical or percentage population variance small enough to be considered *de minimis* and to satisfy the "as nearly as practicable" standard. *Kirkpatrick's* rule was applied by the Court in *White v. Weiser* (1973) to invalidate Texas' redistricting scheme which had a maximum population variance of 4.13%.

Just as *Wesberry* did not require *Kirkpatrick, Kirkpatrick* does not ineluctably lead to the Court's decision today. Although the Court stated that it could see "no nonarbitrary way" to pick a *de minimis* point, the maximum deviation in *Kirkpatrick,* while small, was more than eight times as large as that posed here. Moreover, the deviation in *Kirkpatrick* was not argued to fall within the officially accepted range of statistical imprecision of the census. Accordingly, I do not view the Court's decision today as foreordained by *Kirkpatrick* and *Weiser.*

There can be little question but that the variances in the New Jersey plan are "statistically insignificant." Although the government strives to make the decennial census as accurate as humanly possible, the Census Bureau has never intimated that the results are a perfect count of the American population. The Bureau itself estimates the inexactitude in the taking of the 1970 census at 2.3%, a figure which is considerably larger than the 0.6984% maximum variance in the New Jersey plan, and which dwarfs the 0.2470% difference between the maximum deviations of the selected plan and the leading alternative plan. Because the amount of undercounting differs from district to district, there is no point for a court of law to act under an unproven assumption that such tiny differences between redistricting plans reflect actual differences in population.

Even if the 0.6984% deviation here is not encompassed within the scope of the statistical imprecision of the census, it is miniscule when compared with other variations among the districts inherent in translating census numbers into citizens' votes. First, [d]istrict populations are constantly changing, often at different rates in either direction, up or down. As the Court admits, "the well-known restlessness of the American people means that population counts for particular localities are outdated long before they are completed." Second, far larger differences among districts are introduced because a substantial percentage of the total population is too young to register or is disqualified by alienage. Third, census figures cannot account for the proportion of all those otherwise eligible individuals who fail to register. The differences in the number of eligible voters per district for these reasons overwhelm the minimal variations attributable to the districting plan itself.

Accepting that the census, and the districting plans which are based upon it, cannot be perfect represents no backsliding in our commitment to assuring fair and equal representation in the election of Congress.

If today's decision simply produced an unjustified standard with little practical import, it would be bad enough. Unfortunately, I fear that the Court's insistence that "there are no *de minimis* population variations, which could practicably be avoided, but which nonetheless meet the standard of Art. I, § 2 without justification," invites further litigation of virtually every congressional redistricting plan in the nation. At least twelve states which have completed redistricting on the basis of the 1980 census have adopted plans with a higher deviation than that presented here, and four others have deviations quite similar to New Jersey's. Of course, under the Court's rationale, even Rhode Island's plan—whose two districts have a deviation of 0.02% or about 95 people—would be subject to constitutional attack.

In all such cases, state legislatures will be hard pressed to justify their preference for the selected plan. A good-faith effort to achieve population equality is not enough if the population variances are not "unavoidable." The court must consider whether the population differences could have been further "reduced or eliminated altogether." With the assistance of computers, there will generally be a plan with an even more minimal deviation from the mathematical ideal. Then, "the State must bear the burden of proving that each significant variance between districts was necessary to achieve some legitimate goal." As this case illustrates, literally any variance between districts will be considered "significant."

The state's burden will not be easily met: "the State bears the burden of justifying the differences with particularity." When the state fails to sustain its burden, the result will generally be that a court must select an alternative plan. The choice will often be disputed until the very eve of an election, leaving candidates and voters in a state of confusion.

The only way a legislature or bipartisan commission can hope to avoid litigation will be to dismiss all other legitimate concerns and opt automatically for the districting plan with the smallest deviation. Yet no one can seriously contend that such an inflexible insistence upon mathematical exactness will serve to promote "fair and effective representation." The more likely result of today's extension of *Kirkpatrick* is to move closer to fulfilling Justice Fortas' prophecy that "a legislature might have to ignore the boundaries of common sense, running the congressional district line down the middle of the corridor of an apartment house or even dividing the residents of a single-family house between two districts." Such sterile and mechanistic application only brings the principle of "one man, one vote" into disrepute.

II

One might expect the Court had strong reasons to force this Sisyphean task upon the states. Yet the Court offers no positive virtues that will follow from its decision. No pretense is made that this case follows in the path of *Reynolds* and *Wesberry* in insuring the "fair and effective representation" of citizens. No effort is expended to show that Art. I, § 2's requirement that Congressmen be elected "by the people," *Wesberry v. Sanders*, demands the invalidation of population deviations at this level. Any such absolute requirement, if it did exist, would be irreconcilable with the Court's recognition of certain justifications for population variances. Given no express constitutional basis for the Court's holding, and no showing that the objectives of fair representation are compromised by these minimal disparities, the normal course would be to uphold the actions of the legislature in fulfilling its constitutionally-delegated responsibility to prescribe the manner of holding elections for Senators and Representatives. Doing so would be in keeping with the Court's oft-expressed recognition that apportionment is primarily a matter for legislative judgment.

Instead the Court is purely defensive in support of its decision. The Court refuses to adopt any fixed numerical standard, below which the federal courts would not intervene, asserting that "the principle of population equality for congressional districts has not proved unjust or socially or economically harmful in experience." Of course, the *principle* of population equality is not unjust; the unreasonable *application* of this principle is the rub. Leaving aside that the principle has never been applied with the vengeance witnessed today, there are many, including myself, who take issue with the Court's self-congratulatory assumption that *Kirkpatrick* has been a success. First, a decade of experience with *Kirkpatrick* has shown that the rule of absolute equality is perfectly compatible with "gerrymandering" of the worst sort. With ever more sophisticated computers, legislators can draw countless plans for absolute population equality, but each having its own political ramifications. Although neither a rule of absolute equality nor one of substantial equality can alone prevent deliberate partisan gerrymandering, the former offers legislators a ready justification for disregarding geographical and political boundaries. In addition to providing a patina of respectability for the equipopulous gerrymander, *Kirkpatrick*'s regime assured extensive intrusion of the judiciary into legislative business.

More than a decade's experience with *Kirkpatrick* demonstrates that insistence on precise numerical equality only invites those who lost in the political arena to refight their battles in federal court. Consequently, "[m]ost estimates are that between 25 percent and 35 percent of current house district lines were drawn by the Courts." American Bar Association, Congressional Districting 20 (1981). As I have already noted, by extending *Kirkpatrick* to deviations below even the 1% level, the redistricting plan in every state with more than a single Representative is rendered vulnerable to after-the-fact attack by anyone with a complaint and a calculator.

III

Our cases dealing with state legislative apportionment have taken a more sensible approach. We have recognized that certain small deviations do not, in themselves, ordinarily constitute a *prima facie* constitutional violation. Moreover, we have upheld plans with reasonable variances that were necessary to account for political subdivisions, to preserve the voting strength of minority groups, and to insure political fairness.

Bringing together our legislative and congressional cases does not imply overlooking relevant differences between the two. States normally draw a larger number of legislative districts, which accordingly require a greater margin to account for geographical and political boundaries. "[C]ongressional districts are not so intertwined and freighted with strictly local interests as are state legislative districts." *White v. Weiser*. Furthermore, because Congressional districts are generally much larger than state legislative districts, each percentage point of variation represents a commensurately greater number of people. But these are differences of degree. They suggest that the level at which courts should entertain challenges to districting plans, absent unusual circumstances, should be lower in the congressional cases, but not altogether nonexistent.[14] Although I am not wedded to a precise figure, in light of the current range of population deviations, a 5% cutoff appears reasonable. I would not entertain judicial challenges, absent extraordinary circumstances, where the maximum deviation is less than 5%. Somewhat greater deviations, if rationally related to an important state interest, may also be permissible. Certainly, the maintaining of compact, contiguous districts, the respecting of political subdivisions, and efforts to assure political fairness, constitute such interests.

I would not hold up New Jersey's plan as a model reflection of such interests. Nevertheless, the deviation involved here is *de minimis*, and, regardless of what other infirmities

14. As the law has developed, our congressional cases are rooted in Art. I, § 2 of the Constitution while our legislative cases rely upon the Equal Protection Clause of the Fourteenth Amendment. I am not aware, however, of anything in the respective provisions which justifies, let alone requires, the difference in treatment that has emerged between the two lines of decisions. Our early cases were frequently cross-cited, and the formulation "as nearly of equal population as is practicable" appears in *Reynolds v. Sims*, as well as *Wesberry v. Sanders*.

the plan may have, constitutional or otherwise, there is no violation of Art. I, § 2—the sole issue before us.

Justice POWELL dissenting.

[Omitted]

Figure 1-1

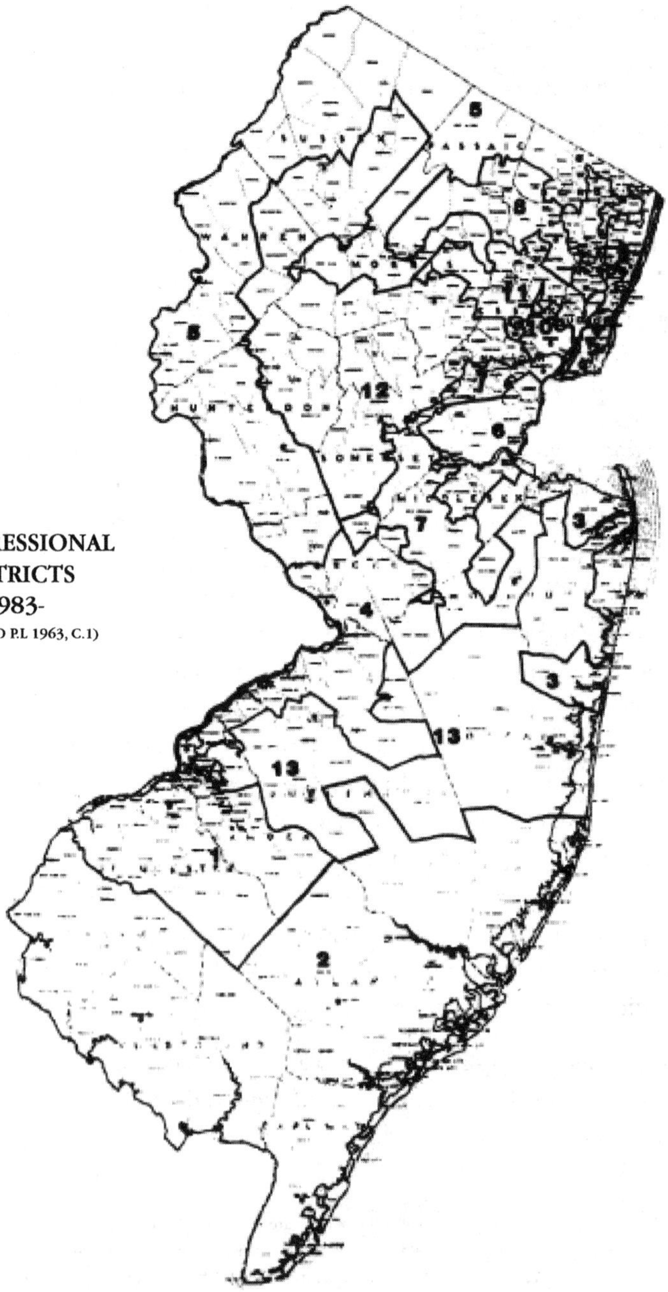

CONGRESSIONAL DISTRICTS 1983-
(Pursuant TO P.L 1963, C.1)

Source: *Daggett v. Kimmelman*, 535 F. Supp. 978, D.C.N.J., 1982.

TENNANT v. JEFFERSON COUNTY COMMISSION

133 S. Ct. 3 (2012)

PER CURIAM.

Plaintiffs in this case claim that West Virginia's 2011 congressional redistricting plan violates the "one person, one vote" principle that we have held to be embodied in Article I, § 2, of the United States Constitution. A three-judge District Court for the Southern District of West Virginia agreed, declaring the plan "null and void" and enjoining West Virginia's Secretary of State from implementing it. The state defendants appealed directly to this Court. Because the District Court misapplied the standard for evaluating such challenges set out in *Karcher v. Daggett*, and failed to afford appropriate deference to West Virginia's reasonable exercise of its political judgment, we reverse.

* * *

Article I, § 2, of the United States Constitution requires that Members of the House of Representatives "be apportioned among the several States . . . according to their respective Numbers" and "chosen every second Year by the People of the several States." In *Wesberry v. Sanders* (1964), we held that these commands require that "as nearly as is practicable one man's vote in a congressional election is to be worth as much as another's." We have since explained that the "as nearly as is practicable" standard does not require that congressional districts be drawn with "precise mathematical equality," but instead that the State justify population differences between districts that could have been avoided by "a good-faith effort to achieve absolute equality." *Karcher*.

Karcher set out a two-prong test to determine whether a State's congressional redistricting plan meets this standard. First, the parties challenging the plan bear the burden of proving the existence of population differences that "could practicably be avoided." If they do so, the burden shifts to the State to "show with some specificity" that the population differences "were necessary to achieve some legitimate state objective." This burden is a "flexible" one, which "depend[s] on the size of the deviations, the importance of the State's interests, the consistency with which the plan as a whole reflects those interests, and the availability of alternatives that might substantially vindicate those interests yet approximate population equality more closely." As we recently reaffirmed, redistricting "ordinarily involves criteria and standards that have been weighed and evaluated by the elected branches in the exercise of their political judgment." *Perry v. Perez*, 565 U.S. ___ (2012) (per curiam). "[W]e are willing to defer to [such] state legislative policies, so long as they are consistent with constitutional norms, even if they require small differences in the population of congressional districts." *Karcher*.

In this case, plaintiffs claim that West Virginia's redistricting plan, adopted following the 2010 decennial United States census, violates Article I, § 2, of the United States Constitution and, separately, the West Virginia Constitution. The 2010 census did not alter West Virginia's allocation of three congressional seats. But due to population shifts within the State, West Virginia nonetheless began redistricting to comply with the requirements in our precedents.

In August 2011, the West Virginia Legislature convened an extraordinary session, and the State Senate formed a 17-member Select Committee on Redistricting. The committee first considered a redistricting plan championed by its chair, Majority Leader John Unger, and dubbed "the Perfect Plan" because it achieved a population difference of a single person between the largest and smallest districts. That appears, however, to have been the only perfect aspect of the Perfect Plan. State legislators expressed concern that the plan contravened the State's longstanding rule against splitting counties, placed two incumbents' residences in the same district, and moved one-third of the State's population from one district to another.

The following day, members of the Redistricting Committee introduced seven additional plans. The committee eventually reported to the full Senate the eighth proposal, referred to as S.B. 1008. The full Senate rejected a ninth proposal offered as an amendment on the floor and adopted S.B. 1008 by a vote of 27 to 4. The House of Delegates approved the bill without debate by a vote of 90 to 5. Governor Bill Tomblin signed the bill into law.

S.B. 1008 does not split county lines, redistrict incumbents into the same district, or require dramatic shifts in the population of the current districts. Indeed, S.B. 1008's chief selling point was that it required very little change to the existing districts: It moved just one county, representing 1.5% of the State's population, from one district to another. This was the smallest shift of any plan considered by the legislature. S.B. 1008, however, has a population variance of 0.79%, the second highest variance of the plans the legislature considered. That is, the population difference between the largest and smallest districts in S.B. 1008 equals 0.79% of the population of the average district.

The Jefferson County Commission and two of its county commissioners sued to enjoin the State from implementing S.B. 1008. At trial, the State conceded that it could have adopted a plan with lower population variations. The State argued, however, that legitimate state policies justified the slightly higher variances in S.B. 1008, citing this Court's statement from *Karcher* that "[a]ny number of consistently applied legislative policies might justify some variance, including, for instance, making districts compact, respecting municipal boundaries, preserving the cores of prior districts, and avoiding contests between incumbent Representatives." The State noted *Karcher*'s approving reference to a District Court opinion upholding a previous West Virginia redistricting plan with a population variance of 0.78%—virtually identical to the variance in S.B. 1008.

The District Court nonetheless granted the injunction, holding that the State's asserted objectives did not justify the population variance. With respect to the objective of not splitting counties, the District Court acknowledged that West Virginia had never in its history divided a county between two or more congressional districts. The court speculated, however, that the practice of other States dividing counties between districts "may portend the eventual deletion" of respecting such boundaries as a potentially legitimate justification for population variances. The court also faulted the West Virginia Legislature for failing "to create a contemporaneous record sufficient to show that S.B. 1008's entire 4,871-person variance—or even a discrete, numerically precise portion thereof—was attributable" to the State's interest in respecting county boundaries and noted that several other plans under consideration also did not split counties.

The court further questioned the State's assertion that S.B. 1008 best preserved the core of existing districts. Preserving the core of a district, the court reasoned, involved respecting the "[s]ocial, cultural, racial, ethnic, and economic interests common to the population of the area," not a "dogged insistence that change be minimized for the benefit of the delicate citizenry." The District Court concluded that although acclimating to a new congressional district and Congressperson "may give rise to a modicum of anxiety and inconvenience, avoiding constituent discomfort at the margins is not among those policies recognized in *Karcher* as capable of legitimizing a variance."

With respect to preventing contests between incumbents, the District Court again faulted the legislature for failing to build a record "linking all or a specific part of the variance" to that asserted interest. And the District Court found that although 0.79% was a minor variation when *Karcher* was decided, the feasibility of achieving smaller variances due to improved technology meant that the same variance must now be considered major.

We stayed the District Court's order pending appeal to this Court, and now reverse.

Given the State's concession that it could achieve smaller population variations, the remaining question under *Karcher* is whether the State can demonstrate that "the population deviations in its plan were necessary to achieve some legitimate state objective." Considering, as *Karcher* instructs, "the size of the deviations, the importance of the State's interests, the consistency with which the plan as a whole reflects those interests, and the availability of alternatives that might substantially vindicate those interests," it is clear that West Virginia has carried its burden.

As an initial matter, the District Court erred in concluding that improved technology has converted a "minor" variation in *Karcher* into a "major" variation today. Nothing about technological advances in redistricting and mapping software has, for example, decreased population variations between a State's counties. Thus, if a State wishes to maintain whole counties, it will inevitably have population variations between districts reflecting the fact that its districts are composed of unevenly populated counties. Despite technological advances, a variance of 0.79% results in no more (or less) vote dilution today than in 1983, when this Court said that such a minor harm could be justified by legitimate state objectives.

Moreover, our cases leave little doubt that avoiding contests between incumbents and not splitting political subdivisions are valid, neutral state districting policies.

The [district court] majority cited no precedent for requiring legislative findings on the "discrete, numerically precise portion" of the variance attributable to each factor, and we are aware of none.

The District Court dismissed the State's interest in limiting the shift of population between old and new districts as "ham-handed," because the State considered only "discrete bounds of geography," rather than "[s]ocial, cultural, racial, ethnic, and economic interests common to the population of the area." According to the District Court, that did not qualify as "preserving the cores of prior districts" under *Karcher*.

Regardless of how to read that language from *Karcher*, however, our opinion made clear that its list of possible justifications for population variations was not exclusive. The desire to minimize population shifts between districts is clearly a valid, neutral state policy. S.B. 1008 achieves significantly lower population shifts than the alternative plans—more than four times lower than the closest alternative, and more than 25 times lower than others.

None of the alternative plans came close to vindicating all three of the State's legitimate objectives while achieving a lower variance. All other plans failed to serve at least one objective as well as S.B. 1008 does; several were worse with respect to two objectives; and the Perfect Plan failed as to all three of the State's objectives. This is not to say that anytime a State must choose between serving an additional legitimate objective and achieving a lower variance, it may choose the former. But here, given the small "size of the deviations," as balanced against "the importance of the State's interests, the consistency with which the plan as a whole reflects those interests," and the lack of available "alternatives that might substantially vindicate those interests yet approximate population equality more closely," *Karcher*, S.B. 1008 is justified by the State's legitimate objectives.

The judgment of the United States District Court for the Southern District of West Virginia is reversed, and the case is remanded for further proceedings consistent with this opinion. (See map at top of next page.)

NOTES ON *BROWN, KARCHER,* AND *TENNANT*

1. *Brown* and *Karcher*, decided the same day, are an odd juxtaposition, as Justice O'Connor acknowledges in her *Brown* concurrence. The Court sustains the Wyoming plan for the state's legislature, even though it deviates sharply from one person, one vote (89 percent maximum deviation). By contrast, the Court invalidates the New Jersey plan for the state's congressional delegation, even though its deviation from one person, one vote is miniscule (0.7 percent).
2. The cases do illustrate a difference in treatment between congressional districts and state legislative districts.

Figure 1-2

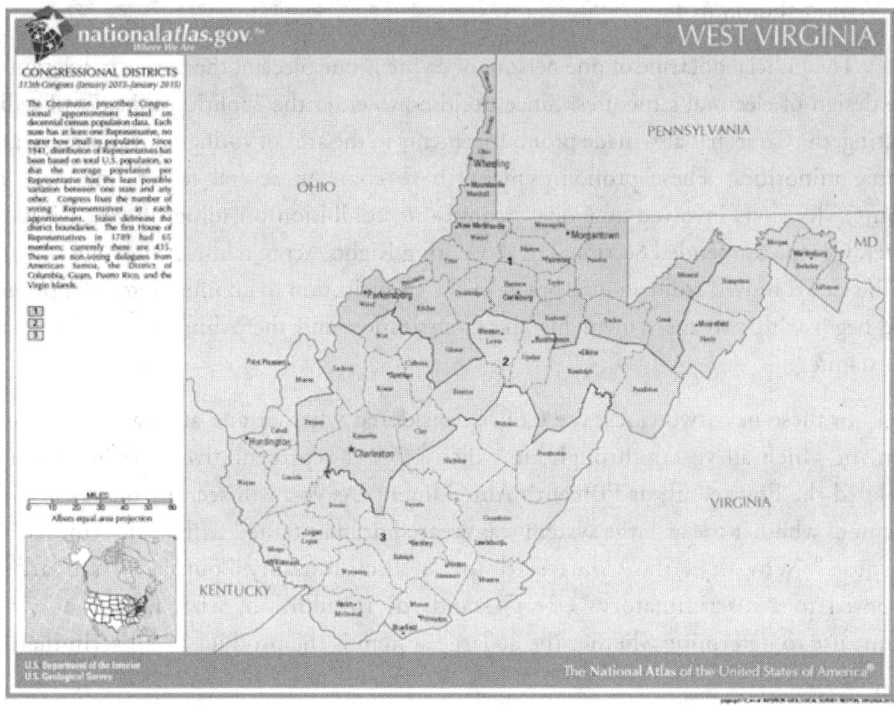

Source: http://nationalatlas.gov/printable/images/pdf/congdist/pagecgd113wv.pdf.

3. When it comes to state legislative (and local) districts, the trend in the cases has been to give state governments a "safe harbor" against a one person, one vote challenge unless the maximum deviation exceeds 10 percent. However, as you will see below in *Larios v. Cox*, 300 F. Supp. 2d. 1320 (N.D. Ga. 2004) (three-judge panel), federal courts have even found state legislative plans that fall below the 10 percent maximum deviation threshold to be unconstitutional. Should the Court create a safe harbor for state legislative districts?
4. When it comes to congressional districts, the trend in the cases—as reflected by *Karcher*—had been to push the deviations toward the minimum. For this reason, during the post-2000 redistricting cycle nearly a third of the states achieved the absolute minimum of population deviation between districts.
5. *Tennant*, however, seems to back off from requiring states to achieve the absolute minimum of population deviation between congressional districts. How much difference is there between *Tennant* and *Karcher*? If there is a difference, is it meaningful? Does *Tennant* give additional flexibility to states in their development of congressional redistricting plans? If so, is providing such flexibility a good idea?

C. Minority Vote Dilution: The Constitution and Section 2 of the Voting Rights Act

The judicial doctrine of one person, one vote is one piece of the puzzle in relation to the design of electoral structures. Since deciding to enter the "political thicket" of redistricting, the Court has also made pronouncements in the area of voting rights for racial and ethnic minorities. These pronouncements have come in several forms. Initially, the Court's decisions involved an Equal Protection prohibition on minority vote dilution. Later, Congress amended Section 2 of the Voting Rights Act to address vote dilution, and so the Court moved from an interpreter of the Constitution to an interpreter of a statute. We begin with two cases involving the Constitution and then shift to cases involving the statute.

In these next two cases, the Court considered whether an "at-large" voting system, in which all voters throughout a district elect representatives for that district, violated the Fourteenth or Fifteenth Amendment. As you will see, the main question becomes whether the at-large system was created or maintained with a "discriminatory purpose." Why does the Court settle on a discriminatory "purpose" standard as opposed to a discriminatory "effect" standard? In addition, what factors does the Court use to determine whether the at-large system is the product of a discriminatory purpose?

CITY OF MOBILE v. BOLDEN

446 U.S. 55 (1980)

Mr. Justice Stewart announced the judgment of the Court and delivered an opinion, in which The Chief Justice, Mr. Justice Powell, and Mr. Justice Rehnquist joined.

The city of Mobile, Ala., has since 1911 been governed by a City Commission consisting of three members elected by the voters of the city at large. The question in this case is whether this at-large system of municipal elections violates the rights of Mobile's Negro voters in contravention of federal statutory or constitutional law.

The appellees brought this suit in the Federal District Court for the Southern District of Alabama as a class action on behalf of all Negro citizens of Mobile.[1] The complaint alleged that the practice of electing the City Commissioners at large unfairly diluted the voting strength of Negroes in violation of § 2 of the Voting Rights Act of 1965, of the Fourteenth Amendment, and of the Fifteenth Amendment. [The district court found for the plaintiffs on both the Fourteenth and Fifteenth Amendment claims and the court of appeals affirmed.]

1. Approximately 35.4 percent of the residents of Mobile are Negro.

I

The three Commissioners jointly exercise all legislative, executive and administrative power in the municipality. They are required after election to designate one of their number as Mayor, a largely ceremonial office, but no formal provision is made for allocating specific executive or administrative duties among the three. As required by the state law enacted in 1911, each candidate for the Mobile City Commission runs for election in the city at large for a term of four years in one of three numbered posts, and may be elected only by a majority of the total vote. This is the same basic electoral system that is followed by literally thousands of municipalities and other local governmental units throughout the Nation.

II

Section 2 of the Voting Rights Act provides:

> "No voting qualification or prerequisite to voting, or standard, practice, or procedure shall be imposed or applied by any State or political subdivision to deny or abridge the right of any citizen of the United States to vote on account of race or color." 42 U.S.C. § 1973.

Assuming, for present purposes, that there exists a private right of action to enforce this statutory provision, it is apparent that the language of § 2 no more than elaborates upon that of the Fifteenth Amendment, and the sparse legislative history of § 2 makes clear that it was intended to have an effect no different from that of the Fifteenth Amendment itself.

III

The Court's early decisions under the Fifteenth Amendment established that it imposes but one limitation on the powers of the States. It forbids them to discriminate against Negroes in matters having to do with voting.

Our decisions, moreover, have made clear that action by a State that is racially neutral on its face violates the Fifteenth Amendment only if motivated by a discriminatory purpose.

The Fifteenth Amendment does not entail the right to have Negro candidates elected, and [precedents of this Court do not] contain[ ] any implication to the contrary. That Amendment prohibits only purposefully discriminatory denial or abridgment by government of the freedom to vote "on account of race, color, or previous condition of servitude." Having found that Negroes in Mobile "register and vote without hindrance," the District Court and Court of Appeals were in error in believing that the appellants invaded the protection of that Amendment in the present case.

IV

The Court of Appeals also agreed with the District Court that Mobile's at-large electoral system violates the Equal Protection Clause of the Fourteenth Amendment. There remains for consideration, therefore, the validity of its judgment on that score.

A

Despite repeated constitutional attacks upon multimember legislative districts, the Court has consistently held that they are not unconstitutional per se. We have recognized, however, that such legislative apportionments could violate the Fourteenth Amendment if their purpose were invidiously to minimize or cancel out the voting potential of racial or ethnic minorities. *See White v. Regester*; *Whitcomb v. Chavis*. To prove such a purpose it is not enough to show that the group allegedly discriminated against has not elected representatives in proportion to its numbers. A plaintiff must prove that the disputed plan was "conceived or operated as [a] purposeful devic[e] to further racial . . . discrimination." [*Whitcomb*.]

This burden of proof is simply one aspect of the basic principle that only if there is purposeful discrimination can there be a violation of the Equal Protection Clause of the Fourteenth Amendment. *See Washington v. Davis*. The Court explicitly indicated in *Washington v. Davis* that this principle applies to claims of racial discrimination affecting voting just as it does to other claims of racial discrimination.

Although dicta may be drawn from a few of the Court's earlier opinions suggesting that disproportionate effects alone may establish a claim of unconstitutional racial voter dilution, the fact is that such a view is not supported by any decision of this Court.

In only one case has the Court sustained a claim that multimember legislative districts unconstitutionally diluted the voting strength of a discrete group. That case was *White v. Regester*. There the Court upheld a constitutional challenge by Negroes and Mexican-Americans to parts of a legislative reapportionment plan adopted by the State of Texas. The plaintiffs alleged that the multimember districts for the two counties in which they resided minimized the effect of their votes in violation of the Fourteenth Amendment, and the Court held that the plaintiffs had been able to "produce evidence to support findings that the political processes leading to nomination and election were not equally open to participation by the group[s] in question." In so holding, the Court relied upon evidence in the record that included a long history of official discrimination against minorities as well as indifference to their needs and interests on the part of white elected officials. The Court also found in each county additional factors that restricted the access of minority groups to the political process. In one county, Negroes effectively were excluded from the process of slating candidates for the Democratic Party, while the plaintiffs in the other county were

Mexican-Americans who "suffer[ed] a cultural and language barrier" that made "participation in community processes extremely difficult, particularly with respect to the political life" of the county.

White v. Regester is thus consistent with "the basic equal protection principle that the invidious equality of a law claimed to be racially discriminatory must ultimately be traced to a racially discriminatory purpose." *Washington v. Davis.*

[I]t is clear that the evidence in the present case fell far short of showing that the appellants "conceived or operated [a] purposeful devic[e] to further racial . . . discrimination."

[T]he District Court based its conclusion of unconstitutionality primarily on the fact that no Negro had ever been elected to the City Commission, apparently because of the pervasiveness of racially polarized voting in Mobile. The trial court also found that city officials had not been as responsive to the interests of Negroes as to those of white persons. On the basis of these findings, the court concluded that the political processes in Mobile were not equally open to Negroes, despite its seemingly inconsistent findings that there were no inhibitions against Negroes becoming candidates, and that in fact Negroes had registered and voted without hindrance. Finally, with little additional discussion, the District Court held that Mobile's at-large electoral system was invidiously discriminating against Negroes in violation of the Equal Protection Clause.

[The evidentiary factors] upon which the District Court and the Court of Appeals relied were most assuredly insufficient to prove an unconstitutionally discriminatory purpose in the present case.

First, the two courts found it highly significant that no Negro had been elected to the Mobile City Commission. From this fact they concluded that the processes leading to nomination and election were not open equally to Negroes. But the District Court's findings of fact, unquestioned on appeal, make clear that Negroes register and vote in Mobile "without hindrance," and that there are no official obstacles in the way of Negroes who wish to become candidates for election to the Commission. It may be that Negro candidates have been defeated but that fact alone does not work a constitutional deprivation.

Second, the District Court relied in part on its finding that the persons who were elected to the Commission discriminated against Negroes in municipal employment and in dispensing public services. If that is the case, those discriminated against may be entitled to relief under the Constitution, albeit of a sort quite different from that sought in the present case. The Equal Protection Clause proscribes purposeful discrimination because of race by any unit of state government, whatever the method of its election. But evidence of discrimination by white officials in Mobile is relevant only as the most tenuous and circumstantial evidence of the constitutional invalidity of the electoral system under which they attained their offices.[20]

Third, the District Court and the Court of Appeals supported their conclusion by drawing upon the substantial history of official racial discrimination in Alabama. But past discrimination cannot, in the manner of original sin, condemn governmental action that is not itself unlawful. The ultimate question remains whether a discriminatory intent has been proved in a given case. More distant instances of official discrimination in other cases are of limited help in resolving that question.

Finally, the District Court and the Court of Appeals pointed to the mechanics of the at-large electoral system itself as proof that the votes of Negroes were being invidiously canceled out. But those features of that electoral system, such as the majority vote requirement, tend naturally to disadvantage any voting minority. They are far from proof that the at-large electoral scheme represents purposeful discrimination against Negro voters.[21]

We turn finally to the arguments advanced in Part I of Mr. Justice Marshall's dissenting opinion. The theory of this dissenting opinion—a theory much more extreme than that espoused by the District Court or the Court of Appeals—appears to be that every "political group," or at least every such group that is in the minority, has a federal constitutional right to elect candidates in proportion to its numbers. Moreover, a political group's "right" to have its candidates elected is said to be a "fundamental interest," the infringement of which may be established without proof that a State has acted with the purpose of impairing anybody's access to the political process. This dissenting opinion finds the "right" infringed in the present case because no Negro has been elected to the Mobile City Commission.

Whatever appeal the dissenting opinion's view may have as a matter of political theory, it is not the law. The Equal Protection Clause of the Fourteenth Amendment does not require proportional representation as an imperative of political organization.

20. Among the difficulties with the District Court's view of the evidence was its failure to identify the state officials whose intent it considered relevant in assessing the invidiousness of Mobile's system of government.

21. According to the District Court, voters in the city of Mobile are represented in the state legislature by three state senators, any one of whom can veto proposed local legislation under the existing courtesy rule. Likewise, a majority of Mobile's 11-member House delegation can prevent a local bill from reaching the floor for debate. Unanimous approval of a local measure by the city delegation, on the other hand, virtually assures passage.

There was evidence in this case that several proposals that would have altered the form of Mobile's municipal government have been defeated in the state legislature, including at least one that would have permitted Mobile to govern itself through a Mayor and City Council with members elected from individual districts within the city. Whether it may be possible ultimately to prove that Mobile's present governmental and electoral system has been retained for a racially discriminatory purpose, we are in no position now to say.

The entitlement that the dissenting opinion assumes to exist simply is not to be found in the Constitution of the United States.

The dissenting opinion erroneously discovers the asserted entitlement to group representation within the "one person, one vote" principle of *Reynolds v. Sims*, and its progeny. Those cases established that the Equal Protection Clause guarantees the right of each voter to "have his vote weighted equally with those of all other citizens." The Court recognized that a voter's right to "have an equally effective voice" in the election of representatives is impaired where representation is not apportioned substantially on a population basis. In such cases, the votes of persons in more populous districts carry less weight than do those of persons in smaller districts. There can be, of course, no claim that the "one person, one vote" principle has been violated in this case, because the city of Mobile is a unitary electoral district and the Commission elections are conducted at large. It is therefore obvious that nobody's vote has been "diluted" in the sense in which that word was used in the *Reynolds* case.

The dissenting opinion places an extraordinary interpretation on these decisions, an interpretation not justified by *Reynolds v. Sims* itself or by any other decision of this Court. It is, of course, true that the right of a person to vote on an equal basis with other voters draws much of its significance from the political associations that its exercise reflects, but it is an altogether different matter to conclude that political groups themselves have an independent constitutional claim to representation. And the Court's decisions hold squarely that they do not.

The fact is that the Court has sternly set its face against the claim, however phrased, that the Constitution somehow guarantees proportional representation. In *Whitcomb v. Chavis*, the trial court had found that a multimember state legislative district had invidiously deprived Negroes and poor persons of rights guaranteed them by the Constitution, notwithstanding the absence of any evidence whatever of discrimination against them. Reversing the trial court, this Court said:

> "The District Court's holding, although on the facts of this case limited to guaranteeing one racial group representation, is not easily contained. It is expressive of the more general proposition that any group with distinctive interests must be represented in legislative halls if it is numerous enough to command at least one seat and represents a majority living in an area sufficiently compact to constitute a single-member district. This approach would make it difficult to reject claims of Democrats, Republicans, or members of any political organization in Marion County who live in what would be safe districts in a single-member district system but who in one year or another, or year after year, are submerged in a one-sided multi-member district vote. There are also union oriented workers, the university community, religious or ethnic groups occupying identifiable areas of our heterogeneous cities and urban areas. Indeed, it would be difficult for a great many, if not

most, multi-member districts to survive analysis under the District Court's view unless combined with some voting arrangement such as proportional representation or cumulative voting aimed at providing representation for minority parties or interests. At the very least, affirmance of the District Court would spawn endless litigation concerning the multi-member district systems now widely employed in this country."

V

The judgment is reversed, and the case is remanded to the Court of Appeals for further proceedings.

It is so ordered.

Mr. Justice BLACKMUN, concurring in the result.

[Justice Blackmun assumed proof of intent was necessary to prevail on a vote dilution claim and was "inclined to agree with" Justice White that purposeful discrimination had been proved in this instance. However, Justice Blackmun concurred in the result because the lower courts had ordered an incorrect remedy.]

Mr. Justice STEVENS, concurring in the judgment.

[Justice Stevens would have found no constitutional violation but would have analyzed the case under a different framework than Justice Stewart.]

Mr. Justice WHITE, dissenting.

In *White v. Regester* (1973), this Court unanimously held the use of multimember districts for the election of state legislators in two counties in Texas violated the Equal Protection Clause of the Fourteenth Amendment because, based on a careful assessment of the totality of the circumstances, they were found to exclude Negroes and Mexican-Americans from effective participation in the political processes in the counties. Without questioning the vitality of *White v. Regester* and our other decisions dealing with challenges to multimember districts by racial or ethnic groups, the Court today inexplicably rejects a similar holding based on meticulous factual findings and scrupulous application of the principles of these cases by both the District Court and the Court of Appeals. The Court's decision is flatly inconsistent with *White v. Regester* and it cannot be understood to flow from our recognition in *Washington v. Davis* that the Equal Protection Clause forbids only purposeful discrimination. Both the District Court and the Court of Appeals properly found that an invidious discriminatory purpose could be inferred from the totality of facts in this case. The Court's cryptic rejection of their conclusions ignores the principles that an invidious discriminatory purpose can be inferred from objective factors of the kind relied on in *White v. Regester* and that the trial courts are in a special position to make such intensely local appraisals.

I

Prior to our decision in *White v. Regester*, we upheld a number of multimember districting schemes against constitutional challenges, but we consistently recognized that such apportionment schemes could constitute invidious discrimination "where the circumstances of a particular case may operate to minimize or cancel out the voting strength of racial or political elements of the voting population." [*Whitcomb.*]

Relying on this principle, in *White v. Regester* we unanimously upheld a District Court's conclusion that the use of multimember districts in Dallas and Bexar Counties in Texas violated the Equal Protection Clause in the face of findings that they excluded Negroes and Mexican-Americans from effective participation in the political processes.

II

In the instant case the District Court and the Court of Appeals faithfully applied the principles of *White v. Regester* in assessing whether the maintenance of a system of at-large elections for the selection of Mobile City Commissioners denied Mobile Negroes their Fourteenth and Fifteenth Amendment rights. Scrupulously adhering to our admonition that "[t]he plaintiffs' burden is to produce evidence to support findings that the political processes leading to nomination and election were not equally open to participation by the group in question," the District Court conducted a detailed factual inquiry into the openness of the candidate selection process to blacks. The court noted that "Mobile blacks were subjected to massive official and private racial discrimination until the Voting Rights Act of 1965" and that "[t]he pervasive effects of past discrimination still substantially affec[t] black political participation." Although the District Court noted that "[s]ince the Voting Rights Act of 1965, blacks register and vote without hindrance," the court found that "local political processes are not equally open" to blacks. Despite the fact that Negroes constitute more than 35% of the population of Mobile, no Negro has ever been elected to the Mobile City Commission. The plaintiffs introduced extensive evidence of severe racial polarization in voting patterns during the 1960's and 1970's with "white voting for white and black for black if a white is opposed to a black," resulting in the defeat of the black candidate or, if two whites are running, the defeat of the white candidate most identified with blacks. Regression analyses covering every City Commission race in 1965, 1969, and 1973, both the primary and general election of the county commission in 1968 and 1972, selected school board races in 1962, 1966, 1970, 1972, and 1974, city referendums in 1963 and 1973, and a countywide legislative race in 1969 confirmed the existence of severe bloc voting. Nearly every active candidate for public office testified that because of racial polarization "it is highly unlikely that anytime in the foreseeable future, under the at-large system, . . . a black can be elected against a white." After single-member districts were created in Mobile County for state legislative elections, "three blacks of the present fourteen member Mobile County delegation have been elected." Based on the foregoing evidence, the District Court found "that the structure of the at-large election of city commissioners combined with strong racial polarization of Mobile's electorate continues to effectively discourage qualified black citizens from seeking office or being elected thereby denying blacks equal access to the slating or candidate selection process."

The District Court also reviewed extensive evidence that the City Commissioners elected under the at-large system have not been responsive to the needs of the Negro community. The court found that city officials have been unresponsive to the interests of Mobile Negroes in municipal employment, appointments to boards and committees, and the provision of municipal services in part because of "the political fear of a white backlash vote when black citizens' needs are at stake." The court also found that there is no clear-cut state policy preference for at-large elections and that past discrimination affecting the ability of Negroes to register and to vote "has helped preclude the effective participation of blacks in the election system today." The adverse impact of the at-large election system on minorities was found to be enhanced by the large size of the citywide election district, the majority vote requirement, the provision that candidates run for positions by place or number, and the lack of any provision for at-large candidates to run from particular geographical subdistricts.

III

Because I believe that the findings of the District Court amply support an inference of purposeful discrimination in violation of the Fourteenth and Fifteenth Amendments, I respectfully dissent.

Mr. Justice BRENNAN, dissenting.

[Justice Brennan would have held that proof of discriminatory impact was sufficient to prove a constitutional violation. In the alternative, Justice Brennan would have found that plaintiffs had proved discriminatory purpose.]

Mr. Justice MARSHALL, dissenting.

[Justice Marshall would have held that discriminatory impact was enough to prove a constitutional violation. Justice Marshall also agreed that even if Justice Stewart's standard for discriminatory purpose were correct, the plaintiffs had proven a discriminatory purpose.]

ROGERS v. LODGE

458 U.S. 613 (1982)

Justice WHITE delivered the opinion of the Court.

The issue in this case is whether the at-large system of elections in Burke County, Ga., violates the Fourteenth Amendment rights of Burke County's black citizens.

I

Burke County is a large, predominately rural county located in eastern Georgia. Eight hundred and thirty-one square miles in area, it is approximately two-thirds the size of the State of Rhode Island. According to the 1980 census, Burke County had a total population of 19,349, of whom 10,385, or 53.6%, were black. The average age of blacks living there is lower than the average age of whites and therefore whites constitute a slight majority of the voting age population. As of 1978, 6,373 persons were registered to vote in Burke County, of whom 38% were black.

The Burke County Board of Commissioners governs the county. It was created in 1911, and consists of five members elected at large to concurrent 4-year terms by all qualified voters in the county. The county has never been divided into districts, either for the purpose of imposing a residency requirement on candidates or for the purpose of requiring candidates to be elected by voters residing in a district. In order to be nominated or elected, a candidate must receive a majority of the votes cast in the primary or general election, and a runoff must be held if no candidate receives a majority in the first primary or general election. Each candidate must run for a specific seat on the Board, and a voter may vote only once for any candidate. No Negro has ever been elected to the Burke County Board of Commissioners.

[The lower courts found that the at-large system was maintained for a discriminatory purpose, and we now affirm.]

II

At-large voting schemes and multimember districts tend to minimize the voting strength of minority groups by permitting the political majority to elect all representatives of the district. A distinct minority, whether it be a racial, ethnic, economic, or political group, may be unable to elect any representatives in an at-large election, yet may be able to elect several representatives if the political unit is divided into single-member districts. The minority's voting power in a multimember district is particularly diluted when bloc voting occurs and ballots are cast along strict majority-minority lines.

Arlington Heights and *Washington v. Davis* both rejected the notion that a law is invalid under the Equal Protection Clause simply because it may affect a greater proportion of one race than another. However, both cases recognized that discriminatory intent need not be proved by direct evidence. "Necessarily, an invidious discriminatory purpose may often be inferred from the totality of the relevant facts, including the fact, if it is true, that the law bears more heavily on one race than another." Thus determining the existence of a discriminatory purpose "demands a sensitive inquiry into such circumstantial and direct evidence of intent as may be available."

[Here, we reject the argument that the lower courts failed to apply the proper legal standard and conclude that the lower courts did apply the discriminatory purpose standard.]

III

A

We are also unconvinced that we should disturb the District Court's finding that the at-large system in Burke County was being maintained for the invidious purpose of diluting the voting strength of the black population.

B

The District Court found that blacks have always made up a substantial majority of the population in Burke County, but that they are a distinct minority of the registered voters. There was also overwhelming evidence of bloc voting along racial lines. Hence, although there had been black candidates, no black had ever been elected to the Burke County Commission. These facts bear heavily on the issue of purposeful discrimination. Voting along racial lines allows those elected to ignore black interests without fear of political consequences, and without bloc voting the minority candidates would not lose elections solely because of their race. Because it is sensible to expect that at least some blacks would have been elected in Burke County, the fact that none have ever been elected is important evidence of purposeful exclusion.

Under our cases, however, such facts are insufficient in themselves to prove purposeful discrimination absent other evidence such as proof that blacks have less opportunity to participate in the political processes and to elect candidates of their choice. Both the District Court and the Court of Appeals thought the supporting proof in this case was sufficient to support an inference of intentional discrimination.

The District Court began by determining the impact of past discrimination on the ability of blacks to participate effectively in the political process. Past discrimination was found to contribute to low black voter registration, because prior to the Voting Rights Act of 1965, blacks had been denied access to the political process by means such as literacy tests, poll taxes, and white primaries. The result was that "Black suffrage in Burke County was virtually non-existent." Black voter registration in Burke County has increased following the Voting Rights Act to the point that some 38% of blacks eligible to vote are registered to do so. On that basis the District Court inferred that "past discrimination has had an adverse effect on black voter registration which lingers to this date." Past discrimination against blacks in education also had the same effect. Not only did Burke County schools discriminate against blacks as recently as 1969, but also some schools still remain essentially segregated and blacks as a group have completed less formal education than whites.

The District Court found further evidence of exclusion from the political process. Past discrimination had prevented blacks from effectively participating in Democratic Party affairs and in primary elections. Until this lawsuit was filed, there had never been a black member of the County Executive Committee of the Democratic Party. There were also property ownership requirements that made it difficult for blacks to serve as chief registrar in the county. There had been discrimination in the selection of grand jurors, the hiring of county employees, and in the appointments to boards and committees which oversee the county government. The District Court thus concluded that historical discrimination had restricted the present opportunity of blacks effectively to participate in the political process. Evidence of historical discrimination is relevant to drawing an inference of purposeful discrimination, particularly in cases such as this one where the evidence shows that discriminatory practices were commonly utilized, that they were abandoned when enjoined by courts or made illegal by civil rights legislation, and that they were replaced by laws and practices which, though neutral on their face, serve to maintain the status quo.

Extensive evidence was cited by the District Court to support its finding that elected officials of Burke County have been unresponsive and insensitive to the needs of the black community, which increases the likelihood that the political process was not equally open to blacks. This evidence ranged from the effects of past discrimination which still haunt the county courthouse to the infrequent appointment of blacks to county boards and committees; the overtly discriminatory pattern of paving county roads; the reluctance of the county to remedy black complaints, which forced blacks to take legal action to obtain school and grand jury desegregation; and the role played by the County Commissioners in the incorporation of an all-white private school to which they donated public funds for the purchase of band uniforms.

The District Court also considered the depressed socio-economic status of Burke County blacks. It found that proportionately more blacks than whites have incomes below the poverty level. Nearly 53% of all black families living in Burke County had incomes equal to or less than three-fourths of a poverty-level income. Not only have blacks completed less formal education than whites, but also the education they have received "was qualitatively inferior to a marked degree." Blacks tend to receive less pay than whites, even for similar work, and they tend to be employed in menial jobs more often than whites. Seventy-three percent of houses occupied by blacks lacked all or some plumbing facilities; only 16% of white-occupied houses suffered the same deficiency. The District Court concluded that the depressed socio-economic status of blacks results in part from "the lingering effects of past discrimination."

Although finding that the state policy behind the at-large electoral system in Burke County was "neutral in origin," the District Court concluded that the policy "has been subverted to invidious purposes." As a practical matter, maintenance of the state statute providing for at-large elections in Burke County is determined by Burke County's state representatives, for the legislature defers to their wishes on matters of purely local application. The court found that Burke County's state representatives "have retained a system which has minimized the ability of Burke County Blacks to participate in the political system."

The trial court considered, in addition, several factors which this Court has indicated enhance the tendency of multimember districts to minimize the voting strength of racial minorities. It found that the sheer geographic size of the county, which is nearly two-thirds the size of Rhode Island, "has made it more difficult for Blacks to get to polling places or to campaign for office." The court concluded, as a matter of law, that the size of the county tends to impair the access of blacks to the political process. The majority vote requirement, was found "to submerge the will of the minority" and thus "deny the minority's access to the system." The court also found the requirement that candidates run for specific seats enhances appellee's lack of access because it prevents a cohesive political group from concentrating on a single candidate. Because Burke County has no residency requirement, "[a]ll candidates could reside in Waynesboro, or in 'lilly-white' [sic] neighborhoods. To that extent, the denial of access becomes enhanced."

None of the District Court's findings underlying its ultimate finding of intentional discrimination appears to us to be clearly erroneous; and as we have said, we decline to overturn the essential finding of the District Court, agreed to by the Court of Appeals, that the at-large system in Burke County has been maintained for the purpose of denying blacks equal access to the political processes in the county.

IV

We also find no reason to overturn the relief ordered by the District Court. Neither the District Court nor the Court of Appeals discerned any special circumstances that would militate against utilizing single-member districts.

The judgment of the Court of Appeals is

Affirmed.

Justice POWELL, with whom Justice REHNQUIST joins, dissenting.

Mobile v. Bolden establishes that an at-large voting system must be upheld against constitutional attack unless maintained for a discriminatory purpose. In *Mobile* we reversed a finding of unconstitutional vote dilution because the lower courts had relied on factors insufficient as a matter of law to establish discriminatory intent. The District Court and Court of Appeals in this case based their findings of unconstitutional discrimination on the same factors held insufficient in *Mobile*. Yet the Court now finds their conclusion unexceptionable. The *Mobile* plurality also affirmed that the concept of "intent" was no mere fiction, and held that the District Court had erred in "its failure to identify the state officials whose intent it considered relevant." Although the courts below did not answer that question in this case, the Court today affirms their decision.

Whatever the wisdom of *Mobile*, the Court's opinion cannot be reconciled persuasively with that case. Because I believe that *Mobile* controls this case, I dissent.

Justice STEVENS, dissenting.

In my opinion, this case raises questions that encompass more than the immediate plight of disadvantaged black citizens. I believe the Court errs by holding the structure of the local governmental unit unconstitutional without identifying an acceptable, judicially manageable standard for adjudicating cases of this kind.

I

The Court's entry into the business of electoral reapportionment in 1962 was preceded by a lengthy and scholarly debate over the role the judiciary legitimately could play in what Justice Frankfurter described as a "political thicket." In that case, decided in 1946, the Court declined to entertain a challenge to single-member congressional districts in Illinois that had been created in 1901 and had become grossly unequal by reason of the great growth in urban population.

In 1962, the Court changed course. In another challenge to the constitutionality of a 1901 districting statute, it held that the political question doctrine did not foreclose judicial review. That decision represents one of the great landmarks in the history of this Court's jurisprudence.

Two aspects of the Court's opinion in *Baker v. Carr* are of special relevance to the case the Court decides today. First, the Court's scholarly review of the political question doctrine focused on the dominant importance of satisfactory standards for judicial determination. Second, the Court's articulation of the relevant constitutional standard made no reference to subjective intent. The host of cases that have arisen in the wake of *Baker v. Carr* have shared these two characteristics. They have formulated, refined, and applied a judicially manageable standard that has become known as the one-person, one-vote rule; they have attached no significance to the subjective intent of the decisionmakers who adopted or maintained the official rule under attack.

In reviewing the constitutionality of the structure of a local government, two quite different methods of analysis could be employed. The Court might identify the specific features of the government that raise constitutional concerns and decide whether, singly or in combination, they are valid. This is the approach the Court has used in testing the constitutionality of rules conditioning the right to vote on payment of a poll tax, imposing burdens on independent candidates, denying new residents or members of the Armed Forces the right to vote, prohibiting crossovers in party primaries, requiring political candidates to pay filing fees, and disadvantaging minority parties in Presidential elections. In none of these cases did the validity of the electoral procedure turn on whether the legislators who enacted the rule subjectively intended to discriminate against minority voters. Under the approach employed by the Court in those cases, the objective circumstances that led to a declaration that an election procedure was unconstitutional would invalidate a similar law wherever it might be found.

Alternatively, the Court could employ a subjective approach under which the constitutionality of a challenged procedure depends entirely on federal judges' appraisals of the reasons why particular localities have chosen to govern themselves in a particular way.

The Constitution would simply protect a right to have an electoral machinery established and maintained without the influence of impermissible factors. Constitutional challenges to identical procedures in neighboring communities could produce totally different results, for the subjective motivations of the legislators who enacted the procedures—or at least the admissible evidence that might be discovered concerning such motivation—could be quite different.

In deciding the question presented in this case, the Court abruptly rejects the former approach and considers only the latter. It starts from the premise that Burke County's at-large method of electing its five county commissioners is, on its face, unobjectionable. The otherwise valid system is unconstitutional, however, because it makes it more difficult for the minority to elect commissioners and because the majority that is now in power has maintained the system for that very reason. Two factors are apparently of critical importance: (1) the intent of the majority to maintain control; and (2) the racial character of the minority.

I am troubled by each aspect of the Court's analysis. In my opinion, the question whether Burke County's at-large system may survive scrutiny under a purely objective analysis is not nearly as easy to answer as the Court implies. Assuming, however, that the system is otherwise valid, I do not believe that the subjective intent of the persons who adopted the system in 1911, or the intent of those who have since declined to change it, can determine its constitutionality. Even if the intent of the political majority were the controlling constitutional consideration, I could not agree that the only political groups that are entitled to protection under the Court's rule are those defined by racial characteristics.

II

At-large voting systems generally tend to maximize the political power of the majority. There are, however, many types of at-large electoral schemes. Three features of Burke County's electoral system are noteworthy, not in my opinion because they shed special light on the subjective intent of certain unidentified people, but rather because they make it especially difficult for a minority candidate to win an election. First, although the qualifications and the duties of the office are identical for all five commissioners, each runs for a separately designated position. Second, in order to be elected, each commissioner must receive a majority of all votes cast in the primary and in the general election; if the leading candidate receives only a plurality, a runoff election must be held. Third, there are no residency requirements; thus, all candidates could reside in a single, all-white neighborhood.

Even if one assumes that a system of local government in which power is concentrated in the hands of a small group of persons elected from the community at large is an acceptable—or perhaps even a preferred—form of municipal government, it is not immediately apparent that these additional features that help to perpetuate the power of an entrenched majority are either desirable or legitimate. If the only purpose these features serve—particularly when viewed in combination—is to assist a dominant party to maintain its political power, they are no more legitimate than the Tennessee districts described in *Baker v. Carr* as "no policy, but simply arbitrary and capricious action." Unless these features are independently justified, they may be invalid simply because there is no legitimate justification for their impact on minority participation in elections.

In this case, appellees have not argued—presumably because they assumed that this Court's many references to the requirement of proving an improper motive in equal protection cases are controlling in this new context—that the special features of Burke County's at-large system have such an adverse impact on the minority's opportunity to participate in the political process that this type of government deprives the minority of equal protection of the law. Nor have the appellants sought to identify legitimate local policies that might justify the use of such rules. As a result, this record does not provide an adequate basis for determining the validity of Burke County's governmental structure on the basis of traditional objective standards.

If the governmental structure were itself found to lack a legitimate justification, inquiry into subjective intent would clearly be unnecessary. Under the Court's analysis, however, the characteristics of the particular form of government under attack are virtually irrelevant. Not only would the Court's approach uphold an arbitrary—but not invidious—system that lacked independent justification, it would invalidate—if a discriminatory intent were proved—a local rule that would be perfectly acceptable absent a showing of invidious intent. The Court's standard applies not only to Burke County and to multimember districts, but to any other form of government as well.

III

Ever since I joined the Court, I have been concerned about the Court's emphasis on subjective intent as a criterion for constitutional adjudication. Although that criterion is often regarded as a restraint on the exercise of judicial power, it may in fact provide judges with a tool for exercising power that otherwise would be confined to the legislature. My principal concern with the subjective-intent standard, however, is unrelated to the quantum of power it confers upon the judiciary. It is based on the quality of that power. For in the long run constitutional adjudication that is premised on a case-by-case appraisal of the subjective intent of local decisionmakers cannot possibly satisfy the requirement of impartial administration of the law that is embodied in the Equal Protection Clause of the Fourteenth Amendment.

The costs and the doubts associated with litigating questions of motive, which are often significant in routine trials, will be especially so in cases involving the "motives" of legislative bodies. Often there will be no evidence that the governmental system was adopted for a discriminatory reason. The reform movement in municipal government or an attempt to comply with the strictures of *Reynolds v. Sims*, may account for the enactment of countless at-large systems. In such a case the question becomes whether the system was maintained for a discriminatory purpose. Whose intentions control? Obviously not the voters, although they may be most responsible for the attitudes and actions of local government. Assuming that it is the intentions of the "state actors" that is critical, how will their mental processes be discovered? Must a specific proposal for change be defeated? What if different motives are held by different legislators or, indeed, by a single official? Is a selfish desire to stay in office sufficient to justify a failure to change a governmental system?

The Court avoids these problems by failing to answer the very question that its standard asks. Presumably, according to the Court's analysis, the Burke County governmental structure is unconstitutional because it was maintained at some point for an invidious purpose. Yet the Court scarcely identifies the manner in which changes to a county governmental structure are made. There is no reference to any unsuccessful attempt to replace the at-large system with single-member districts. It is incongruous that subjective intent is identified as the constitutional standard and yet the persons who allegedly harbored an improper intent are never identified or mentioned. Undoubtedly, the evidence relied on by the Court proves that racial prejudice has played an important role in the history of Burke County and has motivated many wrongful acts by various community leaders. But unless that evidence is sufficient to prove that every governmental action was motivated by a racial animus—and may be remedied by a federal court—the Court has failed under its own test to demonstrate that the governmental structure of Burke County was maintained for a discriminatory purpose.

Moreover, in my opinion the Court is incorrect in assuming that the intent of elected officials is invidious when they are motivated by a desire to retain control of the local political machinery. For such an intent is surely characteristic of politicians throughout the country. But if a political majority's intent to maintain control of a legitimate local government is sufficient to invalidate any electoral device that makes it more difficult for a minority group to elect candidates—regardless of the nature of the interest that gives the minority group cohesion—the Court is not just entering a "political thicket"; it is entering a vast wonderland of judicial review of political activity.

IV

I respectfully dissent.

NOTES ON *BOLDEN* AND *ROGERS*

1. As *Bolden* and *Rogers* indicate, the contours of the constitutional right prohibiting vote dilution have progressed in a nonlinear fashion. Initially, in *Whitcomb v. Chavis*, 403 U.S. 124 (1971), the Court recognized an equal protection right to an undiluted vote for minority voters. However, in that case, which involved a challenge by African-American plaintiffs to at-large elections used to elect state legislators in Marion County, Indiana, the Court declined to find a constitutional violation. The primary rationale for the Court's decision in

Whitcomb was that the minority plaintiffs were losing not for racial reasons but rather for political reasons. In other words, plaintiffs were losing elections not because they were African-Americans but because they were Democrats and Republicans were winning.

2. A couple of years later, though, in *White v. Regester*, 412 U.S. 755 (1973), the Court found vote dilution in the context of a challenge to the election of state legislators in two regions of Texas—Dallas and Bexar Counties (Bexar County encompasses San Antonio). In that case, the Court looked at a panoply of factors to conclude that minority vote dilution had occurred. Both *Whitcomb* and *White* are discussed in the *Bolden* opinions you read.
3. Justice White's dissent in *Bolden* criticizes Justice Stewart's plurality opinion for abandoning the approach the Court had previously taken in *White v. Regester*. In *Bolden*, both Justice Stewart and Justice White are applying the same legal standard—a standard of discriminatory purpose. What is the difference in the application of those standards in their opinions?
4. The approach by Justice Stewart in *Bolden* was highly criticized. In 1982, Congress amended Section 2 of the Voting Rights Act. Under amended Section 2, a court should find vote dilution whenever there discriminatory "results."
5. Since passage of amended Section 2, most of the action in redistricting litigation related to vote dilution has been resolved under the statutory framework of the Voting Rights Act rather than the Equal Protection Clause. (The next two cases in this book involve vote dilution claims under Section 2 of the Voting Rights Act.) The fact that most litigation has been resolved under Section 2 does not, however, mean that vote dilution under the Equal Protection Clause has no modern relevance. As you will see when you read about Sections 5 and 3(c) of the Voting Rights Act in the next section of this casebook, discriminatory purpose under the Constitution still has a role to play in Voting Rights Act cases.
6. *Rogers* is interesting because it is the Supreme Court's most recent direct statement about what constitutes discriminatory purpose in the redistricting context. In addition, as Justice Powell notes, *Rogers* seems to be directly contrary to the plurality opinion in *Bolden* even though it does not overrule *Bolden*. Which approach is best—Justice Stewart's in *Mobile*, Justice White's in both cases, or Justice Stevens's opinion in *Rogers* that searches for a standard not tethered to discriminatory purpose?

As you just read, in *City of Mobile v. Bolden*, a plurality of the Supreme Court held that Section 2 of the Voting Rights Act as originally passed in 1965 could be used only to strike down laws involving individual electoral participation (i.e., laws aimed directly at voter registration and casting ballots at polling places) that were adopted with a purpose to discriminate. Congress reacted to *Bolden* by amending Section 2 to allow challenges to electoral structures that have discriminatory "results." As you will see in *Holder v. Hall*, though, Justice Clarence Thomas disputes that the amendment of Section 2 allows plaintiffs to successfully attack electoral structures such as at-large elections and redistricting plans.

Even if one disagrees with Justice Thomas's assessment as to whether the amendment of Section 2 was intended to allow for attacks on electoral structures, it is safe to say that Congress did not provide much clarity on what it intended the "results" test to mean. Instead, what essentially happened was that Congress passed an amendment and then left it to the federal courts to make sense of the "results" test.

The Supreme Court's first opportunity to engage in a substantial interpretation of what the "results" test meant came in *Thornburg v. Gingles*, 478 U.S. 30 (1986). In *Gingles*, minority plaintiffs attacked the North Carolina state legislature's use of multimember districts. While no one full opinion could garner five votes, Justice William Brennan's opinion did receive a majority for the basic sketch of how the courts should implement the "results" test. In essence, courts are to ensure that plaintiffs challenging an electoral structure prove what have come to be known as the three *Gingles* preconditions and then prove that under the "totality of the circumstances" the electoral structure is discriminatory in "results." As you read the next cases, make sure to note what the three *Gingles* preconditions are and what factors the courts use when assessing the totality of the circumstances.

In the years that immediately followed the *Gingles* decision, many of the challenges brought by plaintiffs resembled the challenges the Supreme Court had heard under the Equal Protection Clause in *White v. Regester* (1973), *City of Mobile v. Bolden* (1980), and *Rogers v. Lodge* (1983). Plaintiffs were often attacking at-large or multimember electoral structures in areas that had, among other things, racially polarized voting, a long history of discrimination, and where African-American or Latino candidates had rarely, if ever, been elected. Under these circumstances, courts often found violations of Section 2 or the jurisdictions (such as counties, cities, and school districts) settled cases with consent decrees that switched from at-large or multimember to single-member districts, some of which were designed to allow minority voters to control the outcomes of elections.

In the early 1990s, however, the focus began to turn away from Section 2 lawsuits involving at-large and multimember election systems; instead, plaintiffs used Section 2 to challenge single-member districting plans. The next two cases involve redistricting cases arising under Section 2—one about statewide maps, the other about local districts. Be sure to note the test the Court employs and the most important factors in applying that test.

It will be helpful to your understanding of these decisions to have knowledge of two different redistricting techniques that can be used to diminish the political influence of a cohesive group of voters: "packing" and "cracking" (which is also known as "fragmenting"). Basically, a cohesive group is "packed" when its members are overwhelmingly placed in one district, thereby diminishing the ability of that group to have electoral power in additional districts. In contrast, a group is "cracked" (or "fragmented") when its members are divided among multiple districts so that the group cannot elect a candidate in any one single district.

It will also be helpful to your understanding of this doctrine to be familiar with four different types of districts that are discussed in Voting Rights Act cases:

- "Majority-minority" or "safe" districts are districts in which "a minority group composes a numerical, working majority of the voting-age population."
- "Crossover" districts are districts in which "minority voters make up less than a majority of the voting-age population . . . [but where the minority population], at least potentially, is large enough to elect the candidate of its choice with help from voters who are members of the majority and who cross over to support the minority's preferred candidate."
- "Coalition" districts are districts in which "two minority groups [e.g., African Americans and Latinos] form a coalition to elect the candidate of the coalition's choice."
- "Influence" districts are districts in which "a minority group can influence the outcome of an election even if its preferred candidate cannot be elected."

Bartlett v. Strickland, 556 U.S. 1, 13 (2009).

JOHNSON v. DE GRANDY

512 U.S. 998 (1994)

Justice SOUTER delivered the opinion of the Court.

[This case is] about the meaning of vote dilution and the facts required to show it, when § 2 of the Voting Rights Act of 1965 is applied to challenges to single-member legislative districts. We hold that no violation of § 2 can be found here, where, in spite of continuing discrimination and racial bloc voting, minority voters form effective voting majorities in a number of districts roughly proportional to the minority voters' respective shares in the voting-age population. While such proportionality is not dispositive in a challenge to single-member districting, it is a relevant fact in the totality of circumstances to be analyzed when determining whether members of a minority group have less opportunity than other members of the electorate to participate in the political process and to elect representatives of their choice.

I

On the first day of Florida's 1992 legislative session, a group of Hispanic voters including Miguel De Grandy (De Grandy plaintiffs) [filed a complaint alleging] that the districts from which Florida voters had chosen their state representatives since 1982 were malapportioned, failing to reflect changes in the State's population during the ensuing decade.

Several months after the first complaint was filed, on April 10, 1992, the state legislature adopted Senate Joint Resolution 2-G (SJR 2-G), providing the reapportionment plan currently at issue. The plan called for dividing Florida into 120 single-member House districts based on population data from the 1990 census.

The De Grandy plaintiffs responded to SJR 2-G by amending their federal complaints to charge the new reapportionment plan with violating § 2. They claimed that SJR 2-G "unlawfully fragments cohesive minority communities and otherwise impermissibly submerges their right to vote and to participate in the electoral process," and they pointed to areas around the State where Hispanic populations could have formed a voting majority in a politically cohesive, reasonably compact district (or in more than one), if SJR 2-G had not fragmented [Hispanic populations] among several districts or packed it into just a few.

At the end of the hearing, on July 1, 1992, the District Court ruled from the bench. It held the plan's provisions for state House districts to be in violation of § 2 because "more than [SJR 2-G's] nine Hispanic districts may be drawn without having or creating a regressive effect upon black voters," and it imposed a remedial plan offered by the De Grandy plaintiffs calling for 11 majority-Hispanic House districts.

In a later, expanded opinion the court reviewed the totality of circumstances as required by § 2 and *Thornburg v. Gingles.* In explaining Dade County's "tripartite politics," in which "ethnic factors . . . predominate over all other[s]," the court found political cohesion within each of the Hispanic and black populations but none between the two, and a tendency of non-Hispanic whites to vote as a bloc to bar minority groups from electing their chosen candidates except in a district where a given minority makes up a voting majority.[6] The court further found that the nearly one million Hispanics in the Dade County area could be combined into 11 House districts, each one relatively compact and with a functional majority of Hispanic voters, whereas SJR 2-G created fewer majority-Hispanic districts. Noting that Florida's [Hispanic population] bore the social, economic, and political effects of past discrimination, the court concluded that SJR 2-G impermissibly diluted the voting strength of Hispanics in its House districts.

II

[Omitted]

III

On the merits of the vote dilution claims covering the House districts, the crux of the State's argument is the power of Hispanics under SJR 2-G to elect candidates of their choice in a number of districts that mirrors their share of the Dade County area's voting-age population (*i.e.,* 9 out of 20 House districts); this power, according to the State, bars

6. The Court recognizes that the terms "black," "Hispanic," and "white" are neither mutually exclusive nor collectively exhaustive. We follow the practice of the District Court in using them as rough indicators of south Florida's three largest racial and linguistic minority groups.

any finding that the plan dilutes Hispanic voting strength. The District Court is said to have missed that conclusion by mistaking our precedents to require the plan to maximize the number of Hispanic-controlled districts.

The State's argument takes us back to ground covered last Term in two cases challenging single-member districts. *See Voinovich v. Quilter*; *Growe v. Emison*. In *Growe,* we held that a claim of vote dilution in a single-member district requires proof meeting the same three threshold conditions for a dilution challenge to a multimember district: that a minority group be "sufficiently large and geographically compact to constitute a majority in a single-member district"; that it be "politically cohesive"; and that "the white majority vot[e] sufficiently as a bloc to enable it . . . usually to defeat the minority's preferred candidate." (quoting *Thornburg v. Gingles*). Of course, as we reflected in *Voinovich* and amplify later in this opinion, "the *Gingles* factors cannot be applied mechanically and without regard to the nature of the claim."

In *Voinovich* we explained how manipulation of district lines can dilute the voting strength of politically cohesive minority group members, whether by fragmenting the minority voters among several districts where a bloc-voting majority can routinely outvote them, or by packing them into one or a small number of districts to minimize their influence in the districts next door. Section 2 prohibits either sort of line-drawing where its result, "interact[ing] with social and historical conditions, impairs the ability of a protected class to elect its candidate of choice on an equal basis with other voters."

A

[Omitted]

B

The District Court found that the three *Gingles* preconditions were satisfied, and that Hispanics had suffered historically from official discrimination, the social, economic, and political effects of which they generally continued to feel. Without more, and on the apparent assumption that what could have been done to create additional Hispanic supermajority districts should have been done, the District Court found a violation of § 2. But the assumption was erroneous, and more is required, as a review of *Gingles* will show.

1

Thornburg v. Gingles prompted this Court's first reading of § 2 of the Voting Rights Act of 1965 after its 1982 amendment.[8] Section 2(a) of the amended Act prohibits any "standard, practice, or procedure . . . which results in a denial or abridgement of the right of any citizen of the United States to vote on account of race or color [or membership in a language minority group]. . . . " Section 2(b) provides that a denial or abridgment occurs where,

8. Congress amended the statute to reach cases in which discriminatory intent is not identified, adding new language designed to codify *White v. Regester* 412 U.S. 755 (1973).

> "based on the totality of circumstances, it is shown that the political processes leading to nomination or election in the State or political subdivision are not equally open to participation by members of a class of citizens protected by subsection (a) of this section in that its members have less opportunity than other members of the electorate to participate in the political process and to elect representatives of their choice. The extent to which members of a protected class have been elected to office in the State or political subdivision is one circumstance which may be considered: *Provided*, That nothing in this section establishes a right to have members of a protected class elected in numbers equal to their proportion in the population." 42 U.S.C. § 1973(b).

Gingles provided some structure to the statute's "totality of circumstances" test in a case challenging multimember legislative districts. The Court listed the factors put forward as relevant in the Senate Report treating the 1982 amendments,[9] and held that

> "[w]hile many or all of [them] may be relevant to a claim of vote dilution through submergence in multimember districts, unless there is a conjunction of the following circumstances, the use of multimember districts generally will not impede the ability of minority voters to elect representatives of their choice. Stated succinctly, a bloc voting majority must *usually* be able to defeat candidates supported by a politically cohesive, geographically insular minority group."

The Court thus summarized the three now-familiar *Gingles* factors (compactness/numerousness, minority cohesion or bloc voting, and majority bloc voting) as "necessary preconditions" for establishing vote dilution by use of a multimember district.

But if *Gingles* so clearly identified the three as generally necessary to prove a § 2 claim, it just as clearly declined to hold them sufficient in combination, either in the sense that a court's examination of relevant circumstances was complete once the three factors were found to exist, or in the sense that the three in combination necessarily and in all circumstances demonstrated dilution. This was true not only because bloc voting was a matter of degree, with a variable legal significance depending on other facts, but also because the ultimate conclusions about equality or inequality of opportunity were intended by Congress to be judgments resting on comprehensive, not limited, canvassing of relevant facts. Lack of electoral success is evidence of vote dilution, but courts must also examine other

9. As summarized in *Gingles*: [T]he Senate Report specifies factors which typically may be relevant to a § 2 claim: the history of voting-related discrimination in the State or political subdivision; the extent to which voting in the elections of the State or political subdivision is racially polarized; the extent to which the State or political subdivision has used voting practices or procedures that tend to enhance the opportunity for discrimination against the minority group, such as unusually large election districts, majority vote requirements, and prohibitions against bullet voting; the exclusion of members of the minority group from candidate slating processes; the extent to which minority group members bear the effects of past discrimination in areas such as education, employment, and health which hinder their ability to participate effectively in the political process; the use of overt or subtle racial appeals in political campaigns; and the extent to which members of the minority group have been elected to public office in the jurisdiction. The Report also notes that evidence demonstrating that elected officials are unresponsive to the particularized needs of the minority group and that the policy underlying the State's or the political subdivision's use of the contested practice or structure is tenuous may have probative value.

evidence in the totality of circumstances, including the extent of the opportunities minority voters enjoy to participate in the political processes.

2

If the three *Gingles* factors may not be isolated as sufficient, standing alone, to prove dilution in every multimember district challenge, *a fortiori* they must not be when the challenge goes to a series of single-member districts, where dilution may be more difficult to grasp. Plaintiffs challenging single-member districts may claim, not total submergence, but partial submergence; not the chance for some electoral success in place of none, but the chance for more success in place of some. When the question thus comes down to the reasonableness of drawing a series of district lines in one combination of places rather than another, judgments about inequality may become closer calls. As facts beyond the ambit of the three *Gingles* factors loom correspondingly larger, fact finders cannot rest uncritically on assumptions about the force of the *Gingles* factors in pointing to dilution.

The cases now before us, of course, fall on this more complex side of the divide, requiring a court to determine whether provision for somewhat fewer majority-minority districts than the number sought by the plaintiffs was dilution of the minority votes. The District Court was accordingly required to assess the probative significance of the *Gingles* factors critically after considering the further circumstances with arguable bearing on the issue of equal political opportunity. We think that in finding dilution here the District Court misjudged the relative importance of the *Gingles* factors and of historical discrimination, measured against evidence tending to show that in spite of these facts, SJR 2-G would provide minority voters with an equal measure of political and electoral opportunity.

The District Court did not, to be sure, commit the error of treating the three *Gingles* conditions as exhausting the enquiry required by § 2. Consistently with *Gingles,* the court received evidence of racial relations outside the immediate confines of voting behavior and found a history of discrimination against Hispanic voters continuing in society generally to the present day. But the District Court was not critical enough in asking whether a history of persistent discrimination reflected in the larger society and its bloc-voting behavior portended any dilutive effect from a newly proposed districting scheme, whose pertinent features were majority-minority districts in substantial proportion to the minority's share of voting-age population. The court failed to ask whether the totality of facts, including those pointing to proportionality,[11] showed that the new scheme would deny minority voters equal political opportunity.

11. "Proportionality" as the term is used here links the number of majority-minority voting districts to minority members' share of the relevant population. The concept is distinct from the subject of the proportional representation clause of § 2, which provides that "nothing in this section establishes a right to have members of a protected class elected in numbers equal to their proportion in the population." 42 U.S.C. § 1973(b). This proviso speaks to the success of minority candidates, as distinct from the political or electoral power of minority voters. And the proviso also confirms what is otherwise clear from the text of the statute, namely, that the ultimate right of § 2 is equality of opportunity, not a guarantee of electoral success for minority-preferred candidates of whatever race.

Treating equal political opportunity as the focus of the enquiry, we do not see how these district lines, apparently providing political effectiveness in proportion to voting-age numbers, deny equal political opportunity. The record establishes that Hispanics constitute 50 percent of the voting-age population in Dade County and under SJR 2-G would make up supermajorities in 9 of the 18 House districts located primarily within the county. Likewise, if one considers the 20 House districts located at least in part within Dade County, the record indicates that Hispanics would be an effective voting majority in 45 percent of them (*i.e.,* nine), and would constitute 47 percent of the voting-age population in the area. In other words, under SJR 2-G Hispanics in the Dade County area would enjoy substantial proportionality. On this evidence, we think the State's scheme would thwart the historical tendency to exclude Hispanics, not encourage or perpetuate it. Thus in spite of that history and its legacy, including the racial cleavages that characterize Dade County politics today, we see no grounds for holding in these cases that SJR 2-G's district lines diluted the votes cast by Hispanic voters.

The De Grandy plaintiffs urge us to put more weight on the District Court's findings of packing and fragmentation, allegedly accomplished by the way the State drew certain specific lines: "[T]he line of District 116 separates heavily Hispanic neighborhoods in District 112 from the rest of the heavily Hispanic Kendall Lakes area and the Kendall area," so that the line divides "neighbors making up the same housing development in Kendall Lakes," and District 114 "packs" Hispanic voters, while Districts 102 and 109 "fragmen[t]" them. We would agree that where a State has split (or lumped) minority neighborhoods that would have been grouped into a single district (or spread among several) if the State had employed the same line-drawing standards in minority neighborhoods as it used elsewhere in the jurisdiction, the inconsistent treatment might be significant evidence of a § 2 violation, even in the face of proportionality. The district court, however, made no such finding. Indeed, the propositions the Court recites on this point are not even phrased as factual findings, but merely as recitations of testimony offered by plaintiffs' expert witness. While the District Court may well have credited the testimony, the court was apparently wary of adopting the witness's conclusions as findings. But even if one imputed a greater significance to the accounts of testimony, they would boil down to findings that several of SJR 2-G's district lines separate portions of Hispanic neighborhoods, while another district line draws several Hispanic neighborhoods into a single district. This, however, would be to say only that lines could have been drawn elsewhere, nothing more. But some dividing by district lines and combining within them is virtually inevitable and befalls any population group of substantial size. Attaching the labels "packing" and "fragmenting" to these phenomena, without more, does not make the result vote dilution when the minority group enjoys substantial proportionality.

3

It may be that the significance of the facts under § 2 was obscured by the rule of thumb apparently adopted by the District Court, that anything short of the maximum number of majority-minority districts consistent with the *Gingles* conditions would violate § 2, at least where societal discrimination against the minority had occurred and continued to occur. But reading the first *Gingles* condition in effect to define dilution as a failure to maximize in the face of bloc voting (plus some other incidents of societal bias to be expected where bloc voting occurs) causes its own dangers, and they are not to be courted.

Assume a hypothetical jurisdiction of 1,000 voters divided into 10 districts of 100 each, where members of a minority group make up 40 percent of the voting population and voting is totally polarized along racial lines. With the right geographic dispersion to satisfy the compactness requirement, and with careful manipulation of district lines, the minority voters might be placed in control of as many as 7 of the 10 districts. Each such district could be drawn with at least 51 members of the minority group, and whether the remaining minority voters were added to the groupings of 51 for safety or scattered in the other three districts, minority voters would be able to elect candidates of their choice in all seven districts.[12] The point of the hypothetical is not, of course, that any given district is likely to be open to such extreme manipulation, or that bare majorities are likely to vote in full force and strictly along racial lines, but that reading § 2 to define dilution as any failure to maximize tends to obscure the very object of the statute and to run counter to its textually stated purpose. One may suspect vote dilution from political famine, but one is not entitled to suspect (much less infer) dilution from mere failure to guarantee a political feast. However prejudiced a society might be, it would be absurd to suggest that the failure of a districting scheme to provide a minority group with effective political power 75 percent above its numerical strength[13] indicates a denial of equal participation in the political process. Failure to maximize cannot be the measure of § 2.

4

While, for obvious reasons, the State agrees that a failure to leverage minority political strength to the maximum possible point of power is not definitive of dilution in bloc-voting societies, it seeks to impart a measure of determinacy by applying a definitive rule of its own: that as a matter of law no dilution occurs whenever the percentage of single-member districts in which minority voters form an effective majority mirrors the minority voters' percentage of the relevant population.[14] Proportionality so defined would thus be a safe harbor for any districting scheme.

12. Minority voters might instead be denied control over a single seat, of course. Each district would need to include merely 51 members of the majority group; minority voters fragmented among the 10 districts could be denied power to affect the result in any district.

13. When 40 percent of the population determines electoral outcomes in 7 out of 10 districts, the minority group can be said to enjoy effective political power 75 percent above its numerical strength.

14. The parties dispute whether the relevant figure is the minority group's share of the population, or of some subset of the population, such as those who are eligible to vote, in that they are United States citizens, over 18 years of age, and not registered at another address (as students and members of the military often are). Because we do not elevate this proportion to the status of a magic parameter, and because it is not dispositive here, we do not resolve that dispute.

The safety would be in derogation of the statutory text and its considered purpose, however, and of the ideal that the Voting Rights Act of 1965 attempts to foster. An inflexible rule would run counter to the textual command of § 2, that the presence or absence of a violation be assessed "based on the totality of circumstances." The need for such "totality" review springs from the demonstrated ingenuity of state and local governments in hobbling minority voting power. In a substantial number of voting jurisdictions, that past reality has included such reprehensible practices as ballot box stuffing, outright violence, discretionary registration, property requirements, the poll tax, and the white primary; and other practices censurable when the object of their use is discriminatory, such as at-large elections, runoff requirements, anti-single-shot devices, gerrymandering, the impeachment of office-holders, the annexation or deannexation of territory, and the creation or elimination of elective offices. Some of those expedients could occur even in a jurisdiction with numerically demonstrable proportionality; the harbor safe for States would thus not be safe for voters. It is, in short, for good reason that we have been, and remain, chary of entertaining a simplification of the sort the State now urges upon us.

Even if the State's safe harbor were open only in cases of alleged dilution by the manipulation of district lines, however, it would rest on an unexplored premise of highly suspect validity: that in any given voting jurisdiction (or portion of that jurisdiction under consideration), the rights of some minority voters under § 2 may be traded off against the rights of other members of the same minority class. Under the State's view, the most blatant racial gerrymandering in half of a county's single-member districts would be irrelevant under § 2 if offset by political gerrymandering in the other half, so long as proportionality was the bottom line.

Finally, we reject the safe harbor rule because of a tendency the State would itself certainly condemn, a tendency to promote and perpetuate efforts to devise majority-minority districts even in circumstances where they may not be necessary to achieve equal political and electoral opportunity. Because in its simplest form the State's rule would shield from § 2 challenge a districting scheme in which the number of majority-minority districts reflected the minority's share of the relevant population, the conclusiveness of the rule might be an irresistible inducement to create such districts. It bears recalling, however, that for all the virtues of majority-minority districts as remedial devices, they rely on a quintessentially race-conscious calculus aptly described [by some commentators] as the "politics of second best". . . . If the lesson of *Gingles* is that society's racial and ethnic cleavages sometimes necessitate majority-minority districts to ensure equal political and electoral opportunity, that should not obscure the fact that there are communities in which minority citizens are able to form coalitions with voters from other racial and ethnic groups, having no need to be a majority within a single district in order to elect candidates of their choice. Those candidates may not represent perfection to every minority voter, but minority voters are not immune from the obligation to pull, haul, and trade to find common political ground, the virtue of which is not to be slighted in applying a statute meant to hasten the waning of racism in American politics.

It is enough to say that, while proportionality in the sense used here is obviously an indication that minority voters have an equal opportunity, in spite of racial polarization, "to participate in the political process and to elect representatives of their choice," 42 U.S.C. § 1973(b), the degree of probative value assigned to proportionality may vary with other facts. No single statistic provides courts with a shortcut to determine whether a set of single-member districts unlawfully dilutes minority voting strength.

5

While the United States concedes the relevance of proportionality to a § 2 claim, it would confine proportionality to an affirmative defense, and one to be made only on a statewide basis in cases that challenge districts for electing a body with statewide jurisdiction. In this litigation, the United States would have us treat any claim that evidence of proportionality supports the State's plan as having been waived because the State made no argument in the District Court that the proportion of districts statewide in which Hispanics constitute an effective voting majority mirrors the proportion of statewide Hispanic population.

The argument has two flaws. . . . There is, first, no textual reason to segregate some circumstances from the statutory totality, to be rendered insignificant unless the defendant pleads them by way of affirmative defense. Second, and just as importantly, the argument would recast these cases as they come to us, in order to bar consideration of proportionality except on statewide scope, whereas up until now the dilution claims have been litigated on a smaller geographical scale. It is, indeed, the plaintiffs themselves, including the United States, who passed up the opportunity to frame their dilution claim in statewide terms. While the United States points to language in its complaint alleging that the redistricting plans dilute the votes of "Hispanic citizens in the State of Florida," the complaint identifies "several areas of the State" where such violations of § 2 are said to occur, and then speaks in terms of Hispanics in the Dade County area. Nowhere do the allegations indicate that claims of dilution "in the State of Florida" are not to be considered in terms of the areas specifically mentioned. The complaint alleges no facts at all about the contours, demographics, or voting patterns of any districts outside the Dade County area[], and neither the evidence at trial nor the opinion of the District Court addressed white bloc voting and political cohesion of minorities statewide. The De Grandy plaintiffs even voluntarily dismissed their claims of Hispanic vote dilution outside the Dade County area. Thus we have no occasion to decide which frame of reference should have been used if the parties had not apparently agreed in the District Court on the appropriate geographical scope for analyzing the alleged § 2 violation and devising its remedy.

6

In sum, the District Court's finding of dilution did not address the statutory standard of unequal political and electoral opportunity, and reflected instead a misconstruction of § 2 that equated dilution with failure to maximize the number of reasonably compact majority-minority districts. Because the ultimate finding of dilution in districting for the Florida House was based on a misreading of the governing law, we hold it to be clearly erroneous.

Justice O'CONNOR, concurring.

[Omitted]

Justice KENNEDY, concurring in part and concurring in the judgment.

[Omitted]

Justice THOMAS, with whom Justice SCALIA joins, dissenting.

[Omitted]

GONZALEZ v. CITY OF AURORA

535 F.3d 594 (7th Cir. 2008)

EASTERBROOK, Chief Judge.

In the 2000 Census, 32.6% of the population in the City of Aurora, Illinois, identified itself as Hispanic, but of the City's residents who are citizens and old enough to vote only 16.3% are Hispanic. Aurora has 10 single-seat wards, only one of which reliably elects Latino candidates to the City Council. Another ward, although about 66% Latino, has twice elected a black alderman since the redistricting that followed the 2000 Census. When the record was compiled, 2 of the 12 aldermen (there are 2 at-large seats in addition to the 10 wards) were Hispanic. One was elected and the second appointed. Plaintiffs contend in this suit under § 2 of the Voting Rights Act that these numbers are insufficient. They want an injunction compelling the City to redraw the ward boundaries so that Aurora's Latino population is concentrated in three wards, each of which then would be likely to elect a Latino candidate (would be, as plaintiffs say, "Latino effective").

Plaintiffs start with the proposition that it takes 70% or more Latino population to ensure the election of a Latino candidate. Whatever rule of thumb courts may have used in the 1960s and 1970s for black voters does not apply to Latinos, plaintiffs contend, because Latinos are younger and less likely to be citizens than are blacks and other minorities. Although the City used the rule of thumb that 65% population is enough to make a district "effective" for a minority group, plaintiffs are sure that this won't work. This table shows why 65% may not be enough:

	Latino Population	Latino Voting-Age Population	Latino Voting-Age Citizen Population
Ward 2	74.54%	71%	47.5%
Ward 7	66.27%	62.9%	43%
Ward 3	52.61%	48%	28%

These figures, all from 2000, are the right ones to use. Plaintiffs' estimates about population in 2005 don't matter, because apportionment is based on Census returns. The district court concluded that a ward with 65% or more Latino residents should be deemed sufficient no matter who it elects. If Latinos vote for candidates of other ethnic backgrounds, this means that Aurora is not afflicted by racial bloc voting, rather than that the map deprives Latinos' votes of full effect. The judge added that, with 16% of the eligible population, Latinos would receive 2 seats in a 12-seat legislature under proportional representation. As 2 of the existing 12 members were Latino, the district judge saw no problem under § 2 and granted summary judgment for the City.

The most striking thing about plaintiffs' brief on appeal is that it neither quotes from nor analyzes the text of § 2. Instead it leaps straight to the "*Gingles* factors" (from *Thornburg v. Gingles*) and language in a Senate committee report. The statute is not self-defining, so it is understandable that lawyers would turn to secondary sources such as judicial decisions and legislative history. But neither is it irrelevant. It is worth quoting. Section 2(a) says that governments cannot adopt standards, practices, or procedures that "result[ ] in a denial or abridgement of the right of any citizen of the United States to vote on account of race or color." This sounds like a rule that race and color cannot be used to prevent anyone from voting, or to disregard a vote once cast. Section 2(b), 42 U.S.C. § 1973(b), then adds this famously elliptical language:

> A violation of subsection (a) of this section is established if, based on the totality of circumstances, it is shown that the political processes leading to nomination or election in the State or political subdivision are not equally open to participation by members of a class of citizens protected by subsection (a) of this section in that its members have less opportunity than other members of the electorate to participate in the political process and to elect representatives of their choice. The extent to which members of a protected class have been elected to office in the State or political subdivision is one circumstance which may be considered: *Provided*, That nothing in this section establishes a right to have members of a protected class elected in numbers equal to their proportion in the population.

What does it mean to "have less opportunity than other members of the electorate to participate in the political process and to elect representatives of their choice"? *Gingles* held that gerrymandering district borders can have this effect even though everyone is entitled to vote, and all votes are counted equally. The Court set out circumstances (the "*Gingles* factors") under which clever map-drawing could have this effect and then turned to the Senate committee report for factors to consider if the conditions are met. The district judge found, and we shall assume, that these conditions are satisfied in Aurora: Latinos are sufficiently concentrated geographically that they can form a majority in some districts; Latinos are politically cohesive; and, without a large bloc of voters, Latino candidates rarely prevail. This just sets the stage.

Plaintiffs leap from satisfaction of the *Gingles* factors to the proposition that the City must do what is possible to maximize Latino voters' ability to elect Latino candidates (euphemistically "candidates of their choice"). But neither § 2 nor *Gingles* nor any later decision of the Supreme Court speaks of maximizing the influence of any racial or ethnic group. Section 2 requires an electoral process "equally open" to all, not a process that favors one group over another. One cannot maximize Latino influence without minimizing some other group's influence. A map drawn to advantage Latino candidates at the expense of black (or white ethnic) candidates violates § 2 as surely as a map drawn to maximize the influence of those groups at the expense of Latinos.

The Supreme Court emphasized in *League of United Latin American Citizens v. Perry* (2006) (*LULAC*), its most recent § 2 redistricting case, that the Voting Rights Act protects the rights of individual voters, not the rights of groups. There is a serious problem with any proposal to employ black or Asian or white citizens of some other ethnic background as "fill" in districts carefully drawn to ensure three 70%-Latino wards—wards in which the remaining 30% are (by design) never going to be able to elect a candidate of their choice. How could one explain to this 30% that the political process was "equally open" to them, as § 2 commands? A problem under § 2 arises whenever any person is moved from one district to another to minimize the value of his vote and give an advantage to someone else.

Section 2's requirement of an "equally open" process usually is described as including a prohibition of vote dilution by redistricting. Plaintiffs want the court to reduce the influence of others to produce an advantage for Latino voters. That may be necessary as a remedy for some earlier vote-dilution exercise, but the first question we need to ask is whether Latino votes have been diluted by Aurora's map. Diluted relative to what benchmark? Not the maximum influence Latinos could have, surely; as we've explained, no group is entitled to that (and all groups cannot enjoy maximum influence simultaneously). Nor is proportional representation the benchmark. *Gingles* holds that this is not the statute's objective—that it is not necessary and, *LULAC* adds, is not sufficient either, if a minority group in one part of a jurisdiction has been thrown to the wolves.

So what benchmarks are possible? One would be the outcome of a race-neutral process in which all districts are compact. Cases in which the Supreme Court has found a problem under § 2 all involve transparent gerrymandering that boosts one group's chances at the expense of another's. Nothing remotely similar happened in Aurora. A glance at the 2002 ward map reveals that the districts are compact and regular, with the few rough edges needed to ensure that they have equal population.

Still, although many opinions, of which *LULAC* is the most recent, emphasize compact districts as the benchmark for a map that does not dilute any group's influence, it is possible to locate even compact districts for political advantage.

Given the very large number of ways that reasonably compact districts of equal population can be drawn, how can a court tell whether a jurisdiction has chosen a particular arrangement in order to advantage one ethnic group over another, diluting the influence of the disfavored group? When the Voting Rights Act was enacted, the answer would have depended on the intent of those who drew the map. *See City of Mobile v. Bolden*. The 1982 amendments replaced intent with effect as the rule of decision, see *Gingles*, but did not supply a means to test whether a given map was ordinary or abnormal. Today, however, computers can use census data to generate many variations on compact districts with equal population. One could do this exercise a hundred or a thousand times, each time placing the center of the first (or "seed") district in a different location. That would generate a hundred or a thousand different maps, and the software could easily check these to determine the ethnic makeup of the districts.

Suppose that after 1,000 different maps of Aurora's wards have been generated, 10% have two or three "safe" districts for Latinos and the other 90% look something like the actual map drawn in 2002: one safe district and two "influence districts" where no candidate is likely to win without substantial Latino support. Then we could confidently conclude that Aurora's map did not dilute the effectiveness of the Latino vote. But suppose, instead, that Latinos are sufficiently concentrated that the random, race-blind exercise we have proposed yields three "Latino effective" districts at least 50% of the time. Then a court might sensibly conclude that Aurora had diluted the Latino vote by undermining the normal effects of the choices that Aurora's citizens had made about where to live. Redistricting software can not answer all hard questions, but it provides a means to implement a pure effects test without demanding proportional representation.

Plaintiffs did not conduct such an exercise, however (or, if they did, they didn't put the results in the record). What we can see from the record suggests that Latinos are not concentrated enough to support three "Latino effective" districts without serious gerrymandering. Ward 2 has 2,453 voting-age citizens who identified themselves as Hispanic in the 2000 Census. Wards 7 and 3 have fewer. Wards 1, 4, and 6 all have more than 1,000 citizen, voting-age Latinos. Ward 5 has another 668. In other words, the Latino population is not concentrated in a way that neutrally drawn compact districts would produce three "Latino effective" wards. That may be why plaintiffs have staked their all on a proposal that Latinos are entitled at least to proportional representation via two Latino-effective districts no matter what the consequences of race-blind districting would be. The Voting Rights Act does not require either outcome.

Because plaintiffs lack any evidence of dilution, there is no point in traipsing through the multiple factors mentioned in the 1982 committee reports. Although plaintiffs briefly mention the City's two at-large districts—at-large districts are a traditional means of reducing the influence of minority groups—they did not make much of them in the district court or here, devoting less than two pages of their brief to the subject. The at-large districts predate the 2002 reapportionment and, for all we know, long predate the presence of a substantial Latino population in Aurora. After the 2000 Census, the City increased the number of single-member districts from 8 to 10, reducing the effect of the 2 at-large districts. Any contention that the at-large districts violate § 2 of the Voting Rights Act has been forfeited.

And plaintiffs have no other arguments. They ignore the fact that several wards—at least Wards 3 and 7, and likely wards 1, 4, and 6 as well—contain enough Latino citizens to produce substantial influence. (Many cases, of which *LULAC* is again the most recent example, hold that "influence districts" count in any assessment of vote dilution. *See also, e.g., Johnson v. De Grandy*.) Plaintiffs tried for the big prize (three safe districts) but did not build the sort of factual record that creates a genuine issue for trial, even under the balancing approach of *Gingles*. They thought, wrongly, that all they had to do to prevail is to show that Ward 7 is not "Latino effective." That's not enough to condemn the current map. The district court's judgment therefore is affirmed.

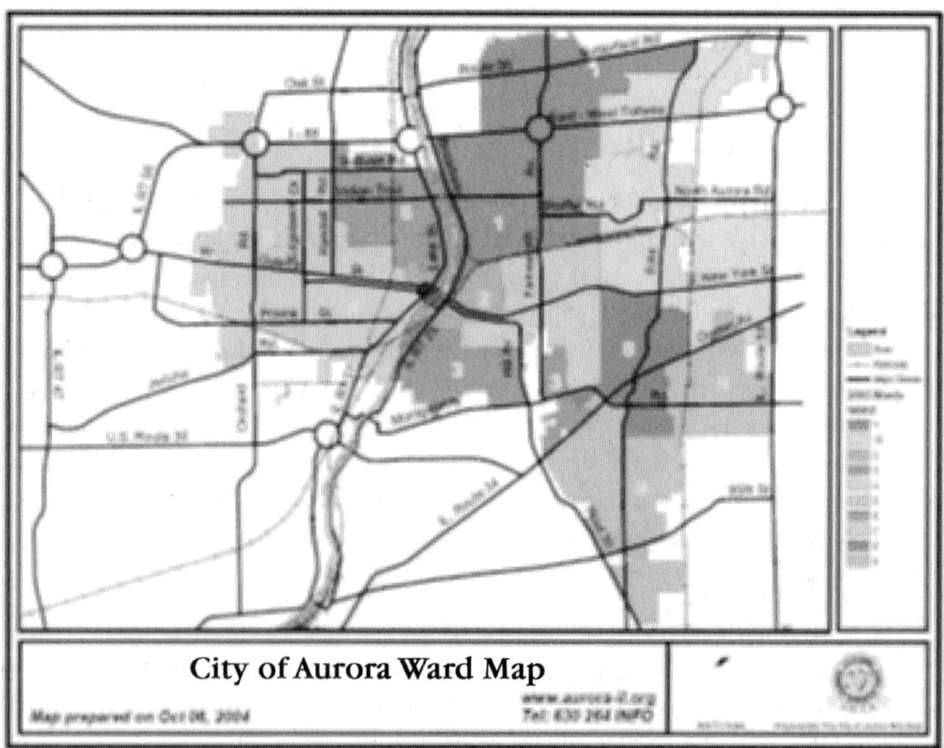

NOTES ON *DE GRANDY, GONZALEZ,* AND SECTION 2 OF THE VOTING RIGHTS ACT

1. Section 2 of the Voting Rights Act creates a "results" test for vote dilution. As the opinions you just read demonstrate, the Court has struggled to define the contours of the results test.
2. In *Gingles v. Thornburg* (1986), Justice Brennan's plurality opinion created the basic framework that courts still use today. Courts first decide whether the three *Gingles* preconditions are met. Those preconditions are: (1) a minority group must be sufficiently large and geographically compact to comprise a majority of the district; (2) the minority group must be politically cohesive (it must demonstrate a pattern of voting for the same candidates); and, (3) white voters must vote sufficiently as a bloc usually to defeat the minority group's preferred candidate. If the plaintiff can establish these three pre-conditions when challenging a redistricting plan, then the courts move to a "totality of the circumstances" test. *Gingles* said courts could use the so-called "Senate Factors" (mentioned in footnote 9 of *De Grandy*) as a guide in the totality of circumstances analysis.
3. Does the first *Gingles* analysis require that a minority group be at least 50 percent in a hypothetical single-member district, or can it have less than a numerical majority but still elect a candidate of its choice with "crossover" votes from white voters? In *Bartlett v. Strickland* (2009), the Court held that "crossover" districts do not satisfy the first *Gingles* precondition. Therefore, to establish a § 2 violation, a plaintiff must show that the minority group would actually be a majority in a single-member district without support from white voters. Does this result make sense? Why not allow minority voters to rely on crossover white voters to establish that they could comprise a majority of the district and thereby elect candidates of their choice?
4. What does *De Grandy* add to the "results" test analysis? Note the use of "proportionality." How does the Court define "proportionality," and how does that differ from proportional representation? Is proportionality even the right factor to consider?
5. Notice how Judge Easterbrook's *Gonzalez* opinion seems to criticize the plaintiffs for "neither quot[ing] nor analyz[ing]" the statutory text of Section 2. Judge Easterbrook quotes the text, but does he engage in any textual analysis?
6. Consider how vague and amorphous the "totality of circumstances" test is. Does it give the Court the freedom to decide whatever it wants with respect to the issue of minority vote dilution? If this amount of judicial discretion is a problem, is it a problem of the Court's own making—or instead a consequence of the statute enacted by Congress?
7. How should courts go about analyzing challenges under the Section 2 results test in the context of single-member districts?

For many years, a majority of the Court has held that the Equal Protection Clause and amended Section 2 of the Voting Rights Act allow plaintiffs to challenge electoral structures for their failure to provide adequate representation (i.e., because the structures cause "vote dilution"). These holdings, though, are not without their critics. Perhaps the most comprehensive critique in a judicial opinion of both the constitutional and statutory decisions of the Court was written by Justice Clarence Thomas in *Holder v. Hall.*

Here is some background to assist you a bit with the specific context of the case. *Holder v. Hall* was a Section 2 challenge to the system of electing the county government in Bleckley County, Georgia. Bleckley County was 20 percent African American and had a single-commissioner form of government—which meant that a single individual elected at-large constituted the "governing body" for the county. Plaintiffs challenged the use of the single-commissioner form of government, alleging that the one-person size was a violation of Section 2 and seeking the establishment of a larger-sized governing body that would be elected by single-member districts.

Justice Anthony Kennedy wrote the lead opinion joined in substantial part by Chief Justice William Rehnquist. Justice Sandra Day O'Connor wrote a concurrence. These three Justices all rejected the plaintiffs' challenge, although for different reasons. The details of the reasoning of the opinions by Justices Kennedy and O'Connor are not important to our purposes here, except to note that both Justices decided the case on far narrower grounds than Justice Thomas would have.

HOLDER v. HALL

512 U.S. 874 (1994)

Justice THOMAS, with whom Justice SCALIA joins, concurring in the judgment.

We are asked in this case to determine whether the size of a local governing body is subject to challenge under § 2 of the Voting Rights Act of 1965 as a "dilutive" practice. While I agree with Justices Kennedy and O'Connor that the size of a governing body cannot be attacked under § 2, I do not share their reasons for reaching that conclusion.

I would explicitly anchor analysis in this case in the statutory text. Only a "voting qualification or prerequisite to voting, or standard, practice, or procedure" can be challenged under § 2. I would hold that the size of a governing body is not a "standard, practice, or procedure" within the terms of the Act. In my view, however, the only principle limiting the scope of the terms "standard, practice, or procedure" that can be derived from the text of the Act would exclude, not only the challenge to size advanced today, but also challenges to allegedly dilutive election methods that we have considered within the scope of the Act in the past.

I believe that a systematic reassessment of our interpretation of § 2 is required in this case. The broad reach we have given the section might suggest that the size of a governing body, like an election method that has the potential for diluting the vote of a minority group, should come within the terms of the Act. But the gloss we have placed on the words "standard, practice, or procedure" in cases alleging dilution is at odds with the terms of the statute and has proved utterly unworkable in practice. A review of the current state of our cases shows that by construing the Act to cover potentially dilutive electoral mechanisms, we have immersed the federal courts in a hopeless project of weighing questions of political theory—questions judges must confront to establish a benchmark concept of an "undiluted" vote. Worse, in pursuing the ideal measure of voting strength, we have devised a remedial mechanism that encourages federal courts to segregate voters into racially designated districts to ensure minority electoral success. In doing so, we have collaborated in what may aptly be termed the racial "balkaniz[ation]" of the Nation.

I can no longer adhere to a reading of the Act that does not comport with the terms of the statute and that has produced such a disastrous misadventure in judicial policymaking. I would hold that the size of a government body is not a "standard, practice, or procedure" because, properly understood, those terms reach only state enactments that limit citizens' access to the ballot.

I

If one surveys the history of the Voting Rights Act, one can only be struck by the sea change that has occurred in the application and enforcement of the Act since it was passed in 1965. The statute was originally perceived as a remedial provision directed specifically at eradicating discriminatory practices that restricted blacks' ability to register and vote in the segregated South. Now, the Act has grown into something entirely different. In construing the Act to cover claims of vote dilution, we have converted the Act into a device for regulating, rationing, and apportioning political power among racial and ethnic groups. In the process, we have read the Act essentially as a grant of authority to the federal judiciary to develop theories on basic principles of representative government, for it is only a resort to political theory that can enable a court to determine which electoral systems provide the "fairest" levels of representation or the most "effective" or "undiluted" votes to minorities.

Before I turn to an analysis of the text of § 2 to explain why, in my view, the terms of the statute do not authorize the project that we have undertaken in the name of the Act, I intend first simply to describe the development of the basic contours of vote dilution actions under the Voting Rights Act.[2] An examination of the current state of our decisions should make obvious a simple fact that for far too long has gone unmentioned: Vote dilution cases have required the federal courts to make decisions based on highly political judgments—judgments that courts are inherently ill-equipped to make. A clear understanding of the

2. Of course, many of the basic principles I will discuss are equally applicable to constitutional vote dilution cases. Indeed, prior to the amendment of the Voting Rights Act in 1982, dilution claims typically were brought under the Equal Protection Clause. *See, e.g., White v. Regester* (1973); *Whitcomb v. Chavis* (1971).

destructive assumptions that have developed to guide vote dilution decisions and the role we have given the federal courts in redrawing the political landscape of the Nation should make clear the pressing need for us to reassess our interpretation of the Act.

As it was enforced in the years immediately following its enactment, the Voting Rights Act of 1965 was perceived primarily as legislation directed at eliminating literacy tests and similar devices that had been used to prevent black voter registration in the segregated South.

The Act was immediately and notably successful in removing barriers to registration and ensuring access to the ballot. For example, in Mississippi, black registration levels skyrocketed from 6.7% to 59.8% in a mere two years; in Alabama the increase was from 19.3% to 51.6% in the same time period.

The Court's decision in *Allen v. State Bd. of Elections* (1969), however, marked a fundamental shift in the focal point of the Act. In an opinion dealing with four companion cases, the *Allen* Court determined that the Act should be given "the broadest possible scope." The decision in *Allen* thus ensured that the terms "standard, practice, or procedure" would extend to encompass a wide array of electoral practices or voting systems that might be challenged for reducing the potential impact of minority votes.

As a consequence, *Allen* also ensured that courts would be required to confront a number of complex and essentially political questions in assessing claims of vote dilution under the Voting Rights Act. The central difficulty in any vote dilution case, of course, is determining a point of comparison against which dilution can be measured. As Justice Frankfurter observed several years before *Allen*, "[t]alk of 'debasement' or 'dilution' is circular talk. One cannot speak of 'debasement' or 'dilution' of the value of a vote until there is first defined a standard of reference as to what a vote should be worth." *Baker v. Carr.* But in setting the benchmark of what "undiluted" or fully "effective" voting strength should be, a court must necessarily make some judgments based purely on an assessment of principles of political theory. As Justice Harlan pointed out in his dissent in *Allen*, the Voting Rights Act supplies no rule for a court to rely upon in deciding, for example, whether a multimember at-large system of election is to be preferred to a single-member district system; that is, whether one provides a more "effective" vote than another. "Under one system, Negroes have some influence in the election of all officers; under the other, minority groups have *more* influence in the selection of *fewer* officers." *Allen.* The choice is inherently a political one, and depends upon the selection of a theory for defining the fully "effective" vote—at bottom, a theory for defining effective participation in representative government. In short, what a court is actually asked to do in a vote dilution case is to choose among competing bases of representation—ultimately, really, among competing theories of political philosophy.

Perhaps the most prominent feature of the philosophy that has emerged in vote dilution decisions since *Allen* has been the Court's preference for single-member districting schemes, both as a benchmark for measuring undiluted minority voting strength and as a remedial mechanism for guaranteeing minorities undiluted voting power. Indeed, commentators surveying the history of voting rights litigation have concluded that it has been the objective of voting rights plaintiffs to use the Act to attack multimember districting schemes and to replace them with single-member districting systems drawn with majority-minority districts to ensure minority control of seats.

It should be apparent, however, that there is no principle inherent in our constitutional system, or even in the history of the Nation's electoral practices, that makes single-member districts the "proper" mechanism for electing representatives to governmental bodies or for giving "undiluted" effect to the votes of a numerical minority. On the contrary, from the earliest days of the Republic, multimember districts were a common feature of our political systems. The Framers left unanswered in the Constitution the question whether congressional delegations from the several States should be elected on a general ticket from each State as a whole or under a districting scheme and left that matter to be resolved by the States or by Congress. It was not until 1842 that Congress determined that Representatives should be elected from single-member districts in the States. Single-member districting was no more the rule in the States themselves, for the Constitutions of most of the 13 original States provided that representatives in the state legislatures were to be elected from multimember districts. Today, although they have come under increasing attack under the Voting Rights Act, multimember district systems continue to be a feature on the American political landscape, especially in municipal governments.

The obvious advantage the Court has perceived in single-member districts, of course, is their tendency to enhance the ability of any numerical minority in the electorate to gain control of seats in a representative body. But in choosing single-member districting as a benchmark electoral plan on that basis the Court has made a political decision and, indeed, a decision that itself depends on a prior political choice made in answer to Justice Harlan's question in *Allen*. Justice Harlan asked whether a group's votes should be considered to be more "effective" when they provide influence over a greater number of seats, or control over a lesser number of seats. In answering that query, the Court has determined that the purpose of the vote—or of the fully "effective" vote—is controlling seats. In other words, in an effort to develop standards for assessing claims of dilution, the Court has adopted the view that members of any numerically significant minority are denied a fully effective use of the franchise unless they are able to control seats in an elected body. Under this theory, votes that do not control a representative are essentially wasted; those who cast them go unrepresented and are just as surely disenfranchised as if they had been barred from registering. Such conclusions, of course, depend upon a certain theory of the "effective" vote, a theory that is not inherent in the concept of representative democracy itself.[6]

6. Undoubtedly, one factor that has prompted our focus on control of seats has been a desire, when confronted with an abstract question of political theory concerning the measure of effective participation in government, to seize upon an objective standard for deciding cases, however much it may oversimplify the issues before us. If using control of seats as our standard does not reflect a very nuanced theory of political participation, it at least has the superficial advantage of appealing to the most easily measured indicia of political power.

In fact, it should be clear that the assumptions that have guided the Court reflect only one possible understanding of effective exercise of the franchise, an understanding based on the view that voters are "represented" only when they choose a delegate who will mirror their views in the legislative halls. But it is certainly possible to construct a theory of effective political participation that would accord greater importance to voters' ability to influence, rather than control, elections. And especially in a two-party system such as ours, the influence of a potential "swing" group of voters composing 10% to 20% of the electorate in a given district can be considerable. Even such a focus on practical influence, however, is not a necessary component of the definition of the "effective" vote. Some conceptions of representative government may primarily emphasize the formal value of the vote as a mechanism for participation in the electoral process, whether it results in control of a seat or not. Under such a theory, minorities unable to control elected posts would not be considered essentially without a vote; rather, a vote duly cast and counted would be deemed just as "effective" as any other. If a minority group is unable to control seats, that result may plausibly be attributed to the inescapable fact that, in a majoritarian system, numerical minorities lose elections.

In short, there are undoubtedly an infinite number of theories of effective suffrage, representation, and the proper apportionment of political power in a representative democracy that could be drawn upon to answer the questions posed in *Allen*. I do not pretend to have provided the most sophisticated account of the various possibilities; but such matters of political theory are beyond the ordinary sphere of federal judges. And that is precisely the point. The matters the Court has set out to resolve in vote dilution cases are questions of political philosophy, not questions of law. As such, they are not readily subjected to any judicially manageable standards that can guide courts in attempting to select between competing theories.

But the political choices the Court has had to make do not end with the determination that the primary purpose of the "effective" vote is controlling seats or with the selection of single-member districting as the mechanism for providing that control. In one sense, these were not even the most critical decisions to be made in devising standards for assessing claims of dilution, for, in itself, the selection of single-member districting as a benchmark election plan will tell a judge little about the number of minority districts to create. Single-member districting tells a court "how" members of a minority are to control seats, but not "how many" seats they should be allowed to control.

But "how many" is the critical issue. Once one accepts the proposition that the effectiveness of votes is measured in terms of the control of seats, the core of any vote dilution claim is an assertion that the group in question is unable to control the "proper" number of seats—that is, the number of seats that the minority's percentage of the population would enable it to control in the benchmark "fair" system. The claim is inherently based on ratios between the numbers of the minority in the population and the numbers of seats controlled. As a result, only a mathematical calculation can answer the fundamental question posed by a claim of vote dilution. And once again, in selecting the proportion that will be used to define the undiluted strength of a minority—the ratio that will provide the principle for decision in a vote dilution case—a court must make a political choice.

The ratio for which this Court has opted, and thus the mathematical principle driving the results in our cases, is undoubtedly direct proportionality. Indeed, four Members of the Court candidly recognized in *Gingles* that the Court had adopted a rule of roughly proportional representation, at least to the extent proportionality was possible given the geographic dispersion of minority populations. While in itself that choice may strike us intuitively as the fairest or most just rule to apply, opting for proportionality is still a political choice, not a result required by any principle of law.

B

The dabbling in political theory that dilution cases have prompted, however, is hardly the worst aspect of our vote dilution jurisprudence. Far more pernicious has been the Court's willingness to accept the one underlying premise that must inform every minority vote dilution claim: the assumption that the group asserting dilution is not merely a racial or ethnic group, but a group having distinct political interests as well. Of necessity, in resolving vote dilution actions we have given credence to the view that race defines political interest. We have acted on the implicit assumption that members of racial and ethnic groups must all think alike on important matters of public policy and must have their own "minority preferred" representatives holding seats in elected bodies if they are to be considered represented at all.

[O]perating under that assumption, we have assigned federal courts the task of ensuring that minorities are assured their "just" share of seats in elected bodies throughout the Nation.

To achieve that result through the currently fashionable mechanism of drawing majority-minority single-member districts, we have embarked upon what has been aptly characterized as a process of "creating racially 'safe boroughs.'" We have involved the federal courts, and indeed the Nation, in the enterprise of systematically dividing the country into electoral districts along racial lines—an enterprise of segregating the races into political homelands that amounts, in truth, to nothing short of a system of "political apartheid." Blacks are drawn into "black districts" and given "black representatives"; Hispanics are drawn into Hispanic districts and given "Hispanic representatives"; and so on. Worse still, it is not only the courts that have taken up this project. In response to judicial decisions and the promptings of the Justice Department, the States themselves, in an attempt to avoid costly and disruptive Voting Rights Act litigation, have begun to gerrymander electoral districts according to race.

The assumptions upon which our vote dilution decisions have been based should be repugnant to any nation that strives for the ideal of a color-blind Constitution.

As a practical political matter, our drive to segregate political districts by race can only serve to deepen racial divisions by destroying any need for voters or candidates to build bridges between racial groups or to form voting coalitions. "Black-preferred" candidates are assured election in "safe black districts"; white-preferred candidates are assured election in "safe white districts." Neither group needs to draw on support from the other's constituency to win on election day.

C

While the results we have already achieved under the Voting Rights Act might seem bad enough, we should recognize that our approach to splintering the electorate into racially designated single-member districts does not by any means mark a limit on the authority federal judges may wield to rework electoral systems under our Voting Rights Act jurisprudence. On the contrary, in relying on single-member districting schemes as a touchstone, our cases so far have been somewhat arbitrarily limited to addressing the interests of minority voters who are sufficiently geographically compact to form a majority in a single-member district. There is no reason *a priori*, however, that our focus should be so constrained. The decision to rely on single-member geographic districts as a mechanism for conducting elections is merely a political choice—and one that we might reconsider in the future. Indeed, it is a choice that has undoubtedly been influenced by the adversary process: In the cases that have come before us, plaintiffs have focused largely upon attacking multimember districts and have offered single-member schemes as the benchmark of an "undiluted" alternative.

But as the destructive effects of our current penchant for majority-minority districts become more apparent, courts will undoubtedly be called upon to reconsider adherence to geographic districting as a method for ensuring minority voting power. Already, some advocates have criticized the current strategy of creating majority-minority districts and have urged the adoption of other voting mechanisms—for example, cumulative voting[15] or a system using transferable votes[16] that can produce proportional results without requiring division of the electorate into racially segregated districts.

Such changes may seem radical departures from the electoral systems with which we are most familiar. Indeed, they may be unwanted by the people in the several States who

15. Under a cumulative voting scheme, a system commonly used in corporations to protect the interests of minority shareholders, each voter has as many votes as there are posts to be filled, and the voter may cast as many of his votes as he wishes for a single candidate. The system thus allows a numerical minority to concentrate its voting power behind a given candidate without requiring that the minority voters themselves be concentrated into a single district.

16. A system utilizing transferable votes is designed to ensure proportional representation with "mathematical exactness." Under such a system, each voter rank orders his choices of candidates. To win, a candidate must receive a fixed quota of votes, which may be set by any of several methods. Ballots listing a given candidate as the voter's first choice are counted for that candidate until the candidate has secured the quota of votes necessary for election. Remaining first-choice ballots for that candidate are then transferred to another candidate, usually the one listed as the second choice on the ballot. Like cumulative voting, the system allows a minority group to concentrate its voting power without requiring districting, and it has the additional advantage of ensuring that "surplus" votes are transferred to support the election of the minority voters' next preference.

purposely have adopted districting systems in their electoral laws. But nothing in our present understanding of the Voting Rights Act places a principled limit on the authority of federal courts that would prevent them from instituting a system of cumulative voting as a remedy under § 2, or even from establishing a more elaborate mechanism for securing proportional representation based on transferable votes.

D

A full understanding of the authority that our current interpretation of the Voting Rights Act assigns to the federal courts, and of the destructive effects that our exercise of that authority is presently having upon our body politic, compels a single conclusion: A systematic reexamination of our interpretation of the Act is required.

II

Section 2(a) of the Voting Rights Act provides that "[n]o voting qualification or prerequisite to voting or standard, practice, or procedure shall be imposed or applied by any State or political subdivision in a manner which results in a denial or abridgement of the right of any citizen of the United States to vote" on account of race, color, or membership in one of the language minority groups defined in the Act. Respondents contend that the terms "standard, practice, or procedure" should extend to cover the size of a governmental body. An examination of the text of § 2 makes it clear, however, that the terms of the Act do not reach that far; indeed, the terms of the Act do not allow many of the challenges to electoral mechanisms that we have permitted in the past. Properly understood, the terms "standard, practice, or procedure" in § 2(a) refer only to practices that affect minority citizens' access to the ballot. Districting systems and electoral mechanisms that may affect the "weight" given to a ballot duly cast and counted are simply beyond the purview of the Act.

A

In determining the scope of § 2(a), as when interpreting any statute, we should begin with the statutory language. Under the plain terms of the Act, § 2(a) covers only a defined category of state actions. Only "voting qualification[s]," "prerequisite[s] to voting," or "standard[s], practice[s], or procedure[s]" are subject to challenge under the Act. The first two items in this list clearly refer to conditions or tests applied to regulate citizens' access to the ballot. They would cover, for example, any form of test or requirement imposed as a condition on registration or on the process of voting on election day.

Taken in isolation, the last grouping of terms—"standard, practice, or procedure"—may seem somewhat less precise. If we give the words their ordinary meanings, however—for they have no technical significance and are not defined in the Act—they would not normally be understood to include the size of a local governing body. Common sense indicates that the size of a governing body and other aspects of government structure do not comfortably fit within the terms "standard, practice, or procedure." Moreover, we need not simply treat the terms in isolation; indeed, it would be a mistake to do so. Reading the words in context strongly suggests that § 2(a) must be understood as referring to any standard, practice, or procedure with respect to voting.

But under our precedents, we have already stretched the terms "standard, practice, or procedure" beyond the limits of ordinary meaning. We have concluded, for example, that the choice of a certain set of district lines is a "procedure," or perhaps a "practice," concerning voting subject to challenge under the Act, even though the drawing of a given set of district lines has nothing to do with the basic process of allowing a citizen to vote—that is, the process of registering, casting a ballot, and having it counted. Similarly, we have determined that the use of multimember districts, rather than single-member districts, can be challenged under the Act.

If we return to the Act to reexamine the terms setting out the actions regulated by § 2, a careful reading of the statutory text will reveal a good deal more about the limitations on the scope of the section than suggested above. The terms "standard, practice, or procedure" appear to have been included in § 2 as a sort of catchall provision. They seem phrased with an eye to eliminating the possibility of evasion. Nevertheless, they are catchall terms that round out a list, and a sensible and long-established maxim of construction limits the way we should understand such general words appended to an enumeration of more specific items. The principle of *ejusdem generis* suggests that such general terms should be understood to refer to items belonging to the same class that is defined by the more specific terms in the list.

Here, the specific items described in § 2(a) ("voting qualification[s]" and "prerequisite[s] to voting") indicate that Congress was concerned in this section with any procedure, however it might be denominated, that regulates citizens' access to the ballot—that is, any procedure that might erect a barrier to prevent the potential voter from casting his vote. In describing the laws that would be subject to § 2, Congress focused attention upon provisions regulating the interaction between the individual voter and the voting process—on hurdles the citizen might have to cross in the form of "prerequisites" or "qualifications." The general terms in the section are most naturally understood, therefore, to refer to any methods for conducting a part of the voting process that might similarly be used to interfere with a citizen's ability to cast his vote, and they are undoubtedly intended to ensure that the entire voting process—a process that begins with registration and includes the casting of a ballot and having the ballot counted—is covered by the Act. Simply by including general terms in § 2(a) to ensure the efficacy of the restriction imposed, Congress should not be understood to have expanded the scope of the restriction beyond the logical limits implied in the specific terms of the statute.

Moreover, it is not only in the terms describing the practices regulated under the Act that § 2(a) focuses on the individual voter. The section also speaks only in the singular of the right of "any citizen" to vote. Giving the terms "standard, practice, or procedure" an expansive interpretation to reach potentially dilutive practices, however, would distort that focus on the individual, for a vote dilution claim necessarily depends on the assertion of a group right. At the heart of the claim is the contention that the members of a group collectively have been unable to exert the influence that their numbers suggest they might under an alternative system. Such a group right, however, finds no grounding in the terms of § 2(a).

Finally, as our cases have shown, reading § 2(a) to reach beyond laws that regulate in some way citizens' access to the ballot turns the section into a command for courts to evaluate abstract principles of political theory in order to develop rules for deciding which votes are "diluted" and which are not. Common sense would suggest that we should not lightly interpret the Act to require courts to address such matters so far outside the normal bounds of judicial competence, and the mere use of three more general terms at the end of the list of regulated practices in § 2(a) cannot properly be understood to incorporate such an expansive command into the Act.

Properly understood, therefore, § 2(a) is a provision designed to protect access to the ballot, and in regulating "standard[s], practice[s], and procedure[s]," it reaches only those state laws that [relate to] either voter qualifications or the manner in which elections are conducted. The section thus covers all manner of registration requirements, the practices surrounding registration (including the selection of times and places where registration takes place and the selection of registrars), the locations of polling places, the times polls are open, the use of paper ballots as opposed to voting machines, and other similar aspects of the voting process that might be manipulated to deny any citizen the right to cast a ballot and have it properly counted. The section does not cover, however, the choice of a multi-member over a single-member districting system or the selection of one set of districting lines over another, or any other such electoral mechanism or method of election that might reduce the weight or influence a ballot may have in controlling the outcome of an election.

Of course, this interpretation of the terms "standard, practice, or procedure" effectively means that § 2(a) does not provide for any claims of what we have called vote "dilution." But that is precisely the result suggested by the text of the statute. Section 2(a) nowhere uses the term "vote dilution" or suggests that its goal is to ensure that votes are given their proper "weight." And an examination of § 2(b) does not suggest any different result. It is true that in construing § 2 to reach vote dilution claims in *Thornburg v. Gingles*, the Court relied largely on the gloss on § 2(b) supplied in the legislative history of the 1982 amendments to the Act. But the text of § 2(b) supplies a weak foundation indeed for reading the Act to reach such claims.

As the Court concluded in *Gingles*, the 1982 amendments incorporated into the Act, and specifically into § 2(b), a "results" test for measuring violations of § 2(a). That test was intended to replace, for § 2 purposes, the "intent" test the Court had announced in *Bolden* for voting rights claims under § 2 of the Voting Rights Act and under the Fourteenth and Fifteenth Amendments. Section 2(a) thus prohibits certain state actions that may "resul[t] in a denial or abridgement" of the right to vote, and § 2(b) incorporates virtually the exact language of the "results test" employed by the Court in *White v. Regester*, and applied in constitutional voting rights cases before our decision in *Bolden*. The section directs courts to consider whether "based on the totality of circumstances," a state practice results in members of a minority group "hav[ing] less opportunity than other members of the electorate to participate in the political process and to elect representatives of their choice."

But the mere adoption of a "results" test, rather than an "intent" test, says nothing about the type of state laws that may be challenged using that test. On the contrary, the type of state law that may be challenged under § 2 is addressed explicitly in § 2(a). While § 2(a) defines and explicitly limits the type of voting practice that may be challenged under the Act, § 2(b) provides only "the test for determining the legality of such a practice." Thus, as an initial matter, there is no reason to think that § 2(b) could serve to expand the scope of the prohibition in § 2(a), which, as I described above, does not extend by its terms to electoral mechanisms that might have a dilutive effect on group voting power.

Even putting that concern aside for the moment, it should be apparent that the incorporation of a results test into the amended section does not necessarily suggest that Congress intended to allow claims of vote dilution under § 2. A results test is useful to plaintiffs whether they are challenging laws that restrict access to the ballot or laws that accomplish some diminution in the "proper weight" of a group's vote. Nothing about the test itself suggests that it is inherently tied to vote dilution claims. A law, for example, limiting the times and places at which registration can occur might be adopted with the purpose of limiting black voter registration, but it could be extremely difficult to prove the discriminatory intent behind such a facially neutral law. The results test would allow plaintiffs to mount a successful challenge to the law under § 2 without such proof.

Moreover, nothing in the language § 2(b) uses to describe the results test particularly indicates that the test was intended to be used under the Act for assessing claims of dilution. Section 2(b) directs courts to consider whether, under the "totality of circumstances," members of a minority group "have less opportunity than other members of the electorate to participate in the political process and to elect representatives of their choice." The most natural reading of that language would suggest that citizens have an equal "opportunity" to participate in the electoral process and an equal "opportunity" to elect representatives when they have been given the same free and open access to the ballot as other citizens and their votes have been properly counted. The section speaks in terms of an opportunity—a chance—to participate and to elect, not an assured ability to attain any particular result. And since the ballot provides the formal mechanism for obtaining access to the political process and for electing representatives, it would seem that one who has had the same chance as others to register and to cast his ballot has had an equal opportunity to participate and to elect, whether or not any of the candidates he chooses is ultimately successful.

To be sure, the test in § 2(b) could be read to apply to claims of vote dilution as well. But to conclude, for example, that a multimember districting system had denied a group of voters an equal opportunity to participate in the political process and to elect representatives, a court would have to embark on the extended project in political theory that I described above in Part I of this opinion. In other words, a court would have to develop some theory of the benchmark undiluted voting system that provides minorities with the "fairest" or most "equitable" share of political influence. Undoubtedly, a dizzying array of concepts of political equality might be described to aid in that task, and each could be used to attribute different values to different systems of election. But the statutory command to determine whether members of a minority have had an equal "opportunity . . . to participate in the political process and to elect representatives" provides no guidance concerning which one of the possible standards setting undiluted voting strength should be chosen over the others. And it would be contrary to common sense to read § 2(b)'s reference to equal opportunity as a charter for federal courts to embark on the ambitious project of developing a theory of political equality to be imposed on the Nation.

It is true that one factor courts may consider under the results test might fit more comfortably with an interpretation of the Act that reaches vote dilution claims. Section 2(b) provides that "one circumstance" that may be considered in assessing the results test is the "extent to which members of a protected class have been elected to office." Obviously, electoral outcomes would be relevant to claims of vote dilution (assuming, of course, that control of seats has been selected as the measure of effective voting). But in some circumstances, results in recent elections might also be relevant for demonstrating that a particular practice concerning registration or polling has served to suppress minority voting. Better factors to consider would be figures for voter registration or turnout at the last election, broken down according to race. But where such data are not readily available, election results may certainly be "one circumstance" to consider in determining whether a challenged practice has resulted in denying a minority group access to the political process. The Act merely directs courts not to ignore such evidence of electoral outcomes altogether.

Moreover, the language providing that electoral outcomes may be considered as "one circumstance" in the results test is explicitly qualified by the provision in § 2(b) that most directly speaks to the question whether § 2 was meant to reach claims of vote dilution—and which suggests that dilution claims are not covered by the section. The last clause in the subsection states in unmistakable terms that "nothing in this section establishes a right to have members of a protected class elected in numbers equal to their proportion in the population." As four Members of the Court observed in *Gingles*, there is "an inherent tension" between this disclaimer of proportional representation and an interpretation of § 2 that encompasses vote dilution claims. As I explained above, dilution claims, by their very nature, depend upon a mathematical principle. The heart of the claim is an assertion that the plaintiff group does not hold the "proper" number of seats. As a result, the principle for deciding the case must be supplied by an arithmetic ratio. Either the group has attained the "proper" number of seats under the current election system, or it has not.

By declaring that the section provides no right to proportional representation, § 2(b) necessarily commands that the existence or absence of proportional electoral results should not become the deciding factor in assessing § 2 claims. But in doing so, § 2(b) removes from consideration the most logical ratio for assessing a claim of vote dilution. To resolve a dilution claim under § 2, therefore, a court either must arbitrarily select a different ratio to represent the "undiluted" norm, a ratio that would have less intuitive appeal than direct proportionality, or it must effectively apply a proportionality test in direct contravention of the text of the Act—hence the "inherent tension" between the text of the Act and vote dilution claims. Given that § 2 nowhere speaks in terms of "dilution," an explicit disclaimer removing from the field of play the most natural deciding principle in dilution cases is surely a strong signal that such claims do not fall within the ambit of the Act.

It is true that the terms "standard, practice, or procedure" in § 5 of the Act have been construed to reach districting systems and other potentially dilutive electoral mechanisms, and Congress has reenacted § 5 subsequent to our decisions adopting that expansive interpretation. Nevertheless, the text of the section suggests precisely the same focus on measures that relate to access to the ballot that appears in § 2.

B

From the foregoing, it should be clear that, as far as the text of the Voting Rights Act is concerned, "§ 2 does not speak in terms of vote dilution." *Gingles* (O'Connor, J., concurring in judgment). One might wonder, then, why we have consistently concluded that "[w]e know that Congress intended to allow vote dilution claims to be brought under § 2." *Id.* The juxtaposition of the two statements surely makes the result in our cases appear extraordinary, since it suggests a sort of statutory construction through divination that has allowed us to determine that Congress "really meant" to enact a statute about vote dilution even though Congress did not do so explicitly. In truth, our method of construing § 2 has been only little better than that, for the only source we have relied upon for the expansive meaning we have given § 2 has been the legislative history of the Act.

We first considered the amended § 2 in *Thornburg v. Gingles*. Although the precise scope of the terms "standard, practice, or procedure" was not specifically addressed in that case, *Gingles* nevertheless established our current interpretation of the amended section as a provision that addresses vote dilution, and in particular it fixed our understanding that the results test in § 2(b) is intended to measure vote dilution in terms of electoral outcomes.

In approaching § 2, the *Gingles* Court, based on little more than a bald assertion that "the authoritative source for legislative intent lies in the Committee Reports on the bill," bypassed a consideration of the text of the Act and proceeded to interpret the section based almost exclusively on its legislative history. It was from the legislative history that the Court culled its understanding that § 2 is a provision encompassing claims that an electoral system has diluted a minority group's vote and its understanding that claims of dilution are to be evaluated based upon how closely electoral outcomes under a given system approximate the outcomes that would obtain under an alternative, undiluted norm.

Contrary to the remarkable "legislative history first" method of statutory construction pursued in *Gingles*, however, I had thought it firmly established that the "authoritative source" for legislative intent was the text of the statute passed by both Houses of Congress and presented to the President, not a series of partisan statements about purposes and objectives collected by congressional staffers and packaged into a committee report. As outlined above, had the Court addressed the text, it would have concluded that the terms of the Act do not address matters of vote "dilution."

Of course, as mentioned above, *Gingles* did not directly address the meaning of the terms "standard, practice, or procedure" in § 2(a). The understanding that those terms extend to a State's laws establishing various electoral mechanisms dates to our decision in *Allen*, in which we construed the identical terms in § 5 of the Act. But the Court's method of statutory construction in *Allen* was little different from that pursued in *Gingles*, and as the analysis of the text of § 5 above demonstrates, it similarly yielded an interpretation in tension with the terms of the Act.

Thus, to the extent that *Allen* implicitly has served as the basis for our subsequent interpretation of the terms of § 2, it hardly can be thought to provide any surer rooting in the language of the Act than the method of statutory construction pursued in *Gingles*.

C

"*Stare decisis* is not an inexorable command," *Payne v. Tennessee* (1991). Indeed, when governing decisions are unworkable or are badly reasoned, this Court has never felt constrained to follow precedent. The discussion above should make clear that our decision in *Gingles* interpreting the scope of § 2 was badly reasoned; it wholly substituted reliance on legislative history for analysis of statutory text. In doing so, it produced a far more expansive interpretation of § 2 than a careful reading of the language of the statute would allow.

Our interpretation of § 2 has also proved unworkable. As I outlined above, it has mired the federal courts in an inherently political task—one that requires answers to questions that are ill-suited to principled judicial resolution. Under § 2, we have assigned the federal judiciary a project that involves, not the application of legal standards to the facts of various cases or even the elaboration of legal principles on a case-by-case basis, but rather the creation of standards from an abstract evaluation of political philosophy.

In my view, our current practice should not continue. Not for another Term, not until the next case, not for another day. The disastrous implications of the policies we have adopted under the Act are too grave; the dissembling in our approach to the Act too damaging to the credibility of the Federal Judiciary. The "inherent tension"—indeed, I would call it an irreconcilable conflict—between the standards we have adopted for evaluating vote dilution claims and the text of the Voting Rights Act would itself be sufficient in my view to warrant overruling the interpretation of § 2 set out in *Gingles*. When that obvious conflict is combined with the destructive effects our expansive reading of the Act has had in involving the Federal Judiciary in the project of dividing the Nation into racially segregated electoral districts, I can see no reasonable alternative to abandoning our current unfortunate understanding of the Act.

I cannot adhere to the construction of § 2 embodied in our decision in *Thornburg v. Gingles*. I reject the assumption implicit in that case that the terms "standard, practice, or procedure" in § 2(a) of the Voting Rights Act can be construed to cover potentially dilutive electoral mechanisms. Understood in context, those terms extend the Act's prohibitions only to state enactments that regulate citizens' access to the ballot or the processes for counting a ballot. The terms do not include a State's or political subdivision's choice of one districting scheme over another.

III

[Omitted]

NOTES ON JUSTICE THOMAS'S OPINION IN *HOLDER v. HALL*

1. Justice Thomas passionately attacks the Court's decisions to allow vote dilution challenges under both the Constitution (footnote 1) and the Voting Rights Act. Do you agree or disagree with his criticisms? Do you agree or disagree with his approach to interpreting the statutory language of amended Section 2?
2. Justice Thomas raises the prospect of the Court opting to order into effect a system of proportional representation (e.g., cumulative voting) rather than single-member districts as a remedy for vote dilution under Section 2. Even though Justice Thomas would not support the federal judiciary using Section 2 to install a system of proportional representation as a remedy for vote dilution, would you?
3. What does Justice Thomas's opinion (which reads like a dissent but is actually an opinion concurring in the judgment) add to the debate regarding the Court's role in resolving election disputes? Is there any way for the Court to decide redistricting cases without becoming too enmeshed in the "political thicket"? More specifically, Justice Thomas criticizes prior precedent for taking sides in what he ultimately concludes is a debate about political philosophy. Why does he think it is improper for the Court to determine, as a matter of law, what kinds of governmental structures pass muster either under the Constitution or the Voting Rights Act?

D. Section 5 of the Voting Rights Act

The Voting Rights Act of 1965 contains another important provision related to redistricting: Section 5. As you will learn, Section 5 is quite distinct from Section 2. Section 5, however, was essentially rendered dormant by the U.S. Supreme Court's 2013 decision in *Shelby County v. Holder.* With the decision in *Shelby County*, you may wonder why it is necessary to learn about Section 5 at all. There are several reasons: (1) it is possible that Congress will address some of the constitutional concerns expressed by the Court in *Shelby County* and revive Section 5; (2) the Section 5 process—which will be described in detail below—may be revived through the use of Section 3(c) of the Voting Rights Act (which will also be described below); (3) it is possible that some of the substantive principles from Section 5—most notably Section 5's non-retrogression principle—will be imported into Section 2 litigation; (4) the decision in *Shelby County* may have implications for the constitutionality of Section 2 of the Voting Rights Act; and (5) Section 5 appeared to play an important role in the development of racial gerrymandering doctrine—which is the next topic we will tackle in relation to redistricting.

With that as an introduction, we will proceed with a somewhat lengthy description of Section 5 so as to provide adequate context for the two opinions from *Shelby County* that you will read—Chief Justice Roberts's opinion for a five-member majority and Justice Ginsburg's dissent.*

The Reason Section 5 was Created. Section 5 was part of the original Voting Rights Act of 1965. The history of Section 5 will be described in the *Shelby County* opinions, but for now it suffices to know that it was a response to what might be termed "massive resistance" on the part of Southern jurisdictions to the enfranchisement of African Americans. Prior to passage of the Voting Rights Act, many Southern jurisdictions refused to allow African-American citizens to register to vote—often through the discriminatory application of literacy tests by county boards of registrars. And even when successful lawsuits would be brought to enjoin existing discriminatory registration practices, the jurisdictions would then switch to a new discriminatory tactic not covered by the injunction. For instance, after receiving a court order to stop engaging in disparate treatment of white and African-American voters during the voter registration process, local registrars would just permanently close the voter registration office.

In reaction to these events, Congress developed Section 5. Section 5 had several features—each of which will be described in more detail below. First, Section 5 did not apply nationwide; instead, it applied only to certain jurisdictions. Second, a jurisdiction subject to Section 5 could "bail out" and a jurisdiction not subject to Section 5 could be "bailed in." Third, Section 5 froze into place the existing voting laws, including redistricting plans, in these covered jurisdictions. Fourth, to change their existing voting laws, the covered jurisdictions would have to obtain "preclearance" from the federal government. Fifth, the federal government would review any voting changes to prevent racial discrimination. Sixth, Section 5 had a built-in sunset provision, but every time it was scheduled to

* The description of Section 5 that follows is based largely on two law review articles: Michael J. Pitts, *Section 5 of the Voting Rights Act: A Once and Future Remedy?*, 81 Denv. U. L. Rev. 225 (2003) and Michael J. Pitts, *Redistricting and Discriminatory Purpose*, 59 Am. U. L. Rev. 1575 (2010).

lapse, Congress extended it. Seventh, Section 5's constitutionality was upheld four times by the Supreme Court prior to *Shelby County*.

Section 5 Coverage/Section 4 of the Voting Rights Act. Unlike amended Section 2 of the Voting Rights Act—which applies nationwide—Section 5 applied only to certain portions of the country (primarily states and counties), commonly referred to as the "covered jurisdictions." Jurisdictions were covered by Section 5 through a formula found in Section 4 of the Voting Rights Act that was designed to target places where voting discrimination had occurred. That formula, developed in 1965, focused on the combination of the use of a literacy test (or similar device) plus reduced participation in the election process as evidenced by low voter registration or low voter turnout rates. Originally (in 1965), the coverage formula captured the entire states of Alabama, Alaska, Georgia, Louisiana, Mississippi, South Carolina, and Virginia, along with 40 counties in North Carolina and a few other counties in Arizona, Hawaii, and Idaho.

Importantly, when a covered jurisdiction became subject to Section 5, all of the political subdivisions within the covered jurisdiction also fell within Section 5's ambit. For example, when the State of Alabama was covered by Section 5, the state was covered but so was every county, city, school district, and so forth within Alabama. Similarly, when Onslow County, North Carolina, was covered, the county was covered but so was every city, town, school district, and the like within Onslow County.

The coverage formula was updated in 1970 and 1975. The update in 1970 was not very significant. The update in 1975, though, expanded the notion of what a "literacy test" was to include the holding of elections solely in English where a critical mass of voters was from a single language-minority group (e.g., Spanish speakers). Notably, this change in the coverage formula resulted in, among other things, the States of Arizona and Texas becoming subject to Section 5.

The coverage formula did not undergo any changes after 1975, and this fact will become important for the majority in *Shelby County*. As of 2008 (one of the last dates on which the Department of Justice publicly published a map), the covered jurisdictions were as shown in Figure 1-4.

"**Bail out.**" Once covered by Section 5, a jurisdiction could later escape coverage through a process known as "bail out." To bail out of Section 5, a covered jurisdiction had to file for a declaratory judgment from a three-judge panel of the U.S. District Court for the District of Columbia and, essentially, prove that it had not engaged in voting-related discrimination for the previous ten years. Historically, relatively few covered jurisdictions bailed out, but, as you can see from the note in the bottom corner of the map in Figure 1-4, the number of jurisdictions bailing out increased quite a bit after 2000.

"Bail in" (Section 3(c) of the Voting Rights Act). A jurisdiction not originally covered by Section 5 can essentially be bailed into coverage under Section 3(c) of the

Figure 1-4

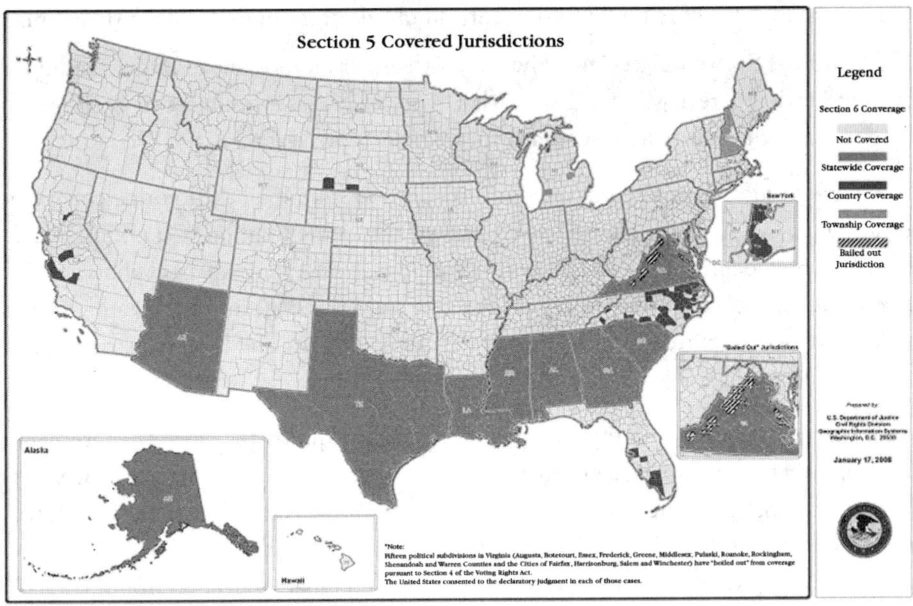

Source: U.S. Department of Justice.

Voting Rights Act. A court can order Section 3(c) coverage after "the court finds that violations of the fourteenth and fifteenth amendment justifying equitable relief have occurred" within the jurisdiction. 42 U.S.C. § 1973a. Historically, only a very few jurisdictions were "bailed in" under Section 3(c). However, with the decision in *Shelby County*, Section 3(c) may well take on greater prominence in future voting rights litigation.

Freezing of Law Until "Preclearance" Obtained. Having learned how jurisdictions were subjected to or escaped Section 5, it is time to turn to what Section 5 actually did. Section 5 froze into place the voting laws of the covered jurisdictions as of the date of coverage and required a jurisdiction to obtain "preclearance" from the federal government to implement a voting change. A covered jurisdiction could receive preclearance by litigation or through an administrative process. The litigation route involved obtaining a declaratory judgment from a three-judge panel of the U.S. District Court for the District of Columbia. The administrative process involved the covered jurisdiction submitting the voting change to the U.S. Department of Justice for review. (During Section 5's existence, the vast majority of preclearance activity took place through the administrative process.)

Here's a more concrete scenario about how Section 5 operates. After the State of Georgia passed its legislative redistricting plans following the 1970 Census, it could not immediately implement those plans. Instead, the state had to send its redistricting plans to

Washington, D.C. for federal approval. Once federal approval ("preclearance") was obtained, only then could the State of Georgia hold elections under its redistricting plans.

Scope of Section 5 Review. There are two aspects important to understanding the scope of Section 5 review. The first is what types of laws were subject to Section 5. The second is the substantive standard for Section 5 preclearance.

First, Section 5 required covered jurisdictions to submit all their voting changes for Section 5 review. A voting change could be a switch in the location of a polling place, a change to voter identification laws, a shift in voting machinery from paper ballots to touch-screen machines, or any other aspect of laws that had a direct nexus to the voting process. Importantly for purposes of this section of the casebook, state and local redistricting plans were subject to Section 5.

Second, Section 5, as originally written in 1965, required the federal government to deny approval to any voting change that would have "the purpose . . . or effect of denying or abridging the right to vote" on account of race or language-minority status. In essence, a covered jurisdiction had the burden of satisfying a two-prong test to receive preclearance: First, it had to prove that the voting change was not discriminatory in effect; second, it had to prove that the voting change was not discriminatory in purpose. And each of these substantive prongs underwent doctrinal developments during the 40-plus year history of Section 5.

Discriminatory Effect. Discriminatory effect under Section 5 came to mean something quite distinctive. In *Beer v. United States*, 425 U.S. 130 (1976), the Supreme Court interpreted Section 5 to bar any voting changes that "retrogress" minority voting strength. In the redistricting context, for a time, this meant that a jurisdiction could not eliminate what came to be known as either a "safe," "majority-minority," or "ability to elect" district. Put concretely into a simple hypothetical, if Onslow County, North Carolina, had a majority-minority single-member county commission district that allowed African-American voters to control who was elected from that district, the Section 5 effects prong prevented Onslow County from obtaining preclearance for a redistricting plan that eliminated that ability of African-American voters to elect a candidate from that district.

In 2003, however, the Supreme Court came up with a more nuanced standard for retrogression in *Georgia v. Ashcroft*, 539 U.S. 461 (2003). A simplified description of *Ashcroft* is that the Court made the somewhat groundbreaking pronouncement that "ability to elect" districts could be traded off against so-called "influence" districts—districts where a minority group can influence an electoral outcome even if its preferred candidate cannot be elected. Put more concretely into a simplified hypothetical, a district with, say, 60 percent African-American population that provided African-American voters the ability to elect a candidate could potentially be replaced with districts that had, say, 30 percent African-American population that would not give African-American voters the ability to elect candidates of their choice, so long as African Americans could "influence" who was elected from those district.

However, the "tweak" to retrogression doctrine brought about by *Ashcroft* was short-lived. In 2006, while it extended Section 5, Congress also reversed the Supreme Court's decision in *Ashcroft* (which was a decision of statutory interpretation rather than a constitutional holding). Congress did so by restoring "ability to elect" as the touchstone against which retrogression should be judged in the redistricting context.

Discriminatory Purpose. The broad strokes of the discriminatory purpose prong are much like the discriminatory effect prong: Initially, the discriminatory purpose prong was interpreted one way; then, in the early 2000s, the Supreme Court reinterpreted the purpose prong; and, subsequently, Congress reversed the Supreme Court's reinterpretation to restore the prior *status quo*.

The initial interpretation of the discriminatory purpose prong was that preclearance could be denied to a redistricting plan if it was adopted for *any* discriminatory purpose. What this meant was that preclearance could be denied if a redistricting plan resulted in unconstitutional vote dilution of the type prohibited by a case you have already encountered—*Rogers v. Lodge*. Basically, the result of this interpretation was that Section 5 could be used to compel covered jurisdictions to create additional districts that provided minority voters with the ability to elect candidates of their choice.

The Supreme Court, however, curbed the reach of Section 5's discriminatory purpose prong in *Reno v. Bossier Parish School Board*, 528 U.S. 320 (2000) (*Bossier Parish II*). In that case, the Court engaged in an interpretation of the statutory language to confine denial of preclearance under the purpose prong to redistricting plans that were adopted with a *purpose to retrogress*. Confining the purpose clause in this way ended the ability to use Section 5 to compel the creation of more districts that would allow minority voters to elect candidates of their choice.

Again, though, this shift in the interpretation of the purpose prong was short-lived. In 2006, when deciding whether to extend Section 5, Congress reversed the Supreme Court's decision in *Bossier Parish II*. Congress did so by restoring the ability of the federal government to deny preclearance when a redistricting plan was adopted with *any* discriminatory purpose.

Sunset Provision and Extensions. When it was first enacted in 1965, Section 5 contained a sunset provision that would lead to its lapsing in 1970. In 1970, Congress extended Section 5 for another five years. In 1975, Congress extended Section 5 for another seven years. In 1982, Congress extended Section 5 for another 25 years. And in 2006, Congress extended Section 5 for another 25 years (until 2031). It is this most recent 2006 extension that was at issue in *Shelby County*.

Prior Challenges to Constitutionality. As you may have noticed from the above description, Section 5 was a unique and somewhat extraordinary statute. There is not really an analogous statute anywhere in the U.S. Code. For this reason, the constitutionality of Section 5 itself and all its various facets has been questioned since its initial passage in 1965. A majority of the Supreme Court upheld Section 5 in the seminal decision of *South Carolina v. Katzenbach*, 383 U.S. 301 (1966). The constitutionality of each of the subsequent extensions of Section 5 were also litigated over the years, but—prior to *Shelby County*—each time the Court declined to declare Section 5—or any of its integral component pieces—invalid. *See Georgia v. United States*, 411 U.S. 526 (1973); *City of Rome v. United States*, 446 U.S. 156 (1980); *Lopez v. Monterey County*, 526 U.S. 266 (1999).

Almost immediately after the 2006 extension, a small utility district in Texas brought a lawsuit seeking to bail out of Section 5 and also seeking to have the statute struck down as unconstitutional. *Northwest Austin Municipal Utility District No. One v. Holder*, 557 U.S. 193 (2009) ("*NAMUDNO*"). In that case, a majority of the Court declined to rule on Section 5's constitutionality and instead engaged in an interpretation of the statute that allowed the utility district to bail out. However, in several paragraphs of *dicta*, the Court made plain that Section 5 raised serious constitutional concerns. *Shelby County* then picks up where that *dicta* left off.

SHELBY COUNTY v. HOLDER

133 S.Ct. 2612 (2013)

Chief Justice ROBERTS delivered the opinion of the Court.

The Voting Rights Act of 1965 employed extraordinary measures to address an extraordinary problem. Section 5 of the Act required States to obtain federal permission before enacting any law related to voting—a drastic departure from basic principles of federalism. And § 4 of the Act applied that requirement only to some States—an equally dramatic departure from the principle that all States enjoy equal sovereignty. This was strong medicine, but Congress determined it was needed to address entrenched racial discrimination in voting, "an insidious and pervasive evil which had been perpetuated in certain parts of our country through unremitting and ingenious defiance of the Constitution." *South Carolina v. Katzenbach* (1966). As we explained in upholding the law, "exceptional conditions can justify legislative measures not otherwise appropriate." Reflecting the unprecedented nature of these measures, they were scheduled to expire after five years.

Nearly 50 years later, they are still in effect; indeed, they have been made more stringent, and are now scheduled to last until 2031. There is no denying, however, that the conditions that originally justified these measures no longer characterize voting in the covered jurisdictions. By 2009, the racial gap in voter registration and turnout [was] lower in the States originally covered by § 5 than it [was] nationwide. Since that time, Census Bureau data indicate that African-American voter turnout has come to exceed white voter turnout in five of the six States originally covered by § 5, with a gap in the sixth State of less than one half of one percent.

At the same time, voting discrimination still exists; no one doubts that. The question is whether the Act's extraordinary measures, including its disparate treatment of the States, continue to satisfy constitutional requirements. As we put it a short time ago, "the Act imposes current burdens and must be justified by current needs." *Northwest Austin* [*Municipal Utility District No. One v. Holder*] (2009).

I

A

The Fifteenth Amendment was ratified in 1870, in the wake of the Civil War. It provides that "[t]he right of citizens of the United States to vote shall not be denied or abridged by the United States or by any State on account of race, color, or previous condition of servitude," and it gives Congress the "power to enforce this article by appropriate legislation."

The first century of congressional enforcement of the Amendment, however, can only be regarded as a failure. In the 1890s, Alabama, Georgia, Louisiana, Mississippi, North Carolina, South Carolina, and Virginia began to enact literacy tests for voter registration and to employ other methods designed to prevent African-Americans from voting. Congress passed statutes outlawing some of these practices and facilitating litigation against them, but litigation remained slow and expensive, and the States came up with new ways to discriminate as soon as existing ones were struck down. Voter registration of African-Americans barely improved.

Inspired to action by the civil rights movement, Congress responded in 1965 with the Voting Rights Act. Section 2 was enacted to forbid, in all 50 States, any "standard, practice, or procedure . . . imposed or applied . . . to deny or abridge the right of any citizen of the United States to vote on account of race or color." The current version forbids any "standard, practice, or procedure" that "results in a denial or abridgement of the right of any citizen of the United States to vote on account of race or color." Both the Federal Government and individuals have sued to enforce § 2, and injunctive relief is available in appropriate cases to block voting laws from going into effect. Section 2 is permanent, applies nationwide, and is not at issue in this case.

Other sections [of the Voting Rights Act] targeted only some parts of the country. At the time of the Act's passage, these "covered" jurisdictions were those States or political subdivisions that had maintained a test or device as a prerequisite to voting as of November 1, 1964, and had less than 50 percent voter registration or turnout in the 1964 Presidential election. Such tests or devices included literacy and knowledge tests, good moral character requirements, the need for vouchers from registered voters, and the like. A covered jurisdiction could "bail out" of coverage if it had not used a test or device in the preceding five years "for the purpose or with the effect of denying or abridging the right to vote on account of race or color." In 1965, the covered States included Alabama, Georgia,

Louisiana, Mississippi, South Carolina, and Virginia. The additional covered subdivisions included 39 counties in North Carolina and one in Arizona.

In those jurisdictions, § 4 of the Act banned all such tests or devices. Section 5 [of the Act] provided that no change in voting procedures could take effect until it was approved by federal authorities in Washington, D.C.—either the Attorney General or a court of three judges. A jurisdiction could obtain such "preclearance" only by proving that the change had neither "the purpose [nor] the effect of denying or abridging the right to vote on account of race or color."

Sections 4 and 5 were intended to be temporary; they were set to expire after five years. In *South Carolina v. Katzenbach*, we upheld the 1965 Act against constitutional challenge, explaining that it was justified to address "voting discrimination where it persists on a pervasive scale."

In 1970, Congress reauthorized the Act for another five years, and extended the coverage formula in § 4(b) to jurisdictions that had a voting test and less than 50 percent voter registration or turnout as of 1968. That swept in several counties in California, New Hampshire, and New York. Congress also extended the ban in § 4(a) on tests and devices nationwide.

In 1975, Congress reauthorized the Act for seven more years, and extended its coverage to jurisdictions that had a voting test and less than 50 percent voter registration or turnout as of 1972. Congress also amended the definition of "test or device" to include the practice of providing English-only voting materials in places where over five percent of voting-age citizens spoke a single language other than English. As a result of these amendments, the States of Alaska, Arizona, and Texas, as well as several counties in California, Florida, Michigan, New York, North Carolina, and South Dakota, became covered jurisdictions. Congress correspondingly amended sections 2 and 5 to forbid voting discrimination on the basis of membership in a language minority group, in addition to discrimination on the basis of race or color. Finally, Congress made the nationwide ban on tests and devices permanent.

In 1982, Congress reauthorized the Act for 25 years, but did not alter its coverage formula. Congress did, however, amend the bailout provisions, allowing political subdivisions of covered jurisdictions to bail out. Among other prerequisites for bailout, jurisdictions and their subdivisions must not have used a forbidden test or device, failed to receive preclearance, or lost a § 2 suit, in the ten years prior to seeking bailout.

We upheld each of these reauthorizations against constitutional challenge. *See Georgia v. United States* (1973); *City of Rome v. United States* (1980); *Lopez v. Monterey County* (1999).

In 2006, Congress again reauthorized the Voting Rights Act for 25 years, again without change to its coverage formula. Congress also amended § 5 to prohibit more conduct than before. Section 5 now forbids voting changes with "any discriminatory purpose" as well as voting changes that diminish the ability of citizens, on account of race, color, or language minority status, "to elect their preferred candidates of choice."

Shortly after this reauthorization, a Texas utility district brought suit, seeking to bail out from the Act's coverage and, in the alternative, challenging the Act's constitutionality. *Northwest Austin.* A three-judge District Court explained that only a State or political subdivision was eligible to seek bailout under the statute, and concluded that the utility district was not a political subdivision, a term that encompassed only "counties, parishes, and voter-registering subunits." The District Court also rejected the constitutional challenge.

We reversed. We explained that "normally the Court will not decide a constitutional question if there is some other ground upon which to dispose of the case." Concluding that "underlying constitutional concerns," among other things, "compel[led] a broader reading of the bailout provision," we construed the statute to allow the utility district to seek bailout. In doing so we expressed serious doubts about the Act's continued constitutionality.

We explained that § 5 "imposes substantial federalism costs" and "differentiates between the States, despite our historic tradition that all the States enjoy equal sovereignty." We also noted that "[t]hings have changed in the South. Voter turnout and registration rates now approach parity. Blatantly discriminatory evasions of federal decrees are rare. And minority candidates hold office at unprecedented levels." Finally, we questioned whether the problems that § 5 meant to address were still "concentrated in the jurisdictions singled out for preclearance."

Eight Members of the Court subscribed to these views, and the remaining Member would have held the Act unconstitutional. Ultimately, however, the Court's construction of the bailout provision left the constitutional issues for another day.

B

Shelby County is located in Alabama, a covered jurisdiction. It has not sought bailout, as the Attorney General has recently objected to voting changes proposed from within the county. Instead, in 2010, the county sued the Attorney General in Federal District Court in Washington, D.C., seeking a declaratory judgment that sections 4(b) and 5 of the Voting Rights Act are facially unconstitutional. The District Court ruled against the county and upheld the Act. [The Court of Appeals for the D.C. Circuit affirmed, and the Court granted certiorari.]

II

In *Northwest Austin*, we stated that "the Act imposes current burdens and must be justified by current needs." And we concluded that "a departure from the fundamental principle of equal sovereignty requires a showing that a statute's disparate geographic coverage is sufficiently related to the problem that it targets." These basic principles guide our review of the question before us.[3]

A

The Constitution and laws of the United States are "the supreme Law of the Land." U.S. Const., Art. VI, cl. 2. State legislation may not contravene federal law. The Federal Government does not, however, have a general right to review and veto state enactments before they go into effect. A proposal to grant such authority to "negative" state laws was considered at the Constitutional Convention, but rejected in favor of allowing state laws to take effect, subject to later challenge under the Supremacy Clause.

Outside the strictures of the Supremacy Clause, States retain broad autonomy in structuring their governments and pursuing legislative objectives. Indeed, the Constitution provides that all powers not specifically granted to the Federal Government are reserved to the States or citizens. Amdt. 10. This allocation of powers in our federal system preserves the integrity, dignity, and residual sovereignty of the States. But the federal balance is not just an end in itself: Rather, federalism secures to citizens the liberties that derive from the diffusion of sovereign power.

More specifically, the Framers of the Constitution intended the States to keep for themselves, as provided in the Tenth Amendment, the power to regulate elections. Of course, the Federal Government retains significant control over federal elections. For instance, the Constitution authorizes Congress to establish the time and manner for electing Senators and Representatives. Art. I, § 4, cl. 1. But States have broad powers to determine the conditions under which the right of suffrage may be exercised. And [e]ach State has the power to prescribe the qualifications of its officers and the manner in which they shall be chosen. Drawing lines for congressional districts is likewise primarily the duty and responsibility of the State.

Not only do States retain sovereignty under the Constitution, there is also a "fundamental principle of equal sovereignty" among the States. *Northwest Austin.* Over a hundred years ago, this Court explained that our Nation "was and is a union of States, equal in power, dignity and authority." *Coyle v. Smith* (1911). Indeed, the constitutional equality of the States is essential to the harmonious operation of the scheme upon which the Republic was organized. *Coyle* concerned the admission of new States, and *Katzenbach* rejected the notion that the principle operated as a bar on differential treatment outside that context. At the same time, as we made clear in *Northwest Austin*, the fundamental principle of equal sovereignty remains highly pertinent in assessing subsequent disparate treatment of States.

The Voting Rights Act sharply departs from these basic principles. It suspends all changes to state election law—however innocuous—until they have been precleared by

3. Both the Fourteenth and Fifteenth Amendments were at issue in *Northwest Austin*, and accordingly *Northwest Austin* guides our review under both Amendments in this case.

federal authorities in Washington, D.C. States must beseech the Federal Government for permission to implement laws that they would otherwise have the right to enact and execute on their own, subject of course to any injunction in a § 2 action.

And despite the tradition of equal sovereignty, the Act applies to only nine States (and several additional counties). While one State waits [for preclearance], its neighbor can typically put the same law into effect immediately, through the normal legislative process. Even if a noncovered jurisdiction is sued, there are important differences between those proceedings and preclearance proceedings; the preclearance proceeding not only switches the burden of proof to the supplicant jurisdiction, but also applies substantive standards quite different from those governing the rest of the nation.

All this explains why, when we first upheld the Act in 1966, we described it as "stringent" and "potent." *Katzenbach*. We recognized that it "may have been an uncommon exercise of congressional power," but concluded that "legislative measures not otherwise appropriate" could be justified by "exceptional conditions." We have since noted that the Act authorizes federal intrusion into sensitive areas of state and local policymaking, and represents an extraordinary departure from the traditional course of relations between the States and the Federal Government. As we reiterated in *Northwest Austin*, the Act constitutes "extraordinary legislation otherwise unfamiliar to our federal system."

B

In 1966, we found these departures from the basic features of our system of government justified. The "blight of racial discrimination in voting" had "infected the electoral process in parts of our country for nearly a century." *Katzenbach*. Several States had enacted a variety of requirements and tests specifically designed to prevent African-Americans from voting. Case-by-case litigation had proved inadequate to prevent such racial discrimination in voting, in part because States "merely switched to discriminatory devices not covered by the federal decrees," "enacted difficult new tests," or simply "defied and evaded court orders." *Id.* Shortly before enactment of the Voting Rights Act, only 19.4 percent of African-Americans of voting age were registered to vote in Alabama, only 31.8 percent in Louisiana, and only 6.4 percent in Mississippi. Those figures were roughly 50 percentage points or more below the figures for whites.

In short, we concluded that "[u]nder the compulsion of these unique circumstances, Congress responded in a permissibly decisive manner." *Id.* We also noted then and have emphasized since that this extraordinary legislation was intended to be temporary, set to expire after five years.

At the time, the coverage formula—the means of linking the exercise of the unprecedented authority with the problem that warranted it—made sense. We found that "Congress chose to limit its attention to the geographic areas where immediate action seemed necessary." *Katzenbach*. The areas where Congress found "evidence of actual voting discrimination" shared two characteristics: the use of tests and devices for voter registration, and a voting rate in the 1964 presidential election at least 12 points below the national average. We explained that "[t]ests and devices are relevant to voting discrimination because of their long history as a tool for perpetrating the evil; a low voting rate is pertinent for the obvious reason that widespread disenfranchisement must inevitably affect the number of actual voters." We therefore concluded that "the coverage formula [was] rational in both practice and theory." It accurately reflected those jurisdictions uniquely characterized by voting discrimination "on a pervasive scale," linking coverage to the devices used to effectuate discrimination and to the resulting disenfranchisement. The formula ensured that the "stringent remedies [were] aimed at areas where voting discrimination ha[d] been most flagrant."

C

Nearly 50 years later, things have changed dramatically. Shelby County contends that the preclearance requirement, even without regard to its disparate coverage, is now unconstitutional. Its arguments have a good deal of force. In the covered jurisdictions, "[v]oter turnout and registration rates now approach parity. Blatantly discriminatory evasions of federal decrees are rare. And minority candidates hold office at unprecedented levels." *Northwest Austin.* The tests and devices that blocked access to the ballot have been forbidden nationwide for over 40 years.

Those conclusions are not ours alone. Congress said the same when it reauthorized the Act in 2006, writing that "[s]ignificant progress has been made in eliminating first generation barriers experienced by minority voters, including increased numbers of registered minority voters, minority voter turnout, and minority representation in Congress, State legislatures, and local elected offices." The House Report elaborated that "the number of African-Americans who are registered and who turn out to cast ballots has increased significantly over the last 40 years, particularly since 1982," and noted that "[i]n some circumstances, minorities register to vote and cast ballots at levels that surpass those of white voters." That Report also explained that there have been "significant increases in the number of African-Americans serving in elected offices"; more specifically, there has been approximately a 1,000 percent increase since 1965 in the number of African-American elected officials in the six States originally covered by the Voting Rights Act.

Census Bureau data from the most recent election indicate that African-American voter turnout exceeded white voter turnout in five of the six States originally covered by § 5, with a gap in the sixth State of less than one half of one percent. The preclearance statistics are also illuminating. In the first decade after enactment of § 5, the Attorney General objected to 14.2 percent of proposed voting changes. In the last decade before reenactment, the Attorney General objected to a mere 0.16 percent.

There is no doubt that these improvements are in large part because of the Voting Rights Act. The Act has proved immensely successful at redressing racial discrimination and integrating the voting process. During the "Freedom Summer" of 1964, in Philadelphia, Mississippi, three men were murdered while working in the area to register African-American voters. On "Bloody Sunday" in 1965, in Selma, Alabama, police beat and used tear gas against hundreds marching in support of African-American enfranchisement. Today both of those towns are governed by African-American mayors. Problems remain in these States and others, but there is no denying that, due to the Voting Rights Act, our Nation has made great strides.

Yet the Act has not eased the restrictions in § 5 or narrowed the scope of the coverage formula in § 4(b) along the way. Those extraordinary and unprecedented features were reauthorized—as if nothing had changed. In fact, the Act's unusual remedies have grown even stronger. When Congress reauthorized the Act in 2006, it did so for another 25 years on top of the previous 40—a far cry from the initial five-year period. Congress also expanded the prohibitions in § 5. We had previously interpreted § 5 to prohibit only those redistricting plans that would have the purpose or effect of worsening the position of minority groups. *Bossier II.* In 2006, Congress amended § 5 to prohibit laws that could have favored such groups but did not do so because of a discriminatory purpose. In addition, Congress expanded § 5 to prohibit any voting law "that has the purpose of or will have the effect of diminishing the ability of any citizens of the United States," on account of race, color, or language minority status, "to elect their preferred candidates of choice." § 1973c(b). In light of those two amendments, the bar that covered jurisdictions must clear has been raised even as the conditions justifying that requirement have dramatically improved.

Respondents do not deny that there have been improvements on the ground, but argue that much of this can be attributed to the deterrent effect of § 5, which dissuades covered jurisdictions from engaging in discrimination that they would resume should § 5 be struck down. Under this theory, however, § 5 would be effectively immune from scrutiny; no matter how "clean" the record of covered jurisdictions, the argument could always be made that it was deterrence that accounted for the good behavior.

The provisions of § 5 apply only to those jurisdictions singled out by § 4. We now consider whether that coverage formula is constitutional in light of current conditions.

III

A

When upholding the constitutionality of the coverage formula in 1966, we concluded that it was "rational in both practice and theory." *Katzenbach.* The formula looked to cause (discriminatory tests) and effect (low voter registration and turnout), and tailored the remedy (preclearance) to those jurisdictions exhibiting both.

By 2009, however, we concluded that the "coverage formula raise[d] serious constitutional questions." *Northwest Austin.* As we explained, a statute's "current burdens" must be justified by "current needs," and any "disparate geographic coverage" must be "sufficiently related to the problem that it targets." The coverage formula met that test in 1965, but no longer does so.

Coverage today is based on decades-old data and eradicated practices. The formula captures States by reference to literacy tests and low voter registration and turnout in the 1960s and early 1970s. But such tests have been banned nationwide for over 40 years. And voter registration and turnout numbers in the covered States have risen dramatically in the years since. Racial disparity in those numbers was compelling evidence justifying the preclearance remedy and the coverage formula. There is no longer such a disparity.

In 1965, the States could be divided into two groups: those with a recent history of voting tests and low voter registration and turnout, and those without those characteristics. Congress based its coverage formula on that distinction. Today the Nation is no longer divided along those lines, yet the Voting Rights Act continues to treat it as if it were.

B

The Government's defense of the formula is limited. First, the Government contends that the formula is "reverse-engineered": Congress identified the jurisdictions to be covered and then came up with criteria to describe them. Under that reasoning, there need not be any logical relationship between the criteria in the formula and the reason for coverage; all that is necessary is that the formula happen to capture the jurisdictions Congress wanted to single out.

The Government suggests that *Katzenbach* sanctioned such an approach, but the analysis in *Katzenbach* was quite different. *Katzenbach* reasoned that the coverage formula was rational because the "formula . . . was relevant to the problem": "Tests and devices are relevant to voting discrimination because of their long history as a tool for perpetrating the evil; a low voting rate is pertinent for the obvious reason that widespread disenfranchisement must inevitably affect the number of actual voters."

Here, by contrast, the Government's reverse-engineering argument does not even attempt to demonstrate the continued relevance of the formula to the problem it targets. And in the context of a decision as significant as this one—subjecting a disfavored subset of States to "extraordinary legislation otherwise unfamiliar to our federal system," *Northwest Austin*—that failure to establish even relevance is fatal.

The Government falls back to the argument that because the formula was relevant in 1965, its continued use is permissible so long as any discrimination remains in the States Congress identified back then—regardless of how that discrimination compares to discrimination in States unburdened by coverage. This argument does not look to "current political conditions," *Northwest Austin*, but instead relies on a comparison between the States in 1965. That comparison reflected the different histories of the North and South. It was in the South that slavery was upheld by law until uprooted by the Civil War, that the reign of Jim Crow denied African-Americans the most basic freedoms, and that state and local governments worked tirelessly to disenfranchise citizens on the basis of race. The Court invoked that history—rightly so—in sustaining the disparate coverage of the Voting Rights Act in 1966.

But history did not end in 1965. By the time the Act was reauthorized in 2006, there had been 40 more years of it. In assessing the "current need[ ]" for a preclearance system that treats States differently from one another today, that history cannot be ignored. During that time, largely because of the Voting Rights Act, voting tests were abolished, disparities in voter registration and turnout due to race were erased, and African-Americans attained political office in record numbers. And yet the coverage formula that Congress reauthorized in 2006 ignores these developments, keeping the focus on decades-old data relevant to decades-old problems, rather than current data reflecting current needs.

The Fifteenth Amendment commands that the right to vote shall not be denied or abridged on account of race or color, and it gives Congress the power to enforce that command. The Amendment is not designed to punish for the past; its purpose is to ensure a better future. To serve that purpose, Congress—if it is to divide the States—must identify those jurisdictions to be singled out on a basis that makes sense in light of current conditions. It cannot rely simply on the past. We made that clear in *Northwest Austin*, and we make it clear again today.

C

In defending the coverage formula, the Government, the intervenors, and the dissent also rely heavily on data from the record that they claim justify disparate coverage. Congress compiled thousands of pages of evidence before reauthorizing the Voting Rights Act. The court below and the parties have debated what that record shows. Regardless of how to look at the record, however, no one can fairly say that it shows anything approaching the "pervasive," "flagrant," "widespread," and "rampant" discrimination that faced Congress in 1965, and that clearly distinguished the covered jurisdictions from the rest of the Nation at that time.

But a more fundamental problem remains: Congress did not use the record it compiled to shape a coverage formula grounded in current conditions. It instead reenacted a formula based on 40-year-old facts having no logical relation to the present day. The dissent relies on "second-generation barriers," which are not impediments to the casting of ballots, but rather electoral arrangements that affect the weight of minority votes. That does not cure the problem. Viewing the preclearance requirements as targeting such efforts simply highlights the irrationality of continued reliance on the § 4 coverage formula, which is based on voting tests and access to the ballot, not vote dilution. We cannot pretend that we are reviewing an updated statute, or try our hand at updating the statute ourselves, based on the new record compiled by Congress. Contrary to the dissent's contention, we are not ignoring the record; we are simply recognizing that it played no role in shaping the statutory formula before us today.

The dissent also turns to the record to argue that, in light of voting discrimination in Shelby County, the county cannot complain about the provisions that subject it to preclearance. But that is like saying that a driver pulled over pursuant to a policy of stopping all redheads cannot complain about that policy, if it turns out his license has expired. Shelby County's claim is that the coverage formula here is unconstitutional in all its applications, because of how it selects the jurisdictions subjected to preclearance. The county was selected based on that formula, and may challenge it in court.

D

The dissent proceeds from a flawed premise. It quotes the famous sentence from *McCulloch v. Maryland*, with the following emphasis: "Let the end be legitimate, let it be within the scope of the constitution, and *all means which are appropriate, which are plainly adapted to that end*, which are not prohibited, but consist with the letter and spirit of the constitution, are constitutional." (Emphasis in dissent.) But this case is about a part of the sentence that the dissent does not emphasize—the part that asks whether a legislative means is "consist[ent] with the letter and spirit of the constitution." The dissent states that "[i]t cannot tenably be maintained" that this is an issue with regard to the Voting Rights Act, but four years ago, in an opinion joined by two of today's dissenters, the Court expressly stated that "[t]he Act's preclearance requirement and its coverage formula raise serious constitutional questions." *Northwest Austin*. The dissent does not explain how those "serious constitutional questions" became untenable in four short years.

The dissent treats the Act as if it were just like any other piece of legislation, but this Court has made clear from the beginning that the Voting Rights Act is far from ordinary.

In other ways as well, the dissent analyzes the question presented as if our decision in *Northwest Austin* never happened. For example, the dissent refuses to consider the principle of equal sovereignty, despite *Northwest Austin*'s emphasis on its significance. *Northwest Austin* also emphasized the "dramatic" progress since 1965, but the dissent describes current levels of discrimination as "flagrant," "widespread," and "pervasive." Despite the fact that *Northwest Austin* requires an Act's "disparate geographic coverage" to be "sufficiently related" to its targeted problems, the dissent maintains that an Act's limited coverage actually eases Congress's burdens, and suggests that a fortuitous relationship should suffice. Although *Northwest Austin* stated definitively that "current burdens" must be justified by "current needs," the dissent argues that the coverage formula can be justified by history, and that the required showing can be weaker on reenactment than when the law was first passed.

There is no valid reason to insulate the coverage formula from review merely because it was previously enacted 40 years ago. If Congress had started from scratch in 2006, it plainly could not have enacted the present coverage formula. It would have been irrational for Congress to distinguish between States in such a fundamental way based on 40-year-old data, when today's statistics tell an entirely different story. And it would have been irrational to base coverage on the use of voting tests 40 years ago, when such tests have been illegal since that time. But that is exactly what Congress has done.

3

Striking down an Act of Congress is the gravest and most delicate duty that this Court is called on to perform. We do not do so lightly. That is why, in 2009, we took care to avoid ruling on the constitutionality of the Voting Rights Act when asked to do so, and instead resolved the case then before us on statutory grounds. But in issuing that decision, we expressed our broader concerns about the constitutionality of the Act. Congress could have updated the coverage formula at that time, but did not do so. Its failure to act leaves us today with no choice but to declare § 4(b) unconstitutional. The formula in that section can no longer be used as a basis for subjecting jurisdictions to preclearance.

Our decision in no way affects the permanent, nationwide ban on racial discrimination in voting found in § 2. We issue no holding on § 5 itself, only on the coverage formula. Congress may draft another formula based on current conditions. Such a formula is an initial prerequisite to a determination that exceptional conditions still exist justifying such an extraordinary departure from the traditional course of relations between the States and the Federal Government. Our country has changed, and while any racial discrimination in voting is too much, Congress must ensure that the legislation it passes to remedy that problem speaks to current conditions.

The judgment of the Court of Appeals is reversed.

Justice THOMAS, concurring.

[Omitted]

Justice GINSBURG, with whom Justice BREYER, Justice SOTOMAYOR, and Justice KAGAN join, dissenting.

In the Court's view, the very success of § 5 of the Voting Rights Act demands its dormancy. Congress was of another mind. Recognizing that large progress has been made, Congress determined, based on a voluminous record, that the scourge of discrimination was not yet extirpated. The question this case presents is who decides whether, as currently operative, § 5 remains justifiable[1], this Court, or a Congress charged with the obligation to enforce the post-Civil War Amendments "by appropriate legislation." With overwhelming support in both Houses, Congress concluded that, for two prime reasons, § 5 should continue in force, unabated. First, continuance would facilitate completion of the impressive gains thus far made; and second, continuance would guard against backsliding. Those

1. The Court purports to declare unconstitutional only the coverage formula set out in § 4(b). But without that formula, § 5 is immobilized.

assessments were well within Congress' province to make and should elicit this Court's unstinting approbation.

I

[V]oting discrimination still exists; no one doubts that. But the Court today terminates the remedy that proved to be best suited to block that discrimination. The Voting Rights Act of 1965 (VRA) has worked to combat voting discrimination where other remedies had been tried and failed. Particularly effective is the VRA's requirement of federal preclearance for all changes to voting laws in the regions of the country with the most aggravated records of rank discrimination against minority voting rights.

A century after the Fourteenth and Fifteenth Amendments guaranteed citizens the right to vote free of discrimination on the basis of race, the "blight of racial discrimination in voting" continued to "infec[t] the electoral process in parts of our country." *South Carolina v. Katzenbach*. Early attempts to cope with this vile infection resembled battling the Hydra. Whenever one form of voting discrimination was identified and prohibited, others sprang up in its place.

Congress learned from experience that laws targeting particular electoral practices or enabling case-by-case litigation were inadequate to the task [of attacking racial discrimination in voting]. In the Civil Rights Acts of 1957, 1960, and 1964, Congress authorized and then expanded the power of the Attorney General to seek injunctions against public and private interference with the right to vote on racial grounds. But circumstances reduced the ameliorative potential of these legislative Acts:

> "Voting suits are unusually onerous to prepare, sometimes requiring as many as 6,000 man-hours spent combing through registration records in preparation for trial. Litigation has been exceedingly slow, in part because of the ample opportunities for delay afforded voting officials and others involved in the proceedings. Even when favorable decisions have finally been obtained, some of the States affected have merely switched to discriminatory devices not covered by the federal decrees or have enacted difficult new tests designed to prolong the existing disparity between white and Negro registration. Alternatively, certain local officials have defied and evaded court orders or have simply closed their registration offices to freeze the voting rolls." [*Katzenbach.*]

Patently, a new approach was needed.

Answering that need, the Voting Rights Act became one of the most consequential, efficacious, and amply justified exercises of federal legislative power in our Nation's history. Requiring federal preclearance of changes in voting laws in the covered jurisdictions—those States and localities where opposition to the Constitution's commands were most virulent—the VRA provided a fit solution for minority voters as well as for States. Under the preclearance regime established by § 5 of the VRA, covered jurisdictions must submit proposed changes in voting laws or procedures to the Department of Justice (DOJ). In the alternative, the covered jurisdiction may seek approval by a three-judge District Court in the District of Columbia.

After a century's failure to fulfill the promise of the Fourteenth and Fifteenth Amendments, passage of the VRA finally led to signal improvement on this front. [I]n assessing the overall effects of the VRA in 2006, Congress found that "[s]ignificant progress has been made in eliminating first generation barriers experienced by minority voters, including increased numbers of registered minority voters, minority voter turnout, and minority representation in Congress, State legislatures, and local elected offices. This progress is the direct result of the Voting Rights Act of 1965." On that matter of cause and effects there can be no genuine doubt.

Although the VRA wrought dramatic changes in the realization of minority voting rights, the Act, to date, surely has not eliminated all vestiges of discrimination against the exercise of the franchise by minority citizens. Jurisdictions covered by the preclearance requirement continued to submit, in large numbers, proposed changes to voting laws that the Attorney General declined to approve, auguring that barriers to minority voting would quickly resurface were the preclearance remedy eliminated. Congress also found that as "registration and voting of minority citizens increas[ed], other measures may be resorted to which would dilute increasing minority voting strength." Efforts to reduce the impact of minority votes, in contrast to direct attempts to block access to the ballot, are aptly described as "second-generation barriers" to minority voting.

Second-generation barriers come in various forms. One of the blockages is racial gerrymandering, the redrawing of legislative districts in an "effort to segregate the races for purposes of voting." Another is adoption of a system of at-large voting in lieu of district-by-district voting in a city with a sizable black minority. By switching to at-large voting, the overall majority could control the election of each city council member, effectively eliminating the potency of the minority's votes. Whatever the device employed, this Court has long recognized that vote dilution, when adopted with a discriminatory purpose, cuts down the right to vote as certainly as denial of access to the ballot.

In response to evidence of these substituted barriers, Congress reauthorized the VRA for five years in 1970, for seven years in 1975, and for 25 years in 1982. Each time, this Court upheld the reauthorization as a valid exercise of congressional power. As the 1982 reauthorization approached its 2007 expiration date, Congress again considered whether the VRA's preclearance mechanism remained an appropriate response to the problem of voting discrimination in covered jurisdictions.

Congress did not take this task lightly. Quite the opposite. The 109th Congress that took responsibility for the renewal started early and conscientiously. In October 2005, the House began extensive hearings. In April 2006, the Senate followed suit. [Eventually, the reauthorization of the Voting Rights Act passed the House by a vote of 390 yeas to 33 nays and passed the Senate by a vote of 98 to 0. President Bush signed it on July 27, 2006.]

In the long course of the legislative process, Congress "amassed a sizable record." *Northwest Austin*. The [record] presents countless examples of flagrant racial discrimination since the last reauthorization; Congress also brought to light systematic evidence that intentional racial discrimination in voting remains so serious and widespread in covered jurisdictions that section 5 preclearance is still needed.

After considering the full legislative record, Congress made the following findings: The VRA has directly caused significant progress in eliminating first-generation barriers to ballot access, leading to a marked increase in minority voter registration and turnout and the number of minority elected officials. But despite this progress, "second generation barriers constructed to prevent minority voters from fully participating in the electoral process" continued to exist, as well as racially polarized voting in the covered jurisdictions, which increased the political vulnerability of racial and language minorities in those jurisdictions. Extensive "[e]vidence of continued discrimination," Congress concluded, "clearly show[ed] the continued need for Federal oversight" in covered jurisdictions. The overall record demonstrated to the federal lawmakers that, "without the continuation of the Voting Rights Act of 1965 protections, racial and language minority citizens will be deprived of the opportunity to exercise their right to vote, or will have their votes diluted, undermining the significant gains made by minorities in the last 40 years."

Based on these findings, Congress reauthorized preclearance for another 25 years. The question before the Court is whether Congress had the authority under the Constitution to act as it did.

II

In answering this question, the Court does not write on a clean slate. It is well established that Congress' judgment regarding exercise of its power to enforce the Fourteenth and Fifteenth Amendments warrants substantial deference. The VRA addresses the combination of race discrimination and the right to vote, which is "preservative of all rights." *Yick Wo v. Hopkins* (1886). When confronting the most constitutionally invidious form of discrimination, and the most fundamental right in our democratic system, Congress' power to act is at its height.

The basis for this deference is firmly rooted in both constitutional text and precedent. The Fifteenth Amendment, which targets precisely and only racial discrimination in voting rights, states that, in this domain, "Congress shall have power to enforce this article by appropriate legislation."[2] In choosing this language, the Amendment's framers invoked

2. The Constitution uses the words "right to vote" in five separate places: the Fourteenth, Fifteenth, Nineteenth, Twenty-Fourth, and Twenty-Sixth Amendments. Each of these Amendments contains the same broad empowerment of Congress to enact "appropriate legislation" to enforce the protected right. The implication is unmistakable: Under our

Chief Justice Marshall's formulation of the scope of Congress' powers under the Necessary and Proper Clause:

> "Let the end be legitimate, let it be within the scope of the constitution, and *all means which are appropriate, which are plainly adapted to that end*, which are not prohibited, but consist with the letter and spirit of the constitution, are constitutional." *McCulloch v. Maryland* (1819) (emphasis added).

It cannot tenably be maintained that the VRA, an Act of Congress adopted to shield the right to vote from racial discrimination, is inconsistent with the letter or spirit of the Fifteenth Amendment, or any provision of the Constitution read in light of the Civil War Amendments. Nowhere in today's opinion, or in *Northwest Austin*[3], is there clear recognition of the transformative effect the Fifteenth Amendment aimed to achieve. Notably, the Founders' first successful amendment told Congress that it could make no law over a certain domain; in contrast, the Civil War Amendments used language [that] authorized transformative new federal statutes to uproot all vestiges of unfreedom and inequality and provided sweeping enforcement powers to enact appropriate legislation targeting state abuses.

Until today, in considering the constitutionality of the VRA, the Court has accorded Congress the full measure of respect its judgments in this domain should garner. *South Carolina v. Katzenbach* supplies the standard of review: "As against the reserved powers of the States, Congress may use any rational means to effectuate the constitutional prohibition of racial discrimination in voting." Faced with subsequent reauthorizations of the VRA, the Court has reaffirmed this standard. *City of Rome.* Today's Court does not purport to alter settled precedent establishing that the dispositive question is whether Congress has employed "rational means."

For three reasons, legislation reauthorizing an existing statute is especially likely to satisfy the minimal requirements of the rational-basis test. First, when reauthorization is at issue, Congress has already assembled a legislative record justifying the initial legislation. Congress is entitled to consider that preexisting record as well as the record before it at the time of the vote on reauthorization. This is especially true where, as here, the Court has repeatedly affirmed the statute's constitutionality and Congress has adhered to the very model the Court has upheld.

Second, the very fact that reauthorization is necessary arises because Congress has built a temporal limitation into the Act. It has pledged to review, after a span of years and in light of contemporary evidence, the continued need for the VRA.

---

constitutional structure, Congress holds the lead rein in making the right to vote equally real for all U.S. citizens. These Amendments are in line with the special role assigned to Congress in protecting the integrity of the democratic process in federal elections. U.S. Const., Art. I, § 4 ("[T]he Congress may at any time by Law make or alter" regulations concerning the "Times, Places and Manner of holding Elections for Senators and Representatives.").

3. Acknowledging the existence of "serious constitutional questions," does not suggest how those questions should be answered.

Third, a reviewing court should expect the record supporting reauthorization to be less stark than the record originally made. Demand for a record of violations equivalent to the one earlier made would expose Congress to a catch-22. If the statute was working, there would be less evidence of discrimination, so opponents might argue that Congress should not be allowed to renew the statute. In contrast, if the statute was not working, there would be plenty of evidence of discrimination, but scant reason to renew a failed regulatory regime.

This is not to suggest that congressional power in this area is limitless. It is this Court's responsibility to ensure that Congress has used appropriate means. The question meet for judicial review is whether the chosen means are adapted to carry out the objects the amendments have in view. The Court's role, then, is not to substitute its judgment for that of Congress, but to determine whether the legislative record sufficed to show that Congress could rationally have determined that [its chosen] provisions were appropriate methods.

In summary, the Constitution vests broad power in Congress to protect the right to vote, and in particular to combat racial discrimination in voting. This Court has repeatedly reaffirmed Congress' prerogative to use any rational means in exercise of its power in this area. And both precedent and logic dictate that the rational-means test should be easier to satisfy, and the burden on the statute's challenger should be higher, when what is at issue is the reauthorization of a remedy that the Court has previously affirmed, and that Congress found, from contemporary evidence, to be working to advance the legislature's legitimate objective.

III

The 2006 reauthorization of the Voting Rights Act fully satisfies the standard stated in *McCulloch*.

A

I begin with the evidence on which Congress based its decision to continue the preclearance remedy. The surest way to evaluate whether that remedy remains in order is to see if preclearance is still effectively preventing discriminatory changes to voting laws. On that score, the record before Congress was huge. In fact, Congress found there were more DOJ objections between 1982 and 2004 (626) than there were between 1965 and the 1982 reauthorization (490).

All told, between 1982 and 2006, DOJ objections blocked over 700 voting changes based on a determination that the changes were discriminatory. Congress found that the majority of DOJ objections included findings of discriminatory intent.

In addition to blocking proposed voting changes through preclearance, DOJ may request more information from a jurisdiction proposing a change. In turn, the jurisdiction may modify or withdraw the proposed change. The number of such modifications or withdrawals provides an indication of how many discriminatory proposals are deterred without need for formal objection. Congress received evidence that more than 800 proposed changes were altered or withdrawn since the last reauthorization in 1982.[4]

Congress also received evidence that litigation under § 2 of the VRA was an inadequate substitute for preclearance in the covered jurisdictions. Litigation occurs only after the fact, when the illegal voting scheme has already been put in place and individuals have been elected pursuant to it, thereby gaining the advantages of incumbency. And litigation places a heavy financial burden on minority voters. Congress also received evidence that preclearance lessened the litigation burden on covered jurisdictions themselves, because the preclearance process is far less costly than defending against a § 2 claim, and clearance by DOJ substantially reduces the likelihood that a § 2 claim will be mounted.

The number of discriminatory changes blocked or deterred by the preclearance requirement suggests that the state of voting rights in the covered jurisdictions would have been significantly different absent this remedy. Set out below are characteristic examples of changes blocked in the years leading up to the 2006 reauthorization:

- Following the 2000 census, the City of Albany, Georgia, proposed a redistricting plan that DOJ found to be "designed with the purpose to limit and retrogress the increased black voting strength . . . in the city as a whole."
- In 2006, this Court found that Texas' attempt to redraw a congressional district to reduce the strength of Latino voters bore "the mark of intentional discrimination that could give rise to an equal protection violation," and ordered the district redrawn in compliance with the VRA. *League of United Latin American Citizens v. Perry*. In response, Texas sought to undermine this Court's order by curtailing early voting in the district, but was blocked by an action to enforce the § 5 preclearance requirement.
- In 2003, after African-Americans won a majority of the seats on the school board for the first time in history, Charleston County, South Carolina, proposed an at-large voting mechanism for the board. The proposal, made without consulting any of the African-American members of the school board, was found to be an exact replica of an earlier voting scheme that, a federal court had determined, violated the VRA. DOJ invoked § 5 to block the proposal.
- In 1993, the City of Millen, Georgia, proposed to delay the election in a majority-black district by two years, leaving that district without representation on the city council while the neighboring majority-white district would have three representatives. DOJ blocked the proposal. The county then sought to

4. This number includes only changes actually proposed. Congress also received evidence that many covered jurisdictions engaged in an "informal consultation process" with DOJ before formally submitting a proposal, so that the deterrent effect of preclearance was far broader than the formal submissions alone suggest.

move a polling place from a predominantly black neighborhood in the city to an inaccessible location in a predominantly white neighborhood outside city limits.

- In 1990, Dallas County, Alabama, whose county seat is the City of Selma, sought to purge its voter rolls of many black voters. DOJ rejected the purge as discriminatory, noting that it would have disqualified many citizens from voting "simply because they failed to pick up or return a voter update form, when there was no valid requirement that they do so."

These examples, and scores more like them, fill the pages of the legislative record. The evidence was indeed sufficient to support Congress' conclusion that "racial discrimination in voting in covered jurisdictions [remained] serious and pervasive."

True, conditions in the South have impressively improved since passage of the Voting Rights Act. Congress noted this improvement and found that the VRA was the driving force behind it. But Congress also found that voting discrimination had evolved into subtler second-generation barriers, and that eliminating preclearance would risk loss of the gains that had been made.

B

I turn next to the evidence on which Congress based its decision to reauthorize the coverage formula in § 4(b). Because Congress did not alter the coverage formula, the same jurisdictions previously subject to preclearance continue to be covered by this remedy. The evidence just described, of preclearance's continuing efficacy in blocking constitutional violations in the covered jurisdictions, itself grounded Congress' conclusion that the remedy should be retained for those jurisdictions.

There is no question, moreover, that the covered jurisdictions have a unique history of problems with racial discrimination in voting. Consideration of this long history, still in living memory, was altogether appropriate. The Court criticizes Congress for failing to recognize that "history did not end in 1965." But the Court ignores that "what's past is prologue." And "[t]hose who cannot remember the past are condemned to repeat it." Congress was especially mindful of the need to reinforce the gains already made and to prevent backsliding.

Of particular importance, even after 40 years and thousands of discriminatory changes blocked by preclearance, conditions in the covered jurisdictions demonstrated that the formula was still justified by "current needs." *Northwest Austin.*

Congress learned of these conditions through a report, known as the Katz study, that looked at § 2 suits between 1982 and 2004. Because the private right of action authorized by § 2 of the VRA applies nationwide, a comparison of § 2 lawsuits in covered and noncovered jurisdictions provides an appropriate yardstick for measuring differences between covered and noncovered jurisdictions. If differences in the risk of voting discrimination between covered and noncovered jurisdictions had disappeared, one would expect that the rate of successful § 2 lawsuits would be roughly the same in both areas.[6] The study's findings, however, indicated that racial discrimination in voting remains concentrated in the jurisdictions singled out for preclearance.

Although covered jurisdictions account for less than 25 percent of the country's population, the Katz study revealed that they accounted for 56 percent of successful § 2 litigation since 1982. The Katz study further found that § 2 lawsuits are more likely to succeed when they are filed in covered jurisdictions than in noncovered jurisdictions. From these findings—ignored by the Court—Congress reasonably concluded that the coverage formula continues to identify the jurisdictions of greatest concern.

The evidence before Congress, furthermore, indicated that voting in the covered jurisdictions was more racially polarized than elsewhere in the country. While racially polarized voting alone does not signal a constitutional violation, it is a factor that increases the vulnerability of racial minorities to discriminatory changes in voting law. The reason is twofold. First, racial polarization means that racial minorities are at risk of being systematically outvoted and having their interests underrepresented in legislatures. Second, when political preferences fall along racial lines, the natural inclinations of incumbents and ruling parties to entrench themselves have predictable racial effects. Under circumstances of severe racial polarization, efforts to gain political advantage translate into race-specific disadvantages.

In other words, a governing political coalition has an incentive to prevent changes in the existing balance of voting power. When voting is racially polarized, efforts by the ruling party to pursue that incentive will inevitably discriminate against a racial group. Just as buildings in California have a greater need to be earthquake-proofed, places where there is greater racial polarization in voting have a greater need for prophylactic measures to prevent purposeful race discrimination. This point was understood by Congress and is well recognized in the academic literature.

The case for retaining a coverage formula that met needs on the ground was therefore solid. Congress might have been charged with rigidity had it afforded covered jurisdictions no way out or ignored jurisdictions that needed superintendence. Congress, however, responded to this concern. Critical components of the congressional design are the statutory provisions allowing jurisdictions to "bail out" of preclearance, and for court-ordered "bail ins." The VRA permits a jurisdiction to bail out. It also authorizes a court to subject a noncovered jurisdiction to federal preclearance upon finding that violations of the Fourteenth and Fifteenth Amendments have occurred there.

Congress was satisfied that the VRA's bailout mechanism provided an effective means of adjusting the VRA's coverage over time. The bail-in mechanism has also worked.

6. Because preclearance occurs only in covered jurisdictions and can be expected to stop the most obviously objectionable measures, one would expect a lower rate of successful § 2 lawsuits in those jurisdictions if the risk of voting discrimination there were the same as elsewhere in the country.

This experience exposes the inaccuracy of the Court's portrayal of the Act as static, unchanged since 1965. Congress designed the VRA to be a dynamic statute, capable of adjusting to changing conditions. True, many covered jurisdictions have not been able to bail out due to recent acts of noncompliance with the VRA, but that truth reinforces the congressional judgment that these jurisdictions were rightfully subject to preclearance, and ought to remain under that regime.

IV

Congress approached the 2006 reauthorization of the VRA with great care and seriousness. The same cannot be said of the Court's opinion today. The Court makes no genuine attempt to engage with the massive legislative record that Congress assembled. Instead, it relies on increases in voter registration and turnout as if that were the whole story. Without even identifying a standard of review, the Court dismissively brushes off arguments based on "data from the record," and declines to enter the "debat[e about] what [the] record shows." One would expect more from an opinion striking at the heart of the Nation's signal piece of civil-rights legislation.

I note the most disturbing lapses. First, by what right, given its usual restraint, does the Court even address Shelby County's facial challenge to the VRA? Second, the Court veers away from controlling precedent regarding the "equal sovereignty" doctrine without even acknowledging that it is doing so. Third, hardly showing the respect ordinarily paid when Congress acts to implement the Civil War Amendments, and as just stressed, the Court does not even deign to grapple with the legislative record.

A

Shelby County launched a purely facial challenge to the VRA's 2006 reauthorization. "A facial challenge to a legislative Act," the Court has other times said, "is, of course, the most difficult challenge to mount successfully, since the challenger must establish that no set of circumstances exists under which the Act would be valid." *United States v. Salerno* (1987).

Embedded in the traditional rules governing constitutional adjudication is the principle that a person to whom a statute may constitutionally be applied will not be heard to challenge that statute on the ground that it may conceivably be applied unconstitutionally to others, in other situations not before the Court. Yet the Court's opinion in this case contains not a word explaining why Congress lacks the power to subject to preclearance the particular plaintiff that initiated this lawsuit—Shelby County, Alabama. The reason for the Court's silence is apparent, for as applied to Shelby County, the VRA's preclearance requirement is hardly contestable.

Alabama is home to Selma, site of the "Bloody Sunday" beatings of civil-rights demonstrators that served as the catalyst for the VRA's enactment. Following those events, Martin Luther King, Jr., led a march from Selma to Montgomery, Alabama's capital, where he called for passage of the VRA. If the Act passed, he foresaw, progress could be made even in Alabama, but there had to be a steadfast national commitment to see the task through to completion. In King's words, "the arc of the moral universe is long, but it bends toward justice."

History has proved King right. Although circumstances in Alabama have changed, serious concerns remain. Between 1982 and 2005, Alabama had one of the highest rates of successful § 2 suits, second only to its VRA-covered neighbor Mississippi. In other words, even while subject to the restraining effect of § 5, Alabama was found to have "deni[ed] or abridge[d]" voting rights "on account of race or color" more frequently than nearly all other States in the Union. Alabama's sorry history of § 2 violations alone provides sufficient justification for Congress' determination in 2006 that the State should remain subject to § 5's preclearance requirement.[7]

A few examples suffice to demonstrate that, at least in Alabama, the "current burdens" imposed by § 5's preclearance requirement are "justified by current needs." *Northwest Austin*. In the interim between the VRA's 1982 and 2006 reauthorizations, this Court twice confronted purposeful racial discrimination in Alabama. In *Pleasant Grove v. United States* (1987), the Court held that Pleasant Grove—a city in Jefferson County, Shelby County's neighbor—engaged in purposeful discrimination by annexing all-white areas while rejecting the annexation request of an adjacent black neighborhood.

Two years before *Pleasant Grove*, the Court in *Hunter v. Underwood* (1985), struck down a provision of the Alabama Constitution that prohibited individuals convicted of misdemeanor offenses "involving moral turpitude" from voting. The provision violated the Fourteenth Amendment's Equal Protection Clause, the Court unanimously concluded, because "its original enactment was motivated by a desire to discriminate against blacks on account of race[,] and the [provision] continues to this day to have that effect." *Id.*

Pleasant Grove and *Hunter* were not anomalies. In 1986, a Federal District Judge concluded that the at-large election systems in several Alabama counties violated § 2. *Dillard v. Baldwin Cty. Bd. of Ed.* (MD Ala. 1988). Summarizing its findings, the court stated that "[f]rom the late 1800's through the present, [Alabama] has consistently erected barriers to keep black persons from full and equal participation in the social, economic, and political life of the state."

The *Dillard* litigation ultimately expanded to include 183 cities, counties, and school boards employing discriminatory at-large election systems. One of those defendants

7. This lawsuit was filed by Shelby County, a political subdivision of Alabama, rather than by the State itself. Nevertheless, it is appropriate to judge Shelby County's constitutional challenge in light of instances of discrimination statewide because Shelby County is subject to § 5's preclearance requirement by virtue of Alabama's designation as a covered jurisdiction under § 4(b) of the VRA. In any event, Shelby County's recent record of employing an at-large electoral system tainted by intentional racial discrimination is by itself sufficient to justify subjecting the county to § 5's preclearance mandate.

was Shelby County, which eventually signed a consent decree to resolve the claims against it.

Although the *Dillard* litigation resulted in overhauls of numerous electoral systems tainted by racial discrimination, concerns about backsliding persist. In 2008, for example, the city of Calera, located in Shelby County, requested preclearance of a redistricting plan that would have eliminated the city's sole majority-black district, which had been created pursuant to the consent decree in *Dillard*. Although DOJ objected to the plan, Calera forged ahead with elections based on the unprecleared voting changes, resulting in the defeat of the incumbent African-American councilman who represented the former majority-black district. The city's defiance required DOJ to bring a § 5 enforcement action that ultimately yielded appropriate redress, including restoration of the majority-black district.

A recent FBI investigation provides a further window into the persistence of racial discrimination in state politics. Recording devices worn by state legislators cooperating with the FBI's investigation captured conversations between members of the state legislature and their political allies. The recorded conversations are shocking. Members of the state Senate derisively refer to African-Americans as "Aborigines" and talk openly of their aim to quash a particular gambling-related referendum because the referendum, if placed on the ballot, might increase African-American voter turnout (legislators and their allies expressed concern that if the referendum were placed on the ballot, "[e]very black, every illiterate would be bused [to the polls] on HUD financed buses"). These conversations occurred not in the 1870's, or even in the 1960's, they took place in 2010. The District Judge presiding over the criminal trial at which the recorded conversations were introduced commented that the "recordings represent compelling evidence that political exclusion through racism remains a real and enduring problem" in Alabama. Racist sentiments, the judge observed, "remain regrettably entrenched in the high echelons of state government."

These recent episodes forcefully demonstrate that § 5's preclearance requirement is constitutional as applied to Alabama and its political subdivisions.[8] And under our case law, that conclusion should suffice to resolve this case.

This Court has consistently rejected constitutional challenges to legislation enacted pursuant to Congress' enforcement powers under the Civil War Amendments upon finding that the legislation was constitutional as applied to the particular set of circumstances before the Court. A similar approach is warranted here.

Leaping to resolve Shelby County's facial challenge without considering whether application of the VRA to Shelby County is constitutional can hardly be described as an

8. Congress continued preclearance over Alabama, including Shelby County, after considering evidence of current barriers there to minority voting clout. Shelby County, thus, is no "redhead" caught up in an arbitrary scheme.

exemplar of restrained and moderate decisionmaking. Quite the opposite. Hubris is a fit word for today's demolition of the VRA.

B

The Court stops any application of § 5 by holding that § 4(b)'s coverage formula is unconstitutional. It pins this result, in large measure, to "the fundamental principle of equal sovereignty." In *Katzenbach,* however, the Court held, in no uncertain terms, that the principle "*applies only to the terms upon which States are admitted to the Union,* and not to the remedies for local evils which have subsequently appeared" (emphasis added).

Katzenbach, the Court acknowledges, "rejected the notion that the [equal sovereignty] principle operate[s] as a bar on differential treatment outside [the] context [of the admission of new States]." But the Court clouds that once clear understanding by citing dictum from *Northwest Austin* to convey that the principle of equal sovereignty "remains highly pertinent in assessing subsequent disparate treatment of States." If the Court is suggesting that dictum in *Northwest Austin* silently overruled *Katzenbach*'s limitation of the equal sovereignty doctrine to "the admission of new States," the suggestion is untenable. *Northwest Austin* cited *Katzenbach's* holding in the course of declining to decide whether the VRA was constitutional or even what standard of review applied to the question. In today's decision, the Court ratchets up what was pure dictum in *Northwest Austin*, attributing breadth to the equal sovereignty principle in flat contradiction of *Katzenbach*. The Court does so with nary an explanation of why it finds *Katzenbach* wrong, let alone any discussion of whether *stare decisis* nonetheless counsels adherence to *Katzenbach*'s ruling on the limited "significance" of the equal sovereignty principle.

Today's unprecedented extension of the equal sovereignty principle outside its proper domain—the admission of new States—is capable of much mischief. Federal statutes that treat States disparately are hardly novelties. *See, e.g.*, 28 U.S.C. § 3704 (no State may operate or permit a sports-related gambling scheme, unless that State conducted such a scheme "at any time during the period beginning January 1, 1976, and ending August 31, 1990"); 26 U.S.C. § 142(1) (EPA required to locate green building project in a State meeting specified population criteria); 42 U.S.C. § 3796bb (at least 50 percent of rural drug enforcement assistance funding must be allocated to States with "a population density of fifty-two or fewer persons per square mile or a State in which the largest county has fewer than one hundred and fifty thousand people, based on the decennial census of 1990 through fiscal year 1997"). Do such provisions remain safe given the Court's expansion of equal sovereignty's sway?

Of gravest concern, Congress relied on our pathmarking *Katzenbach* decision in each reauthorization of the VRA. It had every reason to believe that the Act's limited geographical scope would weigh in favor of, not against, the Act's constitutionality. Congress could hardly have foreseen that the VRA's limited geographic reach would render the Act constitutionally suspect.

In the Court's conception, it appears, defenders of the VRA could not prevail upon showing what the record overwhelmingly bears out, i.e., that there is a need for continuing the preclearance regime in covered States. In addition, the defenders would have to disprove the existence of a comparable need elsewhere. I am aware of no precedent for imposing such a double burden on defenders of legislation.

C

[T]he Court strikes § 4(b)'s coverage provision because, in its view, the provision is not based on "current conditions." It discounts, however, that one such condition was the preclearance remedy in place in the covered jurisdictions, a remedy Congress designed both to catch discrimination before it causes harm, and to guard against return to old ways. Volumes of evidence supported Congress' determination that the prospect of retrogression was real. Throwing out preclearance when it has worked and is continuing to work to stop discriminatory changes is like throwing away your umbrella in a rainstorm because you are not getting wet.

Consider once again the components of the record before Congress in 2006. The coverage provision identified a known list of places with an undisputed history of serious problems with racial discrimination in voting. Recent evidence relating to Alabama and its counties was there for all to see. Multiple Supreme Court decisions had upheld the coverage provision, most recently in 1999. There was extensive evidence that, due to the preclearance mechanism, conditions in the covered jurisdictions had notably improved. And there was evidence that preclearance was still having a substantial real-world effect, having stopped hundreds of discriminatory voting changes in the covered jurisdictions since the last reauthorization. In addition, there was evidence that racial polarization in voting was higher in covered jurisdictions than elsewhere, increasing the vulnerability of minority citizens in those jurisdictions. And countless witnesses, reports, and case studies documented continuing problems with voting discrimination in those jurisdictions. In light of this record, Congress had more than a reasonable basis to conclude that the existing coverage formula was not out of sync with conditions on the ground in covered areas. And certainly Shelby County was no candidate for release through the mechanism Congress provided.

The Court holds § 4(b) invalid on the ground that it is "irrational to base coverage on the use of voting tests 40 years ago, when such tests have been illegal since that time." But the Court disregards what Congress set about to do in enacting the VRA. That extraordinary legislation scarcely stopped at the particular tests and devices that happened to exist in 1965. The grand aim of the Act is to secure to all in our polity equal citizenship stature, a voice in our democracy undiluted by race. As the record for the 2006 reauthorization makes abundantly clear, second-generation barriers to minority voting rights have emerged in the covered jurisdictions as attempted substitutes for the first-generation barriers that originally triggered preclearance in those jurisdictions.

The sad irony of today's decision lies in its utter failure to grasp why the VRA has proven effective. The Court appears to believe that the VRA's success in eliminating the specific devices extant in 1965 means that preclearance is no longer needed. With that belief, and the argument derived from it, history repeats itself. The same assumption—that the problem could be solved when particular methods of voting discrimination are identified and eliminated—was indulged and proved wrong repeatedly prior to the VRA's enactment. Unlike prior statutes, which singled out particular tests or devices, the VRA is grounded in Congress' recognition of the "variety and persistence" of measures designed to impair minority voting rights. *Katzenbach*. In truth, the evolution of voting discrimination into more subtle second-generation barriers is powerful evidence that a remedy as effective as preclearance remains vital to protect minority voting rights and prevent backsliding.

Beyond question, the VRA is no ordinary legislation. It is extraordinary because Congress embarked on a mission long delayed and of extraordinary importance: to realize the purpose and promise of the Fifteenth Amendment. For a half century, a concerted effort has been made to end racial discrimination in voting. Thanks to the Voting Rights Act, progress once the subject of a dream has been achieved and continues to be made.

The record supporting the 2006 reauthorization of the VRA is also extraordinary. After exhaustive evidence-gathering and deliberative process, Congress reauthorized the VRA, including the coverage provision, with overwhelming bipartisan support. It was the judgment of Congress that "40 years has not been a sufficient amount of time to eliminate the vestiges of discrimination following nearly 100 years of disregard for the dictates of the 15th amendment and to ensure that the right of all citizens to vote is protected as guaranteed by the Constitution." That determination of the body empowered to enforce the Civil War Amendments "by appropriate legislation" merits this Court's utmost respect. In my judgment, the Court errs egregiously by overriding Congress' decision.

For the reasons stated, I would affirm the judgment of the Court of Appeals.

NOTES ON *SHELBY COUNTY*

1. As a matter of policy, should Congress have extended Section 5 in 2006? Why or why not? Should Congress have amended Section 5—or just updated Section 4 (the coverage formula)? If so, how?
2. At one level, the debate between Chief Justice Roberts and Justice Ginsburg is about how much the Court should defer to Congress's legislative judgment in the context of racial discrimination in voting. Both sides appear to agree that the test is a rational basis test. The two disagree, though, as to whether the coverage formula meets that rationality standard. Who has the better of the rational basis argument? Is Chief Justice Roberts applying a rational basis test or is he implicitly applying a tougher test?

3. Should Congress now pass legislation amending the coverage formula found in Section 4? Why or why not? If so, what should that coverage formula look like? Note that even if Congress enacts a new coverage formula that passes muster with the Court's majority, *Shelby County* leaves open the question of whether Section 5 itself is constitutional. In other words, even with an updated coverage formula, a majority of the Court could still strike down Section 5. In your best judgment, how likely is it that the Court in its current composition would invalidate Section 5, even with an updated coverage formula?
4. The civil rights community vociferously called upon Congress to fix the Voting Rights Act in the wake of *Shelby County*. Yet the politics of voting rights are not what they have been for much of the last century. The passage of the Voting Rights Act in 1965, as well as its repeated extensions—including the most recent one in 2006—have been bipartisan endeavors, with both Democrats and Republicans overwhelmingly supporting the Act. (In 2006 the vote was 390–33 in the House and 98–0 in the Senate, and Republican President George W. Bush signed the reauthorization of the Voting Rights Act to much fanfare.) Yet that bipartisanship appears to have broken down, and with the control of Congress divided between the two parties, most observers expect no congressional fix of the Voting Rights Act after *Shelby County*.

   What has caused this breakdown of bipartisanship on the issue of voting rights, and is it possible to bring it back? How much, if any, of this breakdown is attributable to the fact that the United States elected President Barack Obama as its first African-American president? Or is the lack of bipartisanship on voting rights just a subset of the extreme polarization of politics that has been witnessed in recent years?
5. At oral argument in *Shelby County*, Justice Scalia controversially spoke of Section 5 as a kind of racial entitlement that, once granted, is difficult to dislodge; even if "politically incorrect," is there something valid to the point that the civil rights community, as an interest group, has become unduly enamored of the preclearance regime, which inevitably bred resentment among covered jurisdictions, and is a kind of remedy that one hopes that the nation can outgrow?
6. As a result of the decision in *Shelby County*, the Department of Justice has turned to Section 3(c) of the Voting Rights Act as a mechanism to "recapture" some of the covered jurisdictions into preclearance. Most notably, the Department of Justice has argued that the State of Texas should be subjected to preclearance at least in part because of a federal court finding of discriminatory purpose in the adoption of the state's post–2010 congressional and State House redistricting plans. *See* Statement of Interest of the United States with Respect to Section 3(c) of the Voting Rights Act, Perez v. Texas (W.D. Tex., filed July 25, 2013),

available at http://moritzlaw.osu.edu/electionlaw/litigation/documents/PErez USstatInterestSec3.pdf. Should Texas be recaptured into preclearance? Is litigation under Section 3(c) superior to the coverage formula held to be unconstitutional in *Shelby County*?

E. Race-Based Gerrymanders

In relation to the intersection of race and redistricting, we have seen that the United States Constitution and Section 2 of the Voting Rights Act prohibit the implementation of districting plans that are discriminatory in purpose or result. We have also seen that, up until the summer of 2013, Section 5 of the Voting Rights Act prohibited certain state and local governments from implementing redistricting plans that were discriminatory in purpose or effect (i.e., retrogressive). These requirements were in force in one form or another since the passage of the Voting Rights Act in 1965, the initial constitutional vote dilution cases in the 1970s (*Whitcomb v. Chavis* and *White v. Regester*), and the amendment to Section 2 of the Act in 1982.

In the early 1990s, the Supreme Court added another important piece to the race and redistricting puzzle: the creation of a new constitutional doctrine of racial gerrymandering. As you will see, under certain circumstances, the doctrine of racial gerrymandering bars the use of race in the redistricting process. In this way, the doctrine of racial gerrymandering operates as a potential counterforce to the requirements of the Voting Rights Act.

The Supreme Court's initial statement on the doctrine of racial gerrymandering came in *Shaw v. Reno* (1992). In *Shaw*, a group of North Carolina voters challenged the state's creation of two congressional districts: District 1 and 12. These two congressional districts were drawn to comply with the Voting Rights Act by providing African-American voters the ability to elect candidates of African-American voters' choice. However, the two districts ended up being bizarrely shaped, in the eyes of some. District 1, for example, was vividly described as looking like a "bug splattered on a windshield." District 12 stretched for about 160 miles, much of it along an interstate highway such that one legislator remarked "[i]f you drove down the interstate with both car doors open, you'd kill most of the people in the district." (Figure 1-5 shows both District 1 and 12 as challenged in *Shaw*.)

The *Shaw* plaintiffs claimed that North Carolina's consideration of race in the creation of those districts was an unconstitutional racial gerrymander in violation of the Equal Protection Clause. A federal district court dismissed the racial gerrymandering claim for failure to state a claim upon which relief could be granted, but the Supreme Court reversed. The Supreme Court held that plaintiffs could state a cognizable claim by alleging that the redistricting was "so irrational on its face that it could be understood only as an effort to segregate voters into separate voting districts because of their race, and that the separation lack[ed] sufficient justification."

The Supreme Court set forth a number of reasons for recognizing claims of racial gerrymandering under the Equal Protection Clause. The key rationale appeared in the following two paragraphs:

> A reapportionment plan that includes in one district individuals who belong to the same race, but who are otherwise widely separated by geographical and political boundaries, and who may have little in common with one another but the color of their skin, bears an uncomfortable resemblance to political apartheid. It reinforces the perception that members of the same racial group—regardless of their age, education, economic status, or the community in which they live—think alike, share the same political interests, and will prefer the same candidates at the polls. We have rejected such perceptions elsewhere as impermissible racial stereotypes. By perpetuating such notions, a racial gerrymander may exacerbate the very patterns of racial bloc voting that majority-minority districting is sometimes said to counteract.
>
> The message that such districting sends to elected representatives is equally pernicious. When a district obviously is created solely to effectuate the perceived common interests of one racial group, elected officials are more likely to believe that their primary obligation is to represent only the members of that group, rather than their constituency as a whole. This is altogether antithetical to our system of representative democracy.

Shaw v. Reno, 509 U.S. 630, 647-648 (1992).

In *Shaw,* the Supreme Court recognized a claim for racial gerrymandering but did not decide the merits of the claim. Instead, the Court remanded the case for a determination of whether North Carolina had, indeed, engaged in unconstitutional racial gerrymandering. In essence, while the Supreme Court recognized a constitutional claim, it left the standard for evaluating the claim up in the air. The next case, *Miller v. Johnson,* provides a ruling on the merits of an unconstitutional gerrymandering claim.

Figure 1-5
NORTH CAROLINA CONGRESSIONAL PLAN
Chapter 7 of the 1991 Session Laws (1991 Extra Session)

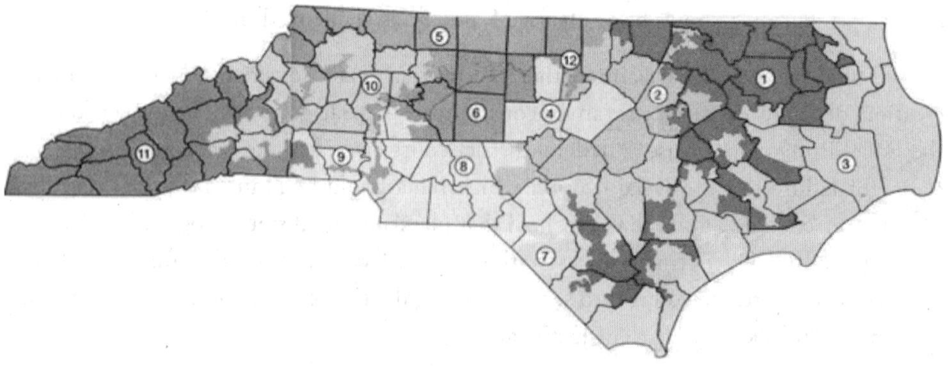

Source: Supreme Court's Appendix to *Shaw v. Reno,* 509 U.S. 630 (1993).

MILLER v. JOHNSON

515 U.S. 900 (1995)

Justice KENNEDY delivered the opinion of the Court.

The constitutionality of Georgia's congressional redistricting plan is at issue here. In *Shaw v. Reno*, we held that a plaintiff states a claim under the Equal Protection Clause by alleging that a state redistricting plan, on its face, has no rational explanation save as an effort to separate voters on the basis of race. The question we now decide is whether Georgia's new Eleventh District gives rise to a valid equal protection claim under the principles announced in *Shaw,* and, if so, whether it can be sustained nonetheless as narrowly tailored to serve a compelling governmental interest.

I

[Section] 5 of the [Voting Rights] Act requires Georgia to obtain either administrative preclearance by the Attorney General or approval by the United States District Court for the District of Columbia of any change in a "standard, practice, or procedure with respect to voting" made after November 1, 1964. 42 U.S.C. § 1973c. The preclearance mechanism applies to congressional redistricting plans, and requires that the proposed change "not have the purpose and will not have the effect of denying or abridging the right to vote on account of race or color."

Between 1980 and 1990, one of Georgia's 10 congressional districts was a majority-black district, that is, a majority of the district's voters were black. The 1990 Decennial Census indicated that Georgia's population of 6,478,216 persons, 27% of whom are black, entitled it to an additional eleventh congressional seat, prompting Georgia's General Assembly to redraw the State's congressional districts. Both the House and the Senate adopted redistricting guidelines which, among other things, required single-member districts of equal population, contiguous geography, nondilution of minority voting strength, fidelity to precinct lines where possible, and compliance with §§ 2 and 5 of the [Voting Rights] Act. Only after these requirements were met did the guidelines permit drafters to consider other ends, such as maintaining the integrity of political subdivisions, preserving the core of existing districts, and avoiding contests between incumbents.

A special session opened in August 1991, and the General Assembly submitted a congressional redistricting plan to the Attorney General for [Section 5] preclearance on October 1, 1991. The legislature's plan contained two majority-minority districts, the Fifth and Eleventh, and an additional district, the Second, in which blacks comprised just over 35% of the voting age population. Despite the plan's increase in the number of majority-black districts from one to two and the absence of any evidence of an intent to discriminate against minority voters, the Department of Justice refused preclearance on January 21, 1992. The Department's objection letter [that refused preclearance] noted a concern that Georgia had created only two majority-minority districts, and that the proposed plan did not "recognize" certain minority populations by placing them in a majority-black district.

The General Assembly returned to the drawing board. A new plan was enacted and submitted for preclearance. This second attempt assigned the black population in Central Georgia's Baldwin County to the Eleventh District and increased the black populations in the Eleventh, Fifth, and Second Districts. The Justice Department refused preclearance again, relying on alternative plans proposing three majority-minority districts. One of the alternative schemes relied on by the Department was the so-called "max-black" plan, drafted by the American Civil Liberties Union (ACLU) for the General Assembly's black caucus. The key to the ACLU's plan was the "Macon/Savannah trade." The dense black population in the Macon region would be transferred from the Eleventh District to the Second, converting the Second into a majority-black district, and the Eleventh District's loss in black population would be offset by extending the Eleventh to include the black populations in Savannah. Pointing to the General Assembly's refusal to enact the Macon/Savannah swap into law, the Justice Department concluded that Georgia had "failed to explain adequately" its failure to create a third majority-minority district. The State did not seek a declaratory judgment from the District Court for the District of Columbia.

Twice spurned, the General Assembly set out to create three majority-minority districts to gain preclearance. Using the ACLU's "max-black" plan as its benchmark, the General Assembly enacted a plan that

> "bore all the signs of [the Justice Department's] involvement: The black population of Meriwether County was gouged out of the Third District and attached to the Second District by the narrowest of land bridges; Effingham and Chatham Counties were split to make way for the Savannah extension, which itself split the City of Savannah; and the plan as a whole split 26 counties, 23 more than the existing congressional districts." See [the district court's opinion].

The new plan also enacted the Macon/Savannah swap necessary to create a third majority-black district. The Eleventh District lost the black population of Macon, but picked up Savannah, thereby connecting the black neighborhoods of metropolitan Atlanta and the poor black populace of coastal Chatham County, though 260 miles apart in distance and worlds apart in culture. In short, the social, political, and economic makeup of the Eleventh District tells a tale of disparity, not community. As the appendices to this opinion attest,

> "[t]he populations of the Eleventh are centered around four discrete, widely spaced urban centers that have absolutely nothing to do with each other, and stretch the district hundreds of miles across rural counties and narrow swamp corridors.

> "The dense population centers of the approved Eleventh District were all majority-black, all at the periphery of the district, and in the case of Atlanta, Augusta and Savannah, all tied to a sparsely populated rural core by even less populated land bridges. Extending from Atlanta to the Atlantic, the Eleventh covered 6,784.2 square miles, splitting eight counties and five municipalities along the way."

The Almanac of American Politics has this to say about the Eleventh District: "Geographically, it is a monstrosity, stretching from Atlanta to Savannah. Its core is the plantation country in the center of the state, lightly populated, but heavily black. It links by narrow corridors the black neighborhoods in Augusta, Savannah and southern DeKalb County." Georgia's plan included three majority-black districts, though, and received Justice Department preclearance on April 2, 1992.

Elections were held under the new congressional redistricting plan on November 4, 1992, and black candidates were elected to Congress from all three majority-black districts. On January 13, 1994, appellees, five white voters from the Eleventh District, filed this action against various state officials in the United States District Court for the Southern District of Georgia. As residents of the challenged Eleventh District, all appellees had standing. Their suit alleged that Georgia's Eleventh District was a racial gerrymander and so a violation of the Equal Protection Clause.

II

A

Finding that the "evidence of the General Assembly's intent to racially gerrymander the Eleventh District is overwhelming, and practically stipulated by the parties involved," the District Court held that race was the predominant, overriding factor in drawing the Eleventh District. Appellants do not take issue with the court's factual finding of this racial motivation. Rather, they contend that evidence of a legislature's deliberate classification of voters on the basis of race cannot alone suffice to state a claim under *Shaw*. They argue that, regardless of the legislature's purposes, a plaintiff must demonstrate that a district's shape is so bizarre that it is unexplainable other than on the basis of race, and that appellees failed to make that showing here. Appellants' conception of the constitutional violation misapprehends our holding in *Shaw* and the equal protection precedent upon which *Shaw* relied.

Shaw recognized a claim "analytically distinct" from a vote dilution claim. Whereas a vote dilution claim alleges that the State has enacted a particular voting scheme as a purposeful device "to minimize or cancel out the voting potential of racial or ethnic minorities," *Mobile v. Bolden,* the essence of the equal protection claim recognized in *Shaw* is that the State has used race as a basis for separating voters into districts. Just as the State may not, absent extraordinary justification, segregate citizens on the basis of race in its public parks, buses, golf courses, beaches, and schools, so did we recognize in *Shaw* that it may not separate its citizens into different voting districts on the basis of race.

When the State assigns voters on the basis of race, it engages in the offensive and demeaning assumption that voters of a particular race, because of their race, "think alike, share the same political interests, and will prefer the same candidates at the polls." *Shaw*. Race-based assignments embody stereotypes that treat individuals as the product of their race, evaluating their thoughts and efforts—their very worth as citizens—according to a criterion barred to the Government by history and the Constitution.

Our observation in *Shaw* of the consequences of racial stereotyping was not meant to suggest that a district must be bizarre on its face before there is a constitutional violation. Nor was our conclusion in *Shaw* that in certain instances a district's appearance (or, to be more precise, its appearance in combination with certain demographic evidence) can give rise to an equal protection claim, a holding that bizarreness was a threshold showing. Our circumspect approach and narrow holding in *Shaw* did not erect an artificial rule barring accepted equal protection analysis in other redistricting cases. Shape is relevant not because bizarreness is a necessary element of the constitutional wrong or a threshold requirement of proof, but because it may be persuasive circumstantial evidence that race for its own sake, and not other districting principles, was the legislature's dominant and controlling rationale in drawing its district lines. The logical implication, as courts applying *Shaw* have recognized, is that parties may rely on evidence other than bizarreness to establish race-based districting.

"In some exceptional cases, a reapportionment plan may be so highly irregular that, on its face, it rationally cannot be understood as anything other than an effort to 'segregat[e] . . . voters' on the basis of race." *Shaw*. In other cases, where the district is not so bizarre on its face that it discloses a racial design, the proof will be more "difficul[t]." Although it was not necessary in *Shaw* to consider further the proof required in these more difficult cases, the logical import of our reasoning is that evidence other than a district's bizarre shape can be used to support the claim.

In sum, we make clear that parties alleging that a State has assigned voters on the basis of race are neither confined in their proof to evidence regarding the district's geometry and makeup nor required to make a threshold showing of bizarreness. Today's litigation requires us further to consider the requirements of the proof necessary to sustain this equal protection challenge.

B

Federal-court review of districting legislation represents a serious intrusion on the most vital of local functions. It is well settled that reapportionment is primarily the duty and responsibility of the State. Electoral districting is a most difficult subject for legislatures, and so the States must have discretion to exercise the political judgment necessary to balance competing interests. Although race-based decision-making is inherently suspect, until a claimant makes a showing sufficient to support that allegation the good faith of a state legislature must be presumed. The courts, in assessing the sufficiency of a challenge to a districting plan, must be sensitive to the complex interplay of forces that enter a legislature's redistricting calculus. Redistricting legislatures will, for example, almost always be aware of racial demographics; but it does not follow that race predominates in the redistricting process. The distinction between being aware of racial considerations and being motivated by them may be difficult to make. This evidentiary difficulty, together with the sensitive nature of redistricting and the presumption of good faith that must be accorded legislative enactments, requires courts to exercise extraordinary caution in adjudicating claims that a State has drawn district lines on the basis of race. The plaintiff's burden is to show, either through circumstantial evidence of a district's shape and demographics or more direct evidence going to legislative purpose, that race was the predominant factor motivating the legislature's decision to place a significant number of voters within or without a particular district. To make this showing, a plaintiff must prove that the legislature subordinated traditional race-neutral districting principles, including but not limited to compactness, contiguity, and respect for political subdivisions or communities defined by actual shared interests, to racial considerations. Where these or other race-neutral considerations are the basis for redistricting legislation, and are not subordinated to race, a State can "defeat a claim that a district has been gerrymandered on racial lines." *Shaw*. These principles inform the plaintiff's burden of proof at trial. Of course, courts must also recognize these principles, and the intrusive potential of judicial intervention into the legislative realm, when assessing under the Federal Rules of Civil Procedure the adequacy of a plaintiff's showing at the various stages of litigation and determining whether to permit discovery or trial to proceed.

In our view, the District Court applied the correct analysis, and its finding that race was the predominant factor motivating the drawing of the Eleventh District was not clearly erroneous. The court found it was "exceedingly obvious" from the shape of the Eleventh District, together with the relevant racial demographics, that the drawing of narrow land bridges to incorporate within the district outlying appendages containing nearly 80% of the district's total black population was a deliberate attempt to bring black populations into the district. Although by comparison with other districts the geometric shape of the Eleventh District may not seem bizarre on its face, when its shape is considered in conjunction with its racial and population densities, the story of racial gerrymandering seen by the District Court becomes much clearer. Although this evidence is quite compelling, we need not determine whether it was, standing alone, sufficient to establish a *Shaw* claim that the Eleventh District is unexplainable other than by race. The District Court had before it considerable additional evidence showing that the General Assembly was motivated by a predominant, overriding desire to assign black populations to the Eleventh District and thereby permit the creation of a third majority-black district in the Second.

The [district] court found that "it became obvious," both from the Justice Department's objection letters and the three preclearance rounds in general, "that [the Justice Department] would accept nothing less than abject surrender to its maximization agenda." It further found that the General Assembly acquiesced and as a consequence was driven by its overriding desire to comply with the Department's maximization demands. The court supported its conclusion not just with the testimony of Linda Meggers, the operator of "Herschel," Georgia's reapportionment computer, and "probably the most knowledgeable person available on the subject of Georgian redistricting," but also with the State's own concessions. The State admitted that it "would not have added those portions of Effingham and Chatham Counties that are now in the [far southeastern extension of the] present Eleventh Congressional District but for the need to include additional black population in that district to offset the loss of black population caused by the shift of predominantly black portions of Bibb County in the Second Congressional District which occurred in response to the Department of Justice's March 20th, 1992, objection letter." It conceded further that "[t]o the extent that precincts in the Eleventh Congressional District are split, a substantial reason for their being split was the objective of increasing the black population of that district." And in its brief to this Court, the State concedes that "[i]t is undisputed that Georgia's eleventh is the product of a desire by the General Assembly to create a majority black district." Hence the trial court had little difficulty concluding that the Justice Department "spent months demanding purely race-based revisions to Georgia's redistricting plans, and that Georgia spent months attempting to comply." On this record, we fail to see how the District Court could have reached any conclusion other than that race was the predominant factor in drawing Georgia's Eleventh District; and in any event we conclude the court's finding is not clearly erroneous.

In light of its well-supported finding, the District Court was justified in rejecting the various alternative explanations offered for the district. Although a legislature's compliance with "traditional districting principles such as compactness, contiguity, and respect for political subdivisions" may well suffice to refute a claim of racial gerrymandering, *Shaw,* appellants cannot make such a refutation where, as here, those factors were subordinated to racial objectives. Georgia's Attorney General objected to the Justice Department's demand for three majority-black districts on the ground that to do so the State would have to "violate all reasonable standards of compactness and contiguity." This statement from a state official is powerful evidence that the legislature subordinated traditional districting principles to race when it ultimately enacted a plan creating three majority-black districts, and justified the District Court's finding that "every [objective districting] factor that could realistically be subordinated to racial tinkering in fact suffered that fate."

Nor can the State's districting legislation be rescued by mere recitation of purported communities of interest. The evidence was compelling that there are no tangible communities of interest spanning the hundreds of miles of the Eleventh District. A comprehensive report demonstrated the fractured political, social, and economic interests within the Eleventh District's black population. It is apparent that it was not alleged shared interests but rather the object of maximizing the district's black population and obtaining Justice Department approval that in fact explained the General Assembly's actions. A State is free to recognize communities that have a particular racial makeup, provided its action is directed toward some common thread of relevant interests.

"[W]hen members of a racial group live together in one community, a reapportionment plan that concentrates members of the group in one district and excludes them from others may reflect wholly legitimate purposes." *Shaw*. But where the State assumes from a group of voters' race that they "think alike, share the same political interests, and will prefer the same candidates at the polls," it engages in racial stereotyping at odds with equal protection mandates. [*Id.*]

Race was, as the District Court found, the predominant, overriding factor explaining the General Assembly's decision to attach to the Eleventh District various appendages containing dense majority-black populations. As a result, Georgia's congressional redistricting plan cannot be upheld unless it satisfies strict scrutiny, our most rigorous and exacting standard of constitutional review.

III

To satisfy strict scrutiny, the State must demonstrate that its districting legislation is narrowly tailored to achieve a compelling interest. Whether or not in some cases compliance with the [Voting Rights] Act, standing alone, can provide a compelling interest independent of any interest in remedying past discrimination, it cannot do so here. As we suggested in *Shaw*, compliance with federal antidiscrimination laws cannot justify race-based districting where the challenged district was not reasonably necessary under a constitutional reading and application of those laws. The congressional plan challenged here was not required by the Act under a correct reading of the statute.

We do not accept the contention that the State has a compelling interest in complying with whatever preclearance mandates the Justice Department issues. When a state governmental entity seeks to justify race-based remedies to cure the effects of past discrimination, we do not accept the government's mere assertion that the remedial action is required. Rather, we insist on a strong basis in evidence of the harm being remedied. Our presumptive skepticism of all racial classifications prohibits us as well from accepting on its face the Justice Department's conclusion that racial districting is necessary under the Act. Where a State relies on the Department's determination that race-based districting is necessary to comply with the Act, the judiciary retains an independent obligation in adjudicating consequent equal protection challenges to ensure that the State's actions are narrowly tailored to achieve a compelling interest. Were we to accept the Justice Department's objection itself as a compelling interest adequate to insulate racial districting from constitutional review, we would be surrendering to the Executive Branch our role in enforcing the constitutional limits on race-based official action. We may not do so.

For the same reasons, we think it inappropriate for a court engaged in constitutional scrutiny to accord deference to the Justice Department's interpretation of the Act. Although we have deferred to the Department's interpretation in certain statutory cases, we have rejected agency interpretations to which we would otherwise defer where they raise serious constitutional questions. When the Justice Department's interpretation of the Act compels race-based districting, it by definition raises a serious constitutional question and should not receive deference.

Georgia's drawing of the Eleventh District was not required under the Act because there was no reasonable basis to believe that Georgia's earlier enacted plans violated § 5. Wherever a plan is "ameliorative," a term we have used to describe plans increasing the number of majority-minority districts, it cannot violate § 5 unless the new apportionment itself so discriminates on the basis of race or color as to violate the Constitution. Georgia's first and second proposed plans increased the number of majority-black districts from 1 out of 10 (10%) to 2 out of 11 (18.18%). These plans were "ameliorative" and could not have violated § 5's nonretrogression principle. Acknowledging as much, the United States now relies on the fact that the Justice Department may object to a state proposal either on the ground that it has a prohibited purpose or a prohibited effect. The Government justifies its preclearance objections on the ground that the submitted plans violated § 5's purpose element. The key to the Government's position is and always has been that Georgia failed to proffer a nondiscriminatory purpose for its refusal in the first two submissions to take the steps necessary to create a third majority-minority district.

The Government's position is insupportable. Georgia's Attorney General provided a detailed explanation for the State's initial decision not to enact the max-black plan. The District Court accepted this explanation and found an absence of any discriminatory intent. The State's policy of adhering to other districting principles instead of creating as many majority-minority districts as possible does not support an inference that the plan so discriminates on the basis of race or color as to violate the Constitution, and thus cannot provide any basis under § 5 for the Justice Department's objection.

[W]e [have] recognized that the purpose of § 5 has always been to insure that no voting-procedure changes would be made that would lead to a retrogression in the position of racial minorities with respect to their effective exercise of the electoral franchise. The Justice Department's maximization policy seems quite far removed from this purpose. We are especially reluctant to conclude that § 5 justifies that policy given the serious constitutional concerns it raises. In *South Carolina v. Katzenbach,* we upheld § 5 as a necessary and constitutional response to some States' "extraordinary stratagem[s] of contriving new rules of various kinds for the sole purpose of perpetuating voting discrimination in the face of adverse federal court decrees." But our belief in *Katzenbach* that the federalism costs exacted by § 5 preclearance could be justified by those extraordinary circumstances does not mean they can be justified in the circumstances of this litigation. And the Justice Department's implicit command that States engage in presumptively unconstitutional race-based districting brings the Act, once upheld as a proper exercise of Congress' authority under § 2 of the Fifteenth Amendment into tension with the Fourteenth Amendment. We need not, however, resolve these troubling and difficult constitutional questions today.

IV

The Act, and its grant of authority to the federal courts to uncover official efforts to abridge minorities' right to vote, has been of vital importance in eradicating invidious discrimination from the electoral process and enhancing the legitimacy of our political institutions. Only if our political system and our society cleanse themselves of that discrimination will all members of the polity share an equal opportunity to gain public office regardless of race. As a Nation we share both the obligation and the aspiration of working toward this end. The end is neither assured nor well served, however, by carving electorates into racial blocs. If our society is to continue to progress as a multi-racial democracy, it must recognize that the automatic invocation of race stereotypes retards that progress and causes continued hurt and injury. It takes a shortsighted and unauthorized view of the Voting Rights Act to invoke that statute, which has played a decisive role in redressing some of our worst forms of discrimination, to demand the very racial stereotyping the Fourteenth Amendment forbids.

Figure 1-6
APPENDIX A
Proposed Eleventh District
Under "Max-Black" Plan

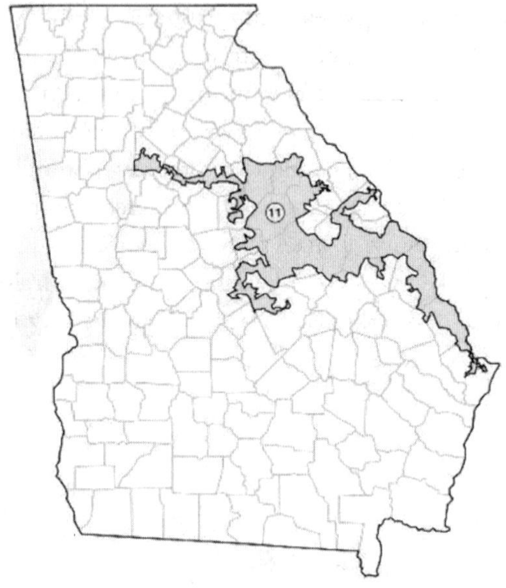

Source: Supreme Court's Appendix to *Miller v. Johnson*, 515 U.S. 900 (1995).

Figure 1-7
APPENDIX B
Current Congressional Districts

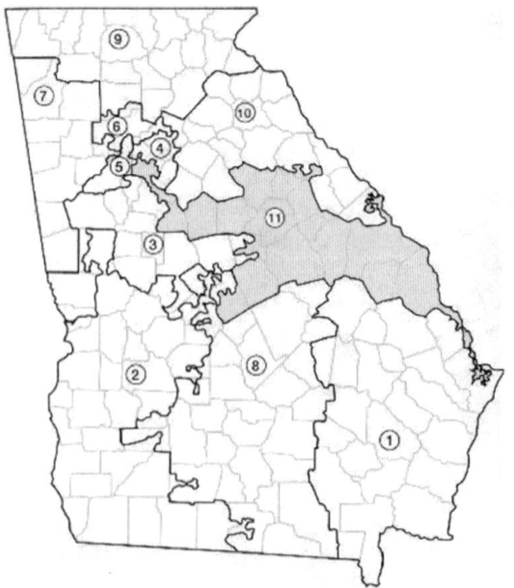

Source: Supreme Court's Appendix to *Miller v. Johnson*, 515 U.S. 900 (1995).

Justice O'CONNOR, concurring.

I understand the threshold standard the Court adopts—that "the legislature subordinated traditional race-neutral districting principles . . . to racial considerations,"—to be a demanding one. To invoke strict scrutiny, a plaintiff must show that the State has relied on race in substantial disregard of customary and traditional districting practices. Those practices provide a crucial frame of reference and therefore constitute a significant governing principle in cases of this kind. The standard would be no different if a legislature had drawn the boundaries to favor some other ethnic group; certainly the standard does not treat efforts to create majority-minority districts *less* favorably than similar efforts on behalf of other groups. Indeed, the driving force behind the adoption of the Fourteenth Amendment was the desire to end legal discrimination against blacks.

Application of the Court's standard does not throw into doubt the vast majority of the Nation's 435 congressional districts, where presumably the States have drawn the boundaries in accordance with their customary districting principles. That is so even though race may well have been considered in the redistricting process. *See Shaw v. Reno*. But application of the Court's standard helps achieve *Shaw*'s basic objective of making extreme instances of gerrymandering subject to meaningful judicial review. I therefore join the Court's opinion.

Justice STEVENS, dissenting.

Our desegregation cases redressed the *exclusion* of black citizens from public facilities reserved for whites. In these cases, in contrast, any voter, black or white, may live in the Eleventh District. What appellees contest is the *inclusion* of too many black voters in the district as drawn. In my view, if appellees allege no vote dilution, that inclusion can cause them no conceivable injury.

The Court's equation of *Shaw* claims with our desegregation decisions is inappropriate for another reason. In each of those cases, legal segregation frustrated the public interest in diversity and tolerance by barring African-Americans from joining whites in the activities at issue. The districting plan here, in contrast, serves the interest in diversity and tolerance by increasing the likelihood that a meaningful number of black representatives will add their voices to legislative debates.

Equally distressing is the Court's equation of traditional gerrymanders, designed to maintain or enhance a dominant group's power, with a dominant group's decision to share its power with a previously underrepresented group. I do not see how a districting plan that favors a politically weak group can violate equal protection. The Constitution does not mandate any form of proportional representation, but it certainly permits a State to adopt a policy that promotes fair representation of different groups.

Justice GINSBURG, with whom Justice STEVENS and Justice BREYER join, and with whom Justice SOUTER joins except as to Part III-B, dissenting.

Today the Court expands the judicial role, announcing that federal courts are to undertake searching review of any district with contours "predominant[ly] motivat[ed]" by race: "[S]trict scrutiny" will be triggered not only when traditional districting practices are abandoned, but also when those practices are "subordinated to"—given less weight than—race. Applying this new "race-as-predominant-factor" standard, the Court invalidates Georgia's districting plan even though Georgia's Eleventh District, the focus of today's dispute, bears the imprint of familiar districting practices. Because I do not endorse the Court's new standard and would not upset Georgia's plan, I dissent.

I

At the outset, it may be useful to note points on which the Court does not divide. First, we agree that federalism and the slim judicial competence to draw district lines weigh heavily against judicial intervention in apportionment decisions; as a rule, the task should remain within the domain of state legislatures. Second, for most of our Nation's history, the franchise has not been enjoyed equally by black citizens and white voters. To redress past wrongs and to avert any recurrence of exclusion of blacks from political processes, federal courts now respond to Equal Protection Clause and Voting Rights Act complaints of state action that dilutes minority voting strength. Third, to meet statutory requirements, state legislatures must sometimes consider race as a factor highly relevant to the drawing of district lines. Finally, state legislatures may recognize communities that have a particular racial or ethnic makeup, even in the absence of any compulsion to do so, in order to account for interests common to or shared by the persons grouped together.

Therefore, the fact that the Georgia General Assembly took account of race in drawing district lines—a fact not in dispute—does not render the State's plan invalid. To offend the Equal Protection Clause, all agree, the legislature had to do more than consider race. How much more, is the issue that divides the Court today.

II

A

The problem in *Shaw* was not the plan architects' consideration of race as relevant in redistricting. Rather, in the Court's estimation, it was the virtual exclusion of other factors from the calculus. Traditional districting practices were cast aside, the Court concluded, with race alone steering placement of district lines.

B

The record before us does not show that race similarly overwhelmed traditional districting practices in Georgia. Although the Georgia General Assembly prominently considered race in shaping the Eleventh District, race did not crowd out all other factors, as the Court found it did in North Carolina's delineation of the *Shaw* district.

In contrast to the snake-like North Carolina district inspected in *Shaw,* Georgia's Eleventh District is hardly "bizarre," "extremely irregular," or "irrational on its face." *Id.* Instead, the Eleventh District's design reflects significant consideration of traditional districting factors (such as keeping political subdivisions intact) and the usual political process of compromise and trades for a variety of nonracial reasons. The district covers a core area in central and eastern Georgia, and its total land area of 6,780 square miles is about average for the State.

Nor does the Eleventh District disrespect the boundaries of political subdivisions. Of the 22 counties in the district, 14 are intact and 8 are divided. That puts the Eleventh District at about the state average in divided counties. Seventy-one percent of the Eleventh District's boundaries track the borders of political subdivisions. Of the State's 11 districts, 5 score worse than the Eleventh District on this criterion, and 5 score better. Eighty-three percent of the Eleventh District's geographic area is composed of intact counties, above average for the State's congressional districts. And notably, the Eleventh District's boundaries largely follow precinct lines.

Evidence at trial similarly shows that considerations other than race went into determining the Eleventh District's boundaries. For a "political reason"—to accommodate the request of an incumbent State Senator regarding the placement of the precinct in which his son lived—the DeKalb County portion of the Eleventh District was drawn to include a particular (largely white) precinct. The corridor through Effingham County was substantially narrowed at the request of a (white) State Representative. In Chatham County, the district was trimmed to exclude a heavily black community in Garden City because a State Representative wanted to keep the city intact inside the neighboring First District. The Savannah extension was configured by "the narrowest means possible" to avoid splitting the city of Port Wentworth.

Georgia's Eleventh District, in sum, is not an outlier district shaped without reference to familiar districting techniques.

C

The Court suggests that it was not Georgia's Legislature, but the U.S. Department of Justice, that effectively drew the lines, and that Department officers did so with nothing but race in mind. Yet the "Max-Black" plan advanced by the Attorney General was not the plan passed by the Georgia General Assembly.

And although the Attorney General refused preclearance to the first two plans approved by Georgia's Legislature, the State was not thereby disarmed; Georgia could have demanded relief from the Department's objections by instituting a civil action in the United States District Court for the District of Columbia, with ultimate review in this Court. Instead of pursuing that avenue, the State chose to adopt the plan here in controversy—a plan the State forcefully defends before us. We should respect Georgia's choice by taking its position as genuine.

D

Along with attention to size, shape, and political subdivisions, the Court recognizes as an appropriate districting principle, "respect for . . . communities defined by actual shared interests." The Court finds no community here, however, because a report in the record showed "fractured political, social, and economic interests within the Eleventh District's black population."

But ethnicity itself can tie people together, as volumes of social science literature have documented—even people with divergent economic interests. For this reason, ethnicity is a significant force in political life.

III

To separate permissible and impermissible use of race in legislative apportionment, the Court orders strict scrutiny for districting plans "predominantly motivated" by race. No longer can a State avoid judicial oversight by giving—as in this case—genuine and measurable consideration to traditional districting practices. Instead, a federal case can be mounted whenever plaintiffs plausibly allege that other factors carried less weight than race. This invitation to litigate against the State seems to me neither necessary nor proper.

A

The Court derives its test from diverse opinions on the relevance of race in contexts distinctly unlike apportionment. The controlling idea, the Court says, is "the simple command [at the heart of the Constitution's guarantee of equal protection] that the Government must treat citizens as individuals, not as simply components of a racial, religious, sexual or national class."

In adopting districting plans, however, States do not treat people as individuals. Apportionment schemes, by their very nature, assemble people in groups. States do not assign voters to districts based on merit or achievement, standards States might use in hiring employees or engaging contractors. Rather, legislators classify voters in groups—by economic, geographical, political, or social characteristics—and then reconcile the competing claims of these groups.

That ethnicity defines some of these groups is a political reality. Until now, no constitutional infirmity has been seen in districting Irish or Italian voters together, for example, so long as the delineation does not abandon familiar apportionment practices. If Chinese-Americans and Russian-Americans may seek and secure group recognition in the delineation of voting districts, then African-Americans should not be dissimilarly treated. Otherwise, in the name of equal protection, we would shut out the very minority group whose history in the United States gave birth to the Equal Protection Clause.

B

Under the Court's approach, judicial review of the same intensity, *i.e.,* strict scrutiny, is in order once it is determined that an apportionment is predominantly motivated by race. It matters not at all, in this new regime, whether the apportionment dilutes or enhances minority voting strength.

Special circumstances justify vigilant judicial inspection to protect minority voters—circumstances that do not apply to majority voters. A history of exclusion from state politics left racial minorities without clout to extract provisions for fair representation in the lawmaking forum. The equal protection rights of minority voters thus could have remained unrealized absent the Judiciary's close surveillance. *Cf. United States v. Carolene Products Co.*, n. 4 (1938) (referring to the "more searching judicial inquiry" that may properly attend classifications adversely affecting "discrete and insular minorities"). The majority, by definition, encounters no such blockage. White voters in Georgia do not lack means to exert strong pressure on their state legislators. The force of their numbers is itself a powerful determiner of what the legislature will do that does not coincide with perceived majority interests.

State legislatures like Georgia's today operate under federal constraints imposed by the Voting Rights Act—constraints justified by history and designed by Congress to make once-subordinated people free and equal citizens. But these federal constraints do not leave majority voters in need of extraordinary judicial solicitude. The Attorney General, who administers the Voting Rights Act's preclearance requirements, is herself a political actor. She has a duty to enforce the law Congress passed, and she is no doubt aware of the political cost of venturing too far to the detriment of majority voters. Majority voters, furthermore, can press the State to seek judicial review if the Attorney General refuses to preclear a plan that the voters favor. Finally, the Act is itself a political measure, subject to modification in the political process.

C

The Court's disposition renders redistricting perilous work for state legislatures. Statutory mandates and political realities may require States to consider race when drawing district lines. But today's decision is a counterforce; it opens the way for federal litigation if "traditional . . . districting principles" arguably were accorded less weight than race. Genuine attention to traditional districting practices and avoidance of bizarre configurations seemed, under *Shaw*, to provide a safe harbor. In view of today's decision, that is no longer the case.

Only after litigation—under either the Voting Rights Act, the Court's new *Miller* standard, or both—will States now be assured that plans conscious of race are safe. Federal judges in large numbers may be drawn into the fray. This enlargement of the judicial role is unwarranted. The reapportionment plan that resulted from Georgia's political process merited this Court's approbation, not its condemnation. Accordingly, I dissent.

NOTES ON *MILLER*

1. Many of the racial gerrymandering cases that the Supreme Court heard in the 1990s emanated from State efforts to secure Section 5 preclearance from the U.S. Department of Justice. Now that preclearance has essentially been rendered a nullity (unless a court orders preclearance as a remedy under Section 3(c)), has

the need for racial gerrymandering doctrine been eliminated? (You may wish to review this question after you have considered *LULAC v. Perry* at the end of Part I.)

2. Focus for a moment on the rationale for the Court's creation of the racial gerrymandering doctrine. Why does the Court entertain claims of racial gerrymandering? Is it because of harms to individual voters? If so, what are those harms? Is it because of harms to groups of voters? If so, what are those harms? Is it because of harms to candidates? If so, what are those harms? Do any of the answers to these questions provide a sufficient justification for the Court's entry into this particular "political thicket"?
3. *Shaw* seemed to provide a standard for determining whether a redistricting represented a racial gerrymander by centering around the "bizarre" shape of a district. *Miller* changes that analysis by noting that the shape of a district is only one evidentiary factor that goes into the determination as to whether race was the "predominant factor" in the drawing of a district. If race is determined by the court to be a predominant factor then the court proceeds to analyze the district based upon strict scrutiny.
4. In essence, the *Miller* Court says that the use of race in redistricting is not *ipso facto* unconstitutional. How does one draw the line between what one might call the "run of the mill" use of race in redistricting and the "excessive" use of race in redistricting? Would it be better to develop a clear rule where a redistricting plan would be held unconstitutional if race played *any role at all* in the drawing of a district?

The twists and turns of the development of the Supreme Court's racial gerrymandering doctrine can be encapsulated in the litigation involving North Carolina's Twelfth Congressional District. That case featured four decisions by a three-judge district court that ended up being reversed by the Supreme Court (an ignominious record if there ever was one!). The first case was *Shaw v. Reno*, which you read about above and involved the creation of a claim of racial gerrymandering based on a bizarrely shaped district. What you are about to read is the fourth opinion in less than a decade from the Supreme Court involving District 12. As you read the case, pay close attention to the history of the litigation and also how this fourth decision might change the playing field in relation to the "law" of racial gerrymandering. Consider also the Supreme Court's role in evaluating a district court's factual findings with respect to a redistricting claim, and how this case represents "precedent" that might apply in future settings.

EASLEY v. CROMARTIE

532 U.S. 234 (2001)

Justice BREYER delivered the opinion of the Court.

In this appeal, we review a three-judge District Court's determination that North Carolina's Legislature used race as the "predominant factor" in drawing its 12th

Congressional District's 1997 boundaries. The court's findings, in our view, are clearly erroneous. We therefore reverse its conclusion that the State violated the Equal Protection Clause.

I

This "racial districting" litigation is before us for the fourth time. Our first two holdings addressed North Carolina's *former* Congressional District 12, one of two North Carolina congressional districts drawn in 1992 that contained a majority of African-American voters. *See Shaw v. Reno,* (1993) (*Shaw I*); *Shaw v. Hunt,* (1996) (*Shaw II*).

A

In *Shaw I,* the Court considered whether plaintiffs' factual allegation—that the legislature had drawn the former district's boundaries for race-based reasons—if true, could underlie a legal holding that the legislature had violated the Equal Protection Clause. The Court held that it could. It wrote that a violation may exist where the legislature's boundary drawing, though "race neutral on its face," nonetheless can be understood only as an effort to "separate voters into different districts on the basis of race," and where the "separation lacks sufficient justification."

In *Shaw II,* the Court reversed a subsequent three-judge District Court's holding that the boundary-drawing law in question did not violate the Constitution. This Court found that the district's "unconventional," snakelike shape, the way in which its boundaries split towns and counties, its predominately African-American racial makeup, and its history, together demonstrated a deliberate effort to create a "majority-black" district in which race "could not be compromised," not simply a district designed to "protec[t] Democratic incumbents." And the Court concluded that the legislature's use of racial criteria was not justified.

B

Our third holding focused on a new District 12, the boundaries of which the legislature had redrawn in 1997. *Hunt v. Cromartie,* (1999). A three-judge District Court, with one judge dissenting, had granted summary judgment in favor of those challenging the district's boundaries. The court found that the legislature again had "used criteria . . . that are facially race driven," in violation of the Equal Protection Clause. It based this conclusion upon "uncontroverted material facts" showing that the boundaries created an unusually shaped district, split counties and cities, and in particular placed almost all heavily Democratic-registered, predominantly African-American voting precincts, inside the district while locating some heavily Democratic-registered, predominantly white precincts, outside the district. This latter circumstance, said the court, showed that the legislature was trying to maximize new District 12's African-American voting strength, not the district's Democratic voting strength.

This Court reversed. We agreed with the District Court that the new district's shape, the way in which it split towns and counties, and its heavily African-American voting population all helped the plaintiffs' case. But neither that evidence by itself, nor when coupled with the evidence of Democratic registration, was sufficient to show, on summary judgment, the unconstitutional race-based objective that plaintiffs claimed. That is because there was a genuine issue of material fact as to whether the evidence also was consistent with a constitutional political objective, namely, the creation of a safe Democratic seat.

We pointed to the affidavit of an expert witness for defendants, Dr. David W. Peterson. Dr. Peterson offered to show that, because North Carolina's African-American voters are overwhelmingly Democratic voters, one cannot easily distinguish a legislative effort to create a majority-African-American district from a legislative effort to create a safely Democratic district. And he also provided data showing that *registration* did not indicate how voters would actually vote. We agreed that data showing how voters actually behave, not data showing only how those voters are registered, could affect the outcome of this litigation. We concluded that the case was "not suited for summary disposition" and we reversed the District Court.

C

On remand, the parties undertook additional discovery. The three-judge District Court held a 3-day trial. And the court again held (over a dissent) that the legislature had unconstitutionally drawn District 12's new 1997 boundaries. It found that the legislature had tried "(1) [to] cur[e] the [previous district's] constitutional defects" while also "(2) drawing the plan to maintain the existing partisan balance in the State's congressional delegation." It added that to "achieve the second goal," the legislature "drew the new plan (1) to avoid placing two incumbents in the same district and (2) to preserve the partisan core of the existing districts." The court concluded that the "plan as enacted largely reflects these directives." But the court also found "as a matter of fact that the General Assembly . . . used criteria . . . that are facially race driven" without any compelling justification for doing so.

The court based its latter, constitutionally critical, conclusion in part upon the district's snakelike shape, the way in which it split cities and towns, and its heavily African-American (47%) voting population—all matters that this Court had considered when it found summary judgment inappropriate. The court also based this conclusion upon a specific finding—absent when we previously considered this litigation—that the legislature had drawn the boundaries in order "to collect precincts with *high racial identification rather than political identification.*"

This last-mentioned finding rested in turn upon five subsidiary determinations:

(1) that "the legislators excluded many heavily-Democratic precincts from District 12, even when those precincts immediately border the Twelfth and would have established a far more compact district";

(2) that "[a]dditionally, Plaintiffs' expert, Dr. Weber, showed time and again how race trumped party affiliation in the construction of the 12th District and how political explanations utterly failed to explain the composition of the district,";
(3) that Dr. Peterson's testimony was "'unreliable' and not relevant,";
(4) that a legislative redistricting leader, Senator Roy Cooper, had alluded at the time of redistricting "to a need for 'racial and partisan' balance,"; and
(5) that the Senate's redistricting coordinator, Gerry Cohen, had sent Senator Cooper an e-mail reporting that Cooper had "moved Greensboro Black community into the 12th, and now need[ed] to take [about] 60,000 out of the 12th."

The State filed a notice of appeal. And we now reverse.

II

The issue in this case is evidentiary. We must determine whether there is adequate support for the District Court's key findings, particularly the ultimate finding that the legislature's motive was predominantly racial, not political. In making this determination, we are aware that, under *Shaw I* and later cases, the burden of proof on the plaintiffs (who attack the district) is a "demanding one." *Miller v. Johnson* (O'Connor, J., concurring). The Court has specified that those who claim that a legislature has improperly used race as a criterion, in order, for example, to create a majority-minority district, must show at a minimum that the legislature subordinated traditional race-neutral districting principles to racial considerations. Race must not simply have been *a* motivation for the drawing of a majority-minority district, but the *predominant* factor motivating the legislature's districting decision. Plaintiffs must show that a facially neutral law is unexplainable on grounds other than race.

The Court also has made clear that the underlying districting decision is one that ordinarily falls within a legislature's sphere of competence. *Miller*. Hence, the legislature "must have discretion to exercise the political judgment necessary to balance competing interests," and courts must "exercise *extraordinary caution* in adjudicating claims that a State has drawn district lines on the basis of race," *id.* Caution is especially appropriate in this case, where the State has articulated a legitimate political explanation for its districting decision, and the voting population is one in which race and political affiliation are highly correlated.

We also are aware that we review the District Court's findings only for "clear error." In applying this standard, we, like any reviewing court, will not reverse a lower court's finding of fact simply because we would have decided the case differently. Rather, a reviewing court must ask whether, on the entire evidence, it is left with the definite and firm conviction that a mistake has been committed.

Where an intermediate court reviews, and affirms, a trial court's factual findings, this Court will not lightly overturn the concurrent findings of the two lower courts. But in this instance there is no intermediate court, and we are the only court of review. Moreover, the trial here at issue was not lengthy and the key evidence consisted primarily of documents and expert testimony. Credibility evaluations played a minor role. Accordingly, we find that an extensive review of the District Court's findings, for clear error, is warranted. That review leaves us "with the definite and firm conviction" that the District Court's key findings are mistaken.

III

The critical District Court determination—the matter for which we remanded this litigation—consists of the finding that race *rather than* politics *predominantly* explains District 12's 1997 boundaries. That determination rests upon three findings (the district's shape, its splitting of towns and counties, and its high African-American voting population) that we previously found insufficient to support summary judgment. Given the undisputed evidence that racial identification is highly correlated with political affiliation in North Carolina, these facts in and of themselves cannot, as a matter of law, support the District Court's judgment. The District Court rested, however, upon five new subsidiary findings to conclude that District 12's lines are the product of no "mer[e] correlat[ion]," but are instead a result of the predominance of race in the legislature's line-drawing process.

In considering each subsidiary finding, we have given weight to the fact that the District Court was familiar with this litigation, heard the testimony of each witness, and considered all the evidence with care. Nonetheless, we cannot accept the District Court's findings as adequate for reasons which we shall spell out in detail and which we can summarize as follows:

First, the primary evidence upon which the District Court relied for its "race, not politics," conclusion is evidence of voting registration, not voting behavior; and that is precisely the kind of evidence that we said was inadequate the last time this case was before us. Second, the additional evidence to which appellees' expert, Dr. Weber, pointed, and the statements made by Senator Cooper and Gerry Cohen, simply do not provide significant additional support for the District Court's conclusion. Third, the District Court, while not accepting the contrary conclusion of appellants' expert, Dr. Peterson, did not (and as far as the record reveals, could not) reject much of the significant supporting factual information he provided. Fourth, in any event, appellees themselves have provided us with charts summarizing evidence of voting behavior and those charts tend to refute the court's "race, not politics," conclusion.

A

The District Court primarily based its "race, not politics," conclusion upon its finding that "the legislators excluded many heavily-Democratic precincts from District 12, even when those precincts immediately border the Twelfth and would have established a far more compact district." This finding, however—insofar as it differs from the remaining four—rests solely upon evidence that the legislature excluded heavily white precincts with high Democratic Party registration, while including heavily African-American precincts with equivalent, or lower, Democratic Party registration. Indeed, the District Court cites at length figures showing that the legislature included "several precincts with racial compositions of 40 to 100 percent African-American," while excluding certain adjacent precincts "with less than 35 percent African-American population" but which contain between 54% and 76% *registered* Democrats.

As we said before, the problem with this evidence is that it focuses upon party registration, not upon voting behavior. And we previously found the same evidence inadequate because registration figures do not accurately predict preference at the polls. In part this is because white voters registered as Democrats "cross-over" to vote for a Republican candidate more often than do African-Americans, who register and vote Democratic between 95% and 97% of the time. A legislature trying to secure a safe Democratic seat is interested in Democratic voting behavior. Hence, a legislature may, by placing reliable Democratic precincts within a district without regard to race, end up with a district containing more heavily African-American precincts, but the reasons would be political rather than racial.

B

The District Court wrote that "[a]dditionally, [p]laintiffs' expert, Dr. Weber, showed time and again how race trumped party affiliation in the construction of the 12th District and how political explanations utterly failed to explain the composition of the district." In support of this conclusion, the court relied upon six different citations to Dr. Weber's trial testimony. We have examined each reference.

1

At the first cited pages of the trial transcript, Dr. Weber says that a reliably Democratic voting population of 60% is sufficient to create a safe Democratic seat. Yet, he adds, the legislature created a more-than-60% reliable Democratic voting population in District 12. Hence (we read Dr. Weber to infer), the legislature likely was driven by race, not politics.

The record indicates, however, that, although Dr. Weber is right that District 12 is more than 60% reliably Democratic, it exceeds that figure by very little. Nor did Dr. Weber ask whether other districts, unchallenged by appellees, were significantly less "safe" than was District 12. In fact, the figures the legislature used showed that District 12 would be 63% reliably Democratic. By the same measures, at least two Republican districts (Districts 6 and 10) are 61% reliably Republican. And, as Dr. Weber conceded, incumbents might have urged legislators (trying to maintain a six/six Democrat/Republican delegation split) to make their seats, not 60% safe, but as safe as possible. In a field such as voting behavior, where figures are inherently uncertain, Dr. Weber's tiny calculated percentage differences are simply too small to carry significant evidentiary weight.

2

The District Court cited two parts of the transcript where Dr. Weber testified about a table he had prepared listing all precincts in the six counties, portions of which make up District 12. Dr. Weber said that District 12 contains between 39% and 56% of the precincts (depending on the county) that are more-than-40% reliably Democratic, but it contains almost every precinct with more-than-40% African-American voters. Why, he essentially asks, if the legislature had had politics primarily in mind, would its effort to place reliably Democratic precincts within District 12 not have produced a greater racial mixture?

Dr. Weber's own testimony provides an answer to this question. As Dr. Weber agreed, the precincts listed in the table were at least *40%* reliably Democratic, but virtually all the African-American precincts included in District 12 were *more* than 40% reliably Democratic. Moreover, *none* of the excluded white precincts were *as* reliably Democratic as the African-American precincts that were included in the district. Yet the legislature sought precincts that were reliably Democratic, not precincts that were *40%* reliably Democratic, for obvious political reasons.

Neither does the table specify whether the excluded white-reliably-Democratic precincts were located near enough to District 12's boundaries or each other for the legislature as a practical matter to have drawn District 12's boundaries to have included them, without sacrificing other important political goals. The contrary is suggested by the fact that Dr. Weber's own proposed alternative plan would have pitted two incumbents against each other (Sue Myrick, a Republican from former District 9 and Mel Watt, a Democrat from former District 12). Dr. Weber testified that such a result—"a very competitive race with one of them losing their seat"—was desirable. But the legislature, for political, not racial, reasons, believed the opposite. And it drew its plan to protect incumbents—a legitimate political goal recognized by the District Court.

For these reasons, Dr. Weber's table offers little insight into the legislature's true motive.

3

The next part of the transcript the District Court cited contains Dr. Weber's testimony about a Mecklenburg County precinct (precinct 77) which the legislature split between Districts 9 and 12. Dr. Weber apparently thought that the legislature did not have to split this precinct, placing the more heavily African-American segment within District 12—unless, of course, its motive was racial rather than political. But Dr. Weber simultaneously conceded that he had not considered whether District 9's incumbent Republican would have wanted the whole of precinct 77 left in her own district where it would have burdened her with a significant additional number of reliably Democratic voters. Nor had Dr. Weber "test[ed]" his conclusion that this split helped to show a racial (rather than political) motive, say, by adjusting other boundary lines and determining the political, or other nonracial, consequences of such adjustments.

The maps in evidence indicate that to have placed all of precinct 77 within District 12 would have created a District 12 peninsula that invaded District 9, neatly dividing that latter district in two—a conclusive nonracial reason for the legislature's decision not to do so.

4

The District Court cited Dr. Weber's conclusion that "race is the predominant factor." But this statement of the conclusion is no stronger than the evidence that underlies it.

5

The District Court's final citation is to Dr. Weber's assertion that there are other ways in which the legislature could have created a safely Democratic district without placing so many primarily African-American districts within District 12. And we recognize that *some* such other ways may exist. But, unless the evidence also shows that these hypothetical alternative districts would have better satisfied the legislature's other nonracial political goals as well as traditional nonracial districting principles, this fact alone cannot show an improper legislative motive. After all, the Constitution does not place an *affirmative* obligation upon the legislature to avoid creating districts that turn out to be heavily, even majority, minority. It simply imposes an obligation not to create such districts for predominantly racial, as opposed to political or traditional, districting motivations. And Dr. Weber's testimony does not, at the pages cited, provide evidence of a politically practical alternative plan that the legislature failed to adopt predominantly for racial reasons.

6

We do not see how Dr. Weber's testimony, taken as a whole, could have provided more than minimal support for the District Court's conclusion that race predominantly underlay the legislature's districting decision.

C

[Omitted]

D

The District Court also relied on two pieces of "direct" evidence of discriminatory intent.

1

The court found that a legislative redistricting leader, Senator Roy Cooper, when testifying before a legislative committee in 1997, had said that the 1997 plan satisfies a "need for 'racial and partisan' balance." The court concluded that the words "racial balance" referred to a 10-to-2 Caucasian/African-American balance in the State's 12-member congressional delegation. Hence, Senator Cooper had admitted that the legislature had drawn the plan with race in mind.

Senator Cooper's full statement reads as follows:

> "Those of you who dealt with Redistricting before realize that you cannot solve each problem that you encounter and everyone can find a problem with this Plan. However, I think that overall it provides for a fair, geographic, racial and partisan balance throughout the State of North Carolina. I think in order to come to an agreement all sides had to give a little bit, but I think we've reached an agreement that we can live with."

We agree that one can read the statement about "racial . . . balance" as the District Court read it—to refer to the current congressional delegation's racial balance. But even as so read, the phrase shows that the legislature considered race, along with other partisan and geographic considerations; and as so read it says little or nothing about whether race played a *predominant* role comparatively speaking.

2

The second piece of "direct" evidence relied upon by the District Court is a February 10, 1997, e-mail sent from Gerry Cohen, a legislative staff member responsible for drafting districting plans, to Senator Cooper and Senator Leslie Winner. Cohen wrote: "I have moved Greensboro Black community into the 12th, and now need to take [about] 60,000 out of the 12th. I await your direction on this."

The reference to race—*i.e.,* "Black community"—is obvious. But the e-mail does not discuss the point of the reference. It does not discuss why Greensboro's African-American voters were placed in the 12th District; it does not discuss the political consequences of failing to do so; it is addressed only to two members of the legislature; and it suggests that the legislature paid less attention to race in respect to the 12th District than in respect to the 1st District, where the e-mail provides a far more extensive, detailed discussion of racial percentages. It is less persuasive than the kinds of direct evidence we have found significant in other redistricting cases. *Miller* (State set out to create majority-minority district). Nonetheless, the e-mail offers some support for the District Court's conclusion.

E

As we have said, we assume that the maps appended to appellees' brief reflect the record insofar as that record describes the relation between District 12's boundaries and reliably Democratic voting behavior. Consequently we shall consider appellees' related claims, made on appeal, that the maps provide significant support for the District Court, in that they show how the legislature might have "swapped" several more heavily African-American District 12 precincts for other less heavily African-American adjacent precincts—without harming its basic "safely Democratic" political objective.

First, appellees suggest, without identifying any specific swap, that the legislature could have brought within District 12 several reliably Democratic, primarily white, precincts in Forsyth County. None of these precincts, however, is more reliably Democratic than the precincts immediately adjacent and within District 12. See Appendix A, *infra* (showing Democratic strength reflected by Republican victories in each precinct). One of them, the Brown/Douglas Recreation Precinct, is heavily African-American. And the remainder form a buffer between the home precinct of Fifth District Representative Richard Burr and the District 12 border, such that their removal from District 5 would deprive Representative Burr of a large portion of his own hometown, making him more vulnerable to a challenge from elsewhere within his district. Consequently the Forsyth County precincts do not significantly help appellees' "race, not politics," thesis.

Second, appellees say that the legislature might have swapped two District 12 Davidson County precincts (Thomasville 1 and Lexington 3) for a District 6 Guilford County precinct (Greensboro 17). Whatever the virtues of such a swap, however, it would have diminished the size of District 12, geographically producing an unusually narrow isthmus linking District 12's north with its south and demographically producing the State's smallest district, deviating by about 1,300 below the legislatively endorsed ideal mean of 552,386 population. Traditional districting considerations consequently militated against any such swap.

Third, appellees suggest that, in Mecklenburg County, two District 12 precincts (Charlotte 81 and LCI-South) be swapped with two District 9 precincts (Charlotte 10 and 21). This suggestion is difficult to evaluate, as the parties provide no map that specifically identifies each precinct in Mecklenburg County by name. Nonetheless, from what we can tell, such a swap would make the district marginally more white (decreasing the African-American population by about 300 persons) while making the shape more questionable, leaving the precinct immediately to the south of Charlotte 81 jutting out into District 9. We are not convinced that this proposal materially advances appellees' claim.

Fourth, appellees argue that the legislature could have swapped two reliably Democratic Greensboro precincts outside District 12 (11 and 14) for four reliably Republican High Point precincts (1, 13, 15, and 19) placed within District 12. The swap would not have improved racial balance significantly, however, for each of the six precincts have an African-American population of less than 35%. Additionally, it too would have altered the shape of District 12 for the worse. And, in any event, the decision to exclude the two Greensboro precincts seems to reflect the legislature's decision to draw boundaries that follow main thoroughfares in Guilford County.

Even if our judgments in respect to a few of these precincts are wrong, a showing that the legislature might have "swapped" a handful of precincts out of a total of 154 precincts, involving a population of a few hundred out of a total population of about half a million, cannot significantly strengthen appellees' case.

IV

We concede the record contains a modicum of evidence offering support for the District Court's conclusion. That evidence includes the Cohen e-mail, Senator Cooper's reference to "racial balance," and to a minor degree, some aspects of Dr. Weber's testimony. The evidence taken together, however, does not show that racial considerations predominated in the drawing of District 12's boundaries. That is because race in this case correlates closely with political behavior. The basic question is whether the legislature drew District 12's boundaries because of race *rather than* because of political behavior (coupled with traditional, nonracial districting considerations). It is not, as the dissent contends, whether a legislature may defend its districting decisions based on a "stereotype" about African-American voting behavior. And given the fact that the party attacking the legislature's decision bears the burden of proving that racial considerations are "dominant and controlling," given the "demanding" nature of that burden of proof, and given the sensitivity, the "extraordinary caution," that district courts must show to avoid treading upon legislative prerogatives, the attacking party has not successfully shown that race, rather than politics, predominantly accounts for the result. The record leaves us with the "definite and firm conviction" that the District Court erred in finding to the contrary. And we do not believe that providing appellees a further opportunity to make their "precinct swapping" arguments in the District Court could change this result.

We can put the matter more generally as follows: In a case such as this one where majority-minority districts (or the approximate equivalent) are at issue and where racial identification correlates highly with political affiliation, the party attacking the legislatively drawn boundaries must show at the least that the legislature could have achieved its legitimate political objectives in alternative ways that are comparably consistent with traditional districting principles. That party must also show that those districting alternatives would have brought about significantly greater racial balance. Appellees failed to make any such showing here. We conclude that the District Court's contrary findings are clearly erroneous. Because of this disposition, we need not address appellants' alternative grounds for reversal.

The judgment of the District Court is

Reversed.

Figure 1-8

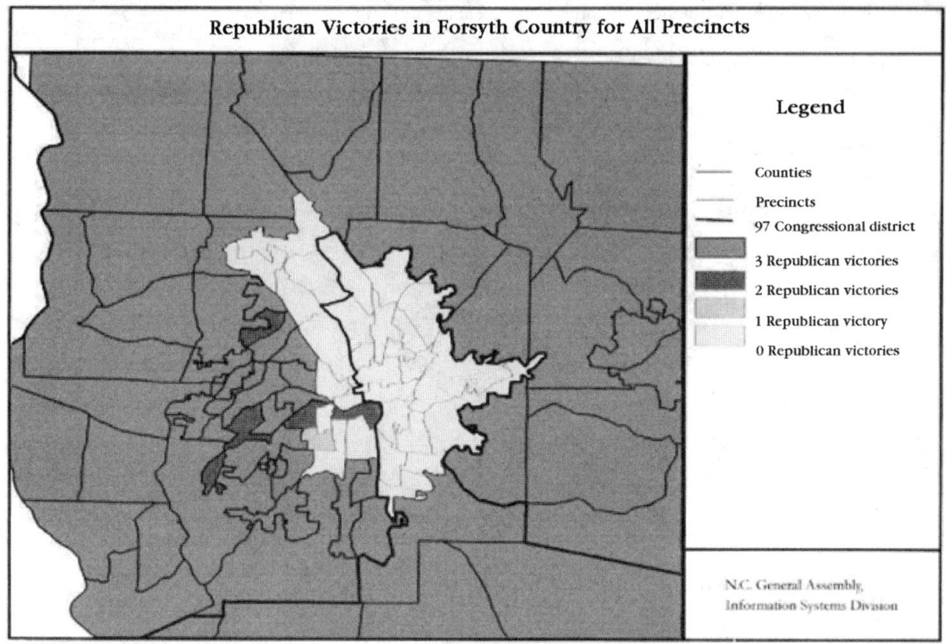

Source: Supreme Court's Appendix to *Easley v. Cromartie*, 532 U.S. 234 (2001).

Figure 1-9

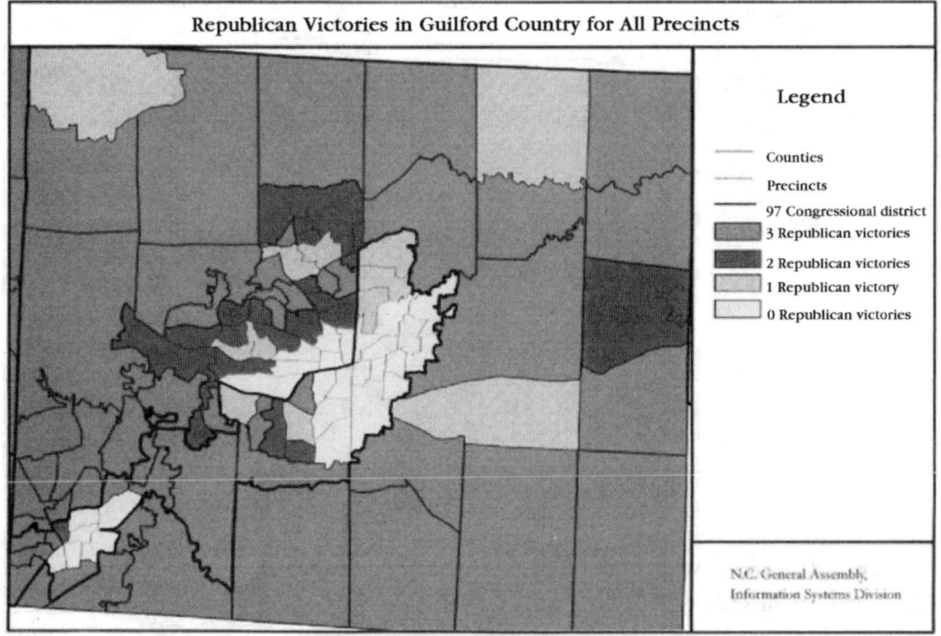

Source: Supreme Court's Appendix to *Easley v. Cromartie*, 532 U.S. 234 (2001).

Figure 1-10

APPENDIX C

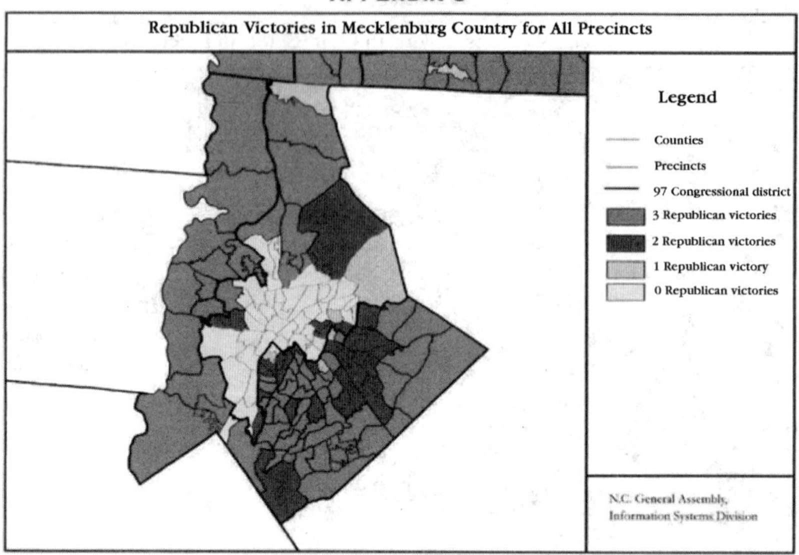

Source: Supreme Court's Appendix to *Easley v. Cromartie*, 532 U.S. 234 (2001).

Figure 1-11

APPENDIX D

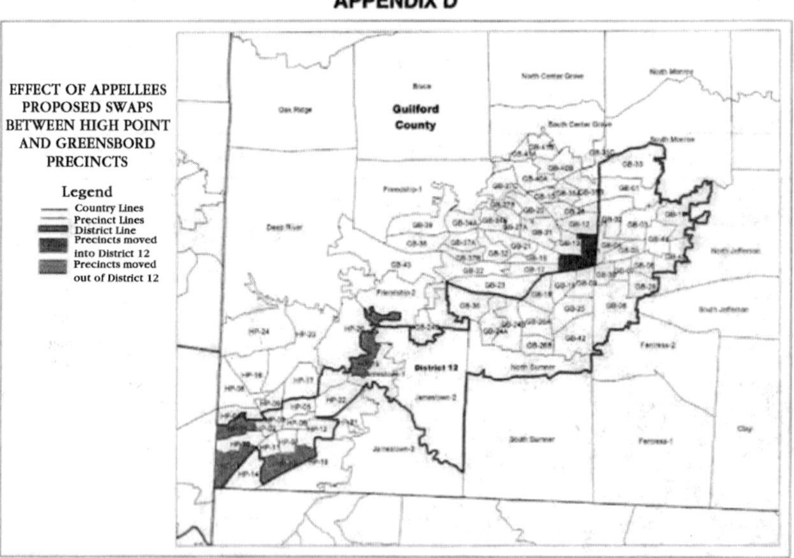

Source: Supreme Court's Appendix to *Easley v. Cromartie*, 532 U.S. 234 (2001).

Justice THOMAS, with whom CHIEF JUSTICE [Rehnquist], Justice SCALIA, and Justice KENNEDY join, dissenting.

The issue for the District Court was whether racial considerations were predominant in the design of North Carolina's Congressional District 12. The issue for this Court is simply whether the District Court's factual finding—that racial considerations did predominate—was clearly erroneous. Because I do not believe the court below committed clear error, I respectfully dissent.

I

The Court does cite cases that address the correct standard of review and does couch its conclusion in "clearly erroneous" terms. But these incantations of the correct standard are empty gestures, contradicted by the Court's conclusion that it must engage in "extensive review." In several ways, the Court ignores its role as a reviewing court and engages in its own fact-finding enterprise. First, the Court suggests that there is some significance to the absence of an intermediate court in this action. This cannot be a legitimate consideration. If it were legitimate, we would have mentioned it in prior redistricting cases. After all, in *Miller* and *Shaw*, we also did not have the benefit of intermediate appellate review.

Second, the Court appears to discount clear error review here because the trial was "not lengthy." Even if considerations such as the length of the trial were relevant in deciding how to review factual findings, an assumption about which I have my doubts, these considerations would not counsel against deference in this action. The trial lasted for three days in which the court heard the testimony of 12 witnesses. And quite apart from the total trial time, the District Court sifted through hundreds of pages of deposition testimony and expert analysis, including statistical analysis. It also should not be forgotten that one member of the panel has reviewed the iterations of District 12 since 1992. If one were to calibrate clear error review according to the trier of fact's familiarity with the case, there is simply no question that the court here gained a working knowledge of the facts of this litigation in myriad ways over a period far longer than three days.

Third, the Court downplays deference to the District Court's finding by highlighting that the key evidence was expert testimony requiring no traditional credibility determinations. As a factual matter, the Court overlooks the District Court's express assessment of the legislative redistricting leader's credibility. It is also likely that the court's interpretation of the e-mail written by Gerry Cohen, the primary drafter of District 12, was influenced by its evaluation of Cohen as a witness. And, as a legal matter, the Court's emphasis on the technical nature of the evidence misses the mark. Although we have recognized that particular weight should be given to a trial court's credibility determinations, we have never held that factual findings based on documentary evidence and expert testimony justify "extensive review." Instead, the rationale for deference extends to all determinations of fact because of the trial judge's "expertise" in making such determinations. Accordingly, deference to the fact finder is the rule, not the exception, and I see no reason to depart from this rule in the case before us now.

Finally, perhaps the best evidence that the Court has emptied clear error review of meaningful content in the redistricting context (and the strongest testament to the fact that the District Court was dealing with a complex fact pattern) is the Court's foray into the minutiae of the record. I do not doubt this Court's ability to sift through volumes of facts or to argue *its* interpretation of those facts persuasively. But I do doubt the wisdom, efficiency, increased accuracy, and legitimacy of an extensive review that is any more searching than clear error review. Thus, I would follow our precedents and simply review the District Court's finding for clear error.

II

Reviewing for clear error, I cannot say that the District Court's view of the evidence was impermissible. First, the court relied on objective measures of compactness, which show that District 12 is the most geographically scattered district in North Carolina, to support its conclusion that the district's design was not dictated by traditional districting concerns. Although this evidence was available when we held that summary judgment was inappropriate, we certainly did not hold that it was irrelevant in determining whether racial gerrymandering occurred. On the contrary, we determined that there was a triable issue of fact. Moreover, although we acknowledged "that a district's unusual shape can give rise to an inference of political motivation," we "doubt[ed] that a bizarre shape *equally* supports a political inference and a racial one." Second, the court relied on the expert opinion of Dr. Weber, who interpreted statistical data to conclude that there were Democratic precincts with low black populations excluded from District 12, which would have created a more compact district had they been included.[4] And contrary to the Court's assertion, Dr. Weber did not merely examine the registration data in reaching his conclusions. Dr. Weber explained that he refocused his analysis on *performance.* He did so in response to our concerns, when we reversed the District Court's summary judgment finding, that voter registration might not be the best measure of the Democratic nature of a precinct. This fact was not lost on the District Court, which specifically referred to those pages of the record covering Dr. Weber's analysis of performance.

Third, the court credited Dr. Weber's testimony that the districting decisions could not be explained by political motives. In the first instance, I, like the Court, might well have concluded that District 12 was not significantly "safer" than several other districts in North Carolina merely because its Democratic reliability exceeded the optimum by only 3 percent. And I might have concluded that it would make political sense for incumbents to adopt a "the more reliable the better" policy in districting. However, I certainly cannot say that the court's inference from the facts was impermissible.

4. I do not think it necessary to impose a new burden on appellees to show that districting alternatives would have brought about "significantly greater racial balance." I cannot say that it was impermissible for the court to conclude that race predominated in this action even if only a slightly better district could be drawn absent racial considerations. The District Court may reasonably have found that racial motivations predominated in selecting one alternative over another even if the net effect on racial balance was not "significant."

Finally, the court found that other evidence demonstrated that race was foremost on the legislative agenda: an e-mail from the drafter of the 1992 and 1997 plans to senators in charge of legislative redistricting, the computer capability to draw the district by race, and statements made by Senator Cooper that the legislature was going to be able to avoid *Shaw*'s majority-minority trigger by ending just short of the majority.[8] The e-mail, in combination with the indirect evidence, is evidence ample enough to support the District Court's finding for purposes of clear error review. The drafter of the redistricting plans reported in the bluntest of terms: "I have moved Greensboro Black community into the 12th [District], and now need to take . . . 60,000 out of the 12th [District]." Certainly the District Court was entitled to believe that the drafter was targeting voters and shifting district boundaries purely on the basis of race. The Court tries to belittle the import of this evidence by noting that the e-mail does not discuss *why* blacks were being targeted. However, the District Court was assigned the task of determining *whether,* not *why,* race predominated. As I see it, this inquiry is sufficient to answer the constitutional question because racial gerrymandering offends the Constitution whether the motivation is malicious or benign. It is not a defense that the legislature merely may have drawn the district based on the stereotype that blacks are reliable Democratic voters.

If I were the District Court, I might have reached the same conclusion that the Court does, that "[t]he evidence taken together . . . does not show that racial considerations predominated in the drawing of District 12's boundaries." But I am not the trier of fact, and it is not my role to weigh evidence in the first instance. The only question that this Court should decide is whether the District Court's finding of racial predominance was clearly erroneous. In light of the direct evidence of racial motive and the inferences that may be drawn from the circumstantial evidence, I am satisfied that the District Court's finding was permissible, even if not compelled by the record.

NOTES ON *EASLEY* AND *THE FUTURE OF SHAW*

1. *Easley* is a difficult case because it seems to run contrary to the trend that the Court started and continued throughout the 1990s in the racial gerrymandering context. During that decade, when presented with a challenge on racial gerrymandering grounds to a plan drawn by a state legislature, the Court tended to find (or agree with a lower court finding) that a racial gerrymander had occurred.
2. *Easley*, however, held that a district court's finding of a racial gerrymander in relation to District 12 was "clearly erroneous." Who has the better of the

8. The court also relied on the statement of legislative redistricting leader Senator Cooper to the North Carolina Legislature, in which the senator mentioned the goals of geographical, political, and *racial* balance. In isolation, this statement does appear to support only the finding that race was *a* motive. Unlike this Court, however, the District Court had the advantage of listening to and watching Senator Cooper testify. I therefore am in no position to question the court's likely analysis that, although Senator Cooper mentioned all three motives, the predominance of race was apparent. This determination was made all the more reasonable by the fact that the District Court found the senator's claim regarding the "happenstance" final composition of the district to lack credibility in light of the e-mail.

argument in relation to whether the district court's finding was clearly erroneous: Justice Stephen Breyer for the majority or Justice Clarence Thomas for the dissenters?

3. How is *Easley* different from the racial gerrymandering decisions that came before it? In particular, how is *Easley* different from *Miller*?
4. Given *Easley*, a state presumably will now always defend against a *Shaw* claim by asserting that, as a factual matter, politics rather than race motivated its decision. If you were an attorney representing a plaintiff bringing a *Shaw*-type claim, what evidence would you need to present to survive a motion for summary judgment filed by the state and, ultimately, to prevail after trial? Would you need some sort of "smoking gun" in the form of an email in which the mapmaker admitted that race was the primary motivation for the district's lines? Would even this kind of "smoking gun" be enough? (Why did the email in *Easley* fail in this respect?) Without a "smoking gun" of this type, would it be possible to win a *Shaw*-type case based solely on expert testimony that race, rather than politics, must have been the mapmaker's primary motivation?
5. It is interesting to note that the Supreme Court has not considered any *Shaw*-type case involving redistricting after the 2000 or 2010 census. As we shall see, the Court has considered other types of claims concerning post–2000 redistricting, but not *Shaw*-type claims (although, as we shall also see, an interesting twist on a *Shaw*-type claim was presented—but not decided—in *LULAC v. Perry*.)

F. Partisan Gerrymanders

At this point, it should come as no surprise that legislative districts are drawn with the knowledge of how those districts will generally perform in future elections. For instance, in the context of the Voting Rights Act, it is possible to draw a district that will ensure that a certain group of voters will have the ability to control the outcome in a district. As one commentator once described it: "All Districting Is 'Gerrymandering.'" Robert D. Dixon, Jr., *Democratic Representation* 462 (1968).

One of the ways districts can be drawn is to elect members of a certain political party. In the United States, this generally boils down to Democrats drawing districts that advantage (i.e., disproportionately elect) Democrats and Republicans drawing districts that advantage Republicans. In addition, it can also lead to districts being drawn to protect incumbents from both political parties—what might be called an "incumbent gerrymander."

Once we recognize the phenomenon of what is known as "partisan gerrymandering," a few key questions arise. First, does partisan gerrymandering represent a problem? Second, if partisan gerrymandering is a problem, should the courts use the U.S. Constitution to do anything about it? Third, if the courts are not going to tackle the issue, is there another way to solve the problem of partisan gerrymandering? All three questions are important, though because this is a casebook about election law litigation, the main focus of our inquiry will be on the second question.

To set the stage for the cases you will be reading, it is helpful to understand the origin of claims of partisan gerrymandering—most notably the case of *Davis v. Bandemer*, 478 U.S. 109 (1986). In *Bandemer*, Democrats in Indiana challenged the state's 1981 legislative redistricting as an unconstitutional partisan gerrymander in violation of the Equal Protection Clause. The Court's response to that challenge involved two steps.

First, the Court needed to decide whether it would recognize an Equal Protection claim of unconstitutional partisan gerrymandering. In other words, the Court needed to decide whether a challenge to a redistricting plan as a partisan gerrymander represented a nonjusticiable political question. In *Bandemer*, six judges decided that no political question barrier existed to the Court's consideration of claims of partisan gerrymandering. Thus, starting in 1986, the courts were open for business in relation to the consideration of claims of partisan gerrymandering.

Second, the Court needed to decide the scope of the constitutional right to prevent unconstitutional gerrymandering. Put simply, the Court had to create a framework for deciding which redistricting plans were unconstitutional partisan gerrymanders and then needed to determine whether Indiana's plan was, indeed, such an unconstitutional gerrymander. At this stage, the *Bandemer* Court spoke with a fragmented voice. In the case you are about to read—*Vieth v. Jubelirer*—Justice Antonin Scalia describes the outlines of that split amongst the *Bandemer* Justices.

In addition to explaining the decision in *Bandemer*, the next case also describes the post-*Bandemer* story of litigation in this area and once again tackles the questions of justiciability, political questions, and manageable standards.

VIETH v. JUBELIRER

541 U.S. 267 (2004)

Justice SCALIA announced the judgment of the Court and delivered an opinion, in which CHIEF JUSTICE [Rehnquist], Justice O'CONNOR, and Justice THOMAS join.

Plaintiffs-appellants Richard Vieth, Norma Jean Vieth, and Susan Furey challenge a map drawn by the Pennsylvania General Assembly establishing districts for the election of congressional Representatives, on the ground that the districting constitutes an unconstitutional political gerrymander.[1] In *Davis v. Bandemer* (1986), this Court held that political gerrymandering claims are justiciable, but could not agree upon a standard to adjudicate

1. The term "political gerrymander" has been defined as "[t]he practice of dividing a geographical area into electoral districts, often of highly irregular shape, to give one political party an unfair advantage by diluting the opposition's voting strength." Black's Law Dictionary (7th ed. 1999).

them. The present appeal presents the questions whether our decision in *Bandemer* was in error, and, if not, what the standard should be.

I

The facts, as alleged by the plaintiffs, are as follows. The population figures derived from the 2000 census showed that Pennsylvania was entitled to only 19 Representatives in Congress, a decrease in 2 from the Commonwealth's previous delegation. Pennsylvania's General Assembly took up the task of drawing a new districting map. At the time, the Republican Party controlled a majority of both state Houses and held the Governor's office. Prominent national figures in the Republican Party pressured the General Assembly to adopt a partisan redistricting plan as a punitive measure against Democrats for having enacted pro-Democrat redistricting plans elsewhere. The Republican members of Pennsylvania's House and Senate worked together on such a plan. On [April 18, 2002] the General Assembly passed its plan, which was signed into law by Governor Schweiker as Act [1].

Plaintiffs, registered Democrats who vote in Pennsylvania, brought suit in the United States District Court for the Middle District of Pennsylvania, seeking to enjoin implementation of Act 1. The complaint alleged that the legislation constituted a political gerrymander, in violation of Article I and the Equal Protection Clause of the Fourteenth Amendment. With regard to [this] contention, the complaint alleged that the districts created by Act 1 were "meandering and irregular," and "ignor[ed] all traditional redistricting criteria, including the preservation of local government boundaries, solely for the sake of partisan advantage."

The District Court reject[ed] the political gerrymandering claim. The plaintiffs appealed the dismissal of their political gerrymandering claim. We noted probable jurisdiction.

II

Political gerrymanders are not new to the American scene. One scholar traces them back to the Colony of Pennsylvania at the beginning of the 18th century, where several counties conspired to minimize the political power of the city of Philadelphia by refusing to allow it to merge or expand into surrounding jurisdictions, and denying it additional representatives. The political gerrymander remained alive and well (though not yet known by that name) at the time of the framing. There were allegations that Patrick Henry attempted (unsuccessfully) to gerrymander James Madison out of the First Congress. And in 1812, of course, there occurred the notoriously outrageous political districting in Massachusetts that gave the gerrymander its name.

It is significant that the Framers provided a remedy for such practices in the Constitution. Article I, § 4, while leaving in state legislatures the initial power to draw districts for federal elections, permitted Congress to "make or alter" those districts if it wished.

Many objected to the congressional oversight established by this provision. In the course of the debates in the Constitutional Convention, Charles Pinkney and John Rutledge moved to strike the relevant language. James Madison responded in defense of the provision that Congress must be given the power to check partisan manipulation of the election process by the States:

> "Whenever the State Legislatures had a favorite measure to carry, they would take care so to mould their regulations as to favor the candidates they wished to succeed. Besides, the inequality of the Representation in the Legislatures of particular States, would produce a like inequality in their representation in the Natl. Legislature, as it was presumable that the Counties having the power in the former case would secure it to themselves in the latter. What danger could there be in giving a controlling power to the Natl. Legislature?"

The power bestowed on Congress to regulate elections, and in particular to restrain the practice of political gerrymandering, has not lain dormant. In the Apportionment Act of 1842, Congress provided that Representatives must be elected from single-member districts "composed of contiguous territory." Congress again imposed these requirements in the Apportionment Act of 1862, and in 1872 further required that districts "contai[n] as nearly as practicable an equal number of inhabitants." In the Apportionment Act of 1901, Congress imposed a compactness requirement. The requirements of contiguity, compactness, and equality of population were repeated in the 1911 apportionment legislation, but were not thereafter continued. Today, only the single-member-district-requirement remains. *See* 2 U.S.C. § 2c. Recent history, however, attests to Congress's awareness of the sort of districting practices appellants protest, and of its power under Article I, § 4 to control them. Since 1980, no fewer than five bills have been introduced to regulate gerrymandering in congressional districting.

Eighteen years ago, we held that the Equal Protection Clause grants judges the power—and duty—to control political gerrymandering, see *Davis v. Bandemer*. It is to consideration of this precedent that we now turn.

III

As Chief Justice Marshall proclaimed two centuries ago, "[i]t is emphatically the province and duty of the judicial department to say what the law is." *Marbury v. Madison*. Sometimes, however, the law is that the judicial department has no business entertaining the claim of unlawfulness—because the question is entrusted to one of the political branches or involves no judicially enforceable rights. Such questions are said to be "non-justiciable," or "political questions."

In *Baker v. Carr*, we set forth six independent tests for the existence of a political question:

> "[1] a textually demonstrable constitutional commitment of the issue to a coordinate political department; or [2] a lack of judicially discoverable and manageable standards for resolving it; or [3] the impossibility of deciding without an initial policy determination of a kind clearly for nonjudicial discretion; or [4] the impossibility of a court's undertaking independent resolution without expressing lack of the respect due coordinate branches of government; or [5] an unusual need for unquestioning adherence to a political decision already made; or [6] the potentiality of embarrassment from multifarious pronouncements by various departments on one question."

These tests are probably listed in descending order of both importance and certainty. The second is at issue here, and there is no doubt of its validity. "The judicial Power" created by Article III, § 1, of the Constitution is not *whatever* judges choose to do. It is the power to act in the manner traditional for English and American courts. One of the most obvious limitations imposed by that requirement is that judicial action must be governed by *standard*, by *rule.* Laws promulgated by the Legislative Branch can be inconsistent, illogical, and ad hoc; law pronounced by the courts must be principled, rational, and based upon reasoned distinctions.

Over the dissent of three Justices, the Court held in *Davis v. Bandemer* that, since it was "not persuaded that there are no judicially discernible and manageable standards by which political gerrymander cases are to be decided," such cases *were* justiciable. The clumsy shifting of the burden of proof for the premise (the Court was "not persuaded" that standards do not exist, rather than "persuaded" that they do) was necessitated by the uncomfortable fact that the six-Justice majority could not discern what the judicially discernable standards might be. There was no majority on that point. Four of the Justices finding justiciability believed that the standard was one thing, two believed it was something else. The lower courts have lived with that assurance of a standard (or more precisely, lack of assurance that there is no standard), coupled with that inability to specify a standard, for the past 18 years. In that time, they have considered numerous political gerrymandering claims; this Court has never revisited the unanswered question of what standard governs.

Nor can it be said that the lower courts have, over 18 years, succeeded in shaping the standard that this Court was initially unable to enunciate. They have simply applied the standard set forth in *Bandemer's* four-Justice plurality opinion. This might be thought to prove that the four-Justice plurality standard has met the test of time—but for the fact that its application has almost invariably produced the same result as would have obtained if the question were nonjusticiable: Judicial intervention has been refused. To think that this lower-court jurisprudence has brought forth "judicially discernible and manageable standards" would be fantasy.

Eighteen years of judicial effort with virtually nothing to show for it justify us in revisiting the question whether the standard promised by *Bandemer* exists. As the following discussion reveals, no judicially discernible and manageable standards for adjudicating political gerrymandering claims have emerged. Lacking them, we must conclude that political gerrymandering claims are nonjusticiable and that *Bandemer* was wrongly decided.

A

We begin our review of possible standards with that proposed by Justice White's plurality opinion in *Bandemer* because, as the narrowest ground for our decision in that case, it has been the standard employed by the lower courts. The plurality concluded that a political gerrymandering claim could succeed only where plaintiffs showed "both intentional discrimination against an identifiable political group and an actual discriminatory effect on that group." As to the intent element, the plurality acknowledged that "[a]s long as redistricting is done by a legislature, it should not be very difficult to prove that the likely political consequences of the reapportionment were intended." However, the effects prong was significantly harder to satisfy. Relief could not be based merely upon the fact that a group of persons banded together for political purposes had failed to achieve representation commensurate with its numbers, or that the apportionment scheme made its winning of elections more difficult. Rather, it would have to be shown that, taking into account a variety of historic factors and projected election results, the group had been "denied its chance to effectively influence the political process" as a whole, which could be achieved even without electing a candidate. It would not be enough to establish, for example, that Democrats had been "placed in a district with a supermajority of other Democratic voters" or that the district "departs from pre-existing political boundaries." Rather, in a challenge to an individual district the inquiry would focus "on the opportunity of members of the group to participate in party deliberations in the slating and nomination of candidates, their opportunity to register and vote, and hence their chance to directly influence the election returns and to secure the attention of the winning candidate." A statewide challenge, by contrast, would involve an analysis of "the voters' direct *or indirect* influence on the elections of the state legislature as a whole." With what has proved to be a gross understatement, the plurality acknowledged this was "of necessity a difficult inquiry."

In her *Bandemer* concurrence, Justice O'Connor predicted that the plurality's standard "will over time either prove unmanageable and arbitrary or else evolve towards some loose form of proportionality." A similar prediction of unmanageability was expressed in Justice Powell's opinion, making it the prognostication of a majority of the Court. That prognostication has been amply fulfilled.

In the lower courts, the legacy of the plurality's test is one long record of puzzlement and consternation. The test has been criticized for its indeterminacy by a host of academic commentators. Because this standard was misguided when proposed, has not been improved in subsequent application, and is not even defended before us today by the appellants, we decline to affirm it as a constitutional requirement.

B

Appellants take a run at enunciating their own workable standard based on Article I, § 2, and the Equal Protection Clause. We consider it at length not only because it reflects the litigant's view as to the best that can be derived from 18 years of experience, but also because it shares many features with other proposed standards, so that what is said of it may be said of them as well. Appellants' proposed standard retains the two-pronged framework of the *Bandemer* plurality—intent plus effect—but modifies the type of showing sufficient to satisfy each.

To satisfy appellants' intent standard, a plaintiff must "show that the mapmakers acted with a *predominant intent* to achieve partisan advantage," which can be shown "by direct evidence or by circumstantial evidence that other neutral and legitimate redistricting criteria were subordinated to the goal of achieving partisan advantage." As compared with the *Bandemer* plurality's test of mere intent to disadvantage the plaintiff's group, this proposal seemingly makes the standard more difficult to meet—but only at the expense of making the standard more indeterminate.

"Predominant intent" to disadvantage the plaintiff's political group refers to the relative importance of that goal as compared with all the other goals that the map seeks to pursue—contiguity of districts, compactness of districts, observance of the lines of political subdivision, protection of incumbents of all parties, cohesion of natural racial and ethnic neighborhoods, compliance with requirements of the Voting Rights Act regarding racial distribution, etc. Appellants contend that their intent test *must* be discernible and manageable because it has been borrowed from our racial gerrymandering cases. *See Miller v. Johnson*; *Shaw v. Reno*. To begin with, in a very important respect that is not so. In the racial gerrymandering context, the predominant intent test has been applied to the challenged district in which the plaintiffs voted. *See Miller*. Here, however, appellants do not assert that an apportionment fails their intent test if any single district does so. Since "it would be quixotic to attempt to bar state legislatures from considering politics as they redraw district lines," Brief for Appellants 3, appellants propose a test that is satisfied only when "partisan advantage was the predominant motivation *behind the entire statewide plan*." Vague as the "predominant motivation" test might be when used to evaluate single districts, it all but evaporates when applied statewide. Does it mean, for instance, that partisan intent must outweigh all other goals—contiguity, compactness, preservation of neighborhoods, etc.—*statewide*? And how is the statewide "outweighing" to be determined? If three-fifths of the map's districts forgo the pursuit of partisan ends in favor of strictly observing political-subdivision lines, and only two-fifths ignore those lines to disadvantage the plaintiffs, is the observance of political subdivisions the "predominant" goal between those two? We are sure appellants do not think so.

Even within the narrower compass of challenges to a single district, applying a "predominant intent" test to *racial* gerrymandering is easier and less disruptive. The Constitution clearly contemplates districting by political entities, see Article I, § 4, and unsurprisingly that turns out to be root-and-branch a matter of politics. By contrast, the purpose of segregating voters on the basis of race is not a lawful one, and is much more rarely encountered. Determining whether the shape of a particular district is so substantially affected by the presence of a rare and constitutionally suspect motive as to invalidate it is quite different from determining whether it is so substantially affected by the excess of an ordinary and lawful motive as to invalidate it. Moreover, the fact that partisan districting is a lawful and common practice means that there is almost *always* room for an election-impeding lawsuit contending that partisan advantage was the predominant motivation; not so for claims of racial gerrymandering. Finally, courts might be justified in accepting a modest degree of unmanageability to enforce a constitutional command which (like the Fourteenth Amendment obligation to refrain from racial discrimination) is clear; whereas they are not justified in inferring a judicially enforceable constitutional obligation (the obligation not to apply *too much* partisanship in districting) which is both dubious and severely unmanageable. For these reasons, to the extent that our racial gerrymandering cases represent a model of discernible and manageable standards, they provide no comfort here.

The effects prong of appellants' proposal replaces the *Bandemer* plurality's vague test of "denied its chance to effectively influence the political process," with criteria that are seemingly more specific. The requisite effect is established when "(1) the plaintiffs show that the districts systematically 'pack' and 'crack' the rival party's voters,[7] *and* (2) the court's examination of the 'totality of circumstances' confirms that the map can thwart the plaintiffs' ability to translate a majority of votes into a majority of seats." This test is loosely based on our cases applying § 2 of the Voting Rights Act to discrimination by race. But a person's politics is rarely as readily discernible—and *never* as permanently discernible—as a person's race. Political affiliation is not an immutable characteristic, but may shift from one election to the next; and even within a given election, not all voters follow the party line. We dare say (and hope) that the political party which puts forward an utterly incompetent candidate will lose even in its registration stronghold. These facts make it impossible to assess the effects of partisan gerrymandering, to fashion a standard for evaluating a violation, and finally to craft a remedy.

Assuming, however, that the effects of partisan gerrymandering can be determined, appellants' test would invalidate the districting only when it prevents a majority of the electorate from electing a majority of representatives. Before considering whether this particular standard is judicially manageable we question whether it is judicially discernible in the sense of being relevant to some constitutional violation. Deny it as appellants may (and do), this standard rests upon the principle that groups (or at least political-action groups) have a right to proportional representation. But the Constitution contains no such principle. It guarantees equal protection of the law to persons, not equal representation in government to equivalently sized groups. It nowhere says that farmers or urban dwellers,

7. "Packing" refers to the practice of filling a district with a supermajority of a given group or party. "Cracking" involves the splitting of a group or party among several districts to deny that group or party a majority in any of those districts.

Christian fundamentalists or Jews, Republicans or Democrats, must be accorded political strength proportionate to their numbers.[9]

Even if the standard were relevant, however, it is not judicially manageable. To begin with, how is a party's majority status to be established? Appellants propose using the results of statewide races as the benchmark of party support. But as their own complaint describes, in the 2000 Pennsylvania statewide elections some Republicans won and some Democrats won. *See* Juris. Statement 137a-138a (describing how Democratic candidates received more votes for President and auditor general, and Republicans received more votes for United States Senator, attorney general, and treasurer). Moreover, to think that majority status in statewide races establishes majority status for district contests, one would have to believe that the only factor determining voting behavior at all levels is political affiliation. That is assuredly not true.

But if we could identify a majority party, we would find it impossible to ensure that that party wins a majority of seats—unless we radically revise the States' traditional structure for elections. In any winner-take-all district system, there can be no guarantee, no matter how the district lines are drawn, that a majority of party votes statewide will produce a majority of seats for that party. The point is proved by the 2000 congressional elections in Pennsylvania, which, according to appellants' own pleadings, were conducted under a judicially drawn district map "free from partisan gerrymandering." On this "neutral playing fiel[d]," the Democrats' statewide majority of the major-party vote (50.6%) translated into a minority of seats (10, versus 11 for the Republicans). Whether by reason of partisan districting or not, party constituents may always wind up "packed" in some districts and "cracked" throughout others. Consider, for example, a legislature that draws district lines with no objectives in mind except compactness and respect for the lines of political subdivisions. Under that system, political groups that tend to cluster (as is the case with Democratic voters in cities) would be systematically affected by what might be called a "natural" packing effect.

Our one-person, one-vote cases have no bearing upon this question, neither in principle nor in practicality. Not in principle, because to say that each individual must have an equal say in the selection of representatives, and hence that a majority of individuals must have a majority say, is not at all to say that each discernible group, whether farmers or urban dwellers or political parties, must have representation equivalent to its numbers. And not in practicality, because the easily administrable standard of population equality adopted by *Reynolds* enables judges to decide whether a violation has occurred (and to remedy it) essentially on the basis of three readily determined factors—where the

9. The Constitution also does not share appellants' alarm at the asserted tendency of partisan gerrymandering to create more partisan representatives. Assuming that assertion to be true, the Constitution does not answer the question whether it is better for Democratic voters to have their State's congressional delegation include 10 wishy-washy Democrats (because Democratic voters are "effectively" distributed so as to constitute bare majorities in many districts), or 5 hardcore Democrats (because Democratic voters are tightly packed in a few districts). Choosing the former "dilutes" the vote of the radical Democrat; choosing the latter does the same to the moderate. Neither Article I, § 2, nor the Equal Protection Clause takes sides in this dispute.

plaintiff lives, how many voters are in his district, and how many voters are in other districts; whereas requiring judges to decide whether a districting system will produce a statewide majority for a majority party casts them forth upon a sea of imponderables, and asks them to make determinations that not even election experts can agree upon.

For these reasons, we find appellants' proposed standards neither discernible nor manageable.

C

For many of the same reasons, we also reject the standard suggested by Justice Powell in *Bandemer.* He agreed with the plurality that a plaintiff should show intent and effect, but believed that the ultimate inquiry ought to focus on whether district boundaries had been drawn solely for partisan ends to the exclusion of "all other neutral factors relevant to the fairness of redistricting." Under that inquiry, the courts should consider numerous factors, though "[n]o one factor should be dispositive." The most important would be "the shapes of voting districts and adherence to established political subdivision boundaries." "Other relevant considerations include the nature of the legislative procedures by which the apportionment law was adopted and legislative history reflecting contemporaneous legislative goals." These factors, which "bear directly on the fairness of a redistricting plan," combined with "evidence concerning population disparities and statistics tending to show vote dilution," make out a claim of unconstitutional partisan gerrymandering.

While Justice Powell rightly criticized the *Bandemer* plurality for failing to suggest a constitutionally based, judicially manageable standard, the standard proposed in his opinion also falls short of the mark. It is essentially a totality-of-the-circumstances analysis, where all conceivable factors, none of which is dispositive, are weighed with an eye to ascertaining whether the particular gerrymander has gone too far—or, in Justice Powell's terminology, whether it is not "fair." "Fairness" does not seem to us a judicially manageable standard. Fairness is compatible with noncontiguous districts, it is compatible with districts that straddle political subdivisions, and it is compatible with a party's not winning the number of seats that mirrors the proportion of its vote. Some criterion more solid and more demonstrably met than that seems to us necessary to enable the state legislatures to discern the limits of their districting discretion, to meaningfully constrain the discretion of the courts, and to win public acceptance for the courts' intrusion into a process that is the very foundation of democratic decision-making.

IV

[Omitted]

V

Justice Kennedy recognizes that we have "demonstrat[ed] the shortcomings of the other standards that have been considered to date." He acknowledges, moreover, that we "lack . . . comprehensive and neutral principles for drawing electoral boundaries," and that there is an "absence of rules to limit and confine judicial intervention." From these premises, one might think that Justice Kennedy would reach the conclusion that political gerrymandering claims are nonjusticiable. Instead, however, he concludes that courts should continue to adjudicate such claims because a standard *may* one day be discovered.

The first thing to be said about Justice Kennedy's disposition is that it is not legally available. The District Court in this case considered the plaintiffs' claims *justiciable* but dismissed them because the standard for unconstitutionality had not been met. It is logically impossible to affirm that dismissal without either (1) finding that the unconstitutional-districting standard applied by the District Court, or some other standard that it *should* have applied, has not been met, or (2) finding (as we have) that the claim is nonjusticiable. Justice Kennedy seeks to affirm '[b]ecause, in the case before us, we have no standard." But it is *our* job, not the plaintiffs', to explicate the standard that makes the facts alleged by the plaintiffs adequate or inadequate to state a claim. We cannot nonsuit *them* for our failure to do so.

Justice Kennedy asserts that to declare nonjusticiability would be incautious. Our rush to such a holding after a mere 18 years of fruitless litigation "contrasts starkly" he says, "with the more patient approach" that this Court has taken in the past. We think not. When it has come to determining what areas fall beyond our Article III authority to adjudicate, this Court's practice, from the earliest days of the Republic to the present, has been more reminiscent of Hannibal than of Hamlet.

The only cases Justice Kennedy cites in defense of his never-say-never approach are *Baker v. Carr* and *Bandemer. Bandemer* provides no cover. There, all of the Justices who concluded that political gerrymandering claims are justiciable proceeded to describe what they regarded as the discernible and manageable standard that rendered it so. The lower courts were set wandering in the wilderness for 18 years not because the *Bandemer* majority thought it a good idea, but because five Justices could not agree upon a single standard, and because the standard the plurality proposed turned out not to work.

As for *Baker v. Carr*: It is true enough that, having had no experience *whatever* in apportionment matters of any sort, the Court there refrained from spelling out the equal-protection standard. (It did so a mere two years later in *Reynolds v. Sims.*) But the judgment under review in *Baker*, unlike the one under review here, did not *demand* the determination of a standard. The lower court in *Baker* had held the apportionment claim of the plaintiffs *nonjusticiable*, and so it was logically possible to dispose of the appeal by simply disagreeing with the nonjusticiability determination. As we observed earlier, that is not possible here, where the lower court has held the claim *justiciable* but unsupported by the facts. We must either enunciate the standard that causes us to agree or disagree with that merits judgment, or else affirm that the claim is beyond our competence to adjudicate.

Justice Kennedy worries that "[a] determination by the Court to deny all hopes of intervention could erode confidence in the courts as much as would a premature decision to intervene." But it is the function of the courts to provide relief, not hope. What we think would erode confidence is the Court's refusal to do its job—announcing that there may well be a valid claim here, but we are not yet prepared to figure it out. Moreover, that course does more than erode confidence; by placing the district courts back in the business of pretending to afford help when they in fact can give none, it deters the political process from affording genuine relief.

Reduced to its essence, Justice Kennedy's opinion boils down to this: "As presently advised, I know of no discernible and manageable standard that can render this claim justiciable. I am unhappy about that, and hope that I will be able to change my opinion in the future." What are the lower courts to make of this pronouncement? We suggest that they must treat it as a reluctant fifth vote against justiciability at district and statewide levels—a vote that may change in some future case but that holds, for the time being, that this matter is nonjusticiable.

VI

We conclude that neither Article I, § 2, nor the Equal Protection Clause, nor (what appellants only fleetingly invoke) Article I, § 4, provides a judicially enforceable limit on the political considerations that the States and Congress may take into account when districting.

Considerations of *stare decisis* do not compel us to allow *Bandemer* to stand. That case involved an interpretation of the Constitution, and the claims of *stare decisis* are at their weakest in that field, where our mistakes cannot be corrected by Congress. They are doubly weak in *Bandemer* because the majority's inability to enunciate the judicially discernible and manageable standard that it thought existed (or did not think did not exist) presaged the need for reconsideration in light of subsequent experience. And they are triply weak because it is hard to imagine how any action taken in reliance upon *Bandemer* could conceivably be frustrated—except the bringing of lawsuits, which is not the sort of primary conduct that is relevant.

While we do not lightly overturn one of our own holdings, when governing decisions are unworkable or are badly reasoned, this Court has never felt constrained to follow precedent. Eighteen years of essentially pointless litigation have persuaded us that *Bandemer* is incapable of principled application. We would therefore overrule that case, and decline to adjudicate these political gerrymandering claims.

The judgment of the District Court is affirmed.

It is so ordered.

Justice KENNEDY, concurring in the judgment.

A decision ordering the correction of all election district lines drawn for partisan reasons would commit federal and state courts to unprecedented intervention in the American political process. The Court is correct to refrain from directing this substantial intrusion into the Nation's political life. While agreeing with the plurality that the complaint the appellants filed in the District Court must be dismissed, and while understanding that great caution is necessary when approaching this subject, I would not foreclose all possibility of judicial relief if some limited and precise rationale were found to correct an established violation of the Constitution in some redistricting cases.

When presented with a claim of injury from partisan gerrymandering, courts confront two obstacles. First is the lack of comprehensive and neutral principles for drawing electoral boundaries. No substantive definition of fairness in districting seems to command general assent. Second is the absence of rules to limit and confine Judicial intervention. With uncertain limits, intervening courts—even when proceeding with best intentions—would risk assuming political, not legal, responsibility for a process that often produces ill will and distrust.

There are, then, weighty arguments for holding cases like these to be nonjusticiable; and those arguments may prevail in the long run. In my view, however, the arguments are not so compelling that they require us now to bar all future claims of injury from a partisan gerrymander. It is not in our tradition to foreclose the judicial process from the attempt to define standards and remedies where it is alleged that a constitutional right is burdened or denied. Nor is it alien to the Judiciary to draw or approve election district lines. Courts, after all, already do so in many instances. A determination by the Court to deny all hopes of intervention could erode confidence in the courts as much as would a premature decision to intervene.

That no such [judicially manageable] standard has emerged in this case should not be taken to prove that none will emerge in the future. Where important rights are involved, the impossibility of full analytical satisfaction is reason to err on the side of caution. Allegations of unconstitutional bias in apportionment are most serious claims, for we have long believed that "the right to vote" is one of "those political processes ordinarily to be relied upon to protect minorities." *United States v. Carolene Products Co.*, n. 4. If a State passed an enactment that declared "All future apportionment shall be drawn so as most to burden Party X's rights to fair and effective representation, though still in accord with one-person, one-vote principles," we would surely conclude the Constitution had been violated. If that is so, we should admit the possibility remains that a legislature might attempt to reach the same result without that express directive. This possibility suggests that in another case a standard might emerge that suitably demonstrates how an apportionment's *de facto* incorporation of partisan classifications burdens rights of fair and effective representation (and so establishes the classification is unrelated to the aims of apportionment and thus is used in an impermissible fashion).

The plurality says that 18 years, in effect, prove the negative. [H]owever, during these past 18 years the lower courts could do no more than follow *Davis v. Bandemer,* which formulated a single, apparently insuperable standard. Moreover, by the timeline of the law 18 years is rather a short period. In addition, the rapid evolution of technologies in the apportionment field suggests yet unexplored possibilities. Computer assisted districting has become so routine and sophisticated that legislatures, experts, and courts can use databases to map electoral districts in a matter of hours, not months. Technology is both a threat and a promise. On the one hand, if courts refuse to entertain any claims of partisan gerrymandering, the temptation to use partisan favoritism in districting in an unconstitutional manner will grow. On the other hand, these new technologies may produce new methods of analysis that make more evident the precise nature of the burdens gerrymanders impose on the representational rights of voters and parties. That would facilitate court efforts to identify and remedy the burdens, with judicial intervention limited by the derived standards.

If suitable standards with which to measure the burden a gerrymander imposes on representational rights did emerge, hindsight would show that the Court prematurely abandoned the field. That is a risk the Court should not take. Instead, we should adjudicate only what is in the papers before us.

Because, in the case before us, we have no standard by which to measure the burden appellants claim has been imposed on their representational rights, appellants cannot establish that the alleged political classifications burden those same rights. Failing to show that the alleged classifications are unrelated to the aims of apportionment, appellants' evidence at best demonstrates only that the legislature adopted political classifications. That describes no constitutional flaw, at least under the governing Fourteenth Amendment standard. As a consequence, appellants' complaint alleges no impermissible use of political classifications and so states no valid claim on which relief may be granted. It must be dismissed as a result.

The plurality thinks I resolve this case with reference to no standard, but that is wrong. The Fourteenth Amendment standard governs; and there is no doubt of that. My analysis only notes that if a subsidiary standard could show how an otherwise permissible classification, as applied, burdens representational rights, we could conclude that appellants' evidence states a provable claim under the Fourteenth Amendment standard.

Though in the briefs and at argument the appellants relied on the Equal Protection Clause as the source of their substantive right and as the basis for relief, I note that the complaint in this case also alleged a violation of First Amendment rights. The First Amendment may be the more relevant constitutional provision in future cases that allege unconstitutional partisan gerrymandering. After all, these allegations involve the First Amendment interest of not burdening or penalizing citizens because of their participation in the electoral process, their voting history, their association with a political party, or their expression of political views. Under general First Amendment principles those burdens in other contexts are unconstitutional absent a compelling government interest. "Representative democracy in any populous unit of governance is unimaginable without the ability of citizens to band together in promoting among the electorate candidates who espouse their political views." *California Democratic Party v. Jones* (2000). As these precedents show, First Amendment concerns arise where a State enacts a law that has the purpose and effect of subjecting a group of voters or their party to disfavored treatment by reason of their views. In the context of partisan gerrymandering, that means that First Amendment concerns arise where an apportionment has the purpose and effect of burdening a group of voters' representational rights.

Where it is alleged that a gerrymander had the purpose and effect of imposing burdens on a disfavored party and its voters, the First Amendment may offer a sounder and more prudential basis for intervention than does the Equal Protection Clause. The equal protection analysis puts its emphasis on the permissibility of an enactment's classifications. This works where race is involved since classifying by race is almost never permissible. It presents a more complicated question when the inquiry is whether a generally permissible classification has been used for an impermissible purpose. That question can only be answered in the affirmative by the subsidiary showing that the classification as applied imposes unlawful burdens. The First Amendment analysis concentrates on whether the legislation burdens the representational rights of the complaining party's voters for reasons of ideology, beliefs, or political association. The analysis allows a pragmatic or functional assessment that accords some latitude to the States.

Finally, I do not understand the plurality to conclude that partisan gerrymandering that disfavors one party is permissible. Indeed, the plurality seems to acknowledge it is not. This is all the more reason to admit the possibility of later suits, while holding just that the parties have failed to prove, under our "well developed and familiar" standard, that these legislative classifications "reflec[t] *no* policy, but simply arbitrary and capricious action." *Baker*. That said, courts must be cautious about adopting a standard that turns on whether the partisan interests in the redistricting process were excessive. Excessiveness is not easily determined. Consider these apportionment schemes: In one State, Party X controls the apportionment process and draws the lines so it captures every congressional seat. In three other States, Party Y controls the apportionment process. It is not so blatant or egregious, but proceeds by a more subtle effort, capturing less than all the seats in each State. Still, the total effect of Party Y's effort is to capture more new seats than Party X captured. Party X's gerrymander was more egregious. Party Y's gerrymander was more subtle. In my view, however, each is culpable.

* * *

The ordered working of our Republic, and of the democratic process, depends on a sense of decorum and restraint in all branches of government, and in the citizenry itself. Here, one has the sense that legislative restraint was abandoned. That should not be thought to serve the interests of our political order. Nor should it be thought to serve our interest in demonstrating to the world how democracy works. Whether spoken with concern or pride, it is unfortunate that our legislators have reached the point of declaring that, when it comes to apportionment: " 'We are in the business of rigging elections'" (quoting a North Carolina state senator).

Still, the Court's own responsibilities require that we refrain from intervention in this instance. The failings of the many proposed standards for measuring the burden a gerrymander imposes on representational rights make our intervention improper. If workable standards do emerge to measure these burdens, however, courts should be prepared to order relief. With these observations, I join the judgment of the Court.

Justice STEVENS, dissenting.

The central question presented by this case is whether political gerrymandering claims are justiciable. Although our reasons for coming to this conclusion differ, five Members of the Court are convinced that the plurality's answer to that question is erroneous. Moreover, as is apparent from our separate writings today, we share the view that, even if these appellants are not entitled to prevail, it would be contrary to precedent and profoundly unwise to foreclose all judicial review of similar claims that might be advanced in the future. That we presently have somewhat differing views—concerning both the precedential value of some of our recent cases and the standard that should be applied in future cases—should not obscure the fact that the areas of agreement set forth in the separate opinions are of far greater significance.

The concept of equal justice under law requires the State to govern impartially. Today's plurality opinion would exempt governing officials from that duty in the context of legislative redistricting and would give license, for the first time, to partisan gerrymanders that are devoid of any rational justification. In my view, when partisanship is the legislature's sole motivation—when any pretense of neutrality is forsaken unabashedly and all traditional districting criteria are subverted for partisan advantage—the governing body cannot be said to have acted impartially.

Although we reaffirm the central holding of the Court in *Davis v. Bandemer*, we have not reached agreement on the standard that should govern partisan gerrymandering claims. I would decide this case on a narrow ground. Plaintiffs-appellants urge us to craft new rules that in effect would authorize judicial review of statewide election results to protect the democratic process from a transient majority's abuse of its power to define voting districts. I agree with the plurality's refusal to undertake that ambitious project. I am persuaded, however, that the District Court failed to apply well-settled propositions of law when it granted the defendants' motion to dismiss plaintiff-appellant Susan Furey's gerrymandering claim.

According to the complaint, Furey is a registered Democrat who resides at an address in Montgomery County, Pennsylvania, that was located under the 1992 districting plan in Congressional District 13. Under the new plan adopted by the General Assembly in 2002,

Furey's address now places her in the "non-compact" District 6. Furey alleges that the new districting plan was created "solely" to effectuate the interests of Republicans, and that the General Assembly relied "exclusively" on a principle of "maximum partisan advantage" when drawing the plan. In my judgment, Furey's allegations are plainly sufficient to establish: (1) that she has standing to challenge the constitutionality of District 6; (2) that her district-specific claim is not foreclosed by the *Bandemer* plurality's rejection of a statewide claim of political gerrymandering; and (3) that she has stated a claim that, at least with respect to District 6, Pennsylvania's redistricting plan violates the equal protection principles enunciated in our voting rights cases both before and after *Bandemer.* The District Court therefore erred when it granted the defendants' motion to dismiss Furey's claim.

I

Prior to our seminal decision in *Baker v. Carr*, a majority of this Court had heeded Justice Frankfurter's repeated warnings about the dire consequences of entering the "political thicket" of legislative districting. *Colegrove v. Green.* As a result, even the most egregious gerrymanders were sheltered from judicial review. It was after *Baker* that we explained that "legislatures . . . should be bodies which are collectively responsive to the popular will," *Reynolds v. Sims*, and we accordingly described "the basic aim of legislative apportionment" as "achieving . . . fair and effective representation for all citizens." Consistent with that goal, we also reviewed claims that the majority had discriminated against particular groups of voters by drawing multimember districts that threatened "to minimize or cancel out the voting strength of racial or political elements of the voting population." *Fortson v. Dorsey* (1965). Such districts were "vulnerable" to constitutional challenge "if racial or political groups ha[d] been fenced out of the political process and their voting strength invidiously minimized." *Gaffney v. Cummings.*

Our holding in *Bandemer,* that partisan gerrymandering claims are justiciable followed ineluctably from the central reasoning in *Baker.* What was true in *Baker* is no less true in this context:

> "The question here is the consistency of state action with the Federal Constitution. We have no question decided, or to be decided, by a political branch of government coequal with this Court. Nor do we risk embarrassment of our government abroad, or grave disturbance at home if we take issue with [Pennsylvania] as to the constitutionality of her action here challenged. Nor need the appellants, in order to succeed in this action, ask the Court to enter upon policy determinations for which judicially manageable standards are lacking. Judicial standards under the Equal Protection Clause are well developed and familiar, and it has been open to courts since the enactment of the Fourteenth Amendment to determine, if on the particular facts they must, that a discrimination reflects *no* policy, but simply arbitrary and capricious action." *Baker.*

At issue in this case, as the plurality states, is *Baker's* second test—the presence or absence of judicially manageable standards. The judicial standards applicable to gerrymandering claims are deeply rooted in decisions that long preceded *Bandemer* and have been refined in later cases. Among those well-settled principles is the understanding that a district's peculiar shape might be a symptom of an illicit purpose in the line-drawing process.

With purpose as the ultimate inquiry, other considerations have supplied ready standards for testing the lawfulness of a gerrymander. In his dissent in *Bandemer*, Justice Powell explained that "the merits of a gerrymandering claim must be determined by reference to the configurations of the districts, the observance of political subdivision lines, and other criteria that have independent relevance to the fairness of redistricting." Applying this three-part standard, Justice Powell first reviewed the procedures used in Indiana's redistricting process and noted that the party in power had excluded the opposition from its deliberations and had placed excessive weight on data concerning party voting trends. Second, Justice Powell pointed to the strange shape of districts that conspicuously ignored traditional districting principles. Third and finally, Justice Powell reviewed other "substantial evidence," including contemporaneous statements and press accounts, demonstrating that the architects of the districts "were motivated solely by partisan considerations."

The Court has made use of all three parts of Justice Powell's standard in its recent racial gerrymandering jurisprudence. In those cases, the Court has examined claims that redistricting schemes violate the equal protection guarantee where they are "so highly irregular" on their face that they "rationally cannot be understood as anything other than an effort" to segregate voters by race, *Shaw v. Reno (Shaw I),* or where "race for its own sake, and not other districting principles, was the legislature's dominant and controlling rationale in drawing its district lines," *Miller v. Johnson*. The *Shaw* line of cases has emphasized that "reapportionment is one area in which appearances do matter," and has focused both on the shape of the challenged districts and the purpose behind the line-drawing in assessing the constitutionality of majority-minority districts under the Equal Protection Clause. These decisions, like Justice Powell's opinion in *Bandemer*, have also considered the process by which the districting schemes were enacted, looked to other evidence demonstrating that purely improper considerations motivated the decision, and included maps illustrating outlandish district shapes.

Given this clear line of precedents, I should have thought the question of justiciability in cases such as this—where a set of plaintiffs argues that a single motivation resulted in a districting scheme with discriminatory effects—to be well settled. The plurality's contrary conclusion cannot be squared with our long history of voting rights decisions. Especially perplexing is the plurality's *ipse dixit* distinction of our racial gerrymandering cases. Notably, the plurality does not argue that the judicially manageable standards that have been used to adjudicate racial gerrymandering claims would not be equally manageable in political gerrymandering cases. Instead, its distinction of those cases rests on its view that race as a districting criterion is "much more rarely encountered" than partisanship, and that determining whether race—"a rare and constitutionally suspect motive"—dominated a districting decision "is quite different from determining whether [such a decision] is so substantially affected by the excess of an ordinary and lawful motive as to [be] invali[d]." But those considerations are wholly irrelevant to the issue of justiciability.

To begin with, the plurality errs in assuming that politics is "an ordinary and lawful motive." We have squarely rejected the notion that a "purpose to discriminate on the basis of politics," is never subject to strict scrutiny. On the contrary, "political belief and association constitute the core of those activities protected by the First Amendment," *Elrod v. Burns* (1976) (plurality opinion), and discriminatory governmental decisions that burden fundamental First Amendment interests are subject to strict scrutiny. In any event, as I understand the plurality's opinion, it seems to agree that if the State goes "too far"—if it engages in "political gerrymandering for politics' sake"—it violates the Constitution in the same way as if it undertakes "racial gerrymandering for race's sake." But that sort of constitutional violation cannot be touched by the courts, the plurality maintains, because the judicial obligation to intervene is "dubious."[14]

II

The plurality opinion in *Bandemer* dealt with a claim that the Indiana apportionment scheme for state legislative districts discriminated against Democratic voters on a statewide basis. In my judgment, the *Bandemer* Court was correct to entertain that statewide challenge because the plaintiffs in that case alleged a group harm that affected members of their party throughout the State. In the subsequent line of racial gerrymandering cases, however, the Court shifted its focus from statewide challenges and required, as a matter of standing, that plaintiffs stating race-based equal protection claims actually reside in the districts they are challenging. *See United States v. Hays* (1995). Because *Hays* has altered the standing rules for gerrymandering claims—and because, in my view, racial and political gerrymanders are species of the same constitutional concern—the *Hays* standing rule requires dismissal of the statewide claim. But that does not end the matter. Challenges to specific districts, such as those considered in the *Shaw* cases, relate to a different type of "representational" harm, and those allegations necessarily must be considered on a district-by-district basis. The complaint in this case alleges injuries of both types—a group harm to Democratic voters throughout Pennsylvania and a more individualized representational injury to Furey as a resident of District 6.

Undergirding the *Shaw* cases is the premise that racial gerrymanders effect a constitutional wrong when they disrupt the representational norms that ordinarily tether elected officials to their constituencies as a whole.

14. The plurality's reluctance to recognize the justiciability of partisan gerrymanders seems driven in part by a fear that recognizing such claims will give rise to a flood of litigation. But in the two decades since *Bandemer*, there has been an average of just three or four partisan gerrymandering cases filed every year. That volume is obviously trivial when compared, for example, to the amount of litigation that followed our adoption of the "one-person, one-vote" rule.

Gerrymanders subvert that representative norm because the winner of an election in a gerrymandered district inevitably will infer that her success is primarily attributable to the architect of the district rather than to a constituency defined by neutral principles.

The risk of representational harms identified in the *Shaw* cases is equally great, if not greater, in the context of partisan gerrymanders. *Shaw I* was borne of the concern that an official elected from a racially gerrymandered district will feel beholden only to a portion of her constituents, and that those constituents will be defined by race. The parallel danger of a partisan gerrymander is that the representative will perceive that the people who put her in power are those who drew the map rather than those who cast ballots, and she will feel beholden not to a subset of her constituency, but to no part of her constituency at all. The problem, simply put, is that the will of the cartographers rather than the will of the people will govern.

III

In evaluating a claim that a governmental decision violates the Equal Protection Clause, we have long required a showing of discriminatory purpose.

Consistent with that principle, our recent racial gerrymandering cases have examined the shape of the district and the purpose of the districting body to determine whether race, above all other criteria, predominated in the line-drawing process. We began by holding in *Shaw I* that a districting scheme could be "so irrational on its face that it [could] be understood only as an effort to segregate voters into separate voting districts because of their race." Then, in *Miller,* we explained that *Shaw I*'s irrational-shape test did not treat the bizarreness of a district's lines itself as a constitutional violation; rather, the irregularity of the district's contours in *Shaw I* was "persuasive circumstantial evidence that race for its own sake, and not other districting principles, was the legislature's dominant and controlling rationale in drawing its district lines." Under the *Shaw* cases, then, the use of race as a criterion in redistricting is not *per se* impermissible, but when race is elevated to paramount status—when it is the be-all and end-all of the redistricting process—the legislature has gone too far. "Race must not simply have been *a* motivation . . . but the *predominant* factor motivating the legislature's districting decision." *Easley.*

Just as irrational shape can serve as an objective indicator of an impermissible legislative purpose, other objective features of a districting map can save the plan from invalidation. We have explained that "traditional districting principles," which include "compactness, contiguity, and respect for political subdivisions," are "important not because they are constitutionally required . . . but because they are objective factors that may serve to defeat a claim that a district has been gerrymandered on racial lines." *Shaw I.* "Where these or other race-neutral considerations are the basis for redistricting legislation, and are not subordinated to race, a State can 'defeat a claim that a district has been gerrymandered on racial lines.'" *Miller* (quoting *Shaw I*).

In my view, the same standards should apply to claims of political gerrymandering, for the essence of a gerrymander is the same regardless of whether the group is identified as political or racial. Gerrymandering always involves the drawing of district boundaries to maximize the voting strength of the dominant political faction and to minimize the strength of one or more groups of opponents. In seeking the desired result, legislators necessarily make judgments about the probability that the members of identifiable groups—whether economic, religious, ethnic, or racial—will vote in a certain way. The overriding purpose of those predictions is political. It follows that the standards that enable courts to identify and redress a racial gerrymander could also perform the same function for other species of gerrymanders.

The plurality reasons that the standards for evaluating racial gerrymanders are not workable in cases such as this because partisan considerations, unlike racial ones, are perfectly legitimate. Until today, however, there has not been the slightest intimation in any opinion written by any Member of this Court that a naked purpose to disadvantage a political minority would provide a rational basis for drawing a district line. On the contrary, our opinions referring to political gerrymanders have consistently assumed that they were at least undesirable, and we always have indicated that political considerations are among those factors that may not dominate districting decisions. Purely partisan motives are "rational" in a literal sense, but there must be a limiting principle. "[T]he word 'rational'—for me at least—includes elements of legitimacy and neutrality that must always characterize the performance of the sovereign's duty to govern impartially." *Cleburne v. Cleburne Living Center, Inc.*, (1985) (Stevens, J., concurring). A legislature controlled by one party could not, for instance, impose special taxes on members of the minority party, or use tax revenues to pay the majority party's campaign expenses. The rational basis for government decisions must satisfy a standard of legitimacy and neutrality; an acceptable rational basis can be neither purely personal nor purely partisan.

The Constitution does not, of course, require proportional representation of racial, ethnic, or political groups. In that I agree with the plurality. We have held, however, that proportional representation of political groups is a permissible objective, *Gaffney*, and some of us have expressed the opinion that a majority's decision to enhance the representation of a racial minority is equally permissible, particularly when the decision is designed to comply with the Voting Rights Act of 1965. Thus, the view that the plurality implicitly embraces today—that a gerrymander contrived for the sole purpose of disadvantaging a political minority is less objectionable than one seeking to benefit a racial minority—is doubly flawed. It disregards the obvious distinction between an invidious and a benign purpose, and it mistakenly assumes that race cannot provide a legitimate basis for making political judgments.

Under my analysis, if no neutral criterion can be identified to justify the lines drawn, and if the only possible explanation for a district's bizarre shape is a naked desire to increase partisan strength, then no rational basis exists to save the district from an equal protection challenge. Such a narrow test would cover only a few meritorious claims, but it would preclude extreme abuses and it would perhaps shorten the time period in which the pernicious effects of such a gerrymander are felt. This test would mitigate the current trend under which partisan considerations are becoming the be-all and end-all in apportioning representatives.

IV

Quite obviously, several standards for identifying impermissible partisan influence are available to judges who have the will to enforce them. It is, instead, a failure of judicial will to condemn even the most blatant violations of a state legislature's fundamental duty to govern impartially.

Accordingly, I respectfully dissent.

Justice SOUTER, with whom Justice GINSBURG joins, dissenting.

[Justice Souter would have adopted a burden-shifting test based on the standard from *McDonall Douglas* (a case about employment discrimination) for partisan gerrymandering claims. His test was focused on uncovering "unfairness" in redistricting, requiring the plaintiff to make out a prima facie case using a five-part test. The burden would then shift to the government defendant to justify the redistricting based on traditional redistricting principles.]

Justice BREYER, dissenting.

The use of purely political considerations in drawing district boundaries is not a "necessary evil" that, for lack of judicially manageable standards, the Constitution inevitably must tolerate. Rather, pure politics often helps to secure constitutionally important democratic objectives. But sometimes it does not. Sometimes purely political "gerrymandering" will fail to advance any plausible democratic objective while simultaneously threatening serious democratic harm. And sometimes when that is so, courts can identify an equal protection violation and provide a remedy. Because the plaintiffs could claim (but have not yet proved) that such circumstances exist here, I would reverse the District Court's dismissal of their complaint.

The plurality focuses directly on the most difficult issue before us. It says, "[n]o test—yea, not even a five-part test—can possibly be successful unless one knows what he is testing *for.*" That is true. Thus, I shall describe a set of circumstances in which the use of purely political districting criteria could conflict with constitutionally mandated democratic requirements—circumstances that the courts should "test for." I shall then explain why I believe it possible to find applicable judicially manageable standards. And I shall illustrate those standards.

I

I start with a fundamental principle. "We the People," who "ordain[ed] and establish[ed]" the American Constitution, sought to create and to protect a workable form of government that is in its principles, structure, and whole mass, basically democratic. In a modern Nation of close to 300 million people, the workable democracy that the Constitution foresees must mean more than a guaranteed opportunity to elect legislators representing equally populous electoral districts. There must also be a method for transforming the will of the majority into effective government.

This Court has explained that political parties play a necessary role in that transformation. At a minimum, they help voters assign responsibility for current circumstances, thereby enabling those voters, through their votes for individual candidates, to express satisfaction or dissatisfaction with the political status quo. Those voters can either vote to support that status quo or vote to "throw the rascals out." A party-based political system that satisfies this minimal condition encourages democratic responsibility. It facilitates the transformation of the voters' will into a government that reflects that will.

Why do I refer to these elementary constitutional principles? Because I believe they can help courts identify at least one abuse at issue in this case. To understand how that is so, one should begin by asking why single-member electoral districts are the norm, why the Constitution does not insist that the membership of legislatures better reflect different political views held by different groups of voters. History, of course, is part of the answer, but it does not tell the entire story. The answer also lies in the fact that a single-member-district system helps to ensure certain democratic objectives better than many "more representative" (*i.e.,* proportional) electoral systems. Of course, single-member districts mean that only parties with candidates who finish "first past the post" will elect legislators. That fact means in turn that a party with a bare majority of votes or even a plurality of votes will often obtain a large legislative majority, perhaps freezing out smaller parties. But single-member districts thereby diminish the need for coalition governments. And that fact makes it easier for voters to identify which party is responsible for government decision-making (and which rascals to throw out), while simultaneously providing greater legislative stability. This is not to say that single-member districts are preferable; it is simply to say that single-member-district systems and more-directly-representational systems reflect different conclusions about the proper balance of different elements of a workable democratic government.

If single-member districts are the norm, however, then political considerations will likely play an important, and proper, role in the drawing of district boundaries.

More important for present purposes, the role of political considerations reflects a surprising mathematical fact. Given a fairly large state population with a fairly large congressional delegation, districts assigned so as to be perfectly random in respect to politics would translate a small shift in political sentiment, say a shift from 51%

Republican to 49% Republican, into a seismic shift in the makeup of the legislative delegation, say from 100% Republican to 100% Democrat. Any such exaggeration of tiny electoral changes—virtually wiping out legislative representation of the minority party—would itself seem highly undemocratic.

Given the resulting need for single-member districts with nonrandom boundaries, it is not surprising that "traditional" districting principles have rarely, if ever, been politically neutral. Rather, because, in recent political memory, Democrats have often been concentrated in cities while Republicans have often been concentrated in suburbs and sometimes rural areas, geographically drawn boundaries have tended to "pac[k]" the former. Neighborhood or community-based boundaries, seeking to group Irish, Jewish, or African-American voters, often did the same. All this is well known to politicians, who use their knowledge about the effects of the "neutral" criteria to partisan advantage when drawing electoral maps. And were it not so, the iron laws of mathematics would have worked their extraordinary volatility-enhancing will.

This is to say that traditional or historically based boundaries are not, and should not be, "politics free." Rather, those boundaries represent a series of compromises of principle—among the virtues of, for example, close representation of voter views, ease of identifying "government" and "opposition" parties, and stability in government. They also represent an uneasy truce, sanctioned by tradition, among different parties seeking political advantage.

As I have said, reference back to these underlying considerations helps to explain why the legislature's use of political boundary drawing considerations ordinarily does *not* violate the Constitution's Equal Protection Clause. The reason lies not simply in the difficulty of identifying abuse or finding an appropriate judicial remedy. The reason is more fundamental: Ordinarily, there simply is no abuse. The use of purely political boundary-drawing factors, even where harmful to the members of one party, will often nonetheless find justification in other desirable democratic ends, such as maintaining relatively stable legislatures in which a minority party retains significant representation.

II

At the same time, these considerations can help identify at least one circumstance where use of purely political boundary-drawing factors can amount to a serious, and remediable, abuse, namely, the *unjustified* use of political factors to entrench a minority in power. By entrenchment I mean a situation in which a party that enjoys only minority support among the populace has nonetheless contrived to take, and hold, legislative power. By *unjustified* entrenchment I mean that the minority's hold on power is purely the result of partisan manipulation and not other factors. These "other" factors that could lead to "justified" (albeit temporary) minority entrenchment include sheer happenstance, the existence of more than two major parties, the unique constitutional requirements of certain representational bodies such as the Senate, or reliance on traditional (geographic, communities of interest, etc.) districting criteria.

The democratic harm of unjustified entrenchment is obvious. As this Court has written in respect to popularly-based electoral districts:

> "Logically, in a society ostensibly grounded on representative government, it would seem reasonable that a majority of the people of a State could elect a majority of that State's legislators. To conclude differently, and to sanction minority control of state legislative bodies, would appear to deny majority rights in a way that far surpasses any possible denial of minority rights that might otherwise be thought to result. Since legislatures are responsible for enacting laws by which all citizens are to be governed, they should be bodies which are collectively responsive to the popular will." *Reynolds*.

Where unjustified entrenchment takes place, voters find it far more difficult to remove those responsible for a government they do not want; and these democratic values are dishonored.

The need for legislative stability cannot justify entrenchment, for stability is compatible with a system in which the loss of majority support implies a loss of power. The need to secure minority representation in the legislature cannot justify entrenchment, for minority party representation is also compatible with a system in which the loss of minority support implies a loss of representation. Constitutionally specified principles of representation, such as that of two Senators per State, cannot justify entrenchment where the House of Representatives or similar state legislative body is at issue. Unless some other justification can be found in particular circumstances, political gerrymandering that so entrenches a minority party in power violates basic democratic norms and lacks countervailing justification. For this reason, whether political gerrymandering does, or does not, violate the Constitution in other instances, gerrymandering that leads to entrenchment amounts to an abuse that violates the Constitution's Equal Protection Clause.

III

Courts need not intervene often to prevent the kind of abuse I have described, because those harmed constitute a political majority, and a majority normally can work its political will. Where a State has improperly gerrymandered legislative or congressional districts to the majority's disadvantage, the majority should be able to elect officials in statewide races—particularly the Governor—who may help to undo the harm that districting has caused the majority's party, in the next round of districting if not sooner. And where a State has improperly gerrymandered congressional districts, Congress retains the power to revise the State's districting determinations.

Moreover, voters in some States, perhaps tiring of the political boundary-drawing rivalry, have found a procedural solution, confiding the task to a commission that is limited in the extent to which it may base districts on partisan concerns. According to the National Conference of State Legislatures, 12 States currently give "first and final authority for [state] legislative redistricting to a group other than the legislature." A number of States use a commission for congressional redistricting: Arizona, Hawaii, Idaho, Montana, New Jersey, and Washington, with Indiana using a commission if the legislature cannot pass a plan and Iowa requiring the district-drawing body not to consider political data. Indeed, where state governments have been unwilling or unable to act, "an informed, civically militant electorate," *Baker v. Carr* (Frankfurter, J., dissenting), has occasionally taken matters into its own hands, through ballot initiatives or referendums. Arizona voters, for example, passed Proposition 106, which amended the State's Constitution and created an independent redistricting commission to draw legislative and congressional districts. Such reforms borrow from the systems used by other countries utilizing single-member districts.

But we cannot always count on a severely gerrymandered legislature itself to find and implement a remedy. The party that controls the process has no incentive to change it. And the political advantages of a gerrymander may become ever greater in the future. The availability of enhanced computer technology allows the parties to redraw boundaries in ways that target individual neighborhoods and homes, carving out safe but slim victory margins in the maximum number of districts, with little risk of cutting their margins too thin. By redrawing districts every 2 years, rather than every 10 years, a party might preserve its political advantages notwithstanding population shifts in the State. The combination of increasingly precise map-drawing technology and increasingly frequent map drawing means that a party may be able to bring about a gerrymander that is not only precise, but virtually impossible to dislodge. Thus, court action may prove necessary.

When it is necessary, a court should prove capable of finding an appropriate remedy. Courts have developed districting remedies in other cases. Moreover, if the dangers of inadvertent political favoritism prove too great, a procedural solution, such as the use of a politically balanced boundary-drawing commission, may prove possible.

The bottom line is that courts should be able to identify the presence of one important gerrymandering evil, the unjustified entrenching in power of a political party that the voters have rejected. They should be able to separate the unjustified abuse of partisan boundary-drawing considerations to achieve that end from their more ordinary and justified use. And they should be able to design a remedy for extreme cases.

IV

I do not claim that the problem of identification and separation is easily solved, even in extreme instances. But courts can identify a number of strong indicia of abuse. The presence of actual entrenchment, while not always unjustified (being perhaps a chance occurrence), is such a sign, particularly when accompanied by the use of partisan boundary drawing criteria in the way that Justice Stevens describes, *i.e.*, a use that both departs from traditional criteria and cannot be explained other than by efforts to achieve partisan advantage. Below, I set forth several sets of circumstances that lay out the indicia of abuse I have in mind. The scenarios fall along a continuum: The more permanently entrenched the minority's hold on power becomes, the less evidence courts will need that the minority engaged in gerrymandering to achieve the desired result.

Consider, for example, the following sets of circumstances. First, suppose that the legislature has proceeded to redraw boundaries in what seem to be ordinary ways, but the entrenchment harm has become obvious. *E.g.,* (a) the legislature has not redrawn district boundaries more than once within the traditional 10-year period; and (b) no radical departure from traditional districting criteria is alleged; but (c) a majority party (as measured by the votes actually cast for all candidates who identify themselves as members of that party in the relevant set of elections; *i.e.,* in congressional elections if a congressional map is being challenged) has *twice* failed to obtain a majority of the relevant legislative seats in elections; and (d) the failure cannot be explained by the existence of multiple parties or in other neutral ways. In my view, these circumstances would be sufficient to support a claim of unconstitutional entrenchment.

Second, suppose that plaintiffs could point to more serious departures from redistricting norms. *E.g.,* (a) the legislature has not redrawn district boundaries more than once within the traditional 10-year period; but (b) the boundary-drawing criteria depart radically from previous or traditional criteria; (c) the departure cannot be justified or explained other than by reference to an effort to obtain partisan political advantage; and (d) a majority party (as defined above) has once failed to obtain a majority of the relevant seats in election using the challenged map (which fact cannot be explained by the existence of multiple parties or in other neutral ways). These circumstances could also add up to unconstitutional gerrymandering.

Third, suppose that the legislature clearly departs from ordinary districting norms, but the entrenchment harm, while seriously threatened, has not yet occurred. *E.g.,* (a) the legislature has redrawn district boundaries more than once within the traditional 10-year census-related period—either, as here, at the behest of a court that struck down an initial plan as unlawful, or of its own accord; (b) the boundary-drawing criteria depart radically from previous traditional boundary-drawing criteria; (c) strong, objective, unrefuted statistical evidence demonstrates that a party with a minority of the popular vote within the State in all likelihood will obtain a majority of the seats in the relevant representative delegation; and (d) the jettisoning of traditional districting criteria cannot be justified or explained other than by reference to an effort to obtain partisan political advantage. To my mind, such circumstances could also support a claim, because the presence of mid-cycle redistricting, for any reason, raises a fair inference that partisan machinations played a major role in the map-drawing process. Where such an inference is accompanied by statistical evidence that entrenchment will be the likely result, a court may conclude that the map crosses the constitutional line we are describing.

The presence of these, or similar, circumstances—where the risk of entrenchment is demonstrated, where partisan considerations render the traditional district-drawing compromises irrelevant, where no justification other than party advantage can be found—seem to me extreme enough to set off a constitutional alarm. The risk of harm to basic democratic principle is serious; identification is possible; and remedies can be found.

V

[Omitted]

VI

I dissent.

NOTES ON *VIETH*

1. We have created a "Political Gerrymandering Hypothetical" (see below) to illustrate how political gerrymandering can work. A key point is that it is possible for the political party in control of the mapmaking process to draw the lines so that it retains control of a majority of legislative seats even after it becomes the minority party in terms of voter popularity. Thus, in the hypothetical, if the Democrats control the districting process, they can gerrymander to assure themselves of six safe seats (out of ten total), even though a shift in public opinion causes Republicans to gain a 55 to 45 percent majority statewide (550,000 Rs; 450,000 Ds). Basically, the idea is to "pack" or concentrate Republicans into fewer districts, so that these Republicans have "wasted" extra votes in these districts (in other words, especially large majorities there), enabling the Democrats to effectively spread themselves over enough districts to control a majority.

Political Gerrymandering Hypothetical

Rs 550,000

Ds 450,000

Total 1,000,000

Need to create 10 Districts

Option A			Option B		
District	Rs	Ds	District	Rs	Ds
1	10	90	1	30	70
2	20	80	2	30	70
3	20	80	3	30	70
4	40	60	4	40	60
5	60	40	5	40	60
6	60	40	6	40	60
7	80	20	7	70	30
8	80	20	8	90	10
9	90	10	9	90	10
10	90	10	10	90	10
T	550	450	T	550	450
6 safe R seats			6 safe D seats		

Assume Option A is more compact and better protects city and county boundaries. Should a court find Option B unconstitutional?

2. The legal question in *Vieth* is: When, if ever, does it violate the U.S. Constitution for a state's mapmaking authority to engage in this kind of political gerrymandering?
3. The plurality led by Justice Scalia says it is "significant" that Congress, if it wished, could prohibit the gerrymandering of congressional districts. But would not the plurality also invoke the political question doctrine to reject judicial consideration of an Equal Protection Clause challenge to the political gerrymandering of a state legislature?
4. Why is Justice Scalia unwilling, and Justice Kennedy hesitant, to subject claims of *political* gerrymandering to strict scrutiny, when both of these Justices are quick to subject claims of *racial* gerrymandering to strict scrutiny? For them, is the difference in the applicable constitutional standard, the cultural difference between race and party affiliation, a combination of these two, or something else? And when reading the *Vieth* dissents, we must ask the same question in reverse: Why are Justices Stevens, Souter, Ginsburg, and Breyer so reluctant to impose strict scrutiny on claims of *racial* gerrymandering, but so willing to impose rigorous judicial review of *political* gerrymandering claims?
5. As we saw with *Shaw*, *Miller*, and *Easley*, the constitutional standard applicable to claims of *racial* gerrymanders is hardly the model of precision: Race must not *predominate* in the drawing of district lines; the consideration of race in districting cannot be *excessive*. According to Justice Scalia, why is it not "judicially manageable" for the courts to implement the same standard with respect to *political* gerrymandering claims? Wouldn't it be just as easy (or equally difficult)

for the courts to determine whether the desire for partisan advantage *predominated* the districting process, or was *excessive*, as for the courts to ascertain whether there was *too much* consideration of race? Does Justice Stevens, who essentially would like to import the test for racial gerrymandering into the political gerrymandering context, have the stronger argument?

6. Justice Breyer's approach is that there is at least one context in which a political gerrymandering claim can be policed by the courts: where a minority is unjustifiably entrenching itself at the expense of the majority. Would Justice Breyer's standard be judicially manageable? Would it be a good idea to implement his standard?
7. In the 2010 redistricting cycle, several states, including California and Arizona, used independent redistricting commissions comprised of citizens to redraw the state's maps. The goal was to minimize partisanship in the redistricting process. Is this the best solution to the perceived problem or can we still rely on courts to remedy the most egregious partisan gerrymanders? If independent commissions are the best solution, how should such commissions be designed?

As you read in *Vieth v. Jubelirer*, the possibility is slim that a plaintiff could successfully challenge a redistricting plan as a partisan gerrymander that violates the U.S. Constitution. Yet the political party that loses the redistricting battle in the legislature would nearly always like to reverse (or at least mitigate) the loss. This, in essence, leads political parties to channel their energies into legal challenges that have a much higher chance of success than a claim of unconstitutional partisan gerrymandering. In other words, the existing legal framework leads the political losers of redistricting battles to challenge redistricting plans using one person, one vote, the Voting Rights Act, or constitutional doctrines related to race and redistricting.

The next case—a decision of a three-judge federal district court panel—deals with Georgia's post–2000 legislative redistricting plans for its House and Senate. As you read the next case, consider whether the following opinion—which purports to be a decision based upon one person, one vote—is really just a partisan gerrymandering ruling in disguise.

LARIOS v. COX

300 F. Supp. 2d 1320 (N.D. Ga. 2004)

Before Marcus, Circuit Judge and Pannell and O'Kelley, District Judges.

[Plaintiffs brought several challenges to the redistricting plans enacted for the Georgia state legislature in 2001 and 2002. At the time the redistricting plans were adopted, Democrats controlled both houses of the state legislature and the governor's office. Plaintiffs asserted numerous claims, alleging partisan and racial gerrymandering in violation of the Equal Protection Clause and a violation of one person, one vote.

The district court dismissed or held in abeyance most of the claims but ruled on the one person, one vote challenge.]

Based upon a thorough review of the record and the applicable law, we conclude:

> Georgia's state legislative reapportionment plans plainly violate the one person, one vote principle embodied in the Equal Protection Clause because each deviates from population equality by a total of 9.98% of the ideal district population and there are no legitimate, consistently applied state policies which justify these population deviations. Instead, the plans arbitrarily and discriminatorily dilute and debase the weight of certain citizens' votes by intentionally and systematically underpopulating districts in rural south Georgia and inner-city Atlanta, correspondingly overpopulating the districts in suburban areas surrounding Atlanta, and by underpopulating the districts held by incumbent Democrats.

I. FINDINGS OF FACT

A. The Reapportionment Process in General

The 2000 Decennial Census reported that the total population of the State of Georgia was 8,186,453 persons. From 1990 to 2000, the population of north Georgia, which is largely comprised of the urban and suburban areas surrounding Atlanta, grew at a much faster rate than the population of south Georgia, which is primarily rural. This population trend has remained consistent for the last several decades. In that same time period, the Republican party has also gained substantial strength in Georgia. In fact, the fastest-growing counties in the state over the past decade are Republican-leaning.

Both houses of the General Assembly used Maptitude software to draw their redistricting plans. With the available technology and the use of this software, redistricting plans in 2001 could have been created with a deviation of 0 to 1 persons. The combination of technology and political data available to legislators and plan drafters also allowed for sophisticated analyses of political performance, so that maps could be drawn and then immediately analyzed politically. Thus, in drafting and considering their proposed maps, members of both houses relied on political performance projections, indicating the percentage of votes Democrats and Republicans would likely receive in future elections based upon an assessment of past election results.

Republicans attempted to influence the redistricting in several ways, with little success. Republicans were not consulted by Democratic legislators regarding the redistricting plans.

B. The Individual Plans

1. The State Legislative Plans

The redistricting guidelines adopted by the House and Senate Reapportionment committees indicated that "[t]he population deviation of [each] plan should not exceed an overall deviation of 10%." Based largely on these guidelines and on the instructions given in previous redistricting cycles, legislators and plan drawers for both houses believed there was a "safe harbor" of ± 5% in the reapportionment of state legislative districts and, therefore, that population deviations not rising to that level did not have to be supported by any legitimate state interest.

The creators of the state plans did not consider such traditional redistricting criteria as district compactness, contiguity, protecting communities of interest, and keeping counties intact. Rather, they had two expressly enumerated objectives: the protection of rural Georgia and inner-city Atlanta against a relative decline in their populations compared with that of the rest of the state and the protection of Democratic incumbents.

a. The House Plan

The House Plan consists of 180 members allocated to 147 districts, with 124 one-member districts, fifteen two-member districts, six three-member districts, and two four-member districts. In the redistricting plan immediately preceding the current plan, the House was comprised of 180 single-member districts. Based on the state's total population according to the 2000 Census, the ideal size of a single-member House district for one person, one vote purposes is 45,480 persons.

The legislative reapportionment staff, and particularly Linda Meggers, worked with individual House members to draft the House Plan. In drawing the districts, Ms. Meggers took into account the political desires of various Democratic incumbents in order to achieve the ninety-one votes required to pass a plan. This was particularly difficult in south Georgia and urban Atlanta, as the districts in those areas were vastly underpopulated at the beginning of the redistricting process and the incumbents in those districts struggled to maintain as many seats as possible. Additionally, incumbents in all areas of the state sought to limit the expansion of their districts to what was considered legally necessary, i.e., a population deviation of ± 5%. At no time did the drafters of the plans nurture the ambition of drawing maps as close to equal in population as was reasonably practicable. In the end, many south Georgia incumbents who had seniority over other House members used their political influence to preserve the representation of rural interests as much as possible, resulting in greater negative population deviations in these areas and, consequently, greater positive population deviations in other areas. Nonetheless, south Georgia still lost seven House districts in the reapportionment plan that ultimately passed.

The resulting House Plan has a total population deviation range of 9.98% and an average deviation of 3.47%. The House districts deviate from ideal equal population by a range of +4.99% to –4.99%, with the largest district having 176,939 persons (in a four-member district) and the smallest district having 43,209 persons. Notably, ninety of the 180 House seats (50.00%) are in districts with population deviations greater than ± 4%. Sixty seats (33.33%) are in districts with deviations greater than ± 4.5%, and twenty seats (11.11%) are in districts with deviations greater than ± 4.9%. The most underpopulated districts are primarily Democratic-leaning, and the most overpopulated districts are primarily Republican-leaning. Moreover, most of the districts with negative deviations of 4% or greater are located either in south Georgia or within inner-city Atlanta. Plainly, redistricting plans could have been easily drawn with smaller population deviations; in fact, some such plans were offered for consideration but were summarily rejected.

The House Plan splits eighty counties into 266 parts. The plan paired forty-two incumbents, including thirty-seven of the seventy-four incumbent Republicans (50% of the Republican caucus), but only nine of the 105 incumbent Democrats (less than 9% of the Democratic caucus). In the 2002 general election, the first general election following enactment of the plan, the composition of the House went from 105 Democrats, 74 Republicans, and 1 Independent to 107 Democrats, 72 Republicans, and 1 Independent.

b. The Senate Plan

The Georgia Senate consists of fifty-six members. The Georgia Constitution requires that the state senate be composed of single-member districts. Therefore, based on the state's total population, the ideal size of a Senate district for one person, one vote purposes according to the 2000 Census is 146,187 persons.

To create a plan, [Democratic] Senator Brown worked with Joseph Stanton and other staff of the legislative reapportionment office, who offered technical assistance. Senator Brown focused his redistricting efforts on five primary goals: (1) drawing districts with population deviations of no greater than ± 5%; (2) ensuring that the districts did not retrogress in violation of Section 5 of the Voting Rights Act; (3) protecting or enhancing opportunities for Democrats to be elected; (4) allowing rural southern Georgia to hold on to as many seats as possible; and (5) obtaining the twenty-nine votes required to pass a plan.

The resulting 2002 Senate Plan has a total population deviation of 9.98% and an average deviation of 3.78%. The Senate districts deviate from ideal equal population by a range of +4.99% to –4.99%, with the largest district having 153,489 persons and the smallest district having 138,894 persons. Thirty-seven of the fifty-six districts (66.07%) have population deviations greater than ± 4%. Thirty-one districts (55.36%) have deviations greater than ± 4.5%, and sixteen districts (28.57%) have deviations greater than ± 4.9%. Not surprisingly, the most underpopulated districts are primarily Democratic-leaning, and the most overpopulated districts are primarily Republican-leaning. Moreover, all of the districts with negative deviations of more than 4% are situated either in south Georgia or within inner-city Atlanta. As in the House, redistricting plans with smaller population deviations were offered for consideration, but were summarily rejected.

The 2002 Senate Plan splits eighty-one counties into 219 parts. The plan also paired twelve incumbents, including ten of the twenty-four incumbent Republicans (42% of the caucus) but only two of the thirty-two incumbent Democrats (6% of the caucus). In the 2002 general election, the first general election following enactment of the plan, the composition of the Senate went from thirty-two Democrats and twenty-four Republicans to thirty Democrats and twenty-six Republicans. Following the election, four Democrats switched allegiance to the Republican Party, giving the Republicans control of the Senate by a margin of 30-26.

c. The Favoring of Rural and Inner-City Interests

Both the explicit admissions of witnesses for the defendant and the circumstantial evidence of the plans themselves leave no doubt that a deliberate and systematic policy of favoring rural and inner-city interests at the expense of suburban areas north, east, and west of Atlanta led to a substantial portion of the 9.98% population deviations in both of the plans.

d. Incumbent Protection

An examination of the entire record also leads us to find that the other major cause of the deviations in both plans was an intentional effort to allow incumbent Democrats to maintain or increase their delegation, primarily by systematically underpopulating the districts held by incumbent Democrats, by overpopulating those of Republicans, and by deliberately pairing numerous Republican incumbents against one another.

While Democratic incumbents who supported the plans were generally protected, Republican incumbents were regularly pitted against one another in an obviously purposeful attempt to unseat as many of them as possible. In the House Plan, forty-seven incumbents were paired. Similarly, the 2002 Senate Plan included six incumbent pairings. In the 2002 general election, eighteen Republican incumbents in the House and four Republican incumbents in the Senate lost their seats due to the pairings, while only three Democratic incumbents in the House and no Democratic incumbents in the Senate lost seats this way.

The numbers largely speak for themselves, but the shapes of many of these districts and the resulting pairings further indicate that there was an intent not only to aid Democratic incumbents in getting re-elected but also to oust many of their Republican incumbent counterparts. For example, one Republican senator (Senator Cable) was drawn into a district with a Democratic incumbent who ultimately won the 2002 general election, while an open district was drawn within two blocks of her residence. Additionally, two of the most senior Republican senators, Senators Burton and Ladd, were drawn into the same district, and a Republican House member, Representative Kaye, who was generally disliked by several of the Democratic incumbents, was paired with another representative in an attempt to unseat him.

Perhaps the most striking example of the manipulation of population deviations at the district level, however, may be what occurred in House District 137, which drew in two Republican incumbents. This district has a positive deviation of 4.45%, although it is located in the southern part of the state, where the vast majority of districts are underpopulated. It borders Districts 132, 133, 135, 136, 138, 139, 140, 141, and 144, which have population deviations of –4.78%, –4.63%, –4.60%, –4.68%, +3.10%, –3.11%, –4.77%, –4.94%, and +2.21%, respectively.

These efforts at selective incumbent protection through the use of population deviations and creative district shapes led to a significant overall partisan advantage for Democrats in the electoral maps. Republican-leaning districts are vastly more overpopulated as a whole than Democratic-leaning districts. Indeed, by one measure, the House Plan contains fifty overpopulated and thirteen underpopulated Republican-leaning districts, compared to only twenty-two overpopulated and fifty-nine underpopulated Democratic-leaning districts, and the 2002 Senate Plan contains nineteen overpopulated and seven underpopulated Republican-leaning districts, compared to only eight overpopulated and twenty-two underpopulated Democratic-leaning districts.

e. Traditional Redistricting Criteria

The Supreme Court has specifically detailed a number of state policies that, when applied in a consistent and nondiscriminatory manner, can justify some level of population deviation. In *Karcher v. Daggett*, discussing population deviations, the Court indicated the kind of policies that might permit some deviation from perfect population equality: "Any number of consistently applied legislative policies might justify some variance, including, for instance, making districts compact, respecting municipal boundaries, preserving the cores of prior districts, and avoiding contests between incumbent Representatives." The last of these, incumbent protection, has already been discussed at length. The other policies were not causes of the population deviations in the House Plan and 2002 Senate Plan; nor indeed, were they priorities at all in drafting the plans. In fact, the defendant has never claimed that they were.

II. Conclusions of Law

The Constitution of the United States requires that congressional and state legislative seats be apportioned equally, so as to ensure that the constitutionally guaranteed right of suffrage is not denied by debasement or dilution of the weight of a citizen's vote. *Reynolds v. Sims.*

While the Court has allowed some flexibility in state legislative reapportionment, the central and invariable objective remains "equal representation for equal numbers of people." Thus, deviations from exact population equality may be allowed in some instances in order to further legitimate state interests such as making districts compact and contiguous, respecting political subdivisions, maintaining the cores of prior districts, and avoiding incumbent pairings. *See Karcher v. Daggett.* However, where population deviations are not supported by such legitimate interests but, rather, are tainted by arbitrariness or discrimination, they cannot withstand constitutional scrutiny.

The population deviations in the Georgia House and Senate Plans are not the result of an effort to further any legitimate, consistently applied state policy. Rather, we have found that the deviations were systematically and intentionally created (1) to allow rural southern Georgia and inner-city Atlanta to maintain their legislative influence even as their rate of population growth lags behind that of the rest of the state; and (2) to protect Democratic incumbents. Neither of these explanations withstands Equal Protection scrutiny. First, forty years of Supreme Court jurisprudence have established that the creation of deviations for the purpose of allowing the people of certain geographic regions of a state to hold legislative power to a degree disproportionate to their population is plainly unconstitutional. Moreover, the protection of incumbents is a permissible cause of population deviations only when it is limited to the avoidance of contests between incumbents and is applied in a consistent and nondiscriminatory manner. The incumbency protection in the Georgia state legislative plans meets neither criterion. Therefore, that interest cannot save the plans from constitutional infirmity. Quite simply, the Georgia plans violate the Equal Protection Clause.

A. The Plaintiffs' One Person, One Vote Challenge to the State Legislative Plans

1. General Principles

Each state is required to "make an honest and good faith effort to construct districts, in both houses of its legislature, as nearly of equal population as is practicable." *Reynolds*. This Equal Protection guarantee, commonly known as the one person, one vote principle, commands that "the seats in both houses of a bicameral state legislature must be apportioned on a population basis." *Reynolds*.

However, the Supreme Court has recognized both that mathematical precision is not a workable constitutional requirement and that it is practically impossible to construct state legislative districts so that each one has an identical number of citizens. Thus, the Court has allowed the states to exercise "[s]omewhat more flexibility" in state legislative redistricting than in congressional redistricting. The Supreme Court has directed:

> So long as the divergences from a strict population standard are based on legitimate considerations incident to the effectuation of a rational state policy, some deviations from the equal-population principle are constitutionally permissible with respect to the apportionment of seats in either or both of the two houses of a bicameral state legislature.

These deviations from perfect equality "may occur in recognizing certain factors that are free from any taint of arbitrariness or discrimination." *Roman v. Sincock* (1964).

In reviewing one person, one vote challenges to state legislative plans, the Supreme Court has adopted a so-called "ten percent rule" for allocating the burden of proof. [T]he Court [has] stated that, as a general matter, "an apportionment plan with a maximum population deviation under 10% falls within this category of minor deviations" that are insufficient to make out a prima facie case of discrimination in violation of the

Fourteenth Amendment. *Brown v. Thomson*. In contrast, a plan with a higher maximum deviation "creates a prima facie case of discrimination and therefore must be justified by the State." *Id.* In considering legitimate justifications, courts must consider "[t]he consistency of application and the neutrality of effect of the nonpopulation criteria" in order to determine whether a state legislative reapportionment plan violates the Fourteenth Amendment. *Id.*

Most lower courts presented with challenges to plans with population deviations of less than 10% have concluded that such plans are not automatically immune from constitutional attack. Thus, for example, the Fourth Circuit has held that the 10% threshold "does not completely insulate a state's districting plan from attack of any type" but, rather, "serves as the determining point for allocating the burden of proof in a one person, one vote case." *Daly v. Hunt* (4th Cir.1996). That court summarized the rule in these terms:

> [I]f the maximum [population] deviation is less than 10%, the population disparity is considered de minimis and the plaintiff cannot rely on it alone to prove invidious discrimination or arbitrariness. To survive summary judgment, the plaintiff would have to produce further evidence to show that the apportionment process had a "taint of arbitrariness or discrimination." In other words, for deviations below 10%, the state is entitled to a presumption that the apportionment plan was the result of an "honest and good faith effort to construct districts . . . as nearly of equal population as is practicable." However, this is a rebuttable presumption.

We agree that state legislative plans with population deviations of less than 10% may be challenged based on alleged violation of the one person, one vote principle. Indeed, the very fact that the Supreme Court has described the ten percent rule in terms of "prima facie constitutional validity" unmistakably indicates that 10% is not a safe harbor. Had the Court intended to foreclose all one person, one vote challenges to plans with population deviations not rising to the 10% level, the Court would undoubtedly have said as much, rather than expressing that such plans are merely "prima facie"—in other words, rebuttably—constitutional. And in this case, because the population deviations in both the House Plan and the 2002 Senate Plan are 9.98%, the ten percent rule applies (albeit barely). In short, the legislative plans are presumptively constitutional, and the burden lies on the plaintiffs to rebut that presumption.

The Supreme Court explained in *Roman* that "the proper judicial approach" to a one person, one vote claim is "to ascertain whether, under the particular circumstances existing in the individual State whose legislative apportionment is at issue, there has been a faithful adherence to a plan of population-based representation, with such minor deviations only as may occur in recognizing certain factors that are free from the taint of arbitrariness or discrimination." The Supreme Court reiterated this sentiment in *Brown*, indicating that the "ultimate inquiry" is "whether the legislature's plan may reasonably be said to advance [a] rational state policy and, if so, whether the population disparities among the districts that have resulted from the pursuit of this plan exceed constitutional limits."

In the redistricting of the Georgia state House and Senate, the drafters of the new electoral maps made no effort to make the districts as nearly of equal population as was practicable. In fact, it is quite apparent on this record that legislators and plan drafters made a concerted effort to contain population deviations to ± 5%, and no further, as they operated on the belief that there was a safe harbor of ± 5%. It is also apparent that any efforts to minimize population deviations ceased once the ± 5% level was reached, even though perfect equality was certainly attainable given current technology.

Such use of a 10% population window as a safe harbor may well violate the fundamental one person, one vote command of *Reynolds*, requiring that states "make an honest and good faith effort to construct districts . . . as nearly of equal population as practicable" and deviate from this principle only where "divergences . . . are based on legitimate considerations incident to the effectuation of a rational state policy." The use of a 10% safe harbor may also conflict with the *Roman* Court's observation that "the constitutionally permissible bounds of discretion in deviating from apportionment according to population" cannot be stated in a uniform mathematical formula, as it assumes that 10% is such a mathematical formula.

We need not decide, however, whether the mere use of a 10% population window renders Georgia's state legislative plans unconstitutional, because the policies the population window was used to promote in this case were not "free from any taint of arbitrariness or discrimination." The record makes abundantly clear that the population deviations in the Georgia House and Senate were not driven by any traditional redistricting criteria such as compactness, contiguity, and preserving county lines. Instead, the defense has put forth two basic explanations for the population deviations. First, witnesses for the defendant have repeatedly asserted—and a look at the redistricting maps does nothing to dispel the notion—that a powerful cause of the deviations in both plans was the concerted effort to allow rural and inner-city Atlanta regions of the state to hold on to their legislative influence (at the expense of suburban Atlanta), even as the rate of population growth in those areas was substantially lower than that of other parts of the state. Second, the deviations were created to protect incumbents in a wholly inconsistent and discriminatory way. On this record, neither explanation can convert a baldly unconstitutional scheme into a lawful one.

2. Regionalism

As we have found, regionalism—namely, a desire by rural and inner-city Atlanta legislators to retain their legislative influence even as the population of these areas has languished in comparison to the high-growth areas of north Georgia—was a major cause of the population deviations in the Georgia House and Senate Plans.

A look at the actual plans also makes it abundantly clear that regional favoritism substantially drove the population deviations, as districts in rural southern Georgia and inner-city Atlanta tended to be substantially underpopulated, while those in other parts of the state were correspondingly overpopulated. In the Senate, every single district that was underpopulated by at least 4% was located either in rural Georgia south of I-20 or in inner-city Atlanta. The correspondingly overpopulated districts were in the more suburban parts of the state. The vast majority of the House districts fit the same pattern, with underpopulated districts in the rural south and inner city and overpopulated ones in suburban areas.

The House and Senate Plans must be struck down on this basis alone, because the Supreme Court has long and repeatedly held that favoring certain geographic regions of a state over other regions is unconstitutional. Discrimination against certain voters based on the fortuity of where in the state they live cannot be reconciled with the command of *Reynolds*.

The *Reynolds* court clearly expressed that, while some deviations from the equal-population principle are permitted in state legislative reapportionment when they are based on "legitimate considerations incident to the effectuation of a rational state policy," geographic interests do not fall within this category of legitimate considerations.

The defendant argues, nonetheless, that the population deviations in this case are permissible because the one person, one vote principle has been relaxed since *Reynolds*, particularly in those cases that have expressed and applied the ten percent rule. We disagree. While the Supreme Court and the lower courts have allowed the states some flexibility in the pursuit of legitimate state interests, the Court has never retreated from the firm command in *Reynolds* that "[d]iluting the weight of votes because of place of residence impairs basic constitutional rights under the Fourteenth Amendment just as much as invidious discriminations based upon factors such as race or economic status."

Rural and inner-city Atlanta voters in Georgia make up a smaller proportion of the population now than they did in the past, primarily because the suburban communities surrounding Atlanta have been growing at a faster rate. Manipulating the legislative districting map to allow rural Georgia and inner-city Atlanta to maintain the number of seats those areas used to have is tantamount to saying that the interests of rural and inner-city voters are simply more important than those of other citizens. Democratic governments are designed for the benefit of the people who live in the state now, not for the benefit of the people who lived there thirty or forty years ago. There are many ways to ensure that the views and desires of the citizens of rural Georgia are heard, but giving them more legislative influence than their population fairly warrants is a kind of electoral dead-hand control: it allows a minority to maintain political power more commensurate with the numbers it used to have than with the numbers it has today.

Simply stated, a state legislative reapportionment plan that systematically and intentionally creates population deviations among districts in order to favor one geographic region of a state over another violates the one person, one vote principle firmly rooted in the Equal Protection Clause. A state cannot dilute or debase the vote of certain citizens based merely on the fortuity of where in the state they reside any more than it can dilute citizens' votes based upon their race, gender, or economic status. While states may employ minor population deviations in redistricting in order to pursue legitimate state interests, such as drawing compact and contiguous districts or preserving the boundaries of the state's political subdivisions, enhancing the political power of large swaths of geography is not such an interest. Thus, in this instance, if the southern and inner-city Atlanta areas of the State of Georgia are in need of some political protection in order to ensure that their economic and other interests are recognized on a statewide basis, that need must be met in some way that does not dilute or debase the fundamental right to vote of citizens living in other parts of the state. In short, the deliberate regional favoritism built into the Georgia House and Senate Plans created more than a taint of arbitrariness and discrimination, violating Equal Protection by diluting the votes of citizens of the suburban and exurban parts of northern Georgia and overweighting the votes of citizens in rural Georgia and inner-city Atlanta.

3. Incumbency Protection

On this record, the creation of population deviations to protect incumbents in the Georgia House and Senate also does not qualify as a legitimate state policy. The incumbency protection in the plans was not consistently applied and went far beyond anything the Supreme Court has ever allowed. Although the plans' drafters were concerned about incumbent protection, insofar as they sought to create "safe districts" for those Democratic incumbents who supported the plans, they plainly did not apply this interest in a manner that is even remotely consistent with the principles set forth in *Reynolds*, *Karcher*, and their progeny.

First, the policy of protecting incumbents was not applied in a consistent and neutral way. On the contrary, it was applied in a blatantly partisan and discriminatory manner, taking pains to protect only Democratic incumbents. The vast majority of districts with negative population deviations were held by Democratic incumbents, while the majority of overpopulated districts were held by Republican incumbents. Moreover, both the House and Senate Plans actually pitted numerous Republican incumbents against one another, while generally protecting their Democratic colleagues.

Far from consistently protecting incumbents, the plans destroyed the reelection hopes of dozens of incumbents. The House Plan created contests between a total of forty-seven incumbents, almost all Republicans. Because six of the affected twenty-one districts were multi-member districts, the end result was that a maximum of twenty-eight of the paired incumbents could be re-elected, while at least nineteen incumbents would be unseated. Likewise, the Senate Plan had six incumbent contests, all involving Republican incumbents facing either other Republican incumbents or, in two instances, Democratic incumbents. These results occurred despite the fact that Republican-leaning areas of the state had a higher rate of population growth, which would suggest that Democrat-Democrat pairings should have been more common than Republican-Republican pairings.

Moreover, many of the districts that created contests between Republican incumbents were not only oddly shaped but also vastly overpopulated. Almost all of these districts bordered at least one underpopulated district, meaning that the deviations could have been avoided if the drafters had simply transferred some of the population from those districts into neighboring districts. Senate District 17, to take one example, had a population deviation of +4.97%, and yet it bordered District 10, which was at –4.96%, and District 43, which was at –4.79%. House District 85, with a deviation of +4.30%, bordered District 59, which was at –4.24%, District 60, at –4.66%, and District 92, at –4.60%. This was the very embodiment of a state policy applied in a discriminatory and arbitrary manner.

A second reason why the protection of incumbents cannot justify the deviations in the state legislative plans is that the protection was overexpansive. The Supreme Court has said only that an interest in avoiding contests between incumbents may justify deviations from exact population equality, not that general protection of incumbents may also justify deviations.

In general, the lower courts have similarly listed only the prevention of contests between incumbents, rather than some broader notion of incumbency protection, as a legitimate state goal supporting population deviations.

In this case, it is clear that many of the incumbent-protecting population deviations were caused not by the legitimate state interest in avoiding contests between incumbents, but, rather by the more aggressive goal of allowing incumbents to avoid taking on more new constituents than was absolutely necessary to stay within 5% of the ideal district size. The defendant has not attempted to present any evidence that any of the population deviations were truly necessary to avoid pairing two incumbents. In short, in this case, the interest of incumbent protection was not applied in a reasonably consistent and nondiscriminatory way and cannot be used to justify the population deviations.

4. Traditional Redistricting Principles

Moreover, there is no evidence that the population deviations in the plans were driven by the neutral and consistent application of any traditional redistricting principles.

The *Reynolds* Court held that states may deviate from population equality in state legislative reapportionment plans for the purpose of constructing districts that are compact and contiguous or that respect the boundaries of the state's various political subdivisions. Moreover, in the congressional one person, one vote context, the Supreme Court has said that certain legislative policies, such as making districts compact, respecting municipal boundaries, preserving the cores of prior districts, and avoiding contests between incumbents, may justify population deviations, so long as these policies are nondiscriminatory and consistently applied. *Karcher.*

The plaintiffs argue that none of these considerations can account for the 9.98% population deviations in either the House Plan or the 2002 Senate Plan, and the defendant does not contradict this assertion. Indeed, the defendant has not attempted to justify the population deviations because of compactness, contiguity, respecting the boundaries of political subdivisions, or preserving the cores of prior districts. And the record evidence squarely forecloses the idea that any of these legitimate reasons could account for the deviations.

First, in considering the interest in compactness, there is not even the slightest suggestion that the population deviations in the House Plan or the 2002 Senate Plan resulted from an attempt to create compact districts. [O]ne can easily discern that just by looking at the maps themselves—in particular at districts such as House Districts 13, 47, 87, 127, and 137, and Senate Districts 16, 17, 24, 28, and 51. Moreover, a more sophisticated analysis of district compactness, calculated by the perimeter-to-area measure or the smallest circle measure, also establishes that compactness was not a factor here. Indeed, quite a few of the districts have shapes that defy Euclidean geometry. The drafters of the House and Senate Plans made no effort to keep districts compact and certainly did not create deviations for the purpose of improving compactness. Finally, we observe that many of the most bizarrely shaped districts are also the ones with the largest population deviations. Clearly, the population deviations in the House and Senate Plans were not caused by a desire to keep districts compact.

Likewise, there is no indication in this record that a regard for contiguity caused the population deviations in the plans. Numerous districts in the House and Senate were kept contiguous only by having them cross bodies of water or by having touch point contiguity. Many of these marginally contiguous districts also had significant population deviations. Notably, the defendant has not attempted to justify the deviations on this basis either. Accordingly, we conclude that the population deviations in the House Plan and the 2002 Senate Plan did not result from an interest in contiguity.

Nor are the population deviations in the plans the result of any attempt to respect the boundaries of the state's various political subdivisions. [N]othing in the testimonial or circumstantial record indicates that the population deviations in the plans were driven by an effort to keep counties (or other political entities) together. The House Plan split 80 of the state's 159 counties, and the 2002 Senate Plan split 81. Both numbers were significantly higher than they had been in the previous redistricting. Therefore, we readily conclude that population deviations in the House Plan and the 2002 Senate Plan did not result from an interest in respecting the boundaries of the state's various political subdivisions.

The population deviations in the state legislative plans were also not motivated by a desire to preserve the cores of all prior districts. To the extent that the cores of prior districts were preserved at all, it was done in a thoroughly disparate and partisan manner, heavily favoring Democratic incumbents while creating new districts for Republican incumbents whose constituency was composed of only a small fraction of their old voters. This was the exact opposite of what one would expect from the rates of population increase in the state, because the populations in Republican-leaning areas have grown at a significantly faster pace than those of Democratic-leaning districts, meaning that Republicans would, in a neutral plan, have to take on fewer new constituents. Moreover, this was not among the factors specifically mentioned in the guidelines for redistricting adopted by the House and Senate reapportionment committees, and it was not offered by the defendant as a justification for the population deviations. Quite simply, the population deviations in the House Plan and the 2002 Senate Plan did not result from a neutral, consistently applied concern for retaining incumbent cores.

Finally, it is unnecessary in this case to decide whether partisan advantage alone would have been enough to justify minor population deviations, although the Supreme Court has never sanctioned partisan advantage as a legitimate justification for population deviations. It is true that the Supreme Court has acknowledged the "reality . . . that districting inevitably has and is intended to have substantial political consequences." *Gaffney*. Moreover, the Supreme Court has recognized that "the goal of fair and effective representation [is not] furthered by making the standards of reapportionment so difficult to satisfy that the reapportionment task is recurringly removed from legislative hands and performed by federal courts." *Id.* (recognizing that minor deviations are insufficient to make out prima facie claim). And it is clear that, according to the strict standard set by *Davis v. Bandemer*, the plaintiffs could not establish a claim of unconstitutional partisan gerrymandering.

However, the Supreme Court's recognition of the politics inherent in districting arose in the context of political gerrymandering. Today, we have no occasion to consider the limits of partisan gerrymandering, but rather the very different set of considerations invoked by a claim that the one person, one vote principle has been violated. The value at issue today is an individualized and personal one, and therefore the offense to Equal Protection that occurred in this case is more readily apparent than in a claim involving gerrymandering. The Supreme Court has recognized the difference by placing greater restrictions on deviations from one person, one vote than on gerrymandering.

We need not resolve the issue of whether or when partisan advantage alone may justify deviations in population, because here the redistricting plans are plainly unlawful. In the state legislative plans at issue in this case, partisan interests are bound up inextricably with the interests of regionalism and incumbent protection. It is simply not possible to draw out and isolate the political goals in these plans from the plainly unlawful objective of regional protection or from the inconsistently applied objective of incumbent protection.

Ultimately, "[t]he showing required to justify population deviations is flexible, depending on the size of the deviations, the importance of the State's interests, the consistency with which the plan as a whole reflects those interests, and the availability of alternatives that might substantially vindicate those interests yet approximate population equality more closely." *Karcher*. In no way do the Georgia plans make such a showing. First, while a 9.98% total deviation is not presumptively unconstitutional, the plans' drafters pushed the deviation as close to the 10% line as they thought they could get away with, conceding the absence of an "honest and good faith effort" to construct equal districts. The 9.98% total deviations are most assuredly not the result of only a small number of outliers; in fact, dozens of districts come close to the 5% line, and the average deviation is well above 3% in both the House and the Senate. Second, each population deviation requires at least some plausible and consistently applied state interest to justify it; yet not one of the legitimate state interests listed by the *Karcher* Court applies in this case, and the defendant's two proffered justifications are plainly impermissible. Third, the record shows not only that the creators of the plans had the technical capability to create maps with substantially smaller population deviations than the plans that were eventually passed but also that the legislators were actually presented with a number of proposed maps with smaller deviations and systematically rejected them. It is readily apparent that alternative plans could have been easily constructed that did not stretch the limits of the one person, one vote principle so far, all the while achieving the state's legitimate interests.

In short, the plaintiffs have shown that the state legislative reapportionment plans enacted by the Georgia Legislature do not represent an "effort to construct districts . . . as nearly of equal population as is practicable." They have also shown that the 9.98% population deviations in those plans are not supported by any legitimate, consistently-applied state interests but, rather, resulted from the arbitrary and discriminatory objective of increasing the political power of southern Georgia and inner-city Atlanta at the expense of voters living in other parts of the state, and from the systematic favoring of Democratic incumbents and the corresponding attempts to eliminate as many Republican incumbents as possible. This represents far more than a "taint of arbitrariness or discrimination." *Roman v. Sincock*.

We therefore conclude that the House Plan and the 2002 Senate Plan violate the Equal Protection Clause by failing to represent "an honest and good faith effort to construct districts . . . as nearly of equal population as is practicable" and by failing to contain only those "divergences from a strict population standard [that] are based on legitimate considerations incident to the effectuation of a rational state policy." *Reynolds*.

NOTES ON *LARIOS*

1. First consider the case from the perspective of the one person, one vote doctrine. *Brown v. Thomson* seems to provide state legislatures with a "safe harbor" from a one person, one vote challenge when the overall relative deviation of state

legislative districts is less than 10 percent. Does the *Larios* court correctly interpret the Supreme Court precedent?

2. Second, consider the case from the perspective of politics as a justification for redistricting choices. The *Larios* case essentially says that political considerations cannot justify Georgia's failure to have lower population deviations in its House and Senate districts. Yet the plurality in *Vieth* says the excessive use of politics does not state a claim upon which relief can be granted. Moreover, a majority of the Supreme Court in *Easley v. Cromartie* accepted politics as the predominant explanation for redistricting choices. (In *Easley*, preservation of incumbent politicians served as a nonracial justification for the composition of North Carolina's congressional District 12.) Is *Larios* distinctive in some way from these cases? If so, how?
3. Toward the end of the opinion, the *Larios* court notes that the harm in a violation of the one person, one vote principle is an "individualized and personal one." What is the individual harm being addressed by the *Larios* court? Perhaps, though, despite the court's statement to the contrary, *Larios* is addressing a group harm. If so, what is the group harm? Perhaps the group harm is to suburbanites, but that might be viewed as saying the group harm is to Republicans. And if the group harm is to Republicans then why isn't this just a decision prohibiting a certain type of partisan gerrymandering?
4. Next, consider the case from the perspective of the search for judicially manageable standards with regard to partisan gerrymandering claims. Because *Larios* involved a constitutional challenge to a statewide redistricting, the district court decision was rendered by a three-judge panel. 28 U.S.C. § 2284. In addition, cases involving constitutional challenges to statewide redistrict plans are allowed a direct appeal to the U.S. Supreme Court. 28 U.S.C. § 1253. In deciding that appeal, the Supreme Court generally does one of the following: (1) notes "probable jurisdiction" and hears the case with a full argument (a process akin to the Supreme Court granting *certiorari* on a case); or (2) summarily affirms the district court decision. In *Larios*, the Supreme Court summarily affirmed.
5. Justices John Paul Stevens and Stephen Breyer wrote a brief concurrence to the Court's summary affirmance of *Larios*. In that concurrence, they argued that the district court's decision in *Larios* demonstrated how "an impermissible partisan gerrymander is visible to the judicial eye and subject to judicially manageable standards." *Cox v. Larios*, 542 U.S. 947, 950 (2004). In addition, they argued that the district court's factual findings in *Larios* "make clear that appellees could satisfy either the standard endorsed by the Court in its racial gerrymandering cases or that advocated in Justice Powell's dissent in *Bandemer*." *Id.*

Larios demonstrates that the federal courts may be indirectly addressing partisan gerrymandering through other doctrines such as one person, one vote. The fact remains, though, that as a result of *Vieth v. Jubelirer*, the federal courts are not in the business of directly addressing claims of partisan gerrymandering.

Up to this point, we have been addressing only the role of the federal constitution in relation to partisan gerrymandering. But there is another possible avenue for the judiciary to constrain partisan gerrymandering. Indeed, one might more accurately say that there are 50 possible avenues for the judiciary to address partisan gerrymandering—each state has its own constitution and judicial branch.

The lack of intervention in this arena by the federal courts using the federal constitution may create opportunities for state courts to intervene using state constitutions. This could occur through interpretations of existing state constitutional provisions or, as the next case demonstrates, through amendments to state constitutions that compel state judiciaries to police partisan gerrymandering.

IN RE SENATE JOINT RESOLUTION OF LEGISLATIVE APPORTIONMENT 1176.

Supreme Court of Florida, 83 So. 3d 597 (2012)

PARIENTE, J.

With the goal of reforming this state's legislative apportionment process, in 2010, the Florida voters approved an amendment to the Florida Constitution establishing stringent new standards for the once-in-a-decade apportionment of legislative districts. After the Legislature draws the apportionment plans, this Court is required by the Florida Constitution to review those plans to ensure their compliance with the constitution.

For the reasons set forth in this opinion, we declare the plan apportioning districts for the Florida House of Representatives to be constitutionally valid under the Florida Constitution. We declare the plan apportioning the districts for the Florida Senate to be constitutionally invalid under the Florida Constitution. The Legislature is now tasked by the Florida Constitution with adopting a new joint resolution of apportionment.

I. INTRODUCTION

Before 2010, this Court held that Florida's constitutional requirements guiding the Legislature during the apportionment process were "not more stringent than the requirements under the United States Constitution."

On November 2, 2010, the voters approved Amendment 5 (Fair Districts Amendment) for inclusion in the Florida Constitution, greatly expanding the standards that govern legislative apportionment.

With the advent of the Fair Districts Amendment, the Florida Constitution now imposes more stringent requirements as to apportionment than the United States

Constitution and prior versions of the state constitution. The new standards enumerated in article III, section 21, are set forth in two tiers, each of which contains three requirements.

On February 9, 2012, the Legislature passed Senate Joint Resolution 1176 (Joint Resolution), apportioning this state into 120 House districts and 40 Senate districts.

II. HISTORICAL EVOLUTION OF ARTICLE III OF THE FLORIDA CONSTITUTION

[Omitted]

III. ANALYSIS

A. Standard and Scope of Review

The new [state constitutional] requirements dramatically alter the landscape with respect to redistricting by prohibiting practices that have been acceptable in the past, such as crafting a plan or district with the intent to favor a political party or an incumbent. By virtue of these additional constitutional requirements, the parameters of the Legislature's responsibilities under the Florida Constitution, and therefore this Court's scope of review, have plainly increased, requiring a commensurately more expanded judicial analysis of legislative compliance.

Because legislative reapportionment is primarily a matter for legislative consideration and determination, this Court will defer to the Legislature's decision to draw a district in a certain way, so long as that decision does not violate the constitutional requirements. With an understanding that the Court's responsibility is limited to ensuring compliance with constitutional requirements, and endeavoring to be respectful to the critically important role of the Legislature, the Court has previously acknowledged that its duty is not to select the best plan, but rather to decide whether the one adopted by the legislature is valid.

B. The Standards Governing Our Analysis

The new standards enumerated in article III, section 21, are set forth in two tiers, each of which contains three requirements. The first tier, contained in section 21(a), lists the following requirements: (1) no apportionment plan or district shall be drawn with the intent to favor or disfavor a political party or an incumbent; (2) districts shall not be drawn with the intent or result of denying or abridging the equal opportunity of racial or language minorities to participate in the political process or to diminish their ability to elect representatives of their choice; and (3) districts shall consist of contiguous territory. The second tier, located in section 21(b), enumerates three additional requirements in drawing district lines, the compliance with which is subordinate to those listed in the first tier of section 21 and to federal law in the event of conflict: (1) districts shall be as nearly equal in population as is practicable; (2) districts shall be compact; and (3) where feasible, districts shall utilize existing political and geographical boundaries. The order in which the constitution lists the standards in tiers one and two is "not [to] be read to establish any priority of one standard over the other within that [tier]." Art. III, § 21(c), Fla. Const.

We interpret the specific constitutional directive that tier two is subordinate to tier one in the event of conflict to mean that the Legislature's obligation is to draw legislative districts that comport with all of the requirements enumerated in Florida's constitution. However, should a conflict in application arise, the Legislature is obligated to adhere to the requirements of section 21(a) (tier one) and then comply with the considerations in section 21(b) (tier two).

1. Tier-One Standards

a. Intent to Favor or Disfavor a Political Party or an Incumbent

The first of the new requirements in our state constitution is the provision in article III, section 21(a), providing that "[n]o apportionment plan or district shall be drawn with the intent to favor or disfavor a political party or an incumbent."

This new requirement in Florida prohibits what has previously been an acceptable practice, such as favoring incumbents and the political party in power.

"The term political gerrymander has been defined as [t]he practice of dividing a geographical area into electoral districts, often of highly irregular shape, to give one political party an unfair advantage by diluting the opposition's voting strength." *Vieth v. Jubelirer*. While some states have sought to minimize the political nature of the apportionment process by establishing independent redistricting commissions to redraw legislative districts, Florida voters have instead chosen to place restrictions on the Legislature by constitutional mandate.

The Florida Constitution now expressly prohibits what the United States Supreme Court has in the past termed a proper, and inevitable, consideration in the apportionment process. *See, e.g., Vieth.*

Florida's express constitutional standard, however, differs from equal protection political gerrymandering claims under either the United States or Florida Constitutions. Political gerrymandering claims under the Equal Protection Clause of the United States Constitution focus on determining when partisan districting as a permissible exercise "has gone too far," *Vieth*, so as to "degrade a voter's or a group of voters' influence on the political process as a whole." *Bandemer.*

In contrast to the federal equal protection standard applied to political gerrymandering, the Florida Constitution prohibits drawing a plan or district with the intent to favor or disfavor a political party or incumbent; there is no acceptable level of improper intent. It does not reference the word "invidious" as the term has been used by the United States Supreme Court in equal protection discrimination cases, *see, e.g., Brown v. Thomson*, and

Florida's provision should not be read to require a showing of malevolent or evil purpose. Moreover, by its express terms, Florida's constitutional provision prohibits intent, not effect, and applies to both the apportionment plan as a whole and to each district individually.

We recognize that any redrawing of lines, regardless of intent, will inevitably have an effect on the political composition of a district and likely whether a political party or incumbent is advantaged or disadvantaged. In short, redistricting will inherently have political consequences, regardless of the intent used in drawing the lines. Thus, the focus of the analysis must be on both direct and circumstantial evidence of intent. *Vill. of Arlington Heights v. Metro. Housing Dev. Corp.* (1977).

This Court has before it objective evidence that can be reviewed in order to perform a facial review of whether the apportionment plans as drawn had the impermissible intent of favoring an incumbent or a political party. While we agree that the standard does not prohibit political effect, the effects of the plan, the shape of district lines, and the demographics of an area are all factors that serve as objective indicators of intent. One piece of evidence in isolation may not indicate intent, but a review of all of the evidence together may lead this Court to the conclusion that the plan was drawn for a prohibited purpose.

With respect to intent to favor or disfavor an incumbent, the inquiry focuses on whether the plan or district was drawn with this purpose in mind.

At the outset, objective indicators of intent to favor or disfavor a political party can be discerned from the Legislature's level of compliance with our own constitution's tier-two requirements, which set forth traditional redistricting principles. A disregard for these principles can serve as indicia of improper intent.

The tier-two requirements of article III, section 21(b), are meant to restrict the Legislature's discretion in drawing irregularly shaped districts; strict compliance with their express terms may serve to undercut or defeat any assertion of improper intent. *Cf. Miller* (stating that in racial gerrymandering context where race-neutral considerations are the basis for redistricting, and are not subordinated to race, a State can "defeat a claim that a district has been gerrymandered on racial lines"). However, where the shape of a district in relation to the demographics is so highly irregular and without justification that it cannot be rationally understood as anything other than an effort to favor or disfavor a political party, improper intent may be inferred.

In making this assessment, we evaluate the shapes of districts together with undisputed objective data, such as the relevant voter registration and elections data, incumbents' addresses, and demographics, as well as any proffered undisputed direct evidence of intent.

Similar to the partisan inquiry, the inquiry for intent to favor or disfavor an incumbent focuses on the shape of the district in relation to the incumbent's legal residence, as well as other objective evidence of intent. Objective indicators of intent may include such factors as the maneuvering of district lines in order to avoid pitting incumbents against one another in new districts or the drawing of a new district so as to retain a large percentage of the incumbent's former district. When analyzing whether the challengers have established an unconstitutional intent to favor an incumbent, we must ensure that this Court does not disregard obvious conclusions from the undisputed facts.

The Court emphasizes that mere access to political data cannot presumptively demonstrate prohibited intent because such data is a necessary component of evaluating whether a minority group has the ability to elect representatives of choice—a required inquiry when determining whether the plan diminishes a protected group's ability to elect a candidate of choice. Likewise, the fact that the Senate or House, or their staff, may or may not have had the incumbents' addresses is not determinative of intent or lack of intent. And, as discussed in the challenges section below, the fact that there were more registered Democrats than registered Republicans in this state, but that there are more Republican-performing districts than Democratic-performing districts in both the newly drawn Senate and House plans, does not permit a conclusion of unlawful intent in this case. Rather, when the Court analyzes the tier-two standards and determines that specific districts violate those standards without any other permissible justification, impermissible intent may be inferred.

C. Challenges to the Apportionment Plans

1. General Challenges

We next proceed to examine the Coalition's [of interest groups] and the FDP's [Florida Democratic Party] arguments that they claim demonstrate improper intent on the part of the Legislature in drawing the apportionment plans.

a. Partisan Imbalance as Demonstrative of Intent

At the time the apportionment plans were drawn in 2012, of the 120 seats in the House, 39 were held by Democrats and 81 by Republicans, and of the 40 seats in the Senate, 12 were held by Democrats and 28 by Republicans. The position of Governor was held by a Republican. The Coalition and the FDP essentially allege that with the Republicans in charge of drawing the apportionment plans, the plans were drawn with the intent to favor the Republican Party.

One of the primary challenges brought by the Coalition and the FDP is that a statistical analysis of the plans reveals a severe partisan imbalance that violates the constitutional prohibition against favoring an incumbent or a political party. The FDP asserts that statistics show an overwhelming partisan bias based on voter registration and election results. Under the circumstances presented to this Court, we are unable to reach the conclusion that improper intent has been shown based on voter registration and election results.

We first address voter registration and acknowledge the reality that based on the 2010 general election data, of the voters in the state who registered with an affiliation with one of the two major parties, 53% were registered as Democrats and 47% were registered as Republicans. The challengers point out that in contrast to the statewide statistics showing that registered Democrats outnumber Republicans, the Senate and House plans contain more districts in which registered Republicans outnumber registered Democrats than vice versa. As of 2010, in the Senate plan there were 18 of 40 Senate districts (45.0%) in which registered Democrats outnumbered registered Republicans, and 22 Senate districts (55.0%) in which registered Republicans outnumbered registered Democrats. In the House plan, there were 59 of 120 House districts in which the registered Democrats outnumber registered Republicans (49.2%), and 61 districts in which registered Republicans outnumber registered Democrats (50.8%).

While Democrats outnumber Republicans statewide in voter registration, this fact does not lead to the conclusions asserted by the challengers that these statistics demonstrate that the plans were drawn with intent to favor Republicans. Although there are more registered Democrats than Republicans, as of 2010, there were over 2.5 million voters who are not registered as Democrats or Republicans. Further, voter registration is not necessarily determinative of actual election results. The actual election results show that the existence of more registered Democrats than registered Republicans statewide has not necessarily translated into Democratic Party victories in statewide elections. To illustrate, Florida last elected a Democratic governor, Lawton Chiles, in 1994.

In further support of their argument that the apportionment plan shows partisan imbalance reflective of impermissible intent to favor a political party, the challengers rely on actual statewide election results. In the 2010 gubernatorial election, Governor Rick Scott, a Republican, received 48.7% of the overall vote and Alex Sink, a Democrat, 47.6% of the overall vote. Of the major-party-affiliated voters, Scott received 50.6% of the vote, and Sink 49.4%. However, under the Senate plan, Governor Scott would have won in 26 Senate districts (65.0%), and Sink in 14 Senate districts (35.0%). Similarly, under the House plan, Scott would have won in 73 House districts (60.8%), and Sink in 47 House districts (39.2%).

In the 2008 presidential election, President Barack Obama, a Democrat, received 50.9% of the overall state vote and Senator John McCain, a Republican, received 48.1% of the overall state vote. Of the major-party-affiliated voters, 51.4% voted for Obama and 48.6% for McCain. Yet in the Senate plan, Obama would have won in 16 Senate districts (40.0%), while McCain would have won in 24 Senate districts (60.0%). Likewise, in the House plan, Obama would have won in 53 House districts (44.2%), while McCain would have won in 67 House districts (55.8%).

We do not agree that the partisan imbalance in the Senate and House plans demonstrates an overall intent to favor Republicans in this case. Explanations other than intent to favor or disfavor a political party could account for this imbalance. First, it has been observed that Democrats tend to cluster in cities, which may result in a natural "packing" effect, regardless of where the lines are drawn. Second, the imbalance could be a result of a legitimate effort to comply with VRA principles or other constitutional requirements. Although the FDP summarily argues that the partisan imbalance cannot be a result of such attempts, it fails to explain why.

We reject any suggestion that the Legislature is required to compensate for a natural packing effect of urban Democrats in order to create a "fair" plan. We also reject the suggestion that once the political results of the plan are known, the Legislature must alter the plan to bring it more in balance with the composition of voters statewide. The Florida Constitution does not require the affirmative creation of a fair plan, but rather a neutral one in which no improper intent was involved.

Although we have rejected the challenge that statewide voter registration and election results demonstrate an overall intent to favor the Republican party, we evaluate these statistics when examining individual districts.

2. The House Plan

a. Overall Challenges

Tier-One Requirements

Intent to favor or disfavor a political party or an incumbent. The first requirement that we address in looking at the overall plan is this important constitutional requirement, the purpose of which is to prevent the drawing of districts designed to protect a political party or an incumbent. We see no overall objective indicia of improper intent with respect to the House plan. It is undisputed that the House plan pits both Democratic and Republican incumbents against each other. While we recognize that the new districts on average retain 59.7% of the population of their predecessor districts, this fact standing alone does not demonstrate intent to favor incumbents.

Finally, as discussed below, the House plan has complied with the tier-two standards, making improper intent less likely. Indeed, the purpose of the tier-two standards—equal population, compactness, and utilizing political and geographical boundaries—is to prohibit political favoritism by constraining legislative discretion.

Tier-Two Requirements

Equal population. In looking at this constitutional requirement, the 2010 census data shows that Florida has a total population of 18,801,310, and the ideal population for each House district is 156,678 individuals. The most populated district in the House plan is District 75, which has a population of 159,978 (an additional 3,300 individuals than the ideal, or a deviation of 2.11%), and the least populated district is District 76, which has a population of 153,745 (2,933 fewer individuals than the ideal, or a deviation of –1.87%). Thus, the total deviation is 3.97%. This is 1.18% higher than the 2.79% population deviation the Court approved in [the previous plan].

The House aptly acknowledges that "[c]onsiderations of compactness and emphasis on county integrity, of course, had to be weighed against other considerations, including population equality." For example, the House explains that it set a population deviation upper limit that would allow Charlotte County, whose population deviated only slightly from the ideal, to remain whole.

Compactness. A visual inspection of the plan reveals that it as a whole appears to be compact and that only a few districts are highly irregular. A visual inspection of the plan reveals that there are districts that are clearly less compact than other districts, with visually unusual shapes. These include Districts 70, 88, and 117. We note that Districts 70, 88, and 117 are majority-minority or minority-opportunity districts, and they are discussed more thoroughly below in conjunction with challenges to individual districts.

Political and geographical boundaries. The House explains that in considering the appropriate balance of equal population, compactness, and adherence to existing boundaries, it emphasized county integrity while adhering to other tier-two standards. As explained in the House's brief: "Where practicable, it sought to keep counties whole within districts, or to wholly locate districts within counties, depending on county populations. Where not feasible, the House sought to 'anchor' districts within a county—tying the geography representing a majority or plurality of the district's residents to one county." The House also considered municipal boundaries and geographical features, but decided that "county lines were usually preferable to other boundaries." The underlying reason for this approach as expressed in the House's brief was that

> [c]ounty boundaries are substantially less likely to change than municipal boundaries, and—unlike municipalities—all counties are contiguous. Moreover, although all Floridians have a home county, millions live outside any incorporated area. Additionally, by using a strategy of keeping counties whole, the House Map necessarily keeps many municipalities whole within districts. And importantly, numerous Floridians advocated an emphasis on county boundaries at the twenty-six public meetings during the summer of 2011.

A review of the House plan reveals that it consistently used county boundaries where feasible, leaving thirty-seven of sixty-seven counties whole.

The House further explained that "[w]here county lines could not serve as the district line, the House relied on municipal boundaries and geographic boundaries such as railways, interstates, state roads, and rivers." As previously discussed, we have adopted the House's view of geographical boundaries as those that are easily ascertainable and commonly understood (e.g., rivers, railways, interstates, and state roads).

Conclusion as to Overall Challenges to the House Plan

A review of the House plan and the record reveals that the House engaged in a consistent and reasoned approach, balancing the tier-two standards by endeavoring to make districts compact and as nearly equal in population as possible, and utilizing political and geographical boundaries where feasible by endeavoring to keep counties and cities together where possible. Although the House plan has a higher population deviation than in the past, the House has explained that this deviation was necessary to achieve other required objectives, such as consistent use of county boundaries. The House further asserts that its "consistent respect for county boundaries provided the additional benefit of creating compact districts."

A facial review of the House plan reveals no objective plan-wide indicia of improper attempt to favor or disfavor a political party or incumbent.

b. Challenges to Individual House Districts

We discuss the challenges to the individual House districts in turn. We conclude that the challengers have not demonstrated that any of these districts violate the Florida Constitution.

House District 38

The FDP summarily alleges that District 38 retains a high percentage of the population from its predecessor district in order to benefit the incumbent in that district. However, the FDP does not point to any additional indicators of improper intent, and we deny this claim.

House District 88

The FDP contends that District 88, located near the east coast of Palm Beach County, was drawn to benefit the Republican Party under the guise of preserving that district as a black majority-minority district. To prove this point, the FDP claims that new District 88 is the least compact of all the House districts, asserting that non-compact districts are often a sign of partisan gerrymanders. The Coalition, on the other hand, does not challenge this district.

District 88 is an odd-shaped, long, and thin district with jagged edges.

District 88 is a black majority-minority district, with a black VAP of 51.8%. The predecessor to District 88, old District 84 in the benchmark plan, was also a black majority-minority district, with a black VAP of 53.5%. This district was drawn differently in 2002, oriented westward and inland from West Palm Beach rather than southward.

The Legislature formed this district with the stated intent to preserve minority voting opportunities. The Legislature explained that its intent was

> to establish State House District 88, which is consistent with Section 2 of the federal Voting Rights Act; does not deny or abridge the equal opportunity of racial or language minorities to participate in the political process or diminish their ability to elect representatives of their choice; is more compact than the comparable district in the benchmark plan; is nearly equal in population as practicable . . . .

The House Staff Analysis further explains that "Palm Beach County has produced a majority-minority Black district in years past and this district recreates that opportunity. However, this district does it in a different manner than the current district."

The tier-two requirement of compactness must yield if it conflicts with the requirement to adhere to Florida's minority voting protection provision. Here, the record reflects that the House considered this interplay. When questioned about whether this district violated the compactness requirement, the record shows the House determined that the configuration of District 88 was more compact than the configuration of its predecessor district and more compact than two potential alternatives. Further, the House conducted an analysis of the voting behavior of minority districts. The FDP does not assert or demonstrate that the district can be drawn more compactly while also adhering to Florida's minority voting protection provision. Accordingly, this claim fails.

House District 99

The Coalition alleges that the Legislature drew District 99 with the intent to disfavor a black Democratic incumbent who currently represents District 93 under the 2002 House plan, a black majority-minority district with a black VAP of 50.9%. Old District 93 is now the equivalent of District 94, which remains a black majority-minority district (black VAP of 54.6%) under the 2012 House plan. The Coalition contends that the incumbent's residence was intentionally placed one block outside of his current district and instead placed in District 99, which neighbors new District 94 to the south, to pit him against another Democratic incumbent. Our review reveals that he has indeed now been drawn into District 99, a majority-white district (white VAP of 54.3% and Hispanic VAP of 29.1%).

However, this may be incidental to wide-sweeping changes made by the House in this region of the state. As compared to the 2002 plan, the 2012 House plan is much more compact with respect to District 94 and its neighboring districts.

The Coalition does not contend that the districts violate the standards of equal population, compactness, or utilizing political and geographical boundaries. We conclude that there are no objective indicia of intent to disfavor an incumbent on this record.

c. Conclusion as to the House Plan

We conclude that the Coalition and the FDP have not successfully demonstrated that the House plan violates one or more of the constitutional standards. In making this determination, we have reviewed the challenges to the House plan as a whole and the challenges to individual districts. [W]e conclude that the House plan is facially valid.

3. The Senate Plan

a. Overall Challenges

In reviewing the Senate plan, we begin by evaluating overall adherence to the constitutional requirements. Then we evaluate a claim that the Senate plan was renumbered for the purpose of favoring incumbents by allowing them to be eligible to serve for longer than they would have otherwise. Finally, we consider the challenges to individual districts.

Tier-One Requirements

Intent to favor or disfavor a political party or an incumbent. In evaluating the Senate plan, we first address this important constitutional requirement, the purpose of which is to prevent the drawing of a plan or districts designed to protect a political party or an incumbent. We conclude that the Senate plan is rife with objective indicators of improper intent which, when considered in isolation do not amount to improper intent, but when viewed cumulatively demonstrate a clear pattern.

First, the Coalition alleges that the Senate plan does not pit incumbents against each other, and the Senate has not contested this. This Court was provided with the addresses of 21 incumbents and has confirmed that of the addresses provided, none of the incumbents would run against another incumbent.

Second, the new districts on average are composed of 64.2% of their predecessor districts. While this percentage is just an average, our below analysis of the individual district challenges reveals that at least some incumbents appear to have been given large percentages of their prior constituencies. These percentages are of even greater concern given that the 2002 Senate plan was drawn at a time when intent to favor a political party or an incumbent was permissible and there were no requirements of compactness or utilizing existing boundaries.

Third, as discussed further below, the Senate admittedly renumbered the Senate plan in order to allow incumbents to be eligible to serve longer than they would have otherwise. Not only do we conclude that this renumbering was improper as it was intended to favor incumbents, but we note that the renumbering process indicates that the Senate specifically considered incumbent information when renumbering the districts.

Fourth, although we do not consider the partisan balance of the plan as evidence of intent, the FDP alleges that the 2012 Senate plan has two fewer Democratic districts than the 2002 plan based on voter registration. However, because voter registration alone is not an accurate measure of how districts perform, we do not consider this as conclusive evidence of improper intent.

Fifth, the majority (70.0%) of under-populated districts are Republican-performing districts when the 2010 gubernatorial and 2008 presidential elections are considered. Thus, it appears that under the Senate plan, individuals residing in Republican-performing districts are over-represented as compared to individuals living in Democratic-performing districts.

Tier-Two Requirements

Equal population. In looking at this constitutional requirement, the 2010 census data shows that Florida has a total population of 18,801,310, and the ideal population for each Senate district is 470,033 individuals. The most populated district in the Senate plan is District 3, which has a population of 474,685 (an additional 4,652 individuals, or a deviation of 0.99%), and the least populated district is District 23, which has a population of 465,343 (4,690 fewer individuals or a deviation of −1.00%). Thus, the total deviation is 1.99%. As to Florida's standard, we must view the population deviation in conjunction with the other tier-two standards.

Compactness. The Senate contends that the Court should find that the Senate plan is facially compact because the plan is now more compact than the 2002 plan. We reject this comparison as evidence of compliance because the 2002 Senate plan had no requirement for compactness and thus cannot serve as an adequate benchmark in establishing adherence to the newly added compactness requirement.

A visual inspection of the plan reveals a number of districts that are clearly less compact than other districts, with visually bizarre and unusual shapes. These districts include Districts 1, 3, 6, 9, 10, 12, 14, 19, 27, 29, 30, and 34.

Political and geographical boundaries. Unlike the House, the Senate did not use any consistent definition of political and geographical boundaries. Some districts adhere to county boundaries (e.g., District 5), while others freely split counties and follow a variety of roads and waterways, including minor residential roads and creeks (e.g., District 1). In some districts, the Senate constantly switched between different types of boundaries within the span of a few miles.

Conclusion as to Overall Challenges to the Senate Plan

We recognize that the Senate did not have the benefit of our opinion when drawing its plan. However, it is clear from a facial review of the Senate plan that the "pick and choose" method for existing boundaries was not balanced with the remaining tier-two requirements, and certainly not in a consistent manner. We again note that while the existing boundaries requirement is stated as "where feasible" and the equal population requirement is stated in terms of "as is practicable," the compactness requirement does not contain those modifiers; rather, the constitutional expression is that "districts shall be compact."

b. Numbering Scheme

We first address the numbering of the Senate plan. Here, the issue we must address is whether the Senate districts were renumbered with the intent to favor incumbents, in violation of [the Florida Constitution].

Specifically, the Coalition contends that by renumbering the apportionment plan so that incumbents eligible for reelection in 2012 would receive a chance to serve for a maximum of ten years, rather than eight, the Senate plan violates the prohibition on favoring incumbents.

Unquestionably, the numbering of a Senate district, whether given an odd or even number, directly affects the length of time a senator may serve.

The Senate's plan plainly favors certain incumbents by renumbering districts to allow them to serve longer than they would otherwise be eligible to serve. Because we conclude that the plan was drawn with the intent to favor incumbents, in violation of article III, section 21(a), we declare the renumbering in the apportionment plan to be invalid.

c. Challenges to the Senate Districts

We now turn to an examination of the challenges raised as to specific Senate districts.

Central Florida: Senate Districts 10 and 12

The Coalition asserts that District 10 was drawn to favor an incumbent, and the FDP contends that District 12 uses Florida's minority voting protection provision as a pretext for partisan favoritism. While the challenges are based on different grounds, we consider these claims in tandem because the Senate justifies the boundaries of District 10 based in part on its assertion that it was required to draw District 12 in the manner that it did in order to ensure minority voting protection. Thus, we start with District 10, then review District 12, and conclude that District 10, as drawn, violates the constitution.

The Coalition asserts that District 10 violates article III, section 21, because this district was gerrymandered into a bizarre shape in order to include a particular incumbent's residence and provide him with a safe Republican seat. The Coalition further asserts that the district barely misses another incumbent's residence that is located on the border between District 10 and District 13, preventing two incumbent Republicans from running against each other.

A visual examination of the challenged districts is set forth below:

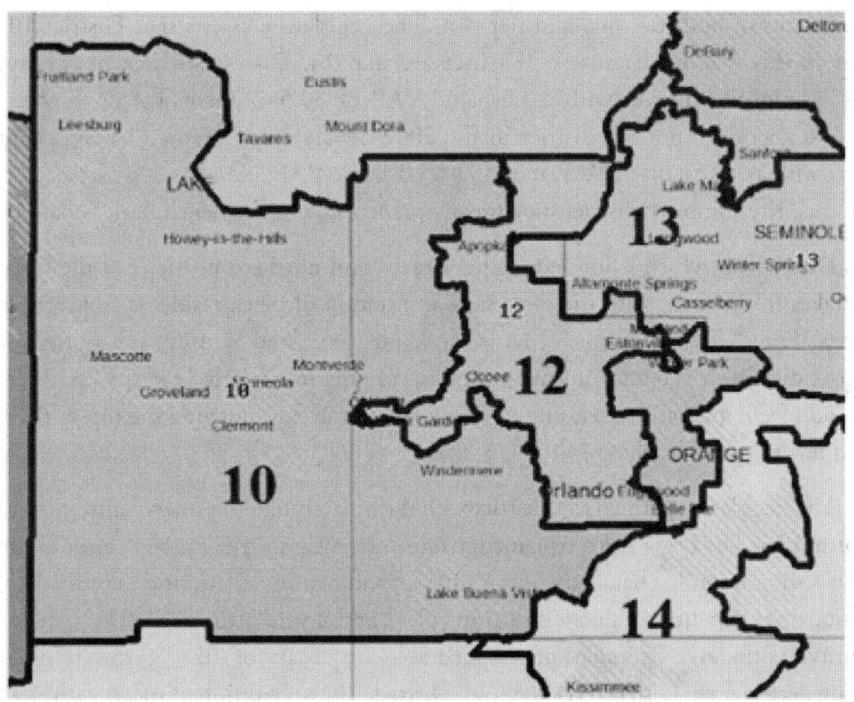

As shown in the above map, District 10 is located mostly on the west side of Orlando, and this portion of the district is fairly compact, following county lines on its west and south sides, continuing until it reaches District 12 on the eastern side, and District 14, which is a Hispanic majority-minority district, on the southeastern side. At that point, District 10 squeezes in between Districts 12 and 14 through a small stretch of land less than half of a mile wide in order to create an odd-shaped appendage that reaches out toward District 13. The appendage is approximately 12 miles long at its longest portion and 8.5 miles wide at its widest, with the majority of the portion being between two and five miles in width. Based on undisputed information provided to this Court in conjunction with this review, an incumbent lives in the appendage. The district line between Districts 10 and 13 stops just short of another Republican incumbent's residence.

Although the [statistical] compactness measures for District 10 reflect that the district is, overall, relatively compact District 10 is visually non-compact as a result of the bizarrely shaped appendage.

The dividing line between the District 10 appendage and surrounding Districts 12, 13, and 14 does not consistently follow any particular political or geographical boundary, sometimes following parts of the city boundaries for Belle Isle, Winter Park, and Edgewood, but other times constantly shifting from major roads to minor roads to railroad tracks. In looking to the population deviation, we note that District 10 is one of the most populated districts with 3,995 people above the ideal population.

Of course, tier-two standards must yield if the Legislature cannot comply with the requirements of both tier one and tier two. The Legislature asserts that District 10 was drawn in this manner because of Districts 12 and 14. District 14 is a new Hispanic majority-minority district with a Hispanic VAP of 50.5%; there was no predecessor Hispanic majority-minority district in the 2002 Senate plan. District 12 is a coalition district with a 40.0% black VAP and 20.9% Hispanic VAP. Notably, District 12 is not a black majority-minority district, nor was its predecessor in the benchmark Senate plan.

District 12, which is located in the western and northern portions of the Orlando area, takes in the areas with the highest concentration of black residents from Orlando, Ocoee, Winter Garden, Apopka, Maitland, Winter Park, and Sanford. It is not a visually compact district. It extends into two counties, running in a relatively narrow path on the west end of Orlando and extending upwards and to the east, hugging the top of the area, with a few portions reaching out.

The Legislature formed this district with the stated intent to preserve minority voting opportunities. The Legislature explained that its intent was to "tie[ ] urban communities of similar socioeconomic characteristics in Orange and Seminole Counties, consistent with traditional, race-neutral redistricting principles" and create a district with "a majority-minority voting-age population, comparable to that of the existing district." The predecessor to District 12 was old District 19, a coalition district with a black

VAP of 33.1% and a Hispanic VAP of 35.5%. District 12 retained 49.0% of its predecessor district.

Although the Legislature contends that District 10 was drawn because of concerns of not diluting minority voting strength in surrounding districts or causing unlawful retrogression, the Senate never performed the analysis necessary to ensure that the reasoning was constitutionally valid.

Based on the objective data before this Court, we conclude that District 10 violates constitutional mandates because it is visually non-compact with an appendage that reaches out to clearly encompass an incumbent, and this bizarre shape cannot be justified based on concerns pertaining to ensuring minority voting strength. District 10 is constitutionally invalid.

Southwest Florida: Senate District 30

The FDP argues that District 30 was drawn with the intent to favor an incumbent in violation of the Florida Constitution. As evidence, the FDP points to the fact that District 30 contains a high percentage of its former constituency, is non-compact, and fails to utilize political and geographical boundaries. After examining all the constitutional requirements, we conclude that the district as drawn violates the Florida constitutional standards that districts "shall be compact" and utilize political and

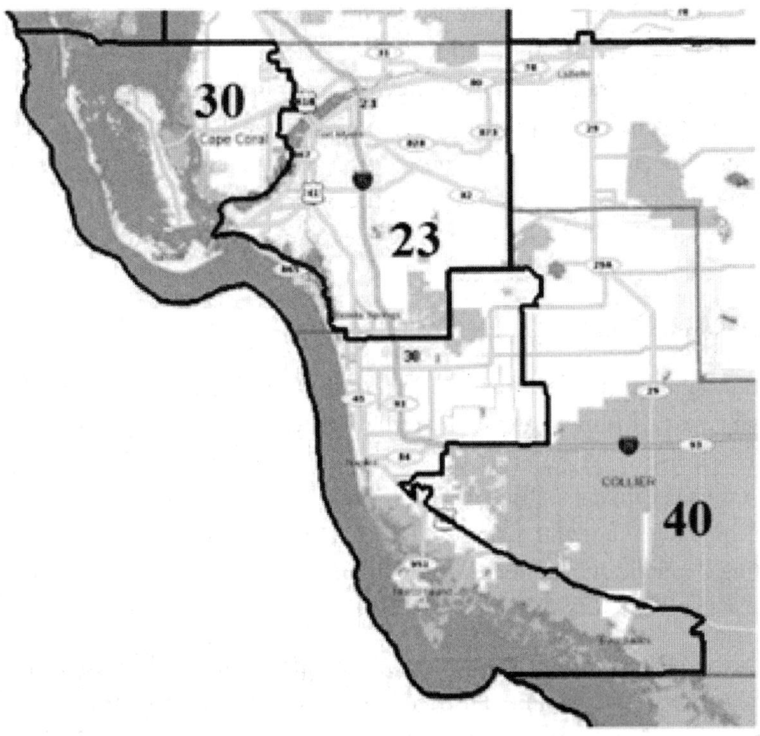

geographical boundaries where feasible. Further, the failure to comply with the tier-two standards, in the absence of any constitutionally valid justification, objectively indicates intent to favor an incumbent.

District 30 is located in Collier and Lee Counties. The map of District 30, best shows its odd-shaped configuration, which resembles an upside-down alligator.

District 30 is a white-majority district (white VAP of 78.4%). District 30 retains 84.9% of its constituency from old District 37 and a shape nearly identical to its predecessor district. It is non-compact.

[I]n addition to being non-compact, District 30 splits counties, municipalities, and geographical features.

In passing the joint resolution, the Legislature stated its intent with respect to this district was to "tie[ ] coastal communities in Lee and Collier Counties."

With the exception of the boundary it shares with District 40, District 30 does not need to be configured to avoid diminishing minority voting strength, and thus the Legislature is required to draw District 30 to be "as nearly equal in population as is practicable," to be "compact," and to "where feasible, utilize existing political and geographical boundaries." Art. III, § 21(b), Fla. Const.

The aforementioned stated legislative intent demonstrates that in creating District 30, the Legislature intended to tie coastal communities together. However, as we have discussed in analyzing the constitutional phrase "compactness" and our discussion of Districts 1 and 3, maintaining communities of interest is not required by the constitution, and comporting with such a principle must not come at the expense of complying with constitutional imperatives. We also consider it significant that District 30 maintained a large percentage of the same constituency as the predecessor district. On this record, there is no valid constitutional justification for the Legislature's decision to draw District 30 in this manner. District 30 is constitutionally invalid.

Southeast Florida: Senate Districts 29 and 34

The FDP and the Coalition contend that Districts 34 and 29 are not compact. Additionally, the Coalition argues that the Senate included as many Democrats as possible into [District 34] in order to dilute their votes elsewhere. The Coalition asserts that this evidences intent to favor an incumbent and a political party. Specifically, the Coalition contends that the decision to draw District 34 this way was a ploy to keep the neighboring Republican incumbent seat safe in District 29 by using minority protection as a pretext for partisan favoritism.

District 34 is a narrow district stretching approximately fifty miles in Broward County. At its narrowest point, District 34 is less than a mere tenth of a mile wide. Following a jagged path south, District 34 slices through cities and neighborhoods, often gathering up residents on one side of a residential street but not the other.

District 29, which is adjacent to District 34, is a long and narrow coastal district. These districts are depicted in the map below.

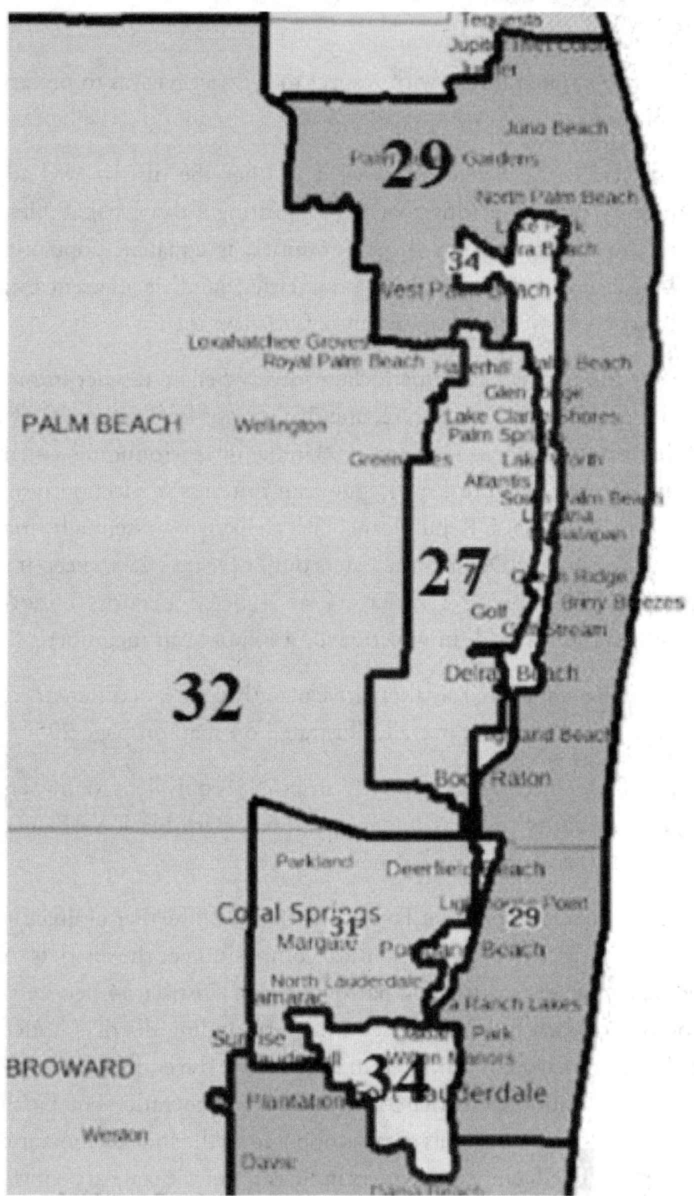

Districts 34 and 29 are clearly not compact. In addition, these districts do not adhere to a consistent boundary as they travel through counties and cities.

Unquestionably, minority protection was an important factor in considering how to draw District 34 because it is a black majority-minority district with a black VAP of 55.8%.

The incumbent for [District 29] is a Republican. It is a white-majority district, having a white VAP of 79.4%.

The Legislature's stated intent with respect to District 34 was to preserve minority voting opportunities.

As to District 29, the Senate acknowledged that the district was adjacent to a minority-opportunity district, stating that it was creating a district that "ties the coastal communities of Broward and Palm Beach Counties; is equal in population to other districts; follows political and geographical boundaries; [and] is adjacent to a minority-opportunity district to its west and the Atlantic Ocean to the east."

We consider the partisan favoritism claim. Every Senate district immediately surrounding District 34 (Districts 27, 31, 32, and 36), except for District 29, is a majority-white district that would perform Democratic. Unlike the surrounding districts, District 29 would remain competitive, but lean Republican in terms of election results, and the incumbent in this district is a Republican. The challengers essentially maintain that District 34 was drawn to take Democratic voters out of District 29 to keep it competitive under the guise of maintaining District 34 as a black majority-minority district. The current configuration would, in effect, favor a Republican incumbent.

The Coalition has submitted an alternative plan that shows a different configuration for this area that is more compact overall, illustrated on map on page 225.

For a point of reference, the Coalition District 29 is equivalent to the Senate District 34 (black majority-minority districts under both plans with black VAPs of 55.7% and 55.8%, respectively). (See map at top of next page.)

In order to evaluate the partisan favoritism claim, we further evaluate the effect of this more compact configuration on the political composition of the districts. As a result of the black Democratic voters in the long narrow strip of District 34 between West Palm Beach and Pompano Beach being dispersed into surrounding districts under the Coalition's plan, rather than being concentrated in District 34, the equivalent to District 29 in the Coalition plan—Coalition District 31—becomes Democratic. The Coalition's plan creates five Democratic districts in this area, as opposed to the four Democratic districts in the 2012 Senate plan. The Democratic voters in this area of the state are concentrated and the area is largely Democratic; the Coalition's plan does not appear to purposefully draw Democratic districts but rather to draw logical, compact districts in a neutral manner.

We conclude that the Senate's decision to draw this region in a less compact manner is indicative of intent to favor an incumbent and a political party by keeping District 29 essentially the same as its predecessor district. Further, in drawing this area of the state, the Senate violated the compactness requirement.

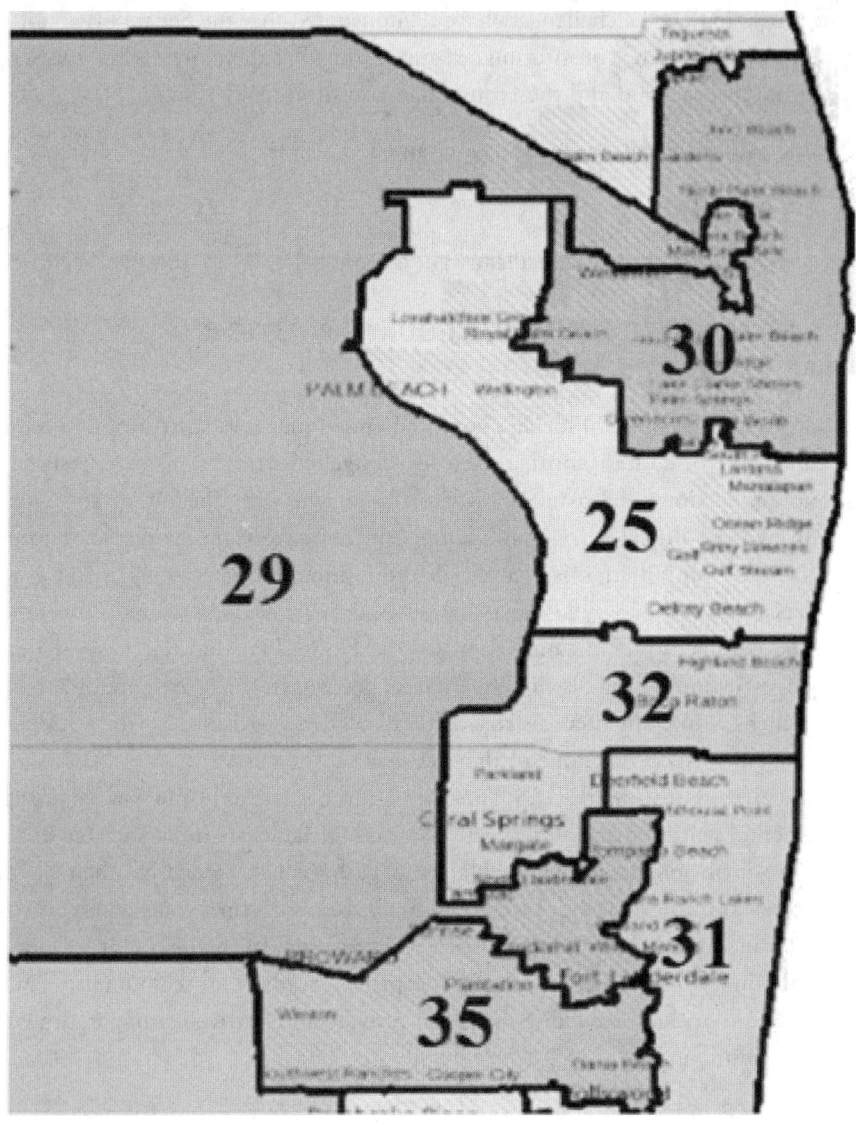

e. Conclusion as to the Senate Plan

We hold that the Senate plan is invalid. [W]e conclude that the Senate plan is rife with objective indicators of improper intent.

IV. CONCLUSION

The Fair Districts Amendment changed the constitutional framework for apportionment, introducing significant reforms in the drawing of legislative districts. Before the passage of the Fair Districts Amendment in 2010, there is no question that the House and Senate plans would have passed constitutional muster and both would have been validated by this Court.

We conclude that the challengers have demonstrated that the Senate plan, but not the House plan, violates the constitutional requirements. We therefore declare the Senate plan constitutionally invalid and the House plan constitutionally valid.

No motion for rehearing shall be entertained. This case is final.

It is so ordered.

LEWIS, QUINCE, LABARGA, and PERRY, JJ., concur.

NOTES ON FLORIDA SUPREME COURT'S POLITICAL GERRYMANDERING CASE

1. As you read, in 2010 Florida's voters amended the state constitution to require that the Florida state courts review legislative redistricting plans to ensure that no "apportionment plan or district [is] drawn with the intent to favor or disfavor a political party or an incumbent." After reading the Florida Supreme Court's opinion in this matter, do you think Florida voters made a wise decision?
2. The Florida Supreme Court approves the House Plan and rejects several challenges to individual districts but rejects the Senate Plan and upholds several challenges to individual districts. Are all of these decisions correct? Are some of them correct? Are none of them correct?
3. As you read in *Vieth*, the U.S. Supreme Court has taken the position, at least as a practical matter, that political gerrymandering claims are nonjusticiable because there is no judicially manageable standard by which to analyze them. (Wait, however, until you read *LULAC v. Perry*, below, before you make your own final judgment about where Justice Kennedy stands on this point.) Does the opinion from Florida's Supreme Court provide support for that nonjusticiability position, or does the Florida opinion provide an effective counterargument to that position?

G. Bringing It All Together

You have separately seen and considered the primary constitutional doctrines and statutory provisions that govern redistricting. It should come as no surprise, however, that modern redistricting cases often involve arguments not just about one of these issues but several of them. To assess your understanding of these doctrines, consider the following problem that is based on the next case you will read—*League of United Latin American Citizens v. Perry*.

A REDISTRICTING PROBLEM

The State of Texas was awarded 30 congressional seats in the apportionment following the 1990 Census. At the time, the Democratic Party controlled all the branches in the legislature and more than two-thirds of Texas's congressional seats. Yet Democrats could see Republicans gaining strength within Texas. For this reason, Democrats used their existing political power to manipulate Texas's congressional districts into what some commentators called the "shrewdest political gerrymander of the 1990s." As a result, Democrats continued to win almost 60 percent of the seats despite garnering only a little more than 40 percent of the statewide vote.

By 2000, though, when Texas was awarded two additional congressional seats (making for a total of 32 seats) through reapportionment, the winds of political change had begun to blow. Republicans had captured a majority of the State Senate. They had also secured the governor's mansion. Yet Democrats still held the State House.

The partisan split in the state legislature led to stalemate when it came to post–2000 congressional redistricting. No redistricting plan emerged from the Texas legislature. Thus, it was left to the federal courts to devise a plan that provided for equal population amongst the districts. In late 2001, the federal court drew a plan that complied with one person, one vote but also essentially left the prior Democratic gerrymander in place. As a result, Democrats in 2002 were still able to capture about 55 percent of the congressional seats despite only capturing about 40 percent of the statewide vote.

In 2003, though, Republicans captured control of all the branches of the Texas state government—the House, the Senate, and the governor's mansion. With their newly gained omnipotent political strength, Republicans decided to redraw Texas's congressional districts. For months, Democrats tried to block passage of the Republican congressional redistricting plan. Ultimately, though, the Republican plan passed in November 2003.

In redrawing the congressional districts, it was clear that the intent of the Republican plan was to increase the number of Republicans elected to Congress from Texas. According to the Lieutenant Governor, a highly regarded Republican member of the State Senate, "Political gain for the Republicans was 110% of the motivation for the Plan—it was the entire motivation." However, some minor changes in lines were made during the redistricting process to accommodate requests from Democrats. The goal of Republicans, however, was to capture 21 of the 32 congressional seats with approximately 58 percent of the statewide vote.

The Republican plan had some very notable features. In relation to the populations of the various districts, the plan used total population data from the 2000 Census. The 2000 Census showed Texas with a total population of 20,851,820. The Republican plan created twenty (20) congressional districts with a total population of 651,619 each, and twelve (12) congressional districts with a population of 651,620 each. In addition, the Republican plan also made major changes in South and West Texas and in the Dallas County area, which are described below.

THE REPUBLICAN PLAN IN SOUTH AND WEST TEXAS

Under the plan that had been adopted by the federal court, there were six congressional districts in South and West Texas. Five of those districts provided Latino voters (who according to the 2000 Census data made up 58 percent of the citizen voting-age population in the South and West Texas region) with an ability to elect their candidate of choice. The sixth district, District 23, had a Latino citizen voting-age majority but elected a Republican who was not the choice of Latino voters.

In contrast, under the Republican plan, South and West Texas had seven congressional districts. Four of those districts clearly provided Latino voters with the ability to elect candidates of choice. Some interesting things were done, however, with the three remaining districts: Districts 23, 25, and 15.

After the 2002 election, it became apparent that District 23 as it existed in the federal court-drawn plan had an increasingly powerful Latino population that threatened to oust the Republican incumbent. Before the 2003 redistricting, the Latino share of the citizen voting-age population in District 23 was 57.5 percent, and the Republican incumbent's support among Latinos had dropped with each successive election since 1996. In 2002, the Republican incumbent captured only 8 percent of the Latino vote, and a mere 51.5 percent of the overall vote. Indeed, District 23's Latino voters were poised to elect their candidate of choice. They were becoming more politically active, with a marked and continuous rise in Latino voter registration. Webb County in particular, with a 94 percent Latino population, spurred the Republican incumbent's near defeat with dramatically increased turnout in 2002.

Faced with this loss of voter support, the Republican plan acted to protect the incumbent by changing the lines—and hence the population mix—of District 23. As originally drawn, District 23 was 500 miles long and extended from the City of El Paso to the City of Laredo. The Republican plan changed District 23 by dividing Webb County and the City of Laredo, on the Mexican border, that formed the county's population base. Webb County, which was 94 percent Latino, had previously rested entirely within District 23; under the Republican plan, nearly 100,000 people were shifted into neighboring District 28. The rest of Webb County, approximately 93,000 people, remained in District 23. To replace the numbers District 23 lost, the state added voters in counties comprising a largely Anglo, Republican area in Central Texas. In the newly drawn District 23, the Latino share of the *citizen* voting-age population dropped to 46 percent, though the Latino share of the total voting-age population remained just over 50 percent.

These changes to shore up District 23 for the Republican incumbent required adjustments elsewhere, of course, so the state created a new district—District 25. District 25 was a long, narrow strip that winded its way from the City of McAllen and the Mexican-border towns in the south to the City of Austin, in the center of the state and 300 miles away. In between it included seven full counties, but 77 percent of its population resided in split counties at the northern and southern ends. Of this 77 percent, roughly half resided in

Hidalgo County, which includes McAllen, and half were in Travis County, which includes parts of Austin. The Latinos in District 25, who comprised 55 percent of the district's citizen voting-age population, were also mostly divided between the two distant areas, north and south. The Latino communities at the opposite ends of District 25 have divergent needs and interests, owing to differences in socioeconomic status, education, employment, health, and other characteristics. There is no doubt, however, that Latino voters will be able to elect a candidate of their choice in District 25.

District 15 was anchored in Hidalgo County. District 15 spanned over 300 miles to Central Texas. Under the plan adopted by the federal court, District 15 had a Latino citizen voting-age population of about 69 percent. However, turnout among Latinos at elections was typically much lower—somewhere in the neighborhood of 54 percent. Under the Republican plan, the Latino citizen voting-age population in District 15 dropped to about 58 percent. The Republican plan changed District 15 by removing some areas of Latino population that had a very high voter turnout and replacing them with some areas of Anglo population that had a very high voter turnout.

A few other facts about South and West Texas and the state as a whole are also helpful to know. First, voting in South and West Texas is racially polarized. Second, it would be possible to draw all seven districts in a way that would provide Latinos with citizen voting-age majorities in all seven districts. However, such a plan would have to take in disparate and distant communities. Third, on a statewide basis in Texas, Latinos made up 22 percent of the citizen voting-age population according to the 2000 Census. In addition, data indicates that as of 2004, Latinos make up 24.5 percent of the state's citizen voting-age population. Fourth, the congressional plan adopted by Republicans does not contain any districts outside of South and West Texas that provide Latino voters with the ability to elect a candidate of their choice.

QUESTIONS

1. Assume you are counsel for the State Democratic Party charged with developing legal theories in relation to a potential challenge to the Republican congressional plan. What constitutional and statutory challenges would you raise against Texas's plan? What arguments would you raise to support your position on the merits of these challenges? [As a hint, the problem raises potential issues in relation to every portion of redistricting law you have studied thus far.]
2. Assume you are counsel for the State Republican Party charged with answering any potential Democratic challenge. What arguments would you counter with in relation to the merits of those Democratic challenges?

The next case—*League of United Latin American Citizens v. Perry*—touches upon nearly every topic we have covered so far: one person, one vote; partisan and racial gerrymandering; the constitutional and Voting Rights Act Section 2 prohibitions on vote dilution; and Section 5 of the Voting Rights Act.

The case concerned the 2003 redistricting of Texas's congressional delegation, a plan that was widely reported to be the brain-child of Rep. Tom DeLay, who was then majority leader of the U.S. House of Representatives. After an extremely complicated set of multiple appeals, the case went directly to the U.S. Supreme Court from a three-judge district court decision that had upheld the plan in its entirety. The case involved essentially two different types of challenges to the plan. First, plaintiffs associated with the Texas Democratic Party brought a *statewide* challenge to the map on the ground that it was an unconstitutional partisan gerrymander. In making these arguments, though, plaintiffs also invoked principles related to one person, one vote. Second, two different groups of minority voters brought separate *district-specific* challenges to the new 2003 map on the ground that these districts violated Section 2 of the Voting Rights Act and were also unconstitutional racial gerrymanders. In analyzing this challenge, several of the opinions also discuss principles related to unconstitutional vote dilution and Section 5.

The Court was extremely fractured in its treatment of these claims, with Justice Kennedy holding the balance of power in the Court's different 5-4 rulings. Joined by Chief Justice Roberts and Justices Scalia, Thomas, and Alito, Justice Kennedy rejected the statewide partisan gerrymandering claim. Justice Kennedy, however, was joined by the four *Vieth* dissenters to reaffirm the justiciability of partisan gerrymandering claims. This latter five-member majority—Justice Kennedy joined by Justices Stevens, Souter, Ginsburg, and Breyer—sustained one of the district-specific claims under the Voting Rights Act, the challenge to District 23 brought by Latino voters. By a separate 5-3 vote—Kennedy again joined by Roberts, Scalia, Thomas, and Alito in the majority—the Court rejected the other district-specific claim under the Voting Rights Act, the challenge to District 24 brought by African-American voters. (Justice Breyer expressed no view regarding the validity of District 24.)

We take the case in two separate parts. The first part considers the partisan gerrymandering claim. The second part considers the claims involving race and redistricting.

LEAGUE OF UNITED LATIN AMERICAN CITIZENS v. PERRY

548 U.S. 399 (2006)

Justice KENNEDY announced the judgment of the Court and delivered the opinion of the Court with respect to Parts II-A and III, an opinion with respect to Parts I and IV, in which THE CHIEF JUSTICE and Justice ALITO join, an opinion with respect to Parts II-B and II-C, and an opinion with respect to Part II-D, in which Justice SOUTER and Justice GINSBURG join.

We affirm the District Court's disposition on the statewide political gerrymandering.

I

[Joined by Chief Justice ROBERTS and Justice ALITO]

To set out a proper framework for the case, we first recount the history of the litigation and recent districting in Texas. An appropriate starting point is not the reapportionment in 2000 but the one from the census in 1990.

The 1990 census resulted in a 30-seat congressional delegation for Texas, an increase of 3 seats over the 27 representatives allotted to the State in the decade before. In 1991 the Texas Legislature drew new district lines. At the time, the Democratic Party controlled both houses in the state legislature, the governorship, and 19 of the State's 27 seats in Congress. Yet change appeared to be on the horizon. In the previous 30 years the Democratic Party's post-Reconstruction dominance over the Republican Party had eroded, and by 1990 the Republicans received 47% of the statewide vote, while the Democrats received 51%.

Faced with a Republican opposition that could be moving toward majority status, the state legislature drew a congressional redistricting plan designed to favor Democratic candidates.

Voters who considered this unfair and unlawful treatment sought to invalidate the 1991 plan as an unconstitutional partisan gerrymander, but to no avail. The 1991 plan realized the hopes of Democrats and the fears of Republicans with respect to the composition of the Texas congressional delegation. The 1990's were years of continued growth for the Texas Republican Party, and by the end of the decade it was sweeping elections for statewide office. Nevertheless, despite carrying 59% of the vote in statewide elections in 2000, the Republicans only won 13 congressional seats to the Democrats' 17.

These events likely were not forgotten by either party when it came time to draw congressional districts in conformance with the 2000 census and to incorporate two additional seats for the Texas delegation. The Republican Party controlled the governorship and the State Senate; it did not yet control the State House of Representatives, however. As so constituted, the legislature was unable to pass a redistricting scheme, resulting in litigation and the necessity of a court-ordered plan to comply with the Constitution's one-person, one-vote requirement. The congressional districting map resulting from the litigation is known as Plan 1151C.

Under Plan 1151C, the 2002 congressional elections resulted in a 17-to-15 Democratic majority in the Texas delegation, compared to a 59% to 40% Republican majority in votes for statewide office in 2000.

The continuing influence of a court-drawn map that perpetuated much of [the 1991] gerrymander, was not lost on Texas Republicans when, in 2003, they gained control of the State House of Representatives and, thus, both houses of the legislature. The Republicans in the legislature set out to increase their representation in the congressional delegation. After a protracted partisan struggle, during which Democratic legislators left the State for a time to frustrate quorum requirements, the legislature enacted a new congressional districting map in October 2003. It is called Plan 1374C. The 2004 congressional elections did not disappoint the plan's drafters. Republicans won 21 seats to the Democrats' 11, while also obtaining 58% of the vote in statewide races against the Democrats' 41%.

Soon after Texas enacted Plan 1374C, appellants challenged it in court. The District Court entered judgment against appellants on all their claims.

II

A

[Majority opinion of Court, joined by Justice STEVENS, SOUTER, GINSBURG, and BREYER]

Based on two similar theories that address the mid-decade character of the 2003 redistricting, appellants now argue that Plan 1374C should be invalidated as an unconstitutional partisan gerrymander. In *Davis v. Bandemer*, the Court held that an equal protection challenge to a political gerrymander presents a justiciable case or controversy, but there was disagreement over what substantive standard to apply. That disagreement persists. A plurality of the Court in *Vieth v. Jubelirer* would have held such challenges to be nonjusticiable political questions, but a majority declined to do so. We do not revisit the justiciability holding but do proceed to examine whether appellants' claims offer the Court a manageable, reliable measure of fairness for determining whether a partisan gerrymander violates the Constitution.

B

[Joined by no other Justice]

Before addressing appellants' arguments on mid-decade redistricting, it is appropriate to note some basic principles on the roles the States, Congress, and the courts play in determining how congressional districts are to be drawn. Article I of the Constitution provides:

> "Section 2. The House of Representatives shall be composed of Members chosen every second Year by the People of the several States. . . .
>
> "Section 4. The Times, Places and Manner of holding Elections for . . . Representatives, shall be prescribed in each State by the Legislature thereof; but the Congress may at any time by Law make or alter such Regulations. . . . "

This text, we have explained, "leaves with the States primary responsibility for apportionment of their federal congressional . . . districts." *Growe v. Emison*. Congress, as the text of the Constitution also provides, may set further requirements, and with respect to districting it has generally required single-member districts. With respect to a mid-decade redistricting to change districts drawn earlier in conformance with a decennial census, the Constitution and Congress state no explicit prohibition.

Although the legislative branch plays the primary role in congressional redistricting, our precedents recognize an important role for the courts when a districting plan violates the Constitution. This litigation is an example, as we have discussed. When Texas did not enact a plan to comply with the one-person, one-vote requirement under the 2000 census, the District Court found it necessary to draw a redistricting map on its own. That the federal courts sometimes are required to order legislative redistricting, however, does not shift the primary locus of responsibility.

> "Legislative bodies should not leave their reapportionment tasks to the federal courts; but when those with legislative responsibilities do not respond, or the imminence of a state election makes it impractical for them to do so, it becomes the unwelcome obligation of the federal court to devise and impose a reapportionment plan pending later legislative action." *Wise v. Lipscomb.*

Quite apart from the risk of acting without a legislature's expertise, and quite apart from the difficulties a court faces in drawing a map that is fair and rational, the obligation placed upon the Federal Judiciary is unwelcome because drawing lines for congressional districts is one of the most significant acts a State can perform to ensure citizen participation in republican self-governance. That Congress is the federal body explicitly given constitutional power over elections is also a noteworthy statement of preference for the democratic process. As the Constitution vests redistricting responsibilities foremost in the legislatures of the States and in Congress, a lawful, legislatively enacted plan should be preferable to one drawn by the courts.

It should follow, too, that if a legislature acts to replace a court-drawn plan with one of its own design, no presumption of impropriety should attach to the legislative decision to act.

C

[Joined by no other Justice]

Appellants claim that Plan 1374C, enacted by the Texas Legislature in 2003, is an unconstitutional political gerrymander. A decision, they claim, to effect mid-decennial redistricting, when solely motivated by partisan objectives, violates equal protection and the First Amendment because it serves no legitimate public purpose and burdens one group because of its political opinions and affiliation. The mid-decennial nature of the redistricting, appellants say, reveals the legislature's sole motivation. Unlike *Vieth,* where the legislature acted in the context of a required decennial redistricting, the Texas Legislature voluntarily replaced a plan that itself was designed to comply with new census data. Because Texas had no constitutional obligation to act at all in 2003, it is hardly surprising, according to appellants, that the District Court found "[t]here is little question but that the single-minded purpose of the Texas Legislature in enacting Plan 1374C was to gain partisan advantage" for the Republican majority over the Democratic minority.

A rule, or perhaps a presumption, of invalidity when a mid-decade redistricting plan is adopted solely for partisan motivations is a salutary one, in appellants' view, for then courts need not inquire about, nor parties prove, the discriminatory effects of partisan gerrymandering—a matter that has proved elusive since *Bandemer*. Adding to the test's simplicity is that it does not quibble with the drawing of individual district lines but challenges the decision to redistrict at all.

For a number of reasons, appellants' case for adopting their test is not convincing. To begin with, the state appellees dispute the assertion that partisan gain was the "sole" motivation for the decision to replace Plan 1151C. There is some merit to that criticism, for the pejorative label overlooks indications that partisan motives did not dictate the plan in its entirety. The legislature does seem to have decided to redistrict with the sole purpose of achieving a Republican congressional majority, but partisan aims did not guide every line it drew. As the District Court found, the contours of some contested district lines were drawn based on more mundane and local interests. The state appellees also contend, and appellants do not contest, that a number of line-drawing requests by Democratic state legislators were honored.

Evaluating the legality of acts arising out of mixed motives can be complex, and affixing a single label to those acts can be hazardous, even when the actor is an individual performing a discrete act. When the actor is a legislature and the act is a composite of manifold choices, the task can be even more daunting. Appellants' attempt to separate the legislature's sole motive for discarding Plan 1151C from the complex of choices it made while drawing the lines of Plan 1374C seeks to avoid that difficulty. We are skeptical, however, of a claim that seeks to invalidate a statute based on a legislature's unlawful motive but does so without reference to the content of the legislation enacted.

Even setting this skepticism aside, a successful claim attempting to identify unconstitutional acts of partisan gerrymandering must do what appellants' sole-motivation theory explicitly disavows: show a burden, as measured by a reliable standard, on the complainants' representational rights. For this reason, a majority of the Court rejected a test proposed in *Vieth* that is markedly similar to the one appellants present today.

The sole-intent standard offered here is no more compelling when it is linked to the circumstance that Plan 1374C is mid-decennial legislation. The text and structure of the Constitution and our case law indicate there is nothing inherently suspect about a legislature's decision to replace mid-decade a court-ordered plan with one of its own. And even if there were, the fact of mid-decade redistricting alone is no sure indication of unlawful political gerrymanders. Under appellants' theory, a highly effective partisan gerrymander that coincided with decennial redistricting would receive less scrutiny than a bumbling, yet solely partisan, mid-decade redistricting. More concretely, the test would leave untouched the 1991 Texas redistricting, which entrenched a party on the verge of minority status, while striking down the 2003 redistricting plan, which resulted in the majority Republican

Party capturing a larger share of the seats. A test that treats these two similarly effective power plays in such different ways does not have the reliability appellants ascribe to it.

Furthermore, compared to the map challenged in *Vieth*, which led to a Republican majority in the congressional delegation despite a Democratic majority in the statewide vote, Plan 1374C can be seen as making the party balance more congruent to statewide party power. To be sure, there is no constitutional requirement of proportional representation, and equating a party's statewide share of the vote with its portion of the congressional delegation is a rough measure at best. Nevertheless, a congressional plan that more closely reflects the distribution of state party power seems a less likely vehicle for partisan discrimination than one that entrenches an electoral minority. By this measure, Plan 1374C can be seen as fairer than the plan that survived in *Vieth* and the two previous Texas plans—all three of which would pass the modified sole-intent test that Plan 1374C would fail.

A brief for one of the *amici* proposes a symmetry standard that would measure partisan bias by "compar[ing] how both parties would fare hypothetically if they each (in turn) had received a given percentage of the vote." Under that standard the measure of a map's bias is the extent to which a majority party would fare better than the minority party should their respective shares of the vote reverse. In our view *amici*'s proposed standard does not compensate for appellants' failure to provide a reliable measure of fairness. The existence or degree of asymmetry may in large part depend on conjecture about where possible vote-switchers will reside. Even assuming a court could choose reliably among different models of shifting voter preferences, we are wary of adopting a constitutional standard that invalidates a map based on unfair results that would occur in a hypothetical state of affairs. Presumably such a challenge could be litigated if and when the feared inequity arose. More fundamentally, the counterfactual plaintiff would face the same problem as the present, actual appellants: providing a standard for deciding how much partisan dominance is too much. Without altogether discounting its utility in redistricting planning and litigation, we conclude asymmetry alone is not a reliable measure of unconstitutional partisanship.

In the absence of any other workable test for judging partisan gerrymanders, one effect of appellants' focus on mid-decade redistricting could be to encourage partisan excess at the outset of the decade, when a legislature redistricts pursuant to its decennial constitutional duty and is then immune from the charge of sole-motivation. If mid-decade redistricting were barred or at least subject to close judicial oversight, opposition legislators would also have every incentive to prevent passage of a legislative plan and try their luck with a court that might give them a better deal than negotiation with their political rivals.

D

[Joined by Justices Souter and Ginsburg]

Appellants' second political gerrymandering theory is that mid-decade redistricting for exclusively partisan purposes violates the one-person, one-vote requirement. They observe that population variances in legislative districts are tolerated only if they "are unavoidable despite a good-faith effort to achieve absolute equality, or for which justification is shown." *Karcher v. Daggett.* Working from this unchallenged premise, appellants contend that, because the population of Texas has shifted since the 2000 census, the 2003 redistricting, which relied on that census, created unlawful interdistrict population variances.

To distinguish the variances in Plan 1374C from those of ordinary, 3-year-old districting plans or belatedly drawn court-ordered plans, appellants again rely on the voluntary, mid-decade nature of the redistricting and its partisan motivation. Appellants do not contend that a decennial redistricting plan would violate equal representation three or five years into the decade if the State's population had shifted substantially. As they must, they concede that States operate under the legal fiction that their plans are constitutionally apportioned throughout the decade, a presumption that is necessary to avoid constant redistricting, with accompanying costs and instability. Appellants agree that a plan implemented by a court in 2001 using 2000 population data also enjoys the benefit of the so-called legal fiction, presumably because belated court-drawn plans promote other important interests, such as ensuring a plan complies with the Constitution and voting rights legislation.

In appellants' view, however, this fiction should not provide a safe harbor for a legislature that enacts a voluntary, mid-decade plan overriding a legal court-drawn plan, thus "unnecessarily" creating population variance "when there was no legal compulsion" to do so. This is particularly so, appellants say, when a legislature acts because of an exclusively partisan motivation. Under appellants' theory this improper motive at the outset seems enough to condemn the map for violating the equal-population principle. For this reason, appellants believe that the State cannot justify under *Karcher v. Daggett* the population variances in Plan 1374C because they are the product of partisan bias and the desire to eliminate all competitive districts.

As the District Court noted, this is a test that turns not on whether a redistricting furthers equal-population principles but rather on the justification for redrawing a plan in the first place. In that respect appellants' approach merely restates the question whether it was permissible for the Texas Legislature to redraw the districting map. Appellants' answer, which mirrors their attack on mid-decennial redistricting solely motivated by partisan considerations, is unsatisfactory for reasons we have already discussed.

Appellants also contend that the legislature intentionally sought to manipulate population variances when it enacted Plan 1374C. There is, however, no District Court finding to that effect, and appellants present no specific evidence to support this serious allegation of bad faith. Because appellants have not demonstrated that the legislature's decision to enact Plan 1374C constitutes a violation of the equal-population requirement, we find unavailing their subsidiary reliance on *Larios v. Cox* (2004). In *Larios,* the District Court reviewed the Georgia Legislature's decennial redistricting of its State Senate and House of Representatives districts and found deviations from the equal-population requirement. The District Court then held the objectives of the drafters, which included partisan interests along with regionalist bias and inconsistent incumbent protection, did not justify those deviations. The *Larios* holding and its examination of the legislature's motivations were relevant only in response to an equal-population violation, something appellants have not established here. Even in addressing political motivation as a justification for an equal-population violation, moreover, *Larios* does not give clear guidance. The panel explained it "need not resolve the issue of whether or when partisan advantage alone may justify deviations in population" because the plans were "plainly unlawful" and any partisan motivations were "bound up inextricably" with other clearly rejected objectives.

In sum, we disagree with appellants' view that a legislature's decision to override a valid, court-drawn plan mid-decade is sufficiently suspect to give shape to a reliable standard for identifying unconstitutional political gerrymanders. We conclude that appellants have established no legally impermissible use of political classifications. For this reason, they state no claim on which relief may be granted for their statewide challenge.

Justice STEVENS, with whom Justice BREYER joins as to Parts I and II, concurring in part and dissenting in part.

This is a suit in which it is perfectly clear that judicially manageable standards enable us to decide the merits of a statewide challenge to a political gerrymander. Applying such standards, I shall explain why the wholly unnecessary replacement of the neutral plan fashioned by the three-judge court with Plan 1374C, which creates districts with less compact shapes, violates the Voting Rights Act, and fragments communities of interest—all for purely partisan purposes—violated the State's constitutional duty to govern impartially. Prior misconduct by the Texas Legislature neither excuses nor justifies that violation. Accordingly, I would hold that Plan 1374C is entirely invalid and direct the District Court to reinstate Plan 1151C.

I

[Omitted]

II

The unique question of law that is raised in this appeal is one that the Court has not previously addressed. That narrow question is whether it was unconstitutional for Texas to replace a lawful districting plan "in the middle of a decade, for the sole purpose of maximizing partisan advantage." This question is both different from, and simpler than, the principal question presented in *Vieth v. Jubelirer*, in which the "lack of judicially discoverable and manageable standards" prevented the plurality from deciding the merits of a statewide challenge to a political gerrymander.

As the State points out, "in every political-gerrymandering claim the Court has considered, the focus has been on the *map* itself, not on the decision to create the map in the first place." In defense of the map itself, rather than the basic decision whether to draw the map in the first place, the State notes that Plan 1374C's district borders frequently follow county lines and other neutral criteria. At what the State describes as the relevant "level of granularity," the State correctly points out that appellants have not even attempted to argue that every district line was motivated solely for partisan gain. Indeed, the multitude of "granular" decisions that are made during redistricting was part of why the *Vieth* plurality concluded, in the context of a statewide challenge to a redistricting plan promulgated in response to a legal obligation to redistrict, that there are no manageable standards to govern whether the predominant motivation underlying the entire redistricting map was partisan.

Unlike *Vieth,* the narrow question presented by the statewide challenge in this litigation is whether the State's decision to draw the map in the first place, when it was under no legal obligation to do so, was permissible. It is undeniable that identifying the motive for making that basic decision is a readily manageable judicial task. Indeed, although the Constitution places no *per se* ban on midcycle redistricting, a legislature's decision to redistrict in the middle of the census cycle, when the legislature is under no legal obligation to do so, makes the judicial task of identifying the legislature's motive simpler than it would otherwise be.

The conclusion that courts can easily identify the motive for redistricting when the legislature is under no legal obligation to act is reinforced by the record in this very case. Indeed, the State itself conceded that "[t]he overwhelming evidence demonstrated that partisan gain was the motivating force behind the decision to redistrict in 2003." In my judgment, there is not even a colorable basis for contending that the relevant intent—in this case a purely partisan intent[3]—cannot be identified on the basis of admissible evidence in the record.

Of course, the conclusions that courts are fully capable of analyzing the intent behind a decision to redistrict, and that desire for partisan gain was the sole factor motivating the decision to redistrict at issue here, do not resolve the question whether proof of a single-minded partisan intent is sufficient to establish a constitutional violation.

The requirements of the Federal Constitution that limit the State's power to rely exclusively on partisan preferences in drawing district lines are the Fourteenth Amendment's prohibition against invidious discrimination, and the First Amendment's protection of citizens from official retaliation based on their political affiliation. The equal protection component of the Fourteenth Amendment requires actions taken by the

3. The State suggests that in the process of drawing districts the architects of Plan 1374C frequently followed county lines, made an effort to keep certain entire communities within a given district and otherwise followed certain neutral principles. But these facts are not relevant to the narrow question presented by these cases: Neutral motivations in the implementation of particular features of the redistricting do not qualify the solely partisan motivation behind the basic decision to adopt an entirely unnecessary plan in the first place.

sovereign to be supported by some legitimate interest, and further establishes that a bare desire to harm a politically disfavored group is not a legitimate interest. Similarly, the freedom of political belief and association guaranteed by the First Amendment prevents the State, absent a compelling interest, from "penalizing citizens because of their participation in the electoral process, . . . their association with a political party, or their expression of political views." *Vieth* (Kennedy, J., concurring in judgment). These protections embodied in the First and Fourteenth Amendments reflect the fundamental duty of the sovereign to govern impartially.

The legislature's decision to redistrict at issue in this litigation was entirely inconsistent with these principles. By taking an action for the sole purpose of advantaging Republicans and disadvantaging Democrats, the State of Texas violated its constitutional obligation to govern impartially.

III

Relying solely on *Vieth*, Justice Kennedy maintains that even if legislation is enacted based solely on a desire to harm a politically unpopular minority, this fact is insufficient to establish unconstitutional partisan gerrymandering absent proof that the legislation did in fact burden "the complainants' representative rights." This conclusion—which clearly goes to the merits, rather than the manageability, of a partisan gerrymandering claim—is not only inconsistent with the constitutional requirement that state action must be supported by a legitimate interest, but also provides an insufficient response to appellants' claim on the merits.

Justice Kennedy argues that adopting "the modified sole-intent test" could "encourage partisan excess at the outset of the decade, when a legislature redistricts pursuant to its decennial constitutional duty and is then immune from the charge of sole-motivation." But this would be a problem of the Court's own making. As the decision in *Cox v. Larios* demonstrates, there are, in fact, readily manageable judicial standards that would allow injured parties to challenge excessive (and unconstitutional) partisan gerrymandering undertaken in response to the release of the decennial census data.[5] Justice Kennedy's concern about a heightened incentive to engage in such excessive partisan gerrymandering would be avoided if the Court were willing to enforce those standards.

In any event, Justice Kennedy's additional requirement that there be proof that the gerrymander did in fact burden the complainants' representative rights is clearly satisfied by the record in this litigation.

5. In *[Larios v.] Cox*, the three-judge District Court undertook a searching review of the entire record in concluding that the population deviations in the state legislative districts created for the Georgia House and Senate after the release of the 2000 census data were not driven by any traditional redistricting criteria, such as compactness or preserving county lines, but were instead driven by the impermissible factors of regional favoritism and the discriminatory protection of Democratic incumbents. If there were no judicially manageable standards to assess whether a State's adoption of a redistricting map was based on valid governmental objectives, we would not have summarily affirmed the decision in *Cox* over the dissent of only one Justice. [Justice Scalia dissented. —Eds.]

In arguing that Plan 1374C does not impose an unconstitutional burden on Democratic voters and candidates, the State takes the position that the plan has resulted in an equitable distribution of political power between the State's two principal political parties. The State emphasizes that in the 2004 elections—held pursuant to Plan 1374C—Republicans won 21 of 32, or 66%, of the congressional seats. That same year, Republicans carried 58% of the vote in statewide elections. Admittedly, these numbers do suggest that the State's congressional delegation was "roughly proportional" to the parties' share of the statewide vote, particularly in light of the fact that our electoral system tends to produce a "seat bonus" in which a party that wins a majority of the vote generally wins an even larger majority of the seats.

That Plan 1374C produced a "roughly proportional" congressional delegation in 2004 does not, however, answer the question whether the plan has a discriminatory effect against Democrats. As appellants point out, whether a districting map is biased against a political party depends upon the bias in the map itself—in other words, it depends upon the opportunities that the map offers each party, regardless of how candidates perform in a given year. And, as the State's expert found in this litigation, Plan 1374C clearly has a discriminatory effect in terms of the opportunities it offers the two principal political parties in Texas. Indeed, that discriminatory effect is severe.

According to the State's expert, Plan 1374C gives Republicans an advantage in 22 of 32 congressional seats. The plaintiffs' expert agreed. He added that, in his view, the only surprise from the 2004 elections was "how far things moved" toward achieving a 22-to-10 pro-Republican split "in a single election year." But this 22-to-10 advantage does not depend on Republicans winning the 58% share of the statewide vote that they received in 2004. Instead, Republicans would be likely to carry 22 of 32 congressional seats if they won only 52% of the statewide vote. Put differently, Plan 1374C ensures that, even if the Democratic Party succeeds in convincing 10% of the people who voted for Republicans in the last statewide elections to vote for Democratic congressional candidates,[8] which would constitute a major electoral shift, there is unlikely to be *any* change in the number of congressional seats that Democrats win. Moreover, Republicans would still have an overwhelming advantage if Democrats achieved full electoral parity. According to Professor Gaddie's analysis, Republicans would be likely to carry 20 of the 32 congressional seats even if they only won 50% (or, for that matter, 49%) of the statewide vote. This demonstrates that Plan 1374C is inconsistent with the symmetry standard, a measure social scientists use to assess partisan bias, which is undoubtedly "a reliable standard" for measuring a "burden . . . on the complainants' representative rights."

The symmetry standard requires that the electoral system treat similarly-situated parties equally, so that each receives the same fraction of legislative seats for a particular vote percentage as the other party would receive if it had received the same percentage.

8. If 10% of Republican voters decided to vote for Democratic candidates, and if there were no other changes in voter turnout or preferences, the Republicans' share of the statewide vote would be reduced from 58% to 52%.

This standard is widely accepted by scholars as providing a measure of partisan fairness in electoral systems. Like other models that experts use in analyzing vote dilution claims, compliance with the symmetry standard is measured by extrapolating from a sample of known data. In this litigation, the symmetry standard was not simply proposed by an *amicus* to this Court, it was also used by the expert for plaintiffs and the expert for the State in assessing the degree of partisan bias in Plans 1151C and 1374C.

Because, as noted above, Republicans would have an advantage in a significant majority of seats even if the statewide vote were equally distributed between Republicans and Democrats, Plan 1374C constitutes a significant departure from the symmetry standard. By contrast, under Plan 1151C the parties were likely to each take 16 congressional seats if they won 50% of the statewide vote.

Plan 1374C then, clearly has a discriminatory impact on the opportunities that Democratic citizens have to elect candidates of their choice. Moreover, this discriminatory effect cannot be dismissed as *de minimis*. According to the State's expert, if each party receives half the statewide vote, under Plan 1374C the Republicans would carry 62.5% (20) of the congressional seats, whereas the Democrats would win 37.5% (12) of those seats. In other words, at the vote distribution point where a politically neutral map would result in zero differential in the percentage of seats captured by each party, Plan 1374C is structured to create a 25% differential. When a redistricting map imposes such a significant disadvantage on a politically salient group of voters, the State should shoulder the burden of defending the map. *Cf. Brown v. Thomson* (holding that the implementation of a redistricting plan for state legislative districts with population deviations over 10% creates a prima facie case of discrimination under the Equal Protection Clause, thus shifting the burden to the State to defend the plan); *Larios v. Cox* (2004) (same, but further pointing out that the "ten percent rule" is not a safe harbor, and concluding that, under the circumstances of the case before it, a state legislative districting plan was unconstitutional even though population deviations were under 10%). At the very least, once plaintiffs have established that the legislature's sole purpose in adopting a plan was partisan—as plaintiffs have established in this action such a severe discriminatory effect should be sufficient to meet any additional burden they have to demonstrate that the redistricting map accomplishes its discriminatory purpose.[9]

9. Justice Kennedy faults proponents of the symmetry standard for not "providing a standard for deciding how much partisan bias is too much," But it is this Court, not proponents of the symmetry standard, that has the judicial obligation to answer the question of how much unfairness is too much. It would, of course, be an eminently manageable standard for the Court to conclude that deviations of over 10% from symmetry create a prima facie case of an unconstitutional gerrymander, just as population deviations among districts of more than 10% create such a prima facie case. Or, the Court could conclude that a significant departure from symmetry is one relevant factor in analyzing whether, under the totality of the circumstances, a districting plan is an unconstitutional partisan gerrymander. At any rate, proponents of the symmetry standard have provided a helpful (though certainly not talismanic) tool in this type of litigation. While I appreciate Justice Kennedy's leaving the door open to the use of the standard in future cases, I believe it is the role of this Court, not social scientists, to determine how much partisan dominance is too much.

In sum, I think it is clear that Plan 1374C has a severe burden on the capacity of Texas Democrats to influence the political process. The plan guarantees that the Republican-dominated membership of the Texas congressional delegation will remain constant notwithstanding significant pro-Democratic shifts in public opinion. Moreover, the harms Plan 1374C imposes on Democrats are not "hypothetical" or "counterfactual," simply because, in the 2004 elections, Republicans won a share of seats roughly proportional to their statewide voting strength. By creating 19-22 safe Republican seats, Plan 1374C has already harmed Democrats because it significantly undermines the likelihood that Republican lawmakers from those districts will be responsive to the interests of their Democratic constituents. In addition, Democrats will surely have a more difficult time recruiting strong candidates, and mobilizing voters and resources, in these safe Republican districts. Thus, appellants have satisfied any requisite obligation to demonstrate that they have been harmed by the adoption of Plan 1374C.

Accordingly, even accepting the Court's view that a gerrymander is tolerable unless it in fact burdens the minority's representative rights, I would hold that Plan 1374C is unconstitutional.[11]

Justice SOUTER, with whom Justice GINSBURG joins, concurring in part and dissenting in part.

I do not share Justice Kennedy's seemingly flat rejection of any test of gerrymander turning on the process followed in redistricting, nor do I rule out the utility of a criterion of symmetry as a test. Interest in exploring this notion is evident. Perhaps further attention could be devoted to the administrability of such a criterion at all levels of redistricting and its review.

Justice BREYER, concurring in part and dissenting in part.

I join Parts II-A and III of the Court's opinion. I also join Parts I and II of Justice Stevens' opinion concurring in part and dissenting in part.

For one thing, the timing of the redistricting (between census periods), the radical departure from traditional boundary-drawing criteria, and the other evidence to which Justice Stevens refers in Parts I and II of his opinion make clear that a desire to maximize partisan advantage was the sole purpose behind the decision to promulgate Plan 1374C.

11. In this litigation expert testimony provided the principal evidence about the effects of the plan that satisfy the test Justice Kennedy would impose. In my judgment, however, most statewide challenges to an alleged gerrymander should be evaluated primarily by examining these objective factors: (1) the number of people who have been moved from one district to another, (2) the number of districts that are less compact than their predecessors, (3) the degree to which the new plan departs from other neutral districting criteria, including respect for communities of interest and compliance with the Voting Rights Act, (4) the number of districts that have been cracked in a manner that weakens an opposition party incumbent, (5) the number of districts that include two incumbents from the opposite party, (6) whether the adoption of the plan gave the opposition party, and other groups, a fair opportunity to have input in the redistricting process, (7) the number of seats that are likely to be safe seats for the dominant party, and (8) the size of the departure in the new plan from the symmetry standard.

For another thing, the evidence to which Justice Stevens refers in Part III of his opinion demonstrates that the plan's effort to maximize partisan advantage encompasses an effort not only to exaggerate the favored party's electoral majority but also to produce a majority of congressional representatives even if the favored party receives only a *minority* of popular votes.

Finally, because the plan entrenches the Republican Party, the State cannot successfully defend it as an effort simply to *neutralize* the Democratic Party's previous political gerrymander. Nor has the State tried to justify the plan on nonpartisan grounds, either as an effort to achieve legislative stability by avoiding legislative exaggeration of small shifts in party preferences, or in any other way.

In sum, the risk of entrenchment is demonstrated, partisan considerations have rendered the traditional district-drawing compromises irrelevant, and no justification other than party advantage can be found. The record reveals a plan that overwhelmingly relies upon the unjustified use of purely partisan line-drawing considerations and which will likely have seriously harmful electoral consequences. For these reasons, I believe the plan in its entirety violates the Equal Protection Clause.

Chief Justice ROBERTS, with whom Justice ALITO joins, concurring in part and concurring in the judgment in part.

With regard to Part II [of Justice Kennedy's opinion], I agree with the determination that appellants have not provided "a reliable standard for identifying unconstitutional political gerrymanders." The question whether any such standard exists—that is, whether a challenge to a political gerrymander presents a justiciable case or controversy—has not been argued in these cases. I therefore take no position on that question, which has divided the Court, see *Vieth v. Jubelirer*, and I join the Court's disposition in Part II without specifying whether appellants have failed to state a claim on which relief can be granted, or have failed to present a justiciable controversy.

Justice SCALIA, with whom Justice THOMAS joins, concurring in the judgment in part.

I

As I have previously expressed, claims of unconstitutional partisan gerrymandering do not present a justiciable case or controversy. See *Vieth v. Jubelirer*. Justice Kennedy's discussion of appellants' political-gerrymandering claims ably demonstrates that, yet again, no party or judge has put forth a judicially discernable standard by which to evaluate them. Unfortunately, the opinion then concludes that the appellants have failed to state a claim as to political gerrymandering, without ever articulating what the elements of such a claim consist of. That is not an available disposition of this appeal. We must either conclude that the claim is nonjusticiable and dismiss it, or else set forth a standard and measure appellant's claim against it. Instead, we again dispose of this claim in a way that provides no guidance to lower-court judges and perpetuates a cause of action with no discernible content. We should simply dismiss appellants' claims as nonjusticiable.

The next portion of *LULAC* we will cover discusses the issues surrounding minority voting rights. Note again how many of the doctrines we have discussed in this redistricting unit intertwine in the Court's analysis.

LEAGUE OF UNITED LATIN AMERICAN CITIZENS v. PERRY

548 U.S. 399 (2006)

Justice KENNEDY delivered the opinion of the Court with respect to Part III:

III

Plan 1374C made changes to district lines in south and west Texas that appellants challenge as violations of § 2 of the Voting Rights Act and the Equal Protection Clause of the Fourteenth Amendment. The most significant changes occurred to District 23 and to District 25.

After the 2002 election, it became apparent that District 23 as then drawn had an increasingly powerful Latino population that threatened to oust the incumbent Republican, Henry Bonilla. Before the 2003 redistricting, the Latino share of the citizen voting-age population was 57.5%, and Bonilla's support among Latinos had dropped with each successive election since 1996. In 2002, Bonilla captured only 8% of the Latino vote, and 51.5% of the overall vote. Faced with this loss of voter support, the legislature acted to protect Bonilla's incumbency by changing the lines—and hence the population mix—of the district. To begin with, the new plan divided Webb County and the city of Laredo, on the Mexican border, that formed the county's population base. Webb County, which is 94% Latino, had previously rested entirely within District 23; under the new plan, nearly 100,000 people were shifted into neighboring District 28. The rest of the county, approximately 93,000 people, remained in District 23. To replace the numbers District 23 lost, the State added voters in counties comprising a largely Anglo, Republican area in central Texas. In the newly drawn district, the Latino share of the citizen voting-age population dropped to 46%, though the Latino share of the total voting-age population remained just over 50%.

These changes required adjustments elsewhere, of course, so the State inserted a third district between the two districts to the east of District 23, and extended all three of them farther north. New District 25 is a long, narrow strip that winds its way from McAllen and the Mexican border towns in the south to Austin, in the center of the State and 300 miles away. In between it includes seven full counties, but 77% of its population resides in split counties at the northern and southern ends. Of this 77%, roughly half reside in Hidalgo County, which includes McAllen, and half are in Travis County, which includes parts of

Austin. The Latinos in District 25, comprising 55% of the district's citizen voting-age population, are also mostly divided between the two distant areas, north and south. The Latino communities at the opposite ends of District 25 have divergent needs and interests, owing to differences in socio-economic status, education, employment, health, and other characteristics.

The District Court summed up the purposes underlying the redistricting in south and west Texas: "The change to Congressional District 23 served the dual goal of increasing Republican seats in general and protecting Bonilla's incumbency in particular, with the additional political nuance that Bonilla would be reelected in a district that had a majority of Latino voting age population—although clearly not a majority of citizen voting age population and certainly not an effective voting majority." The goal in creating District 25 was just as clear: "[t]o avoid retrogression under § 5" of the Voting Rights Act given the reduced Latino voting strength in District 23.

A

The question we address is whether Plan 1374C violates § 2 of the Voting Rights Act. A State violates § 2

> "if, based on the totality of circumstances, it is shown that the political processes leading to nomination or election in the State or political subdivision are not equally open to participation by members of [a racial group] in that its members have less opportunity than other members of the electorate to participate in the political process and to elect representatives of their choice." 42 U.S.C. § 1973(b).

The Court has identified three threshold conditions for establishing a § 2 violation: (1) the racial group is sufficiently large and geographically compact to constitute a majority in a single-member district; (2) the racial group is politically cohesive; and (3) the majority vot[es] sufficiently as a bloc to enable it . . . usually to defeat the minority's preferred candidate. These are the so-called *Gingles* requirements.

If all three *Gingles* requirements are established, the statutory text directs us to consider the "totality of circumstances" to determine whether members of a racial group have less opportunity than do other members of the electorate. The general terms of the statutory standard "totality of circumstances" require judicial interpretation. For this purpose, the Court has referred to the Senate Report on the 1982 amendments to the Voting Rights Act, which identifies factors typically relevant to a § 2 claim, including:

> "the history of voting-related discrimination in the State or political subdivision; the extent to which voting in the elections of the State or political subdivision is racially polarized; the extent to which the State or political subdivision has used voting practices or procedures that tend to enhance the opportunity for discrimination against the minority group . . . ; the extent to which minority group members bear the effects of past discrimination in areas such as education, employment, and health, which hinder

their ability to participate effectively in the political process; the use of overt or subtle racial appeals in political campaigns; and the extent to which members of the minority group have been elected to public office in the jurisdiction. The Report notes also that evidence demonstrating that elected officials are unresponsive to the particularized needs of the members of the minority group and that the policy underlying the State's or the political subdivision's use of the contested practice or structure is tenuous may have probative value." *Gingles*.

Another relevant consideration is whether the number of districts in which the minority group forms an effective majority is roughly proportional to its share of the population in the relevant area. *De Grandy*.

The District Court's determination whether the § 2 requirements are satisfied must be upheld unless clearly erroneous. Where "the ultimate finding of dilution" is based on "a misreading of the governing law," however, there is reversible error. *De Grandy*.

B

Appellants argue that the changes to District 23 diluted the voting rights of Latinos who remain in the district. Specifically, the redrawing of lines in District 23 caused the Latino share of the citizen voting-age population to drop from 57.5% to 46%. The District Court recognized that "Latino voting strength in Congressional District 23 is, unquestionably, weakened under Plan 1374C." The question is whether this weakening amounts to vote dilution.

To begin the *Gingles* analysis, it is evident that the second and third *Gingles* preconditions—cohesion among the minority group and bloc voting among the majority population—are present in District 23. The District Court found "racially polarized voting" in south and west Texas, and indeed "throughout the State." The polarization in District 23 was especially severe: 92% of Latinos voted against Bonilla in 2002, while 88% of non-Latinos voted for him. Furthermore, the projected results in new District 23 show that the Anglo citizen voting-age majority will often, if not always, prevent Latinos from electing the candidate of their choice in the district. For all these reasons, appellants demonstrated sufficient minority cohesion and majority bloc voting to meet the second and third *Gingles* requirements.

The first *Gingles* factor requires that a group be "sufficiently large and geographically compact to constitute a majority in a single-member district." Latinos in District 23 could have constituted a majority of the citizen voting-age population in the district, and in fact did so under Plan 1151C. Though it may be possible for a citizen voting-age majority to lack real electoral opportunity, the Latino majority in old District 23 did possess electoral opportunity protected by § 2.

While the District Court stated that District 23 had not been an effective opportunity district under Plan 1151C, it recognized the district was "moving in that direction."

Indeed, by 2002 the Latino candidate of choice in District 23 won the majority of the district's votes in 13 out of 15 elections for statewide officeholders. And in the congressional race, Bonilla could not have prevailed without some Latino support, limited though it was. State legislators changed District 23 specifically because they worried that Latinos would vote Bonilla out of office.

Furthermore, to the extent the District Court suggested that District 23 was not a Latino opportunity district in 2002 simply because Bonilla prevailed, it was incorrect. The circumstance that a group does not win elections does not resolve the issue of vote dilution. We have said that "the ultimate right of § 2 is equality of opportunity, not a guarantee of electoral success for minority-preferred candidates of whatever race." In old District 23 the increase in Latino voter registration and overall population, the concomitant rise in Latino voting power in each successive election, the near-victory of the Latino candidate of choice in 2002, and the resulting threat to the Bonilla incumbency, were the very reasons that led the State to redraw the district lines. Since the redistricting prevented the immediate success of the emergent Latino majority in District 23, there was a denial of opportunity in the real sense of that term.

Plan 1374C's version of District 23, by contrast is unquestionably not a Latino opportunity district. Latinos, to be sure, are a bare majority of the voting-age population in new District 23, but only in a hollow sense, for the parties agree that the relevant numbers must include citizenship. This approach fits the language of § 2 because only eligible voters affect a group's opportunity to elect candidates. In sum, appellants have established that Latinos could have had an opportunity district in District 23 had its lines not been altered and that they do not have one now.

Considering the district in isolation, the three *Gingles* requirements are satisfied. The State argues, nonetheless, that it met its § 2 obligations by creating new District 25 as an offsetting opportunity district. It is true, of course, that "States retain broad discretion in drawing districts to comply with the mandate of § 2." *Shaw v. Hunt (Shaw II)*. This principle has limits, though. The Court has rejected the premise that a State can always make up for the less-than-equal opportunity of some individuals by providing greater opportunity to others. As set out below, these conflicting concerns are resolved by allowing the State to use one majority-minority district to compensate for the absence of another only when the racial group in each area had a § 2 right and both could not be accommodated.

As to the first *Gingles* requirement, it is not enough that appellants show the possibility of creating a majority-minority district that would include the Latinos in District 23. If the inclusion of the plaintiffs would necessitate the exclusion of others, then the State cannot be faulted for its choice.

The District Court found that the current plan contains six Latino opportunity districts and that seven reasonably compact districts could not be drawn. Appellant

GI Forum presented a plan with seven majority-Latino districts, but the District Court found these districts were not reasonably compact, in part because they took in "disparate and distant communities." While there was some evidence to the contrary, the court's resolution of the conflicting evidence was not clearly erroneous.

A problem remains, though, for the District Court failed to perform a comparable compactness inquiry for Plan 1374C as drawn. *De Grandy* requires a comparison between a challenger's proposal and the "existing number of reasonably compact districts." To be sure, § 2 does not forbid the creation of a noncompact majority-minority district. The noncompact district cannot, however, remedy a violation elsewhere in the State. Simply put, the State's creation of an opportunity district for those without a § 2 right offers no excuse for its failure to provide an opportunity district for those with a § 2 right. And since there is no § 2 right to a district that is not reasonably compact, the creation of a noncompact district does not compensate for the dismantling of a compact opportunity district.

The District Court stated that Plan 1374C created "six *Gingles* Latino" districts, but it failed to decide whether District 25 was reasonably compact for § 2 purposes. It recognized there was a 300-mile gap between the Latino communities in District 25, and a similarly large gap between the needs and interests of the two groups. After making these observations, however, it did not make any finding about compactness. It ruled instead that, despite these concerns, District 25 would be an effective Latino opportunity district because the combined voting strength of both Latino groups would allow a Latino-preferred candidate to prevail in elections. The District Court's general finding of effectiveness cannot substitute for the lack of a finding on compactness, particularly because the District Court measured effectiveness simply by aggregating the voting strength of the two groups of Latinos. Under the District Court's approach, a district would satisfy § 2 no matter how noncompact it was, so long as all the members of a racial group, added together, could control election outcomes.

While no precise rule has emerged governing § 2 compactness, the inquiry should take into account traditional districting principles such as maintaining communities of interest and traditional boundaries. The recognition of nonracial communities of interest reflects the principle that a State may not "assum[e] from a group of voters' race that they 'think alike, share the same political interests, and will prefer the same candidates at the polls.'" *Miller* [*v. Johnson*]. In the absence of this prohibited assumption, there is no basis to believe a district that combines two far-flung segments of a racial group with disparate interests provides the opportunity that § 2 requires or that the first *Gingles* condition contemplates. The purpose of the Voting Rights Act is to prevent discrimination in the exercise of the electoral franchise and to foster our transformation to a society that is no longer fixated on race. We do a disservice to these important goals by failing to account for the differences between people of the same race.

While the District Court recognized the relevant differences, by not performing the compactness inquiry it failed to account for the significance of these differences under § 2. In these cases the District Court's findings regarding the different characteristics, needs, and interests of the Latino community near the Mexican border and the one in and around Austin are well supported and uncontested. Legitimate yet differing communities of interest should not be disregarded in the interest of race. The practical consequence of drawing a district to cover two distant, disparate communities is that one or both groups will be unable to achieve their political goals. Compactness is, therefore, about more than "style points;" it is critical to advancing the ultimate purposes of § 2, ensuring minority groups equal "opportunity . . . to participate in the political process and to elect representatives of their choice." We do not question the District Court's finding that the groups' combined voting strength would enable them to elect a candidate each prefers to the Anglos' candidate of choice. We also accept that in some cases members of a racial group in different areas—for example, rural and urban communities—could share similar interests and therefore form a compact district if the areas are in reasonably close proximity. When, however, the only common index is race and the result will be to cause internal friction, the State cannot make this a remedy for a § 2 violation elsewhere. We emphasize it is the enormous geographical distance separating the Austin and Mexican-border communities, coupled with the disparate needs and interests of these populations—not either factor alone—that renders District 25 noncompact for § 2 purposes. The mathematical possibility of a racial bloc does not make a district compact.

Since District 25 is not reasonably compact, Plan 1374C contains only five reasonably compact Latino opportunity districts. Plan 1151C, by contrast, created six such districts.

Appellants have thus satisfied all three *Gingles* requirements as to District 23, and the creation of new District 25 does not remedy the problem.

C

We proceed now to the totality of the circumstances, and first to the proportionality inquiry, comparing the percentage of total districts that are Latino opportunity districts with the Latino share of the citizen voting-age population. As explained in *De Grandy,* proportionality is "a relevant fact in the totality of circumstances." It does not, however, act as a "safe harbor" for States in complying with § 2.

The State contends that proportionality should be decided on a regional basis, while appellants say their claim requires the Court to conduct a statewide analysis.

We conclude the answer in these cases is to look at proportionality statewide.

Looking statewide, there are 32 congressional districts. The five reasonably compact Latino opportunity districts amount to roughly 16% of the total, while Latinos make up 22% of Texas' citizen voting-age population. Latinos are, therefore, two districts shy of proportional representation. There is, of course, no "magic parameter" and "rough proportionality" must allow for some deviations. We need not decide whether the two-district deficit in these cases weighs in favor of a § 2 violation. Even if Plan 1374C's disproportionality were deemed insubstantial, that consideration would not overcome the other evidence of vote dilution for Latinos in District 23. "[T]he degree of probative value assigned to proportionality may vary with other facts," *De Grandy*, and the other facts in these cases convince us that there is a § 2 violation.

District 23's Latino voters were poised to elect their candidate of choice. They were becoming more politically active, with a marked and continuous rise in Spanish-surnamed voter registration. In successive elections Latinos were voting against Bonilla in greater numbers, and in 2002 they almost ousted him. Webb County in particular, with a 94% Latino population, spurred the incumbent's near defeat with dramatically increased turnout in 2002. In response to the growing participation that threatened Bonilla's incumbency, the State divided the cohesive Latino community in Webb County, moving about 100,000 Latinos to District 28, which was already a Latino opportunity district, and leaving the rest in a district where they now have little hope of electing their candidate of choice.

The changes to District 23 undermined the progress of a racial group that has been subject to significant voting-related discrimination and that was becoming increasingly politically active and cohesive.

[T]he Latinos' diminishing electoral support for Bonilla indicates their belief he was unresponsive to the particularized needs of the members of the minority group. In essence the State took away the Latinos' opportunity because Latinos were about to exercise it. This bears the mark of intentional discrimination that could give rise to an equal protection violation. Even if we accept the District Court's finding that the State's action was taken primarily for political, not racial, reasons, the redrawing of the district lines was damaging to the Latinos in District 23. The State not only made fruitless the Latinos' mobilization efforts but also acted against those Latinos who were becoming most politically active, dividing them with a district line through the middle of Laredo.

Furthermore, the reason for taking Latinos out of District 23, according to the District Court, was to protect Congressman Bonilla from a constituency that was increasingly voting against him. The Court has noted that incumbency protection can be a legitimate factor in districting, but experience teaches that incumbency protection can take various forms, not all of them in the interests of the constituents. If the justification for incumbency protection is to keep the constituency intact so the officeholder is accountable for promises made or broken, then the protection seems to accord with concern for the voters. If, on the other hand, incumbency protection means excluding some voters from the district simply because they are likely to vote against the officeholder, the change is to benefit the officeholder, not the voters. By purposely redrawing lines around those who opposed Bonilla, the state legislature took the latter course. This policy, whatever its validity in the realm of politics, cannot justify the effect on Latino voters. The policy becomes even more suspect when considered in light of evidence suggesting that the State intentionally drew District 23 to have a nominal Latino voting-age majority (without a citizen voting-age majority) for political reasons. This use of race to create the façade of a Latino district also weighs in favor of appellants' claim.

Contrary to The Chief Justice's suggestion that we are reducing the State's needed flexibility in complying with § 2, the problem here is entirely of the State's own making. The State chose to break apart a Latino opportunity district to protect the incumbent congressman from the growing dissatisfaction of the cohesive and politically active Latino community in the district. The State then purported to compensate for this harm by creating an entirely new district that combined two groups of Latinos, hundreds of miles apart, that represent different communities of interest. Under § 2, the State must be held accountable for the effect of these choices in denying equal opportunity to Latino voters. Notwithstanding these facts, The Chief Justice places great emphasis on the District Court's statement that "new District 25 is a more effective Latino opportunity district than Congressional District 23 had been." Even assuming this statement, expressed in the context of summarizing witnesses' testimony, qualifies as a finding of the District Court, two points make it of minimal relevance. First, as previously noted, the District Court measured the effectiveness of District 25 without accounting for the detrimental consequences of its compactness problems. Second, the District Court referred only to how effective District 23 "had been," not to how it would operate today, a significant distinction given the growing Latino political power in the district.

Based on the foregoing, the totality of the circumstances demonstrates a § 2 violation. Even assuming Plan 1374C provides something close to proportional representation for Latinos, its troubling blend of politics and race—and the resulting vote dilution of a group that was beginning to achieve § 2's goal of overcoming prior electoral discrimination—cannot be sustained.

D

Because we hold Plan 1374C violates § 2 in its redrawing of District 23, we do not address appellants' claims that the use of race and politics in drawing that district violates the First Amendment and equal protection. We also need not confront appellants' claim of an equal protection violation in the drawing of District 25. The districts in south and west Texas will have to be redrawn to remedy the violation in District 23, and we have no cause to pass on the legitimacy of a district that must be changed. District 25, in particular, was formed to compensate for the loss of District 23 as a Latino opportunity district, and there is no reason to believe District 25 will remain in its current form once District 23 is brought into compliance with § 2. We therefore vacate the District Court's judgment as to these claims.

Chief Justice ROBERTS, with whom Justice ALITO joins, dissenting in part.

I must dissent from Part III of the Court's opinion. According to the District Court's factual findings, the State's drawing of district lines in south and west Texas caused the area to move from five out of seven effective Latino opportunity congressional districts, with an additional district "moving" in that direction, to *six* out of seven effective Latino opportunity districts. The end result is that while Latinos make up 58% of the citizen voting age population in the area, they control 85% (six of seven) of the districts under the State's plan.

In the face of these findings, the majority nonetheless concludes that the State's plan somehow dilutes the voting strength of Latinos in violation of § 2 of the Voting Rights Act. The majority reaches its surprising result because it finds that Latino voters in one of the State's Latino opportunity districts—District 25—are insufficiently compact, in that they consist of two different groups, one from around the Rio Grande and another from around Austin. According to the majority, this may make it more difficult for certain Latino-preferred candidates to be elected from that district—*even though Latino voters make up 55% of the citizen voting age population in the district and vote as a bloc.* The majority prefers old District 23, despite the District Court determination that new District 25 is "a more effective Latino opportunity district than Congressional District 23 had been." The District Court based that determination on a careful examination of regression analysis showing that "the Hispanic-preferred candidate [would win] *every* primary and general election examined in District 25," compared to the only partial success such candidates enjoyed in former District 23.

The majority dismisses the District Court's careful fact-finding on the ground that the experienced judges did not properly consider whether District 25 was "compact" for purposes of § 2. But the District Court opinion itself clearly demonstrates that the court carefully considered the compactness of the minority group in District 25, just as the majority says it should have. The District Court recognized the very features of District 25 highlighted by the majority and unambiguously concluded, under the totality of the circumstances, that the district was an effective Latino opportunity district, and that no violation of § 2 in the area had been shown.

Unable to escape the District Court's fact-finding, the majority is left in the awkward position of maintaining that its *theory* about compactness is more important under § 2 than the actual prospects of electoral success for Latino-preferred candidates under a State's apportionment plan. And that theory is a novel one to boot. Never before has this or any other court struck down a State's redistricting plan under § 2, on the ground that the plan achieves the maximum number of possible majority-minority districts, but loses on style points, in that the minority voters in one of those districts are not as "compact" as the minority voters would be in another district were the lines drawn differently. Such a basis for liability pushes voting rights litigation into a whole new area—an area far removed from the concern of the Voting Rights Act to ensure minority voters an equal opportunity "to elect representatives of their choice." 42 U.S.C. § 1973(b).

I

We have emphasized, since *Gingles* itself, that a § 2 plaintiff must at least show an apportionment that is likely to perform *better* for minority voters, compared to the existing one. And unsurprisingly, in the context of single-member districting schemes, we have invariably understood this to require the possibility of *additional* single-member districts that minority voters might control.

Here the District Court found that six majority-Latino districts were all that south and west Texas could support. Plan 1374C provides six such districts, just as its predecessor did. This fact, combined with our precedent making clear that § 2 plaintiffs must show an alternative with *better* prospects for minority success, should have resulted in affirmance of the District Court decision on vote dilution in south and west Texas.

The majority avoids this result by finding fault with the District Court's analysis of one of the Latino-majority districts in the State's plan. That district—District 25—is like other districts in the State's plan, like districts in the predecessor plan, and like districts in the *plaintiffs'* proposed seven-district plan, in that it joins population concentrations around the border area with others closer to the center of the State. The District Court explained that such "bacon-strip" districts are inevitable, given the geography and demography of that area of the State.

What is blushingly ironic is that the district preferred by the majority—former District 23—suffers from the same "flaw" the majority ascribes to District 25, except to a greater degree. While the majority decries District 25 because the Latino communities there are separated by "enormous geographical distance," and are "hundreds of miles apart," Latino communities joined to form the voting majority in old District 23 are nearly twice as far apart. Old District 23 runs "from El Paso, over 500 miles, into San Antonio and down into Laredo. It covers a much longer distance than . . . the 300 miles from Travis to McAllen [in District 25]." So much for the significance of "enormous geographical distance." Or perhaps the majority is willing to "assume" that Latinos around San Antonio have common interests with those on the Rio Grande rather than those around Austin, even though San Antonio and Austin are a good bit closer to each other (less than 80 miles apart) than either is to the Rio Grande.

The District Court considered expert evidence on projected election returns and concluded that District 25 would likely perform impeccably for Latino voters, better indeed than former District 23. The District Court also concluded that the other districts in Plan 1374C would give Latino voters a favorable opportunity to elect their preferred candidates. In light of these findings, the District Court concluded that "compared to Plan 1151C . . . Plaintiffs have not shown an impermissible reduction in effective opportunities for Latino electoral control or in opportunities for Latino participation in the political process."

Viewed against this backdrop, the majority's holding that Plan 1374C violates § 2 amounts to this: A State has denied minority voters equal opportunity to "participate in the political process and to elect representatives of their choice," when the districts in the plan a State has created have *better* prospects for the success of minority-preferred candidates than an alternative plan, simply because one of the State's districts combines different minority communities, which, in any event, are likely to vote as a controlling bloc. It baffles me how this could be vote dilution.

II

[Omitted]

III

Even if a plaintiff satisfies the *Gingles* factors, a finding of vote dilution under § 2 does not automatically follow. In *De Grandy,* we identified another important aspect of the totality inquiry under § 2: whether "minority voters form effective voting majorities in a number of districts roughly proportional to the minority voters' respective shares in the voting-age population." A finding of proportionality under this standard can defeat § 2 liability even if a clear *Gingles* violation has been made out.

In south and west Texas, Latinos constitute 58% of the relevant population and control 85% (six out of seven) of the congressional seats in that region. That includes District 25, because the District Court found, without clear error, that Latino voters in that district "will likely control every primary and general election outcome." But even not counting that district as a Latino opportunity district, because of the majority's misplaced compactness concerns, Latinos in south and west Texas still control congressional seats in a markedly greater proportion—71% (five out of seven)—than their share of the population there. In other words, in the only area in which the *Gingles* factors can be satisfied, Latino voters enjoy effective political power 46% above their numerical strength, or, even disregarding District 25 as an opportunity district, 24% above their numerical strength. Surely these figures do not suggest a denial of equal *opportunity* to *participate* in the political process.

The majority's only answer is to shift the focus to statewide proportionality.

In any event, at a statewide level, 6 Latino opportunity districts out of 32, or 19% of the seats, would certainly seem to be "roughly proportional" to the Latino 22% share of the population. The District Court accordingly determined that proportionality suggested the lack of vote dilution, even considered on a statewide basis. The majority avoids that suggestion by disregarding the District Court's factual finding that District 25 is an effective Latino opportunity district. That is not only improper, for the reasons given, but the majority's rejection of District 25 as a Latino opportunity district is also flatly inconsistent with its statewide approach to analyzing proportionality. Under the majority's view, the Latino voters in the northern end of District 25 cannot "count" along with the Latino voters at the southern end to form an effective majority, because they belong to different communities. But Latino voters from everywhere around the State of Texas—even those from areas where the *Gingles* factors are not satisfied—can "count" for purposes of calculating the proportion against which effective Latino electoral power should be measured. Heads the plaintiffs win; tails the State loses.

* * *

The State has drawn a redistricting plan that provides six of seven congressional districts with an effective majority of Latino voting-age citizens in south and west Texas, and it is not possible to provide more. The majority nonetheless faults the state plan because of the *particular mix* of Latino voters forming the majority in one of the six districts—a combination of voters from around the Rio Grande and from around Austin, as opposed to what the majority uncritically views as the more monolithic majority assembled (from more far-flung communities) in old District 23. This despite the express factual findings, from judges far more familiar with Texas than we are, that the State's new district would be a more effective Latino majority district than old District 23 ever was, and despite the fact that *any* plan would necessarily leave *some* Latino voters outside a Latino-majority district.

Whatever the majority believes it is fighting with its holding, it is not vote dilution on the basis of race or ethnicity. I do not believe it is our role to make judgments about which *mixes* of minority voters should count for purposes of forming a majority in an electoral district, in the face of factual findings that the district is an effective majority-minority district. It is a sordid business, this divvying us up by race. When a State's plan already provides the maximum possible number of majority-minority effective opportunity districts, and the minority enjoys effective political power in the area well in *excess* of its proportion of the population, I would conclude that the courts have no further role to play in rejiggering the district lines under § 2.

I respectfully dissent from Part III of the Court's opinion.

Justice SCALIA, with whom Justice THOMAS joins, and with whom THE CHIEF JUSTICE and Justice ALITO join as to Part III, dissenting in part.

II

I would dismiss appellants' vote-dilution claims premised on § 2 of the Voting Rights Act of 1965 for failure to state a claim. The Court's § 2 jurisprudence continues to drift ever further from the Act's purpose of ensuring minority voters equal electoral opportunities.

III

Because I find no merit in either of the claims addressed by the Court, I must consider appellants' race-based equal protection claims. The GI Forum appellants focus on the removal of 100,000 residents, most of whom are Latino, from District 23. They assert that this action constituted intentional vote dilution in violation of the Equal Protection Clause. The Jackson appellants contend that the intentional creation of District 25 as a majority-minority district was an impermissible racial gerrymander. The District Court rejected the equal protection challenges to both districts.

A

The GI Forum appellants contend that the Texas Legislature removed a large number of Latino voters living in Webb County from District 23 with the purpose of diminishing Latino electoral power in that district. Congressional redistricting is primarily a responsibility of state legislatures, and legislative motives are often difficult to discern. We presume, moreover, that legislatures fulfill this responsibility in a constitutional manner. Although a State will almost always be aware of racial demographics when it redistricts, it does not follow from this awareness that the State redistricted on the basis of race. Thus, courts must "exercise extraordinary caution" in concluding that a State has intentionally used race when redistricting. [*Miller*.] Nevertheless, when considerations of race predominate, we do not hesitate to apply the strict scrutiny that the Equal Protection Clause requires.

At the time the legislature redrew Texas's congressional districts, District 23 was represented by Congressman Henry Bonilla, whose margin of victory and support among Latinos had been steadily eroding. In the 2002 election, he won with less than 52 percent of the vote, and received only 8 percent of the Latino vote. The District Court found that the goal of the map-drawers was to adjust the lines of that district to protect the imperiled incumbent: "The record presents undisputed evidence that the Legislature desired to increase the number of Republican votes cast in Congressional District 23 to shore up Bonilla's base and assist in his reelection." To achieve this goal, the legislature extended the district north to include counties in the central part of the State with residents who voted Republican, adding 100,000 people to the district. Then, to comply with the one-person, one-vote requirement, the legislature took one-half of heavily Democratic Webb County, in the southern part of the district, and included it in the neighboring district.

Appellants acknowledge that the State redrew District 23 at least in part to protect Bonilla. They argue, however, that they assert an intentional vote-dilution claim that is analytically distinct from the racial-gerrymandering claim of the sort at issue in *Shaw v. Reno (Shaw I)*. A vote-dilution claim focuses on the majority's intent to harm a minority's voting power; a *Shaw I* claim focuses instead on the State's purposeful classification of individuals by their race, regardless of whether they are helped or hurt. In contrast to a *Shaw I* claim, appellants contend, in a vote-dilution claim the plaintiff need not show that the racially discriminatory motivation *predominated,* but only that the invidious purpose was *a* motivating factor. Whatever the validity of this distinction, on the facts of these cases it is irrelevant. The District Court's conclusion that the legislature was not racially motivated when it drew the plan as a whole, and when it split Webb County, dooms appellants' intentional-vote-dilution claim.

We review a district court's factual finding of a legislature's motivation for clear error. I cannot say that the District Court clearly erred when it found that "[t]he legislative motivation for the division of Webb County between Congressional District 23 and Congressional District 28 in Plan 1374C was political."

B

The District Court's finding with respect to District 25 is another matter. There, too, the District Court applied the approach set forth in *Easley,* in which the Court held that race may be a motivation in redistricting as long as it is not the predominant one. In my view, however, when a legislature intentionally creates a majority-minority district, race is necessarily its predominant motivation and strict scrutiny is therefore triggered. [T]he State's concession here sufficiently establishes that the legislature classified individuals on the basis of their race when it drew District 25: "[T]o avoid retrogression and achieve compliance with § 5 of the Voting Rights Act . . . , the Legislature chose to create a new Hispanic-opportunity district—new CD 25—which would allow Hispanics to actually elect its candidate of choice." Brief for State Appellees. Unquestionably, in my view, the drawing of District 25 triggers strict scrutiny.

Texas must therefore show that its use of race was narrowly tailored to further a compelling state interest. Texas asserts that it created District 25 to comply with its obligations under § 5 of the Voting Rights Act. The purpose of § 5 is to prevent retrogression in the position of racial minorities with respect to their effective exercise of the electoral franchise. Since its changes to District 23 had reduced Latino voting power in that district, Texas asserts that it needed to create District 25 as a Latino-opportunity district in order to avoid § 5 liability.

We have in the past left undecided whether compliance with federal antidiscrimination laws can be a compelling state interest. I would hold that compliance with § 5 of the Voting Rights Act can be such an interest. We long ago upheld the constitutionality of § 5 as a proper exercise of Congress's authority under § 2 of the Fifteenth Amendment to enforce that Amendment's prohibition on the denial or abridgment of the right to vote. *South Carolina v. Katzenbach.* If compliance with § 5 were not a compelling state interest, then a State could be placed in the impossible position of having to choose between compliance with § 5 and compliance with the Equal Protection Clause. Moreover, the compelling nature of the State's interest in § 5 compliance is supported by our recognition in previous cases that race may be used where necessary to remedy identified past discrimination. Congress enacted § 5 for just that purpose and that provision applies only to jurisdictions with a history of official discrimination. In the proper case, therefore, a covered jurisdiction may have a compelling interest in complying with § 5.

To support its use of § 5 compliance as a compelling interest with respect to a particular redistricting decision, the State must demonstrate that such compliance was its "actual purpose" and that it had "'a strong basis in evidence' for believing," that the redistricting decision at issue was "reasonably necessary under a constitutional reading and application of" the Act, *Miller*.[2] Moreover, in order to tailor the use of race narrowly to its purpose of complying with the Act, a State cannot use racial considerations to achieve results beyond those that are required to comply with the statute.

In light of these factors bearing upon the question whether the State had a strong evidentiary basis for believing that the creation of District 25 was reasonably necessary to comply with § 5, I would normally remand for the District Court to undertake that "fact-intensive" inquiry. Appellants concede, however, that the changes made to District 23 "necessitated creating an additional effective Latino district elsewhere, in an attempt to avoid Voting Rights Act liability." This is, of course, precisely the State's position. Nor do appellants charge that in creating District 25 the State did more than what was required by § 5. In light of these concessions, I do not believe a remand is necessary, and I would affirm the judgment of the District Court.

Figure 1-16
PLAN 1151C
Reprinted with permission from the Texas Legislative Council.

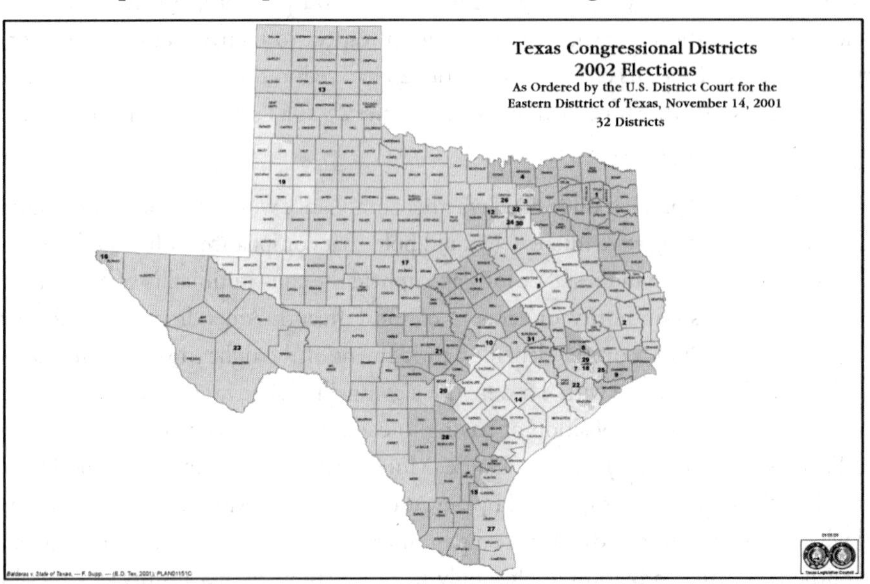

Source: http://www.tlc.state.tx.us/redist/pdf/congress_historical/c_2002.pdf

2. No party here raises a constitutional challenge to § 5 as applied in these cases, and I assume its application is consistent with the Constitution.

Figure 1-17
Plan 1374C
Reprinted with permission from the Texas Legislative Council.

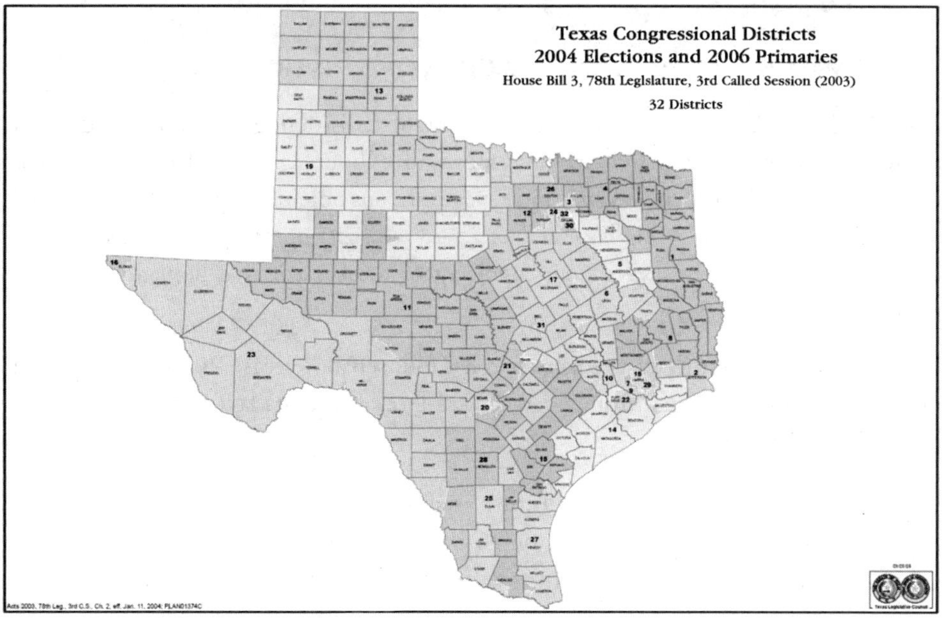

Texas Congressional Districts
2004 Elections and 2006 Primaries
House Bill 3, 78th Legislature, 3rd Called Session (2003)
32 Districts

Source: http://www.tlc.state.tx.us/redist/pdf/congress_historical/c_2004_2006.pdf

NOTES ON *LULAC*

1. Consider initially the partisan gerrymandering aspect of the opinion. In many respects, the discussion just reaffirms previous sentiments expressed in *Vieth*, where a majority of Justices could not agree on a judicially manageable standard. However, *LULAC* presents at least two new wrinkles in the search for a judicially manageable standard—the symmetry standard and a ban on "re-redistricting." Why does Justice Kennedy reject these proposed standards? In light of Justice Kennedy's rejection of these potential standards, does it make sense for him to keep leaving the door slightly ajar to claims of partisan gerrymandering?
2. Consider next the constitutional vote dilution aspect of this case. Justice Kennedy asserts that what the Texas legislature did to Latino voters in District 23 might amount to purposeful racial discrimination that would violate the Constitution. Do you agree?
3. Justice Kennedy's opinion finds a violation of Section 2 in Texas's treatment of Latino voters in District 23. Chief Justice Roberts would find no such violation because of the state's creation of District 25. Who has the better argument? Does it make any sense for Justice Kennedy to focus on the rights of individual voters in District 23 when individual voters cannot elect candidates?

4. Did Texas engage in unconstitutional racial gerrymandering? How do the dissenters analyze that claim? What would be the arguments on the other side?

SUMMARY OF THE LAW OF LEGISLATIVE DISTRICTING

As the *LULAC* case demonstrates, the law of redistricting is complex and multifaceted. Those charged with drawing lines must think about legal considerations at almost every turn, as the "losers" in redistricting have numerous potential legal challenges at their disposal. Yet those who bring legal challenges to redistricting plans also face hurdles of their own, as the courts always seem cognizant of the hazards that lie in the "political thicket."

We began by noting that redistricting has four separate areas (plus Section 5) and it makes sense to briefly recap from a very macro-level where the law stands and where it might be headed:

- One person, one vote is a firmly established doctrine that amounts to a first principle for redistricting actors to consider. Future cases are likely to focus on litigants arguing for a stricter or looser interpretation of the one person, one vote principle rather than for a wholesale dismantling of the doctrine.
- Racial vote dilution under the Constitution and Section 2 of the Voting Rights Act will likely be a dynamic area with continued disputes over the role of the Court and the level of representation that must be provided to minority groups to meet constitutional and statutory dictates. Section 2 may become even more important given the Court's decision in *Shelby County* that, essentially, eliminated Section 5 preclearance (absent further congressional action).
- Section 5 of the Voting Rights Act has been effectively nullified by the Court's *Shelby County* decision declaring that the coverage formula is unconstitutional. In the short term, the Court's decision will lead to: (1) calls for Congress to pass legislation creating a new coverage formula; (2) litigants attempting to reinstate preclearance using Section 3(c); and (3) the channeling of issues that originally would have been handled by Section 5 preclearance into Section 2 litigation.
- Racial gerrymandering doctrine was a very active doctrine in the 1990s but has essentially gone dormant since then. It remains to be seen whether changes in judicial personnel will result in a resurgence of these types of cases.
- Political gerrymandering doctrine seems to be going nowhere at the moment, despite Justice Kennedy leaving the door slightly ajar for the courts to entertain such claims. Future action that attempts to curb partisan gerrymandering will probably be directed more at legislative or referendum/initiative proposals aimed at substituting independent redistricting commissions for legislative control over

redistricting, or will be directed at litigation seeking to have state courts limit partisan gerrymandering through interpretations of state constitutions. This area is one, however, in which a new Justice has the potential of making a major difference in the development of the law—either by slamming the door shut (in agreement with the *Vieth* plurality), or by joining forces with the Court's liberals to fashion some new standard of partisan fairness (whether based on the "symmetry" idea entertained in *LULAC* or some other).

PART II

THE LAW OF NOMINATING CANDIDATES

INTRODUCTION

A major challenge for any electoral process is winnowing the field of potential candidates from many to few to eventually a winner. It is common to see early presidential debates where the stage is crowded with seven or more candidates—and that's just for either the Democratic or Republican party!

In the 2008 presidential election, the list of Democratic Party candidates initially included: (1) Joe Biden, (2) Hillary Clinton, (3) Chris Dodd, (4) John Edwards, (5) Mike Gravel, (6) Barack Obama, (7) Bill Richardson, and (8) Tom Vilsack—with speculation about Al Gore potentially entering the race at a late stage. Similarly, the initial list of Republican candidates included: (1) Sam Brownback, (2) Jim Gilmore, (3) Rudy Giuliani, (4) Mike Huckabee, (5) Duncan Hunter, (6) John McCain, (7) Ron Paul, (8) Mitt Romney, (9) Tom Tancredo, (10) Fred Thompson, and (11) Tommy Thompson. In 2012, there were seven main Republican challengers for the nomination; Mitt Romney eventually won the Republican nod after a fairly heated primary season battle.

There were also third-party and independent candidates for President in 2008. Bob Barr, a former congressman, was the Libertarian party's candidate and potentially could have been a factor in the November 2008 general election. Ralph Nader, who ran again as an independent, also could have affected the results. (Nader was a major factor in the 2000 presidential election: Had his supporters in Florida voted instead for Gore, there would have been no recount controversy that year.) Earlier in 2008, there was significant speculation about New York City's mayor, Michael Bloomberg, entering the race as an independent, but that speculation died down once both major parties chose candidates—McCain and Obama—considered to be appealing to centrist voters. Each presidential election, of course, contains an array of minor-party candidates unlikely to draw any significant support, including those from the Constitution, Prohibition, Socialist, and Socialist Workers parties.

In the United States, we divide the winnowing process into two basic stages: first, primaries, and second, the general election. We do this for presidential elections as well as for other contests (gubernatorial, congressional, state legislative, mayoral, and so forth). But the primary process for presidential elections, because of its uniquely national scope, is quite different from primaries for all other races. Take, for example, the election for governor of any state. The primary process for that election will generally consist of a single date, confined to that single state, and the winner of the party primaries will be placed on the ballot for the general election, along with any third-party or independent candidates who qualify for the ballot through some means other than conducting a party primary (usually by complying with a signature requirement).

The primary process for presidential elections, however, is not so simple. The winner of any state's presidential primary does not necessarily end up on the general election ballot in that state or any other. (Think of all the primaries that Hillary Clinton won in 2008, or the votes cast for Rick Santorum in 2012, and yet neither was on the ballot in the general election in those years.) Instead, presidential primaries (and caucuses) elect delegates to National Party conventions, which nominate candidates based on the total number of delegates for each candidate within the party—and based also on, in the case of the Democratic Party, preferences of so-called "super-delegates," chosen according to party rules. The party nominees, in turn, become candidates on the general election ballot, along with the third-party and independent candidates who qualify through other means.

Whether in its simpler form for gubernatorial (and other nonpresidential) elections, or in its more complicated form for presidential elections, the primary process raises important constitutional questions. To what extent can government, state or federal, regulate these primaries? Or, conversely, to what extent do the political parties control these primaries, immune from governmental regulation, by virtue of their rights to political association protected by the First Amendment? As we shall see, the U.S. Supreme Court has struggled with these questions ever since challenges arose, in what are known as the "White Primary" cases, to the discriminatory exclusion of African Americans from Democratic Party primaries in the South during the post-Reconstruction era of segregation.

This part of the case book considers the laws for nominating candidates. How have the Court's decisions impacted the "many to few to one" process? We first discuss rules governing the primary process, and then we analyze issues involving ballot access for general elections. When reading this material, consider the clash of values and rights between the various stakeholders: voter; major and minor political parties; independent candidates; and the state and federal governments. Also pay attention to whose rights come out on top in the constitutional analysis. Finally, consider what type of primary system makes the most sense for American democracy.

A Preliminary Note on the White Primary Cases

The so-called "White Primary Cases" from the 1940s and 1950s, *Smith v. Allwright*, 321 U.S. 649 (1944), and *Terry v. Adams*, 345 U.S. 461 (1953), were cases in which both the political party and the state government were in agreement that they wanted to exclude

African Americans from the right to vote in primary elections. (At least, the state government wanted to permit the Democratic Party to make this choice for itself. Earlier, the state law itself had banned African Americans from participating in Democratic Party primaries.) The U.S. Supreme Court, however, held that the U.S. Constitution's prohibition on race discrimination with respect to voting trumped the wishes of both the party and the state.

The White Primary Cases were decided on the ground that the primary election was an integral component of the overall electoral process leading up to the general election. Texas law required the Democratic Party to nominate its candidates through a primary election. Texas law also heavily regulated the internal operations of the Democratic Party, including the means by which its officers were chosen. These regulations, according to the Court, made the Party "an agency of the state in so far as it determines the participants in a primary election." *Smith v. Allwright*, 321 U.S. at 663. That is, the Democratic Party was a "state actor" with respect to how it ran its primary.

Is this an accurate description of how political parties operate? Are they public or private organizations? In the White Primary Cases the Court in essence said that the way the Democratic Party in Texas operated made them like an arm of the state. What rationale justifies this conclusion?

The Court was influenced in part by the fact that whoever won the Democratic Party primary in Texas in the 1940s and 1950s also, as a practical matter, had a lock on the general election. Consequently, the Court thought it essential to eliminate race discrimination in the primary election to vindicate the right to vote. This right, the Court said, "is not to be nullified by a state through casting its electoral process in a form which permits a private organization to practice racial discrimination in the election." *Id.* at 664.

It seems clear under the rationale of the White Primary Cases that a political party is a state actor when the party's nominee usually wins the general election and the party is excluding people on the basis of race. But how far does that principle extend? What if there were a political party called the American Christian Party and its internal governing rules denied membership to anyone unwilling to swear an oath that they are Christians? If a voter or candidate challenged that exclusion as unconstitutional religious discrimination, analogous to the unconstitutional racial discrimination in the White Primary Cases, would the claim prevail? If not, why not? Because religion is different than race? Or because the American Christian Party is (presumably) a minor party, in contrast to the Democratic Party? (If either major political party today required its members to swear allegiance to "Judeo-Christian values," would that membership requirement be constitutionally permissible?) Think about what arguments you would make to analyze these hypotheticals in light of the cases that follow. Also consider how these next few cases are different, constitutionally, from the White Primary Cases. Do primaries belong to the political party, the government, or both?

A. Political Party Versus the State

In 2008, a dispute arose over whether the national Democratic Party would seat the delegates from Florida and Michigan at the 2008 National Convention. Those states had decided to hold their presidential primaries in January, earlier than the national party's rules allowed, to enhance their influence in the selection of the party's nominee. (National Party rules dictate when states may hold their presidential primaries, stipulating that New Hampshire shall have the first primary and Iowa shall have the first caucus. Florida and Michigan scheduled their primaries for after these states but still before National Party rules permitted.) As a "punishment," the National Party threatened either not to seat delegates from those states or to give them reduced voting power at the National Convention. Hillary Clinton, who had won those states' Democratic primaries, sought to require the National Party to seat the delegates at the Convention. A federal court eventually ruled that the DNC had a First Amendment right to exclude delegates chosen contrary to DNC rules. *See Nelson v. Dean*, 528 F. Supp. 2d 1271 (N.D. Fla. 2007). Once the primary process concluded and it became clear that Barack Obama would have enough delegates to win the Democratic nomination for president, however, the DNC agreed to seat all of the Florida and Michigan delegates with full voting power.

The Supreme Court had previously decided a case from Wisconsin that resembles in many ways the 2008 dispute over the delegates from Florida and Michigan. As you read the following case, note two distinctions between it and the 2008 dispute: First, the Wisconsin case did not involve the date on which the state's primary was held, but instead the rules for who could vote in the state's primary—and the obligation of the party's convention delegates to follow the results of the primary; and second, neither Florida nor Michigan took legal action in an effort to force the Democratic Party to seat its delegates with full voting power; instead, individual voters who supported Hillary Clinton attempted (unsuccessfully) to sue the Democratic Party on the ground that it was violating their constitutionally protected voting rights. Consequently, as you read this Wisconsin case, ask yourself how either of these two distinctions (or both in combination) affect its status as precedent in a potential future dispute over the date of a state's primary, especially one brought by individual voters who seek full representation for their delegates at the National Convention. To what extent are the national party's rules paramount over a state's desire to regulate its primary process?

DEMOCRATIC PARTY OF THE UNITED STATES v. WISCONSIN EX REL. LA FOLLETTE

450 U.S. 107 (1981)

Justice Stewart delivered the opinion of the Court.

The charter of the appellant Democratic Party of the United States (National Party) provides that delegates to its National Convention shall be chosen through procedures in which only Democrats can participate. The question on this appeal is whether Wisconsin may successfully insist that its delegates to the Convention be seated, even though those delegates are chosen through a process that includes a binding state preference primary election in which voters do not declare their party affiliation. The Wisconsin Supreme Court held that the National Convention is bound by the Wisconsin primary election results, and cannot refuse to seat the delegates chosen in accord with Wisconsin law.

I

Rule 2A of the Democratic Selection Rules for the 1980 National Convention states: "Participation in the delegate selection process in primaries or caucuses shall be restricted to Democratic voters only who publicly declare their party preference and have that preference publicly recorded."

The election laws of Wisconsin allow non-Democrats—including members of other parties and independents—to vote in the Democratic primary without regard to party affiliation and without requiring a public declaration of party preference. The voters in Wisconsin's "open" primary express their choice among Presidential candidates for the Democratic Party's nomination; they do not vote for delegates to the National Convention. Delegates to the National Convention are chosen separately, after the primary, at caucuses of persons who have stated their affiliation with the Party. But these delegates, under Wisconsin law, are bound to vote at the National Convention in accord with the results of the open primary election. Accordingly, while Wisconsin's open Presidential preference primary does not itself violate National Party rules, the State's mandate that the results of the primary shall determine the allocation of votes cast by the State's delegates at the National Convention does.

[The Wisconsin Supreme Court ruled that the National Party had to seat the Wisconsin delegates at the National Convention because the state's system of selecting delegates is constitutional and binding on the National Party. The National Party appealed.]

II

Rule 2A can be traced to efforts of the National Party to study and reform its nominating procedures and internal structure after the 1968 Democratic National Convention. The Convention, the Party's highest governing authority, directed the Democratic National Committee (DNC) to establish a Commission on Party Structure and Delegate Selection. This Commission concluded that a major problem faced by the Party was that rank-and-file Party members had been underrepresented at its Convention, and that the Party should "find methods which would guarantee every American who claims a stake in the Democratic Party the opportunity to make his judgment felt in the presidential nominating process." The Commission stressed that Party nominating procedures should be as open and accessible as possible to all persons who wished to join the Party, but expressed the concern that "a full opportunity for all Democrats to participate is diluted if members of other political parties are allowed to participate in the selection of delegates to the Democratic National Convention."

III

The question in this case is not whether Wisconsin may conduct an open primary election if it chooses to do so, or whether the National Party may require Wisconsin to limit its primary election to publicly declared Democrats. Rather, the question is whether, once Wisconsin has opened its Democratic Presidential preference primary to voters who do not publicly declare their party affiliation, it may then bind the National Party to honor the binding primary results, even though those results were reached in a manner contrary to National Party rules.

The Wisconsin Supreme Court considered the question before it to be the constitutionality of the "open" feature of the state primary election law, as such. Concluding that the open primary serves compelling state interest by encouraging voter participation, the court held the state open primary constitutionally valid. Upon this issue, the Wisconsin Supreme Court may well be correct. In any event there is no need to question its conclusion here. For the rules of the National Party do not challenge the authority of a State to conduct an open primary, so long as it is not binding on the National Party Convention. The issue is whether the State may compel the National Party to seat a delegation chosen in a way that violates the rules of the Party. And this issue was resolved, we believe, in *Cousins v. Wigoda* (1975).

In *Cousins* the Court reviewed the decision of an Illinois court holding that state law exclusively governed the seating of a state delegation at the 1972 Democratic National Convention, and enjoining the National Party from refusing to seat delegates selected in a manner in accord with state law although contrary to National Party rules. Certiorari was granted "to decide the important question . . . whether the [a]ppellate [c]ourt was correct in according primacy to state law over the National Political Party's rules in the determination of the qualifications and eligibility of delegates to the Party's National Convention." The Court reversed the state judgment, holding that "Illinois' interest in protecting the integrity of its electoral process cannot be deemed compelling in the context of the selection of delegates to the National Party Convention." That disposition controls here.

The *Cousins* Court relied upon the principle that "[t]he National Democratic Party and its adherents enjoy a constitutionally protected right of political association." This First Amendment freedom to gather in association for the purpose of advancing shared beliefs is protected by the Fourteenth Amendment from infringement by any State. And the freedom to associate for the common advancement of political beliefs necessarily presupposes the freedom to identify the people who constitute the association, and to limit the association to those people only. Here, the members of the National Party, speaking through their rules, chose to define their associational rights by limiting those who could participate in the processes leading to the selection of delegates to their National Convention. On several occasions this Court has recognized that the inclusion of persons unaffiliated with a political party may seriously distort its collective decisions—thus impairing the party's essential functions—and that political parties may accordingly protect themselves from intrusion by those with adverse political principles. In *Rosario v. Rockefeller*, for example, the Court sustained the constitutionality of a requirement—there imposed by a state statute—that a voter enroll in the party of his choice at least 30 days before the general election in order to vote in the next party primary. The purpose of that statute was "to inhibit party 'raiding,' whereby voters in sympathy with one party designate themselves as voters of another party so as to influence or determine the results of the other party's primary."

The State argues that its law places only a minor burden on the National Party. The National Party argues that the burden is substantial, because it prevents the Party from "screen[ing] out those whose affiliation is . . . slight, tenuous, or fleeting," and that such screening is essential to build a more effective and responsible Party. But it is not for the courts to mediate the merits of this dispute. For even if the State were correct, a State, or a court, may not constitutionally substitute its own judgment for that of the Party. A political party's choice among the various ways of determining the makeup of a State's delegation to the party's national convention is protected by the Constitution.

IV

We must consider, finally, whether the State has compelling interests that justify the imposition of its will upon the appellants. "Neither the right to associate nor the right to participate in political activities is absolute." The State asserts a compelling interest in preserving the overall integrity of the electoral process, providing secrecy of the ballot, increasing voter participation in primaries, and preventing harassment of voters. But all those interests go to the conduct of the Presidential preference primary—not to the imposition of voting requirements upon those who, in a separate process, are eventually selected as delegates. Therefore, the interests advanced by the State do not justify its substantial intrusion into the associational freedom of members of the National Party.

V

The State has a substantial interest in the manner in which its elections are conducted, and the National Party has a substantial interest in the manner in which the delegates to its National Convention are selected. But these interests are not incompatible, and to the limited extent they clash in this case, both interests can be preserved. The National Party rules do not forbid Wisconsin to conduct an open primary. But if Wisconsin does open its primary, it cannot require that Wisconsin delegates to the National Party Convention vote there in accordance with the primary results, if to do so would violate Party rules. Since the Wisconsin Supreme Court has declared that the National Party cannot disqualify delegates who are bound to vote in accordance with the results of the Wisconsin open primary, its judgment is reversed.

Justice Powell, with whom Justice Blackmun and Justice Rehnquist join, dissenting.

Under Wisconsin law, the Wisconsin delegations to the Presidential nominating conventions of the two major political parties are required to cast their votes in a way that reflects the outcome of the State's "open" primary election. That election is conducted without advance party registration or any public declaration of party affiliation, thus allowing any registered voter to participate in the process by which the Presidential preferences of the Wisconsin delegation to the Democratic National Convention are determined. The question in this case is whether, in light of the National Party's rule that only publicly declared Democrats may have a voice in the nomination process, Wisconsin's open primary law infringes the National Party's First Amendment rights of association. Because I believe that this law does not impose a substantial burden on the associational freedom of the National Party, and actually promotes the free political activity of the citizens of Wisconsin, I dissent.

I

The Wisconsin open primary law was enacted in 1903. It was amended two years later to apply to Presidential nominations. As the Wisconsin Supreme Court described in its opinion below:

> "The primary was aimed at stimulating popular participation in politics thereby ending boss rule, corruption, and fraudulent practices which were perceived to be part of the party caucus or convention system. Robert M. La Follette, Sr., supported the primary because he believed that citizens should nominate the party candidates; that the citizens, not the party bosses, could control the party by controlling the candidate selection process; and that the candidates and public officials would be more directly responsible to the citizens."

II

The analysis in this kind of First Amendment case has two stages. If the law can be said to impose a burden on the freedom of association, then the question becomes whether this burden is justified by a compelling state interest. The Court in this case concludes that the Wisconsin law burdens associational freedoms. It then appears to acknowledge that the interests asserted by Wisconsin are substantial, but argues that these interests "go to the conduct of the Presidential preference primary—not to the imposition of voting requirements upon those who, in a separate process, are eventually selected as delegates." In my view, however, any burden here is not constitutionally significant, and the State has presented at least a formidable argument linking the law to compelling state interests.

A

In analyzing the burden imposed on associational freedoms in this case, the Court treats the Wisconsin law as the equivalent of one regulating delegate selection, and, relying on *Cousins v. Wigoda*, concludes that any interference with the National Party's accepted delegate-selection procedures impinges on constitutionally protected rights. It is important to recognize, however, that the facts of this case present issues that differ considerably from those we dealt with in *Cousins.*

In *Cousins,* we reversed a determination that a state court could interfere with the Democratic Convention's freedom to select one delegation from the State of Illinois over another. At issue in the case was the power of the National Party to reject a delegation chosen in accordance with state law because the State's delegate-selection procedures violated party rules regarding participation of minorities, women, and young people, as well as other matters. The state court had ordered the Convention to seat the delegation chosen under state law, rather than the delegation preferred by the Convention itself. In contrast with the direct state regulation of the delegate-selection process at issue in *Cousins,* this case involves a state statutory scheme that regulates delegate selection only indirectly. Under Wisconsin law, the "method of selecting the delegates or alternates [is] determined by the state party organization." Wisconsin simply mandates that each delegate selected, by whatever procedure, must be pledged to represent a candidate who has won in the state primary election the right to delegate votes at the Convention.

In evaluating the constitutional significance of this relatively minimal state regulation of party membership requirements, I am unwilling—at least in the context of a claim by one of the two major political parties—to conclude that every conflict between state law and party rules concerning participation in the nomination process creates a burden on associational rights. Instead, I would look closely at the nature of the intrusion, in light of the nature of the association involved, to see whether we are presented with a real limitation on First Amendment freedoms.

It goes without saying that nomination of a candidate for President is a principal function performed by a national political party, and Wisconsin has, to an extent, regulated the terms on which a citizen may become a "member" of the group of people permitted to influence that decision. If appellant National Party were an organization with a particular ideological orientation or political mission, perhaps this regulation would present a different question. In such a case, the state law might well open the organization to participation by persons with incompatible beliefs and interfere with the associational rights of its founders.

The Democratic Party, however, is not organized around the achievement of defined ideological goals. Instead, the major parties in this country "have been characterized by a fluidity and overlap of philosophy and membership." *Rosario* v. *Rockefeller* (1973) (Powell, J., dissenting). It can hardly be denied that this party generally has been composed of various elements reflecting most of the American political spectrum. The Party does take positions on public issues, but these positions vary from time to time, and there never has been a serious effort to establish for the Party a monolithic ideological identity by excluding all those with differing views. As a result, it is hard to see what the Democratic Party has to fear from an open primary plan. Wisconsin's law may influence to some extent the outcome of a primary contest by allowing participation by voters who are unwilling to affiliate with the Party publicly. It is unlikely, however, that this influence will produce a delegation with preferences that differ from those represented by a substantial number of delegates from other parts of the country. Moreover, it seems reasonable to conclude that, insofar as the major parties do have ideological identities, an open primary merely allows relatively independent voters to cast their lot with the party that speaks to their present concerns. By attracting participation by relatively independent-minded voters, the Wisconsin plan arguably may enlarge the support for a party at the general election.

It is significant that the Democratic Party of Wisconsin, which represents those citizens of Wisconsin willing to take part publicly in Party affairs, is here *defending* the state law. Moreover, the National Party's apparent concern that the outcome of the Wisconsin Presidential primary will be skewed cannot be taken seriously when one considers the alternative delegate-selection methods that are acceptable to the Party under its rules. Delegates pledged to various candidates may be selected by a caucus procedure involving a small minority of Party members, as long as all participants in the process are publicly affiliated. While such a process would eliminate "crossovers," it would be at least as likely as an open primary to reflect inaccurately the views of a State's Democrats. In addition, the National Party apparently is quite willing to accept public affiliation immediately before primary voting, which some States permit. As Party affiliation becomes this easy for a voter to change in order to participate in a particular primary election, the difference between open and closed primaries loses its practical significance.

In sum, I would hold that the National Party has failed to make a sufficient showing of a burden on its associational rights.

B

The Court does not dispute that the State serves important interests by its open primary plan. Instead the Court argues that these interests are irrelevant because they do not support a requirement that the outcome of the primary be binding on delegates chosen for the convention. This argument, however, is premised on the unstated assumption that a nonbinding primary would be an adequate mechanism for pursuing the state interests involved. This assumption is unsupportable because the very purpose of a Presidential primary, as enunciated as early as 1903 when Wisconsin passed its first primary law, was to give control over the nomination process to individual voters. Wisconsin cannot do this, and still pursue the interests underlying an open primary, without making the open primary binding.

III

The history of state regulation of the major political parties suggests a continuing accommodation of the interests of the parties with those of the States and their citizens. In the process, "the States have evolved comprehensive, and in many respects complex, election codes regulating in most substantial ways, with respect to both federal and state elections, the time, place, and manner of holding primary and general elections, the registration and qualifications of voters, and the selection and qualification of candidates."

Today, the Court departs from this process of accommodation. It does so, it seems to me, by upholding a First Amendment claim by one of the two major parties without any serious inquiry into the extent of the burden on associational freedoms and without due consideration of the countervailing state interests.

B. Voter or Candidate versus Political Party

Having considered the clash between the National Party and the state, we next ask whether voters and/or candidates have any federal constitutional rights to insist that a political party's nominating process be structured to provide fair opportunities for participation. The Court answered this question in a case involving New York's nominating process for judicial candidates, elevating the rights of the political party machinery over the "outsider" candidate. As you read this case, consider its implications for other types of nominating processes—including the type of argument Hillary Clinton's supporters might have made to challenge the national Democratic Party's decision not to seat the delegates from Florida and Michigan at the 2008 National Convention. Would the holding and rationale from *López Torres* impact the analysis of this sort of claim?

NEW YORK STATE BOARD OF ELECTIONS v. LÓPEZ TORRES

552 U.S. 196 (2008)

Justice Scalia delivered the opinion of the Court.

The State of New York requires that political parties select their nominees for Supreme Court Justice at a convention of delegates chosen by party members in a primary election. We consider whether this electoral system violates the First Amendment rights of prospective party candidates.

I

A

The Supreme Court of New York is the State's trial court of general jurisdiction, with an Appellate Division that hears appeals from certain lower courts. Under New York's current Constitution, the State is divided into 12 judicial districts, and Supreme Court Justices are elected to 14-year terms in each such district.

Over the years, New York has changed the method by which Supreme Court Justices are selected several times.

In 1911, the New York Legislature enacted a law requiring political parties to select Supreme Court nominees through direct primary elections. The primary system came to be criticized as a "device capable of astute and successful manipulation by professionals," Editorial, The State Convention, N.Y. Times, May 1, 1917, p. 12, and the Republican candidate for Governor in 1920 campaigned against it as "a fraud" that "offered the opportunity for two things, for the demagogue and the man with money." A law enacted in 1921 required parties to select their candidates for the Supreme Court by a convention composed of delegates elected by party members.

New York retains this system of choosing party nominees for Supreme Court Justice to this day. In a September "delegate primary," party members elect delegates from each of New York's 150 assembly districts to attend the party's judicial convention for the judicial district in which the assembly district is located. An individual may run for delegate by submitting to the Board of Elections a designating petition signed by 500 enrolled party members residing in the assembly district, or by five percent of such enrolled members, whichever is less. These signatures must be gathered within a 37-day period preceding the filing deadline, which is approximately two months before the delegate primary. The delegates elected in these primaries are uncommitted; the primary ballot does not specify the judicial nominee whom they will support.

The nominating conventions take place one to two weeks after the delegate primary. Each of the 12 judicial districts has its own convention to nominate the party's Supreme Court candidate or candidates who will run at large in that district in the general election. The general election takes place in November. The nominees from the party conventions appear automatically on the general-election ballot. They may be joined on the general-election ballot by independent candidates and candidates of political organizations that fail to meet the 50,000 vote threshold for "party" status; these candidates gain access to the ballot by submitting timely nominating petitions with (depending on the judicial district) 3,500 or 4,000 signatures from voters in that district or signatures from five percent of the number of votes cast for Governor in that district in the prior election, whichever is less.

B

Respondent López Torres [and others] brought suit in federal court against the New York Board of Elections, which is responsible for administering and enforcing the New York election law. They contended that New York's election law burdened the rights of challengers seeking to run against candidates favored by the party leadership, and deprived voters and candidates of their rights to gain access to the ballot and to associate in choosing their party's candidates. As relevant here, they sought a declaration that New York's convention system for selecting Supreme Court Justices violates their First Amendment rights, and an injunction mandating the establishment of a direct primary election to select party nominees for Supreme Court Justice.

The District Court issued a preliminary injunction granting the relief requested, pending the New York Legislature's enactment of a new statutory scheme. A unanimous panel of the United States Court of Appeals for the Second Circuit affirmed. The Second Circuit's holding effectively returned New York to the system of electing Supreme Court Justices that existed before the 1921 amendments to the election law.

II

A

A political party has a First Amendment right to limit its membership as it wishes, and to choose a candidate-selection process that will in its view produce the nominee who best represents its political platform. These rights are circumscribed, however, when the State gives the party a role in the election process—as New York has done here by giving certain parties the right to have their candidates appear with party endorsement on the general-election ballot. Then, for example, the party's racially discriminatory action may become state action that violates the Fifteenth Amendment. And then also the State acquires a legitimate governmental interest in assuring the fairness of the party's nominating process, enabling it to prescribe what that process must be. We have, for example, considered it to be "too plain for argument" that a State may prescribe party use of primaries or conventions to select nominees who appear on the general-election ballot. *American Party of Tex. v. White* (1974). That prescriptive power is not without limits. In [*California Democratic Party v.*] *Jones* [(2000)], for example, we invalidated on First Amendment grounds California's blanket primary, reasoning that it permitted non-party members to determine the candidate bearing the party's standard in the general election.

In the present case, however, the party's associational rights are at issue (if at all) only as a shield and not as a sword. Respondents are in no position to rely on the right that the First Amendment confers on political parties to structure their internal party processes and to select the candidate of the party's choosing. Indeed, both the Republican and Democratic state parties have intervened from the very early stages of this litigation to defend New York's electoral law. The weapon wielded by these plaintiffs is their *own* claimed associational right not only to join, but to have a certain degree of influence in, the party. They contend that New York's electoral system does not go far enough—does not go as far as the Constitution demands—in assuring that they will have a fair chance of prevailing in their parties' candidate-selection process.

This contention finds no support in our precedents. We have indeed acknowledged an individual's associational right to vote in a party primary without undue state-imposed impediment. In *Kusper v. Pontikes* (1973), we invalidated an Illinois law that required a voter wishing to change his party registration so as to vote in the primary of a different party to do so almost two full years before the primary date. But *Kusper* does not cast doubt on all state-imposed limitations upon primary voting. In *Rosario v. Rockefeller* (1973), we upheld a New York State requirement that a voter have enrolled in the party of his choice at least 30 days before the previous general election in order to vote in the next party primary. In any event, respondents do not claim that they have been excluded from voting in the primary. Moreover, even if we extended *Kusper* to cover not only the right to vote in the party primary but also the right to run, the requirements of the New York law (a 500-signature petition collected during a 37-day window in advance of the primary) are entirely reasonable. Just as States may require persons to demonstrate "a significant modicum of support" before allowing them access to the general-election ballot, lest it become unmanageable, they may similarly demand a minimum degree of support for candidate access to a primary ballot. The signature requirement here is far from excessive.

Respondents' real complaint is not that they cannot vote in the election for delegates, nor even that they cannot run in that election, but that the convention process that follows the delegate election does not give them a realistic chance to secure the party's nomination. The party leadership, they say, inevitably garners more votes for its slate of delegates (delegates uncommitted to any judicial nominee) than the unsupported candidate can amass for himself. And thus the leadership effectively determines the nominees. But this says nothing more than that the party leadership has more widespread support than a candidate not supported by the leadership. No New York law compels election of the leadership's slate—or, for that matter, compels the delegates elected on the leadership's slate to vote the way the leadership desires. And no state law prohibits an unsupported candidate from attending the convention and seeking to persuade the delegates to support her. Our cases invalidating ballot-access requirements have focused on the requirements themselves, and not on the manner in which political actors function under those requirements. Here respondents complain not of the state law, but of the voters' (and their elected delegates') preference for the choices of the party leadership.

To be sure, we have, as described above, permitted States to set their faces against "party bosses" by requiring party-candidate selection through processes more favorable to insurgents, such as primaries. But to say that the State can require this is a far cry from saying that the Constitution demands it. None of our cases establishes an individual's constitutional right to have a "fair shot" at winning the party's nomination. And with good reason. What constitutes a "fair shot" is a reasonable enough question for legislative judgment, which we will accept so long as it does not too much infringe upon the party's associational rights. But it is hardly a manageable constitutional question for judges—especially for judges in our legal system, where traditional electoral practice gives no hint of even the existence, much less the content, of a constitutional requirement for a "fair shot" at party nomination. Party conventions, with their attendant "smoke-filled rooms" and domination by party leaders, have long been an accepted manner of selecting party candidates. Selection by convention has never been thought unconstitutional, even when the delegates were not selected by primary but by party caucuses.

The Second Circuit's judgment finesses the difficulty of saying how much of a shot is a "fair shot" by simply mandating a primary until the New York Legislature acts. This was, according to the Second Circuit, the New York election law's default manner of party-candidate selection for offices whose manner of selection is not otherwise prescribed. Petitioners question the propriety of this mandate, but we need not pass upon that here. Even conceding its propriety, there is good reason to believe that the elected members of the New York Legislature remain opposed to the primary, for the same reasons their predecessors abolished it 86 years ago: because it leaves judicial selection to voters uninformed about judicial qualifications, and places a high premium upon the ability to raise money. Should the New York Legislature persist in that view, and adopt something different from a primary and closer to the system that the Second Circuit invalidated, the question whether *that* provides enough of a "fair shot" would be presented. We are not inclined to open up this new and excitingly unpredictable theater of election jurisprudence. Selection by convention has been a traditional means of choosing party nominees. While a State may determine it is not desirable and replace it, it is not unconstitutional.

B

Respondents put forward, as a special factor which gives them a First Amendment right to revision of party processes in the present case, the assertion that party loyalty in New York's judicial districts renders the general-election ballot "uncompetitive." They argue that the existence of entrenched "one-party rule" demands that the First Amendment be used to impose additional competition in the nominee-selection process of the parties. (The asserted "one-party rule," we may observe, is that of the Democrats in some judicial districts, and of the Republicans in others). This is a novel and implausible reading of the First Amendment.

To begin with, it is hard to understand how the competitiveness of the general election has anything to do with respondents' associational rights in the party's selection process. It makes no difference to the person who associates with a party and seeks its nomination whether the party is a contender in the general election, an underdog, or the favorite. Competitiveness may be of interest to the voters in the general election, and to the candidates who choose to run *against* the dominant party. But we have held that those interests are well enough protected so long as all candidates have an adequate opportunity to appear on the general-election ballot. In *Jenness* [*v. Fortson* (1971)] we upheld a petition-signature requirement for inclusion on the general-election ballot of five percent of the eligible voters, and in *Munro v. Socialist Workers Party* (1986), we upheld a petition-signature requirement of one percent of the vote in the State's primary. New York's general-election balloting procedures for Supreme Court Justice easily pass muster under this standard. Candidates who fail to obtain a major party's nomination via convention can still get on the general-election ballot for the judicial district by providing the requisite number of signatures of voters resident in the district. To our knowledge, outside of the Fourteenth and Fifteenth Amendment contexts [involving racial discrimination], no court has ever made "one-party entrenchment" a basis for interfering with the candidate-selection processes of a party. (Of course, the *lack* of one-party entrenchment will not cause free access to the general-election ballot to validate an otherwise unconstitutional restriction upon participation in a party's nominating process.)

The reason one-party rule is entrenched may be (and usually is) that voters approve of the positions and candidates that the party regularly puts forward. It is no function of the First Amendment to require revision of those positions or candidates. The States can, within limits (that is, short of violating the parties' freedom of association), discourage party monopoly—for example, by refusing to show party endorsement on the election ballot. But the Constitution provides no authority for federal courts to prescribe such a course. The First Amendment creates an open marketplace where ideas, most especially political ideas, may compete without government interference. It does not call on the federal courts to manage the market by preventing too many buyers from settling upon a single product.

Limiting respondents' court-mandated "fair shot at party endorsement" to situations of one-party entrenchment merely multiplies the impracticable lines courts would be called upon to draw. It would add to those alluded to earlier the line at which mere party popularity turns into "one-party dominance." In the case of New York's election system for Supreme Court Justices, that line would have to be drawn separately for each of the 12 judicial districts—and in those districts that are "competitive" the current system would presumably remain valid. But why limit the remedy to *one*-party dominance? Does not the dominance of two parties similarly stifle competing opinions? Once again, we decline to enter the morass.

. . .

New York State has thrice (in 1846, 1911, and 1921) displayed a willingness to reconsider its method of selecting Supreme Court Justices. If it wishes to return to the primary system that it discarded in 1921, it is free to do so; but the First Amendment does not compel that. We reverse the Second Circuit's contrary judgment.

It is so ordered.

Justice STEVENS, with whom Justice SOUTER joins, concurring.

While I join Justice Scalia's cogent resolution of the constitutional issues raised by this case, I think it appropriate to emphasize the distinction between constitutionality and wise policy. Our holding with respect to the former should not be misread as endorsement of the electoral system under review, or disagreement with the findings of the District Court that describe glaring deficiencies in that system and even lend support to the broader proposition that the very practice of electing judges is unwise. But as I recall my esteemed former colleague, Thurgood Marshall, remarking on numerous occasions: "The Constitution does not prohibit legislatures from enacting stupid laws."

NOTES ON *DEMOCRATIC PARTY v. WISCONSIN* AND *LÓPEZ TORRES*

1. The Court in *Wisconsin* relies on *Cousins v. Wigoda*, 419 U.S. 477 (1975), which involved a dispute over the rules for selecting delegates to the Democratic National Convention in 1972. In that case, the National Party chose to seat one slate of delegates from Illinois (who supported George McGovern) over another slate (who supported Chicago Mayor Richard Daley). The McGovern slate was selected according to the National Party's new rules, while the Daley

slate conformed with state law. The Court declared that "[t]he National Democratic Party and its adherents enjoy a constitutionally protected right of political association" and held that Illinois's law must yield to the party's desire to seat delegates in accordance with its own rules. Several Justices in *Cousins* (including Justice Stewart, who wrote the majority opinion in *Wisconsin*) wrote separately to object to the Court's "unnecessarily broad language." How does the holding in *Cousins* relate to the holding in *Wisconsin*? Did the *Wisconsin* Court narrow this holding? How do these two older cases relate to the holding in *López Torres*?

2. What do these cases say about the primacy of political parties' associational rights under the First Amendment? One takeaway seems to be that the rights of political parties are paramount as against both the state and candidates who want to have an effect on the nomination process.
3. Who or what is a political party? Is it the voters? The candidates? The party leaders? Of these groups, whose interests does the majority of the Court find to be paramount in *Wisconsin*? In *López Torres*?
4. Is Justice Powell correct in *Wisconsin* that the Democratic Party is not "organized around the achievement of defined ideological goals"? Would Justice Powell rule differently if this was the "Lower Taxes Party"? Does it make sense to have one set of rules for the major political parties (Democrats and Republicans) and different rules for the minor parties? Put differently, what is the role of political parties? To espouse a particular ideology? If the major parties are perceived as trying to achieve particular ideological outcomes, then may the state still provide them favored status (such as automatic ballot access for their nominees)?
5. In *López Torres*, Justice Scalia did not provide details on how the New York statutory scheme actually worked in practice. The Second Circuit explained that the two-step primary and nominating convention process for delegates was extremely arduous for a judicial candidate without a political machine behind it: The candidate would need to have its slate of delegates obtain between 9,000 and as many as 24,000 signatures (depending on the relevant population in the district) within 37 days to have the delegates appear on the primary election ballot; educate voters in the primary as to which delegates have agreed to vote for the candidate at the convention (because the delegates run technically unpledged to a specific candidate); and then lobby between 64 and as many as 248 elected delegates in the next two weeks after the primary election to vote for the candidate at the nominating convention. Political parties have pre-existing apparatuses in place to assist with these functions, particularly through the county chairs. Further, in reality there is rarely any debate at the nominating conventions, and often no contest at all. Do these facts change the way in which we should analyze Justice Scalia's opinion?

6. Note that Justice Scalia uses the "marketplace of ideas" analogy to reject the candidate's argument: "The First Amendment creates an open marketplace where ideas, most especially political ideas, may compete without government interference. It does not call on the federal courts to manage the market by preventing too many buyers from settling upon a single product." But what if the structure of the "market" (nomination process) means that there is really only one "product" (candidate) available?

C. Washington's "Top-Two" Primary and the Limits of Party Autonomy

Insofar as the *Wisconsin* case from 1981 signaled that the U.S. Supreme Court would protect vigorously a political party's autonomy from interfering state legislation, that signal became even stronger in *California Democratic Party v. Jones*, 530 U.S. 567 (2000). In *Jones*, the Court relied heavily on the *Wisconsin* precedent to hold that a state may not use a so-called "blanket" primary where doing so would deprive a party of its freedom to nominate the candidate of its own choice for the general election. A blanket primary is one in which a voter can choose any candidate from any party for any office on the ballot. Think of it as an "open primary on steroids": In an "open" primary, the voter can choose whichever party he or she wants that day, but must vote from only among that party's candidates for all of the races on the ballot; by contrast, in a blanket primary, the voter can choose one of the Democratic candidates for president, one of the Republican candidates for governor, go back to one of the Democratic candidates for senator, then back to one of the Republican candidates for House representative, and so forth.

The flaw that the U.S. Supreme Court found in California's version of the blanket primary was that the top vote-recipient from each party for each office moved on to the general election as the nominee of the political party with which they were affiliated in the primary. Thus, voters who were not party members and who had voted for a different party's candidate for a different office could have a significant say in selecting the party's nominee. Had voting for the party's candidate for each office been confined solely to party members, a different primary candidate might have been the winner. In the Court's judgment, this interference with the party's autonomy to identify its own nominee for the general election violated the First Amendment. But the Court pointed out how a state could achieve the goals of a blanket primary without violating the First Amendment: Simply make it a *nonpartisan* blanket primary, in which the top two vote-recipients move on to the general election ballot (making it a kind of run-off election) but without identifying either of these general election candidates as the official nominee of a political party.

In the wake of *Jones*, the State of Washington modified its own version of the blanket primary to comply with the Court's instructions. But were the modifications sufficient? That's the subject of the next case.

WASHINGTON STATE GRANGE v. WASHINGTON STATE REPUBLICAN PARTY

552 U.S. 442 (2008)

Justice THOMAS delivered the opinion of the Court.

In 2004, voters in the State of Washington passed an initiative changing the State's primary election system. The People's Choice Initiative of 2004, or Initiative 872 (I-872), provides that candidates for office shall be identified on the ballot by their self-designated "party preference"; that voters may vote for any candidate; and that the top two votegetters for each office, regardless of party preference, advance to the general election. The Court of Appeals for the Ninth Circuit held I-872 facially invalid as imposing an unconstitutional burden on state political parties' First Amendment rights. Because I-872 does not on its face impose a severe burden on political parties' associational rights, and because respondents' arguments to the contrary rest on factual assumptions about voter confusion that can be evaluated only in the context of an as-applied challenge, we reverse.

I.

For most of the past century, Washington voters selected nominees for state and local offices using a blanket primary.[1] From 1935 until 2003, the State used a blanket primary that placed candidates from all parties on one ballot and allowed voters to select a candidate from any party. Under this system, the candidate who won a plurality of votes within each major party became that party's nominee in the general election. California used a nearly identical primary in its own elections until our decision in *California Democratic Party v. Jones* (2000).

In *Jones*, four political parties challenged California's blanket primary, arguing that it unconstitutionally burdened their associational rights by forcing them to associate with voters who did not share their beliefs. We agreed and struck down the blanket primary as inconsistent with the First Amendment. In so doing, we emphasized the importance of the nomination process as "the crucial juncture at which the appeal to common principles may be translated into concerted action, and hence to political power in the community." We observed that a party's right to exclude is central to its freedom of association, and is never "more important than in the process of selecting its nominee." California's blanket primary, we concluded, severely burdened the parties' freedom of association because it forced them to allow nonmembers to participate in selecting the parties' nominees. That the parties retained the right to endorse their preferred candidates did not render the burden any less severe, as "[t]here is simply no substitute for a party's selecting its own candidates."

Because California's blanket primary severely burdened the parties' associational rights, we subjected it to strict scrutiny, carefully examining each of the state interests

1. The term "blanket primary" refers to a system in which "any person, regardless of party affiliation, may vote for a party's nominee." *California Democratic Party v. Jones* (2000). A blanket primary is distinct from an "open primary," in which a person may vote for any party's nominees, but must choose among that party's nominees for all offices, and the more traditional "closed primary" in which "only persons who are members of the political party . . . can vote on its nominee," *id.*

offered by California in support of its primary system. We rejected as illegitimate three of the asserted interests: "producing elected officials who better represent the electorate," "expanding candidate debate beyond the scope of partisan concerns," and ensuring "the right to an effective vote" by allowing nonmembers of a party to vote in the majority party's primary in "safe" districts. We concluded that the remaining interests—promoting fairness, affording voters greater choice, increasing voter participation, and protecting privacy—were not compelling on the facts of the case. Even if they were, the partisan California primary was not narrowly tailored to further those interests because a nonpartisan blanket primary, in which the top two votegetters advance to the general election regardless of party affiliation, would accomplish each of those interests without burdening the parties' associational rights. The nonpartisan blanket primary had "all the characteristics of the partisan blanket primary, save the constitutionally crucial one: Primary voters [were] not choosing a party's nominee."

After our decision in *Jones* the Court of Appeals for the Ninth Circuit struck down Washington's primary as "materially indistinguishable from the California scheme." The Washington State Grange promptly proposed I-872 as a replacement. It passed with nearly 60% of the vote and became effective in December 2004.

Under I-872, all elections for "partisan offices" are conducted in two stages: a primary and a general election. To participate in the primary, a candidate must file a "declaration of candidacy" form, on which he declares his "major or minor party preference, or independent status." Each candidate and his party preference (or independent status) is in turn designated on the primary election ballot. A political party cannot prevent a candidate who is unaffiliated with, or even repugnant to, the party from designating it as his party of preference. In the primary election, voters may select "any candidate listed on the ballot, regardless of the party preference of the candidates or the voter."

The Court of Appeals noted a "constitutionally significant distinction between ballots and other vehicles for political expression," reasoning that the risk of perceived association is particularly acute when ballots include party labels because such labels are typically used to designate candidates' views on issues of public concern. And it determined that the State's interests underlying I-872 were not sufficiently compelling to justify the severe burden on the parties' association. Concluding that the provisions of I-872 providing for the party-preference designation on the ballot were not severable, the court struck down I-872 in its entirety. We granted certiorari, to determine whether I-872, on its face, violates the political parties' associational rights.

II

Respondents object to I-872 not in the context of an actual election, but in a facial challenge. Under *United States* v. *Salerno* (1987), a plaintiff can only succeed in a facial challenge by "establish[ing] that no set of circumstances exists under which the Act would be valid," i.e., that the law is unconstitutional in all of its applications. While some

Members of the Court have criticized the *Salerno* formulation, all agree that a facial challenge must fail where the statute has a plainly legitimate sweep. Washington's primary system survives under either standard, as we explain below. In determining whether a law is facially invalid, we must be careful not to go beyond the statute's facial requirements and speculate about "hypothetical" or "imaginary" cases. The State has had no opportunity to implement I-872, and its courts have had no occasion to construe the law in the context of actual disputes arising from the electoral context, or to accord the law a limiting construction to avoid constitutional questions. Exercising judicial restraint in a facial challenge frees the Court not only from unnecessary pronouncement on constitutional issues, but also from premature interpretations of statutes in areas where their constitutional application might be cloudy.

Facial challenges are disfavored for several reasons. Claims of facial invalidity often rest on speculation. As a consequence, they raise the risk of "premature interpretation of statutes on the basis of factually barebones records." *Sabri* v. *United States* (2004). Facial challenges also run contrary to the fundamental principle of judicial restraint that courts should neither "anticipate a question of constitutional law in advance of the necessity of deciding it nor formulate a rule of constitutional law broader than is required by the precise facts to which it is to be applied." *Ashwander v. TVA* (1936) (Brandeis, J., concurring). Finally, facial challenges threaten to short circuit the democratic process by preventing laws embodying the will of the people from being implemented in a manner consistent with the Constitution. We must keep in mind that "[a] ruling of unconstitutionality frustrates the intent of the elected representatives of the people." *Ayotte v. Planned Parenthood of Northern New Eng.* (2006). It is with these principles in view that we turn to the merits of respondents' facial challenge to I-872.

A

Election regulations that impose a severe burden on associational rights are subject to strict scrutiny, and we uphold them only if they are "narrowly tailored to serve a compelling state interest." If a statute imposes only modest burdens, however, then "the State's important regulatory interests are generally sufficient to justify reasonable, nondiscriminatory restrictions" on election procedures. *Anderson v. Celebrezze* (1983). "Accordingly, we have repeatedly upheld reasonable, politically neutral regulations that have the effect of channeling expressive activity at the polls." *Burdick v. Takushi* (1992).

The parties do not dispute these general principles; rather, they disagree about whether I-872 severely burdens respondents' associational rights. That disagreement begins with *Jones*. Petitioners argue that the I-872 primary is indistinguishable from the alternative *Jones* suggested would be constitutional. In *Jones* we noted that a nonpartisan blanket primary, where the top two votegetters proceed to the general election regardless of their party, was a less restrictive alternative to California's system because such a primary does not nominate candidates.

That question is now squarely before us. Respondents argue that I-872 is unconstitutional under *Jones* because it has the same "constitutionally crucial" infirmity that doomed California's blanket primary: it allows primary voters who are unaffiliated with a party to choose the party's nominee. Respondents claim that candidates who progress to the general election under I-872 will become the *de facto* nominees of the parties they prefer, thereby violating the parties' right to choose their own standard-bearers, and altering their messages.

The flaw in this argument is that, unlike the California primary, the I-872 primary does not, by its terms, choose parties' nominees. The essence of nomination—the choice of a party representative—does not occur under I-872. The law never refers to the candidates as nominees of any party, nor does it treat them as such. To the contrary, the election regulations specifically provide that the primary "does not serve to determine the nominees of a political party but serves to winnow the number of candidates to a final list of two for the general election." The top two candidates from the primary election proceed to the general election regardless of their party preferences. Whether parties nominate their own candidates outside the state-run primary is simply irrelevant. In fact, parties may now nominate candidates by whatever mechanism they choose because I-872 repealed Washington's prior regulations governing party nominations.[7]

Respondents counter that, even if the I-872 primary does not actually choose parties' nominees, it nevertheless burdens their associational rights because voters will assume that candidates on the general election ballot are the nominees of their preferred parties. This brings us to the heart of respondents' case—and to the fatal flaw in their argument. At bottom, respondents' objection to I-872 is that voters will be confused by candidates' party-preference designations. Respondents' arguments are largely variations on this theme. Thus, they argue that even if voters do not assume that candidates on the general election ballot are the nominees of their parties, they will at least assume that the parties associate with, and approve of, them. This, they say, compels them to associate with candidates they do not endorse, alters the messages they wish to convey, and forces them to engage in counterspeech to disassociate themselves from the candidates and their positions on the issues.

We reject each of these contentions for the same reason: They all depend, not on any facial requirement of I-872, but on the possibility that voters will be confused as to the meaning of the party-preference designation. But respondents' assertion that voters will misinterpret the party-preference designation is sheer speculation. It depends upon the belief that voters can be "misled" by party labels. But [o]ur cases reflect a greater faith in the

7. It is true that parties may no longer indicate their nominees on the ballot, but that is unexceptionable: The First Amendment does not give political parties a right to have their nominees designated as such on the ballot. *See Timmons v. Twin Cities Area New Party* (1997) ("We are unpersuaded, however, by the party's contention that it has a right to use the ballot itself to send a particularized message, to its candidate and to the voters, about the nature of its support for the candidate"). Parties do not gain such a right simply because the State affords candidates the opportunity to indicate their party preference on the ballot. "Ballots serve primarily to elect candidates, not as forums for political expression." *Id.*

ability of individual voters to inform themselves about campaign issues. There is simply no basis to presume that a well-informed electorate will interpret a candidate's party-preference designation to mean that the candidate is the party's chosen nominee or representative or that the party associates with or approves of the candidate. This strikes us as especially true here, given that it was the voters of Washington themselves, rather than their elected representatives, who enacted I-872.

Of course, it is *possible* that voters will misinterpret the candidates' party-preference designations as reflecting endorsement by the parties. [But this case involves] a facial challenge, and we cannot strike down I-872 on its face based on the mere possibility of voter confusion. Because respondents brought their suit as a facial challenge, we have no evidentiary record against which to assess their assertions that voters will be confused. Indeed, because I-872 has never been implemented, we do not even have ballots indicating how party preference will be displayed. It stands to reason that whether voters will be confused by the party-preference designations will depend in significant part on the form of the ballot. The Court of Appeals assumed that the ballot would not place abbreviations like "D" and "R," or "Dem." and "Rep." after the names of candidates, but would instead "clearly state that a particular candidate 'prefers' a particular party." It thought that even such a clear statement did too little to eliminate the risk of voter confusion.

But we see no reason to stop there. As long as we are speculating about the form of the ballot—and we can do no more than speculate in this facial challenge—we must, in fairness to the voters of the State of Washington who enacted I-872 and in deference to the executive and judicial officials who are charged with implementing it, ask whether the ballot could conceivably be printed in such a way as to eliminate the possibility of widespread voter confusion and with it the perceived threat to the First Amendment.

It is not difficult to conceive of such a ballot. For example, petitioners propose that the actual I-872 ballot could include prominent disclaimers explaining that party preference reflects only the self-designation of the candidate and not an official endorsement by the party. They also suggest that the ballots might note preference in the form of a candidate statement that emphasizes the candidate's personal determination rather than the party's acceptance of the candidate, such as "my party preference is the Republican Party." Additionally, the State could decide to educate the public about the new primary ballots through advertising or explanatory materials mailed to voters along with their ballots.[8] We are satisfied that there are a variety of ways in which the State could implement I-872 that would eliminate any real threat of voter confusion. And without the specter of widespread voter confusion, respondents' arguments about forced association and compelled speech fall flat.

8. Washington counties have broad authority to conduct elections entirely by mail ballot rather than at in-person polling places. As a result, over 90% of Washington voters now vote by mail.

Our conclusion that these implementations of I-872 would be consistent with the First Amendment is fatal to respondents' facial challenge. Each of their arguments rests on factual assumptions about voter confusion, and each fails for the same reason: In the absence of evidence, we cannot assume that Washington's voters will be misled. That factual determination must await an as-applied challenge. On its face, I-872 does not impose any severe burden on respondents' associational rights.

B

Because we have concluded that I-872 does not severely burden respondents, the State need not assert a compelling interest. The State's asserted interest in providing voters with relevant information about the candidates on the ballot is easily sufficient to sustain I-872. *See Anderson* ("There can be no question about the legitimacy of the State's interest in fostering informed and educated expressions of the popular will in a general election").

Respondents ask this Court to invalidate a popularly enacted election process that has never been carried out. Immediately after implementing regulations were enacted, respondents obtained a permanent injunction against the enforcement of I-872. The First Amendment does not require this extraordinary and precipitous nullification of the will of the people. Because I-872 does not on its face provide for the nomination of candidates or compel political parties to associate with or endorse candidates, and because there is no basis in this facial challenge for presuming that candidates' party-preference designations will confuse voters, I-872 does not on its face severely burden respondents' associational rights. We accordingly hold that I-872 is facially constitutional. The judgment of the Court of Appeals is reversed.

Chief Justice ROBERTS, with whom Justice ALITO joins, concurring.

I share Justice Scalia's concern that permitting a candidate to identify his political party preference on an official election ballot—regardless of whether the candidate is endorsed by the party or is even a member—may effectively force parties to accept candidates they do not want, amounting to forced association in violation of the First Amendment.

I do think, however, that whether voters *perceive* the candidate and the party to be associated is relevant to the constitutional inquiry. Our other forced-association cases indicate as much. In *Boy Scouts of America v. Dale* (2000), we said that Dale's presence in the Boy Scouts would "force the organization to send a message . . . [to] the world" that the Scouts approved of homosexuality. In other words, accepting Dale would lead outsiders to believe the Scouts endorsed homosexual conduct. Largely for that reason, we held that the First Amendment entitled the Scouts to exclude Dale. Similarly, in *Hurley v. Irish-American Gay, Lesbian and Bisexual Group of Boston, Inc.* (1995), we allowed the organizers of Boston's St. Patrick's Day Parade to exclude a pro-gay rights float because the float's presence in the parade might create the impression that the organizers agreed with the float-sponsors' message.

Voter perceptions matter, and if voters do not actually believe the parties and the candidates are tied together, it is hard to see how the parties' associational rights are adversely implicated. After all, individuals frequently claim to favor this or that political party; these preferences, without more, do not create an unconstitutional forced association.

What makes these cases different, as Justice Scalia explains, is the place where the candidates express their party preferences: on the ballot. And what makes the ballot "special" is precisely the effect it has on voter impressions. But because respondents brought this challenge before the State of Washington had printed ballots for use under the new primary regime, we have no idea what those ballots will look like. Petitioners themselves emphasize that the content of the ballots in the pertinent respect is yet to be determined.

If the ballot is designed in such a manner that no reasonable voter would believe that the candidates listed there are nominees or members of, or otherwise associated with, the parties the candidates claimed to "prefer," the I-872 primary system would likely pass constitutional muster. I cannot say on the present record that it would be impossible for the State to design such a ballot. Assuming the ballot is so designed, voters would not regard the listed candidates as "party" candidates, any more than someone saying "I like Campbell's soup" would be understood to be associated with Campbell's. Voters would understand that the candidate does not speak on the party's behalf or with the party's approval. On the other hand, if the ballot merely lists the candidates' preferred parties next to the candidates' names, or otherwise fails clearly to convey that the parties and the candidates are not necessarily associated, the I-872 system would not survive a First Amendment challenge.

Justice Scalia complains that "[i]t is hard to know how to respond" to such mistaken views, but he soldiers on nonetheless. He would hold that a party is burdened by a candidate's statement of preference even if no reasonable voter believes from the ballot that the party and the candidate are associated. I take his point to be that a particular candidate's "endorsement" of a party might alter the party's message, and this violates the party's freedom of association.

But there is no general right to stop an individual from saying, "I prefer this party," even if the party would rather he not. Normally, the party protects its message in such a case through responsive speech of its own. What makes this case different of course is that the State controls the content of the ballot, which we have never considered a public forum. Neither the candidate nor the party dictates the message conveyed by the ballot. In such a case, it is important to know what the ballot actually says—both about the candidate and about the party's association with the candidate. It is possible that no reasonable voter in Washington State will regard the listed candidates as members of, or otherwise associated with, the political parties the candidates claim to prefer. Nothing in my analysis requires the parties to produce studies regarding voter perceptions on this score, but I would wait to see what the ballot says before deciding whether it is unconstitutional.

Still, I agree with Justice Scalia that the history of the challenged law suggests the State is not particularly interested in devising ballots that meet these constitutional requirements. But this record simply does not allow us to say with certainty that the election system created by I-872 is unconstitutional. Accordingly, I agree with the Court that respondents' present challenge to the law must fail, and I join the Court's opinion.

Justice SCALIA, with whom Justice KENNEDY joins, dissenting.

The electorate's perception of a political party's beliefs is colored by its perception of those who support the party; and a party's defining act is the selection of a candidate and advocacy of that candidate's election by conferring upon him the party's endorsement. When the state-printed ballot for the general election causes a party to be associated with candidates who may not fully (if at all) represent its views, it undermines both these vital aspects of political association. The views of the self-identified party supporter color perception of the party's message, and that self-identification on the ballot, with no space for party repudiation or party identification of its own candidate, impairs the party's advocacy of its standard bearer. Because Washington has not demonstrated that this severe burden upon parties' associational rights is narrowly tailored to serve a compelling interest—indeed, because it seems to me Washington's only plausible interest is precisely to reduce the effectiveness of political parties—I would find the law unconstitutional.

I

Among the First Amendment rights that political parties possess is the right to associate with the persons whom they choose and to refrain from associating with persons whom they reject. Also included is the freedom to choose and promote the "standard bearer who best represents the party's ideologies and preferences." *Eu v. San Francisco County Democratic Central Comm.* (1989).

When an expressive organization is compelled to associate with a person whose views the group does not accept, the organization's message is undermined; the organization is understood to embrace, or at the very least tolerate, the views of the persons linked with them.

A political party's expressive mission is not simply, or even primarily, to persuade voters of the party's views. Parties seek principally to promote the election of candidates who will implement those views. That is achieved in large part by marking candidates with the party's seal of approval. Parties devote substantial resources to making their names trusted symbols of certain approaches to governance. They then encourage voters to cast their votes for the candidates that carry the party name. Parties' efforts to support candidates by marking them with the party trademark, so to speak, have been successful enough to make the party name, in the words of one commentator, "the most important resource that the party possesses." And all evidence suggests party labels are indeed a central consideration for most voters.

II

A

The State of Washington need not like, and need not favor, political parties. It is entirely free to decline running primaries for the selection of party nominees and to hold nonpartisan general elections in which party labels have no place on the ballot. Parties would then be left to their own devices in both selecting and publicizing their candidates. But Washington has done more than merely decline to make its electoral machinery available for party building. Recognizing that parties draw support for their candidates by giving them the party imprimatur, Washington seeks to reduce the effectiveness of that endorsement by allowing *any* candidate to use the ballot for drawing upon the goodwill that a party has developed, while preventing the party from using the ballot to reject the claimed association or to identify the genuine candidate of its choice. This does not merely place the ballot off limits for party building; it makes the ballot an instrument by which party building is impeded, permitting unrebutted associations that the party itself does not approve.

These cases cannot be decided without taking account of the special role that a state-printed ballot plays in elections. The ballot comes into play "at the most crucial stage in the electoral process—the instant before the vote is cast." *Anderson v. Martin* (1964). It is the only document that all voters are guaranteed to see, and it is "the last thing the voter sees before he makes his choice," *Cook v. Gralike* (2001) (Rehnquist, C.J., concurring in judgment).

The Court makes much of the fact that the party names shown on the Washington ballot may be billed as mere statements of candidate "preference." To be sure, the party is not itself forced to display favor for someone it does not wish to associate with, as the Boy Scouts were arguably forced to do by employing the homosexual scoutmaster in *Dale*, and as the political parties were arguably forced to do by lending their ballot-endorsement as party nominee in *Jones*. But thrusting an unwelcome, self-proclaimed association upon the party on the election ballot itself is amply destructive of the party's associational rights. An individual's endorsement of a party shapes the voter's view of what the party stands for, no less than the party's endorsement of an individual shapes the voter's view of what the individual stands for. That is why party nominees are often asked (and regularly agree) to repudiate the support of persons regarded as racial extremists. On Washington's ballot, such repudiation is impossible. And because the ballot is the only document voters are guaranteed to see, and the last thing they see before casting their vote, there is "no means of replying" that "would be equally effective with the voter." *Cook* (Rehnquist, C. J., concurring in judgment).

Not only is the party's message distorted, but its goodwill is hijacked. There can be no dispute that candidate acquisition of party labels on Washington's ballot—even if billed as self-identification—is a means of garnering the support of those who trust and agree with the party. The "I prefer the D's" and "I prefer the R's" will not be on the ballot for esthetic reasons; they are designed to link candidates to unwilling parties (or at least parties who are unable to express their revulsion) and to encourage voters to cast their ballots based in part on the trust they place in the party's name and the party's philosophy. These harms will be present no matter how Washington's law is implemented. There is therefore "no set of circumstances" under which Washington's law would not severely burden political parties, and no good reason to wait until Washington has undermined its political parties to declare that it is forbidden to do so.

B

The Chief Justice would wait to see if the law is implemented in a manner that no more harms political parties than allowing a person to state that he "like[s] Campbell's soup" would harm the Campbell Soup Company. It is hard to know how to respond. First and most fundamentally, there is simply no comparison between statements of "preference" for an expressive association and statements of "preference" for soup. The robust First Amendment freedom to associate belongs only to groups "engage[d] in 'expressive association,'" *Dale*. The Campbell Soup Company does not exist to promote a message, and "there is only minimal constitutional protection of the freedom of commercial association," *Roberts v. United States Jaycees* (1984) (O'Connor, J., concurring in part and concurring in judgment).

Second, I assuredly do not share The Chief Justice's view that the First Amendment will be satisfied so long as the ballot "is designed in such a manner that no reasonable voter would believe that the candidates listed there are nominees or members of, or otherwise associated with, the parties the candidates claimed to 'prefer.'" To begin with, it seems to me quite impossible for the ballot to satisfy a reasonable voter that the candidate is not "associated with" the party for which he has expressed a preference. He has associated himself with the party by his very expression of a preference—and that indeed is the whole purpose of allowing the preference to be expressed. If all the Chief Justice means by "associated with" is that the candidate "does not speak on the party's behalf or with the party's approval," none of my analysis in this opinion relies upon that misperception, nor upon the misperception that the candidate is a member or the nominee of the party. Avoiding those misperceptions is far from enough. Is it enough to say on the ballot that a notorious and despised racist who says that the party is his choice does not speak with the party's approval? Surely not. His unrebutted association of that party with his views distorts the image of the party nonetheless. And the fact that the candidate who expresses a "preference" for one or another party is shown not to be the nominee of that party does not deprive him of the boost from the party's reputation which the party wishes to confer only on its nominee. The Chief Justice claims that "the content of the ballots in the pertinent respect is yet to be determined." I disagree. We know all we need to know about the form of ballot. When pressed, Washington's Attorney General assured us at oral argument that the ballot will not say whether the party for whom the candidate expresses a preference claims or disavows him. (Of course it will not, for that would enable the party expression that it is the very object of this legislation to impair.)

And finally, while The Chief Justice earlier expresses his awareness that the special character of the ballot is what makes these cases different, his Campbell's Soup example seems to forget that. If we must speak in terms of soup, Washington's law is like a law that encourages Oscar the Grouch (Sesame Street's famed bad-taste resident of a garbage can) to state a "preference" for Campbell's at every point of sale, while barring the soup company from disavowing his endorsement, or indeed using its name at all, in those same crucial locations. Reserving the most critical communications forum for statements of "preference" by a potentially distasteful speaker alters public perceptions of the entity that is "preferred"; and when this privileged connection undermines not a company's ability to identify and promote soup but an expressive association's ability to identify and promote its message and its standard bearer, the State treads on the constitutionally protected freedom of association.

The majority opinion and The Chief Justice's concurrence also endorse a wait-and-see approach on the grounds that it is not yet evident how the law will affect voter perception of the political parties. But contrary to the Court's suggestion, it is not incumbent on the political parties to adduce "evidence" that forced association affects their ability to advocate for their candidates and their causes. We have never put expressive groups to this perhaps-impossible task. Rather, we accept their own assessments of the matter. It does not take a study to establish that when statements of party connection are the sole information listed next to candidate names on the ballot, those statements will affect voters' perceptions of what the candidate stands for, what the party stands for, and whom they should elect.

III

The right to associate for the election of candidates is fundamental to the operation of our political system, and state action impairing that association bears a heavy burden of justification. Washington's electoral system permits individuals to appropriate the parties' trademarks, so to speak, at the most crucial stage of election, thereby distorting the parties' messages and impairing their endorsement of candidates. The State's justification for this (to convey a "modicum of relevant information") is not only weak but undeserving of credence. We have here a system which, like the one it replaced, does not merely refuse to assist, but positively impairs, the legitimate role of political parties. I dissent from the Court's conclusion that the Constitution permits this sabotage.

NOTES ON *WASHINGTON STATE GRANGE*

1. Much of Justice Thomas's majority opinion focuses on the difference between facial and as-applied challenges. In a facial challenge, the plaintiff is claiming that the law is unconstitutional in every instance, regardless of how it operates with respect to that plaintiff specifically. In an as-applied challenge, by contrast, the plaintiff is asserting only that the law is unconstitutional as it affects that plaintiff (and those similarly situated). That is, a facial challenge is a challenge to the law in its entirety.

An as-applied challenge is narrower, as a court could rule the law unconstitutional with respect to that plaintiff but not to others with different circumstances. Why is the difference so significant here? Should the plaintiffs have waited for an actual election to challenge the law so there was evidence on how the law operated? What sort of evidence might they need to bring a successful as-applied challenge? One implication of this opinion might be that the political party must suffer a potential constitutional violation for at least one election before it can secure judicial relief.

2. Does a designation that a candidate "Prefers Democratic Party" really tell a voter that the affiliation is only one way? How do most voters decide who to vote for in down-ballot elections? Many voters use political party affliation as a useful proxy. This decision therefore puts a lot of faith in voters' knowledge that a party does not endorse a candidate even if the candidate prefers the party. Is it realistic to expect voters to understand this distinction? On the other hand, perhaps a top-two primary is useful for branches of one of the major parties, such as the Tea Party movement. A candidate could prefer "Tea Party" instead of "Republican Party" to indicate his or her specific views.

READ: Each candidate for partisan office may state a political party that he or she prefers. A candidate's preference does not imply that the candidate is nominated or endorsed by the party, or that the party approves of or associates with that candidate.

FEDERAL

United States Representative
Congressional District No. 7
Partisan Office
Vote for One

- **Goodspaceguy Nelson** (Prefers Democratic Party)
- **Mark A. Goldman** (States No Party Preference)
- **Donovan Rivers** (Prefers Democratic Party)
- **Al Schaefer** (States No Party Preference)
- **Steve Beren** (Prefers Republican Party)
- **Jim McDermott** (Prefers Democratic Party)
- Write-in

STATE OF WASHINGTON

Governor
Partisan Office
Vote for One

- **Dino Rossi** (Prefers G.O.P. Party)
- **Will Baker** (Prefers Reform Party)
- **Christine Gregoire** (Prefers Democratic Party)
- **Duff Badgley** (Prefers Green Party)
- **John W. Aiken, Jr.** (Prefers Republican Party)
- **Christian Pierre Joubert** (Prefers Democratic Party)
- **Christopher A. Tudor** (States No Party Preference)
- **Javier O. Lopez** (Prefers Republican Party)
- **Mohammad Hasan Said** (States No Party Preference)
- **James White** (Prefers Independent Party)
- Write-in

Source: King County, (WA) Department of Elections.

3. On page 292 is a copy of part of the "sample ballot" that King County, Washington distributed to voters before the 2008 election. This is the ballot the Department of Elections designed in the wake of Washington's new top-two law. Does seeing the ballot alter your views on whether it would confuse voters about a political party's endorsement of a candidate?
4. Imagine you represent the Democratic Party. Rush Limbaugh, a noted conservative talk radio host, decides to run for office in Washington State and declares his party preference for the ballot as Democratic Party, perhaps to take away votes from the "true" Democrats in the election. What would you advise the party to do?
5. Does this decision pull back on the seeming primacy of political parties from *Democratic Party v. Wisconsin*? Further, how can we reconcile the role of political parties envisioned in *López Torres* with the role of political parties envisioned in *Washington State Grange*?
6. In 2010, taking advantage of the *Washington State Grange* decision, California adopted its own version of the top-two primary (as distinct from its earlier blanket primary invalidated in *California Democratic Party v. Jones*). Because California is the nation's largest state (and is especially multicultural in its demographics), politicians and pundits are watching closely to see how Top Two operates there, and whether the combined experience of California and Washington serves as a catalyst for adopting this reform in other states. Meanwhile, a three-judge panel of the Ninth Circuit unanimously upheld California's new law against a First Amendment challenge. *Chamness v. Brown*, 722 F.3d 1110 (9th Cir. 2013). In that case, a candidate unaffiliated with any political party complained that the California law only gave him the option of stating "No Party Designation" on the primary ballot, rather than the label "Independent," which he preferred. The court held that because the ballot belonged to the state, and because the label "Independent" might cause confusion with the "American Independent" party (one of the six political parties qualified for party designation under California's law), the state's rule was a reasonable regulation. The candidate of course remained free to describe himself as an "Independent" in his own campaign communications.

D. Inviting Nonmembers to the Party (or at Least to Its Primary)

As *California Democratic Party* and *Washington State Grange* show, often a political party does not want to permit nonmembers to affect the choice of which candidate from the party carries the party's banner in the general election. In 2008, for example, some Democrats feared that—after John McCain clinched the Republican nomination but the battle between Barack Obama and Hillary Clinton waged on in states like Ohio—Republicans would "cross-over" or "raid" the remaining Democratic Party primaries to vote for Clinton because they thought she would be easier for McCain to beat in the general election. Whatever its motive, the cross-over vote in Ohio may have contributed to the prolonged fight between Obama and Clinton, which could have used up Obama's resources before he won the nomination and entered the general election campaign.

Sometimes, however, political parties like to welcome nonmembers to vote in their primaries. The strategy is to appeal to centrist voters early, so that the party's nominees are not chosen solely by its "base" and thus are less likely to be polarizing choices in November. In *Tashjian v. Republican Party of Connecticut*, 479 U.S. 208 (1986), Connecticut law mandated a "closed" primary in that state, meaning that only party members were permitted to vote in a party's primary. The Republican Party in the state wanted to permit independents to vote in its primary and thus sued to invalidate the state law on First Amendment grounds. The party prevailed in the U.S. Supreme Court.

The reach of *Tashjian* as precedent was the focus of this important case, which failed to produce a clear majority opinion. Pay special attention to Justice O'Connor's concurrence, asking yourself why she and Justice Breyer refused to join Justice Thomas's opinion in full, and how their disagreement might prove significant in future litigation.

CLINGMAN v. BEAVER

544 U.S. 581 (2005)

Justice THOMAS delivered the opinion of the Court, except as to Part II-A.

Oklahoma has a semi-closed primary system, in which a political party may invite only its own party members and voters registered as Independents to vote in the party's primary. [Members of other political parties are excluded.] The Court of Appeals held that this system violates the right to freedom of association of the Libertarian Party of Oklahoma (LPO) and several Oklahomans who are registered members of the Republican and Democratic parties. We hold that it does not.

I

In May 2000, the LPO notified the secretary of the Oklahoma State Election Board that it wanted to open its upcoming primary to all registered Oklahoma voters, without regard to their party affiliation. [T]he secretary agreed as to Independent voters, but not as to voters registered with other political parties. The LPO and several Republican and Democratic voters then sued for declaratory and injunctive relief . . . , alleging that Oklahoma's semi-closed primary law unconstitutionally burdens their First Amendment right to freedom of political association.

II

The Constitution grants States "broad power to prescribe the 'Time, Places and Manner of holding Elections for Senators and Representatives,' Art. I, § 4, cl. 1, which power is matched by state control over the election process for state offices." *Tashjian v. Republican Party of Conn.* (1986). We have held that the First Amendment, among other things, protects the right of citizens "to band together in promoting among the electorate candidates who espouse their political views." *California Democratic Party v. Jones* (2000). Regulations that impose severe burdens on associational rights must be narrowly tailored to serve a compelling state interest. However, when regulations impose lesser burdens, "a State's important regulatory interests will usually be enough to justify reasonable, nondiscriminatory restrictions."

In *Tashjian*, this Court struck down, as inconsistent with the First Amendment, a closed primary system that prevented a political party from inviting Independent voters to vote in the party's primary. This case presents a question that *Tashjian* left open: whether a State may prevent a political party from inviting registered voters of other parties to vote in its primary. As *Tashjian* acknowledged, opening a party's primary "to all voters, including members of other parties, . . . raise[s] a different combination of considerations." We are persuaded that any burden Oklahoma's semi-closed primary imposes is minor and justified by legitimate state interests.

A

[Plurality, Justice THOMAS joined by Chief Justice REHNQUIST, Justice SCALIA, and Justice KENNEDY]

At the outset, we note that Oklahoma's semi-closed primary system is unlike other laws this Court has held to infringe associational rights. Oklahoma has not sought through its electoral system to discover the names of the LPO's members; to interfere with the LPO by restricting activities central to its purpose; to disqualify the LPO from public benefits or privileges; or to compel the LPO's association with unwanted members or voters. The LPO is free to canvass the electorate, enroll or exclude potential members, nominate the candidate of its choice, and engage in the same electoral activities as every other political party in Oklahoma. Oklahoma merely prohibits the LPO from leaving the selection of its candidates to people who are members of another political party. Nothing prevents members of other parties from switching their registration to the LPO or to Independent status.[2] The question is whether the Constitution requires that voters who are registered in other parties be allowed to vote in the LPO's primary.

In other words, the Republican and Democratic voters who have brought this action do not want to associate with the LPO, at least not in any formal sense. They wish to remain registered with the Republican, Democratic, or Reform parties, and yet to assist in selecting the Libertarian Party's candidates for the general election. Their interest is in casting a vote for a Libertarian candidate in a particular primary election, rather than in

2. Respondents argue, for the first time before this Court, that Oklahoma election statutes other than § 1-104 make it difficult for voters to disaffiliate from their parties of first choice and register as Libertarians or Independents (either of which would allow them to vote in the LPO primary). [Because respondents raised this argument for the first time their merits brief to this Court,] we decline to consider this aspect of respondents' challenge.

banding together with fellow citizens committed to the LPO's political goals and ideas. And the LPO is happy to have their votes, if not their membership on the party rolls.

However, a voter who is unwilling to disaffiliate from another party to vote in the LPO's primary forms little "association" with the LPO—nor the LPO with him. That same voter might wish to participate in numerous party primaries, or cast ballots for several candidates, in any given race. The issue is not "dual associations," but seemingly boundless ones. "If the concept of freedom of association is extended" to a voter's every desire at the ballot box, "it ceases to be of any analytic use." *Tashjian* (Scalia, J., dissenting).

But even if Oklahoma's semi-closed primary system burdens an associational right, the burden is less severe than others this Court has upheld as constitutional. For instance, in *Timmons*, we considered a Minnesota election law prohibiting multiparty, or "fusion," candidacies in which a candidate appears on the ballot as the nominee of more than one party. Minnesota's law prevented the New Party, a minor party under state law, from putting forward the same candidate as a major party. The New Party challenged the law as unconstitutionally burdening its associational rights. This Court concluded that the burdens imposed by Minnesota's law—"though not trivial—[were] not severe."

The burdens were not severe because the New Party and its members remained free to govern themselves internally and to communicate with the public as they wished. Minnesota had neither regulated the New Party's internal decision-making process, nor compelled it to associate with voters of any political persuasion. The New Party and its members simply could not nominate as their candidate any of "those few individuals who both have already agreed to be another party's candidate and also, if forced to choose, themselves prefer that other party."

The same reasons underpinning our decision in *Timmons* show that Oklahoma's semi-closed primary system burdens the LPO only minimally. As in *Timmons*, Oklahoma's law does not regulate the LPO's internal processes, its authority to exclude unwanted members, or its capacity to communicate with the public. And just as in *Timmons*, in which Minnesota conditioned the party's ability to nominate the candidate of its choice on the candidate's willingness to disaffiliate from another political party, Oklahoma conditions the party's ability to welcome a voter into its primary on the voter's willingness to dissociate from his current party of choice. If anything, it is "[t]he moment of choosing the party's nominee" that matters far more, for that is "the crucial juncture at which the appeal to common principles may be translated into concerted action, and hence to political power in the community," *Jones*. If a party may be prevented from associating with the candidate of its choice—its desired "standard bearer,"—because that candidate refuses to disaffiliate from another political party, a party may also be prevented from associating with a voter who refuses to do the same.

B

Respondents argue that this case is no different from *Tashjian*. According to respondents, the burden imposed by Oklahoma's semi-closed primary system is no less severe than the burden at issue in *Tashjian,* and hence we must apply strict scrutiny as we did in *Tashjian.* We disagree. At issue in *Tashjian* was a Connecticut election statute that required voters to register with a political party before participating in its primary. The State's Republican Party, having adopted a rule that allowed Independent voters to participate in its primary, contended that Connecticut's closed primary infringed its right to associate with Independent voters. Applying strict scrutiny, this Court found that the interests Connecticut advanced to justify its ban were not compelling, and thus that the State could not constitutionally prevent the Republican Party from inviting into its primary willing Independent voters.

Respondents' reliance on *Tashjian* is unavailing. As an initial matter, *Tashjian* applied strict scrutiny with little discussion of the magnitude of the burdens imposed by Connecticut's closed primary on parties' and voters' associational rights. But not every electoral law that burdens associational rights is subject to strict scrutiny. Instead, as our cases since *Tashjian* have clarified, strict scrutiny is appropriate only if the burden is severe. In *Tashjian* itself, Independent voters could join the Connecticut Republican Party as late as the day before the primary. As explained above, requiring voters to register with a party prior to participating in the party's primary minimally burdens voters' associational rights.

Nevertheless, *Tashjian* is distinguishable. Oklahoma's semi-closed primary imposes an even less substantial burden than did the Connecticut closed primary at issue in *Tashjian.* In *Tashjian,* this Court identified two ways in which Connecticut's closed primary limited citizens' freedom of political association. The first and most important was that it required Independent voters to affiliate publicly with a party to vote in its primary. That is not true in this case. At issue here are voters who have *already* affiliated publicly with one of Oklahoma's political parties. These voters need not register as Libertarians to vote in the LPO's primary; they need only declare themselves Independents, which would leave them free to participate in any party primary that is open to registered Independents.

The second and less important burden imposed by Connecticut's closed primary system was that political parties could not "broaden opportunities for joining . . . by their own act, without any intervening action by potential voters." *Tashjian.* Voters also had to act by registering themselves in a particular party. That is equally true of Oklahoma's semi-closed primary system: Voters must register as Libertarians or Independents to participate in the LPO's primary. However, *Tashjian* did not characterize this burden alone as severe, and with good reason. Many electoral regulations, including voter registration generally, require that voters take some action to participate in the primary process. Election laws invariably "affec[t]—at least to some degree—the individual's right to vote and his right to associate with others for political ends." *Anderson v. Celebrezze* (1983).

These minor barriers between voter and party do not compel strict scrutiny. To deem ordinary and widespread burdens like these severe would subject virtually every electoral regulation to strict scrutiny, hamper the ability of States to run efficient and equitable elections, and compel federal courts to rewrite state electoral codes. The Constitution does not require that result, for it is beyond question "that States may, and inevitably must, enact reasonable regulations of parties, elections, and ballots to reduce election- and campaign-related disorder." *Timmons*. Oklahoma's semi-closed primary system does not severely burden the associational rights of the state's citizenry.

C

When a state electoral provision places no heavy burden on associational rights, "a State's important regulatory interests will usually be enough to justify reasonable, non-discriminatory restrictions." *Timmons*. Here, Oklahoma's semi-closed primary advances a number of regulatory interests that this Court recognizes as important: It preserves political parties as viable and identifiable interest groups; enhances parties' electioneering and party-building efforts; and guards against party raiding and "sore loser" candidacies by spurned primary contenders.

First, [t]he LPO wishes to open its primary to registered Republicans and Democrats, who may well vote in numbers that dwarf the roughly 300 registered LPO voters in Oklahoma. If the LPO is permitted to open its primary to all registered voters regardless of party affiliation, the candidate who emerges from the LPO primary may be "unconcerned with, if not . . . hostile to," the political preferences of the majority of the LPO's members. It does not matter that the LPO is willing to risk the surrender of its identity in exchange for electoral success. Oklahoma's interest is independent and concerns the integrity of its primary system. The State wants to "avoid primary election outcomes which would tend to confuse or mislead the general voting population to the extent [it] relies on party labels as representative of certain ideologies."

Moreover, this Court has found that in facilitating the effective operation of a democratic government, a state might reasonably classify voters or candidates according to political affiliations. But for that classification to mean much, Oklahoma must be allowed to limit voters' ability to roam among parties' primaries. The purpose of party registration is to provide a minimal demonstration by the voter that he has some "commitment" to the party in whose primary he wishes to participate. That commitment is lessened if party members may retain their registration in one party while voting in another party's primary. Opening the LPO's primary to all voters not only would render the LPO's *imprimatur* an unreliable index of its candidate's actual political philosophy, but it also would make registered party affiliations significantly less meaningful in the Oklahoma primary election system. Oklahoma reasonably has concluded that opening the LPO's primary to all voters regardless of party affiliation would undermine the crucial role of political parties in the primary process.

Second, Oklahoma's semi-closed primary system, by retaining the importance of party affiliation, aids in parties' electioneering and party-building efforts. It is common experience that direct solicitation of party members—by mail, telephone, or face-to-face contact, and by the candidates themselves or by their active supporters—is part of any primary election campaign. Yet parties' voter turnout efforts depend in large part on accurate voter registration rolls.

When voters are no longer required to disaffiliate before participating in other parties' primaries, voter registration rolls cease to be an accurate reflection of voters' political preferences. And without registration rolls that accurately reflect likely or potential primary voters, parties risk expending precious resources to turn out party members who may have decided to cast their votes elsewhere. If encouraging citizens to vote is an important state interest, then Oklahoma is entitled to protect parties' ability to plan their primaries for a stable group of voters.

Third, Oklahoma has an interest in preventing party raiding, or "the organized switching of blocs of voters from one party to another in order to manipulate the outcome of the other party's primary election." *Anderson.* For example, if the outcome of the Democratic Party primary were not in doubt, Democrats might vote in the LPO primary for the candidate most likely to siphon off votes from the Republican candidate in the general election. Or a Democratic primary contender who senses defeat might launch a "sore loser" candidacy by defecting to the LPO primary, taking with him loyal Democratic voters, and thus undermining the Democratic Party in the general election. Oklahoma has an interest in "temper[ing] the destabilizing effects" of precisely this sort of "party-splintering and excessive factionalism." *Timmons.* Oklahoma's semi-closed primary system serves that interest by discouraging voters from temporarily defecting from another party to vote in the LPO primary. While the State's interest will not justify "unreasonably exclusionary restrictions," we have "repeatedly upheld reasonable, politically neutral regulations" like Oklahoma's semi-closed primary law. [*Id.*]

III

[Omitted.]

. . .

Oklahoma remains free to allow the LPO to invite registered voters of other parties to vote in its primary. But the Constitution leaves that choice to the democratic process, not to the courts. The judgment of the Court of Appeals is reversed, and the case is remanded for further proceedings.

Justice O'CONNOR, with whom Justice BREYER joins except as to Part III, concurring in part and concurring in the judgment.

I join the Court's opinion except for Part II-A. Although I agree with most of the Court's reasoning, I write separately to emphasize two points. First, I think respondents' claim implicates important associational interests, and I see no reason to minimize those interests to dispose of this case. Second, I agree with the Court that only Oklahoma's semi-closed primary law is properly before us, that standing alone it imposes only a modest, nondiscriminatory burden on respondents' associational rights, and that this burden is justified by the State's legitimate regulatory interests. I note, however, that there are some grounds for concern that other state laws may unreasonably restrict voters' ability to change party registration so as to participate in the Libertarian Party of Oklahoma's (LPO) primary. A realistic assessment of regulatory burdens on associational rights would, in an appropriate case, require examination of the cumulative effects of the State's overall scheme governing primary elections; and any finding of a more severe burden would trigger more probing review of the justifications offered by the State.

I

Nearly every State in the Nation now mandates that political parties select their candidates for national or statewide office by means of primary elections. Primaries constitute both a crucial juncture in the electoral process, and a vital forum for expressive association among voters and political parties. It is here that the parties invite voters to join in selecting their standard bearers. The outcome is pivotal, of course, for it dictates the range of choices available at—and often the presumptive winner of—the general election.

"No right is more precious in a free country than that of having a voice in the election of those who make the laws under which, as good citizens, we must live," *Wesberry v. Sanders*, and the right to associate with the political party of one's choice is an integral part of this basic constitutional freedom. The Court has repeatedly reaffirmed that the First and Fourteenth Amendments protect the rights of voters and parties to associate through primary elections. Indeed, constitutional protection of associational rights is especially important in this context because the aggregation of votes is, in some sense, the essence of the electoral process. To have a meaningful voice in this process, the individual voter must join together with likeminded others at the polls. And the choice of who will participate in selecting a party's candidate obviously plays a critical role in determining both the party's message and its prospects of success in the electoral contest.

The majority questions whether the LPO and voters registered with another party have any constitutionally cognizable interest in associating with one another through the LPO's primary. Its doubts on this point appear to stem from two implicit premises: first, that a voter forms a cognizable association with a political party only by registering with that party; and second, that a voter can only form a cognizable association with one party at a time. Neither of these premises is sound, in my view. As to the first, registration with a political party surely may signify an important personal commitment, which may be accompanied by faithful voting and even activism beyond the polls. But for many voters, registration serves principally as a mandatory (and perhaps even ministerial) prerequisite to participation in the party's primaries. The act of casting a ballot in a given primary may, for both the voter and the party, constitute a form of association that is at least as important as the act of registering. The fact that voting is episodic does not, in my judgment, undermine its associational significance; it simply reflects the special character of the electoral process, which allows citizens to join together at regular intervals to shape government through the choice of public officials.

As to the question of dual associations, I fail to see why registration with one party should negate a voter's First Amendment interest in associating with a second party. We surely would not say, for instance, that a registered Republican or Democrat has no protected interest in associating with the Libertarian Party by attending meetings or making political contributions. The validity of voters' and parties' interests in dual associations seems particularly clear where minor parties are concerned. For example, a voter may have a longstanding affiliation with a major party that she wishes to maintain, but she may nevertheless have a substantial interest in associating with a minor party during particular election cycles or in elections for particular offices. The voter's refusal to disaffiliate from the major party may reflect her abiding commitment to that party (which is not necessarily inconsistent with her desire to associate with a second party), the objective costs of disaffiliation or both. The minor party, for its part, may have a significant interest in augmenting its voice in the political process by associating with sympathetic members of the major parties.

None of this is to suggest that the State does not have a superseding interest in restricting certain forms of association. We have never questioned, for example, the States' authority to restrict voters' public registration to a single party or to limit each voter to participating in a single party's primary. But the fact that a State's regulatory authority may ultimately trump voters' or parties' associational interests in a particular context is no reason to dismiss the validity of those interests. As a more general matter, I question whether judicial inquiry into the genuineness, intensity, or duration of a given voter's association with a given party is a fruitful way to approach constitutional challenges to regulations like the one at issue here. Primary voting is an episodic and sometimes isolated act of association, but it is a vitally important one and should be entitled to some level of constitutional protection. Accordingly, where a party invites a voter to participate in its primary and the voter seeks to do so, we should begin with the premise that there are significant associational interests at stake. From this starting point, we can then ask to what extent and in what manner the State may justifiably restrict those interests.

II

[Omitted.]

III

In briefing and oral argument before this Court, respondents raise for the first time the claim that Oklahoma's semi-closed primary law severely burdens their associational rights not through the law's own operation, but rather because *other* state laws make it quite difficult for voters to reregister as Independents or Libertarians so as to participate in the LPO primary. Respondents characterize Oklahoma's regulatory scheme as follows.

Partisan primaries in Oklahoma are held on the last Tuesday in July of each even-numbered year. To field a party candidate in an election, the LPO must obtain "recognized" party status. This requires it to submit, no later than May 1 of any even-numbered year (*i.e.*, any election year), a petition with the signatures of registered voters equal to at least five percent of the total votes cast in the most recent gubernatorial or Presidential election. The State Election Board then has 30 days to determine whether the petition is sufficient. The LPO has attained recognized party status in this fashion in every Presidential election year since 1980. However, unless the party's candidate receives at least 10 percent of the total votes cast for Governor or President in the general election (which no minor party has been able to do in any State in recent history), it loses recognized party status. To regain party status, the group must go through the petition process again.

When a party loses its recognized status, as the LPO has after every general election in which it has participated, the affiliation of any voter registered with the party is changed to Independent. As the District Court noted, "it is highly likely that the ranks of independents, and, indeed, of registered Republicans and Democrats, contain numerous voters who sympathize with the LPO but who simply do not wish to go through the motions of re-registering every time they are purged from the rolls." And the Republican and Democratic parties in Oklahoma, as it turns out, do not permit voters registered as Independents to participate in their primaries.

Most importantly, according to respondents, the deadline for changing party affiliation makes it quite difficult for the LPO to invite voters to reregister in order to participate in its primary. Assuming the LPO submits its petition for recognized party status on the May 1 deadline, the State has until May 31 to determine whether party status will be conferred. But in order to participate in the LPO primary, a voter registered with another party must change her party affiliation to Independent or Libertarian no later than June 1. Moreover, no candidate for office is permitted officially to declare her candidacy with the State Election Board until the period between the first Monday in June and the next succeeding Wednesday.

If this characterization of state law is accurate, a registered Democrat or Republican sympathetic to the LPO or to an LPO candidate in a given election year would seem to face a genuine dilemma. On the one hand, she may stick with her major party registration and forfeit the opportunity to participate in the LPO primary. Alternatively, she may reregister as a Libertarian or Independent, thus forfeiting her opportunity to participate in the major party primary, though no candidate will have officially declared yet and the voter may not yet know whether the LPO will even be permitted to conduct a primary. Moreover, she must make this choice roughly eight weeks before the primaries, at a time when most voters have not yet even tuned in to the election, much less decided upon a candidate. That might pose a special difficulty for voters attracted to minor party candidates, for whom support may not coalesce until comparatively late in the election cycle.

Throughout the proceedings in the lower courts, which included a full bench trial before the District Court, respondents made no attempt to challenge these other electoral requirements or to argue that they were relevant to respondents' challenge to the semi-closed primary law. The lower courts, accordingly, gave little or no consideration to how these various regulations interrelate or operate in practice, nor did the State seek to justify them. Given this posture, I agree with the Court that it would be neither proper nor prudent for us to rule on the reformulated claim that respondents now urge.

Nevertheless, respondents' allegations are troubling, and, if they had been properly raised, the Court would want to examine the *cumulative* burdens imposed by the *overall* scheme of electoral regulations upon the rights of voters and parties to associate through primary elections. A panoply of regulations, each apparently defensible when considered alone, may nevertheless have the combined effect of severely restricting participation and competition. Even if each part of a regulatory regime might be upheld if challenged separately, one or another of these parts might have to fall if the overall scheme unreasonably curtails associational freedoms. Oklahoma's requirement that a voter register as an Independent or a Libertarian in order to participate in the LPO's primary is not itself unduly onerous; but that is true only to the extent that the State provides reasonable avenues through which a voter can change her registration status. The State's regulations governing changes in party affiliation are not properly before us now. But if it were shown, in an appropriate case, that such regulations imposed a weighty or discriminatory restriction on voters' ability to participate in the LPO's or some other party's primary, then more probing scrutiny of the State's justifications would be required.

Justice STEVENS, with whom Justice GINSBURG joins, and with whom Justice SOUTER joins as to Parts I, II, and III, dissenting.

The Court's decision today diminishes the value of two important rights protected by the First Amendment: the individual citizen's right to vote for the candidate of her choice and a political party's right to define its own mission.

I

In rejecting the individual respondents' claims, the majority focuses on their associational interests. While the voters in this case certainly have an interest in associating with the LPO, they are primarily interested in voting for a particular candidate, who happens to be in the LPO. Indeed, I think we have lost sight of the principal purpose of a primary: to nominate a candidate for office.

Because our recent cases have focused on the associational interest of voters, rather than the right to vote itself, it is important to identify three basic precepts. First, it is clear that the right to vote includes the right to vote in a primary election. When the State makes the primary an integral part of the procedure of choice, every eligible citizen's right to vote should receive the same protection as in the general election. Second, the right to vote, whether in the primary or the general election, is the right to vote for the candidate of one's choice. Finally, in assessing burdens on that right—burdens that are not limited to absolute denial of the right—we should focus on the realities of the situation, not on empty formalism.

Here, the impact of the Oklahoma statute on the voters' right to vote for the candidate of their choosing is not a mere "burden"; it is a prohibition. By virtue of the fact that their preferred candidate is a member of a different party, respondents are absolutely precluded from voting for him or her in the primary election. It is not an answer that the voters could participate in another primary (*i.e.*, the primary for the party with which they are registered) since the individual for whom they wish to vote is not a candidate in that primary.

This is not to say that voters have an absolute right to participate in whatever primary they desire. For instance, the parties themselves have a strong associational interest in determining which individuals may vote in their primaries, and that interest will normally outweigh the interest of the uninvited voter. But in the ordinary case the State simply has no interest in classifying voters by their political party and in limiting the elections in which voters may participate as a result of that classification. Just as we held in *Reynolds* that all voters of a State stand in the same relation to the State regardless of where they live, and that the State must thus not make their vote count more or less depending upon that factor, so too do citizens stand in the same relation *to the State* regardless of the political party to which they belong. The State may thus not deny them participation in a primary of a party that seeks their participation absent a state interest of overriding importance.

II

In addition to burdening the individual respondent's right to vote, the Oklahoma scheme places a heavy burden on the LPO's associational rights. While Oklahoma permits independent voters to participate in the LPO's primary elections, it refuses to allow registered Republicans or Democrats to do so. That refusal has a direct impact on the LPO's selection of candidates for public office, the importance of which cannot be overstated. A primary election plays a critical role in enabling a party to disseminate its message to the public. It is through its candidates that a party is able to give voice to its political views, to engage other candidates on important issues of the day, and to affect change in the government of our society. Our cases "vigorously affirm the special place the First Amendment reserves for, and the special protection it accords, the process by which a political party selects a standard bearer who best represents the party's ideologies and preferences." [*Jones*.]

The LPO's desire to include Democrats and Republicans is undoubtedly informed by the fact that, given the stringent requirements of Oklahoma law, the LPO ceases to become a formally recognized party after each election cycle, and its members automatically revert to being independents. Because the LPO routinely loses its status as a recognized party, many voters who might otherwise register as Libertarians instead register as

Democrats or Republicans. Thus, the LPO's interest in inviting registered Republicans and Democrats to participate in the selection of its standard-bearer has even greater force than did the Republican Party's desire to invite independents to associate with it in *Tashjian.*

III

As justification for the State's abridgment of the constitutionally protected interests asserted by the LPO and the voters, the majority relies on countervailing state interests that are either irrelevant or insignificant. Neither separately nor in the aggregate do these interests support the Court's decision.

First, the Court makes the remarkable suggestion that by opening up its primary to Democrats and Republicans, the LPO will be saddled with so many non-libertarian voters that the ultimate candidate will not be, in any sense, "libertarian." But the LPO is *seeking* the crossover voting of Republicans and Democrats. Rightly or wrongly, the LPO feels that the best way to produce a viable candidate is to invite voters from other parties to participate in its primary. That may dilute what the Court believes to be the core of the Libertarian philosophy, but it is no business of the State to tell a political party what its message should be, how it should select its candidates, or how it should form coalitions to ensure electoral success.

Second, the majority expresses concern that crossover voting may create voter confusion. This paternalistic concern is belied by the District Court's finding that no significant voter confusion would occur.

Third, the majority suggests that crossover voting will impair the State's interest in properly classifying candidates and voters. As an empirical matter, a crossover voter may have a lesser commitment to the party with which he is registered if he votes in another party's primary. Nevertheless, the State does not have a valid interest in defining what it means to be a Republican or a Democrat, or in attempting to ensure the political orthodoxy of party members simply for the convenience of those parties. Even if participation in the LPO's primary causes a voter to be a less committed "Democrat" or "Republican" (a proposition I reject), the dilution of that commitment does not justify abridgment of the fundamental rights at issue in this case. While party identity is important in our political system, it should not be immunized from the risk of change.

Fourth, the majority argues that opening up the LPO primary to members of the Republican and Democratic parties might interfere with electioneering and party-building efforts. It is clear, of course, that the majority here is concerned only with the Democratic and Republican parties, since party building is precisely what the LPO is attempting to accomplish. Nevertheless, that concern is misplaced. Even if, as the majority claims, the Republican and Democratic voter rolls, mailing lists, and phone banks are not as accurate as they would otherwise be, the administrative inconvenience of the major parties does not outweigh the right to vote or the associational interests of those voters and the LPO. At its core, this argument is based on a fear that the LPO might be successful in convincing Democratic or Republican voters to participate more fully in the LPO. Far from being a compelling interest, it is an impermissible one.

Finally, the majority warns against the possibility of raiding by which voters of another party maliciously vote in a primary in order to change the outcome of the primary, either to nominate a particularly weak candidate, a "sore-loser" candidate, or a candidate who would siphon votes from another party. The District Court, whose factual findings are entitled to substantial deference, found as a factual and legal matter that the State's argument concerning raiding was "unpersuasive."

Even if raiding were a possibility, however, the state interests are remote. The possibility of harm to the LPO itself is insufficient to overcome the LPO's associational rights. If the LPO is willing to take the risk that its party may be "hijacked" by individuals who hold views opposite to their own, the State has little interest in second-guessing the LPO's decision.

With respect to the possibility that Democratic or Republican voters might raid the LPO to the detriment of their own or another party, neither the State nor the majority has identified any evidence that voters are sufficiently organized to achieve such a targeted result. Such speculation is not, in my view, sufficient to override the real and acknowledged interest of the LPO and the voters who wish to participate in its primary.[11]

In the end, the balance of interests clearly favors the LPO and those voters who wish to participate in its primary. The associational interests asserted—the right to select a standard bearer that the party thinks has the best chance of success, the ability to associate at the crucial juncture of selecting a candidate, and the desire to reach out to voters of other parties—are substantial and undoubtedly burdened by Oklahoma's statutory scheme. Any doubt about that fact is clearly answered by *Tashjian.* On the other side, the interests asserted by the State are either entirely speculative or simply protectionist measures that benefit the parties in power. No matter what the standard, they simply do not outweigh the interests of the LPO and its voters.

IV

The Libertarian Party of Oklahoma is not the only loser in this litigation. Other minor parties and voters who have primary allegiance to one party but sometimes switch their support to rival candidates are also harmed by this decision. In my judgment, however, the real losers include all participants in the political market. Decisions that give undue deference to the interest in preserving the two-party system, like decisions that

11. The flimsy character of the state interests in this case confirms my view that today's decision rests primarily on a desire to protect the two-party system. In *Jones,* the Court concluded that the associational interests of the parties trumped state interests that were much more compelling than those asserted in this case. Here, by contrast, where the associational interests are being asserted by a minor party rather than by one of the dominant parties, the Court has reversed course and rejected those associational interests as insubstantial compared to the interests asserted by the State.

encourage partisan gerrymandering, enhance the likelihood that so-called "safe districts" will play an increasingly predominant role in the electoral process. Primary elections are already replacing general elections as the most common method of actually determining the composition of our legislative bodies. The trend can only increase the bitter partisanship that has already poisoned some of those bodies that once provided inspiring examples of courteous adversary debate and deliberation.

The decision in this case, like the misguided decisions in *Timmons* and *Jones*, attaches overriding importance to the interest in preserving the two-party system. In my view, there is over a century of experience demonstrating that the two major parties are fully capable of maintaining their own positions of dominance in the political marketplace without any special assistance from the state governments that they dominate or from this Court. Whenever they receive special advantages, the offsetting harm to independent voters may be far more significant than the majority recognizes.

Because the Court's holding today has little to support it other than a naked interest in protecting the two major parties, I respectfully dissent.

NOTES ON *CLINGMAN*

1. Is *Clingman* distinguishable from *Tashjian*? Note that the majority in *Clingman* strongly suggests that *Tashjian* was incorrect, but it still attempts to distinguish rather than overrule *Tashjian*.
2. Justice Thomas states, "[t]o deem ordinary and widespread burdens like these severe would subject virtually every electoral regulation to strict scrutiny, hamper the ability of States to run efficient and equitable elections, and compel federal courts to rewrite state electoral codes." Subsequent courts have relied heavily on this statement to uphold state election regulations. Is he going too far? Is he giving states too much power to regulate the electoral process? Or is he correct that states need wide leeway in running elections and that applying strict scrutiny would entail too much judicial oversight?
3. What do the different opinions suggest about the role of the major political parties versus minor political parties? Is there a thumb on the scale in favor of the Republican and Democratic parties? If so, is this acceptable?
4. What does Justice O'Connor's opinion suggest about the proper way to craft a challenge to a state's election rules?

E. Candidate v. State: The State's Control over the Content of the General Election Ballot

In the cases that we have read so far in Part II of this book, the disputes have concerned the rules governing primary elections—and the consequences of those rules for the placement of a candidate's name on the general election ballot. The remainder of the cases in Part II cover disputes over a candidate's placement on the general election ballot through means other than prevailing in a primary election. Most of these cases are about the requirements that a candidate must satisfy to qualify for a general election ballot either as an independent candidate or as the candidate of a "minor" political party that did not participate in the state's primary election. But first we should examine two U.S. Supreme Court cases that set a general framework for analyzing this category of "ballot access" cases: The first of these two cases involves a state's prohibition against "write-in" candidates, while the second involves the desire of candidates to be listed on the ballot as the nominee of more than one political party. In both cases, the state prevails against the claim that these laws governing the content of the state's general election ballot violate the First Amendment rights of candidates and their supporters.

BURDICK v. TAKUSHI

504 U.S. 428 (1992)

Justice WHITE delivered the opinion of the Court.

The issue in this case is whether Hawaii's prohibition on write-in voting unreasonably infringes upon its citizens' rights under the First and Fourteenth Amendments. Petitioner contends that the Constitution requires Hawaii to provide for the casting, tabulation, and publication of write-in votes. The Court of Appeals for the Ninth Circuit disagreed, holding that the prohibition, taken as part of the State's comprehensive election scheme, does not impermissibly burden the right to vote. We affirm.

I

[Omitted.]

II

Petitioner proceeds from the erroneous assumption that a law that imposes any burden upon the right to vote must be subject to strict scrutiny. Our cases do not so hold.

It is beyond cavil that "voting is of the most fundamental significance under our constitutional structure." *Illinois Bd. of Elections v. Socialist Workers Party* (1979). It does not follow, however, that the right to vote in any manner and the right to associate for political purposes through the ballot are absolute. The Constitution provides that States may prescribe "[t]he Times, Places and Manner of holding Elections for Senators and Representatives," Art. I, § 4, cl. 1, and the Court therefore has recognized that States retain the power to regulate their own elections. Common sense, as well as constitutional law, compels the conclusion that government must play an active role in structuring elections; "as a practical matter, there must be a substantial regulation of elections if they are to be fair and honest and if some sort of order, rather than chaos, is to accompany the democratic processes." *Storer v. Brown* (1974).

Election laws will invariably impose some burden upon individual voters. Each provision of a code, "whether it governs the registration and qualifications of voters, the selection and eligibility of candidates, or the voting process itself, inevitably affects—at least to some degree—the individual's right to vote and his right to associate with others for political ends." *Anderson v. Celebrezze* (1983). Consequently, to subject every voting regulation to strict scrutiny and to require that the regulation be narrowly tailored to advance a compelling state interest, as petitioner suggests, would tie the hands of States seeking to assure that elections are operated equitably and efficiently. Accordingly, the mere fact that a State's system "creates barriers . . . tending to limit the field of candidates from which voters might choose . . . does not of itself compel close scrutiny." *Bullock v. Carter* (1972).

Instead, as the full Court agreed in *Anderson*, a more flexible standard applies. A court considering a challenge to a state election law must weigh "the character and magnitude of the asserted injury to the rights protected by the First and Fourteenth Amendments that the plaintiff seeks to vindicate" against "the precise interests put forward by the State as justifications for the burden imposed by its rule," taking into consideration "the extent to which those interests make it necessary to burden the plaintiff's rights."

Under this standard, the rigorousness of our inquiry into the propriety of a state election law depends upon the extent to which a challenged regulation burdens First and Fourteenth Amendment rights. Thus, as we have recognized when those rights are subjected to "severe" restrictions, the regulation must be "narrowly drawn to advance a state interest of compelling importance." *Norman v. Reed* (1992). But when a state election law provision imposes only "reasonable, nondiscriminatory restrictions" upon the First and Fourteenth Amendment rights of voters, "the State's important regulatory interests are generally sufficient to justify" the restrictions.

A

There is no doubt that the Hawaii election laws, like all election regulations, have an impact on the right to vote, but it can hardly be said that the laws at issue here unconstitutionally limit access to the ballot by party or independent candidates or unreasonably interfere with the right of voters to associate and have candidates of their choice placed on the ballot. Indeed, petitioner understandably does not challenge the manner in which the State regulates candidate access to the ballot.

To obtain a position on the November general election ballot, a candidate must participate in Hawaii's open primary, in which all registered voters may choose in which party primary to vote. The State provides three mechanisms through which a voter's candidate-of-choice may appear on the primary ballot.

[The Court discussed the three mechanisms, which included filing a party petition with enough signatures for new parties, filing nominating papers for candidates for "established" parties, and appearing on the designated nonpartisan ballot and receiving 10 percent of the primary vote to advance to the general election.]

Although Hawaii makes no provision for write-in voting in its primary or general elections, the system outlined above provides for easy access to the ballot until the cutoff date for the filing of nominating petitions, two months before the primary. Consequently, any burden on voters' freedom of choice and association is borne only by those who fail to identify their candidate of choice until days before the primary.

Because he has characterized this as a voting rights rather than ballot access case, petitioner submits that the write-in prohibition deprives him of the opportunity to cast a meaningful ballot, conditions his electoral participation upon the waiver of his First Amendment right to remain free from espousing positions that he does not support, and discriminates against him based on the content of the message he seeks to convey through his vote. At bottom, he claims that he is entitled to cast and Hawaii required to count a "protest vote" for Donald Duck, and that any impediment to this asserted "right" is unconstitutional.

Petitioner's argument is based on two flawed premises. First, in *Bullock v. Carter*, we minimized the extent to which voting rights cases are distinguishable from ballot access cases, stating that "the rights of voters and the rights of candidates do not lend themselves to neat separation." Second, the function of the election process is "to winnow out and finally reject all but the chosen candidates," not to provide a means of giving vent to "short-range political goals, pique, or personal quarrel[s]." *Storer.* Attributing to elections a more generalized expressive function would undermine the ability of States to operate elections fairly and efficiently.

Accordingly, we have repeatedly upheld reasonable, politically neutral regulations that have the effect of channeling expressive activity at the polls. Petitioner offers no persuasive reason to depart from these precedents. Reasonable regulation of elections *does not* require voters to espouse positions that they do not support; it *does* require them to act in a timely fashion if they wish to express their views in the voting booth. And there is nothing content based about a flat ban on all forms of write-in ballots.

The appropriate standard for evaluating a claim that a state law burdens the right to vote is set forth in *Anderson.* Applying that standard, we conclude that, in light of the adequate ballot access afforded under Hawaii's election code, the State's ban on write-in voting imposes only a limited burden on voters' rights to make free choices and to associate politically through the vote.

B

We turn next to the interests asserted by Hawaii to justify the burden imposed by its prohibition of write-in voting. Because we have already concluded that the burden is slight, the State need not establish a compelling interest to tip the constitutional scales in its direction. Here, the State's interests outweigh petitioner's limited interest in waiting until the eleventh hour to choose his preferred candidate.

Hawaii's interest in "avoid[ing] the possibility of unrestrained factionalism at the general election," *Munro*, provides adequate justification for its ban on write-in voting in November. The primary election is "an integral part of the entire election process," and the State is within its rights to reserve "[t]he general election ballot . . . for major struggles . . . [and] not a forum for continuing intraparty feuds." *Storer*. The prohibition on write-in voting is a legitimate means of averting divisive sore-loser candidacies. Hawaii further promotes the two-stage, primary-general election process of winnowing out candidates by permitting the unopposed victors in certain primaries to be designated office-holders. This focuses the attention of voters upon contested races in the general election. This would not be possible, absent the write-in voting ban.

Hawaii also asserts that its ban on write-in voting at the primary stage is necessary to guard against "party raiding." *Tashjian*. Party raiding is generally defined as "the organized switching of blocs of voters from one party to another in order to manipulate the outcome of the other party's primary election." *Anderson*. Petitioner suggests that, because Hawaii conducts an open primary, this is not a cognizable interest. We disagree. While voters may vote on any ticket in Hawaii's primary, the State requires that party candidates be "member[s] of the party," and prohibits candidates from filing "nomination papers both as a party candidate and as a nonpartisan candidate." Hawaii's system could easily be circumvented in a party primary election by mounting a write-in campaign for a person who had not filed in time or who had never intended to run for election. It could also be frustrated at the general election by permitting write-in votes for a loser in a party primary or for an independent who had failed to get sufficient votes to make the general election ballot. The State has a legitimate interest in preventing these sorts of maneuvers, and the write-in voting ban is a reasonable way of accomplishing this goal.

We think these legitimate interests asserted by the State are sufficient to outweigh the limited burden that the write-in voting ban imposes upon Hawaii's voters.

III

[Omitted.]

Justice KENNEDY, with whom Justice BLACKMUN and Justice STEVENS join, dissenting.

The record demonstrates the significant burden that Hawaii's write-in ban imposes on the right of voters such as petitioner to vote for the candidates of their choice. In the election that triggered this lawsuit, petitioner did not wish to vote for the one candidate who ran for state representative in his district. Because he could not write in the name of a candidate he preferred, he had no way to cast a meaningful vote. Petitioner's dilemma is a recurring, frequent phenomenon in Hawaii because of the State's ballot access rules and the circumstance that one party, the Democratic Party, is predominant. It is critical to understand that petitioner's case is not an isolated example of a restriction on the free choice of candidates. The very ballot access rules the Court cites as mitigating his injury in fact compound it system wide.

The majority suggests that it is easy for new parties to petition for a place on the primary ballot because they must obtain the signatures of only one percent of the State's registered voters. This ignores the difficulty presented by the early deadline for gathering these signatures: 150 days (5 months) before the primary election. Meeting this deadline requires considerable organization at an early stage in the election, a condition difficult for many small parties to meet.

If the party petition is unsuccessful or not completed in time, or if a candidate does not wish to be affiliated with a party, he may run as an independent. While the requirements to get on the nonpartisan ballot are not onerous (15 to 25 signatures, 60 days before the primary), the non-partisan ballot presents voters with a difficult choice. This is because each primary voter can choose only a single ballot for all offices. Hence, a voter who wishes to vote for an independent candidate for one office must forgo the opportunity to vote in an established party primary in every other race. Since there might be no independent candidates for most of the other offices, in practical terms the voter who wants to vote for one independent candidate forfeits the right to participate in the selection of candidates for all other offices. This rule, the very ballot access rule that the Court finds to be curative, in fact presents a substantial disincentive for voters to select the nonpartisan ballot. A voter who wishes to vote for a third-party candidate for only one particular office faces a similar disincentive to select the third party's ballot.

The dominance of the Democratic Party magnifies the disincentive because the primary election is dispositive in so many races. In effect, a Hawaii voter who wishes to vote for any independent candidate must choose between doing so and participating in what will be the dispositive election for many offices. This dilemma imposes a substantial burden on voter choice. It explains also why so few independent candidates secure enough primary votes to advance to the general election. As the majority notes, only eight independent candidates have succeeded in advancing to the general election in the past 10 years. That is, less than one independent candidate per year on average has in fact run in a general election in Hawaii.

Aside from constraints related to ballot access restrictions, the write-in ban limits voter choice in another way. Write-in voting can serve as an important safety mechanism in those instances where a late-developing issue arises or where new information is disclosed about a candidate late in the race. In these situations, voters may become disenchanted with the available candidates when it is too late for other candidates to come forward and qualify for the ballot. The prohibition on write-in voting imposes a significant burden on voters, forcing them either to vote for a candidate whom they no longer support or to cast a blank ballot. Write-in voting provides a way out of the quandary, allowing voters to switch their support to candidates who are not on the official ballot. Even if there are other mechanisms to address the problem of late-breaking election developments (unsuitable candidates who win an election can be recalled), allowing write-in voting is the only way to preserve the voters' right to cast a meaningful vote in the general election.

TIMMONS v. TWIN CITIES AREA NEW PARTY

520 U.S. 351 (1997)

Chief Justice REHNQUIST delivered the opinion of the Court.

Most States prohibit multiple-party, or "fusion," candidacies for elected office.[1] The Minnesota laws challenged in this case prohibit a candidate from appearing on the ballot as the candidate of more than one party. We hold that such a prohibition does not violate the First and Fourteenth Amendments to the United States Constitution.

Respondent is a chartered chapter of the national New Party. Petitioners are Minnesota election officials. In April 1994, Minnesota State Representative Andy Dawkins was running unopposed in the Minnesota Democratic-Farmer-Labor Party's (DFL) primary. That same month, New Party members chose Dawkins as their candidate for the same office in the November 1994 general election. Neither Dawkins nor the DFL objected, and Dawkins signed the required affidavit of candidacy for the New Party. Minnesota, however, prohibits fusion candidacies. Because Dawkins had already filed as a candidate for the DFL's nomination, local election officials refused to accept the New Party's nominating petition.

The New Party filed suit in United States District Court, contending that Minnesota's antifusion laws violated the party's associational rights under the First and Fourteenth Amendments. The District Court granted summary judgment for the state defendants[.]

The Court of Appeals reversed. We granted certiorari and now reverse.

Fusion was a regular feature of Gilded Age American politics. Particularly in the West and Midwest, candidates of issue-oriented parties like the Grangers, Independents, Greenbackers, and Populists often succeeded through fusion with the Democrats, and vice versa. Republicans, for their part, sometimes arranged fusion candidacies in the South, as part of a general strategy of encouraging and exploiting divisions within the dominant Democratic Party.

Fusion was common in part because political parties, rather than local or state governments, printed and distributed their own ballots. These ballots contained only the names of a particular party's candidates, and so a voter could drop his party's ticket

1. "Fusion," also called "cross-filing" or "multiple-party nomination," is "the electoral support of a single set of candidates by two or more parties." Argersinger, "A Place on the Ballot": Fusion Politics and Antifusion Laws, 85 Am. Hist. Rev. 287, 288 (1980); *see also Twin Cities Area New Party v. McKenna* (8th Cir. 1996) (Fusion is "the nomination by more than one political party of the same candidate for the same office in the same general election").

in the ballot box without even knowing that his party's candidates were supported by other parties as well. But after the 1888 presidential election, which was widely regarded as having been plagued by fraud, many States moved to the "Australian ballot system." Under that system, an official ballot, containing the names of all the candidates legally nominated by all the parties, was printed at public expense and distributed by public officials at polling places. By 1896, use of the Australian ballot was widespread. During the same period, many States enacted other election-related reforms, including bans on fusion candidacies. Minnesota banned fusion in 1901. This trend has continued and, in this century, fusion has become the exception, not the rule. Today, multiple-party candidacies are permitted in just a few States, and fusion plays a significant role only in New York.

The First Amendment protects the right of citizens to associate and to form political parties for the advancement of common political goals and ideas.

On the other hand, it is also clear that States may, and inevitably must, enact reasonable regulations of parties, elections, and ballots to reduce election- and campaign-related disorder.

When deciding whether a state election law violates First and Fourteenth Amendment associational rights, we weigh the character and magnitude of the burden the State's rule imposes on those rights against the interests the State contends justify that burden, and consider the extent to which the State's concerns make the burden necessary. Regulations imposing severe burdens on plaintiffs' rights must be narrowly tailored and advance a compelling state interest. Lesser burdens, however, trigger less exacting review, and a State's important regulatory interests will usually be enough to justify reasonable, nondiscriminatory restrictions. No bright line separates permissible election-related regulation from unconstitutional infringements on First Amendment freedoms.

The New Party's claim that it has a right to select its own candidate is uncontroversial, so far as it goes. That is, the New Party, and not someone else, has the right to select the New Party's "standard bearer." It does not follow, though, that a party is absolutely entitled to have its nominee appear on the ballot as that party's candidate. A particular candidate might be ineligible for office, unwilling to serve, or, as here, another party's candidate. That a particular individual may not appear on the ballot as a particular party's candidate does not severely burden that party's associational rights.

The New Party relies on *Eu v. San Francisco County Democratic Central Comm.* [(1989)] and *Tashjian v. Republican Party of Conn.* [(1986)]. In *Eu*, we struck down California election provisions that prohibited political parties from endorsing candidates in party primaries and regulated parties' internal affairs and structure. And in *Tashjian*, we held that Connecticut's closed-primary statute, which required voters in a party primary to be registered party members, interfered with a party's associational rights by limiting "the group of registered voters whom the Party may invite to participate in the basic function of selecting the Party's candidates." But while *Tashjian* and *Eu* involved regulation of political parties' internal affairs and core associational activities, Minnesota's fusion ban does not. The ban, which applies to major and minor parties alike, simply precludes one party's candidate from appearing on the ballot, as that party's candidate, if already nominated by another party. Respondent is free to try to convince Representative Dawkins to be the New Party's, not the DFL's, candidate. Whether the party still wants to endorse a candidate who, because of the fusion ban, will not appear on the ballot as the party's candidate, is up to the party.

The Court of Appeals also held that Minnesota's laws "keep the New Party from developing consensual political alliances and thus broadening the base of public participation in and support for its activities." The burden on the party was, the court held, severe because "[h]istory shows that minor parties have played a significant role in the electoral system where multiple party nomination is legal, but have no meaningful influence where multiple party nomination is banned." In the view of the Court of Appeals, Minnesota's fusion ban forces members of the New Party to make a "no-win choice" between voting for "candidates with no realistic chance of winning, defect[ing] from their party and vot[ing] for a major party candidate who does, or declin[ing] to vote at all."

But Minnesota has not directly precluded minor political parties from developing and organizing. Nor has Minnesota excluded a particular group of citizens, or a political party, from participation in the election process. The New Party remains free to endorse whom it likes, to ally itself with others, to nominate candidates for office, and to spread its message to all who will listen.

The Court of Appeals emphasized its belief that, without fusion-based alliances, minor parties cannot thrive. This is a predictive judgment which is by no means self-evident.[9] But, more importantly, the supposed benefits of fusion to minor parties do not require that Minnesota permit it. Many features of our political system—*e.g.*, single-member districts, "first past the post" elections, and the high costs of campaigning—make it difficult for third parties to succeed in American politics. But the Constitution does not require States to permit fusion any more than it requires them to move to proportional-representation elections or public financing of campaigns.

9. Between the First and Second World Wars, for example, various radical, agrarian, and labor-oriented parties thrived, without fusion, in the Midwest. One of these parties, Minnesota's Farmer-Labor Party, displaced the Democratic Party as the Republicans' primary opponent in Minnesota during the 1930's. As one historian has noted: "The Minnesota Farmer-Labor Party elected its candidates to the governorship on four occasions, to the U.S. Senate in five elections, and to the U.S. House in twenty-five campaigns. . . . Never less than Minnesota's second strongest party, in 1936 Farmer-Laborites dominated state politics. . . . The Farmer-Labor Party was a success despite its independence of America's two dominant national parties and despite the sometimes bold anticapitalist rhetoric of its platforms." It appears that factionalism within the Farmer-Labor Party, the popular successes of New Deal programs and ideology, and the gradual movement of political power from the States to the National Government contributed to the party's decline. Eventually, a much-weakened Farmer-Labor Party merged with the Democrats, forming what is now Minnesota's Democratic-Farmer-Labor Party, in 1944.

The New Party contends that the fusion ban burdens its "right . . . to communicate its choice of nominees on the ballot on terms equal to those offered other parties, and the right of the party's supporters and other voters to receive that information," and insists that communication on the ballot of a party's candidate choice is a "critical source of information for the great majority of voters . . . who . . . rely upon party 'labels' as a voting guide."

It is true that Minnesota's fusion ban prevents the New Party from using the ballot to communicate to the public that it supports a particular candidate who is already another party's candidate. In addition, the ban shuts off one possible avenue a party might use to send a message to its preferred *candidate* because, with fusion, a candidate who wins an election on the basis of two parties' votes will likely know more—if the parties' votes are counted separately—about the particular wishes and ideals of his constituency. We are unpersuaded, however, by the party's contention that it has a right to use the ballot itself to send a particularized message, to its candidate and to the voters, about the nature of its support for the candidate. Ballots serve primarily to elect candidates, not as forums for political expression. Like all parties in Minnesota, the New Party is able to use the ballot to communicate information about itself and its candidate to the voters, so long as that candidate is not already someone else's candidate. The party retains great latitude in its ability to communicate ideas to voters and candidates through its participation in the campaign, and party members may campaign for, endorse, and vote for their preferred candidate even if he is listed on the ballot as another party's candidate.

In sum, Minnesota's laws do not restrict the ability of the New Party and its members to endorse, support, or vote for anyone they like. The laws do not directly limit the party's access to the ballot. They are silent on parties' internal structure, governance, and policymaking. Instead, these provisions reduce the universe of potential candidates who may appear on the ballot as the party's nominee only by ruling out those few individuals who both have already agreed to be another party's candidate and also, if forced to choose, themselves prefer that other party. They also limit, slightly, the party's ability to send a message to the voters and to its preferred candidates. We conclude that the burdens Minnesota imposes on the party's First and Fourteenth Amendment associational rights—though not trivial—are not severe.

The Court of Appeals determined that Minnesota's fusion ban imposed "severe" burdens on the New Party's associational rights, and so it required the State to show that the ban was narrowly tailored to serve compelling state interests. We disagree; given the burdens imposed, the bar is not so high. Instead, the State's asserted regulatory interests need only be "sufficiently weighty to justify the limitation" imposed on the party's rights. Nor do we require elaborate, empirical verification of the weightiness of the State's asserted justifications.

The Court of Appeals acknowledged Minnesota's interests in avoiding voter confusion and overcrowded ballots, preventing party splintering and disruptions of the two-party system, and being able to clearly identify the election winner. Minnesota argues here that its fusion ban is justified by its interests in avoiding voter confusion, promoting candidate competition (by reserving limited ballot space for opposing candidates), preventing electoral distortions and ballot manipulations, and discouraging party splintering and "unrestrained factionalism."

States certainly have an interest in protecting the integrity, fairness, and efficiency of their ballots and election processes as means for electing public officials. Petitioners contend that a candidate or party could easily exploit fusion as a way of associating his or its name with popular slogans and catchphrases. For example, members of a major party could decide that a powerful way of "sending a message" via the ballot would be for various factions of that party to nominate the major party's candidate as the candidate for the newly-formed "No New Taxes," "Conserve Our Environment," and "Stop Crime Now" parties. In response, an opposing major party would likely instruct its factions to nominate that party's candidate as the "Fiscal Responsibility," "Healthy Planet," and "Safe Streets" parties' candidate.

Whether or not the putative "fusion" candidates' names appeared on one or four ballot lines, such maneuvering would undermine the ballot's purpose by transforming it from a means of choosing candidates to a billboard for political advertising. The New Party responds to this concern, ironically enough, by insisting that the State could avoid such manipulation by adopting more demanding ballot-access standards rather than prohibiting multiple-party nomination. However, as we stated above, because the burdens the fusion ban imposes on the party's associational rights are not severe, the State need not narrowly tailor the means it chooses to promote ballot integrity. The Constitution does not require that Minnesota compromise the policy choices embodied in its ballot-access requirements to accommodate the New Party's fusion strategy.

Relatedly, petitioners urge that permitting fusion would undercut Minnesota's ballot-access regime by allowing minor parties to capitalize on the popularity of another party's candidate, rather than on their own appeal to the voters, in order to secure access to the ballot. That is, voters who might not sign a minor party's nominating petition based on the party's own views and candidates might do so if they viewed the minor party as just another way of nominating the same person nominated by one of the major parties. Thus, Minnesota fears that fusion would enable minor parties, by nominating a major party's candidate, to bootstrap their way to major-party status in the next election and circumvent the State's nominating-petition requirement for minor parties. The State surely has a valid interest in making sure that minor and third parties who are granted access to the ballot are bona fide and actually supported, on their own merits, by those who have provided the statutorily required petition or ballot support.

States also have a strong interest in the stability of their political systems. This interest does not permit a State to completely insulate the two-party system from minor parties' or independent candidates' competition and influence; nor is it a paternalistic license for States to protect political parties from the consequences of their own internal disagreements. That said, the States' interest permits them to enact reasonable election regulations that may, in practice, favor the traditional two-party system, and that temper the destabilizing effects of party-splintering and excessive factionalism. The Constitution permits the Minnesota Legislature to decide that political stability is best served through a healthy two-party system. And while an interest in securing the perceived benefits of a stable two-party system will not justify unreasonably exclusionary restrictions, States need not remove all of the many hurdles third parties face in the American political arena today.

We conclude that the burdens Minnesota's fusion ban imposes on the New Party's associational rights are justified by "correspondingly weighty" valid state interests in ballot integrity and political stability. In deciding that Minnesota's fusion ban does not unconstitutionally burden the New Party's First and Fourteenth Amendment rights, we express no views on the New Party's policy-based arguments concerning the wisdom of fusion. It may well be that, as support for new political parties increases, these arguments will carry the day in some States' legislatures. But the Constitution does not require Minnesota, and the approximately 40 other States that do not permit fusion, to allow it. The judgment of the Court of Appeals is reversed.

Justice STEVENS, with whom Justice GINSBURG joins, and with whom Justice SOUTER joins as to Parts I and II, dissenting.

The Court's conclusion that the Minnesota statute prohibiting multiple-party candidacies is constitutional rests on three dubious premises: (1) that the statute imposes only a minor burden on the Party's right to choose and to support the candidate of its choice; (2) that the statute significantly serves the State's asserted interests in avoiding ballot manipulation and factionalism; and (3) that, in any event, the interest in preserving the two-party system justifies the imposition of the burden at issue in this case. I disagree with each of these premises.

I

The members of a recognized political party unquestionably have a constitutional right to select their nominees for public office and to communicate the identity of their nominees to the voting public. Both the right to choose and the right to advise voters of that choice are entitled to the highest respect.

The Minnesota statutes place a significant burden on both of those rights. The Court's recital of burdens that the statute does not inflict on the Party does nothing to minimize the severity of the burdens that it does impose. The fact that the Party may nominate its second choice surely does not diminish the significance of a restriction that denies it the right to have the name of its first choice appear on the ballot. Nor does the point that it may use some of its limited resources to publicize the fact that its first choice is the nominee of some other party provide an adequate substitute for the message that is conveyed to every person who actually votes when a party's nominees appear on the ballot.

As to the first point, the State contends that the fusion ban in fact limits by only a few candidates the range of individuals a party may nominate, and that the burden is therefore quite small. But the *number* of candidates removed from the Party's reach cannot be the determinative factor. The ban leaves the Party free to nominate any eligible candidate except the particular "standard bearer who best represents the party's ideologies and preferences."

The State next argues that—instead of nominating a second-choice candidate—the Party could remove itself from the ballot altogether, and publicly endorse the candidate of another party. But the right to be on the election ballot is precisely what separates a political party from any other interest group. The Court relies on the fact that the Party remains free "to spread its message to all who will listen" through forums other than the ballot. Given the limited resources available to most minor parties, and the less-than-universal interest in the messages of third parties, it is apparent that the Party's message will, in this manner, reach a much smaller audience than that composed of all voters who can read the ballot in the polling booth.

In this case, and presumably in most cases, the burden of a statute of this kind is imposed upon the members of a minor party, but its potential impact is much broader. Popular candidates like Andy Dawkins sometimes receive nation-wide recognition. Fiorello LaGuardia, Earl Warren, Ronald Reagan, and Franklin D. Roosevelt are names that come readily to mind as candidates whose reputations and political careers were enhanced because they appeared on election ballots as fusion candidates. A statute that denied a political party the right to nominate any of those individuals for high office simply because he had already been nominated by another party would, in my opinion, place an intolerable burden on political expression and association.

II

Minnesota argues that the statutory restriction on the Party's right to nominate the candidate of its choice is justified by the State's interests in avoiding voter confusion, preventing ballot clutter and manipulation, encouraging candidate competition, and minimizing intraparty factionalism. None of these rationales can support the fusion ban because the State has failed to explain how the ban actually serves the asserted interests.

I believe that the law significantly abridges First Amendment freedoms and that the State therefore must shoulder a correspondingly heavy burden of justification if the law is to survive judicial scrutiny. But even accepting the majority's view that the burdens imposed by the law are not weighty, the State's asserted interests must at least bear some plausible relationship to the burdens it places on political parties. Although the Court today suggests that the State does not have to support its asserted justifications for the fusion ban with evidence that they have any empirical validity, we have previously required more than a bare assertion that some particular state interest is served by a burdensome election requirement. While the State describes some imaginative theoretical sources of voter confusion that could result from fusion candidacies, in my judgment the argument that the burden on First Amendment interests is justified by this concern is meritless and severely underestimates the intelligence of the typical voter.

The State's concern about ballot manipulation, readily accepted by the majority, is similarly farfetched. The possibility that members of the major parties will begin to create dozens of minor parties with detailed, issue-oriented titles for the sole purpose of nominating candidates under those titles is entirely hypothetical. The majority dismisses out-of-hand the Party's argument that the risk of this type of ballot manipulation and crowding is more easily averted by maintaining reasonably stringent requirements for the creation of minor parties. In fact, though, the Party's point merely illustrates the idea that a State can place some kinds—but not every kind—of limitation on the abilities of small parties to thrive. If the State wants to make it more difficult for any group to achieve the legal status of being a political party, it can do so within reason and still not run up against the First Amendment. But once the State has established a standard for achieving party status, forbidding an acknowledged party to put on the ballot its chosen candidate clearly frustrates core associational rights.[5]

The State argues that the fusion ban promotes political stability by preventing intraparty factionalism and party raiding. States do certainly have an interest in maintaining a stable political system. But the State has not convincingly articulated how the fusion ban will prevent the factionalism it fears. Unlike the law at issue in *Storer v. Brown*, for example, this law would not prevent sore-loser candidates from defecting with a disaffected segment of a major party and running as an opposition candidate for a newly formed minor party. Nor does this law, like those aimed at requiring parties to show a modicum of support in order to secure a place on the election ballot, prevent the formation of numerous small parties. Indeed, the activity banned by Minnesota's law is the formation of coalitions, not the division and dissension of "splintered parties and unrestrained factionalism."

As for the State's argument that the fusion ban encourages candidate competition, this claim treats "candidates" as fungible goods, ignoring entirely each party's interest in nominating not just any candidate, but the candidate who best represents the party's views. Minnesota's fusion ban simply cannot be justified with reference to this or any of the above-mentioned rationales. I turn, therefore, to what appears to be the true basis for the Court's holding—the interest in preserving the two-party system.

5. A second "ballot manipulation" argument accepted by the majority is that minor parties will attempt to "capitalize on the popularity of another party's candidate, rather than on their own appeal to the voters, in order to secure access to the ballot." What the majority appears unwilling to accept is that *Andy Dawkins was the Party's chosen candidate.* The Party was not trying to capitalize on his status as someone else's candidate, but to identify him as their own choice.

III

In most States, perhaps in all, there are two and only two major political parties. It is not surprising, therefore, that most States have enacted election laws that impose burdens on the development and growth of third parties. The law at issue in this case is undeniably such a law. The fact that the law was both intended to disadvantage minor parties and has had that effect is a matter that should weigh against, rather than in favor of, its constitutionality.

Our jurisprudence in this area reflects a certain tension: On the one hand, we have been clear that political stability is an important state interest and that incidental burdens on the formation of minor parties are reasonable to protect that interest; on the other, we have struck down state elections laws specifically because they give "the two old, established parties a decided advantage over any new parties struggling for existence," *Williams v. Rhodes* (1968). Between these boundaries, we have acknowledged that there is "no litmus-paper test for separating those restrictions that are valid from those that are invidious. . . .
The rule is not self-executing and is no substitute for the hard judgments that must be made." *Storer*.

Nothing in the Constitution prohibits the States from maintaining single-member districts with winner-take-all voting arrangements. And these elements of an election system do make it significantly more difficult for third parties to thrive. But these laws are different in two respects from the fusion bans at issue here. First, the method by which they hamper third-party development is not one that impinges on the associational rights of those third parties; minor parties remain free to nominate candidates of their choice, and to rally support for those candidates. The small parties' relatively limited likelihood of ultimate success on election day does not deprive them of the right to try. Second, the establishment of single-member districts correlates directly with the States' interests in political stability. Systems of proportional representation, for example, may tend toward factionalism and fragile coalitions that diminish legislative effectiveness. In the context of fusion candidacies, the risks to political stability are extremely attenuated. Of course, the reason minor parties so ardently support fusion politics is because it allows the parties to build up a greater base of support, as potential minor party members realize that a vote for the smaller party candidate is not necessarily a "wasted" vote. Eventually, a minor party might gather sufficient strength that—were its members so inclined—it could successfully run a candidate not endorsed by any major party, and legislative coalition building will be made more difficult by the presence of third-party legislators. But the risks to political stability in that scenario are speculative at best.

In some respects, the fusion candidacy is the best marriage of the virtues of the minor party challenge to entrenched viewpoints and the political stability that the two-party system provides. The fusion candidacy does not threaten to divide the legislature and create significant risks of factionalism, which is the principal risk proponents of the two-party system point to. But it does provide a means by which voters with viewpoints not adequately represented by the platforms of the two major parties can indicate to a particular candidate that—in addition to his support for the major party views—he should be responsive to the views of the minor party whose support for him was demonstrated where political parties demonstrate support—on the ballot.

The strength of the two-party system—and of each of its major components—is the product of the power of the ideas, the traditions, the candidates, and the voters that constitute the parties. It demeans the strength of the two-party system to assume that the major parties need to rely on laws that discriminate against independent voters and minor parties in order to preserve their positions of power. Indeed, it is a central theme of our jurisprudence that the entire electorate, which necessarily includes the members of the major parties, will benefit from robust competition in ideas and governmental policies that "is at the core of our electoral process and of the First Amendment freedoms." *Anderson.*

In my opinion legislation that would otherwise be unconstitutional because it burdens First Amendment interests and discriminates against minor political parties cannot survive simply because it benefits the two major parties. Accordingly, I respectfully dissent.

Justice SOUTER, dissenting.

[Omitted.]

NOTES ON *BURDICK AND TIMMONS*

1. Note the common themes between these two cases: In both cases, the Court weighs the burdens on the individual and political party with the state's interests; both cases discuss the role and purpose of the ballot (as a form of expression or simply to allow the state to winnow the candidates and decide the race); in both cases the concern of favoring the two-party system plays a prominent role in the analysis; and in both cases the Court elevates the state's interests in regulating a free and fair election over the burdens imposed on voters and political parties.
2. Note also the continuing debate on the proper level of scrutiny for a law that impacts electoral rights. The majority in *Burdick* states, "to subject every voting regulation to strict scrutiny and to require that the regulation be narrowly tailored to advance a compelling state interest, as petitioner suggests, would tie the hands of States seeking to assure that elections are operated equitably and efficiently." Is this a sound rationale for rejecting strict scrutiny and employing a balancing test dependent on the "burdens" the law imposes? The "severe burden" framework from both *Burdick and Anderson v. Celebrezze* (our next case) is often referred to as the "*Anderson-Burdick* balancing test." We will see this test employed again in many of the cases in Part IV of this case book.
3. Make sure to understand the state's asserted interests for the law in each case. Are these interests sufficient to sustain the laws?

4. Is there an absolute or fundamental right to be a candidate? What does the holding in *Burdick* suggest? Imagine a case in which a state law precluded current public office holders (such as County Judges) from running for state legislature if their term overlapped with the legislative term to which they aspired. Even resigning would not allow them to run for state legislative office: They would have to wait until the set term for their current office was complete before they could run. What arguments would you make to challenge the constitutionality of the law? In *Clements v. Fashing*, 457 U.S. 957 (1982), which presented these facts, the Supreme Court ruled that there is no absolute right for someone to run for a particular office, and that the state had legitimate reasons for prohibiting current office holders from running for other offices. Given the discussion in the cases presented thus far, what valid interests would the state have in placing this limitation on candidates?
5. What is the role of a ballot? Should it be to allow parties and voters to engage in a particular expression, or is it merely for the purpose of deciding who wins a race?
6. Should the state be allowed to create rules that favor the two-party system? What does this say about the role of minor parties in our democracy? Is this just a function of entrenchment?

F. Independent Candidates on the General Election Ballot

Given the debate on the role of maintaining a two-party system in the previous cases, a further question arises regarding ballot access on the presidential general election ballot for independent candidates. What rules should dictate whether these candidates may appear on the ballot? To what extent can a state limit ballot access for independent candidates in an effort to ward off "sore loser" candidacies for those candidates who embark on the political primary process, see the writing on the wall that they will not secure the party's nomination, and decide to mount an independent candidacy? The next case considers these questions.

ANDERSON v. CELEBREZZE

460 U.S. 780 (1983)

Justice Stevens delivered the opinion of the Court.

On April 24, 1980, petitioner John Anderson announced that he was an independent candidate for the office of President of the United States. Thereafter, his supporters—by gathering the signatures of registered voters, filing required documents, and submitting filing fees—were able to meet the substantive requirements for having his name placed on the ballot for the general election in November 1980 in all 50 States and the District of Columbia. On April 24, however, it was already too late for Anderson to qualify for a position on the ballot in Ohio and certain other states because the statutory deadlines for filing a statement of candidacy had already passed. The question presented by this case is whether Ohio's early filing deadline placed an unconstitutional burden on the voting and associational rights of Anderson's supporters.

The facts are not in dispute. On May 16, 1980, Anderson's supporters tendered a nominating petition containing approximately 14,500 signatures and a statement of candidacy to respondent Celebrezze, the Ohio Secretary of State. These documents would have entitled Anderson to a place on the ballot if they had been filed on or before March 20, 1980. Respondent refused to accept the petition solely because it had not been filed within the time required by § 3513.257 of the Ohio Revised Code. Three days later Anderson and three voters, two registered in Ohio and one in New Jersey, commenced this action in the United States District Court for the Southern District of Ohio, challenging the constitutionality of Ohio's early filing deadline for independent candidates. The District Court granted petitioners' motion for summary judgment and ordered respondent to place Anderson's name on the general election ballot.

The Secretary of State promptly appealed and unsuccessfully requested expedited review in both the Court of Appeals and this Court, but apparently did not seek to stay the District Court's order. The election was held while the appeal was pending. In Ohio Anderson received 254,472 votes, or 5.9 percent of the votes cast; nationally, he received 5,720,060 votes or approximately 6.6 percent of the total.

The Court of Appeals reversed. It held that Ohio's early deadline "ensures that voters making the important choice of their next president have the opportunity for a careful look at the candidates, a chance to see how they withstand the close scrutiny of a political campaign."

In other litigation brought by Anderson challenging early filing deadlines in Maine and Maryland, the Courts of Appeals for the First and Fourth Circuits affirmed District Court judgments ordering Anderson's name placed on the ballot. The conflict among the Circuits on an important question of constitutional law led us to grant certiorari. We now reverse.

I

After a date toward the end of March, even if intervening events create unanticipated political opportunities, no independent candidate may enter the Presidential race and seek to place his name on the Ohio general election ballot. Thus the direct impact of Ohio's early filing deadline falls upon aspirants for office. Nevertheless, as we have recognized, "the rights of voters and the rights of candidates do not lend themselves to neat separation; laws that affect candidates always have at least some theoretical, correlative effect on voters." *Bullock v. Carter* (1972). Our primary concern is with the tendency of ballot access restrictions "to limit the field of candidates from which voters might choose." Therefore, "[i]n approaching candidate restrictions, it is essential to examine in a realistic light the extent and nature of their impact on voters."

Although [the] rights of voters are fundamental, not all restrictions imposed by the States on candidates' eligibility for the ballot impose constitutionally-suspect burdens on voters' rights to associate or to choose among candidates. We have recognized that, "as a practical matter, there must be a substantial regulation of elections if they are to be fair and honest and if some sort of order, rather than chaos, is to accompany the democratic processes." *Storer v. Brown* (1974). To achieve these necessary objectives, States have enacted comprehensive and sometimes complex election codes. Each provision of these schemes, whether it governs the registration and qualifications of voters, the selection and eligibility of candidates, or the voting process itself, inevitably affects—at least to some degree—the individual's right to vote and his right to associate with others for political ends. Nevertheless, the state's important regulatory interests are generally sufficient to justify reasonable, nondiscriminatory restrictions.[9]

Constitutional challenges to specific provisions of a State's election laws therefore cannot be resolved by any "litmus-paper test" that will separate valid from invalid restrictions. Instead, a court must resolve such a challenge by an analytical process that parallels its work in ordinary litigation. It must first consider the character and magnitude of the asserted injury to the rights protected by the First and Fourteenth Amendments that the plaintiff seeks to vindicate. It then must identify and evaluate the precise interests put forward by the State as justifications for the burden imposed by its rule. In passing judgment, the Court must not only determine the legitimacy and strength of each of those interests; it also must consider the extent to which those interests make it necessary to burden the plaintiff's rights. Only after weighing all these factors is the reviewing court in a position to decide whether the challenged provision is unconstitutional. The results of this evaluation will not be automatic; as we have recognized, there is "no substitute for the hard judgments that must be made." *Storer v. Brown.*

II

An early filing deadline may have a substantial impact on independent-minded voters. In election campaigns, particularly those which are national in scope, the candidates and the issues simply do not remain static over time. Various candidates rise and fall in popularity; domestic and international developments bring new issues to center stage and may affect voters' assessments of national problems. Such developments will certainly affect the strategies of candidates who have already entered the race; they may also create opportunities for new candidacies. Yet Ohio's filing deadline prevents persons who wish to be independent candidates from entering the significant political arena established in the State by a Presidential election campaign—and creating new political coalitions of Ohio voters—at any time after mid-to-late March. At this point developments in campaigns for

9. We have upheld generally-applicable and evenhanded restrictions that protect the integrity and reliability of the electoral process itself. The State has the undoubted right to require candidates to make a preliminary showing of substantial support in order to qualify for a place on the ballot, because it is both wasteful and confusing to encumber the ballot with the names of frivolous candidates.

the major-party nominations have only begun, and the major parties will not adopt their nominees and platforms for another five months. Candidates and supporters within the major parties thus have the political advantage of continued flexibility; for independents, the inflexibility imposed by the March filing deadline is a correlative disadvantage because of the competitive nature of the electoral process.

If the State's filing deadline were later in the year, a newly-emergent independent candidate could serve as the focal point for a grouping of Ohio voters who decide, after mid-March, that they are dissatisfied with the choices within the two major parties. As we recognized in *Williams v. Rhodes*, "Since the principal policies of the major parties change to some extent from year to year, and since the identity of the likely major party nominees may not be known until shortly before the election, this disaffected 'group' will rarely if ever be a cohesive or identifiable group until a few months before the election." Indeed, several important third-party candidacies in American history were launched after the two major parties staked out their positions and selected their nominees at national conventions during the summer. But under § 3513.257, a late-emerging Presidential candidate outside the major parties, whose positions on the issues could command widespread community support, is excluded from the Ohio general election ballot. The "Ohio system thus denies the 'disaffected' not only a choice of leadership but a choice on the issues as well." *Williams v. Rhodes.*

Not only does the challenged Ohio statute totally exclude any candidate who makes the decision to run for President as an independent after the March deadline. It also burdens the signature-gathering efforts of independents who decide to run in time to meet the deadline. When the primary campaigns are far in the future and the election itself is even more remote, the obstacles facing an independent candidate's organizing efforts are compounded. Volunteers are more difficult to recruit and retain, media publicity and campaign contributions are more difficult to secure, and voters are less interested in the campaign.

It is clear, then, that the March filing deadline places a particular burden on an identifiable segment of Ohio's independent-minded voters. As our cases have held, it is especially difficult for the State to justify a restriction that limits political participation by an identifiable political group whose members share a particular viewpoint, associational preference, or economic status.

A burden that falls unequally on new or small political parties or on independent candidates impinges, by its very nature, on associational choices protected by the First Amendment. It discriminates against those candidates and—of particular importance—against those voters whose political preferences lie outside the existing political parties. By limiting the opportunities of independent-minded voters to associate in the electoral arena to enhance their political effectiveness as a group, such restrictions threaten to reduce diversity and competition in the marketplace of ideas. Historically political figures outside the two major parties have been fertile sources of new ideas and new programs; many of their challenges to the status quo have in time made their way into the political mainstream. In short, the primary values protected by the First Amendment—"a profound national commitment to the principle that debate on public issues should be uninhibited, robust, and wide-open," *New York Times Co. v. Sullivan*—are served when election campaigns are not monopolized by the existing political parties.

Furthermore, in the context of a Presidential election, state-imposed restrictions implicate a uniquely important national interest. For the President and the Vice President of the United States are the only elected officials who represent all the voters in the Nation. Moreover, the impact of the votes cast in each State is affected by the votes cast for the various candidates in other States. Thus in a Presidential election a State's enforcement of more stringent ballot access requirements, including filing deadlines, has an impact beyond its own borders.[20] Similarly, the State has a less important interest in regulating Presidential elections than statewide or local elections, because the outcome of the former will be largely determined by voters beyond the State's boundaries. This Court, striking down a state statute unduly restricting the choices made by a major party's Presidential nominating convention, observed that such conventions serve "the pervasive national interest in the selection of candidates for national office, and this national interest is greater than any interest of an individual State." *Cousins v. Wigoda*. The Ohio filing deadline challenged in this case does more than burden the associational rights of independent voters and candidates. It places a significant state-imposed restriction on a nationwide electoral process.

III

The State identifies three separate interests that it seeks to further by its early filing deadline for independent Presidential candidates: voter education, equal treatment for partisan and independent candidates, and political stability. We now examine the legitimacy of these interests and the extent to which the March filing deadline serves them.

Voter Education

There can be no question about the legitimacy of the State's interest in fostering informed and educated expressions of the popular will in a general election. Moreover, the Court of Appeals correctly identified that interest as one of the concerns that motivated the Framers' decision not to provide for direct popular election of the President. We are persuaded, however, that the State's important and legitimate interest in voter education does not justify the specific restriction on participation in a Presidential election that is at issue in this case.

20. In approximately two-thirds of the States and the District of Columbia, filing deadlines for independent Presidential candidates occur in August or September. The deadlines in a number of other States are in June or July. Anderson was barred by early filing deadlines in Ohio and four other States; he succeeded in obtaining court orders requiring placement on the ballot in all five.

The passage of time since the Constitutional Convention in 1787 has brought about two changes that are relevant to the reasonableness of Ohio's statutory requirement that independents formally declare their candidacy at least seven months in advance of a general election. First, although it took days and often weeks for even the most rudimentary information about important events to be transmitted from one part of the country to another in 1787, today even trivial details about national candidates are instantaneously communicated nationwide in both verbal and visual form. Second, although literacy was far from universal in 18th-century America, today the vast majority of the electorate not only is literate but is informed on a day-to-day basis about events and issues that affect election choices and about the ever-changing popularity of individual candidates. In the modern world it is somewhat unrealistic to suggest that it takes more than seven months to inform the electorate about the qualifications of a particular candidate simply because he lacks a partisan label.

Our cases reflect a greater faith in the ability of individual voters to inform themselves about campaign issues. In *Dunn v. Blumstein*, the Court considered the validity of a Tennessee statute requiring residence in the State for one year and in the county for three months as a prerequisite for registration to vote. The Court held the statute unconstitutional, specifically rejecting the argument that the requirements were justified by the State's interest in voter education.

This reasoning applies with even greater force to a Presidential election, which receives more intense publicity. Nor are we persuaded by the State's assertion that, unless a candidate actually files a formal declaration of candidacy in Ohio by the March deadline, Ohio voters will not realize that they should pay attention to his candidacy. The validity of this asserted interest is undermined by the State's willingness to place major-party nominees on the November ballot even if they never campaigned in Ohio.

It is also by no means self-evident that the interest in voter education is served at all by a requirement that independent candidates must declare their candidacy before the end of March in order to be eligible for a place on the ballot in November. Had the requirement been enforced in Ohio, petitioner Anderson might well have determined that it would be futile for him to allocate any of his time and money to campaigning in that State. The Ohio electorate might thereby have been denied whatever benefits his participation in local debates could have contributed to an understanding of the issues. A State's claim that it is enhancing the ability of its citizenry to make wise decisions by restricting the flow of information to them must be viewed with some skepticism.

Equal Treatment

We also find no merit in the State's claim that the early filing deadline serves the interest of treating all candidates alike. It is true that a candidate participating in a primary election must declare his candidacy on the same date as an independent. But both the burdens and the benefits of the respective requirements are materially different, and the reasons for requiring early filing for a primary candidate are inapplicable to independent candidates in the general election.

The consequences of failing to meet the statutory deadline are entirely different for party primary participants and independents. The name of the nominees of the Democratic and Republican parties will appear on the Ohio ballot in November even if they did not decide to run until after Ohio's March deadline had passed, but the independent is simply denied a position on the ballot if he waits too long.[26] Thus, under Ohio's scheme, the major parties may include all events preceding their national conventions in the calculus that produces their respective nominees and campaign platforms, but the independent's judgment must be based on a history that ends in March.

The early filing deadline for a candidate in a party's primary election is adequately justified by administrative concerns. Seventy-five days appears to be a reasonable time for processing the documents submitted by candidates and preparing the ballot. The primary date itself must be set sufficiently in advance of the general election; furthermore, a Presidential preference primary must precede the national convention, which is regularly held during the summer. Finally, the successful participant in a party primary generally acquires the automatic support of an experienced political organization; in the Presidential contest he obtains the support of convention delegates.

Neither the administrative justification nor the benefit of an early filing deadline is applicable to an independent candidate. Ohio does not suggest that the March deadline is necessary to allow petition signatures to be counted and verified or to permit November general election ballots to be printed.[28] In addition, the early deadline does not correspond to a potential benefit for the independent, as it does for the party candidate. After filing his statement of candidacy, the independent does not participate in a structured intraparty contest to determine who will receive organizational support; he must develop support by other means. In short, "equal treatment" of partisan and independent candidates simply is not achieved by imposing the March filing deadline on both. As we have written, "[s]ometimes the grossest discrimination can lie in treating things that are different as though they were exactly alike." *Jenness v. Fortson.*

26. It is true, of course, that Ohio permits "write-in" votes for independents. We have previously noted that this opportunity is not an adequate substitute for having the candidate's name appear on the printed ballot.

28. Respondent conceded in the District Court that the nominating petitions filed on March 20 remain unprocessed in his office until June 15, when he transmits them to county boards of election. The boards do not begin to verify the signatures until the period July 1 to July 15. Finally, the Secretary of State does not certify the names of Presidential candidates, including independents, for inclusion on the ballot until late August, after the party nominating conventions. According to the District Court, based on the stipulated facts, it appears that no more than 75 days are necessary to perform these tasks.

Political Stability

The State's brief explains that the State has a substantial interest in protecting the two major political parties from "damaging intraparty feuding." According to the State, a candidate's decision to abandon efforts to win the party primary and to run as an independent "can be very damaging to state political party structure." Anderson's decision to run as an independent, the State argues, threatened to "splinter" the Ohio Republican party "by drawing away its activists to work in his 'independent' campaign."

Ohio's asserted interest in political stability amounts to a desire to protect existing political parties from competition—competition for campaign workers, voter support, and other campaign resources—generated by independent candidates who have previously been affiliated with the party. Our evaluation of this interest is guided by two of our prior cases, *Williams v. Rhodes* and *Storer v. Brown.*

In *Williams v. Rhodes* we squarely held that protecting the Republican and Democratic parties from external competition cannot justify the virtual exclusion of other political aspirants from the political arena. Thus in *Williams v. Rhodes* we concluded that First Amendment values outweighed the State's interest in protecting the two major political parties.

On the other hand, in *Storer v. Brown* we upheld two California statutory provisions that restricted access by independent candidates to the general election ballot. Under California law, a person could not run as an independent in November if he had been defeated in a party primary that year or if he had been registered with a political party within one year prior to that year's primary election. We stated that "California apparently believes with the Founding Fathers that splintered parties and unrestrained factionalism may do significant damage to the fabric of government," and that destruction of "the political stability of the system of the State" could have "profound consequences for the entire citizenry." Further, we approved the State's goals of discouraging "independent candidacies prompted by short-range political goals, pique, or personal quarrel."

Ohio's challenged restriction is substantially different from the California provisions upheld in *Storer.* As we have noted, the early filing deadline does discriminate against independents. And the deadline is neither a "sore loser" provision nor a disaffiliation statute. Furthermore, it is important to recognize that *Storer* upheld the State's interest in avoiding political fragmentation in the context of elections wholly within the boundaries of California. The State's interest in regulating a nationwide Presidential election is not nearly as strong; no State could singlehandedly assure "political stability" in the Presidential context. The Ohio deadline does not serve any state interest in "maintaining the integrity of the various routes to the ballot" for the Presidency, because Ohio's Presidential preference primary does not serve to narrow the field for the general election. A major party candidate who loses the Ohio primary, or who does not even run in Ohio, may nonetheless appear on the November general election ballot as the party's nominee.

In addition, the national scope of the competition for delegates at the Presidential nominating conventions assures that "intraparty feuding" will continue until August.

More generally, the early filing deadline is not precisely drawn to protect the parties from "intraparty feuding," whatever legitimacy that state goal may have in a Presidential election. If the deadline is designed to keep intraparty competition within the party structure, its coverage is both too broad and too narrow. It is true that in this case § 3513.257 was applied to a candidate who had previously competed in party primaries and then sought to run as an independent. But the early deadline applies broadly to independent candidates who have not been affiliated in the recent past with any political party. On the other hand, as long as the decision to run is made before the March deadline, Ohio does not prohibit independent candidacies by persons formerly affiliated with a political party, or currently participating in intraparty competition in other States—regardless of the effect on the political party structure.

We conclude that Ohio's March filing deadline for independent candidates for the office of President of the United States cannot be justified by the State's asserted interest in protecting political stability.

IV

We began our inquiry by noting that our primary concern is not the interest of candidate Anderson, but rather, the interests of the voters who chose to associate together to express their support for Anderson's candidacy and the views he espoused. Under any realistic appraisal, the "extent and nature" of the burdens Ohio has placed on the voters' freedom of choice and freedom of association, in an election of nationwide importance, unquestionably outweigh the State's minimal interest in imposing a March deadline.

The judgment of the Court of Appeals is *Reversed.*

Justice REHNQUIST, with whom Justice WHITE, Justice POWELL, and Justice O'CONNOR join, dissenting.

Article II of the Constitution provides that "[e]ach State shall appoint, in such Manner as the Legislature thereof may direct, a Number of Electors" who shall select the President of the United States. U.S. Const., art. II, § 1, cl. 2. This provision, one of few in the Constitution that grants an express plenary power to the States, conveys "the broadest power of determination" and "[i]t recognizes that [in the election of a President] the people act through their representatives in the legislature, and *leaves it to the legislature exclusively to define the method of effecting the object.*"

In exercising this power, the Ohio legislature has provided alternative routes to its general election ballot for capture of Ohio's Presidential electoral votes. *Political parties* can earn the right to field a Presidential candidate in the general election in one of two ways. Parties that obtained at least 5% of the vote in the preceding gubernatorial or Presidential election are automatically entitled to have a candidate on the general election ballot. Other political parties are required to file 120 days before the primary election (in 1980 the date was February 4) a statement of intent to participate in the primary, together with petitions containing signatures of voters equal to 1% of the votes cast in the last gubernatorial or Presidential election (in 1980 approximately 28,000 signatures would have been required).

Ohio also offers *candidates* different routes to the general election ballot. Should a candidate decide to seek the nomination of a political party participating in Ohio's primary election by capturing delegate votes for the party's national convention, the candidate must file a declaration of candidacy and a nominating petition bearing signatures from 1,000 members of the party; the filing must occur no later than the 75th day before the first Tuesday after the first Monday in June of the election year (in 1980 the date was March 20). Of course, because a political party has earned the right to put on the ballot a candidate chosen at its national convention, a candidate seeking the nomination of that party could forgo the Ohio primary process and, if he should win at the national convention, still be placed on the ballot as a party candidate. If a candidate chooses to run as a nonparty candidate, he must file, by the same date as a party candidate participating in the primary, a statement of candidacy and a nominating petition bearing the signatures of 5,000 qualified voters. Since a nonparty candidate does not participate in a national convention, obviously he cannot benefit from the routes made available to political parties.

Today the Court holds that the filing deadline for nonparty candidates in this statutory scheme violated the First Amendment rights of 1980 Presidential hopeful John Anderson and Anderson's supporters. Certainly, absent a court injunction ordering that his name be placed on the ballot, Anderson and his supporters would have been injured by Ohio's ballot access requirements; by failing to comply with the filing deadline for nonparty candidates Anderson would have been excluded from Ohio's 1980 general election ballot.[1] But the Constitution does not require that a State allow any particular Presidential candidate to be on its ballot, and so long as the Ohio ballot access laws are rational and allow nonparty candidates reasonable access to the general election ballot, this Court should not interfere with Ohio's exercise of its Article II, § 1, cl. 2 power. Since I believe that the Ohio laws meet these criteria, I dissent.

On the record before us, the effect of the Ohio filing deadline is quite easily summarized: it requires that a candidate, who has already decided to run for President, decide by March 20 which route his candidacy will take. He can become a nonparty candidate by filing a nominating petition with 5,000 signatures and assure himself a place on the general election ballot. Or, he can become a party candidate and take his chances in securing a position on the general election ballot by seeking the nomination of a party's national convention. Anderson chose the latter route and submitted in a timely fashion his

1. Anderson would not have been totally excluded from participating in the general election since Ohio allows for "write-in" candidacies. The Court suggests, however, that this is of no relevance because a write-in procedure "is not an adequate substitute for having the candidate's name appear on the printed ballot." Until today the Court had not squarely so held and in fact in earlier decisions the Court had treated the availability of write-in candidacies as quite relevant. *See Storer v. Brown.*

nominating petition for Ohio's Republican Primary. Then, realizing that he had no chance for the Republican nomination, Anderson sought to change the form of this candidacy. The Ohio filing deadline prevented him from making this change. Quite clearly, rather than prohibiting him from seeking the Presidency, the filing deadline only prevented Anderson from having two shots at it in the same election year.

Refusing to own up to the conflict its opinion creates with *Storer*, the Court tries to distinguish it[.] "Ohio's asserted interest in political stability," says the Court, "amounts to a desire to protect existing political parties from competition." But this simply is not the case. The Ohio filing deadline in no way makes it "virtually impossible" for new parties or nonparty candidates to secure a position on the general election ballot. It does require early decisions. But once a decision is made, there is no claim that the additional requirements for new parties and nonparty candidates are too burdensome. In fact, past experience has shown otherwise. What the Ohio filing deadline prevents is a candidate such as Anderson from seeking a party nomination and then, finding that he is rejected by the party, bolting from the party to form an independent candidacy. This is precisely the same behavior that California sought to prevent by the disaffiliation statute this Court upheld in *Storer.*

The Court makes other attempts to distinguish this case from the obviously similar *Storer* case. The Court says Ohio has no interest in preventing "intraparty feuding" because by the nature of the Presidential nominating conventions "'intraparty feuding' will continue until August."[4] This is certainly no different than the situation in *Storer.* Essentially all of the battles for party nominations in California would have taken place during the 12 months before the party primaries; the period during which an independent candidate had to be disaffiliated with any party.

The Court further notes that "*Storer* upheld the State's interest in avoiding political fragmentation in the context of elections wholly within the boundaries of California. The State's interest in regulating a nationwide Presidential election is not nearly as strong." The Court's characterization of the election simply is incorrect. The Ohio general election in 1980, among other things, was for the appointment of Ohio's representatives to the Electoral College. U.S. Const., art. II, § 1, cl. 2. The Court throughout its opinion fails to come to grips with this fact. While Ohio may have a lesser interest in who is ultimately selected by the Electoral College, its interest in who is supported by its own Presidential electors must be at least as strong as its interest in electing other representatives. While the Presidential electors may serve a short term and may speak only one time on behalf of the voters they represent, their role in casting Ohio's electoral votes for a President may be second to none in importance.

4. The Court seeks comfort from the idea that the filing deadline is not a "sore loser" statute which prevents a candidate who is defeated in a primary from running as an independent candidate. But the effect of the deadline in this case is much the same. Under the Court's approach, so long as a candidate pulls out of his party race before the votes of the party are counted, he must be recognized as a "newly-emergent independent candidate" whose candidacy is created by a dramatic change in national events. To the contrary, I submit that such a candidate is no more than a "sore loser" who ducked out before putting his popularity to the vote of his party.

The point the Court misses is that in cases like this and *Storer*, we have never required that States meet some kind of "narrowly tailored" standard in order to pass constitutional muster. In reviewing election laws like Ohio's filing deadline, we have said before that a court's job is to ensure that the State "in no way freezes the status quo, but implicitly recognizes the potential fluidity of American political life." *Jenness v. Fortson*. If it does not freeze the status quo, then the State's laws will be upheld if they are "tied to a particularized legitimate purpose, and [are] in no sense invidious or arbitrary." *Rosario v. Rockefeller*. The Court tries to avoid the rules set forth in some of these cases, saying that such rules were "applicable only to party primaries" and that "this case involves restrictions on access to the general election ballot." The fallacy in this reasoning is quite apparent: one cannot restrict access to the primary ballot without also restricting access to the general election ballot. As the Court said in *Storer v. Brown*: "The direct party primary in California is not merely an exercise or warm-up for the general election but an integral part of the entire election process, the initial stage in a two-stage process by which the people choose their public officers. It functions to winnow out and finally reject all but the chosen candidates."

The Ohio filing deadline easily meets the test described above. In the interest of the "stability of its political system," Ohio must be "free to assure itself that [a nonparty] candidate is a serious contender, *truly independent*, and with a satisfactory level of community support." *Storer v. Brown*. This interest alone is sufficient to support Ohio ballot access laws which require that candidates for Presidential electors choose their route early, thus preventing a person who has decided to run for a party nomination from switching to a nonparty candidacy after he discovers that he is not the favorite of his party. But this is not the only interest furthered by Ohio's laws.

Ohio maintains that requiring an early declaration of candidacy gives its voters a better opportunity to take a careful look at the candidates and see how they withstand the close scrutiny of a political campaign. The Court does not dispute the legitimacy of this interest. But the Court finds that "the State's important and legitimate interest in voter education does not justify the specific restriction on participation in a Presidential election that is at issue in this case." The Court explains that "[i]n the modern world it is somewhat unrealistic to suggest that it takes more than seven months to inform the electorate about the qualifications of a particular candidate. . . . Our cases reflect a greater faith in the ability of individual voters to inform themselves about campaign issues."

I cannot agree with the suggestion that the early deadline reflects a lack of "faith" in the voters. That Ohio wants to give its voters as much time as possible to gather information on the potential candidates would seem to lead to the contrary conclusion. There is nothing improper about wanting as much time as possible in which to evaluate all available information when making an important decision. Besides, the Court's assertion that it does not take seven months to inform the electorate is difficult to explain in light of the fact that Anderson allowed himself some 19 months to complete this task; and we are all well aware that Anderson's decision to make an early go of it is not atypical.

Ohio also has an interest in assisting its citizens in apportioning their resources among various candidates running for the Presidency. The supply of resources needed for operating a political campaign is limited; this is especially true of two of the most important commodities, money and volunteers. By doing its best to present the field of candidates by Spring, right at the time that campaigns begin to intensify, Ohio allows those of its citizens who want to provide support other than voting adequate time to decide how to divide up that support. While the Court does not give attention to this interest, it is certainly a legitimate one and an important one in terms of the effective campaigning of Presidential candidates.

The Court's decision in this case is not necessary for the protection of like-minded voters who want to support an independent candidate; Ohio laws already protect such voters. This case presents a completely different story. John Anderson decided some 19 months before the 1980 general election to run for President. He decided to run as a Republican Party candidate. When Anderson sought to get on the Ohio ballot after the March 20 deadline, he was not a "newly-emergent independent candidate" whose candidacy had been created by dramatic changes in the election campaign. He was a party candidate who saw impending rejection by his party and rather than throw his support to the party's candidate or some other existing candidacy, Anderson wanted to bolt and have a second try.

The Court's opinion protects this particular kind of candidate—an individual who decides well in advance to become a Presidential candidate, decides which route to follow in seeking a position on the general election ballot, and, after seeing his hopes turn to ashes, wants to try another route. The Court's opinion draws no line; I presume that a State must wait until all party nominees are chosen and then allow all unsuccessful party candidates to refight their party battles by forming an "independent" candidacy. I find nothing in the Constitution which requires this result. For this reason I would affirm the judgment of the Court of Appeals.

NOTES ON *ANDERSON*

1. *Anderson* presents the initial "balancing of interests" framework that, along with *Burdick v. Takushi*, eventually became known as the "severe burden" test. This was one of the first indications that laws restricting voting rights would not necessarily require strict scrutiny review.
2. Note that the Court construes the plaintiffs' claims as challenging the law's impact on voters, even though the law does not regulate voters directly. Are laws impacting candidates tantamount to laws burdening voters?
3. Justice Stevens discusses the "practical difficulties" independent candidates face, particularly in gathering signatures and seeking money early in the campaign season. Justice Rehnquist responds that Anderson himself did not actually face any problems because he was able to obtain the signatures and finance a robust campaign. To what extent should the practical realities of the situation before the

Court play into the analysis? Is it more important to consider the facts of that case, the rule to apply in the future, or the theoretical underpinnings of the analysis? In some ways this debate foreshadows the discussion of facial and as-applied challenges in more recent cases such as *Washington State Grange* (presented earlier in this Part) and *Crawford v. Marion County Election Board* (presented in Part IV of this book).

4. What are the state's asserted interests? Justice Stevens categorizes them as voter education, equal treatment between candidates, and political stability. Are these legitimate state interests? If so, why does Justice Stevens strike down the law? How is the early filing deadline tailored to these interests?
5. Is Justice Stevens' opinion faithful to the constitutional grant of authority to states to determine how to choose its presidential electors? Justice Rehnquist focuses his dissent on this constitutional provision; Justice Stevens largely ignores it.
6. Note also how Justice Rehnquist construes the early filing deadline: it primarily serves as a sore loser law. Is that true?

G. Minor Party Candidates on the General Election Ballot

How do the Supreme Court's ballot access cases apply today to independent or minor party candidates? The following two cases are representative examples. Note the problems inherent in discerning whether the laws impose a "severe burden" in each case, and how the determination of whether the burden is "severe" dictates the level of scrutiny and often the ultimate outcome of the case. Also note the tension between the right of voters to have candidates of their choice on the ballot and the right of states to regulate the electoral process.

NADER v. KEITH

385 F.3d 729 (7th Cir. 2004)

Before Posner, Wood, and Evans, Circuit Judges.

Posner, Circuit Judge.

Ralph Nader, joined by his campaign committee and two registered Illinois voters who support his candidacy, brought this suit to require the State of Illinois to place his name on the ballot for the forthcoming Presidential election. He appeals to us from the district court's denial of a preliminary injunction that would order the state to do that.

The suit challenges, as violations of the First and Fourteenth Amendments, three provisions of the Illinois Election Code that have in combination prevented Nader from qualifying for a place on the ballot. The first provision requires any candidate who has not been nominated by a party that received at least 5 percent of the votes in the most recent statewide election to obtain nominating petitions signed by at least 25,000 qualified voters. The second provision requires that the address on each petition be the address at which the petitioner is registered to vote. And the third requires that the petitions be submitted to the state board of elections at least 134 days before the election. The deadline this year was thus June 21. Only two states, Texas and Arizona, had an earlier deadline.

Nader declared his candidacy on February 22, which gave him four months to drum up support for his presidential bid, though a provision of the election code that he does not challenge required him to wait until the ninetieth day before the expiration of the June 21 deadline to begin circulating the actual petition forms for signature. On June 21 he turned in 32,437 petitions. More than 19,000 of these were challenged by defendant John Tully, whom Nader describes as a "minion" of the Illinois Democratic Party. The principal ground for challenging a petition was that the petitioner wasn't registered to vote at the address shown on it. After state administrative hearings, 12,327 petitions were struck, which brought Nader's total below 25,000. Nader's campaign continued to obtain petitions after the June 21 deadline, and by August 19, when the district court held a hearing on the motion for a preliminary injunction, another 7,000 or so had been collected, but the election authorities refused to consider them because they were untimely.

Nader argues that the three rules that in combination ruled him off the ballot impose an unreasonable burden on third-party and independent (nonparty) candidacy (though the Libertarian Party's candidate was able to qualify), and if this is so the rules are unconstitutional. Nader emphasizes the role that third parties have played in American democracy. The Republican Party started as a third party; and such third parties as the Progressive Party of Theodore Roosevelt, LaFollette's Progressive Party, and the Reform Party have made significant contributions to political competition, whether by injecting new ideas or, in the case of the Republican Party, by actually displacing one of the major parties.

So the barriers to the entry of third parties must not be set too high; yet the two major parties, who between them exert virtually complete control over American government, are apt to collude to do just that. For like other duopolists they would prefer not to be challenged by some upstart—although if a major party believes that a third party will take more votes from the other party than from itself, it will support that third party (surreptitiously, because it's supporting an ideological opponent), and the other party will oppose it (also surreptitiously, because it's opposing an ideological ally).

It doesn't follow from what we said about the importance of preserving opportunities for the entry of new parties into the political arena that it would be a good thing if there were no barriers at all to third-party candidacies. A multiplication of parties would make our politics more ideological by reducing the influence of the median voter (who in a two-party system determines the outcome of most elections), and this could be a very bad thing. More mundanely, terminal voter confusion might ensue from having a multiplicity of Presidential candidates on the ballot—for think of the confusion caused by the "butterfly" ballot used in Palm Beach County, Florida in the 2000 Presidential election. That fiasco was a consequence of the fact that the ballot listed ten Presidential candidates. The butterfly ballot was a folded punchcard ballot in which the ten candidates for

President were listed on facing pages. This unusual design was innocently adopted in order to enable the candidates' names to be printed in large type, in consideration of the number of elderly voters in the county, while at the same time placing all the candidates for each office in sight of the voter at one time so that he would be less likely to overvote. Another ballot design might have effectively disfranchised voters who had poor eyesight, or who cast their vote before realizing there were additional candidates for the same office on the next page of the ballot, or who cast two votes for candidates for the same office because they didn't realize that candidates for the same office appeared on different pages. But with names on each side and the chads (the places in the ballot that the voter punches out in order to vote) in the middle, it was easy to punch the chad of the candidate on one of the facing pages meaning to vote for the candidate on the opposite page. Apparently a significant number of voters did just that: intending to vote for Al Gore, they voted for Patrick Buchanan. With fewer candidates, the "butterfly" design and resulting confusion would have been avoided.

Less obviously, third-party candidates would themselves be harmed if there were no barriers to including such candidates on the ballot. It is to the Libertarian Party's advantage that if Nader's challenge fails, its candidate will be the only independent candidate for President on the ballot. If there were 98 independent candidates, none could hope for a nontrivial vote.

So there have to be hurdles to getting on the ballot and the requirement of submitting a minimum number of nominating petitions is a standard one. In a state the size of Illinois—the population exceeds 12 million, of whom more than 7 million are registered voters—requiring a third-party candidate to obtain 25,000 signed nominating petitions cannot be thought excessive. *Jenness v. Fortson* (1971) upheld a Georgia law that required petitions from 5 percent of the registered voters—in Illinois that would mean 350,000 petitions!

And especially in a state as notorious for election fraud as Illinois, the fact that the nominating petitions that a candidate submits have actually been signed by registered voters has to be verified. If the petition were not required to contain any identifying information (such as date of birth, mother's maiden name, or, the identifier that Illinois has chosen, the address at which the petitioner is registered to vote), there would be no practical impediment to a person's signing the name of anyone he knew to be a registered voter.

Of course a law requiring verification could require so much or such esoteric information that most petitions would be invalidated. The best way of evaluating this danger is to determine the total number of petitions that a third party would have to submit in order to be reasonably confident of having enough valid ones to get on the ballot. Almost one-third of the Nader petitions were invalidated. So if instead of 32,000 petitions his campaign had collected 37,500 and a third had been invalidated, there would have been 25,000 valid petitions, and Nader would be on the ballot. If 25,000 is not an excessive number to require, neither is 40,000 (to provide an extra margin of error), for that is only slightly more than one-half of one percent of the number of registered voters in Illinois.

But is it reasonable to require that the required number of nominating petitions all be collected by June 21 when the election is not until November 2? June 21 preceded both major parties' conventions, and depending on what occurred there a third-party candidacy might generate a degree of support that it could not have attracted earlier. The problem is that time has to be allowed between the deadline for petitions and the election to enable challenges to the validity of the petitions to be made and adjudicated and then to enable a ballot to be printed and distributed that will contain the names of all the candidates—and the ballot must be printed well before the election so that it can be distributed to registered voters who vote by absentee ballot.

But how much time? One hundred thirty-four days—almost four and a half months—seems awfully long. Too long, seems to be the judgment of 47 of the other 49 states. In *Anderson v. Celebrezze*, on which the plaintiffs primarily rely, the Court invalidated a seven-month deadline, and though it was much longer than Illinois's 134 days and Ohio had not argued that it needed that much time "to allow petition signatures to be counted and verified or to permit November general election ballots to be printed," the Court noted, though non-committally, that the district court had found that 75 days should be enough. The Court also emphasized that deadlines that states set for qualifying to be a candidate in a national election must be scrutinized with particular care because such deadlines have effects outside the states imposing them; a strong third-party showing could sway the outcome of the Presidential election.

Restrictions on candidacy must, moreover, be considered together rather than separately. (This, incidentally, makes it difficult to rely heavily on precedent in evaluating such restrictions, because there is great variance among the states' schemes.) The fewer the petitions required to put a candidate on the ballot and the harder it is to challenge a petition (and so the lower the number of petitions above the minimum that a candidate must submit in order to be on the safe side), the shorter the deadline for submitting petitions can be made without unduly burdening aspiring candidates. Illinois requires a substantial though not paralyzing number of petitions, makes challenges easy rather than hard (since a discrepancy between the address on the petition and the address at which the petitioner is registered is likely to be pretty common even without fraud), and sets a tight deadline for submitting a qualifying number. In these circumstances, the tightness of the deadline can be questioned.

But we must not overlook another variable in a system of ballot access, and that is the procedure for resolving challenges to nominating petitions. The more extensive the procedure that a state provides, the more time the state will need in order to determine whether a candidate has qualified. Illinois, perhaps out of sensitivity to the state's history of voting fraud, has decided to allow candidates to respond to challenges, and this decision requires pushing back the deadline for submitting petitions by increasing the amount of time required to determine whether the candidate has obtained the requisite number of valid petitions. A state that employed a purely ex parte procedure for resolving challenges could set a later deadline for submission of petitions. But Nader does not question the appropriateness of the state's entitling him to rebut challenges to his nominating petitions. With 19,000 challenges to consider one by one and the Nader campaign entitled to rebut all 19,000, the board of elections needed a significant amount of time for resolving challenges and only after doing so could it print up the ballots (unless it printed a double set of ballots—one with, one without, Nader's name—an expedient that has not been suggested). At argument Nader's lawyer claimed that the 19,000 challenges could all have been resolved within five to eight days. That seems preposterous and in any event no attempt has been made to substantiate the figure.

Well, even given the expanded procedure, is 134 days *really* a reasonable period for resolving challenges and printing and distributing ballots? Couldn't that be done quicker? Maybe so, but Nader has not presented evidence that would enable a court to prescribe a shorter period. We cannot micromanage the regulation of the electoral process to the degree he seeks.

Even if he has a better case on the merits than we think, he has not made a persuasive case for the extraordinary remedy of a preliminary injunction against a state agency. Remember that between the expiration of the statutory deadline and August 19, his campaign collected another 7,000 petitions. Were August 19 the deadline instead of June 21, we do not think it would be argued that the deadline was still too tight; nor do we understand Nader to be making such an argument, or to be arguing that if that were the deadline he would have collected more than 39,437 petitions (32,437 + 7,000). If a third of those are invalid, he is perilously close to the 25,000 minimum. Yet he argues not that the state election board should verify the 7,000, but that that number, though it undoubtedly includes many invalid petitions, should be added to his 20,182 total of verified petitions, carrying him above the 25,000 threshold. That is an improper procedure; his proposing it suggests that he is pessimistic that he actually has 25,000 valid petitions.

It also is unlikely that the 134-day rule, though it could prevent some third-party candidates, and perhaps even Nader in different circumstances, from having a reasonable shot at collecting the qualifying number of nominating petitions, could have made a difference to Nader's ability to collect petitions in this year's election campaign. Long before the June deadline it was not only certain who the major parties' candidates would be but their positions were well known, the candidates were campaigning vigorously, there was a high level of public interest in the campaign, Nader himself had been campaigning since February, and he has long been a well-known national figure with more name recognition than Senator Kerry had before Kerry entered the Democratic primary. If he could not obtain nominating petitions from (realistically, to supply a comfortable margin of error) 40,000 of Illinois's 7 million registered voters, the implication is that his popular appeal in Illinois in the forthcoming election is slight. With 90 days to collect the 40,000 petitions, and 100 canvassers working to collect them, each canvasser would have to collect an average of only 4 to 5 a day (40,000 / 90 / 100 = 4.44). If Nader could not recruit 100 canvassers in Illinois, his electoral prospects were dismal indeed.

Moreover, it would be inequitable to order preliminary relief in a suit filed so gratuitously late in the campaign season. It wasn't filed until June 27, only a little more than four months before the election. If when he declared his candidacy back in February Nader had thought as he now does that the Illinois Election Code unconstitutionally impaired his chances of getting a place on the ballot, he could easily have filed suit at the same time that he declared his candidacy—especially as he had filed a similar suit the last time he ran for President, in 2000, when he obtained a preliminary injunction that got him on the Illinois ballot by allowing him to submit petitions collected after the deadline.

By waiting as long as he did to sue, and despite the strenuous efforts by the district court and this court to expedite the litigation, Nader created a situation in which any remedial order would throw the state's preparations for the election into turmoil. Absentee ballots have already been mailed to voters who will be overseas on election day, and the remaining absentee ballots will be mailed on September 23. At argument Nader's lawyer offered no reason for the delay in filing the suit.

We are mindful that the right to stand for office is to some extent derivative from the right of the people to express their opinions by voting; it was doubtless to remind us of this that Nader's lawyers added two prospective voters as plaintiffs. But nothing is more common than for the denial of an injunction to harm innocent nonparties, such as people who would like to vote for Nader but unlike the two voter plaintiffs are not complicit in his decision on the timing of the suit. But there are innocents on the other side as well—namely the people who will be harmed if a last-minute injunction disrupts the Presidential election in Illinois. And Nader's supporters can of course cast write-in votes for him in November.

So, all things considered, we cannot say that the district judge abused his discretion in refusing to issue a preliminary injunction.

Affirmed.

LIBERTARIAN PARTY OF OHIO v. BLACKWELL

462 F.3d 579 (6th Cir. 2006)

Before: CLAY, GIBBONS, and GRIFFIN, Circuit Judges.

JULIA SMITH GIBBONS, Circuit Judge.

The LPO's claim is that the combination of two Ohio election regulations—the requirement that all political parties nominate their candidates via primary election and the requirement that all minor political parties file a petition with the Secretary 120 days in advance of the primary—imposes an unconstitutional burden on its First and Fourteenth Amendment rights of free association, by effectively preventing it from gaining access to the general election ballot in the twelve months preceding a presidential election. Following the analytical framework set forth by the Supreme Court in *Anderson v. Celebrezze* (1983), and its progeny, we find that the combination of these two requirements imposes a severe burden on the constitutional rights of the LPO, its members, and its potential voter-supporters. As the regulations are not narrowly tailored and do not advance a compelling state interest, Ohio's system for registering new political parties violates the Constitution. Thus, we reverse the ruling of the district court.

I.

This case presents a conflict between the constitutional rights of minor political parties and the authority of a state to regulate its elections and ensure the state's relevance in the modern presidential election cycle. As the nominees of the "major" political parties[1] become known earlier in the election year, states have pushed back the dates of their primary elections to the beginning of the primary election cycle. Over the last twenty-five years, the primary date in Ohio in presidential election years has moved from the first Tuesday in June to the first Tuesday in March. As a result, the date by which a political party must file to qualify for the primary also has moved, from the end of March in the year of the election to the beginning of November in the preceding year. The issue in this case is whether the move to accommodate the major parties has placed an impermissible burden on the constitutional rights of minor parties, including the LPO, and the supporters of these minor parties.

The Ohio Constitution requires that all political parties, including minor parties, nominate their candidates at primary elections. By statute, primaries are held the first Tuesday after the first Monday in May, except in presidential election years, when the primaries are held the first Tuesday after the first Monday in March. The 2004 primaries were held on March 2 of that year.

Ohio law provides two methods by which a party can qualify for the primary election. Any party that, in the preceding state election, receives at least five percent of the vote for its candidate for governor or president automatically qualifies for the next statewide election. All other parties must file a petition no later than 120 days prior to the date of the primary election that contains the number of signatures equal to one percent of the total votes cast in the previous election—32,290 in 2004. A party that does not file a petition by this date cannot participate in the primary and is thus prevented from appearing on the general election ballot. To be on the ballot for the November 2, 2004 general

1. Throughout this opinion, the Republican and Democratic parties will be referred to as the "major" political parties. All other political parties will be known as "minor" political parties. Judge Griffin correctly notes that the language of Ohio Rev. Code § 3517.01 makes no distinction between "major" and "minor" political parties. However, as will be discussed in Part III.A.1, the practical effect of the state's election law has been to limit the rights of parties other than the Republican and Democratic Parties from appearing on the general election ballot, making them the de facto "major" parties.

election, minor parties like the LPO were required to submit a petition no later than November 3, 2003.

The LPO failed to qualify as a political party and was unable to participate in the March 2, 2004, primary election. As a result, the party and its candidates were prohibited from appearing on the ballot for the 2004 general election.

On January 6, 2004, the LPO filed suit under 42 U.S.C. § 1983, claiming a violation of the rights guaranteed under the First and Fourteenth Amendments and seeking declaratory and injunctive relief. On June 1, the LPO and the State filed cross-motions for summary judgment. The court granted the State's motion and denied the LPO's motion. The LPO filed a timely appeal. We review a district court's grant of summary judgment de novo.

II.

[Omitted.]

III.

We turn to the merits—whether the combined effect of the Ohio election laws being challenged impermissibly burdens the plaintiffs' rights to free speech and association under the First Amendment. When analyzing the statutes, we are cognizant that "the state laws place burdens on two different, although overlapping, kinds of rights—the right of individuals to associate for the advancement of political beliefs and the right of qualified voters, regardless of their political persuasion, to cast their votes effectively." *Williams v. Rhodes*; *see also Anderson v. Celebrezze* ("[T]he rights of voters and the rights of candidates do not lend themselves to neat separation; laws that affect candidates always have at least some theoretical correlative effect on voters."). The right to cast an effective vote "is of the most fundamental significance under our constitutional structure." *Burdick v. Takushi*. The rights of political association and free speech occupy a similarly hallowed place in the constitutional pantheon. *See California Democratic Party v. Jones* ("Representative democracy in any populous unit of governance is unimaginable without the ability of citizens to band together in promoting among the electorate candidates who espouse their political views.").

This does not mean, however, that all state restrictions on political parties and elections violate the Constitution. The Supreme Court has clearly stated that states "may, and inevitably must, enact reasonable regulations of parties, elections, and ballots to reduce election- and campaign-related disorder." *Timmons v. Twin Cities Area New Party*. Thus, voting regulations are not automatically subjected to heightened scrutiny. The Supreme Court has set forth the appropriate analytical framework in *Anderson* and *Burdick*. First, the court looks at the "character and magnitude of the asserted injury" to petitioner's constitutional rights. *Anderson*. The court must then "identify and evaluate the precise interests put forward by the State as justifications for the burden imposed by its rule." If petitioner's rights are subjected to "severe" restrictions, "the regulation must be 'narrowly drawn to advance a state interest of compelling importance.'" *Burdick*. But if the state law imposes only "reasonable, nondiscriminatory restrictions" upon the protected rights, then the interests of the state in regulating elections is "generally sufficient to justify" the restrictions.

A.

The first step under the *Anderson/Burdick* framework is to determine whether this burden on the associational rights of political parties is "severe." In order to accurately apply this test, we must first determine the exact nature of the burden placed upon minor political parties and their voter-supporters. The LPO challenges the Ohio regulations that: (1) mandate that parties not meeting the five percent vote threshold in the previous election file a petition 120 days in advance of the primary election in order to qualify; and (2) require that parties participate in the March primary in order to appear on the general election ballot. Our inquiry is not whether each law individually creates an impermissible burden but rather whether the combined effect of the applicable election regulations creates an unconstitutional burden on First Amendment rights.

Deadlines early in the election cycle require minor political parties to recruit supporters at a time when the major party candidates are not known and when the populace is not politically energized. In this case, the LPO needed to find more than thirty thousand Ohio residents to sign its petition to appear on the 2004 ballot more than one year in advance of the election. Early deadlines also have the effect of ensuring that any contentious issue raised in the same year as an election cannot be responded to by the formation of a new political party. The combination of these burdens impacts the party's ability to appear on the general election ballot, and thus, its opportunity to garner votes and win the right to govern. The LPO's argument, thus, is that the ballot-access restrictions resulting from the filing deadline one year in advance of the general election imposes a severe burden on the First Amendment rights of the party, its members, and its potential voter-supporters.

1.

In determining the magnitude of the burden imposed by a state's election laws, the Supreme Court has looked to the associational rights at issue, including whether alternative means are available to exercise those rights; the effect of the regulations on the voters, the parties and the candidates; evidence of the real impact the restriction has on the process; and the interests of the state relative to the scope of the election.

The key factor in determining the level of scrutiny to apply is the importance of the associational right burdened. Restrictions that do not affect a political party's ability to perform its primary functions—organizing and developing, recruiting supporters, choosing a candidate, and voting for that candidate in a general election—have not been held to impose a severe burden. [*See, e.g.*, *Timmons*, *Burdick*, and *Clingman*.]

As noted above, however, the statutes at issue in this case do not merely affect the rights of the LPO to associate with non-members or select a certain candidate to be its standard-bearer. Certainly, both of these interests are implicated, but Ohio's regulations limit a far more important function of a political party—its ability to appear on the general election ballot.

The ability of a political party to appear on the general election ballot affects not only the party's rights, but also the First Amendment rights of voters. *See Tashjian v. Republican Party of Conn.* (noting the fundamental importance of "[t]he right to associate with the political party of one's choice"). It is true that a voter does not have an absolute right to vote for a candidate of her choice, especially when that candidate or party has not complied with reasonable state regulations. However, when a candidate wishes to appear as one party's standard-bearer and voters want to exercise their constitutional right to cast a ballot for this candidate, the Court has viewed state-imposed restrictions on this fundamental process with great skepticism. [*See Anderson.*]

The evidence in the record shows that in Ohio, elections have indeed been monopolized by two parties, and thus, the burdens imposed by the state's election laws are "far from remote." *Jones.* In *Jones*, the Supreme Court noted the importance of evidence that the burden imposed was a "clear and present danger" and not merely the product of speculation. The LPO has put forth evidence showing that Ohio is among the most restrictive, if not the most restrictive, state in granting minor parties access to the ballot. Of the eight most populous states, Ohio has had by far the fewest minor political parties on its general election ballot. From 1992-2002, the other states in this group averaged four minor political parties on the ballot each year. In contrast, Ohio averaged one per year, and no minor political parties qualified for the ballot, in any race, in 1992, 1994, 2002 and 2004. This is a product of not only the primary requirement and filing deadline, but also of the laws providing for automatic party qualification.

In addition, of the seven states that require all political parties to nominate their candidates in the state's primary election, Ohio imposes the most burdensome restrictions of both automatic qualification and petition qualification; as a result, it has seen the fewest number of minor parties on the ballot. California is the only other state with a filing deadline more than a year before the general election; however, its qualification requirements are much lower than Ohio's, and the state had seven political parties automatically qualify for the ballot in 2004. The same is true of Mississippi, which has a January filing deadline, but requires only that a party certify a list of statewide party officers in each of the state's four congressional districts in order to qualify. It, too, had seven ballot-eligible political parties in 2004.[10] Ohio had no minor political parties on its 2004 ballot. Forty-three other states, including Texas, New York, Illinois and Pennsylvania, permit minor political parties to nominate their candidates via convention or petition and provide far more flexibility in the date by which a party must qualify. While not conclusive in and of itself, the Supreme Court has noted that a historical record of parties and candidates being unable to meet the state's ballot-access requirements is a helpful guide in determining their constitutionality. *Storer*; *see also Jones.*

10. Only four other states require minor political parties to nominate their candidates in a primary election; all four have filing deadlines in April or later.

Put simply, the restrictions at issue in this case serve to prevent a minor political party from engaging in the most fundamental of political activities—recruiting supporters, selecting a candidate, and placing that candidate on the general election ballot in hopes of winning votes and ultimately, the right to govern. The evidence in the record indicates the negative impact these laws have had on minor parties and on political activity as a whole in Ohio. As such, we find that the Ohio system for registering minor political parties imposes a severe burden on associational rights.

Ohio's deadline in the November preceding the election is the earliest of any deadline reviewed by a federal court. It is 120 days in advance of the primary election and 364 days ahead of the general election for which the party wishes to appear on the ballot. This deadline imposes a severe burden on the First Amendment rights of the LPO.

2.

The State makes several arguments that the burdens imposed by the regulations are not severe.

The first contention is that the laws place no limit on key First Amendment rights of recruiting new members and engaging in political speech. We find this argument unpersuasive. First, the laws in question may indeed place limits on these other associational rights. The requirement that a fledgling political party rally support more than a year in advance of an election, when the major party candidates are not known and the majority of the country is not focused on the election, is an exceedingly difficult task. This easily could mute the party's message and limit its ability to recruit new members. Even if the statutes leave some associational rights unimpeded, this is not sufficient to establish that no burden is imposed.

Moreover, the rights left unimpeded by the Ohio regulations are not the ones most central to the goals of a political party. Recruiting members and engaging in political speech are important rights, but a political party's aims are far higher. The LPO does not aspire simply to assemble in public meeting places and engage in speech activities that further their beliefs. Certainly, this is a cherished First Amendment right and one that is jealously guarded. But the goal of a political party and its supporters is to govern. A party cannot lead if not elected and cannot be elected if not on the ballot. As the Supreme Court stated thirty years ago, "[t]he right to form a party for the advancement of political goals means little if a party can be kept off the election ballot. . . ." *Williams.* The statutes at issue in this case affect the ability of a political party to appear on the ballot and thus to exercise its most fundamental of rights.

Next, the State notes that Ohio law permits a candidate of a minor political party to appear on the ballot without participating in the primary election. To do so, a candidate need only file a nominating petition 75 days prior to the general election (August 18 in 2004), and he or she will be listed without party affiliation—as an independent or under "Other Party." This argument also misses the mark. Political parties, especially for national elections, aim to gather members together under a common title and common ideological beliefs. On many ballots, the option of a "straight-ticket" vote is even available, which allows an individual to mark one box that automatically selects the candidates from one of the major parties. Thus, in many cases party affiliation has the same, if not more, importance than the identity of the candidate. The Supreme Court has noted that "the political party and the independent candidate approaches to political activity are entirely different and neither is a satisfactory substitute for the other." *Storer.* A candidate's appearance without party affiliation is not a substitute for appearing under a party name, and it does not lessen the burden imposed by Ohio's restrictions on minor parties.

We make one additional observation about the State's arguments. The State analyzes the burdens imposed by the challenged statutes separately, rather than addressing their collective impact. For example, it argues that *Jones*, is controlling on the question of whether states may require political parties to nominate their candidates in a primary election. Putting aside the issue of whether *Jones* actually stands for this proposition, such reliance misses the point. The LPO does not challenge the primary requirement alone, but rather in combination with the 120-day filing deadline. It is this combined burden on the party's rights that we must address.

The State has not convinced us that the burden imposed by the filing deadline and primary requirement is not severe. There are few greater burdens that can be placed on a political party than being denied access to the ballot. In this case, the combination of the laws challenged by the LPO acted to impose just such a burden. We hold that the combination of Ohio laws that require a political party to file a registration petition twelve months in advance of the general election in order to appear on the ballot imposes a severe burden on the First Amendment rights of the LPO and its potential voter-supporters. As such, any regulation of this right "must be narrowly drawn to advance a state interest of compelling importance." *Burdick.*

B.

The State has made no clear argument regarding the precise interests it feels are protected by the regulations at issue in the case, relying instead on generalized and hypothetical interests identified in other cases. Reliance on suppositions and speculative interests is not sufficient to justify a severe burden on First Amendment rights. In the interest of a full and fair review, however, we have mined the State's brief and argument to identify its proffered rationales for the primary requirement and filing deadline. To determine if these interests are compelling, we examine each "in the circumstances of this case." *Jones.*

The State argues that a filing deadline 120 days in advance of the primary election allows a reasonable amount of time to process a petition for the registration of a political party. In that 120 days, the State must certify the signatures on the petition; allow for administrative appeals; print, distribute, and proof ballots; and prepare and mail absentee ballots. It is true that a 120-day period may be a reasonable amount of time to process the registration of a political party; however, this is not the inquiry before us. Rather, we must examine whether mandating that this 120-day period take place in advance of a March primary, resulting in a filing deadline one year in advance of the general election, promotes a compelling state interest. We find it does not.

The primary interests asserted by the State include preserving the integrity and fairness of the electoral process and ensuring that minor parties given access to the ballot have established bona fide support. Both the Supreme Court and this court have recognized the viability of these interests, but the State has provided no evidence that its registration procedure for minor parties in any way protects these interests. The State makes no argument that a filing deadline one year in advance of the general election is needed to ensure electoral fairness, and it would be difficult to do so. Forty-eight states have filing deadlines for minor parties later in the election cycle, and forty-three states allow minor parties to nominate candidates in a manner other than the primary election.

The State also asserts an interest in regulating the number of candidates in order to promote political stability, encourage compromise that limits the number of candidates with short-range goals, and avoid voter confusion. Again, the State has put forth no evidence that these interests are compelling or that they are advanced by the early filing deadline. There is some question as to whether this rationale is even reasonable. A state may not legitimately claim that preventing other parties from accessing the ballot is needed to protect political stability. The deadline in this case serves only to prevent the registration of new political parties unless those parties can mobilize more than a year before the election in which they wish to run. This system serves to protect the two major parties at the expense of political dialogue and free expression, which is not justified, much less compelling.

Moreover, the regulations arguably have a negative effect on limiting short-range candidates and preventing voter confusion. Political parties are organizations with short and long-term political objectives, as well as a desire for continuity and growth. By making it more difficult for parties to access the political arena, the state actually increases the possibility that issue-specific independent candidates will emerge to fill this void. These candidates do not offer the stability of a political party, and the sheer number leads to a greater likelihood of political instability and voter confusion.

The State has made no showing that the voters of Ohio, who are able to cast an effective ballot featuring several independent candidates, would be flummoxed by a ballot featuring multiple political parties.

Finally, it is important to note that the state's interests in regulating an election cannot trump the national interest in having presidential candidates appear on the ballot in each state. In the context of the presidential election, "state-imposed restrictions implicate a uniquely important national interest." *Anderson*. Strict ballot access requirements imposed by states have an impact beyond their own borders, placing some limits on a state's prerogative to regulate its elections. Moreover, as opposed to state or local elections, the outcome of a presidential election largely will be determined by voters outside a state's borders, reducing the importance of the state's administrative concerns. The combination of restrictions in this case "does more than burden the associational rights of . . . voters and candidates. It places a significant state-imposed restriction on a nationwide electoral process." *Anderson.*

Moving the filing deadline closer to the date of the primary or allowing parties to choose their candidates in another manner may impose some additional costs on the state, but this is the price imposed by the First Amendment. Ohio is well within its authority to mandate primary elections, to limit all parties to one primary date, or to require filing a petition in advance of the primary for administrative purposes. Viewed individually, each of these requirements may only impose a reasonable burden on constitutional rights. In practice, however, the combination of these laws imposes a severe burden on the associational rights of the LPO, its members, and its potential voter-supporters. As the State has not shown that these laws are narrowly tailored to protect a compelling state interest, we find that the Ohio system for minor party qualification violates the First Amendment of the Constitution.

IV.

There is an inherent constitutional tension between the rights of states to conduct and regulate elections and the rights of political parties and voters to exercise their First Amendment rights. We do not presume to dictate how Ohio must run its elections, except to say that the system must fall within the outer boundaries established by the Constitution. The filing deadline and primary requirement challenged by the LPO, when viewed in combination, fall outside these constitutional limits.

For these reasons, we reverse the judgment of the district court.

CLAY, Circuit Judge, concurring in part and dissenting in part.

[Omitted.]

GRIFFIN, Circuit Judge, dissenting.

[T]he majority erroneously subjects the disputed Ohio election regulations to a strict scrutiny analysis which, in turn, compels the majority to rule the laws unconstitutional. Because the challenged election rules are a reasonable non-discriminatory use of Ohio's regulatory power, I would . . . uphold the laws as constitutional.

Although the majority purportedly undertakes the requisite balancing required by the Supreme Court's decision in *Anderson,* it declines to recognize that a party challenging a State's reasonable and nondiscriminatory regulatory interests bears "a heavy constitutional burden." Rather than highlight this "heavy constitutional burden," alongside the wide discretion a state has to regulate its election system, the majority cites several decisions that allegedly represent the "weight" of authority disapproving of early filing deadlines. In doing so, however, it declines to note the significant distinction between those cases and this case; i.e., that the language of Ohio's laws in this case refer to a political party, as opposed to singling out minor parties or independent candidates. Indeed, the decisions cited by the majority for the proposition that early filing deadlines impose a severe burden predominantly deal with cases in which the deadline for independents (or minor parties) to file was substantially in advance of the primary election.

Unlike those decisions, the Ohio election regulations in this case impose equal obligations on all political parties. Ohio therefore "retains the right to ensure that candidates claiming to represent a political party meet the statutory requirements necessary to establish that the putative party has obtained 'some preliminary showing of a significant modicum of support' before appearing on the ballot as a candidate of that party."

Most problematically, Judge Gibbons arbitrarily characterizes "major parties" as Republican and Democrat and "minor parties" as all other political parties, despite the lack of any such distinction in Ohio's election laws. By framing the issue in these terms, the opinion glosses over the laws' equal treatment and applicability to all political parties.

In isolation, or in tandem, the Ohio requirements of primary election and 120-day preelection filing of petitions are reasonable. These election regulations do not impose a "severe" burden on plaintiffs' First and Fourteenth Amendment rights. In fact, the only evidence in the record on this issue is that [in the past], plaintiff LPO was able to comply with these election requirements. Moreover, according to plaintiffs' expert Richard Winger, in 1996 the Natural Law Party and the Reform Party qualified for the Ohio ballot, in 1998 the Libertarian Party and the Reform Party, and in 2000 the Libertarian Party and the Natural Law Party.

Finally, the majority's reliance on the "minor" party history of other states is misplaced. Each of our fifty states has its unique political dynamic. Consider the success of the Conservative and Liberal parties in New York and the Green Party and Libertarian Party in some states. The failure of third or fourth parties to thrive in Ohio is not likely the result of the challenged requirements of primary election and 120-day pre-election petition filing, but rather voter ideology, traditional party loyalty to the Republican and Democrat parties, and the unchallenged five percent automatic ballot access threshold.

In conclusion, absent a constitutional violation, it is the province of the legislature, not the courts, to write our election laws. Here, the challenged Ohio election regulations treat the LPO the same as any other political party. The primary election required by the Ohio Constitution and petition filing time requirements chosen by the Ohio General Assembly are not severe, but reasonable, in order to insure a fair, honest, and orderly election. Therefore, the challenged Ohio election regulations do not violate the Constitution of the United States.

For these reasons, I respectfully dissent.

NOTES ON *NADER v. KEITH* AND *LPO v. BLACKWELL*

1. Is there a way to reconcile *Nader v. Keith* and *LPO v. Blackwell*? That is, is there a unifying thread in the analyses in the cases? One thing these cases demonstrate is that determining whether an election law poses a "severe" burden is context- and fact-specific, and that the Supreme Court's ballot access cases can be difficult to apply. How would you synthesize the rules coming out of these cases?
2. How would you determine whether the burden of a ballot access law is "severe"? That is, what factors should go into the analysis of discerning the difference between a "severe" and "not severe" ballot access requirement? Note that you must balance, on the one hand, the desire to allow access for candidates and parties that can show they have a modicum of support, and on the other hand, administrative ease for those who run elections.
3. The cases also demonstrate once again that determining the "threshold" of whether the law imposes a severe burden is often the most important part of the analysis. If the law is severe, the court will apply strict scrutiny and likely (although not always) invalidate the election practice. If the law does not pose a severe burden, the court will use a lower level of scrutiny and is more likely to uphold the law.
4. Imagine that after the Sixth Circuit's decision in 2006, the secretary of state puts the LPO's candidate on the ballot. But the Ohio legislature fails to change the law. It is now 2008, and the LPO again seeks ballot access. You are the Ohio secretary of state. What do you do? Are you authorized to put the LPO on the ballot, even though the Ohio statute (that the Sixth Circuit struck down in the context of the 2006 election) would not grant ballot access? Do you have any other solutions?

SUMMARY OF THE LAW OF NOMINATING CANDIDATES

The cases in this Part II had several overarching themes. Among them included:

- Discerning the best way to go from "many to few to one" in selecting a party nominee (or independent candidate) and then eventual winner
- Determining the permissible requirements for ballot access
- Employing the severe burden test to determine the proper level of scrutiny—which often ultimately decided the constitutionality of the law under review
- The concern of entrenchment and the protection of the two major political parties

The cases showed that major political parties have a robust First Amendment right to freedom of association and have wide discretion in choosing the method for selecting their nominee. In addition, national political parties seem to have more discretion than state political parties, especially when the issue involves party autonomy. But we also found that states have wide leeway in enacting regulations for ballot access—such as imposing write-in bans (*Burdick*), antifusion laws (*Timmons*), and signature requirements for independent candidates (*Anderson*)—so long as there are legitimate state interests. We learned about different kinds of primaries: open, closed, semi-closed, and top two. We studied a political party's interest in avoiding party raiding and sore loser candidacies, and the way in which these interests impact the constitutionality of ballot access rules. We discussed the difference between facial and as-applied challenges in litigation involving election laws. Through it all, we realized that in many of these cases it is difficult to locate a reconciling principle beyond determining the severity of the burden and weighing that burden against the importance of the state's interests.

Therefore, one of the more important aspects of this material to master is the *Anderson-Burdick* "severe burden" test and how courts employ (or, some might say, manipulate) it to determine the level of scrutiny. We will see courts use this test again in issues involving election administration in Part IV. You should also consider the clash between stakeholders in this area: candidates and their supporters, state political parties, national political parties, minor parties, and the state in its regulation of the political process. We see, in cases such as *Democratic Party v. Wisconsin* and *Lopez Torres*, that the Court highly values a political party's right to associational autonomy. But this right is not absolute, as the *Washington State Grange* and *Clingman* decisions demonstrate, as in both cases the state was allowed greater leeway to regulate the political process. With respect to independent candidates securing ballot access for the general election, the Court requires the path to the ballot to be open, but states can impose modest constraints such as reasonable signature requirements. Once again, then, we circle back to the application of the "severe burden" balancing test in an attempt to reconcile this area of law.

PART III

The Law of Campaign Practices

Introduction

Now that we have defined a constituency to elect a person through redistricting and determined how a candidate appears on the ballot, the next step in the electoral process is running the campaign. This involves two main topics: (1) laws involving the conduct of the campaign itself (such as campaign ads, last-minute campaigning at the polls, or even more egregious efforts to persuade a voter to cast a ballot for a particular candidate, such as financial inducements); and (2) laws about the regulation of money used to pay for campaign activities, or (in other words) campaign finance.

During the most recent election cycles, there have been many allegations of campaign practices that seemed to push the limits of permissible activity. There were reports of flyers distributed to poor, largely African-American communities claiming that Election Day had been moved to Wednesday (the day after the actual Election Day). There were also reports of unlawful "vote buying" across the country. In 2010, thousands of Nevada voters awoke at 1:00 A.M. to a "robocall" from Justice Sandra Day O'Connor urging them to vote for a ballot initiative that would change the method of selecting Nevada judges from an election to appointment by a commission. The firm placing the calls had meant to have them go out at 1:00 P.M. But this raises the question: To what extent may states regulate robocalls? Beyond illegal or untoward campaign activities, every election entails questions regarding the permissible scope of advertising, campaigning, and get-out-the-vote efforts.

On the campaign finance front, the past few years have been extremely volatile. The amount of money in politics has skyrocketed as the Supreme Court has struck down various campaign finance limitations. In part as a result of the Supreme Court's 2010 decision in *Citizens United v. FEC*, the 2010 midterm elections were the most expensive in history. The 2012 general election surpassed this record. Indeed, the debate regarding campaign finance laws has spilled out into the public arena, with even President Obama inserting himself into the discussion by criticizing the Supreme Court's decision during his 2010 State of the Union address.*

* The line between "campaign" regulations, addressed in this Part of the book, and "voting" regulations, addressed in Part IV, is inevitably blurry at the margins. For example, the regulation of campaign activities that occur at polling places on Election Day itself could be considered in either category. The same can be said of laws that prohibit the payment of a financial inducement in exchange for the promise to vote for a particular candidate. We have chosen to include these particular topics in Part III, rather than Part IV, because we want to focus attention in this Part on the extent to which the law may constrain candidates and their campaigns from attempting to influence a voter's choice. In Part IV, by contrast, we focus on the

Throughout the materials in this Part, consider the manner in which courts allow federal or state governments to regulate campaign practices. To what extent are there limits on the ability of candidates and campaigns to interact with voters? When does a plea to vote become harassing? How does the constitutional right to vote conflict with the First Amendment right to freedom of speech, and what falls under the rubric of allowed "speech" for campaign purposes? In justifying their laws, the federal and state governments usually point to interests in election integrity, ensuring open and equal access to the ballot, and limiting corruption and fraud. When are these interests sufficient? As in the other Parts of this book, there are usually no easy answers, and the analysis depends largely on the clash of rights between stakeholders in the electoral arena.

A. False or Misleading Campaign Ads

Few would dispute that our politics have become extremely vitriolic. Negative ads are a routine part of campaigns. In fact, studies have demonstrated that "going negative" often works in a campaign, especially to make up ground in a close race. Do states have an interest in promoting civil discourse during elections by regulating the kinds of permissible campaign advertisements? Is limiting misleading or even downright false campaign statements consistent with the First Amendment rights of candidates? When does an advertisement cross the line from being a fair attack on an opponent's record to being inaccurate or even a lie, and is there anything a state can do about advertisements that go too far? The next set of cases present opposing views on these issues.*

As a backdrop to these cases, you should know that the U.S. Supreme Court has permitted the punishment of intentional or reckless falsehoods in the context of defamation law, which is designed to protect against injury to reputation. Should the same First Amendment (freedom of speech) standard apply when the state is asserting the different interest of protecting the electoral process? Defamation law is inapplicable when a candidate lies about facts relevant to a policy issue ("Gas prices tripled in the last three years"—when in fact they rose by only 30 percent), or when candidates falsely inflate their own records ("I received the Medal of Honor for bravery under fire in the Iraq War"—when in fact the candidate never saw combat). That is, based on well-settled doctrine, a defamation lawsuit is unavailable for false statements about a policy matter or when the candidate lies about him or herself.

As you read these next cases, consider whether the First Amendment should distinguish among types of campaign falsehoods for the purpose of a candidate's potential liability. Moreover, what sorts of punishments would be permissible for the state to impose

---

regulation of casting and counting ballots even when there is no issue concerning improper influence on the voter's free electoral choice.

* Just before this book went to press, the U.S. Supreme Court granted certiorari in a case that involves the same Ohio law as in the *McKimm* case that follows: *Susan B. Anthony List v. Driehaus*, No. 13-193 (cert. granted Jan. 10, 2014). Obviously, the Court's treatment of this new case may affect significantly our understanding of the jurisprudence on this issue—although, given the posture of the particular case, it is also possible that the Court will consider only justiciability issues concerning the timing of First Amendment challenges to the enforceability of Ohio's law.

if and when a court finds a speaker liable for a false or misleading campaign ad? For example, would it be permissible for a court to disqualify a candidate from holding office, or only to impose a modest fine? Finally, if you conclude that campaign ads should be entirely protected from liability, except in the context of a defamation lawsuit, are there any other steps that the government can take in an effort to protect the public from the intentional lies of unscrupulous politicians?

MCKIMM v. OHIO ELECTIONS COMMISSION*

729 N.E.2d 364 (Ohio 2000)

[Justice COOK delivered the unanimous opinion of the Ohio Supreme Court.]

[Facts]

In the November 1995 election for Jackson Township Trustee, Dan McKimm challenged the incumbent candidate, Randy Gonzalez. McKimm won the election. A few days before the voting took place, McKimm had mailed a campaign brochure to township voters. A full page of McKimm's brochure consisted of "[a] multiple-choice quiz to help you select the best candidate." The quiz contained eighteen multiple-choice questions, and several of these were accompanied by small, cartoon-like illustrations. [See Figures 3-1 and 3-2.] McKimm suggested the "correct" answers to the questions by indicating them in bold print. Most of McKimm's questions mentioned Gonzalez by name and discussed Gonzalez's actions during his tenure as trustee. At the top of the page, the brochure indicated to township voters that "[r]esearch documentation" was available and provided the telephone number of McKimm's campaign chairman.

After reading the brochure, Gonzalez filed a complaint with the Ohio Elections Commission, alleging that McKimm violated Ohio's election laws by disseminating several of the statements included in the brochure. Specifically, Gonzalez alleged that McKimm violated R.C. 3517.21, which provides:

> "(B) No person, during the course of any campaign for nomination or election to public office or office of a political party, by means of campaign materials, . . . shall knowingly and with intent to affect the outcome of such campaign do any of the following:
>
> . . .
>
> "(10) Post, publish, circulate, distribute, or otherwise disseminate a false statement concerning a candidate, either knowing the same to be false or with reckless disregard of whether it was false or not, if the statement is designed to promote the election, nomination, or defeat of the candidate."

Question No. 7 and its accompanying illustration were among the items Gonzalez challenged in his affidavit. Question No. 7 read as follows:

* [Editors' note: Professor Foley, one of the authors of this casebook, participated in the state's defense of its law in this case, as the author was serving as the State Solicitor at the time.]

"**7. Which of the following is true?**
"A. Trustees have a policy of bidding **all** contracts greater than $10,000.
"B. Randy Gonzalez **ignored** bidding policy. He voted to contract an architect for $51,000 to design the Social Hall (pavilion) ***without taking bids.***
"**C.** This one is tricky. Both A and B are true." (Emphasis *sic.*)

An illustration accompanied the text of Question No. 7. In the drawing, a human hand extends toward the reader from underneath the corner of a table. The hand holds a bundle of cash, and small lines drawn around the bundle give the reader the impression of motion—as if the hand is waving the cash back and forth underneath the table. For the convenience of the reader, we have appended a reproduction of Question No. 7 and its accompanying illustration to the end of this opinion, as well as a reproduction of the "quiz" page of McKimm's brochure.

In his affidavit to the commission, Gonzalez alleged that Question No. 7 "indicates by representation that [Gonzalez] accepted money under the table, or solicited a bribe or kickback in return for awarding the contract referred to." Gonzalez denied that he ever received, solicited, or encouraged a bribe in relation to the contract. In a written response, McKimm disagreed with Gonzalez's characterization of the illustration. McKimm maintained that "[t]he drawing included with Item No. 7 of the Circular depicts my personal belief that the decision of complainant Gonzalez to disregard the Board's own policy . . . and to instead award a contract to a contractor on the basis of personal preference, and unsubstantiated 'freebies,' . . . is fairly characterized as underhanded, less than open, and hidden beneath the table of secrecy if you will."

At a hearing before the Elections Commission, McKimm conceded that he distributed the brochure intending to affect the outcome of the campaign and to promote his candidacy. When Gonzalez's attorney asked McKimm why he included illustrations in the brochure, McKimm testified that he intended the drawings "to lend, if you will, substance or credibility to the [adjacent] text."

When the parties turned specifically to Question No. 7 and its accompanying illustration, McKimm initially argued that the drawing did not actually depict a hand waving money *under* the table. He testified that the hand was drawn either behind or to the side of the table. Nevertheless, McKimm answered affirmatively when Gonzalez's attorney asked him to refer to the exhibit depicting "the money under the table." And Commissioner Duncan stated on the record that the drawing "clearly" depicted a hand waving cash underneath the table.

McKimm conceded that he had heard of the phrase "passing money under the table," while denying that he intended the cartoon to suggest that Gonzalez had taken a bribe. When asked if he had any evidence that Gonzalez had ever taken a bribe during his tenure as trustee, McKimm replied, "No, sir."

For his part, Gonzalez testified that his vote on the unbid construction contract was a legal action that occurred at a public meeting.

Commissioner Webster urged the commission to find that McKimm's brochure "in its totality," and by clear and convincing evidence, violated Ohio's election laws, and his motion passed by a vote of five to two. Though the commission declined to refer the matter to a prosecutor, the commission issued a reprimand letter. The two commissioners who voted against the motion described the cartoon as "sleazy" and "offensive," but concluded that all of the challenged statements in the brochure were protected by the First Amendment.

[The Franklin County Court of Common Pleas affirmed the commission's order, but only insofar as the illustration accompanying Question No. 7 was concerned. The court determined that the constitutional guarantees of free speech protected the *text* of Question No. 7. The Franklin County Court of Appeals reversed the decision of the trial court. The appellate court decided that the evidence failed to show that McKimm published the illustration with knowledge that it was false or in reckless disregard of its falsity.]

The cause is now before this court upon the allowance of a discretionary appeal.

[Law]

The cartoon drawing at the heart of this case presents this court with an opportunity to clarify the relationship between Ohio's election laws and the constitutional guarantees of free speech. The General Assembly empowered the Ohio Elections Commission to investigate allegations regarding the dissemination of false and misleading statements by candidates for public office in Ohio, and to take appropriate action when it concludes that a violation has occurred. The commission may exercise its authority, however, only when that authority does not clash with the freedoms of speech and press independently recognized by the United States and Ohio Constitutions.

The trial court determined that the commission properly reprimanded Dan McKimm for publishing the illustration contained in his campaign brochure. But the court of appeals reversed, holding that the commission's order violated the First Amendment to the United States Constitution. Because we determine that the court of appeals erred in its analysis of the constitutional issues in this case, we reverse.

The Elements of R.C. 3517.21(B)(10)

At the commission hearing, McKimm conceded that he distributed the brochure intending to affect the outcome of the campaign and to promote his candidacy. All that remained for the commission to determine, therefore, was whether McKimm disseminated (1) a false statement about his opponent, (2) "knowing the same to be false or with reckless disregard of whether it was false or not." R.C. 3517.21(B)(10).[1]

The court of appeals reversed the decision of the trial court on the basis of the second element (termed "actual malice"), holding that the record did not contain clear and

1. The commission must apply a standard of clear and convincing evidence with respect to findings under R.C. 3517.21. R.C. 3517.155(D).

convincing evidence that McKimm distributed the cartoon with actual malice. Because we analyze the evidentiary requirements differently than the court of appeals, we conclude that the evidence supports the commission's findings regarding both elements.

In Part A, below, we agree with the trial court that, to the reasonable reader, McKimm's cartoon constitutes a false statement of fact: that Gonzalez accepted a bribe or received an illegal kickback when he voted to award the unbid contract. In Part B, we conclude that, since there was sufficient evidence for the Elections Commission to draw the reasonable inference that McKimm *intended* to convey the very message that he *did* convey about Gonzalez's "crime," and since McKimm admitted that he had no basis to believe that Gonzalez committed bribery during his tenure as trustee, McKimm disseminated the brochure containing this reasonable connotation of bribery with actual malice.

A. McKimm's Money-Under-the-Table Cartoon: to the Reasonable Reader, A False Statement that Gonzalez Committed Bribery

The common pleas court determined that the illustration accompanying Question No. 7 made "a clear and obvious implication that [Gonzalez], in voting to violate township policy, received money—under the table—in return." We agree. Under both the United States and Ohio Constitutions, courts assess the meaning of an allegedly libelous statement under an objective standard—that of the reasonable reader.

[Subsections 1 and 2 are omitted.]

3. Application of the Reasonable-Reader Standard to McKimm's Cartoon

In the case at bar, the Elections Commission could not reprimand McKimm for the illustration accompanying Question No. 7 unless the cartoon, to the reasonable reader, constituted a false statement of fact about Gonzalez. We conclude that the commission and trial court correctly assessed the meaning of McKimm's cartoon from the perspective of the reasonable reader and that the average reader would view the cartoon as a false factual assertion that Gonzalez accepted cash in exchange for his vote to award the unbid construction contract.

Commissioner Duncan explicitly referred to the appropriate standard when he said, "[O]ne wonders what it was that a *reasonable reader* would perceive after having seen this cartoon." (Emphasis added.) Shortly thereafter, Commissioner Duncan concluded—along with the other commissioners who voted to reprimand McKimm—that the cartoon unambiguously depicted Gonzalez engaging in unlawful activity. Likewise, the common pleas judge determined that McKimm's illustration was "capable of only one *reasonable* interpretation: which is [that Gonzalez] took money under the table to award a contract without competitive bidding and therefore was guilty of bribery." (Emphasis added.)

The phrase "passing money under the table" connotes an illegal transaction made for personal gain. The drawing depicting this illegal conduct appeared adjacent to text in a "quiz" that made serious and specific allegations about Gonzalez's conduct as a trustee. The quiz even included a phone number for voters to call for documentation—suggesting that the statements therein could be proven true. And a political cartoon that falsely depicts a public official engaging in illegal conduct will not be exempt from legal redress merely because the charge is depicted graphically rather than verbally.

As the commission notes in its merit brief, "We all know what a hand under a table holding cash implies, particularly . . . in the context of a discussion about a government contract being let contrary to standard policy and without competitive bidding." McKimm's cartoon implied to the reasonable reader that Gonzalez actually accepted cash for his vote to award the lucrative, unbid construction contract.

[Subsection 4 is omitted.]

B. McKimm Disseminated the Cartoon with Actual Malice

Having determined that McKimm's cartoon was defamatory, we turn to the only remaining issue: whether McKimm published the cartoon with actual malice—that is, either knowing that it was false or acting in reckless disregard of whether it was false or not.*

1. The Role of the Actual-Malice Standard

By permitting liability only for those false statements about public officials made with actual malice, courts promote robust criticism of public officials in their conduct of governmental affairs. Public officials will often be subject to "vehement, caustic, and sometimes unpleasantly sharp attacks." *New York Times* [*Co. v. Sullivan* (1964)]. By prohibiting the imposition of strict liability for false statements made against public figures, the actual-malice standard provides essential "breathing space" for the criticism that is inevitable in free debate and crucial to our democratic system.

On the other hand, the actual-malice standard is not an impenetrable shield for the benefit of those who engage in false speech about public figures. "[F]alse speech, even political speech, does not merit constitutional protection if the speaker knows of the falsehood or recklessly disregards the truth." *Pestrak* [*v. Ohio Elections Comm.* (6th Cir. 1991)]. "[T]he use of the known lie as a tool is at once at odds with the premises of democratic government and with the orderly manner in which economic, social, or political change is to be effected. . . . Hence the knowingly false statement and the false statement made with reckless disregard of the truth, do not enjoy constitutional protection." *Garrison* [*v. Louisiana* (1964)].

2. The Evidentiary Requirements of the Actual-Malice Standard

Whether the evidence in the record supports a finding of actual malice is a question of law. To answer this question, we are obliged to undertake an independent review of the record. We may not infer the existence of actual malice from evidence of personal spite or

* [Editors' note: "Actual malice" is a term of art within defamation law; it means specifically an intentional or reckless falsehood and does not necessarily entail ill will or spite, although it often includes such emotion.]

ill will alone; rather, our focus is on the publisher's attitude toward the truth or falsity of the publication.

We conclude that the record in this case clearly and convincingly confirms that McKimm's conduct surpassed the actual-malice threshold. McKimm's testimony before the commission amply supported that body's conclusion—and our own—that McKimm *intended* to convey to township voters the false message that the drawing *did* convey to the reasonable reader of his brochure.

McKimm knew that Gonzalez and the other trustees were not legally obliged to solicit bids for the construction contract before awarding it, and knew that the trustees awarded the unbid contract only after discussion in an open meeting. McKimm also testified, however, that he personally disapproved of Gonzalez's vote, and that he felt a wrongdoing had occurred. In this, McKimm saw an opportunity—for he testified that, if township voters were aware of what happened, "they would have reacted in the same fashion that I did."

But instead of merely disseminating his brochure with the bare facts that appeared in the text of Question No. 7, McKimm chose to accompany those facts with a cartoon. That cartoon, as we have already determined, unambiguously depicts a hand passing money under the table—a concept with which McKimm admitted he was personally familiar. McKimm, however, also admitted that he had *no basis* to believe that Gonzalez had engaged in any illegal conduct during his tenure as trustee. As the trial court determined, McKimm chose "to illustrate the right of the voters to question [Gonzalez's] conduct by illustrating a criminal act, where no evidence exists to support such an act."

When called to answer for his choice before the commission, McKimm admitted that he knew of the phrase "passing money under the table," and that he had no basis to believe that Gonzalez had participated in such an act—or any illegal acts—during his tenure as trustee. McKimm also testified implausibly by insisting that the hand in his drawing appeared either on the "other side of the table," or "behind the table," but "not under the table." After our independent review of this record, we agree with the commission and the trial court that McKimm disseminated his cartoon well aware of its false implication. McKimm conveyed a message to the reasonable reader that he knew had no basis in fact.

Conclusion

The commission properly acted in this case to recognize society's "pervasive and strong interest in preventing and redressing attacks upon reputation." *Rosenblatt v. Baer* (1966).

For the foregoing reasons, we hold that when a candidate for public office distributes a campaign brochure containing an illustration with accompanying text that imply to the reasonable reader that the candidate's opponent committed an illegal act while in office, and the candidate lacks any basis to believe that the opponent committed the act depicted in the brochure, the Ohio Elections Commission may constitutionally determine that the candidate violated R.C. 3517.21(B)(10). Accordingly, we reverse the decision of the court of appeals, and reinstate the decision of the trial court.

Judgment reversed.

Figure 3-1

APPENDIX 1

7. Which of the following is true?

A. Trustees have a policy of bidding **all** contracts greater than $10,000.

B. Randy Gonzalez **ignored** bidding policy. He voted to contract an architect for $51,000 to design the Social Hall (pavilion) ***without taking bids.***

C. This one is tricky. Both A.... and B. are true.

Source: Ohio Supreme Court's Appendix to *McKimm v. Ohio Elections Commission*, 729 N.E.2d 364 (Ohio 2000)

Figure 3-2

APPENDIX 2

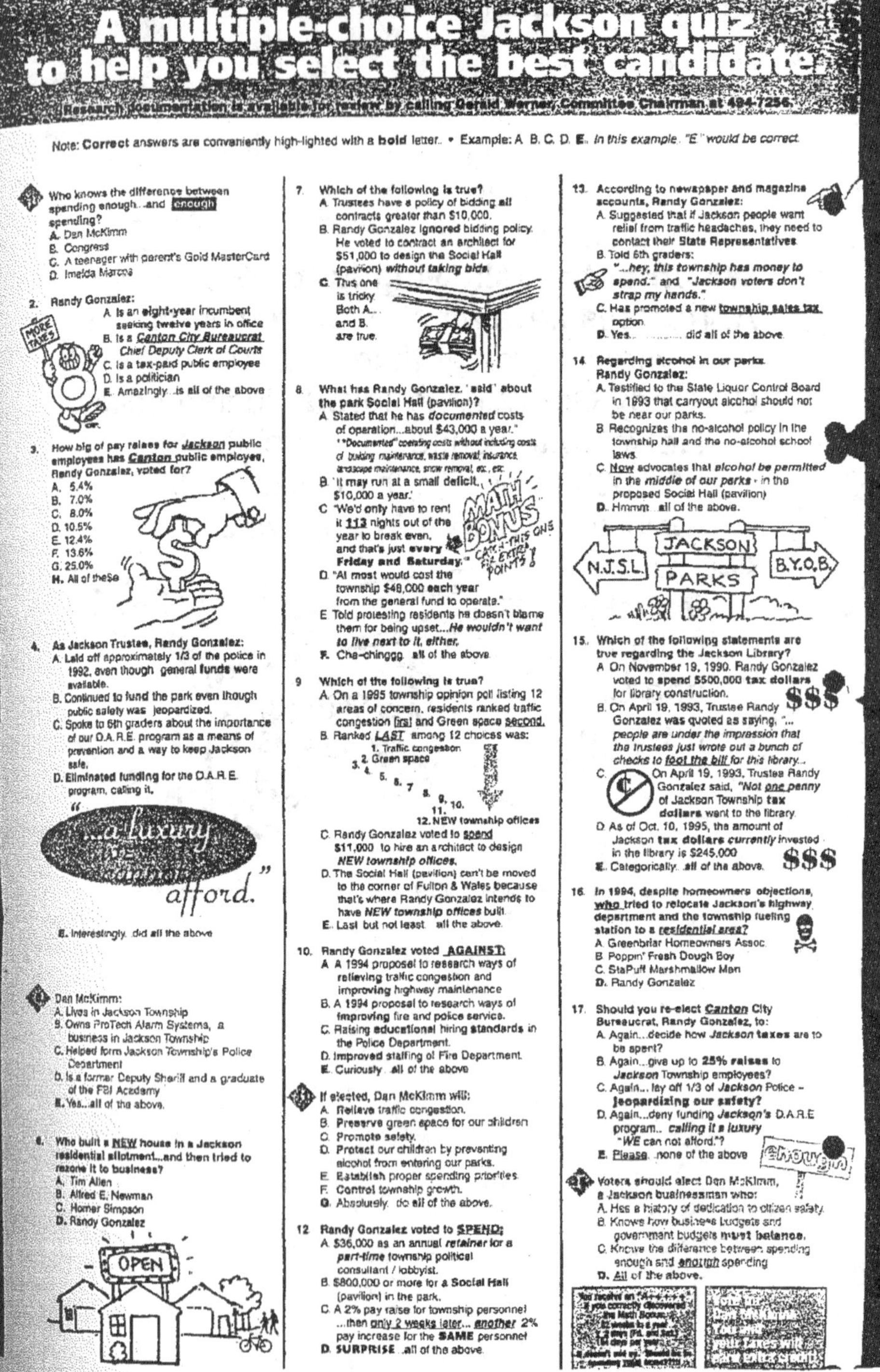

A multiple-choice Jackson quiz to help you select the best candidate.

(Research documentation is available for review by calling Gerald Werner, Committee Chairman at 494-7256.)

Note: **Correct** answers are conveniently high-lighted with a **bold** letter.. • Example: A B. C. D. **E**. *In this example. "E" would be correct.*

Who knows the difference between spending enough...and enough spending?
A. Dan McKimm
B. Congress
C. A teenager with parent's Gold MasterCard
D. Imelda Marcos

2. **Randy Gonzalez:**
A. Is an **eight-year** incumbent **seeking twelve years** in office
B. Is a *Canton City Bureaucrat Chief Deputy Clerk of Courts*
C. Is a tax-paid public employee
D. Is a politician
E. Amazingly...is **all** of the above

3. **How big of pay raises for *Jackson* public employees has *Canton* public employee, Randy Gonzalez, voted for?**
A. 5.4%
B. 7.0%
C. 8.0%
D. 10.5%
E. 12.4%
F. 13.6%
G. 25.0%
H. All of these

4. **As Jackson Trustee, Randy Gonzalez:**
A. **Laid off** approximately 1/3 of the police in 1992, even though general **funds** were available.
B. **Continued** to fund the park even though public safety was jeopardized.
C. **Spoke** to 6th graders about the importance of our D.A.R.E. program as a means of prevention and a way to keep Jackson safe.
D. **Eliminated funding** for the D.A.R.E. program, calling it,

"...a luxury we cannot afford."

E. Interestingly...did **all** the above

Dan McKimm:
A. Lives in Jackson Township
B. Owns ProTech Alarm Systems, a business in Jackson Township
C. Helped form Jackson Township's Police Department
D. Is a former Deputy Sheriff and a graduate of the FBI Academy
E. Yes...all of the above.

6. **Who built a NEW house in a Jackson residential allotment...and then tried to rezone it to business?**
A. Tim Allen
B. Alfred E. Newman
C. Homer Simpson
D. Randy Gonzalez

7. **Which of the following is true?**
A. Trustees have a policy of bidding **all** contracts greater than $10,000.
B. Randy Gonzalez **ignored** bidding policy. He voted to contract an architect for **$51,000 to design the Social Hall** (pavilion) ***without taking bids.***
C. This one is tricky. Both A... and B. are true.

8. **What has Randy Gonzalez 'said' about the park Social Hall (pavilion)?**
A. Stated that he has *documented* costs of operation...about $43,000 a year."
*"Documented" operating costs without including costs of building maintenance, waste removal, insurance, landscape maintenance, snow removal, etc., etc.
B. "It **may** run at a small **deficit**, $10,000 a year."
C. "We'd **only** have to rent it **113** nights out of the year to break even, and that's just **every Friday and Saturday.**"
D. "**At most** would cost the township $48,000 **each year** from the general fund to operate."
E. Told protesting residents he doesn't blame them for being upset...***He wouldn't want to live next to it, either.***
F. Cha-chinggg...**all** of the above

9. **Which of the following is true?**
A. On a 1995 township opinion poll listing 12 areas of concern, residents ranked traffic congestion first and Green space second.
B. Ranked *LAST* among 12 choices was:
1. Traffic congestion
2. Green space
3. 4. 5. 6. 7 8. 9. 10. 11.
12. **NEW township offices**
C. Randy Gonzalez voted to spend **$11,000** to hire an architect to design ***NEW township offices.***
D. The Social Hall (pavilion) can't be moved to the corner of Fulton & Wales because that's where Randy Gonzalez intends to have ***NEW township offices*** built.
E. Last but not least...all the above.

10. **Randy Gonzalez voted AGAINST:**
A. A 1994 proposal to research ways of **relieving** traffic congestion and **improving** highway maintenance
B. A 1994 proposal to research ways of **improving** fire and police service.
C. Raising **educational** hiring **standards** in the Police Department.
D. **Improved** staffing of Fire Department.
E. Curiously...**all** of the above

If elected, Dan McKimm will:
A. **Relieve** traffic congestion.
B. **Preserve** green space for our children
C. **Promote** safety.
D. **Protect** our children by preventing alcohol from entering our parks.
E. **Establish** proper spending priorities
F. **Control** township growth.
G. Absolutely...do **all** of the above.

12. **Randy Gonzalez voted to SPEND:**
A. $36,000 as an annual *retainer* for a *part-time* township political consultant / lobbyist.
B. $800,000 or more for **a Social Hall** (pavilion) in the park.
C. A 2% pay raise for township personnel ...then only 2 weeks later... *another* 2% pay increase for the **SAME** personnel
D. **SURPRISE**...all of the above.

13. **According to newspaper and magazine accounts, Randy Gonzalez:**
A. Suggested that if Jackson people want relief from traffic headaches, they need to contact their **State Representatives**
B. Told 6th graders:
"...hey, this township has money to spend." and ***"Jackson voters don't strap my hands."***
C. Has promoted a new township sales tax option
D. Yes... ...did **all** of the above.

14. **Regarding alcohol in our parks. Randy Gonzalez:**
A. Testified to the State Liquor Control Board in 1993 that carryout alcohol should not be near our parks.
B. Recognizes the no-alcohol policy in the township hall and the no-alcohol school laws.
C. Now advocates that ***alcohol be permitted*** in the ***middle of our parks*** - in the proposed Social Hall (pavilion)
D. Hmmm...**all** of the above.

15. **Which of the following statements are true regarding the Jackson Library?**
A. On November 19, 1990. Randy Gonzalez voted to **spend $500,000 tax dollars** for library construction.
B. On April 19, 1993, Trustee Randy Gonzalez **was** quoted as saying, "... *people are under the impression that the trustees just wrote out a bunch of checks to foot the bill for this library...*
C. On April 19, 1993, Trustee Randy Gonzalez said, ***"Not one penny*** of Jackson Township **tax dollars** went to the library.
D. As of Oct. 10, 1995, the amount of Jackson **tax dollars** ***currently*** invested in the library is $245,000
E. Categorically...**all** of the above.

16. ***In 1994, despite homeowners objections, who tried to relocate Jackson's highway department and the township fueling station to a residential area?***
A. Greenbriar Homeowners Assoc.
B. Poppin' Fresh Dough Boy
C. StaPuff Marshmallow Man
D. Randy Gonzalez

17. **Should you re-elect *Canton* City Bureaucrat, Randy Gonzalez, to:**
A. Again...decide how ***Jackson* taxes** are to be spent?
B. Again...give up to **25% raises** to ***Jackson*** Township employees?
C. Again... lay off 1/3 of ***Jackson*** Police - **jeopardizing our safety?**
D. Again...deny funding ***Jackson's*** D.A.R.E program.. ***calling it a luxury*** "*WE* can not afford."?
E. Please...none of the above

Voters should elect Dan McKimm, a Jackson businessman who:
A. Has a history of dedication to citizen safety.
B. Knows how business budgets and government budgets **must balance.**
C. Knows the difference between spending enough and ***enough*** spending
D. All of the above.

Source: Ohio Supreme Court's Appendix to *McKimm v. Ohio Elections Commission*, 729 N.E.2d 364 (Ohio 2000)

THE TEAM WORKING FOR YOU v. OHIO ELECTIONS COMMISSION

754 N.E.2d 273 (Ohio Ct. App. 2001)

[Before the Ohio Court of Appeals, Tenth District.]

BOWMAN, Judge.

In November 1997, Peggy Spraggins filed a complaint with appellee, Ohio Elections Commission ("commission"), alleging that appellants, The Team Working for You, Nick Molnar, James Predovic, Anna Hejduk, Clarence E. Johnson, and The News Leader newspaper, were responsible for publishing an advertisement on October 22, 1997, which contained false statements.[1] Spraggins, Molnar, Predovic, Hejduk, and Johnson were all candidates for Macedonia City Council. Molnar, Predovic, Hejduk, and Johnson formed a committee known as The Team Working for You to promote their candidacy.

The commission and the trial court found the statements at issue to be a violation of R.C. 3517.21(B)(10), which provides as follows:

> "(B) No person, during the course of any campaign for nomination or election to public office or office of a political party, by means of campaign materials, including sample ballots, an advertisement on radio or television or in a newspaper or periodical, a public speech, press release, or otherwise, shall knowingly and with intent to affect the outcome of such campaign do any of the following:
>
> . . .
>
> "(10) Post, publish, circulate, distribute, or otherwise disseminate a false statement concerning a candidate, either knowing the same to be false or with reckless disregard of whether it was false or not, if the statement is designed to promote the election, nomination, or defeat of the candidate."

In this case, Spraggins, a city council candidate, was a public figure, and, therefore, we must conduct an independent review of the entire record and determine whether the statements were false and made with actual malice, that is, either the statements were made with knowledge that they were false or with reckless disregard as to the falsity.

The first statement that the commission found to be a violation of R.C. 3517.21 was that Spraggins "is currently campaigning against industrial growth and overdevelopment in Macedonia." Spraggins testified that, in 1997, she did not develop a platform for her campaign and focused more on her credentials. She disseminated only a card and a letter as campaign materials, neither of which discuss industrial growth in Macedonia.

1. A copy of the advertisement is set forth in the Appendix [Figure 3-3].

During her mayoral campaign in 1995, she made comments about industrial growth and development. In 1995, she was against tax abatements, but her position in both 1995 and 1997 was to seek planned growth not to campaign against growth. Spraggins admitted at the hearing that, in 1995, she did make comments about industrial growth and development in Macedonia. She also admitted that, in 1995, she did adopt statements that she wanted to preserve the quiet quality of life of Macedonia and she stated that she was "committed to helping our community keep its small town atmosphere while moving forward into the next century." Thus, at the time of the 1997 campaign, which is the subject of this case, Spraggins was not opposed to growth but did not favor growth supported by taxpayers through tax abatements.

[Rosaline Koren, the treasurer of Team Working For You,] testified that the members of the team met at several meetings and exchanged personal experiences, researched newspaper articles, campaign materials and minutes of city council meetings and other official documents to develop the advertisement. Hejduk testified essentially the same. Molnar and Johnson testified that they were present at some of the meetings but did not review the advertisement before it was published. Predovic did not testify. Koren testified that her definition of "campaign" was "assist," and when asked her definition of "currently campaigning," she testified: "My definition of currently campaigning was in the past." All of the appellants who testified stated that they believed that the information that was published was true.

Appellants contend that the statement is grounded in fact because Spraggins was against overdevelopment and tax abatements, and increased traffic or threats to the small town atmosphere of Macedonia. Appellants further contend that, since the statement is not absolutely false, no liability may be found.

However, the advertisement read that Spraggins "is currently campaigning against industrial growth" and, in 1997, she was not campaigning as such. "Currently" means occurring or existing in the present time, not two years prior. Also, a statement against tax abatements does not equate to being against industrial growth. Thus, while appellants may have testified that they believed that the statements to be true, they displayed a reckless disregard for the truth by using inaccurate words in the advertisement. Molnar and Johnson also displayed reckless disregard in failing to review the advertisement before it was published.

[T]he judgment of the Franklin County Court of Common Pleas is affirmed.

Peggy, L., Bryant, P.J., and Deshler, J., concur.

Figure 3-3
APPENDIX

Pd Pol Adv

RESIDENTS, REMEMBER THESE FACTS WHEN YOU VOTE ON NOVEMBER 4:

Peggy Spraggins has a checkered political history in Macedonia. Over the years, she has developed a habit of telling voters one thing, then doing another.

1. She is currently campaigning against industrial growth and overdevelopment in Macedonia.

• However, when she ran for council in 1985, she actively supported rezoning of the corner of Rt. 82 and S. Bedford Road for apartment buildings. Fortunately, she lost and the apartments were not built.

• In 1987, she worked with an out-of-town developer to rezone several acres of wooded property on Highland Road from residential to industrial. Spraggins, actively advised and campaigned for the developer despite the protest of residents who lived in the area and did not want industrial development.

• Recently, she has been paid to promote industry in another suburb. This action is in complete contradiction to her alleged concerns for our city.

• Her campaign platform concerning"proper planning" is no longer relevant. An individual claiming to have been "active" in the city should be aware comprehensive plans for growth were started back in 1980 when Jim Lutz was mayor. The development occurring now has been in accordance with plans put in place 10 to 15 years ago.

2. She put the passage of the fire levy in jeopardy by misleading the voters about the City's finances. (NEWS LEADER 4-23-97.) The City's Finance Directory immediately issued a rebuttal with accurate figures. The failure of the issue would have meant no third shift in the Fire Department. Again she lost, and the residents won when informed voters passed the issue.

3. In 1994, Spraggins stopped a referendum petition that would have given the residents a vote on Environmental Services proposed increase in our sewer rates. Prosecutor Lynn Slaby's letter addressed to Ms. Spraggins dated 4-7-94 indicated that he was responding to her..."request." Because the referendum was stopped, our sewer rates were increased without voters' input.

4. Currently, Spraggins was involved with bringing suit against the City to stop the golf course. She claimed the City was rushing the issue past the voters; yet, for the past 11 years she has been aware that a golf course has been planned. **Never once, until now, was there a request to put the issue on the ballot. She lost again when the courts ruled in favor of the City.** However, the suit cost the taxpayers $10,000 to defend the case. Now, Spraggins and others, unhappy with the court's ruling have appealed the court's decision which will cost the City additional legal fees.

5. This action against the golf course will have a big impact on future development of our parks and on the Field of Dreams Committee to provide additional recreation. All of the revenue from the golf course was earmarked for the Parks Department. The golf course developer would have had to install sewer lines to the Park at no cost to the City. The $125,000 saved would have gone to the Field of Dreams Committee. Because of this legal action and delay in Twinsburg, the developer may withdraw.

Elect

"THE TEAM WORKING FOR YOU"

ANNA **HEJDUK** ☑

CLARENCE **JOHNSON** ☑

NICK **MOLNAR** ☑

JIM **PREDOVIC** ☑

POSITIVE, PROGRESSIVE CANDIDATES WORKING *for the* PEOPLE

PAID FOR BY "THE TEAM WORKING FOR YOU"

ROSALIE KOREN, TREASURER, 9460 WOODVIEW MACEDONIA, OHIO 44056

RICKERT v. STATE PUBLIC DISCLOSURE COMMISSION

168 P.3d 826 (Wash. 2007)

J.M. JOHNSON, J.

The United States and Washington Constitutions both protect the right of free speech, and political speech is the core of that right. The notion that a censorship scheme like RCW 42.17.530(1)(a) [the statute at issue in this case, as described below] may be constitutionally enforced by a government agency erroneously "presupposes [that] the State possesses an independent right to determine truth and falsity in political debate." *State ex rel. Pub. Disclosure Comm'n v. 119 Vote No! Comm.* (Wash. 1998) (plurality opinion). Yet, "'[t]he very purpose of the First Amendment is to foreclose public authority from assuming a guardianship of the public mind.'" *Id. (internal quotation marks omitted) (quoting Meyer v. Grant* (1988)). This court has previously agreed that state censorship is not allowed: "The State cannot 'substitute its judgment as to how best to speak for that of speakers and listeners; free and robust debate cannot thrive if directed by the government.'" *Id.* (quoting *Riley v. Nat'l Fed'n of Blind, Inc.* (1988)). The present case provides an opportunity to vigorously reaffirm the law on this vital constitutional issue.

FACTS AND PROCEDURAL HISTORY

In 2002, Ms. Rickert challenged incumbent Senator Tim Sheldon in the election for state senator from Washington's 35th Legislative District. During the campaign, Ms. Rickert sponsored a mailing that included a brochure comparing her positions to those of Senator Sheldon. In part, the brochure stated that Ms. Rickert "[s]upports social services for the most vulnerable of the state's citizens." By way of comparison, the brochure stated that Senator Sheldon "voted to close a facility for the developmentally challenged in his district." In response to the latter statement, Senator Sheldon filed a complaint with the Public Disclosure Commission (PDC), alleging a violation of RCW 42.17.530(1)(a).

RCW 42.17.530(1) provides, in relevant part:

> It is a violation of this chapter for a person to sponsor with actual malice:
>
> (a) Political advertising or an electioneering communication that contains a false statement of material fact about a candidate for public office. However, this subsection (1)(a) does not apply to statements made by a candidate or the candidate's agent about the candidate himself or herself.

"Actual malice" means "to act with knowledge of falsity or with reckless disregard as to truth or falsity." RCW 42.17.020(1). A violation of RCW 42.17.530(1)(a) must be proven by clear and convincing evidence. RCW 42.17.530(2).

The PDC held a hearing regarding Senator Sheldon's complaint on July 29, 2003, months after Senator Sheldon handily defeated Ms. Rickert in the 2002 election. The PDC found that Ms. Rickert's brochure contained two false statements: "(a) Senator Sheldon voted to close the Mission Creek Youth Camp, and (b) . . . Mission Creek was a facility for the developmentally challenged." Additionally, the PDC concluded that the statements were material, that Ms. Rickert sponsored the brochure with actual malice, and that her violation of RCW 42.17.530(1)(a) had been established by clear and convincing evidence. The PDC imposed a $1,000 penalty on Ms. Rickert.

The superior court affirmed the PDC's final order. Ms. Rickert then appealed to the Court of Appeals, which reversed. The Court of Appeals held that RCW 42.17.530(1)(a) violates the First Amendment because it cannot survive strict scrutiny. We agree and, accordingly, affirm.

ANALYSIS

A. RCW 42.17.530(1)(A) Extends to Protected Speech, Hence, Strict Scrutiny Applies

"[T]he First Amendment 'has its fullest and most urgent application' to speech uttered during a campaign for political office." *Burson v. Freeman* (1992) (plurality opinion). Accordingly, any statute that purports to regulate such speech based on its content is subject to strict scrutiny. Under this standard, the State must demonstrate that RCW 42.17.530(1)(a) is necessary to serve a compelling state interest and that it is narrowly drawn to achieve that end.

The text of RCW 42.17.530(1)(a) suggests that the legislature may have intended to limit the scope of its prohibition to the unprotected category of political defamation speech identified by the United States Supreme Court in *New York Times Co. v. Sullivan* (1964). However, as correctly noted by the Court of Appeals, "[U]nder *New York Times*, only *defamatory* statements . . . are not constitutionally protected speech." Because RCW 42.17.530(1)(a) does not require proof of the defamatory nature of the statements it prohibits, its reach is not limited to the very narrow category of unprotected speech identified in *New York Times* and its progeny. Thus, RCW 42.17.530(1)(a) extends to protected political speech and strict scrutiny must apply.

B. RCW 42.17.530(1)(A) Cannot Survive Strict Scrutiny

1. Protecting candidates is not a compelling government interest here, and RCW 42.17.530(1)(a) is not narrowly tailored to further that interest

The plain language of RCW 42.17.530(1)(a) provides that the law's purpose is "to provide protection for candidates for public office." [T]he State claims that it may prohibit false statements of fact contained in political advertisements. However, this claim presupposes the State possesses an independent right to determine truth and falsity in political debate, a proposition fundamentally at odds with the principles embodied in the First Amendment. Moreover, it naively assumes that the government is capable of correctly and consistently negotiating the thin line between fact and opinion in political speech. Yet, political speech is usually as much opinion as fact. ("Spinning" is a common term used to describe putting different perspectives on facts.) Every person must be his own watchman for truth, because the forefathers did not trust any government to separate the truth from the false for us.

Particularly relevant here is the fundamental First Amendment principle forbidding censorship or coerced silence in the context of political debate. "The First Amendment exists precisely to protect against laws . . . which suppress ideas and inhibit free discussion of governmental affairs." [Court of Appeals' decision] Hence, the Sedition Act of 1798, which censored speech about government, has been subject to nearly unanimous historical condemnation. For similar reasons, RCW 42.17.530(1)(a) is deserving of condemnation, lacks a compelling justification, and thus must be declared unconstitutional.

The Supreme Court has recognized a legitimate, and at times compelling, interest in "compensating private individuals for wrongful injury to reputation." *Gertz v. Robert Welch, Inc.* (1974). However, this interest cannot justify a government-enforced censorship scheme like RCW 42.17.530(1)(a). The statute may protect candidates from criticism, but it has no mechanism for compensation for damage to reputations. More importantly, there is no requirement that the statements subject to sanction under RCW 42.17.530(1)(a) be of the kind that tend to cause harm to an individual's reputation, i.e., defamatory.

In sum, the interest asserted by the legislature—protecting political candidates (including themselves)—is not a compelling interest in support of RCW 42.17.530(1)(a). Accordingly, the statute fails under strict scrutiny.

2. Preserving the integrity of elections is not a compelling government interest here, and RCW 42.17.530(1)(a) is not narrowly tailored to further that interest

At argument below and before this court, the PDC suggests that preserving the integrity of the election process is the primary government interest furthered by RCW 42.17.530(1)(a). However, this was not the interest asserted by the legislature in enacting RCW 42.17.530(1)(a). Under strict scrutiny, a law burdening speech may not be upheld for any conceivable purpose but must be evaluated according to its actual purpose. Thus, it is arguably inappropriate to even consider the PDC's argument based on this belated, alternative interest.

Even assuming it were proper to consider a state interest asserted for the first time at argument, the PDC's claim still fails. The government may have a compelling interest in preventing direct harm to elections. *See, e.g., Burson.* However, that interest is not advanced in any significant manner by prosecuting Ms. Rickert, and other similarly situated individuals, under RCW 42.17.530(1)(a). Rather, the PDC's claim that it must prohibit arguably false, but nondefamatory, statements about political candidates to save our elections conflicts with the fundamental principles of the First Amendment. Therefore, "preserving the integrity of the election process" cannot be deemed a compelling interest in the context of a scheme like RCW 42.17.530(1)(a).

Furthermore, even if such an interest were valid, RCW 42.17.530(1)(a) would remain unconstitutional because it is not narrowly tailored. The statute is underinclusive because it does not apply to many statements that pose an equal threat to the State's alleged interest in protecting elections. Specifically, the statute exempts all statements made by a candidate (or his supporters) about himself. Basically, a candidate is free to lie about himself, while an opponent will be sanctioned. Yet, "[t]he PDC presents no compelling reason why a candidate would be less likely to deceive the electorate on matters concerning him- or herself and [thus] compromise the integrity of the elections process." [Court of Appeals' decision.]

In sum, RCW 42.17.530(1)(a)'s exemption for candidates' false speech about themselves demonstrates that the statute is not narrowly tailored to serve the State's alleged interest in preserving the integrity of elections. Because RCW 42.17.530(1)(a) is not narrowly tailored, the statute cannot survive under strict scrutiny.

3. The faulty procedural mechanisms of RCW 42.17.530(1)(a) confirm that the law is not narrowly tailored and, thus, fails under strict scrutiny

RCW 42.17.530(1)(a) is also fatally flawed due to its enforcement procedures, which are likely to have a chilling effect on speech. These procedural defects further indicate that the statute is not the least restrictive alternative to achieve the compelling interests it allegedly furthers. Ultimately, these defects support the conclusion that any statute permitting censorship by a group of unelected government officials is inherently unconstitutional.

The members of the PDC, the administrative body that enforces RCW 42.17.530(1)(a), are appointed by the governor, a political officer. This group of unelected individuals is empowered not only to review alleged false statements made in political campaigns but also to impose sanctions. Finally, there is no requirement that a reviewing court conduct an independent, de novo review as to whether there is clear and convincing evidence the respondent uttered the statements with actual malice.

The chilling effects resulting from this procedural scheme are manifest. A sitting governor may appoint a majority of the PDC's members. When this same governor seeks reelection, the governor's own appointees will decide whether to sanction the speech of campaign opponents. The campaign opponents will not be guaranteed a jury trial or independent, de novo judicial review. The mere threat of such a process will chill political speech. Likewise, the prospect of such a proceeding justifiably undermines the public's confidence in the propriety of Washington's electoral process—the very interest which the PDC purports to serve. Because of the risks to liberty inherent in RCW 42.17.530(1)(a)'s enforcement mechanisms, the statute cannot survive strict scrutiny.

Conclusion

Our constitutional election system already contains the solution to the problem that RCW 42.17.530(1)(a) is meant to address. "In a political campaign, a candidate's factual blunder is unlikely to escape the notice of, and correction by, the erring candidate's political opponent. The preferred First Amendment remedy of 'more speech, not enforced silence,' thus has special force." *Brown v. Hartlage* (1982) (quoting *Whitney v. California* (1927) (Brandeis, J., concurring)). In other words, the best remedy for false or unpleasant speech is more speech, not less speech. The importance of this constitutional principle is illustrated by the very real threats to liberty posed by allowing an unelected government censor like the PDC to act as an arbiter of truth.

In the case at bar, Ms. Rickert made knowingly false or reckless statements about Senator Sheldon, a man with an outstanding reputation. Senator Sheldon and his (many) supporters responded to Ms. Rickert's false statements with the truth. As a consequence, Ms. Rickert's statements appear to have had little negative impact on Senator Sheldon's successful campaign and may even have increased his vote. *See* [Court of Appeals' decision] (noting that "Senator Sheldon was reelected . . . by approximately 79 percent of the vote."). Were there injury to Senator Sheldon's reputation, compensation would be available through a defamation action. As it is, Ms. Rickert was singled out by the PDC for punishment, six months after the election, based on statements that had no apparent impact on the government interests allegedly furthered by the statute. That the statute may be applied in such a manner proves that it is fatally flawed under the First Amendment.

There can be no doubt that false personal attacks are too common in political campaigns, with wide-ranging detrimental consequences. However, government censorship such as RCW 42.17.530(1)(a) is not a constitutionally permitted remedy. We hold that this statute, which allows a government agency to censor political speech, is unconstitutional and affirm the decision of the Court of Appeals.

We concur: Charles W. JOHNSON, Susan OWENS, Richard B. SANDERS.

JJ. ALEXANDER, C.J. concurring.

[Omitted.]

MADSEN, J. dissenting.

The impression left by the majority's rhetoric, that oppressive government regulation is at issue in this case, is simply wrong. When cases decided by the United States Supreme Court are properly applied, it is obvious that RCW 42.17.530(1)(a) infringes on no First Amendment rights.

Unfortunately, the majority's decision is an invitation to lie with impunity. The majority opinion advances the efforts of those who would turn political campaigns into contests of the best stratagems of lies and deceit, to the end that honest discourse and honest candidates are lost in the maelstrom. The majority does no service to the people of Washington when it turns the First Amendment into a shield for the "unscrupulous . . . and skillful" liar to use knowingly false statements as an "effective political tool" in election campaigns. *See Garrison v. Louisiana* (1964). It is little wonder that so many view political campaigns with distrust and cynicism.

The majority is wrong when it says that state government cannot constitutionally regulate truth or falsity of political speech. No such blanket rule exists under the First Amendment. There is no question that the First and Fourteenth Amendments embody our "profound national commitment to the principle that debate on public issues should be uninhibited, robust, and wide-open, and that it may well include vehement, caustic, and sometimes unpleasantly sharp attacks on government and public officials." *New York Times Co. v. Sullivan* (1964). But it is equally true that the use of calculated falsehood is not constitutionally protected. "Neither the intentional lie nor the careless error materially advances society's interest in 'uninhibited, robust, and wide-open' debate on public issues." *Gertz v. Robert Welch, Inc.* (1974) (quoting *New York Times*).

The United States Supreme Court has made it absolutely clear that the deliberate lie in political debate has no protected place under the First Amendment because such lies do not advance the free political process but rather subvert it[.]

The majority's premise that there can be no regulation of political speech whatsoever cannot be squared with the United States Supreme Court's conclusion that under the First Amendment:

> *Calculated falsehood falls into that class of utterances which "are no essential part of any exposition of ideas, and are of such slight social value as a step to truth that any benefit that may be derived from them is clearly outweighed by the social interest in order and morality. . . ." Chaplinsky v. New Hampshire* [(1942)]. Hence the knowingly false statement and the false statement made with reckless disregard of the truths do not enjoy constitutional protection.

[*Garrison*] (emphasis added).

The majority is also wrong when it asserts that the only time that a false statement about a candidate for office can be burdened is when the statement constitutes civil defamation, actionable in tort law. This premise is no more accurate than the majority's conclusion that government cannot regulate political speech by proscribing the known lie.

Because the majority declines to follow precedent holding that false statements under the actual malice standard are not protected speech, it engages in a strict scrutiny analysis of RCW 42.17.530(1)(a)'s constitutionality. However, if the actual malice standard is met the speech falls within a class of speech that is not constitutionally protected. Therefore, a statute that proscribes speech under this standard does not have to meet the strict scrutiny/compelling governmental interest test that applies to statutes regulating protected political speech.

Further, the majority refuses to recognize that the actual malice standard is an exceedingly high standard to meet. Most political speech does not even approach being subject to regulation under this standard; the standard prohibits only the very worst untruths—those made with knowledge of their falsity or with reckless disregard to truth or falsity. In addition, the burden of proof is also high—proof must be by clear and convincing evidence. The actual malice standard is deliberately difficult to satisfy, precisely because free speech rights are at issue. Therefore, much nuanced speech, and all speech that constitutes opinion rather than fact, will simply fall short of it.

Finally, while the majority would prefer that no entity have authority to make final decisions on whether speech may be regulated and whether any regulations that are enacted conform to First Amendment requirements, this authority is constitutionally vested in the courts. Under RCW 42.17.530(1) the courts will continue to act as the final arbiter of any administrative decision.

Ultimately, the majority's claim of government censorship does not reflect the statute or the legislature's attempt to prohibit unprotected speech. Accordingly, I dissent.

The calculated falsehood in the course of an election campaign can distort the electoral process by misinforming the voters and so interfere with the process "upon which democracy is based." William P. Marshall, *False Campaign Speech and the First Amendment*, 153 U. Pa. L. Rev. 285, 294 (2004). As Marshall notes, and quoted above, using the known lie as a tool is at odds with the premises of democratic government and the orderly way in which change is to be effected. False statements can lower the quality of campaign discourse and debate, generating response to the attacks rather than engagement on major issues. False advertising also may give rise to or exacerbate voter alienation and distrust of the political process.

In light of these interests, there is no reason to treat the calculated falsehood with any greater protection in the context of a campaign than the Court said is constitutionally required in a defamation action involving a public official or public figure and a matter of public concern, or in the other contexts where it has applied the standard. These interests justify the actual malice standard in the context of political campaigns. They also warrant the conclusion that the calculated lie about a candidate for office during an election campaign is not subject to correction only through more speech or only through private defamation actions.

I believe that the actual malice standard is both a necessary and a sufficient standard for regulating false campaign speech.

In sum, RCW 42.17.530(1)(a) prohibits false statements of facts that are material to the election campaign. By limiting the statute's reach to facts, the legislature has avoided unconstitutionally infringing on opinions and ideas.

The majority, however, finds constitutional infirmity in the fact that the statute does not apply to statements made by a candidate, or his or her agent, about the candidate. In the course of its erroneous strict scrutiny analysis the majority agrees with Ms. Rickert's contention that the statute is not narrowly tailored because it does not apply to such statements.

Here, the basis for the discrimination consists entirely of the reasons that the calculated falsehood may be proscribed, and therefore no significant danger of viewpoint discrimination exists. As explained, lies about public officials are clearly outweighed by "'the social interest in order and morality,'" *Garrison* (quoting *Chaplinsky*), because they undermine the integrity and reliability of the election process, distort the political process through untrue and inaccurate speech that misinforms the voters and so interferes with the democratic process and the orderly way that change should be effected, lower the quality of campaign discourse and debate by generating response to the attacks rather than engagement on major issues, lead to public cynicism and apathy toward the electoral process, and cause or increase voter alienation and distrust of the political process. These reasons "have special force" when the statements are made about a candidate for office (not including false statements by a candidate about himself or herself).

The majority also finds unconstitutionality in the procedural aspects of the statute because liability under the statute is determined by an administrative agency rather than a jury. Aside from the majority's general disparaging remarks about nonelected officials and its unwarranted claims of censorship, the thrust of the majority's dissatisfaction is that the Public Disclosure Commission determines in the first instance whether there is a violation and, the majority says, there is no requirement that a reviewing court conduct an independent, de novo review, assessing whether the actual malice standard was satisfied. The majority says, in fact, that "[t]he campaign opponents will not be guaranteed . . . independent, de novo judicial review."

Whether RCW 42.17.530 (or any other statute) expressly provides for independent, de novo judicial review, such review unquestionably applies as a matter of constitutional law. A court is required to "make an independent examination of the whole record, so as to assure [itself] that the judgment does not constitute a forbidden intrusion on the field of free expression." *Bose* [*Corp. v. Consumers Union* (1984)]. The independent review rule is "a rule of federal constitutional law." [*Id.*] Thus, irrespective of whether there is a statutory requirement for independent, de novo judicial review, the *Constitution* mandates such review. Accordingly, the absence of a statutory provision for independent judicial review does not chill free speech rights as the majority asserts.

CONCLUSION

I would reverse the Court of Appeals' holding that RCW 42.17.530(1)(a) is facially unconstitutional. The statute accurately sets forth the *New York Times* standard for determining that certain false statements are not protected speech under the First Amendment, and this standard may constitutionally be applied to regulate candidates' speech during election campaigns.

I dissent.

We concur: TOM CHAMBERS, MARY E. FAIRHURST, BOBBE J. BRIDGE, JJ.

NOTES ON *McKIMM, THE TEAM WORKING FOR YOU,* AND *RICKERT*

1. As the opinions discuss, the Supreme Court recognized the First Amendment protection for false or misleading speech in *New York Times v. Sullivan*, 376 U.S. 254 (1964). The First Amendment protection of campaign speech is quite extensive because it is based on the premise that there is "a profound national commitment to the principle that debate on public issues should be uninhibited, robust, and wide-open, and that it may well include vehement, caustic, and sometimes unpleasantly sharp attacks on government and public officials." Thus, the First Amendment protects negligently made false statements during a campaign. Similarly, if a statement is made with a good-faith belief of its truthfulness, it receives constitutional protection.
2. What about outright lies? In *United States v. Alvarez*, 132 S. Ct. 2537 (2012), the Supreme Court struck down the "Stolen Valor Act," which made it a crime to lie about receiving the Congressional Medal of Honor. The defendant was a board member of a local water board and lied during a public meeting about receiving the Medal of Honor. The Court rejected the government's argument that the law was needed to protect the sanctity of the nation's highest military award. Might the analysis differ if the law was limited to lying in a political campaign about receiving the Medal of Honor? Or do statutes like Ohio's work only if they are targeted at making false statements about the candidate's opponent?
3. Notice the First Amendment debate in these cases. In Ohio, the courts applied the law and ruled that the ads, to a "reasonable" viewer, were false and disseminated with actual malice. In Washington, the Justices debated vigorously whether the First Amendment protects false political advertisements. Part of the problem with the law, according to the majority in *Rickert*, is that it swept in both constitutionally protected speech and unlawful defamation.
4. What do you think of the majority's formulation in *Rickert* of the proper remedy for false ads: more speech? Is this really the right solution? Did "more" speech

help John Kerry respond to the "Swift Boat Veterans for Truth" ads during the 2004 presidential election campaign? Did it help Mitt Romney respond to questions about his financial holdings in 2012?

5. In *McKimm*, the only actual punishment was a "reprimand letter"—essentially the government's official statement (akin to a declaratory judgment) that the candidate had committed an intentional or reckless falsehood. Should this form of punishment be considered "counterspeech" on the part of the government—in keeping with Justice Brandeis's admonition (echoed by the *Rickert* majority) that falsehoods should be countered with the truth? If so, should the government's imposition of a reprimand letter even be subject to any First Amendment constraints at all? In other words, as long as the government's only "punishment" is for the government to say what it thinks is the truth, may the candidate stop the government from speaking out in this way? Or is it problematic for the government to attempt to referee in any kind of official way the competing claims of opposing candidates? Although newspapers and other private-sector organizations (like Factcheck.org) can speak out to condemn campaign ads as false—Politifact.org labels the most egregious of them as "Pants on Fire"—should the government stay out of the "Truth Squad" business?
6. Alternatively, would imposing a fine be the right type of remedy? What about overturning the results of the election? Is there a sufficiently satisfying remedy?
7. Do negative ads have an adverse effect on political tenor? If so, are legislatures the right entities to tackle this problem? Even if we lament negative ads, especially when they are intentionally deceptive, would any cure the legislature adopts be worse than the disease? Part of the problem is that any standard the legislature chooses would need to be enforced by bureaucrats or judges; can they be entirely impartial between competing candidates? In addition, might legislatures and executives enact incumbent-friendly laws—such as Washington's regime of allowing the governor's appointees to determine the truthfulness of campaign statements during the governor's re-election campaign—in an effort to entrench themselves?
8. What if an intentional falsehood is dropped into the campaign at the very end, with no time for an opponent (or others) to respond? The next case is directly relevant to that particular problem.

B. Last-Minute and Harassing Campaign Tactics

What happens when the exercise of First Amendment rights clashes with the fundamental right to vote? The next case presents the question of whether a state may create a "campaign-free" zone around a polling place. During the days leading up to Election Day, streets and sidewalks sometimes become cluttered with campaign signs. In some states, campaign workers set up tables outside of the polls to disseminate literature on their candidates. Political parties might hand out a "sample ballot" with their preferred choices for voters to follow as they vote. Candidates themselves often spend time at the busiest polling places shaking hands and seeking last-minute support. In this case, Tennessee sought to give voters a reprieve from these campaign messages—as well as other more overt forms of campaigning—directly around the polling site. The underlying purpose, according to the state, was to protect the right to vote and to limit fraud and intimidation.

Indeed, the United States has a long history of actual or perceived election fraud. This case provides a detailed explanation for the main reason behind secret balloting: to limit the possibility of undue influence or intimidation infiltrating the voting process. In the early days of our democracy, political parties printed ballots listing their nominees, and voters simply took the party's ballot they preferred with them to the polls. Concerns about vote buying and fraud led most states to adopt the "Australian" ballot, in which the government prints the ballot of all parties' nominees and voters make their selections via secret ballot. Does a campaign-free zone serve the same purposes as a secret ballot?

Further, given the state's interest in rooting out fraud, is the restriction on campaigning near the polls consistent with a candidate's First Amendment right to disseminate a political message? Consider how the Supreme Court reconciles the right to vote with the right to freedom of speech in this case.

Figure 3-4

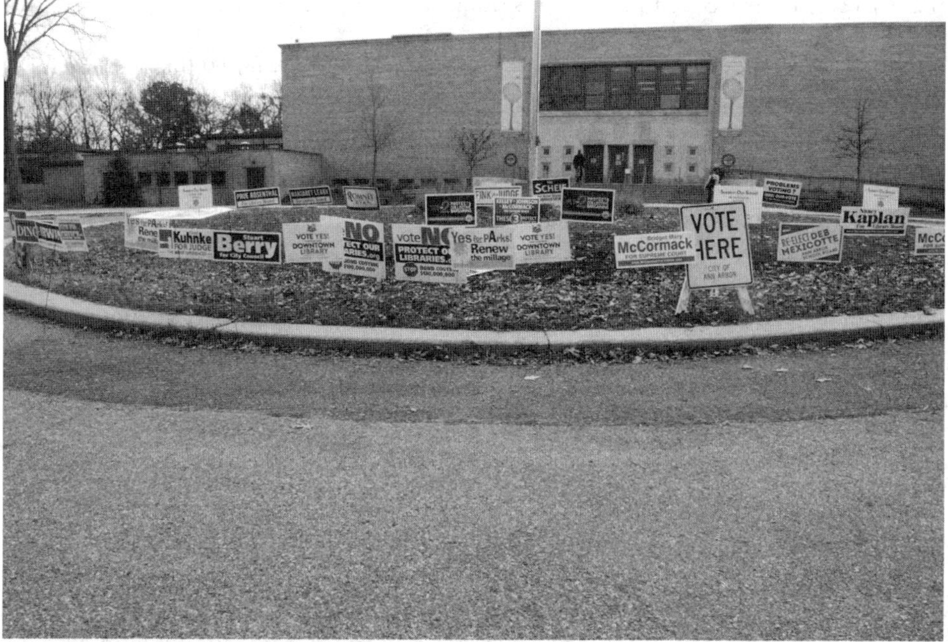

Reprinted with permission from the *Ann Arbor Chronicle.*

As Figure 3-4 shows, polling places often become cluttered with campaign signs. The law at question in *Burson v. Freeman* attempted to limit this kind of campaigning outside of the polls.

BURSON v. FREEMAN

504 U.S. 191 (1992)

Justice BLACKMUN announced the judgment of the Court and delivered an opinion, in which Chief Justice REHNQUIST, Justice WHITE, and Justice KENNEDY join.

Twenty-six years ago, this Court struck down a state law that made it a crime for a newspaper editor to publish an editorial on election day urging readers to vote in a particular way. *Mills v. Alabama* (1966). While the Court did not hesitate to denounce the statute as an "obvious and flagrant abridgment" of First Amendment rights, it was quick to point out that its holding "in no way involve[d] the extent of a State's power to regulate conduct in and around the polls in order to maintain peace, order and decorum there[.]" [*Id.*]

Today, we confront the issue carefully left open in *Mills.* The question presented is whether a provision of the Tennessee Code, which prohibits the solicitation of votes and the display or distribution of campaign materials within 100 feet of the entrance to a polling place, violates the First and Fourteenth Amendments.

I

The State of Tennessee has carved out an election-day "campaign-free zone" through § 2-7-111(b) of its election code. That section reads in pertinent part:

> "Within the appropriate boundary as established in subsection (a) [100 feet from the entrances], and the building in which the polling place is located, the display of campaign posters, signs or other campaign materials, distribution of campaign materials, and solicitation of votes for or against any person or political party or position on a question are prohibited." Tenn. Code Ann. § 2-7-111(b) (Supp. 1991).

Violation of § 2-7-111(b) is a Class C misdemeanor punishable by a term of imprisonment not greater than 30 days or a fine not to exceed $50, or both. Tenn. Code Ann. §§ 2-19-119 and 40-35-111(e)(3) (1990).

II

Respondent Mary Rebecca Freeman has been a candidate for office in Tennessee, has managed local campaigns, and has worked actively in statewide elections. In 1987, she was the treasurer for the campaign of a city-council candidate in Metropolitan Nashville-Davidson County.

Asserting that §§ 2-7-111(b) and 2-19-119 limited her ability to communicate with voters, respondent brought a facial challenge to these statutes in Davidson County Chancery Court. She sought a declaratory judgment that the provisions were unconstitutional under both the United States and the Tennessee Constitutions. She also sought a permanent injunction against their enforcement.

The Chancellor ruled that the statutes did not violate the United States or Tennessee Constitutions and dismissed respondent's suit. He determined that § 2-7-111(b) was a content-neutral and reasonable time, place, and manner restriction; that the 100-foot boundary served a compelling state interest in protecting voters from interference, harassment, and intimidation during the voting process; and that there was an alternative channel for respondent to exercise her free speech rights outside the 100-foot boundary.

The Tennessee Supreme Court, by a 4-to-1 vote, reversed. The court first held that § 2-7-111(b) was content based "because it regulates a specific subject matter, the solicitation of votes and the display or distribution of campaign materials, and a certain category of speakers, campaign workers." The court then held that such a content-based statute could not be upheld unless (i) the burden placed on free speech rights is justified by a compelling state interest and (ii) the means chosen bear a substantial relation to that interest and are the least intrusive to achieve the State's goals. While the Tennessee Supreme Court found that the State unquestionably had shown a compelling interest in banning solicitation of voters and distribution of campaign materials within the polling place itself, it concluded that the State had not shown a compelling interest in regulating the premises around the polling place. Accordingly, the court held that the 100-foot limit was not narrowly tailored to protect the demonstrated interest. The court also held that the statute was not the least restrictive means to serve the State's interests. The court found less restrictive the current Tennessee statutes prohibiting interference with an election or the use of violence or intimidation to prevent voting. Finally, the court noted that if the State were able to show a compelling interest in preventing congestion and disruption at the entrances to polling places, a shorter radius "might perhaps pass constitutional muster."

Because of the importance of the issue, we granted certiorari. We now reverse the Tennessee Supreme Court's judgment that the statute violates the First Amendment of the United States Constitution.

III

The Tennessee statute implicates three central concerns in our First Amendment jurisprudence: regulation of political speech, regulation of speech in a public forum, and regulation based on the content of the speech. The speech restricted by § 2-7-111(b) obviously is political speech. [T]his Court has recognized that "the First Amendment 'has its fullest and most urgent application' to speech uttered during a campaign for political office." *Eu v. San Francisco Cty. Democratic Central Comm.* (1989) (quoting *Monitor Patriot Co. v. Roy* (1971)).

The second important feature of § 2-7-111(b) is that it bars speech in quintessential public forums. These forums include those places "which by long tradition or by government fiat have been devoted to assembly and debate," such as parks, streets, and sidewalks. *Perry Ed. Assn. v. Perry Local Educators' Assn.* (1983). At the same time, however, expressive activity, even in a quintessential public forum, may interfere with other important activities for which the property is used. Accordingly, this Court has held that the government may regulate the time, place, and manner of the expressive activity, so long as such restrictions are content neutral, are narrowly tailored to serve a significant governmental interest, and leave open ample alternatives for communication.

The Tennessee restriction under consideration, however, is not a facially content-neutral time, place, or manner restriction. Whether individuals may exercise their free speech rights near polling places depends entirely on whether their speech is related to a political campaign. The statute does not reach other categories of speech, such as commercial solicitation, distribution, and display. This Court has held that the First Amendment's hostility to content-based regulation extends not only to a restriction on a particular viewpoint, but also to a prohibition of public discussion of an entire topic.

As a facially content-based restriction on political speech in a public forum, § 2-7-111(b) must be subjected to exacting scrutiny: The State must show that the "regulation is necessary to serve a compelling state interest and that it is narrowly drawn to achieve that end." *Perry Ed. Assn. v. Perry Local Educators' Assn.*

Despite the ritualistic ease with which we state this now-familiar standard, its announcement does not allow us to avoid the truly difficult issues involving the First Amendment. Perhaps foremost among these serious issues are cases that force us to reconcile our commitment to free speech with our commitment to other constitutional rights embodied in government proceedings. *See, e.g., Sheppard v. Maxwell* (1966) (outlining restrictions on speech of trial participants that courts may impose to protect an accused's right to a fair trial). This case presents us with a particularly difficult reconciliation: the accommodation of the right to engage in political discourse with the right to vote—a right at the heart of our democracy.

IV

Tennessee asserts that its campaign-free zone serves two compelling interests. First, the State argues that its regulation serves its compelling interest in protecting the right of its citizens to vote freely for the candidates of their choice. Second, Tennessee argues that its restriction protects the right to vote in an election conducted with integrity and reliability.

The interests advanced by Tennessee obviously are compelling ones. This Court has recognized that the "right to vote freely for the candidate of one's choice is of the essence of a democratic society." *Reynolds v. Sims* (1964). Indeed,

> "[n]o right is more precious in a free country than that of having a voice in the election of those who make the laws under which, as good citizens, we must live. Other rights, even the most basic, are illusory if the right to vote is undermined." *Wesberry v. Sanders* (1964).

Accordingly, this Court has concluded that a State has a compelling interest in protecting voters from confusion and undue influence.

The Court also has recognized that a State "indisputably has a compelling interest in preserving the integrity of its election process." [*Eu.*] The Court thus has "upheld generally applicable and evenhanded restrictions that protect the integrity and reliability of the electoral process itself." *Anderson v. Celebrezze* (1983) (collecting cases). In other words, it has recognized that a State has a compelling interest in ensuring that an individual's right to vote is not undermined by fraud in the election process.

To survive strict scrutiny, however, a State must do more than assert a compelling state interest—it must demonstrate that its law is necessary to serve the asserted interest. While we readily acknowledge that a law rarely survives such scrutiny, an examination of the evolution of election reform, both in this country and abroad, demonstrates the necessity of restricted areas in or around polling places.

During the colonial period, many government officials were elected by the *viva voce* method or by the showing of hands, as was the custom in most parts of Europe. That voting scheme was not a private affair, but an open, public decision, witnessed by all and improperly influenced by some. The opportunities that the *viva voce* system gave for bribery and intimidation gradually led to its repeal.

Within 20 years of the formation of the Union, most States had incorporated the paper ballot into their electoral system. Initially, this paper ballot was a vast improvement. Individual voters made their own handwritten ballots, marked them in the privacy of their homes, and then brought them to the polls for counting. But the effort of making out such a ballot became increasingly more complex and cumbersome.

Wishing to gain influence, political parties began to produce their own ballots for voters. These ballots were often printed with flamboyant colors, distinctive designs, and emblems so that they could be recognized at a distance. State attempts to standardize the ballots were easily thwarted—the vote buyer could simply place a ballot in the hands of the bribed voter and watch until he placed it in the polling box. Thus, the evils associated with the earlier *viva voce* system reinfected the election process; the failure of the law to secure secrecy opened the door to bribery[6] and intimidation.[7]

6. One writer described the conditions as follows: "This sounds like exaggeration, but it is truth; and these are facts so notorious that no one acquainted with the conduct of recent elections now attempts a denial—that the raising of colossal sums for the purpose of bribery has been rewarded by promotion to the highest offices in the Government; that systematic organization for the purchase of votes, individually and in blocks, at the polls, has become a recognized factor in the machinery of the parties; that the number of voters who demand money compensation for their ballots has grown greater with each recurring election." J. Gordon, The Protection of Suffrage 13 (1891) (quoted in Evans 11).

Evans reports that the bribery of voters in Indiana in 1880 and 1888 was sufficient to determine the results of the election and that "[m]any electors, aware that the corrupt element was large enough to be able to turn the election, held aloof altogether."

7. According to a report of a committee of the 46th Congress, men were frequently marched or carried to the polls in their employers' carriages. They were then furnished with ballots and compelled to hold their hands up with their ballots in them so they could easily be watched until the ballots were dropped into the box. S. Rep. No. 497, 46th Cong., 2d Sess., 9-10 (1880).

Approaching the polling place under this system was akin to entering an open auction place. As the elector started his journey to the polls, he was met by various party ticket peddlers "who were only too anxious to supply him with their party tickets." Evans, [*A History of the Australia Ballot System in the United States* (1917), at] 9. Often the competition became heated when several such peddlers found an uncommitted or wavering voter. Sham battles were frequently engaged in to keep away elderly and timid voters of the opposition.

The problems with voter intimidation and election fraud that the United States was experiencing were not unique. Several other countries were attempting to work out satisfactory solutions to these same problems. Some Australian provinces adopted a series of reforms intended to secure the secrecy of an elector's vote. The most famous feature of the Australian system was its provision for an official ballot, encompassing all candidates of all parties on the same ticket. But this was not the only measure adopted to preserve the secrecy of the ballot. The Australian system also provided for the erection of polling booths (containing several voting compartments) open only to election officials, two "scrutinees" for each candidate, and electors about to vote.

The Australian system was enacted in England in 1872 after a study by the committee of election practices identified Australia's ballot as the best possible remedy for the existing situation. Belgium followed England's example in 1877. Like the Australian provinces, both England and Belgium excluded the general public from the entire polling room.

After several failed attempts to adopt the Australian system in Michigan and Wisconsin, the Louisville, Kentucky, municipal government, the Commonwealth of Massachusetts, and the State of New York adopted the Australian system in 1888. The Louisville law prohibited all but voters, candidates or their agents, and electors from coming within 50 feet of the voting room inclosure. The Louisville law also provided that candidates' agents within the restricted area "were not allowed to persuade, influence, or intimidate any one in the choice of his candidate, or to attempt doing so. . . ." Wigmore [*The Australian Ballot System Embodied in the Legislation of Various Countries* (1889)]. The Massachusetts and New York laws differed somewhat from the previous Acts in that they excluded the general public only from the area encompassed within a guardrail constructed six feet from the voting compartments. This modification was considered an improvement because it provided additional monitoring by members of the general public and independent candidates, who in most States were not allowed to be represented by separate inspectors. Otherwise, "in order to perpetrate almost every election fraud it would only be necessary to buy up the election officers of the other party." *Id.* Finally, New York also prohibited any person from "electioneering on election day within any polling-place, or within one hundred feet of any polling place." *Id.*

The success achieved through these reforms was immediately noticed and widely praised. One commentator remarked of the New York law of 1888:

> "We have secured secrecy; and intimidation by employers, party bosses, police officers, saloonkeepers and others has come to an end.
>
> "In earlier times our polling places were frequently, to quote the litany, 'scenes of battle, murder, and sudden death.' This also has come to an end, and until nightfall, when the jubilation begins, our election days are now as peaceful as our Sabbaths.
>
> "The new legislation has also rendered impossible the old methods of frank, hardy, straightforward and shameless bribery of voters at the polls." W. Ivins, The Electoral System of the State of New York, Proceedings of the 29th Annual Meeting of the New York State Bar Association (1906).

The triumphs of 1888 set off a rapid and widespread adoption of the Australian system in the United States. By 1896, almost 90 percent of the States had adopted the Australian system. This accounted for 92 percent of the national electorate.

The roots of Tennessee's regulation can be traced back to two provisions passed during this period of rapid reform. Tennessee passed the first relevant provision in 1890 as part of its switch to an Australian system. In its effort to "secur[e] the purity of elections," Tennessee provided that only voters and certain election officials were permitted within the room where the election was held or within 50 feet of the entrance. The Act did not provide any penalty for violation and applied only in the more highly populated counties and cities.

The second relevant provision was passed in 1901 as an amendment to Tennessee's "Act to preserve the purity of elections, and define and punish offenses against the elective franchise." The original Act, passed in 1897, made it a misdemeanor to commit various election offenses, including the use of bribery, violence, or intimidation in order to induce a person to vote or refrain from voting for any particular person or measure. The 1901 amendment made it a misdemeanor for any person, except the officers holding the elections, to approach nearer than 30 feet to any voter or ballot box. This provision applied to all Tennessee elections.

These two laws remained relatively unchanged until 1967, when Tennessee added yet another proscription to its secret ballot law. This amendment prohibited the distribution of campaign literature "on the same floor of a building, or within one hundred (100) feet thereof, where an election is in progress."

In 1972, the State enacted a comprehensive code to regulate the conduct of elections. The code included a section that proscribed the display and the distribution of campaign material and the solicitation of votes within 100 feet of the entrance to a polling place. The 1972 "campaign-free zone" is the direct precursor of the restriction challenged in the present litigation.

Today, all 50 States limit access to the areas in or around polling places. The National Labor Relations Board also limits activities at or near polling places in union-representation elections.

In sum, an examination of the history of election regulation in this country reveals a persistent battle against two evils: voter intimidation and election fraud. After an unsuccessful experiment with an unofficial ballot system, all 50 States, together with numerous other Western democracies, settled on the same solution: a secret ballot secured in part by a restricted zone around the voting compartments. We find that this widespread and time-tested consensus demonstrates that some restricted zone is necessary in order to serve the States' compelling interests in preventing voter intimidation and election fraud.

Respondent and the dissent advance three principal challenges to this conclusion. First, respondent argues that restricted zones are overinclusive because States could secure these same compelling interests with statutes that make it a misdemeanor to interfere with an election or to use violence or intimidation to prevent voting. We are not persuaded. Intimidation and interference laws fall short of serving a State's compelling interests because they "deal with only the most blatant and specific attempts" to impede elections. *Cf. Buckley v. Valeo* (1976) (existence of bribery statute does not preclude need for limits on contributions to political campaigns). Moreover, because law enforcement officers generally are barred from the vicinity of the polls to avoid any appearance of coercion in the electoral process, many acts of interference would go undetected. These undetected or less than blatant acts may nonetheless drive the voter away before remedial action can be taken.

Second, respondent and the dissent argue that Tennessee's statute is underinclusive because it does not restrict other types of speech, such as charitable and commercial solicitation or exit polling, within the 100-foot zone. We agree that distinguishing among types of speech requires that the statute be subjected to strict scrutiny. We do not, however, agree that the failure to regulate all speech renders the statute fatally underinclusive. In fact, as one early commentator pointed out, allowing members of the general public access to the polling place makes it more difficult for political machines to buy off all the monitors. *See* Wigmore. But regardless of the need for such additional monitoring, there is, as summarized above, ample evidence that political candidates have used campaign workers to commit voter intimidation or electoral fraud. In contrast, there is simply no evidence that political candidates have used other forms of solicitation or exit polling to commit such electoral abuses. States adopt laws to address the problems that confront them. The First Amendment does not require States to regulate for problems that do not exist.

Finally, the dissent argues that we confuse history with necessity. Yet the dissent concedes that a secret ballot was necessary to cure electoral abuses. Contrary to the dissent's contention, the link between ballot secrecy and some restricted zone surrounding the voting area is not merely timing—it is common sense. The only way to preserve the secrecy of the ballot is to limit access to the area around the voter. Accordingly, we hold that *some* restricted zone around the voting area is necessary to secure the State's compelling interest.

The real question then is *how large* a restricted zone is permissible or sufficiently tailored. Respondent and the dissent argue that Tennessee's 100-foot boundary is not narrowly drawn to achieve the State's compelling interest in protecting the right to vote. We disagree.

As a preliminary matter, the long, uninterrupted and prevalent use of these statutes makes it difficult for States to come forward with the sort of proof the dissent wishes to require. The majority of these laws were adopted originally in the 1890s, long before States engaged in extensive legislative hearings on election regulations. The prevalence of these laws, both here and abroad, then encouraged their reenactment without much comment. The fact that these laws have been in effect for a long period of time also makes it difficult for the States to put on witnesses who can testify as to what would happen without them. Finally, it is difficult to isolate the exact effect of these laws on voter intimidation and election fraud. Voter intimidation and election fraud are successful precisely because they are difficult to detect.

Furthermore, because a government has such a compelling interest in securing the right to vote freely and effectively, this Court never has held a State "to the burden of demonstrating empirically the objective effects on political stability that [are] produced" by the voting regulation in question. *Munro v. Socialist Workers Party* (1986).[11] Elections vary from year to year, and place to place. It is therefore difficult to make specific findings about the effects of a voting regulation. Moreover, the remedy for a tainted election is an imperfect one. Rerunning an election would have a negative impact on voter turnout. Thus, requiring proof that a 100-foot boundary is perfectly tailored to deal with voter intimidation and election fraud

> "would necessitate that a State's political system sustain some level of damage before the legislature could take corrective action. Legislatures, we think, should be permitted to respond to potential deficiencies in the electoral process with foresight rather than reactively, provided that the response is reasonable and does not *significantly impinge* on constitutionally protected rights." *Id.* (emphasis added).

We do not think that the minor geographic limitation prescribed by § 2-7-111(b) constitutes such a significant impingement. Thus, we simply do not view the question whether the 100-foot boundary line could be somewhat tighter as a question of "constitutional dimension." *Id.* Reducing the boundary to 25 feet, as suggested by the Tennessee Supreme Court, is a difference only in degree, not a less restrictive alternative in kind. As was pointed out in the dissenting opinion in the Tennessee

11. This modified "burden of proof" does not apply to all cases in which there is a conflict between First Amendment rights and a State's election process—instead, it applies only when the First Amendment right threatens to interfere with the act of voting itself, *i.e.*, cases involving voter confusion from overcrowded ballots, like *Munro*, or cases such as this one, in which the challenged activity physically interferes with electors attempting to cast their ballots. Thus, for example, States must come forward with more specific findings to support regulations directed at intangible "influence," such as the ban on election-day editorials struck down in *Mills v. Alabama* (1966).

Supreme Court, it "takes approximately 15 seconds to walk 75 feet." The State of Tennessee has decided that these last 15 seconds before its citizens enter the polling place should be their own, as free from interference as possible. We do not find that this is an unconstitutional choice.[13]

At some measurable distance from the polls, of course, governmental regulation of vote solicitation could effectively become an impermissible burden akin to the statute struck down in *Mills v. Alabama* (1966). In reviewing challenges to specific provisions of a State's election laws, however, this Court has not employed any "'litmus-paper test' that will separate valid from invalid restrictions." *Anderson v. Celebrezze*. Accordingly, it is sufficient to say that in establishing a 100-foot boundary, Tennessee is on the constitutional side of the line.

In conclusion, we reaffirm that it is the rare case in which we have held that a law survives strict scrutiny. This, however, is such a rare case. Here, the State, as recognized administrator of elections, has asserted that the exercise of free speech rights conflicts with another fundamental right, the right to cast a ballot in an election free from the taint of intimidation and fraud. A long history, a substantial consensus, and simple common sense show that some restricted zone around polling places is necessary to protect that fundamental right. Given the conflict between these two rights, we hold that requiring solicitors to stand 100 feet from the entrances to polling places does not constitute an unconstitutional compromise.

The judgment of the Tennessee Supreme Court is reversed, and the case is remanded for further proceedings not inconsistent with this opinion.

Justice THOMAS took no part in the consideration or decision of this case.

Justice KENNEDY, concurring.

[T]here is a narrow area in which the First Amendment permits freedom of expression to yield to the extent necessary for the accommodation of another constitutional right. Voting is one of the most fundamental and cherished liberties in our democratic system of government. The State is not using this justification to suppress legitimate expression.

13. Respondent also raises two more specific challenges to the tailoring of the Tennessee statute. First, she contends that there may be some polling places so situated that the 100-foot boundary falls in or on the other side of a highway. Second, respondent argues that the inclusion of quintessential public forums in some campaign-free zones could result in the prosecution of an individual for driving by in an automobile with a campaign bumper sticker. At oral argument, petitioner denied that the statute would reach this latter, inadvertent conduct, since this would not constitute "display" of campaign material. In any event, these arguments are "as applied" challenges that should be made by an individual prosecuted for such conduct. If successful, these challenges would call for a limiting construction rather than a facial invalidation. In the absence of any factual record to support respondent's contention that the statute has been applied to reach such circumstances, we do not entertain the challenges in this case.

Justice SCALIA, concurring in the judgment.

If the category of "traditional public forum" is to be a tool of analysis rather than a conclusory label, it must remain faithful to its name and derive its content from *tradition.* Because restrictions on speech around polling places on election day are as venerable a part of the American tradition as the secret ballot, Tenn. Code Ann. § 2-7-111 does not restrict speech in a traditional public forum, and the "exacting scrutiny" that the plurality purports to apply, is inappropriate. Instead, I believe that § 2-7-111, though content-based, is constitutional because it is a reasonable, viewpoint-neutral regulation of a nonpublic forum.

Justice STEVENS, with whom Justice O'CONNOR and Justice SOUTER join, dissenting.

The speech and conduct prohibited in the campaign-free zone created by Tenn. Code Ann. § 2-7-111 is classic political expression. Therefore, I fully agree with the plurality that Tennessee must show that its "'regulation is necessary to serve a compelling state interest and that it is narrowly drawn to achieve that end.'" I do not agree, however, that Tennessee has made anything approaching such a showing.

I

Statutes creating campaign-free zones outside polling places serve two quite different functions—they protect orderly access to the polls and they prevent last-minute campaigning. There can be no question that the former constitutes a compelling state interest and that, in light of our decision in *Mills v. Alabama* (1966), the latter does not. Accordingly, a State must demonstrate that the particular means it has fashioned to ensure orderly access to the polls do not unnecessarily hinder last-minute campaigning.

Campaign-free zones are noteworthy for their broad, antiseptic sweep. The Tennessee zone encompasses at least 30,000 square feet around each polling place; in some States, such as Kentucky and Wisconsin, the radius of the restricted zone is 500 feet—silencing an area of over 750,000 square feet. Even under the most sanguine scenario of participatory democracy, it is difficult to imagine voter turnout so complete as to require the clearing of hundreds of thousands of square feet simply to ensure that the path to the polling-place door remains open and that the curtain that protects the secrecy of the ballot box remains closed.

The fact that campaign-free zones cover such a large area in some States unmistakably identifies censorship of election-day campaigning as an animating force behind these restrictions. That some States have no problem maintaining order with zones of 50 feet or less strongly suggests that the more expansive prohibitions are not necessary to maintain access and order. Indeed, on its face, Tennessee's statute appears informed by political concerns. Although the statute initially established a 100-foot zone, it was later amended to establish a 300-foot zone in 12 of the State's 95 counties. As the State Attorney General observed, "there is not a rational basis" for this special treatment, for there is no "discernable reason why an extension of the boundary . . . is necessary in" those 12 counties.

Moreover, the Tennessee statute does not merely regulate conduct that might inhibit voting; it bars the simple "display of campaign posters, signs, or other campaign materials." § 2-7-111(b). Bumper stickers on parked cars and lapel buttons on pedestrians are taboo. The notion that such sweeping restrictions on speech are necessary to maintain the freedom to vote and the integrity of the ballot box borders on the absurd.

The evidence introduced at trial to demonstrate the necessity for Tennessee's campaign-free zone was exceptionally thin. Although the State's sole witness explained the need for special restrictions *inside* the polling place itself, she offered no justification for a ban on political expression *outside* the polling place. On this record it is far from surprising that the Tennessee Supreme Court—which surely is more familiar with the State's electoral practices and traditions than we are—concluded that the 100-foot ban outside the polling place was not justified by regulatory concerns. This conclusion is bolstered by Tennessee law, which indicates that normal police protection is completely adequate to maintain order in the area more than *10* feet from the polling place.

Perhaps in recognition of the poverty of the record, the plurality—without briefing, or legislative or judicial factfinding—looks to history to assess whether Tennessee's statute is in fact necessary to serve the State's interests.

This analysis is deeply flawed; it confuses history with necessity, and mistakes the traditional for the indispensable. The plurality's reasoning combines two logical errors: First, the plurality assumes that a practice's long life itself establishes its necessity; and second, the plurality assumes that a practice that was once necessary remains necessary until it is ended.

With regard to the first, the fact that campaign-free zones were, as the plurality indicates, introduced as part of a broader package of electoral reforms does not demonstrate that such zones were *necessary.* The abuses that affected the electoral system could have been cured by the institution of the secret ballot and by the heightened regulation of the polling place alone, without silencing the political speech *outside* the polling place.[4] In my opinion, more than mere timing is required to infer necessity from tradition.

We have never regarded tradition as a proxy for necessity where necessity must be demonstrated. To the contrary, our election-law jurisprudence is rich with examples of traditions that, though longstanding, were later held to be unnecessary. For example, "[m]ost of the early Colonies had [poll taxes]; many of the States have had them during much of their histories. . . ." *Harper v. Virginia Bd. of Elections* (1966) (Harlan, J., dissenting). Similarly, substantial barriers to candidacy, such as stringent petition requirements, see *Williams v. Rhodes* (1968), property-ownership requirements, see *Turner v.*

4. The plurality's suggestion that "[t]he only way to preserve the secrecy of the ballot is to limit access to the area around the voter" is specious. First, there are obvious and simple means of preserving voter secrecy (*e.g.*, opaque doors or curtains on the voting booth) that do not involve the suppression of political speech. Second, there is no disagreement that the restrictions on campaigning *within the polling place* are constitutional; the issue is not whether the State may limit access to the "area *around the voter*" but whether the State may limit speech in the area *around the polling place.*

Fouche (1970), and onerous filing fees, see *Lubin v. Panish* (1974), were all longstanding features of the electoral labyrinth.

Never have we indicated that tradition was synonymous with necessity.

Even if we assume that campaign-free zones were once somehow "necessary," it would not follow that, 100 years later, those practices remain necessary. Much in our political culture, institutions, and practices has changed since the turn of the century: Our elections are far less corrupt, far more civil, and far more democratic today than 100 years ago. These salutary developments have substantially eliminated the need for what is, in my opinion, a sweeping suppression of core political speech.

Although the plurality today blithely dispenses with the need for factual findings to determine the necessity of "traditional" restrictions on speech, courts that have made such findings with regard to other campaign-free zones have, without exception, found such zones unnecessary. [citing cases] All of these courts, having received evidence on this issue, were far better situated than we are to assess the contemporary necessity of campaign-free zones. All of these courts concluded that such suppression of expression is unnecessary, suggesting that such zones were something of a social atavism. To my mind, this recent history, developed in the context of an adversarial search for the truth, indicates that, whatever the original historical basis for campaign-free zones may have been, their continued "necessity" has not been established. Especially when we deal with the First Amendment, when the reason for a restriction disappears, the restriction should as well.

II

In addition to sweeping too broadly in its reach, Tennessee's campaign-free zone selectively prohibits speech based on content. Within the zone, § 2-7-111 silences all campaign-related expression, but allows expression on any other subject: religious, artistic, commercial speech, even political debate and solicitation concerning issues or candidates not on the day's ballot. Indeed, as I read it, § 2-7-111 does not prohibit exit polling, which surely presents at least as great a potential interference with orderly access to the polls as does the distribution of campaign leaflets, the display of campaign posters, or the wearing of campaign buttons. This discriminatory feature of the statute severely undercuts the credibility of its purported law-and-order justification.

Tennessee's content-based discrimination is particularly problematic because such a regulation will inevitably favor certain groups of candidates. As the testimony in this case illustrates, several groups of candidates rely heavily on last-minute campaigning. Candidates with fewer resources, candidates for lower visibility offices, and "grassroots" candidates benefit disproportionately from last-minute campaigning near the polling place.

Access to, and order around, the polls would be just as threatened by the congregation of citizens concerned about a local environmental issue not on the ballot as by the congregation of citizens urging election of their favored candidate. Similarly, assuming that disorder immediately outside the polling place could lead to the commission of errors or the perpetration of fraud, such disorder could just as easily be caused by a religious dispute sparked by a colporteur as by a campaign-related dispute sparked by a campaign worker. In short, Tennessee has failed to point to any legitimate interest that would justify its selective regulation of campaign-related expression.

III

[Omitted.]

IV

In my opinion, the presence of campaign workers outside a polling place is, in most situations, a minor nuisance. But we have long recognized that "'the fact that society may find speech offensive is not a sufficient reason for suppressing it.'" *Hustler Magazine, Inc. v. Falwell* (1988). Although we often pay homage to the electoral process, we must be careful not to confuse sanctity with silence. The hubbub of campaign workers outside a polling place may be a nuisance, but it is also the sound of a vibrant democracy.

In silencing that sound, Tennessee "trenches upon an area in which the importance of First Amendment protections is 'at its zenith.'" *Meyer v. Grant* (1988). For that reason, Tennessee must shoulder the burden of demonstrating that its restrictions on political speech are no broader than necessary to protect orderly access to the polls. It has not done so.

I therefore respectfully dissent.

Unwanted Political Campaigning: A Hypo on Robocalls

Indiana's Automated Dialing Machine Statute (IADMS) provides, in relevant part,

(a) This section does not apply to messages:
  (1) from school districts to students, parents, or employees;
  (2) to subscribers with whom the caller has a current business or personal relationship; or
  (3) advising employees of work schedules.
(b) A caller may not use or connect to a telephone line an automatic dialing–announcing device unless:
  (1) The subscriber has knowingly or voluntarily requested, consented to, permitted, or authorized receipt of the message; or
  (2) The message is immediately preceded by a live operator who obtains the subscriber's consent before the message is delivered.

A violation of the IADMS constitutes a Class C misdemeanor.

Indiana asserts that its interest in the law is, among others, protecting residential privacy, ensuring that voters are not subjected to harassing campaign messages, and promoting live discussion among people during a campaign (as opposed to through automated messages). It also contends that its law improves political discourse.

Given the discussion in the false advertising cases and in *Burson*, what is the best argument that this provision violates the First Amendment? What is the best argument to uphold the law? How would the current Supreme Court analyze this issue? Would it adopt the *Burson* Court's formulation, or have the tides shifted to the dissent's view?

Note: A federal district court will be reviewing the constitutionality of Indiana's law. This issue is therefore *one* to keep watching. *See Patriotic Veterans, Inc. v. Indiana*, No. 11-3265 (7th Cir. 2013).

C. Election Crimes

The Court in *Burson* recounted how U.S. states and localities adopted the "Australian" secret ballot in an effort to root out fraud, intimidation, and vote buying. Protecting the integrity of electoral processes is often a key consideration in promulgating an election law. How does the criminal justice system respond to unlawful election activities? The first two cases in this section present opposing views on the construction of a federal law that criminalizes election fraud, particularly in the context of absentee balloting before Election Day. As you read the cases, consider which one you find most persuasive. Also think about the reforms you might suggest to minimize this kind of fraud. After these two cases, we will read a third case about a Texas criminal statute that attempts to combat voter fraud on absentee ballot applications. Does the First Amendment right to association encompass a right to engage in voter assistance efforts, especially for those who may have a harder time voting (such as the elderly or those with a disability)? How does the balance between voter mobilization and rooting out fraud play out in these cases?

UNITED STATES v. SALISBURY

983 F.2d 1369 (6th Cir. 1993)

Celebrezze, Senior Circuit Judge.

Defendant Betty Salisbury appeals her conviction and sentence on one count of voting and assisting others in voting more than once in violation of 42 U.S.C. § 1973i(e) and 18 U.S.C. § 2.

Upon review, we find compelling reasons to order the reversal and vacation of defendant's conviction.

During the latter part of 1990, the Federal Bureau of Investigation began examining the Pike County [Ohio] electoral process in response to citizens' complaints concerning the administration of absentee ballot voting. The testimony adduced at trial described how defendant Salisbury, a Pike County Republican Party operative and committee chairperson, usually accompanied by co-defendant Judith Scott, went to the homes of county residents to solicit applications for absentee ballot registration. Upon delivery by mail of the ballot packets at the homes, the defendants would immediately appear, ostensibly to assist the voters in filling out the ballots.* Trial testimony revealed that the assistance frequently consisted of Salisbury reading aloud to the voter the identification numbers of the Republican candidates she supported, while the voter punched the numbers corresponding to those candidates on the ballot card. Numerous voters "helped" by the defendants told the court that Salisbury never asked any of them whom they wished to vote for and never offered alternative choices to the candidates she personally endorsed. In a few instances, where voters expressed interest in voting for a particular candidate not personally endorsed by Salisbury, Salisbury would disparage the character, motivation and skill of the politician and instead offer those voters only the identification number of the candidate she supported. Upon completing the ballot card, the voter would sign the form and often Salisbury would take the ballot, seal the envelope, and convey it to the Board of Elections.

Salisbury and Scott conducted their activities from April 3, 1990 through election day, May 8, 1990. Though the duo normally read aloud the identification numbers of their endorsed candidates and instructed the voters to punch the corresponding numbers on the ballot cards, in some instances the defendants punched the ballot cards themselves, ostensibly on behalf of the voter. Further, Salisbury frequently prohibited voters from seeing the entire list of candidates enclosed in the absentee voter ballot packets, forcing them to rely on her oral recitation of identification numbers. In at least one instance, Republican Party operative Salisbury drove an absentee voter to the Board of Elections in order to exchange the voter's Democratic Party ballot for a Republican Party ballot. In another instance, Salisbury assisted one voter in obtaining and completing absentee ballots on behalf of the voter's sons, all of whom resided out of state.

At trial, the prosecution attempted to raise an inference that Salisbury preyed on unsophisticated voters, with little knowledge of the voting process, because Salisbury assisted an eighteen year old first time voter and a ninety-two year old nursing home resident in the sparsely populated and rural Pike County. Salisbury testified in her own defense and denied all the conduct upon which the charges against her were based.

* The evidence presented at trial disclosed that the defendants, at times, would actually circle a neighborhood by car until they saw the mail carrier deposit an absentee ballot packet at a particular voter's home.

A number of the voters whom Salisbury "helped" were disgruntled by her assistance, which many felt had actually amounted to coercion to vote absentee and to vote for Salisbury's slate of Republican candidates. The letters of these voters to the Board of Elections resulted in some of these contested ballots not being counted and prompted the investigation which led to this case against the co-defendants.

Upon conviction, the court sentenced Salisbury to eighteen months incarceration, a $1,000 fine and two years of supervised release.

Defendant first avers that the district court erroneously failed to dismiss count two of the indictment as unconstitutionally vague because it did not set forth the specific occurrences which purportedly constituted the multiple voting crime charged.

Count two of the indictment states:

> On or about the period April 3, 1990, through May 8, 1990, in the Southern District of Ohio, the defendant, BETTY SALISBURY, did vote and cause others to vote more than once each in the May 8, 1990 primary election, which election was held in part for the purpose of selecting and nominating candidates for the office of Representative to Congress from the Sixth Congressional District of Ohio.
> In violation of 42 U.S.C. § 1973i(e) and 18 U.S.C. § 2.

18 U.S.C. § 2 permits defendant to be charged as a principal for her commission and encouragement of the commission of the prohibited activity of voting more than once in an election, as set forth in 42 U.S.C. § 1973i(e).[2] In the instant case, however, the defendant's conduct, as detailed by the government, is not so clearly "voting more than once."

As will be more fully discussed in subsequent pages, 42 U.S.C. § 1973i(e) does not define the phrase "voting more than once" to completely and unambiguously prohibit the conduct exhibited in the instant case. In fact, the statute does not even define "voting more than once" except to exclude from its ambit the situation where a voter casts an additional ballot after having a previous ballot invalidated.

The factual basis of the indictment in the instant case consisted of a litany of actions which purportedly constituted "voting more than once." None of the listed actions, however, clearly exemplifies multiple voting. For instance, the indictment enumerates, in specific detail, the following actions: 1) the co-defendants caused a third party to punch

2. 42 U.S.C. § 1973i(e) sets forth:
(1) Whoever votes more than once in an election referred to in paragraph (2) shall be fined no more than $10,000 or imprisoned not more than five years, or both.
(2) The prohibition of this subsection applies with respect to any general, special or primary election held solely or in part for the purpose of selecting or electing any candidate for the office of President, Vice President, presidential elector, Member of the United States Senate, Member of the United States House of Representatives, Delegate from the District of Columbia, Guam, or the Virgin Islands, or Resident Commissioner of the Commonwealth of Puerto Rico.
(3) As used in this subsection, the term "votes more than once" does not include the casting of an additional ballot if all prior ballots of that voter were invalidated, nor does it include the voting in two jurisdictions under section 1973aa-1 of the title, to the extent two ballots are not cast for an election to the same candidacy or office.

holes in the ballot of an absentee voter without his "active participation"; 2) defendant Salisbury "caused" a Democrat to apply for a Republican absentee ballot; 3) defendant Salisbury "voted" the ballots of absentee voters without their permission; 4) defendants, on several occasions, instructed an absentee voter to punch a certain set of holes on his absentee ballot without allowing him to identify the corresponding candidates; and 5) defendant "voted" an absentee ballot on behalf of a person she knew was no longer a resident of Pike County.

The indictment, like the statute, does not set forth a clear and unambiguous definition of the term "vote" or the phrase "voting more than once." It also does not describe which of Salisbury's activities specifically constitutes "voting" or "voting more than once." For example, Salisbury's actions, such as reading candidates' names aloud to an absentee voter while the absentee voter physically punched the holes on the ballot and signed the form, do not seem to comport with our common understanding of what constitutes voting. We note that the indictment does not even clearly allege that Salisbury voted on her own behalf. Thus, we hold that count two of the indictment, even in the context of the entire indictment, fails to adequately notify the defendant of the specific occurrences which constituted the charge against her.

[The defendant next challenges the district court's jury instructions.]

The district court confused the issue for the jury by not clarifying whether the jury had to find defendant herself voted multiple times and/or assisted others in doing so. Related to this, the district court enhanced the confusion by its failure to define "voting" as well as "voting more than once." While we acknowledge that there is little case authority on the subject, we must note that the language of the statute fails to explain at what point in the ballot process, particularly the absentee ballot process, the act of voting has occurred. The court needed to define what specific activity constitutes voting. For example, the jury, without guidance, could assume a person "votes" at the time she punches the hole next to the number identifying her selected candidate, when she signs her name, when she mails her absentee ballot or when the ballot is officially counted.

The Eleventh Circuit Court of Appeals, in *United States v. Hogue* [(11th Cir. 1987)], provides the sort of guidance the district court could have used in instructing the jury in the instant case. The *Hogue* court provided the following explanation of voting:

> [F]irst, for a defendant to mark a candidate selection on the ballot of some other voter in a race where that voter has not marked a candidate selection, without the expressed or implied consent of that voter, constitutes voting; and second, for a defendant to change or alter the mark on the ballot of some other voter to vote for some candidate different from the candidate selected by that voter, without the expressed or implied consent of that voter, constitutes voting.

The *Hogue* instruction further mandated a unanimous jury determination that defendant had voted more than once in either of the two manners enumerated.

We concede, though, that even the *Hogue* instruction would have been insufficient in the instant case, without additional guidance defining "consent"[4] as well as a precise statement of whether a person may "vote" another's ballot without actually "marking a candidate selection" or signing the ballot.

Our review of the preceding issues has led this panel to the inescapable conclusion that the fundamental issue in this case, though not directly raised by the parties, is whether defendant received fair notice that her activities were encompassed by the 42 U.S.C. § 1973i(e) prohibition against voting more than once.

The due process clauses of the Fifth and Fourteenth Amendments require criminal statutes to provide notice to the accused of the nature and specific elements of the crime charged. The "void for vagueness" doctrine requires that a statutory prohibition be sufficiently defined so that ordinary people, exercising ordinary common sense, can understand it and avoid conduct which is prohibited, without encouragement of arbitrary and discriminatory enforcement. The law must be specific enough to give reasonable and fair notice in order to warn people to avoid conduct with criminal consequences. In addition to notice, a statute must also establish minimal guidelines to govern enforcement.

Due process is violated where a statute provides no definite standard of conduct, thereby giving law enforcement officers, courts and jurors unfettered freedom to act on nothing but their own preferences and beliefs.

To illustrate why 42 U.S.C. § 1973i(e) is unconstitutionally void for vagueness as applied to Salisbury, we must examine the statute in the context of its judicial constructions. We have found only two cases which provide insight into the scope of 42 U.S. § 1973i(e): *United States v. Lewis* [(D.C. Pa. 1981)] and *United States v. Hogue. United States v. Lewis* applies 42 U.S.C. § 1973i(e) to a clear cut case of a voter casting multiple ballots and, thus, does not enlarge the scope of the prohibition against multiple voting. In contrast, as we noted earlier, *United States v. Hogue* defines multiple voting to include a person marking, changing or altering a candidate selection of another voter without the express or implied consent of that other voter. This, however, gives us no indication whether a person can illegally vote on behalf of another without physically marking the ballot or, whether a person can vote on behalf of another without consent where that other person signed the absentee ballot form.

We next turn to the legislative history of 42 U.S.C. § 1973i(e) to determine whether the prohibition against "voting more than once" is unconstitutionally void for vagueness as applied to Salisbury's conduct in this case.

4. For example, an important issue in the instant case is whether the voters consented to Salisbury's input in their voting decisions by signing the ballots.

Our review of the legislative history reveals that 42 U.S.C. § 1973 et seq. was instituted by Pub. L. 97-205, entitled Voting Rights Act Amendments of 1982, to provide an enforcement mechanism for the Voting Rights Act of 1965. The exclusive reference to multiple voting appears in S. Rep. No. 97-417, 97th Cong., 2nd Cong., 2nd Sess. (1982), which established a prohibition against " . . . various criminal offenses with regard to failure to register voters, or count votes, intimidating or threatening voters, providing false registration information, and voting more than once." The legislature has provided no other insight.

On its face, the 42 U.S.C. § 1973i(e) statute simply proscribes "voting more than once." This language clearly prohibits a voter from entering a voting booth twice in order to fill out two separate ballots on her own behalf during the same election. It also prohibits marking another person's ballot in addition to one's own or multiple other persons' ballots without consent. *United States v. Hogue.* Beyond this, however, it is unclear what conduct the statute prohibits. For instance, it remains unclear, as we have already noted, whether, pursuant to 42 U.S.C. § 1973i(e), an accused has actually voted on behalf of another if the accused has not physically marked the ballot. Likewise, it is unclear whether an accused can vote on behalf of another without consent where that other person signed the ballot form.

There is no legislative or case authority indicating that Congress intended to proscribe a spouse from advising his/her partner how to vote or a political operative from encouraging a citizen to vote for a particular party or candidate. There are, we note, other laws prohibiting such a person from using threats, deceit, fraud or coercion to obtain votes for a particular candidate, issue or party. In the instant case, the entire written record and oral argument have made it abundantly clear that the parties, the district court and this court, are uncertain as to what constitutes multiple voting and whether 42 U.S.C. § 1973i(e) proscribes Salisbury's conduct in this case. Absent an amendment or judicial construction defining the act of voting more than once, the statute, as presently constituted, subjected Salisbury to criminal liability via a standard so indefinite that law enforcement personnel, the district court, and the jury were free to react to nothing more than their own individual definitions of what constitutes voting more than once to the prejudice of Salisbury. 42 U.S.C. § 1973i(e), in light of the scant interpretive authority that exists, sets forth no standard with sufficient particularity for determining whether Salisbury's activities constituted voting more than once and, thus, is unconstitutionally void for vagueness as applied to this case.

We hold that 42 U.S.C. § 1973i(e) is unconstitutionally void for vagueness as applied in this case.

The judgment of the district court is hereby reversed and vacated.

KENNEDY, Circuit Judge, concurring in part and dissenting in part.

[Omitted.]

UNITED STATES v. COLE

41 F.3d 303 (7th Cir. 1994)

Godbold, Circuit Judge.*

Davis Cole was convicted by a jury of one count of conspiracy to commit election fraud in violation of 18 U.S.C. § 371 and one count of multiple voting in violation of 42 U.S.C. § 1973i(e) and (c). He was sentenced to 46 months imprisonment. We affirm the conviction and the sentence.

BACKGROUND

Cole was a deputy voter registrar in Springfield, Illinois, and, as such, he was authorized to register voters and to assist qualified voters in obtaining absentee ballots. In March 1990 he was a candidate in the Democratic primary election for Democratic precinct committeeman for a Springfield precinct. The incumbent, Edna Tyler, opposed him. The primary was a joint state and federal election, but there were only two candidates for federal office on the ballot, one for the Democratic nomination for U.S. senator and the other for the Democratic nomination for a U.S. House of Representatives seat. Each was unopposed. Cole won his race with 100 votes to Tyler's 75. Eighty-eight votes were cast in the form of absentee ballots.

At trial the government called 19 witnesses who testified that in the primary Cole and/or one of his associates improperly influenced their voting by absentee ballots. Most of these witnesses testified that Cole instructed them on how to apply for an absentee ballot, and that he came to their residences a second time after the ballot arrived in the mail. Absentee voters testified that they signed only their names on the ballots while Cole, or his associate, or an unknown person, filled in the remaining information and votes by punching the ballot. Additionally, several witnesses testified that they were given beer or cigarettes from Cole or his associate, and one witness testified she also received a dollar in addition to cigarettes.

DISCUSSION

[Section 1 is omitted.]

2. Constitutionality of § 1973I(E)-Void for Vagueness

The court did not commit plain error by applying § 1973i(e), the multiple voter statute, which Cole says is void for vagueness as applied. Cole contends that the statute does not adequately define the phrase "voting more than once" to prohibit his conduct. Where an indictment does not enumerate the necessary elements of the alleged crime clearly and fully, the statute must set forth the elements. "[T]he void-for-vagueness

* The Honorable John C. Godbold, Circuit Judge for the United States Court of Appeals for the Eleventh Circuit, is sitting by designation.

doctrine requires that a penal statute define the criminal offense with sufficient definiteness that ordinary people can understand what conduct is prohibited and in a manner that does not encourage arbitrary and discriminatory enforcement." *Kolender v. Lawson* (1983). The primary concern of the doctrine is that legislatures establish clear guidelines to govern the discretion of law enforcement officials.

In pertinent part § 1973i(e) states that "[w]hoever votes more than once in an election . . . shall be fined not more than $10,000 or imprisoned not more than five years, or both." 42 U.S.C. § 1973i(e)(1). Subsection 3 clarifies slightly the term "votes more than once" by specifying that the term does not include a subsequent vote by a voter whose prior vote was deemed invalid. However, to understand fully the term "vote," one must look to § 1973l (c)(1):

> The terms 'vote' or 'voting' shall include all action necessary to make a vote effective in any primary, special, or general election, including, but not limited to, registration, listing pursuant to this subchapter, or other action required by law prerequisite to voting, casting a ballot, and having such ballot counted properly and included in the appropriate totals of votes cast with respect to candidates for public or party office and propositions for which votes are received in an election.

In common parlance "vote" is defined as "the expression of one's will, preference, or choice," Black's Law Dictionary 1576 (6th ed. 1990), or "to express the will or a preference in a matter by ballot, voice, etc.," Webster's New World Dictionary 1593 (2d College ed. 1984). Ordinary people can conclude that Cole's behavior is prohibited by § 1973i(e). Most of the government witnesses testified that Cole or one of his associates marked their ballots. One witness testified that she thought Cole was registering her to vote; she did not realize that he was voting for her. Ordinary people can conclude that the absentee voters were not expressing their wills or preferences, i.e., that Cole was using the absentee voters' ballots to vote his will and preferences.

In *U.S. v. Salisbury* (6th Cir. 1993), the defendants solicited applications for absentee ballots door-to-door. When the ballots were received by the residents, the defendants appeared to "assist" the residents in completing the ballots. Frequently Salisbury would read aloud the numbers of the Republican candidates she supported and the absentee voter would punch the ballot accordingly. Occasionally the defendants would actually punch the absentee ballots themselves, ostensibly on behalf of the absentee voters. Salisbury actively discouraged voters from voting for candidates that she did not support. After punching the ballot, the absentee voter would sign it, and then oftentimes hand it over to Salisbury. The Sixth Circuit determined that neither the indictment nor § 1973i(e) "set forth a clear and unambiguous definition of the term 'vote' or the phrase 'voting more than once.'" The court then held that the statute did not adequately inform Salisbury of the elements of her alleged crime, thus holding that § 1973i(e) was unconstitutionally vague as applied to Salisbury. *Salisbury* is similar to this case, but we will not follow it. The Sixth

Circuit, in looking for a definition of "vote," looked only to § 1973i(e) and the indictment; the court seemingly did not consider the definition laid out at § 1973l (c). Section 1973l(c) adequately defines "vote," and that definition is supported by the common understanding of the word.

CONCLUSION

The conviction and sentence are affirmed.

RAY v. TEXAS

Civil Action No. 2-06-CV-385 (E.D. Tex. 2008)

T. John Ward, District Judge

1. Introduction

A Texas statute makes it a criminal offense for any person to sign as a witness for more than one early voting ballot application, subject to limited exceptions. The question presented in this case is whether the Texas law is consistent with the First and Fourteenth Amendments [to the U.S. Constitution]. For the reasons assigned in this opinion, the court concludes that the statute is constitutional.

2. Background and Procedural Posture

Title 7 of the Texas Election Code establishes the statutory scheme for early voting. A voter may participate in early voting either by mail or in-person. *See* Tex. Elec. Code § 84.001(a). If general voter eligibility requirements are met, a voter may vote early by mail if: (a) the voter expects to be absent from the country of the voter's residence on election day and during the regular hours for conducting early voting at the main early voting polling place; (b) the voter has a disability that prevents the voter from appearing at the polling place on election day; (c) the voter is 65 years old or older on election day; or (d) the voter is confined in jail on election day. The plaintiffs' claims in this case relate to provisions (b) and (c).

To be entitled to vote early by mail, an eligible voter must apply for an early voting ballot. In circumstances where a person by reason of disability or illiteracy cannot sign an application, then another person may sign as a witness. If a witness signs the application, then the application must indicate the witness's relationship to the applicant, or, if unrelated, indicate that fact.

If an applicant for early voting by mail satisfies the statutory requirements, the early voting clerk will mail that person the ballot material. After receiving the ballot material, the voter must mark the ballot in accordance with the instructions on the ballot envelope. The voter must then place the ballot in the official ballot envelope, seal the envelope, place the ballot envelope in the official carrier envelope, seal the carrier envelope, and sign the certificate on the carrier envelope.

If the voter needs help in preparing the ballot, he or she may select an authorized person to provide such assistance. Any person other than the voter's employer, an agent of the voter's employer, or an officer or agent of a labor union to which the voter belongs may assist the voter. This assistance may include: (a) reading the ballot to the voter; (b) directing the voter to read the ballot; (c) marking the voter's ballot; or (d) directing the voter to mark the ballot.

The challenged provision relates to the process by which a putative early voter applies for an application and specifically the need to have a witness for the application if a person is unable to sign his or her own application. § 84.004 of the Texas Election Code provides as follows:

> (a) A person commits an offense if, in the same election, the person signs an early voting ballot application as a witness for more than one applicant.
> (b) It is an exception to the application of Subsection (a) that the person signed early voting ballot applications for more than one applicant:
> (1) as an early voting clerk or deputy early voting clerk; or
> (2) and the person is related to the additional applicants as a parent, grandparent, spouse, child, or sibling.
> (c) A violation of this section does not affect the validity of an application involved in the offense.
> (d) Each application signed by the witness in violation of this section constitutes a separate offense.
> (e) An offense under this section is a Class B misdemeanor

The plaintiffs contend that § 84.004 has had a chilling effect on Democratic Party activists who have assisted mail-in voters in the past, but have stopped due to their fear of prosecution and/or confusion concerning the statute's scope. In turn, this lack of assistance has resulted in the disenfranchisement of elderly and disabled voters. The State argues that § 84.004 combats election fraud and is reasonably tailored in scope. In response, the plaintiffs note that other laws—that are not as oppressive as § 84.004—exist to fight election fraud.

The evidence in support of the plaintiffs' claims includes testimony concerning the impact § 84.004 has had, and will have, on voters and those who assist voters. For example, Willie Ray notes that she has been unable to serve as a witness to multiple voters who have asked for her assistance because of § 84.004. Ms. Ray suggests that if she (or someone similarly situated) is unable to witness a signature for an application, the applicant likely will not seek further assistance and will not vote.

The record includes more concrete examples of the impact of § 84.004: Plaintiff Minniweather was interviewed by an investigator from the Attorney General's office in relation to assistance she provided for mail-in voters. The State did not pursue the criminal prosecution, but Minniweather stopped assisting with mail-in voting as a result of the investigation. The State also investigated Plaintiff Meeks in connection with assisting mail-in voters, but there is no indication that she stopped assisting voters as a result.

3. Discussion

"Voting is of the most fundamental significance under our constitutional structure." *Illinois Bd. of Elections v. Socialist Workers Party* (1979). However, the right to vote and the right to associate for political purposes are not absolute. *See Munro v. Socialist Workers Party* (1986). The Constitution allows the states to regulate the time, places, and manner of holding elections for members of congress. "Common sense, as well as constitutional law, compels the conclusion that government must play an active role in structuring elections; 'as a practical matter, there must be a substantial regulation of elections if they are to be fair and honest and if some sort of order, rather than chaos, is to accompany the democratic process.'" *Burdick* [*v. Takushi* (1992)] (citing *Storer v. Brown* (1974)).

The State argues that § 84.004 is justified by the State's interest in preventing election fraud. Specifically, the State argues that the statute was intended to prevent elderly and disabled individuals from being unwitting victims of voting fraud perpetuated through the use of fraudulent absentee ballot applications. This interest is certainly important and recognized by the Supreme Court. This court accepts the State's representation that § 84.004 is intended to combat election fraud. . . . The legislative history includes testimony that individuals fraudulently obtained absentee ballots for nursing home residents and testimony of complaints about fraudulent applications for absentee ballots. Accordingly, it appears that § 84.004 was enacted at least in part to combat election fraud.

The present plaintiffs focus on the effect of § 84.004 on elderly and disabled voters. The plaintiffs offer their deposition testimony which includes logical deductions that § 84.004 has the effect of decreasing the numbers of volunteers willing to assist with the early voting ballot application. With one exception, [however,] the plaintiffs admit that they will continue to provide assistance to voters. The court appreciates the logical conclusion that precluding volunteers from witnessing more than one ballot application could reduce voter participation to some extent. However, the record lacks concrete evidence that § 84.004 has had an appreciable impact on elderly and disabled voter participation. On this record, the court cannot conclude that § 84.004 has had a "chilling effect" on voters or that § 84.004 has "disenfranchised" the voting public to any appreciable extent.

The State may impose reasonable non-discriminatory restrictions on a person's right to vote. Section 84.004 reasonably and non-discriminatorially restricts the number of applications for early balloting a person may witness.

4. Conclusion

The challenged restriction is not contrary to the First or Fourteenth Amendments. . . .

NOTES ON *SALISBURY, COLE,* AND *RAY*

1. As you just read, the Sixth Circuit in *Salisbury* ruled that the federal statute did not define the meaning of "vote" with enough precision, while the Seventh Circuit in *Cole* used the common meaning of that term. Which court had the better argument? Suppose you are a legislative aide to a member of Congress who wants to respond to the Sixth Circuit's decision by curing the constitutional defect. What definition would you use for the word "vote"?
2. *Salisbury* and *Cole* represent the most common form of voter fraud: through absentee balloting. What kinds of electoral reforms would you suggest to root out absentee ballot fraud like this? Does the state have the burden of providing actual evidence of the fraud it is trying to combat, or do those challenging the laws need to show why the criminal sanctions will lead to disenfranchisement? In *Ray*, the court seemed to credit the state's justifications over the plaintiff's assertions that the law limiting witnesses for absentee ballot applications would lead to fewer citizens being able to vote. But perhaps there is a broader doctrinal theme to consider: Is there a First Amendment value in voter mobilization that a law such as Texas's infringes? That is, does part of the right to political association include the right to help others vote? If there is a First Amendment right in voter mobilization, how does that relate to the associational rights of political parties discussed in Part II of this book?
3. A less frequent (although still existing) type of voter fraud is through vote buying. In this scenario, candidates and campaigns literally pay voters to cast their ballots in a particular way. Sometimes those involved enlist poll workers to ensure that voters cast their ballots for the candidate that is buying their votes, or have poll workers manipulate the machines to change votes after the voters leave. A recent judicial opinion sheds some light on how this works:

> Political candidates pooled money to buy votes and to pay "vote haulers" to deliver voters whose votes could be bought. In order to be paid, voters had to vote for a particular set of candidates, known as a "slate" or "ticket." To ensure that these voters actually voted for the correct slate, co-conspiring election officers and poll workers reviewed voters' ballots—a practice known in this case as "voting the voter." Once the proper slate was confirmed, a token (such as a raffle ticket) or marking was given to the voters to confirm that they did in fact vote for the proper slate. Voters with the token or marking were then paid by members of the conspiracy in a location away from the polls. Conspirators retained lists of voters to avoid double payments and to keep track of whose votes could be bought in ensuing elections.
>
> In addition to hiring vote haulers, defendants allegedly utilized other methods of buying votes. Absentee voting and voter-assistance forms helped minimize the difficulty of checking paid voters' ballots. In the latter case, co-conspiring poll workers were permitted to be in the voting booth under the

> pretext that they were assisting voters; in reality, co-conspiring poll workers were confirming that voters chose the proper slates. When electronic voting machines were introduced to Clay County in the 2006 election, the conspiracy both stole and bought votes. To steal votes, conspirators, typically poll workers, purposefully misinformed voters that they did not need to click "cast ballot" on a screen that appeared after voters had selected candidates for whom they wished to vote. Co-conspiring poll workers would enter the voting booth after the voter exited and change the electronic ballot to reflect the slate before finally casting the ballot.

United States v. Adams, 722 F.3d 788 (6th Cir. 2013). Are criminal laws sufficient to deter vote buying of this kind? The court in *Adams* reversed the defendants' criminal convictions based on errors the district court made in admitting certain evidence, but the government indicated that it would re-try the defendants.

D. Campaign Finance

Politics is expensive. The amount of money in campaigns has continued to skyrocket. As the costs to run for office have increased, so too has a candidate's need to solicit and spend money to stay viable.

Where do candidates find this money? The main sources are the candidate's own pockets (if the candidate is wealthy enough); political parties, individual voters, or organized interest groups sympathetic to the candidate's views; and (where applicable) the public itself through public financing. Moreover, outside groups (and even corporations) may spend money on their own electioneering communications to support or oppose a candidate. The cases in this section are organized loosely around the concept of who is spending the money: candidates, individuals, political parties, corporations and unions, the public through public financing, and political action committees (PACs), which are nonprofit organizations created to be generally independent of candidates and which engage in electioneering activities. Consider the way in which the rules differ for different kinds of political actors.

In addition to focusing on the *who*, it is important to consider *what* the actors are doing with their money. As you will see, the Supreme Court has made a fundamental conceptual distinction between *donations* to a candidate, a political party, or a PAC, and *independent expenditures* to advocate for or against a candidate's election. (This distinction will become clearer as you read the Court's cases.) But even within the realm of independent spending to support or oppose a candidate, there is the further distinction between *express advocacy*, which explicitly declares its support or opposition to a candidate's election, and *issue advocacy*, which discusses issues of public policy and might even mention the name of a candidate—thereby seeming implicitly to support or oppose the candidate's election, but without an explicit statement of electoral advocacy. Moreover, because the distinction between federal and state elections matters for campaign finance law, in some contexts it is important to know whether a political party has paid for activities that specifically benefit their federal candidates or, instead, has paid for campaign activities that benefit both their federal and state candidates.

With increased money in campaigns comes concerns about potential corruption or undue influence of those who contribute. Might a politician favor those who contributed to his or her campaign when passing legislation? Will those who give money have greater access to influence the politician? Does the increase of money in politics mean that only wealthy individuals, or those backed by wealthy groups, have a chance to win?

Enter Congress and state legislatures, which have sought to regulate this area. Since the 1970s, in response to the egregious and well-documented corruption that occurred as part of President Nixon's efforts to win reelection in 1972 (usually referred to as "Watergate," although the break-in of the Democratic Party's headquarters was just one piece of the overall corruption), Congress became more active in passing laws that place parameters around the use of money in politics. In particular, Congress has sought to impose limits on the amount of money individuals can contribute, the amount candidates can spend, and the amount individuals or groups not affiliated with a campaign may spend (independent expenditures). Generally, Congress has espoused the goals of eliminating corruption or the appearance of corruption, ensuring political actors cannot circumvent valid campaign finance restrictions, and equalizing the opportunities for electoral success by reducing the skyrocketing cost of campaigns. As you read through the cases, consider to what extent courts deem these interests valid. We start with the seminal case in this area, *Buckley v. Valeo*.

1. The Buckley *Foundation*

The United States has regulated campaign finance for over a century. In 1907, Congress passed the Tillman Act, which prohibited corporations from contributing to national political campaigns. Congress followed with additional regulation through the Federal Corrupt Practices Act, the Hatch Act, the Smith-Connolly Act, and the Taft-Hartley Act. All of these laws sought to regulate spending in campaigns for federal office. But none provided a comprehensive solution, and in practice there was little regulation of money in campaigns. Congress, perceiving abuses in the financing of campaigns and concerned about the rising costs of campaigning, enacted the Federal Election Campaign Act (FECA) of 1971. Congress found, in passing FECA, that "the unchecked rise in campaign expenditures coupled with the absence of limitations on contributions and expenditures, has increased the dependence of candidates on special interest groups and large contributors. Under the present law the impression persists that a candidate can buy an election by simply spending large sums in a campaign." FECA itself was substantially amended just a few years later, after the Watergate abuses showed that the original version of the statute was inadequate to achieve its anticorruption goals.

For our purposes, FECA introduced three major changes to the financing of campaigns. First, the law imposed a limit on how much individuals could contribute to campaigns. Second, FECA set limits on independent expenditures—money not given to a campaign, and spent without any coordination with the campaign, but still advocating for a certain result. In essence, a contribution is writing a check to the campaign itself; an independent expenditure is spending your own money directly on campaign activities. Finally, the law imposed disclosure requirements.

Opponents of the law immediately challenged these aspects of FECA. The Supreme Court's decision, upholding the contribution limits and disclosure requirements but striking down the independent expenditure limitations, forms the foundation for today's campaign finance regime. As you read *Buckley*, consider the way in which the analysis for contributions as opposed to independent expenditures is or should be different. Also note how the Court deems campaign spending a form of "speech" that requires robust First Amendment protection.

BUCKLEY v. VALEO

424 U.S. 1 (1976)

PER CURIAM.

These appeals present constitutional challenges to the key provisions of the Federal Election Campaign Act of 1971 (Act), as amended in 1974.

The statutes at issue summarized in broad terms, contain the following provisions: individual political contributions are limited to $1,000 to any single candidate per election, with an overall annual limitation of $25,000 by any contributor;* independent expenditures by individuals and groups "relative to a clearly identified candidate" are limited to $1,000 a year; campaign spending by candidates for various federal offices and spending for national conventions by political parties are subject to prescribed limits.

I. CONTRIBUTION AND EXPENDITURE LIMITATIONS

The intricate statutory scheme adopted by Congress to regulate federal election campaigns includes restrictions on political contributions and expenditures that apply broadly to all phases of and all participants in the election process. The major contribution and expenditure limitations in the Act prohibit individuals from contributing more than $25,000 in a single year or more than $1,000 to any single candidate for an election

* [Editors' note: The contribution limits are indexed for inflation; today, the contribution limit for individuals is $2,600 per candidate in an election, with an overall biennial limitation by any contributor to all candidates of $48,600. Individuals may also give to the national, state, or local parties, with separate ceilings for these contributions. To see a chart listing these limits, visit http://www.fec.gov/pages/brochures/contriblimits.shtml.]

campaign and from spending more than $1,000 a year "relative to a clearly identified candidate." Other provisions restrict a candidate's use of personal and family resources in his campaign and limit the overall amount that can be spent by a candidate in campaigning for federal office.

The constitutional power of Congress to regulate federal elections is well established and is not questioned by any of the parties in this case. Thus, the critical constitutional questions presented here go not to the basic power of Congress to legislate in this area, but to whether the specific legislation that Congress has enacted interferes with First Amendment freedoms

A. General Principles

The Act's contribution and expenditure limitations operate in an area of the most fundamental First Amendment activities. Discussion of public issues and debate on the qualifications of candidates are integral to the operation of the system of government established by our Constitution. The First Amendment affords the broadest protection to such political expression in order "to assure (the) unfettered interchange of ideas for the bringing about of political and social changes desired by the people." *Roth v. United States* (1957). Although First Amendment protections are not confined to "the exposition of ideas," "there is practically universal agreement that a major purpose of that Amendment was to protect the free discussion of governmental affairs. . . . of course includ(ing) discussions of candidates. . . ." *Mills v. Alabama* (1966). This no more than reflects our "profound national commitment to the principle that debate on public issues should be uninhibited, robust, and wide-open," *New York Times Co. v. Sullivan* (1964). In a republic where the people are sovereign, the ability of the citizenry to make informed choices among candidates for office is essential, for the identities of those who are elected will inevitably shape the course that we follow as a nation. As the Court observed in *Monitor Patriot Co. v. Roy* (1971), "it can hardly be doubted that the constitutional guarantee has its fullest and most urgent application precisely to the conduct of campaigns for political office."

It is with these principles in mind that we consider the primary contentions of the parties with respect to the Act's limitations upon the giving and spending of money in political campaigns. Appellees contend that what the Act regulates is conduct, and that its effect on speech and association is incidental at most. Appellants respond that contributions and expenditures are at the very core of political speech, and that the Act's limitations thus constitute restraints on First Amendment liberty that are both gross and direct.

Some forms of communication made possible by the giving and spending of money involve speech alone, some involve conduct primarily, and some involve a combination of the two. Yet this Court has never suggested that the dependence of a communication on the expenditure of money operates itself to introduce a nonspeech element or to reduce the exacting scrutiny required by the First Amendment.

Even if the categorization of the expenditure of money as conduct were accepted, the limitations challenged here . . . involve "suppressing communication." The interests served by the Act include restricting the voices of people and interest groups who have money to spend and reducing the overall scope of federal election campaigns. Although the Act does not focus on the ideas expressed by persons or groups subject to its regulations, it is aimed in part at equalizing the relative ability of all voters to affect electoral outcomes by placing a ceiling on expenditures for political expression by citizens and groups.

A restriction on the amount of money a person or group can spend on political communication during a campaign necessarily reduces the quantity of expression by restricting the number of issues discussed, the depth of their exploration, and the size of the audience reached.[18] This is because virtually every means of communicating ideas in today's mass society requires the expenditure of money. The distribution of the humblest handbill or leaflet entails printing, paper, and circulation costs. Speeches and rallies generally necessitate hiring a hall and publicizing the event. The electorate's increasing dependence on television, radio, and other mass media for news and information has made these expensive modes of communication indispensable instruments of effective political speech.

The expenditure limitations contained in the Act represent substantial rather than merely theoretical restraints on the quantity and diversity of political speech. The $1,000 ceiling on spending "relative to a clearly identified candidate" would appear to exclude all citizens and groups except candidates, political parties, and the institutional press from any significant use of the most effective modes of communication. Although the Act's limitations on expenditures by campaign organizations and political parties provide substantially greater room for discussion and debate, they would have required restrictions in the scope of a number of past congressional and Presidential campaigns and would operate to constrain campaigning by candidates who raise sums in excess of the spending ceiling.

By contrast with a limitation upon expenditures for political expression, a limitation upon the amount that any one person or group may contribute to a candidate or political committee entails only a marginal restriction upon the contributor's ability to engage in free communication. A contribution serves as a general expression of support for the candidate and his views, but does not communicate the underlying basis for the support. The quantity of communication by the contributor does not increase perceptibly with the size of his contribution, since the expression rests solely on the undifferentiated, symbolic act of contributing. At most, the size of the contribution provides a very rough index of the intensity of the contributor's support for the candidate. A limitation on the amount of money a person may give to a candidate or campaign organization thus involves little direct restraint on his political communication, for it permits the symbolic expression of support evidenced by a contribution but does not in any way infringe the contributor's freedom to discuss candidates and issues. While contributions may result in political expression if

18. Being free to engage in unlimited political expression subject to a ceiling on expenditures is like being free to drive an automobile as far and as often as one desires on a single tank of gasoline.

spent by a candidate or an association to present views to the voters, the transformation of contributions into political debate involves speech by someone other than the contributor.

Given the important role of contributions in financing political campaigns, contribution restrictions could have a severe impact on political dialogue if the limitations prevented candidates and political committees from amassing the resources necessary for effective advocacy. There is no indication, however, that the contribution limitations imposed by the Act would have any dramatic adverse effect on the funding of campaigns and political associations. The overall effect of the Act's contribution ceilings is merely to require candidates and political committees to raise funds from a greater number of persons and to compel people who would otherwise contribute amounts greater than the statutory limits to expend such funds on direct political expression, rather than to reduce the total amount of money potentially available to promote political expression.

The Act's contribution and expenditure limitations also impinge on protected associational freedoms. Making a contribution, like joining a political party, serves to affiliate a person with a candidate. In addition, it enables like-minded persons to pool their resources in furtherance of common political goals. The Act's contribution ceilings thus limit one important means of associating with a candidate or committee, but leave the contributor free to become a member of any political association and to assist personally in the association's efforts on behalf of candidates. And the Act's contribution limitations permit associations and candidates to aggregate large sums of money to promote effective advocacy. By contrast, the Act's $1,000 limitation on independent expenditures "relative to a clearly identified candidate" precludes most associations from effectively amplifying the voice of their adherents, the original basis for the recognition of First Amendment protection of the freedom of association. *See NAACP v. Alabama* [(1958)].

In sum, although the Act's contribution and expenditure limitations both implicate fundamental First Amendment interests, its expenditure ceilings impose significantly more severe restrictions on protected freedoms of political expression and association than do its limitations on financial contributions.

B. Contribution Limitations

1. The $1,000 Limitation on Contributions by Individuals and Groups to Candidates and Authorized Campaign Committees

Section 608(b) provides, with certain limited exceptions, that "no person shall make contributions to any candidate with respect to any election for Federal office which, in the aggregate, exceed $1,000." The $1,000 ceiling applies regardless of whether the contribution is given to the candidate, to a committee authorized in writing by the candidate to accept contributions on his behalf, or indirectly via earmarked gifts passed through an intermediary to the candidate. The restriction applies to aggregate amounts contributed to the candidate for each election with primaries, run-off elections, and general elections counted separately, and all Presidential primaries held in any calendar year treated together as a single election campaign.

Appellants contend that the $1,000 contribution ceiling unjustifiably burdens First Amendment freedoms, employs overbroad dollar limits, and discriminates against candidates opposing incumbent officeholders. We address each of these claims of invalidity in turn.

(a)

As the general discussion in Part I-A indicated, the primary First Amendment problem raised by the Act's contribution limitations is their restriction of one aspect of the contributor's freedom of political association. In view of the fundamental nature of the right to associate, governmental "action which may have the effect of curtailing the freedom to associate is subject to the closest scrutiny." *NAACP v. Alabama*. Yet, it is clear that "(n)either the right to associate nor the right to participate in political activities is absolute." *CSC v. Letter Carriers* (1973). Even a "'significant interference' with protected rights of political association" may be sustained if the State demonstrates a sufficiently important interest and employs means closely drawn to avoid unnecessary abridgment of associational freedoms.

Appellees argue that the Act's restrictions on large campaign contributions are justified by three governmental interests. [T]he primary interest served by the limitations and, indeed, by the Act as a whole, is the prevention of corruption and the appearance of corruption spawned by the real or imagined coercive influence of large financial contributions on candidates' positions and on their actions if elected to office. Two "ancillary" interests underlying the Act are also allegedly furthered by the $1,000 limits on contributions. First, the limits serve to mute the voices of affluent persons and groups in the election process and thereby to equalize the relative ability of all citizens to affect the outcome of elections.[26] Second, it is argued, the ceilings may to some extent act as a brake on the skyrocketing cost of political campaigns and thereby serve to open the political system more widely to candidates without access to sources of large amounts of money.

It is unnecessary to look beyond the Act's primary purpose to limit the actuality and appearance of corruption resulting from large individual financial contributions in order to find a constitutionally sufficient justification for the $1,000 contribution limitation. Under a system of private financing of elections, a candidate lacking immense personal or family wealth must depend on financial contributions from others to provide the resources necessary to conduct a successful campaign. The increasing importance of the communications media and sophisticated mass-mailing and polling operations to effective campaigning make the raising of large sums of money an ever more essential ingredient of an

26. Contribution limitations alone would not reduce the greater potential voice of affluent persons and well-financed groups, who would remain free to spend unlimited sums directly to promote candidates and policies they favor in an effort to persuade voters.

effective candidacy. To the extent that large contributions are given to secure a political quid pro quo from current and potential office holders, the integrity of our system of representative democracy is undermined. Although the scope of such pernicious practices can never be reliably ascertained, the deeply disturbing examples surfacing after the 1972 election demonstrate that the problem is not an illusory one.

Of almost equal concern as the danger of actual quid pro quo arrangements is the impact of the appearance of corruption stemming from public awareness of the opportunities for abuse inherent in a regime of large individual financial contributions. Congress could legitimately conclude that the avoidance of the appearance of improper influence is also critical if confidence in the system of representative Government is not to be eroded to a disastrous extent.

Appellants contend that the contribution limitations must be invalidated because bribery laws and narrowly drawn disclosure requirements constitute a less restrictive means of dealing with "proven and suspected quid pro quo arrangements." But laws making criminal the giving and taking of bribes deal with only the most blatant and specific attempts of those with money to influence governmental action. And while disclosure requirements serve many salutary purposes, Congress was surely entitled to conclude that disclosure was only a partial measure, and that contribution ceilings were a necessary legislative concomitant to deal with the reality or appearance of corruption inherent in a system permitting unlimited financial contributions, even when the identities of the contributors and the amounts of their contributions are fully disclosed.

The Act's $1,000 contribution limitation focuses precisely on the problem of large campaign contributions the narrow aspect of political association where the actuality and potential for corruption have been identified while leaving persons free to engage in independent political expression, to associate actively through volunteering their services, and to assist to a limited but nonetheless substantial extent in supporting candidates and committees with financial resources. Significantly, the Act's contribution limitations in themselves do not undermine to any material degree the potential for robust and effective discussion of candidates and campaign issues by individual citizens, associations, the institutional press, candidates, and political parties.

We find that, under the rigorous standard of review established by our prior decisions, the weighty interests served by restricting the size of financial contributions to political candidates are sufficient to justify the limited effect upon First Amendment freedoms caused by the $1,000 contribution ceiling.

(b)

Appellants' first overbreadth challenge to the contribution ceilings rests on the proposition that most large contributors do not seek improper influence over a candidate's position or an officeholder's action. Although the truth of that proposition may be assumed, it does not undercut the validity of the $1,000 contribution limitation.

Not only is it difficult to isolate suspect contributions, but, more importantly, Congress was justified in concluding that the interest in safeguarding against the appearance of impropriety requires that the opportunity for abuse inherent in the process of raising large monetary contributions be eliminated.

A second, related overbreadth claim is that the $1,000 restriction is unrealistically low because much more than that amount would still not be enough to enable an unscrupulous contributor to exercise improper influence over a candidate or officeholder, especially in campaigns for statewide or national office. While the contribution limitation provisions might well have been structured to take account of the graduated expenditure limitations for congressional and Presidential campaigns, Congress' failure to engage in such fine tuning does not invalidate the legislation. If it is satisfied that some limit on contributions is necessary, a court has no scalpel to probe, whether, say, a $2,000 ceiling might not serve as well as $1,000. Such distinctions in degree become significant only when they can be said to amount to differences in kind.

(c)

Apart from these First Amendment concerns, appellants argue that the contribution limitations work such an invidious discrimination between incumbents and challengers that the statutory provisions must be declared unconstitutional on their face. In considering this contention, it is important at the outset to note that the Act applies the same limitations on contributions to all candidates regardless of their present occupations, ideological views, or party affiliations. Absent record evidence of invidious discrimination against challengers as a class, a court should generally be hesitant to invalidate legislation which on its face imposes evenhanded restrictions.

There is no such evidence to support the claim that the contribution limitations in themselves discriminate against major-party challengers to incumbents. Challengers can and often do defeat incumbents in federal elections. Major-party challengers in federal elections are usually men and women who are well known and influential in their community or State. Often such challengers are themselves incumbents in important local, state, or federal offices. Statistics in the record indicate that major-party challengers as well as incumbents are capable of raising large sums for campaigning. Indeed, a small but nonetheless significant number of challengers have in recent elections outspent their incumbent rivals. And, to the extent that incumbents generally are more likely than challengers to attract very large contributions, the Act's $1,000 ceiling has the practical effect of benefiting challengers as a class. Contrary to the broad generalization drawn by the appellants, the practical impact of the contribution ceilings in any given election will clearly depend upon the amounts in excess of the ceilings that, for various reasons, the candidates in that election would otherwise have received and the utility of these additional amounts to the candidates. To be sure, the limitations may have a significant effect on particular challengers or incumbents, but the record provides no basis for predicting that such adventitious factors will invariably and invidiously benefit incumbents as a class.

Since the danger of corruption and the appearance of corruption apply with equal force to challengers and to incumbents, Congress had ample justification for imposing the same fundraising constraints upon both.

In view of these considerations, we conclude that the impact of the Act's $1,000 contribution limitation on major-party challengers and on minor-party candidates does not render the provision unconstitutional on its face.

2. The $5,000 Limitation on Contributions by Political Committees

Section 608(b)(2) permits certain committees, designated as "political committees," to contribute up to $5,000 to any candidate with respect to any election for federal office. In order to qualify for the higher contribution ceiling, a group must have been registered with the [Federal Election] Commission as a political committee for not less than six months, have received contributions from more than 50 persons, and, except for state political party organizations, have contributed to five or more candidates for federal office. Appellants argue that these qualifications unconstitutionally discriminate against ad hoc organizations in favor of established interest groups and impermissibly burden free association. The argument is without merit. Rather than undermining freedom of association, the basic provision enhances the opportunity of bona fide groups to participate in the election process, and the registration, contribution, and candidate conditions serve the permissible purpose of preventing individuals from evading the applicable contribution limitations by labeling themselves committees.

3. Limitations on Volunteers' Incidental Expenses

[Omitted.]

4. The $25,000 Limitation on Total Contributions During any Calendar Year

In addition to the $1,000 limitation on the nonexempt contributions that an individual may make to a particular candidate for any single election, the Act contains an overall $25,000 limitation on total contributions by an individual during any calendar year. A contribution made in connection with an election is considered, for purposes of this subsection, to be made in the year the election is held. The overall $25,000 ceiling does impose an ultimate restriction upon the number of candidates and committees with which an individual may associate himself by means of financial support. But this quite modest restraint upon protected political activity serves to prevent evasion of the $1,000 contribution limitation by a person who might otherwise contribute massive amounts of money to a particular candidate through the use of unearmarked contributions to political committees likely to contribute to that candidate, or huge contributions to the candidate's political party. The limited, additional restriction on associational freedom imposed by the overall ceiling is thus no more than a corollary of the basic individual contribution limitation that we have found to be constitutionally valid.

C. Expenditure Limitations

The Act's expenditure ceilings impose direct and substantial restraints on the quantity of political speech. The most drastic of the limitations restricts individuals and groups . . . to an expenditure of $1,000 "relative to a clearly identified candidate during a calendar year." Other expenditure ceilings limit spending by candidates, their campaigns, and political parties in connection with election campaigns. It is clear that a primary effect of these expenditure limitations is to restrict the quantity of campaign speech by individuals, groups, and candidates. The restrictions, while neutral as to the ideas expressed, limit political expression "at the core of our electoral process and of the First Amendment freedoms." *Williams v. Rhodes* (1968).

1. The $1,000 Limitation on Expenditures "Relative to a Clearly Identified Candidate"

Section 608(e)(1) provides that "(n)o person may make any expenditure . . . relative to a clearly identified candidate during a calendar year which, when added to all other expenditures made by such person during the year advocating the election or defeat of such candidate, exceeds $1,000."[45] The plain effect of § 608(e)(1) is to prohibit all individuals, who are neither candidates nor owners of institutional press facilities, and all groups, except political parties and campaign organizations, from voicing their views "relative to a clearly identified candidate" through means that entail aggregate expenditures of more than $1,000 during a calendar year. The provision, for example, would make it a federal criminal offense for a person or association to place a single one-quarter page advertisement "relative to a clearly identified candidate" in a major metropolitan newspaper.

Before examining the interests advanced in support of § 608(e)(1)'s expenditure ceiling, consideration must be given to appellants' contention that the provision is unconstitutionally vague. Close examination of the specificity of the statutory limitation is required where, as here, the legislation imposes criminal penalties in an area permeated by First Amendment interests. The test is whether the language of § 608(e)(1) affords the "(p)recision of regulation (that) must be the touchstone in an area so closely touching our most precious freedoms." *NAACP v. Button* [(1963)].

The key operative language of the provision limits "any expenditure . . . relative to a clearly identified candidate." Although "expenditure," "clearly identified," and "candidate" are defined in the Act, there is no definition clarifying what expenditures are "relative to" a candidate. The use of so indefinite a phrase as "relative to" a candidate fails to clearly mark the boundary between permissible and impermissible speech, unless other portions of § 608(e)(1) make sufficiently explicit the range of expenditures covered by the limitation. The section prohibits "any expenditure . . . relative to a clearly identified candidate during a calendar year which, when added to all other expenditures . . . *advocating the*

45. The statute provides some limited exceptions [including] "any news story, commentary, or editorial distributed through the facilities of any broadcasting station, newspaper, magazine, or other periodical publication, unless such facilities are owned or controlled by any political party, political committee, or candidate."

election or defeat of such candidate, exceeds, $1,000." This context clearly permits, if indeed it does not require, the phrase "relative to" a candidate to be read to mean "advocating the election or defeat of" a candidate.

But while such a construction of § 608(e)(1) refocuses the vagueness question, the distinction between discussion of issues and candidates and advocacy of election or defeat of candidates may often dissolve in practical application. Candidates, especially incumbents, are intimately tied to public issues involving legislative proposals and governmental actions. Not only do candidates campaign on the basis of their positions on various public issues, but campaigns themselves generate issues of public interest.

The constitutional deficiencies can be avoided only by reading § 608(e)(1) as limited to communications that include explicit words of advocacy of election or defeat of a candidate. This is the reading of the provision suggested by the non-governmental appellees in arguing that "(f)unds spent to propagate one's views on issues without expressly calling for a candidate's election or defeat are thus not covered." We agree that in order to preserve the provision against invalidation on vagueness grounds, § 608(e)(1) must be construed to apply only to expenditures for communications that in express terms advocate the election or defeat of a clearly identified candidate for federal office.[52]

We turn then to the basic First Amendment question whether § 608(e)(1), even as thus narrowly and explicitly construed, impermissibly burdens the constitutional right of free expression.

The discussion in Part I-A explains why the Act's expenditure limitations impose far greater restraints on the freedom of speech and association than do its contribution limitations. The markedly greater burden on basic freedoms caused by § 608(e)(1) thus cannot be sustained simply by invoking the interest in maximizing the effectiveness of the less intrusive contribution limitations. Rather, the constitutionality of § 608(e)(1) turns on whether the governmental interests advanced in its support satisfy the exacting scrutiny applicable to limitations on core First Amendment rights of political expression.

We find that the governmental interest in preventing corruption and the appearance of corruption is inadequate to justify § 608(e)(1)'s ceiling on independent expenditures. First, assuming, arguendo, that large independent expenditures pose the same dangers of actual or apparent quid pro quo arrangements as do large contributions, § 608(e)(1) does not provide an answer that sufficiently relates to the elimination of those dangers. Unlike the contribution limitations' total ban on the giving of large amounts of money to candidates, § 608(e)(1) prevents only some large expenditures. So long as persons and groups eschew expenditures that in express terms advocate the election or defeat of a clearly identified candidate, they are free to spend as much as they want to promote the candidate

52. This construction would restrict the application of § 608(e)(1) to communications containing express words of advocacy of election or defeat, such as "vote for," "elect," "support," "cast your ballot for," "Smith for Congress," "vote against," "defeat," "reject."

and his views. The exacting interpretation of the statutory language necessary to avoid unconstitutional vagueness thus undermines the limitation's effectiveness as a loophole-closing provision by facilitating circumvention by those seeking to exert improper influence upon a candidate or office-holder. It would naively underestimate the ingenuity and resourcefulness of persons and groups desiring to buy influence to believe that they would have much difficulty devising expenditures that skirted the restriction on express advocacy of election or defeat but nevertheless benefited the candidate's campaign. Yet no substantial societal interest would be served by a loophole-closing provision designed to check corruption that permitted unscrupulous persons and organizations to expend unlimited sums of money in order to obtain improper influence over candidates for elective office.

Second, quite apart from the shortcomings of § 608(e)(1) in preventing any abuses generated by large independent expenditures, the independent advocacy restricted by the provision does not presently appear to pose dangers of real or apparent corruption comparable to those identified with large campaign contributions. The parties defending § 608(e)(1) contend that it is necessary to prevent would-be contributors from avoiding the contribution limitations by the simple expedient of paying directly for media advertisements or for other portions of the candidate's campaign activities. They argue that expenditures controlled by or coordinated with the candidate and his campaign might well have virtually the same value to the candidate as a contribution and would pose similar dangers of abuse. Yet such controlled or coordinated expenditures are treated as contributions rather than expenditures under the Act. Section 608(b)'s contribution ceilings rather than § 608(e)(1)'s independent expenditure limitation prevent attempts to circumvent the Act through prearranged or coordinated expenditures amounting to disguised contributions. By contrast, § 608(e)(1) limits expenditures for express advocacy of candidates made totally independently of the candidate and his campaign. Unlike contributions, such independent expenditures may well provide little assistance to the candidate's campaign and indeed may prove counterproductive. The absence of prearrangement and coordination of an expenditure with the candidate or his agent not only undermines the value of the expenditure to the candidate, but also alleviates the danger that expenditures will be given as a quid pro quo for improper commitments from the candidate. Rather than preventing circumvention of the contribution limitations, § 608(e)(1) severely restricts all independent advocacy despite its substantially diminished potential for abuse.

While the independent expenditure ceiling thus fails to serve any substantial governmental interest in stemming the reality or appearance of corruption in the electoral process, it heavily burdens core First Amendment expression. Advocacy of the election or defeat of candidates for federal office is no less entitled to protection under the First Amendment than the discussion of political policy generally or advocacy of the passage or defeat of legislation.

It is argued, however, that the ancillary governmental interest in equalizing the relative ability of individuals and groups to influence the outcome of elections serves to justify the limitation on express advocacy of the election or defeat of candidates imposed by § 608(e)(1)'s expenditure ceiling. But the concept that government may restrict the speech of some elements of our society in order to enhance the relative voice of others is wholly foreign to the First Amendment, which was designed "to secure 'the widest possible dissemination of information from diverse and antagonistic sources,'" and "'to assure unfettered interchange of ideas for the bringing about of political and social changes desired by the people.'" *New York Times Co. v. Sullivan.* The First Amendment's protection against governmental abridgment of free expression cannot properly be made to depend on a person's financial ability to engage in public discussion.

For the reasons stated, we conclude that § 608(e)(1)'s independent expenditure limitation is unconstitutional under the First Amendment.[56]

2. Limitation on Expenditures by Candidates from Personal or Family Resources

The Act also sets limits on expenditures by a candidate "from his personal funds, or the personal funds of his immediate family, in connection with his campaigns during any calendar year." These ceilings vary from $50,000 for Presidential or Vice Presidential candidates to $35,000 for senatorial candidates, and $25,000 for most candidates for the House of Representatives.

[For essentially the same reasons that the independent expenditure limitation is unconstitutional, we] hold that § 608(a)'s restriction on a candidate's personal expenditures is unconstitutional.

3. Limitations on Campaign Expenditures

Section 608(c) places limitations on overall campaign expenditures by candidates seeking nomination for election and election to federal office.

No governmental interest that has been suggested is sufficient to justify the restriction on the quantity of political expression imposed by § 608(c)'s campaign expenditure limitations. The major evil associated with rapidly increasing campaign expenditures is the danger of candidate dependence on large contributions. The interest in alleviating the corrupting influence of large contributions is served by the Act's contribution limitations and disclosure provisions rather than by § 608(c)'s campaign expenditure ceilings.

The campaign expenditure ceilings appear to be designed primarily to serve the governmental interests in reducing the allegedly skyrocketing costs of political campaigns. [T]he mere growth in the cost of federal election campaigns in and of itself provides no

56. The Act exempts most elements of the institutional press, limiting only expenditures by institutional press facilities that are owned or controlled by candidates and political parties. But, whatever differences there may be between the constitutional guarantees of a free press and of free speech, it is difficult to conceive of any principled basis upon which to distinguish § 608(e)(1)'s limitations upon the public at large and similar limitations imposed upon the press specifically. [Footnote relocated]—EDS.

basis for governmental restrictions on the quantity of campaign spending and the resulting limitation on the scope of federal campaigns.

For these reasons we hold that § 608(c) is constitutionally invalid.

In sum, the provisions of the Act that impose a $1,000 limitation on contributions to a single candidate, a $5,000 limitation on contributions by a political committee to a single candidate, and a $25,000 limitation on total contributions by an individual during any calendar year, are constitutionally valid. These limitations, along with the disclosure provisions, constitute the Act's primary weapons against the reality or appearance of improper influence stemming from the dependence of candidates on large campaign contributions. The contribution ceilings thus serve the basic governmental interest in safeguarding the integrity of the electoral process without directly impinging upon the rights of individual citizens and candidates to engage in political debate and discussion. By contrast, the First Amendment requires the invalidation of the Act's independent expenditure ceiling, its limitation on a candidate's expenditures from his own personal funds, and its ceilings on overall campaign expenditures. These provisions place substantial and direct restrictions on the ability of candidates, citizens, and associations to engage in protected political expression, restrictions that the First Amendment cannot tolerate.

Mr. Chief Justice BURGER, concurring in part and dissenting in part.

The contribution limitations infringe on First Amendment liberties and suffer from the same infirmities that the Court correctly sees in the expenditure ceilings.

More broadly, the Court's result does violence to the intent of Congress in this comprehensive scheme of campaign finance. By dissecting the Act bit by bit, and casting off vital parts, the Court fails to recognize that the whole of this Act is greater than the sum of its parts. Congress intended to regulate all aspects of federal campaign finances, but what remains after today's holding leaves no more than a shadow of what Congress contemplated. I question whether the residue leaves a workable program.

CONTRIBUTION AND EXPENDITURE LIMITS

I agree fully with that part of the Court's opinion that holds unconstitutional the limitations the Act puts on campaign expenditures which "place substantial and direct restrictions on the ability of candidates, citizens, and associations to engage in protected political expression, restrictions that the First Amendment cannot tolerate." Yet when it approves similarly stringent limitations on contributions, the Court ignores the reasons it finds so persuasive in the context of expenditures. For me contributions and expenditures are two sides of the same First Amendment coin.

[THE STATUTE AS A WHOLE]

I cannot join in the attempt to determine which parts of the Act can survive review here. The statute as it now stands is unworkable and inequitable.

Given the unfortunate record of past attempts to draw distinctions of this kind, it is not too much to predict that the Court's holding will invite avoidance, if not evasion of the intent of the Act, with "independent" committees undertaking "unauthorized" activities in order to escape the limits on contributions.

Mr. Justice WHITE, concurring in part and dissenting in part.

I am in agreement with the Court's judgment upholding the limitations on contributions. I dissent, however, from the Court's view that the expenditure limitations violate the First Amendment.

It would make little sense to me, and apparently made none to Congress, to limit the amounts an individual may give to a candidate or spend with his approval but fail to limit the amounts that could be spent on his behalf. Yet the Court permits the former while striking down the latter limitation. No more than $1,000 may be given to a candidate or spent at his request or with his approval or cooperation; but otherwise, apparently, a contributor is to be constitutionally protected in spending unlimited amounts of money in support of his chosen candidate or candidates.

I would take the word of those who know that limiting independent expenditures is essential to prevent transparent and widespread evasion of the contribution limits.

It is also important to restore and maintain public confidence in federal elections. It is critical to obviate or dispel the impression that federal elections are purely and simply a function of money, that federal offices are bought and sold or that political races are reserved for those who have the facility and the stomach for doing whatever it takes to bring together those interests, groups, and individuals that can raise or contribute large fortunes in order to prevail at the polls.

As with the campaign expenditure limits, Congress was entitled to determine that personal wealth ought to play a less important role in political campaigns than it has in the past. Nothing in the First Amendment stands in the way of that determination.

For these reasons I respectfully dissent from the Court's [decision striking down the independent expenditure limitation, the total campaign expenditure limitation, and the limitation on the amount of money that a candidate or his family may spend on his campaign.]

Mr. Justice MARSHALL, concurring in part and dissenting in part.

I join in all of the Court's opinion except Part I-C-2, which deals with 18 U.S.C. § 608(a) (1970 ed., Supp. IV). That section limits the amount a candidate may spend from his personal funds, or family funds under his control, in connection with his campaigns during any calendar year. The Court invalidates § 608(a) as violative of the candidate's First Amendment rights.

To be sure, § 608(a) affects the candidate's exercise of his First Amendment rights. But unlike the other expenditure limitations contained in the Act and invalidated by the

Court, the limitations on expenditures by candidates from personal resources contained in § 608(a) need never prevent the speaker from spending another dollar to communicate his ideas. Section 608(a) imposes no overall limit on the amount a candidate can spend; it simply limits the "contribution" a candidate may make to his own campaign. The candidate remains free to raise an unlimited amount in contributions from others. So long as the candidate does not contribute to his campaign more than the amount specified in § 608(a), and so long as he does not accept contributions from others in excess of the limitations imposed by § 608(b), he is free to spend without limit on behalf of his campaign.

The Court views "(t)he ancillary interest in equalizing the relative financial resources of candidates" as the relevant rationale for § 608(a), and deems that interest insufficient to justify § 608(a). In my view the interest is more precisely the interest in promoting the reality and appearance of equal access to the political arena. [This provision] emerges not simply as a device to reduce the natural advantage of the wealthy candidate, but as a provision providing some symmetry to a regulatory scheme that otherwise enhances the natural advantage of the wealthy. I therefore respectfully dissent from the Court's invalidation of § 608(a).

Mr. Justice REHNQUIST, concurring in part and dissenting in part. [Omitted; Justice Rehnquist dissented on an aspect of the majority's opinion dealing with minor political parties and independent candidates.]

Mr. Justice BLACKMUN, concurring in part and dissenting in part. [Omitted; same position as C.J. BURGER.]

NOTES ON *BUCKLEY*

1. Count the votes: Seven Justices (all but Burger and Blackmun) voted to uphold the contribution limitations; eight Justices (all but White) voted to strike down the independent expenditure limitations.
2. Is spending money on elections a form of "speech" that the First Amendment must protect? The "money equals speech" proposition from *Buckley* is generally well-settled. But need it be so? Are there any arguments against construing campaign spending as speech? *Buckley* might be dependent on the proposition that spending money is itself expressive activity that the First Amendment protects, but it also could rely on the notion that money is critically instrumental to the production and dissemination of expression—including books, films, or any other medium of expression. Which, if either, is a better justification for the decision?

   Would the First Amendment tolerate limits on spending money for speech unrelated to campaigns—for example, money to produce Hollywood movies or TV shows (even ones with political themes, like "The Campaign" or "The West Wing")? Or would the First Amendment tolerate limits on the amount of money a university or think tank could spend to develop innovative public policy proposals? Or for a newspaper to report on, and editorialize about, politics? If not, then why might the First Amendment permit spending limits with respect to campaign-specific speech? Is the answer (at least for those who disagree with *Buckley* on this point) that campaign speech is tantamount to a public debate on which candidate should win and therefore subject to "equal time" rules analogous to other forms of public debate? After all, at a Supreme Court oral argument, each side has exactly 30 minutes to make its case; neither side is permitted to purchase extra time. The same is true for the formal debates between presidential candidates, or debates in Congress. Is the debate analogy legitimate with respect to campaign advertisements purchased to support or oppose a candidate's election?

3. Is there a clear line between contributions and independent expenditures? One potential problem arises if a candidate controls someone else's expenditures that purport to be independent but in fact are not. Suppose an individual says to a candidate, "Rather than my donating money to your campaign, tell me what you'd like me to do with my money." This would be an obvious end-run around the contribution limit. Consequently, FECA deems such "coordinated expenditures" to be "contributions" and thus to fall within the contribution limitations. In other words, "independent" expenditures must truly be independent of the campaign, making them the speaker's own speech. But what if, without direct coordination, candidates are able to signal to their outside supporters what kinds of ads they would like to be run through independent expenditures? In the current era of the Internet and the 24-hour news cycle, this kind of signaling may be much easier than in the past. In the 2012 election, all of the spending by the so-called "super PACs" was supposed to be independent and uncoordinated with a candidate's own campaign (more on "super PACs" later), but is the "independence" of this spending entirely a fiction? If so, has the fundamental conceptual distinction in *Buckley* between contributions and independent expenditures completely broken down?
4. One recurring theme of those who oppose campaign finance regulations is that they are unnecessary because criminal sanctions and disclosure laws can handle corruption or the appearance of corruption. As the majority in *Buckley* notes, however, Congress determined that more direct regulations are required. Keep this debate in mind as you move through the material that follows.
5. Note Chief Justice Burger's prediction that political operatives will still be able to spend large amounts of money on political campaigns regardless of FECA's contribution limitations, particularly by channeling money through independent expenditures. Put differently, if one goal of contribution limitations is to reduce the amount of money in politics, that plainly has not occurred, as campaigns have become more and more expensive. Is this a problem of our electoral system, or a virtue?

2. "Soft Money" and Political Party Spending

After almost three decades under the FECA system, Congress realized that candidates and political parties had found ways around FECA's contribution limitations. Part of the culprit was the Federal Election Commission's "allocation" regime, which construed political parties' mixed-purpose activities—generic party activities such as get-out-the-vote drives that benefit both the party and federal candidates—as not constituting "contributions" under FECA. Thus, parties were allowed to raise and spend unlimited amounts of this so-called "soft money," which is money not expressly directed solely at the election or defeat of a federal candidate. That is, "soft money" was considered "nonfederal" because it was not tied explicitly to the election of a federal candidate and therefore was raised outside of the limits and prohibitions of federal campaign finance law. Of course, however, many party-building "nonfederal" purposes have a significant effect on federal candidates. In addition, there was a tremendous rise in unlimited "issue advertising" that omitted the use of "magic words" (expressly advocating the election or defeat of a candidate) so as not to fall within FECA's regulation. Congress sought to close both of these loopholes in the Bipartisan Campaign Reform Act of 2002 (BCRA), sometimes referred to as McCain-Feingold after its two main sponsors, Senators John McCain and Russ Feingold. The most significant portions of BCRA banned the national political parties from raising or spending "soft money" and limited corporate and union independent expenditures.

The next case presents the initial constitutional challenge to BCRA and its consideration of the Act's various limitations on soft money. Later, in *Citizens United*, we will analyze BCRA's prohibition on "electioneering communication."

The Court ruled, 5-4, to uphold the soft money limitations, with the more "liberal" Justices (along with Justice O'Connor) in the majority. By contrast, Justice Kennedy in dissent would have struck down the soft money ban as an unconstitutional expenditure limitation. One of the main disputes between the majority and the dissent in this case is whether a soft money ban is more like a contribution limitation or an expenditure limitation. As we know from *Buckley*, a contribution limitation receives less scrutiny than an independent expenditure limitation, which is generally unconstitutional.

As you are reading this case, pay attention to the discussion of the rise of "soft money" in elections. Where does this money come from? Was the goal of BCRA's soft money regulations simply to limit the influence of political parties in how they can spend money? Indeed, the most significant part of BCRA Title I is § 323(a), which prohibits National Party committees and their agents from soliciting, receiving, directing, or spending any soft money. What is the governmental interest in this provision? Is it trying to root out the same type of corruption that the government sought to eliminate in *Buckley*? Or has the conception of corruption shifted?

In particular, think about the Court's construction of Congress's main interest in passing BCRA: to eliminate corruption and the appearance of corruption in campaigns.

Should "corruption" have a broad or narrow definition? How do the majority and dissenting opinions differ in their definitions of corruption? Congress had a further goal of anticircumvention: the desire to create rules to ensure that candidates and political parties cannot circumvent valid contribution limitations, that is, to close loopholes in the law.

Finally, consider what Congress was really trying to do here: (1) prevent the corruption of candidates (or its appearance) through soft money gifts to parties; and (2) limit campaign spending by corporations, unions, and wealthy individuals on both sides of the aisle, again in the name of preventing corruption or the appearance of corruption. The majority states that limiting donations from wealthy individuals and groups will increase the number of donors a candidate or party must solicit, thus opening up the campaign to many more people. Moreover, Congress determined—based in part on evidence in the years after *Buckley*—that large donations to incumbents create an unacceptably high risk of corruption or at least the appearance of corruption. Is the dissent's response to this evidence to deny it factually, or instead to argue that officeholders inevitably will become beholden to financial interests and that this influence-peddling is a necessary offspring of First Amendment freedom?

McCONNELL v. FEDERAL ELECTION COMMISSION

540 U.S. 93 (2003)†

Justice STEVENS and Justice O'CONNOR delivered the opinion of the Court with respect to BCRA Titles I and II.*

The Bipartisan Campaign Reform Act of 2002 (BCRA), contains a series of amendments to the Federal Election Campaign Act of 1971 (FECA or Act), and other portions of the United States Code, that are challenged in these cases. In this opinion we discuss Titles I and II of BCRA. [What follows here is the Court's discussion of the background of BCRA and its legal analysis of Title I, the "soft money" part of the statute. We have omitted the portion of the Court's opinion addressing Title II and the "electioneering communications" part of the statute, as the Court overruled that portion of *McConnell* in 2010 in *Citizens United v. FEC.*]

I

BCRA is the most recent federal enactment designed to purge national politics of what was conceived to be the pernicious influence of "big money" campaign contributions.

Three important developments in the years after our decision in *Buckley* persuaded Congress that further legislation was necessary to regulate the role that corporations, unions, and wealthy contributors play in the electoral process. As a preface to our discussion of the specific provisions of BCRA, we comment briefly on the increased importance

† [Disclosure: One of the casebook authors served as a consultant to the attorneys representing Senators McCain and Feingold and the other legislative sponsors of the statute, who were Intervenor-Defendants in the case.—EDS.]

* Justice SOUTER, Justice GINSBURG, and Justice BREYER join this opinion in its entirety.

of "soft money," the proliferation of "issue ads," and the disturbing findings of a Senate investigation into campaign practices related to the 1996 federal elections.

Soft Money

Under FECA, "contributions" must be made with funds that are subject to the Act's disclosure requirements and source and amount limitations. Such funds are known as "federal" or "hard" money. FECA defines the term "contribution," however, to include only the gift or advance of anything of value "made by any person for the purpose of influencing any election for *Federal* office." 2 U.S.C. § 431(8)(A)(i) (emphasis added). Donations made solely for the purpose of influencing state or local elections are therefore unaffected by FECA's requirements and prohibitions. As a result, prior to the enactment of BCRA, federal law permitted corporations and unions, as well as individuals who had already made the maximum permissible contributions to federal candidates, to contribute "nonfederal money"—also known as "soft money"—to political parties for activities intended to influence state or local elections.

Shortly after *Buckley* was decided, questions arose concerning the treatment of contributions intended to influence both federal and state elections. Although a literal reading of FECA's definition of "contribution" would have required such activities to be funded with hard money, the FEC ruled that political parties could fund mixed-purpose activities—including get-out-the-vote drives and generic party advertising—in part with soft money. In 1995 the FEC concluded that the parties could also use soft money to defray the costs of "legislative advocacy media advertisements," even if the ads mentioned the name of a federal candidate, so long as they did not expressly advocate the candidate's election or defeat.

As the permissible uses of soft money expanded, the amount of soft money raised and spent by the national political parties increased exponentially. Of the two major parties' total spending, soft money accounted for 5% ($21.6 million) in 1984, 11% ($45 million) in 1988, 16% ($80 million) in 1992, 30% ($272 million) in 1996, and 42% ($498 million) in 2000. The national parties transferred large amounts of their soft money to the state parties, which were allowed to use a larger percentage of soft money to finance mixed-purpose activities under FEC rules. In the year 2000, for example, the national parties diverted $280 million—more than half of their soft money—to state parties.

Many contributions of soft money were dramatically larger than the contributions of hard money permitted by FECA. For example, in 1996 the top five corporate soft-money donors gave, in total, more than $9 million in nonfederal funds to the two national party committees. In the most recent election cycle the political parties raised almost $300 million—60% of their total soft-money fundraising—from just 800 donors, each of which contributed a minimum of $120,000. Moreover, the largest corporate donors often made substantial contributions to both parties. Such practices corroborate evidence indicating that many corporate contributions were motivated by a desire for access to candidates and a fear of being placed at a disadvantage in the legislative process relative to other contributors, rather than by ideological support for the candidates and parties.

The solicitation, transfer, and use of soft money thus enabled parties and candidates to circumvent FECA's limitations on the source and amount of contributions in connection with federal elections.

Issue Advertising

In *Buckley* we construed FECA's disclosure and reporting requirements, as well as its expenditure limitations, "to reach only funds used for communications that expressly advocate the election or defeat of a clearly identified candidate." As a result of that strict reading of the statute, the use or omission of "magic words" such as "Elect John Smith" or "Vote Against Jane Doe" marked a bright statutory line separating "express advocacy" from "issue advocacy." Express advocacy was subject to FECA's limitations and could be financed only using hard money. The political parties, in other words, could not use soft money to sponsor ads that used any magic words, and corporations and unions could not fund such ads out of their general treasuries. So-called issue ads, on the other hand, not only could be financed with soft money, but could be aired without disclosing the identity of, or any other information about, their sponsors.

While the distinction between "issue" and express advocacy seemed neat in theory, the two categories of advertisements proved functionally identical in important respects. Both were used to advocate the election or defeat of clearly identified federal candidates, even though the so-called issue ads eschewed the use of magic words. Little difference existed, for example, between an ad that urged viewers to "vote against Jane Doe" and one that condemned Jane Doe's record on a particular issue before exhorting viewers to "call Jane Doe and tell her what you think." Indeed, campaign professionals testified that the most effective campaign ads, like the most effective commercials for products such as Coca-Cola, should, and did, avoid the use of the magic words.

Because FECA's disclosure requirements did not apply to so-called issue ads, sponsors of such ads often used misleading names to conceal their identity. "Citizens for Better Medicare," for instance, was not a grassroots organization of citizens, as its name might suggest, but was instead a platform for an association of drug manufacturers. And "Republicans for Clean Air," which ran ads in the 2000 Republican Presidential primary, was actually an organization consisting of just two individuals—brothers who together spent $25 million on ads supporting their favored candidate.

While the public may not have been fully informed about the sponsorship of so-called issue ads, the record indicates that candidates and officeholders often were. A former Senator confirmed that candidates and officials knew who their friends were and "sometimes suggest[ed] that corporations or individuals make donations to interest groups that run 'issue ads.'" As with soft-money contributions, political parties and candidates used the availability of so-called issue ads to circumvent FECA's limitations, asking donors who contributed their permitted quota of hard money to give money to nonprofit corporations to spend on "issue" advocacy.

Senate Committee Investigation

In 1998 the Senate Committee on Governmental Affairs issued a six-volume report summarizing the results of an extensive investigation into the campaign practices in the 1996 federal elections. The report gave particular attention to the effect of soft money on the American political system, including elected officials' practice of granting special access in return for political contributions.

The committee's principal findings relating to Democratic Party fundraising were set forth in the majority's report, while the minority report primarily described Republican practices. The two reports reached consensus, however, on certain central propositions. They agreed that the "soft money loophole" had led to a "meltdown" of the campaign finance system that had been intended "to keep corporate, union and large individual contributions from influencing the electoral process." One Senator stated that "the hearings provided overwhelming evidence that the twin loopholes of soft money and bogus issue advertising have virtually destroyed our campaign finance laws, leaving us with little more than a pile of legal rubble."

The report was critical of both parties' methods of raising soft money, as well as their use of those funds. It concluded that both parties promised and provided special access to candidates and senior Government officials in exchange for large soft-money contributions. The committee majority described the White House coffees that rewarded major donors with access to President Clinton, and the courtesies extended to an international businessman named Roger Tamraz, who candidly acknowledged that his donations of about $300,000 to the DNC and to state parties were motivated by his interest in gaining the Federal Government's support for an oil-line project in the Caucasus. The minority described the promotional materials used by the RNC's two principal donor programs, "Team 100" and the "Republican Eagles," which promised "special access to high-ranking Republican elected officials, including governors, senators, and representatives." One fundraising letter recited that the chairman of the RNC had personally escorted a donor on appointments that "turned out to be very significant in legislation affecting public utility holding companies" and made the donor "a hero in his industry."

In 1996 both parties began to use large amounts of soft money to pay for issue advertising designed to influence federal elections. The committee found such ads highly problematic for two reasons. Since they accomplished the same purposes as express advocacy (which could lawfully be funded only with hard money), the ads enabled unions, corporations, and wealthy contributors to circumvent protections that FECA was intended to provide. Moreover, though ostensibly independent of the candidates, the ads were often actually coordinated with, and controlled by, the campaigns. The ads thus provided a means for evading FECA's candidate contribution limits.

The report also emphasized the role of state and local parties. While the FEC's allocation regime permitted national parties to use soft money to pay for up to 40% of the costs of both generic voter activities and issue advertising, they allowed state and local parties to use larger percentages of soft money for those purposes. For that reason, national parties often made substantial transfers of soft money to "state and local political parties for 'generic voter activities' that in fact ultimately benefit[ed] federal candidates because the funds for all practical purposes remain[ed] under the control of the national committees." The report concluded that "[t]he use of such soft money thus allow[ed] more corporate, union treasury, and large contributions from wealthy individuals into the system."

The report discussed potential reforms, including a ban on soft money at the national and state party levels and restrictions on sham issue advocacy by nonparty groups. The majority expressed the view that a ban on the raising of soft money by national party committees would effectively address the use of union and corporate general treasury funds in the federal political process only if it required that candidate-specific ads be funded with hard money. The minority similarly recommended the elimination of soft-money contributions to political parties from individuals, corporations, and unions, as well as "reforms addressing candidate advertisements masquerading as issue ads."

II

In BCRA, Congress enacted many of the committee's proposed reforms. BCRA's central provisions are designed to address Congress' concerns about the increasing use of soft money and issue advertising to influence federal elections. Title I regulates the use of soft money by political parties, officeholders, and candidates.

III

Title I is Congress' effort to plug the soft-money loophole. The cornerstone of Title I is new FECA § 323(a), which prohibits national party committees and their agents from soliciting, receiving, directing, or spending any soft money. In short, § 323(a) takes national parties out of the soft-money business.

Plaintiffs mount a facial First Amendment challenge to new FECA § 323, as well as challenges based on the Elections Clause, U.S. Const., Art. I, § 4, principles of federalism, and the equal protection component of the Due Process Clause. We address these challenges in turn.

A

In *Buckley* and subsequent cases, we have subjected restrictions on campaign expenditures to closer scrutiny than limits on campaign contributions. In these cases we have recognized that contribution limits, unlike limits on expenditures, "entai[l] only a marginal restriction upon the contributor's ability to engage in free communication."

Because the communicative value of large contributions inheres mainly in their ability to facilitate the speech of their recipients, we have said that contribution limits impose serious burdens on free speech only if they are so low as to "preven[t] candidates and political committees from amassing the resources necessary for effective advocacy."

Like the contribution limits we upheld in *Buckley*, § 323's restrictions have only a marginal impact on the ability of contributors, candidates, officeholders, and parties to engage in effective political speech. Complex as its provisions may be, § 323, in the main, does little more than regulate the ability of wealthy individuals, corporations, and unions to contribute large sums of money to influence federal elections, federal candidates, and federal officeholders.

Plaintiffs contend that we must apply strict scrutiny to § 323 because many of its provisions restrict not only contributions but also the spending and solicitation of funds raised outside of FECA's contribution limits. But for purposes of determining the level of scrutiny, it is irrelevant that Congress chose in § 323 to regulate contributions on the demand rather than the supply side. The relevant inquiry is whether the mechanism adopted to implement the contribution limit, or to prevent circumvention of that limit, burdens speech in a way that a direct restriction on the contribution itself would not. That is not the case here.

For example, while § 323(a) prohibits national parties from receiving or spending nonfederal money, and § 323(b) prohibits state party committees from spending non-federal money on federal election activities, neither provision in any way limits the total amount of money parties can spend. Rather, they simply limit the source and individual amount of donations. That they do so by prohibiting the spending of soft money does not render them expenditure limitations.

Section 323 thus shows "due regard for the reality that solicitation is characteristically intertwined with informative and perhaps persuasive speech seeking support for particular causes or for particular views." *Schaumburg v. Citizens for a Better Environment* (1980). The fact that party committees and federal candidates and officeholders must now ask only for limited dollar amounts or request that a corporation or union contribute money through its PAC in no way alters or impairs the political message "intertwined" with the solicitation. And rather than chill such solicitations, the restriction here tends to increase the dissemination of information by forcing parties, candidates, and officeholders to solicit from a wider array of potential donors. As with direct limits on contributions, therefore, § 323's spending and solicitation restrictions have only a marginal impact on political speech.

Finally, plaintiffs contend that the type of associational burdens that § 323 imposes are fundamentally different from the burdens that accompanied *Buckley*'s contribution limits, and merit the type of strict scrutiny we have applied to attempts to regulate the internal processes of political parties. *E.g.*, *California Democratic Party v. Jones* (2000).

In making this argument, plaintiffs greatly exaggerate the effect of § 323, contending that it precludes *any* collaboration among national, state, and local committees of the same party in fundraising and electioneering activities. We do not read the provisions in that way. Section 323 merely subjects a greater percentage of contributions to parties and candidates to FECA's source and amount limitations. *Buckley* has already acknowledged that such limitations "leave the contributor free to become a member of any political association and to assist personally in the association's efforts on behalf of candidates." The modest impact that § 323 has on the ability of committees within a party to associate with each other does not independently occasion strict scrutiny. None of this is to suggest that the alleged associational burdens imposed on parties by § 323 have no place in the First Amendment analysis; it is only that we account for them in the application, rather than the choice, of the appropriate level of scrutiny.

With these principles in mind, we apply the less rigorous scrutiny applicable to contribution limits to evaluate the constitutionality of new FECA § 323. Because the five challenged provisions of § 323 implicate different First Amendment concerns, we discuss them separately. We are mindful, however, that Congress enacted § 323 as an integrated whole to vindicate the Government's important interest in preventing corruption and the appearance of corruption.

New FECA § 323(a)'s Restrictions on National Party Committees

The core of Title I is new FECA § 323(a), which provides that "national committee[s] of a political party . . . may not solicit, receive, or direct to another person a contribution, donation, or transfer of funds or any other thing of value, or spend any funds, that are not subject to the limitations, prohibitions, and reporting requirements of this Act." 2 U.S.C. § 441i(a)(1) (Supp. 2003). The prohibition extends to "any officer or agent acting on behalf of such a national committee, and any entity that is directly or indirectly established, financed, maintained, or controlled by such a national committee." § 441i(a)(2).

The main goal of § 323(a) is modest. In large part, it simply effects a return to the scheme that was approved in *Buckley* and that was subverted by the creation of the FEC's allocation regime, which permitted the political parties to fund federal electioneering efforts with a combination of hard and soft money. Under that allocation regime, national parties were able to use vast amounts of soft money in their efforts to elect federal candidates. Consequently, as long as they directed the money to the political parties, donors could contribute large amounts of soft money for use in activities designed to influence federal elections. New § 323(a) is designed to put a stop to that practice.

1. Governmental Interests Underlying New FECA § 323(a)

The Government defends § 323(a)'s ban on national parties' involvement with soft money as necessary to prevent the actual and apparent corruption of federal candidates and officeholders. Our cases have made clear that the prevention of corruption or its appearance constitutes a sufficiently important interest to justify political contribution limits. We have not limited that interest to the elimination of cash-for-votes exchanges. In *Buckley*, we expressly rejected the argument that antibribery laws provided a less restrictive alternative to FECA's contribution limits, noting that such laws "deal[t] with only the most blatant and specific attempts of those with money to influence governmental action." Thus, "[i]n speaking of 'improper influence' and 'opportunities for abuse' in addition to '*quid pro quo* arrangements,' we [have] recognized a concern not confined to bribery of public officials, but extending to the broader threat from politicians too compliant with the wishes of large contributors." [*Nixon v. Shrink Missouri Government PAC* (2000)]; *see also* [*FEC v. Colorado Republican Campaign Committee* (2001) (*Colorado II*)] (acknowledging that corruption extends beyond explicit cash-for-votes agreements to "undue influence on an officeholder's judgment").

Of "almost equal" importance has been the Government's interest in combating the appearance or perception of corruption engendered by large campaign contributions. Take away Congress' authority to regulate the appearance of undue influence and "the cynical assumption that large donors call the tune could jeopardize the willingness of voters to take part in democratic governance." *Shrink Missouri.* And because the First Amendment does not require Congress to ignore the fact that candidates, donors, and parties test the limits of the current law, these interests have been sufficient to justify not only contribution limits themselves, but laws preventing the circumvention of such limits.

The idea that large contributions to a national party can corrupt or, at the very least, create the appearance of corruption of federal candidates and officeholders is neither novel nor implausible. For nearly 30 years, FECA has placed strict dollar limits and source restrictions on contributions that individuals and other entities can give to national, state, and local party committees for the purpose of influencing a federal election. The premise behind these restrictions has been, and continues to be, that contributions to a federal candidate's party in aid of that candidate's campaign threaten to create—no less than would a direct contribution to the candidate—a sense of obligation. This is particularly true of contributions to national parties, with which federal candidates and officeholders enjoy a special relationship and unity of interest. This close affiliation has placed national parties in a unique position, "whether they like it or not," to serve as "agents for spending on behalf of those who seek to produce obligated officeholders." *Colorado II.*

The question for present purposes is whether large *soft-money* contributions to national party committees have a corrupting influence or give rise to the appearance of corruption. Both common sense and the ample record in these cases confirm Congress' belief that they do. [T]he FEC's allocation regime has invited widespread circumvention of FECA's limits on contributions to parties for the purpose of influencing federal elections. Under this system, corporate, union, and wealthy individual donors have been free to contribute substantial sums of soft money to the national parties, which the parties can spend for the specific purpose of influencing a particular candidate's federal election. It is not only plausible, but likely, that candidates would feel grateful for such donations and that donors would seek to exploit that gratitude.

The evidence in the record shows that candidates and donors alike have in fact exploited the soft-money loophole, the former to increase their prospects of election and the latter to create debt on the part of officeholders, with the national parties serving as willing intermediaries. Thus, despite FECA's hard-money limits on direct contributions to candidates, federal officeholders have commonly asked donors to make soft-money donations to national and state committees solely in order to assist federal campaigns, including the officeholder's own. Parties kept tallies of the amounts of soft money raised by each officeholder, and "the amount of money a Member of Congress raise[d] for the national political party committees often affect[ed] the amount the committees g[a]ve to assist the Member's campaign." Donors often asked that their contributions be credited to particular candidates, and the parties obliged, irrespective of whether the funds were hard or soft. National party committees often teamed with individual candidates' campaign committees to create joint fundraising committees, which enabled the candidates to take advantage of the party's higher contribution limits while still allowing donors to give to their preferred candidate. Even when not participating directly in the fundraising, federal officeholders were well aware of the identities of the donors: National party committees would distribute lists of potential or actual donors, or donors themselves would report their generosity to officeholders.

For their part, lobbyists, CEOs, and wealthy individuals alike all have candidly admitted donating substantial sums of soft money to national committees not on ideological grounds, but for the express purpose of securing influence over federal officials.

Particularly telling is the fact that, in 1996 and 2000, more than half of the top 50 soft-money donors gave substantial sums to *both* major national parties, leaving room for no other conclusion but that these donors were seeking influence, or avoiding retaliation, rather than promoting any particular ideology.

The evidence from the federal officeholders' perspective is similar. For example, one former Senator described the influence purchased by nonfederal donations as follows:

> "Too often, Members' first thought is not what is right or what they believe, but how it will affect fundraising. Who, after all, can seriously contend that a $100,000 donation does not alter the way one thinks about—and quite possibly votes on—an issue? . . . When you don't pay the piper that finances your campaigns, you will never get any more money from that piper. Since money is the mother's milk of politics, you never want to be in that situation." [Lower court opinion] (quoting declaration of former Sen. Alan Simpson).

Plaintiffs argue that without concrete evidence of an instance in which a federal officeholder has actually switched a vote (or, presumably, evidence of a specific instance where the public believes a vote was switched), Congress has not shown that there exists real or apparent corruption. But the record is to the contrary. The evidence connects soft money to manipulations of the legislative calendar, leading to Congress' failure to enact, among other things, generic drug legislation, tort reform, and tobacco legislation. To claim that such actions do not change legislative outcomes surely misunderstands the legislative process.*

More importantly, plaintiffs conceive of corruption too narrowly. Our cases have firmly established that Congress' legitimate interest extends beyond preventing simple cash-for-votes corruption to curbing "undue influence on an officeholder's judgment, and the appearance of such influence." *Colorado II.* Many of the "deeply disturbing examples" of corruption cited by this Court in *Buckley* to justify FECA's contribution limits were not episodes of vote buying, but evidence that various corporate interests had given substantial donations to gain access to high-level government officials. Even if that access did not secure actual influence, it certainly gave the "appearance of such influence."

The record in the present case is replete with similar examples of national party committees peddling access to federal candidates and officeholders in exchange for large soft-money donations.

Despite this evidence and the close ties that candidates and officeholders have with their parties, Justice Kennedy would limit Congress' regulatory interest *only* to the prevention of the actual or apparent *quid pro quo* corruption "inherent in" contributions made directly to, contributions made at the express behest of, and expenditures made in coordination with, a federal officeholder or candidate. Regulation of any other donation or expenditure—regardless of its size, the recipient's relationship to the candidate or officeholder, its potential impact on a candidate's election, its value to the candidate, or its unabashed and explicit intent to purchase influence—would, according to Justice Kennedy, simply be out of bounds. This crabbed view of corruption, and particularly of the appearance of corruption, ignores precedent, common sense, and the realities of political fundraising exposed by the record in this litigation.

In sum, there is substantial evidence to support Congress' determination that large soft-money contributions to national political parties give rise to corruption and the appearance of corruption.

* [Editors' note: The Court based its factual determination in this paragraph, at least in part, on evidence contained in a sealed, undisclosed record of specific instances in which soft-money contributions to political parties affected the legislative behavior of Members of Congress. Even though the Court could not discuss this evidence in detail, it seems plausible that it was influential in persuading Justice O'Connor, who had been skeptical of the government's position at oral argument—but who herself had been a member of Arizona's state legislature before becoming a judge and thus appreciated the risk of improper financial influence on legislative behavior—to provide the fifth vote to uphold the constitutionality of BCRA's soft-money provisions.]

2. New FECA § 323(a)'s Restriction on Spending and Receiving Soft Money

Plaintiffs and Chief Justice [Rehnquist] contend that § 323(a) is impermissibly overbroad because it subjects *all* funds raised and spent by national parties to FECA's hard-money source and amount limits, including, for example, funds spent on purely state and local elections in which no federal office is at stake. Such activities, Chief Justice [Rehnquist] asserts, pose "little or no potential to corrupt . . . federal candidates and officeholders." This observation is beside the point. Section 323(a), like the remainder of § 323, regulates contributions, not activities. As the record demonstrates, it is the close relationship between federal officeholders and the national parties, as well as the means by which parties have traded on that relationship, that have made all large soft-money contributions to national parties suspect.

Given this close connection and alignment of interests, large soft-money contributions to national parties are likely to create actual or apparent indebtedness on the part of federal officeholders, regardless of how those funds are ultimately used.

This close affiliation has also placed national parties in a position to sell access to federal officeholders in exchange for soft-money contributions that the party can then use for its own purposes. Access to federal officeholders is the most valuable favor the national party committees are able to give in exchange for large donations. The fact that officeholders comply by donating their valuable time indicates either that officeholders place substantial value on the soft-money contribution themselves, without regard to their end use, or that national committees are able to exert considerable control over federal officeholders. Either way, large soft-money donations to national party committees are likely to buy donors preferential access to federal officeholders no matter the ends to which their contributions are eventually put. Congress had sufficient grounds to regulate the appearance of undue influence associated with this practice. The Government's strong interests in preventing corruption, and in particular the appearance of corruption, are thus sufficient to justify subjecting all donations to national parties to the source, amount, and disclosure limitations of FECA.

3. New FECA § 323(a)'s Restriction on Soliciting or Directing Soft Money

[The Court rejected the Plaintiffs' contention that § 323(a)'s prohibition on National Parties' soliciting or directing soft-money contributions was substantially overbroad. The Court explained that National Party committees could still solicit hard money, and that officers of National Parties could still solicit soft money in their individual capacities. "A national committee is likely to respond favorably to a donation made at its request regardless of whether the recipient is the committee itself or another entity."]

4. New FECA § 323(a)'s Application to Minor Parties

[The Court rejected the argument that § 323(a) is substantially overbroad because it impermissibly infringes the speech and associational rights of minor parties who are unlikely to pose a threat of corruption. The Court explained, "the relevance of the interest in avoiding actual or apparent corruption is not a function of the number of legislators a given party manages to elect. It applies as much to a minor party that manages to elect only one of its members to federal office as it does to a major party whose members make up a majority of Congress."]

5. New FECA § 323(a)'s Associational Burdens

[The Court rejected the Plaintiffs' argument that "§ 323(a) is unconstitutional because it impermissibly interferes with the ability of national committees to associate with state and local committees," reasoning that even under § 323(a) National and state party officers can still engage in "joint planning and electioneering activity."]

Accordingly, we reject the plaintiffs' First Amendment challenge to new FECA § 323(a).

New FECA § 323(b)'s Restrictions on State and Local Party Committees

In constructing a coherent scheme of campaign finance regulation, Congress recognized that, given the close ties between federal candidates and state party committees, BCRA's restrictions on national committee activity would rapidly become ineffective if state and local committees remained available as a conduit for soft-money donations. Section 323(b) is designed to foreclose wholesale evasion of § 323(a)'s anticorruption measures by sharply curbing state committees' ability to use large soft-money contributions to influence federal elections. The core of § 323(b) is a straightforward contribution regulation: It prevents donors from contributing nonfederal funds to state and local party committees to help finance "Federal election activity." 2 U.S.C. § 441i(b)(1). The term "Federal election activity" encompasses four distinct categories of electioneering: (1) voter registration activity during the 120 days preceding a regularly scheduled federal election; (2) voter identification, get-out-the-vote (GOTV), and generic campaign activity[54] that is "conducted in connection with an election in which a candidate for Federal office appears on the ballot"; (3) any "public communication" that "refers to a clearly identified candidate for Federal office" and "promotes," "supports," "attacks," or "opposes" a candidate for that office; and (4) the services provided by a state committee employee who dedicates more than 25% of his or her time to "activities in connection with a Federal election." §§ 431(20)(A)(i)-(iv). The Act explicitly excludes several categories of activity from this definition: public communications that refer solely to nonfederal candidates; contributions to nonfederal candidates; state and local political conventions; and the cost of grassroots campaign materials like bumper stickers that refer only to state candidates. All activities that fall within the statutory definition must be funded with hard money.

1. Governmental Interests Underlying New FECA § 323(b)

We begin by noting that, in addressing the problem of soft-money contributions to state committees, Congress both drew a conclusion and made a prediction. Its conclusion,

54. Generic campaign activity promotes a political party rather than a specific candidate. 2 U.S.C. § 431(21).

based on the evidence before it, was that the corrupting influence of soft money does not insinuate itself into the political process solely through national party committees. Rather, state committees function as an alternate avenue for precisely the same corrupting forces. Indeed, both candidates and parties already ask donors who have reached the limit on their direct contributions to donate to state committees. There is at least as much evidence as there was in *Buckley* that such donations have been made with the intent—and in at least some cases the effect—of gaining influence over federal officeholders. Section 323(b) thus promotes an important governmental interest by confronting the corrupting influence that soft-money donations to political parties already have.

Congress also made a prediction. Having been taught the hard lesson of circumvention by the entire history of campaign finance regulation, Congress knew that soft-money donors would react to § 323(a) by scrambling to find another way to purchase influence. It was neither novel nor implausible for Congress to conclude that political parties would react to § 323(a) by directing soft-money contributors to the state committees, and that federal candidates would be just as indebted to these contributors as they had been to those who had formerly contributed to the national parties. We "must accord substantial deference to the predictive judgments of Congress," *Turner Broadcasting System, Inc. v. FCC* (1994) (plurality opinion), particularly when, as here, those predictions are so firmly rooted in relevant history and common sense. Preventing corrupting activity from shifting wholesale to state committees and thereby eviscerating FECA clearly qualifies as an important governmental interest.

2. New FECA § 323(b)'s Tailoring

Plaintiffs argue that even if some legitimate interest might be served by § 323(b), the provision's restrictions are unjustifiably burdensome and therefore cannot be considered "closely drawn" to match the Government's objectives.

Plaintiffs assert that § 323(b) represents a new brand of pervasive federal regulation of state-focused electioneering activities that cannot possibly corrupt or appear to corrupt federal officeholders and thus goes well beyond Congress' concerns about the corruption of the federal electoral process. We disagree.

It is true that § 323(b) captures some activities that affect state campaigns for nonfederal offices. But these are the same sorts of activities that already were covered by the FEC's pre-BCRA allocation rules, and thus had to be funded in part by hard money, because they affect federal as well as state elections. As a practical matter, BCRA merely codifies the principles of the FEC's allocation regime while at the same time justifiably adjusting the formulas applicable to these activities in order to restore the efficacy of FECA's longtime statutory restriction—approved by the Court and eroded by the FEC's allocation regime—on contributions to state and local party committees for the purpose of influencing federal elections.

The first two categories of "Federal election activity," voter registration efforts, and voter identification, GOTV, and generic campaign activities conducted in connection with a federal election, clearly capture activity that benefits federal candidates. Common sense dictates, and it was "undisputed" below, that a party's efforts to register voters sympathetic to that party directly assist the party's candidates for federal office. It is equally clear that federal candidates reap substantial rewards from any efforts that increase the number of like-minded registered voters who actually go to the polls.

The record also makes quite clear that federal officeholders are grateful for contributions to state and local parties that can be converted into GOTV-type efforts.

Because voter registration, voter identification, GOTV, and generic campaign activity all confer substantial benefits on federal candidates, the funding of such activities creates a significant risk of actual and apparent corruption. Section 323(b) is a reasonable response to that risk. Its contribution limitations are focused on the subset of voter registration activity that is most likely to affect the election prospects of federal candidates: activity that occurs within 120 days before a federal election. Appropriately, in implementing this subsection, the FEC has categorically excluded all activity that takes place during the run up to elections when no federal office is at stake. The prohibition on the use of soft money in connection with these activities is therefore closely drawn to meet the sufficiently important governmental interests of avoiding corruption and its appearance.

"Public communications" that promote or attack a candidate for federal office—the third category of "Federal election activity," § 301(20)(A)(iii)—also undoubtedly have a dramatic effect on federal elections. Such ads were a prime motivating force behind BCRA's passage. As explained below, any public communication that promotes or attacks a clearly identified federal candidate directly affects the election in which he is participating. The record on this score could scarcely be more abundant. Given the overwhelming tendency of public communications, as carefully defined in § 301(20)(A)(iii), to benefit directly federal candidates, we hold that application of § 323(b)'s contribution caps to such communications is also closely drawn to the anticorruption interest it is intended to address.

As for the final category of "Federal election activity," § 301(20)(A)(iv), we find that Congress' interest in preventing circumvention of § 323(b)'s other restrictions justifies the requirement that state and local parties spend federal funds to pay the salary of any employee spending more than 25% of his or her compensated time on activities in connection with a federal election. In the absence of this provision, a party might use soft money to pay for the equivalent of a full-time employee engaged in federal electioneering, by the simple expedient of dividing the federal workload among multiple employees. Plaintiffs have suggested no reason for us to strike down this provision. Accordingly, we give "deference to [the] congressional determination of the need for [this] prophylactic rule." [*Fed. Election Comm'n v.*] *National Conservative Political Action Comm* [(1985)].

We accordingly conclude that § 323(b), on its face, is closely drawn to match the important governmental interests of preventing corruption and the appearance of corruption.

New FECA § 323(d)'s Restrictions on Parties' Solicitations for, and Donations to, Tax-Exempt Organizations

1. New FECA § 323(d)'s Regulation of Solicitations

[The Court upheld the restriction on parties soliciting donations to third-party tax-exempt organizations as preventing circumvention of Title I's limits on contributions of soft money to national, state, and local party committees. "Section 323(d)'s solicitation restriction is closely drawn to prevent political parties from using tax-exempt organizations as soft-money surrogates."]

2. New FECA § 323(d)'s Regulation of Donations

[The Court upheld the prohibition of national, state, and local party committees from making or directing donations to tax-exempt organizations, again explaining that the regulation served to prevent circumvention of § 323(a)'s antisolicitation restrictions. However, the Court construed this provision to apply only to donations of funds not raised in compliance with the FECA, not hard money. If political parties could direct soft-money donations to tax-exempt organizations but could not raise their own soft money, they would just do so through organizations that support the party and its candidates, thereby thwarting § 323(a).]

New FECA § 323(e)'s Restrictions on Federal Candidates and Officeholders

[The Court upheld § 323(e), which regulates the raising and soliciting of soft money by federal candidates and officeholders, as a valid anticircumvention measure. "Without some restriction on solicitations, federal candidates and officeholders could easily avoid FECA's contribution limits by soliciting funds from large donors and restricted sources to like-minded organizations engaging in federal election activities."]

New FECA § 323(f)'s Restrictions on State Candidates and Officeholders

[The Court upheld the BCRA's restriction on candidates for local office, or state or local officeholders, from spending soft money to fund "public communications" that refer to a candidate for federal office. The Court explained that this provision is geared toward preventing the circumvention of valid contribution limits.]

B

[Omitted.]

C

Finally, plaintiffs argue that Title I violates the equal protection component of the Due Process Clause of the Fifth Amendment because it discriminates against political parties in favor of special interest groups such as the National Rifle Association, American Civil Liberties Union, and Sierra Club. As explained earlier, BCRA imposes numerous restrictions on the fundraising abilities of political parties, of which the soft-money ban is only the most prominent. Interest groups, however, remain free to raise soft money to fund voter registration, GOTV activities, mailings, and broadcast advertising (other than electioneering communications). We conclude that this disparate treatment does not offend the Constitution.

As an initial matter, we note that BCRA actually favors political parties in many ways. Most obviously, party committees are entitled to receive individual contributions that substantially exceed FECA's limits on contributions to nonparty political committees; individuals can give $25,000 to political party committees whereas they can give a maximum of $5,000 to nonparty political committees. In addition, party committees are entitled in effect to contribute to candidates by making coordinated expenditures, and those expenditures may greatly exceed the contribution limits that apply to other donors.

More importantly, however, Congress is fully entitled to consider the real-world differences between political parties and interest groups when crafting a system of campaign finance regulation. Interest groups do not select slates of candidates for elections. Interest groups do not determine who will serve on legislative committees, elect congressional leadership, or organize legislative caucuses. Political parties have influence and power in the Legislature that vastly exceeds that of any interest group. As a result, it is hardly surprising that party affiliation is the primary way by which voters identify candidates, or that parties in turn have special access to and relationships with federal officeholders. Congress' efforts at campaign finance regulation may account for these salient differences. Taken seriously, plaintiffs' equal protection arguments would call into question not just Title I of BCRA, but much of the pre-existing structure of FECA as well. We therefore reject those arguments.

[Based on the foregoing reasoning, the Court rejected the plaintiffs' facial challenge to BCRA's soft-money provisions.]

McCONNELL v. FEC DISSENTS

As you read the dissents* in this case, keep a few things in mind: (1) What definition of "corruption" do the dissents embrace? (2) What is the role of political parties in relationship to their candidates? (3) What is the relationship between national and state parties, and does BCRA unconstitutionally infringe on state parties' rights? (4) To what extent is BCRA an incumbent-protection measure? (5) Is a law like BCRA needed to ferret out "bad" money in politics?

---

* Editors' note: the dissents have been re-ordered to aid comprehension.

Justice KENNEDY, dissenting in part with respect to BCRA Title I, [in which Chief Justice REHNQUIST and Justice SCALIA joined in relevant part].

The First Amendment guarantees our citizens the right to judge for themselves the most effective means for the expression of political views and to decide for themselves which entities to trust as reliable speakers. Significant portions of Titles I and II of the Bipartisan Campaign Reform Act of 2002 (BCRA or Act) constrain that freedom. These new laws force speakers to abandon their own preference for speaking through parties and organizations. And they provide safe harbor to the mainstream press, suggesting that the corporate media alone suffice to alleviate the burdens the Act places on the rights and freedoms of ordinary citizens.

Today's decision upholding these laws purports simply to follow *Buckley v. Valeo* (1976) and to abide by *stare decisis*; but the majority, to make its decision work, must abridge free speech where *Buckley* did not. *Buckley* did not authorize Congress to decide what shapes and forms the national political dialogue is to take. To reach today's decision, the Court surpasses *Buckley*'s limits and expands Congress' regulatory power. In so doing, it replaces discrete and respected First Amendment principles with new, amorphous, and unsound rules, rules which dismantle basic protections for speech.

Our precedents teach, above all, that Government cannot be trusted to moderate its own rules for suppression of speech. The dangers posed by speech regulations have led the Court to insist upon principled constitutional lines and a rigorous standard of review. The majority now abandons these distinctions and limitations.

I. TITLE I AND COORDINATION PROVISIONS

Even a cursory review of the speech and association burdens these laws create makes their First Amendment infirmities obvious:

Title I bars individuals with shared beliefs from pooling their money above limits set by Congress to form a new third party.

Title I bars national party officials from soliciting or directing soft money to state parties for use on a state ballot initiative. This is true even if no federal office appears on the same ballot as the state initiative.

A national party's mere involvement in the strategic planning of fundraising for a state ballot initiative risks a determination that the national party is exercising "indirect control" of the state party. If that determination is made, the state party must abide by federal regulations. And this is so even if the federal candidate on the ballot, if there is one, runs unopposed or is so certain of election that the only voter interest is in the state and local campaigns.

Title I compels speech. Party officials who want to engage in activity such as fundraising must now speak magic words to ensure the solicitation cannot be interpreted as anything other than a solicitation for hard, not soft, money.

Title I prohibits the national parties from giving any sort of funds to nonprofit entities, even federally regulated hard money, and even if the party hoped to sponsor the interest group's exploration of a particular issue in advance of the party's addition of it to their platform.

By express terms, Title I imposes multiple different forms of spending caps on parties, candidates, and their agents.

A. Constitutionally Sufficient Interest

In *Buckley*, the Court held that one, and only one, interest justified the significant burden on the right of association involved there: eliminating, or preventing, actual corruption or the appearance of corruption stemming from contributions to candidates.

In parallel, *Buckley* concluded the expenditure limitations in question were invalid because they did not advance that same interest.

Thus, though *Buckley* subjected expenditure limits to strict scrutiny and contribution limits to less exacting review, it held neither could withstand constitutional challenge unless it was shown to advance the anticorruption interest. In these consolidated cases, unless *Buckley* is to be repudiated, we must conclude that the regulations further that interest before considering whether they are closely drawn or narrowly tailored. If the interest is not advanced, the regulations cannot comport with the Constitution, quite apart from the standard of review.

Buckley made clear, by its express language and its context, that the corruption interest only justifies regulating candidates' and officeholders' receipt of what we can call the "*quids*" in the *quid pro quo* formulation. The Court rested its decision on the principle that campaign finance regulation that restricts speech without requiring proof of particular corrupt action withstands constitutional challenge only if it regulates conduct posing a demonstrable *quid pro quo* danger[.]

Placing *Buckley*'s anticorruption rationale in the context of the federal legislative power yields the following rule: Congress' interest in preventing corruption provides a basis for regulating federal candidates' and officeholders' receipt of *quids*, whether or not the candidate or officeholder corruptly received them. Conversely, the rule requires the Court to strike down campaign finance regulations when they do not add regulation to "actual or apparent *quid pro quo* arrangements."

The Court ignores these constitutional bounds and in effect interprets the anticorruption rationale to allow regulation not just of "actual or apparent *quid pro quo* arrangements," but of any conduct that wins goodwill from or influences a Member of Congress. It is not that there is any quarrel between this opinion and the majority that the inquiry since *Buckley* has been whether certain conduct creates "undue influence." On that we agree. The very aim of *Buckley*'s standard, however, was to define undue influence by reference to the presence of *quid pro quo* involving the officeholder. The Court, in contrast, concludes that access, without more, proves influence is undue. Access, in the Court's view, has the same legal ramifications as actual or apparent corruption of officeholders. This new definition of corruption sweeps away all protections for speech that lie in its path.

The majority also ignores that in *Buckley*, and ever since, those party contributions that have been subject to congressional limit were not general party-building contributions but were only contributions used to influence particular elections. That is, they were contributions that flowed to a particular candidate's benefit, again posing a *quid pro quo* danger.

Access in itself, however, shows only that in a general sense an officeholder favors someone or that someone has influence on the officeholder. There is no basis, in law or in fact, to say favoritism or influence in general is the same as corrupt favoritism or influence in particular.

The generic favoritism or influence theory articulated by the Court is at odds with standard First Amendment analyses because it is unbounded and susceptible to no limiting principle. Any given action might be favored by any given person, so by the Court's reasoning political loyalty of the purest sort can be prohibited.

Though the majority cites common sense as the foundation for its definition of corruption, in the context of the real world only a single definition of corruption has been found to identify political corruption successfully and to distinguish good political responsiveness from bad—that is *quid pro quo.* Favoritism and influence are not, as the Government's theory suggests, avoidable in representative politics. It is in the nature of an elected representative to favor certain policies, and, by necessary corollary, to favor the voters and contributors who support those policies. It is well understood that a substantial and legitimate reason, if not the only reason, to cast a vote for, or to make a contribution to, one candidate over another is that the candidate will respond by producing those political outcomes the supporter favors. Democracy is premised on responsiveness. *Quid pro quo* corruption has been, until now, the only agreed upon conduct that represents the bad form of responsiveness and presents a justiciable standard with a relatively clear limiting principle: Bad responsiveness may be demonstrated by pointing to a relationship between an official and a *quid.*

The majority attempts to mask its extension of *Buckley* under claims that BCRA prevents the appearance of corruption, even if it does not prevent actual corruption, since some assert that any donation of money to a political party is suspect. Under *Buckley*'s holding that Congress has a valid "interest in stemming the reality or appearance of corruption," however, the inquiry does not turn on whether some persons assert that an appearance of corruption exists. Rather, the inquiry turns on whether the Legislature has established that the regulated conduct has inherent corruption potential, thus justifying the inference that regulating the conduct will stem the appearance of real corruption. *Buckley* was guided and constrained by this analysis. In striking down expenditure limits the Court in

Buckley did not ask whether people thought large election expenditures corrupt, because clearly at that time many persons, including a majority of Congress and the President, did. Instead, the Court asked whether the Government had proved that the regulated conduct, the expenditures, posed inherent *quid pro quo* corruption potential.

From that it follows that the Court today should not ask, as it does, whether some persons, even Members of Congress, conclusorily assert that the regulated conduct appears corrupt to them. Following *Buckley*, it should instead inquire whether the conduct now prohibited inherently poses a real or substantive *quid pro quo* danger, so that its regulation will stem the appearance of *quid pro quo* corruption.

1. New FECA §§ 323(a), (b), (d), and (f)

Sections 323(a), (b), (d), and (f), cannot stand because they do not add regulation to conduct that poses a demonstrable *quid pro quo* danger. They do not further *Buckley*'s corruption interest.

The majority, with a broad brush, paints § 323(a) as aimed at limiting contributions possessing federal officeholder corruption potential. From there it would justify § 323's remaining provisions as necessary complements to ensure the national parties cannot circumvent § 323(a)'s prohibitions. The broad brush approach fails, however, when the provisions are reviewed under *Buckley*'s proper definition of corruption potential.

On its face § 323(a) does not regulate federal candidates' or officeholders' receipt of *quids* because it does not regulate contributions to, or conduct by, candidates or officeholders.

The realities that underlie the statute, furthermore, do not support the majority's interpretation. Before BCRA's enactment, parties could only use soft money for a candidate's "benefit" (*e.g.*, through issue ads, which all parties now admit may influence elections) independent of that candidate. And, as discussed later, § 323(e) validly prohibits federal candidate and officeholder solicitation of soft money party donations. Section 323(a), therefore, only adds regulation to soft money party donations not solicited by, or spent in coordination with, a candidate or officeholder.

These donations (noncandidate or officeholder solicited soft money party donations that are independently spent) do not pose the *quid pro quo* dangers that provide the basis for restricting protected speech. Though the government argues § 323(a) does regulate federal candidates' and officeholders' receipt of *quids*, it bases its argument on this flawed reasoning:

(1) "[F]ederal elected officeholders are inextricably linked to their political parties,"
(2) All party receipts must be connected to, and must create, corrupt donor favoritism among these officeholders.
(3) Therefore, regulation of party receipts equals regulation of *quids* to the party's officeholders.

The reasoning is flawed because the Government's reasoning only establishes the first step in its chain of logic: that a party is a proxy for its candidates generally. It does not establish the second step: that as a proxy for its candidates generally, *all* moneys the party receives (not just candidate solicited-soft money donations, or donations used in coordinated activity) represent *quids* for all the party's candidates and officeholders.

The piece of record evidence the Government puts forward on this score comes by way of deposition testimony from former Senator Simon and Senator Feingold. Senator Simon reported an unidentified colleague indicated frustration with Simon's opposition to legislation that would benefit a party contributor on the grounds that "'we've got to pay attention to who is buttering our bread'" and testified he did not think there was any question "'this'" (*i.e.*, "donors getting their way") was why the legislation passed. Senator Feingold, too, testified an unidentified colleague suggested he support the legislation because "'they [*i.e.*, the donor] just gave us [*i.e.*, the party] $100,000.'"

That evidence in fact works against the Government. These two testifying Senators expressed disgust toward the favoring of a soft money giver, and not the good will one would have expected under the Government's theory. That necessarily undercuts the inference of corruption the Government would have us draw from the evidence.

Even more damaging to the Government's argument from the testimony is the absence of testimony that the Senator who allegedly succumbed to corrupt influence had himself solicited soft money from the donor in question. Equally, there is no indication he simply favored the company with his vote because it had, without any involvement from him, given funds to the party to which he belonged. This fact is crucial. If the Senator himself had been the solicitor of the soft money funds in question, the incident does nothing more than confirm that Congress' efforts at campaign finance reform ought to be directed to conduct that implicates *quid pro quo* relationships. Only if there was some evidence that the officeholder had not solicited funds from the donor could the Court extrapolate from this episode that general party contributions function as *quids*, inspiring corrupt favoritism among party members. The episode is the single one of its type reported in the record and does not seem sufficient basis for major incursions into settled practice. Given the Government's claim that the corrupt favoritism problem is widespread, its inability to produce more than a single instance purporting to illustrate the point demonstrates the Government has not fairly characterized the general attitudes of Members towards soft money donors from whom they have not solicited.

In light of all this, § 323(a) has no valid anticorruption interest. The anticircumvention interests the Government offers in defense of §§ 323(b), (d), and (f) must also fall with the interests asserted to justify § 323(a). Any anticircumvention interest can be only as compelling as the interest justifying the underlying regulation.

None of these other sections has an independent justifying interest.

When one recognizes that §§ 323(a), (b), (d), and (f) do not serve the interest the anticorruption rationale contemplates, Title I's entirety begins to look very much like an incumbency protection plan. The controlling point, of course, is the practical burden on challengers. That the prohibition applies to both incumbents and challengers in no way establishes that it burdens them equally in that regard. Name recognition and other advantages held by incumbents ensure that as a general rule incumbents will be advantaged by the legislation the Court today upholds.

The Government identifies no valid anticorruption interest justifying §§ 323(a), (b), (d), and (f). The very nature of the restrictions imposed by these provisions makes one all the more skeptical of the Court's explanation of the interests at stake. These provisions cannot stand under the First Amendment.

2. New FECA § 323(e)

Ultimately, only one of the challenged Title I provisions satisfies *Buckley*'s anticorruption rationale and the First Amendment's guarantee. It is § 323(e). This provision is the sole aspect of Title I that is a direct and necessary regulation of federal candidates' and officeholders' receipt of *quids.* Section 323(e) governs "candidate[s], individual[s] holding Federal office, agent[s] of a candidate or an individual holding Federal office, or an entity directly or indirectly established, financed, maintained or controlled by or acting on behalf of 1 or more candidates or individuals holding Federal office." These provisions, and the regulations that follow, limit candidates' and their agents' solicitation of soft money. The regulation of a candidate's receipt of funds furthers a constitutionally sufficient interest. More difficult, however, is the question whether regulation of a candidate's solicitation of funds also furthers this interest if the funds are given to another.

I agree with the Court that the broader solicitation regulation does further a sufficient interest. The making of a solicited gift is a *quid* both to the recipient of the money and to the one who solicits the payment (by granting his request). Rules governing candidates' or officeholders' solicitation of contributions are, therefore, regulations governing their receipt of *quids.* This regulation fits under *Buckley*'s anticorruption rationale.

B. Standard of Review

It is common ground between the majority and this opinion that a speech-suppressing campaign finance regulation, even if supported by a sufficient Government interest, is unlawful if it cannot satisfy our designated standard of review. In *Buckley*, we applied "closely drawn" scrutiny to contribution limitations and strict scrutiny to expenditure limitations. Against that backdrop, the majority assumes that because *Buckley* applied the rationale in the context of contribution and expenditure limits, its application gives Congress and the Court the capacity to classify any challenged campaign finance regulation as either a contribution or an expenditure limit. Thus, it first concludes Title I's regulations are contributions limits and then proceeds to apply the lesser scrutiny.

Though the majority's analysis denies it, Title I's dynamics defy this facile, initial classification.

Title I's provisions prohibit the receipt of funds; and in most instances, but not all, this can be defined as a contribution limit. They prohibit the spending of funds; and in most instances this can be defined as an expenditure limit. They prohibit the giving of funds to nonprofit groups; and this falls within neither definition as we have ever defined it. Finally, they prohibit fundraising activity; and the parties dispute the classification of this regulation (the challengers say it is core political association, while the Government says it ultimately results only in a limit on contribution receipts).

The majority's classification overlooks these competing characteristics and exchanges *Buckley*'s substance for a formulaic caricature of it. Despite the parties' and the majority's best efforts on both sides of the question, it ignores reality to force these regulations into one of the two legal categories as either contribution or expenditure limitations. Instead, these characteristics seem to indicate Congress has enacted regulations that are neither contribution nor expenditure limits, or are perhaps both at once.

Even if the laws could be classified in broad terms as only contribution limits, as the majority is inclined to do, that still leaves the question what "contribution limits" can include if they are to be upheld under *Buckley. Buckley*'s application of a less exacting review to contribution limits must be confined to the narrow category of money gifts that are directed, in some manner, to a candidate or officeholder. Any broader definition of the category contradicts *Buckley*'s *quid pro quo* rationale and overlooks *Buckley*'s language, which contemplates limits on contributions to a candidate or campaign committee in explicit terms.

The Court, it must be acknowledged, both in *Buckley* and on other occasions, has described contribution limits due some more deferential review in less than precise terms. At times it implied that donations to political parties would also qualify as contributions whose limitation too would be subject to less exacting review.

These seemingly conflicting statements are best reconciled by reference to *Buckley*'s underlying rationale for applying less exacting review. In a similar, but more imperative, sense proper application of the standard of review to regulations that are neither contribution nor expenditure limits (nor which are both at once) can only be determined by reference to that rationale.

Buckley's underlying rationale is this: Less exacting review applies to Government regulations that "significantly interfere" with First Amendment rights of association. But any regulation of speech or associational rights creating "markedly greater interference" than such significant interference receives strict scrutiny.

The majority makes *Buckley*'s already awkward and imprecise test all but meaningless in its application. If one is viewing BCRA through *Buckley*'s lens, as the majority purports to do, one must conclude the Act creates markedly greater associational burdens than the significant burden created by contribution limitations and, unlike contribution limitations, also creates significant burdens on speech itself. While BCRA contains federal contribution limitations, which significantly burden association, it goes even further. The Act entirely reorders the nature of relations between national political parties and their candidates, between national political parties and state and local parties, and between national political parties and nonprofit organizations.

The many and varied aspects of Title I's regulations impose far greater burdens on the associational rights of the parties, their officials, candidates, and citizens than do regulations that do no more than cap the amount of money persons can contribute to a political candidate or committee. The evidence shows that national parties have a long tradition of engaging in essential associational activities, such as planning and coordinating fundraising with state and local parties, often with respect to elections that are not federal in nature. This strengthens the conclusion that the regulations now before us have unprecedented impact. It makes impossible, moreover, the contrary conclusion—which the Court's standard of review determination necessarily implies—that BCRA's soft money regulations will not much change the nature of association between parties, candidates, nonprofit groups, and the like. Similarly, Title I now compels speech by party officials. These officials must be sure their words are not mistaken for words uttered in their official capacity or mistaken for soliciting prohibited soft, and not hard, money. Few interferences with the speech, association, and free expression of our people are greater than attempts by Congress to say which groups can or cannot advocate a cause, or how they must do it.

Congress has undertaken this comprehensive reordering of association and speech rights in the name of enforcing contribution limitations. Here, however, as in *Buckley*, "[t]he markedly greater burden on basic freedoms caused by [BCRA's pervasive regulation] cannot be sustained simply by invoking the interest in maximizing the effectiveness of the less intrusive contribution limitations." BCRA fundamentally alters, and thereby burdens, protected speech and association throughout our society. Strict scrutiny ought apply to review of its constitutionality. Under strict scrutiny, the congressional scheme, for the most part, cannot survive. This is all but acknowledged by the Government, which fails even to argue that strict scrutiny could be met.

1. New FECA § 323(e)

Because most of the Title I provisions discussed so far do not serve a compelling or sufficient interest, the standard of review analysis is only dispositive with respect to new FECA § 323(e). As to § 323(e), I agree with the Court that this provision withstands constitutional scrutiny.

Section 323(e) is directed solely to federal candidates and their agents; it does not ban all solicitation by candidates, but only their solicitation of soft money contributions; and it incorporates important exceptions to its limits (candidates may receive, solicit, or direct funds that comply with hard money standards; candidates may speak at fundraising events; candidates may solicit or direct unlimited funds to organizations not involved with federal election activity; and candidates may solicit or direct up to $20,000 per individual per year for organizations involved with certain federal election activity (*e.g.*, GOTV, voter registration)). These provisions help ensure that the law is narrowly tailored to satisfy First Amendment requirements. For these reasons, I agree § 323(e) is valid.

2. New FECA §§ 323(a), (b), (d), and (f)

Though these sections do not survive even the first test of serving a constitutionally valid interest, it is necessary as well to examine the vast overbreadth of the remainder of Title I, so the import of the majority's holding today is understood. Sections 323(a), (b), (d), and (f), are not narrowly tailored, cannot survive strict scrutiny, and cannot even be considered closely drawn, unless that phrase is emptied of all meaning.

First, the sections all possess fatal overbreadth. By regulating conduct that does not pose *quid pro quo* dangers, they are incursions on important categories of protected speech by voters and party officials.

[Justice Kennedy discussed each of the sections in turn. Section 323(a), he asserted, is overbroad because it regulates all National Parties, even if they do not present candidates in federal elections, and even during odd-numbered years that have only state and local elections. Section 323(b), he asserted, reaches speech by the state parties on nonfederal issues, such as a state or local party saying, "The Democratic slate for state assembly opposes President Bush's tax policy . . . Elect the Republican slate to tell Washington, D.C. we don't want higher taxes." Section 323(b), he noted, also is overbroad because it proscribes the use of soft money for all state party voter registration efforts occurring within 120 days of a federal election, meaning that "the vagaries of election timing, not any real interest related to corruption, will control whether state parties can spend nonfederally regulated funds on ballot efforts." Sections 323(d) and 323(f), according to Justice Kennedy, also are not narrowly tailored.]

Compared to the narrowly tailored effort of § 323(e), which addresses in direct and specific terms federal candidates' and officeholders' quest for dollars, these sections cast a wide net not confined to the critical categories of federal candidate or officeholder involvement. They are not narrowly tailored; they are not closely drawn; they flatly violate the First Amendment; and even if they do encompass some speech that poses a regulable *quid pro quo* danger, that little assurance does not justify or permit a regime which silences so many legitimate voices in this protected sphere.

Chief Justice REHNQUIST, dissenting with respect to BCRA Title I, [in which Justice SCALIA and KENNEDY joined].

Although I join Justice Kennedy's opinion in full, I write separately to highlight my disagreement with the Court on Title I of the [BCRA].

I

The issue presented by Title I is not, as the Court implies, whether Congress can permissibly regulate campaign contributions to candidates, *de facto* or otherwise, or seek to eliminate corruption in the political process. Rather, the issue is whether Congress can permissibly regulate much speech that has no plausible connection to candidate contributions or corruption to achieve those goals. Under our precedent, restrictions on political contributions implicate important First Amendment values and are constitutional only if they are "closely drawn" to reduce the corruption of federal candidates or the appearance of corruption. *Buckley v. Valeo*. Because, in reality, Title I is much broader than the Court allows, regulating a good deal of speech that does *not* have the potential to corrupt federal candidates and officeholders, I dissent.

The linchpin of Title I, new FECA § 323(a), prohibits national political party committees from "solicit[ing]," "receiv[ing]," "direct[ing] to another person," and "spend[ing]" *any* funds not subject to federal regulation, even if those funds are used for nonelection related activities. [Section] 323(a) does not regulate only donations given to influence a particular federal election; it regulates *all donations* to national political committees, no matter the use to which the funds are put.

The Court attempts to sidestep the unprecedented breadth of this regulation by stating that the "close relationship between federal officeholders and the national parties" makes all donations to the national parties "suspect." But a close association with others, especially in the realm of political speech, is not a surrogate for corruption; it is one of our most treasured First Amendment rights. The Court's willingness to impute corruption on the basis of a relationship greatly infringes associational rights and expands Congress' ability to regulate political speech. And there is nothing in the Court's analysis that limits congressional regulation to national political parties. In fact, the Court relies in part on this closeness rationale to regulate *nonprofit organizations.* Who knows what association will be deemed too close to federal officeholders next. When a donation to an organization has no potential to corrupt a federal officeholder, the relationship between the officeholder and the organization is simply irrelevant.

The Court fails to recognize that the national political parties are exemplars of political speech at all levels of government, in addition to effective fundraisers for federal candidates and officeholders. For sure, national political party committees exist in large part to elect federal candidates, but they also promote coordinated political messages and participate in public policy debates unrelated to federal elections, promote, even in off-year elections, state and local candidates and seek to influence policy at those levels, and increase public participation in the electoral process.

As these activities illustrate, political parties often foster speech crucial to a healthy democracy, and fulfill the need for like-minded individuals to band together and promote a political philosophy. When political parties engage in pure political speech that has little or no potential to corrupt their federal candidates and officeholders, the Government cannot constitutionally burden their speech any more than it could burden the speech of individuals engaging in these same activities. Notwithstanding the Court's citation to the numerous abuses of FECA, under any definition of "exacting scrutiny," the means chosen by Congress, restricting all donations to national parties no matter the purpose for which they are given or are used, are not "closely drawn to avoid unnecessary abridgment of associational freedoms." *Buckley*.

BCRA's overinclusiveness is not limited to national political parties. To prevent the circumvention of the ban on the national parties' use of nonfederal funds, BCRA extensively regulates state parties, primarily state elections, and state candidates. For example, new FECA § 323(b) prohibits state parties from using nonfederal funds for general partybuilding activities such as voter registration, voter identification, and get out the vote for state candidates even if federal candidates are not mentioned. New FECA § 323(d) prohibits state and local political party committees, like their national counterparts, from soliciting and donating "any funds" to nonprofit organizations such as the National Rifle Association or the National Association for the Advancement of Colored People (NAACP). And, new FECA § 323(f) requires a state gubernatorial candidate to abide by federal funding restrictions when airing a television ad that tells voters that, if elected, he would oppose the President's policy of increased oil and gas exploration within the State because it would harm the environment.

Although these provisions are more focused on activities that may *affect* federal elections, there is scant evidence in the record to indicate that federal candidates or officeholders are corrupted or would appear corrupted by donations for these activities. Nonetheless, the Court concludes that because these activities *benefit* federal candidates and officeholders, or prevent the circumvention of pre-existing or contemporaneously enacted restrictions, it must defer to the predictive judgments of Congress.

Yet the Court cannot truly mean what it says. Newspaper editorials and political talk shows *benefit* federal candidates and officeholders every bit as much as a generic voter registration drive conducted by a state party; there is little doubt that the endorsement of a major newspaper *affects* federal elections, and federal candidates and officeholders are surely "grateful," for positive media coverage. I doubt, however, the Court would seriously contend that we must defer to Congress' judgment if it chose to reduce the influence of political endorsements in federal elections. *See Miami Herald Publishing Co. v. Tornillo* (1974) (holding unconstitutional a state law that required newspapers to provide "right to reply" to any candidate who was personally or professionally assailed in order to eliminate the "abuses of bias and manipulative reportage" by the press).

It is also true that any circumvention rationale ultimately must rest on the circumvention itself leading to the corruption of federal candidates and officeholders. All political speech that is not sifted through federal regulation circumvents the regulatory scheme to some degree or another, and thus by the Court's standard would be a "loophole" in the current system. Unless the Court would uphold federal regulation of all funding of political speech, a rationale dependent on circumvention alone will not do. By untethering its inquiry from corruption or the appearance of corruption, the Court has removed the touchstone of our campaign finance precedent and has failed to replace it with any logical limiting principle.

But such an untethering is necessary to the Court's analysis. Only by using amorphous language to conclude a federal interest, however vaguely defined, exists can the Court avoid the obvious fact that new FECA §§ 323(a), (b), (d), and (f) are vastly overinclusive. Any campaign finance law aimed at reducing corruption will almost surely affect federal elections or prohibit the circumvention of federal law, and if broad enough, most laws will generally reduce some appearance of corruption. Indeed, it is precisely because broad laws are likely to nominally further a legitimate interest that we require Congress to tailor its restrictions; requiring all federal candidates to self-finance their campaigns would surely reduce the appearance of donor corruption, but it would hardly be constitutional. In allowing Congress to rely on general principles such as affecting a federal election or prohibiting the circumvention of existing law, the Court all but eliminates the "closely drawn" tailoring requirement and meaningful judicial review.

No doubt Congress was convinced by the many abuses of the current system that something in this area must be done. Its response, however, was too blunt. Many of the abuses described by the Court involve donations that were made for the "purpose of influencing a federal election," and thus are already regulated. Congress could have sought to have the existing restrictions enforced or to enact other restrictions that are "closely drawn" to its legitimate concerns. But it should not be able to broadly restrict political speech in the fashion it has chosen. Today's decision, by not requiring tailored restrictions, has significantly reduced the protection for political speech having little or nothing to do with corruption or the appearance of corruption.

Justice THOMAS, dissenting with respect to BCRA Title I, [in which Justice SCALIA joined].

[T]he Court today upholds what can only be described as the most significant abridgment of the freedoms of speech and association since the Civil War. With breathtaking scope, the [BCRA] directly targets and constricts core political speech. In response to this assault on the free exchange of ideas and with only the slightest consideration of the appropriate standard of review or of the Court's traditional role of protecting First Amendment freedoms, the Court has placed its *imprimatur* on these unprecedented restrictions. The very "purpose of the First Amendment [is] to preserve an uninhibited marketplace of ideas in which truth will ultimately prevail." *Red Lion Broadcasting Co. v. FCC* (1969). Yet today the fundamental principle that "the best test of truth is the power of the thought to get itself accepted in the competition of the market," *Abrams v. United States* (1919) (Holmes, J., dissenting), is cast aside in the purported service of preventing "corruption," or the mere "appearance of corruption." *Buckley v. Valeo.*

I

A

"[C]ampaign finance laws are subject to strict scrutiny," *Federal Election Comm'n v. Beaumont* (Thomas, J., dissenting), and thus Title I must satisfy that demanding standard even if it were (incorrectly) conceived of as nothing more than a contribution limitation. [A]s I have previously noted, it is unclear why "[b]ribery laws [that] bar precisely the *quid pro quo* arrangements that are targeted here" and "disclosure laws" are not "less restrictive means of addressing [the government's] interest in curtailing corruption." *Shrink Missouri.*

The joint opinion not only continues the errors of *Buckley v. Valeo*, by applying a low level of scrutiny to contribution ceilings, but also builds upon these errors by expanding the anticircumvention rationale beyond reason.

Rather than permit this never-ending and self-justifying process, I would require that the Government explain why proposed speech restrictions are needed in light of actual Government interests, and, in particular, why the bribery laws are not sufficient.

B

But Title I falls even on the joint opinion's terms. A donation to a political party is a clumsy method by which to influence a candidate, as the party is free to spend the donation however it sees fit, and could easily spend the money as to provide no help to the candidate. And, a soft-money donation to a party will be of even less benefit to a candidate, "because of legal restrictions on how the money may be spent." Brief for FEC. It follows that the defendants bear an especially heavy empirical burden in justifying Title I.

The evidence cited by the joint opinion does not meet this standard and would barely suffice for anything more than rational-basis review. The first category of the joint opinion's evidence is evidence that "federal officeholders have commonly asked donors to make soft-money donations to national and state committees solely in order to assist federal campaigns, including the officeholder's own." But to the extent that donors and federal officeholders have collaborated so that donors could give donations to a national party committee "for the purpose of influencing any election for Federal office," the alleged soft-money donation is in actuality a regular "contribution" as already defined and regulated by FECA. Neither the joint opinion nor the defendants present evidence that enforcement of pre-BCRA law has proved to be impossible, ineffective, or even particularly difficult.

The second category is evidence that "lobbyists, CEOs, and wealthy individuals" have "donat[ed] substantial sums of soft money to national committees not on ideological grounds, but for the express purpose of securing influence over federal officials." Even if true (and the cited evidence consists of nothing more than vague allegations of wrongdoing), it is unclear why existing bribery laws could not address this problem. Again, neither the joint opinion nor the defendants point to evidence that the enforcement of bribery laws has been or would be ineffective. If the problem has been clear and widespread, as the joint opinion suggests, I would expect that convictions, or at least prosecutions, would be more frequent.

The joint opinion also places a substantial amount of weight on the fact that "in 1996 and 2000, more than half of the top 50 soft-money donors gave substantial sums to *both* major national parties," and suggests that this fact "leav[es] room for no other conclusion but that these donors were seeking influence, or avoiding retaliation, rather than promoting any particular ideology." But that is not necessarily the case. The two major parties are not perfect ideological opposites, and supporters or opponents of certain policies or ideas might find substantial overlap between the two parties. If donors feel that both major parties are in general agreement over an issue of importance to them, it is unremarkable that such donors show support for both parties. This commonsense explanation surely belies the joint opinion's too-hasty conclusion drawn from a relatively innocent fact.

Justice SCALIA, [dissenting with report to Title I].

This is a sad day for the freedom of speech. Who could have imagined that the same Court which, within the past four years, has sternly disapproved of restrictions upon such inconsequential forms of expression as virtual child pornography, tobacco advertising, dissemination of illegally intercepted communications, and sexually explicit cable programming, would smile with favor upon a law that cuts to the heart of what the First Amendment is meant to protect: the right to criticize the government. For that is what the most offensive provisions of this legislation are all about. We are governed by Congress, and this legislation prohibits the criticism of Members of Congress by those entities most capable of giving such criticism loud voice: national political parties and corporations, both of the commercial and the not-for-profit sort. It forbids national-party use of "soft" money to fund "issue ads" that incumbents find so offensive.

To be sure, the legislation is evenhanded: It similarly prohibits criticism of the candidates who oppose Members of Congress in their reelection bids. But as everyone knows, this is an area in which evenhandedness is not fairness. If *all* electioneering were evenhandedly prohibited, incumbents would have an enormous advantage. Likewise, if incumbents and challengers are limited to the same quantity of electioneering, incumbents are favored. In other words, any restriction upon a type of campaign speech that is equally available to challengers and incumbents tends to favor incumbents.

Beyond that, however, the present legislation targets for prohibition certain categories of campaign speech that are particularly harmful to incumbents. Is it accidental, do you think, that incumbents raise about three times as much "hard money"—the sort of funding generally not restricted by this legislation—as do their challengers? Or that lobbyists (who seek the favor of incumbents) give 92 percent of their money in "hard" contributions? And is it mere happenstance, do you estimate, that national-party funding, which is severely limited by the Act, is more likely to assist cash-strapped challengers than flush-with-hard-money incumbents? Was it unintended, by any chance, that incumbents are free personally to receive some soft money and even to solicit it for other organizations, while national parties are not? See new FECA §§ 323(a) and (e).

This litigation is about preventing criticism of the government. I cannot say for certain that many, or some, or even any, of the Members of Congress who voted for this legislation did so not to produce "fairer" campaigns, but to mute criticism of their records and facilitate reelection. Indeed, I will stipulate that all those who voted for BCRA believed they were acting for the good of the country. There remains the problem of the Charlie Wilson Phenomenon, named after Charles Wilson, former president of General Motors, who is supposed to have said during the Senate hearing on his nomination as Secretary of Defense that "what's good for General Motors is good for the country." Those in power, even giving them the benefit of the greatest good will, are inclined to believe that what is good for them is good for the country. Whether in prescient recognition of the Charlie Wilson Phenomenon, or out of fear of good old-fashioned, malicious, self-interested manipulation, "[t]he fundamental approach of the First Amendment . . . was to assume the worst, and to rule the regulation of political speech 'for fairness' sake' simply out of bounds." *Austin* [*v. Michigan Chamber of Commerce* (1990)] (Scalia, J., dissenting). Having abandoned that approach to a limited extent in *Buckley*, we abandon it much further today.

We will unquestionably be called upon to abandon it further still in the future. The most frightening passage in the lengthy floor debates on this legislation is the following assurance given by one of the cosponsoring Senators to his colleagues:

> "This is a modest step, it is a first step, it is an essential step, but it does not even begin to address, in some ways, the fundamental problems that exist with the hard money aspect of the system." 148 Cong. Rec. S2101 (Mar. 20, 2002) (statement of Sen. Feingold).

The system indeed. The first instinct of power is the retention of power, and, under a Constitution that requires periodic elections, that is best achieved by the suppression of election-time speech. We have witnessed merely the second scene of Act I of what promises to be a lengthy tragedy. In scene 3 the Court, having abandoned most of the First Amendment weaponry that *Buckley* left intact, will be even less equipped to resist the incumbents' writing of the rules of political debate. The federal election campaign laws, which are already (as today's opinions show) so voluminous, so detailed, so complex, that no ordinary citizen dare run for office, or even contribute a significant sum, without hiring an expert adviser in the field, can be expected to grow more voluminous, more detailed, and more complex in the years to come—and always, always, with the objective of reducing the excessive amount of speech.

NOTES ON *McCONNELL v. FEC*

1. Notice the different constructions of "corruption" between the majority and dissenting opinions. The majority defined corruption broadly to encompass the securing of *access* to elected officials in exchange for soft-money contributions. The dissents, by contrast, limit "corruption" to quid-pro-quo arrangements. Which is more consistent with today's political realities? Does the First Amendment, whether from an originalist or a philosophically sound perspective, compel choosing the latter view of corruption (as Justice Kennedy seems to believe)?
2. Justice Kennedy and the other dissenters question the strength of the government's evidence. Is it possible for the public to evaluate the dispute between the Justices on this point, given the fact that the key relevant evidence was kept secret in the sealed record in the case? Did the dissenters deny the facts as the majority understood them, or instead did the dissenters simply disagree about the constitutional implications of those facts?
3. Justice Thomas obviously thinks *Buckley* was incorrectly decided and that Congress should not be able to impose contribution limits. Instead, he believes that bribery and disclosure laws can root out undue influence. Is he correct? Keep this debate in mind for the *Citizens United* discussion later in this Part.
4. Justice Scalia's opinion concurring in part and dissenting in part addressed (in a portion we omitted) what he termed "fallacious" propositions that he saw supporters of BCRA explicitly or implicitly endorsing: that "money is not speech," that "pooling money is not speech," and that "speech by corporations can be abridged." The last proposition relates more to BCRA's "electioneering communications" provision, discussed below in *Citizens United*. What about the first two? Is spending money a form of speech, and is there (or should there be) a First Amendment right to pool money together to influence the political process?
5. Given that Justice Alito has replaced Justice O'Connor, are the soft-money holdings of *McConnell*, which secured only a five-Justice majority (including Justice O'Connor) vulnerable to overruling? The Court rejected an invitation to do so in *Republican National Committee (RNC) v. FEC*, 130 S. Ct. 3544 (2010), summarily affirming 698 F. Supp. 2d 150 (D.D.C. 2010), but perhaps the Court's unwillingness in that case is just a matter of timing. The Court had already overruled a huge portion of *McConnnell* in *Citizens United* when *RNC v. FEC* arrived at its doorstep, and maybe the Court did not have the stomach for overruling the soft-money part of *McConnell* so quickly thereafter. But once *Citizens United* is a few years old, will the Court be ready to adopt as its majority view what Justice Kennedy wrote in his dissent on the soft-money issues?

3. Political Parties and "Coordinated" Expenditures

In *Buckley* and *McConnell*, the Court explained that when a candidate coordinates with a political party, the resulting expenditure is deemed to be a "coordinated" expenditure and therefore becomes subject to the contribution limitations of the law. That is, unlimited (and unregulated) independent expenditures must truly be independent—at least in theory. As the Court explained in *Buckley*, designating coordinated expenditures as contributions is required to ensure that candidates cannot circumvent the valid contribution limitations simply by funneling their spending through political parties.

Moreover, in *Colorado Republican Fed. Campaign Comm. v. FEC*, 518 U.S. 604 (1996) ("*Colorado I*"), the Court held that political parties may spend unlimited amounts in support of a candidate (that is, make unlimited independent expenditures) so long as that spending is truly independent. The Court thus sustained an as-applied challenge to the portion of the law that limited political parties' independent expenditures. But in *FEC v. Colorado Republican Fed. Campaign Comm.*, 533 U.S. 431, 465 (2001) ("*Colorado II*"), the Court rejected a facial challenge to the law and found that "a party's coordinated expenditures, unlike expenditures truly independent, may be restricted to minimize circumvention of contribution limits." Given these two holdings, political parties have created internal units, separated from their operations that work directly with their candidates, so that these separate units may engage in unlimited "independent expenditures" in support of their candidates. Indeed, in the 2012 election cycle political parties made over $255 million in independent expenditures.

Joseph Cao was a Member of Congress from Louisiana who was running for reelection in 2008. The Republican National Committee sought to run its own ad supporting Cao's candidacy but wanted to coordinate with Cao regarding the best timing for the ad. Could the party do so without having the ad be considered a regulated "coordinated" expenditure? That is the topic of this next case, from the United States Court of Appeals for the Fifth Circuit. The Supreme Court denied certiorari in this case, so the Fifth Circuit's decision is the most recent (and for now, determinative) opinion on this issue.

IN RE CAO

619 F.3d 410 (5th Cir. 2010) (en banc)

W. Eugene Davis and Benavides, Circuit Judges:

The challenges raised in the present case require this court to decide whether certain provisions of the Federal Election Campaign Act ("FECA" or "the Act") of 1971 violate the Plaintiffs' right to free speech under the First Amendment. Applying Supreme Court precedent, we conclude that each of the challenged FECA provisions constitutes a constitutionally permissible regulation of political parties' campaign contributions and coordinated expenditures. Accordingly, we find that none of the challenged provisions unconstitutionally infringe upon the rights of the Plaintiffs to engage in political debate and discussion.

I

Plaintiff Anh "Joseph" Cao is the United States Representative for the Second Congressional District of Louisiana, and Plaintiff Republican National Committee ("RNC") is the national political party committee of the Republican Party. Generally, the Plaintiffs challenge the statutory provisions limiting the RNC's contributions to, and expenditures made in coordination with, Cao's 2008 congressional campaign.

[T]he district court began by discussing the general contribution and expenditure limitations FECA places on political parties. Specifically examining how FECA affected the RNC's contributions and expenditures related to the 2008 Cao campaign, the district court then found that the RNC spent all of the $42,100 it was allowed to spend on coordinated expenditures under the Party Expenditure Provision, 2 U.S.C. § 441a(d)(2)(3),[5] and reached its $5,000 contribution limit under § 441a(a)(2)(A). Additionally, the district court found that the RNC would have spent additional money on speech expressly advocating the election of Cao had it been permitted to spend beyond FECA limitations.

[The district court certified four constitutional questions to the en banc court of appeals under the procedure outlined in 2 U.S.C. § 437h.]

II

This appeal requires us to address the intersection of congressional campaign finance reform with the fundamental right to free speech under the First Amendment. Since the landmark decision of *Buckley v. Valeo* (1976), the Supreme Court on a number of occasions has evaluated the limitations that the First Amendment imposes on the Government's ability to preserve the integrity of the democratic election process through its regulation of campaign expenditures and contributions made to federal candidates.

In . . . articulating the constitutional distinction between contributions and expenditures, the Court [in *Buckley*] carefully distinguished independent expenditures from those expenditures that are "prearranged or coordinated" with a particular candidate. Following the terminology used in FECA, the *Buckley* Court considered that for purposes of First Amendment scrutiny, "prearranged or coordinated expenditures" are constitutionally equivalent to contributions. According to the Court, it followed that coordinated expenditures are subject to the same limitations and scrutiny that apply to contributions. Although the facts of the challenge and nature of the Court's analysis in *Buckley* gave the Court no reason to specifically address the level of scrutiny for coordinated expenditures, the *Buckley* Court implicitly recognized that limitations on coordinated expenditures would be, like contribution limitations, subject to a lower level of constitutional scrutiny than limitations on independent expenditures.

5. [Section 441a(d)(2)(3), the "Party Expenditure Provision," provides limits on the amount political parties may expend in connection with the general election campaign of candidates for various offices—Eds.]

III

The second question certified to the en banc court asks:

> Do the expenditure and contribution limits and contribution provision in 2 U.S.C. §§ 441a(a)(23), 441a(a)(2)(A), and 441a(a)(7)(B)(i) violate the First Amendment rights of one or more of [the] plaintiffs as applied to coordinated communications that convey the basis for the expressed support?

This question arose out of the RNC's desire to spend in excess of the amount allowed for coordinated campaign expenditures under the Party Expenditure Provision. Particularly, the RNC wanted to expend its funds to run a radio advertisement in support of Cao (hereinafter "the Cao ad"). The proposed Cao ad said:

> Why We Support Cao
>
> The Republican National Committee has long stood for certain core principles, which we believe are the fundamentals of good government. When it comes to the issues of lower taxes, individual freedoms and a strong national defense, we need leaders who will stand with the American people and defend those issues.
>
> We need leaders who understand that our economy is in a recession, our individual freedoms are constantly under attack and we continue to fight the global war on terrorism to keep our families safe.
>
> Joseph Cao understands and fights for those issues. And, that is why we ask you to join us in supporting him on December 6. It's important for Louisiana and important for the country.

The RNC wanted to coordinate with the Cao campaign as to the "best timing" for the Cao ad. However, the RNC's involvement with the Cao campaign amounted to coordination, and the RNC already had spent the entire amount it was allowed to spend on coordinated campaign expenditures under FECA. Therefore, the RNC concluded that it could not coordinate with the Cao campaign to run the Cao ad without violating FECA. Ultimately, the RNC chose to not expend its funds to air the Cao ad and brought this challenge to FECA's restrictions on coordinated expenditures.

Because we are a court of error and only decide issues the parties bring to us, it is important at the outset to identify the RNC's sole argument on this certified question. The RNC argues and only argues that §§ 441a(d)(2)(3), 441a(a)(2)(A), and 441a(a)(7)(B)(i) violate its First Amendment rights because the provisions regulate the RNCs "own speech." The RNC asserts that its own speech may not be regulated, regardless of whether the speech is coordinated. "Own speech" is defined by the RNC as speech that is "attributable" to the RNC and includes speech the candidate writes and decides how the speech is to be disseminated. In other words, the RNC argues that speech it adopts is attributed to it and therefore exempt from regulation regardless of the extent of coordination with the candidate.

To evaluate the merit of the Plaintiffs' expansive "own speech" argument, we return to *Buckley v. Valeo*, the first case to discuss coordinated expenditures under FECA. In *Buckley*, the Supreme Court examined, *inter alia*, then-18 U.S.C. § 608(e)(1) which limited individuals' ability to make independent expenditures. The Government argued that Congress could restrict independent expenditures because independent expenditures could be used to circumvent contribution limits. The *Buckley* Court rejected the Government's argument. In finding that independent expenditures could not be regulated, the Court compared § 608(e)(1) with § 608(b), the provision that regulated expenditures coordinated with a candidate. The *Buckley* Court stated:

> . . . [C]ontrolled or coordinated expenditures are treated as contributions rather than expenditures under the Act. Section 608(b)'s contribution ceilings rather than § 608(e)(1)'s independent expenditure limitation prevent attempts to circumvent the Act through prearranged or coordinated expenditures amounting to disguised contributions. By contrast, § 608(e)(1) limits expenditures for express advocacy of candidates made totally independently of the candidate and his campaign. Unlike contributions, such independent expenditures may well provide little assistance to the candidate's campaign and indeed may prove counterproductive. The absence of prearrangement and coordination of an expenditure with the candidate or his agent not only undermines the value of the expenditure to the candidate, but also alleviates the danger that expenditures will be given as a quid pro quo for improper commitments from the candidate.

Thus, the *Buckley* Court concluded that although Congress was unable to regulate individuals' independent expenditures, Congress could regulate individuals' coordinated expenditures.

Building on and embracing its analysis in *Buckley*, the Court in *Colorado I* and *Colorado II* further examined the limitations on coordinated and independent expenditures as applied to political parties. In *Colorado I*, the Colorado Republican Party ("CRP") brought an as-applied challenge to the Party Expenditure Provision arguing that restricting a party's independent expenditures was unconstitutional. The *Colorado I* Court followed the *Buckley* rationale and found that "the constitutionally significant fact . . . is the lack of coordination between the candidate and the source of the expenditure." *Colorado I*. In holding that the restraint on an independent expenditure was unconstitutional, the Court distinguished between coordinated expenditures and independent expenditures, stating:

> . . . [T]he Court's cases have found a "fundamental constitutional difference between money spent to advertise one's views independently of the candidate's campaign and money contributed to the candidate to be spent on his campaign." . . . [R]easonable contribution limits directly and materially advance the Government's interest in preventing exchanges of large financial contributions for political favors.
> . . . [L]imitations on independent expenditures are less directly related to preventing corruption, since "the absence of prearrangement and coordination of an expenditure

> with the candidate . . . not only undermines the value of the expenditure to the candidate, but also alleviates the danger that expenditures will be given as a quid pro quo for improper commitments from the candidate."

Thus, the *Colorado I* Court found that the Party Expenditure Provision was unconstitutional as applied to the CRP's independent expenditures.

In *Colorado I,* the CRP also raised a facial challenge to the application of the Party Expenditure Provision to coordinated expenditures. The *Colorado I* Court remanded this facial challenge because the lower courts had not considered the issue. The remanded issue of whether Congress could restrict coordinated expenditures reached the Supreme Court five years later as *Colorado II.* After analyzing its precedents in *Buckley* and *Colorado I,* the *Colorado II* Court found that "a party's coordinated expenditures, unlike expenditures truly independent, may be restricted to minimize circumvention of contribution limits." In examining whether coordinated expenditures could be restricted, the Court applied the intermediate scrutiny standard announced in *Buckley*: the restriction must be closely drawn to match a important government interest. The Court found that Congress could regulate coordinated expenditures as contributions because of the sufficiently important governmental interest in preventing the potential for political corruption by circumvention of campaign finance laws. The Court stated:

> There is no significant functional difference between a party's coordinated expenditure and a direct party contribution to the candidate, and there is good reason to expect that a party's right of unlimited coordinated spending would attract increased contributions to parties to finance exactly that kind of spending. Coordinated expenditures of money donated to a party are tailor-made to undermine contribution limits. Therefore the choice here is not, as in *Buckley* and *Colorado I,* between a limit on pure contributions and pure expenditures. The choice is between limiting contributions and limiting expenditures whose special value as expenditures is also the source of their power to corrupt. Congress is entitled to its choice.

Though the *Colorado II* Court unambiguously found the application of the Party Expenditure Provision to coordinated expenditures to be facially constitutional, the Plaintiffs argue that "*Colorado II* expressly left open the as-applied question of whether parties' own speech may be limited as contributions."

Assuming that the *Colorado II* Court left open the possibility for an as-applied challenge to the Party Expenditure Provision's application to coordinated spending, the facts and arguments in the instant case do not present this court with that question. Acceptance of the Plaintiffs' "own speech" argument would effectively eviscerate the Supreme Court's holding in *Colorado II,* which dealt only with coordinated expenditures. The Court in *Colorado II* expressly recognized that Congress has the power to regulate coordinated expenditures in order to combat circumvention of the contribution limits and political corruption.

The *Colorado II* Court stated:

> . . . [T]he question is whether experience under the present law confirms a serious threat of abuse from the unlimited coordinated party spending as the Government contends. It clearly does. Despite years of enforcement of the challenged limits, substantial evidence demonstrates how candidates, donors, and parties test the limits of the current law, and it shows beyond serious doubt how contribution limits would be eroded if inducement to circumvent them were enhanced by declaring parties' coordinated spending wide open.

If this court were to accept the Plaintiffs' exceedingly broad argument, we would be reaching a conclusion inconsistent with the *Colorado II* Court's teaching that coordinated expenditures may be restricted. The RNC's sole argument throughout has been that there is no limit to its claim that Congress cannot regulate a party's own speech regardless of the degree of coordination with the candidate. The district court succinctly identified the Plaintiffs' argument: "Plaintiffs claim that a party coordinated communication disclosed as paid for by the party is the party's 'own speech' even if a candidate indicates in the communication that he has approved the message." Moreover, "Plaintiffs claim that a party coordinated communication disclosed as having been paid for by the party is the party's 'own speech' even if the candidate or her campaign actually creates the communication and passes it along to the party." Thus, under the Plaintiffs' standard, all coordinated expenditures paid for and adopted by the party would be considered a party's own speech and not subject to restriction. As demonstrated above, the *Colorado II* Court, as well as the Court's earlier cases, clearly held that coordinated expenditures may be restricted to prevent circumvention and corruption.

We find the *Colorado II* Court's concern with corruption particularly important since, in the present case, the Plaintiffs admit that they themselves have already taken steps to circumvent the Act's individual donor contribution limits. The district court found that "[t]he RNC encourages its candidates to tell their 'maxed out' donors to contribute to the RNC." Representative Cao confirmed in his deposition this behavior by the RNC. "Congressman Cao has personally suggested to donors who had given the maximum amount to his campaign that they could also contribute to the party." [Citation to district court's opinion.] Furthermore, the district court found that "the party has shared [its] donor list" with its federal candidates, and that "[t]he sharing of information also happens in the other direction[, since the party] receives information from federal candidates about who has contributed to their campaigns." The district court also found that "the RNC organizes 'fulfillment' events to which individuals who have made a large contribution to the RNC of a specified amount are invited" so that they can have special access to federal lawmakers. The *Colorado II* Court warned that "[i]f the effectiveness of party spending could be enhanced by limitless coordination, the ties of straitened candidates to prosperous ones and, vicariously, to large donors would be reinforced as well." The above facts demonstrate the potential corruption and abuse that concerned *Colorado II*.

Colorado II certainly left open the possibility for an as-applied challenge to the Party Expenditure Provision as it applies to coordinated expenditures; it is well-established that the facial upholding of a law does not prevent future as-applied challenges. However, simply characterizing the challenge as an as-applied challenge does make it one. "While rejection of a facial challenge to a statute does not preclude all as-applied attacks, surely it precludes one resting upon the same asserted principle of law." *Penry v. Lynaugh* (1989) (Scalia, J., dissenting).

The argument raised by the Plaintiffs in this case rests not on a sufficiently developed factual record, but rather, on the same general principles rejected by the Court in *Colorado II*, namely the broad position that coordinated expenditures may not be regulated. Finding for the Plaintiffs would require us to hold that Congress cannot limit a party's expenditures on a campaign ad, the content of which the party adopts, regardless of the degree of coordination with the candidate. Because such a conclusion would effectually overrule all restrictions on coordinated expenditures, the RNC's argument must fail in light of *Colorado II.*

The Plaintiffs' "own speech" argument cannot be reconciled with *Colorado II.* As such, we find that the expenditure and contribution limits and contribution provision in 2 U.S.C. §§ 441a(a)(2)(3), 441a(a)(2)(A), and 441a(a)(7)(B)(I) do not violate the First Amendment rights of one or more of the Plaintiffs as applied to coordinated communications that convey the basis for the party's expressed support.

IV

The principal disagreement we have with the dissents is over the scope of Plaintiffs' argument with respect to the constitutionality of contribution restrictions relative to coordinated expenditures. Based on the record, briefs and oral argument, we have explained above why we conclude that the only issue Plaintiffs presented to us for decision is whether the RNC's "own speech" is subject to regulation and restriction under FECA. As we read Chief Judge Jones's dissent, she agrees that *Colorado II* answers this question and authorizes regulation of RNC's own speech generally. Chief Judge Jones's principal argument is that Plaintiffs also presented for decision whether the Act can constitutionally restrict expenditures for the Cao Ad involved in this case when that ad was coordinated between the RNC and the candidate as to "timing only."

[The majority recounts its determination, based on the briefs and oral argument, that the Plaintiffs conceded that the ad in question amounted to a coordinated expenditure.]

Even if we further consider that Plaintiffs made and did not abandon the argument that the coordination between the candidate and the party was de minimis, based on the stipulation and admission of counsel the coordination cannot be considered de minimis. At oral argument, Plaintiffs' counsel conceded that the RNC intended to coordinate the

Cao Ad with Cao not only with regard to timing, but also by providing Cao with advance knowledge of the Cao Ad's content.

This "content awareness" stipulation has significance that the dissents completely overlook. For instance, given advance knowledge of the Cao Ad's content, if Cao approved of the content and found it favorable to his campaign, he may have told or requested the RNC to run the ad frequently during prime hours. If Cao disapproved of the Cao Ad's content and found it unfavorable to his campaign, he may have told or requested the party to run it infrequently during off hours, or perhaps not at all. This degree of coordination of campaign expenditures contrasts sharply with the Supreme Court's functional definition of independent expenditures. Whereas the Supreme Court has explained that an independent expenditure representing the party's own views may at times work against the candidate's interests, timing-plus-content-awareness coordination may ensure that a party's message virtually always works in the candidate's favor.

For these reasons we cannot agree with Chief Judge Jones's conclusion that "there is no functional difference between the Cao Ad and a constitutionally protected independent expenditure." As we have explained above, knowledge of content plus timing coordination makes a huge difference relative to the benefit of the ad to the candidate that the dissent fails to recognize—namely, the candidate's ability to direct approved content for maximum impact and redirect disapproved content for minimum impact on his campaign.

This type of coordinated activity, moreover, implicates the same corruption and circumvention concerns of the *Colorado II* Court. Therefore, based on what we know of the extent of the proposed coordination on this scant record, it is reasonable to infer that the coordination of the Cao Ad between the candidate and the party as to timing with the candidate's prior knowledge of the ad's content would amount to a coordinated expenditure subject to restriction under *Colorado II*.

JONES, Chief Judge, concurring in part and dissenting in part:

The first object of the First Amendment is to protect robust political debate that underpins free citizens' ability to govern ourselves. "Speech is an essential mechanism of democracy, for it is the means to hold officials accountable to the people. . . . The First Amendment has its fullest and most urgent application to speech uttered during a campaign for political office." *Citizens United v. FEC* (2010). Yet the majority hold that Congress may forbid a political party from broadcasting an advertisement explaining why the party supports its own congressional candidate merely because the advertisement was coordinated with the candidate as to timing.

We dissent. The Cao Ad cannot be suppressed by the FEC on the facts before us.

Substantively, the majority['s] analysis, flawed by its overbroad premises, ultimately begs the primary question before us—at what point does "coordination" between a candidate and a political party transform the party's communicative speech into a mere "contribution" subject to strict dollar limits? This question was left open by the Supreme Court. *Colorado II* (2001). In light of subsequent Supreme Court decisions, courts must begin to deal with it.

I. A Narrow Fact-Based Challenge Is Before the Court

Despite the majority's contentions, the court is obliged to address the facts that have actually been presented—specifically, whether this particular ad can be regulated as a de facto contribution even though the coordination regarded solely the timing of its broadcast.

It is important to stress just how minimal was the level of coordination. When the Supreme Court has interpreted the term "coordinated expenditures," it described a spectrum, at one end of which political parties would simply foot the candidate's bills. The present scenario stands at the other end.

The ad was produced and approved by the RNC, on its own initiative, without any input from Cao. Cao and the RNC intended to cooperate only as to the timing of the ad. Timing constituted the only coordination. There is no evidence that Cao suggested, instigated or requested the ad. There is no evidence that he or his campaign wrote it or provided their views on its content. There is no evidence that the ad might have caused Cao to spend his campaign funds any differently. Thus, whether or not such de minimis coordination allows the Cao Ad to be banned as a "coordinated expenditure" is before the court for decision.

II. The Court Must Address Narrow Issues First

[Omitted.]

III. Evaluating Cao's As-Applied Challenge

In this as-applied attack on the coordinated expenditure limit that would ban broadcast of the Cao Ad, this court must first determine the appropriate level of scrutiny and then evaluate the evidence concerning the government's regulation. Two levels of scrutiny govern campaign finance regulations: strict scrutiny and, unique to campaign finance jurisprudence, "closely drawn" scrutiny. *Buckley v. Valeo* (1976). The former has been applied to candidates' speech and independent expenditures, while the latter applies to contributions and facially to "coordinated expenditures." Which standard pertains to the government's regulation of the Cao Ad depends on whether the ad is core political speech or a functional contribution. This court is not bound by the government's simply labeling the speech "coordinated[.]"

Buckley held that contributions to a candidate may be regulated, because contributions, unlike communicative independent expenditures, express merely a general support for a candidate. The FECA defines contributions as including "expenditures made by any person in cooperation, consultation, or concert, with, or at the request or suggestion of, a candidate." 2 U.S.C. § 441a(a)(7)(B)(i). While the Supreme Court has placed great importance on whether speech is coordinated, and thus regarded as a contribution, it has offered no guidance except to acknowledge that the sweeping term "coordinated expenditures" covers a wide range of activities with varying constitutional attributes:

> The principal opinion in *Colorado I* noted that coordinated expenditures "share some of the constitutionally relevant features of independent expenditures." But it also observed that "many [party coordinated expenditures] are . . . virtually indistinguishable from simple contributions." Coordinated spending by a party, in other words, covers a spectrum of activity, as does coordinated spending by other political actors.

Colorado II.

There is no doubt that, standing alone, the Cao Ad is core political speech. The Cao Ad is more than "a general expression of support for the candidate." *Buckley.* The ad expressly advocates for Cao, "communicate[s] the underlying basis for [the RNC's] support," and increases "the quantity of communication." [*Id.*]

Further, the ad hews closely to the independent expenditure side of the spectrum. The RNC independently produced the Cao Ad without input from Cao; the RNC created the ad at its own initiative; the RNC planned the ad's message; the RNC produced the ad; the RNC approved the final version of the ad; and the RNC decided to air the ad. Like the ads in *Colorado I,* the Cao Ad "was developed by the [party] independently and not pursuant to any general or particular understanding with a candidate." *Colorado I.* It unambiguously "reflects [the RNC's] members' views about the philosophical and governmental matters that bind them together [and] also seeks to convince others to join those members in a practical democratic task, the task of creating a government that voters can instruct and hold responsible for subsequent success or failure." [*Id.*]

At the opposite end of the coordination spectrum are instances in which a party simply pays its candidate's bills. Apparently rejecting the spectrum approach, the FEC asserts that the Cao Ad is functionally the same as a cash contribution to the candidate. This is inaccurate. The critical differences between the Cao Ad and a direct contribution or "footing the candidate's bills" include the ad's initiator, message, quality, ultimate source of approval, and decision to air. The Cao Ad is not "virtually identical" to one that Cao might produce. Further, despite the timing coordination, the ads "may well provide little assistance to the candidate's campaign and indeed may prove counterproductive." *Buckley.* Because the party decides to create and air the ad of its own initiative, the candidate cannot depend on it. The candidate will not know whether the ad is effective. If the ad is useful to the candidate, then it is useful only because the interests of the party and the candidate coincide. On all these grounds, there is no significant functional difference between the Cao Ad and a constitutionally protected independent expenditure.

Compared with the *Colorado II* pronouncement that the coordinated expenditure limits are facially valid, this case presents the narrow question whether de minimis coordination transforms otherwise constitutionally protected core political speech into something less. We believe it does not. Because the Cao Ad represents core political speech, it should be evaluated under the traditional strict scrutiny test. Alternatively, even if "closely drawn" scrutiny is required because of *Colorado II*, the Cao Ad cannot be subjected to dollar limits.

A. Applying Strict Scrutiny

That a statute has been held facially valid does not answer whether it may be constitutionally applied in a specific circumstance. Instead "[a] court applying strict scrutiny must ensure that a compelling interest supports each application of a statute restricting speech." [*FEC v. Wisconsin Right to Life, Inc.* (2007) (*WRTL*).] Moreover, the government bears the burden to demonstrate that the law is constitutional as applied to plaintiffs' speech.

The government contends that regulating timing-only coordination furthers its compelling interest in preventing corruption or its appearance or circumvention of the contribution limits. The FEC also argues that an expansive definition of "coordination" is necessary to ensure that it can regulate all coordinated expenditures that truly are de facto contributions.

The import of [the Supreme Court's precedents] is clear. Even if the record afforded some support for regulating timing-only coordination, which it does not, it clearly does not support treating the Cao Ad as the "functional equivalent" of a mere monetary contribution. The expressive content of the ad prevents that. In addition, the risk of circumvention of campaign contribution limits is not appreciably greater here than it is with "independent" expenditures. The candidate lacks control or influence over the initiation, production, and content of the party ad. The party decides whether or not an ad will be made, what it will say, what it will look like, and whether it will air. The candidate may or may not approve of the ad or find it useful.

Consequently, this expenditure will be useful to the candidate only to the extent that his and the party's interests coincide. Should the candidate "encourage" donors to give money to the party, he cannot be certain whether these party donations will be more useful to him than an independent expenditure. Without some link of candidate control or influence, neither the quid pro quo corruption nor appearance of corruption that justifies contribution limits can occur.

The FEC essentially argues . . . that expansive definitions of coordination and coordinated expenditures are needed to ensure that coordinating solely the broadcast timing of the party's ad does not circumvent the rule against coordinated expenditures which in turn helps to prevent circumvention of contribution limits which culminates in preventing quid pro quo corruption or the appearance of such corruption. It is an overly broad approach that here sweeps up protected speech.

B. Applying "Closely Drawn" Scrutiny

Even if the regulation of the Cao Ad must be evaluated under *Buckley*'s "closely drawn" standard because of its de minimis coordination, the government still must affirmatively demonstrate some sufficiently important interest—preventing corruption, the appearance of corruption, or circumvention. The government remains obliged to present evidence that the interest applies to the facts before us. Not to require some level of proof by the government would allow censorship of the party's ad based on nothing more than the general proof offered to sustain the statute's facial validity in *Colorado II*.

The FEC offered no evidence or argument that coordination of the Cao Ad as to broadcast timing will appreciably increase the risk or appearance of corruption or circumvention of contribution limits. Overall, the record evidence proves that money plays a primary role in political campaigns, that parties and party leaders are significantly involved in political fund-raising, and that independent groups have played an increasing role in recent years. More money than ever is being raised, and election advertising has become more important and more of a science than ever before. Frequently, this money, whether it travels through campaigns, parties, or independent groups, opens up opportunities for access to candidates and politicians. In short, despite FECA, as amended by McCain-Feingold, money and politics remain inextricably linked, and may be more entangled than they were at the time of FECA's passage.

None of this, however, demonstrates that the specific type of coordination at issue in this case, concerning the timing of otherwise-independent expenditures, has any propensity to increase quid pro quo corruption or the appearance of corruption or to promote circumvention of contribution limits. Indeed, the voluminous evidentiary record contains only a few, incidental references to timing coordination. For example, a campaign finance expert opines that "Giving candidates a direct say in whether, when, and how often a party's speech is broadcast essentially gives them a direct say in the content of what the voters get to hear." Content, however, is not at issue in this case. A former politician states that party advertisements in the final days of a campaign can make the difference between winning and losing. Coordination is hardly necessary to draw that conclusion. One campaign consultant complained that "the clutter on television during the last few weeks of the campaign really prevented our message from getting through as clearly as we would have liked." No doubt. What is absent from the record is any discussion or evaluation (let alone evidence) on whether timing coordination increases the risk of corruption or its appearance. Instead, the record simply includes blanket conclusions that any coordination increases the risk.

In contrast, the general evidence demonstrating risks of circumvention presented in *Colorado II* involved situations where the candidate retained real control over the party's coordinated expenditures. Candidates controlled the message and its presentation and, ultimately, approved of those coordinated expenditures. Here, Cao had no influence over the RNC's speech save what time it would air. The candidate does not even have input into whether or on what stations the ad will air, only when it will air, and he cannot be certain that the party will heed his advice. If there is any heightened possibility of corruption or circumvention in this arrangement, the government has not pointed to it, and we ought not to invent some conceivable interest that the government itself is unable to articulate or prove.

Nor, in this instance, are entirely uncoordinated expenditures an adequate alternative to minimally coordinated speech. The record demonstrates that FEC's coordination-regulation regime prevents party leaders from exercising any degree of control over their party's advertisements in support of a candidate. Because party leaders inevitably associate with candidates, to avoid the taint of coordination parties must establish "independent expenditure programs" staffed by hired consultants who are responsible for all aspects of the party's communications, from polling and research to writing the scripts, but for the topline budget. In effect, a party has no control over its own message. The party leaders must make a Hobson's choice between talking to their own candidates and controlling their own party's message. The government justifies this regime by reference to the risk of "circumvention." But by prohibiting speech subject to de minimis coordination, the FEC severely abridges parties' constitutionally protected right to engage in independent expenditures—in other words, to speak in public in support of their own candidates.

"Closely drawn" scrutiny has to mean something when applied to censorship of core political speech. Where the government cannot demonstrate a compelling interest, and the effect of regulation in this case is to ban the Cao Ad, the regulation cannot be "closely drawn."

IV. The Majority Opinion

[Omitted.]

V. Conclusion

The constitutional rules governing campaign finance law are presently in a state of flux, but there is a clear trend favoring the protection of political speech. [T]he Supreme Court has, in measured steps, protected political speech while leaving the scaffolding of *Buckley* in place. It has cast aside both recently enacted speech restrictions and decades-old speech restrictions. Lower courts have conformed to this trend.

In each of those instances, the Supreme Court has demanded, to justify banning speech, that the government provide strong evidence of a compelling interest in preventing the appearance or occurrence of corruption. Where there is uncertainty about the government's interest, "the First Amendment requires us to err on the side of protecting political speech rather than suppressing it." *WRTL*. [T]he Cao Ad is core political speech. The RNC wishes to coordinate with Cao on its broadcast timing, but the Supreme Court has never spoken on what degree of contact makes expressive political speech "coordinated" such that it may be suppressed. The Supreme Court's recent decisions demand much more from the government than it has presented here—essentially nothing. Even if the government were to meet its burden, it seems inconceivable that in this country founded on the hope and reality of free and open political debate, otherwise independent political speech could be banned because its speakers have asked a candidate, "When do we air the ad?"

It is not our place to revisit whether the government may generally regulate coordinated expenditures. Still less is it our place to approve the banning of a specific political ad simply because the Court has held that when coordinated expenditures are generally analogous to paying the candidate's bills, they may be regulated. But when it comes to defining what speech qualifies as coordinated expenditures subject to such regulation—the issue we do have to decide—we should follow Chief Justice Roberts's admonition in *WRTL*:

> [W]e give the benefit of the doubt to speech, not censorship. The First Amendment's command that "Congress shall make no law . . . abridging the freedom of speech" demands at least that.

We respectfully dissent.

BROWN CLEMENT, Circuit Judge, concurring in part and dissenting in part:

I join the Chief Judge's dissent because I believe the Party Expenditure Provision cannot be constitutionally applied to the Cao ad. I write separately to note that I would go further than the Chief Judge in fashioning a standard that protects political speech that is not the functional equivalent of a campaign contribution.

I see no reason that timing alone makes any difference in the constitutional analysis, and question whether a de minimis standard provides a line bright enough to avoid chilling protected speech through the threat of an enforcement action. The Supreme Court has drawn the relevant distinction between an expenditure and a contribution: a contribution "serves as a general expression of support for the candidate and his views," while an expenditure "communicate[s] the underlying basis for the support." *Buckley v. Valeo* (1976). The Court has also identified the goal of the anti-coordination rules: preventing circumvention of the contribution limits by expenditures that amount to simply paying a candidate's bills. A "timing only" standard does nothing to capture the difference between these two constitutionally distinct forms of communication. The same could be said of other standards based on the manner of coordination, such as medium (radio versus television); venue (the local Spanish-language channel versus the soft rock channel); or region (the Lower Ninth Ward versus Uptown New Orleans).

Likewise, a de minimis standard is difficult to apply and interpret. The FEC would be required to develop extensive regulations drawing lines between de minimis and prohibited coordination. Courts attempting to adjudicate the application of these regulations to specific factual situations would find themselves drawn into similar hair splitting.

Litigants would be forced to respond to extensive discovery on the substance of their contacts with the candidate. A speaker contemplating engaging in speech such as the Cao ad would face a "burdensome, expert-driven inquiry, with an indeterminate result." *WRTL* (2007). Despite the best intentions of such a standard, "it will unquestionably chill a substantial amount of political speech." *Id.*

What does make a difference in the constitutional analysis, however, is coordination as to the content of the ad. The Cao ad is the RNC's own speech, expressing its views on political issues, and identifying Cao as a candidate who supports those views. Cao did not provide input on its content and was not asked to provide his consent to run the ad. If he had, that would indeed raise a suspicion that the parties were attempting to circumvent the rules against coordination so that the RNC could pay the bill for Cao's speech—the evil at which the coordination rules are aimed.

Accordingly, I would propose a two-pronged standard that is "content-driven," rather than one that turns on the degree of coordination. Specifically, I would propose the following: An advertisement is functionally identical to a contribution only if it is susceptible of no other reasonable interpretation than as a general expression of support for the candidate, and the ad was not generated by the candidate. Under this standard, the speaker could only take refuge in the safe harbor of a content-driven standard if the speech conveys the underlying basis of the support, and was not merely adopted speech indistinguishable from paying a candidate's advertising bills. This approach . . . is clear, objective, and content-driven, and because it is relatively simple for both speakers and regulators to understand and apply, will not chill speech through the threat of litigation. It limits discovery to a factual issue that is relatively easy to ascertain, i.e., whether the ad was generated by or its content approved by the candidate or the political party. It references the fundamental distinction the Court drew between contributions and expenditures in *Buckley*, and exempts from its protection expenditures that amount to a party merely paying a candidate's bills. The standard would also align more closely than other possible standards with the actual definition of a coordinated expenditure, which prohibits spending "*at the request or suggestion of*, a candidate." 2 U.S.C. § 441a(a)(7)(B)(I) (emphasis added).

Applying this standard, the Cao ad is not functionally identical to a campaign contribution. The ad was generated by the RNC. It expresses not merely the kind of generalized sentiment—"Vote for Joseph Cao"—that the Court has described as the hallmark of a contribution, but expresses the RNC's view on important matters of public concern and urges a vote for Cao because he shares the same views. While the "takeaway" message of this advertisement may be one urging support for Cao, the message is anchored and inspired not by the RNC's support for Cao, but by Cao's support for the views expressed by the RNC. The ad thus communicates the underlying basis for the support, making it more like an expenditure protected by strict scrutiny. This is far from the archetypal coordination described in *Buckley*: effectively paying a candidate's advertising bills. The Cao ad can reasonably be interpreted as something other than a general expression of support for a candidate and was not generated by Cao, and as such, strict scrutiny should apply to laws regulating this ad.

The Court has emphasized that political parties have the First Amendment right to speak on political issues and explicitly acknowledged that coordinated expenditures "share some of the constitutionally relevant features of independent expenditures." *Colorado I.* Speech that articulates a set of political views and explains the speaker's support of a candidate in terms of that candidate's endorsement of those views—i.e., speech that conveys the underlying basis of support—is speech that implicates the strongest and most compelling First Amendment interests.

In any case dealing with campaign finance law it is easy to mystify oneself—and one's audience—with talk of "coordination," "circumvention," "functional equivalent," and the like. These bland phrases mask the import of the absolutist position the majority has taken today. The standard I have proposed makes distinctions and is consistent with the Court's often difficult precedents in this area, but it proceeds from a fairly simple impulse: If the First Amendment means anything, it means that political speech is not the same thing as paying a candidate's bills for travel, or salaries, or for hamburgers and balloons. In this case, a group of citizens has banded together to express their views on important public matters. Congress has abridged their freedom to do so. This the Constitution does not permit. I respectfully dissent.

NOTES ON *CAO*

1. Do coordinated expenditures pose the same kind of corruption concern as contributions? Put differently, if political parties and candidates can coordinate as to timing and discuss the content of the party's ad, will this open the door to circumvention of valid contribution limits? That, in essence, is the crux of the debate: Is the coordinated expenditure limitation a needed measure for anticircumvention?
2. Notice how the majority and dissents are in essence talking past each other about what is even in dispute. At oral argument and in postargument briefs, the Republican Party emphatically conceded that it was not challenging whether this ad was a coordinated ad. They made this concession by stipulating that discussion of the timing of the ad with Cao would qualify the ad as a coordinated expenditure. Why do you think the plaintiffs conceded this point? Was this a wise strategy? And should this concession preclude the court from deciding whether the Cao Ad qualifies as a coordinated expenditure (the majority's position), or, as Chief Judge Jones posits, can the court resolve whether this ad is still "core political speech" that the First Amendment protects?
3. What do you think of the standard Judge Clement proposes? As a lower court of appeals judge, is she in a position to suggest such a standard? More importantly, is

there a meaningful way to distinguish between a political party's "own speech" and speech that it coordinates with a candidate? Put differently, is there a way to distinguish "good" coordination from "bad" coordination?

4. The legality of spending by nominally independent entities will likely be fodder for litigation in the coming years. During the 2012 presidential election campaign, both Mitt Romney and Barack Obama had "independent" organizations that supported their candidacies. These political action committees, known as Super PACs, were created in the wake of the Supreme Court's decision in *Citizens United* (discussed below), and their purpose was to make only independent expenditures (that is, not on behalf of or coordinated with the candidate or campaign) for their "own" electioneering. Should this activity be considered "coordinated" spending? Consider that former Romney aides, who had worked on Romney's 2008 presidential campaign, created the pro-Romney Super PAC, Restore Our Future; similarly, former Obama campaign officials ran the pro-Obama Super PAC, Priorities USA Action. In theory neither Super PAC coordinated their spending with the campaigns they supported. Is it realistic to think that the former aides, who were personally close to each candidate, were not discussing their campaign strategies or spending initiatives with the campaign? How should the Federal Election Commission or the courts determine if this kind of spending is "coordinated" and therefore should be subject to the expenditure limitations of federal law? If you were a lawyer for one of these Super PACs, what kinds of "walls" or other strategies would you advise to ensure that the spending is not considered "coordinated"? (We will revisit these issues at the end of this Part after the *SpeechNow* case.)

4. Corporate and Union Independent Expenditures

The Supreme Court's 2010 opinion in *Citizens United v. FEC* was probably the most controversial decision since *Bush v. Gore* (which we will read in Part IV of this book), and perhaps even more so. This case considered the constitutionality of BCRA's ban on corporations and unions using money from their general treasuries to fund their own campaign ads.

The opinion spanned 183 pages. We will consider the opinion in three parts. First, we will look at Justice Kennedy's majority opinion for five Justices (the typical "conservatives"—Roberts, Scalia, Kennedy, Thomas, and Alito). Second, we will read Justice Stevens's lengthy dissent for the four traditionally "liberal" Justices (Stevens, Breyer, Ginsburg, and Sotomayor). Finally, later in this Part, we will consider a portion of Justice Kennedy's majority opinion and Justice Thomas's dissent with respect to the law's disclosure and disclaimer requirements.

Some background may be useful before reading the opinions. Congress first prohibited corporations from making contributions to candidates in 1907 in the Tillman Act. As Justice Stevens says in his dissent in *Citizens United*, Congress was concerned with "the enormous power corporations had come to wield in federal elections, with the accompanying threat of both actual corruption and a public perception of corruption" and "a respect for the interest of shareholders and members in preventing the use of their money to support candidates they opposed." In 1947, Congress passed the Taft-Hartley Act, which extended the prohibition on corporate support of candidates to include independent expenditures.

As you know, Congress banned individuals from making more than $1,000 of independent expenditures in FECA, and the Court in *Buckley* struck down that provision as unconstitutional. Federal law (beginning with the Taft-Hartley Act of 1947) also included a separate ban on corporate and union independent expenditures, but the Court did not consider that provision in *Buckley*.

The Court subsequently rendered several opinions on laws involving corporate independent expenditure bans. In *First Nat. Bank of Boston v. Bellotti*, 435 U.S. 765 (1978), by a 5-4 vote, the Court struck down a Massachusetts law that criminalized a corporate expenditure advocating the adoption or defeat of a referendum or other ballot question submitted directly to the voters. The particular ballot question in the case concerned whether to raise taxes, and the bank wanted to spend its money to broadcast ads opposing this measure. In essence, the Court said that Massachusetts could not limit corporate independent expenditures in ballot initiative campaigns because there was little concern about corruption in that type of election. The Court did not address whether the state could ban corporate independent expenditures for candidate elections.

Then, in *Federal Election Comm'n v. Massachusetts Citizens for Life, Inc.*, 479 U.S. 238 (1986) (*MCFL*), the Court carved out an as-applied exception to FECA ban on corporate independent expenditures, determining that it could not validly apply to nonprofit corporations that (1) were formed for the sole purpose of promoting political ideas, (2) did not engage in business activities, and (3) did not accept contributions from for-profit corporations or labor unions. The Court determined that this type of nonprofit organization did not pose a danger of corruption that would justify the ban, or at least that the First Amendment interests in permitting this type of entity to engage in the advocacy outweighed whatever risks of corruption the express electoral activity might create.

In *Austin v. Michigan Chamber of Commerce*, 494 U.S. 652 (1990), (5-4) the Court upheld a Michigan law that banned corporations from using their general treasury funds to make independent expenditures. The case involved the Michigan Chamber of Commerce, which could not qualify for the First Amendment protection identified in *MCFL* because the Chamber accepted funds from for-profit business corporations. The majority opinion in *Austin* was concerned with the ability of business corporations to use the wealth they aggregated from their business activities, with the benefit of the corporate form, to unduly influence public debate over which candidates deserve election to public office. *Austin* was widely recognized as a major decision that permitted the regulation of campaign finance in the interest of protecting the perceived integrity of the electoral process. Opponents of *Austin*, including Justices Kennedy and Scalia dissenting in that case, saw it as anathema to the free marketplace of political ideas—in which corporations as much as individual citizens, in their view, are entitled to participate.

The next major development was the passage of BCRA in 2003. As the *Citizens United* opinion explains, that law prohibited corporations and unions from using their general treasury funds to make "electioneering communications" within 30 days of a primary or 60 days of a general election. In this respect, BCRA extended the prohibition in Taft-Hartley from the narrower category of express electoral advocacy (considered by some at the time to be limited to ads containing specific "magic words" like "Vote for" or "Vote against") to the broader category of "electioneering communications" as defined in the new statute. Part of the facial challenge to BCRA in *McConnell* (which you read above regarding soft money) included an argument that the electioneering communications ban was unconstitutional. The Court upheld the law on its face, by an unexpected 5-4 vote (with Justice O'Connor providing the key fifth vote for the majority even though she had dissented in *Austin*), and Justice Kennedy writing a vigorous dissent.

Then, in *Federal Election Comm'n v. Wisconsin Right to Life, Inc.*, 551 U.S. 449 (2007) (*WRTL*), the Court sustained an as-applied challenge to the law. The Court determined that the law could not apply validly to a nonprofit corporation's "issue advocacy." The Court stated that the "electioneering communication" ban could apply only to "express advocacy," which the Court defined as an ad that is "susceptible of no reasonable interpretation other than as an appeal to vote for or against a specific candidate." Thus, the opinion in *WRTL* significantly narrowed the scope of BCRA's ban on corporate independent expenditures, saying that it applied only to a corporation's "express ads" and not to their "issue ads," thereby essentially confining the statutory prohibition to what was enacted in the 1947 Taft-Hartley law rather than the broader BCRA formulation. This set up the Court's decision in *Citizens United*, in which it sustained a facial challenge to the law as violating the First Amendment, thus overruling *Austin* as well as a portion of *McConnell* and rendering the Taft-Hartley law (and not just BCRA) unconstitutional as written.

Citizens United originally was another attempt to chip away at the law incrementally through an as-applied challenge, at least as the lawyers who filed the complaint initially intended. The plaintiff nonprofit corporation, which had aired a "video-on-demand" film critical of Hillary Clinton at the time she was running for President, sought to create another exception similar to the one from *MCFL* or *WRTL*. The Court heard oral argument in the case in March 2009. On the last day of the Term, the Supreme Court declined to issue an opinion and instead set the case for a new oral argument for September 2009 (before the new Term was to start). To prepare for the re-argument, the Court asked the parties to file additional briefs on whether it should overrule its decisions in *Austin* and *McConnell.* The re-argument was Justice Sotomayor's first case on the Court.

What changed between *Austin* (decided in 1990), *McConnell* (decided in 2003), and the Court's consideration of *Citizens United* in 2009? Supporters of the majority's decision would note that *Austin* and *McConnell* were simply wrong from the start and that the Court merely corrected its error. Cynics of the decision might counter that the personnel on the Court changed; in particular, Justice Alito, who voted with the majority in *Citizens United* to strike down the law, replaced Justice O'Connor, who had voted to uphold the law in *McConnell.*

Also in the background of this case was the Supreme Court's decision the year before in *Caperton v. Massey Coal,* in which it ruled, 5-4, that the failure of an elected judge to recuse himself from a case that involved one of his main donors "created a constitutionally intolerable probability of actual bias." *Caperton v. A.T. Massey Coal Co.*, 556 U.S. 868 (2009). This case was not about federal campaign finance law but still provided some insights on the Court's views regarding independent expenditures and their actual or apparent corrupting influence. The donor had contributed the maximum amount to the judge's campaign for the West Virginia Supreme Court and also had given almost $2.5 million to a "527 organization" (a tax-exempt political group that is technically unaffiliated with a candidate) that ran ads targeting the judge's opponent. That is, the donor helped to fund independent expenditures that assisted the judge in his election. The Court found that the judge's failure to recuse in a case involving the donor's company raised a specter of *quid pro quo* corruption, even if there was no evidence that the judge's vote in the case was because of the favorable expenditures. Thus, the Court recognized that independent expenditures could bring about an appearance of corruption, at least when it involved a judicial election. But this was a due process case about the appearance of fairness in litigation based on donations to a judge, not the rights of an individual or corporation to make those independent expenditures. The remedy in *Caperton* was not to limit the expenditures themselves but to require the judge to recuse. Justice Kennedy authored the majority opinion, joined by the four typically "liberal" Justices; he also wrote the majority opinion (joined by the four "conservatives") in *Citizens United* that invalidated the independent expenditure limitation. Essentially, then, Justice Kennedy's vote made the difference in requiring recusal in *Caperton* but striking down the independent expenditure limitation in *Citizens United.* Given that Justice Kennedy wrote both opinions, think about how he might reconcile these views.

As you are reading *Citizens United,* be sure to understand the government's main arguments and why the Court rejects them. What were the justifications behind the law? Why were they insufficient? Also consider the implications of the holding: that corporations and unions have a similar First Amendment right to freedom of speech as individuals in the political arena. What impact will this have on campaigns? Then consider Justice Stevens's response in his dissent. Was there a narrower ground to resolve this dispute?

Were the government's stated interests valid? Did the government make any strategic mistakes in arguing this case? Finally, consider the role of stare decisis. Was the Court justified in overruling precedents that were only 7 (*McConnell*) and 20 (*Austin*) years old?

CITIZENS UNITED v. FEDERAL ELECTION COMMISSION

558 U.S. 310 (2010)

Justice KENNEDY delivered the opinion of the Court.

Federal law prohibits corporations and unions from using their general treasury funds to make independent expenditures for speech defined as an "electioneering communication" or for speech expressly advocating the election or defeat of a candidate. 2 U.S.C. § 441b. Limits on electioneering communications were upheld in *McConnell v. Federal Election Comm'n* (2003). The holding of *McConnell* rested to a large extent on an earlier case, *Austin v. Michigan Chamber of Commerce* (1990). *Austin* had held that political speech may be banned based on the speaker's corporate identity.

In this case we are asked to reconsider *Austin* and, in effect, *McConnell.* It has been noted that "*Austin* was a significant departure from ancient First Amendment principles," *Federal Election Comm'n v. Wisconsin Right to Life, Inc.* (2007) *(WRTL)* (Scalia, J., concurring in part and concurring in judgment). We agree with that conclusion and hold that *stare decisis* does not compel the continued acceptance of *Austin.* The Government may regulate corporate political speech through disclaimer and disclosure requirements, but it may not suppress that speech altogether.

I

A

Citizens United is a nonprofit corporation [with] an annual budget of about $12 million. Most of its funds are from donations by individuals; but, in addition, it accepts a small portion of its funds from for-profit corporations.

In January 2008, Citizens United released a film entitled *Hillary: The Movie.* We refer to the film as *Hillary.* It is a 90-minute documentary about then-Senator Hillary Clinton, who was a candidate in the Democratic Party's 2008 Presidential primary elections. *Hillary* mentions Senator Clinton by name and depicts interviews with political commentators and other persons, most of them quite critical of Senator Clinton. *Hillary* was released in theaters and on DVD, but Citizens United wanted to increase distribution by making it available through video-on-demand.

Video-on-demand allows digital cable subscribers to select programming from various menus, including movies, television shows, sports, news, and music. The viewer can watch the program at any time and can elect to rewind or pause the program. In December 2007, a cable company offered, for a payment of $1.2 million, to make *Hillary* available on a video-on-demand channel called "Elections '08." Some video-on-demand services require viewers to pay a small fee to view a selected program, but here the proposal was to make *Hillary* available to viewers free of charge.

B

Before the Bipartisan Campaign Reform Act of 2002 (BCRA), federal law prohibited—and still does prohibit—corporations and unions from using general treasury funds to [either (1)] make direct contributions to candidates or [(2) make] independent expenditures that expressly advocate the election or defeat of a candidate, through any form of media, in connection with certain qualified federal elections. 2 U.S.C. § 441b (2000 ed.); *see McConnell*; *Federal Election Comm'n v. Massachusetts Citizens for Life, Inc.*, (1986) (*MCFL*). BCRA § 203 amended § 441b to prohibit [the use of corporate or union general treasury funds to be used for] any "electioneering communication" as well. 2 U.S.C. § 441b(b)(2) (2006 ed.). An electioneering communication is defined as "any broadcast, cable, or satellite communication" that "refers to a clearly identified candidate for Federal office" and is made within 30 days of a primary or 60 days of a general election. § 434(f)(3)(A). The Federal Election Commission's (FEC) regulations further define an electioneering communication as a communication that is "publicly distributed." 11 CFR § 100.29(a)(2) (2009). "In the case of a candidate for nomination for President . . . *publicly distributed* means" that the communication "[c]an be received by 50,000 or more persons in a State where a primary election . . . is being held within 30 days." § 100.29(b)(3)(ii). Corporations and unions are barred from using their general treasury funds for express advocacy or electioneering communications. They may establish, however, a "separate segregated fund" (known as a political action committee, or PAC) for these purposes. 2 U.S.C. § 441b(b)(2). The moneys received by the segregated fund are limited to donations from stockholders and employees of the corporation or, in the case of unions, members of the union.

C

Citizens United wanted to make *Hillary* available through video-on-demand within 30 days of the 2008 primary elections. It feared, however, that both the film and the ads would be covered by § 441b's ban on corporate-funded independent expenditures, thus subjecting the corporation to civil and criminal penalties under § 437g. In December 2007, Citizens United sought declaratory and injunctive relief against the FEC. It argued that (1) § 441b is unconstitutional as applied to *Hillary*; and (2) BCRA's disclaimer and disclosure requirements, BCRA §§ 201 and 311, are unconstitutional as applied to *Hillary* and to three ads for the movie.

II

Before considering whether *Austin* should be overruled, we first address whether Citizens United's claim that § 441b cannot be applied to *Hillary* may be resolved on other, narrower grounds.

A

[Omitted.]

B

[Omitted.]

C

Citizens United contends that § 441b should be invalidated as applied to movies shown through video-on-demand, arguing that this delivery system has a lower risk of distorting the political process than do television ads. On what we might call conventional television, advertising spots reach viewers who have chosen a channel or a program for reasons unrelated to the advertising. With video-on-demand, by contrast, the viewer selects a program after taking "a series of affirmative steps": subscribing to cable; navigating through various menus; and selecting the program.

While some means of communication may be less effective than others at influencing the public in different contexts, any effort by the Judiciary to decide which means of communications are to be preferred for the particular type of message and speaker would raise questions as to the courts' own lawful authority. Substantial questions would arise if courts were to begin saying what means of speech should be preferred or disfavored. And in all events, those differentiations might soon prove to be irrelevant or outdated by technologies that are in rapid flux.

Courts, too, are bound by the First Amendment. We must decline to draw, and then redraw, constitutional lines based on the particular media or technology used to disseminate political speech from a particular speaker. It must be noted, moreover, that this undertaking would require substantial litigation over an extended time, all to interpret a law that beyond doubt discloses serious First Amendment flaws. The interpretive process itself would create an inevitable, pervasive, and serious risk of chilling protected speech pending the drawing of fine distinctions that, in the end, would themselves be questionable.

D

Citizens United also asks us to carve out an exception to § 441b's expenditure ban for nonprofit corporate political speech funded overwhelmingly by individuals. As an alternative to reconsidering *Austin*, the Government also seems to prefer this approach. This line of analysis, however, would be unavailing.

In *MCFL*, the Court found unconstitutional § 441b's restrictions on corporate expenditures as applied to nonprofit corporations that were formed for the sole purpose of promoting political ideas, did not engage in business activities, and did not accept contributions from for-profit corporations or labor unions. Citizens United does not qualify for the *MCFL* exemption, however, since some funds used to make the movie were donations from for-profit corporations.

The Government suggests we could [extend *MCFL* to nonprofits that receive only a negligible amount of funds from for-profit corporations]. If the Court decided to create a *de minimis* exception to *MCFL*, the result would be to allow for-profit corporate general treasury funds to be spent for independent expenditures that support candidates. There is no principled basis for doing this without rewriting *Austin*'s holding that the Government can restrict corporate independent expenditures for political speech.

Though it is true that the Court should construe statutes as necessary to avoid constitutional questions, [here this approach] would be difficult to take in view of the language of the statute. In addition to those difficulties the Government's suggestion is troubling for still another reason. The Government does not say that it agrees with the interpretation it wants us to consider. *See* Supp. Brief for Appellee 3, n. 1 ("Some courts" have implied a *de minimis* exception, and "appellant would appear to be covered by these decisions"). Presumably it would find textual difficulties in this approach too. The Government, like any party, can make arguments in the alternative; but it ought to say if there is merit to an alternative proposal instead of merely suggesting it. This is especially true in the context of the First Amendment. As the Government stated, this case "would require a remand" to apply a *de minimis* standard. Tr. of Oral Arg. 39 (Sept. 9, 2009). Applying this standard would thus require case-by-case determinations. But archetypical political speech would be chilled in the meantime. "'First Amendment freedoms need breathing space to survive.'" *WRTL* (opinion of Roberts, C.J.) (quoting *NAACP v. Button* (1963)). We decline to adopt an interpretation that requires intricate case-by-case determinations to verify whether political speech is banned, especially if we are convinced that, in the end, this corporation has a constitutional right to speak on this subject.

E

As the foregoing analysis confirms, the Court cannot resolve this case on a narrower ground without chilling political speech, speech that is central to the meaning and purpose of the First Amendment. It is not judicial restraint to accept an unsound, narrow argument just so the Court can avoid another argument with broader implications. Indeed, a court would be remiss in performing its duties were it to accept an unsound principle merely to avoid the necessity of making a broader ruling. Here, the lack of a valid basis for an alternative ruling requires full consideration of the continuing effect of the speech suppression upheld in *Austin*.

III

The First Amendment provides that "Congress shall make no law . . . abridging the freedom of speech." The law before us is an outright ban, backed by criminal sanctions. Section 441b makes it a felony for all corporations—including nonprofit advocacy corporations—either to expressly advocate the election or defeat of candidates or to broadcast electioneering communications within 30 days of a primary election and 60 days of a general election. Thus, the following acts would all be felonies under § 441b: The Sierra

Club runs an ad, within the crucial phase of 60 days before the general election, that exhorts the public to disapprove of a Congressman who favors logging in national forests; the National Rifle Association publishes a book urging the public to vote for the challenger because the incumbent U.S. Senator supports a handgun ban; and the American Civil Liberties Union creates a Web site telling the public to vote for a Presidential candidate in light of that candidate's defense of free speech. These prohibitions are classic examples of censorship.

Section 441b is a ban on corporate speech notwithstanding the fact that a PAC created by a corporation can still speak. A PAC is a separate association from the corporation. So the PAC exemption from § 441b's expenditure ban does not allow corporations to speak. Even if a PAC could somehow allow a corporation to speak—and it does not—the option to form PACs does not alleviate the First Amendment problems with § 441b. PACs are burdensome alternatives; they are expensive to administer and subject to extensive regulations. For example, every PAC must appoint a treasurer, forward donations to the treasurer promptly, keep detailed records of the identities of the persons making donations, preserve receipts for three years, and file an organization statement and report changes to this information within 10 days.

PACs have to comply with these regulations just to speak. This might explain why fewer than 2,000 of the millions of corporations in this country have PACs. PACs, furthermore, must exist before they can speak. Given the onerous restrictions, a corporation may not be able to establish a PAC in time to make its views known regarding candidates and issues in a current campaign.

Section 441b's prohibition on corporate independent expenditures is thus a ban on speech. As a "restriction on the amount of money a person or group can spend on political communication during a campaign," that statute "necessarily reduces the quantity of expression by restricting the number of issues discussed, the depth of their exploration, and the size of the audience reached." *Buckley v. Valeo* (1976). Were the Court to uphold these restrictions, the Government could repress speech by silencing certain voices at any of the various points in the speech process. If § 441b applied to individuals, no one would believe that it is merely a time, place, or manner restriction on speech. Its purpose and effect are to silence entities whose voices the Government deems to be suspect.

Speech is an essential mechanism of democracy, for it is the means to hold officials accountable to the people. The right of citizens to inquire, to hear, to speak, and to use information to reach consensus is a precondition to enlightened self-government and a necessary means to protect it. The First Amendment "'has its fullest and most urgent application' to speech uttered during a campaign for political office." *Eu v. San Francisco County Democratic Central Comm.* (1989) (quoting *Monitor Patriot Co. v. Roy* (1971)).

For these reasons, political speech must prevail against laws that would suppress it, whether by design or inadvertence. Laws that burden political speech are "subject to strict scrutiny," which requires the Government to prove that the restriction "furthers a compelling interest and is narrowly tailored to achieve that interest." *WRTL* (opinion of Roberts, C.J.). While it might be maintained that political speech simply cannot be banned or restricted as a categorical matter, the quoted language from *WRTL* provides a sufficient framework for protecting the relevant First Amendment interests in this case. We shall employ it here.

Premised on mistrust of governmental power, the First Amendment stands against attempts to disfavor certain subjects or viewpoints. Prohibited, too, are restrictions distinguishing among different speakers, allowing speech by some but not others. *See First Nat. Bank of Boston v. Bellotti* (1978). As instruments to censor, these categories are interrelated: Speech restrictions based on the identity of the speaker are all too often simply a means to control content.

Quite apart from the purpose or effect of regulating content, moreover, the Government may commit a constitutional wrong when by law it identifies certain preferred speakers. By taking the right to speak from some and giving it to others, the Government deprives the disadvantaged person or class of the right to use speech to strive to establish worth, standing, and respect for the speaker's voice. The Government may not by these means deprive the public of the right and privilege to determine for itself what speech and speakers are worthy of consideration. The First Amendment protects speech and speaker, and the ideas that flow from each.

The Court has upheld a narrow class of speech restrictions that operate to the disadvantage of certain persons, but these rulings were based on an interest in allowing governmental entities to perform their functions. *See, e.g., Bethel School Dist. No. 403 v. Fraser* (1986) (protecting the "function of public school education"); *Jones v. North Carolina Prisoners' Labor Union, Inc.* (1977) (furthering "the legitimate penological objectives of the corrections system"); *Parker v. Levy* (1974) (ensuring "the capacity of the Government to discharge its [military] responsibilities"); *Civil Service Comm'n v. Letter Carriers* (1973) ("[F]ederal service should depend upon meritorious performance rather than political service"). The corporate independent expenditures at issue in this case, however, would not interfere with governmental functions, so these cases are inapposite.* These precedents stand only for the proposition that there are certain governmental functions that cannot operate without some restrictions on particular kinds of speech. By contrast, it is inherent in the nature of the political process that voters must be free to obtain information from diverse sources in order to determine how to cast their votes. At least before *Austin*, the Court had not allowed the exclusion of a class of speakers from the general public dialogue.

* [Editors' note: Ask yourself whether the Court would distinguish a case involving a corporation with particularly extensive ties to the government; for example, a banking corporation that is a member of the Federal Reserve system, or a defense contractor that depends on the military for most of its revenues. *Cf. Lebron v. National Railroad Passenger Corporation*, 513 U.S. 374 (1995) (holding that Amtrak, although technically a corporation, counts as part of the federal government for First Amendment purposes). *Lebron* also explores the history of governmental corporations and explains why they must be treated to a functional rather than a formalistic analysis under the First Amendment.]

We find no basis for the proposition that, in the context of political speech, the Government may impose restrictions on certain disfavored speakers. Both history and logic lead us to this conclusion.

A

1

The Court has recognized that First Amendment protection extends to corporations. *Bellotti*. This protection has been extended by explicit holdings to the context of political speech. Under the rationale of these precedents, political speech does not lose First Amendment protection "simply because its source is a corporation." *Bellotti*. The Court has thus rejected the argument that political speech of corporations or other associations should be treated differently under the First Amendment simply because such associations are not "natural persons." [*Id.*]

[The Court discussed some of its previous cases that touched upon this issue, but none had dealt directly with the constitutional question regarding a ban on corporate independent expenditures. In most of these cases, a separate concurring or dissenting opinion had mentioned that those Justices would reach the constitutional issues.]

2

[The Court discussed in detail two of its prior cases relating to this issue. In *Buckley v. Valeo*, the Court struck down an independent expenditure ban. The *Buckley* Court, however, "did not consider § 610's separate ban on corporate and union independent expenditures. Had § 610 been challenged in the wake of *Buckley*, however, it could not have been squared with the reasoning and analysis of that precedent."

Four months after *Buckley* was decided, Congress recodified § 610's corporate and union expenditure ban at 2 U.S.C. § 441b, which is the precursor to the law being challenged in *Citizens United*.

Shortly after deciding *Buckley*, the Court in *First Nat. Bank of Boston v. Bellotti* '765 (1978) struck down a state-law prohibition on corporate independent expenditures related to referenda (as opposed to candidate elections). "*Bellotti* did not address the constitutionality of the State's ban on corporate independent expenditures to support candidates. In our view, however, that restriction would have been unconstitutional under *Bellotti*'s central principle: that the First Amendment does not allow political speech restrictions based on a speaker's corporate identity."]

3

Thus the law stood until *Austin*. *Austin* "uph[eld] a direct restriction on the independent expenditure of funds for political speech for the first time in [this Court's] history." [*Austin v. Michigan Chamber of Commerce* (1990)] (Kennedy, J., dissenting). There, the Michigan Chamber of Commerce sought to use general treasury funds to run a newspaper ad supporting a specific candidate. Michigan law, however, prohibited corporate independent expenditures that supported or opposed any candidate for state office. A violation of the law was punishable as a felony. The Court sustained the speech prohibition.

To bypass *Buckley* and *Bellotti*, the *Austin* Court identified a new governmental interest in limiting political speech: an antidistortion interest. *Austin* found a compelling governmental interest in preventing "the corrosive and distorting effects of immense aggregations of wealth that are accumulated with the help of the corporate form and that have little or no correlation to the public's support for the corporation's political ideas."

B

The Court is thus confronted with conflicting lines of precedent: a pre-*Austin* line that forbids restrictions on political speech based on the speaker's corporate identity and a post-*Austin* line that permits them. No case before *Austin* had held that Congress could prohibit independent expenditures for political speech based on the speaker's corporate identity. Before *Austin* Congress had enacted legislation for this purpose, and the Government urged the same proposition before this Court [but never] did the Court adopt the proposition.

In its defense of the corporate-speech restrictions in § 441b, the Government notes the antidistortion rationale on which *Austin* and its progeny rest in part, yet it all but abandons reliance upon it. It argues instead that two other compelling interests support *Austin*'s holding that corporate expenditure restrictions are constitutional: an anticorruption interest and a shareholder-protection interest. We consider the three points in turn.

1

As for *Austin*'s antidistortion rationale, the Government does little to defend it. And with good reason, for the rationale cannot support § 441b.

If the First Amendment has any force, it prohibits Congress from fining or jailing citizens, or associations of citizens, for simply engaging in political speech. If the antidistortion rationale were to be accepted, however, it would permit Government to ban political speech simply because the speaker is an association that has taken on the corporate form. The Government contends that *Austin* permits it to ban corporate expenditures for almost all forms of communication stemming from a corporation. If *Austin* were correct, the Government could prohibit a corporation from expressing political views in media beyond those presented here, such as by printing books. The Government responds "that the FEC has never applied this statute to a book," and if it did, "there would be quite [a] good as-applied challenge." Tr. of Oral Arg. 65 (Sept. 9, 2009). This troubling assertion of brooding governmental power cannot be reconciled with the confidence and stability in civic discourse that the First Amendment must secure.

Political speech is "indispensable to decisionmaking in a democracy, and this is no less true because the speech comes from a corporation rather than an individual." *Bellotti.* This protection for speech is inconsistent with *Austin*'s antidistortion rationale. *Austin* sought to defend the antidistortion rationale as a means to prevent corporations from obtaining "'an unfair advantage in the political marketplace'" by using "'resources amassed in the economic marketplace.'" *Austin* (quoting *MCFL*). But *Buckley* rejected the premise that the Government has an interest "in equalizing the relative ability of individuals and groups to influence the outcome of elections." *Buckley* was specific in stating that "the skyrocketing cost of political campaigns" could not sustain the governmental prohibition. The First Amendment's protections do not depend on the speaker's "financial ability to engage in public discussion." [*Id.*]

Either as support for its antidistortion rationale or as a further argument, the *Austin* majority undertook to distinguish wealthy individuals from corporations on the ground that "[s]tate law grants corporations special advantages—such as limited liability, perpetual life, and favorable treatment of the accumulation and distribution of assets." This does not suffice, however, to allow laws prohibiting speech. "It is rudimentary that the State cannot exact as the price of those special advantages the forfeiture of First Amendment rights." *Id.* (Scalia, J., dissenting).

It is irrelevant for purposes of the First Amendment that corporate funds may "have little or no correlation to the public's support for the corporation's political ideas." *Id.* (majority opinion). All speakers, including individuals and the media, use money amassed from the economic marketplace to fund their speech. The First Amendment protects the resulting speech, even if it was enabled by economic transactions with persons or entities who disagree with the speaker's ideas.

Austin's antidistortion rationale would produce the dangerous, and unacceptable, consequence that Congress could ban political speech of media corporations. Media corporations are now exempt from § 441b's ban on corporate expenditures. *See* 2 U.S.C. §§ 431(9)(B)(i), 434(f)(3)(B)(i). Yet media corporations accumulate wealth with the help of the corporate form, the largest media corporations have "immense aggregations of wealth," and the views expressed by media corporations often "have little or no correlation to the public's support" for those views. *Austin.* Thus, under the Government's reasoning, wealthy media corporations could have their voices diminished to put them on par with other media entities. There is no precedent for permitting this under the First Amendment.

The media exemption discloses further difficulties with the law now under consideration. There is no precedent supporting laws that attempt to distinguish between corporations which are deemed to be exempt as media corporations and those which are not. "We have consistently rejected the proposition that the institutional press has any constitutional privilege beyond that of other speakers." *Id.* (Scalia, J., dissenting). With the advent of the Internet and the decline of print and broadcast media, moreover, the line between the media and others who wish to comment on political and social issues becomes far more blurred.

The law's exception for media corporations is, on its own terms, all but an admission of the invalidity of the antidistortion rationale. And the exemption results in a further, separate reason for finding this law invalid: Again by its own terms, the law exempts some corporations but covers others, even though both have the need or the motive to communicate their views. The exemption applies to media corporations owned or controlled by corporations that have diverse and substantial investments and participate in endeavors other than news. So even assuming the most doubtful proposition that a news organization has a right to speak when others do not, the exemption would allow a conglomerate that owns both a media business and an unrelated business to influence or control the media in order to advance its overall business interest. At the same time, some other corporation, with an identical business interest but no media outlet in its ownership structure, would be forbidden to speak or inform the public about the same issue. This differential treatment cannot be squared with the First Amendment.

Austin interferes with the "open marketplace" of ideas protected by the First Amendment. It permits the Government to ban the political speech of millions of associations of citizens. *See* Statistics of Income 2 (5.8 million for-profit corporations filed 2006 tax returns). Most of these are small corporations without large amounts of wealth. *See* Supp. Brief for Chamber of Commerce of the United States of America as *Amicus Curiae* 1, 3 (96% of the 3 million businesses that belong to the U.S. Chamber of Commerce have fewer than 100 employees); M. Keightley, Congressional Research Service Report for Congress, Business Organizational Choices: Taxation and Responses to Legislative Changes 10 (2009) (more than 75% of corporations whose income is taxed under federal law, see 26 U.S.C. § 301, have less than $1 million in receipts per year). This fact belies the Government's argument that the statute is justified on the ground that it prevents the "distorting effects of immense aggregations of wealth." *Austin*. It is not even aimed at amassed wealth.

The purpose and effect of this law is to prevent corporations, including small and nonprofit corporations, from presenting both facts and opinions to the public. This makes *Austin*'s antidistortion rationale all the more an aberration. "[T]he First Amendment protects the right of corporations to petition legislative and administrative bodies." *Bellotti*. Corporate executives and employees counsel Members of Congress and Presidential administrations on many issues, as a matter of routine and often in private. An *amici* brief filed on behalf of Montana and 25 other States notes that lobbying and corporate communications with elected officials occur on a regular basis. When that phenomenon is coupled with § 441b, the result is that smaller or nonprofit corporations cannot raise a voice to object when other corporations, including those with vast wealth, are cooperating with the Government. That cooperation may sometimes be voluntary, or it may be at the demand of a Government official who uses his or her authority, influence, and power to threaten corporations to support the Government's policies. Those kinds of interactions are often unknown and unseen. The speech that § 441b forbids, though, is public, and all can judge its content and purpose. References to massive corporate treasuries should not mask the real operation of this law. Rhetoric ought not obscure reality.

Even if § 441b's expenditure ban were constitutional, wealthy corporations could still lobby elected officials, although smaller corporations may not have the resources to do so. And wealthy individuals and unincorporated associations can spend unlimited amounts on independent expenditures. Yet certain disfavored associations of citizens—those that have taken on the corporate form—are penalized for engaging in the same political speech.

When Government seeks to use its full power, including the criminal law, to command where a person may get his or her information or what distrusted source he or she may not hear, it uses censorship to control thought. This is unlawful. The First Amendment confirms the freedom to think for ourselves.

2

What we have said also shows the invalidity of other arguments made by the Government. For the most part relinquishing the antidistortion rationale, the Government falls back on the argument that corporate political speech can be banned in order to prevent corruption or its appearance. In *Buckley*, the Court found this interest "sufficiently important" to allow limits on contributions but did not extend that reasoning to expenditure limits. When *Buckley* examined an expenditure ban, it found "that the governmental interest in preventing corruption and the appearance of corruption [was] inadequate to justify [the ban] on independent expenditures."

With regard to large direct contributions, *Buckley* reasoned that they could be given "to secure a political *quid pro quo*," and that "the scope of such pernicious practices can never be reliably ascertained." The practices *Buckley* noted would be covered by bribery laws, *see, e.g.*, 18 U.S.C. § 201, if a *quid pro quo* arrangement were proved. The Court, in consequence, has noted that restrictions on direct contributions are preventative, because few if any contributions to candidates will involve *quid pro quo* arrangements. The *Buckley* Court, nevertheless, sustained limits on direct contributions in order to ensure against the reality or appearance of corruption. That case did not extend this rationale to independent expenditures, and the Court does not do so here.

"The absence of prearrangement and coordination of an expenditure with the candidate or his agent not only undermines the value of the expenditure to the candidate, but also alleviates the danger that expenditures will be given as a *quid pro quo* for improper commitments from the candidate." *Buckley* (independent expenditures have a "substantially diminished potential for abuse"). Limits on independent expenditures, such as § 441b, have a chilling effect extending well beyond the Government's interest in preventing *quid pro quo* corruption. The anticorruption interest is not sufficient to displace the speech here in question. Indeed, 26 States do not restrict independent expenditures by for-profit corporations. The Government does not claim that these expenditures have corrupted the political process in those States.

When *Buckley* identified a sufficiently important governmental interest in preventing corruption or the appearance of corruption, that interest was limited to *quid pro quo* corruption. The fact that speakers may have influence over or access to elected officials does not mean that these officials are corrupt:

> "Favoritism and influence are not . . . avoidable in representative politics. It is in the nature of an elected representative to favor certain policies, and, by necessary corollary, to favor the voters and contributors who support those policies. It is well understood that a substantial and legitimate reason, if not the only reason, to cast a vote for, or to make a contribution to, one candidate over another is that the candidate will respond by producing those political outcomes the supporter favors. Democracy is premised on responsiveness." *McConnell* (opinion of Kennedy, J.).

Reliance on a "generic favoritism or influence theory . . . is at odds with standard First Amendment analyses because it is unbounded and susceptible to no limiting principle." *Id.*

The appearance of influence or access, furthermore, will not cause the electorate to lose faith in our democracy. By definition, an independent expenditure is political speech presented to the electorate that is not coordinated with a candidate. The fact that a corporation, or any other speaker, is willing to spend money to try to persuade voters presupposes that the people have the ultimate influence over elected officials. This is inconsistent with any suggestion that the electorate will refuse "'to take part in democratic governance'" because of additional political speech made by a corporation or any other speaker. *McConnell.*

The *McConnell* record was "over 100,000 pages" long, yet it "does not have any direct examples of votes being exchanged for . . . expenditures." [Citation to lower court opinion] (opinion of Kollar-Kotelly, J.). This confirms *Buckley*'s reasoning that independent expenditures do not lead to, or create the appearance of, *quid pro quo* corruption. In fact, there is only scant evidence that independent expenditures even ingratiate. Ingratiation and access, in any event, are not corruption. BCRA record establishes that certain donations to political parties, called "soft money," were made to gain access to elected officials. This case, however, is about independent expenditures, not soft money. When Congress finds that a problem exists, we must give that finding due deference; but Congress may not choose an unconstitutional remedy. If elected officials succumb to improper influences from independent expenditures; if they surrender their best judgment; and if they put expediency before principle, then surely there is cause for concern. We must give weight to attempts by Congress to seek to dispel either the appearance or the reality of these influences. The remedies enacted by law, however, must comply with the

First Amendment; and, it is our law and our tradition that more speech, not less, is the governing rule. An outright ban on corporate political speech during the critical preelection period is not a permissible remedy. Here Congress has created categorical bans on speech that are asymmetrical to preventing *quid pro quo* corruption.

3

The Government contends further that corporate independent expenditures can be limited because of its interest in protecting dissenting shareholders from being compelled to fund corporate political speech. This asserted interest, like *Austin*'s antidistortion rationale, would allow the Government to ban the political speech even of media corporations. Assume, for example, that a shareholder of a corporation that owns a newspaper disagrees with the political views the newspaper expresses. Under the Government's view, that potential disagreement could give the Government the authority to restrict the media corporation's political speech. The First Amendment does not allow that power. There is, furthermore, little evidence of abuse that cannot be corrected by shareholders "through the procedures of corporate democracy." *Bellotti.*

Those reasons are sufficient to reject this shareholder-protection interest; and, moreover, the statute is both underinclusive and overinclusive. As to the first, if Congress had been seeking to protect dissenting shareholders, it would not have banned corporate speech in only certain media within 30 or 60 days before an election. A dissenting shareholder's interests would be implicated by speech in any media at any time. As to the second, the statute is overinclusive because it covers all corporations, including nonprofit corporations and for-profit corporations with only single shareholders. As to other corporations, the remedy is not to restrict speech but to consider and explore other regulatory mechanisms. The regulatory mechanism here, based on speech, contravenes the First Amendment.

4

We need not reach the question whether the Government has a compelling interest in preventing foreign individuals or associations from influencing our Nation's political process. *Cf.* 2 U.S.C. § 441e (contribution and expenditure ban applied to "foreign national[s]"). Section 441b is not limited to corporations or associations that were created in foreign countries or funded predominately by foreign shareholders. Section 441b therefore would be overbroad even if we assumed, *arguendo*, that the Government has a compelling interest in limiting foreign influence over our political process.*

* [Editors' note: This paragraph was the basis of the dispute between President Barack Obama and Justice Alito at Obama's 2010 State of the Union address. Obama stated that the Court's decision would "open the floodgates for special interests—including foreign companies—to spend without limit in our elections," and Alito visibly mouthed "not true." This set off a vigorous debate regarding whether the President should criticize a Supreme Court decision during the State of the Union speech with the Justices sitting in the front row.]

C

For the reasons above, it must be concluded that *Austin* was not well reasoned. Austin is [further] undermined by experience since its announcement. Political speech is so ingrained in our culture that speakers find ways to circumvent campaign finance laws. Our Nation's speech dynamic is changing, and informative voices should not have to circumvent onerous restrictions to exercise their First Amendment rights. Speakers have become adept at presenting citizens with sound bites, talking points, and scripted messages that dominate the 24-hour news cycle. Corporations, like individuals, do not have monolithic views. On certain topics corporations may possess valuable expertise, leaving them the best equipped to point out errors or fallacies in speech of all sorts, including the speech of candidates and elected officials.

Rapid changes in technology—and the creative dynamic inherent in the concept of free expression—counsel against upholding a law that restricts political speech in certain media or by certain speakers. Today, 30-second television ads may be the most effective way to convey a political message. Soon, however, it may be that Internet sources, such as blogs and social networking Web sites, will provide citizens with significant information about political candidates and issues. Yet, § 441b would seem to ban a blog post expressly advocating the election or defeat of a candidate if that blog were created with corporate funds. The First Amendment does not permit Congress to make these categorical distinctions based on the corporate identity of the speaker and the content of the political speech.

Due consideration leads to this conclusion: *Austin* should be and now is overruled. We return to the principle established in *Buckley* and *Bellotti* that the Government may not suppress political speech on the basis of the speaker's corporate identity. No sufficient governmental interest justifies limits on the political speech of nonprofit or for-profit corporations.

D

Austin is overruled, so it provides no basis for allowing the Government to limit corporate independent expenditures. As the Government appears to concede, overruling *Austin* "effectively invalidate[s] not only BCRA Section 203, but also 2 U.S.C. 441b's prohibition on the use of corporate treasury funds for express advocacy." Brief for Appellee 33, n. 12. Section 441b's restrictions on corporate independent expenditures are therefore invalid and cannot be applied to *Hillary*.

Given our conclusion we are further required to overrule the part of *McConnell* that upheld BCRA § 203's extension of § 441b's restrictions on corporate independent expenditures. The *McConnell* Court relied on the antidistortion interest recognized in *Austin* to uphold a greater restriction on speech than the restriction upheld in *Austin*, and we have found this interest unconvincing and insufficient. This part of *McConnell* is now overruled.

IV

[This Part of the opinion considered the disclosure and disclaimer requirements and is presented below.]

V

When word concerning the plot of the movie *Mr. Smith Goes to Washington* reached the circles of Government, some officials sought, by persuasion, to discourage its distribution. Under *Austin*, though, officials could have done more than discourage its distribution—they could have banned the film. After all, it, like *Hillary*, was speech funded by a corporation that was critical of Members of Congress.* *Mr. Smith Goes to Washington* may be fiction and caricature; but fiction and caricature can be a powerful force.

Modern day movies, television comedies, or skits on Youtube.com might portray public officials or public policies in unflattering ways. Yet if a covered transmission during the blackout period creates the background for candidate endorsement or opposition, a felony occurs solely because a corporation, other than an exempt media corporation, has made the "purchase, payment, distribution, loan, advance, deposit, or gift of money or anything of value" in order to engage in political speech. 2 U.S.C. § 431(9)(A)(i). Speech would be suppressed in the realm where its necessity is most evident: in the public dialogue preceding a real election. Governments are often hostile to speech, but under our law and our tradition it seems stranger than fiction for our Government to make this political speech a crime. Yet this is the statute's purpose and design.

Some members of the public might consider *Hillary* to be insightful and instructive; some might find it to be neither high art nor a fair discussion on how to set the Nation's course; still others simply might suspend judgment on these points but decide to think more about issues and candidates. Those choices and assessments, however, are not for the Government to make. "The First Amendment underwrites the freedom to experiment and to create in the realm of thought and speech. Citizens must be free to use new forms, and new forums, for the expression of ideas. The civic discourse belongs to the people, and the Government may not prescribe the means used to conduct it." *McConnell* (opinion of Kennedy, J.).

The judgment of the District Court is reversed with respect to the constitutionality of 2 U.S.C. § 441b's restrictions on corporate independent expenditures.

* [Editors' note: The Court's claim that under *Austin* Congress could have banned the movie *Mr. Smith Goes to Washington* is incorrect or at least very misleading. This movie did not cross the line from *Bellotti* to *Austin*, from "issue" advocacy to "express candidate" advocacy. Therefore, the movie would have been protected under *Bellotti* even if *Austin* remained good law.]

CITIZENS UNITED v. FEC DISSENT

Justice STEVENS, with whom Justice GINSBURG, Justice BREYER, and Justice SOTOMAYOR join, concurring in part and dissenting in part.

The real issue in this case concerns how, not if, the appellant may finance its electioneering. Citizens United is a wealthy nonprofit corporation that runs a political action committee (PAC) with millions of dollars in assets. Under the Bipartisan Campaign Reform Act of 2002 (BCRA), it could have used those assets to televise and promote *Hillary: The Movie* wherever and whenever it wanted to. It also could have spent unrestricted sums to broadcast *Hillary* at any time other than the 30 days before the last primary election. Neither Citizens United's nor any other corporation's speech has been "banned." All that the parties dispute is whether Citizens United had a right to use the funds in its general treasury to pay for broadcasts during the 30-day period. The notion that the First Amendment dictates an affirmative answer to that question is, in my judgment, profoundly misguided. Even more misguided is the notion that the Court must rewrite the law relating to campaign expenditures by *for-profit* corporations and unions to decide this case.

The basic premise underlying the Court's ruling is its iteration, and constant reiteration, of the proposition that the First Amendment bars regulatory distinctions based on a speaker's identity, including its "identity" as a corporation. While that glittering generality has rhetorical appeal, it is not a correct statement of the law. Nor does it tell us when a corporation may engage in electioneering that some of its shareholders oppose. It does not even resolve the specific question whether Citizens United may be required to finance some of its messages with the money in its PAC. The conceit that corporations must be treated identically to natural persons in the political sphere is not only inaccurate but also inadequate to justify the Court's disposition of this case.

In the context of election to public office, the distinction between corporate and human speakers is significant. Although they make enormous contributions to our society, corporations are not actually members of it. They cannot vote or run for office. Because they may be managed and controlled by nonresidents, their interests may conflict in fundamental respects with the interests of eligible voters. The financial resources, legal structure, and instrumental orientation of corporations raise legitimate concerns about their role in the electoral process. Our lawmakers have a compelling constitutional basis, if not also a democratic duty, to take measures designed to guard against the potentially deleterious effects of corporate spending in local and national races.

Although I concur in the Court's decision to sustain BCRA's disclosure provisions and join Part IV of its opinion, I emphatically dissent from its principal holding.[1]

1. Specifically, Part I addresses the procedural history of the case and the narrower grounds of decision the majority has bypassed. Part II addresses *stare decisis*. Part III addresses the Court's assumptions that BCRA "bans" corporate speech, that identity-based distinctions may not be drawn in the political realm, and that *Austin* and *McConnell* were outliers in our First Amendment tradition. Part IV addresses the Court's treatment of the anticorruption, antidistortion, and shareholder protection rationales for regulating corporate electioneering. [Footnote relocated—EDS.]

I

The Court's ruling threatens to undermine the integrity of elected institutions across the Nation. The path it has taken to reach its outcome will, I fear, do damage to this institution. Before turning to the question whether to overrule *Austin* and part of *McConnell*, it is important to explain why the Court should not be deciding that question.

Narrower Grounds

Consider just three of the narrower grounds of decision that the majority has bypassed. First, the Court could have ruled, on statutory grounds, that a feature-length film distributed through video-on-demand does not qualify as an "electioneering communication" under § 203 of BCRA, 2 U.S.C. § 441b. BCRA defines that term to encompass certain communications transmitted by "broadcast, cable, or satellite." § 434(f)(3)(A). When Congress was developing BCRA, the video-on-demand medium was still in its infancy, and legislators were focused on a very different sort of programming: short advertisements run on television or radio. The sponsors of BCRA acknowledge that the FEC's implementing regulations do not clearly apply to video-on-demand transmissions. *See* Brief for Senator John McCain et al. as *Amici Curiae*. In light of this ambiguity, the distinctive characteristics of video-on-demand, and "[t]he elementary rule . . . that every reasonable construction must be resorted to, in order to save a statute from unconstitutionality," *Hooper v. California* (1895), the Court could have reasonably ruled that § 203 does not apply to *Hillary*.

Second, the Court could have expanded the *MCFL* exemption to cover § 501(c)(4) nonprofits that accept only a *de minimis* amount of money from for-profit corporations. Citizens United professes to be such a group: Its brief says it "is funded predominantly by donations from individuals who support [its] ideological message." Brief for Appellant. Numerous Courts of Appeal have held that *de minimis* business support does not, in itself, remove an otherwise qualifying organization from the ambit of *MCFL*. This Court could have simply followed their lead.

Finally, let us not forget Citizens United's as-applied constitutional challenge. Precisely because Citizens United looks so much like the *MCFL* organizations we have exempted from regulation, while a feature-length video-on-demand film looks so unlike the types of electoral advocacy Congress has found deserving of regulation, this challenge is a substantial one. As the appellant's own arguments show, the Court could have easily limited the breadth of its constitutional holding had it declined to adopt the novel notion that speakers and speech acts must always be treated identically—and always spared expenditures restrictions—in the political realm. Yet the Court nonetheless turns its back on the as-applied review process that has been a staple of campaign finance litigation since *Buckley v. Valeo* (1976).

This brief tour of alternative grounds on which the case could have been decided is not meant to show that any of these grounds is ideal, though each is perfectly "valid," (majority opinion).[16] It is meant to show that there were principled, narrower paths that a Court that was serious about judicial restraint could have taken. There was also the straightforward path: applying *Austin* and *McConnell*, just as the District Court did in holding that the funding of Citizens United's film can be regulated under them. The only thing preventing the majority from affirming the District Court, or adopting a narrower ground that would retain *Austin*, is its disdain for *Austin*.

II

The final principle of judicial process that the majority violates is the most transparent: *stare decisis*. I am not an absolutist when it comes to *stare decisis*, in the campaign finance area or in any other. No one is. But if this principle is to do any meaningful work in supporting the rule of law, it must at least demand a significant justification, beyond the preferences of five Justices, for overturning settled doctrine. "[A] decision to overrule should rest on some special reason over and above the belief that a prior case was wrongly decided." *Planned Parenthood of Southeastern Pa. v. Casey* (1992). No such justification exists in this case, and to the contrary there are powerful prudential reasons to keep faith with our precedents.

The Court's central argument for why *stare decisis* ought to be trumped is that it does not like *Austin*. The opinion "was not well reasoned," our colleagues assert, and it conflicts with First Amendment principles. This, of course, is the Court's merits argument, the many defects in which we will soon consider. I am perfectly willing to concede that if one of our precedents were dead wrong in its reasoning or irreconcilable with the rest of our doctrine, there would be a compelling basis for revisiting it. But neither is true of *Austin*, as I explain at length in Parts III and IV [of this dissent], and restating a merits argument with additional vigor does not give it extra weight in the *stare decisis* calculus.

In the end, the Court's rejection of *Austin* and *McConnell* comes down to nothing more than its disagreement with their results. Virtually every one of its arguments was made and rejected in those cases, and the majority opinion is essentially an amalgamation of resuscitated dissents. The only relevant thing that has changed since *Austin* and *McConnell* is the composition of this Court. Today's ruling thus strikes at the vitals of *stare decisis*, "the means by which we ensure that the law will not merely change erratically, but will develop in a principled and intelligible fashion" that "permits society to presume that bedrock principles are founded in the law rather than in the proclivities of individuals." *Vasquez v. Hillery* (1986).

16. The Chief Justice finds our discussion of these narrower solutions "quite perplexing" because we suggest that the Court should "latch on to one of them in order to avoid reaching the broader constitutional question," without doing the same ourselves. There is nothing perplexing about the matter, because we are not similarly situated to our colleagues in the majority. We do not share their view of the First Amendment. Our reading of the Constitution would not lead us to strike down any statutes or overturn any precedents in this case, and we therefore have no occasion to practice constitutional avoidance or to vindicate Citizens United's as-applied challenge. Each of the arguments made above is surely at least as strong as the statutory argument the Court accepted in last year's Voting Rights Act case, *Northwest Austin Municipal Util. Dist. No. One v. Holder* (2009).

III

The novelty of the Court's procedural dereliction and its approach to *stare decisis* is matched by the novelty of its ruling on the merits. The ruling rests on several premises. First, the Court claims that *Austin* and *McConnell* have "banned" corporate speech. Second, it claims that the First Amendment precludes regulatory distinctions based on speaker identity, including the speaker's identity as a corporation. Third, it claims that *Austin* and *McConnell* were radical outliers in our First Amendment tradition and our campaign finance jurisprudence. Each of these claims is wrong.

The So-Called "Ban"

Pervading the Court's analysis is the ominous image of a "categorical ba[n]" on corporate speech. Indeed, the majority invokes the specter of a "ban" on nearly every page of its opinion. This characterization is highly misleading, and needs to be corrected.

In fact it already has been. Our cases have repeatedly pointed out that, "[c]ontrary to the [majority's] critical assumptions," the statutes upheld in *Austin* and *McConnell* do "not impose an *absolute* ban on all forms of corporate political spending." *Austin*; *see also McConnell*. For starters, both statutes provide exemptions for PACs, separate segregated funds established by a corporation for political purposes. "The ability to form and administer separate segregated funds," we observed in *McConnell*, "has provided corporations and unions with a constitutionally sufficient opportunity to engage in express advocacy. That has been this Court's unanimous view."

Under BCRA, any corporation's "stockholders and their families and its executive or administrative personnel and their families" can pool their resources to finance electioneering communications. 2 U.S.C. § 441b(b)(4)(A)(i). A significant and growing number of corporations avail themselves of this option; during the most recent election cycle, corporate and union PACs raised nearly a billion dollars. Administering a PAC entails some administrative burden, but so does complying with the disclaimer, disclosure, and reporting requirements that the Court today upholds, and no one has suggested that the burden is severe for a sophisticated for-profit corporation. To the extent the majority is worried about this issue, it is important to keep in mind that we have no record to show how substantial the burden really is, just the majority's own unsupported factfinding. Like all other natural persons, every shareholder of every corporation remains entirely free under *Austin* and *McConnell* to do however much electioneering she pleases outside of the corporate form. The owners of a "mom & pop" store can simply place ads in their own names, rather than the store's. If ideologically aligned individuals wish to make unlimited expenditures through the corporate form, they may utilize an *MCFL* organization that has policies in place to avoid becoming a conduit for business or union interests.

The laws upheld in *Austin* and *McConnell* leave open many additional avenues for corporations' political speech.

At the time Citizens United brought this lawsuit, the only types of speech that could be regulated under § 203 were: (1) broadcast, cable, or satellite communications; (2) capable of reaching at least 50,000 persons in the relevant electorate; (3) made within 30 days of a primary or 60 days of a general federal election; (4) by a labor union or a non-*MCFL*, nonmedia corporation; (5) paid for with general treasury funds; and (6) susceptible of no reasonable interpretation other than as an appeal to vote for or against a specific candidate. The category of communications meeting all of these criteria is not trivial, but the notion that corporate political speech has been "suppress[ed] . . . altogether," that corporations have been "exclu[ded] . . . from the general public dialogue," or that a work of fiction such as *Mr. Smith Goes to Washington* might be covered, is nonsense.

In many ways, then, § 203 functions as a source restriction or a time, place, and manner restriction. It applies in a viewpoint-neutral fashion to a narrow subset of advocacy messages about clearly identified candidates for federal office, made during discrete time periods through discrete channels. In the case at hand, all Citizens United needed to do to broadcast *Hillary* right before the primary was to abjure business contributions or use the funds in its PAC, which by its own account is "one of the most active conservative PACs in America."

So let us be clear: Neither *Austin* nor *McConnell* held or implied that corporations may be silenced; the FEC is not a "censor"; and in the years since these cases were decided, corporations have continued to play a major role in the national dialogue. Laws such as § 203 target a class of communications that is especially likely to corrupt the political process, that is at least one degree removed from the views of individual citizens, and that may not even reflect the views of those who pay for it. Such laws burden political speech, and that is always a serious matter, demanding careful scrutiny. But the majority's incessant talk of a "ban" aims at a straw man.

Identity-Based Distinctions

[Justice Stevens discounted the majority's argument that Congress cannot make distinctions based on the speaker, especially as between individuals and corporations.]

Our First Amendment Tradition

A third fulcrum of the Court's opinion is the idea that *Austin* and *McConnell* are radical outliers, "aberration[s]," in our First Amendment tradition. The Court has it exactly backwards. It is today's holding that is the radical departure from what had been settled First Amendment law.

[Discussion omitted.]

IV

Having explained why this is not an appropriate case in which to revisit *Austin* and *McConnell* and why these decisions sit perfectly well with "First Amendment principles,"

I come at last to the interests that are at stake. The majority recognizes that *Austin* and *McConnell* may be defended on anticorruption, antidistortion, and shareholder protection rationales. It badly errs both in explaining the nature of these rationales, which overlap and complement each other, and in applying them to the case at hand.

The Anticorruption Interest

Undergirding the majority's approach to the merits is the claim that the only "sufficiently important governmental interest in preventing corruption or the appearance of corruption" is one that is "limited to *quid pro quo* corruption." This is the same "crabbed view of corruption" that was espoused by Justice Kennedy in *McConnell* and squarely rejected by the Court in that case. While it is true that we have not always spoken about corruption in a clear or consistent voice, the approach taken by the majority cannot be right, in my judgment. It disregards our constitutional history and the fundamental demands of a democratic society.

On numerous occasions we have recognized Congress' legitimate interest in preventing the money that is spent on elections from exerting an "'undue influence on an officeholder's judgment'" and from creating " 'the appearance of such influence,'" beyond the sphere of *quid pro quo* relationships. [*McConnell*]. Corruption can take many forms. Bribery may be the paradigm case. But the difference between selling a vote and selling access is a matter of degree, not kind. And selling access is not qualitatively different from giving special preference to those who spent money on one's behalf. Corruption operates along a spectrum, and the majority's apparent belief that *quid pro quo* arrangements can be neatly demarcated from other improper influences does not accord with the theory or reality of politics. It certainly does not accord with the record Congress developed in passing BCRA, a record that stands as a remarkable testament to the energy and ingenuity with which corporations, unions, lobbyists, and politicians may go about scratching each other's backs—and which amply supported Congress' determination to target a limited set of especially destructive practices.

Quid Pro Quo *Corruption*

There is no need to take my side in the debate over the scope of the anticorruption interest to see that the Court's merits holding is wrong. Even under the majority's "crabbed view of corruption," *McConnell*, the Government should not lose this case.

"The importance of the governmental interest in preventing [corruption through the creation of political debts] has never been doubted." *Bellotti*. Even in the cases that have construed the anticorruption interest most narrowly, we have never suggested that such *quid pro quo* debts must take the form of outright vote buying or bribes, which have long been distinct crimes. Rather, they encompass the myriad ways in which outside parties may induce an officeholder to confer a legislative benefit in direct response to, or anticipation of, some outlay of money the parties have made or will make on behalf of the officeholder. It has likewise never been doubted that "[o]f almost equal concern as the danger of actual *quid pro quo* arrangements is the impact of the appearance of corruption." *Id.* A democracy cannot function effectively when its constituent members believe laws are being bought and sold.

In theory, our colleagues accept this much. As applied to BCRA § 203, however, they conclude "[t]he anticorruption interest is not sufficient to displace the speech here in question."

The legislative and judicial proceedings relating to BCRA generated a substantial body of evidence suggesting that, as corporations grew more and more adept at crafting "issue ads" to help or harm a particular candidate, these nominally independent expenditures began to corrupt the political process in a very direct sense. The sponsors of these ads were routinely granted special access after the campaign was over; "candidates and officials knew who their friends were[.]" *McConnell.* Many corporate independent expenditures, it seemed, had become essentially interchangeable with direct contributions in their capacity to generate *quid pro quo* arrangements. In an age in which money and television ads are the coin of the campaign realm, it is hardly surprising that corporations deployed these ads to curry favor with, and to gain influence over, public officials.

The majority appears to think it decisive that BCRA record does not contain "direct examples of votes being exchanged for . . . expenditures." It would have been quite remarkable if Congress had created a record detailing such behavior by its own Members. Proving that a specific vote was exchanged for a specific expenditure has always been next to impossible: Elected officials have diverse motivations, and no one will acknowledge that he sold a vote. Yet, even if "[i]ngratiation and access . . . are not corruption" themselves, they are necessary prerequisites to it; they can create both the opportunity for, and the appearance of, *quid pro quo* arrangements. The influx of unlimited corporate money into the electoral realm also creates new opportunities for the mirror image of *quid pro quo* deals: threats, both explicit and implicit. Starting today, corporations with large war chests to deploy on electioneering may find democratically elected bodies becoming much more attuned to their interests. The majority both misreads the facts and draws the wrong conclusions when it suggests that BCRA record provides "only scant evidence that independent expenditures . . . ingratiate," and that, "in any event," none of it matters.

[T]he consequences of today's holding will not be limited to the legislative or executive context. The majority of the States select their judges through popular elections. At a time when concerns about the conduct of judicial elections have reached a fever pitch, the Court today unleashes the floodgates of corporate and union general treasury spending in these races. Perhaps "*Caperton* motions" [seeking recusal of a Judge who received contributions or significant independent expenditures from a party in a suit before that Judge] will catch some of the worst abuses. This will be small comfort to those States that, after today, may no longer have the ability to place modest limits on corporate electioneering even if they believe such limits to be critical to maintaining the integrity of their judicial systems.

Austin and Corporate Expenditures

Just as the majority gives short shrift to the general societal interests at stake in campaign finance regulation, it also overlooks the distinctive considerations raised by the regulation of *corporate* expenditures. The majority fails to appreciate that *Austin*'s antidistortion rationale is itself an anticorruption rationale, tied to the special concerns raised by corporations. Understood properly, "antidistortion" is simply a variant on the classic governmental interest in protecting against improper influences on officeholders that debilitate the democratic process. It is manifestly not just an "equalizing" ideal in disguise.

1. *Antidistortion*

The fact that corporations are different from human beings might seem to need no elaboration, except that the majority opinion almost completely elides it. *Austin* set forth some of the basic differences. Unlike natural persons, corporations have "limited liability" for their owners and managers, "perpetual life," separation of ownership and control, "and favorable treatment of the accumulation and distribution of assets . . . that enhance their ability to attract capital and to deploy their resources in ways that maximize the return on their shareholders' investments." [*Austin*]. Unlike voters in U.S. elections, corporations may be foreign controlled. Unlike other interest groups, business corporations have been "effectively delegated responsibility for ensuring society's economic welfare"; they inescapably structure the life of every citizen. "'[T]he resources in the treasury of a business corporation,'" furthermore, "'are not an indication of popular support for the corporation's political ideas.'" [*Austin*] (quoting *MCFL*). "'They reflect instead the economically motivated decisions of investors and customers. The availability of these resources may make a corporation a formidable political presence, even though the power of the corporation may be no reflection of the power of its ideas.'" [*Id.* (quoting *MCFL*)].

It might also be added that corporations have no consciences, no beliefs, no feelings, no thoughts, no desires. Corporations help structure and facilitate the activities of human beings, to be sure, and their "personhood" often serves as a useful legal fiction. But they are not themselves members of "We the People" by whom and for whom our Constitution was established.

It is an interesting question "who" is even speaking when a business corporation places an advertisement that endorses or attacks a particular candidate. Presumably it is not the customers or employees, who typically have no say in such matters. It cannot realistically be said to be the shareholders, who tend to be far removed from the day-to-day decisions of the firm and whose political preferences may be opaque to management. Perhaps the officers or directors of the corporation have the best claim to be the ones speaking, except their fiduciary duties generally prohibit them from using corporate funds for personal ends. Some individuals associated with the corporation must make the decision to place the ad, but the idea that these individuals are thereby fostering their self-expression or cultivating their critical faculties is fanciful. It is entirely possible that the corporation's electoral message will *conflict* with their personal convictions. Take away the ability to use general treasury funds for some of those ads, and no one's autonomy, dignity, or political equality has been impinged upon in the least.

"[C]orporate participation" in elections, any business executive will tell you, "is more transactional than ideological." Supp. Brief for Committee for Economic Development as *Amicus Curiae*. In this transactional spirit, some corporations have affirmatively urged Congress to place limits on their electioneering communications. These corporations fear that officeholders will shake them down for supportive ads, that they will have to spend increasing sums on elections in an ever-escalating arms race with their competitors, and that public trust in business will be eroded. A system that effectively forces corporations to use their shareholders' money both to maintain access to, and to avoid retribution from, elected officials may ultimately prove more harmful than beneficial to many corporations. It can impose a kind of implicit tax.

In short, regulations such as § 203 and the statute upheld in *Austin* impose only a limited burden on First Amendment freedoms not only because they target a narrow subset of expenditures and leave untouched the broader "public dialogue," but also because they leave untouched the speech of natural persons. Recognizing the weakness of a speaker-based critique of *Austin*, the Court places primary emphasis not on the corporation's right to electioneer, but rather on the listener's interest in hearing what every possible speaker may have to say. The Court's central argument is that laws such as § 203 have "'deprived [the electorate] of information, knowledge and opinion vital to its function,'" and this, in turn, "interferes with the 'open marketplace' of ideas protected by the First Amendment."

There are many flaws in this argument. If the overriding concern depends on the interests of the audience, surely the public's perception of the value of corporate speech should be given important weight. That perception today is the same as it was a century ago when Theodore Roosevelt delivered the speeches to Congress that, in time, led to the limited prohibition on corporate campaign expenditures that is overruled today. The distinctive threat to democratic integrity posed by corporate domination of politics was recognized at "the inception of the republic" and "has been a persistent theme in American political life" ever since. It is only certain Members of this Court, not the listeners themselves, who have agitated for more corporate electioneering.

Austin recognized that there are substantial reasons why a legislature might conclude that unregulated general treasury expenditures will give corporations "unfai[r] influence" in the electoral process and distort public debate in ways that undermine rather than advance the interests of listeners. The legal structure of corporations allows them to amass and deploy financial resources on a scale few natural persons can match. The structure of a business corporation, furthermore, draws a line between the corporation's economic interests and the political preferences of the individuals associated with the corporation; the corporation must engage the electoral process with the aim "to enhance the profitability of the company, no matter how persuasive the arguments for a broader or conflicting set of priorities," Brief for American Independent Business Alliance as *Amicus Curiae*. In a state election such as the one at issue in *Austin*, the interests of nonresident corporations may be fundamentally adverse to the interests of local voters. Consequently, when corporations grab up the prime broadcasting slots on the eve of an election, they can flood the market with advocacy that bears "little or no correlation" to the ideas of natural persons or to any broader notion of the public good. [*Austin*]. The opinions of real people may be marginalized. "The expenditure restrictions of [2 U.S.C.] § 441b are thus meant to ensure that competition among actors in the political arena is truly competition among ideas." *MCFL*.

In addition to this immediate drowning out of noncorporate voices, there may be deleterious effects that follow soon thereafter. Corporate "domination" of electioneering can generate the impression that corporations dominate our democracy. When citizens turn on their televisions and radios before an election and hear only corporate electioneering, they may lose faith in their capacity, as citizens, to influence public policy. A Government captured by corporate interests, they may come to believe, will be neither responsive to their needs nor willing to give their views a fair hearing. The predictable result is cynicism and disenchantment: an increased perception that large spenders "call the tune" and a reduced "willingness of voters to take part in democratic governance." *McConnell*. To the extent that corporations are allowed to exert undue influence in electoral races, the speech of the eventual winners of those races may also be chilled. Politicians who fear that a certain corporation can make or break their reelection chances may be cowed into silence about that corporation. On a variety of levels, unregulated corporate electioneering might diminish the ability of citizens to "hold officials accountable to the people" and disserve the goal of a public debate that is "uninhibited, robust, and wide-open," *New York Times Co. v. Sullivan* (1964). At the least, I stress again, a legislature is entitled to credit these concerns and to take tailored measures in response.

The majority's unwillingness to distinguish between corporations and humans similarly blinds it to the possibility that corporations' "war chests" and their special "advantages" in the legal realm may translate into special advantages in the market for legislation. When large numbers of citizens have a common stake in a measure that is under consideration, it may be very difficult for them to coordinate resources on behalf of their position. The corporate form, by contrast, "provides a simple way to channel rents to only those who have paid their dues, as it were. If you do not own stock, you do not benefit from the larger dividends or appreciation in the stock price caused by the passage of private interest legislation." Sitkoff, *Corporate Political Speech, Political Extortion, and the Competition for Corporate Charters*, 69 U. Chi. L. Rev. 1103, 1113 (2002). Corporations, that is, are uniquely equipped to seek laws that favor their owners, not simply because they have a lot of money but because of their legal and organizational structure. Remove all restrictions on their electioneering, and the door may be opened to a type of rent seeking that is "far more destructive" than what noncorporations are capable of. It is for reasons such as these that our campaign finance jurisprudence has long appreciated that "the 'differing structures and purposes' of different entities 'may require different forms of regulation in order to protect the integrity of the electoral process.'" [*Federal Election Comm'n v. National Right to Work Committee* (1982) (*NRWC*)].

The Court's facile depiction of corporate electioneering assumes away all of these complexities. Our colleagues ridicule the idea of regulating expenditures based on "nothing more" than a fear that corporations have a special "ability to persuade," as if corporations were our society's ablest debaters and viewpoint-neutral laws such as § 203 were created to suppress their best arguments. In their haste to knock down yet another straw man, our colleagues simply ignore the fundamental concerns of the *Austin* Court and the legislatures that have passed laws like § 203: to safeguard the integrity, competitiveness, and democratic responsiveness of the electoral process. All of the majority's theoretical arguments turn on a proposition with undeniable surface appeal but little grounding in evidence or experience, "that there is no such thing as too much speech."[74] If individuals in our society had infinite free time to listen to and contemplate every last bit of speech uttered by anyone, anywhere; and if broadcast advertisements had no special ability to influence elections apart from the merits of their arguments (to the extent they make any); and if legislators always operated with nothing less than perfect virtue; then I suppose the majority's premise would be sound. In the real world, we have seen, corporate domination of the airwaves prior to an election may decrease the average listener's exposure to relevant viewpoints, and it may diminish citizens' willingness and capacity to participate in the democratic process.

None of this is to suggest that corporations can or should be denied an opportunity to participate in election campaigns or in any other public forum (much less that a work of art such as *Mr. Smith Goes to Washington* may be banned), or to deny that some corporate speech may contribute significantly to public debate. What it shows, however, is that *Austin*'s "concern about corporate domination of the political process," reflects more than a concern to protect governmental interests outside of the First Amendment. It also reflects a concern to *facilitate* First Amendment values by preserving some breathing room around the electoral "marketplace" of ideas, the marketplace in which the actual people of this Nation determine how they will govern themselves. The majority seems oblivious to the simple truth that laws such as § 203 do not merely pit the anticorruption interest against the First Amendment, but also pit competing First Amendment values against each other. There are, to be sure, serious concerns with any effort to balance the First Amendment rights of speakers against the First Amendment rights of listeners. But when the speakers in question are not real people and when the appeal to "First Amendment principles" depends almost entirely on the listeners' perspective, it becomes necessary to consider how listeners will actually be affected.

74. Of course, no presiding person in a courtroom, legislature, classroom, polling place, or family dinner would take this hyperbole literally.

In critiquing *Austin*'s antidistortion rationale and campaign finance regulation more generally, our colleagues place tremendous weight on the example of media corporations. Yet it is not at all clear that *Austin* would permit § 203 to be applied to them. The press plays a unique role not only in the text, history, and structure of the First Amendment but also in facilitating public discourse; as the *Austin* Court explained, "media corporations differ significantly from other corporations in that their resources are devoted to the collection of information and its dissemination to the public." Our colleagues have raised some interesting and difficult questions about Congress' authority to regulate electioneering by the press, and about how to define what constitutes the press. *But that is not the case before us.* Section 203 does not apply to media corporations, and even if it did, Citizens United is not a media corporation. There would be absolutely no reason to consider the issue of media corporations if the majority did not invent the theory that legislatures must eschew all "identity"-based distinctions and treat a local nonprofit news outlet exactly the same as General Motors.[75] This calls to mind George Berkeley's description of philosophers: "[W]e have first raised a dust and then complain we cannot see." Principles of Human Knowledge/Three Dialogues (R. Woolhouse ed. 1988).

The Court's blinkered and aphoristic approach to the First Amendment may well promote corporate power at the cost of the individual and collective self-expression the Amendment was meant to serve. It will undoubtedly cripple the ability of ordinary citizens, Congress, and the States to adopt even limited measures to protect against corporate domination of the electoral process. Americans may be forgiven if they do not feel the Court has advanced the cause of self-government today.

2. *Shareholder Protection*

There is yet another way in which laws such as § 203 can serve First Amendment values. Interwoven with *Austin*'s concern to protect the integrity of the electoral process is a concern to protect the rights of shareholders from a kind of coerced speech: electioneering expenditures that do not "reflec[t] [their] support." When corporations use general treasury funds to praise or attack a particular candidate for office, it is the shareholders, as the residual claimants, who are effectively footing the bill. Those shareholders who disagree with the corporation's electoral message may find their financial investments being used to undermine their political convictions.

The PAC mechanism, by contrast, helps assure that those who pay for an electioneering communication actually support its content and that managers do not use general treasuries to advance personal agendas. It "'allows corporate political participation without the temptation to use corporate funds for political influence, quite possibly at odds with the sentiments of some shareholders or members.'" *McConnell.* A rule that privileges the

75. Under the majority's view, the legislature is thus damned if it does and damned if it doesn't. If the legislature gives media corporations an exemption from electioneering regulations that apply to other corporations, it violates the newly minted First Amendment rule against identity-based distinctions. If the legislature does not give media corporations an exemption, it violates the First Amendment rights of the press. The only way out of this invented bind: no regulations whatsoever.

use of PACs thus does more than facilitate the political speech of like-minded shareholders; it also curbs the rent seeking behavior of executives and respects the views of dissenters. *Austin*'s acceptance of restrictions on general treasury spending "simply allows people who have invested in the business corporation for purely economic reasons"—the vast majority of investors, one assumes—"to avoid being taken advantage of, without sacrificing their economic objectives." Winkler, *Beyond* Bellotti, 32 Loyola (LA) L. Rev. 133, 201 (1998).

The concern to protect dissenting shareholders and union members has a long history in campaign finance reform. It provided a central motivation for the Tillman Act in 1907 and subsequent legislation, and it has been endorsed in a long line of our cases. Indeed, we have unanimously recognized the governmental interest in "protect[ing] the individuals who have paid money into a corporation or union for purposes other than the support of candidates from having that money used to support political candidates to whom they may be opposed." *NRWC*.

The Court dismisses this interest on the ground that abuses of shareholder money can be corrected "through the procedures of corporate democracy" and, it seems, through Internet-based disclosures.[76] I fail to understand how this addresses the concerns of dissenting union members, who will also be affected by today's ruling, and I fail to understand why the Court is so confident in these mechanisms. By "corporate democracy," presumably the Court means the rights of shareholders to vote and to bring derivative suits for breach of fiduciary duty. In practice, however, many corporate lawyers will tell you that "these rights are so limited as to be almost nonexistent," given the internal authority wielded by boards and managers and the expansive protections afforded by the business judgment rule. Modern technology may help make it easier to track corporate activity, including electoral advocacy, but it is utopian to believe that it solves the problem. Most American households that own stock do so through intermediaries such as mutual funds and pension plans, which makes it more difficult both to monitor and to alter particular holdings. Studies show that a majority of individual investors make no trades at all during a given year. Moreover, if the corporation in question operates a PAC, an investor who sees the company's ads may not know whether they are being funded through the PAC or through the general treasury.

If and when shareholders learn that a corporation has been spending general treasury money on objectionable electioneering, they can divest. Even assuming that they reliably learn as much, however, this solution is only partial. The injury to the shareholders' expressive rights has already occurred; they might have preferred to keep that corporation's stock in their portfolio for any number of economic reasons; and they may incur a capital gains tax or other penalty from selling their shares, changing their pension plan, or the like.

76. I note that, among the many other regulatory possibilities it has left open, ranging from new versions of § 203 supported by additional evidence of *quid pro quo* corruption or its appearance to any number of tax incentive or public financing schemes, today's decision does not require that a legislature rely solely on these mechanisms to protect shareholders. Legislatures remain free in their incorporation and tax laws to condition the types of activity in which corporations may engage, including electioneering activity, on specific disclosure requirements or on prior express approval by shareholders or members.

The shareholder protection rationale has been criticized as underinclusive, in that corporations also spend money on lobbying and charitable contributions in ways that any particular shareholder might disapprove. But those expenditures do not implicate the selection of public officials, an area in which "the interests of unwilling . . . corporate shareholders [in not being] forced to subsidize that speech" "are at their zenith." *Austin*. And in any event, the question is whether shareholder protection provides a basis for regulating expenditures in the weeks before an election, not whether additional types of corporate communications might similarly be conditioned on voluntariness.

Recognizing the limits of the shareholder protection rationale, the *Austin* Court did not hold it out as an adequate and independent ground for sustaining the statute in question. Rather, the Court applied it to reinforce the antidistortion rationale, in two main ways. First, the problem of dissenting shareholders shows that even if electioneering expenditures can advance the political views of some members of a corporation, they will often compromise the views of others. Second, it provides an additional reason, beyond the distinctive legal attributes of the corporate form, for doubting that these "expenditures reflect actual public support for the political ideas espoused." The shareholder protection rationale, in other words, bolsters the conclusion that restrictions on corporate electioneering can serve both speakers' and listeners' interests, as well as the anticorruption interest. And it supplies yet another reason why corporate expenditures merit less protection than individual expenditures.

V

Today's decision is backwards in many senses. It elevates the majority's agenda over the litigants' submissions, broad constitutional theories over narrow statutory grounds, individual dissenting opinions over precedential holdings, assertion over tradition, absolutism over empiricism, rhetoric over reality. Our colleagues have arrived at the conclusion that *Austin* must be overruled and that § 203 is unconstitutional only after mischaracterizing both the reach and rationale of those authorities, and after bypassing or ignoring rules of judicial restraint used to cabin the Court's lawmaking power. Their conclusion that the societal interest in avoiding corruption and the appearance of corruption does not provide an adequate justification for regulating corporate expenditures on candidate elections relies on an incorrect description of that interest, along with a failure to acknowledge the relevance of established facts and the considered judgments of state and federal legislatures over many decades.

In a democratic society, the longstanding consensus on the need to limit corporate campaign spending should outweigh the wooden application of judge-made rules. The majority's rejection of this principle "elevate[s] corporations to a level of deference which has not been seen at least since the days when substantive due process was regularly used to invalidate regulatory legislation thought to unfairly impinge upon established economic interests." *Bellotti* (White, J., dissenting). At bottom, the Court's opinion is thus a rejection of the common sense of the American people, who have recognized a need to prevent corporations from undermining self-government since the founding, and who have fought against the distinctive corrupting potential of corporate electioneering since the days of Theodore Roosevelt. It is a strange time to repudiate that common sense. While American democracy is imperfect, few outside the majority of this Court would have thought its flaws included a dearth of corporate money in politics.

I would affirm the judgment of the District Court.

CITIZENS UNITED v. FEC CONCURRENCES

The concurrences in this case sought largely to respond to Justice Stevens's dissent. Chief Justice Roberts wrote to explain why overruling recent precedent was required in this case. Justice Scalia wrote to respond to Justice Stevens's argument regarding the "Original Understandings" of the First Amendment (which we largely omitted from his opinion above). We have included a few paragraphs from each concurrence just so you have a flavor of the arguments.

Chief Justice ROBERTS, with whom Justice ALITO joins, concurring.

The Government urges us in this case to uphold a direct prohibition on political speech. It asks us to embrace a theory of the First Amendment that would allow censorship not only of television and radio broadcasts, but of pamphlets, posters, the Internet, and virtually any other medium that corporations and unions might find useful in expressing their views on matters of public concern. Its theory, if accepted, would empower the Government to prohibit newspapers from running editorials or opinion pieces supporting or opposing candidates for office, so long as the newspapers were owned by corporations—as the major ones are. First Amendment rights could be confined to individuals, subverting the vibrant public discourse that is at the foundation of our democracy.

It is only because the majority rejects Citizens United's statutory claim that it proceeds to consider the group's various constitutional arguments, beginning with its narrowest claim (that *Hillary* is not the functional equivalent of express advocacy) and proceeding to its broadest claim (that *Austin* should be overruled).

The dissent advocates an approach to addressing Citizens United's claims that I find quite perplexing. It presumably agrees with the majority that Citizens United's narrower statutory and constitutional arguments lack merit—otherwise its conclusion that the group should lose this case would make no sense. Despite agreeing that these narrower arguments fail, however, the dissent argues that the majority should nonetheless latch on to one of them in order to avoid reaching the broader constitutional question of whether *Austin* remains good law. It even suggests that the Court's failure to adopt one of these concededly meritless arguments is a sign that the majority is not "serious about judicial restraint."

This approach is based on a false premise: that our practice of avoiding unnecessary (and unnecessarily broad) constitutional holdings somehow trumps our obligation faithfully to interpret the law. It should go without saying, however, that we cannot embrace a narrow ground of decision simply because it is narrow; it must also be right.

The Court properly rejects that theory, and I join its opinion in full. The First Amendment protects more than just the individual on a soapbox and the lonely pamphleteer. I write separately to address the important principles of judicial restraint and *stare decisis* implicated in this case.

[*S*]*tare decisis* is neither an "inexorable command," *Lawrence v. Texas* (2003), nor "a mechanical formula of adherence to the latest decision," *Helvering v. Hallock* (1940), especially in constitutional cases. If it were, segregation would be legal, minimum wage laws would be unconstitutional, and the Government could wiretap ordinary criminal suspects without first obtaining warrants. As the dissent properly notes, none of us has viewed *stare decisis* in such absolute terms.

Stare decisis is instead a "principle of policy." *Helvering*. When considering whether to reexamine a prior erroneous holding, we must balance the importance of having constitutional questions *decided* against the importance of having them *decided right*. As Justice Jackson explained, this requires a "sober appraisal of the disadvantages of the innovation as well as those of the questioned case, a weighing of practical effects of one against the other." Jackson, Decisional Law and *Stare Decisis*, 30 A.B.A.J. 334 (1944).

In conducting this balancing, we must keep in mind that *stare decisis* is not an end in itself. It is instead "the means by which we ensure that the law will not merely change erratically, but will develop in a principled and intelligible fashion." *Vasquez v. Hillery* (1986). Its greatest purpose is to serve a constitutional ideal—the rule of law. It follows that in the unusual circumstance when fidelity to any particular precedent does more to damage this constitutional ideal than to advance it, we must be more willing to depart from that precedent.

[Chief Justice Roberts then discussed why he believed the balancing required the Court to overrule *Austin*.]

Justice Scalia, with whom Justice Alito joins, and with whom Justice Thomas joins in part, concurring.

I write separately to address Justice Stevens' discussion of "*Original Understandings*." This section of the dissent purports to show that today's decision is not supported by the original understanding of the First Amendment. The dissent attempts this demonstration, however, in splendid isolation from the text of the First Amendment. It never shows why "the freedom of speech" that was the right of Englishmen did not include the freedom to speak in association with other individuals, including association in the corporate form. To be sure, in 1791 (as now) corporations could pursue only the objectives set forth in their charters; but the dissent provides no evidence that their speech in the pursuit of those objectives could be censored.

Instead of taking this straightforward approach to determining the Amendment's meaning, the dissent embarks on a detailed exploration of the Framers' views about the "role of corporations in society." The Framers didn't like corporations, the dissent concludes, and therefore it follows (as night the day) that corporations had no rights of free speech. Of course the Framers' personal affection or disaffection for corporations is relevant only insofar as it can be thought to be reflected in the understood meaning of the text they enacted—not, as the dissent suggests, as a freestanding substitute for that text. But the dissent's distortion of proper analysis is even worse than that. Though faced with a constitutional text that makes no distinction between types of speakers, the dissent feels no necessity to provide even an isolated statement from the founding era to the effect that corporations are *not* covered, but places the burden on petitioners to bring forward statements showing that they *are* ("there is not a scintilla of evidence to support the notion that anyone believed [the First Amendment] would preclude regulatory distinctions based on the corporate form").

. . .

Historical evidence relating to the textually similar clause "the freedom of . . . the press" also provides no support for the proposition that the First Amendment excludes conduct of artificial legal entities from the scope of its protection. The freedom of "the press" was widely understood to protect the publishing activities of individual editors and printers. But these individuals often acted through newspapers, which (much like corporations) had their own names, outlived the individuals who had founded them, could be bought and sold, were sometimes owned by more than one person, and were operated for profit. Their activities were not stripped of First Amendment protection simply because they were carried out under the banner of an artificial legal entity. And the notion which follows from the dissent's view, that modern newspapers, since they are incorporated, have free-speech rights only at the sufferance of Congress, boggles the mind.[6]

. . .

But to return to, and summarize, my principal point, which is the conformity of today's opinion with the original meaning of the First Amendment. The Amendment is written in terms of "speech," not speakers. Its text offers no foothold for excluding any category of speaker, from single individuals to partnerships of individuals, to unincorporated associations of individuals, to incorporated associations of individuals—and the dissent offers no evidence about the original meaning of the text to support any such

6. The dissent seeks to avoid this conclusion (and to turn a liability into an asset) by interpreting the Freedom of the Press Clause to refer to the institutional press (thus demonstrating, according to the dissent, that the Founders "did draw distinctions—explicit distinctions—between types of 'speakers,' or speech outlets or forms"). It is passing strange to interpret the phrase "the freedom of speech, or of the press" to mean, not everyone's right to speak or publish, but rather everyone's right to speak or the institutional press's right to publish. No one thought that is what it meant.

exclusion. We are therefore simply left with the question whether the speech at issue in this case is "speech" covered by the First Amendment. No one says otherwise. A documentary film critical of a potential Presidential candidate is core political speech, and its nature as such does not change simply because it was funded by a corporation. Nor does the character of that funding produce any reduction whatever in the "inherent worth of the speech" and "its capacity for informing the public," *First Nat. Bank of Boston v. Bellotti* (1978). Indeed, to exclude or impede corporate speech is to muzzle the principal agents of the modern free economy. We should celebrate rather than condemn the addition of this speech to the public debate.

---

5. *Contribution Limitations*

As you are well aware, in *Buckley* and subsequent cases the Supreme Court upheld the ability of Congress to enact contribution limitations to prevent corruption or the appearance of corruption. Is there a level of contributions that is so de minimis as not to raise a corruption concern? Moreover, might setting a contribution limit at an extremely low level raise First Amendment problems in that the limitation in essence precludes donors from having any "voice" in politics or thwarts candidates from having any chance to campaign effectively? The next two cases address these issues in the context of state campaign finance laws. Note that—having won a challenge to independent expenditure limitations for corporations (in *Citizens United*, discussed above), the "antiregulation" movement is now setting its sights on eliminating any regulation of contributions. How successful are they likely to be?

As you are reading these cases, keep the following issues in mind: (1) Is *Buckley*'s holding regarding contributions sustainable? (2) Is there a guiding principle on what level of contribution limits are too low? (3) Must contribution limitations be indexed to inflation? (4) What kind of evidence must plaintiffs present to demonstrate that contribution limits are too low? Notice also that these cases are in some ways outliers in that the courts apply the "lower" level of scrutiny for contribution limitations but still strike down both laws.

RANDALL v. SORRELL

548 U.S. 230 (2006)

Justice BREYER announced the judgment of the Court and delivered an opinion, in which THE CHIEF JUSTICE joins, and in which Justice ALITO joins except as to Parts II-B-1 and II-B-2.

We here consider the constitutionality of a Vermont campaign finance statute that limits both (1) the amounts that candidates for state office may spend on their campaigns (expenditure limitations) and (2) the amounts that individuals, organizations, and political parties may contribute to those campaigns (contribution limitations). Vt. Stat. Ann., Tit.

17, § 2801 et seq. (2002). We hold that both sets of limitations are inconsistent with the First Amendment. Well-established precedent makes clear that the expenditure limits violate the First Amendment. The contribution limits are unconstitutional because in their specific details (involving low maximum levels and other restrictions) they fail to satisfy the First Amendment's requirement of careful tailoring. That is to say, they impose burdens upon First Amendment interests that (when viewed in light of the statute's legitimate objectives) are disproportionately severe.

I

A

Prior to 1997, Vermont's campaign finance law imposed no limit upon the amount a candidate for state office could spend. It did, however, impose limits upon the amounts that individuals, corporations, and political committees could contribute to the campaign of such a candidate. Individuals and corporations could contribute no more than $1,000 to any candidate for state office. Political committees, excluding political parties, could contribute no more than $3,000. The statute imposed no limit on the amount that political parties could contribute to candidates.

In 1997, Vermont enacted a more stringent campaign finance law, [Act 64,] the statute at issue here.

Act 64 . . . imposes strict contribution limits. The amount any single individual can contribute to the campaign of a candidate for state office during a "two-year general election cycle" [(which encompasses the primary and general elections)] is limited as follows: governor, lieutenant governor, and other statewide offices, $400; state senator, $300; and state representative, $200. Unlike its expenditure limits, Act 64's contribution limits are not indexed for inflation.

A political committee is subject to these same limits. So is a political party, defined broadly to include "any subsidiary, branch or local unit" of a party, as well as any "national or regional affiliates" of a party (taken separately or together). § 2801(5). Thus, for example, the statute treats the local, state, and national affiliates of the Democratic Party as if they were a single entity and limits their total contribution to a single candidate's campaign for governor (during the primary and the general election together) to $400.

The Act also imposes a limit of $2,000 upon the amount any individual can give to a political party during a 2-year general election cycle.

The Act defines "contribution" broadly in approximately the same way it defines "expenditure." Any expenditure made on a candidate's behalf counts as a contribution to the candidate if it is "intentionally facilitated by, solicited by or approved by" the candidate. §§ 2809(a), (c). And a party expenditure that "primarily benefits six or fewer candidates who are associated with the" party is "presumed" to count against the party's contribution limits. §§ 2809(a), (d).

There are a few exceptions. A candidate's own contributions to the campaign and those of the candidate's family fall outside the contribution limits. Volunteer services do not count as contributions. Nor does the cost of a meet-the-candidate function, provided that the total cost for the function amounts to $100 or less.

B

[Omitted.]

II

[The Court struck down the expenditure limitation in Vermont's law as violating the First Amendment. The Court rejected the state's invitation to overrule the part of *Buckley* that struck down the FECA's independent expenditure limits and ruled that *Buckley* is indistinguishable from this case with respect to independent expenditures.]

III

We turn now to a more complex question, namely, the constitutionality of Act 64's contribution limits. The parties, while accepting *Buckley*'s approach, dispute whether, despite *Buckley*'s general approval of statutes that limit campaign contributions, Act 64's contribution limits are so severe that in the circumstances its particular limits violate the First Amendment.

A

As with the Act's expenditure limits, we begin with *Buckley*. In that case, the Court upheld the $1,000 contribution limit before it. *Buckley* recognized that contribution limits, like expenditure limits, "implicate fundamental First Amendment interests," namely, the freedoms of "political expression" and "political association." But, unlike expenditure limits (which "necessarily reduc[e] the quantity of expression by restricting the number of issues discussed, the depth of their exploration, and the size of the audience reached,") contribution limits "involv[e] little direct restraint on" the contributor's speech. They do restrict "one aspect of the contributor's freedom of political association," namely, the contributor's ability to support a favored candidate, but they nonetheless "permi[t] the symbolic expression of support evidenced by a contribution," and they do "not in any way infringe the contributor's freedom to discuss candidates and issues."

Consequently, the Court wrote, contribution limitations are permissible as long as the Government demonstrates that the limits are "closely drawn" to match a "sufficiently important interest." It found that the interest advanced in the case, "prevent[ing] corruption" and its "appearance," was "sufficiently important" to justify the statute's contribution limits.

The Court also found that the contribution limits before it were "closely drawn." It recognized that, in determining whether a particular contribution limit was "closely drawn," the amount, or level, of that limit could make a difference. Indeed, it wrote that "contribution restrictions could have a severe impact on political dialogue if the limitations prevented candidates and political committees from amassing the resources necessary for effective advocacy." But the Court added that such "distinctions in degree become significant only when they can be said to amount to differences in kind." Pointing out that it had "'no scalpel to probe, whether, say, a $2,000 ceiling might not serve as well as $1,000,'" the Court found "no indication" that the $1,000 contribution limitations imposed by the Act would have "any dramatic adverse effect on the funding of campaigns." It therefore found the limitations constitutional.

B

Following *Buckley*, we must determine whether Act 64's contribution limits prevent candidates from "amassing the resources necessary for effective [campaign] advocacy"; whether they magnify the advantages of incumbency to the point where they put challengers to a significant disadvantage; in a word, whether they are too low and too strict to survive First Amendment scrutiny. In answering these questions, we recognize, as *Buckley* stated, that we have "'no scalpel to probe'" each possible contribution level. We cannot determine with any degree of exactitude the precise restriction necessary to carry out the statute's legitimate objectives. In practice, the legislature is better equipped to make such empirical judgments, as legislators have "particular expertise" in matters related to the costs and nature of running for office. *McConnell*. Thus ordinarily we have deferred to the legislature's determination of such matters.

Nonetheless, as *Buckley* acknowledged, we must recognize the existence of some lower bound. At some point the constitutional risks to the democratic electoral process become too great. After all, the interests underlying contribution limits, preventing corruption and the appearance of corruption, "directly implicate the integrity of our electoral process." *McConnell*. Yet that rationale does not simply mean "the lower the limit, the better." That is because contribution limits that are too low can also harm the electoral process by preventing challengers from mounting effective campaigns against incumbent officeholders, thereby reducing democratic accountability. Were we to ignore that fact, a statute that seeks to regulate campaign contributions could itself prove an obstacle to the very electoral fairness it seeks to promote. Thus, we see no alternative to the exercise of independent judicial judgment as a statute reaches those outer limits. And, where there is strong indication in a particular case, i.e., danger signs, that such risks exist (both present in kind and likely serious in degree), courts, including appellate courts, must review the record independently and carefully with an eye toward assessing the statute's "tailoring," that is, toward assessing the proportionality of the restrictions.

We find those danger signs present here. As compared with the contribution limits upheld by the Court in the past, and with those in force in other States, Act 64's limits are sufficiently low as to generate suspicion that they are not closely drawn. The Act sets its limits per election cycle, which includes both a primary and a general election. Thus, in a gubernatorial race with both primary and final election contests, the Act's contribution limit amounts to $200 per election per candidate (with significantly lower limits for contributions to candidates for State Senate and House of Representatives). These limits apply both to contributions from individuals and to contributions from political parties, whether made in cash or in expenditures coordinated (or presumed to be coordinated) with the candidate.

These limits are well below the limits this Court upheld in *Buckley*. Indeed, in terms of real dollars (i.e., adjusting for inflation), the Act's $200 per election limit on individual contributions to a campaign for governor is slightly more than one-twentieth of the limit on contributions to campaigns for federal office before the Court in *Buckley*.

Moreover, considered as a whole, Vermont's contribution limits are the lowest in the Nation. Act 64 limits contributions to candidates for statewide office (including governor) to $200 per candidate per election. We have found no State that imposes a lower per election limit. Indeed, we have found only seven States that impose limits on contributions to candidates for statewide office at or below $500 per election, more than twice Act 64's limit.* We are aware of no State that imposes a limit on contributions from political parties to candidates for statewide office lower than Act 64's $200 per candidate per election limit. Similarly, we have found only three States that have limits on contributions to candidates for state legislature below Act 64's $150 and $100 per election limits.** And we are aware of no State that has a lower limit on contributions from political parties to state legislative candidates.

Finally, Vermont's limit is well below the lowest limit this Court has previously upheld, the limit of $1,075 per election (adjusted for inflation every two years) for candidates for Missouri state auditor. [*Nixon v. Shrink Missouri Government PAC* (2000)]. The comparable Vermont limit of roughly $200 per election, not adjusted for inflation, is less than one-sixth of Missouri's current inflation-adjusted limit ($1,275).

In sum, Act 64's contribution limits are substantially lower than both the limits we have previously upheld and comparable limits in other States. These are danger signs that Act 64's contribution limits may fall outside tolerable First Amendment limits. We consequently must examine the record independently and carefully to determine whether Act 64's contribution limits are "closely drawn" to match the State's interests.

C

Our examination of the record convinces us that, from a constitutional perspective, Act 64's contribution limits are too restrictive. We reach this conclusion based not merely on the low dollar amounts of the limits themselves, but also on the statute's effect on political parties and on volunteer activity in Vermont elections. Taken together, Act 64's substantial restrictions on the ability of candidates to raise the funds necessary to run a

* [These states are Arizona, Colorado, Florida, Maine, Massachusetts, Montana, South Dakota.—Eds.]

** [These states are Arizona, Montana, and South Dakota.—Eds.]

competitive election, on the ability of political parties to help their candidates get elected, and on the ability of individual citizens to volunteer their time to campaigns show that the Act is not closely drawn to meet its objectives. In particular, five factors together lead us to this decision.

First, the record suggests, though it does not conclusively prove, that Act 64's contribution limits will significantly restrict the amount of funding available for challengers to run competitive campaigns. For one thing, the petitioners' expert, Clark Bensen, conducted a race-by-race analysis of the 1998 legislative elections (the last to take place before Act 64 took effect) and concluded that Act 64's contribution limits would have reduced the funds available in 1998 to Republican challengers in competitive races in amounts ranging from 18% to 53% of their total campaign income.

For another thing, the petitioners' expert witnesses produced evidence and analysis showing that Vermont political parties (particularly the Republican Party) "target" their contributions to candidates in competitive races, that those contributions represent a significant amount of total candidate funding in such races, and that the contribution limits will cut the parties' contributions to competitive races dramatically. Their statistics showed that the party contributions accounted for a significant percentage of the total campaign income in those races. And their studies showed that Act 64's contribution limits would cut the party contributions by between 85% (for the legislature on average) and 99% (for governor).

The respondents did not contest these figures. Rather, they presented evidence that focused, not upon strongly contested campaigns, but upon the funding amounts available for the average campaign. The respondents' expert, Anthony Gierzynski, concluded, for example, that Act 64 would have a "minimal effect on . . . candidates' ability to raise funds." But he rested this conclusion upon his finding that "only a small proportion of" all contributions to all campaigns for state office "made during the last three elections would have been affected by the new limits."

The respondents' evidence leaves the petitioners' evidence unrebutted in certain key respects. That is because the critical question concerns not simply the average effect of contribution limits on fundraising but, more importantly, the ability of a candidate running against an incumbent officeholder to mount an effective challenge. And information about average races, rather than competitive races, is only distantly related to that question, because competitive races are likely to be far more expensive than the average race.

Rather, the petitioners' studies, taken together with low average Vermont campaign expenditures and the typically higher costs that a challenger must bear to overcome the name-recognition advantage enjoyed by an incumbent, raise a reasonable inference that the contribution limits are so low that they may pose a significant obstacle to candidates in competitive elections. Information about average races does not rebut that inference.

Consequently, the inference amounts to one factor (among others) that here counts against the constitutional validity of the contribution limits.

Second, Act 64's insistence that political parties abide by exactly the same low contribution limits that apply to other contributors threatens harm to a particularly important political right, the right to associate in a political party.

The Act applies its $200 to $400 limits—precisely the same limits it applies to an individual—to virtually all affiliates of a political party taken together as if they were a single contributor. That means, for example, that the Vermont Democratic Party, taken together with all its local affiliates, can make one contribution of at most $400 to the Democratic gubernatorial candidate, one contribution of at most $300 to a Democratic candidate for State Senate, and one contribution of at most $200 to a Democratic candidate for the State House of Representatives. The Act includes within these limits not only direct monetary contributions but also expenditures in kind: stamps, stationery, coffee, doughnuts, gasoline, campaign buttons, and so forth. Indeed, it includes all party expenditures "intended to promote the election of a specific candidate or group of candidates" as long as the candidate's campaign "facilitate[s]," "solicit[s]," or "approve[s]" them. §§ 2809(a), (c). And a party expenditure that "primarily benefits six or fewer candidates who are associated with the" party is "presumed" to count against the party's contribution limits. § 2809(d).

In addition to the negative effect on "amassing funds" that we have described, the Act would severely limit the ability of a party to assist its candidates' campaigns by engaging in coordinated spending on advertising, candidate events, voter lists, mass mailings, even yard signs. And, to an unusual degree, it would discourage those who wish to contribute small amounts of money to a party, amounts that easily comply with individual contribution limits. Suppose that many individuals do not know Vermont legislative candidates personally, but wish to contribute, say, $20 or $40, to the State Republican Party, with the intent that the party use the money to help elect whichever candidates the party believes would best advance its ideals and interests—the basic object of a political party. Or, to take a more extreme example, imagine that 6,000 Vermont citizens each want to give $1 to the State Democratic Party because, though unfamiliar with the details of the individual races, they would like to make a small financial contribution to the goal of electing a Democratic state legislature. And further imagine that the party believes control of the legislature will depend on the outcome of three (and only three) House races. The Act prohibits the party from giving $2,000 (of the $6,000) to each of its candidates in those pivotal races. Indeed, it permits the party to give no more than $200 to each candidate, thereby thwarting the aims of the 6,000 donors from making a meaningful contribution to state politics by giving a small amount of money to the party they support. Thus, the Act would severely inhibit collective political activity by preventing a political party from using contributions by small donors to provide meaningful assistance to any individual candidate.

We consequently agree with the District Court that the Act's contribution limits "would reduce the voice of political parties" in Vermont to a "whisper." And we count the special party-related harms that Act 64 threatens as a further factor weighing against the constitutional validity of the contribution limits.

Third, the Act's treatment of volunteer services aggravates the problem. Like its federal statutory counterpart, the Act excludes from its definition of "contribution" all "services provided without compensation by individuals volunteering their time on behalf of a candidate." Vt. Stat. Ann., Tit. 17, § 2801(2) (2002). But the Act does not exclude the expenses those volunteers incur, such as travel expenses, in the course of campaign activities. The Act's broad definitions would seem to count those expenses against the volunteer's contribution limit, at least where the spending was facilitated or approved by campaign officials. And, unlike the Federal Government's treatment of comparable requirements, the State has not (insofar as we are aware) created an exception excluding such expenses.

The absence of some such exception may matter in the present context, where contribution limits are very low. That combination, low limits and no exceptions, means that a gubernatorial campaign volunteer who makes four or five round trips driving across the State performing volunteer activities coordinated with the campaign can find that he or she is near, or has surpassed, the contribution limit. So too will a volunteer who offers a campaign the use of her house along with coffee and doughnuts for a few dozen neighbors to meet the candidate, say, two or three times during a campaign. Such supporters will have to keep careful track of all miles driven, postage supplied (500 stamps equals $200), pencils and pads used, and so forth. And any carelessness in this respect can prove costly, perhaps generating a headline, "Campaign laws violated," that works serious harm to the candidate.

These sorts of problems are unlikely to affect the constitutionality of a limit that is reasonably high. But Act 64's contribution limits are so low, and its definition of "contribution" so broad, that the Act may well impede a campaign's ability effectively to use volunteers, thereby making it more difficult for individuals to associate in this way. Again, the very low limits at issue help to transform differences in degree into difference in kind. And the likelihood of unjustified interference in the present context is sufficiently great that we must consider the lack of tailoring in the Act's definition of "contribution" as an added factor counting against the constitutional validity of the contribution limits before us.

Fourth, unlike the contribution limits we upheld in *Shrink*, Act 64's contribution limits are not adjusted for inflation. Its limits decline in real value each year. Indeed, in real dollars the Act's limits have already declined by about 20% ($200 in 2006 dollars has a real value of $160.66 in 1997 dollars). A failure to index limits means that limits which are already suspiciously low will almost inevitably become too low over time. It means that future legislation will be necessary to stop that almost inevitable decline, and it thereby imposes the burden of preventing the decline upon incumbent legislators who may not diligently police the need for changes in limit levels to ensure the adequate financing of electoral challenges.

Fifth, we have found nowhere in the record any special justification that might warrant a contribution limit so low or so restrictive as to bring about the serious associational and expressive problems that we have described. Rather, the basic justifications the State has advanced in support of such limits are those present in *Buckley*. The record contains no indication that, for example, corruption (or its appearance) in Vermont is significantly more serious a matter than elsewhere. Indeed, other things being equal, one might reasonably believe that a contribution of, say, $250 (or $450) to a candidate's campaign was less likely to prove a corruptive force than the far larger contributions at issue in the other campaign finance cases we have considered.

These five sets of considerations, taken together, lead us to conclude that Act 64's contribution limits are not narrowly tailored. Rather, the Act burdens First Amendment interests by threatening to inhibit effective advocacy by those who seek election, particularly challengers; its contribution limits mute the voice of political parties; they hamper participation in campaigns through volunteer activities; and they are not indexed for inflation. Vermont does not point to a legitimate statutory objective that might justify these special burdens. We understand that many, though not all, campaign finance regulations impose certain of these burdens to some degree. We also understand the legitimate need for constitutional leeway in respect to legislative line-drawing. But our discussion indicates why we conclude that Act 64 in this respect nonetheless goes too far. It disproportionately burdens numerous First Amendment interests, and consequently, in our view, violates the First Amendment.

[T]he judgment of the Court of Appeals is reversed, and the cases are remanded for further proceedings.

It is so ordered.

Justice ALITO, concurring in part and concurring in the judgment.

[Omitted.]

Justice KENNEDY, concurring in the judgment.

[Omitted.]

Justice THOMAS, with whom Justice SCALIA joins, concurring in the judgment.

[Justice Thomas indicated that he would overrule *Buckley*'s holding with respect to contribution limitations, stating that there is no meaningful distinction between a contribution and an independent expenditure. He would thus subject both contribution and expenditure limitations to strict scrutiny review.]

Justice STEVENS, dissenting.

[Justice Stevens stated that he would overrule *Buckley's* holding with respect to independent expenditures and allow Congress to regulate them. Justice Stevens noted the "fundraising straitjacket" that the lack of independent expenditure limitations engenders.]

Justice SOUTER, with whom Justice GINSBURG joins, and with whom Justice STEVENS joins as to Parts II and III, dissenting.

In 1997, the Legislature of Vermont passed Act 64 after a series of public hearings persuaded legislators that rehabilitating the State's political process required campaign finance reform. A majority of the Court today decides that the expenditure and contribution limits enacted are irreconcilable with the Constitution's guarantee of free speech. I would adhere to the Court of Appeals's decision to remand for further enquiry bearing on the limitations on candidates' expenditures, and I think the contribution limits satisfy controlling precedent. I respectfully dissent.

I

[Omitted.]

II

I believe the Court of Appeals correctly rejected the challenge to the contribution limits. Low though they are, one cannot say that "the contribution limitation[s are] so radical in effect as to render political association ineffective, drive the sound of a candidate's voice below the level of notice, and render contributions pointless." *Nixon v. Shrink Missouri Government PAC* (2000).

To place Vermont's contribution limits beyond the constitutional pale, therefore, is to forget not only the facts of *Shrink*, but also our self-admonition against second-guessing legislative judgments about the risk of corruption to which contribution limits have to be fitted. And deference here would surely not be overly complaisant. Vermont's legislators themselves testified at length about the money that gets their special attention, see Legislative Findings (finding that "[s]ome candidates and elected officials, particularly when time is limited, respond and give access to contributors who make large contributions in preference to those who make small or no contributions"); [Lower court opinion] (testimony of Elizabeth Ready: "If I have only got an hour at night when I get home to return calls, I am much more likely to return [a donor's] call than I would [a non-donor's]. . . . [W]hen you only have a few minutes to talk, there are certain people that get access" (alterations in original)). The record revealed the amount of money the public sees as suspiciously large. And testimony identified the amounts high enough to pay for effective campaigning in a State where the cost of running tends to be on the low side.

Still, our cases do not say deference should be absolute. We can all imagine dollar limits that would be laughable, and per capita comparisons that would be meaningless because aggregated donations simply could not sustain effective campaigns. The plurality thinks that point has been reached in Vermont, and in particular that the low contribution limits threaten the ability of challengers to run effective races against incumbents. Thus, the plurality's limit of deference is substantially a function of suspicion that political incumbents in the legislature set low contribution limits because their public recognition and easy access to free publicity will effectively augment their own spending power beyond anything a challenger can muster. The suspicion is, in other words, that incumbents cannot be trusted to set fair limits, because facially neutral limits do not in fact give challengers an even break. But this received suspicion is itself a proper subject of suspicion. The petitioners offered, and the plurality invokes, no evidence that the risk of a pro-incumbent advantage has been realized. The Legislature of Vermont evidently tried to account for the realities of campaigning in Vermont, and I see no evidence of constitutional miscalculation sufficient to dispense with respect for its judgments.

III

Four issues of detail call for some attention, the first being the requirement that a volunteer's expenses count against the person's contribution limit. The plurality certainly makes out the case that accounting for these expenses will be a colossal nuisance, but there is no case here that the nuisance will noticeably limit volunteering, or that volunteers whose expenses reach the limit cannot continue with their efforts subject to charging their candidates for the excess. Granted, if the provisions for contribution limits were teetering on the edge of unconstitutionality, Act 64's treatment of volunteers' expenses might be the finger-flick that gives the fatal push, but it has no greater significance than that.

Second, the failure of the Vermont law to index its limits for inflation is even less important. This challenge is to the law as it is, not to a law that may have a different impact after future inflation if the state legislature fails to bring it up to economic date.

Third, subjecting political parties to the same contribution limits as individuals does not condemn the Vermont scheme. What we said in *Federal Election Comm'n v. Colorado Republican Federal Campaign Comm.* (2001), dealing with regulation of coordinated expenditures, goes here, too. The capacity and desire of parties to make large contributions to competitive candidates with uphill fights are shared by rich individuals, and the risk that large party contributions would be channels to evade individual limits cannot be eliminated. Nor are these reasons to support the party limits undercut by claims that the restrictions render parties impotent, for the parties are not precluded from uncoordinated spending to benefit their candidates. That said, I acknowledge the suggestions in the petitioners' briefs that such restrictions in synergy with other influences weakening party power would justify a wholesale reexamination of the situation of party organization today. But whether such a comprehensive reexamination belongs in courts or only in legislatures is not an issue presented by these cases.

[Justice Souter's fourth point here is omitted.]

IV

Because I would not pass upon the constitutionality of Vermont's expenditure limits prior to further enquiry into their fit with the problem of fundraising demands on candidates, and because I do not see the contribution limits as depressed to the level of political inaudibility, I respectfully dissent.

FOSTER v. DILGER

Civil Action No. 3:10-41 (E.D. Ky. 2010)

DANNY C. REEVES, District Judge.

Plaintiffs Benjamin Foster and Edward Britton have filed a Motion for a Preliminary Injunction. Plaintiffs argue that Kentucky Revised Statutes ("KRS") § 121.150(6) is unconstitutional and Defendant Dilger and the Kentucky Registry of Election Finance ("Registry") should be enjoined from enforcing the statute's limits on contributions by individuals. For the following reasons, the motion will be granted.

I. Background and Findings of Fact

Plaintiffs are individuals who wish to contribute more than $100 to local school board election campaigns, but cannot do so for fear of criminal prosecution. At the current time, a donor may not contribute more than $100 to each school board candidate. The pertinent portion of KRS § 121.150(6) states:

> No person, permanent committee, or contributing organization shall contribute more than one thousand dollars ($1,000) to any one (1) candidate, campaign committee, political issues committee, nor anyone acting on their behalf, in any one (1) election; except that no person shall contribute more than one hundred dollars ($100) and no permanent committee or contributing organization shall contribute more than two hundred dollars ($200) to any one (1) school board candidate, his campaign committee, nor anyone acting on their behalf, in any one (1) election.

A violation of KRS § 121.150(6) carries a criminal penalty. Plaintiffs claim that the provision limiting donations to candidates for school board unconstitutionally violates their First Amendment rights of expression and association.

The most salient facts in this case are those from Jefferson County. In Jefferson County, campaigns for school board have become increasingly expensive as a result of large independent expenditures by the Jefferson County Teachers Association ("JCTA").

In 2008, JCTA spent nearly $150,000 in support of a single candidate. Plaintiffs highlighted numerous other races where JCTA spent well over $100,000 in support of individual candidates. In contrast, candidates who rely on individual donations must raise support in $100 increments. The Registry confirmed that the overwhelming majority of candidates raise less than $3,000 per campaign from individual donors. Plaintiffs argue that the $100 limit is unconstitutional because, when viewed in contrast with the increasing amounts of independent expenditures and cost of campaigns, it drives the candidate's voice below the point of notice and effectively nullifies their ability to mount a campaign based on individual donations.

II. Analysis

A. Preliminary Injunction Standard

The Sixth Circuit has developed a well-settled, four-factor test to direct the Court's inquiry. The Court should consider: (1) whether there is a strong or substantial likelihood of success on the merits; (2) whether an injunction is necessary to prevent irreparable harm to the plaintiff; (3) whether granting the injunction will cause harm to others, including the defendant; and (4) whether the public interest favors granting the injunction.

B. Irreparable Injury

Plaintiffs correctly contend that they will suffer irreparable harm if the Court does not enjoin enforcement of KRS § 121.150(6). The violation of an individual's constitutional guarantees is intolerable and undoubtably causes irreparable injury. The Supreme Court has recognized that "the loss of First Amendment freedoms, for even minimal periods of time, unquestionably constitutes irreparable injury." *Elrod v. Burns* (1976). If KRS § 121.150(6) does in fact violate Plaintiffs' constitutional freedom of association or speech, allowing its continued operation would cause Plaintiffs irreparable harm.

C. Likelihood of Success on the Merits

The question then becomes whether KRS § 121.150(6) violates Plaintiffs' constitutional right or, in other words, whether Plaintiffs are likely to succeed on the merits of their challenge. After considering the respective arguments, the Court concludes that the Plaintiffs have shown a substantial likelihood of success on their constitutional challenge.

1. Standard of Scrutiny

The initial issue in determining whether Plaintiffs are likely to succeed on the merits is what standard of scrutiny should be applied to the provision they challenge. Under Supreme Court precedent, there is a distinction between the standard of scrutiny applied to regulations of campaign expenditures and those limiting campaign contributions. *Buckley v. Valeo* (1976). Despite Plaintiffs' contention that this distinction is "dubious" and "meaningless," both the Supreme Court and Sixth Circuit have continued to apply it in their holdings. While limits on expenditures are subject to strict scrutiny, limits on contributions are subject to "less rigorous scrutiny," *McConnell.* Contribution limits must be "closely drawn to match a sufficiently important [governmental] interest." [citation omitted] (quoting *McConnell*). KRS § 121.150(6) limits direct contributions. Therefore, to withstand constitutional scrutiny, the regulation must be closely drawn to a sufficiently important governmental interest.

2. The Government's Interest

Defendant asserts that the regulation's purpose is to prevent corruption or the appearance of corruption. This interest is clearly important. The Court in *Citizens United* explained that the anti-corruption rationale is limited to the prevention of actual quid pro quo corruption or the appearance of such. *Citizens United* (2010). Defendant has provided a sufficiently important justification for KRS § 121.150(6), because it is intended to prevent quid pro quo corruption or the appearance of such corruption.

3. Whether the Regulation is "Closely Drawn" to Prevent Quid Pro Quo Corruption

While there is little doubt about the sufficiency of the government's interest, the question becomes whether KRS § 121.150(6) is closely drawn to achieve its stated purpose. A statute is closely drawn when its enforcement does not substantially burden an individual's rights more than is necessary to further the government's legitimate interests.

Plaintiffs contend that the $100 limit is so small that it impermissibly burdens Plaintiffs' associational rights more than is necessary to simply prevent corruption. This argument has substantial merit. While the Court has held that the dollar amount of a contribution "need not be 'fine tuned,'" *Nixon* [*v. Shrink Missouri Government PAC* (2000)] (citing *Buckley*), there is a point at which a limit is so low as to effectively abridge an individual contributor's associational rights. The Court in *Nixon* recognized that some limits may be "so radical in effect as to render political association ineffective, drive the sound of a candidate's voice below the level of notice, and render contributions pointless." The issue, the Court held, "must go to the power to mount a campaign with all the dollars likely to be forthcoming."

Plaintiffs have produced evidence which shows a substantial likelihood that the statute's $100 limit is so low as to make individual contributors' political association ineffective.

At the outset, a regulation limiting contributions over $100 cannot be per se too low. The Sixth Circuit approved a $100 contribution limit for the City of Akron's municipal elections. *Frank v. City of Akron* (6th Cir. 2002). However, the Sixth Circuit's holding in *Frank* is distinguishable from the case at bar. The amendment to the City of Akron's charter limited contributions for elections in one locality: Akron. The court explained that the limit did not fall below the *Nixon* threshold because it did not inhibit candidates from accumulating substantial war chests. The limit did not drive the voice of the candidate below notice because candidates in Akron elections rarely used mass media or television in the way candidates in larger campaigns did. The court found the $100 limit closely drawn to prevent quid pro quo corruption in the Akron municipal elections.

The same cannot be said for a $100 limit for all school board elections across the Commonwealth. Other courts have considered equally low limits and found that they were not "closely drawn." *See Russel v. Burris* (8th Cir. 1998) (striking down contribution limits of $100 and $300 for statewide candidates); *Carver v. Nixon* (8th Cir. 1995) (striking down a system of tiered contribution limits based on the size of the district, where districts with fewer than 100,000 residents were subject to a $100 contribution limit); *Nat'l Black Police Ass'n v. Dist. or Columbia Bd. of Elections and Ethics* (D.D.C. 1996) (holding a $100 contribution limit for mayoral elections unconstitutional).

Defendants have not shown that any of the factors which distinguished *Frank* from this line of precedents are present in this case. First, Jefferson County is significantly larger than the City of Akron. Campaigns in Jefferson County have become increasingly expensive and candidates who rely on individual donations cannot compete. Well-funded candidates regularly utilize expensive mass-media to support their campaigns. Large independent expenditures have driven up the costs of campaigns and made it unrealistic to mount a campaign based solely on individual contributions. The facts which the court found persuasive in *Frank* do not apply to school board elections in counties such as Jefferson County. Plaintiffs' constitutional rights are in danger because KRS § 121.150(6)'s $100 limit threatens to make their individual contributions, and political association, absolutely ineffective. As the *Nixon* court stated, the issue is the power to mount a campaign with the dollars likely to be forthcoming. Here, the Plaintiffs have shown that mounting a campaign on individual contributions is nearly impossible in Jefferson County. Defendant argues that in smaller counties, such as Clay County or Breathitt County, raising the limit to $1,000 is imprudent because that amount "could buy contributors considerable influence." They demonstrate the tailoring problem precisely. While a $100 limit may be necessary to prevent quid pro quo corruption in smaller counties, a $100 contribution is insignificant in Jefferson County. If the purpose is to prevent quid pro quo corruption, the potential for such corruption at a particular dollar amount cannot be the same in every county of every size statewide. The charter amendment in *Frank* was upheld because it was closely drawn to the need to prevent corruption in a particular city election. The Registry has not provided evidence to show that a limit as low as $100 is closely drawn to prevent quid pro quo in places such as Jefferson County. In those counties, such a limit is so low as to nullify Plaintiffs' associational exercise.

Based upon the foregoing analysis, the Plaintiffs have made a sufficient showing that they have a substantial likelihood of success on the merits of their constitutional challenge.

D. Injury to Others

Defendant argues that the Registry and other candidates for school board will be harmed by the granting of a preliminary injunction. He asserts that an injunction will harm the Registry because the Registry has already printed materials outlining the current guidelines and changing the guidelines would cause confusion and expense. Defendant also argues other candidates will be injured who had "planned their campaign strategies taking into account the $100 contribution limit." The Court does not find either of these arguments persuasive.

The harm and difficulty of changing a regulation cannot be said to outweigh the violation of constitutional rights it perpetuates. It would be far worse that an election continue under an unconstitutional regime than the Registry experience difficulty or expense in altering that regime. Further, it is unlikely any individual candidate will be harmed by an injunction. First, the Defendant has offered no proof to support his contention that all candidates have built their campaign strategies around $100 limits. Second, the change in regulations will apply to all candidates. No one candidate will suddenly be on stronger footing than another. All will be allowed to solicit $1,000 donations. It is unlikely that the availability of an extra $900 per donor, by being able to solicit $1,000 rather than $100, will cause harm to an individual candidate. When the potential harm to Plaintiffs is the violation of their constitutional rights and the potential harms to Defendant and others are small, the balance of hardships weighs in favor of granting the injunction.

E. The Public Interest

"It is in the public interest not to perpetuate the unconstitutional application of a statute." *Martin-Marietta Corp. v. Bendix Corp.* (6th Cir. 1982). Every citizen of Kentucky, not just the individual plaintiffs, has a constitutionally-protected interest in political association. When a statute potentially violates that interest, the public interest weighs in favor of enjoining its enforcement. Here, Plaintiffs have met their burden of showing that they have a substantial likelihood of success on the merits of their challenge, and the public interest weighs in favor of enjoining the continued enforcement of the potentially unconstitutional provision.

F. Scope of Injunction

When a court confronts a constitutional flaw in a statute, the court should "fit the solution to the problem" and enjoin only the unconstitutional applications while leaving the other applications in force. *Ayotte v. Planned Parenthood* (2006). Accordingly, there is no need for the Court to enjoin the enforcement of KRS § 121.150(6) altogether. The Court will limit the scope of its injunction to the enforcement of the $100 contribution limit for individual donors to school board campaigns. The $1,000 limit on contributions stands and now governs campaigns for school board as well.

III. Conclusion

Plaintiffs have met their burden of showing that a preliminary injunction is proper. They have proven that their constitutional right of association is in danger and that they will suffer irreparable harm if the Court does not issue an injunction. They have also demonstrated a substantial likelihood of success on the merits of their constitutional challenge to KRS § 121.150(6). They have further shown that an injunction would not cause undue harm to others and that the public interest supports an injunction. For these reasons, it is hereby

Ordered that Plaintiffs' Motion for a Preliminary Injunction is granted. The Court preliminarily enjoins the Registry from enforcing KRS § 121.150(6)'s $100 contribution limit in school board campaigns or prosecuting individuals for contributing amounts above that limit.

[Note: The court eventually converted its preliminary injunction to a permanent injunction and entered a declaratory judgment that KRS § 121.150(6)'s $100 contribution limit for school board campaigns violates the First Amendment.]

NOTES ON *RANDALL* AND *FOSTER*

1. Note how the analyses in these cases are extremely fact-specific. The courts thus far have eschewed bright-line rules in the contribution context, instead explaining that the constitutionality of a contribution limitation will depend largely on the context of the elections in the locality. But ask yourself whether the analysis will be the same in the future in light of two factors: (1) the replacement of Justice O'Connor with Justice Alito and the consequent rightward shift of the Court on campaign finance regulation; and (2) the Court's consideration of *McCutcheon v. FEC*, which raises the possibility that this new conservative majority may for the first time since *Buckley* apply a more rigorous standard of judicial review to a kind of contribution limit (an aggregate limit on total contributions and thus a contribution limit with close affinity to a spending limit). On *McCutcheon*, see the note below.
2. The *Buckley* Court seemed to suggest that contribution limitations are usually valid because they must meet only a lower ("closely drawn") level of scrutiny. Given that both courts struck down contribution limitations under that "lower" threshold, do these cases call that holding into question? Note that other lower courts have generally upheld contribution limitations under closely drawn scrutiny. That is, most contribution limitations are probably constitutional, so long as they are not so low as to actually preclude a candidate from mounting a successful campaign.
3. The court in *Foster* failed to rely on *Randall v. Sorrell* in its analysis. Why do you think this is? Does it say anything about the type of arguments that are most persuasive regarding contribution limits, or was this just an oversight by the District Judge?
4. *Foster* is also a good illustration of how the preliminary injunction standard operates in the context of an election law dispute.
5. In a portion of *Randall* that we omitted, the Court invalidated Vermont's expenditure limitations, refusing the state's invitation to overrule *Buckley*.

It also disagreed with Vermont's alternative argument for imposing an expenditure limitation: to reduce the amount of time candidates must spend raising money. Vermont asserted that, without an expenditure limitation, candidates would have to spend more time raising money to combat the expenditures against them and therefore less time meeting voters. The Court rejected this rationale, saying that a desire to protect a candidate's time from fundraising did not undermine *Buckley*'s reasoning regarding the First Amendment implications of an expenditure limitation.

6. Imagine you are in the Kentucky legislature. What kind of bill would you propose to maintain a sufficiently low contribution limit for school board elections but still follow the *Foster* court's requirements? Put more broadly, what is the best way to tailor a contribution limitation?

A NOTE ON *MCCUTCHEON v. FEC*

During the 2013-2014 Term, the Supreme Court will decide an important case involving a challenge to the Federal Election Campaign Act's (FECA) aggregate contribution limitations. Federal law limits the total amount an individual may contribute to all candidates or political committees during a two-year election cycle. Under FECA (as subsequently amended), an individual may contribute a total of $48,600 to all federal candidates combined, and a total of $74,600 to all noncandidate political committees such as national or state political parties or PACs, during a two-year election cycle. (The aggregate contribution limits are indexed for inflation.) *See* 2 U.S.C. § 441a. These aggregate limits are in addition to the law's base contribution limits for individuals, which are currently set at $2,600 per election to a federal candidate, $10,000 per year to a state or local political party, $32,400 per year to a national political party, and $5,000 per year to any other political committee.

The aggregation limits, however, do not apply to so-called "Super PACs," which promise to make only independent expenditures rather than making contributions of their own to candidates. In the wake of *Citizens United* and *SpeechNow* (to be addressed later in this Part), the Federal Election Commission has decided not to enforce any limits on the amount of money individuals may give to these Super PACs, which in turn are free to spend as much as they wish on express advocacy to support a candidate.

The Court in *Buckley* had upheld FECA's original aggregate contribution limits but did not provide much explanation. Here is the crux of the analysis from *Buckley*:

> The over-all [contribution] ceiling does impose an ultimate restriction upon the number of candidates and committees with which an individual may associate himself by means of financial support. But this quite modest restraint upon protected political activity serves to prevent evasion of the [individual] contribution limitation by a person who

> might otherwise contribute massive amounts of money to a particular candidate through the use of unearmarked contributions to political committees likely to contribute to that candidate, or huge contributions to the candidate's political party. The limited, additional restriction on associational freedom imposed by the over-all ceiling is thus no more than a corollary of the basic individual contribution limitation that we have found to be constitutionally valid.

Buckley v. Valeo, 424 U.S. 1, 38 (1976).

Plaintiffs in *McCutcheon*, including an individual who wanted to contribute more than the aggregate amount would allow, and the Republican National Committee, which wanted to receive this money, challenged the constitutionality of FECA's current aggregate contribution limits. The plaintiffs argued that the aggregate contribution limits burdened core First Amendment speech and therefore should be subject to strict scrutiny. They also argued that the base contribution limits for individuals were sufficient to ward off corruption or the appearance of corruption. Additionally, the plaintiffs contended that the line between contributions and independent expenditures is sufficiently blurry and that the aggregate contribution limits are more like expenditure limitations because they limit the total amount an individual can *spend* on an election through donations (although of course the individual still would be free to make unlimited independent expenditures). However, the lower court, following *Buckley v. Valeo*, upheld the law under closely drawn scrutiny. Indeed, this lawsuit can be seen as a direct challenge to this particular portion of *Buckley*, although the plaintiffs claim that *Buckley* is distinguishable since the overall architecture of campaign finance regulation has changed since then.

The Supreme Court agreed to hear the case, with a decision expected soon after this book goes to print. What might the Supreme Court do? Although it is always risky to read the "tea leaves" from the oral argument in a case, it appears that a majority of the Court (likely noting 5-4 ideological lines) is poised to invalidate at least some of these aggregate contribution limits. Most vulnerable, it would seem, is the aggregate limit on the amount an individual donor can give to multiple candidates. Chief Justice Roberts, in particular, expressed reservations during the oral argument about the idea that Congress could prevent an individual from contributing to more than nine separate congressional candidates—which would happen under the current statute if the individual donor gave the maximum allowed to each of the nine. On the other hand, Chief Justice Roberts—as well as Justice Alito—expressed some sympathy with the idea that Congress might wish to prevent a wealthy donor from spreading millions of dollars among a proliferation of "conduit PACs," which unlike Super PACs, can turn around and transfer the funds to candidates through direct contributions. The prospect of one donor circumventing in this way the limit on contributing to the candidate directly suggests that it is possible that the Court might uphold an aggregate limit applicable solely to these "conduit PACs." If the Court does reach some sort of split decision along these lines, it suggests that the Court would be less likely to use *McCutcheon* as a vehicle for making a broad pronouncement about the basic *Buckley* distinction between expenditure and contribution limits. Still, even this sort of split decision could be seen as eroding (or chipping away at) the contribution-expenditure distinction from *Buckley*, depending in particular on exactly how the majority (or plurality) opinion is written.

As you anticipate the arrival of *McCutcheon*, and as you prepare for your career in the practice of law, imagine yourself in the position of needing to give advice to a client about the meaning and implications of *McCutcheon*, particularly concerning its relationship to the foundational *Buckley* precedent. What would you be looking for in reading *McCutcheon* for the first time, and how best could you review the existing cases (including Buckley) to prepare you for that assignment?

6. *Public Financing*

In an effort to reduce the amount of outside money in campaigns and to try to equalize the opportunity for nonwealthy candidates to compete, both Congress and some state legislatures have passed public financing regimes. Typically, to accept public funds, a candidate must agree to certain conditions, such as a cap on the amount of money their campaigns will raise in contributions or will spend on campaigning. BCRA included what has been termed the "Millionaire's Amendment": If a nonpublically financed candidate spent more than $350,000 of his or her personal funds on the campaign, a publically financed opponent could collect three times the normal contribution amount. The Court struck down this provision in *Davis v. FEC*, 544 U.S. 724 (2008). The Court held that the increased contribution cap for a publicly financed candidate unconstitutionally forced a nonpublically financed candidate "to choose between the First Amendment right to engage in unfettered political speech and subjection to discriminatory fundraising limitations." *Id.* at 739.

Arizona had a similar public financing scheme, but instead of increasing the contribution limits, it actually gave the publicly financed candidate more state money for the campaign if a privately financed candidate spent over a certain amount. Was that provision unconstitutional under the Court's decision in *Davis*, or were there unique features of the Arizona system that would allow it to pass constitutional muster? That question is the subject of the next case. As you are reading, note the strong divide between the majority and dissent. What is the point of public financing systems? Are they viable if rich candidates can devote their personal wealth to being elected? That is, why would a candidate ever accept public financing (and the accompanying strings on contribution limits) if they know a wealthy candidate will be able to raise and spend as much as he or she wants? Does this mean that less-wealthy candidates have no shot at winning an election? Also note the continued adherence to the anticorruption rationale that the Court requires to sustain a campaign finance regulation. Finally, why are the opinions so pointed and caustic toward each other? Are the two sides exhibiting incompatible worldviews regarding the financing of elections?

ARIZONA FREE ENTERPRISE CLUB'S FREEDOM CLUB PAC v. BENNETT

131 S. Ct. 2806 (2011)

Chief Justice ROBERTS delivered the opinion of the Court.

Under Arizona law, candidates for state office who accept public financing can receive additional money from the State in direct response to the campaign activities of privately financed candidates and independent expenditure groups. Once a set spending limit is exceeded, a publicly financed candidate receives roughly one dollar for every dollar spent by an opposing privately financed candidate. The publicly financed candidate also receives roughly one dollar for every dollar spent by independent expenditure groups to support the privately financed candidate, or to oppose the publicly financed candidate. We hold that Arizona's matching funds scheme substantially burdens protected political speech without serving a compelling state interest and therefore violates the First Amendment.

I

A

The Arizona Citizens Clean Elections Act, passed by initiative in 1998, created a voluntary public financing system to fund the primary and general election campaigns of candidates for state office. All eligible candidates for Governor, secretary of state, attorney general, treasurer, superintendent of public instruction, the corporation commission, mine inspector, and the state legislature (both the House and Senate) may opt to receive public funding. Eligibility is contingent on the collection of a specified number of five-dollar contributions from Arizona voters, and the acceptance of certain campaign restrictions and obligations. Publicly funded candidates must agree, among other things, to limit their expenditure of personal funds to $500; participate in at least one public debate; adhere to an overall expenditure cap; and return all unspent public moneys to the State.

In exchange for accepting these conditions, participating candidates are granted public funds to conduct their campaigns. In many cases, this initial allotment may be the whole of the State's financial backing of a publicly funded candidate. But when certain conditions are met, publicly funded candidates are granted additional "equalizing" or matching funds.

Matching funds are available in both primary and general elections. In a primary, matching funds are triggered when a privately financed candidate's expenditures, combined with the expenditures of independent groups made in support of the privately financed candidate or in opposition to a publicly financed candidate, exceed the primary election allotment of state funds to the publicly financed candidate. During the general election, matching funds are triggered when the amount of money a privately financed candidate receives in contributions, combined with the expenditures of independent groups made in support of the privately financed candidate or in opposition to a publicly financed candidate, exceed the general election allotment of state funds to the publicly financed candidate. A privately financed candidate's expenditures of his personal funds are counted as contributions for purposes of calculating matching funds during a general election.

Once matching funds are triggered, each additional dollar that a privately financed candidate spends during the primary results in one dollar in additional state funding to his publicly financed opponent (less a 6% reduction meant to account for fundraising expenses). During a general election, every dollar that a candidate receives in contributions—which includes any money of his own that a candidate spends on his campaign—results in roughly one dollar in additional state funding to his publicly financed opponent. In an election where a privately funded candidate faces multiple publicly financed candidates, one dollar raised or spent by the privately financed candidate results in an almost one dollar increase in public funding to each of the publicly financed candidates.

Once the public financing cap is exceeded, additional expenditures by independent groups can result in dollar-for-dollar matching funds as well. Spending by independent groups on behalf of a privately funded candidate, or in opposition to a publicly funded candidate, results in matching funds. Independent expenditures made in support of a publicly financed candidate can result in matching funds for other publicly financed candidates in a race. The matching funds provision is not activated, however, when independent expenditures are made in opposition to a privately financed candidate. Matching funds top out at two times the initial authorized grant of public funding to the publicly financed candidate.

Under Arizona law, a privately financed candidate may raise and spend unlimited funds, subject to state-imposed contribution limits and disclosure requirements. Contributions to candidates for statewide office are limited to $840 per contributor per election cycle and contributions to legislative candidates are limited to $410 per contributor per election cycle.

An example may help clarify how the Arizona matching funds provision operates. Arizona is divided into 30 districts for purposes of electing members to the State's House of Representatives. Each district elects two representatives to the House biannually. In the last general election, the number of candidates competing for the two available seats in each district ranged from two to seven. Arizona's Fourth District had three candidates for its two available House seats. Two of those candidates opted to accept public funding; one candidate chose to operate his campaign with private funds.

In that election, if the total funds contributed to the privately funded candidate, added to that candidate's expenditure of personal funds and the expenditures of supportive independent groups, exceeded $21,479—the allocation of public funds for the general election in a contested State House race—the matching funds provision would be triggered. At that point, a number of different political activities could result in the distribution of matching funds. For example:

- If the privately funded candidate spent $1,000 of his own money to conduct a direct mailing, each of his publicly funded opponents would receive $940 ($1,000 less the 6% offset).
- If the privately funded candidate held a fundraiser that generated $1,000 in contributions, each of his publicly funded opponents would receive $940.
- If an independent expenditure group spent $1,000 on a brochure expressing its support for the privately financed candidate, each of the publicly financed candidates would receive $940 directly.
- If an independent expenditure group spent $1,000 on a brochure opposing one of the publicly financed candidates, but saying nothing about the privately financed candidate, the publicly financed candidates would receive $940 directly.
- If an independent expenditure group spent $1,000 on a brochure supporting one of the publicly financed candidates, the other publicly financed candidate would receive $940 directly, but the privately financed candidate would receive nothing.
- If an independent expenditure group spent $1,000 on a brochure opposing the privately financed candidate, no matching funds would be issued.

A publicly financed candidate would continue to receive additional state money in response to fundraising and spending by the privately financed candidate and independent expenditure groups until that publicly financed candidate received a total of $64,437 in state funds (three times the initial allocation for a State House race).[3]

B

[Omitted.]

II

"Discussion of public issues and debate on the qualifications of candidates are integral to the operation" of our system of government. *Buckley v. Valeo* (1976). As a result, the First Amendment "'has its fullest and most urgent application' to speech uttered during a campaign for political office." *Eu v. San Francisco County Democratic Central Comm.* (1989) (quoting *Monitor Patriot Co. v. Roy* (1971)). "Laws that burden political speech are" accordingly "subject to strict scrutiny, which requires the Government to prove that the restriction furthers a compelling interest and is narrowly tailored to achieve that interest." *Citizens United v. Federal Election Comm'n* (2010).

Although the speech of the candidates and independent expenditure groups that brought this suit is not directly capped by Arizona's matching funds provision, those

3. Maine and North Carolina have both passed matching funds statutes that resemble Arizona's law. Minnesota, Connecticut, and Florida have also adopted matching funds provisions, but courts have enjoined the enforcement of those schemes after concluding that their operation violates the First Amendment.

parties contend that their political speech is substantially burdened by the state law in the same way that speech was burdened by the law we recently found invalid in *Davis v. Federal Election Comm'n* (2008). In *Davis*, we considered a First Amendment challenge to the so-called "Millionaire's Amendment" of the Bipartisan Campaign Reform Act of 2002. Under that Amendment, if a candidate for the United States House of Representatives spent more than $350,000 of his personal funds, "a new, asymmetrical regulatory scheme [came] into play." The opponent of the candidate who exceeded that limit was permitted to collect individual contributions up to $6,900 per contributor—three times the normal contribution limit of $2,300. The candidate who spent more than the personal funds limit remained subject to the original contribution cap. Davis argued that this scheme "burden[ed] his exercise of his First Amendment right to make unlimited expenditures of his personal funds because" doing so had "the effect of enabling his opponent to raise more money and to use that money to finance speech that counteract[ed] and thus diminishe[d] the effectiveness of Davis' own speech."

In addressing the constitutionality of the Millionaire's Amendment, we acknowledged that the provision did not impose an outright cap on a candidate's personal expenditures. We nonetheless concluded that the Amendment was unconstitutional because it forced a candidate "to choose between the First Amendment right to engage in unfettered political speech and subjection to discriminatory fundraising limitations." Any candidate who chose to spend more than $350,000 of his own money was forced to "shoulder a special and potentially significant burden" because that choice gave fundraising advantages to the candidate's adversary. We determined that this constituted an "unprecedented penalty" and "impose[d] a substantial burden on the exercise of the First Amendment right to use personal funds for campaign speech," and concluded that the Government had failed to advance any compelling interest that would justify such a burden.

A

1

The logic of *Davis* largely controls our approach to this case. Much like the burden placed on speech in *Davis*, the matching funds provision "imposes an unprecedented penalty on any candidate who robustly exercises [his] First Amendment right[s]." Under that provision, "the vigorous exercise of the right to use personal funds to finance campaign speech" leads to "advantages for opponents in the competitive context of electoral politics."

Once a privately financed candidate has raised or spent more than the State's initial grant to a publicly financed candidate, each personal dollar spent by the privately financed candidate results in an award of almost one additional dollar to his opponent. That plainly forces the privately financed candidate to "shoulder a special and potentially significant burden" when choosing to exercise his First Amendment right to spend funds on behalf of his candidacy. If the law at issue in *Davis* imposed a burden on candidate speech, the Arizona law unquestionably does so as well.

The penalty imposed by Arizona's matching funds provision is different in some respects from the penalty imposed by the law we struck down in *Davis*. But those differences make the Arizona law more constitutionally problematic, not less. First, the penalty in *Davis* consisted of raising the contribution limits for one of the candidates. The candidate who benefited from the increased limits still had to go out and raise the funds. He may or may not have been able to do so. The other candidate, therefore, faced merely the possibility that his opponent would be able to raise additional funds, through contribution limits that remained subject to a cap. And still the Court held that this was an "unprecedented penalty," a "special and potentially significant burden" that had to be justified by a compelling state interest—a rigorous First Amendment hurdle. Here the benefit to the publicly financed candidate is the direct and automatic release of public money. That is a far heavier burden than in *Davis*.

Second, depending on the specifics of the election at issue, the matching funds provision can create a multiplier effect. In the Arizona Fourth District House election previously discussed, if the spending cap were exceeded, each dollar spent by the privately funded candidate would result in an additional dollar of campaign funding to each of that candidate's publicly financed opponents. In such a situation, the matching funds provision forces privately funded candidates to fight a political hydra of sorts. Each dollar they spend generates two adversarial dollars in response. Again, a markedly more significant burden than in *Davis*.

Third, unlike the law at issue in *Davis*, all of this is to some extent out of the privately financed candidate's hands. Even if that candidate opted to spend less than the initial public financing cap, any spending by independent expenditure groups to promote the privately financed candidate's election—regardless whether such support was welcome or helpful—could trigger matching funds. What is more, that state money would go directly to the publicly funded candidate to use as he saw fit. That disparity in control—giving money directly to a publicly financed candidate, in response to independent expenditures that cannot be coordinated with the privately funded candidate—is a substantial advantage for the publicly funded candidate. That candidate can allocate the money according to his own campaign strategy, which the privately financed candidate could not do with the independent group expenditures that triggered the matching funds.

2

Arizona, the Clean Elections Institute, and the United States offer several arguments attempting to explain away the existence or significance of any burden imposed by matching funds. None is persuasive.

Arizona contends that the matching funds provision is distinguishable from the law we invalidated in *Davis*. The State correctly points out that our decision in *Davis* focused on the asymmetrical contribution limits imposed by the Millionaire's Amendment. But that is not because—as the State asserts—the reach of that opinion is limited to asymmetrical contribution limits. It is because that was the particular burden on candidate speech we faced in *Davis*. And whatever the significance of the distinction in general, there can be no doubt that the burden on speech is significantly greater in this case than in *Davis*: That means that the law here—like the one in *Davis*—must be justified by a compelling state interest.

The State argues that the matching funds provision actually results in more speech by "increas[ing] debate about issues of public concern" in Arizona elections and "promot[ing] the free and open debate that the First Amendment was intended to foster." In the State's view, this promotion of First Amendment ideals offsets any burden the law might impose on some speakers.

Not so. Any increase in speech resulting from the Arizona law is of one kind and one kind only—that of publicly financed candidates. The burden imposed on privately financed candidates and independent expenditure groups reduces their speech; "restriction[s] on the amount of money a person or group can spend on political communication during a campaign necessarily reduces the quantity of expression." *Buckley*. Thus, even if the matching funds provision did result in more speech by publicly financed candidates and more speech in general, it would do so at the expense of impermissibly burdening (and thus reducing) the speech of privately financed candidates and independent expenditure groups. This sort of "beggar thy neighbor" approach to free speech—"restrict[ing] the speech of some elements of our society in order to enhance the relative voice of others"—is "wholly foreign to the First Amendment." *Id.*

The State correctly asserts that the candidates and independent expenditure groups "do not . . . claim that a single lump sum payment to publicly funded candidates," equivalent to the maximum amount of state financing that a candidate can obtain through matching funds, would impermissibly burden their speech. The State reasons that if providing all the money up front would not burden speech, providing it piecemeal does not do so either. And the State further argues that such incremental administration is necessary to ensure that public funding is not under- or over-distributed.

These arguments miss the point. It is not the amount of funding that the State provides to publicly financed candidates that is constitutionally problematic in this case. It is the manner in which that funding is provided—in direct response to the political speech of privately financed candidates and independent expenditure groups. And the fact that the State's matching mechanism may be more efficient than other alternatives—that it may help the State in "finding the sweet-spot" or "fine-tuning" its financing system to avoid a drain on public resources—is of no moment; "the First Amendment does not permit the State to sacrifice speech for efficiency." *Riley v. National Federation of Blind of N.C., Inc.* (1988).

B

Because the Arizona matching funds provision imposes a substantial burden on the speech of privately financed candidates and independent expenditure groups, "that provision cannot stand unless it is 'justified by a compelling state interest,'" *id.* (quoting *Massachusetts Citizens for Life*).

There is a debate between the parties in this case as to what state interest is served by the matching funds provision. The privately financed candidates and independent expenditure groups contend that the provision works to "level[ ] electoral opportunities" by equalizing candidate "resources and influence." The State and the Clean Elections Institute counter that the provision "furthers Arizona's interest in preventing corruption and the appearance of corruption."

1

There is ample support for the argument that the matching funds provision seeks to "level the playing field" in terms of candidate resources. The clearest evidence is of course the very operation of the provision: It ensures that campaign funding is equal, up to three times the initial public funding allotment. The text of the Citizens Clean Elections Act itself confirms this purpose. The statutory provision setting up the matching funds regime is titled "Equal funding of candidates." Ariz. Rev. Stat. Ann. § 16-952. The Act refers to the funds doled out after the Act's matching mechanism is triggered as "equalizing funds." See §§ 16-952(C)(4), (5). And the regulations implementing the matching funds provision refer to those funds as "equalizing funds" as well. *See* Citizens Clean Elections Commission, Ariz. Admin. Rule R2-20-113.[10]

We have repeatedly rejected the argument that the government has a compelling state interest in "leveling the playing field" that can justify undue burdens on political speech. In *Davis*, we stated that discriminatory contribution limits meant to "level electoral opportunities for candidates of different personal wealth" did not serve "a legitimate government objective," let alone a compelling one. And in *Buckley*, we held that limits on overall campaign expenditures could not be justified by a purported government "interest in equalizing the financial resources of candidates." After all, equalizing campaign resources "might serve not to equalize the opportunities of all candidates, but to handicap a candidate who lacked substantial name recognition or exposure of his views before the start of the campaign." *Id.*

"Leveling the playing field" can sound like a good thing. But in a democracy, campaigning for office is not a game. It is a critically important form of speech. The First Amendment embodies our choice as a Nation that, when it comes to such speech, the guiding principle is freedom—the "unfettered interchange of ideas"—not whatever the State may view as fair. [*Id.*]

10. Prior to oral argument in this case, the Citizens Clean Elections Commission's Web site stated that "'The Citizens Clean Elections Act was passed by the people of Arizona in 1998 to level the playing field when it comes to running for office.' " AFEC Brief 10, n. 3 (quoting http://www.azcleanelections.gov/about-us/get-involved.aspx). The Web site now says that "The Citizens Clean Elections Act was passed by the people of Arizona in 1998 to restore citizen participation and confidence in our political system." [Footnote relocated.—EDS.]

2

As already noted, the State and the Clean Elections Institute disavow any interest in "leveling the playing field." They instead assert that the "Equal funding of candidates" provision serves the State's compelling interest in combating corruption and the appearance of corruption.

Burdening a candidate's expenditure of his own funds on his own campaign does not further the State's anticorruption interest. Indeed, we have said that "reliance on personal funds reduces the threat of corruption" and that "discouraging [the] use of personal funds[ ] disserves the anticorruption interest." *Davis.* That is because "the use of personal funds reduces the candidate's dependence on outside contributions and thereby counteracts the coercive pressures and attendant risks of abuse" of money in politics. *Buckley.* The matching funds provision counts a candidate's expenditures of his own money on his own campaign as contributions, and to that extent cannot be supported by any anticorruption interest.

Arizona already has some of the most austere contribution limits in the United States. Arizona also has stringent fundraising disclosure requirements. In the face of such ascetic contribution limits, strict disclosure requirements, and the general availability of public funding, it is hard to imagine what marginal corruption deterrence could be generated by the matching funds provision.

III

"[T]here is practically universal agreement that a major purpose of" the First Amendment "was to protect the free discussion of governmental affairs," "includ[ing] discussions of candidates." *Buckley.* That agreement "reflects our 'profound national commitment to the principle that debate on public issues should be uninhibited, robust, and wide-open.'" [*Id.*] (quoting *New York Times Co. v. Sullivan* (1964)). True when we said it and true today. Laws like Arizona's matching funds provision that inhibit robust and wide-open political debate without sufficient justification cannot stand.

Justice KAGAN, with whom Justice GINSBURG, Justice BREYER, and Justice SOTOMAYOR join, dissenting.

Imagine two States, each plagued by a corrupt political system. In both States, candidates for public office accept large campaign contributions in exchange for the promise that, after assuming office, they will rank the donors' interests ahead of all others. As a result of these bargains, politicians ignore the public interest, sound public policy languishes, and the citizens lose confidence in their government.

Recognizing the cancerous effect of this corruption, voters of the first State, acting through referendum, enact several campaign finance measures previously approved by this Court. They cap campaign contributions; require disclosure of substantial donations; and create an optional public financing program that gives candidates a fixed public subsidy if they refrain from private fundraising. But these measures do not work. Individuals who "bundle" campaign contributions become indispensable to candidates in need of money. Simple disclosure fails to prevent shady dealing. And candidates choose not to participate in the public financing system because the sums provided do not make them competitive with their privately financed opponents. So the State remains afflicted with corruption.

Voters of the second State, having witnessed this failure, take an ever-so-slightly different tack to cleaning up their political system. They too enact contribution limits and disclosure requirements. But they believe that the greatest hope of eliminating corruption lies in creating an effective public financing program, which will break candidates' dependence on large donors and bundlers. These voters realize, based on the first State's experience, that such a program will not work unless candidates agree to participate in it. And candidates will participate only if they know that they will receive sufficient funding to run competitive races. So the voters enact a program that carefully adjusts the money given to would-be officeholders, through the use of a matching funds mechanism, in order to provide this assurance. The program does not discriminate against any candidate or point of view, and it does not restrict any person's ability to speak. In fact, by providing resources to many candidates, the program creates more speech and thereby broadens public debate. And just as the voters had hoped, the program accomplishes its mission of restoring integrity to the political system. The second State rids itself of corruption.

A person familiar with our country's core values—our devotion to democratic self-governance, as well as to "uninhibited, robust, and wide-open" debate, *New York Times Co. v. Sullivan* (1964)—might expect this Court to celebrate, or at least not to interfere with, the second State's success. But today, the majority holds that the second State's system—the system that produces honest government, working on behalf of all the people—clashes with our Constitution. The First Amendment, the majority insists, requires us all to rely on the measures employed in the first State, even when they have failed to break the stranglehold of special interests on elected officials.

I disagree. The First Amendment's core purpose is to foster a healthy, vibrant political system full of robust discussion and debate. Nothing in Arizona's anti-corruption statute, the Arizona Citizens Clean Elections Act, violates this constitutional protection. To the contrary, the Act promotes the values underlying both the First Amendment and our entire Constitution by enhancing the "opportunity for free political discussion to the end that government may be responsive to the will of the people." *Id.* I therefore respectfully dissent.

I

A

[P]ublic financing systems today dot the national landscape. Almost one-third of the States have adopted some form of public financing, and so too has the Federal

Government for presidential elections. The federal program—which offers presidential candidates a fixed public subsidy if they abstain from private fundraising—originated in the campaign finance law that Congress enacted in 1974 on the heels of the Watergate scandal. Congress explained at the time that the "potentia[l] for abuse" inherent in privately funded elections was "all too clear." S. Rep. No. 93-689, p. 4 (1974).

We declared the presidential public financing system constitutional in *Buckley v. Valeo*. Congress, we stated, had created the program "for the 'general welfare'—to reduce the deleterious influence of large contributions on our political process," as well as to "facilitate communication by candidates with the electorate, and to free candidates from the rigors of fundraising." We thus gave state and municipal governments the green light to adopt public financing systems along the presidential model.

But this model, which distributes a lump-sum grant at the beginning of an election cycle, has a significant weakness: It lacks a mechanism for setting the subsidy at a level that will give candidates sufficient incentive to participate, while also conserving public resources. Public financing can achieve its goals only if a meaningful number of candidates receive the state subsidy, rather than raise private funds. But a public funding program must be voluntary to pass constitutional muster, because of its restrictions on contributions and expenditures. And candidates will choose to sign up only if the subsidy provided enables them to run competitive races. If the grant is pegged too low, it puts the participating candidate at a disadvantage: Because he has agreed to spend no more than the amount of the subsidy, he will lack the means to respond if his privately funded opponent spends over that threshold. So when lump-sum grants do not keep up with campaign expenditures, more and more candidates will choose not to participate.[1] But if the subsidy is set too high, it may impose an unsustainable burden on the public fisc. At the least, hefty grants will waste public resources in the many state races where lack of competition makes such funding unnecessary.

The difficulty, then, is in finding the Goldilocks solution—not too large, not too small, but just right. And this in a world of countless variables—where the amount of money needed to run a viable campaign against a privately funded candidate depends on, among other things, the district, the office, and the election cycle. A state may set lump-sum grants district-by-district, based on spending in past elections; but even that approach leaves out many factors—including the resources of the privately funded candidate—that alter the competitiveness of a seat from one election to the next. In short, the dynamic nature of our electoral system makes ex ante predictions about campaign expenditures almost impossible. And that creates a chronic problem for lump-sum public financing programs, because inaccurate estimates produce subsidies that either dissuade candidates

1. The problem is apparent in the federal system. In recent years, the number of presidential candidates opting to receive public financing has declined because the subsidy has not kept pace with spending by privately financed candidates. The last election cycle offers a stark example: Then-candidate Barack Obama raised $745.7 million in private funds in 2008, in contrast with the $105.4 million he could have received in public funds.

from participating or waste taxpayer money. And so States have made adjustments to the lump-sum scheme that we approved in *Buckley*, in attempts to more effectively reduce corruption.

B

[Omitted.]

II

Arizona's statute does not impose a "restriction" or "substantia[l] burde[n]" on expression. [Citation to majority opinion.] The law has quite the opposite effect: It subsidizes and so produces more political speech. We recognized in *Buckley* that, for this reason, public financing of elections "facilitate[s] and enlarge[s] public discussion," in support of First Amendment values. And what we said then is just as true today. Except in a world gone topsy-turvy, additional campaign speech and electoral competition is not a First Amendment injury.

A

At every turn, the majority tries to convey the impression that Arizona's matching fund statute is of a piece with laws prohibiting electoral speech. The majority invokes the language of "limits," "bar[s]," and "restraints." It equates the law to a "restrictio[n] on the amount of money a person or group can spend on political communication during a campaign." It insists that the statute "restrict[s] the speech of some elements of our society" to enhance the speech of others. And it concludes by reminding us that the point of the First Amendment is to protect "against unjustified government restrictions on speech."

There is just one problem. Arizona's matching funds provision does not restrict, but instead subsidizes, speech. By enabling participating candidates to respond to their opponents' expression, the statute expands public debate, in adherence to "our tradition that more speech, not less, is the governing rule." *Citizens United.* What the law does—all the law does—is fund more speech.

This suit, in fact, may merit less attention than any challenge to a speech subsidy ever seen in this Court. In the usual First Amendment subsidy case, a person complains that the government declined to finance his speech, while bankrolling someone else's; we must then decide whether the government differentiated between these speakers on a prohibited basis—because it preferred one speaker's ideas to another's. But the candidates bringing this challenge do not make that claim—because they were never denied a subsidy. Arizona, remember, offers to support any person running for state office. Petitioners here refused that assistance. So they are making a novel argument: that Arizona violated their First Amendment rights by disbursing funds to other speakers even though they could have received (but chose to spurn) the same financial assistance. Some people might call that *chutzpah.*

Indeed, what petitioners demand is essentially a right to quash others' speech through the prohibition of a (universally available) subsidy program. Petitioners are able to convey their ideas without public financing—and they would prefer the field to themselves, so that they can speak free from response. To attain that goal, they ask this Court to prevent Arizona from funding electoral speech—even though that assistance is offered to every state candidate, on the same (entirely unobjectionable) basis. And this Court gladly obliges.

If an ordinary citizen, without the hindrance of a law degree, thought this result an upending of First Amendment values, he would be correct. [T]o invalidate a statute that restricts no one's speech and discriminates against no idea—that only provides more voices, wider discussion, and greater competition in elections—is to undermine, rather than to enforce, the First Amendment.

B

The majority has one, and only one, way of separating this case from *Buckley* and our other, many precedents involving speech subsidies. According to the Court, the special problem here lies in Arizona's matching funds mechanism, which the majority claims imposes a "substantia[l] burde[n]" on a privately funded candidate's speech.

[D]oes [the supposed effect of the matching provision in leading a privately funded candidate to stop spending in an election] count as a severe burden on expression? By the measure of our prior decisions—which have upheld campaign reforms with an equal or greater impact on speech—the answer is no.

Number one: *Any* system of public financing, including the lump-sum model upheld in *Buckley*, imposes a similar burden on privately funded candidates. Suppose Arizona were to do what all parties agree it could under *Buckley*—provide a single upfront payment (say, $150,000) to a participating candidate, rather than an initial payment (of $50,000) plus 94% of whatever his privately funded opponent spent, up to a ceiling (the same $150,000). That system would "diminis[h] the effectiveness" of a privately funded candidate's speech at least as much, and in the same way: It would give his opponent, who presumably would not be able to raise that sum on his own, more money to spend. And so too, a lump-sum system may deter speech. A person relying on private resources might well choose not to enter a race at all, because he knows he will face an adequately funded opponent. And even if he decides to run, he likely will choose to speak in different ways—for example, by eschewing dubious, easy-to-answer charges—because his opponent has the ability to respond. Indeed, privately funded candidates may well find the lump-sum system more burdensome than Arizona's (assuming the lump is big enough). Pretend you are financing your campaign through private donations. Would you prefer that your opponent receive a guaranteed, upfront payment of $150,000, or that he receive only $50,000, with the possibility—a possibility that you mostly get to control—of collecting another $100,000 somewhere down the road? Me too. That's the first reason the burden on speech cannot command a different result in this case than in *Buckley*.

Number two: Our decisions about disclosure and disclaimer requirements show the Court is wrong. Like a disclosure rule, the matching funds provision may occasionally deter, but "impose[s] no ceiling" on electoral expression. [*Citizens United.*]

Number three: Any burden that the Arizona law imposes does not exceed the burden associated with contribution limits, which we have also repeatedly upheld. I doubt I have to reiterate that the Arizona statute imposes no restraints on any expressive activity. So the majority once again has no reason here to reach a different result.

In this way, our campaign finance cases join our speech subsidy cases in supporting the constitutionality of Arizona's law. Both sets of precedents are in accord that a statute funding electoral speech in the way Arizona's does imposes no First Amendment injury.

C

The majority thinks it has one case on its side—*Davis v. Federal Election Comm'n*—and it pegs everything on that decision. But *Davis* relies on principles that fit securely within our First Amendment law and tradition—most unlike today's opinion.

Under the First Amendment, the similarity between *Davis* and this case matters far less than the differences. Here is the similarity: In both cases, one candidate's campaign expenditure triggered . . . something. Now here are the differences: In *Davis*, the candidate's expenditure triggered a discriminatory speech restriction, which Congress could not otherwise have imposed consistent with the First Amendment; by contrast, in this case, the candidate's expenditure triggers a non-discriminatory speech subsidy, which all parties agree Arizona could have provided in the first instance. In First Amendment law, that difference makes a difference—indeed, it makes all the difference.

But what of the trigger mechanism—in *Davis*, as here, a candidate's campaign expenditures? That, after all, is the only thing that this case and *Davis* share. If *Davis* had held that the trigger mechanism itself violated the First Amendment, then the case would support today's holding. But *Davis* said nothing of the kind. It made clear that the trigger mechanism could not rescue the discriminatory contribution limits from constitutional invalidity; that the limits went into effect only after a candidate spent substantial personal resources rendered them no more permissible under the First Amendment. But *Davis* did not call into question the trigger mechanism itself. Indeed, *Davis* explained that Congress could have used that mechanism to activate a non-discriminatory (i.e., across-the-board) increase in contribution limits; in that case, the Court stated, "Davis' argument would plainly fail." The constitutional infirmity in *Davis* was not the trigger mechanism, but rather what lay on the other side of it—a discriminatory speech restriction.

III

For all these reasons, the Court errs in holding that the government action in this case substantially burdens speech and so requires the State to offer a compelling interest. But in any event, Arizona has come forward with just such an interest, explaining that the

Clean Elections Act attacks corruption and the appearance of corruption in the State's political system. The majority's denigration of this interest—the suggestion that it either is not real or does not matter—wrongly prevents Arizona from protecting the strength and integrity of its democracy.

A

Our campaign finance precedents leave no doubt: Preventing corruption or the appearance of corruption is a compelling government interest. And so too, these precedents are clear: Public financing of elections serves this interest.

And that interest justifies the matching funds provision at issue because it is a critical facet of Arizona's public financing program. The provision is no more than a disbursement mechanism; but it is also the thing that makes the whole Clean Elections Act work. As described earlier, public financing has an Achilles heel—the difficulty of setting the subsidy at the right amount. Too small, and the grant will not attract candidates to the program; and with no participating candidates, the program can hardly decrease corruption. Too large, and the system becomes unsustainable, or at the least an unnecessary drain on public resources. But finding the sweet-spot is near impossible because of variation, across districts and over time, in the political system. Enter the matching funds provision, which takes an ordinary lump-sum amount, divides it into thirds, and disburses the last two of these (to the extent necessary) via a self-calibrating mechanism. That provision is just a fine-tuning of the lump-sum program approved in *Buckley*—a fine-tuning, it bears repeating, that prevents no one from speaking and discriminates against no message. But that fine-tuning can make the difference between a wholly ineffectual program and one that removes corruption from the political system.[12] If public financing furthers a compelling interest—and according to this Court, it does—then so too does the disbursement formula that Arizona uses to make public financing effective. The one conclusion follows directly from the other.

B

The majority instead devotes most of its energy to trying to show that "level[ing] the playing field," not fighting corruption, was the State's real goal. But the majority's distaste for "leveling" provides no excuse for striking down Arizona's law.

1

For starters, the Court has no basis to question the sincerity of the State's interest in rooting out political corruption. As I have just explained, that is the interest the State has

12. For this reason, the majority is quite wrong to say that the State's interest in combating corruption does not support the matching fund provision's application to a candidate's expenditure of his own money or to an independent expenditure. The point is not that these expenditures themselves corrupt the political process. Rather, Arizona includes these, as well as all other, expenditures in the program to ensure that participating candidates receive the funds necessary to run competitive races—and so to attract those candidates in the first instance. That is in direct service of the State's anti-corruption interest.

asserted in this Court; it is the interest predominantly expressed in the "findings and declarations" section of the statute; and it is the interest universally understood (stretching back to Teddy Roosevelt's time) to support public financing of elections. As against all this, the majority claims to have found three smoking guns that reveal the State's true (and nefarious) intention to level the playing field. But the only smoke here is the majority's, and it is the kind that goes with mirrors.

The majority first observes that the matching funds provision is titled "'Equal funding of candidates'" and that it refers to matching grants as "'equalizing funds.'" Well, yes. The statute provides for matching funds (above and below certain thresholds); a synonym for "match" is "equal"; and so the statute uses that term. In sum, the statute describes what the statute does. But the relevant question here (according to the majority's own analysis) is why the statute does that thing—otherwise said, what interest the statute serves. The State explains that its goal is to prevent corruption, and nothing in the Act's descriptive terms suggests any other objective.

Next, the majority notes that the Act allows participating candidates to accept private contributions if (but only if) the State cannot provide the funds it has promised (for example, because of a budget crisis). That provision, the majority argues, shows that when push comes to shove, the State cares more about "leveling" than about fighting corruption. But this is a plain misreading of the law. All the statute does is assure participating candidates that they will not be left in the lurch if public funds suddenly become unavailable. That guarantee helps persuade candidates to enter the program by removing the risk of a state default. And so the provision directly advances the Act's goal of combating corruption.

Finally, the Court remarks in a footnote that the Clean Elections Commission's website once stated that the "'Act was passed by the people of Arizona . . . to level the playing field.'" I can understand why the majority does not place much emphasis on this point. Some members of the majority have ridiculed the practice of relying on subsequent statements by legislators to demonstrate an earlier Congress's intent in enacting a statute. *See, e.g., Sullivan v. Finkelstein* (1990) (Scalia, J., concurring in part); *United States v. Hayes* (2009) (Roberts, C.J., dissenting). Yet here the majority makes a much stranger claim: that a statement appearing on a government website in 2011 (written by who-knows-whom?) reveals what hundreds of thousands of Arizona's voters sought to do in 1998 when they enacted the Clean Elections Act by referendum. Just to state that proposition is to know it is wrong.

So the majority has no evidence—zero, none—that the objective of the Act is anything other than the interest that the State asserts, the Act proclaims, and the history of public financing supports: fighting corruption.

2

[Omitted.]

IV

[Omitted. Justice Kagan ended her dissent by saying: "Truly, democracy is not a game. I respectfully dissent."]

NOTES ON *ARIZONA FREE ENTERPRISE v. BENNETT*

1. In a part of Justice Kagan's dissent that we omitted, she recounted the evidence of massive corruption in Arizona's politics. Before enacting the public financing scheme that was the subject of this case, Arizona had passed, by referendum, a contribution limitation. Five years after the implementation of that campaign finance regulation, Arizona suffered "the worst public corruption scandal in its history," in which nearly 10 percent of the state's legislators were caught accepting campaign contributions or bribes in exchange for favorable legislative votes. Following that scandal the voters of Arizona passed the public financing/matching system. Should this history make a difference in the analysis?
2. Do public finance regimes root out corruption or the appearance of corruption? Make sure you can articulate both the majority and dissent's views on this point.
3. To what extent are public funding programs such as Arizona's a valid response to entrenchment—the concern that incumbents will naturally favor policies to help their own electoral chances and keep them in office? That is, a public financing regime might help "outside" candidates remain viable against well-financed and wealthy incumbents. Should Arizona's legislature be applauded for enacting this kind of anti-entrenchment measure? Should the Court have considered this potential rationale?
4. Imagine you are a legislator in Arizona who supports this kind of law. What kind of new bill might you propose to respond to the Court's concerns in this case but still achieve the state's goals?

7. Disclosure and Disclaimer Requirements

Along with limits on expenditures and contributions, the third main pillar of campaign finance law that has seen the most judicial activity is disclosure and disclaimer requirements. Once again, *Buckley* provides the foundation. Part of the Federal Election Campaign Act imposed various disclosure and disclaimer requirements on those who spent money on elections. The goal, as in the other parts of FECA, was to reduce the pernicious influence of money in politics, and in addition to shed light on who was spending on campaigns.

Congress first passed a campaign finance disclosure law in 1910. It then broadened the disclosure requirements in 1925 as part of the Federal Corrupt Practices Act. However, as the Court notes in *Buckley*, these disclosure provisions were "widely circumvented."

Congress therefore made the disclosure requirements in FECA more robust. Those opposed to FECA challenged these disclosure provisions along with the other parts of the Act.

The government asserted three main interests in supporting disclosure laws. First, there is an informational interest: giving voters information about the source of political funding. Second, there is the familiar "corruption or the appearance of corruption" rationale. Third, disclosure laws can help to detect violations of valid contribution limitations. As you are reading this portion of *Buckley*, think about why the Court expanded the permissible justifications for disclosure laws, as opposed to its narrower construction of the required governmental interests for contribution and expenditure laws.

Then consider whether—with the shifting landscape of campaign finance law, most notably from *Citizens United*—the Court might now construe disclosure laws more strictly. Are the same three justifications listed above still valid governmental interests in the wake of *Citizens United*? The Court rejected a constitutional attack to BCRA's disclaimer and disclosure laws in *Citizens United*. What does this suggest about the scope of campaign finance regulation moving forward? Finally, we will read a post-*Citizens United* decision from the D.C. Circuit presenting a slightly different challenge to BCRA's disclosure provisions. What does this case suggest about how plaintiffs should proceed in challenging disclosure laws?

BUCKLEY v. VALEO

424 U.S. 1 (1976)

Per Curiam

II. REPORTING AND DISCLOSURE REQUIREMENTS

Unlike the limitations on contributions and expenditures imposed by 18 U.S.C. § 608, the disclosure requirements of the Act, 2 U.S.C. § 431 et seq. are not challenged by appellants as per se unconstitutional restrictions on the exercise of First Amendment freedoms of speech and association. Indeed, appellants argue that "narrowly drawn disclosure requirements are the proper solution to virtually all of the evils Congress sought to remedy." The particular requirements embodied in the Act are attacked as overbroad both in their application to minor-party and independent candidates and in their extension to contributions as small as $11 or $101. Appellants also challenge the provision for disclosure by those who make independent contributions and expenditures. The Court of Appeals found no constitutional infirmities in the provisions challenged here. We affirm the determination on overbreadth and hold that § 434(e), if narrowly construed, also is within constitutional bounds.

The Act presently under review replaced all prior disclosure laws. Its primary disclosure provisions impose reporting obligations on "political committees" and candidates.

"Political committee" is defined in § 431(d) as a group of persons that receives "contributions" or makes "expenditures" of over $1,000 in a calendar year. "Contributions" and "expenditures" are defined in lengthy parallel provisions. Both definitions focus on the use of money or other objects of value "for the purpose of . . . influencing" the nomination or election of any person to federal office. § 431(e)(1), (f)(1).

Each political committee is required to register with the Commission, and to keep detailed records of both contributions and expenditures. These records must include the name and address of everyone making a contribution in excess of $10, along with the date and amount of the contribution. If a person's contributions aggregate more than $100, his occupation and principal place of business are also to be included. These files are subject to periodic audits and field investigations by the Commission

Each committee and each candidate also is required to file quarterly reports. The reports are to contain detailed financial information, including the full name, mailing address, occupation, and principal place of business of each person who has contributed over $100 in a calendar year, as well as the amount and date of the contributions. They are to be made available by the Commission "for public inspection and copying." § 438(a)(4). Every candidate for federal office is required to designate a "principal campaign committee," which is to receive reports of contributions and expenditures made on the candidate's behalf from other political committees and to compile and file these reports, together with its own statements, with the Commission.

Every individual or group, other than a political committee or candidate, who makes "contributions" or "expenditures" of over $100 in a calendar year "other than by contribution to a political committee or candidate" is required to file a statement with the Commission. Any violation of these record-keeping and reporting provisions is punishable by a fine of not more than $1,000 or a prison term of not more than a year, or both.

A. General Principles

Unlike the overall limitations on contributions and expenditures, the disclosure requirements impose no ceiling on campaign-related activities. But we have repeatedly found that compelled disclosure, in itself, can seriously infringe on privacy of association and belief guaranteed by the First Amendment.

We long have recognized that significant encroachments on First Amendment rights of the sort that compelled disclosure imposes cannot be justified by a mere showing of some legitimate governmental interest. Since *NAACP v. Alabama* [(1958)] we have required that the subordinating interests of the State must survive exacting scrutiny. We also have insisted that there be a "relevant correlation" or "substantial relation" between the governmental interest and the information required to be disclosed. [Citations omitted.] This type of scrutiny is necessary even if any deterrent effect on the exercise of First Amendment rights arises, not through direct government action, but indirectly as an unintended but inevitable result of the government's conduct in requiring disclosure.

The strict test established by *NAACP v. Alabama* is necessary because compelled disclosure has the potential for substantially infringing the exercise of First Amendment rights. But we have acknowledged that there are governmental interests sufficiently important to outweigh the possibility of infringement, particularly when the "free functioning of our national institutions" is involved. *Communist Party v. Subversive Activities Control Bd.* (1961).

The governmental interests sought to be vindicated by the disclosure requirements are of this magnitude. They fall into three categories. First, disclosure provides the electorate with information "as to where political campaign money comes from and how it is spent by the candidate" in order to aid the voters in evaluating those who seek federal office. It allows voters to place each candidate in the political spectrum more precisely than is often possible solely on the basis of party labels and campaign speeches. The sources of a candidate's financial support also alert the voter to the interests to which a candidate is most likely to be responsive and thus facilitate predictions of future performance in office.

Second, disclosure requirements deter actual corruption and avoid the appearance of corruption by exposing large contributions and expenditures to the light of publicity. This exposure may discourage those who would use money for improper purposes either before or after the election. A public armed with information about a candidate's most generous supporters is better able to detect any post-election special favors that may be given in return. And, as we recognized in *Burroughs v. United States* [(1934)], Congress could reasonably conclude that full disclosure during an election campaign tends "to prevent the corrupt use of money to affect elections." In enacting these requirements it may have been mindful of Mr. Justice Brandeis' advice:

> "Publicity is justly commended as a remedy for social and industrial diseases. Sunlight is said to be the best of disinfectants; electric light the most efficient policeman."[80]

Third, and not least significant, recordkeeping, reporting, and disclosure requirements are an essential means of gathering the data necessary to detect violations of the contribution limitations described above.

The disclosure requirements, as a general matter, directly serve substantial governmental interests. In determining whether these interests are sufficient to justify the requirements we must look to the extent of the burden that they place on individual rights.

It is undoubtedly true that public disclosure of contributions to candidates and political parties will deter some individuals who otherwise might contribute. In some instances, disclosure may even expose contributors to harassment or retaliation. These are not insignificant burdens on individual rights, and they must be weighed carefully against the interests which Congress has sought to promote by this legislation. In this

80. L. Brandeis, Other People's Money 62 (National Home Library Foundation ed. 1933).

process, we note and agree with appellants' concession that disclosure requirements certainly in most applications appear to be the least restrictive means of curbing the evils of campaign ignorance and corruption that Congress found to exist.

B. Application to Minor Parties and Independents

[Omitted.]

C. Section 434(E)

Section 434(e) requires "(e)very person (other than a political committee or candidate) who makes contributions or expenditures" aggregating over $100 in a calendar year "other than by contribution to a political committee or candidate" to file a statement with the Commission. Unlike the other disclosure provisions, this section does not seek the contribution list of any association. Instead, it requires direct disclosure of what an individual or group contributes or spends.

1. The Role of § 434(e)

The Court of Appeals upheld § 434(e) as necessary to enforce the independent-expenditure ceiling imposed by 18 U.S.C. § 608(e)(1). It said:

> "If . . . Congress has both the authority and a compelling interest to regulate independent expenditures under section 608(e), surely it can require that there be disclosure to prevent misuse of the spending channel."

We have found that § 608(e)(1) unconstitutionally infringes upon First Amendment rights. If the sole function of § 434(e) were to aid in the enforcement of that provision, it would no longer serve any governmental purpose.

But the two provisions are not so intimately tied. The legislative history on the function of § 434(e) is bare, but it was clearly intended to stand independently of § 608(e)(1). It was enacted with the general disclosure provisions in 1971 as part of the original Act, while § 608(e)(1) was part of the 1974 amendments. Like the other disclosure provisions, § 434(e) could play a role in the enforcement of the expanded contribution and expenditure limitations included in the 1974 amendments, but it also has independent functions. Section 434(e) is part of Congress' effort to achieve "total disclosure" by reaching "every kind of political activity" in order to insure that the voters are fully informed and to achieve through publicity the maximum deterrence to corruption and undue influence possible. The provision is responsive to the legitimate fear that efforts would be made, as they had been in the past, to avoid the disclosure requirements by routing financial support of candidates through avenues not explicitly covered by the general provisions of the Act.

2. Vagueness Problems

In its effort to be all-inclusive, however, the provision raises serious problems of vagueness, particularly treacherous where, as here, the violation of its terms carries criminal penalties and fear of incurring these sanctions may deter those who seek to exercise protected First Amendment rights.

Section 434(e) applies to "(e)very person . . . who makes contributions or expenditures." "Contributions" and "expenditures" are defined in parallel provisions in terms of the use of money or other valuable assets "for the purpose of . . . influencing" the nomination or election of candidates for federal office. It is the ambiguity of this phrase that poses constitutional problems.

In enacting the legislation under review Congress addressed broadly the problem of political campaign financing. It wished to promote full disclosure of campaign-oriented spending to insure both the reality and the appearance of the purity and openness of the federal election process. Our task is to construe "for the purpose of . . . influencing," incorporated in § 434(e) through the definitions of "contributions" and "expenditures," in a manner that precisely furthers this goal.

In Part I we discussed what constituted a "contribution" for purposes of the contribution limitations set forth in 18 U.S.C. § 608(b). We construed that term to include not only contributions made directly or indirectly to a candidate, political party, or campaign committee, and contributions made to other organizations or individuals but earmarked for political purposes, but also all expenditures placed in cooperation with or with the consent of a candidate, his agents, or an authorized committee of the candidate. The definition of "contribution" in § 431(e) for disclosure purposes parallels the definition in Title 18 almost word for word, and we construe the former provision as we have the latter. So defined, "contributions" have a sufficiently close relationship to the goals of the Act, for they are connected with a candidate or his campaign.

When we attempt to define "expenditure" in a similarly narrow way we encounter line-drawing problems of the sort we faced in 18 U.S.C. § 608(e)(1). Although the phrase, "for the purpose of . . . influencing" an election or nomination, differs from the language used in § 608(e)(1), it shares the same potential for encompassing both issue discussion and advocacy of a political result. The general requirement that "political committees" and candidates disclose their expenditures could raise similar vagueness problems, for "political committee" is defined only in terms of amount of annual "contributions" and "expenditures," and could be interpreted to reach groups engaged purely in issue discussion. The lower courts have construed the words "political committee" more narrowly. To fulfill the purposes of the Act they need only encompass organizations that are under the control of a candidate or the major purpose of which is the nomination or election of a candidate. Expenditures of candidates and of "political committees" so construed can be assumed to fall within the core area sought to be addressed by Congress. They are, by definition, campaign related.

But when the maker of the expenditure is not within these categories when it is an individual other than a candidate or a group other than a "political committee" the relation of the information sought to the purposes of the Act may be too remote. To insure that the reach of § 434(e) is not impermissibly broad, we construe "expenditure" for purposes of that section in the same way we construed the terms of § 608(e) to reach only funds used for communications that expressly advocate the election or defeat of a clearly identified candidate. This reading is directed precisely to that spending that is unambiguously related to the campaign of a particular federal candidate.

In summary, § 434(e), as construed, imposes independent reporting requirements on individuals and groups that are not candidates or political committees only in the following circumstances: (1) when they make contributions earmarked for political purposes or authorized or requested by a candidate or his agent, to some person other than a candidate or political committee, and (2) when they make expenditures for communications that expressly advocate the election or defeat of a clearly identified candidate.

Unlike 18 U.S.C. § 608(e)(1), § 434(e), as construed, bears a sufficient relationship to a substantial governmental interest. As narrowed, § 434(e), like § 608(e)(1), does not reach all partisan discussion for it only requires disclosure of those expenditures that expressly advocate a particular election result. This might have been fatal if the only purpose of § 434(e) were to stem corruption or its appearance by closing a loophole in the general disclosure requirements. But the disclosure provisions, including § 434(e), serve another, informational interest, and even as construed § 434(e) increases the fund of information concerning those who support the candidates. It goes beyond the general disclosure requirements to shed the light of publicity on spending that is unambiguously campaign related but would not otherwise be reported because it takes the form of independent expenditures or of contributions to an individual or group not itself required to report the names of its contributors. By the same token, it is not fatal that § 434(e) encompasses purely independent expenditures uncoordinated with a particular candidate or his agent. The corruption potential of these expenditures may be significantly different, but the informational interest can be as strong as it is in coordinated spending, for disclosure helps voters to define more of the candidates' constituencies.

D. Thresholds

[Omitted.]

In summary, we find no constitutional infirmities in the recordkeeping reporting, and disclosure provisions of the Act.

CITIZENS UNITED v. FEC

130 S. Ct. 876 (2010)

Justice KENNEDY's majority opinion on disclaimer and disclosure portion of BCRA:*

* This portion of the opinion garnered eight votes: all but Justice Thomas agreed with Justice Kennedy's decision regarding the disclosure and disclaimer requirements [—EDS.].

IV

A

Citizens United next challenges BCRA's disclaimer and disclosure provisions as applied to *Hillary* and three advertisements for the movie. Under BCRA § 311, televised electioneering communications funded by anyone other than a candidate must include a disclaimer that "'______________ is responsible for the content of this advertising.'" 2 U.S.C. § 441d(d)(2). The required statement must be made in a "clearly spoken manner," and displayed on the screen in a "clearly readable manner" for at least four seconds. It must state that the communication "is not authorized by any candidate or candidate's committee"; it must also display the name and address (or Web site address) of the person or group that funded the advertisement. § 441d(a)(3). Under BCRA § 201, any person who spends more than $10,000 on electioneering communications within a calendar year must file a disclosure statement with the FEC. That statement must identify the person making the expenditure, the amount of the expenditure, the election to which the communication was directed, and the names of certain contributors.

Disclaimer and disclosure requirements may burden the ability to speak, but they "impose no ceiling on campaign-related activities," *Buckley*, and "do not prevent anyone from speaking," *McConnell.* The Court has subjected these requirements to "exacting scrutiny," which requires a "substantial relation" between the disclosure requirement and a "sufficiently important" governmental interest. *Buckley*.

In *Buckley*, the Court explained that disclosure could be justified based on a governmental interest in "provid[ing] the electorate with information" about the sources of election-related spending. The *McConnell* Court applied this interest in rejecting facial challenges to BCRA §§ 201 and 311. There was evidence in the record that independent groups were running election-related advertisements "while hiding behind dubious and misleading names." The Court therefore upheld BCRA §§ 201 and 311 on the ground that they would help citizens "make informed choices in the political marketplace." [*Id.*]

Although both provisions were facially upheld, the Court acknowledged that as-applied challenges would be available if a group could show a "reasonable probability'" that disclosure of its contributors' names "will subject them to threats, harassment, or reprisals from either Government officials or private parties." *Id.*

For the reasons stated below, we find the statute valid as applied to the ads for the movie and to the movie itself.

B

Citizens United sought to broadcast one 30-second and two 10-second ads to promote *Hillary*. Under FEC regulations, a communication that "[p]roposes a commercial transaction" was not subject to 2 U.S.C. § 441b's restrictions on corporate or union funding of electioneering communications. 11 CFR § 114.15(b)(3)(ii). The regulations, however, do not exempt those communications from the disclaimer and disclosure requirements in BCRA §§ 201 and 311.

Citizens United argues that the disclaimer requirements in § 311 are unconstitutional as applied to its ads. It contends that the governmental interest in providing information to the electorate does not justify requiring disclaimers for any commercial advertisements, including the ones at issue here. We disagree. The ads fall within BCRA's definition of an "electioneering communication": They referred to then-Senator Clinton by name shortly before a primary and contained pejorative references to her candidacy. The disclaimers required by § 311 "provid[e] the electorate with information," *McConnell*, and "insure that the voters are fully informed" about the person or group who is speaking, *Buckley*; *see also Bellotti* ("Identification of the source of advertising may be required as a means of disclosure, so that the people will be able to evaluate the arguments to which they are being subjected"). At the very least, the disclaimers avoid confusion by making clear that the ads are not funded by a candidate or political party.

Citizens United argues that § 311 is underinclusive because it requires disclaimers for broadcast advertisements but not for print or Internet advertising. It asserts that § 311 decreases both the quantity and effectiveness of the group's speech by forcing it to devote four seconds of each advertisement to the spoken disclaimer. We rejected these arguments in *McConnell*. And we now adhere to that decision as it pertains to the disclosure provisions.

As a final point, Citizens United claims that, in any event, the disclosure requirements in § 201 must be confined to speech that is the functional equivalent of express advocacy. We reject this contention. The Court has explained that disclosure is a less restrictive alternative to more comprehensive regulations of speech. In *Buckley*, the Court upheld a disclosure requirement for independent expenditures even though it invalidated a provision that imposed a ceiling on those expenditures. In *McConnell*, three Justices who would have found § 441b to be unconstitutional nonetheless voted to uphold BCRA's disclosure and disclaimer requirements. *McConnell* (opinion of Kennedy, J., joined by Rehnquist, C.J., and Scalia, J.). And the Court has upheld registration and disclosure requirements on lobbyists, even though Congress has no power to ban lobbying itself. *United States v. Harriss* (1954) (Congress "has merely provided for a modicum of information from those who for hire attempt to influence legislation or who collect or spend funds for that purpose"). For these reasons, we reject Citizens United's contention that the disclosure requirements must be limited to speech that is the functional equivalent of express advocacy.

Citizens United also disputes that an informational interest justifies the application of § 201 to its ads, which only attempt to persuade viewers to see the film. Even if it disclosed the funding sources for the ads, Citizens United says, the information would not help viewers make informed choices in the political marketplace. This is similar to the argument rejected above with respect to disclaimers. Even if the ads only pertain to a commercial transaction, the public has an interest in knowing who is speaking about a candidate shortly before an election. Because the informational interest alone is sufficient to justify application of § 201 to these ads, it is not necessary to consider the Government's other asserted interests.

Last, Citizens United argues that disclosure requirements can chill donations to an organization by exposing donors to retaliation. Some *amici* point to recent events in which donors to certain causes were blacklisted, threatened, or otherwise targeted for retaliation. In *McConnell*, the Court recognized that § 201 would be unconstitutional as applied to an organization if there were a reasonable probability that the group's members would face threats, harassment, or reprisals if their names were disclosed. The examples cited by *amici* are cause for concern. Citizens United, however, has offered no evidence that its members may face similar threats or reprisals. To the contrary, Citizens United has been disclosing its donors for years and has identified no instance of harassment or retaliation.

Shareholder objections raised through the procedures of corporate democracy can be more effective today because modern technology makes disclosures rapid and informative. A campaign finance system that pairs corporate independent expenditures with effective disclosure has not existed before today. It must be noted, furthermore, that many of Congress' findings in passing BCRA were premised on a system without adequate disclosure. With the advent of the Internet, prompt disclosure of expenditures can provide shareholders and citizens with the information needed to hold corporations and elected officials accountable for their positions and supporters. Shareholders can determine whether their corporation's political speech advances the corporation's interest in making profits, and citizens can see whether elected officials are "'in the pocket' of so-called moneyed interests." *McConnell* (opinion of Scalia, J.). The First Amendment protects political speech; and disclosure permits citizens and shareholders to react to the speech of corporate entities in a proper way. This transparency enables the electorate to make informed decisions and give proper weight to different speakers and messages.

C

For the same reasons we uphold the application of BCRA §§ 201 and 311 to the ads, we affirm their application to *Hillary*. We find no constitutional impediment to the application of BCRA's disclaimer and disclosure requirements to a movie broadcast via video-on-demand. And there has been no showing that, as applied in this case, these requirements would impose a chill on speech or expression.

Justice THOMAS, concurring in part and dissenting in part.

I join all but Part IV of the Court's opinion.

Political speech is entitled to robust protection under the First Amendment. Section 203 of the Bipartisan Campaign Reform Act of 2002 (BCRA) has never been reconcilable with that protection. By striking down § 203, the Court takes an important first step toward restoring full constitutional protection to speech that is "indispensable to the effective and intelligent use of the processes of popular government." *McConnell* (Thomas, J., concurring in part, concurring in judgment in part, and dissenting in part). I dissent from Part IV of the Court's opinion, however, because the Court's constitutional analysis does not go far enough. The disclosure, disclaimer, and reporting requirements in BCRA §§ 201 and 311 are also unconstitutional.

Congress may not abridge the "right to anonymous speech" based on the "simple interest in providing voters with additional relevant information," *id.* (quoting *McIntyre v. Ohio Elections Comm'n* (1995)). In continuing to hold otherwise, the Court misapprehends the import of "recent events" that some *amici* describe "in which donors to certain causes were blacklisted, threatened, or otherwise targeted for retaliation." The Court properly recognizes these events as "cause for concern," but fails to acknowledge their constitutional significance. In my view, *amici*'s submissions show why the Court's insistence on upholding §§ 201 and 311 will ultimately prove as misguided (and ill fated) as was its prior approval of § 203.

Before the 2008 Presidential election, a "newly formed nonprofit group . . . plann[ed] to confront donors to conservative groups, hoping to create a chilling effect that will dry up contributions." Luo, Group Plans Campaign Against G.O.P. Donors, N.Y. Times, Aug. 8, 2008, p. A15. Its leader, "who described his effort as 'going for the jugular,'" detailed the group's plan to send a "warning letter . . . alerting donors who might be considering giving to right-wing groups to a variety of potential dangers, including legal trouble, public exposure and watchdog groups digging through their lives."

These instances of retaliation sufficiently demonstrate why this Court should invalidate mandatory disclosure and reporting requirements. But *amici* present evidence of yet another reason to do so—the threat of retaliation from *elected officials*. For example, a candidate challenging an incumbent state attorney general reported that some members of the State's business community feared donating to his campaign because they did not want to cross the incumbent; in his words, "'I go to so many people and hear the same thing: "I sure hope you beat [the incumbent], but I can't afford to have my name on your records. He might come after me next."'" Strassel, Challenging Spitzerism at the Polls, Wall Street Journal, Aug. 1, 2008, p. A11. The incumbent won reelection in 2008.

My point is to demonstrate—using real-world, recent examples—the fallacy in the Court's conclusion that "[d]isclaimer and disclosure requirements . . . impose no ceiling on campaign-related activities, and do not prevent anyone from speaking." Of course they do. Disclaimer and disclosure requirements enable private citizens and elected officials to implement political strategies *specifically calculated* to curtail campaign-related activity and prevent the lawful, peaceful exercise of First Amendment rights.

The Court nevertheless insists that as-applied challenges to disclosure requirements will suffice to vindicate those speech rights, as long as potential plaintiffs can "show a reasonable probability that disclosure . . . will subject them to threats, harassment, or reprisals from either Government officials or private parties." But the Court's opinion itself proves the irony in this compromise. In correctly explaining why it must address the facial constitutionality of § 203, the Court recognizes that "[t]he First Amendment does not permit laws that force speakers to . . . seek declaratory rulings before discussing the most salient political issues of our day," that as-applied challenges to § 203 "would require substantial litigation over an extended time" and result in an "interpretive process [that] itself would create an inevitable, pervasive, and serious risk of chilling protected speech pending the drawing of fine distinctions that, in the end, would themselves be questionable," that "a court would be remiss in performing its duties were it to accept an unsound principle merely to avoid the necessity of making a broader ruling," and that avoiding a facial challenge to § 203 "would prolong the substantial, nation-wide chilling effect" that § 203 causes. This logic, of course, applies equally to as-applied challenges to §§ 201 and 311.

Irony aside, the Court's promise that as-applied challenges will adequately protect speech is a hollow assurance. Now more than ever, §§ 201 and 311 will chill protected speech because "the advent of the Internet" enables "prompt disclosure of expenditures," which "provide[s]" political opponents "with the information needed" to intimidate and retaliate against their foes. Thus, "disclosure permits citizens . . . to react to the speech of [their political opponents] in a proper"—or undeniably *improper*—"way" long before a plaintiff could prevail on an as-applied challenge.

I cannot endorse a view of the First Amendment that subjects citizens of this Nation to death threats, ruined careers, damaged or defaced property, or pre-emptive and threatening warning letters as the price for engaging in "core political speech, the primary object of First Amendment protection." *McConnell* (Thomas, J., concurring in part, concurring in judgment in part, and dissenting in part). Accordingly, I respectfully dissent from the Court's judgment upholding BCRA §§ 201 and 311.

SPEECHNOW.ORG v. FEC

599 F.3d 686 (D.C. Cir. 2010) (en banc)

SENTELLE, Chief Judge:

David Keating is president of an unincorporated nonprofit association, SpeechNow.org (SpeechNow), that intends to engage in express advocacy supporting candidates for federal office who share his views on First Amendment rights of free speech and freedom to assemble. In January 2008, the Federal Election Committee (FEC) issued a draft advisory opinion concluding that under the Federal Election Campaign Act (FECA), SpeechNow would be required to organize as a "political committee" as defined by 2 U.S.C. § 431(4) and would be subject to all the requirements and restrictions concomitant with that designation. Keating and four other individuals availed themselves of 2 U.S.C. § 437h, under which an individual may seek declaratory judgment to construe the constitutionality of any provision of FECA. As required by that provision, the district court certified the constitutional questions directly to this court for en banc determination. Thereafter, the Supreme Court decided *Citizens United v. FEC* (2010), which resolves this appeal. In accordance with that decision, we hold that the contribution limits of 2 U.S.C. § 441a(a)(1)(C) and 441a(a)(3) are unconstitutional as applied to individuals' contributions to SpeechNow. However, we also hold that the reporting requirements of 2 U.S.C. §§ 432, 433, and 434(a) and the organizational requirements of 2 U.S.C. § 431(4) and 431(8) can constitutionally be applied to SpeechNow.

I. Background

SpeechNow is an unincorporated nonprofit association registered as a "political organization" under § 527 of the Internal Revenue Code. Its purpose is to promote the First Amendment rights of free speech and freedom to assemble by expressly advocating for federal candidates whom it views as supporting those rights and against those whom it sees as insufficiently committed to those rights. It intends to acquire funds solely through donations by individuals. SpeechNow further intends to operate exclusively through "independent expenditures." FECA defines "independent expenditures" as expenditures "expressly advocating the election or defeat of a clearly identified candidate" that are "not made in concert or cooperation with or at the request or suggestion of such candidate, the candidate's authorized political committee, or their agents, or a political party committee or its agents." 2 U.S.C. § 431(17). SpeechNow has five members, two of whom are plaintiffs in this case: David Keating, who is also SpeechNow's president and treasurer, and Edward Crane. Keating makes the operational decisions for SpeechNow, including in which election campaigns to run advertisements, which candidates to support or oppose, and all administrative decisions.

Believing that subjecting SpeechNow to all the restrictions imposed on political committees would be unconstitutional, SpeechNow and the five individual plaintiffs filed a complaint in the district court requesting declaratory relief against the FEC.

The district court made findings of fact, and certified to this court five questions:

[Questions 1 through 3 are related to the contribution and expenditure limitations and are discussed below in the reading on PACs.]

4. Whether the organizational, administrative, and continuous reporting requirements set forth in 2 U.S.C. §§ 432, 433, and 434(a) violate the First Amendment by requiring David Keating, SpeechNow.org's president and treasurer, to register SpeechNow.org as a political committee, to adopt the organizational structure of a political committee, and to comply with the continuous reporting requirements that apply to political committees.
5. Whether 2 U.S.C. §§ 431(4) and 431(8) violate the First Amendment by requiring David Keating, SpeechNow.org's president and treasurer, to register

> SpeechNow.org as a political committee and comply with the organizational and continuous reporting requirements for political committees before SpeechNow.org has made any expenditures or broadcast any advertisements.

Under FECA, a political committee is "any committee, club, association, or other group of persons" that receives contributions of more than $1000 in a year or makes expenditures of more than $1000 in a year. 2 U.S.C. § 431(4). A political committee . . . must comply with all applicable recordkeeping and reporting requirements of 2 U.S.C. §§ 432, 433, and 434(a). Under those sections, if the FEC regulates SpeechNow as a political committee, SpeechNow would be required to, among other things: appoint a treasurer; maintain a separately designated bank account; keep records for three years that include the name and address of any person who makes a contribution in excess of $50; keep records for three years that include the date, amount, and purpose of any disbursement and the name and address of the recipient; register with the FEC within ten days of becoming a political committee; file with the FEC quarterly or monthly reports during the calendar year of a general election detailing cash on hand, total contributions, the identification of each person who contributes an annual aggregate amount of more than $200, independent expenditures, donations to other political committees, any other disbursements, and any outstanding debts or obligations; file a pre-election report and a post-election report detailing the same; file semiannual or monthly reports with the same information during years without a general election; and file a written statement in order to terminate the committee.

II. Analysis

A. Contribution Limits (Certified Questions 1-3)

[Omitted here. This portion of the opinion is included below in the unit on PACs.]

B. Organizational and Reporting Requirements (Certified Questions 4 & 5)

Disclosure requirements also burden First Amendment interests because "compelled disclosure, in itself, can seriously infringe on privacy of association and belief." *Buckley*. However, in contrast with limiting a person's ability to spend money on political speech, disclosure requirements "impose no ceiling on campaign-related activities," *id.*, and "do not prevent anyone from speaking," *McConnell.* Because disclosure requirements inhibit speech less than do contribution and expenditure limits, the Supreme Court has not limited the government's acceptable interests to anti-corruption alone. Instead, the government may point to any "sufficiently important" governmental interest that bears a "substantial relation" to the disclosure requirement. *Citizens United.* Indeed, the Court has approvingly noted that "disclosure is a less restrictive alternative to more comprehensive regulations of speech." [*Id.*]

The Supreme Court has consistently upheld organizational and reporting requirements against facial challenges. In *Buckley*, the Court upheld FECA's disclosure requirements, including the requirements of §§ 432, 433, and 434(a) at issue here, based on a governmental interest in "provid[ing] the electorate with information" about the sources of political campaign funds, not just the interest in deterring corruption and enforcing anti-corruption measures. In *McConnell*, the Court upheld similar requirements for organizations engaging in electioneering communications for the same reasons. *Citizens United* upheld disclaimer and disclosure requirements for electioneering communications as applied to Citizens United, again citing the government's interest in providing the electorate with information. And while the Court in *Davis v. FEC* found that a certain disclosure requirement violated the First Amendment, it only did so because that disclosure triggered the application of an unconstitutional provision which imposed asymmetrical contribution limits on candidates based on how much of their personal funds they planned to spend. Because the asymmetrical limits were unconstitutional, there was no justification for the disclosure requirement.

Plaintiffs do not disagree that the government may constitutionally impose reporting requirements, and SpeechNow intends to comply with the disclosure requirements that would apply even if it were not a political committee. *See* 2 U.S.C. § 434(c) (reporting requirements for individuals or groups that are not political committees that make independent expenditures); § 441d (disclaimer requirements for independent expenditures and electioneering communications). Instead, plaintiffs argue that the additional burden that would be imposed on SpeechNow if it were required to comply with the organizational and reporting requirements applicable to political committees is too much for the First Amendment to bear. We disagree.

SpeechNow, as we have said, intends to comply with the disclosure requirements applicable to those who make independent expenditures but are not organized as political committees. Those disclosure requirements include, for example, reporting much of the same data on contributors that is required of political committees; information about each independent expenditure, such as which candidate the expenditure supports or opposes; reporting within 24 hours expenditures of $1000 or more made in the twenty days before an election; and reporting within 48 hours any expenditures or contracts for expenditures of $10,000 or more made at any other time.

Because SpeechNow intends only to make independent expenditures, the additional reporting requirements that the FEC would impose on SpeechNow if it were a political committee are minimal. Indeed, at oral argument, plaintiffs conceded that "the reporting is not really going to impose an additional burden" on SpeechNow. Oral Arg. Tr. at 14 ("Judge Sentelle: So, just calling you a [PAC] and not making you do anything except the reporting is not really going to impose an additional burden on you right? . . . Mr. Simpson: I think that's true. Yes."). Nor do the organizational requirements that SpeechNow protests, such as designating a treasurer and retaining records, impose much of an additional burden upon SpeechNow, especially given the relative simplicity with which SpeechNow intends to operate.

Neither can SpeechNow claim to be burdened by the requirement to organize as a political committee as soon as it receives $1000, as required by the definition of "political committee," 2 U.S.C. § 431(4), 431(8), rather than waiting until it expends $1000. Plaintiffs argue that such a requirement forces SpeechNow to comply with the burdens of political committees without knowing if it is going to have enough money to make its independent expenditures. This is a specious interpretation of the facts before us. As the district court found, SpeechNow already has $121,700 in planned contributions from plaintiffs alone, with dozens more individuals claiming to want to donate. SpeechNow can hardly compare itself to "ad hoc groups that want to create themselves on the spur of the moment," as plaintiffs attempted at oral argument. In addition, plaintiffs concede that in practice the burden is substantially the same to *any* group whether the FEC imposes reporting requirements at the point of the money's receipt or at the point of its expenditure. A group raising money for political speech will, we presume, always hope to raise enough to make it worthwhile to spend it. Therefore, groups would need to collect and keep the necessary data on contributions even before an expenditure is made; it makes little difference to the burden of compliance *when* the group must comply as long as it anticipates complying at some point.

We cannot hold that the organizational and reporting requirements are unconstitutional. If SpeechNow were not a political committee, it would not have to report contributions made exclusively for administrative expenses. But the public has an interest in knowing who is speaking about a candidate and who is funding that speech, no matter whether the contributions were made towards administrative expenses or independent expenditures. Further, requiring disclosure of such information deters and helps expose violations of other campaign finance restrictions, such as those barring contributions from foreign corporations or individuals. These are sufficiently important governmental interests to justify requiring SpeechNow to organize and report to the FEC as a political committee.

We therefore answer the last two certified questions in the negative. The FEC may constitutionally require SpeechNow to comply with 2 U.S.C. §§ 432, 433, and 434(a), and it may require SpeechNow to start complying with those requirements as soon as it becomes a political committee under the current definition of § 431(4).

NOTES ON DISCLOSURE LAWS

1. What do these three cases say about the landscape of disclaimer and disclosure laws? Are they the only hope for any sort of campaign finance "reform" given the Court's recent deregulation decisions?
2. Disclosure laws may be the next major political battlefield in campaign finance. After *Citizens United*, Democrats in Congress proposed a new disclosure law, the DISCLOSE Act (Democracy is Stronger by Casting Light on Spending in Elections Act). The law was intended to strengthen disclosure requirements for

corporate campaign contributions and place limits on political contributions from foreign corporations. The law also would have required CEOs and heads of interest groups to appear on camera in a political ad to endorse the group's message. Senate Republicans succeeded in blocking the bill, claiming it would have violated corporations' and other groups' free speech rights. What compromise solution can you envision?

3. Although not in the campaign finance context, the Court in *Doe v. Reed*, 130 S. Ct. 2811 (2010), upheld the public disclosure of the names of those who signed a petition to place a referendum on the ballot. Relying in part on the discussion of disclosure laws in *Buckley* and *Citizen United*, the Court held that public disclosure of petition signatures is tied to the government's compelling interest in achieving "transparency and accountability in the electoral process." The Court explained the public disclosure of signatures helps to preserve the integrity of the election, particularly because it makes it easier to ferret out fraudulent or invalid signatures. The Court left the door open to an as-applied challenge to public disclosure if there was actual evidence of harassment from the disclosure.
4. Assume you represent an individual or entity that opposes disclosure laws. How might you present your argument in light of the courts' decisions in these cases? What kind of evidence must you gather?

8. Looking Forward: The (Uncertain) Status of PACs and Other Advocacy Organizations

One of the most significant aspects of the post-*Citizens United* climate is the rise in "outside" groups spending money on politics. The 2012 election cycle saw outside groups spend over $1.2 billion, on both sides of the aisle, often through political action committees (PACs).

PACs have existed for years. A PAC is an organization of individuals that is created, generally independent of a particular candidate, for the purpose of engaging in political advocacy. Under federal law, PACs must register, file certain disclosures, and are subject to other restrictions. The question after *Citizens United* was whether various campaign finance regulations, such as contribution limits, still applied to these organizations. In *SpeechNow*, the D.C. Circuit considered the application of *Citizens United* to organizations created solely to make independent expenditures during a campaign—often referred to as a Super PAC. (In this respect, a Super PAC is different from a conventional PAC, often created to channel contributions to particular candidates. A Super PAC, by contrast, promises to make no contributions to, or coordinated expenditures with, any candidate.) You read above that the court in *SpeechNow* upheld disclosure obligations on independent expenditure-only groups. The portion of the case that you will read below is considered to be the most important analysis to date on funding restrictions as applied to outside advocacy groups. FECA, which by its own terms does not distinguish between conventional PACs and Super PACs, limits permissible contributions to PACs to $5,000. But what about the applicability of this $5,000 limit to Super PACs? As long as a Super PAC makes no contributions of its own, should it not be able to receive as much money as its donors wish to give it—as a means of collectively engaging in the right to make unlimited independent expenditures (as upheld in *Citizens United*)? At least that's the argument considered in the case; can you formulate a counterargument?

Moreover, PACs have additional limitations and reporting requirements, as compared to nonprofit organizations that are not designated as "political organizations." In the second case below, *Real Truth*, we will consider how the Federal Election Commission (FEC) designates a group as a "political organization." As you are reading, think about the best way to determine if a group is "political enough" to fall under the FEC's regulations. Also ask yourself whether it is better to have clearly defined or more context-specific rules for this question.

SPEECHNOW.ORG v. FEC

599 F.3d 686 (D.C. Cir. 2010) (en banc)

SENTELLE, Chief Judge:

[You have already read part of this opinion above, in the unit on disclosure laws. A portion of the beginning of the opinion is also included here for context.]

SpeechNow is an unincorporated nonprofit association registered as a "political organization" under § 527 of the Internal Revenue Code. Its purpose is to promote the First Amendment rights of free speech and freedom to assemble by expressly advocating for federal candidates whom it views as supporting those rights and against those whom it sees as insufficiently committed to those rights. It intends to acquire funds solely through donations by individuals. SpeechNow further intends to operate exclusively through "independent expenditures." FECA defines "independent expenditures" as expenditures "expressly advocating the election or defeat of a clearly identified candidate" that are "not made in concert or cooperation with or at the request or suggestion of such candidate, the candidate's authorized political committee, or their agents, or a political party committee or its agents." SpeechNow has five members, two of whom are plaintiffs in this case: David Keating, who is also SpeechNow's president and treasurer, and Edward Crane. Keating makes the operational decisions for SpeechNow, including in which election campaigns to run advertisements, which candidates to support or oppose, and all administrative decisions.

Though it has not yet begun operations, SpeechNow has made plans both for fundraising and for making independent expenditures. All five of the individual plaintiffs—Keating, Crane, Fred Young, Brad Russo, and Scott Burkhardt—are prepared to donate to SpeechNow. Keating proposes to donate $5500. Crane proposes to donate $6000. Young, who is otherwise unaffiliated with SpeechNow, proposes to donate

$110,000. Russo and Burkhardt want to make donations of $100 each. In addition, as of August 2008, seventy-five other individuals had indicated on SpeechNow's website that they were interested in making donations. As for expenditures, SpeechNow planned ads for the 2008 election cycle against two incumbent candidates for federal office who, in the opinion of SpeechNow, did not sufficiently support First Amendment rights. These ads would have cost around $12,000 to produce. Keating intended to place the ads so that the target audience would view the ads at least ten times, which would have cost around $400,000. As SpeechNow never accepted any donations, it never produced or ran these ads. However, SpeechNow intends to run similar ads for the 2010 election cycle if it is not subject to the contribution limits of § 441a(a) at issue in this case.

Believing that subjecting SpeechNow to all the restrictions imposed on political committees would be unconstitutional, SpeechNow and the five individual plaintiffs filed a complaint in the district court requesting declaratory relief against the FEC.

The district court made findings of fact, and certified to this court five questions:

1. Whether the contribution limits contained in 2 U.S.C. §§ 441a(a)(1)(C) and 441a(a)(3) violate the First Amendment by preventing David Keating, SpeechNow.org's president and treasurer, from accepting contributions to SpeechNow.org in excess of the limits contained in §§ 441a(a)(1)(C) and 441a(a)(3).
2. Whether the contribution limit mandated by 2 U.S.C. § 441a(a)(1)(C) violates the First Amendment by preventing the individual plaintiffs from making contributions to SpeechNow.org in excess of $5000 per calendar year.
3. Whether the biennial aggregate contribution limit mandated by 2 U.S.C. § 441a(a)(3) violates the First Amendment by preventing Fred Young from making contributions to SpeechNow.org that would exceed his individual biennial aggregate limit.

[Questions 4 and 5 relate to the disclosure provisions and are discussed above in the unit on disclosure.]

Under FECA, a political committee is "any committee, club, association, or other group of persons" that receives contributions of more than $1000 in a year or makes expenditures of more than $1000 in a year. Once a group is so designated, contributions to the committee are restricted by 2 U.S.C. § 441a(a)(1)(C) and 441a(a)(3). The first provision limits an individual's contribution to a political committee to $5000 per calendar year; the second limits an individual's total contributions to all political committees to $69,900 biennially.[2]

2. Subject to exceptions not here relevant, FECA defines "contributions" as "any gift, subscription, loan, advance, or deposit of money or anything of value made by any person for the purpose of influencing any election for Federal office." 2 U.S.C. § 431(8)(A)(i). Again subject to exceptions, the Act defines "expenditure" as "any purchase, payment, distribution, loan, advance, deposit, or gift of money or anything of value, made by any person for the purpose of influencing any election for Federal office; and [ ] a written contract, promise, or agreement to make an expenditure." 2 U.S.C. § 431(9)(A)(i)-(ii).

II. Analysis

A. *Contribution Limits (Certified Questions 1-3)*

The First Amendment mandates that "Congress shall make no law . . . abridging the freedom of speech." In *Buckley v. Valeo*, the Supreme Court held that, although contribution limits do encroach upon First Amendment interests, they do not encroach upon First Amendment interests to as great a degree as expenditure limits. In *Buckley*, the Supreme Court first delineated the differing treatments afforded contribution and expenditure limits. In that case, the Court struck down limits on an individual's expenditures for political advocacy, but upheld limits on contributions to political candidates and campaigns. In making the distinction, the Court emphasized that in "contrast with a limitation upon expenditures for political expression, a limitation upon the amount that any one person or group may contribute to a candidate or political committee entails only a marginal restriction upon the contributor's ability to engage in free communication." However, contribution limits still do implicate fundamental First Amendment interests.

When the government attempts to regulate the financing of political campaigns and express advocacy through contribution limits, therefore, it must have a countervailing interest that outweighs the limit's burden on the exercise of First Amendment rights. Thus a "contribution limit involving significant interference with associational rights must be closely drawn to serve a sufficiently important interest." *Davis v. FEC* (2008) (quoting *McConnell v. FEC* (2003)). The Supreme Court has recognized only one interest sufficiently important to outweigh the First Amendment interests implicated by contributions for political speech: preventing corruption or the appearance of corruption. The Court has rejected each of the few other interests the government has, at one point or another, suggested as a justification for contribution or expenditure limits. Equalization of differing viewpoints is not a legitimate government objective. *Davis*. An informational interest in "identifying the sources of support for and opposition to" a political position or candidate is not enough to justify the First Amendment burden. *Citizens Against Rent Control v. City of Berkeley* (1981). And, though this rationale would not affect an unincorporated association such as SpeechNow, the Court has also refused to find a sufficiently compelling governmental interest in preventing "the corrosive and distorting effects of immense aggregations of wealth that are accumulated with the help of the corporate form." *Citizens United.*

Given this precedent, the only interest we may evaluate to determine whether the government can justify contribution limits as applied to SpeechNow is the government's anticorruption interest. Because of the Supreme Court's recent decision in *Citizens United v. FEC*, the analysis is straightforward. There, the Court held that the government has no anti-corruption interest in limiting independent expenditures.[3]

3. Of course, the government still has an interest in preventing quid pro quo corruption. However, after *Citizens United*, independent expenditures do not implicate that interest.

Citizens United involved a nonprofit corporation that in January 2008 produced a film that was highly critical of then-Senator Hillary Clinton, a candidate in the Democratic Party's 2008 Presidential primary elections. The film was, "in essence, . . . a feature-length negative advertisement that urges viewers to vote against Senator Clinton for President." As such, the film was subject to the restrictions of 2 U.S.C. § 441b. That provision made it unlawful for any corporation or union to use general treasury funds to make independent expenditures as defined by 2 U.S.C. § 431(17) or expenditures for speech defined as "electioneering communications," which are certain types of political ads aired shortly before an election or primary, 2 U.S.C. § 434(f)(3). The Supreme Court declared this expenditure ban unconstitutional, holding that corporations may not be prohibited from spending money for express political advocacy when those expenditures are independent from candidates and uncoordinated with their campaigns.

The independence of independent expenditures was a central consideration in the Court's decision. By definition, independent expenditures are "not made in concert or cooperation with or at the request or suggestion of such candidate, the candidate's authorized political committee, or their agents, or a political party committee or its agents." 2 U.S.C. § 431(17). As the *Buckley* Court explained when it struck down a limit on independent expenditures, "[t]he absence of prearrangement and coordination of an expenditure with the candidate or his agent . . . alleviates the danger that expenditures will be given as a quid pro quo for improper commitments from the candidate." However, the *Buckley* Court left open the possibility that the future might bring data linking independent expenditures to corruption or the appearance of corruption. The Court merely concluded that independent expenditures "do [ ] not presently appear to pose dangers of real or apparent corruption comparable to those identified with large campaign contributions."

Over the next several decades, Congress and the Court gave little further guidance respecting *Buckley*'s reasoning that a lack of coordination diminishes the possibility of corruption. Just a few months after *Buckley*, Congress codified a ban on corporations' independent expenditures at 2 U.S.C. § 441b. In 1978, in *First National Bank of Boston v. Bellotti*, the Court "struck down a state-law prohibition on corporate independent expenditures related to referenda," but did not "address the constitutionality of the State's ban on corporate independent expenditures to support candidates." *Citizens United.* Though the *Bellotti* Court sweepingly rejected "the proposition that speech that otherwise would be within the protection of the First Amendment loses that protection simply because its source is a corporation," it limited the implications of that rejection by opining in a footnote that "Congress might well be able to demonstrate the existence of a danger of real or apparent corruption in independent expenditures by corporations to influence candidate elections." Then, in *Austin*, the Court expressly upheld a Michigan law that prohibited corporate independent expenditures. And in *McConnell*, the Court relied on *Austin* to uphold the Bipartisan Campaign Reform Act of 2002's (BCRA's) extension of § 441b's ban on corporate expenditures to electioneering communications.

The *Citizens United* Court reevaluated this line of cases and found them to be incompatible with *Buckley*'s original reasoning. The Court overruled *Austin* and the part of *McConnell* that upheld BCRA's amendments to § 441b. More important for this case, the Court did so by expressly deciding the question left open by the footnoted caveat in *Bellotti*. The Court stated, "[W]e now conclude that independent expenditures, including those made by corporations, do not give rise to corruption or the appearance of corruption." *Citizens United.*

The Court came to this conclusion by looking to the definition of corruption and the appearance of corruption. For several decades after *Buckley*, the Court's analysis of the government's anti-corruption interest revolved largely around the "hallmark of corruption," "financial quid pro quo: dollars for political favors." However, in a series of cases culminating in *McConnell*, the Court expanded the definition to include "the appearance of undue influence" created by large donations given for the purpose of "buying access." The *McConnell* Court concluded that limiting the government's anticorruption interest to preventing quid pro quo was a "crabbed view of corruption, and particularly of the appearance of corruption" that "ignores precedent, common sense, and the realities of political fundraising." The *Citizens United* Court retracted this view of the government's interest, saying that "[t]he fact that speakers may have influence over or access to elected officials does not mean that these officials are corrupt." The Court returned to its older definition of corruption that focused on quid pro quo, saying that "[i]ngratiation and access . . . are not corruption." Therefore, without any evidence that independent expenditures "lead to, or create the appearance of, quid pro quo corruption," and only "scant evidence" that they even ingratiate, the Court concluded that independent expenditures do not corrupt or create the appearance of corruption.

In light of the Court's holding as a matter of law that independent expenditures do not corrupt or create the appearance of quid pro quo corruption, contributions to groups that make only independent expenditures also cannot corrupt or create the appearance of corruption. The Court has effectively held that there is no corrupting "quid" for which a candidate might in exchange offer a corrupt "quo."

Given this analysis from *Citizens United*, we must conclude that the government has no anti-corruption interest in limiting contributions to an independent expenditure group such as SpeechNow. This simplifies the task of weighing the First Amendment interests implicated by contributions to SpeechNow against the government's interest in limiting such contributions. Thus, we do not need to quantify to what extent contributions to SpeechNow are an expression of core political speech. We do not need to answer whether giving money is speech per se, or if contributions are merely symbolic expressions of general support, or if it matters in this case that just one person, David Keating, decides what the group will say. All that matters is that the First Amendment cannot be encroached upon for naught.

At oral argument, the FEC insisted that *Citizens United* does not disrupt *Buckley*'s longstanding decision upholding contribution limits. This is literally true. But, as *Citizens United* emphasized, the limits upheld in *Buckley* were limits on contributions made directly to candidates. Limits on direct contributions to candidates, "unlike limits on independent expenditures, have been an accepted means to prevent quid pro quo corruption." *Citizens United.*

The FEC argues that the analysis of *Citizens United* does not apply because that case involved an expenditure limit while this case involves a contribution limit. Alluding to the divide between expenditure limits and contribution limits established by *Buckley*, the FEC insists that contribution limits are subject to a lower standard of review than expenditure limits, so that "what may be insufficient to justify an expenditure limit may be sufficient to justify a contribution limit." Plaintiffs, on the other hand, argue that *Citizens United* stands for the proposition that "burdensome laws trigger strict scrutiny." We do not find it necessary to decide whether the logic of *Citizens United* has any effect on the standard of review generally afforded contribution limits. The *Citizens United* Court avoided "reconsider[ing] whether contribution limits should be subjected to rigorous First Amendment scrutiny," and so do we. Instead, we return to what we have said before: because *Citizens United* holds that independent expenditures do not corrupt or give the appearance of corruption as a matter of law, then the government can have no anti-corruption interest in limiting contributions to independent expenditure-only organizations. No matter which standard of review governs contribution limits, the limits on contributions to SpeechNow cannot stand.

We therefore answer in the affirmative each of the first three questions certified to this Court. The contribution limits of 2 U.S.C. § 441a(a)(1)(C) and 441a(a)(3) violate the First Amendment by preventing plaintiffs from donating to SpeechNow in excess of the limits and by prohibiting SpeechNow from accepting donations in excess of the limits. We should be clear, however, that we only decide these questions as applied to contributions to SpeechNow, an independent expenditure-only group. Our holding does not affect, for example, § 441a(a)(3)'s limits on direct contributions to candidates.

THE REAL TRUTH ABOUT ABORTION, INC. v. FEDERAL ELECTION COMM'N

681 F.3d 544 (4th Cir. 2012)

NIEMEYER, Circuit Judge:

The Real Truth About Abortion, Inc. (formerly known as The Real Truth About Obama, Inc.), a Virginia non-profit corporation organized under § 527 of the Internal Revenue Code to provide "accurate and truthful information about the public policy positions of Senator Barack Obama," commenced this action against the Federal Election Commission and the Department of Justice, contending that it was "chilled" from posting information about then-Senator Obama because of the vagueness of a Commission regulation and a Commission policy relating to whether Real Truth has to make disclosures or is a "political committee" (commonly referred to as a political action committee or PAC). Real Truth asserts that it is not subject to regulation but fears the Commission could take steps to regulate it because of the vagueness of 11 C.F.R. § 100.22(b) and the policy of the Commission to determine whether an organization is a PAC by applying the "major purpose" test on a case-by-case basis. It alleges that the regulation and policy are unconstitutionally broad and vague, both facially and as applied to it, in violation of the First and Fifth Amendments.

On cross-motions for summary judgment, the district court found both the regulation and the policy constitutional. And, applying the "exacting scrutiny" standard applicable to disclosure provisions, we affirm.

I

Real Truth was organized on July 24, 2008, as an "issue-[advocacy] '527' organization" under § 527 of the Internal Revenue Code. In its IRS filing, Real Truth stated that its purpose was to provide truthful information about the public positions taken by Senator Barack Obama but that it would not "expressly advocate the election or defeat" of any political candidate or "make any contribution" to a candidate.

Within a few days of its incorporation, Real Truth commenced this action challenging . . . the Commission's regulations implementing the Federal Election Campaign Act ("FECA")—11 C.F.R. § 100.22(b) (defining when a communication expressly advocates the election or defeat of a clearly identified candidate. In addition, Real Truth challenged the Commission's policy of determining PAC status by using a "major purpose" test on a case-by-case basis. It asserted that these regulations and the policy were unconstitutional, facially and as applied, in that they were overbroad and vague, in violation of the First and Fifth Amendments to the Constitution.

[T]he district court granted summary judgment to the Commission and the Department of Justice, holding that 11 C.F.R. § 100.22(b) and the Commission's case-by-case policy for determining whether an organization was a PAC were constitutional, both facially and as applied to Real Truth. More particularly, the court found that § 100.22(b) was consistent with the "appeal-to-vote" test articulated in *Federal Election Commission v. Wisconsin Right to Life, Inc.* (2007), and that the Commission was entitled to use a multifactor approach on a case-by-case basis for determining PAC status because "ascertaining an organization's single major purpose is an inherently comparative task and requires consideration of the full range of an organization's activities."

II

At the outset, we address Real Truth's contention that, in reviewing the Commission's regulation and policy, we should apply the strict scrutiny standard. Real Truth argues that the regulation and policy place onerous burdens on speech similar to the burdens to which the Supreme Court applied strict scrutiny in *Citizens United*.

The Commission contends instead that because the challenged regulation and policy only implicate disclosure requirements and do not restrict either campaign activities or speech, we should apply the less stringent "exacting scrutiny" standard. Under this standard, the government must demonstrate only a "substantial relation" between the disclosure requirement and "sufficiently important government interest."

Regulation 100.22(b), which Real Truth challenges as too broad and vague, implements the statutory definition of "independent expenditure," 2 U.S.C. § 431(17), which in turn determines whether a person must make disclosures as required by 2 U.S.C. § 434(c). The definition could also contribute to the determination of whether Real Truth is a PAC because it is an organization with expenditures of more than $1,000, which would impose not only disclosure requirements, but also organizational requirements. Similarly, the Commission's policy for applying the "major purposes" test to organizations, which Real Truth also challenges, would also determine whether Real Truth is a PAC, again implicating disclosure and organizational requirements.

Such disclosure and organizational requirements, however, are not as burdensome on speech as are limits imposed on campaign activities or limits imposed on contributions to and expenditures by campaigns. Indeed, the Supreme Court has noted that "disclosure requirements certainly in most applications appear to be the least restrictive means of curbing the evils of campaign ignorance and corruption that Congress found to exist." *Buckley v. Valeo*. Accordingly, an intermediate level of scrutiny known as "exacting scrutiny" is the appropriate standard to apply in reviewing provisions that impose disclosure requirements, such as the regulation and policy.

In sum, we conclude that even after *Citizens United*, it remains the law that provisions imposing disclosure obligations are reviewed under the intermediate scrutiny level of "exacting scrutiny." We will accordingly review the Commission's regulation 100.22(b) and its policy for determining the major purpose of an organization under the exacting scrutiny standard.

III

Turning to the challenge of 11 C.F.R. § 100.22, Real Truth contends that the regulation's second definition of "expressly advocating," as contained in subsection (b), is fatally broader and more vague than the restrictions imposed on the definition of "expressly advocating" by *Buckley*.

Regulation 100.22 defines "expressly advocating" as the term is used in 2 U.S.C. § 431(17), which in turn defines "independent expenditure" as an expenditure by a person "*expressly advocating* the election or defeat of a clearly identified candidate" and not made by or in coordination with a candidate or political party. (Emphasis added.) Subsection (a) defines "expressly advocating" in the manner stated by the Supreme Court in *Buckley* and thus includes communications that use phrases "which in context can have no other reasonable meaning than to urge the election or defeat" of a candidate, 11 C.F.R. § 100.22(a)—words such as "vote for," "elect," "defeat," or "reject," which are often referred to as the express advocacy "magic words." *See McConnell v. Fed. Election Comm'n.* Subsection (b), on the other hand, defines "expressly advocating" more contextually, without using the "magic words." This subsection, which is the subject of Real Truth's challenge, provides in relevant part:

> Expressly advocating means any communication that—
> (b) When taken as a whole and with limited reference to external events, such as the proximity to the election, could only be interpreted by a reasonable person as containing advocacy of the election or defeat of one or more clearly identified candidate(s) because—
> (1) The electoral portion of the communication is unmistakable, unambiguous, and suggestive of only one meaning; and
> (2) Reasonable minds could not differ as to whether it encourages actions to elect or defeat one or more clearly identified candidate(s) or encourages some other kind of action.

A

Real Truth first challenges § 100.22(b) as facially overbroad. The Commission's approach of defining "expressly advocating" with the magic words of *Buckley* in subsection (a) and with their functional equivalent in subsection (b) was upheld by the Supreme Court in considering a facial over-breadth challenge to the BCRA, which included a provision defining express advocacy for purposes of electioneering communications. *See McConnell.* In rejecting the challenge, the *McConnell* Court noted that *Buckley*'s narrow construction of the FECA to require express advocacy was a function of the vagueness of the original statutory definition of "expenditure," not an absolute First Amendment imperative. The Court accordingly held that Congress could permissibly regulate not only communications containing the "magic words" of *Buckley*, but also communications that were "the functional equivalent" of express advocacy.

Later, in *Federal Election Commission v. Wisconsin Right to Life, Inc.* (2007), the Chief Justice's controlling opinion further elaborated on the meaning of *McConnell*'s "functional equivalent" test. The Chief Justice held that where an "ad is susceptible of no reasonable interpretation other than as an appeal to vote for or against a specific candidate," it could be regulated in the same manner as express advocacy. The Chief Justice explicitly rejected the argument, raised by Justice Scalia's concurring opinion, that the only permissible test for express advocacy is a magic words test.

Contrary to Real Truth's assertions, *Citizens United* also supports the Commission's use of a functional equivalent test in defining "express advocacy." In the course of striking down FECA's spending prohibitions on certain corporate election expenditures, the *Citizens*

United majority first considered whether those regulations applied to the communications at issue in the case. Using *Wisconsin Right to Life*'s "functional equivalent" test, the Court concluded that one advertisement—Hillary: The Movie—qualified as the functional equivalent of express advocacy because it was "in essence . . . a feature-length negative advertisement that urges viewers to vote against Senator [Hillary] Clinton for President." But more importantly for our decision, the Court also upheld BCRA's disclosure requirements for all electioneering communications—including those that are not the functional equivalent of express advocacy. In this portion of the opinion, joined by eight Justices, the Court explained that because disclosure "is a less restrictive alternative to more comprehensive regulations of speech," mandatory disclosure requirements are constitutionally permissible even if ads contain no direct candidate advocacy and "only pertain to a commercial transaction." If mandatory disclosure requirements are permissible when applied to ads that merely mention a federal candidate, then applying the same burden to ads that go further and are the functional equivalent of express advocacy cannot automatically be impermissible.

B

In addition to its overbreadth argument, Real Truth argues that even if express advocacy is not limited to communications using *Buckley*'s magic words, § 100.22(b) is nonetheless unconstitutionally vague. Here again, however, Real Truth's arguments run counter to an established Supreme Court precedent. The language of § 100.22(b) is consistent with the test for the "functional equivalent of express advocacy" that was adopted in *Wisconsin Right to Life*, a test that the controlling opinion specifically stated was not "impermissibly vague." Moreover, just as the "functional equivalent" test is objective, so too is the similar test contained in § 100.22(b).

Both standards are also restrictive, in that they limit the application of the disclosure requirements solely to those communications that, in the estimation of any reasonable person, would constitute advocacy. Although it is true that the language of § 100.22(b) does not exactly mirror the functional equivalent definition in *Wisconsin Right to Life*—e.g., § 100.22(b) uses the word "suggestive" while *Wisconsin Right to Life* used the word "susceptible"—the differences between the two tests are not meaningful. Indeed, the test in § 100.22(b) is likely narrower than the one articulated in *Wisconsin Right to Life*, since it requires a communication to have an "electoral portion" that is "unmistakable" and "unambiguous."

The Supreme Court has routinely recognized that because disclosure requirements occasion a lesser burden on speech, it is constitutionally permissible to require disclosure for a wider variety of speech than mere electioneering. *Citizens United* only confirmed the breadth of Congress' power in this regard.

C

At bottom, we conclude that § 100.22(b) is constitutional, facially and as applied to Real Truth's intended advertisements. The regulation is consistent with the test developed in *Wisconsin Right to Life* and is not unduly vague.

IV

Finally, Real Truth contends that the Commission's policy for applying the "major purpose" test in determining whether an organization is a PAC is unconstitutional because it "weigh[s] various vague and overbroad factors with undisclosed weight." It maintains that the only permissible methods of analyzing PAC status are (1) examining an organization's expenditures to see if campaign-related speech amounts to 50% of all expenditures; or (2) reviewing "the organization's central purpose revealed by its organic documents."

The FECA defines a "political committee" or PAC, as we have called it, as any "committee, club, association, or other group of persons" that makes more than $1,000 in political expenditures or receives more than $1,000 in contributions during a calendar year. The terms "expenditures" and "contributions" are in turn defined to encompass any spending or fundraising "for the purpose of influencing any election for Federal office."

In *Buckley*, the Supreme Court concluded that defining PACs "only in terms of amounts of annual 'contributions' and 'expenditures'" might produce vagueness issues. Accordingly, the Court limited the applicability of FECA's PAC requirements to organizations controlled by a candidate or whose "major purpose" is the nomination or election of candidates. An organization that is not controlled by a candidate must therefore register as a PAC if its contributions or expenditures exceed $1,000 and its "major purpose" is the nomination or election of a federal candidate.

Following *Buckley*, the Commission adopted a policy of determining PAC status on a case-by-case basis. Under this approach, the Commission first considers a group's political activities, such as spending on a particular electoral or issue-advocacy campaign, and then it evaluates an organization's "major purpose," as revealed by that group's public statements, fundraising appeals, government filings, and organizational documents.

In March 2004, the Commission published a Notice of Proposed Rulemaking that, among other things, requested comments on whether the Commission should adopt a regulatory definition of "political committee" or PAC. After receiving public comments and holding several hearings, the Commission issued a Final Rule stating that it would not alter its existing method of determining PAC status.

When the Commission's decision not to adopt a statutory definition of a PAC was challenged in [the D.C. district] court, the court rejected the plaintiffs' request to require the Commission to commence a new rulemaking. It found, however, that the Commission had "failed to present a reasoned explanation for its decision" to regulate § 527 organizations through case-by-case adjudication rather than a rulemaking. Therefore, it remanded the case to the Commission "to explain its decision or institute a new rulemaking."

The Commission responded in February 2007 by publishing in the Federal Register a "Supplemental Explanation and Justification," as part of the 2007 Notice, where it gave notice of its decision not to promulgate a new definition of "political committee" and discussed the reasons it would not do so but instead would continue to apply a case-by-case approach. The Commission stated that "[a]pplying the major purpose doctrine . . . requires the flexibility of a case-by-case analysis of an organization's conduct that is incompatible with a one-size-fits-all rule." The 2007 Notice also "explain[ed] the framework for establishing political committee status under FECA" and "discusse[d] several recently resolved administrative matters that provide considerable guidance to all organizations regarding . . . political committee status."

Although *Buckley* did create the major purpose test, it did not mandate a particular methodology for determining an organization's major purpose. And thus the Commission was free to administer FECA political committee regulations either through categorical rules or through individualized adjudications.

We conclude that the Commission had good and legal reasons for taking the approach it did. The determination of whether the election or defeat of federal candidates for office is the major purpose of an organization, and not simply *a* major purpose, is inherently a comparative task, and in most instances it will require weighing the importance of some of a group's activities against others. As the district court noted in upholding the case-by-case approach in *Shays v. Federal Election Commission* (D.D.C. 2007)

> an organization . . . may engage in many non-electoral activities so that determining its major purpose requires a very close examination of various activities and statements. Or an organization may be engaging in substantial amounts of both federal and non-federal electoral activity, again requiring a detailed analysis of its various activities.

The necessity of a contextual inquiry is supported by judicial decisions applying the major purpose test, which have used the same fact-intensive analysis that the Commission has adopted.

Real Truth's argument that the major purpose test requires a bright-line, two-factor test relies heavily on *Massachusetts Citizens for Life*. But [this case] can[not] bear the weight Real Truth ascribes to it. In *Massachusetts Citizens for Life*, the Court suggested in dicta (inasmuch as Massachusetts Citizens for Life was not a PAC) that an organization's independent spending could "become so extensive that the organization's major purpose may be regarded as campaign activity." This statement indicates that the amount of independent spending is a relevant factor in determining PAC status, but it does not imply that the Commission may only consider spending. Indeed, the Court in *Massachusetts Citizens for Life* implicitly endorsed the Commission's approach when it examined the entire record to conclude that the plaintiff did not satisfy the "major purpose" test.

Thus, although cases since *Buckley* have indicated that certain facts may be particularly relevant when assessing an organization's major purpose, those decisions do not foreclose the Commission from using a more comprehensive methodology.

Despite Real Truth's protestations, we see little risk that the Commission's existing major purpose test will chill political expression. In the First Amendment context, a statute may be found overbroad if a "substantial number of [the statute's] applications are unconstitutional, judged in relation to the statute's plainly legitimate sweep." *United States v. Stevens* (2010) (quoting *Wash. State Grange v. Wash. State Republican Party* (2008)). Real Truth has failed to explain why the Commission's test would prevent any party from speaking, especially in view of the fact that the application of the test to find that an organization is a PAC would subject the organization only to "minimal" reporting and organizational obligations.

We should note that the class of speakers who would be subject to FECA's PAC regulations would be significantly smaller than the totality of groups that speak on political subjects. In most cases the Commission would only begin to consider a group's "major purpose" after confirming that the group had either made $1,000 in expenditures or received more than $1,000 in contributions. The expenditure or contribution threshold means that some groups whose "major purpose" was indisputably the nomination or election of federal candidates would not be designated PACs.

And even if an organization were to find itself subject to a major-purpose investigation, that investigation would not necessarily be an intrusive one. Much of the information the Commission would consider would already be available in that organization's government filings or public statements. If additional information were required, the Commission's Federal Register notices, advisory opinions, and other policy documents would provide the organization with ample guidance as to the criteria the Commission might consider.

At bottom, we conclude that the Commission, in its policy, adopted a sensible approach to determining whether an organization qualifies for PAC status. And more importantly the Commission's multi-factor major-purpose test is consistent with Supreme Court precedent and does not unlawfully deter protected speech. Accordingly, we find the policy constitutional.

NOTES ON *SPEECHNOW* AND *REAL TRUTH*

1. Does the decision in *SpeechNow* inextricably flow from *Citizens United*? The court in *SpeechNow* says that *Citizens United* stated "as a matter of law" that independent expenditures do not lead to corruption. But is that an accurate reading of *Citizens United*? Or was the Court in *Citizens United* instead making a factual determination that independent expenditures usually do not lead to corruption, but that the law might be valid if there is evidence of *quid pro quo* corruption based on independent expenditures? In a challenge to a Montana law prohibiting corporate independent expenditures, the Montana Supreme Court upheld the law and ruled that Montana's unique history of corporate corruption distinguished *Citizens United* as a factual matter. The Supreme Court issued a

5-4 summary reversal, holding that *Citizens United* applies to Montana. *American Tradition Partnership v. Bullock*, 132 S. Ct. 2490 (2012).

2. Think about the real-world implications of the decision in *Real Truth*. Can an organization ever be secure that it is or is not subject to FECA's regulations? Is the "major purpose" test clear enough that you would be able to advise a client regarding whether it must comply? If the "major purpose" test is too murky, how would you revise it? What are the pitfalls of having a stricter test? Presumably, organizations would go right up to the line of whatever that test is before they fell under the regulation's strictures. Which is better in this area: bright-line rules or context-specific tests?
3. As a result of the decision in *SpeechNow*, new organizations began to pop up for both the 2010 and 2012 election cycles: Super PACs. A Super PAC is an independent expenditure-only organization. In essence, it is a political committee that is separate from a candidate and exists solely to make independent expenditures. Technically speaking, Super PACs are completely separate from political candidates; in reality, most Super PACs are at least aligned with a particular candidate even though there is no formal "coordination."
4. How should the Federal Election Commission and the courts determine if a Super PAC's spending qualifies as an independent expenditure or instead is being coordinated with a campaign? The FEC's website, citing the relevant regulation, provides that "a payment for a communication is 'coordinated' if it is made in cooperation, consultation or concert with, or at the request or suggestion of, a candidate, a candidate's authorized committee or their agents, or a political party committee or its agents." Is this standard helpful? The FEC has also created a three-part test to determine if a communication is "coordinated," all three of which must be satisfied for the communication to be coordinated and therefore subject to BCRA's contribution limitations. First, under the "payment" prong, the communication simply needs to be paid for by someone other than the candidate or political party committee. Second, under the "content" prong, the communication essentially must be about the candidate or the campaign. Finally, under the "conduct" prong, the person paying for the communication and the candidate or campaign must have some interaction, such as having substantial discussions between the entity paying for the ad and the candidate or campaign about the content or timing of the ad, or employing the same vendor when that vendor uses material information it has learned about the campaign's plans or activities in the creation, production, or distribution of the ad. Does this adequately capture the kind of communications that the Constitution allows the government to limit? For a detailed explanation of the three-prong test, visit the FEC's website at http://www.fec.gov/pages/brochures/indexp.shtml#CC. *See also* 11 C.F.R. § 109.21. Note that some of these regulations themselves have been the subject of judicial decisions, meaning that the law in this area is still ever-changing.

5. The rise of Super PACs in the wake of *Citizens United* led to the widely reported "scandal" in 2013 over IRS scrutiny of certain political groups. Some political operatives who wanted to keep their donors secret created new political groups, organizing them as tax-exempt 501(c)(4) entities. Under this provision of the tax code, 501(c)(4) groups need not disclose the identity of their donors. The section defines an eligible organization as "civic leagues, social welfare organizations, and local associations of employees." Generally accepted guidance is that an organization falls within the definition of a "social welfare organization" so long as its primary purpose—that is, at least 50 percent of its activities—is nonpolitical, i.e., related to social welfare. The IRS, suspecting that many of these so-called social welfare groups were actually political groups in disguise, began to scrutinize some groups' tax-exempt status applications more closely based on the groups' names. In particular, there were allegations that the IRS picked out groups whose names included certain terms, such as "tea party," for closer scrutiny. The scandal erupted because it appeared that the IRS was focusing on some groups over others based on their perceived political affiliations. In the wake of this controversy, the Obama administration has proposed new regulations on the political activities of 501(c)(4) organizations.

SUMMARY OF THE LAW OF CAMPAIGN PRACTICES

We have woven our way through the intricacies of the law of campaign practices, which has covered campaign ads, election crimes, and campaign finance. The recurring themes of the cases included:

- The clash of the First Amendment right to free speech with the desire to regulate false or misleading campaign ads, and the corresponding degree of regulation permissible to achieve better discourse in campaigning.
- A discussion of the best ways to ferret out improper or illegal campaign practices, such as manipulating absentee ballots or stopping "harassment" at the polls.
- The concern about deterring election fraud and corruption.
- The push-and-pull of regulating money in politics.

Specifically regarding campaign finance, we saw that the cases usually turn on both the type of money spent (contribution or independent expenditure), as well as who is spending it (the candidate, political party, individual, corporation or union, the public through public financing, or a political organization such as a PAC). The key question is whether the money spent would lead to actual or apparent corruption, defined (at least for the current majority of the Supreme Court) solely as *quid pro quo* corruption. Spending money on elections is a form of speech, so it receives constitutional protection under the First Amendment. But legislatures have an interest in limiting (to an extent) the improper influence of money in politics.

Current doctrine (as a general matter) states that legislatures cannot limit any kind of independent expenditures, as those are "independent" of any candidate and therefore cannot lead to a sufficient risk of corruption or the appearance of corruption, which is the only valid governmental interest to justify constraints on the freedom to engage in such electoral advocacy. These laws must pass strict scrutiny review. Contribution limits are usually tolerable, to an extent, as courts review them under the lower "close scrutiny" standard. But they cannot be so low as to preclude any effective political expression. Disclosure laws are usually valid, again under close scrutiny. Public financing regimes cannot treat candidates unequally, even if the candidates have preexisting unequal resources. There is also a continuing debate regarding the level of coordination allowed between candidates and so-called "outside" groups such as PACs. As the doctrine reveals, this is an ever-changing field, especially as campaigns become even more expensive. If anything, then, this unit demonstrated the extent to which courts can influence greatly the ways in which campaigns are run.

PART IV

The Law of Voting

Introduction

We now reach the last portion of our journey through the election cycle: casting and counting the ballots. This Part deals with the myriad aspects involved in actually voting for a candidate and tallying the results. Many of the issues discussed in this Part fall under the umbrella of "election administration," but the doctrine encompasses more than just the nuts-and-bolts of running an election. There are constitutional considerations regarding the right to vote, political concerns about how to register voters and run the polls—both with early voting and on Election Day—and practical aspects of resolving an election that goes into overtime.

The issues in this Part are sometimes the most contested, often appearing on the front pages of newspapers as an election nears. We will consider, for example, voter purges of registration lists, photo ID laws, and postelection disputes—including the most famous, *Bush v. Gore*. Also, in the lead up to the 2012 presidential election, early voting became a major issue, with the Obama campaign winning a key lawsuit in Ohio that left the polls open for all voters on the weekend before Election Day. Especially given that many African-American churches employed "souls to the polls" campaigns to bus voters to early voting sites after church on Sunday, this potentially could have helped to tip the balance for Obama in that state. (As it turned out, Obama's margin in the state, as well as the nation, did not make the votes cast on that Sunday decisive, but of course no one knew that ahead of time.) Provisional ballots often become the subject of lawsuits, especially when whether to count them will decide who won an election. Along the same lines, we will also consider the way in which our electoral system is one close election away from another *Bush v. Gore*—and how we can resolve it when it happens.

As with the other parts of this book, there are few easy answers to these difficult questions. But a few themes emerge. As you are reading this material, consider the following:

- What is the proper judicial test for the constitutional right to vote?
- Should we allow partisan operatives to run our elections? If so, is the judiciary an effective check?
- To what extent are the rules of election administration too incumbent-friendly, and should that concern us?

- How can we avoid another postelection meltdown?
- How should we resolve these postelection disputes?

Many of the cases in this Part come from the last four presidential election cycles (2000, 2004, 2008, 2012), meaning that the law in this area is both recent and ever-changing. The Law of Voting will likely continue to prove tumultuous in the years ahead. Although there are few clear answers, by the end of this Part you will at least have a firm grasp on the judiciary's role in the voting process.

A. Voter Eligibility

1. *Foundations*

The "right to vote" is not explicitly enumerated within the federal Constitution. In addition, the federal Constitution did not originally constrain a state's choice about which of its citizens were entitled to vote in state elections. Indeed, the Constitution piggybacked on state law to determine who was eligible to vote for U.S. House of Representatives: "The electors in each state shall have the qualifications requisite for the electors of the most numerous branch of the state legislature."*

Nor was the Fourteenth Amendment originally understood to constrain a state's choice concerning the qualifications necessary for voting. In *Minor v. Happersett*, 88 U.S. 162 (1874), decided just six years after the Fourteenth Amendment's ratification, the Supreme Court specifically rejected the claim that the Fourteenth Amendment required states to extend voting rights equally to women and men. Instead, it was thought necessary to add more amendments to the federal Constitution to limit a state's ability to differentiate among citizens in determining who may exercise the right to vote. Thus, the Fifteenth Amendment prohibits states from denying the right to vote "on account of race," while the Nineteenth Amendment explicitly did what *Minor v. Happersett* refused: give women the same voting rights as men.

Moreover, the Twenty-Fourth Amendment, ratified in 1964, prohibits a state from making the payment of a poll tax a prerequisite to voting in an election for *federal* office, although by its terms it imposes no constraint on poll taxes as a prerequisite for voting in an election for *state* office. The Twenty-Sixth Amendment, ratified in 1971, prohibits a state from making age a barrier to voting for any citizen at least 18 years old.

In light of this history, and specifically the intentionally limited language of the Twenty-Fourth Amendment, how do you understand the following case, *Harper v. Virginia Bd. of Elections*, which in 1966—just two years after the Twenty-Fourth Amendment's adoption—interpreted the Fourteenth Amendment to prohibit states from making the payment of a poll tax a prerequisite for voting in a *state* election? Is *Harper* a legitimate exercise of constitutional *interpretation*, or instead an illegitimate act of constitutional

* The Seventeenth Amendment contains this same language with respect to U.S. Senate elections.

amendment undertaken by the Supreme Court unilaterally (without following the amendment process in Article V of the federal Constitution)?

Whatever your view of *Harper*, it is here to stay. As the case after *Harper*, *Kramer v. Union Free School Dist. No. 15*, demonstrates, *Harper* was part of a series of cases that the Warren Court decided in the 1960s concerning the right to vote. These cases, which included the "one person, one vote" doctrine of *Reynolds v. Sims* and related reapportionment decisions, gave voting rights strict federal constitutional protections. The U.S. Supreme Court, even as it has become successively more conservative, has repeatedly reaffirmed—and even extended—the Warren Court's voting rights jurisprudence. As you will see, *Bush v. Gore* cites *Harper* and *Reynolds* as the key precedents for its own Equal Protection holding. Thus, unlike some Warren Court precedents in other areas of constitutional law, no one thinks that *Harper* (or *Kramer*) is vulnerable to overruling—although the Court may tinker with the application of these precedents (as the Court arguably did in the voter ID case you will soon read).

HARPER v. VIRGINIA STATE BOARD OF ELECTIONS

383 U.S. 663 (1966)

[Virginia law imposed a $1.50 annual poll tax on all citizens of voting age. Failure to pay the poll tax disqualified a person from voting. The revenue from the tax was used to pay for public schools and other local government functions. Suit was brought in federal district court to declare the poll tax unconstitutional under the Equal Protection Clause of the Fourteenth Amendment. The suit was dismissed on the authority of *Breedlove v. Suttles*, 302 U.S. 277 (1937), which had rejected an Equal Protection challenge to a state poll tax. Plaintiffs appealed directly to the Supreme Court.]

Justice Douglas delivered the opinion of the Court.

We conclude that a State violates the Equal Protection Clause whenever it makes the affluence of the voter or payment of any fee an electoral standard. Voter qualifications have no relation to wealth nor to paying or not paying this or any other tax.

Long ago in *Yick Wo v. Hopkins* (1886), the Court referred to "the political franchise of voting" as a "fundamental political right, because preservative of all rights." Recently in *Reynolds v. Sims* (1964), we said, "Undoubtedly, the right of suffrage is a fundamental matter in a free and democratic society. Especially since the right to exercise the franchise in a free and unimpaired manner is preservative of other basic civil and political rights, any alleged infringement of the right of citizens to vote must be carefully and meticulously scrutinized." There we were considering charges that voters in one part of the State had greater representation per person in the State Legislature than voters in another part of the State. We concluded: "A citizen, a qualified voter, is no more nor no less so because he lives in the city or on the farm."

We say the same whether the citizen, otherwise qualified to vote, has $1.50 in his pocket or nothing at all, pays the fee or fails to pay it. The principle that denies the State the right to dilute a citizen's vote on account of his economic status or other such factors by analogy bars a system which excludes those unable to pay a fee to vote or who fail to pay.

It is argued that a State may exact fees from citizens for many different kinds of licenses; that if it can demand from all an equal fee for a driver's license, it can demand from all an equal poll tax for voting. But we must remember that the interest of the State, when it comes to voting, is limited to the power to fix qualifications. Wealth, like race, creed, or color, is not germane to one's ability to participate intelligently in the electoral process. Lines drawn on the basis of wealth or property, like those of race, are traditionally disfavored. To introduce wealth or payment of a fee as a measure of a voter's qualifications is to introduce a capricious or irrelevant factor. The degree of the discrimination is irrelevant. In this context that is, as a condition of obtaining a ballot the requirement of fee paying causes an "invidious" discrimination that runs afoul of the Equal Protection Clause. Levy "by the poll," as stated in *Breedlove v. Suttles* is an old familiar form of taxation; and we say nothing to impair its validity so long as it is not made a condition to the exercise of the franchise. *Breedlove v. Suttles* sanctioned its use as "a prerequisite of voting." To that extent the *Breedlove* case is overruled.

We agree, of course, with Mr. Justice Holmes that the Due Process Clause of the Fourteenth Amendment "does not enact Mr. Herbert Spencer's Social Statics" (*Lochner v. People of State of New York* [(1905)]). Likewise, the Equal Protection Clause is not shackled to the political theory of a particular era. In determining what lines are unconstitutionally discriminatory, we have never been confined to historic notions of equality, any more than we have restricted due process to a fixed catalogue of what was at a given time deemed to be the limits of fundamental rights. Notions of what constitutes equal treatment for purposes of the Equal Protection Clause do change. This Court in 1896 held that laws providing for separate public facilities for white and Negro citizens did not deprive the latter of the equal protection and treatment that the Fourteenth Amendment commands. *Plessy v. Ferguson* [(1896)]. When, in 1954 more than a half-century later we repudiated the "separate-but-equal" doctrine of *Plessy* as respects public education we stated: "In approaching this problem, we cannot turn the clock back to 1868 when the Amendment was adopted, or even to 1896 when *Plessy v. Ferguson* was written." *Brown v. Board of Education* [(1954)].

We have long been mindful that where fundamental rights and liberties are asserted under the Equal Protection Clause, classifications which might invade or restrain them must be closely scrutinized and carefully confined. *See, e.g.*, *Skinner v. State of Oklahoma*, [(1942)].

Those principles apply here. For to repeat, wealth or fee paying has, in our view, no relation to voting qualifications; the right to vote is too precious, too fundamental to be so burdened or conditioned.

Reversed.

Mr. Justice HARLAN, whom Mr. Justice STEWART joins, dissenting.

The final demise of state poll taxes, already totally proscribed by the Twenty-Fourth Amendment with respect to federal elections and abolished by the States themselves in all but four States with respect to state elections,[8] is perhaps in itself not of great moment. But that fact that the coup de grace has been administered by this Court instead of being left to the affected States or to the federal political process should be a matter of continuing concern to all interested in maintaining the proper role of this tribunal under our scheme of government.

My disagreement with the present decision is that in holding the Virginia poll tax violative of the Equal Protection Clause the Court has departed from long-established standards governing the application of that clause.

The Equal Protection Clause prevents States from arbitrarily treating people differently under their laws. Whether any such differing treatment is to be deemed arbitrary depends on whether or not it reflects an appropriate differentiating classification among those affected; the clause has never been thought to require equal treatment of all persons despite differing circumstances. The test evolved by this Court for determining whether an asserted justifying classification exists is whether such a classification can be deemed to be founded on some rational and otherwise constitutionally permissible state policy. This standard reduces to a minimum the likelihood that the federal judiciary will judge state policies in terms of the individual notions and predilections of its own members, and until recently it has been followed in all kinds of "equal protection" cases.

Reynolds v. Sims, among its other breaks with the past, also marked a departure from these traditional and wise principles. Unless its "one man, one vote" thesis of state legislative apportionment is to be attributed to the unsupportable proposition that "Equal Protection" simply means indiscriminate equality, it seems inescapable that what *Reynolds* really reflected was but this Court's own views of how modern American representative government should be run. For it can hardly be thought that no other method of apportionment may be considered rational.

[T]oday in holding unconstitutional state poll taxes and property qualifications for voting and overruling *Breedlove v. Suttles*, the Court [continues] the highly subjective judicial approach manifested by *Reynolds*. In substance the Court's analysis of the equal protection issue goes no further than to say that the electoral franchise is "precious" and "fundamental," and to conclude that "(t)o introduce wealth or payment of a fee as a measure of a voter's qualifications is to introduce a capricious or irrelevant factor." These are of course captivating phrases, but they are wholly inadequate to satisfy the standard governing adjudication of the equal protection issue: Is there a rational basis

8. Alabama, Mississippi, Texas, and Virginia.

for Virginia's poll tax as a voting qualification? I think the answer to that question is undoubtedly "yes."

Property qualifications and poll taxes have been a traditional part of our political structure. [W]ith property qualifications, it is only by fiat that it can be said, especially in the context of American history, that there can be no rational debate as to their advisability. Most of the early Colonies had them; many of the States have had them during much of their histories; and, whether one agrees or not, arguments have been and still can be made in favor of them. For example, it is certainly a rational argument that payment of some minimal poll tax promotes civic responsibility, weeding out those who do not care enough about public affairs to pay $1.50 or thereabouts a year for the exercise of the franchise. It is also arguable, indeed it was probably accepted as sound political theory by a large percentage of Americans through most of our history, that people with some property have a deeper stake in community affairs, and are consequently more responsible, more educated, more knowledgeable, more worthy of confidence, than those without means, and that the community and Nation would be better managed if the franchise were restricted to such citizens. Nondiscriminatory and fairly applied literacy tests, upheld by this Court in *Lassiter v. Northampton County Board of Elections* (1959), find justification on very similar grounds.

These viewpoints, to be sure, ring hollow on most contemporary ears. Their lack of acceptance today is evidenced by the fact that nearly all of the States, left to their own devices, have eliminated property or poll-tax qualifications; by the cognate fact that Congress and three-quarters of the States quickly ratified the Twenty-Fourth Amendment.

Property and poll-tax qualifications, very simply, are not in accord with current egalitarian notions of how a modern democracy should be organized. It is of course entirely fitting that legislatures should modify the law to reflect such changes in popular attitudes. However, it is all wrong, in my view, for the Court to adopt the political doctrines popularly accepted at a particular moment of our history and to declare all others to be irrational and invidious, barring them from the range of choice by reasonably minded people acting through the political process. It was not too long ago that Mr. Justice Holmes felt impelled to remind the Court that the Due Process Clause of the Fourteenth Amendment does not enact the laissez-faire theory of society, *Lochner v. People of State of New York*. The times have changed, and perhaps it is appropriate to observe that neither does the Equal Protection Clause of that Amendment rigidly impose upon America an ideology of unrestrained egalitarianism.

Mr. Justice Black, dissenting.

[Justice Black dissented for essentially the same reasons that Justices Harlan and Stewart did. He added these points:]

All voting laws treat some persons differently from others in some respects. Some bar a person from voting who is under 21 years of age; others bar those under 18. Some bar convicted felons or the insane, and some have attached a freehold or other property qualification for voting. And in *Lassiter v. Northampton Election Board* (1959)], this Court held that state laws which disqualified the illiterate from voting did not violate the Equal Protection Clause. [I]t is clear that some discriminatory voting qualifications can be imposed without violating the Equal Protection Clause.

Another reason for my dissent from the Court's judgment and opinion is that it seems to be using the old "natural-law-due-process formula" to justify striking down state laws as violations of the Equal Protection Clause. I have heretofore had many occasions to express my strong belief that there is no constitutional support whatever for this Court to use the Due Process Clause as though it provided a blank check to alter the meaning of the Constitution as written so as to add to it substantive constitutional changes which a majority of the Court at any given time believes are needed to meet present-day problems. If basic changes as to the respective powers of the state and national governments are needed, I prefer to let those changes be made by amendment as Article V of the Constitution provides. For a majority of this Court to undertake that task, whether purporting to do so under the Due Process or the Equal Protection Clause amounts, in my judgment, to an exercise of power the Constitution makers with foresight and wisdom refused to give the Judicial Branch of the Government.

The Court denies that it is using the "natural-law-due-process formula." I find no statement in the Court's opinion, however, which advances even a plausible argument as to why the alleged discriminations which might possibly be effected by Virginia's poll tax law are "irrational," "unreasonable," "arbitrary," or "invidious" or have no relevance to a legitimate policy which the State wishes to adopt. The Court gives no reason at all to discredit the long-standing beliefs that making the payment of a tax a prerequisite to voting is an effective way of collecting revenue and that people who pay their taxes are likely to have a far greater interest in their government. The Court's failure to give any reasons to show that these purposes of the poll tax are "irrational," "unreasonable," "arbitrary," or "invidious" is a pretty clear indication to me that none exist. I can only conclude that the primary, controlling, predominate, if not the exclusive reason for declaring the Virginia law unconstitutional is the Court's deep-seated hostility and antagonism, which I share, to making payment of a tax a prerequisite to voting.

The Court's justification for consulting its own notions rather than following the original meaning of the Constitution, as I would, apparently is based on the belief of the majority of the Court that for this Court to be bound by the original meaning of the Constitution is an intolerable and debilitating evil; that our Constitution should not be "shackled to the political theory of a particular era," and that to save the country from the original Constitution the Court must have constant power to renew it and keep it abreast of this Court's more enlightening theories of what is best for our society. It seems to me that this is an attack not only on the great value of our Constitution itself but also on the concept of a written constitution which is to survive through the years as originally written unless changed through the amendment process which the Framers wisely provided. Moreover, when a "political theory" embodied in our Constitution becomes outdated, it seems to me that a majority of the nine members of this Court are not only without constitutional power but are far less qualified to choose a new constitutional political theory than the people of this country proceeding in the manner provided by Article V.

The people have not found it impossible to amend their Constitution to meet new conditions. The Equal Protection Clause itself is the product of the people's desire to use their constitutional power to amend the Constitution to meet new problems. Moreover, the people, in § 5 of the Fourteenth Amendment, designated the governmental tribunal they wanted to provide additional rules to enforce the guarantees of that Amendment. The branch of Government they chose was not the Judicial Branch but the Legislative. I have no doubt at all that Congress has the power under § 5 to pass legislation to abolish the poll tax in order to protect the citizens of this country if it believes that the poll tax is being used as a device to deny voters equal protection of the laws.

KRAMER v. UNION FREE SCHOOL DISTRICT NO. 15

395 U.S. 621 (1969)

Mr. Chief Justice WARREN delivered the opinion of the Court.

In this case we are called on to determine whether § 2012 of the New York Education Law is constitutional. The legislation provides that in certain New York school districts residents who are otherwise eligible to vote in state and federal elections may vote in the school district election only if they (1) own (or lease) taxable real property within the district, or (2) are parents (or have custody of) children enrolled in the local public schools. Appellant, a bachelor who neither owns nor leases taxable real property, filed suit in federal court claiming that § 2012 denied him equal protection of the laws in violation of the Fourteenth Amendment. With one judge dissenting, a three-judge District Court dismissed appellant's complaint. Finding that § 2012 does violate the Equal Protection Clause of the Fourteenth Amendment, we reverse.

At the outset, it is important to note what is not at issue in this case. The requirements of § 2012 that school district voters must (1) be citizens of the United States, (2) be bona fide residents of the school district, and (3) be at least 21 years of age are not challenged. Appellant agrees that the States have the power to impose reasonable citizenship, age, and residency requirements on the availability of the ballot. The sole issue in this case is whether the additional requirements of § 2012, which prohibit some district residents who are otherwise qualified by age and citizenship from participating in district meetings and school board elections, violate equal protection.

"In determining whether or not a state law violates the Equal Protection Clause, we must consider the facts and circumstances behind the law, the interests which the State claims to be protecting, and the interests of those who are disadvantaged by the classification." *Williams v. Rhodes* (1968). And, in this case, we must give the statute a close and exacting examination. "(S)ince the right to exercise the franchise in a free and unimpaired manner is preservative of other basic civil and political rights, any alleged infringement of the right of citizens to vote must be carefully and meticulously scrutinized." *Reynolds v. Sims* (1964). This careful examination is necessary because statutes distributing the franchise constitute the foundation of our representative society. Any unjustified discrimination in determining who may participate in political affairs or in the selection of public officials undermines the legitimacy of representative government.

Thus, state apportionment statutes, which may dilute the effectiveness of some citizens' votes, receive close scrutiny from this Court. No less rigid an examination is applicable to statutes denying the franchise to citizens who are otherwise qualified by residence and age. Statutes granting the franchise to residents on a selective basis always pose the danger of denying some citizens any effective voice in the governmental affairs which substantially affect their lives. Therefore, if a challenged state statute grants the right to vote to some bona fide residents of requisite age and citizenship and denies the franchise to others, the Court must determine whether the exclusions are necessary to promote a compelling state interest.

And, for these reasons, the deference usually given to the judgment of legislators does not extend to decisions concerning which resident citizens may participate in the election of legislators and other public officials. Those decisions must be carefully scrutinized by the Court to determine whether each resident citizen has, as far as is possible, an equal voice in the selections. Accordingly, when we are reviewing statutes which deny some residents the right to vote, the general presumption of constitutionality afforded state statutes and the traditional approval given state classifications if the Court can conceive of a "rational basis" for the distinctions made are not applicable. *See Harper v. Virginia State Bd. of Elections* (1966). The presumption of constitutionality and the approval given "rational" classifications in other types of enactments are based on an assumption that the institutions of state government are structured so as to represent fairly all the people. However, when the challenge to the statute is in effect a challenge of this basic assumption, the assumption can no longer serve as the basis for presuming constitutionality. And, the assumption is no less under attack because the legislature which decides who may participate at the various levels of political choice is fairly elected. Legislation which delegates decision making to bodies elected by only a portion of those eligible to vote for the legislature can cause unfair representation. Such legislation can exclude a minority of voters from any voice in the decisions just as effectively as if the decisions were made by legislators the minority had no voice in selecting.

The need for exacting judicial scrutiny of statutes distributing the franchise is undiminished simply because, under a different statutory scheme, the offices subject to election might have been filled through appointment. States do have latitude in determining whether certain public officials shall be selected by election or chosen by appointment and whether various questions shall be submitted to the voters. In fact, we have held that where a county school board is an administrative, not legislative, body, its members need not be elected. *Sailors v. Kent County Bd. of Education* (1967). However, "once the franchise is granted to the electorate, lines may not be drawn which are inconsistent with the Equal Protection Clause of the Fourteenth Amendment." *Harper.*

Nor is the need for close judicial examination affected because the district meetings and the school board do not have "general" legislative powers. Our exacting examination is not necessitated by the subject of the election; rather, it is required because some resident citizens are permitted to participate and some are not. For example, a city charter might well provide that the elected city council appoint a mayor who would have broad administrative powers. Assuming the council were elected consistent with the commands of the Equal Protection Clause, the delegation of power to the mayor would not call for this Court's exacting review. On the other hand, if the city charter made the office of mayor subject to an election in which only some resident citizens were entitled to vote, there would be presented a situation calling for our close review.

Besides appellant and others who similarly live in their parents' homes, the statute also disenfranchises the following persons (unless they are parents or guardians of children enrolled in the district public school): senior citizens and others living with children or relatives; clergy, military personnel, and others who live on tax-exempt property; boarders and lodgers; parents who neither own nor lease qualifying property and whose children are too young to attend school; parents who neither own nor lease qualifying property and whose children attend private schools.

Appellant asserts that excluding him from participation in the district elections denies him equal protection of the laws. He contends that he and others of his class are substantially interested in and significantly affected by the school meeting decisions. All members of the community have an interest in the quality and structure of public education, appellant says, and he urges that "the decisions taken by local boards . . . may have grave consequences to the entire population." Appellant also argues that the level of property taxation affects him, even though he does not own property, as property tax levels affect the price of goods and services in the community.

We turn therefore to question whether the exclusion is necessary to promote a compelling state interest. First appellees argue that the State has a legitimate interest in limiting the franchise in school district elections to "members of the community of interest"—those "primarily interested in such elections." Second, appellees urge that the State may reasonably and permissibly conclude that "property taxpayers" (including lessees of taxable property who share the tax burden through rent payments) and parents of the children enrolled in the district's schools are those "primarily interested" in school affairs.

We do not understand appellees to argue that the State is attempting to limit the franchise to those "subjectively concerned" about school matters. Rather, they appear to argue that the State's legitimate interest is in restricting a voice in school matters to those "directly affected" by such decisions. The State apparently reasons that since the schools are financed in part by local property taxes, persons whose out-of-pocket expenses are "directly" affected by property tax changes should be allowed to vote. Similarly, parents of children in school are thought to have a "direct" stake in school affairs and are given a vote.

Appellees argue that it is necessary to limit the franchise to those "primarily interested" in school affairs because "the ever increasing complexity of the many interacting phases of the school system and structure make it extremely difficult for the electorate fully to understand the whys and wherefores of the detailed operations of the school system." Appellees say that many communications of school boards and school administrations are sent home to the parents through the district pupils and are "not broadcast to the general public"; thus, nonparents will be less informed than parents. Further, appellees argue, those who are assessed for local property taxes (either directly or indirectly through rent) will have enough of an interest "through the burden on their pocketbooks, to acquire such information as they may need."

We need express no opinion as to whether the State in some circumstances might limit the exercise of the franchise to those "primarily interested" or "primarily affected." Of course, we therefore do not reach the issue of whether these particular elections are of the type in which the franchise may be so limited. For, assuming, arguendo, that New York legitimately might limit the franchise in these school district elections to those "primarily interested in school affairs," close scrutiny of the § 2012 classifications demonstrates that they do not accomplish this purpose with sufficient precision to justify denying appellant the franchise.

Whether classifications allegedly limiting the franchise to those resident citizens "primarily interested" deny those excluded equal protection of the laws depends, inter alia, on whether all those excluded are in fact substantially less interested or affected than those the statute includes. In other words, the classifications must be tailored so that the exclusion of appellant and members of his class is necessary to achieve the articulated state goal.[14] Section 2012 does not meet the exacting standard of precision we require of statutes which selectively distribute the franchise. The classifications in § 2012 permit inclusion of many persons who have, at best, a remote and indirect interest, in school affairs and, on the other hand, exclude others who have a distinct and direct interest in the school meeting decisions.[15]

Nor do appellees offer any justification for the exclusion of seemingly interested and informed residents—other than to argue that the § 2012 classifications include those "whom the State could understandably deem to be the most intimately interested in

14. Of course, if the exclusions are necessary to promote the articulated state interest, we must then determine whether the interest promoted by limiting the franchise constitutes a compelling state interest. We do not reach that issue in this case.

15. For example, appellant resides with his parents in the school district, pays state and federal taxes and is interested in and affected by school board decisions; however, he has no vote. On the other hand, an uninterested unemployed young man who pays no state or federal taxes, but who rents an apartment in the district, can participate in the election.

actions taken by the school board," and urge that "the task of . . . balancing the interest of the community in the maintenance of orderly school district elections against the interest of any individual in voting in such elections should clearly remain with the Legislature." But the issue is not whether the legislative judgments are rational. A more exacting standard obtains. The issue is whether the § 2012 requirements do in fact sufficiently further a compelling state interest to justify denying the franchise to appellant and members of his class. The requirements of § 2012 are not sufficiently tailored to limiting the franchise to those "primarily interested" in school affairs to justify the denial of the franchise to appellant and members of his class.

Mr. Justice STEWART, with whom Mr. Justice BLACK, and Mr. Justice HARLAN join, dissenting.

[T]he appellant explicitly concedes, as he must, the validity of voting requirements relating to residence, literacy, and age. Yet he argues—and the Court accepts the argument—that the voting qualifications involved here somehow have a different constitutional status. I am unable to see the distinction.

Clearly a State may reasonably assume that its residents have a greater stake in the outcome of elections held within its boundaries than do other persons. Likewise, it is entirely rational for a state legislature to suppose that residents, being generally better informed regarding state affairs than are nonresidents, will be more likely than nonresidents to vote responsibly. And the same may be said of legislative assumptions regarding the electoral competence of adults and literate persons on the one hand, and of minors and illiterates on the other. It is clear, of course, that lines thus drawn can not infallibly perform their intended legislative function. Just as illiterate people may be intelligent voters, nonresidents or minors might also in some instances be interested, informed, and intelligent participants in the electoral process. Persons who commute across a state line to work may well have a great stake in the affairs of the State in which they are employed; some college students under 21 may be both better informed and more passionately interested in political affairs than many adults. But such discrepancies are the inevitable concomitant of the line drawing that is essential to law making. So long as the classification is rationally related to a permissible legislative end, therefore—as are residence, literacy, and age requirements imposed with respect to voting—there is no denial of equal protection.

Thus judged, the statutory classification involved here seems to me clearly to be valid. New York has made the judgment that local educational policy is best left to those persons who have certain direct and definable interests in that policy: those who are either immediately involved as parents of school children or who, as owners or lessees of taxable property are burdened with the local cost of funding school district operations. True, persons outside those classes may be genuinely interested in the conduct of a school district's business—just as commuters from New Jersey may be genuinely interested in the outcome of a New York City election. But unless this Court is to claim a monopoly of wisdom regarding the sound operation of school systems in the 50 States, I see no way to justify the conclusion that the legislative classification involved here is not rationally related to a legitimate legislative purpose.

With good reason, the Court does not really argue the contrary. Instead, it strikes down New York's statute by asserting that the traditional equal protection standard is inapt in this case, and that a considerably stricter standard—under which classifications relating to "the franchise" are to be subjected to "exacting judicial scrutiny"—should be applied. But the asserted justification for applying such a standard cannot withstand analysis.

The Court is quite explicit in explaining why it believes this statute should be given "close scrutiny":

> "The presumption of constitutionality and the approval given 'rational' classifications in other types of enactments are based on an assumption that the institutions of state government are structured so as to represent fairly all the people. However, when the challenge to the statute is in effect a challenge of this basic assumption, the assumption can no longer serve as the basis for presuming constitutionality." (Footnote omitted.)

I am at a loss to understand how such reasoning is at all relevant to the present case. The voting qualifications at issue have been promulgated, not by Union Free School District No. 15, but by the New York State Legislature, and the appellant is of course fully able to participate in the election of representatives in that body. There is simply no claim whatever here that the state government is not "structured so as to represent fairly all the people," including the appellant.

Nor is there any other jurisdiction for imposing the Court's "exacting" equal protection test. This case does not involve racial classifications, which in light of the genesis of the Fourteenth Amendment have traditionally been viewed as inherently "suspect." And this statute is not one that impinges upon a constitutionally protected right, and that consequently can be justified only by a "compelling" state interest. For "the Constitution of the United States does not confer the right of suffrage upon any one . . . ." *Minor v. Happerset* [(1875)].

In any event, it seems to me that under any equal protection standard, short of a doctrinaire insistence that universal suffrage is somehow mandated by the Constitution, the appellant's claim must be rejected. First of all, it must be emphasized despite the Court's undifferentiated references to what it terms "the franchise" that we are dealing here, not with a general election, but with a limited, special purpose election.[9] The appellant is eligible to vote in all state, local, and federal elections in which general governmental policy is determined. He is fully able, therefore, to participate not only in the

9. Special-purpose governmental authorities such as water, lighting, and sewer districts exist in various sections of the country, and participation in such districts is undoubtedly limited in many instances to those who partake of the agency's services and are assessed for its expenses. The constitutional validity of such a policy is, it seems to me, unquestionable. And while it is true, as the appellant argues, that a school system has a more pervasive influence in the community than do most other such special-purpose authorities, I cannot agree that that difference in degree presents anything approaching a distinction of constitutional dimension.

processes by which the requirements for school district voting may be changed, but also in those by which the levels of state and federal financial assistance to the District are determined. He clearly is not locked into any self-perpetuating status of exclusion from the electoral process.

Secondly, the appellant is of course limited to asserting his own rights, not the purported rights of hypothetical childless clergymen or parents of preschool children, who neither own nor rent taxable property. The appellant's status is merely that of a citizen who says he is interested in the affairs of his local public schools. If the Constitution requires that he must be given a decision-making role in the governance of those affairs, then it seems to me that any individual who seeks such a role must be given it.

2. The Voting Rights of the Mentally Infirm

Just how extensive is the federal constitutional protection of the right to vote? Would it limit a state's power to deny the right to vote to individuals adjudicated to be mentally incompetent, by reason of either severe mental retardation or severe mental illness? As you read the next case on voter eligibility, which involves New Jersey law, ask yourself whether the Fourteenth Amendment in light of *Harper* and *Kramer* would have required the New Jersey court to reach the same result on federal constitutional grounds as the court did under state law.

This issue is not merely theoretical. It has increasingly practical importance in the specific context of senility and voting by nursing home patients, as the large "baby boomer" generation becomes elderly. Obviously a sensitive subject, the question still must be asked whether the Fourteenth Amendment would limit a state's effort to prevent ballots cast on behalf of mentally incompetent nursing home residents, who might be manipulated by staff or others to vote in ways they would not want or do not understand. The New Jersey case shows that state constitutional and statutory law will have an important role to play in addressing this topic, even apart from the Fourteenth Amendment jurisprudence of *Harper* and *Kramer*.

IN MATTER OF ABSENTEE BALLOTS CAST BY FIVE RESIDENTS OF TRENTON PSYCHIATRIC HOSPITAL

750 A.2d 790 (2000) (Superior Court of New Jersey, Appellate Division)

The opinion of the court was delivered by [Judge] RODRIGUEZ.

In this appeal, we hold that voters who are involuntarily committed residents of a psychiatric hospital are presumed competent to vote. Therefore, they cannot be challenged as voters nor their ballots segregated, absent a particularized showing of incompetence.

On November 3, 1998, a general election day, the attorney for the Mercer County Republican Committee wrote a letter to the Mercer County Board of Elections

(Board) challenging any absentee ballot cast by residents of Trenton Psychiatric Hospital. The attorney asserted that he had [become] aware that "there was an organized effort to register voters that have been committed by a judge to Trenton Psychiatric Hospital." Seven absentee ballots were identified as being cast by residents of the hospital. The Attorney General advised the Board that, absent an adjudication of insanity or other documentary evidence of insanity or incompetency, the ballots should be counted. The Board rejected two of the ballots on grounds other than competency. However, the Board was deadlocked regarding the remaining five absentee ballots. The Board referred the challenge of these ballots to the [trial court].

The judge decided that the ballots should remain unopened and segregated. The judge reasoned that the "safe approach" was to segregate the ballots now, and only allow the ballots to be opened if the voter was later determined competent.

On appeal, [it is] contended that: (1) a challenge based on residency at the psychiatric hospital alone is illegal; (2) the voters were deprived of their fundamental right to vote because their ballots were segregated; and (3) the judge erred by not placing the burden on the challengers to show by clear and convincing evidence that the voters were ineligible to vote. We agree with all three contentions.

The New Jersey Constitution sets forth the qualifications for being a voter. A voter must be a United States citizen, eighteen years old or older, and satisfy a thirty-day State or County residency requirement. However, "[n]o idiots or insane person shall enjoy the right of suffrage." However, there is no statutory definition of the terms "idiot" or "insane."

Generally, a voter may be subject to a challenge of his or her right to vote. Nonetheless, there are specific limitations on the powers of challengers in order to effectuate the overriding public policy in favor of enfranchisement. Such policy derives from the basic precept that the right to vote is quintessential to our democratic process. It follows, then, that all challenges to an individual's right to vote be carefully scrutinized.

New Jersey's commitment statute sets forth the framework for involuntary commitment of mentally ill and mentally retarded persons to state institutions designed for their care. However, the legislature specifically guaranteed that the right of suffrage not be deprived to an individual receiving treatment in psychiatric hospitals. Specifically, *N.J.S.A.* 30:4-24.2a provides:

> Subject to any provisions of law and the Constitution of New Jersey and the United States, no patient shall be deprived of any civil right solely by reason of his receiving treatment under the provisions of this Title nor shall such treatment modify or vary any legal or civil right of any such patient including but not limited to the right to register and to vote at elections. . . .

In *Carroll v. Cobb* (N.J. App. Div. 1976), we held that residence at a state school for the mentally retarded did not per se render an individual, who otherwise meets all other voting requirements, ineligible to vote. We concluded that as long as the voters were bona fide residents of the township, "were properly registered and were not otherwise disqualified, they were entitled to vote." *Id.* This holding did not "foreclose the county board of elections, *on an individual basis and for specifically stated reasons,* from reviewing and challenging the voting qualifications of any member of the class, so long as it is done in the manner provided by law." [*Id.*] (emphasis supplied.)

In *Carroll,* we underscored the need for a particularized showing of incompetence by expert testimony by observing,

> It should be abundantly evident that a lay person is completely unequipped to determine whether an applicant is either an "idiot" or an "insane person," as those terms are used in the Constitution and the statute, and thus disenfranchised. Indeed we suspect that those imprecise terms may be troublesome to experts in the fields of psychiatry or psychology.

We reasoned "that a mentally retarded person need not be an 'idiot,' and a mentally ill person need not be 'insane.'" *Id.* Thus, we reaffirmed the principle set forth in the commitment statute that no presumption of incompetence arises from being treated at a mental institution. A separate adjudication of incompetence is required. We note that for purposes of challenging any voter, on competing or any other ground, a complete list of the names and addresses of all registered voters is made available to any voter. In addition, once every calendar year, the State Committee of each political party may request the registry list.

Here, no evidence was adduced regarding the competency of the challenged voters. Therefore, the judge had no option but to reject the challenge. Their ballots should have been counted.

[The] second contention is that the burden of proof falls on those seeking to challenge the patients' right to vote. Again, we agree. Voting is a fundamental right. As with all fundamental rights, there can be no interference with an individual's right to vote, "unless a compelling state interest to justify the restriction is shown." *Worden v. Mercer County Bd. of Elections* (N.J. 1972). Similarly, the burden of demonstrating that an individual is incompetent requires proof that is clear and convincing. *See In Re Grady* (N.J. 1981). Therefore, those who seek to deprive an individual of a fundamental right must meet a clear and convincing burden of proof.

Applying that principle here, it follows that the burden fell on the challengers to prove the patient's incompetence. Because there was no evidence presented as to the competence of the voters, the trial judge erred by segregating the ballots. These ballots should be opened and counted.

3. *Felon Disenfranchisement*

Most states deny the right to vote to their citizens who have been convicted of a felony, at least during the time in which they are serving their prison sentence.* As a result, more than 5 million U.S. citizens, who otherwise would be qualified to vote, are ineligible to do so.** Because this number has grown in recent years, due to the increasing percentage of U.S. citizens behind bars (largely as a consequence of the "war on drugs"), the widespread practice of felon disenfranchisement has come under attack in the past decade.

Moreover, because African Americans are incarcerated at much higher rates than the U.S. population as a whole—almost one in ten African-American adults is in prison, whereas fewer than one in thirty of all American adults are (correspondingly, almost 40 percent of the prison population is African American, whereas African Americans are only 12.5 percent of the U.S. population as a whole)—felon disenfranchisement laws inevitably have a disproportionately adverse effect on African Americans. Generally speaking, Section 2 of the Voting Rights Act (as amended in 1982) prohibits voting qualification rules that disproportionately burden African Americans. Therefore, the question necessarily arises whether felon disenfranchisement laws violate the "results" test found in Section 2 of the Voting Rights Act.

The federal judiciary has struggled with this question in the last decade. This struggle takes on two parts. The first is whether Congress intended Section 2 to apply at all to felon disenfranchisement laws. Several appellate courts have found historical evidence to indicate Congress never intended the Voting Rights Act to apply to felon disenfranchisement laws. The most recent of these appellate decisions include *Simmons v. Galvin*, 575 F.3d 24, 41 (1st Cir. 2009), which the U.S. Supreme Court refused to review, and *Farrakhan v. Gregoire*, 623 F.3d 990 (9th Cir. 2010), where an eleven-member "en banc panel" of the Ninth Circuit overruled a three-member panel that went the other way.

If Section 2 were found to speak on the issue of felon disenfranchisement laws, then a second issue arises: Which felon disenfranchisement laws violate the "results" test? Does any felon disenfranchisement law that has a disparate impact on, say, African Americans or Latinos violate the results test, or would a plaintiff in such a case need to prove something more? If a plaintiff needs to prove something more, what additional facts would a plaintiff need to emerge as victorious on the merits of a Section 2 claim against a felon disenfranchisement statute?

The federal circuits have consistently made it difficult for plaintiffs to use Section 2 to attack state felon disenfranchisement laws—either finding that Section 2 does not apply at all or that plaintiffs have not provided enough evidence to prove a violation of the "results" test. But the consistency of the federal circuits masks the significant dissent among judges within each circuit. Two other circuits, besides the Ninth, needed to take the issue

* Only Maine and Vermont do not disenfranchise felons even while they are serving their prison term.

** Nicole Porter, Expanding the Vote: State Felony Disenfranchisement Reform, 1997-2010 (The Sentencing Project Oct. 2010), at 3.

"en banc" to resolve it. And, as one of these cases will now show, several of the nation's most prominent jurists refused to accept the majority view of this issue. Judge Calabresi, who dissented from the Second Circuit's decision that we will now read, is well known for serving as Dean of the Yale Law School (and being a leading scholar) before taking the bench. And, of course, Judge Sotomayor, who also dissented in the same case, now sits on the Supreme Court. In making these observations, the editors of this casebook do not mean to say that they believe that Judges Calabresi and Sotomayor had the better of the argument; only that strong arguments could be made on both sides of the question. By the way, the split among the thirteen Second Circuit judges in this case was 8-5.

HAYDEN v. PATAKI

449 F.3d 305 (2d Cir. 2006) (en banc)

José A. Cabranes, Circuit Judge.

We have granted en banc review in order to decide whether plaintiffs can state a claim for violation of Section 2 of the Voting Rights Act ("VRA"), 42 U.S.C. § 1973, based on allegations that a New York State statute that disenfranchises currently incarcerated felons and parolees, N.Y. Election Law § 5-106, results in unlawful vote denial and vote dilution.

We hold that the Voting Rights Act does not encompass these felon disenfranchisement provisions. Our holding is based on our conclusion that Congress did not intend or understand the Voting Rights Act to encompass such felon disenfranchisement statutes, that application of the Voting Rights Act to felon disenfranchisement statutes such as these would alter the constitutional balance between the States and the Federal Government, and that Congress at the very least did not clearly indicate that it intended the Voting Rights Act to alter the federal balance in this way.

I

Plaintiffs' amended complaint challenges "New York State's discriminatory practice of denying suffrage to persons who are incarcerated or on parole for a felony conviction and the resulting discriminatory impact that such denial of suffrage has on Blacks and Latinos in the State." Plaintiffs allege both vote denial and vote dilution claims under Section 2 of the Voting Rights Act.

[T]he District Court grant[ed] defendants' motion for judgment on the pleadings and dismiss[ed] all of plaintiffs' claims. [We affirm.]

II

A. Statutory Provisions

Section 5-106 of the New York Election Law provides that no person convicted of a felony "shall have the right to register for or vote at any election" unless he has been pardoned, his maximum sentence of imprisonment has expired, or he has been discharged from parole.[5]

Felon disenfranchisement has a long history in New York. The New York State Constitution of 1821 authorized the state legislature to enact laws disenfranchising those convicted of "infamous crimes." The state legislature passed such a law the next year. This law, as revised, has been in effect in the State ever since. It was modified in 1971 to provide that those convicted of felonies would automatically regain the right to vote once their maximum sentence had been served or they had been discharged from parole. In 1973, New York again amended the statute to ensure that felons were only disenfranchised if they were sentenced to a term of imprisonment and not if they were sentenced to fines, probation, or conditional discharge.

Section 2 of the Voting Rights Act provides: "No voting qualification or prerequisite to voting or standard, practice, or procedure shall be imposed or applied by any State or political subdivision in a manner which results in a denial or abridgement of the right of any citizen of the United States to vote on account of race or color." 42 U.S.C. § 1973(a). Section 1973(b), originally enacted in 1982, states, in relevant part, that "[a] violation of subsection (a) . . . is established if, based on the totality of circumstances, it is shown that . . . members [of protected minority groups] have less opportunity than other members of the electorate to participate in the political process and to elect representatives of their choice."

The current language of § 1973 was enacted by Congress as part of the Voting Rights Act Amendments of 1982, largely in response to the Supreme Court's decision in *City of Mobile v. Bolden* (1980). In *Bolden,* a plurality of the Court held that racially neutral state action violates § 1973 only if it is motivated by a discriminatory purpose. The amended version of § 1973 eliminates this "discriminatory purpose" requirement and, instead, prohibits any voting qualification or standard that "results" in the denial of the right to vote "on account of" race.

B

[Omitted.]

C. VOTE DENIAL

We confront the question whether the VRA applies to a claim that a prisoner disenfranchisement statute such as § 5-106, acting in combination with historic racial discrimination allegedly afflicting the New York criminal justice system as well as society at large, results in the denial to Black and Latino prisoners of the right to vote "on account of race or color."[8] [W]e must first determine whether the Act applies to such statutes at all. If

5. Although § 5-106 disenfranchises felons on parole as well as incarcerated felons, for ease of reference we refer to the class of felons disenfranchised by § 5-106 as "incarcerated felons."

8. We note that, despite plaintiffs' claim that racial discrimination infects the whole of the criminal justice system such that non-racially motivated felon disenfranchisement laws violate the VRA, counsel for plaintiffs insisted at oral argument that they do not allege any discrimination in plaintiffs' particular convictions.

the VRA does not encompass such statutes, that would end our inquiry; if, conversely, we conclude that it may apply to felon disenfranchisement laws, we would then need to evaluate such an interpretation of the VRA in light of its implications for our constitutional jurisprudence and the structure of our federal system.

We thus consider the scope of § 1973. There is no question that the language of § 1973 is extremely broad—any "voting qualification or prerequisite to voting or standard, practice, or procedure" that adversely affects the right to vote—and could be read to include felon disenfranchisement provisions if the phrase is read without the benefit of context and background assumptions supplied by other statutory and Constitutional wording, by history, and by the manifestations of intent by Congress at the time of the VRA's enactment and thereafter.

We are not convinced that the use of broad language in the statute necessarily means that the statute is unambiguous with regard to its application to felon disenfranchisement laws. In any event, our interpretation of a statute is not in all circumstances limited to any apparent "plain meaning." As Justice Holmes has observed, "[i]t is said that when the meaning of language is plain we are not to resort to evidence in order to raise doubts. That is rather an axiom of experience than a rule of law, and does not preclude consideration of persuasive evidence if it exists." *Boston Sand & Gravel Co. v. United States* (1928). Here, there are persuasive reasons to believe that Congress did not intend to include felon disenfranchisement provisions within the coverage of the Voting Rights Act, and we must therefore look beyond the plain text of the statute in construing the reach of its provisions. These reasons include (1) the explicit approval given such laws in the Fourteenth Amendment;[10] (2) the long history and continuing prevalence of felon disenfranchisement provisions throughout the United States; (3) the statements in the House and Senate Judiciary Committee Reports and on the Senate floor explicitly excluding felon disenfranchisement laws from provisions of the statute; (4) the absence of any affirmative consideration of felon disenfranchisement laws during either the 1965 passage of the Act or its 1982 revision; (5) the introduction thereafter of bills specifically intended to include felon disenfranchisement provisions within the VRA's coverage; (6) the enactment of a felon disenfranchisement statute for the District of Columbia by Congress soon after the passage of the Voting Rights Act; and (7) the subsequent passage of statutes designed to facilitate the removal of convicted felons from the voting rolls. We therefore conclude that § 1973 was not intended to—and thus does not—encompass felon disenfranchisement provisions.

10. Contrary to the suggestion of our colleagues in dissent, we do not rely on the Fourteenth Amendment for the proposition that felon disenfranchisement statutes are "always constitutional" or somehow "immune from congressional regulation." Nor do we suggest that the Voting Rights Act was enacted pursuant to Congress's power under the Fourteenth Amendment, rather than the Fifteenth Amendment. Instead, our inquiry into Congressional intent is simply informed by the historic nature of felon disenfranchisement statutes and by the Fourteenth Amendment's explicit approval of such laws.

D. Felon Disenfranchisement

The starting point for our analysis is the explicit approval given felon disenfranchisement provisions in the Constitution. Section 2 of the Fourteenth Amendment provides that "when the right to vote at any [federal] election . . . is denied to any of the male inhabitants of [a] State . . . or in any way abridged, *except for participation in rebellion, or other crime,* the basis of representation therein shall be reduced . . . ." U.S. Const. amend. XIV, § 2 (emphasis added). The Supreme Court has ruled that, as a result of this language, felon disenfranchisement provisions are presumptively constitutional. *Richardson v. Ramirez* (1974) (rejecting a nonracial Equal Protection challenge to the felon disenfranchisement provision of California's constitution).[11]

Indeed, the practice of disenfranchising those convicted of crimes is of ancient origin. Professor Mirjan R. Damaska of the Yale Law School, among others, has recounted that in ancient Athens, the penalty for certain crimes was placement in a state of "infamy," which entailed the loss of those rights that enabled a citizen to participate in public affairs, such as the rights to vote, to attend assemblies, to make speeches, and to hold public office. Mirjan R. Damaska, *Adverse Legal Consequences of Conviction and their Removal: A Comparative Study,* 59 J. Crim. L., Criminology & Police Sci. 347, 351 (1968). The Roman Republic also employed infamy as a penalty for those convicted of crimes involving moral turpitude. *Id.*

Similar laws disenfranchising felons were adopted in the American Colonies and the Early American Republic as well. [E]leven state constitutions adopted between 1776 and 1821 prohibited or authorized the legislature to prohibit exercise of the franchise by convicted felons, and twenty-nine states had such provisions when the Fourteenth Amendment was adopted in 1868. Today, likewise, every state except Maine and Vermont disenfranchises felons. As the Eleventh Circuit noted, "considering the prevalence of felon disenfranchisement [provisions] in every region of the country since the Founding, it seems unfathomable that Congress would silently amend the Voting Rights Act in a way that would affect them." *Johnson* [*v. Gov. of State of Florida* (11th Cir. 2005) (en banc)]. We now proceed to determine whether Congress in fact intended to do so.[13]

11. The Fourteenth Amendment, as interpreted by the Supreme Court, does not completely insulate felon disenfranchisement provisions from constitutional scrutiny. It is clear, for example, that if a State disenfranchises felons "with the intent of disenfranchising blacks," that State has run afoul of Section 1 of the Fourteenth Amendment. *See Hunter v. Underwood,* (1985) (invalidating disenfranchisement provision of Alabama Constitution passed with discriminatory intent). Our conclusion that § 1973 does not encompass prisoner disenfranchisement laws such as that of New York thus does not mean that there is no remedy for laws of this type that were passed with the intent to disenfranchise members of minority groups, as these laws are already unconstitutional under the Fourteenth Amendment.

13. Our dissenting colleagues dismiss our analysis of the historical origins of felon disenfranchisement statutes as mere "[h]istorical anecdotes," likening such statutes to other longstanding voting qualifications such as literacy tests and poll taxes. Yet we do not suggest that felon disenfranchisement laws fall outside the scope of the Voting Rights Act simply because they are deeply rooted in American history and in the Western tradition more broadly. Rather, we argue that it is unlikely that Congress would have invalidated such laws—which have been widely used since the origins of the Republic—without any discussion of the matter. By contrast, section 4(c) of the Voting Rights Act explicitly prohibits literacy tests. Likewise, in 1964, a year prior to

E. Congressional Intent in the Voting Rights Act

The Voting Rights Act "was designed by Congress to banish the blight of racial discrimination in voting, which has infected the electoral process in parts of our country for nearly a century." *South Carolina v. Katzenbach* (1966). It is indisputable that the Congress intended "to give the Act the broadest possible scope." *Allen v. State Bd. of Elections* (1969).

We do not believe that this general intent answers the specific question regarding whether the Act covers felon disenfranchisement laws, as it is equally indisputable that Congress did not explicitly consider felon disenfranchisement laws to be covered by the Act and indeed affirmatively stated that such laws were *not* implicated by provisions of the statute. In discussing Section 4(c) of the Voting Rights Act, which banned any "test or device" that limited the ability to vote to those individuals with "good moral character," the Senate Judiciary Committee Report stated that the provision "would not result in the proscription of the frequent requirement of States and political subdivisions that an applicant for voting or registration for voting be free of conviction of a felony or mental disability." S. Rep. No. 89-162, at 24 (1965), *see also* H.R. Rep. No. 89-439, at 25-26 (1965), ("This subsection does not proscribe a requirement of a State or any political subdivision of a State that an applicant for voting or registration for voting be free of conviction of a felony or mental disability."). Senator Joseph D. Tydings of Maryland "emphasize[d]" on the Senate floor that Section 4(c) was not intended to prohibit "a requirement that an applicant for voting or registration for voting be free of conviction of a felony or mental disability. Those grounds for disqualification are objective, easily applied, and do not lend themselves to fraudulent manipulation." 111 Cong. Rec. S8366 (daily ed. April 23, 1965).

Though these statements were made in the context of a particular VRA provision not at issue here—the provision banning any "test or device"—it is apparent to us that Congress's effort to highlight the exclusion of felon disenfranchisement laws from a VRA provision that otherwise would likely be read to invalidate such laws is indicative of its broader intention to exclude such laws from the reach of the statute. Indeed, the emphatic language chosen to provide assurance that felon disenfranchisement laws remain unaffected by the statute suggests that these statements be read to indicate that "*not even this section* applies to felon disenfranchisement laws," rather than "*this section* does not apply to felon disenfranchisement laws, but other sections might," as plaintiffs argue.

Further indications that Congress in 1965 did not intend or understand the Voting Rights Act (or its subsequent amendments) to apply to felon disenfranchisement provisions come from the unsuccessful attempts in the early 1970s to amend the statute to apply

---

Congress's passage of the Voting Rights Act, poll taxes had been expressly forbidden by the 24th Amendment. The explicit treatment, either in the Voting Rights Act or in the Constitution, of *other* similarly longstanding and widely-practiced voting qualifications only serves to confirm our view that Congress did not amend the Voting Rights Act in a way that brought felon disenfranchisement laws within its purview.

to such provisions. Following hearings by the House Judiciary Committee in 1972 to address "The Problems of the Ex-Offender," several notable proponents of the VRA jointly introduced a bill designed "[t]o amend the Voting Rights Act of 1970 to prohibit the States from denying the right to vote in Federal elections to former criminal offenders who have not been convicted of any offense related to voting or elections and who are not confined in a correctional institution." H.R. 15049, 92d Cong. (1972). The bill was thus expressly intended to *amend* the Voting Rights Act to encompass the very laws that plaintiffs in the instant case insist were already covered by the 1965 Act. Apparently, no further action was taken on this bill.

In the next Congress, in 1973, Representative Kastenmeier, a supporter of the Voting Rights Act of 1965 and a "principal architect" of the re-authorization of the Voting Rights Act in 1968 as well as the enactment of the Civil Rights Act of 1964, introduced a new bill with the identical text. H.R. 9020, 93d Cong. (1973). A hearing on the proposed bill was entirely predicated on the understanding that the Voting Rights Act did not cover felon disenfranchisement laws. Accordingly, the hearing focused on whether such an amendment to the VRA would be constitutional and whether it was sound policy. None of the Representatives who spoke at the hearing so much as intimated that the proposed bill was made unnecessary by the fact that the statute already encompassed felon disenfranchisement laws.

The proposed bills of 1972 and 1973 thus reveal that the law was not understood by those most familiar with it to encompass felon disenfranchisement provisions. Furthermore, because these proposed bills only sought to add Voting Rights Act coverage to those who were no longer "confined in a correctional institution," it is yet more implausible that the Voting Rights Act was understood to apply to prisoner disenfranchisement statutes.

In this regard, it is also telling that during this same period, Congress affirmatively enacted a felon disenfranchisement statute in the District of Columbia, over which it had plenary power before the conferral of "home rule" in 1974. It is highly implausible that shortly after passing a statute (the VRA) purportedly intended to limit such laws, Congress would have enacted for its local jurisdiction a new statute doing exactly what it had supposedly forbidden on a national level.

The 1982 amendment of the Voting Rights Act also gives no indication that the law is to apply to felon disenfranchisement provisions. Congress's intention in amending § 1973 was to target those electoral laws, practices, and procedures that resulted in diluting the strength of the votes of members of racial and ethnic minorities but did not on their face deny any individuals the vote. The addition of § 1973(b) further demonstrates that Congress's particular focus was these vote-diluting practices. Section 1973(b) provides that a violation of the VRA can be established if "the political processes leading to nomination or election in the State or political subdivision are not equally open to participation" by members of a protected class of citizens such that "its members have less opportunity than other members of the electorate to participate in the political process and to elect representatives of their choice." 42 U.S.C. § 1973(b). There is no question that incarcerated persons cannot "fully participate in the political process"—they cannot petition, protest, campaign, travel, freely associate, or raise funds. It follows that Congress did not have this subpopulation in mind when the VRA section at issue took its present form in 1982.

Subsequent Congressional actions provide additional evidence that Congress has not understood the Voting Rights Act to cover felon disenfranchisement laws. For example, the National Voter Registration Act, enacted in 1993, explicitly provides for "criminal conviction" as a basis upon which voters' names may be removed from lists of eligible voters. The Help America Vote Act of 2002 directs States to remove disenfranchised felons from their lists of those eligible to vote in federal elections. Finally, a number of bills have been proposed in the past several years that would limit States' ability to disenfranchise felons. These bills further indicate that Congress itself continues to assume that the Voting Rights Act does not apply to felon disenfranchisement provisions.

In light of this wealth of persuasive evidence that Congress has never intended to extend the coverage of the Voting Rights Act to felon disenfranchisement provisions, we deem this one of the "rare cases [in which] the literal application of a statute will produce a result demonstrably at odds with the intentions of its drafters." *United States v. Ron Pair Enters., Inc.* (1989). We accordingly construe the statute to not encompass felon disenfranchisement laws.

III

A. Clear Statement Rule

Our decision not to apply § 1973 to felon disenfranchisement provisions is confirmed and supported by the operation of the clear statement rule (also known as the "plain statement rule"), a canon of interpretation which requires Congress to make its intent "unmistakably clear" when enacting statutes that would alter the usual constitutional balance between the Federal Government and the States. *Gregory v. Ashcroft* (1991).

For the clear statement rule to apply here in defendants' favor, we would therefore need to conclude (1) that applying § 1973 to prisoner disenfranchisement laws would alter the constitutional balance between the States and the Federal Government and (2) that Congress has not made its intention to alter that balance *unmistakably clear.*

B. Threshold Question: Does the Clear Statement Rule Apply?

Given the "sensitive topic" at issue, we would expect Congress to have specified that felon disenfranchisement provisions are covered by the Voting Rights Act if that were its intent.

C. Application of the Clear Statement Rule

In applying the clear statement rule, we must first decide whether bringing felon disenfranchisement laws within the scope of the Voting Rights Act would "alter the usual constitutional balance between the States and the Federal Government." *Gregory*. As a preliminary matter, plaintiffs argue that the application of the Voting Rights Act to felon disenfranchisement provisions could not affect the "federal balance" because that balance was already changed by the passage of the Fourteenth and Fifteenth Amendments, and the sole task of the Voting Rights Act is to effectuate those constitutional provisions. We do not find this argument persuasive, for, while it undoubtedly rings true for the Voting Rights Act in general, Section 2 of the Fourteenth Amendment explicitly leaves the federal balance intact with regard to felon disenfranchisement laws specifically. Therefore, extending the coverage of the Voting Rights Act to these provisions would introduce a change in the federal balance not contemplated by the framers of the Fourteenth Amendment.

D. Has Congress Made a Clear Statement?

[O]ur review of the legislative history of both the 1965 enactment and 1982 revision of the Voting Rights Act as well as our examination of other proposed legislation on this issue compel us to conclude that Congress unquestionably did not manifest an "unmistakably clear" intent to include felon disenfranchisement laws under the VRA. As a result, we hold that the requirements of the clear statement rule are not met, and we will accordingly not construe the Voting Rights Act to reach these laws.

* * *

Accordingly, we conclude that plaintiffs' vote denial claim, which seeks to challenge New York's prisoner disenfranchisement statute under the Voting Rights Act, must be dismissed.

IV

Vote Dilution Claim

[P]laintiffs have also raised a vote dilution claim based on "the disproportionate disfranchisement under New York State Election Law § 5-106(2) of Black and Latino persons who are incarcerated or on parole for a felony conviction." In light of our conclusion that the Voting Rights Act does not encompass felon disenfranchisement provisions and that plaintiffs thus cannot state a vote denial claim under the statute, it is clear that plaintiffs also cannot state a claim for vote dilution based on the assertion that the denial of the vote to incarcerated felons and parolees dilutes the voting strength of minority communities. Accordingly, this claim is likewise dismissed.

John M. Walker, Jr., Chief Judge, concurring, with whom Judge Jacob joins.

[E]ven if Section 2 of the VRA applies to Section 5-106 and no contrary congressional intent were evident, then I believe that, as applied, the VRA would be unconstitutional because Congress would have exceeded its enforcement power under the Reconstruction Amendments. As the majority demonstrates, the case can be resolved without reaching this issue, but I believe it provides yet another sound basis for rejecting the dissent's position. [This concurrence then applied the "congruence and proportionality" test to conclude that bringing felon disenfranchisement statutes with the scope of the VRA would be beyond congressional power.]

STRAUB, Circuit Judge, with whom Judge SACK joins, concurring in part and concurring in judgment.

We concur in the result reached by the majority and in its reasoning that the evidence of legislative intent weighs decisively against applying the Voting Rights Act to New York Election Law § 5-106. We do not join in any holding that a clear statement rule applies here, as we believe such a rule, in addition to being unnecessary to the disposition of this case, would be inappropriate in the voting rights context.

CALABRESI, Circuit Judge, dissenting.

The majority opinion is learned, thoroughly researched, well-written, and restrained but it is almost totally irrelevant to the question presented in this case. The majority demonstrates beyond peradventure that Congress did not intend the Voting Rights Act to prohibit felon disenfranchisement *categorically,* as that statute *categorically* prohibits, for instance, the use of literacy tests and "good moral character" requirements in certain jurisdictions. And if the plaintiffs were, in fact, arguing that the Voting Rights Act erects a *per se* ban on felon disenfranchisement, I would readily join the majority. But, of course, this is not the plaintiffs' position. Rather, they contend that the Voting Rights Act prohibits felon disenfranchisement laws *that result in the denial or dilution of voting rights on the basis of race.* Their complaint alleges that New York Election Law § 5-106 has precisely this result, and we are bound to accept this allegation as the gospel truth for purposes of New York's motion for judgment on the pleadings. Nothing in the majority opinion—nor, for that matter, in the concurrences—gives a single reason to suggest that Congress did not intend the Voting Rights Act to do what its plain language says and bar felon disenfranchisement statutes *that result in racial discrimination.* I, therefore, see no basis for depriving the plaintiffs of the right to prove their allegations.

I

The majority makes much of legislative history showing that Congress did not intend § 4(c) to forbid felon disenfranchisement. True enough. Felon disenfranchisement is *not* prohibited in the absence of a showing that it brings about discriminatory results. But the statements in legislative history that felon disenfranchisement is not banned by § 4(c) cannot be taken to imply a wholesale carve-out that exempts felon disenfranchisement from Voting Rights Act scrutiny altogether, as the majority asserts. The fact that race-neutral felon disenfranchisement is permissible under § 4(c) tells us nothing at all about whether § 2 allows *racially discriminatory* felon disenfranchisement. And the language of § 2(a) makes perfectly plain that such discriminatory disenfranchisement *is* barred.

The majority also tells us that some members of Congress tried, unsuccessfully, to amend the Voting Rights Act "to prohibit the States from denying the right to vote in

Federal elections to former criminal offenders who have not been convicted of any offense related to voting or elections and who are not confined in a correctional institution." Once again, this does indeed imply that the Voting Rights Act does not, of itself, prohibit *all* felon disenfranchisement—a fact that no one disputes. How the majority moves from the fact that Congress declined to proscribe *race-neutral* felon disenfranchisement to the conclusion that Congress intended to exempt *racially discriminatory* felon disenfranchisement from the coverage of the Voting Rights Act is beyond me. It is perfectly clear that voting practices and procedures that are not *per se* impermissible under the Voting Rights Act—at-large voting and multi-member districts, for instance—violate the statute when they produce discriminatory results. And so it is with felon disenfranchisement laws. The majority has shown that some members of Congress thought felon disenfranchisement to be so inimical to voting rights as to try to forbid the practice even in the absence of discriminatory effects. The idea that such congressional efforts somehow imply the existence of a "safe harbor" for felon disenfranchisement statutes that *do* result in racially discriminatory denials or dilutions of voting rights is, it seems to me, risible.

Nor do subsequent enactments that presuppose the validity of felon disenfranchisement laws (*e.g.,* a provision of the Help America Vote Act of 2002), or bills that seek to limit felon disenfranchisement (*e.g.*, the Ex-Offenders Voting Rights Act of 2005), suggest in the slightest that Congress understands *discriminatory* felon disenfranchisement to be consistent with the Voting Rights Act.

Still, the majority concludes, largely based on the statutory history recounted above, that "the Voting Rights Act does not apply to felon disenfranchisement provisions." What is behind this remarkable decision to buck text, context, and legislative history in order to insulate a particular racially discriminatory practice from an anti-discrimination rule of general applicability?

II

I believe the majority opinion [is] motivated in large part by skepticism that Congress could have intended the result that the plaintiffs urge. But it is important here, in talking about congressional intent, to distinguish between the enacting Congress and the current Congress. It is, of course, the legislative intent of the enacting Congress—not the current Congress—that is controlling. And I see no reason to think that the 97th Congress, which was responsible for the "dramatic substantive transformation" of the Voting Rights Act in 1982, meant the expansive prohibition of discriminatory results it enacted to apply in any other way than precisely as written. The fact that the 109th Congress in the year 2006, if asked, might very well choose not to invalidate felon disenfranchisement laws that produce discriminatory results in no way indicates that the very different Congress of a generation ago made, or would now make, the same choice.

SOTOMAYOR, Circuit Judge, dissenting.

It is plain to anyone reading the Voting Rights Act that it applies to all "voting qualification[s]." And it is equally plain that § 5-106 disqualifies a group of people from voting. These two propositions should constitute the entirety of our analysis. Section 2 of the Act by its unambiguous terms subjects felony disenfranchisement and all other voting qualifications to its coverage.

The duty of a judge is to follow the law, not to question its plain terms. I do not believe that Congress wishes us to disregard the plain language of any statute or to invent exceptions to the statutes it has created. The majority's "wealth of persuasive evidence" that Congress intended felony disenfranchisement laws to be immune from scrutiny under § 2 of the Act includes not a single legislator actually saying so. But even if Congress had doubts about the wisdom of subjecting felony disenfranchisement laws to the results test of § 2, I trust that Congress would prefer to make any needed changes itself, rather than have courts do so for it.

KATZMANN, Circuit Judge, dissenting.

[I]f I saw clear evidence in the authoritative legislative history that the Congress that enacted it intended to exclude felon disenfranchisement policies from its reach, I would so construe it. But when we look to the authoritative legislative history, we find complete silence as to whether Congress intended to exclude felon disenfranchisement policies from its reach. Surely, the silence of enacting legislators cannot overcome the unambiguous and broadly worded provisions of a statute that was meant to apply to a multitude of state policies not specifically enumerated in its text.

B.D. PARKER, Jr., Circuit Judge, dissenting.

The majority concludes that felon disenfranchisement laws are immune from VRA scrutiny, no matter how discriminatory the effects of those laws might be. No one disputes that states have the right to disenfranchise felons: § 2 of the Fourteenth Amendment makes that clear. But the fact that felon disenfranchisement statutes may sometimes be constitutional does not mean they are always constitutional. In any event, this case is largely about the Fifteenth, not the Fourteenth Amendment. Section 1 of the Fifteenth Amendment makes it clear that states may not disenfranchise on the basis of race. Section 2 of the VRA, as amended in 1982, also makes it clear that states may not disenfranchise on the basis of race, *even unintentionally.*

[VRA] § 4 and § 2(a) employ starkly different language that dramatically distinguishes their scope. Section 4's use of the narrow terms "any test or device," is not comparable to § 2(a)'s use of the broad language "[n]o voting qualification or prerequisite to voting or standard, practice, or procedure." Second, § 4 and § 2 serve separate functions and operate differently. Section 4 imposes an outright ban on tests or devices, while § 2(a) creates a "results" test, which requires investigating and weighing numerous factors. Given this outright ban, one can understand why Congress would want to narrow the category of voting mechanisms falling under § 4(c) relative to § 2(a), where a plaintiff need only demonstrate discriminatory results. Third, the legislative history of one provision enacted in 1965 (§ 4) has nothing to say about Congress's intentions when amending a different provision (§ 2), seventeen years later in 1982. Equivocal fragments from legislative history should not obscure the fact that, from its inception and particularly through its amendment in 1982, Congress intended that § 2, unlike § 4, be given the broadest possible reach, as the text it chose makes clear.

For several reasons, the clear statement rule does not apply. First, for it to apply, ambiguity must exist, and § 2(a) is unambiguous. Second, even if VRA § 2(a) were ambiguous, the clear statement rule would still not apply because the provision is broadly worded, and the rule does not apply to broadly worded remedial statutes. Congress used language in § 2 that was deliberately broad and generic. Congress could hardly have been expected to have enumerated every conceivable voting qualification, prerequisite, practice, or procedure to which the statute could apply in the text, or even the legislative history, of § 2(a). To do so would have left the states free to devise new means to discriminate that were not listed. To hold that Congress did not intend the VRA to cover felon disenfranchisement statutes is to hold that Congress actually intended to allow some forms of race-based voter disenfranchisement. Such a result I find improbable—indeed inconceivable.

Third, the clear statement rule cannot be justified by contending that unless it is applied, the VRA would improperly interfere with "sensitive domains" such as the core state function of regulating the franchise. This contention overlooks the quite obvious fact that the very purpose of the VRA was to impose Congressional regulation on the traditional state function of regulating voting. *See Lopez v. Monterey County* (1999) ("In short, the Voting Rights Act, by its nature, intrudes on state sovereignty. The Fifteenth Amendment permits this intrusion, however"). Felon disenfranchisement is no more a core state function than any of these examples.

Fourth, while it is correct that the states possess the primary authority for defining and enforcing the criminal law, the short and conclusive answer is that New York Election Law § 5-106 is not a criminal law. It is a voting law found in New York's Election code, not among its criminal laws. As Judge Friendly pointed out, "[d]epriving convicted felons of the franchise is not a punishment but rather is a nonpenal exercise of the power to regulate the franchise." *Green v. Bd. of Elections* (2d Cir. 1967).

Fifth, the clear statement rule is particularly inappropriate in the context of the VRA, which was enacted and amended pursuant to Congress's powers under *both* the Fourteenth *and* Fifteenth Amendments. Contrary to the suggestion of some members of this Court, the seismic shift created by the Fourteenth and Fifteenth Amendments clearly altered the federal-state balance in an attempt to address a truly compelling national interest namely, reducing racial discrimination perpetuated by the states. Indeed, these Amendments "were specifically designed as an expansion of federal power and an intrusion on state sovereignty." *Gregory*. In sum, any shift in the federal-state balance of power that would purportedly result from applying VRA § 2 to New York Election Law § 5-106 would not occur as a result of the resolution of this case. That shift occurred more than 130 years ago when the Reconstruction Amendments were passed and ratified.

[Moreover], were a clear statement required, VRA § 2(a) supplies it. Since § 2(a) covers all voting qualifications, it indisputably covers felon disenfranchisement laws like New York Election Law § 5-106. If anything is clear from the legislative history of the VRA it is that Congress intended to eliminate all race-based disfranchisement, no matter the means by which it was achieved.

[Finally], Judge Walker's view that Congress lacks the authority to reach felon disenfranchisement statutes that result in the denial of the right to vote on account of race is wrong. To adopt that view is to conclude that there are some forms of race-based voter discrimination that are beyond Congress's reach, a proposition that is not correct.

NOTE ON FELON DISENFRANCHISEMENT IN FLORIDA

In 2012, Florida led all 50 states in the percentage of adult citizens ineligible to vote because of a felony conviction: 10.4 percent. Florida also had the nation's highest percentage of African Americans disenfranchised because of a felony: 23 percent.* Because Florida is the fourth largest state—and one of the leading battlegrounds in presidential elections—this disenfranchisement of a large portion of the state's potential electorate has national as well as state-specific significance. In 2007, then-Governor Charlie Crist (at the time a Republican, but now a Democrat) used his clemency powers to make it much easier for ex-felons, who had completed their sentences, to have their voting rights restored. In 2011, however, the new governor Rick Scott, a more conservative Republican, reversed this policy, and Florida now requires a waiting period of at least five years after completion of a sentence before an ex-felon can become eligible for restoration of voting rights.

Back in 2005, the en banc Eleventh Circuit ruled—like the Second Circuit in *Hayden v. Pataki*—that Florida's current felon disenfranchisement law, adopted in 1968, did not violate Section 2 of the Voting Rights Act. The Eleventh Circuit also held that this current law was not motivated by a racially discriminatory bias (even if Florida's previous disenfranchisement of felons, adopted a century earlier, was so motivated). *See Johnson v. Governor*, 405 F.3d 2014 (11th Cir. 2005). It remains to be seen whether a plausible case could be made that the renewed stringency of Florida's felon disenfranchisement regime under Governor Scott, after Governor Crist's period of relative leniency, was motivated by unlawful racial animus, in violation of the Voting Rights Act and/or the Fourteenth and Fifteenth Amendments to the U.S. Constitution. One significant obstacle to such a claim is that even if Governor Scott's increased stringency was

* William E. Gibson, *Florida Leads U.S. in Barring Ex-Felons from Voting*, Orlando Sentinel, July 13, 2012, A3.

motivated by a desire to disenfranchise more *Democrats*, and even if many of these Democrats are African American, this *correlation* between race and partisanship does not establish a desire to disenfranchise *because of* race rather than partisanship. This issue of proving improper racial animus is an issue that is much broader than the context of felon disenfranchisement specifically. As we have seen in connection with *LULAC v. Perry* (in Part I of this book), it has the potential of surfacing any time a claim is made that the government has restricted voting rights because of race. The government's response may be that it was merely motivated by partisanship, not race, and the correlation of the two was incidental to motive.

B. Voter Registration and Identification

1. *Historical Overview and the Basis of State and Federal Power*

Since the presidential election of 2000, which was extraordinarily close and controversial, the United States has undertaken an extensive reexamination of many of its rules that govern the casting of ballots. Most of these rules are enacted by state legislatures, rather than by Congress, although Congress has imposed some constraints on the voting rules that states may adopt.

Much of this legislative reform has been motivated by a genuine desire to improve the voting process. But some appears to derive from partisan desires to tilt the electoral playing field in a way that would favor one party's candidates, or the other's, over their competitors. Right or wrong, there is a widespread perception among political professionals that Democrats generally favor voting rules that make it easier to cast ballots even at the risk that some of those ballots may be illegitimate, while Republicans prefer voting rules that make it tougher to cast an invalid ballot but also make it harder for eligible voters to cast their valid ballots. There is even the cynical view that some Republican politicians would like to impose more rigorous voting requirements solely to reduce turnout among certain groups of voters, like minorities and lower-income individuals, who tend to vote for Democrats—while, conversely, Democratic politicians would like to reduce the barriers to casting a ballot simply because doing so would make it more likely for Democrats to win elections. The partisan fights over the rules of the voting process have intensified, and become nastier, over the last decade and consequently have been dubbed "The Voting Wars."*

If we take a historical perspective, however, these voting wars are nothing new. The two dominant political parties have been fighting over the rules for casting ballots for just about as long as our political system has had two dominant political parties, which is to say for almost as long as the Republic has been in existence. In the nineteenth century, the fight initially was over whether there would be voter registration requirements. With the expansion of the franchise associated with the removal of property qualifications, there

* *See* Richard L. Hasen, The Voting Wars: From Florida 2000 to the Next Meltdown (2012).

became increasing pressure to adopt requirements that potential voters register in advance of the day on which they would be entitled to cast their ballots. Poll workers could use the registration lists to ensure that individuals arriving at the polling place to cast ballots were indeed eligible to vote. Opponents of the new registration requirements argued that they were unconstitutional (under state constitutional provisions) on the ground that the obligation to register in advance added an extra eligibility prerequisite inconsistent with the constitutional specification of the entitlement to the franchise. (In other words, if the state constitution said that all male citizens over the age of 21 were entitled to vote, then opponents of the new registration requirement said that it was an extra limitation on the franchise not specified in the state constitution.) State courts generally rejected this argument on the ground that the registration requirement was not a limitation on who was eligible to vote, but instead a regulation of the method by which eligible voters exercised the franchise. As you will see, this longstanding distinction figures prominently in a new case from the U.S. Supreme Court, *Arizona v. Intertribal Council,* which is a major statement delineating the relationship of state and federal power over the regulation of the voting process.

Another aspect of the current voting wars echoes old historical patterns. In the early twentieth century, registration rules were used to make it more difficult for recent immigrants to become registered. Requirements to register in person, rather than by mail, or even limiting the opportunity to register to a single day, were particularly onerous for workers whose jobs did not give them the flexibility to go register during working hours. And especially in the South, a whole variety of practices were developed to prevent African Americans from voting. In Part I, we saw that the drawing of legislative districts can be manipulated to curtail the influence of African-American voters. But other outright barriers, like literacy tests, were erected during the Jim Crow era to disenfranchise African Americans.

The impotency of the Fifteenth Amendment in protecting against these racially discriminatory measures was best illustrated by *Giles v. Harris*, 189 U.S. 475 (1903), in which Justice Oliver Wendell Holmes (writing for the Court) refused to grant injunctive relief to stop even blatantly overt and systematic discrimination against African Americans in the registration of new voters in Alabama. Justice Holmes said that if the racial discrimination was as systematic as the plaintiffs alleged, then the federal judiciary would be powerless to remedy the wrong unless it took over control of the state's entire voting apparatus—something the Supreme Court in 1903 was unprepared to undertake. Today one can understand *Giles* only by recognizing that, after the abandonment of Reconstruction in the last decades of the nineteenth century, there was no national will to protect African Americans from the renewed thoroughgoing subjugation of Jim Crow.

The Voting Rights Act of 1965, arguably the greatest of all the achievements of the Civil Rights movement, resulted in great strides being made in enfranchising African Americans. It did so, at least in part, by banning literacy tests—first in the places where discrimination against African Americans was most rampant, and then nationwide. The Voting Rights Act (VRA) also included Section 5 preclearance, which served as a check on election administration changes that would discriminate against African Americans and language minorities in the jurisdictions (mostly in the South and Southwest) covered by Section 5.

Yet we saw in Part I of this book that the Supreme Court just recently, in *Shelby County v. Holder*, rendered Section 5 dormant. One of the major unanswered questions of the current voting wars is the extent to which the remainder of the VRA will be effective in preventing any newly erected barriers to casting ballots that are racially discriminatory in either intent or effect. *Shelby County* left standing Section 2 of the VRA, which prohibits any voting "practice" or "procedure" that "results in a denial or abridgement of the right of any citizen of the United States to vote on account of race." But as *Hayden v. Pataki* illustrated, this statutory text will not necessarily be broadly interpreted. Instead, the federal judiciary is still in the process of developing a standard for determining when a voting rule that imposes a differentially heavier burden on minority voters is a violation of the results test of the VRA's Section 2.

The number one issue over which the current voting wars have been fought is voter identification—what sort of evidence should voters be required to present when they cast their ballots to demonstrate who they are? Voter identification is closely related to voter registration, as *Arizona v. Intertribal Council* will show. There is arguably no need to register in advance if voters can show up at the polls on Election Day with adequate proof of their identity, which establishes their eligibility to vote. Indeed, several states have adopted this policy, which is usually called Election Day Registration, because citizens can register and vote at the same time on Election Day.

Conversely, if citizens establish their eligibility when they register, then arguably the identification requirement can be less onerous when they show up to cast their ballot on Election Day. In this situation, they do not need to prove their eligibility all over again; they only need to confirm that they are the same person who previously registered. In the twentieth century, after registering in advance had become a widespread requirement, it was often thought adequate for voters simply to sign their names in a poll book listing registered voters. This signature, when checked against the one on file, would confirm the identity of the registered voter. Since 2000, however, there has been increasing sentiment that some additional documentary proof of identity should be required when a voter casts a ballot. *Crawford v. Marion County Election Board*, which we will read after *Arizona v. Intertribal Council*, concerns how strict or lenient this identification requirement should be.

But first let's examine the basic question of how and when voters establish the fundamental eligibility requirement of citizenship. Should it be sufficient for voters simply to sign a statement, under penalty of perjury (or the equivalent) that they are in fact U.S. citizens? Or should voters be required to show documentary proof of their citizenship, such as a birth certificate or naturalization papers? And, if so, when? Is it better to have the voters present this documentary proof of citizenship when they register in advance? Or should voters be required to bring this documentary proof of citizenship with them to the polls on Election Day?

Arizona enacted a law that requires documentary proof of citizenship at the time of registration. Arguably, this law is less onerous than one that would require the same documentary proof of citizenship at the time of voting. But the legal question arose whether Arizona's law conflicted with the National Voter Registration Act (NVRA), which Congress passed in 1993 (and which is often colloquially called the "Motor Voter" law). And if Arizona's law does conflict with the federal statute, which one must give way under the federal Constitution—specifically, the Elections Clause of Article I, Section 4? These were the legal and constitutional questions that the U.S. Supreme Court addressed in the following, potentially far-reaching case.

ARIZONA v. INTER TRIBAL COUNCIL OF ARIZONA, INC.

133 S. Ct. 2247 (2013)

Justice SCALIA delivered the opinion of the Court.

The National Voter Registration Act [NVRA] requires States to "accept and use" a uniform federal form to register voters for federal elections. The contents of that form (colloquially known as the Federal Form) are prescribed by a federal agency, the Election Assistance Commission. The Federal Form developed by the EAC does not require documentary evidence of citizenship; rather, it requires only that an applicant aver, under penalty of perjury, that he is a citizen. Arizona law requires voter-registration officials to "reject" any application for registration, including a Federal Form, that is not accompanied by concrete evidence of citizenship. The question is whether Arizona's evidence-of-citizenship requirement, as applied to Federal Form applicants, is pre-empted by the Act's mandate that States "accept and use" the Federal Form.

I

Over the past two decades, Congress has erected a complex superstructure of federal regulation atop state voter-registration systems. The NVRA "requires States to provide simplified systems for registering to vote in *federal* elections." *Young v. Fordice* (1997). The Act requires each State to permit prospective voters to "register to vote in elections for Federal office" by any of three methods: simultaneously with a driver's license application, in person, or by mail.

This case concerns registration by mail. Section 1973gg-4 requires States to "accept and use" a standard federal registration form. The Election Assistance Commission is invested with rulemaking authority to prescribe the contents of that Federal Form. The EAC is explicitly instructed, however, to develop the Federal Form "in consultation with the chief election officers of the States." The Federal Form thus contains a number of state-specific instructions, which tell residents of each State what additional information they must provide and where they must submit the form. *See* National Mail Voter Registration Form.* Each state-specific instruction must be approved by the EAC before it is included on the Federal Form.

To be eligible to vote under Arizona law, a person must be a citizen of the United States. This case concerns Arizona's efforts to enforce that qualification. In 2004, Arizona voters adopted Proposition 200, a ballot initiative designed in part "to combat voter fraud by requiring voters to present proof of citizenship when they register to vote and to present identification when they vote on election day." *Purcell v. Gonzalez* (2006). Proposition 200 amended the State's election code to require county recorders to "reject any application for registration that is not accompanied by satisfactory evidence of United States citizenship." Ariz. Rev. Stat. Ann. § 16-166(F). The proof-of-citizenship requirement is satisfied by (1) a photocopy of the applicant's passport or birth certificate, (2) a driver's license number, if the license states that the issuing authority verified the holder's U.S. citizenship, (3) evidence of naturalization, (4) tribal identification, or (5) "[o]ther documents or methods of proof . . . established pursuant to the Immigration Reform and Control Act of 1986." The EAC did not grant Arizona's request to include this new requirement among the state-specific instructions for Arizona on the Federal Form. Consequently, the Federal Form includes a statutorily required attestation, subscribed to under penalty of perjury, that an Arizona applicant meets the State's voting requirements (including the citizenship requirement), but does not require concrete evidence of citizenship.

[P]laintiffs [sued] seeking to enjoin the voting provisions of Proposition 200. A panel of the Ninth Circuit [ruled] that "Proposition 200's documentary proof of citizenship requirement conflicts with the NVRA's text, structure, and purpose." The en banc Court of Appeals agreed.

II

The Elections Clause, Art. I, § 4, cl. 1, provides:

> "The Times, Places and Manner of holding Elections for Senators and Representatives, shall be prescribed in each State by the Legislature thereof; but the Congress may at any time by Law make or alter such Regulations, except as to the places of chusing [*sic*] Senators."

The Clause empowers Congress to pre-empt state regulations governing the "Times, Places and Manner" of holding congressional elections. The question here is whether the federal statutory requirement that States "accept and use" the Federal Form pre-empts Arizona's state-law requirement that officials "reject" the application of a prospective voter who submits a completed Federal Form unaccompanied by documentary evidence of citizenship.

* *Available at* http://www.eac.gov/assets/1/Documents/Federal%20Voter%Registration_1209_en9242012.pdf.

A

The Elections Clause has two functions. Upon the States it imposes the duty ("*shall* be prescribed") to prescribe the time, place, and manner of electing Representatives and Senators; upon Congress it confers the power to alter those regulations or supplant them altogether. This grant of congressional power was the Framers' insurance against the possibility that a State would refuse to provide for the election of representatives to the Federal Congress.

The Clause's substantive scope is broad. "Times, Places, and Manner," we have written, are "comprehensive words," which "embrace authority to provide a complete code for congressional elections," including, as relevant here and as petitioners do not contest, regulations relating to "registration." *Smiley v. Holm* (1932). In practice, the Clause functions as "a default provision; it invests the States with responsibility for the mechanics of congressional elections, but only so far as Congress declines to pre-empt state legislative choices." *Foster v. Love* (1997). The power of Congress over the "Times, Places and Manner" of congressional elections "is paramount, and may be exercised at any time, and to any extent which it deems expedient; and so far as it is exercised, and no farther, the regulations effected supersede those of the State which are inconsistent therewith." *Ex parte Siebold* (1880).

B

The straightforward textual question here is whether Ariz. Rev. Stat. Ann. § 16-166(F), which requires state officials to "reject" a Federal Form unaccompanied by documentary evidence of citizenship, conflicts with the NVRA's mandate that Arizona "accept and use" the Federal Form. If so, the state law, "so far as the conflict extends, ceases to be operative." *Siebold.* In Arizona's view, these seemingly incompatible obligations can be read to operate harmoniously: The NVRA, it contends, requires merely that a State receive the Federal Form willingly and use that form as one element in its (perhaps lengthy) transaction with a prospective voter.

Taken in isolation, the mandate that a State "accept and use" the Federal Form is fairly susceptible of two interpretations. It might mean that a State must accept the Federal Form as a complete and sufficient registration application; or it might mean that the State is merely required to receive the form willingly and use it *somehow* in its voter registration process. Both readings—"receive willingly" and "accept as sufficient"—are compatible with the plain meaning of the word "accept." *See* 1 Oxford English Dictionary 70 (2d ed. 1989) ("To take or receive (a thing offered) willingly"; "To receive as sufficient or adequate"); Webster's New International Dictionary 14 (2d ed. 1954) ("To receive (a thing offered to or thrust upon one) with a consenting mind"; "To receive with favor; to approve"). And we take it as self-evident that the "elastic" verb "use," read in isolation, is broad enough to encompass Arizona's preferred construction. In common parlance, one might say that a restaurant accepts and uses credit cards even though it requires customers to show matching identification when making a purchase.

"Words that can have more than one meaning are given content, however, by their surroundings." *Whitman v. American Trucking Assns., Inc.* (2001). And reading "accept" merely to denote willing receipt seems out of place in the context of an official mandate to accept and use something for a given purpose. The implication of such a mandate is that its object is to be accepted *as sufficient* for the requirement it is meant to satisfy. For example, a government *diktat* that "civil servants shall accept government IOUs for payment of salaries" does not invite the response, "sure, we'll accept IOUs—if you pay us a ten percent down payment in cash." Many federal statutes contain similarly phrased commands, and they contemplate more than mere willing receipt.[3]

Arizona's reading is also difficult to reconcile with neighboring provisions of the NVRA. Section 1973gg-6(a)(1)(B) provides that a State shall "ensure that any eligible applicant is registered to vote in an election . . . if the *valid voter registration form* of the applicant is postmarked" not later than a specified number of days before the election. (Emphasis added.) Yet Arizona reads the phrase "accept and use" in § 1973gg-4(a)(1) as permitting it to *reject* a completed Federal Form if the applicant does not submit additional information required by state law. That reading can be squared with Arizona's obligation under § 1973gg-6(a)(1) only if a completed Federal Form is not a "valid voter registration form," which seems unlikely. The statute empowers the EAC to create the Federal Form, requires the EAC to prescribe its contents within specified limits, and requires States to "accept and use" it. It is improbable that the statute envisions a completed copy of the form it takes such pains to create as being anything less than "valid."

The Act also authorizes States, "*[i]n addition to* accepting and using the" Federal Form, to create their own, state-specific voter-registration forms, which can be used to register voters in both state and federal elections. (Emphasis added). These state-developed forms may require information the Federal Form does not. (For example, unlike the Federal Form, Arizona's registration form includes Proposition 200's proof-of-citizenship requirement.) This permission works in tandem with the requirement that States "accept and use" the Federal Form. States retain the flexibility to design and use their own registration forms, but the Federal Form provides a backstop: No matter what procedural hurdles a State's own form imposes, the Federal Form guarantees that a simple means of registering to vote in federal elections will be available.[4] Arizona's reading would permit a State to demand of Federal Form applicants every additional piece of information the State

3. The dissent accepts that a State may not impose additional requirements that render the Federal Form *entirely* superfluous; it would require that the State "us[e] the form as a meaningful part of the registration process." The dissent does not tell us precisely how large a role for the Federal Form suffices to make it "meaningful": One step out of two? Three? Ten? There is no easy answer, for the dissent's "meaningful part" standard is as indeterminate as it is atextual. [Footnote relocated. —EDS.]

4. In the face of this straightforward explanation, the dissent maintains that it would be "nonsensical" for a less demanding federal form to exist alongside a more demanding state form. But it is the dissent's alternative explanation for § 1973gg-4(a)(2) that makes no sense. The "purpose" of the Federal Form, it claims, is "to facilitate interstate voter registration drives. Thanks to the federal form, volunteers distributing voter registration materials at a shopping mall in Yuma can give a copy of the same form to every person they meet without attempting to distinguish between residents of Arizona and California." But in the dissent's world, a volunteer in Yuma would have to give every prospective voter not only a Federal Form, but also a separate set of either Arizona- or California-specific instructions detailing the additional information the applicant must submit to the State. In ours, every eligible voter can be assured that if he does what the Federal Form says, he will be registered. The dissent therefore provides yet another compelling reason to interpret the statute our way.

requires on its state-specific form. If that is so, the Federal Form ceases to perform any meaningful function, and would be a feeble means of "increas[ing] the number of eligible citizens who register to vote in elections for Federal office." § 1973gg(b).

Finally, Arizona appeals to the presumption against pre-emption sometimes invoked in our Supremacy Clause cases. *See, e.g., Gregory v. Ashcroft* (1991). Where it applies, "we start with the assumption that the historic police powers of the States were not to be superseded by the Federal Act unless that was the clear and manifest purpose of Congress." *Rice v. Santa Fe Elevator Corp.* (1947). That rule of construction rests on an assumption about congressional intent: that "Congress does not exercise lightly" the "extraordinary power" to "legislate in areas traditionally regulated by the States." *Gregory.* We have never mentioned such a principle in our Elections Clause cases. *Siebold,* for example, simply said that Elections Clause legislation, "so far as it extends and conflicts with the regulations of the State, necessarily supersedes them." There is good reason for treating Elections Clause legislation differently: The assumption that Congress is reluctant to pre-empt does not hold when Congress acts under that constitutional provision, which empowers Congress to "make or alter" state election regulations. Art. I, § 4, cl. 1. When Congress legislates with respect to the "Times, Places and Manner" of holding congressional elections, it *necessarily* displaces some element of a pre-existing legal regime erected by the States. Because the power the Elections Clause confers is none other than the power to pre-empt, the reasonable assumption is that the statutory text accurately communicates the scope of Congress's pre-emptive intent. Moreover, the federalism concerns underlying the presumption in the Supremacy Clause context are somewhat weaker here. Unlike the States' "historic police powers," the States' role in regulating congressional elections—while weighty and worthy of respect—has always existed subject to the express qualification that it "terminates according to federal law." *Buckman Co. v. Plaintiffs' Legal Comm.* (2001). In sum, there is no compelling reason not to read Elections Clause legislation simply to mean what it says.

We conclude that the fairest reading of the statute is that a state-imposed requirement of evidence of citizenship not required by the Federal Form is inconsistent with the NVRA's mandate that States "accept and use" the Federal Form. If this reading prevails, the Elections Clause requires that Arizona's rule give way.

We note, however, that while the NVRA forbids States to demand that an applicant submit additional information beyond that required by the Federal Form, it does not preclude States from "deny[ing] registration based on information in their possession establishing the applicant's ineligibility." Brief for United States as *Amicus Curiae* 24. The NVRA clearly contemplates that not every submitted Federal Form will result in registration. *See* § 1973gg-7(b)(1) (Federal Form "may require only" information "necessary to enable the appropriate State election official to *assess the eligibility of the applicant*" (emphasis added)); § 1973gg-6(a)(2) (States must require election officials to "send notice to each applicant of the disposition of the application").

III

Arizona contends, however, that its construction of the phrase "accept and use" is necessary to avoid a conflict between the NVRA and Arizona's constitutional authority to establish qualifications (such as citizenship) for voting. Arizona is correct that the Elections Clause empowers Congress to regulate *how* federal elections are held, but not *who* may vote in them.* The Constitution prescribes a straightforward rule for the composition of the federal electorate. Article I, § 2, cl. 1, provides that electors in each State for the House of Representatives "shall have the Qualifications requisite for Electors of the most numerous Branch of the State Legislature," and the Seventeenth Amendment adopts the same criterion for senatorial elections. One cannot read the Elections Clause as treating implicitly what these other constitutional provisions regulate explicitly. "It is difficult to see how words could be clearer in stating what Congress can control and what it cannot control. Surely nothing in these provisions lends itself to the view that voting qualifications in federal elections are to be set by Congress." *Oregon v. Mitchell* (1970) (Harlan, J., concurring in part and dissenting in part).[8]

Prescribing voting qualifications, therefore, "forms no part of the power to be conferred upon the national government" by the Elections Clause, which is "expressly restricted to the regulation of the *times,* the *places,* and the *manner* of elections." The Federalist No. 60, at 371 (A. Hamilton). This allocation of authority sprang from the Framers' aversion to concentrated power. A Congress empowered to regulate the qualifications of its own electorate, Madison warned, could "by degrees subvert the Constitution." 2 Records of the Federal Convention of 1787, p. 250 (M. Farrand rev. 1966). At the same time, by tying the federal franchise to the state franchise instead of simply placing it within the unfettered discretion of state legislatures, the Framers avoided "render[ing] too dependent on the State governments that branch of the federal government which ought to be dependent on the people alone." The Federalist No. 52, at 326 (J. Madison).

Since the power to establish voting requirements is of little value without the power to enforce those requirements, Arizona is correct that it would raise serious constitutional

* [Editors' note: The statement in this sentence and the ones that follow—which stipulate that Congress may dictate *how* elections are run but not *who* may vote in them—are extremely important, in that they delineate the balance of power between the federal and state governments in promulgating election regulations. In essence, Justice Scalia is saying that Congress has some, but not complete, authority and that states also have significant power.]

8. In *Mitchell,* the judgment of the Court was that Congress could compel the States to permit 18-year-olds to vote in federal elections. Of the five Justices who concurred in that outcome, only Justice Black was of the view that congressional power to prescribe this age qualification derived from the Elections Clause, while four Justices relied on the Fourteenth Amendment, *id.* (opinion of Douglas, J.), (joint opinion of Brennan, White, and Marshall, JJ.). That result, which lacked a majority rationale, is of minimal precedential value here. Five Justices took the position that the Elections Clause did *not* confer upon Congress the power to regulate voter qualifications in federal elections. *Mitchell* (opinion of Douglas, J.), (opinion of Harlan, J.), (opinion of Stewart, J., joined by Burger, C.J., and Blackmun, J.). (Justices Brennan, White, and Marshall did not address the Elections Clause.) This last view, which commanded a majority in *Mitchell,* underlies our analysis here. Five Justices also agreed that the Fourteenth Amendment did not empower Congress to impose the 18-year-old-voting mandate. *See Mitchell* (opinion of Black, J.), (opinion of Harlan, J.), (opinion of Stewart, J.).

doubts if a federal statute precluded a State from obtaining the information necessary to enforce its voter qualifications.[9] If, but for Arizona's interpretation of the "accept and use" provision, the State would be precluded from obtaining information necessary for enforcement, we would have to determine whether Arizona's interpretation, though plainly not the best reading, is at least a possible one. *Cf. Crowell v. Benson* (1932) (the Court will "ascertain whether a construction of the statute *is fairly possible* by which the [constitutional] question may be avoided" (emphasis added)). Happily, we are spared that necessity, since the statute provides another means by which Arizona may obtain information needed for enforcement.

Section 1973gg-7(b)(1) of the Act provides that the Federal Form "may require only such identifying information (including the signature of the applicant) and other information (including data relating to previous registration by the applicant), as is necessary to enable the appropriate State election official to assess the eligibility of the applicant and to administer voter registration and other parts of the election process." At oral argument, the United States expressed the view that the phrase "may require only" in § 1973gg-7(b)(1) means that the EAC "*shall require* information that's necessary, but may only require that information." (emphasis added). That is to say, § 1973gg-7(b)(1) acts as both a ceiling and a floor with respect to the contents of the Federal Form. We need not consider the Government's contention that despite the statute's statement that the EAC "may" require on the Federal Form information "necessary to enable the appropriate State election official to assess the eligibility of the applicant," other provisions of the Act indicate that such action is statutorily required. That is because we think that—by analogy to the rule of statutory interpretation that avoids questionable constitutionality—validly conferred discretionary executive authority is properly exercised (as the Government has proposed) to avoid serious constitutional doubt. That is to say, it is surely permissible if not requisite for the Government to say that necessary information which *may* be required *will* be required.

Since, pursuant to the Government's concession, a State may request that the EAC alter the Federal Form to include information the State deems necessary to determine eligibility, and may challenge the EAC's rejection of that request in a suit under the Administrative Procedure Act, no constitutional doubt is raised by giving the "accept and use" provision of the NVRA its fairest reading. That alternative means of enforcing its constitutional power to determine voting qualifications remains open to Arizona here. In 2005, the EAC divided 2-to-2 on the request by Arizona to include the evidence-of-citizenship requirement among the state-specific instructions on the Federal Form, which meant that no action could be taken. Arizona did not challenge that agency action (or rather inaction) by seeking APA review in federal court, but we are aware of nothing that

9. In their reply brief, petitioners suggest for the first time that "registration is itself a qualification to vote." We resolve this case on the theory on which it has hitherto been litigated: that *citizenship* (not registration) is the voter qualification Arizona seeks to enforce.

prevents Arizona from renewing its request.[10] Should the EAC's inaction persist, Arizona would have the opportunity to establish in a reviewing court that a mere oath will not suffice to effectuate its citizenship requirement and that the EAC is therefore under a nondiscretionary duty to include Arizona's concrete evidence requirement on the Federal Form. Arizona might also assert (as it has argued here) that it would be arbitrary for the EAC to refuse to include Arizona's instruction when it has accepted a similar instruction requested by Louisiana.

We hold that 42 U.S.C. § 1973gg-4 precludes Arizona from requiring a Federal Form applicant to submit information beyond that required by the form itself. Arizona may, however, request anew that the EAC include such a requirement among the Federal Form's state-specific instructions, and may seek judicial review of the EAC's decision under the Administrative Procedure Act.

The judgment of the Court of Appeals is affirmed.

Justice KENNEDY, concurring in part and concurring in the judgment.

The opinion for the Court insists on stating a proposition that, in my respectful view, is unnecessary for the proper disposition of the case and is incorrect in any event. The Court concludes that the normal "starting presumption that Congress does not intend to supplant state law" does not apply here because the source of congressional power is the Elections Clause and not some other provision of the Constitution.

There is no sound basis for the Court to rule, for the first time, that there exists a hierarchy of federal powers so that some statutes pre-empting state law must be interpreted by different rules than others, all depending upon which power Congress has exercised.

Whether the federal statute concerns congressional regulation of elections or any other subject proper for Congress to address, a court must not lightly infer a congressional directive to negate the States' otherwise proper exercise of their sovereign power. This case illustrates the point. The separate States have a continuing, essential interest in the integrity and accuracy of the process used to select both state and federal officials. The States pay the costs of holding these elections, which for practical reasons often overlap so that the two sets of officials are selected at the same time, on the same ballots, by the same voters. It seems most doubtful to me to suggest that States have some lesser concern when what is involved is their own historic role in the conduct of elections. [To the contrary,] the State's undoubted interest in the regulation and conduct of elections must be taken into account and ought not to be deemed by this Court to be a subject of secondary importance.

10. The EAC currently lacks a quorum—indeed, the Commission has not a single active Commissioner. If the EAC proves unable to act on a renewed request, Arizona would be free to seek a writ of mandamus to "compel agency action unlawfully withheld or unreasonably delayed." 5 U.S.C. § 706(1). It is a nice point, which we need not resolve here, whether a court can compel agency action that the agency itself, for lack of the statutorily required quorum, is incapable of taking. If the answer to that is no, Arizona might then be in a position to assert a constitutional right to demand concrete evidence of citizenship apart from the Federal Form.

Here, in my view, the Court is correct to conclude that the National Voter Registration Act of 1993 is unambiguous in its pre-emption of Arizona's statute. For this reason, I concur in the judgment and join all of the Court's opinion except its discussion of the presumption against pre-emption.

Justice THOMAS, dissenting.

I think that both the plain text and the history of the Voter Qualifications Clause, U.S. Const., Art. I, § 2, cl. 1, and the Seventeenth Amendment authorize States to determine the qualifications of voters in federal elections, which necessarily includes the related power to determine whether those qualifications are satisfied. To avoid substantial constitutional problems created by interpreting § 1973gg-4(a)(1) to permit Congress to effectively countermand this authority, I would construe the law as only requiring Arizona to accept and use the form as part of its voter registration process, leaving the State free to request whatever additional information it determines is necessary to ensure that voters meet the qualifications it has the constitutional authority to establish.

The United States argues that Congress has the authority under Article I, § 4, "to set the rules for voter registration in federal elections." Neither the text nor the original understanding of Article I, § 4, supports that position.

Prior to the Constitution's ratification, the phrase "manner of election" was commonly used in England, Scotland, Ireland, and North America to describe the entire election process. Natelson, The Original Scope of the Congressional Power to Regulate Elections, 13 U. Pa. J. Constitutional L. 1, 10-18 (2010). But there are good reasons for concluding that Article I, § 4's use of "Manner" is considerably more limited. The Constitution does not use the word "Manner" in isolation; rather, "after providing for qualifications, times, and places, the Constitution described the residuum as 'the Manner of holding Elections.' This precise phrase seems to have been newly coined to denote a subset of traditional 'manner' regulation." Consistent with this view, during the state ratification debates, the "Manner of holding Elections" was construed to mean the circumstances under which elections were held and the mechanics of the actual election. *See* 4 Debates in the Several State Conventions on the Adoption of the Federal Constitution 71 (J. Elliot 2d ed. 1863) (hereafter Elliot's Debates) ("The power over the manner of elections does not include that of saying who shall vote . . . the power over the manner only enables them to determine *how* those electors shall elect—whether by ballot, or by vote, or by any other way" (John Steele at the North Carolina ratification debates)). The text of the Times, Places and Manner Clause, therefore, cannot be read to authorize Congress to dictate voter eligibility to the States.

Respondents and the United States point out that *Smiley v. Holm* (1932), mentioned "registration" in a list of voting-related subjects it believed Congress could regulate under Article I, § 4. *Id.* (listing "notices, *registration,* supervision of voting, protection of voters, prevention of fraud and corrupt practices, counting of votes, duties of inspectors and canvassers, and making and publication of election returns" (emphasis added). But that statement was dicta because *Smiley* involved congressional redistricting, not voter registration. Cases since *Smiley* have similarly not addressed the issue of voter qualifications but merely repeated the word "registration" without further analysis.

It is, thus, difficult to maintain that the Times, Places and Manner Clause gives Congress power beyond regulating the casting of ballots and related activities, even as a matter of precedent.

I would interpret § 1973gg-4(a)(1) to avoid the constitutional problems discussed above.

I cannot, therefore, adopt the Court's interpretation that § 1973gg-4(a)(1)'s "accept and use" provision requires states to register anyone who completes and submits the form. Arizona sets citizenship as a qualification to vote, and it wishes to verify citizenship, as it is authorized to do under Article 1, § 2. It matters not whether the United States has specified one way in which *it* believes Arizona might be able to verify citizenship; Arizona has the independent constitutional authority to verify citizenship in the way it deems necessary. By requiring Arizona to register people who have not demonstrated to Arizona's satisfaction that they meet its citizenship qualification for voting, the NVRA, as interpreted by the Court, would exceed Congress' powers under Article I, § 4, and violate Article 1, § 2.

Fortunately, Arizona's alternative interpretation of § 1973gg-4(a)(1) avoids this problem. It is plausible that Arizona "accept[s] and use[s]" the federal form under § 1973gg-4(a)(1) so long as it receives the form and considers it as part of its voter application process. Given States' exclusive authority to set voter qualifications and to determine whether those qualifications are met, I would hold that Arizona may request whatever additional information it requires to verify voter eligibility.

I would not require Arizona to seek approval for its registration requirements from the Federal Government, for, as I have shown, the Federal Government does not have the constitutional authority to withhold such approval. Accordingly, it does not have the authority to command States to seek it. As a result, the majority's proposed solution does little to avoid the serious constitutional problems created by its interpretation.

Justice ALITO, dissenting.

The Court reads an ambiguous federal statute in a way that brushes aside the constitutional authority of the States and produces truly strange results.

Under the Constitution, the States, not Congress, have the authority to establish the qualifications of voters in elections for Members of Congress. The States also have the default authority to regulate federal voter registration. Exercising its right to set federal voter qualifications, Arizona, like every other State, permits only U.S. citizens to vote in federal elections, and Arizona has concluded that this requirement cannot be effectively enforced unless applicants for registration are required to provide proof of citizenship.

According to the Court, however, the National Voter Registration Act of 1993 (NVRA) deprives Arizona of this authority. I do not think that this is what Congress intended.

I also doubt that Congress meant for the success of an application for voter registration to depend on which of two valid but substantially different registration forms the applicant happens to fill out and submit, but that is how the Court reads the NVRA. The Court interprets one provision, 42 U.S.C. § 1973gg-6(a)(1)(B), to mean that, if an applicant fills out the federal form, a State must register the applicant without requiring proof of citizenship. But the Court does not question Arizona's authority under another provision of the NVRA, § 1973gg-4(a)(2), to create its own application form that demands proof of citizenship; nor does the Court dispute Arizona's right to refuse to register an applicant who submits that form without the requisite proof. I find it very hard to believe that this is what Congress had in mind.

These results are not required by the NVRA. Proper respect for the constitutional authority of the States demands a clear indication of a congressional intent to pre-empt state laws enforcing voter qualifications. And while the relevant provisions of the Act are hardly models of clarity, their best reading is that the States need not treat the federal form as a complete voter registration application.

I would begin by applying a presumption against pre-emption of the Arizona law requiring voter registration applicants to submit proof of citizenship. Under the Elections Clause, the States have the authority to specify the times, places, and manner of federal elections except to the extent that Congress chooses to provide otherwise. And in recognition of this allocation of authority, it is appropriate to presume that the States retain this authority unless Congress has clearly manifested a contrary intent. The presumption against pre-emption applies with full force when Congress legislates in a "field which the States have traditionally occupied," and the NVRA was the first significant federal regulation of voter registration enacted under the Elections Clause since Reconstruction.

The NVRA does not come close to manifesting the clear intent to pre-empt that we should expect to find when Congress has exercised its Elections Clause power in a way that is constitutionally questionable. Indeed, even if neither the presumption against pre-emption nor the canon of constitutional avoidance applied, the better reading of the Act would be that Arizona is free to require those who use the federal form to supplement their applications with proof of citizenship.

I agree with the Court that the phrase "accept and use," when read in isolation, is ambiguous, but I disagree with the Court's conclusion that § 1973gg-4(a)(1)'s use of that phrase means that a State must treat the federal form as a complete application and must either grant or deny registration without requiring that the applicant supply additional information. Instead, I would hold that a State "accept[s] and use [s]" the federal form so long as it uses the form as a meaningful part of the registration process.

The Court begins its analysis of § 1973gg-4(a)(1)'s context by examining unrelated uses of the word "accept" elsewhere in the United States Code. But a better place to start is to ask what it normally means to "accept and use" an application form. When the phrase is used in that context, it is clear that an organization can "accept and use" a form that it does not treat as a complete application. For example, many colleges and universities accept and use the Common Application for Undergraduate College Admission but also require that applicants submit various additional forms or documents. Similarly, the Social Security Administration undoubtedly "accepts and uses" its Social Security card application form even though someone applying for a card must also prove that he or she is a citizen or has a qualifying immigration status. As such examples illustrate, when an organization says that it "accepts and uses" an application form, it does not necessarily mean that the form constitutes a complete application.

Although § 1973gg-4(a)(1) forbids States from requiring applicants who use the federal form to submit a duplicative state form, nothing in that provision's text prevents Arizona from insisting that federal form applicants supplement their applications with additional information.

That understanding of § 1973gg-4(a)(1) is confirmed by § 1973gg-4(a)(2), which allows States to design and use their own voter registration forms "[i]n addition to accepting and using" the federal form. The Act clearly permits States to require proof of citizenship on their own forms, *see* §§ 1973gg-4(a)(2) and 1973gg-7(b)—a step that Arizona has taken and that today's decision does not disturb. Thus, under the Court's approach, whether someone can register to vote in Arizona without providing proof of citizenship will depend on the happenstance of which of two alternative forms the applicant completes. That could not possibly be what Congress intended; it is as if the Internal Revenue Service issued two sets of personal income tax forms with different tax rates.

We could avoid this nonsensical result by holding that the Act lets the States decide for themselves what information "is necessary . . . to assess the eligibility of the applicant"—both by designing their own forms and by requiring that federal form applicants provide supplemental information when appropriate. The Act's provision for state forms shows that the purpose of the federal form is not to supplant the States' authority in this area but to facilitate interstate voter registration drives. Thanks to the federal form, volunteers distributing voter registration materials at a shopping mall in Yuma can give a copy of the same form to every person they meet without attempting to distinguish between residents of Arizona and California. The federal form was meant to facilitate voter registration drives, not to take away the States' traditional authority to decide what information registrants must supply.[3]

3. The Court argues that the federal form would not accomplish this purpose under my interpretation because "a volunteer in Yuma would have to give every prospective voter not only a Federal Form, but also a separate set of either Arizona- or California-specific instructions." But this is exactly what Congress envisioned. Eighteen of the federal form's 23 pages are state-specific instructions.

The Court purports to find support for its contrary approach in § 1973gg-6(a)(1)(B), which says that a State must "ensure that any eligible applicant is registered to vote in an election . . . if the valid voter registration form of the applicant is post-marked" within a specified period. The Court understands § 1973gg-6(a)(1)(B) to mean that a State must register an eligible applicant if he or she submits a "valid voter registration form." But when read in context, that provision simply identifies the time within which a State must process registration applications; it says nothing about whether a State may require the submission of supplemental information. The Court's more expansive interpretation of § 1973gg-6(a)(1)(B) sneaks in a qualification that is nowhere to be found in the text. The Court takes pains to say that a State need not register an applicant who properly completes and submits a federal form but is known by the State to be ineligible. But the Court takes the position that a State may not demand that an applicant supply any additional information to confirm voting eligibility. Nothing in § 1973gg-6(a)(1)(B) supports this distinction.

What is a State to do if it has reason to doubt an applicant's eligibility but cannot be sure that the applicant is ineligible? Must the State either grant or deny registration without communicating with the applicant? Or does the Court believe that a State may ask for additional information in individual cases but may not impose a categorical requirement for all applicants? If that is the Court's position, on which provision of the NVRA does it rely? The Court's reading of § 1973gg-6(a)(1)(B) is atextual and makes little sense.

Properly interpreted, the NVRA permits Arizona to require applicants for federal voter registration to provide proof of eligibility.

QUESTIONS ON *ARIZONA v. INTER TRIBAL COUNCIL*

1. How important is the Court's qualification that Arizona can ask the U.S. Election Assistance Commission to include the documentation-of-citizenship requirement as part of the Federal Form? If the EAC denied that request, would the NVRA then be unconstitutional as-applied for interfering with Arizona's constitutional authority to set the basic requirements for voter eligibility? Or can Arizona adequately enforce its citizenship eligibility requirement by other means?
2. Is the debate between Justices Scalia and Kennedy over whether there should be a "presumption against preemption" under the Elections Clause of practical, or only theoretical, significance?
3. What do you make of the fact that Justices Scalia and Roberts, two of the Court's conservative members, joined the Court's four liberals to make up the majority opinion (and with Kennedy also joining almost all of it), leaving the case essentially a 7-2 split?
4. Virtually every state constitution includes an explicit grant of the right to vote to its state citizens. As Justice Scalia explains, the Election Clause contemplates the states determining voter eligibility. What role does this suggest state courts

should play in construing their state constitutional provisions? Should they follow U.S. Supreme Court guidance on the question or give their state constitutions some kind of independent interpretation? If the latter, what factors should go into the meaning of the state constitutional right to vote?

2. *Voter Identification and Equal Protection*

From the media's treatment of the voting wars, one might think that the issue of voter identification (ID) is purely dichotomous, like an on-off switch—either you are for it or against it, and there are no middle-ground positions. But that simplistic view is grossly inaccurate. Even a signature is a form of identification, and thus anyone who believes that voters should be required to sign a poll register when they go to cast their ballots is in favor of at least one form of voter identification. At the other end of the spectrum, conversely, supporting a strict requirement that only one particular type of identification—for example, a photo ID issued by a state's department of motor vehicles—as a satisfactory prerequisite to casting a countable ballot is a very different view on the voter identification issue. In between these two polar positions, there are lots of different points on the spectrum concerning what different forms of ID might suffice—like bank statements or utility bills or library cards, and the like—and what is the consequence of not being able to present an ID at the time of casting one's ballot. For example, some states permit voters without an ID to sign an affidavit as an alternative; other states do not permit this affidavit option.

Congress weighed in on this debate in a limited way in the Help America Vote Act of 2002 (HAVA), requiring identification of first-time voters who register to vote by mail. But Congress permitted a wide range of documents (including pay checks or bank statements) to satisfy this limited federal voter ID requirement. Apart from this requirement, Congress has otherwise left the issue to the states—assuming, of course, that voter ID rules do not discriminate on the basis of race in violation of the federal Voting Rights Act (an issue that is under litigation in Texas and may end up being further litigated in other places). The states have responded by enacting various different types of voter ID laws, some much stricter than others.

The Supreme Court was involved in the voter ID debate in the following case, although the Court was fractured in deciding it, with the nine Justices splintering into three groups of three: the plurality (Stevens, with Roberts and Kennedy), a concurrence (Scalia, with Thomas and Alito), and the dissenters (Breyer, Souter, and Ginsburg, in two separate dissents). As you wade through the opinions, ask yourself what is the relationship of this case to the canonical voter eligibility cases of *Harper* and *Kramer*. Is voter identification a form of voting qualification, like the payment of a poll tax in *Harper*, since an individual is ineligible to cast a ballot that counts if the individual fails to provide the required ID? In fact, is a voter ID rule actually a kind of unconstitutional poll tax, in violation of *Harper* itself, if it costs the individual money to obtain the ID (or, to complicate the issue, as you will see soon, if it costs the individual money to obtain an underlying document, like a birth certificate, to obtain the necessary voter

ID)? Or, alternatively, as long as a voter ID rule does not operate as a wealth qualification in violation of *Harper*, then is a voter ID rule really not an eligibility requirement at all, but just a procedure the voter must follow—like going to the voter's correct polling place to cast a ballot, or signing the poll book before voting? (This division between eligibility requirements, on the one hand, and "manner of voting" rules, on the other, tracks the distinction the Court drew in *Arizona v. Intertribal Council.*)

These questions raise more broadly the issue of what standard of review the Court should apply to a voter ID rule. As you will see, the Justices diverge on this issue. Is that because they differ on how to think about the voter ID rule specifically, or do they have a more general jurisprudential disagreement about the role of the federal judiciary in voting cases (a disagreement we have seen before, and will see again in cases that have nothing to do with voter ID itself)? Similarly, are some of the Justices more faithful to the legacy of *Harper* and *Kramer* than others, or are they all on board with *Harper* and *Kramer* as far as those precedents go, but the Justices just diverge as they move farther along the journey of adjudicating voting rights cases?

A few more things to think about as you read this very important case: (1) Why is Justice Stevens, usually a "liberal," grouped here with Roberts and Kennedy, who are usually more conservative than Stevens? (2) To what extent does it matter that this case involved a "facial" rather than "as-applied" challenge (and what difference might this distinction make in future cases)? (3) How important is the factual debate over the extent to which "voter fraud" exists and might be thwarted by voter ID rules (in other words, how often do individuals attempt to cast ballots pretending to be someone they are not, such that an ID rule would stop them from doing so)? (4) As a factual matter, how many persons does a voter ID law actually disenfranchise?

CRAWFORD v. MARION COUNTY ELECTION BOARD

553 U.S. 181 (2008)

Justice STEVENS announced the judgment of the Court and delivered an opinion in which THE CHIEF JUSTICE and Justice KENNEDY join.

At issue is the constitutionality of an Indiana statute requiring citizens voting in person on election day, or casting a ballot in person at the office of the circuit court clerk prior to election day, to present photo identification issued by the government.

Referred to as either the "Voter ID Law" or "SEA 483," the statute applies to in-person voting at both primary and general elections. The requirement does not apply to absentee ballots submitted by mail, and the statute contains an exception for persons living and voting in a state-licensed facility such as a nursing home. A voter who is indigent or has a religious objection to being photographed may cast a provisional ballot that will be counted only if she executes an appropriate affidavit before the circuit court clerk within 10 days following the election. A voter who has photo identification but is unable to present that identification on election day may file a provisional ballot that will be counted if she brings her photo identification to the circuit county clerk's office within 10 days. No photo identification is required in order to register to vote, and the State offers free photo identification to qualified voters able to establish their residence and identity.

We are persuaded that the District Court and the Court of Appeals correctly concluded that the evidence in the record is not sufficient to support a facial attack on the validity of the entire statute, and thus affirm.

I

In *Harper v. Virginia Bd. of Elections* (1966), the Court held that Virginia could not condition the right to vote in a state election on the payment of a poll tax of $1.50. We rejected the dissenters' argument that the interest in promoting civic responsibility by weeding out those voters who did not care enough about public affairs to pay a small sum for the privilege of voting provided a rational basis for the tax. Applying a stricter standard, we concluded that a State "violates the Equal Protection Clause of the Fourteenth Amendment whenever it makes the affluence of the voter or payment of any fee an electoral standard." We used the term "invidiously discriminate" to describe conduct prohibited under that standard. Although the State's justification for the tax was rational, it was invidious because it was irrelevant to the voter's qualifications. Thus, under the standard applied in *Harper*, even rational restrictions on the right to vote are invidious if they are unrelated to voter qualifications. In *Anderson v. Celebrezze*, however, we confirmed the general rule that "evenhanded restrictions that protect the integrity and reliability of the electoral process itself" are not invidious and satisfy the standard set forth in *Harper*. Rather than applying any "litmus test" that would neatly separate valid from invalid restrictions, we concluded that a court must identify and evaluate the interests put forward by the State as justifications for the burden imposed by its rule, and then make the "hard judgment" that our adversary system demands.

Later, in *Burdick v. Takushi* (1992), we applied *Anderson*'s standard for "reasonable, nondiscriminatory restrictions" and upheld Hawaii's prohibition on write-in voting despite the fact that it prevented a significant number of "voters from participating in Hawaii elections in a meaningful manner." *Id.* (Kennedy, J., dissenting). We reaffirmed *Anderson*'s requirement that a court evaluating a constitutional challenge to an election regulation weigh the asserted injury to the right to vote against the "precise interests put forward by the State as justifications for the burden imposed by its rule." (quoting *Anderson*).[8]

In neither [*Anderson*] nor *Burdick* did we identify any litmus test for measuring the severity of a burden that a state law imposes on a political party, an individual voter, or a

8. Contrary to Justice Scalia's suggestion, our approach remains faithful to *Anderson* and *Burdick*. The *Burdick* opinion was explicit in its endorsement and adherence to *Anderson* and repeatedly cited *Anderson*. To be sure, *Burdick* rejected the argument that strict scrutiny applies to all laws imposing a burden on the right to vote; but in its place, the Court applied the "flexible standard" set forth in *Anderson*. *Burdick* surely did not create a novel "deferential 'important regulatory interests' standard."

discrete class of voters. However slight that burden may appear, as *Harper* demonstrates, it must be justified by relevant and legitimate state interests sufficiently weighty to justify the limitation.

II

The State has identified several state interests that arguably justify the burdens that SEA 483 imposes on voters and potential voters. While petitioners argue that the statute was actually motivated by partisan concerns and dispute both the significance of the State's interests and the magnitude of any real threat to those interests, they do not question the legitimacy of the interests the State has identified. Each is unquestionably relevant to the State's interest in protecting the integrity and reliability of the electoral process.

The first is the interest in deterring and detecting voter fraud. The State has a valid interest in participating in a nationwide effort to improve and modernize election procedures that have been criticized as antiquated and inefficient. The State also argues that it has a particular interest in preventing voter fraud in response to a problem that is in part the product of its own maladministration—namely, that Indiana's voter registration rolls include a large number of names of persons who are either deceased or no longer live in Indiana. Finally, the State relies on its interest in safeguarding voter confidence. Each of these interests merits separate comment.

Election Modernization

[N]either HAVA nor NVRA required Indiana to enact SEA 483, but they do indicate that Congress believes that photo identification is one effective method of establishing a voter's qualification to vote and that the integrity of elections is enhanced through improved technology.

Voter Fraud

The only kind of voter fraud that SEA 483 addresses is in-person voter impersonation at polling places. The record contains no evidence of any such fraud actually occurring in Indiana at any time in its history. Moreover, petitioners argue that provisions of the Indiana Criminal Code punishing such conduct as a felony provide adequate protection against the risk that such conduct will occur in the future. It remains true, however, that flagrant examples of such fraud in other parts of the country have been documented throughout this Nation's history by respected historians and journalists,[11] that occasional

11. One infamous example is the New York City elections of 1868. William (Boss) Tweed set about solidifying and consolidating his control of the city. One local tough who worked for Boss Tweed, "Big Tim" Sullivan, insisted that his "repeaters" (individuals paid to vote multiple times) have whiskers:

> "When you've voted 'em with their whiskers on, you take 'em to a barber and scrape off the chin fringe. Then you vote 'em again with the side lilacs and a mustache. Then to a barber again, off comes the sides and you vote 'em a third time with the mustache. If that ain't enough and the box can stand a few more ballots, clean off the mustache and vote 'em plain face. That makes every one of 'em good for four votes." A. Callow, THE TWEED RING 210 (1966) (quoting M. Werner, TAMMANY HALL 439 (1928)).

examples have surfaced in recent years, and that Indiana's own experience with fraudulent voting in the 2003 Democratic primary for East Chicago Mayor—though perpetrated using absentee ballots and not in-person fraud—demonstrate that not only is the risk of voter fraud real but that it could affect the outcome of a close election.

There is no question about the legitimacy or importance of the State's interest in counting only the votes of eligible voters. Moreover, the interest in orderly administration and accurate recordkeeping provides a sufficient justification for carefully identifying all voters participating in the election process. While the most effective method of preventing election fraud may well be debatable, the propriety of doing so is perfectly clear.

[T]he State argues that the inflation of its voter rolls provides further support for its enactment of SEA 483. Even though Indiana's own negligence may have contributed to the serious inflation of its registration lists when SEA 483 was enacted, the fact of inflated voter rolls does provide a neutral and nondiscriminatory reason supporting the State's decision to require photo identification.

Safeguarding Voter Confidence

Finally, the State contends that it has an interest in protecting public confidence "in the integrity and legitimacy of representative government." While that interest is closely related to the State's interest in preventing voter fraud, public confidence in the integrity of the electoral process has independent significance, because it encourages citizen participation in the democratic process. As the Carter-Baker Report [a bipartisan report conducted by former President Jimmy Carter and former Secretary of State James Baker] observed, the "electoral system cannot inspire public confidence if no safeguards exist to deter or detect fraud or to confirm the identity of voters."

III

A photo identification requirement imposes some burdens on voters that other methods of identification do not share. For example, a voter may lose his photo identification, may have his wallet stolen on the way to the polls, or may not resemble the photo in the identification because he recently grew a beard. Burdens of that sort arising from life's vagaries, however, are neither so serious nor so frequent as to raise any question about the constitutionality of SEA 483; the availability of the right to cast a provisional ballot provides an adequate remedy for problems of that character.

The burdens that are relevant to the issue before us are those imposed on persons who are eligible to vote but do not possess a current photo identification that complies with the requirements of SEA 483. The fact that most voters already possess a valid driver's license, or some other form of acceptable identification, would not save the statute under our reasoning in *Harper,* if the State required voters to pay a tax or a fee to obtain a new photo identification. But just as other States provide free voter registration cards, the photo identification cards issued by Indiana's BMV are also free. For most voters who need them, the inconvenience of making a trip to the BMV, gathering the required documents, and posing for a photograph surely does not qualify as a substantial burden on the right to vote, or even represent a significant increase over the usual burdens of voting.[17]

Both evidence in the record and facts of which we may take judicial notice, however, indicate that a somewhat heavier burden may be placed on a limited number of persons. They include elderly persons born out-of-state, who may have difficulty obtaining a birth certificate; persons who because of economic or other personal limitations may find it difficult either to secure a copy of their birth certificate or to assemble the other required documentation to obtain a state-issued identification; homeless persons; and persons with a religious objection to being photographed. If we assume, as the evidence suggests, that some members of these classes were registered voters when SEA 483 was enacted, the new identification requirement may have imposed a special burden on their right to vote.

The severity of that burden is, of course, mitigated by the fact that, if eligible, voters without photo identification may cast provisional ballots that will ultimately be counted. To do so, however, they must travel to the circuit court clerk's office within 10 days to execute the required affidavit. It is unlikely that such a requirement would pose a constitutional problem unless it is wholly unjustified. And even assuming that the burden may not be justified as to a few voters, that conclusion is by no means sufficient to establish petitioners' right to the relief they seek in this litigation.

IV

Given the fact that petitioners have advanced a broad attack on the constitutionality of SEA 483, seeking relief that would invalidate the statute in all its applications, they bear a heavy burden of persuasion. Only a few weeks ago we held that the Court of Appeals for the Ninth Circuit had failed to give appropriate weight to the magnitude of that burden when it sustained a preelection, facial attack on a Washington statute regulating that State's primary election procedures. *Washington State Grange v. Washington State Republican Party* (2008). Our reasoning in that case applies with added force [here].

Petitioners ask this Court, in effect, to perform a unique balancing analysis that looks specifically at a small number of voters who may experience a special burden under the statute and weighs their burdens against the State's broad interests in protecting election integrity. Petitioners urge us to ask whether the State's interests justify the burden imposed on voters who cannot afford or obtain a birth certificate and who must make a second trip to the circuit court clerk's office after voting. But on the basis of the evidence in the record it is not possible to quantify either the magnitude of the burden on this narrow class of voters or the portion of the burden imposed on them that is fully justified.

17. To obtain a photo identification card a person must present at least one "primary" document, which can be a birth certificate, certificate of naturalization, U.S. veterans photo identification, U.S. military photo identification, or a U.S. passport. Indiana, like most States, charges a fee for obtaining a copy of one's birth certificate. This fee varies by county and is currently between $3 and $12. Some States charge substantially more.

First, the evidence in the record does not provide us with the number of registered voters without photo identification. Further, the evidence does not provide any concrete evidence of the burden imposed on voters who currently lack photo identification. [Also,] although it may not be a completely acceptable alternative, the elderly in Indiana are able to vote absentee without presenting photo identification.

The record says virtually nothing about the difficulties faced by either indigent voters or voters with religious objections to being photographed. The record does contain the affidavit of one homeless woman who has a copy of her birth certificate, but was denied a photo identification card because she did not have an address. But that single affidavit gives no indication of how common the problem is.

In sum, we cannot conclude that the statute imposes "excessively burdensome requirements" on any class of voters. *See Storer v. Brown* (1974).[20] A facial challenge must fail where the statute has a plainly legitimate sweep. When we consider only the statute's broad application to all Indiana voters we conclude that it "imposes only a limited burden on voters' rights." *Burdick.* The precise interests advanced by the State are therefore sufficient to defeat petitioners' facial challenge to SEA 483.

Finally we note that petitioners have not demonstrated that the proper remedy—even assuming an unjustified burden on some voters—would be to invalidate the entire statute. When evaluating a neutral, nondiscriminatory regulation of voting procedure, "[w]e must keep in mind that a ruling of unconstitutionality frustrates the intent of the elected representatives of the people." *Ayotte v. Planned Parenthood of Northern New Eng.* [(2006)].

V

In their briefs, petitioners stress the fact that all of the Republicans in the General Assembly voted in favor of SEA 483 and the Democrats were unanimous in opposing it. It is fair to infer that partisan considerations may have played a significant role in the decision to enact SEA 483. If such considerations had provided the only justification for a photo identification requirement, we may also assume that SEA 483 would suffer the same fate as the poll tax at issue in *Harper.*

But if a nondiscriminatory law is supported by valid neutral justifications, those justifications should not be disregarded simply because partisan interests may have provided one motivation for the votes of individual legislators. The state interests identified as justifications for SEA 483 are both neutral and sufficiently strong to require us to reject petitioners' facial attack on the statute. The application of the statute to the vast majority of Indiana voters is amply justified by the valid interest in protecting "the integrity and reliability of the electoral process." *Anderson.*

20. While it is true that obtaining a birth certificate carries with it a financial cost, the record does not provide even a rough estimate of how many indigent voters lack copies of their birth certificates. Supposition based on extensive Internet research is not an adequate substitute for admissible evidence subject to cross-examination in constitutional adjudication.

Justice SCALIA, with whom Justice THOMAS and Justice ALITO join, concurring in the judgment.

The lead opinion assumes petitioners' premise that the voter-identification law "may have imposed a special burden on" some voters, but holds that petitioners have not assembled evidence to show that the special burden is severe enough to warrant strict scrutiny. That is true enough, but for the sake of clarity and finality (as well as adherence to precedent), I prefer to decide these cases on the grounds that petitioners' premise is irrelevant and that the burden at issue is minimal and justified.

To evaluate a law respecting the right to vote—whether it governs voter qualifications, candidate selection, or the voting process—we use the approach set out in *Burdick v. Takushi* (1992). This calls for application of a deferential "important regulatory interests" standard for nonsevere, nondiscriminatory restrictions, reserving strict scrutiny for laws that severely restrict the right to vote. The lead opinion resists the import of *Burdick* by characterizing it as simply adopting "the balancing approach" of *Anderson v. Celebrezze* (1983). Although *Burdick* liberally quoted *Anderson*, *Burdick* forged *Anderson*'s amorphous "flexible standard" into something resembling an administrable rule. Since *Burdick*, we have repeatedly reaffirmed the primacy of its two-track approach. "[S]trict scrutiny is appropriate only if the burden is severe." [*Clingman v. Beaver*, (2005).] Thus, the first step is to decide whether a challenged law severely burdens the right to vote. Ordinary and widespread burdens, such as those requiring "nominal effort" of everyone, are not severe. Burdens are severe if they go beyond the merely inconvenient.

Of course, we have to identify a burden before we can weigh it. The Indiana law affects different voters differently, but what petitioners view as the law's several light and heavy burdens are no more than the different impacts of the single burden that the law uniformly imposes on all voters. To vote in person in Indiana, everyone must have and present a photo identification that can be obtained for free. The State draws no classifications, let alone discriminatory ones, except to establish optional absentee and provisional balloting for certain poor, elderly, and institutionalized voters and for religious objectors. Nor are voters who already have photo identifications exempted from the burden, since those voters must maintain the accuracy of the information displayed on the identifications, renew them before they expire, and replace them if they are lost.

The Indiana photo-identification law is a generally applicable, nondiscriminatory voting regulation, and our precedents refute the view that individual impacts are relevant to determining the severity of the burden it imposes. Indeed, *Clingman*'s holding that burdens are not severe if they are ordinary and widespread would be rendered meaningless if a single plaintiff could claim a severe burden.

Insofar as our election-regulation cases rest upon the requirements of the Fourteenth Amendment, weighing the burden of a nondiscriminatory voting law upon each voter and concomitantly requiring exceptions for vulnerable voters would effectively turn back decades of equal-protection jurisprudence. A voter complaining about such a law's effect on him has no valid equal-protection claim because, without proof of discriminatory intent, a generally applicable law with disparate impact is not unconstitutional. *See, e.g., Washington v. Davis* (1976). The Fourteenth Amendment does not regard neutral laws as invidious ones, even when their burdens purportedly fall disproportionately on a protected class. A fortiori it does not do so when, as here, the classes complaining of disparate impact are not even protected.

Even if I thought that *stare decisis* did not foreclose adopting an individual-focused approach, I would reject it as an original matter. This is an area where the dos and don'ts need to be known in advance of the election, and voter-by-voter examination of the burdens of voting regulations would prove especially disruptive. A case-by-case approach naturally encourages constant litigation. Very few new election regulations improve everyone's lot, so the potential allegations of severe burden are endless. A State reducing the number of polling places would be open to the complaint it has violated the rights of disabled voters who live near the closed stations. Indeed, it may even be the case that some laws already on the books are especially burdensome for some voters.

That sort of detailed judicial supervision of the election process would flout the Constitution's express commitment of the task to the States. It is for state legislatures to weigh the costs and benefits of possible changes to their election codes, and their judgment must prevail unless it imposes a severe and unjustified overall burden upon the right to vote, or is intended to disadvantage a particular class. Judicial review of their handiwork must apply an objective, uniform standard that will enable them to determine, ex ante, whether the burden they impose is too severe.

The lead opinion's record-based resolution of these cases, which neither rejects nor embraces the rule of our precedents, provides no certainty, and will embolden litigants who surmise that our precedents have been abandoned. There is no good reason to prefer that course.

* * *

The universally applicable requirements of Indiana's voter-identification law are eminently reasonable. The burden of acquiring, possessing, and showing free photo identification is simply not severe, because it does not even represent a significant increase over the usual burdens of voting. And the State's interests are sufficient to sustain that minimal burden. That should end the matter. That the State accommodates some voters by permitting (not requiring) the casting of absentee or provisional ballots, is an indulgence—not a constitutional imperative that falls short of what is required.

Justice SOUTER, with whom Justice GINSBURG joins, dissenting.

Indiana's "Voter ID Law" threatens to impose nontrivial burdens on the voting right of tens of thousands of the State's citizens, and a significant percentage of those individuals are likely to be deterred from voting. The statute is unconstitutional under the balancing standard of *Burdick v. Takushi* (1992): a State may not burden the right to vote merely by invoking abstract interests, be they legitimate, or even compelling, but must make a particular, factual showing that threats to its interests outweigh the particular impediments it has imposed. The State has made no such justification here, and as to some aspects of its law, it has hardly even tried.

I

Voting-rights cases raise two competing interests, the one side being the fundamental right to vote. The Judiciary is obliged to train a skeptical eye on any qualification of that right. *See Reynolds.*

As against the unfettered right, however, lies the "[c]ommon sense, as well as constitutional law . . . that government must play an active role in structuring elections; as a practical matter, there must be a substantial regulation of elections if they are to be fair and honest and if some sort of order, rather than chaos, is to accompany the democratic processes." *Burdick.*

Given the legitimacy of interests on both sides, we have avoided pre-set levels of scrutiny in favor of a sliding-scale balancing analysis: the scrutiny varies with the effect of the regulation at issue. And whatever the claim, the Court has long made a careful, ground-level appraisal both of the practical burdens on the right to vote and of the State's reasons for imposing those precise burdens.

The lead opinion does not disavow these basic principles. But I think it does not insist enough on the hard facts that our standard of review demands.

II

A

The first set of burdens shown in these cases is the travel costs and fees necessary to get one of the limited variety of federal or state photo identifications needed to cast a regular ballot under the Voter ID Law. The travel is required for the personal visit to the BMV, which is demanded of anyone applying for a driver's license or non-driver photo identification. Poor, old, and disabled voters who do not drive a car may find the trip prohibitive.[4]

4. The State asserts that the elderly and disabled are adequately accommodated through their option to cast absentee ballots, and so any burdens on them are irrelevant. There are crucial differences between the absentee and regular ballot. Voting by absentee ballot leaves an individual without the possibility of receiving assistance from poll workers, and thus increases the likelihood of confusion and error. More seriously, Indiana law "treats absentee voters differently from the way it treats Election Day voters," in the important sense that "an absentee ballot may not be recounted in situations where clerical error by an election officer rendered it invalid." *Horseman v. Keller,* 841 N.E.2d 164, 171 (Ind. 2006). The State itself notes that "election officials routinely reject absentee ballots on suspicion of forgery." The record indicates that voters in Indiana are not unaware of these risks. It is one thing (and a commendable thing) for the State to make absentee voting available to the elderly and disabled; but it is quite another to suggest that, because the more convenient but less reliable absentee ballot is available, the State may freely deprive the elderly and disabled of the option of voting in person.

The burden of traveling to a more distant BMV office rather than a conveniently located polling place is probably serious for many of the individuals who lack photo identification. They almost certainly will not own cars, and public transportation in Indiana is fairly limited.

For those voters who can afford the roundtrip, a second financial hurdle appears: in order to get photo identification for the first time, they need to present "a birth certificate, a certificate of naturalization, U.S. veterans photo identification, U.S. military photo identification, or a U.S. passport." As the lead opinion says, the two most common of these documents come at a price: Indiana counties charge anywhere from \$3 to \$12 for a birth certificate (and in some other States the fee is significantly higher), and that same price must usually be paid for a first-time passport, since a birth certificate is required to prove U.S. citizenship by birth. The total fees for a passport are up to about \$100. As with the travel costs, these fees are far from shocking on their face, but in the *Burdick* analysis it matters that both the travel costs and the fees are disproportionately heavy for, and thus disproportionately likely to deter, the poor, the old, and the immobile.

B

To be sure, Indiana has a provisional-ballot exception to the ID requirement for individuals the State considers "indigent" as well as those with religious objections to being photographed, and this sort of exception could in theory provide a way around the costs of procuring an ID. But Indiana's chosen exception does not amount to much relief.

[T]o have the provisional ballot counted, a voter must appear in person before the circuit court clerk or county election board within 10 days of the election, to sign an affidavit attesting to indigency or religious objection to being photographed (or to present an ID at that point). Forcing these people to travel to the county seat every time they try to vote is particularly onerous.

That the need to travel to the county seat each election amounts to a high hurdle is shown in the results of the 2007 municipal elections in Marion County, to which Indiana's Voter ID Law applied. Thirty-four provisional ballots were cast, but only two provisional voters made it to the County Clerk's Office within the 10 days. All 34 of these aspiring voters appeared at the appropriate precinct; 33 of them provided a signature, and every signature matched the one on file; and 26 of the 32 voters whose ballots were not counted had a history of voting in Marion County elections.

C

Indiana's Voter ID Law thus threatens to impose serious burdens on the voting right, and the next question under *Burdick* is whether the number of individuals likely to be affected is significant as well. Record evidence and facts open to judicial notice answer yes.

Although the District Court found that petitioners failed to offer any reliable empirical study of numbers of voters affected, we may accept that court's rough calculation that 43,000 voting-age residents lack the kind of identification card required by Indiana's law.

The State, in fact, shows no discomfort with the District Court's finding that an "estimated 43,000 individuals" (about 1% of the State's voting-age population) lack a qualifying ID. If the State's willingness to take that number is surprising, it may be less so in light of the District Court's observation that "several factors . . . suggest the percentage of Indiana's voting age population with photo identification is actually lower than 99%," a suggestion in line with national surveys showing roughly 6-10% of voting-age Americans without a state-issued photo-identification card.

The upshot is this. Tens of thousands of voting-age residents lack the necessary photo identification. A large proportion of them are likely to be in bad shape economically.[25] The Voter ID Law places hurdles in the way of either getting an ID or of voting provisionally, and they translate into nontrivial economic costs. There is accordingly no reason to doubt that a significant number of state residents will be discouraged or disabled from voting.

Thus, petitioners' case is clearly strong enough to prompt more than a cursory examination of the State's asserted interests. And the fact that Indiana's photo identification requirement is one of the most restrictive in the country makes a critical examination of the State's claims all the more in order.

III

Because the lead opinion finds only "limited" burdens on the right to vote, it avoids a hard look at the State's claimed interests. As the lead opinion sees it, the State has offered four related concerns that suffice to justify the Voter ID Law: modernizing election procedures, combating voter fraud, addressing the consequences of the State's bloated voter rolls, and protecting public confidence in the integrity of the electoral process. On closer look, however, it appears that the first two (which are really just one) can claim modest weight at best, and the latter two if anything weaken the State's case.

A

1

There is no denying the abstract importance, the compelling nature, of combating voter fraud. But it takes several steps to get beyond the level of abstraction here.

25. Studies in other States suggest that the burdens of an ID requirement may also fall disproportionately upon racial minorities. *See* Overton, *Voter Identification*, 105 Mich. L. Rev. 631, 659 (2007) ("In 1994, the U.S. Department of Justice found that African-Americans in Louisiana were four to five times less likely than white residents to have government-sanctioned photo identification"); *id.*, at 659-660 (describing June 2005 study by the Employment and Training Institute at the University of Wisconsin-Milwaukee, which found that while 17% of voting-age whites lacked a valid driver's license, 55% of black males and 49% of black females were unlicensed, and 46% of Latino males and 59% of Latino females were similarly unlicensed).

To begin with, requiring a voter to show photo identification before casting a regular ballot addresses only one form of voter fraud: in-person voter impersonation. The photo ID requirement leaves untouched the problems of absentee-ballot fraud, which (unlike in-person voter impersonation) is a documented problem in Indiana; of registered voters voting more than once (but maintaining their own identities) in different counties or in different States; of felons and other disqualified individuals voting in their own names; of vote buying; or, for that matter, of ballot-stuffing, ballot miscounting, voter intimidation, or any other type of corruption on the part of officials administering elections.

[Moreover,] the State has not come across a single instance of in-person voter impersonation fraud in all of Indiana's history. The State responds to the want of evidence with the assertion that in-person voter impersonation fraud is hard to detect. But this is like saying the "man who wasn't there" is hard to spot, and to know whether difficulty in detection accounts for the lack of evidence one at least has to ask whether in-person voter impersonation is (or would be) relatively harder to ferret out than other kinds of fraud (*e.g.*, by absentee ballot) which the State has had no trouble documenting. The answer seems to be no; there is reason to think [according to the relevant federal agency] that "impersonation of voters is . . . the most likely type of fraud to be discovered." U.S. Election Assistance Commission, Election Crimes: An Initial Report and Recommendations for Future Study 9 (Dec. 2006).

2

For that matter, the deterrence argument can do only so much work, since photo identification is itself hardly a failsafe against impersonation. Indiana knows this, and that is why in 2007 the State began to issue redesigned driver's licenses with digital watermarking. The State has made this shift precisely because, in the words of its BMV, "visual inspection is not adequate to determine the authenticity" of driver's licenses. Indeed, the BMV explains that the digital watermarks (which can be scanned using equipment that, so far, Indiana does not use at polling places) is needed to "tak[e] the guesswork out of inspection." So, at least until polling places have the machines and special software to scan the new driver's licenses, and until all the licenses with the older designs expire, Indiana's law does no more than assure that any in-person voter fraud will take place with fake IDs, not attempted signature forgery.

Despite all this, I will readily stipulate that a State has an interest in responding to the risk (however small) of in-person voter impersonation. But the ultimate valuation of the particular interest a State asserts has to take account of evidence against it as well as legislative judgments for it (certainly when the law is one of the most restrictive of its kind), and on this record it would be unreasonable to accord this assumed state interest more than very modest significance.

3

What is left of the State's claim must be downgraded further for one final reason: regardless of the interest the State may have in adopting a photo identification requirement as a general matter, that interest in no way necessitates the particular burdens the Voter ID Law imposes on poor people and religious objectors. Individuals unable to get photo identification are forced to travel to the county seat every time they wish to exercise the franchise, and they have to get there within 10 days of the election. Nothing about the State's interest in fighting voter fraud justifies this requirement of a post-election trip to the county seat instead of some verification process at the polling places.

In briefing this Court, the State responds by pointing to an interest in keeping lines at polling places short. But this argument fails on its own terms, for whatever might be the number of individuals casting a provisional ballot, the State could simply allow voters to sign the indigency affidavit at the polls subject to review there after the election.

Indeed, the State's argument more than fails; it backfires, in implicitly conceding that a not-insignificant number of individuals will need to rely on the burdensome provisional-ballot mechanism. What is more, as the District Court found, the Voter ID Law itself actually increases the likelihood of delay at the polls. Since any minor discrepancy between a voter's photo identification card and the registration information may lead to a challenge, "the opportunities for presenting challenges ha[ve] increased as a result of the photo identification requirements." [District court opinion.]

B

The State's asserted interests in modernizing elections and combating fraud are decidedly modest; at best, they fail to offset the clear inference that thousands of Indiana citizens will be discouraged from voting. The two remaining justifications, meanwhile, actually weaken the State's case.

[Justice Souter addresses Indiana's contention that it imposed the Voter ID law in part in response to its own failure to maintain accurate voter registration lists.]

How any of this can justify restrictions on the right to vote is difficult to say. The State is simply trying to take advantage of its own wrong: if it is true that the State's fear of in-person voter impersonation fraud arises from its bloated voter checklist, the answer to the problem is in the State's own hands.

The State's final justification, its interest in safeguarding voter confidence, similarly collapses. The problem with claiming this interest lies in its connection to the bloated voter rolls; the State has come up with nothing to suggest that its citizens doubt the integrity of the State's electoral process, except its own failure to maintain its rolls. The answer to this problem is not to burden the right to vote, but to end the official negligence.

It should go without saying that none of this is to deny States' legitimate interest in safeguarding public confidence. It is simply not plausible to assume here, with no evidence of in-person voter impersonation fraud in a State, and very little of it nationwide, that a public perception of such fraud is nevertheless "inherent" in an election system providing severe criminal penalties for fraud and mandating signature checks at the polls.

C

If more were needed to condemn this law, our own precedent would provide it, for the calculation revealed in the Indiana statute crosses a line when it targets the poor and the weak. The State's requirements here, that people without cars travel to a motor vehicle registry and that the poor who fail to do that get to their county seats within 10 days of every election, translate into unjustified economic burdens uncomfortably close to the outright $1.50 fee we struck down 42 years ago [in *Harper*]. Like that fee, the onus of the Indiana law is illegitimate just because it correlates with no state interest so well as it does with the object of deterring poorer residents from exercising the franchise.

Justice BREYER, dissenting.

I believe the statute is unconstitutional because it imposes a disproportionate burden upon those eligible voters who lack a driver's license or other statutorily valid form of photo ID. I share the general view of the lead opinion insofar as it holds that the Constitution does not *automatically* forbid Indiana from enacting a photo ID requirement. I cannot agree, however, with Justice Stevens' or Justice Scalia's assessment of the burdens imposed by the statute. The Carter-Baker Commission *conditioned* its recommendation upon the States' willingness to ensure that the requisite photo IDs "be easily available and issued free of charge" and that the requirement be "phased in" over two federal election cycles, to ease the transition. Indiana's law fails to satisfy these aspects of the Commission's recommendation.

By way of contrast, two other States—Florida and Georgia—have put into practice photo ID requirements significantly less restrictive than Indiana's. Under the Florida law, the range of permissible forms of photo ID is substantially greater than in Indiana. Moreover, a Florida voter who lacks photo ID may cast a provisional ballot at the polling place that will be counted if the State determines that his signature matches the one on his voter registration form.

Georgia restricts voters to a more limited list of acceptable photo IDs than does Florida, but accepts in addition to proof of voter registration a broader range of underlying documentation than does Indiana. While Indiana allows only certain groups such as the elderly and disabled to vote by absentee ballot, in Georgia *any* voter may vote absentee without providing any excuse, and (except where required by federal law) need not present a photo ID in order to do so. Finally, neither Georgia nor Florida insists, as Indiana does, that indigent voters travel each election cycle to potentially distant places for the purposes of signing an indigency affidavit.

NOTE ON VOTER ID LAWS SINCE *CRAWFORD*

In 2011 and 2012, in advance of the presidential election in which Barack Obama would be seeking a second term, 15 state legislatures passed new voter ID laws, although governors in three states prevented the enactment of them. Moreover, notwithstanding *Crawford*, in none of the states that adopted strict forms of photo-only voter ID laws did the judiciary permit those laws to take effect for the 2012 election. For example, a federal court denied preclearance under section 5 of the Voting Rights Act to Texas's new strict photo ID law, finding it to have a retrogressive effect (this decision predated the Supreme Court's 2013 decision in *Shelby County*). Following *Shelby County* and Texas's announcement that it would implement its voter ID law, the Obama Administration sued Texas, claiming that its voter ID law violates Section 2 of the VRA.

In addition, state courts in Pennsylvania and Wisconsin blocked enforcement of those states' voter ID laws on state constitutional grounds. The essence of the Pennsylvania court's reasoning was that the purported benefits of the new law, in terms of reducing the risk of voter fraud, did not outweigh the burdens that the law imposed. In other words, the Pennsylvania court conducted a balancing test similar to the one employed by the plurality in *Crawford*, but it simply reached the opposite conclusion (as did, of course, the *Crawford* dissenters)—at least with respect to the state's desire to implement the law for the 2012 election. This litigation is ongoing, however, and the court (or a Pennsylvania appellate court) might ultimately uphold the law once the state can prove that it will sufficiently implement the law so as not to disenfranchise too many voters. Similarly, two Wisconsin judges determined that its state constitution grants the right to vote subject only to certain criteria (such as citizenship in the state, residency in the electoral district, and age) and that the voter ID law was an additional qualification beyond what the state constitution expressly allows. These state judges may have believed that they had greater latitude in protecting the right to vote more vigorously (as compared to federal jurisprudence) because the Pennsylvania and Wisconsin constitutions, unlike the federal Constitution, explicitly protect the fundamental right to vote as an entitlement of adult citizenship. (In fact, virtually all state constitutions explicitly grant the right to vote to their citizens.) The Wisconsin cases are under appeal (with one court of appeals already reversing on narrow, fact-specific grounds), and the Wisconsin Supreme Court has agreed to hear these appeals.

Moreover, Wisconsin's voter ID law is under consideration in federal court, where a trial has occurred on both *Crawford*-type Equal Protection claims applicable to all voters regardless of race and VRA-specific claims concerning the racially discriminatory effect of the law. This federal court litigation over Wisconsin's voter ID law is receiving considerable attention not only because of Wisconsin's status as a prominent battleground state in presidential elections, but also because Wisconsin is within the Seventh Circuit—the same one as Indiana and thus the one from which *Crawford* came. When *Crawford* was in the Seventh Circuit, Judge Richard Posner (the especially prominent and prolific jurist) wrote the appellate court's opinion upholding the law. Since then, Judge Posner has backed away from his opinion, saying that it was based on the absence of evidence concerning the degree of burden imposed by the ID requirement, and thereby suggesting that the outcome might well be different in a case with a different record.* The federal-court litigation over Wisconsin's ID law has included an eight-day evidentiary trial, and thus there has been speculation about how Judge Posner will assess the record in that case if and when it comes before him in the Seventh Circuit (either as part of a three-judge panel or upon en banc consideration).

In most states, these new voter ID laws were adopted by legislatures in which the Republican Party had a majority of both houses, and these laws were widely perceived as a partisan effort to tilt the electoral playing field in favor of Republicans. Indeed, in Pennsylvania, the Republican leader in the state's House of Representatives, Mike Turzai, was caught on tape in a closed-door GOP meeting, bragging: "Voter ID, which is gonna allow Governor Romney to win the state of Pennsylvania, done." Although the courts did not cite the partisan motives behind the new voter ID laws as a justification for blocking their enforcement in 2012, it seems clear that the courts saw their role as preventing partisan and unwarranted disenfranchisement of valid voters as a consequence of these new voter ID laws. For example, the Pennsylvania judge who blocked enforcement of that state's law specifically invoked the "disenfranchisement" that the law would cause as the reason for his ruling.

The enactment of strict new voter ID laws did not end in 2012. Since then, Arkansas, North Carolina, and Virginia have adopted photo-only versions of voter ID. North Carolina's law was enacted in the aftermath of *Shelby County* and is part of an omnibus package of new voting rules that are seen by many as a Republican effort to make it more difficult for Democratic supporters to vote. Immediately upon its enactment, various voting rights groups filed multiple lawsuits to challenge the law's validity as violating both federal and state constitutional law as well as Section 2 of the VRA.

This flurry of new voter ID laws, followed by widespread judicial nullification of those laws (at least temporarily), indicates that the American electoral system is in a state of

* In a new book, Judge Posner writes: "I plead guilty to having written the majority opinion (affirmed by the Supreme Court) upholding Indiana's requirement that prospective voters prove their identity with a photo ID—a type of law now widely regarded as a means of voter suppression rather than of fraud prevention." Richard Posner, Reflections on Judging 84-85 (2013) (citation omitted). In a subsequent *New Republic* essay, however, Judge Posner elaborated upon that single sentence from the book:

> I did not say that my decision, and the Supreme Court's decision affirming it (written, be it noted, by the notably liberal Justice Stevens), were wrong, only that, in common with many other judges, I could not be confident that it was right, since I am one of the judges who doesn't understand the electoral process sufficiently well to be able to gauge the consequences of decisions dealing with that process. . . .
> We judges weren't given, in *Crawford*, the data we would have needed to balance the good and bad effects of the Indiana law. . . . Given such empirical uncertainty, we naturally were reluctant to invalidate the law in the name of the Constitution; to have done so would have plunged the federal courts deeply into the management of the electoral process—a managerial responsibility that sections 1 and 4 of Article I of the Constitution actually consign to the states.

Richard Posner, *I Did Not "Recant" on Voter ID Laws*, New Republic, Oct.27, 2013, ***available at*** http://www.newrepublic.com/article/115363/richard-posner-i-did-not-recant-my-opinion-voter-id. But the *New Republic* essay (which Posner has since described as "the fullest and most accurate summary of my views on the matter") also acknowledges that "I may well have been wrong in *Crawford*," and in a subsequent MSNBC interview Posner described *Crawford* as mere "guesswork" at best: "We just didn't know. . . . The fact is we just didn't have the information." The various permutations of Posner's reflections on *Crawford* sparked much commentary in the blogosphere, but perhaps the most important takeaway for a student of election law is to recognize the opportunity to relitigate an issue based on new evidence.

disequilibrium with respect to the issue of voter identification. It remains to be seen whether the system can achieve equilibrium, with courts willing to let these voter ID laws take effect in advance of the 2016 presidential election because they are not unduly burdensome, or instead whether (notwithstanding *Crawford*) the strictest versions of these laws remain legally unenforceable.

---

3. The Accuracy of Voter Registration Lists

Historically, one of the biggest weaknesses of America's electoral system has been the significant inaccuracies in state and local voter registration lists. These lists have been riddled with duplications and outdated entries, with some names remaining on the rolls long after the individual has died or moved out-of-state. Sometimes the registrations lists have been bloated with so many "phantom" entries that a locality will have more registered voters than residents as indicated by the most recent census. These problems invite the suspicion that "ghost voters" will be turned into manufactured ballots that can wrongfully sway an election.

Erroneously bloated registration rolls can also lead to efforts to cleanse or "purge" the rolls of these errors, and this purging can backfire with disastrous consequences. That is one of the major problems that surfaced in Florida's mishandling of the 2000 presidential election. Thousands of eligible voters were wrongfully purged from the rolls, and when some of them went to the polls to cast their ballots they were turned away—improperly disenfranchised—because the poll workers did not see them as registered voters on the "cleansed" lists.

The federal Help America Vote Act of 2002 (HAVA) responded to this situation with several measures. First, HAVA requires states to give voters provisional ballots even if their names do not appear in the poll books, and these provisional ballots are entitled to be counted if it turns out that the state made a mistake that caused their names to be omitted (through either erroneous purging or any other administrative error). Second, HAVA contains various mechanisms and incentives designed to help states improve the accuracy of their voter registration lists in advance, so as to reduce the need to rely on risky purging procedures. One of these sections of HAVA calls for states to verify the accuracy of their voter registration databases by checking corresponding information in the state's motor vehicle registry.

The following two cases concern HAVA's database-matching protocols. The first, from Florida, addresses the consequence to a would-be voter of an unfixed mismatch upon submission of a new registration form. The second, from Ohio, addresses whether a state has an obligation to take certain steps to redress a mismatch. These suits, in other words, attack the administration of a state's database-matching practices from opposite perspectives: The plaintiffs in the Florida case, reflecting the experience of Florida in 2000, want to protect voters from being disenfranchised as a consequence of an erroneous mismatch; by contrast, the plaintiffs in the Ohio case want to protect the accuracy (and, by implication, integrity) of the state's electoral process from the consequence of having mismatched (and thus potentially unconfirmed) entries in the state's voter registration database.

Despite coming at the issue of database matching from opposite perspectives, these two cases have important features in common. Both were decided in 2008, a major presidential election year. Both involve the two most prominent "swing states" in recent presidential elections, Florida and Ohio, which have become legal as well as political battlegrounds in the quadrennial fight to win the White House. Both these decisions were decided by federal courts of appeals—the Eleventh Circuit in the Florida case and the Sixth Circuit in the Ohio case—and both decisions reveal the difficulty federal judges had that year in deciding this kind of case without the appearance of partisanship tainting their judicial reasoning. In the Florida case, the three-judge appellate panel split 2-1; the two judges in the majority were appointed by Republican presidents, and the dissenter by a Democratic president. The partisan divide among the appellate judges in the Ohio case, which was decided by the full Sixth Circuit "en banc," was even more pronounced (and will be further described when we discuss that case).

FLORIDA NAACP v. BROWNING

522 F.3d 1153 (11th Cir. 2008)

TJOFLAT, Circuit Judge:

This is an appeal of a preliminary injunction barring enforcement of a Florida voter registration statute as being preempted by two different federal statutes. The state law would require as a precondition of registering to vote for the first time in Florida that the voter disclose her driver's license number or the last four digits of her Social Security number on the registration application, and that this number match up with the number for this voter contained in the state driver's license database or the Social Security Administration's database, respectively. The district court held that plaintiffs, several organizations representing the interests of minority communities in Florida, had standing to challenge the statute, would likely succeed at trial on the merits of their claim that federal law preempts the enforcement of the state law, and would suffer irreparable injury absent relief. We affirm the district court's decision on plaintiffs' standing to prosecute this action and reverse its decision granting the preliminary injunction.

I

Title III of HAVA mandates that each state create a centralized, periodically updated database for its registration rolls, and that each registered voter must be linked to a unique identification number in this database. *See* 42 U.S.C. § 15483(a). Voters are required to provide on their registration application forms either the last four digits of their Social Security numbers or their driver's license numbers; if a voter has been issued neither number, then the state is required to assign to that voter a unique identification number for entry into the database. *See id.* at § 15483(a)(5)(A). HAVA also directs each state to determine according to its own laws whether the information provided by the registrant "is sufficient to meet the [federal] requirements." *Id.* at § 15483(a)(5)(A)(iii).

The state statute challenged in this case, Florida Statutes § 97.053(6) ("Subsection 6"), was enacted as part of Florida's implementation of HAVA. As amended, Subsection 6 imposes a new verification process as a precondition of voter registration for first-time registrants in Florida. Under Florida law, valid registration is a prerequisite to voting in elections. To be eligible to register to vote, a person must be a citizen of the United States, a permanent resident of Florida, over the age of eighteen, and not have been convicted of a felony or adjudicated mentally incapacitated. *See* Fla. Stat. § 97.041. Florida law also requires the voter to file her registration application at least twenty-nine days before a scheduled election, the so-called book closing date, in order to be eligible to vote in that election. *See* Fla. Stat. § 97.053(3)-(4); § 97.055.

To complete a registration form, the applicant must disclose certain personal identifying information, including the applicant's name, home address, and date of birth. Additionally, both Subsection 6 and HAVA require each applicant to provide either her Florida driver's license (or state-issued non-driver identification) number or the last four digits of the applicant's Social Security number when registering to vote. Subsection 6 also requires that before an application is accepted and the voter is listed as registered, the Florida Department of State must first verify or match the number provided in the application with the number assigned to the applicant's name by the state Department of Highway Safety and Motor Vehicles ("DHSMV") or the Social Security Administration ("SSA").

The consequences of the matching procedure are at the center of this controversy. After a voter completes the registration application form and turns it in to the county election officials, the Department of State takes the information on the application form and compares it electronically against the information contained in the DHSMV and SSA databases. If the information the applicant fills out on her registration form cannot be matched to the information held by the DHSMV or the SSA, the registration will not be completed and the applicant will receive a brief and generic notification through the mail to that effect.

What the voter must do to correct the mistake depends on the nature of the error, which unfortunately is not always made known to the applicant before she goes to correct it. If an error was made by the Department of State, e.g., during the data entry or matching process someone transposes two digits of a driver's license number, then the applicant needs to present documentary proof, like a copy of her driver's license or Social Security card, to the county Supervisor of Elections showing that the identification information she submitted in her application was correct. The voter can do this either before election day, or she can go to the polls on election day and cast a provisional ballot and then within two days bring the proof to the Supervisor of Elections. *See* Fla. Stat. § 97.053(6); § 101.048 (specifying the procedure for validating a provisional ballot).

However, if the error was made by the applicant herself—either by transposing digits in the entry of the driver's license number or by entering a nickname or maiden name instead of the precise spelling of her legal name—then the only way to cure the defect and be eligible to vote in the upcoming election is by filing a new application with the correct information *before the book closing date*.[4] There is no post-election way to fix an applicant-side error, and the provisional ballot cast by such a voter would not be counted because the voter would have failed to register in time. *See* Fla. Stat. § 101.048(2)(b)2 ("If it is determined that the person voting the provisional ballot was not registered, then the provisional ballot shall not be counted").

II

Plaintiffs filed this suit in the United States District Court for the Northern District of Florida and simultaneously moved for a preliminary injunction against the Florida Secretary of State, seeking to block the enforcement of Subsection 6 prior to the book closing date for the primary election held on January 29, 2008. The amended complaint raises a host of claims for relief under 42 U.S.C. § 1983, alleging that Subsection 6 violates the fundamental right to vote contained in the First and Fourteenth Amendments, the Equal Protection Clause of the Fourteenth Amendment, and the Due Process Clause of the Fourteenth Amendment. It also raises statutory claims, alleging that Subsection 6 conflicts with and is preempted by the following: section 303 of HAVA, 42 U.S.C. § 15483; section 2 of the Voting Rights Act of 1965, 42 U.S.C. § 1973; Title I of the Civil Rights Act of 1964, 42 U.S.C. § 1971(a)(2)(B); and the National Voter Registration Act, 42 U.S.C. § 1973gg-6.

[T]he district court granted plaintiffs' motion for preliminary injunction. It found that plaintiffs are likely to succeed on the merits of their conflict preemption claims under HAVA and Title I of the Civil Rights Act of 1964, 42 U.S.C. § 1971, and that without a remedy the plaintiffs would likely suffer irreparable harm once the book closing date passed.

Because the statutory claims under HAVA and § 1971 were sufficient to grant plaintiffs' motion, the court avoided deciding whether the constitutional challenges were likely to succeed on the merits. On plaintiffs' remaining two statutory claims—under Section 2 of the Voting Rights Act and under the National Voter Registration Act—the court granted the Secretary's motion to dismiss. The Secretary now appeals the district court's order granting the preliminary injunction.

4. This rule has the practical effect of moving back the date before each election by which voters must register, which is currently set at twenty-nine days before the election. *See* Fla. Stat. § 97.055. Since there is always a risk of making a mistake on the form, applicants must know to file the application early enough so that they can be notified of a mismatch and refile the application before the book closing date.

III

[Standing discussion omitted.]

IV

Because we conclude that the federal statutes do not conflict with and preempt Subsection 6, and therefore that plaintiffs [cannot] prevail on the merits of these claims, we need not discuss the [equitable] factors of the preliminary injunction analysis. This Part [of the opinion] addresses preemption under HAVA; Part V [of the opinion] discusses § 1971 of the Civil Rights Act of 1964.

At bottom this is a case about statutory interpretation, viz., whether Congress intended either HAVA or § 1971(a)(2) of the Civil Rights Act to displace state laws like Subsection 6. The Secretary urges us to apply a presumption against preemption because states have traditionally regulated elections. Although his observation of the states' traditional role is well-taken, in practice it is difficult to understand what a presumption in preemption cases amounts to, as we are surely not requiring Congress to state expressly that a given state law is preempted using some formula or magic words. Either Congress intended to displace certain state laws or it did not. Federal law is not obliged to bend over backwards to accommodate contradictory state laws, as should be clear from the Supremacy Clause's blanket instruction that federal law is the "supreme Law of the land . . . any Thing in the Constitution or Laws of any State to the Contrary notwithstanding." U.S. Const. art. VI, cl. 2. Thus, whether an area of law is one of traditional state regulation does not affect whether we will put a thumb on the scale against giving effect to what Congress intended. But hewing to congressional intent cuts both ways. Although we will not apply a presumption to give less preemptive effect than Congress intended, we will also not apply an overly broad construction of the statute's supposed objectives to give more than Congress intended.

HAVA represents Congress's attempt to strike a balance between promoting voter access to ballots on the one hand and preventing voter impersonation fraud on the other. Plaintiffs argue that Subsection 6 conflicts with this balance in three separate instances. First, plaintiffs argue that HAVA section 303(a) conflicts with Subsection 6. Section 303(a) sets forth the requirements for the creation of new state voter registration databases. It requires states to keep up-to-date and accurate rolls of registered voters and to eliminate redundant entries. Another provision of the subparagraph also requires registration applicants to provide a unique identification number—either a driver's license number, a Social Security number, or a unique number assigned specifically for this purpose—and requires the state to verify this number on new voter registration applications in accordance with a procedure of the state's choosing. *See* [42 U.S.C.] § 15483(a)(5).

Plaintiffs contend that the objective of section 303(a) is to ensure that states keep accurate records of registered voters, and that it was not intended to prescribe matching as a federal precondition for voter registration. Further, plaintiffs argue that Florida misunderstood what section 303(a) required and consequently acted as though HAVA mandated matching as a precondition to registration, resulting in the enactment of Subsection 6. The negative implication of section 303(a)'s actual objective is, so it goes, that HAVA prohibits states from using the identification verification process as a basis for excluding otherwise eligible voters. Assuming that plaintiffs are right that section 303(a)(5) of HAVA does not impose matching as a requirement of voter registration, it also does not seem to prohibit states from implementing it. *See* 42 U.S.C. § 15483(a)(5)(A)(iii) ("The State shall determine whether the information provided by an individual is sufficient to meet the requirements of this subparagraph, in accordance with State law."). It [also] is certainly possible to comply with both HAVA section 303(a) and Subsection 6. Indeed, if plaintiffs are correct that section 303(a) is really just concerned with managing databases, then it has nothing whatsoever to do with the registration requirements of Subsection 6 and cannot be in conflict with it. Plaintiffs have failed to show how making matching a prerequisite to registration undermines the functioning of the database itself, which is, under plaintiffs' own interpretation of the statute, the only objective of section 303(a).

Second, plaintiffs argue that HAVA section 303(b) also conflicts with Subsection 6. At the outset, it is important to point out a crucial difference between the subject matter of Subsection 6 and of section 303(b). Section 303(b) deploys HAVA's provisions against voter impersonation fraud by imposing additional restrictions on those individuals who registered by mail before they can *vote* either a regular or a provisional ballot. It is not a federal *registration* provision. Every command in section 303(b) applies only to voters who have already registered—specifically, registered by mail instead of in person—according to the laws of that voter's state. Simplified, section 303(b) requires voters who registered by mail to verify their identity in any one of three ways before casting a regular ballot. First, the voter can present some form of identification from a pre-approved statutory list at the polling location (or send a copy of the identification with her mail-in vote). *See* 42 U.S.C. § 15483(b)(2)(A). The second and third ways of verifying identity in order to vote occur at the point of registration, but they are not registration requirements under section 303(b). A voter can verify her identity either by presenting the same forms of acceptable identification or by matching up one of her identification numbers (driver's license or Social Security) when she registers to vote. *Id.* § 15483(b)(3)(A)-(B). Nothing in this provision states or suggests that Congress intended to alter state registration requirements, and certainly nothing in the section suggests that voters can bypass state registration requirements entirely as long as they satisfy federal identification requirements for voting a regular ballot.

To succeed on this argument, plaintiffs would have to demonstrate how a provision dealing exclusively with voting requirements can be transformed to conflict with a state statute on registration requirements. The only argument made for a textual conflict is that upholding Subsection 6 would render HAVA section 303(b)(3)(B) superfluous. Plaintiffs contend that this section, which exempts those voters who pass the matching requirement at registration from showing identification at voting, would be unnecessary if Subsection 6 stands because every voter would need to match their Social Security or driver's license numbers at registration. This utterly misapplies the familiar canon of construction that "a statute ought, upon the whole, to be so construed that, if it can be prevented, no clause, sentence, or word shall be superfluous, void, or insignificant." *TRW Inc. v. Andrews* (2001). This canon applies when courts are discerning the meanings of different provisions of the same statute, and it instructs that no portion of the statute should be read that would make another part unnecessary. Clearly this is not the case here. Plaintiffs offer no authority or reason to support an application of this canon to two different statutes from two separate sovereigns, and such an approach would be untenable anyway. If courts were to adopt plaintiffs' interpretive method, then every federal statute that is consistent and parallel with a state statute would, paradoxically, have the opposite effect of preempting the state statute since the state statute would otherwise make the federal statute superfluous.

Third, plaintiffs argue that Subsection 6 conflicts with HAVA section 303(b)(2)(B)'s so-called fail-safe voting provision, which states that "[a]n individual who desires to vote in person, but who does not meet the [identification] requirements . . . may cast a provisional ballot" as described in section 302(a) of HAVA. Section 302(a) of HAVA, in turn, provides that a voter who "does not appear on the official list of eligible voters for the polling place" or who is claimed by the election official not to be an eligible voter, can cast a provisional ballot upon affirming that the voter is registered and is eligible to vote. *See* 42 U.S.C. § 15482(a). Once the provisional ballot is cast, the election official is to determine whether the individual is "eligible under State law to vote," and the official must count the ballot if the voter is eligible. *See id.* § 15482(a)(4).

It is not entirely clear what plaintiffs' interpretation of HAVA's provisional ballot provisions is, or where they think the conflict with Subsection 6 lies. HAVA section 302(a) describes general procedures for casting and reviewing provisional ballots; it does not impose any federal standards on voter registration or voter eligibility, both of which remain state decisions. Subsection 6 itself states that a voter who has failed to register due to a mismatch of the identification numbers can cast a provisional ballot, which will be counted if the voter can verify the information provided within two days of the election date. *See* Fla. Stat. § 97.053(6). HAVA section 302(a) expressly states that a provisional ballot be counted only if the voter is eligible under state law to vote in that particular election. Registration is an eligibility requirement under the Florida constitution and statutes. Subsection 6's provisional ballot measures are consistent with HAVA section 302(a), as both statutes would count only those provisional ballots cast by voters who were eligible—in Florida, registered—to vote in the election.

Perhaps plaintiffs interpret HAVA to mean that any voter eligible *to register* under state law is entitled to have her provisional ballot count under section 302(a). Commentators have called this interpretation the "substantive vision of provisional voting," which means that "the provisional ballot should count whenever the individual who casts the ballot is someone who substantively has the qualifications necessary to be a registered voter." Edward B. Foley, *The Promise and Problems of Provisional Voting,* 73 GEO. WASH. L. REV. 1193, 1194 (2005).[18] Such an interpretation would turn section 302 into a sweeping federal invalidation of state voter registration requirements, and while textually plausible it is not, in our judgment, the intent of Congress in enacting HAVA section 302.

Section 302 states that a voter wishing to cast a provisional ballot must be "registered" to vote in her state and must execute a written affirmation to that effect. It is only after the voter affirms that she is registered and is eligible to vote that she can even fill out a provisional ballot. These parts of section 302 in clear terms indicate that Congress did not intend to do away with the importance and consequences of state registration requirements. Once the provisional ballot has been cast, the state election officials must then "determine[ ] that the individual is eligible" to vote before counting the ballot. 42 U.S.C. § 15482(a)(4).

It is worth noting that although Congress drew a distinction between a voter being registered and a voter being eligible earlier in the same subsection, *see id.*§ 15482(a)(2)(A)-(B), the verification subsection speaks only of determining whether a voter is "eligible under State law," not whether the voter ever successfully registered. It is plausible to interpret this subsection, and its omission of two words like "and registered," to mean that Congress rewrote all state voter registration law to be nonmandatory for voters wishing to cast a (provisional) ballot, in effect adopting the procedural* vision of provisional voting, *see supra* note 18. Indeed this seems to be the dissent's understanding of Congress's intent behind this provision. But an equally plausible textual interpretation that is more consistent with congressional intent evidenced by the rest of HAVA is that by the term "eligible under State law," Congress intended to incorporate state law on the issue instead of creating a federal standard. In other words, section 302(a) lets the states decide whether a voter who is not registered but is otherwise eligible to vote should have her provisional ballot counted anyway. *Cf. Sandusky County Democratic Party v. Blackwell* (6th Cir. 2004) (discussing state law that may permit voters to cast provisional ballots outside of their registered precincts). Thus, under HAVA section 302, states can still choose whether they will effectively waive the registration requirement for voters casting provisional ballots. Florida has chosen not to do so, and that decision conflicts with neither section 302(a) nor with section 303(b)(2)(B) of HAVA.

18. Contrast this with the "procedural vision" of provisional voting, which means that "if the local election board never officially registered an individual because of an incomplete registration form . . . the individual is out of luck." Edward B. Foley, *The Promise and Problems of Provisional Voting,* 73 GEO. WASH. L. REV. 1193, 1195 (2005); *see also id.* ("The procedural vision of provisional voting . . . mean[s] that if an omission were to be caused by voter error . . . the individual would be stuck with the consequences.").

* [Editors' note: The opinion says "procedural" here, but in context it seems as if the court meant instead that Congress adopted the "substantive" vision of provisional voting.]

It is appropriate now to look through a wider lens, lest we miss the forest of Congress's intent for the trees of HAVA's clumsy subsections and clauses. Plaintiffs' preemption argument comes down to the claim that HAVA presents a fixed federal standard for the identification requirements that states may impose on individual voters, and that any state standard more demanding or burdensome must give way. Subsection 6 is and was intended to be such an identity verification provision that is unquestionably more demanding and less flexible than the alternative methods of identity verification provided by HAVA. The question remains whether Subsection 6 sufficiently impedes HAVA's objectives as to be preempted by it. Plaintiffs argue that HAVA's standards for voter identification are in effect the national maximum (and presumably minimum as well) that any state may impose on voters.

Reading HAVA Title III as a whole, we are not convinced that its objectives are to federalize voter identification standards. First, at multiple points throughout the statute, HAVA dynamically incorporates state law requirements instead of promulgating national standards. Second, section 304 of HAVA states explicitly that "[t]he requirements established by this subchapter are minimum requirements." *Id.* § 15484. Plaintiffs point out that the section goes on to say that stricter state requirements for "election technology and administration" cannot be "inconsistent with the Federal requirements." *Id.* Although this congressional hedge means that HAVA section 304 is not a silver bullet for the Secretary's position, it also throws some doubt on plaintiffs' claim that HAVA evinces a uniform national voter identification policy as it clearly contemplates the existence of requirements more restrictive than the federal minimum. [P]laintiffs have been unable to show how Subsection 6 is inconsistent with any of the specific "requirements" of HAVA. Their argument that it is inconsistent with some more nebulous conception of HAVA's objective fails once we recognize that on issues relating to voter registration and identification not specifically addressed by HAVA, Congress essentially punted to the states.

Third, if HAVA were intended to preempt all state laws like Subsection 6, then we would expect to see a more comprehensive regulation of voter registration and identification. Instead, what we actually have in HAVA section 303(b) is a provision covering only mail-in registrants. There is nothing at all in the statute that discusses the requirements and procedures for establishing eligibility and identity of in-person registrants. Thus, so far as the specific requirements of HAVA section 303(b) are concerned, we must conclude that Congress left it entirely up to the states to prescribe the requirements for in-person registrants. Under plaintiffs' own interpretation, section 303(b) would preempt Subsection 6 as applied to mail-in registrants whose Social Security and drivers' license numbers failed to match, but not as applied to in-person registrants who had the same problem. Yet this would mean that section 303(b) would be more protective of mail-in registrants—the very group upon whom Congress imposed additional federal identification requirements to counteract greater perceived risks of impersonation fraud—than of in-person registrants in states like Florida. If Congress had wanted the verification methods described in section 303(b) to apply to all voters nationally, it would have said so. If it had intended even less demanding methods to apply nationally for in-person registrants, it would have said that as well. The fact that the statute addresses only one specific subgroup of registrants is more consistent with the Secretary's interpretation of HAVA—that it created some minimum verification procedures for one specific group where concerns of fraud were particularly high but otherwise left the states free to draw up their own voter identification measures.

V

We next consider whether Subsection 6 conflicts with § 1971(a) of the Civil Rights Act.[20] As with the analysis of HAVA, the task with § 1971(a) is determining whether Subsection 6 stands as an obstacle to the objectives of the federal statute. We conclude that it does not.

Section 1971(a)(2)(B) was originally enacted as part of Title I of the Civil Rights Act of 1964. The measure was at the time the latest entry in a spurt of federal enforcement of voting rights after a long slumber following syncopated efforts during Reconstruction. Statutes enacted in 1870, 1871, 1957, and 1960 had all been unsuccessful attempts to counteract state and local government tactics of using, among other things, burdensome registration requirements to disenfranchise African-Americans. This latest addition to federal law was "necessary to sweep away such tactics as disqualifying an applicant who failed to list the exact number of months and days in his age." Such trivial information served no purpose other than as a means of inducing voter-generated errors that could be used to justify rejecting applicants.

The requirements of Subsection 6 are, of course, not trivial or irrelevant in the way that the specific kinds of information requests targeted by Congress in enacting § 1971(a)(2)(B) were trivial. Although Subsection 6 does not present a paradigmatic violation of § 1971(a)(2)(B), we recognize that Congress in combating specific evils might choose a broader remedy. The text of the resulting statute, and not the historically motivating examples of intentional and overt racial discrimination, is thus the appropriate starting point of inquiry in discerning congressional intent.

The text of § 1971(a)(2)(B) prohibits denying the right to vote based on errors or omissions that are not material in determining voter eligibility. *See* 42 U.S.C. § 1971(a)(2)(B). The term "material" not surprisingly signifies different degrees of importance in different legal contexts. In constitutionalized criminal procedure, exculpatory evidence is "material only if there is a reasonable probability that, had the evidence

20. The relevant portion of the statute reads:

(2) No person acting under color of state law shall-

(B) deny the right of any individual to vote in any election because of an error or omission on any record or paper relating to any application [or] registration . . . if such error or omission is not material in determining whether [the] individual is qualified under State law to vote in such election. 42 U.S.C. § 1971(a)(2)(B).

been disclosed to the defense, the result of the proceeding would have been different." *United States v. Bagley* (1985). In the voluminous jurisprudence of section 10b of the 1934 Securities Exchange Act and Rule 10b-5, a misrepresentation or omission is material if and only if there is a "substantial likelihood that the disclosure of the omitted fact would have been viewed by the reasonable investor as having significantly altered the 'total mix' of information made available." *TSC Indus., Inc. v. Northway, Inc.* (1976).

However, in the federal criminal mail and wire fraud context, materiality seems to take on a much lower evidentiary threshold, for "a false statement is material if it has a natural tendency to influence, or is capable of influencing, the decision of the decision making body to which it was addressed." *United States v. Gray* (11th Cir. 2004). Similarly, in the context of sentencing range enhancements for concealing evidence under the federal Sentencing Guidelines, we have observed that the threshold for materiality is "conspicuously low," such that material information is "information that, if believed, would tend to influence or affect the issue under determination." *United States v. Dedeker* (11th Cir. 1992).

Roughly speaking, there appears to be two kinds of "materiality," one similar to minimal relevance and the other closer to outcome-determinative. If materiality in the context of § 1971(a)(2)(B) means minimal relevance, then it is clear that a failure to match the information required under Subsection 6 is "material" to determining voter eligibility. An application that fails to match up the identification numbers tends to make it more likely that the applicant is not a qualified voter than if the numbers had matched.

If materiality means something more like outcome-determinative, then the Secretary would have to meet a higher burden in demonstrating that the information required to make a match is necessary or sufficient, along with other information available, to determining eligibility. Fortunately for the Secretary, Congress has already resolved this potentially difficult issue in his favor by enacting HAVA section 303(a). The fact that HAVA section 303(a) requires states to obtain the applicant's identification numbers before accepting a registration application and also to "determine whether the information provided . . . is sufficient to meet [that] requirement[ ]" indicates that Congress deemed the identification numbers material to determining eligibility to register and to vote.[21] 42 U.S.C. § 15483(a)(5)(A)(iii). Moreover, the section 303(a)(5) issues this directive to states "notwithstanding any other provision of law," which of course includes the temporally prior § 1971(a)(2)(B). We doubt that Congress would mandate the gathering of information—indeed, that it would make that a precondition for accepting registration application—that it also deems immaterial. Read together, HAVA section 303(a) removes

21. To be sure, HAVA also does not require that states authenticate these numbers by matching them against existing databases. It is explicit that states are to make determinations of validity in accordance with state law. States are therefore free to accept the numbers provided on application form, which at least in Florida are completed with an oath or affirmation under penalty of perjury, as self-authenticating. This does not alter the materiality of the information itself.

specific kinds of information from § 1971(a)'s domain by making those kinds of information automatically material.[22]

Plaintiffs argue that whether or not the underlying information sought by the registration is material, an error caused by a typo cannot be material because it does not reflect the absence of any actual, substantive element that makes the applicant ineligible. The mistaken premise in this argument is that the materiality provision refers to the nature of the error rather than the nature of the underlying information requested. If plaintiffs were correct and materiality refers to the fact of the error itself, then no error would ever be material because an error by definition mistakenly and *incorrectly* represents the underlying substantive element of eligibility. A more sound interpretation of § 1971(a)(2)(B) asks whether, accepting the error *as true and correct,* the information contained in the error is material to determining the eligibility of the applicant. As discussed above, HAVA makes that information material.[23]

Ultimately, the thrust of plaintiffs' argument is not that the information sought by HAVA and Subsection 6 are immaterial, but that the likelihood of error combined with the consequences are unjustifiably burdensome on the applicant in light of other available and more error-tolerant ways of verifying identity, and in light of the overall balance of effects on social utility. That is an argument for another day. Section 1971(a)(2)(B) does not establish a least-restrictive-alternative test for voter registration applications in the plain text of the statute. Finding no conflict between Subsection 6 and § 1971(a)(2)(B) of the Civil Rights Act, we conclude that the Florida law is not preempted.

VI

For the foregoing reasons, we reverse the district court's decision granting plaintiffs a preliminary injunction. The case is remanded for further proceedings not inconsistent herewith.

22. In a way, this issue in this case is the mirror image of the one decided in *Schwier v. Cox* (N.D. Ga. 2005), aff'd (11th Cir. 2006). *Schwier* involved a challenge to Georgia's Voter Registration Form, which had required the plaintiff applicants to disclose their full Social Security numbers to be verified. The district court held, and we affirmed, that the Georgia law conflicted with § 1971(a)(2)(B)'s materiality provision because Congress had made it illegal in a different statute, section 7(b) of the Privacy Act, 5 U.S.C. § 552a (note), to mandate the disclosure of one's complete Social Security number without providing certain information and notice to the individual. Because the Georgia registration form ran afoul of the section 7(b) of the Privacy Act, the Social Security number was per se immaterial under § 1971(a)(2)(B). Here, because Congress required the identification numbers to be on voter registration applications, they are per se material under § 1971(a)(2)(B).

23. The standard that the dissent proposes, that an error is immaterial if it would not "preclude a reasonable election official from identifying the applicant," works only when the applicant has brought it to the election official's attention that the mismatch is in fact an error by presenting proof of her identity and eligibility. Without this additional identifying information, such as a copy of the applicant's driver's license, it would be impossible to tell whether the applicant's error was major, minor, or indeed an error at all (as opposed to an actual attempt at fraudulently registering). However, with this additional information, the election official will always be able to verify identity of the applicant. It is this additional information exclusively—and not the degree to which that new information deviates from the information on the registration application form, or the "nature of the error"—that enables the election official to ascertain the identity of the voter. Thus, under this approach no error can ever be material.

BARKETT, Circuit Judge, dissenting.

I dissent from the majority's determination that Plaintiffs are not entitled to a preliminary injunction against the enforcement of Florida Statutes § 97.053(6) ("Subsection 6"), which impermissibly disenfranchises Florida citizens.

Florida and the majority read this provision to say that the match from the official database must be, not to the actual and valid driver's license or social security card, but to the name and number placed on the registration application. Under the majority's interpretation of this provision, regardless of an applicant's proof of eligibility, any provisional vote legitimately cast in an election will not be counted if an applicant's name or number is erroneously *copied* onto the application form. An individual's ability to cast a provisional ballot therefore turns not on whether he or she is *eligible* to vote, but on whether the name or number on the registration application contains a mistake.

Such a requirement for voting violates the Help America Vote Act of 2002 ("HAVA"), the Voting Rights Act, and the First and Fourteenth Amendments of the Constitution. Moreover, I cannot believe that this interpretation was intended by the Florida legislature. It is inconceivable that a state would intend that a typographical or transpositional error on a registration application could not be corrected through irrefutable proof of a valid driver's license or social security card to permit a Florida citizen's vote to be counted. [But if] Subsection 6 [is interpreted this way], Florida has impermissibly deprived a class of over 14,000 citizens—the vast majority of whom are minorities[4]—th[e] fundamental right [to vote].

I. FLORIDA'S "MATCHING" REQUIREMENT

The state and the majority take the position that such a provisional ballot may be counted *only* if the state made the mistake in the matching process but *not* if that very same mistake was made by the applicant. If an election official transposes two numbers or omits a letter, hyphen, or suffix from a name on a registration application when entering that information into the state's voter database, resulting in a non-match with either the DHSMV or SSA database, that applicant's provisional ballot will be counted upon presentation of a valid driver's license or social security card. *Id.* § 97.053(6). However, if the applicant makes the very same mistake on her application, then no matter what irrefutable proof she provides of her identity and eligibility to vote, including a valid driver's license or social security card, her provisional ballot will *never* be counted.

4. For example, African-Americans make up 13% of the applicant pool, but 26% of the unmatched voter pool. Similarly, Hispanic-Americans comprise 15% of the applicant pool, but 39% of the unmatched voter pool. To show the sharp contrast and illustrate how Subsection 6 affects minorities to a much larger extent, whites make up 66% of the applicant pool but only 17% of the unmatched voter pool. Because minority communities often have names that are unfamiliar to data-entry processors, and because they are more likely than whites to have hyphenated or compound names, the database entries are more likely to not match for minorities.

This inconsistency in the treatment of provisional ballots is compounded by the fact that there is no provision under Florida law that addresses disputes regarding whether the mistake was made by the applicant or by an election official. For example, an applicant may well argue that her application is correct, but that an election official misread the application by seeing a "7" where the applicant wrote the number "1," or by construing the number "5" as the letter "S."

[P]ermitting Florida to disenfranchise voters under this scheme violates both federal law and the Constitution.

II. SUBSECTION 6 CONFLICTS WITH HAVA

Subsection 6 completely eviscerates provisional balloting for a group of otherwise eligible voters who make a minor mistake on their registration applications. Subsection 6 permits voters to cast a provisional ballot which will be counted *only* if applicants present evidence—their driver's license or social security card—which verifies the number "provided *on [their] application*," Fla. Stat. § 97.053(6) (emphasis added). This is impossible if an applicant has made a minor mistake in writing her name or number on her application. An actual, valid driver's license or social security number will never match the registration application upon which two numbers might have been transposed, or upon which a letter or hyphen might have been inadvertently omitted from a name. According to the state, it is the match itself, not the validity of the requested information, that is determinative of a vote being counted. Thus, when an applicant makes a minor mistake on her registration application, the majority says that Florida is free to disregard HAVA's provisions for provisional balloting.

The majority reads HAVA as authorizing the administrative matching of numbers and letters as a precondition to registration. This misreading clearly conflicts with HAVA's objectives of promoting accessible and non-discriminatory methods of voting that minimize voter disenfranchisement. These objectives preclude states from using the identification-verification process as a basis for excluding actually qualified voters. While I certainly agree that states have the right to "determine whether the information provided by an individual is sufficient to meet the requirements [for voter registration under HAVA], in accordance with State law," *see* 42 U.S.C. § 15483(a)(5)(A)(iii), they cannot do so in a way that would prevent a clearly and undisputedly eligible voter from having her vote counted.

Although the majority states that we should look at HAVA through a "wider lens" so that we do not overlook Congress' intent in enacting HAVA at the expense of "HAVA's clumsy subsections and clauses," the majority fails to do what it says: to specifically look at Subsection 6 in light of HAVA's purposes. Instead, the majority begs the question by holding that Subsection 6 is permissible because Congress did not intend to prescribe uniform national standards for both voter registration and identification.

The majority reasons that because Congress did not impose uniform national standards for voter registration when it enacted HAVA, the implication is that Congress left room for states to "supplement" HAVA's provisions with laws such as Subsection 6. But HAVA does not need to prescribe uniform national standards for voter registration in order for HAVA to preempt Subsection 6. Although not preempting *all* state registration and identification laws, HAVA will preempt those state laws that act as "obstacle[s] to the accomplishment and execution of the *full* purposes and objectives of Congress." *Hines* [v. v. *Davidowitz* (1941)] (emphasis added).

Furthermore, by interpreting HAVA as allowing Florida to make administrative matching and verification a precondition of eligibility, Subsection 6 fails to pass constitutional muster. Given the choice between two interpretations of a federal statute, we should choose the one that does not deprive citizens of their fundamental constitutional rights. If we are to seriously strive in upholding the integrity of elections, citizens must be given at a bare minimum a *fair* opportunity to vote. The state's concern with fraud is not a one-way street: not only must the government make sure that individuals are not voting fraudulently, but the government must not fraudulently deprive its citizens of their lawful right to vote. With no evidence of voter fraud in Florida, and with the undisputed fact that over 14,000 individuals to date have been denied their right to vote simply because their applications have not been administratively matched, even though they may be able to prove their eligibility to vote, Subsection 6 conflicts with HAVA and is preempted by it.

III. SUBSECTION 6 VIOLATES THE VOTING RIGHTS ACT

Florida's matching scheme also violates the materiality provision of the Voting Rights Act ("VRA"). 42 U.S.C. § 1971(a)(2)(B). Although the majority acknowledges that Congress enacted [this provision] as a means of combating "burdensome [state] registration requirements to disenfranchise African-Americans," its test of "materiality" pays only lip-service to, and would frustrate, that very purpose.

To determine whether an error is material, the majority's test ignores the nature of the error and asks solely whether the underlying information containing the error is relevant in determining an applicant's eligibility to vote. I agree that this is a necessary first step. If the information is not material in determining the eligibility of the applicant, it follows that any error or omission in reporting that information necessarily would not be material and there would be no need for further analysis.*See, e.g., Schwier v. Cox* (11th Cir. 2006). But Congress recognized in passing the VRA that discriminatory registration requirements are more sophisticated and pernicious than simply asking applicants for immaterial information. Its concern was not merely with overtly discriminatory requirements that ask for irrelevant information, but also with requirements that ask for relevant information but disproportionately penalize applicants for trivial mistakes.

For example, Congress intended the VRA to eliminate the practice of disqualifying applicants who make mistakes when asked to "list the exact number of months and days in [their] age." *Condon v. Reno* (D. S.C. 1995). The majority recognizes that Congress sought to end such insidious practices, but under its test for materiality, it would have to find th[is] practice *permissible* because the underlying substantive information sought—the age of the applicant—is material in determining whether the applicant is eligible. As this application of the majority's test makes clear, it is insufficient to look solely at the "nature of the underlying information requested" to determine the materiality of an error or omission.

Therefore, even taking as true the majority's contention that an applicant's driver's license or social security number is per se material because of HAVA, (which I do not),[17] that fact alone does not end the materiality inquiry in assessing errors under Florida's matching scheme. The nature of the error must also be considered. Under Florida's scheme, an applicant with a hyphenated last name would have her application denied if the databases did not include the hyphen; similarly, an applicant who failed to include a suffix such as "Jr." or "Sr." would have his application denied. Even though the information sought is clearly relevant, these small inconsistencies would not preclude a reasonable election official from identifying the applicant and, thus, should not be considered a material error or omission.[18] Similarly, the accidental transposition of two numbers from a driver's license or social security number is not a material error under the VRA. These are the very mistakes that Congress intended to prevent states from using as "burdensome" barriers to registration.

Furthermore, the state's own practices confirm that a minor error on an application, in and of itself, is not immutably material. At oral argument, the state admitted that when it makes similar mistakes, applicants are allowed to cure those mistakes after casting a provisional ballot. Thus, if an applicant is able to correct an error made by the state, a similar error made by a voter without a meaningful opportunity to cure that error cannot be material in determining eligibility.

The VRA simply does not countenance the inhumanly strict precision demanded by Florida's matching scheme.

17. I do not believe this to be the case as HAVA does not require states to verify an applicant's identifying number. If a state is not required to verify an applicant's identifying number, then HAVA does not automatically make such information material because an individual in a state without a matching scheme could provide her driver's license or social security number and even though she may have transposed two numbers of her application, that immaterial error would not prevent her from voting in that state. Furthermore, the information cannot be per se material because HAVA provides for the assignment of a unique identifying number, which does not have to be matched, for those individuals who do not have a driver's license or social security number. The information also cannot be per se material if a state such as North Dakota is allowed to hold federal elections without any registration requirements.

18. The majority argues that this standard that an error is immaterial if it does not preclude a reasonable election official from identifying the applicant only works if the applicant presents proof of her identity or eligibility. This is simply not true. If all of an applicant's registration information matches a database but for a missing hyphen, this minor error would not preclude a reasonable election official from determining that a voter is eligible based solely on the information provided on the application itself, not based on the applicant presenting additional identifying information.

NOTE ON THE CONSTITUTIONAL QUESTIONS IN FLORIDA *NAACP v. BROWNING*

The Eleventh Circuit's majority opinion did not address the plaintiffs' constitutional claims because the district court had not reached them. Judge Barkett's dissent, however, did so. She would have found Subsection 6, in addition to being preempted by HAVA and the VRA, to be a violation of the Fourteenth Amendment. The essence of her reasoning was that Subsection 6 was "patently unfair" and thus unconstitutional because it did not provide voters with an adequate opportunity to correct minor clerical errors on their registration forms to avoid disenfranchisement. On remand from the Eleventh Circuit, however, the district court rejected the plaintiffs' constitutional claims, thereby disagreeing with Judge Barkett. The district court ruled that the matching requirement of Subsection 6 was reasonably related to the state's valid goal of avoiding voter fraud and that it was not constitutionally required for Florida to notify voters of clerical mistakes that the voters made on their registration applications, or that voters must be given the opportunity to correct those errors after the deadline for registration has passed. In doing so, the district court cited the 2008 decision in *Diaz v. Cobb* (see p. 671, below) and essentially reached the same decision, only with respect to a different specific registration prerequisite (the matching of identification numbers, instead of completed "check boxes"). *See Florida NAACP v. Browning*, 569 F. Supp. 2d 1237 (N.D. Fla. 2008). The plaintiffs did not appeal the district court's rejection of their constitutional claim, perhaps anticipating that the majority of the Eleventh Circuit would do so as well (and thus wishing to avoid more adverse precedent at the appellate level).

4. Judicial Partisanship Over HAVA Enforcement

The case you are about to read was one of many filed in Ohio in the weeks preceding the casting of ballots in the November 2008 general election. Because Ohio was perceived as a potential "swing state" in the 2008 presidential election, as it had been in 2004, lawyers on each side of the partisan divide used litigation as a tool to potentially alter the voting process to give their side a perceived benefit that might increase the chance that their presidential candidate would win. This case was the most prominent of these "election eve" lawsuits in 2008, going all the way to the U.S. Supreme Court after being decided by the full "en banc" U.S. Court of Appeals for the Sixth Circuit. Until the U.S. Supreme Court ruled unanimously in nullifying the "en banc" Sixth Circuit's order, the case exposed deep partisan divisions among the federal judges involved. It started with the Ohio Republican Party successfully obtaining an emergency Temporary Restraining Order (TRO) against Ohio's Democratic Secretary of State at the time, Jennifer Brunner, from a federal district judge who had been appointed by President Reagan. Brunner then appealed to the Sixth Circuit, where a three-judge panel split 2-1 along party lines in granting her request to stay the TRO. The Ohio Republican Party then took the case to the full Sixth Circuit, which split 10-6 in deciding to reinstate the TRO. Nine of the ten judges in the en banc majority, who ruled in favor of the Ohio Republican Party, had been appointed by Republican presidents, and five of the six judges in the en banc dissent (and who thus supported the position taken by both the Democratic Secretary of State Brunner as well as the Ohio Democratic Party, which participated in the case in support of Brunner) were appointed by Democratic presidents. The unseemly nature of this partisan split raises the question whether federal judges are capable of deciding this kind of election case "objectively" or "on the merits," without regard to their own partisan backgrounds (and the case indicates that this question can be asked equally of federal judges coming from both Republican and Democratic backgrounds). Fortunately, however, the U.S. Supreme Court was able to maintain unanimity in the case, thus avoiding a similar partisan split among its members. What follows are the principal majority and dissenting opinions at the en banc stage, as well as the Supreme Court's short unanimous order. As you read the two en banc opinions, ask yourself whether you can tell if the majority and dissent are influenced by partisanship, or instead are both sides able to clothe their positions in objective-sounding legal analysis (even if they are motivated, intentionally or unintentionally, by partisanship)?

OHIO REPUBLICAN PARTY v. BRUNNER

544 F.3d 711 (6th Cir. 2008) (en banc)

ORDER

A majority of the Judges of the Court in regular active service have voted to hear this case *en banc* and to deny the motion of the Appellant Secretary of State to vacate or stay the district court's TRO.

SUTTON, Circuit Judge, joined by Chief Judge BOGGS and Judges BATCHELDER, GILMAN, GIBBONS, COOK, MCKEAGUE, GRIFFIN and KETHLEDGE. [Judge ROGERS's separate concurrence is omitted.]

As this case comes (rapidly) to the court, the parties share some common ground. No one disputes that federal law, as described in the Help America Vote Act ("HAVA"), helps Americans cast votes and helps to ensure that their votes count in two distinct respects. In one respect, the Act makes it easier for individuals to cast ballots by establishing a vote-first-challenge-later approach to dealing with disputes about an individual's eligibility to vote, the most obvious feature of which is the right to cast a provisional ballot when an election official questions an individual's eligibility to vote. In another respect, the Act helps to ensure that those votes count, or to put it another way the Act helps to ensure that those votes are not diluted by guarding against voter fraud. The one goal complements the other: Enabling the casting of one vote does little good if another voter fraudulently cancels it out. *See Crawford v. Marion County Election Bd.* (2008); *Purcell v. Gonzalez* (2006).

No one disputes that one of the tools that HAVA creates to address fraud is found in 42 U.S.C. § 15483(a)(5)(B)(i). It says:

> (5) Verification of voter registration information
>
> . . .
>
> (B) Requirements for State officials.
>
> (i) Sharing information in databases.
>
> The chief State election official and the official responsible for the State motor vehicle authority of a State shall enter into an agreement to match information in the database of the statewide voter registration system with information in the database of the motor vehicle authority to the extent required to enable each such official to verify the accuracy of the information provided on applications for voter registration.

No one disputes that this provision places mandatory duties on the Secretary of State. At a minimum, it requires the Secretary of State, together with the head of Ohio's Bureau of Motor Vehicles ("BMV"), to agree to "match" information in BMV's database with information in the Statewide Voter Registration Database ("SWVRD"). No one disputes that the purpose of this matching is "to enable [officials] to verify the accuracy of the information provided on applications for voter registration." *Id.*

And no one disputes that the Secretary of State has put together an SWVRD System Manual, which is designed to implement these obligations. The pertinent section of that manual says the following:

> 15.4. BMV Not Confirmed (this process is currently turned off)
>
> Upon receipt of a voter registration record or update, the [Secretary of State] SWVRD will validate certain voter information with the BMV. If the [Secretary] and BMV validation is unable to match the voter record, it may not be confirmed. If this occurs the [Secretary] SWVRD sends the [county boards of election] a message stating that the record may not be "confirmed." Voter records that are not confirmed **must** have their information updated and resent to the [Secretary] SWVRD and validation with the BMV will be reattempted.

According to the Secretary of State's manual, that office at one point implemented § 15483(a)(5)(B)(i) in this way: first, if there was not a match between the Secretary's and BMV's records, the Secretary would send the county boards of elections a message indicating that the voter's registration record cannot be "confirmed"; second, after that happened, the Secretary required unconfirmed voter records to be updated and resent to the Secretary for another effort to validate them with the BMV records.

The apparent "turn[ing] off" of this voter-registration-verification process, or at least the discovery that it had been turned off, prompted this dispute. For reasons that the record does not reveal and at a time the record does not reveal, the Secretary of State apparently chose to deactivate at least part of the process, if not all of the process, described in section 15.4 of her manual. In particular, she concedes that at some point she stopped communicating with the county boards about mismatches and stopped renewing validation requests with the BMV after obtaining a mismatch. The Ohio

Republican Party ("ORP") and Larry Wolpert, a state representative, supported by affidavits from two officials of different county boards of election, challenge the Secretary's interpretation of her duties under HAVA. As they see it, § 15483(a)(5)(B)(i) requires the Secretary to do what she formerly did under section 15.4 of her manual or at least requires her to share county-by-county records of mismatches with the local boards of election. If the statute requires the Secretary only to identify mismatches but does not require her to share this information in a meaningful way with the county boards, they add, then the purpose of verifying voter records with driver's license records would be defeated, and one of HAVA's tools for ferreting out voter fraud would become an empty gesture. The Secretary responds that the county boards of election technically still have "access" to this information because they have access to the SWVRD, which permits them to check each absentee voter (or any other type of voter) for mismatches. But, in contrast to being given a list of mismatches by county or having the Secretary assist them in addressing mismatch problems, the plaintiffs say that general access to the SWVRD system is essentially useless—not unlike asking for a drink of water and being given access to a fire hose at full volume—and will do nothing to address the anti-fraud objective of this provision of HAVA.

This dispute and several others apparently grew out of the Secretary's August order to allow simultaneous registration and voting for six days in Ohio in late September and early October. In resolving today's dispute, the district court on October 10, 2008, entered a temporary restraining order ("TRO") directing the Secretary to ensure that "HAVA's matching requirements are not rendered meaningless" and to do so either by providing lists of mismatches to the county boards of elections or by providing the county boards of election with a method to search the SWVRD so that they "can isolate and review the mismatches and take appropriate action."

A panel of this court vacated the order later that same day—October 10. While I tend to agree with some aspects of the panel's decision and sympathize with the lack of time it had to address these issues (12 hours or so), I disagree with its key premises for vacating the district court's TRO.

Before addressing those issues, it is important to point out why en banc review of the panel's decision is appropriate in this matter. While in the normal course it often will be unwise and inefficient to grant en banc review of decisions like this one, this is not a normal case—as the panel's interlocutory reversal of the district court's TRO itself establishes. Section 1292(a)(1) does not give courts of appeals authority to review temporary restraining orders but only "injunctions." 28 U.S.C. § 1292(a)(1). We have correctly construed that authority to extend to TROs in limited cases, namely when a TRO effectively operates as a litigation-altering and litigation-ending injunction because it gives the parties no "meaningful appellate options" about a significant issue of law given the imminence of an irreversible event—say an execution or as here an election. The same considerations that justify the panel's decision to review this TRO—the imminence of a national election and the significance of the issues presented—provide ample justifications for the en banc court to consider doing the same.

There are three problems with the Secretary's request to stay the district court's TRO. In the first place, her interpretation of § 15483(a)(5)(B)(i) is not convincing. The key likelihood-of-success inquiry is this: does the provision permit the Secretary only to identify matches on the database (and effectively keep them to herself or, as plaintiffs put it, "throw them in the trash"), or does it require her also to verify the registration mismatches either by doing the verification herself or in cooperation with the county boards of election? So far as this record is concerned, the Secretary has given no tenable explanation why her current interpretation of the statute, as opposed to the office's prior implementation of the law, remotely furthers the anti-fraud objective of the law. A mismatch that she does not track down and that she does not allow the county boards of election meaningfully to track down is not a usable mismatch. When the Secretary argues in her papers that she has no duty to provide the most "user-friendly" system of HAVA compliance, that is something of a euphemism. As far as we can tell, the problem with the current system is not that it is insufficiently user-friendly but that it is effectively useless.

But there is another problem with the Secretary's interpretation: It straddles the two competing interpretive options presented by the provision rather than embracing one interpretation or the other. The most ruthlessly literal interpretation of the provision is this: the law requires the Secretary and the BMV only to enter into an agreement to match information in their databases and, once they have done that, they have satisfied HAVA's obligations—meaning that, other than the duty to share their data with each other, they have no duty to share mismatches with anyone else, to provide access to data showing the mismatches to anyone else or to investigate mismatches. The other interpretation of the provision is this: in addition to creating the two databases and in addition to identifying mismatches between them, the Secretary must "verify the accuracy of the information provided on applications for voter registration," 42 U.S.C. § 15483(a)(5)(B)(i), by correcting mismatches either at the Secretary's level or at the county board's level in order to ensure that the "voter registration records in the State are accurate and are updated regularly" and in order to ensure that the State's "system of file maintenance . . . makes a reasonable effort to remove registrants who are ineligible to vote," *id.* § 15483(a)(4)(A). The former interpretation does not require the Secretary to provide "access" to mismatch data contained in the system; only the latter interpretation does.

The Secretary picks neither option by itself. She adopts option one in the main but then borrows from option two by conceding that she must provide "access" to the data containing evidence of mismatches. Only then does she draw a line found nowhere in the statute—that the county boards must be given access; they just need not be given meaningful access. Call that interpretation what you will, but it is hardly a construction of the law mandated by its "plain language." In picking option two, the district court embraced a sensible and coherent interpretation of these provisions, one sufficiently likely to succeed that it deserves our respect.

Contrary to the dissent's and amici's interpretation, *Washington Ass'n of Churches v. Reed* (W.D. Wash. 2006), and *Florida State Conference of the NAACP v. Browning* (11th Cir. 2008), offer no support for a contrary interpretation. These cases deal with whether HAVA preempts state laws that *require* successful matching before a would-be voter can *register* to vote. *Reed* and *Browning* are thus two steps removed from today's case: (1) We are not dealing with any precondition on voter registration, and (2) no one is arguing that a successful match is a necessary precondition to anything. Put simply, neither case addressed, in holding or dicta, the issue presented here: namely, whether § 15483(a)(5)(B)(i), together with other provisions of HAVA, require the Secretary to provide local election officials with meaningful access to mismatches identified in the SWVRD.

Nor, it bears emphasizing, is anyone arguing that a mismatch necessarily requires that a registered voter be removed from the rolls. At most, the identification of a mismatch allows a county board to investigate whether the mismatch has a legitimate explanation (say, a recent change of address. Nothing about this case or the relief plaintiffs seek will allow them to prevent a single voter from casting a ballot in the November election. At most, the relief could prompt an inquiry into the bona fides of an individual's registration, and at most it could require an individual to cast a provisional ballot. At that point, the validity of the voter's registration will be determined and, with it, the validity of his or her vote. That is not only sensible but it is also fair—and it also furthers both objectives of HAVA rather than just one of them.

In the second place, the risks of harm to each party and above all the risks of harm to the public support the TRO. HAVA, all recognize, attempts to balance competing interests: enhancing access to the ballot on the one hand while preserving the value of each vote from the diluting effects of fraud on the other. In doing so, the Act no doubt imposes burdens on the States to further these goals, but the policy interests and hardship concerns that HAVA puts front and center are those affecting the *rights of voters.* Once we balance *those* interests, they point unmistakably in one direction. The window to detect and deal with vote-diluting fraud in Ohio begins to close on October 25, when the county boards of election open the first absentee-ballot envelopes. All this order does is ensure that the county boards may, if they wish, investigate voter-registration discrepancies by that date—in part by using the SWVRD (or information already derived from that database) that was designed for this purpose. If that information becomes available after October 25, when the absentee-ballot opening begins, the opportunity to follow up on voter-registration mismatches will be irretrievably lost, a concern that affects all Ohio voters. At the same time, nothing about Judge Smith's [TRO] order will limit a single individual's right to vote in the normal process or at a minimum through a provisional ballot.

The Secretary's risk-of-harm arguments focus principally on burdens that the district court's TRO imposes on her, not on burdens or risks that the order imposes on Ohio voters. She raises two burdens: that it will be difficult for her office to develop a computer program to get access to this information and that any changes to the SWVRD at this late stage in the election risk creating other problems in the election process. But why all of this is so is never explained, much less supported by affidavits from the Secretary or her office. The bureaucrat's lament—that this will be difficult to do—is a hard sell given that the Secretary's office previously shared this kind of information with the county boards. And if the question is who will have a harder time obtaining meaningful access to the voter-registration mismatches—the Secretary or the county boards of election—it is difficult to see how anyone can argue that the Secretary faces the harder task. So far as the record shows, the only way the county boards can use the database would be to enter each name of every registered voter in the database to determine whether there was a mismatch for that voter. By contrast, the Secretary told the district court that she could put the program together in two to three days. As between these burdens, I am hard-pressed to understand why the Secretary's alleged difficulties outweigh the counties'.

The Secretary also argues that running such a program at this stage could create other problems for the election. Here, too, her argument raises more questions than it answers because she again never explains why this is so, much less supports her position with affidavits from someone who would know. The past practices of the Secretary's office—in providing this kind of information to the county boards before—again suggest that she can mitigate these risks in the same ways she mitigated them before. And if for some reason that is not the case, she has not explained why the TRO does not require relatively modest adjustments to the program—one of which would filter the data to identify mismatched records and one of which would capture the mismatches for each of the 88 counties in the State. As for risks to the database when it comes to other uses of the system during the election, it is not clear why running a report or copy of the database *before* making these adjustments would not compartmentalize, and thereby eliminate, any risks to the SWVRD. But if all of these things are exceedingly difficult for the Secretary, or worse if they would create a meaningful risk of harm to other parts of the database at this stage in the year, she needs to explain why rather than allowing her attorneys to speculate why. The record on all of this is ear-splittingly silent—all the more conspicuously so given that it is the key risk of harm identified on the Secretary's side of the case and it is the one risk that must be balanced against the risk (come October 25) of allowing potentially fraudulent votes to be forever counted.

In the third place, the Secretary mistakenly claims that the timing exigencies created by this case should be laid at the feet of the plaintiffs. All of this came to a head, the complaint alleges, when the Secretary issued her August advisory. Because state officials had spoken publicly about trying to resolve election disputes through alternative dispute resolution rather than the courts (still a good idea by the way), we should not punish the plaintiffs for failing to run to court the day after the issuance of the advisory. To this day, it remains unclear when the Secretary told the public that she had changed the office's prior policy on implementing § 15483(a)(5)(B)(i), when she told the public why she made these changes and whether she has made additional changes to the policy since. On this record, there is no cognizable basis for punishing the plaintiffs for bringing this challenge when they did.

As for the notion that courts should hesitate to alter election procedures on the eve of an election, that is true—so far as it goes. When an election is "imminen[t]" and when there is "inadequate time to resolve . . . factual disputes," it will often be the case that courts will decline to grant an injunction to alter a State's established practice. *Purcell.* But that will not always be the case. This generalization surely does not control many election-related disputes—keeping polls open past their established times *on* election day or altering the rules for casting ballots or provisional ballots *during* election week—and it is unclear why it ought to control this one. The question here is whether there is sufficient time to resolve these fact disputes when absentee-vote processing starts on October 25, and the district court determined that it will take two to three days to get the information, not that it cannot be done. Nor, it seems clear, are the plaintiffs challenging an *established* election practice of the State. The established practice in this case is the one the State used in the last national election, not the Secretary's innovation of it for this one.

At the panel stage, in deciding to vacate the district court's TRO, this court did not rely on the Secretary's position that the plaintiffs may not vindicate these rights through a private right of action under § 1983. At the en banc stage, however, the dissent has now embraced the Secretary's position as a ground for decision and maintains that plaintiffs have no right to bring a federal cause of action under this statute to enforce these provisions of HAVA. There is nothing wrong with this change of heart, particularly given how little time the panel had to address the issue, but it should prompt similar empathy for a district court judge forced to do the same thing: make a quick likelihood-of-success decision about what can only be described as a deeply intricate issue.

At this stage in the case, there are several reasons for accepting the district court's probability-of-success prediction on this issue. Since *Maine v. Thiboutot* (1980), the Supreme Court has made it clear that § 1983 empowers claimants to file lawsuits against state officials who violate their constitutional *and* statutory rights because the provision covers "rights . . . secured by the Constitution *and laws*" of the United States. 42 U.S.C. § 1983 (emphasis added). In deciding whether a claimant may enforce a given statute through a § 1983 action, we consider three factors: (1) Did Congress "intend[ ] the provision in question" to "benefit" the claimant? (2) is the asserted right so "vague and amorphous" as to "strain judicial competence"? and (3) is the asserted right "couched in mandatory, rather than precatory, terms"? *Blessing v. Freestone* (1997). There is no doubt that the HAVA provisions at issue satisfy the second and third prongs of the test: In enacting the matching-and-verification requirements, Congress did not merely express an aspiration that state officials would cooperate in sharing information; it mandated that they "*shall* enter into an agreement to match information" for the purpose of "enabl[ing] [the officials] to verify the accuracy of the information provided on applications for voter registration." 42 U.S.C. § 15483(a)(5)(B)(i) (emphasis added). The statute thus imposes binding, enforceable duties on the Secretary that do not "strain judicial competence."

What is difficult is the first inquiry: Did the statute intend to benefit the claimants? In one sense, the answer to that question seems straightforward. In *Sandusky County Democratic Party v. Blackwell* (6th Cir. 2004), we held that another provision of HAVA—dealing with provisional ballots, 42 U.S.C. § 15482(a)—was intended to benefit individuals, and it would seem strange to infer that Congress wished to pull apart the threads of HAVA by permitting individual enforcement of some of its mandatory provisions but not others. There also seems to be little doubt that a tool designed to facilitate governmental efforts to identify voter fraud is a tool that redounds to the benefit of individuals. The whole point of curbing fraud is to prevent the dilution of individuals' votes, not to mandate anti-fraud requirements for their own stake.

What makes this question close and presumably what prompted the panel not to rely on this consideration as a basis for vacating the district court's TRO is the impact of the Supreme Court's decision in *Gonzaga University v. Doe* (2002), on this analysis. There, in discussing the first prong of the right-of-action test, the Court emphasized that "it is *rights,* not the broader or vaguer 'benefits' or 'interests,' that may be enforced" under § 1983 and that such rights must be "unambiguously conferred . . . to support a cause of action brought under § 1983." Picking up on this language, the Secretary argues that the HAVA provision at issue in *Sandusky County*—"[t]he individual shall be permitted to cast a provisional ballot," 42 U.S.C. § 15482(a)(2)—differs from the language at issue here. Even though the language in each case is mandatory and even though the language in each case identifies judicially enforceable obligations, the Secretary argues that the matching-and-verification requirements do not expressly identify any one individual or group of individuals as beneficiaries of the statutory obligation in the same way as this other provision of HAVA does.

This is a fair argument, one that this court will have to resolve with finality at some point. But it is not an argument with just one plausible answer or even a clear answer. The problem with contending that there is only one way to look at this issue is that the Secretary assumes *Gonzaga* requires individual-rights-granting language even when there is no individual to whom such language could apply. The beneficiary of every eliminated instance of voter fraud is never any one individual because the individual whose vote would have been diluted—the individual, if you will, whose "right" to vote is impaired—is never known or knowable. Perhaps when a statute effectively benefits everyone but no one in particular, a right of action still may exist, all other things being equal; perhaps it may not. But, either way, it is hard to maintain that the district court should have understood that *Gonzaga* resolved this point since it did not address, much less discuss, *this* issue. Nor did *Gonzaga* overrule earlier holdings that generally permitted the beneficiaries of federal statutes to enforce them through § 1983.

There is one more oddity with accepting the Secretary's position. The right-of-action inquiry requires a court to ascertain what Congress meant in imposing certain mandatory duties on States—to "determine whether Congress *intended to create a federal right.*" [*Gonzaga.*] To accept the Secretary's position in this case, however, we would have to infer that Congress meant to make both halves of HAVA mandatory—the ease of voting and casting provisional ballots on the one hand and the anti-fraud provisions on the other—yet wished to allow citizens to enforce just one half of those policies. There is no indication in the statute, or for that matter in the legislative history, that this is what Congress meant, and the fact that *all* of HAVA's relevant provisions may be enforced by the United States Attorney General or through administrative processes at the state level, 42 U.S.C. §§ 15511-12, suggests that all mandates should be privately enforceable or none should be. In the final analysis, the most that can be said about the Secretary's argument is that it raises a difficult issue. The "close" answer to this question, together with the reality that all of the other risks of error support the plaintiffs, weigh in favor of denying the Secretary's motion to stay the TRO.

That brings us to one final point. As the panel pointed out in vacating the district court's TRO, the record in this case is far from ample. That is true, but it will almost always be true in the context of a TRO, the nature of which requires rapid decisionmaking. That is what makes the standard of review—abuse of discretion—so relevant to the disposition of this emergency appeal. The point is not just that we give substantial discretion to the district court's ring-side view of the case in reviewing an order already issued; it is that we entrust the district court to deal fairly with future implementation issues implicated by that order. When it comes to applying abuse-of-discretion review here, one of the key obstacles to the Secretary's request for relief is the lack of any affidavit or other factual support for her arguments that altering the relevant computer programs will be difficult or will create material risks to other aspects of the election process. In upholding the district court's October 10 order and its October 17 deadline, it is appropriate to assume what we should always assume in denying interim relief—that the district court will respond fairly to requests to adjust the TRO if the Secretary offers reasonable bases for doing so. With that assumption in mind and with the view that this court should now allow the district court to do its job in handling this difficult case, we deny the Secretary's motion to stay the district court's October 10th TRO.

Karen Nelson Moore, Circuit Judge, [joined by Martin, Daughtrey, Cole, and Clay,] dissenting from hearing en banc and from reinstating the district court's Temporary Restraining Order. [Judge White's separate dissent is omitted.]

This case is wholly inappropriate for initial or immediate hearing en banc. Not only have the criteria for initial hearing or rehearing en banc not been satisfied, but also the en banc court is particularly ill-suited to consider in the first instance swiftly developing election-law issues in the compressed time period now available. The majority's action is judicial activism in the extreme.

I. OPPOSITION TO GRANT OF EN BANC REVIEW

The panel assigned to this case pursuant to Sixth Circuit rules has considered carefully the materials filed on behalf of both sides in this dispute and has issued an order staying the temporary restraining order improperly entered by the district court. The motion for hearing en banc filed by the Ohio Republican Party and Larry Wolpert (collectively "ORP") at this time is nothing more than a blatant attempt of ORP to overturn the duly authorized panel's decision to stay the district court's order that required the Secretary of State to likely violate both the Help America Vote Act ("HAVA") and the National Voter Registration Act ("NVRA").

The Secretary should not be required by various federal judges to violate those federal statutes, nor should she be required to reconfigure and reprogram the state's computers and practices this close to an election. Because the granting of en banc hearing and the simultaneous reinstatement of the district court's temporary restraining order will throw the election process in Ohio into total chaos, I dissent.

On October 10, 2008, the Sixth Circuit panel stayed the district court's temporary restraining order. In our opinion, we explained our reasoning and concluded as follows:

> It is clear that the district court's four specific orders insert the federal court into the delicate balance struck by HAVA. We have expressed our concern that under established law ORP does not have a private right of action under 42 U.S.C. § 15483(a)(5)(B)(i). Assuming ORP has the right to bring such an action, we believe that the Secretary is likely to succeed on the merits of the issue of the proper interpretation of HAVA; HAVA does not mandate that the Secretary undertake the particularized matching required by the district court's TRO. Further, the irreparable harm caused by the district court's TRO is significant. With less than a month until the election, and less than two weeks until the beginning of counting absentee ballots, the Secretary cannot be required to undertake the extensive reprogramming and other changes to the election mechanics without complete disruption of the electoral process in Ohio. The irreparable harm to the voting public caused by the district court's order is equally clear. Finally, the intrusion into the state's processes by the federal courts with the ensuing confusion regarding the applicable process weighs heavily against the district court's order.
>
> As the Supreme Court wrote in *Purcell,* "Given the imminence of the election and the inadequate time to resolve the factual disputes, our action today shall of necessity allow the election to proceed without an injunction" altering the state's established practice. *Purcell [v. Gonzalez]* [2006]. We hereby stay the district court's TRO. . . .

ORP asserts that hearing this case initially en banc and bypassing the duly assigned panel (or rehearing en banc) is appropriate because of the importance of the issues presented and the press of time. The time pressures in this case are entirely caused by ORP's last-minute challenges to the procedures initiated by the Secretary of State's office before the current Secretary began her position in 2007. While the Secretary's procedures have been known and in effect for a considerable time, ORP waited to file its suit in the district court until September 26, 2008, and did not file its motion for this temporary restraining order until October 5, 2008. If ORP had truly wanted to have review of the methods and procedures used by the Secretary, it should have brought its action much earlier. More importantly, the NVRA specifically requires that "any program the purpose of which is to systematically remove the names of ineligible voters from the official lists of eligible voters" must be completed at least 90 days prior to a federal election. 42 U.S.C. § 1973gg-6(c)(2)(A). HAVA provides for removing voters in accordance with the NVRA, and the latter does not permit registered voters to be removed based on computer matching. 42 U.S.C. § 15483(a)(2)(A)(i); 42 U.S.C. § 1973gg-6.

Thus ORP has brought its action too late to obtain its requested relief; ORP's claimed press of time is both self-created and self-defeating. The press of time is not a valid basis for obtaining hearing en banc in this case.

The other reason asserted by ORP for hearing en banc is that the case "is an extraordinary case, involving the integrity of the election for President of the United States . . . in a state vital to both candidates' chances at victory." The Federal Rules of Appellate Procedure allow hearing or rehearing en banc where "the proceeding involves one or more *questions of exceptional importance, each of which must be concisely stated.*" Fed. R. App. P. 35(b)(1)(B) (emphasis added). Yet ORP completely fails to comply with the requirements of this Rule: it has not specified in its motion for hearing en banc ANY specific question of exceptional importance. ORP's utter failure to comply with the Federal Rules of Appellate Procedure suggests that its effort to obtain hearing en banc concerning this temporary restraining order is based on ORP's dissatisfaction with the panel's composition or with the merits of the decision of the duly assigned Sixth Circuit panel to stay the previous temporary restraining order issued by the district judge in this case. ORP is simply trying to get a different result by having a different forum within the Sixth Circuit.

In summary, a hearing en banc in this case is wholly unwarranted and entirely unjustified. Granting a hearing en banc on this flawed motion and in light of the circumstances of this litigation is unsound intellectually and without any valid justification. Any lawyer reading the plaintiffs/appellees' motion for initial hearing en banc or its renewed motion can see that substantively it is baseless and procedurally it violates the Federal Rules of Appellate Procedure. I dissent from the majority's rash and meritless decision to grant en banc review and to reinstate the district court's TRO.

II. ORP HAS NO PRIVATE RIGHT OF ACTION

In addition to disagreeing with this court's decision to grant en banc review, I must dissent from its decision to reinstate the district court's temporary restraining order. On its face, HAVA does not create a private right of action. Supreme Court precedent makes it absolutely clear that the provisions of HAVA at issue here, 42 U.S.C. §§ 15483(a)(1)(A) &

(a)(5)(B)(i), do not create federal rights enforceable by private plaintiffs under 42 U.S.C. § 1983. For a statute to be enforced via § 1983, Congress must have unambiguously intended to create an individual right. *Gonzaga Univ. v. Doe* (2002). However, these provisions of HAVA regulate the conduct of *officials* involved in the voting process; they do not create rights enforceable by individual voters. In sharp contrast to the statutory provisions that the Supreme Court and this circuit have recognized as establishing privately enforceable rights, the HAVA provisions at issue in this case contain absolutely no rights-creating language. It is not surprising, therefore, that *no* court has interpreted these provisions as conferring a right enforceable by private plaintiffs under § 1983. Instead HAVA provides its own enforcement mechanisms, specifying that the U.S. Attorney General may bring suit to enforce HAVA. 42 U.S.C. § 15511. The U.S. Attorney General has not brought suit.

A statute is enforceable via a private right of action under § 1983 only if contains "an unambiguously conferred right." *Gonzaga*. "[I]t is *rights,* not the broader or vaguer 'benefits' or 'interests,' that may be enforced under the authority of that section." *Id.* If a "statute by its terms grants no private rights to any identifiable class," then Congress did not intend to create a private right of action. *Id.* This inquiry begins with the text of the statute. "For a statute to create such private rights, its text must be 'phrased in terms of the persons benefited.'" *Id.* By contrast, statutes that "speak only in terms of institutional policy and practice" or that "have an 'aggregate' focus" do not confer a right that may be enforced via § 1983. *Id.* Similarly, "[s]tatutes that focus on the person regulated rather than the individuals protected" do not confer enforceable rights. *Alexander v. Sandoval* (2001).

The provisions of HAVA at issue here contain absolutely no rights-creating language. Instead, they impose an obligation on state officials to establish a voter-registration system meeting certain criteria. Section 15483(a)(1)(A) requires each state to "implement . . .a . . . computerized statewide voter registration list . . . that contains the name and registration information of every legally registered voter in the State and assigns a unique identifier to each legally registered voter in the State. . . . " 42 U.S.C. § 15483(a)(1)(A). Section 15483(a)(5)(B)(i) further requires that "[t]he chief State election official and the official responsible for the State motor vehicle authority of a State shall enter into an agreement to match information in the database of the statewide voter registration system with information in the database of the motor vehicle authority to the extent required to enable each such official to verify the accuracy of the information provided on applications for voter registration." 42 U.S.C. § 15483(a)(5)(B)(i). These provisions focus on the administration of federal elections and the duties of state *officials* to establish institutional mechanisms meeting certain criteria. Nothing in these provisions contains the sort of rights-focused language that the Supreme Court has required to establish a privately enforceable right.

[T]he HAVA provisions in this case speak only to government *officials.* HAVA directs that state election officials "implement . . . a computerized statewide voter registration list," 42 U.S.C. § 15483(a)(1)(A), and that they "enter into an agreement to match information in the database of the statewide voter registration system with information in the database of the motor vehicle authority to the extent required to enable each such official to verify the accuracy of the information provided on applications for voter registration," 42 U.S.C. § 15483(a)(5)(B)(i). In other words, these provisions require state officials to maintain a centralized statewide computerized voter registration list and to maintain that list according to certain standards. Nothing in these provisions refers to the "rights" of "individuals" or "voters."

The HAVA provisions at issue in this case also differ dramatically from the rights-creating language contained in HAVA § 302(a)(2), which we have held creates a private right enforceable via § 1983. *See Sandusky County Democratic Party v. Blackwell* (6th Cir. 2004). The provision at issue in *Sandusky,* HAVA § 302(a)(2), provides that upon making the required affirmation, an "*individual shall be permitted* to cast a provisional ballot." 42 U.S.C. § 15482(a)(2) (emphasis added). In *Sandusky,* we concluded that "[t]his language mirrors the rights-creating language of Title VI of the Civil Rights Act of 1964 and Title IX of the Education Amendments of 1972." We further noted that "this language markedly differs from the statutory language found by the Supreme Court in *Gonzaga* to be insufficiently focused on the benefited class to create an individually enforceable right." *Id.* We also stated that § 302 of HAVA "refers explicitly to the '*right of an individual to cast a provisional ballot,*' . . . and requires states to post information at polling places about this right along with 'instructions on how to contact the appropriate officials if *these rights* are alleged to have been violated.'" *Id.* (emphasis in original) (citing 42 U.S.C. § 15482(b)(2)(E)). By contrast, the HAVA provisions at issue in this case do not so much as mention "individuals" or "rights." Instead, these provisions are directed solely at regulating the conduct of state election officials.

Finally, nothing in HAVA's legislative history indicates that Congress intended to create a private right of action to enforce the provisions at issue in this case, 42 U.S.C. §§ 15483(a)(1)(A) & (a)(5)(B)(i). If anything, the legislative history weighs against the recognition of privately enforceable rights under HAVA, because Congress apparently considered, and rejected, the creation of an express private right of action under HAVA. Senator Christopher Dodd, a sponsor of HAVA and principal Senate author of the conference report, stated that "[w]hile [he] would have preferred that we extend [a] private right of action . . . , the House simply would not entertain such an enforcement provision[ ]. Nor would they accept federal judicial review of any adverse decision by a State administrative body." 148 Cong. Rec. S10505 (daily ed. Oct. 16, 2002) (statement of Sen. Dodd).

Therefore, pursuant to well-established Supreme Court and Sixth Circuit precedent, ORP has no explicit or implied private right of action to bring this lawsuit or to seek the relief granted by the district court and the en banc majority. I would dismiss this action because plaintiffs have failed to state a claim on which relief can be granted.

III. THE MOTION TO VACATE THE TRO SHOULD BE GRANTED

Even assuming that a private right of action exists under HAVA, I believe that *Northeast Ohio Coalition for Homeless v. Blackwell* (6th Cir. 2006), demands that this court issue a stay and vacate the district court's temporary restraining order.

A. Success on the Merits

The Help America Vote Act, known as HAVA, [provides:]

> The chief State election official and the official responsible for the State motor vehicle authority of a State shall enter into an agreement to match information in the database of the statewide voter registration system with information in the database of the motor vehicle authority to the extent required to enable each such official to verify the accuracy of the information provided on applications for voter registration.

42 U.S.C. § 15483(a)(5)(B)(i).

Under the plain language of the statute, it is clear that all that this section requires is that a state: (1) have an agreement between the election official and the motor vehicle authority official to share and compare information in the statewide voter registration system with information in the motor vehicle authority database; and (2) give the state election official and the motor vehicle official the ability to check voter registration information in the system. There is absolutely no language that imposes an affirmative duty on any state official to enable a purge of voters by either scouring the database to locate mismatches or by providing a system that would allow a person to make such a search. "It is clear from the language of the statute and by looking at legislative history that HAVA's matching requirement was intended as an administrative safeguard for 'storing and managing the official list of registered voters,' and not as a restriction on voter eligibility." *Washington Ass'n of Churches v. Reed* (W.D. Wash. 2006). In fact, the two federal courts to consider the provision in question here, *Reed* and *Florida NAACP v. Browning* (11th Cir. 2008), both rejected the argument asserted by ORP that HAVA requires matching to be used to verify eligible voters. The *Reed* court stressed that the matching system is simply one way that a new voter who registered by mail could be verified. *Reed* went on to explain that a system that made matching the only way to verify voter identity would violate HAVA. In *Browning*, the Eleventh Circuit acknowledged that, while HAVA would allow a state to require that an individual have a match to be eligible to vote, HAVA did not compel such a requirement.

Though *Browning* and *Reed* disagree as to whether a state can choose to base voter eligibility solely on matching, they agree on the issue before this court: HAVA does not compel states to use a certain type of match system to verify voters. All that HAVA requires is that election officials have some method by which to verify registrations. The language of HAVA does not mandate what system the states must use to match or verify votes, leaving such decisions to the discretion of the states. The majority of this circuit thus conflicts with the Eleventh Circuit and creates a circuit split that should be resolved by the Supreme Court.

It boggles the mind that the majority can distort this simple language to force a state to implement a specific type of match system. This conclusion flies in the face of HAVA's own directive that the *State gets to choose* how to implement HAVA. 42 U.S.C. § 15485 ("The specific choices on the methods of complying with the requirements of this subchapter shall be left to *the discretion of the State.*" (emphasis added).) I cannot comprehend why the majority is going to such lengths to force this strained interpretation into the case law, and I dissent from the majority's violation of the plain statutory language.

Moreover, the majority's view would require the Secretary to violate the National Voter Registration Act ("NVRA") and HAVA. HAVA specifically provides for the removal of voters "in accordance with the provision of the National Voter Registration Act of 1993." 42 U.S.C. § 15483(a)(2)(A)(i). NVRA, however, does not permit registered voters to be removed based on computer matching. *See* 42 U.S.C. § 1973gg-6. Indeed, the NVRA requires that "any program the purpose of which is to systematically remove the names of ineligible voters from the official lists of eligible voters" must be completed at least 90 days prior to a federal election. § 1973gg-6(c)(2)(A). The stated purpose of the TRO is to allow for an "effective way to access and review the mismatches" located in the current database, because, allegedly, "some mismatches will reflect voter fraud." Thus, the TRO demands a "program the purpose of which is to systematically remove the names of ineligible voters from the official lists of eligible voters." § 1973gg-6(c)(2)(A). Therefore, the TRO, now sanctioned by the majority's forced interpretation of HAVA, mandates that the Secretary violate federal law. Congress cannot have intended HAVA to be read in such a way.

Applying the correct interpretation of this statute to the facts in this case, I believe Ohio is likely in compliance with HAVA. Currently, the Secretary has a database which matches the information a voter provided when registering to vote with the information contained in the Ohio Bureau of Motor Vehicles database. If there is a mismatch, the database notes the mismatch. This record of mismatches in the database is accessible by both the Secretary and the individual boards of election in Ohio. The individual boards of election can query a voter's match status in real time in order to verify registration. This is all HAVA requires. It is true that the statewide voter database does not provide for a list of these mismatches, but HAVA does not require that level of user-friendliness. To be sure, it might be nice if the system printed out a list of individuals within, for example, a particular precinct, that did not match, but I refuse to manipulate the clear language of Congress in HAVA to require Ohio to comply with a particular interested private party's view of what type of match system would be best. For all these reasons, I conclude that the likelihood that the Secretary will succeed on the merits is great.

B. Irreparable Harm

The district court found that there would be no harm to others, including the Secretary, if it issued the TRO that ORP sought. This determination is wholly unsubstantiated and contrary to the realities of the TRO issued. In a week, the database that the district court has ordered to be reprogrammed "will be used to generate the Election Day poll books." Secretary Br. at 19. The district court made its reprogramming order without hearing any evidence pertaining to how such a reprogramming would affect the existing election system and, more importantly, how long it would take to test the reprogrammed system, retrain personnel, and ensure that the new reprogramming did not cause problems. The Supreme Court has exhorted courts to exercise "proper judicial restraint" before making "precipitate changes" to election procedures and policies when "an impending election is imminent and a State's election machinery is already in progress." *Reynolds v. Sims* (1964); *see also Purcell v. Gonzalez* (2006). Election procedures are matters of state law, and federal courts should hesitate to interfere, particularly when operating on limited information in the weeks preceding an election.

The Secretary must handle all problems related to the reprogramming that is required under the district court's novel order embraced by the majority of the en banc court. The most alarming possible side-effect of reprogramming would be that a programming glitch could cause validly registered voters to be inadvertently purged from poll books. Such a glitch would leave the Secretary with a database that can no longer be trusted for use in generating the poll books required for the election, causing "delays and inaccuracies in the creation of the poll books." Secretary Br. at 19. The short timeframe available to comply with the TRO amplifies the risk of programming errors, one of numerous significant problems presented by the requirements imposed by the district court on short notice.

Additionally, even if the court-ordered reprogramming works perfectly, the Secretary will be faced with a large number of mismatches to contend with at the last minute. Because of the time limitations, voters whose information does not match may not be aware that there is any question about their registration and may not have or be able to obtain the documents necessary to further verify their registration. It is unlikely that the state can properly investigate all of the mismatches created by the TRO, and as a result, properly registered voters will likely be forced to cast provisional ballots, will believe that they cannot vote, or will be turned away at the polling places. *See Purcell* (demanding "careful consideration" of any legal challenge that involves "the possibility that qualified voters might be turned away from the polls"). It is worth noting that the procedures each county uses to deal with these mismatches may not be uniform and could result in disproportionate disenfranchisement. *See Bush v. Gore* (2000) (noting importance of statewide standards for resolving questions of voting procedure). This confusion over what HAVA requires in terms of matching would affect not only Ohio, but every state in the country.

Moreover, at a time when the Secretary is already busy with routine election procedures, the TRO will require the Secretary to expend significant scarce resources on the reprogramming and matching effort. This diversion of resources could leave the state unable to respond to routine election issues such as broken voting machines and lines at polling places. If significant energies are devoted to matching issues, the orderly administration of the election will suffer. For all these reasons, I conclude that the Secretary would suffer irreparable injury if we do not grant a stay and vacate the district court's TRO.

C. Substantial Harm to Others and Public Interest

Given the fact that hurriedly reprogramming the database could lead to the purging of validly registered voters, a stay of the district court's intrusive TRO is necessary to protect the voters of Ohio. Though I agree with the district court's conclusion that "safeguarding the legitimacy of the election of the President of the United States" is of great public importance, the TRO is not required to protect that interest. It is striking that both the district court and the majority of this court have determined that the TRO is the proper remedy without any factfinding. The district court stressed that the public, as well as ORP, would be injured by voter fraud if a TRO were not granted. This is the kind of inquiry that demands extensive factfinding. *See Purcell.* However, rather than undertake such factfinding, the district court, citing two newspaper articles, merely assumed that there will be widespread voter fraud absent the issuing of a TRO. Numerous other newspaper articles quote election officials who distinguish voter-registration fraud from actual voter fraud, and who indicate that actual improper voter registrations are already being detected. Given the shaky ground on which the district court's suggestion of voter-fraud rests, I believe that this unsubstantiated fear does not warrant the district court's intrusion into the established state practice.

Additionally, available evidence indicates that this intrusive TRO will cause more harm than it seeks to address. Computer matching is not a reliable way to verify voter eligibility. Indeed, evidence from other states indicates that human error, not fraud, causes most mismatches. Data suggests that when the database match is conducted, anywhere from 15 to 30 percent of registered voters will fail to match. Disturbingly, mismatches have been shown to bar non-white voters more frequently than white voters. Data from the Secretary of State shows that there are at least 485,000 new registered voters in Ohio this year. Given these numbers, the TRO issued by the district court and revived by today's result, could result in anywhere between 72,750 to 145,500 registered voters being removed from voting rolls, being forced to cast provisional ballots, or being otherwise wrongly disenfranchised.

In contrast to these concrete projections, ORP has failed to present evidence that any voters, including those who have registered in the last year, have committed actual voting fraud. Indeed, data collected by the Brennan Center, the same non-partisan organization that studied the failure rate of data matching, indicates that actual voter fraud is extremely rare. The Brennan Center noted that "claims of voter fraud are frequently used to justify policies that do not solve the alleged wrongs, but that could well disenfranchise legitimate voters." Similarly, the League of Women Voters of Ohio and the Coalition on Homelessness and Housing in Ohio studied the 9 million votes cast in Ohio between 2002 and 2004, and found only *four fraudulent ballots*. Therefore, the matching policy mandated by the TRO purportedly to eliminate voter fraud is actually likely to cause mismatches which will erroneously be labeled voter fraud, thereby disenfranchising individual voters and undermining public confidence in election results.[7] The likelihood that this last-minute TRO will undermine confidence in the election results and will adversely affect, and perhaps even disenfranchise, a large number of voters is greater and more disturbing than the possibility that fraudulent votes will dilute the strength of legitimate ballots.

On the eve of the presidential election, ORP asks this court to derail election procedures that have been months in the making. The stay that the majority has vacated would simply have preserved the status quo and allowed Ohio to conduct its elections in the orderly method it had planned. The majority's ruling today upends all order, injects the potential for erroneous disenfranchisement of qualified voters into the election, and creates confusion surrounding voting rights on the unverified specter of potential fraud.

The harm that the TRO will inflict on the Secretary, the voters, and the public is clear: elections in Ohio will be chaotic at best, blatantly unfair at worst, and doubt will fall on the validity of election results across the state. The mere specter of voter fraud, often raised but seldom proven, is the only injury that ORP asserts, and this unfounded threat cannot be used to coerce courts into acceding to the eleventh-hour demands of a partisan group that is intimately concerned with the results of the election it seeks to control. Accordingly, I would hold, as I did previously, that we should stay the TRO originally issued by the district court.

IV. CONCLUSION

Accordingly, I would hold that: (1) granting of en banc is inappropriate; (2) there is no private right of action and thus ORP's claims must be dismissed; and (3) on the merits, we should **GRANT** the Secretary's motion to vacate the district judge's intrusive and invalid temporary restraining order. I dissent.

7. Members of the majority lightly assume that reinstating the TRO will not harm individual voters. This short-sighted assessment ignores the reality that voters do not always know they have a right to cast a provisional ballot and even when they do, may not understand the procedure or be able to wait for necessary assistance. Notably, some who cast provisional ballots in Ohio are required to bring verifying information to the board of elections within ten days or else their votes will not be counted. This is a burden that many individuals cannot bear. Additionally, there is no guarantee that such ballots will be counted in time to affect the election. Daniel P. Tokaji, *An Unsafe Harbor: Recounts, Contests, and the Electoral College,* 106 Mich. L. Rev. First Impressions 84, 87 (2008) ("One of the major steps before a final vote total can be ascertained is determining which provisional ballots should be counted, a process that would almost surely become heated in a tight election. It is difficult to see how the process of verification of ballots, let alone any judicial proceedings that might take place over the canvassing and recounting of ballots, could be completed by the safe harbor date.").

BRUNNER v. OHIO REPUBLICAN PARTY

555 U.S. 5 (2008)

PER CURIAM.

On October 9, 2008, the United States District Court for the Southern District of Ohio entered a temporary restraining order (TRO) directing Jennifer Brunner, the Ohio Secretary of State, to update Ohio's Statewide Voter Registration Database (SWVRD) to comply with Section 303 of the Help America Vote Act of 2002 (HAVA), 42 U.S.C. § 15483(a)(5)(B)(i). The United States Court of Appeals for the Sixth Circuit denied the Secretary's motion to vacate the TRO. The Secretary has filed an application to stay the TRO with Justice Stevens as Circuit Justice for the Sixth Circuit, and he has referred the matter to the Court. The Secretary argues both that the District Court had no jurisdiction to enter the TRO and that its ruling on the merits was erroneous. We express no opinion on the question whether HAVA is being properly implemented. Respondents, however, are not sufficiently likely to prevail on the question whether Congress has authorized the District Court to enforce Section 303 in an action brought by a private litigant to justify the issuance of a TRO. *See Gonzaga Univ. v. Doe* (2002); *Alexander v. Sandoval,* 532 U.S. 275, 286 (2001). We therefore grant the application for a stay and vacate the TRO.

5. Additional Voter Registration Litigation

Various state practices concerning voter registration have been the subject of litigation around the country during the last decade of the voting wars. Battleground states like Colorado and Michigan have seen their share of cases on this topic, none more so than Florida—the proverbial "mother" of all battleground states. In addition to *NAACP v. Browning* (above), the federal judiciary has sustained Florida's requirement that new registrants both check boxes associated with prerequisites of eligibility (citizenship, adulthood, mental competence) and sign an affirmation of eligibility. *Diaz v. Cobb*, 435 F. Supp. 2d 1206 (S.D. Fla. 2006). The same court also ruled that, for voters who submit their registration forms on time but who inadvertently fail to check a required box, federal law does not require Florida to give these voters extra time beyond the deadline to fix the mistake. *Diaz v. Cobb*, 541 F. Supp. 2d 1319 (S.D. Fla. 2008). Finally, the Eleventh Circuit has an important pending case concerning the validity of Florida's most recent practices for the "purging" of its voter registration lists. *See Arcia v. Detzner*, http://moritzlaw.osu.edu/electionlaw/litigation/arciaVdetzner.php.

C. EARLY VOTING

One of the most significant developments in the way Americans vote since 2000 is the rapid rise in alternatives to the traditional method of casting a ballot at a neighborhood polling place on Election Day. One increasingly prevalent alternative is "no excuse" vote-by-mail. Traditionally, absentee voting was limited to only those voters with a specifically authorized need to vote by mail: away on business, a disability, or the like. In recent years, however, many states have changed their laws to permit any registered voter to choose to vote by mail, if that method is the one that the voter prefers, and some western states have moved to all vote-by-mail elections (meaning that they have eliminated neighborhood polling places entirely on Election Day, although they do permit voters to deliver their ballots personally to specifically designated locations rather than submitting them to the U.S. Postal Service).

Another recent development in so-called "convenience" voting is the establishment of "early voting," whereby voters may go in person to cast their ballots for a period of time prior to Election Day. Early voting locations are not nearly as numerous as neighborhood polling places on Election Day; indeed, sometimes they are limited to one per county. But often early voting locations offer voters the same kind of voting machine that would be used in their neighborhood polling location, so the voter's experience of casting a ballot at an early voting location is similar to the voting experience on Election Day (just several days earlier). States that offer early voting differ in the number of days and hours in which they make it available.

It turns out that voters in different demographic groups have different preferences for these alternative methods of voting. In 2008, it became apparent that many in the African-American community liked to take advantage of in-person early voting, particularly on Sunday after church services in a practice known as "souls to the polls." In the two presidential swing states of Florida and Ohio, the GOP-controlled legislatures passed laws in advance of the 2012 election to reduce the availability of early voting in comparison to what had occurred in 2008. Civil rights groups viewed these cutbacks in early voting as an effort to suppress African-American turnout in 2012, and President Obama's reelection campaign saw these cutbacks as a direct threat to his chances at victory. The Florida cutback in early voting was subject to preclearance under Section 5 of the Voting Rights Act, and a three-judge federal court denied preclearance on the ground that Florida could not prove that the cutback would not have a retrogressive discriminatory effect on the opportunity of African Americans to participate in the 2012 election. Ohio is not subject to preclearance under Section 5 of the Voting Rights Act. Instead, the Obama campaign sued under the Equal Protection Clause of the Fourteenth Amendment to undo Ohio's rollback of early voting.

When the Obama campaign filed this lawsuit, commentators were divided on its chances of success. Reportedly, one of Obama's senior legal advisors bet the campaign's general counsel that their side would lose. The general counsel won both the bet and the lawsuit. Not a single federal judge ruled against the Obama campaign. The district court granted a preliminary injunction that restored the days of early voting that the legislature had taken away, the court of appeals affirmed that injunction (although the three judges on the panel differed in their reasoning, and on the precise scope of the injunction, as you will soon see), and the U.S. Supreme Court, without comment or dissent, declined to hear the state's appeal.

As you read the appellate opinions in the case, ask yourself about the nature of the Equal Protection analysis that the judges use to justify their ruling. Is the *Anderson-Burdick* test used here the same one that the Supreme Court used in *Crawford*? You will see that the Sixth Circuit cites *Bush v. Gore* in support of its decision. You have not yet read *Bush v. Gore*, but it is enough for now to know that the case controversially ended the ballot-counting dispute in the 2000 presidential election and, in doing so, apparently established an Equal Protection principle that no election law may "arbitrarily" treat voters differently from each other. What, if anything, does this "no arbitrariness" principle add to the *Anderson-Burdick* balancing test, and does it help to explain the outcome of this case on early voting?

OBAMA FOR AMERICA v. HUSTED

697 F.3d 423 (6th Cir. 2012)

CLAY, Circuit Judge.

Defendants Jon Husted, the Secretary of State of Ohio, and Mike DeWine, the Attorney General of Ohio (collectively the "State"), joined by Intervenors representing numerous military service associations ("Intervenors"), appeal from the district court's order granting Plaintiffs' motion for a preliminary injunction. The district court enjoined the State from enforcing Ohio Rev. Code § 3509.03 to the extent that it prevents some Ohio voters from casting in-person early ballots during the three days before the November 2012 election on the basis that the statute violates the Equal Protection Clause of the Fourteenth Amendment. For the reasons set forth below, we affirm the district court's order granting the preliminary injunction.

BACKGROUND

I. Procedural History

On July 17, 2012, Plaintiffs Obama for America, the Democratic National Committee, and the Ohio Democratic Party filed a complaint alleging that Ohio Rev. Code § 3509.03 was unconstitutional insofar as it imposes on non-military voters a deadline of 6:00 p.m. on the Friday before Election Day for in-person early voting.[1] On the same day, Plaintiffs moved for a preliminary injunction preventing the statute's enforcement. They argued that the relevant statutory provisions "burden the fundamental right to vote but are not necessary to any sufficiently weighty state interest."

1. All references to the election or Election Day refer to the November 6, 2012 election. The three-day period prior to Election Day specifically refers to Saturday, November 3, 2012; Sunday, November 4, 2012; and Monday, November 5, 2012. "Military and overseas voters" are those voters identified in the federal Uniformed and Overseas Citizens Absentee Voting Act of 1986, 42 U.S.C. § 1973ff ("UOCAVA"), as amended by the Military and Overseas Voter Empowerment Act, Pub.L. 111-84, 123 Stat. 2190 (2009) ("MOVE Act"), and corresponding sections of the Ohio Election Code, Ohio Rev. Code § 3511.01. "Non-military voters" are all other eligible voters.

On August 1, 2012, numerous military service associations filed a motion to intervene, and the district court granted the motion. The State and Intervenors opposed Plaintiffs' motion for a preliminary injunction. They argued that the State's interest in providing military voters with added in-person early voting time and the burden on local boards of elections of providing that same extra time for all voters justified imposing a different deadline on military and overseas voters than all other voters.

The district court conducted a hearing on Plaintiffs' motion on August 15, 2012. The parties filed numerous exhibits, including legislative history, declarations of career military officers and voting experts, and statistical and demographic studies by various governmental agencies and non-governmental organizations. On August 31, 2012, the district court issued an opinion and order granting Plaintiffs' motion for a preliminary injunction. The district court concluded that § 3509.03 violated the Equal Protection Clause to the extent that it set a different in-person early voting deadline for non-military voters because "the State's interests are insufficiently weighty to justify the injury to Plaintiffs." The preliminary injunction ensures that all Ohio voters—military, overseas, and non-military—are afforded the same opportunity for in-person early voting that was available to them prior to the enactment of § 3509.03.

The State and Intervenors now appeal the district court's order granting a preliminary injunction. On September 12, 2012, the district court denied the State's motion to stay its order pending appeal, and the preliminary injunction remains in effect.

II. Facts

A. *In-Person Early Voting in Ohio*

Ohio introduced in-person early voting largely in response to the myriad problems faced by voters during the 2004 election. During that election, Ohio voters faced long lines and wait-times that, at some polling places, stretched into the early morning of the following day. To prevent similar problems from disenfranchising voters in the future and to ease the strain of accommodating all voters on a single day, the State established no-fault absentee voting in October 2005. The new rules eliminated the need for absentee voters to have an excuse for not voting on election day. After the creation of in-person early voting, any registered voter could cast an absentee ballot at the appropriate board of elections office through the Monday before the election.

The evidence considered by the district court showed that a large number of Ohio voters chose to utilize the new early voting procedures in elections from 2006 through 2010. Early voting peaked during the 2008 election, when approximately 1.7 million Ohioans cast their ballots before election day, amounting to 20.7% of registered voters and 29.7% of the total votes cast. In Ohio's twelve largest counties, approximately 340,000 voters, or about 9% of the total votes cast in those counties, chose to vote early at a local board of elections office. Using data from seven of Ohio's largest counties, one study projected that, in 2008, approximately 105,000 Ohioans cast their ballots in person during the final three days before the election. In 2010, approximately 1 million Ohioans voted early, and 17.8% of them chose to cast their ballots in person. In a poll conducted after the 2010 election, 29.6% of early voters reported voting within one week of election day.

Voters who chose to cast their ballots early tended to be members of different demographic groups than those who voted on election day. Early voters were "more likely than election-day voters to be women, older, and of lower income and education attainment." Data from Cuyahoga and Franklin Counties suggests that early voters were disproportionately African-American and that a large majority of early in-person votes (82% in Franklin County) were cast after hours on weekdays, on the weekend, or on the Monday before the election.

B. Legislative Changes to In-Person Early Voting

On July 1, 2011, Ohio Governor John Kasich signed Amended Substitute House Bill 194, an omnibus bill that made broad changes to Ohio election law. Among other things, the Ohio legislature apparently intended to change the deadlines for in-person early voting from the Monday before the election to 6:00 p.m. on the Friday before the election. Instead, H.B. 194 created two separate and contradictory deadlines: one on Friday and one on Monday. For non-military voters, Ohio Rev.Code § 3509.03 contained the former Monday deadline, but an amended § 3509.01 imposed the new Friday deadline. Military and overseas voters found themselves in much the same position, with § 3511.02 containing the former deadline, and an amended § 3511.10 containing the new one.

In an attempt to correct its mistake, the Ohio General Assembly passed Amended Substitute House Bill 224, which became effective on October 27, 2011. H.B. 224 fixed the inconsistent deadlines in § 3509.03 and § 3511.02, changing the deadlines for all voters to 6:00 p.m. on the Friday before the election. Before the technical corrections in H.B. 224 could take effect, however, a petition with more than 300,000 signatures was filed to put the omnibus election law, H.B. 194, to a referendum. The referendum petition was certified by the Secretary of State on December 9, 2011, and pursuant to the Ohio Constitution, the implementation of H.B. 194 was suspended for the 2012 election cycle.

On May 8, 2012, the General Assembly repealed the then-suspended H.B. 194 through Substitute Senate Bill 295. However, neither the organizers of the referendum petition nor the Ohio legislature thought to attack or repeal the bill containing the technical changes, H.B. 224, which remained in effect. Therefore, even though the original bill, H.B. 194, was repealed, the technical changes contained in H.B. 224 remained in place, and Ohio voters were still left with inconsistent deadlines. Nonmilitary voters could cast ballots in-person until 6:00 p.m. on the Friday before the election. But military and overseas voters had two deadlines: Friday at 6:00 p.m. pursuant to § 3511.02, and the close of the polls on election day pursuant to § 3511.10.

In order to correct this confusion, Defendant Husted construed the statute to apply the more generous deadline contained in § 3511.10 to military and overseas voters. Attempts by local boards of elections to provide in-person early voting to non-military voters through the Monday before the election were denied by the Secretary of State on the grounds that the statute does not permit it. On August 15, 2012, Defendant Husted issued Directive 2012-35, instructing the local boards of election that they were to maintain regular business hours between October 2, 2012 and November 2, 2012. This directive eliminated the local boards' discretion to be open on weekends during that period. Between October 2, 2012 and October 19, 2012, the boards must close at 5:00 p.m. During the last two weeks of the election, the boards will remain open until 7:00 p.m. but may not remain open afterwards or on the weekends. The directive does not address office hours on the final three-day period before Election Day, when, according to the statute, only military and overseas voters can cast ballots in person.

DISCUSSION

I.

[Omitted.]

II. Likelihood of Succeed on the Merits

A. Equal Protection in the Voting Context

The right to vote is a "precious" and "fundamental" right. *Harper v. Va. State Bd. of Elections* (1966). "Other rights, even the most basic, are illusory if the right to vote is undermined." *Wesberry v. Sanders* (1964);*see also Yick Wo v. Hopkins* (1886) (finding that the right to vote is "preservative of all rights"). "'The right to vote is protected in more than the initial allocation of the franchise. Equal protection applies as well to the manner of its exercise.'" *League of Women Voters v. Brunner* (6th Cir. 2008) (quoting *Bush v. Gore* (2000)). "[A] citizen has a constitutionally protected right to participate in elections on an equal basis with other citizens in the jurisdiction." *Dunn v. Blumstein* (1972). "Having once granted the right to vote on equal terms, the State may not, by later arbitrary and disparate treatment, value one person's vote over that of another." *Bush*; *see also Wesburry* ("Our Constitution leaves no room for classification of people in a way that unnecessarily abridges [the right to vote.]").

The Equal Protection Clause applies when a state either classifies voters in disparate ways, *see Bush* (arbitrary and disparate treatment of votes violates equal protection), or places restrictions on the right to vote, *see League of Women Voters* (voting system that burdens the exercise of the right to vote violates equal protection). The precise character of the state's action and the nature of the burden on voters will determine the appropriate equal protection standard. *See Biener v. Cailo* (3d Cir. 2004) ("The scrutiny test depends on the [regulation's] effect on [the plaintiff's] rights.").

If a plaintiff alleges only that a state treated him or her differently than similarly situated voters, without a corresponding burden on the fundamental right to vote, a straightforward rational basis standard of review should be used. *See McDonald v. Bd. of Election Comm'rs* (1969) (applying rational basis to a state statute that prohibited plaintiffs' access to absentee ballots where no burden on the right to vote was shown); *Biener* (applying rational basis where there was no showing of an "infringement on the fundamental right to vote"). On the other extreme, when a state's classification "severely" burdens the fundamental right to vote, as with poll taxes, strict scrutiny is the appropriate standard. *Burdick v. Takushi* (1992); *see also Harper* ("We have long been mindful that where fundamental rights and liberties are asserted under the Equal Protection Clause, classifications which might invade or restrain them must be closely scrutinized and carefully confined.").

Most cases fall in between these two extremes. When a plaintiff alleges that a state has burdened voting rights through the disparate treatment of voters, we review the claim using the "flexible standard" outlined in *Anderson v. Celebrezze* (1983), and *Burdick v. Takushi* (1992). Although *Anderson* and *Burdick* were both ballot-access cases, the Supreme Court has confirmed their vitality in a much broader range of voting rights contexts. *See Crawford* (Scalia, J., concurring) ("To evaluate a law respecting the right to vote—whether it governs voter qualifications, candidate selection, or the voting process—we use the approach set out in *Burdick. . . .* "). The *Burdick* Court stated the standard as follows:

> A court considering a challenge to a state election law must weigh "the character and magnitude of the asserted injury to the rights protected by the First and Fourteenth Amendments that the plaintiff seeks to vindicate" against "the precise interests put forward by the State as justifications for the burden imposed by its rule," taking into consideration "the extent to which those interests make it necessary to burden the plaintiffs' rights."

Burdick (quoting *Anderson*)).

This standard is sufficiently flexible to accommodate the complexities of state election regulations while also protecting the fundamental importance of the right to vote. There is no "litmus test" to separate valid from invalid voting regulations; courts must weigh the burden on voters against the state's asserted justifications and "make the 'hard judgment' that our adversary system demands." *Crawford* (Stevens, J., announcing the judgment of the Court).

The district court applied the *Anderson-Burdick* standard and ultimately concluded that the justifications proffered by the State were insufficient to outweigh the burden on Plaintiffs' voting rights. Instead of the *Anderson-Burdick* standard, the State and Intervenors urge us to apply a rational basis standard of review to the early voting restriction at issue. Because Plaintiffs' complaint alleges a straightforward equal protection violation, they argue, a straightforward equal protection analysis should follow. However, when a state regulation is found to treat voters differently in a way that burdens the fundamental right to vote, the *Anderson-Burdick* standard applies.

The State and Intervenors argue that the *Anderson-Burdick* standard is applicable only when a state regulation is alleged to have violated the free association and due process guarantees of the First and Fourteenth Amendments, not when a plaintiff alleges only an equal protection violation. The State seeks to disconnect and isolate these areas of constitutional law as they apply to voting rights, but its approach would create inflexible doctrinal silos. The Supreme Court in *Anderson* explicitly imported the analysis used in equal protection cases to evaluate voting rights challenges brought under the First Amendment thus creating a single standard for evaluating challenges to voting restrictions. The Supreme Court confirmed this approach in *Crawford* by directly connecting its equal protection voting rights jurisprudence in *Harper v. Va. State Bd. of Elections* (1966), with *Anderson* and *Burdick,* and finally applying the standard derived from those cases to a state statute allegedly burdening the right to vote. Plaintiffs have demonstrated that their right to vote is unjustifiably burdened by the changes in Ohio's early voting regime. The *Anderson-Burdick* standard therefore applies.

The State relies heavily on *McDonald v. Bd. of Election Comm'rs* (1969) for the proposition that rational basis is the appropriate standard when a state denies absentee ballots to some citizens and not others. In *McDonald,* unsentenced Illinois inmates were denied access to absentee ballots because they were not among the categories of voters that were provided those ballots under Illinois law. The Court applied a rational basis standard of review, reasoning that the state had not classified the inmates based on race or wealth, nor was there any evidence "in the record to indicate that the Illinois statutory scheme has an impact on appellants' ability to exercise the fundamental right to vote." *Id.* The Court found no fundamental right to receive an absentee ballot as such, and stated, "[W]e cannot lightly assume, with nothing in the record to support such an assumption, that Illinois has in fact precluded appellants from voting." *Id.* The *McDonald* plaintiffs failed to make out a claim for heightened scrutiny because they had presented no evidence to support their allegation that they were being prevented from voting. *See O'Brien v. Skinner* (1974) ("Essentially the Court's disposition of the claims in *McDonald* rested on failure of proof."); *Goosby v. Osser* (finding that *McDonald* itself suggested a different result if plaintiffs had presented evidence that the state was effectively preventing them from voting).

On the contrary, Plaintiffs introduced extensive evidence that a significant number of Ohio voters will in fact be precluded from voting without the additional three days of in-person early voting.* The district court credited statistical studies that estimated approximately 100,000 Ohio voters would choose to vote during the three-day period before Election Day, and that these voters are disproportionately "women, older, and of lower income and education attainment." The district court concluded that the burden on

* [Editors' note: This assertion of "extensive evidence that a significant number of Ohio voters will in fact be precluded from voting without the additional three days of in-person early voting" was vigorously disputed by Husted and DeWine in their subsequent effort to convince the U.S. Supreme Court to block the injunction. You should also pay close attention to what Judge White's separate opinion says about this assertion.]

Plaintiffs was "particularly high" because their members, supporters, and constituents represent a large percentage of those who participated in early voting in past elections. The State did not dispute the evidence presented by Plaintiffs, nor did it offer any evidence to contradict the district court's findings of fact. Plaintiffs did not need to show that they were legally prohibited from voting, but only that "burdened voters have few alternate means of access to the ballot." *Citizens for Legislative Choice v. Miller* (6th Cir. 1998) (citing *Burdick*).

The State argues that the burden on non-military voters is slight because they have "ample" other means to cast their ballots, including by requesting and mailing an absentee ballot, voting in person prior to the final weekend before Election Day, or on Election Day itself. However, the district court concluded that because early voters have disproportionately lower incomes and less education than election day voters, and because all evening and weekend voting hours prior to the final weekend were eliminated by Directive 2012-35, "thousands of voters who would have voted during those three days will not be able to exercise their right to cast a vote in person." Based on the evidence in the record, this conclusion was not clearly erroneous. Because the district court found that Plaintiffs' right to vote was burdened, it properly applied the *Anderson-Burdick* standard. Therefore, if Plaintiffs can show that the State's burden on their voting rights is not sufficiently justified, they are likely to succeed on their claim that the State has violated the Equal Protection Clause.

B. Ohio's Justifications

The State offers two justifications for eliminating in-person early voting for non-military voters during the three days before Election Day. First, it asserts that local county boards of elections are too busy preparing for Election Day to accommodate early voters after 6:00 p.m. on the Friday before the election. Second, the State claims that the unique challenges faced by military service members and their families justify maintaining in-person early voting for them but not for other Ohio voters.

The State correctly argues that its two justifications are relevant to two separate aspects of the equal protection analysis: the first justification—the burden on local boards of elections—should be considered in relation to the State's restriction of voting rights, while the second justification—the need to accommodate military voters and their families—should be considered in relation to the State's disparate treatment of military and non-military voters. These two strands are part of the same equal protection analysis. If the State merely placed "nonsevere, nondiscriminatory restrictions" on all voters, the restrictions would survive if they could be sufficiently justified. *See Crawford* (discussing the application of the *Anderson-Burdick* standard to "reasonable, nondiscriminatory restrictions"). On the other hand, if the State merely classified voters disparately but placed no restrictions on their right to vote, the classification would survive if it had a rational basis. *See McDonald* (applying rational basis review where no burden on the right to vote was shown). However, the State has done both; it has classified voters disparately and has burdened their right to vote. Therefore, both justifications proffered by the State must be examined to determine whether the challenged statutory scheme violates equal protection. We will address each proposed justification in turn.

1. Burden on Local Boards of Elections

The State contends that halting in-person early voting at 6:00 p.m. on the Friday before the election is necessary to give local county boards of elections enough time to prepare for Election Day. The State introduced the affidavit of Deputy Assistant Secretary of State Matthew Damschroder, who explained the myriad tasks that the boards must complete during the Saturday, Sunday, and Monday before the election. Among these duties are: (1) validating, scanning, and tabulating absentee ballots that have been cast in-person or received by mail prior to the final weekend, (2) securing all the necessary ballots, instruction cards, registration forms, and other materials for use by voters, (3) ensuring that each polling place has the proper voting equipment, tables, chairs, and signs, (4) ensuring that each polling place is accessible and making any temporary improvements that are necessary, such as installing ramps, (5) preparing the official lists of registered voters, including notations for those voters who have already requested absentee ballots, and (6) handling any last-minute issues that arise, including moving polling places and replacing poll workers who are suddenly unable to serve.

Granted, the list of responsibilities of the boards of elections is long, and the staff and volunteers who prepare for and administer elections undoubtedly have much to accomplish during the final few days before the election. But the State has shown no evidence indicating how this election will be more onerous than the numerous other elections that have been successfully administered in Ohio since early voting was put into place in 2005. During that time, the Ohio boards of elections have effectively conducted a presidential election and a gubernatorial election, not to mention many other statewide and local elections, all while simultaneously handling in-person early voting during the three days prior to the election. The State has not shown that any problems arose as a result of the added responsibilities of administering early voting, and in fact, it seems that one of the primary motivations behind instituting early voting was to relieve local boards of the strain caused by all voters casting their ballots on a single day. *See League of Women Voters* (describing the many problems faced by voters during the November 2004 election in Ohio, including extremely long lines and wait-times on Election Day).

The district court considered evidence from several of Ohio's counties that contradicts the State's assertions. Ohio's most populous county, Cuyahoga County, asserted that maintaining in-person early voting would actually alleviate some of its burden by spreading out the demand for voting over more days, thus reducing lines and wait times at polling places on Election Day. Further evidence showed that several more Ohio counties have already allocated funding for early voting, thus allaying concerns about the financial hardship that early voting might cause. While these counties cannot speak for all of

Ohio's counties, the State introduced no specific evidence to refute any of their assertions, nor has it suggested that the experience of these counties is unique.

Under the *Anderson-Burdick* standard, we must weigh "the character and magnitude of the asserted injury" against the "precise interests put forward by the State . . . taking into consideration the extent to which those interests make it *necessary* to burden the plaintiff's rights." *Burdick* (emphasis added). The State must propose an "interest sufficiently weighty to justify the limitation." *Norman v. Reed* (1992). The burden on Plaintiffs' voting rights is surely real, as the district court found, but the elimination of in-person early voting during the three-day period prior to the election does not absolutely prohibit early voters from voting. However, because early voters tend to be members of demographic groups that may be unable to vote on Election Day or during the workday at local boards of elections because of work schedules, their ability to cast a ballot is impeded by Ohio's statutory scheme. The burden on non-military Ohio voters is not severe, but neither is it slight.

The State's proffered interest in smooth election administration must be "sufficiently weighty" to justify the elimination of in-person early voting for non-military voters during the three-day period in question. If the State had enacted a generally applicable, nondiscriminatory voting regulation that limited in-person early voting for all Ohio voters, its "important regulatory interests" would likely be sufficient to justify the restriction. *See Burdick.* However, Ohio's statutory scheme is not generally applicable to all voters, nor is the State's justification sufficiently "important" to excuse the discriminatory burden it has placed on some but not all Ohio voters. The State advances only a vague interest in the smooth functioning of local boards of elections. The State simply indicates that allowing in-person early voting, as was done in the past, "*could* make it much more difficult for the boards of elections to prepare for Election Day." (emphasis added). With no evidence that local boards of elections have struggled to cope with early voting in the past, no evidence that they may struggle to do so during the November 2012 election, and faced with several of those very local boards in opposition to its claims, the State has not shown that its regulatory interest in smooth election administration is "important," much less "sufficiently weighty" to justify the burden it has placed on nonmilitary Ohio voters.

2. Unique Challenges to Military Service Members and Their Families

The State's asserted goal of accommodating the unique situation of members of the military, who may be called away at a moment's notice in service to the nation, is certainly a worthy and commendable goal. However, while there is a compelling reason to provide more opportunities for military voters to cast their ballots, there is no corresponding satisfactory reason to prevent non-military voters from casting their ballots as well.

Federal and state law makes numerous exceptions and special accommodations for members of the military, within the voting context and without, and no one argues that these exceptions are somehow constitutionally suspect. By and large, these statutes and regulations—from UOCAVA and the MOVE Act to the Uniformed Services Employment and Reemployment Act—are based on highly relevant distinctions between service members and the civilian population, and they confer benefits accordingly. For example, UOCAVA's accommodations for military and overseas voters are based almost entirely on the difficulties that arise from being physically located outside the United States. To address communication difficulties, Ohio law permits absent military and overseas voters to request an absentee ballot by mail, fax, email, or in person, while other voters may only do so by mail or in person. To account for inconsistencies and delays in foreign mail systems, UOCAVA, as amended by the MOVE Act, requires states to provide absentee ballots to absent military and overseas voters at least 45 days prior to an election. 42 U.S.C. § 1973ff-1(a)(8). These special accommodations are tailored to address the problems that arise from being overseas.

Providing more time for military and overseas voters to cast their ballots in-person is not a response to the problem of these voters being absent, because absent voters obviously cannot cast ballots in person. Rather, the State argues that these voters need more time to vote early because they could be called away from the jurisdiction in an emergency with little notice. We acknowledge the difficult circumstances of members of the military and their families, who constantly face the possibility of a sudden and unexpected deployment, and we admire their dedication and sacrifice. For that reason, Ohio's commitment to providing as many opportunities as possible for service members and their families to vote early is laudable. However, the State has offered no justification for not providing similarly situated voters those same opportunities. *See S.S. v. E. Ky. Univ.* (6th Cir. 2008) ("In essence, a State must 'treat similarly situated individuals in a similar manner.'" (quoting *Buchanan v. City of Bolivar* (6th Cir. 1996)).

The State asserts that military and overseas voters are not similarly situated to other Ohio voters for equal protection purposes. "The Equal Protection Clause does not forbid classifications. It simply keeps governmental decisionmakers from treating differently persons who are in all *relevant* respects alike." *Nordlinger v. Hahn* (1992) (emphasis added). In many respects, absent military and overseas voters are not similarly situated to other Ohio voters. Typically, their absence from the country is the factor that makes them distinct, and this is reflected in the exceptions and special accommodations afforded to these voters under federal and state law.

With respect to in-person early voting, however, there is no relevant distinction between the two groups. The State argues that military voters need extra early voting time because they could be suddenly deployed. But any voter could be suddenly called away and prevented from voting on Election Day. At any time, personal contingencies like medical emergencies or sudden business trips could arise, and police officers, firefighters and other first responders could be suddenly called to serve at a moment's notice. There is no reason to provide these voters with fewer opportunities to vote than military voters, particularly when there is no evidence that local boards of elections will be unable to cope with more early voters. While we readily acknowledge the need to provide military voters more time to vote, we see no corresponding justification for giving others less time.

The State and Intervenors worry about the logical extensions and practical implications of Plaintiffs' position. If states are forced to provide the same accommodations to every voter that they currently provide to military and overseas voters, such as added flexibility and extra time, states may simply eliminate these special accommodations altogether. However, virtually all of the special voting provisions in federal and Ohio law address problems that arise when military and overseas voters are *absent* from their voting jurisdictions. They are not similarly situated to all other voters in this respect, and states are justified in accommodating their particular needs. With respect to in-person voting, the two groups are similarly situated, and the State has not shown that it would be burdensome to extend early voting to all voters. Its argument to the contrary is not borne out by the evidence.

Equally worrisome would be the result if states were permitted to pick and choose among groups of similarly situated voters to dole out special voting privileges. Partisan state legislatures could give extra early voting time to groups that traditionally support the party in power and impose corresponding burdens on the other party's core constituents. *See Clingman v. Beaver* (2005) (O'Connor, J., concurring) ("[P]articularly where [voting restrictions] have discriminatory effects, there is increasing cause for concern that those in power may be using electoral rules to erect barriers to electoral competition."). To avoid this dangerous result, courts must carefully weigh the asserted injury against the "precise interests" proffered by the State. *Burdick*. Although the State argues that it has justifiably given more early voting time to military and overseas voters, in fact, the time available to those voters has not changed and will not be affected by the district court's order. Rather, the State must show that its decision to reduce the early voting time of non-military voters is justified by a "sufficiently weighty" interest. The State has proposed no interest which would justify reducing the opportunity to vote by a considerable segment of the voting population.

Having found that neither interest proposed by the State is sufficient to justify the limitation on in-person early voting imposed on all non-military Ohio voters, we find that Plaintiffs are likely to succeed on their claim that Ohio Rev. Code § 3509.03, as implemented by the Ohio Secretary of State, violates the Equal Protection Clause.

III. Equitable Factors

Plaintiffs, their members and constituents, and all non-military Ohio voters would be irreparably injured absent a preliminary injunction. When constitutional rights are threatened or impaired, irreparable injury is presumed. A restriction on the fundamental right to vote therefore constitutes irreparable injury.

The balance of equities and the public interest also weigh in plaintiff's favor. The burden on non-military Ohio voters' ability to cast ballots, particularly when many of those voters will likely be unable to vote on Election Day or during the day at local boards of elections because of work schedules, outweighs any corresponding burden on the State, which has not shown that local boards will be unable to cope with three extra days of in-person early voting—as they have successfully done in past elections. While states have "a strong interest in their ability to enforce state election law requirements," *Hunter*, the public has a "strong interest in exercising the 'fundamental political right' to vote." *Purcell v. Gonzalez* (2006) (quoting *Dunn*). "That interest is best served by favoring enfranchisement and ensuring that qualified voters' exercise of their right to vote is successful." *Hunter*. The public interest therefore favors permitting as many qualified voters to vote as possible. Because the district court properly found that the equitable factors favor Plaintiffs, its decision to issue a preliminary injunction was appropriate.

IV. District Court's Remedy

The State argues that the district court's remedy was overbroad because it could be read to affirmatively require the State to mandate early voting hours during the three-day period prior to the election. We do not read the district court's order in this way. The order clearly restores the *status quo ante,* returning discretion to local boards of elections to allow all Ohio voters to vote during Saturday, November 3, 2012; Sunday, November 4, 2012; and Monday, November 5, 2012. Because Ohio Rev. Code § 3509.03 is unconstitutional to the extent that it prohibits non-military voters from voting during this period, the State is enjoined from preventing those voters from participating in early voting. But the State is not affirmatively required to order the boards to be open for early voting. Under the district court's order, the boards have discretion, just as they had before the enactment of § 3509.03. The district court's remedy was therefore appropriate.

CONCLUSION

For the foregoing reasons, we affirm the district court's order granting a preliminary injunction.

Helene N. WHITE, Circuit Judge (concurring in part and dissenting in part).

Except with respect to the remedy, I join in the affirmance but arrive there by a different route.

I

[Omitted.]

II

There is no constitutional right to an absentee ballot. This is made clear in *McDonald v. Board of Election Commissioners* (1969). The Constitution protects the right to vote, and it is only when there is no alternative vehicle for voting that the Supreme Court has found a right to an absentee ballot. [The Court's] absentee-ballot cases applied the rational-basis test to claims of entitlement to an absentee ballot as well as to equal protection challenges based on differentiations between voters with regard to absentee ballots, and recognized the state interest in regulating elections. One may understandably ask, then, how Ohio's restrictions on in-person absentee voting can violate the Constitution. For me, the answer is that the Supreme Court has since applied the *Anderson/Burdick* balancing test in evaluating a state's interest in the regulation of elections, and that in applying that test, it is proper to look at the facts on the ground in Ohio.

III

The instant case raises several preliminary questions that affect the result. The first is which standard governs our consideration of plaintiffs' claims—the rational-basis test employed in the absentee-ballot cases, or the more recent *Anderson/Burdick* balancing test, which weighs the burden on the right to vote against the state's important regulatory interests. The Supreme Court has not decided an absentee-ballot case since the *Anderson/Burdick* test was announced, but two circuit courts have, and both applied the balancing test. In *Price v. New York State Board of Elections* (2d Cir. 2008), the Second Circuit considered a challenge to New York statutes that permitted absentee voting in all elections except county party committee elections. The court rejected New York's argument that rational-basis review should apply, analyzed the case under *Anderson/Burdick,* and found New York's interests did not justify the burden on voters. In *Griffin v. Roupas* (7th Cir. 2004), the Seventh Circuit considered a challenge brought by Illinois working mothers who asserted a constitutional right to vote by absentee ballot (or some other alternative means) on the same basis as other voters who were granted the right to vote by absentee ballot because, like the other voters, they too had great difficulty voting between 6 a.m. and 7 p.m. on election day. Although the court denied the challenge, it applied the *Anderson/Burdick* balancing test.

Thus, I agree with the district court and the majority that the *Anderson/Burdick* balancing test is, indeed, the proper test. The Supreme Court has applied this test in its election jurisprudence since *Anderson, see, e.g., Crawford* (2008), and the test is flexible enough to approximate the rational-basis test when appropriate, i.e., where the burden is slight, the required showing by the state is correspondingly light.

IV

In applying this balancing test, I cannot agree with the majority's assertion that "Plaintiffs introduced extensive evidence that a significant number of Ohio voters will in fact be precluded from voting without the additional three days of in-person early voting." If that were in fact the case, this would be a simple matter. The burden would be great and the rationales offered by Ohio, which are plausible and rational on their face but find little support in the record, would not outweigh the burden on those precluded from exercising their right to vote. However, though the record clearly establishes that a significant number of Ohio voters found it most convenient to vote after hours and the weekend before the election, the study did not consider the extent to which these voters would or could avail themselves of other voting options, either by mail ballot or in-person absentee ballot at other times, or in-person voting on election day. Convenience cannot be equated with necessity without more. Thus, it cannot be fairly said that there was evidence that a significant number of Ohio voters will be precluded from voting unless weekend and after-hours voting is restored.

Nevertheless, the burden may be substantial without being preclusive. A report by the Franklin County Board of Elections concluded that in-person early voting accounted for 9 percent of all ballots cast in the 2008 election, that a disproportionately higher number of African-Americans voted early and, most significantly, that 82 percent of all early in-person votes were cast either after hours on weekdays, on weekends, or the Monday before the election. A study by a voter advocacy group indicating that restrictions on in-person early voting would disproportionately affect African-American voters in Cuyahoga County revealed that African-Americans in that county had voted in disproportionately large numbers during extended hours and weekends, and in the three days before the 2008 general election, although they had the option of voting by mail and in-person during regular business hours; and that restricting in-person early voting in 2012 would likely lead to crowded conditions during regular board hours, raising concern that voters would find it necessary to abandon their attempts to vote due to extremely long wait times. To be sure, these studies as well do not establish that voters will be precluded from voting if after-hours and weekend in-person absentee voting is not restored. But they are strong evidence that a significant number of voters in Ohio's two largest counties have come to depend on after-hours and weekend voting as a vehicle for exercising their right to vote.[7]

Still, no case has held that voting has to be convenient. The question then is whether the elimination of in-person after-hours and weekend voting should be viewed in a vacuum—as if plaintiffs were simply asserting that because of their long work hours and other demographics they should be able to vote after hours and on weekends so that they can get the full benefit of early in-person voting—or in the context of Ohio voting over the last decade, which includes Ohio's remedial grant of such extended in-person absentee-voting opportunities, the substantial exercise of that right, and the boards of Ohio's largest counties' reliance on the availability of such voting. If the weighing must be done in the abstract, I would be compelled to dissent because the election case law does not support the proposition that there is a constitutional right to have voting on terms that

7. Justices Scalia, Thomas and Alito would hold that the weighing of the burden on voters against the state's legitimate regulatory interests must be conducted by looking at the electorate at large, not a particular group of voters who may be burdened disproportionately by an otherwise nondiscriminatory law. *See Crawford* (Scalia, J., concurring). However, Justice Stevens' opinion in *Crawford* (the narrowest opinion, thus the controlling one for our purposes) examined the evidence and concluded that, "on the basis of the record that has been made in this litigation, we cannot conclude that the statute imposes 'excessively burdensome requirements' on any class of voters." *Id*. (quoting *Storer v. Brown* (1974)). Justice Stevens' opinion does not reveal any disinclination to evaluate evidence of an excessive burden; rather, the purely anecdotal evidence did not support that the voter-ID statute at issue imposed such a burden. *See Crawford.*

are equally convenient for all voters. I conclude, however, that the *Anderson/Burdick* balancing in this case should not be divorced from reality, and that both the burden and the legitimate regulatory interest should be evaluated in context.

V

The key distinguishing factor here is that Ohio voters were granted the statutory right to in-person absentee voting through the close of business hours on the Monday before election day, and the election boards of the largest counties broadly embraced and facilitated that right, in response to the unacceptably burdensome situation at many Ohio polling sites during the 2004 election where, in some counties, voters were required to stand in line for long hours and until late at night. Thus, section 3509.03(I), as originally enacted, was intended to relieve the pressure on the system resulting from heavy turnout on election day. Further, experience shows that Ohio voters have taken increasing advantage of in-person absentee voting. In the last presidential election, close to 500,000 Ohio voters cast in-person absentee ballots, of which it appears a little over 100,000 were cast the weekend before the election. Further, in the 2008 election, the residents of Ohio's two largest counties, Cuyahoga and Franklin, cast over 100,000 in-person absentee votes, the vast majority during after-hours and on weekends. These counties have budgeted and planned for the expected extended hours and weekend in-person absentee voting, especially the weekend before the election. They have not budgeted or planned for any increase in election-day voting caused by the elimination of weekend and after-hours voting, and fear that the restrictions on the hours for in-person absentee voting will cause some citizens not to vote and others to vote on election day, leading to long lines and unreasonable delays at the polls, which in turn will cause some voters to abandon their attempts at voting, as happened in 2004.

Although states are permitted broad discretion in devising the election scheme that fits best with the perceived needs of the state, and there is no abstract constitutional right to vote by absentee ballot, eleventh-hour changes to remedial voting provisions that have been in effect since 2005 and have been relied on by substantial numbers of voters for the exercise of their franchise are properly considered as a burden in applying *Anderson/Burdick* balancing. To conclude otherwise is to ignore reality. This does not mean that states cannot change their voting schemes, only that in doing so they must consider the burden the change and the manner of implementing the change places on the exercise of the right to vote.

VI

Defendants argue that the new restricted in-person absentee voting hours are necessary to relieve election workers and election officials from the burdens of in-person absentee voting immediately before the election, and to assure uniformity in absentee-voting hours throughout the state. These are legitimate regulatory interests; but neither bears any relation to the elimination of all after-hours and weekend voting preceding the final weekend. Regarding the final weekend, these concerns provide little explanation for the elimination of the right to obtain an absentee ballot in person the Saturday before the election, when election workers are still honoring mail requests for absentee ballots until noon pursuant to statute. And in weighing the elimination of in-person absentee voting the remainder of the weekend, the record shows that many of the specific complaints voiced by election officials stemmed from in-person absentee voting the Monday before the election, not the entire weekend. The desire for uniformity has little to do with the elimination of all weekend and after-hours in-person voting. Defendants offer no explanation for curtailing hours other than on the final weekend, and uniformity without some underlying reason for the chosen rule is not a justification in and of itself. Nor is there a showing that eliminating all weekend and after-hours voting will in fact produce uniform access, as opposed to uniform hours.

Given the studies presented regarding the heavy use of in-person after-hours and weekend voting, and the legitimate concerns of Ohio's largest counties and their voters regarding the smooth and efficient running of the 2012 presidential election, I conclude that defendants' legitimate regulatory interests do not outweigh the burden on voters.

Finally, I conclude that this is the unusual case where distinctions between UOCAVA and non-UOCAVA voters cannot support the disparate treatment at issue. The record adequately supports the district court's conclusion that the State's proffered reason for the distinction between UOCAVA and non-UOCAVA voters—concern that military voters might be deployed sometime between Friday evening and election day—had no relation to the statutory distinction.

VII

Turning to the question of remedy, I understand the district court to have required Secretary Husted to restore in-person absentee voting through the Monday preceding election day. I would remand the matter with instructions to give the Secretary and the General Assembly a short and finite period in which cure the constitutional defects, with the understanding that a failure to do so will result in the reinstatement of the preliminary injunction.

NOTE ON THE REDUCTION OF EARLY VOTING IN NORTH CAROLINA

As part of the comprehensive set of changes to North Carolina's voting laws adopted in 2013, the legislature eliminated the first week of early voting that had previously existed (causing early voting to start now on the second Thursday before Election Day, rather than the third Thursday beforehand) and required that early voting end by 1 P.M. on Saturday before Election Day. This curtailment of early voting is now under litigation in federal court, and this case will be a test of the precedent established in *Obama for America v. Husted.* The North Carolina law does not differentiate between military and nonmilitary voters in the availability of early voting; will this fact make a difference in the outcome of the pending litigation?

Moreover, in addition to arguing that the new North Carolina law violates Equal Protection, the pending lawsuit also claims that it violates Section 2 of the Voting Rights Act because it imposes a discriminatory burden on African-American voters, who as a group rely upon early voting (particularly the last Sunday before Election Day) more heavily than white voters. What do you think are the chances of success of this particular claim, and what kind (and degree) of evidence would plaintiffs need to show to prevail?

D. "Election Eve" Litigation

In *Ohio Republican Party v. Brunner*, we saw an example of "election eve" litigation—a lawsuit filed shortly before Election Day in an effort to affect the conduct of the voting process for the upcoming election. Although the substantive issue in that case concerned voter registration databases, and specifically whether Ohio's Secretary of State was obligated to share certain information about database "mismatches" with local boards of elections, the timing of the litigation raised additional procedural issues concerning whether it was appropriate for the federal judiciary to issue a temporary restraining order (TRO) so close in time to the casting of ballots (and thus whether it was appropriate for the appellate court to vacate that TRO).

The leading case concerning "election eve" litigation is *Purcell v. Gonzales*, 549 U.S. 1 (2006), which was prominently cited by both sides in *Ohio Republican Party v. Brunner*. We have already read a later phase of the same lawsuit as *Purcell v. Gonzales*: *Arizona v. Intertribal Council*, about the validity of Arizona's requirement that voters prove their citizenship when they register to vote, was the subsequent substantive decision on the merits long after the preliminary procedural ruling in *Purcell v. Gonzales*. Thus, *Purcell* (like *Ohio Republican Party v. Brunner*) illustrates how different substantive issues can be intertwined with similar procedural issues. Indeed, after reading *Purcell* itself, we will consider some additional "election eve" litigation that concerned other types of substantive issues, including the rules for "polling place challenges," which occur when someone at a polling place argues that a particular individual who wants to vote is ineligible to do so.

PURCELL v. GONZALEZ

549 U.S. 1 (2006)

Per Curiam.

The State of Arizona and officials from four of its counties seek relief from an interlocutory injunction entered by a two-judge motions panel of the Court of Appeals for the Ninth Circuit. Justice Kennedy has referred the applicants' filings to the Court. We construe the filings of the State and the county officials as petitions for certiorari; we grant the petitions; and we vacate the order of the Court of Appeals.

I

In 2004, Arizona voters approved Proposition 200. The measure sought to combat voter fraud by requiring voters to present proof of citizenship when they register to vote and to present identification when they vote on election day.

The election procedures implemented to effect Proposition 200 do not necessarily result in the turning away of qualified, registered voters by election officials for lack of proper identification. A voter who arrives at the polls on election day without identification may cast a conditional provisional ballot. For that ballot to be counted, the voter is allowed five business days to return to a designated site and present proper identification. In addition any voter who knows he or she cannot secure identification within five business days of the election has the option to vote before election day during the early voting period. The State has determined that, because there is adequate time during the early voting period to compare the voters' signatures on the ballot with their signatures on the registration rolls, voters need not present identification if voting early.

In the District Court the plaintiffs in this action are residents of Arizona; Indian tribes; and various community organizations. In May 2006, these plaintiffs brought suit challenging Proposition 200's identification requirements. On September 11, 2006, the District Court denied their request for a preliminary injunction, but it did not at that time issue findings of fact or conclusions of law. These findings were important because resolution of legal questions in the Court of Appeals required evaluation of underlying factual issues.

The plaintiffs appealed the denial, and the Clerk of the Court of Appeals set a briefing schedule that concluded on November 21, two weeks after the upcoming November 7 election. The plaintiffs then requested an injunction pending appeal. Pursuant to the Court of Appeals' rules, the request for an injunction was assigned to a two-judge motions/screening panel. On October 5, after receiving lengthy written responses from the State and the county officials but without oral argument, the panel issued a four-sentence order enjoining Arizona from enforcing Proposition 200's provisions pending [appeal]. The Court of Appeals offered no explanation or justification for its order.

Despite the time-sensitive nature of the proceedings and the pendency of a request for emergency relief in the Court of Appeals, the District Court did not issue its findings of fact and conclusions of law until October 12. It then concluded that "plaintiffs have shown a possibility of success on the merits of some of their arguments but the Court cannot say that at this stage they have shown a strong likelihood." The District Court then found the balance of the harms and the public interest counseled in favor of denying the injunction.

II

"A State indisputably has a compelling interest in preserving the integrity of its election process." *Eu v. San Francisco County Democratic Central Comm.* (1989). Confidence in the integrity of our electoral processes is essential to the functioning of our participatory democracy. Voter fraud drives honest citizens out of the democratic process and breeds distrust of our government. Voters who fear their legitimate votes will be outweighed by fraudulent ones will feel disenfranchised. "[T]he right of suffrage can be denied by a debasement or dilution of the weight of a citizen's vote just as effectively as by wholly prohibiting the free exercise of the franchise." *Reynolds v. Sims* (1964). Countering the State's compelling interest in preventing voter fraud is the plaintiffs' strong interest in exercising the "fundamental political right" to vote. *Dunn v. Blumstein* (1972). Although the likely effects of Proposition 200 are much debated, the possibility that qualified voters might be turned away from the polls would caution any district judge to give careful consideration to the plaintiffs' challenges.

Faced with an application to enjoin operation of voter identification procedures just weeks before an election, the Court of Appeals was required to weigh, in addition to the harms attendant upon issuance or nonissuance of an injunction, considerations specific to election cases and its own institutional procedures. Court orders affecting elections, especially conflicting orders, can themselves result in voter confusion and consequent incentive to remain away from the polls. As an election draws closer, that risk will increase. So the Court of Appeals may have deemed this consideration to be grounds for prompt action. Furthermore, it might have given some weight to the possibility that the nonprevailing parties would want to seek en banc review. In the Ninth Circuit that procedure, involving voting by all active judges and an en banc hearing by a court of 15, can consume further valuable time. These considerations, however, cannot be controlling here. It was still necessary, as a procedural matter, for the Court of Appeals to give deference to the discretion of the District Court. We find no indication that it did so, and we conclude this was error.

Although at the time the Court of Appeals issued its order the District Court had not yet made factual findings to which the Court of Appeals owed deference, by failing to provide any factual findings or indeed any reasoning of its own the Court of Appeals left this Court in the position of evaluating the Court of Appeals' bare order in light of the District Court's ultimate findings. There has been no explanation given by the Court of Appeals showing the ruling and findings of the District Court to be incorrect. In view of the impending election, the necessity for clear guidance to the State of Arizona, and our conclusion regarding the Court of Appeals' issuance of the order, we vacate the order of the Court of Appeals.

We underscore that we express no opinion here on the correct disposition, after full briefing and argument, of the appeals from the District Court's September 11 order or on the ultimate resolution of these cases. As we have noted, the facts in these cases are hotly contested, and "[n]o bright line separates permissible election-related regulation from unconstitutional infringements." *Timmons v. Twin Cities Area New Party* (1997). Given the imminence of the election and the inadequate time to resolve the factual disputes, our action today shall of necessity allow the election to proceed without an injunction suspending the voter identification rules.

The order of the Court of Appeals is vacated, and the cases are remanded for further proceedings consistent with this opinion.

1. The Immediate Fight over the Meaning of Purcell

Only 11 days after the Supreme Court issued its decision in *Purcell v. Gonzales*, a Sixth Circuit panel split 2-1 over how to apply it to another "election eve" case that same year. Whereas in *Purcell* the district court had refused to enjoin a voter identification rule challenged just before the casting of ballots was about to begin, and the Supreme Court had rebuked the Ninth Circuit for failing to defer to the district court, here the district court had enjoined the challenged rule. Thus, on appeal, the question was whether *Purcell* was more about giving deference to the district court (which would have supported upholding the district court's injunction), or more about the federal judiciary's need to refrain from interfering with the operation of election procedures during the last few days before the casting of ballots (which would serve as a reason to overturn the district court's injunction in this case). Perhaps not surprisingly, the 2-1 split in this case tracked the partisan background of the three judges: The two Republican appointees in the majority favored the "no last-minute interference" interpretation of *Purcell*, whereas the one Democratic appointee preferred the "deference to the district court" interpretation.

NORTHEAST OHIO COALITION FOR THE HOMELESS v. BLACKWELL

467 F.3d 999 (6th Cir. 2006)

JULIA SMITH GIBBONS, Circuit Judge.

J. Kenneth Blackwell, in his official capacity as the Secretary of State of Ohio, moves this court to stay or vacate a temporary restraining order ("TRO") [blocks] enforcement of certain absentee voter identification provisions under Ohio Rev. Code Ann. §§ 3509.03(E)(1)-(3), 3509.04, 3509.05(A).

I

[Ohio statutory law requires absentee voters to provide either their driver's license number, the last four digits of their Social Security number, or a copy of one of several different types of identifying documents. The plaintiffs in this case challenged these requirements on the ground that they were unconstitutionally imprecise in various ways. For example, an Ohio driver's license actually contains two numbers, one more prominently displayed than the other, but the less prominent of the two is the only one that state law considers to be the official driver's license number.]

II

After a hearing on October 26, 2006, the district court issued a TRO restraining the enforcement of the absentee voting identification requirements. Specifically, the district court concluded the phrases "current," "other government document," "military identification," and "driver's license number" were unconstitutionally vague and were being unequally applied by the Boards of Elections. In addition to enjoining enforcement of these provisions, the district court ordered the Secretary to issue a directive to the Boards of Elections requiring that they not enforce the enjoined provisions, preserve all absentee ballots in their present form, and inform absentee voters that compliance with the enjoined provisions was not required.

III

The TRO at issue in this case both threatens to inflict irretrievable harm before it expires and acts as a mandatory injunction that does not preserve the status quo. The TRO requires the Secretary to direct County Boards of Elections not to enforce the disputed voter identification requirements and, in fact, to instruct voters affirmatively that they need not comply with the identification requirements. Any absentee ballot cast during the operation of the TRO must necessarily be considered valid, regardless of whether the voter has complied with the identification requirements. As it will be difficult, if not impossible, to equitably enforce the voter identification requirements retroactively for these ballots, the TRO permanently exempts these ballots from the disputed law, regardless of the ultimate resolution of this case, inflicting an irretrievable harm on the State of Ohio. Thus the TRO goes far beyond preserving the status quo, which could be achieved by restraining the State from discarding any ballots that it found to be in violation of the identification requirements. The nature and effect of this TRO necessitate an immediate interlocutory appeal.

IV

[Omitted.]

V

The district court's decision to grant a temporary restraining order, when appealable, is reviewed by this court for abuse of discretion. To determine whether a TRO should be stayed, the court considers the same factors considered in determining whether to issue a TRO or preliminary injunction. Those factors are (1) whether the movant has a strong likelihood of success on the merits, (2) whether the movant would suffer irreparable injury absent a stay, (3) whether granting the stay would cause substantial harm to others, and (4) whether the public interest would be served by granting the stay. "These factors are not prerequisites that must be met, but are interrelated considerations that must be balanced together." *Mich. Coal. of Radioactive Material Users, Inc. v. Griepentrog* (6th Cir. 1991). For example, the probability of success that must be demonstrated is inversely proportional to the amount of irreparable injury the movants will suffer absent the stay.

[Because the Secretary has issued a Directive clarifying the statutory terms that the plaintiffs claim to be unconstitutionally imprecise,] there is reason to question whether they are likely to prevail. Count One alleges a due process violation arising from the vagueness of the laws, causing the election to be conducted in an unfair manner due to nonuniform application of the law and chilling voters' willingness to exercise their right to vote. Count Two alleges that the vagueness and nonuniform application constitute an equal protection violation. The Directive addresses various provisions that were the subject of plaintiffs' claims of nonuniform application, including the meanings of the terms "current," "government document," and "driver's license number."[5] Thus, the Directive appears to largely obviate the [plaintiffs'] concerns with respect to absentee ballots submitted after its issuance. Certainly, its issuance reduces the scope of the disputed issues to a set far smaller than those the TRO encompasses.

Plaintiffs do not challenge the Secretary's authority to issue the Directive. Nor do they deny that it will at least prospectively obviate many of their vagueness and inconsistent treatment concerns. Plaintiffs argue, however, that the Directive may have the effect of disadvantaging or disenfranchising some who have already cast their absentee ballots. This speculation is insufficient to satisfy plaintiffs' burden of demonstrating a strong likelihood of success on the merits. Furthermore, plaintiffs' contention that confusion stemming from the pre-Directive vagueness of terms and inconsistent practices will have had a deterrent or chilling effect on absentee voters is unsubstantiated and too speculative to be cognizable.

The remaining factors we must consider strongly support staying the district court's orders. The balance of harms in this case significantly favors granting a stay of the TRO. Each day the TRO is in effect, the Secretary is forced to accept absentee ballots that do not comply with the voter identification requirements enacted by the General Assembly. Should the Secretary prevail after a full adjudication of the merits, it will be difficult, if not impossible, for the voter identification requirements to be applied retroactively to those absentee ballots casts [*sic*] during the TRO. "[T]he State will be irreparably injured in its ability to execute valid laws, which are presumed constitutional, for keeping ineligible voters from voting."[6] *Summit County* [*Democratic Central and Executive Committee v. Blackwell* (6th Cir. 2004)]. However, the State suffers no harm by being required to preserve all absentee ballots. As to the potential harm facing the [plaintiffs], if they

5. The Attorney General states that he is willing to work with plaintiffs to resolve any issues not clarified by the Directive. An amicable resolution of the dispute is obviously far preferable to last-minute litigation that disrupts ongoing electoral processes.

6. In fact, the TRO has already potentially harmed the State by enabling absentee ballots to be submitted without complying with the enjoined provisions. After full adjudication of the merits, if the Secretary prevails and the voter requirements are deemed enforceable, the district court and the parties will have to address how these ballots should be handled to comport with due process and equal protection concerns.

were to prevail on the claims at issue, the vagueness and nonuniformity of the absentee ballot requirements, they would be irreparably harmed only if any noncomplying ballots were disposed of or destroyed and could not later be counted. However, the [plaintiffs] suffer no injury from the continued enforcement of the voter identification requirements to absentee ballots pending a full resolution on the merits. If the [plaintiffs] prevail, all absentee ballots can be counted without regard to the identification requirements. Plaintiffs' concerns that the Directive may have the effect of disadvantaging or disenfranchising some who have already cast their absentee ballots can be completely protected by preserving the ballots without further injunctive relief. Therefore, the balance of harms significantly favors granting a stay of the TRO, except for its requirement that the Boards of Elections preserve all absentee ballots in their present form.

The public interest weighs in favor of granting a stay of the TRO. There is a strong public interest in allowing every registered voter to vote. *See Purcell v. Gonzalez* (2006). There is also a strong public interest in permitting legitimate statutory processes to operate to preclude voting by those who are not entitled to vote. Finally, there is a strong public interest in smooth and effective administration of the voting laws that militates against changing the rules in the middle of the submission of absentee ballots. As the Supreme Court recently recognized, court orders affecting elections can themselves result in voter confusion and cause the very chilling effect that plaintiffs claim they seek to avoid. *See Purcell.* The TRO issued by the district court needlessly creates disorder in electoral processes, without any concomitant benefit to the public.

After weighing all the factors required, the court concludes that the district court abused its discretion by granting the TRO.

Arthur J. TARNOW, District Judge [sitting by designation], dissenting.

I dissent from the Majority's opinion that the district court abused its discretion when it granted the Plaintiffs' request for a temporary restraining order. [I]n a recent voting rights case involving a temporary restraining order, the Supreme Court stated that "it was still necessary, as a procedural matter, for the Court of Appeals to give deference to the discretion of the District Court." *Purcell v. Gonzalez* (2006). I am of the opinion that the Majority has failed to give this required deference to the district court's decision.

2. Voter Eligibility Challenges

In the last few days leading up to the 2004 presidential election in Ohio, there were two rounds of intense litigation concerning the Republican Party's publicly announced desire to challenge the eligibility of up to 35,000 names of newly registered voters in the state. The first round, at issue in the next case, concerned the possibility that local boards of elections would hold hearings prior to Election Day on the eligibility of individual voters. By this decision, the federal judiciary prohibited any such hearings. As a result, the time and place for challenging the eligibility of individual voters would occur on Election Day itself at the polls. The possibility that Republicans would engage in a large number of polling place challenges then prompted the second round of litigation, addressed by the Sixth Circuit in *Summit County Democratic Central and Executive Committee v. Blackwell*, and ultimately resolved by Justice Stevens in *Spencer v. Pugh*, discussed below.

MILLER v. BLACKWELL

348 F. Supp. 2d 916 (S.D. Ohio 2004)

DLOTT, District Judge.

Plaintiffs in this case are the Ohio Democratic Party [and the class of individuals whose eligibility to vote the Ohio Republican Party (ORP) has indicated that it wishes to challenge]. Defendants in the case are J. Kenneth Blackwell, the Ohio Secretary of State, in his official capacity, as well as the Lawrence, Scioto, Cuyahoga, Franklin, Medina, and Trumbull County Boards of Elections, [which plan to hold hearings before Election Day on the ORP's challenges]. Plaintiffs allege that the timing and manner in which Defendants intend to hold hearings regarding pre-election challenges violate both the National Voter Registration Act and the Due Process Clause of the Constitution. The challenges alleged that the voters were ineligible to vote because a nonforwardable mailing that was sent to each of the voters from the Ohio Republican Party was returned, which shows that these voters intend to vote in a precinct in which they are ineligible to vote.

Plaintiffs Miller and Haddix [two of the individuals whose eligibility to vote has been challenged] each signed an affidavit attesting that she is a registered voter residing in the precinct in which she is registered. Both attest that they have not received notice of a hearing regarding the challenge to their respective voter eligibility, but that they were aware that the Medina County Board of Elections scheduled a hearing regarding the challenges on Thursday, October 28, 2004, which neither can attend.

The Court conducted a telephone conference with counsel for all parties on the morning of October 27, 2004. Counsel for each of the County Boards of Elections advised the Court that their respective clients had sent notice or intended to send notice to between 14 and 17,000 challenged voters within their respective counties advising them that their voter registration had been challenged and that a hearing would be held on their eligibility pursuant to Ohio Revised Code Section 3503.24.[4] Counsel advised the Court that these

4. Section 3503.24 provides:

> Any qualified elector of the county may challenge the right to vote of any registered elector not later than eleven days prior to the election. Upon receiving such a challenge, the director must set a time and date for a hearing before the county board of elections and send notice to the challenged voter. The notice must be sent by first class mail no later than three days before the day of any scheduled hearing, and the hearing must be held no later than two days prior to any election. Finally, if the board decides that the voter is in fact not entitled to have his or her name on the voter registration list, the board must remove that person's name from the list.

hearings had been set for various times, ranging from later that afternoon, Wednesday, October 27, 2004, at 4:30 p.m. to Saturday, October 30, at 8 a.m. Counsel also advised the Court that the notices were or would be sent to the address that the Counties had on file—presumably the same address as that on the returned mail that is the basis of these challenges.

ANALYSIS

The timing and manner in which the Defendants intend to send notice and conduct hearings raise grave due process concerns. The Due Process Clause requires notice that is "reasonably calculated, under all the circumstances, to apprise interested parties of the pendency of the action and afford them an opportunity to present their objections." *Dusenbery v. United States* (2002). The Defendants' intended timing and manner of sending notice is not reasonably calculated to apprise Plaintiff Voters of the hearing regarding the challenge to their registrations, nor to give them the opportunity to present their objections, as demonstrated by the individual situations of Plaintiffs Miller and Haddix. The notice here provides too little time for Plaintiff Voters' to receive the notice—if notice is received at all—given that it seems that Defendants intend to send the notice to an address which has already been demonstrated to be faulty.

Additionally, the timing and manner in which Defendants intend to send notice may discourage Plaintiff Voters from exercising th[e] fundamental right [to vote] by leading them to believe that they are not eligible to vote. Consequently, Plaintiffs have demonstrated a substantial likelihood of success on the merits of their claim. They have made a strong showing that Defendants' intended actions regarding pre-election challenges to voter eligibility abridge the Plaintiffs' fundamental right to vote and violate the Due Process Clause.

CONCLUSION

Because Plaintiffs have demonstrated a strong likelihood of success on the merits regarding an alleged violation of their constitutional rights, the other factors to consider in granting a temporary restraining order automatically weigh in Plaintiffs' favor. The Court hereby **ENJOINS** Defendant County Boards of Elections from issuing notices or conducting hearings, including those already scheduled, regarding the pre-election challenges to voter eligibility at issue in this case, and **ENJOINS** Defendant Blackwell from mandating or enforcing such procedures.

NOTE ON WHAT HAPPENED NEXT

Two days later, in *Miller v. Blackwell*, 388 F.3d 546 (Oct. 29, 2004), a three-judge panel of the Sixth Circuit unanimously refused to stay the foregoing TRO:

> This Court is mindful of the practical difficulty of the County Boards of Elections arranging and conducting literally thousands of hearings for all challenged voters between today's date and November 2, 2004 in a manner that complies with all legal prerequisites of county and state election laws without contravening the requirements of the Due Process Clause of the Fourteenth Amendment to the United States Constitution and the National Voter Registration Act, 42 U.S.C. §§ 1973gg *et. seq.* After considering the difficulties posed by the competing concerns of not discouraging or preventing legal voting, on the one hand, and minimizing false registrations and election fraud, on the other hand, this Court hereby [leaves the district court's TRO in place and defers further consideration of the merits until after additional evidentiary proceedings in the district court].

The practical effect of the Sixth Circuit's denial of a stay in *Miller* was to cause the fight over the Republican Party's intended challenges to the eligibility of 35,000 newly registered voters to move to the second round of litigation, this time concerning the possibility of challenges at the polling places on Election Day. This opinion is how the Sixth Circuit handled that second round:

SUMMIT COUNTY DEMOCRATIC CENTRAL AND EXECUTIVE COMMITTEE v. BLACKWELL

388 F.3d 547 (6th Cir. 2004)

ROGERS, Circuit Judge.

Ohio Revised Code § 3505.20 provides that "Any person offering to vote may be challenged at the polling place by any challenger, any elector then lawfully in the polling place, or by any judge or clerk of elections." The challengers referred to in § 3505.20 are provided for in § 3505.21, which provides:

> At any primary, special, or general election, any political party supporting candidates to be voted upon at such election may appoint to any of the polling places in the county or city one person, a qualified elector, who shall serve as challenger for such party during the casting of the ballots.

[This opinion, which concerns tomorrow's presidential election, covers two consolidated cases. One] is an appeal from an order entered on October 31, 2004, by the United States District Court for the Northern District of Ohio, which granted a motion for a temporary restraining order, ordering that "persons appointed as challengers may not be present at the polling place for the sole purpose of challenging the qualifications of other voters" on November 2, 2004, the date of the Ohio general election. The [other] is an appeal from an order entered on November 1, 2004, by the United States District Court for the Southern District of Ohio, which granted a motion for injunctive relief, enjoining "all Defendants from allowing any challengers other than election judges and other electors into the polling places throughout the state of Ohio on Election Day." The district court found that

> "[t]he evidence before the Court shows that in Tuesday's election, the polling places will be crowded with a bewildering array of participants—people attempting to vote, challengers (Republican, Democrat, and issue proponents or opponents), and precinct judges. In the absence of any statutory guidance whatsoever governing the procedures and limitations for challenging voters by challengers, and the questionable enforceability of the State's and County's policies regarding good faith challenges and ejection of disruptive challengers from the polls, there exists an enormous risk of chaos, delay, intimidation, and pandemonium inside the polls and in the lines out the door."

The factors to be considered in determining whether an order should be stayed are the same factors considered in determining whether to issue a temporary restraining order or a preliminary injunction. These factors are (1) whether the movant has a 'strong' likelihood of success on the merits; (2) whether the movant would otherwise suffer irreparable injury; (3) whether issuance of a preliminary injunction would cause substantial harm to others; and (4) whether the public interest would be served by issuance of a preliminary injunction.

Although it is possible that the plaintiffs will succeed on the merits, it is not likely. Neither district court relied upon racial discrimination as a basis for finding a likelihood of success on the merits. Instead, the courts below found a likelihood that the right to vote would be unconstitutionally burdened by having challengers present at the polling place, and that the presence of such challengers was not a sufficiently narrowly tailored way to accomplish legitimate government interests. Of course if we assume that the presence of challengers burdens the right to vote, it may certainly be argued that a more narrowly tailored approach is available. But the plaintiffs do not appear likely to succeed on the necessary primary finding that the presence of challengers burdens the right to vote. Challengers may only *initiate* an inquiry process by precinct judges, judges who are of the majority party of the precinct. The lower court orders do not rely on the likelihood of success of plaintiffs' challenges to the procedure that will be used by precinct judges once a challenge has been made. Longer lines may of course result from delays and confusion when one side in a political controversy employs a statutorily prescribed polling place procedure more vigorously than in previous elections. But such a possibility does not amount to the severe burden upon the right to vote that requires that the statutory authority for the procedure be declared unconstitutional.

The balance of harms in this case is close. If plaintiffs are correct in their view of the law, they will suffer irreparable harm. On the other hand, if the plaintiffs are not correct in their view of the law, the State will be irreparably injured in its ability to execute valid laws, which are presumed constitutional, for keeping ineligible voters from voting. In particular, the State's interest in not having its voting processes interfered with, assuming that such processes are legal and constitutional, is great. It is particularly harmful to such interests to have the rules changed at the last minute.

On balance, the public interest weighs against the granting of the preliminary injunction. There is a strong public interest in allowing every registered voter to vote freely. There is also a strong public interest in permitting legitimate statutory processes to operate to preclude voting by those who are not entitled to vote. Finally, there is a strong public interest in smooth and effective administration of the voting laws that militates against changing the rules in the hours immediately preceding the election.

[Accordingly, the two district court orders under review are hereby stayed.]

RYAN, Circuit Judge, concurring.

The statute authorizing the presence of challengers at the polling places is presumed to be constitutional. The plaintiffs have offered no evidence that the injury they allege will occur tomorrow, has ever occurred before in an Ohio election or that there has been any threat by the defendants or anyone else that such injury will occur. The "injury" the district courts found that the plaintiffs will suffer tomorrow is wholly speculative, conjectural, and hypothetical.

R. GUY COLE, Jr., Circuit Judge, dissenting.

We have before us today a matter of historic proportions. In this appeal, partisan challengers, for the first time since the civil rights era, seek to target precincts that have a majority African-American population, and without any legal standards or restrictions, challenge the voter qualifications of people as they stand waiting to exercise their fundamental right to vote.

When the fundamental right to vote without intimidation or undue burden is pitted against the rights of those seeking to prevent voter fraud, we must err on the side of those exercising the franchise. In this case, we need not go so far as to balance these interests in a vacuum, however, because here, the rights of those seeking to prevent voter fraud are already well protected by the election protocols established by the state: at each polling place, there are election officials, election judges, and ordinary voters who can challenge potential voter fraud.

The movant in this case bears the burden to show why this Court should reverse the well-reasoned decisions by two district court judges, appointed by a Democrat and Republican President respectively. Each judge independently came to the conclusion that a Temporary Restraining Order ("TRO") against the Challengers was constitutionally required. The Republican Ohio Secretary of State, J. Kenneth Blackwell, has publicly stated that he wants all Challengers banned from the polls on election day. Now, this Court steps in to overturn the district court, permitting Challengers to go to any polls they wish to target tomorrow. As troubling as the public policy ramifications from this decision are, the legal implications are equally astonishing.

The factors which this Court must consider in deciding whether to grant a preliminary injunction have all been met in this case. Here, two separate district courts each heard testimony and reviewed evidence to support explicit factual findings that such a procedure may lead to suppression, intimidation, and chaos at the polls. Nonetheless, without the benefit of reviewing any of this testimony or evidence, the lead opinion would reverse the decisions of two trial courts on the grounds that evidence establishes only a "questionable" burden. But our standard of review clearly indicates that in cases where the evidence is "questionable," we will defer to the reasoned discretion of the district court.

The burden on the right to vote is evident. In this case, we anticipate the arrival of hundreds of Republican lawyers to challenge voter registrations at the polls. Behind them will be hundreds of Democrat lawyers to challenge these Challengers' challenges. This is a recipe for confusion and chaos. Further, although the district courts did not render their decisions on Equal Protection grounds, Plaintiffs' evidence on this point is relevant to show the harm that will naturally ensue from the presence of the partisan Challengers. Numerous studies have documented the dramatic effect of poll watchers on African-American voters.

The Supreme Court's decision in *Burson v. Freeman* (1992), is also instructive. In that case, the Supreme Court found that allowing vote solicitation near the polls would cause voter intimidation. This case is similar. In fact, in this case, voter intimidation is likely to be even greater because the partisan operatives at the polls will be challenging the right to vote itself, rather than merely campaigning for a particular candidate or issue. There is no question that this poses a burden.

Second, the balance of harms is not at all close in this case. The magnitude of burden imposed on voters is great. Although the State of Ohio does have a compelling interest in preventing voter fraud, that interest is served by election officials, election judges, and other voters lawfully at the polling place. The statute providing for additional Challengers at the poll is not narrowly tailored to serve this interest, and is not the least restrictive means for doing so. The harm caused by the chaos and uncertainty imposed by hundreds of additional Challengers at the poll far outweighs any minor decrease in voter fraud as a result of the Challengers' presence. The election judges and other voters perform the same function as these Challengers.

Third, the public interest weighs in favor of allowing registered voters to vote freely. The freedom to vote is best served by allowing election officials, election judges, and citizens to protect against voter fraud. Permitting hundreds of election Challengers to challenge voters at particular polls will promote chaos and uncertainty; it will divert the attention of election judges; and most importantly, it will create a level of voter frustration that could deter citizens from exercising their constitutional right to vote. Election Judges represent both parties, with no one party having more than 50% of the judges. This requirement alleviates any fear that the appellants have in this case. There is no reason to believe that these election judges, many of whom are members of the same party that insists on sending more lawyers to the polls, will fail to detect voter fraud, especially when it is their job to do so.

The majority indicates that the procedures for partisan political operatives to challenge an Ohio citizen's right to vote will not result in voter suppression, intimidation, or chaos at the polls. I deeply and sincerely hope they are right. However, as voting is the very foundation of this Republic, our Constitution requires more than mere hope. Rather, the citizens of Ohio have the right to vote without the threat of suppression, intimidation, or chaos sown by partisan political operatives. I therefore dissent.

NOTE ON OVERNIGHT LITIGATION IN THE U.S. SUPREME COURT

After the Sixth Circuit issued the immediately preceding 2-1 decision, the plaintiffs sought emergency relief in the U.S. Supreme Court. Justice Stevens, as Circuit Justice for the Sixth Circuit, issued this order in the early hours of Election Day.

SPENCER v. PUGH

543 U.S. 1301 (2004)

Justice STEVENS, Circuit Justice.

In two suits brought in the Federal District Courts of Ohio, plaintiffs allege that Ohio Republicans plan to send hundreds of challengers into predominantly African-American neighborhoods to mount indiscriminate challenges at polling places, which they claim will cause voter intimidation and inordinate delays in voting.

After taking evidence, the District Courts granted partial relief, reasoning that the "severe burden" that these challengers would place on the rights of voters was not justified by the State's interest in preventing fraud. The courts, however, refused to enjoin the challenge process completely, but, consistently with a memorandum issued by the secretary of state, ordered the challengers to stay out of polling places or (under the other court order) to remain in polling places only as witnesses.

While the secretary of state—the official charged with administering the State's election code—did not appeal the District Courts' orders, various Republican voters, who intervened in the District Court proceedings, sought relief from the Sixth Circuit Court of Appeals. Over a dissent, the Court of Appeals granted their motions for an emergency stay. *Summit Cty. Democratic Central and Executive Comm. v. Blackwell* (6th Cir. 2004). With just several hours left before the first voters will make their way to the polls, the plaintiffs have applied to me in my capacity as Circuit Justice to enter an order reinstating the District Courts' injunctions. While I have the power to grant the relief requested, I decline to do so for prudential reasons.

Although the hour is late and time is short, I have reviewed the District Court opinions and the opinions of the Circuit Judges. That reasonable judges can disagree about the issues is clear enough.

The allegations of abuse made by the plaintiffs are undoubtedly serious—the threat of voter intimidation is not new to our electoral system—but on the record before me it is impossible to determine with any certainty the ultimate validity of the plaintiffs' claims.

Practical considerations, such as the difficulty of digesting all of the relevant filings and cases, and the challenge of properly reviewing all of the parties' submissions as a full Court in the limited timeframe available, weigh heavily against granting the extraordinary type of relief requested here. Moreover, I have faith that the elected officials and numerous election volunteers on the ground will carry out their responsibilities in a way that will enable qualified voters to cast their ballots.

Because of the importance of providing the parties with a prompt decision, I am simply denying the applications to vacate stays without referring them to the full Court.

NOTE ON LONG LINES AT POLLING PLACES

One of the fears expressed in the litigation over polling place challenges in Ohio's 2004 presidential election was the risk that these challenges would create long lines at the polls, causing would-be voters to leave without casting a ballot and thus suffering a kind of disenfranchisement. The same fear has justified other forms of "election eve" judicial intervention. For example, in Pennsylvania, less than a week before the November 4, 2008 presidential election, a federal district judge ordered the Secretary of State to issue a directive that would require every precinct in the state to make emergency paper ballots available to voters if 50 percent of the electronic voting machines in that precinct became inoperable. *NAACP v. Cortes*, 591 F. Supp. 2d 757 (E.D. Pa. 2008). The Secretary had already directed precincts to provide emergency paper ballots when 100 percent of the electronic voting machines were inoperable, but the district court ruled that this was not good enough. Based on testimony of the long lines that caused voters to leave their polling places without casting a ballot during the 2008 primary election in Pennsylvania, even when less than 100 percent of the electronic voting machines became inoperable in particular precincts, the district court found that it "is likely to cause unacceptably long lines" in the November 2008 general election even if only half of a precinct's electronic machines become inoperable.

3. *"Last Minute" Litigation to Extend Polling Hours*

Even where there has been no "election eve" litigation, if long lines or other problems actually occur at polling places on Election Day, then there is also the possibility of lawsuits filed that day seeking to keep polls open later than their originally scheduled closing time. Many states have statutory provisions that require officials to permit voters who are standing in line at the time polls are scheduled to close to cast ballots that will be counted at the end of the day. But sometimes courts find this kind of provision inadequate: For example, if the problem that caused excessively long lines occurred early in the morning, when voters attempted to cast ballots before going to work, judges may wish to give these voters extra hours in the evening when they can show up to cast a ballot.

This kind of judicial extension of polling hours, however, can cause its own difficulties. If limited only to some precincts, does it give an extra advantage to voters in those precincts that is not available to voters in other precincts? Usually, a judicial order extending polling hours does not require that voters who take advantage of the extension show that they personally suffered the problem that triggered the extension. Thus, especially when they are limited to precincts where one political party has an advantage, this kind of extension can be abused: The favored party can target their Election Day campaigning to round up additional voters to cast ballots during the extended hours. Accordingly, HAVA requires any ballot cast pursuant to a judicial extension of polling hours to be a provisional ballot. Beyond that, state law can require the disqualification of these ballots if the extension was unwarranted.

For an example of a state-court decision that disapproved the extension of polling hours for those who were not already in line at the time the polls were scheduled to close, see *State ex rel. Bush-Cheney 2000, Inc. v. Baker*, 34 S.W.3d 410 (Mo. Ct. App. 2000). There the court rejected the problem of long lines as a justification for the extension of polling hours:

> Although the lines may be long and the number of working machines less than desirable, anyone in line at seven o'clock [the statutorily designated closing time] will eventually be permitted to vote no matter how late the hour and their vote will count. If any voters in line at seven o'clock are unwilling or unable to stay and vote, their inconvenience will not be lessened by extending the hours in which new voters can join the line. Extending the hours of voting simply permits voting by persons not entitled to vote due to their failure to come to the polls on time. [The trial court] has no authority to authorize voters who did not come to the polls during the hours established by the legislature to participate in the election.

E. The Counting of Ballots

1. Ballot-Counting Disputes in the States

There have been significant disputes over the counting of ballots since the 13 original states declared their independence from Britain. One major early dispute concerned New York's gubernatorial election of 1792. John Jay was willing to leave his position as the first Chief Justice of the United States to challenge the incumbent governor, George Clinton—a career move that shows the relative importance of the two offices at the time! America's first two-party system was beginning to emerge, with Jay representing the Federalists against the Jeffersonians (who were the forerunners of today's Democrats). The election was extremely close, as are all elections in which a dispute over the counting of specific ballots could make a difference in determining the winner. Jay would have won if ballots from Cooperstown, the future home of baseball's hall of fame, had been counted. But the town's ballots were disqualified by the state's canvassing committee, which split 7-4 along newly formed party lines. The reason the Jeffersonians gave for disqualifying the ballots was the fact that state law required the town's ballots to be delivered to the secretary of state by the local sheriff, but the Cooperstown sheriff's commission had expired and therefore he was no longer legally qualified to deliver the ballots (as he had done). The Federalists cried foul, believing that the election had been stolen from them based on a purely partisan pretext. They took to the streets, and for a while considered calling a new constitutional convention in the state to undo the result, but ultimately they acquiesced. The experience, however, left many of the Founders—above all Jay himself—believing that their own constitutional handiwork had been inadequate in a key moment in the life of a republic: when it is time to count ballots in a close election for a major office.*

Ballot-counting disputes that will determine the outcome of a major election continue to cause problems for state legal systems. Consider, for example, the dispute over the 2004 election for governor in the State of Washington. The dispute lasted seven months, until June 6, 2005, when the Republican candidate conceded after a state trial court rejected his challenge to the Democratic candidate's victory—a result that embittered many Republicans in the state.

A recount completed on December 30, 2004 showed the Democrat winning by just 127 votes, but the trial court found that 1,678 votes had been unlawfully cast and should not have been counted. (Most of these unlawful votes had been cast by felons, who were not entitled to participate in the election under Washington law. But several hundred were provisional ballots that should have been disqualified but were erroneously counted. There were also 19 ballots fraudulently cast on behalf of deceased voters, and six individuals who each illegally cast two ballots.)

The trial court, however, refused to order any remedy, neither voiding the election on the ground that the number of unlawful ballots far exceeded the Democrat's certified margin of victory, nor awarding the election to the Republican candidate based on a statistical calculation that most of the unlawful ballots had been cast in Democratic-leaning precincts. The trial court ruled, instead, that the Republican candidate was

* If you are interested in learning further details of this 1792 dispute (although doing so is not necessary for this introductory Election Law course), see Edward B. Foley, *The Founders' Bush v. Gore: The 1792 Election Dispute and Its Continuing Relevance*, 44 IND. L. REV. 23 (2010).

obligated to prove that enough unlawful ballots had actually been cast for the Democrat to erase the 127-vote margin. It did not matter that this burden of proof was a practical impossibility, as it would be extremely difficult for him to find and bring all of the unlawful voters to court and convince them to testify that they had voted illegally, and coercing them to testify would have violated the secrecy of the ballot by requiring them to testify under oath which candidate they supported. Absent this additional evidence, according to the trial court, the result of the election must stand even though the number of unlawful ballots was over ten times larger than the certified margin of victory.

Courts in other states would not necessarily agree with the Washington trial court's ruling. Reading precedents from around the country suggests that some state courts would be willing to void the election in this situation, whereas others might entertain the kind of statistical analysis that the Washington trial court refused to consider.

But one must be cautious when reading these other precedents because they did not involve a gubernatorial election, where the stakes are especially high. Even though the doctrine articulated in the precedents does not distinguish between gubernatorial and other types of elections, judges cannot help but be aware of the political context in which they adjudicate a particular ballot-counting dispute. When the consequence of voiding an election would leave a state without a newly elected governor, or would require the expense of holding another statewide vote, a state court may balk even if the state's most relevant judicial precedents would seem to require that result. Thus, as you read the following cases, ask yourself whether the opinions and outcomes would have been the same if the elections involved had been, like in Washington, for governor rather than a local office.

GECY v. BAGWELL

642 S.E.2d 569 (S.C. 2007)

PER CURIAM [unanimous].

Appellant Tammy Bagwell, candidate for Simpsonville City Council, contested the results of the municipal election which resulted in respondent, Robert Gecy, being declared winner. The Simpsonville Election Commission ("Commission") invalidated the results and ordered a new election. The circuit court overturned the ruling of the Commission and reinstated Gecy as winner of the Simpsonville City Council seat. We reverse.

FACTS

On November 8, 2005, the city of Simpsonville held an election to fill three seats on its city council. The two candidates on the ballot for the Ward IV race were Bagwell and Gecy. The final vote tally was 430-427 in favor of Gecy, with one write-in vote for another individual.

On November 10, 2005, Bagwell filed a timely protest of the election. The Commission [after a hearing] decided that two illegal votes had been cast, and these votes rendered doubtful the result of the election. One of the illegal votes was cast by a voter who moved from her residence in one precinct to a residence in another precinct, and the other illegal vote came from a Simpsonville resident who voted in a precinct where his old business was located. The two illegal votes were subtracted from Gecy's total, leaving him with a total of 428 votes, preventing him from garnering a majority of the total votes cast [because Bagwell's 427 votes plus the one write-in equaled that number]. The Commission then ordered a new election.

Gecy appealed the Commission's ruling to the circuit court, [which] overturned the Commission. Bagwell appeals the order of the circuit court and seeks a new election for the contested seat.

ANALYSIS

Bagwell argues that the votes cast in the wrong precinct were illegal, and as a result, a new election should have been held. We agree.

In this case, two voters cast a ballot in a precinct where they previously were registered, but they no longer had a valid address in that precinct at the time of the election. Both parties agree that these two votes were not properly cast, and the question becomes whether these illegal votes should be thrown out, which would require a new election.

The election process is exclusively controlled by statute. S.C. Const. Art. II, § 10. We have recognized that perfect compliance with the election statutes is unlikely, and this Court will not nullify an election based on minor violations of technical requirements.

As a general rule, statutory provisions are mandatory when the statute expressly declares that a particular act is essential to the validity of an election. However, the Court may [also] deem such provisions to be mandatory, and thus non-compliance may nullify the results, when the provisions substantially affect the determination of the results, an essential element of the election, or the fundamental integrity of the election. Where there is a total disregard of the statute, the violation cannot be treated as an irregularity, but it must be held and adjudicated to be cause for declaring the election void and illegal. The Court will not sanction practices which circumvent the plain purposes of the law and open the door to fraud.

The use of precincts in our election process is a fundamental part of our statutory scheme. [The court cited various portions of the state's election code, including S.C. Code Ann. § 7-5-440 (Supp. 2005) (outlining specific procedures for voting by an elector who has moved to a new precinct but has not notified the county registration board).]

The disregard of the election statutes requiring electors to be residents of the precincts in which they vote, as well as failing to follow the procedure outlined in S.C. Code

Ann. § 7-5-440 for those voters who have moved to a new precinct, constitutes more than a mere irregularity or illegality. The precinct system is an essential element of our voting process, and the failure of the two voters to adhere to the statutory requirements for registration and voting requires their votes to be rejected. Because the rejection of these two votes results in Gecy no longer carrying a majority of the total votes cast, a new election must be held.

Gecy also contends that S.C. Code Ann. § 7-13-810, which allows for post-election challenges based on after-discovered evidence, requires the protesting party to exercise due diligence in obtaining information that could have been acquired prior to the election. Gecy argues that because Bagwell could have determined before the election that the two illegal voters no longer lived in the precinct where they were registered, her protest fails because it was not based on after-discovered evidence. We disagree.

Although this Court has defined after-discovered evidence in other contexts, the applicable election statute clearly provides:

> A candidate may protest an election in which he is a candidate pursuant to 7-17-30 when the protest is based in whole or in part on evidence discovered after the election. This evidence may include, but is not limited to, after-discovered evidence of voters who have voted in a precinct or for a district office other than the one in which they are entitled by law to vote.

S.C. Code Ann. § 7-13-810. In this case, evidence of the two voters who cast their ballots in a precinct where they no longer resided qualifies as after-discovered evidence allowed by § 7-13-810. Even though Bagwell could have discovered the evidence on which she bases her challenge before the election, we decline to require a candidate to review all registration books and match each registered voter with his current address before the election.

CONCLUSION

We reverse the circuit court's decision to reinstate Gecy as the winner of the Simpsonville City Council seat. The two illegal votes cannot be counted, and a new election is required.

IN RE MIAMI MAYORAL ELECTION OF 1997
DISTRICT COURT OF APPEAL OF FLORIDA, THIRD DISTRICT

707 So.2d 1170 (Fla. Dist. Ct. App. 1998)

PER CURIAM.

This appeal involves an election contest [over Miami's 1997 election for mayor]. After considering the evidence, the lower tribunal issued a Final Judgment which found that the evidence demonstrated an extensive "pattern of fraudulent, intentional and criminal conduct that resulted in such an extensive abuse of the absentee ballot laws that it can fairly be said that the intent of these laws was totally frustrated." The lower court ordered that the appropriate remedy was to declare the entire Mayoral election void and order that a new election be held within sixty (60) days. While we find that substantial competent evidence existed to support the trial court's findings of massive fraud in the absentee ballots, we disagree as to the appropriateness of the trial court's remedy in ordering a new election.

On November 4, 1997, a general election was held for the position of Mayor, with Joe Carollo and Xavier Suarez as two of the contenders. Carollo received a majority of the precinct votes (51.41%) and Suarez received a majority of the absentee votes (61.48%), resulting in Carollo receiving 49.65% of the votes and Suarez receiving 46.80% of the votes when the absentee ballot votes were combined with the machine precinct votes.

Since neither of the parties received a majority of the overall votes, a run-off election was held on November 13, 1997. In that election, Suarez defeated Carollo in both precinct votes and the absentee votes. On November 14, 1997, the results of the November 13, 1997, election were certified and Suarez assumed the position of Mayor. On the same day, Carollo filed a protest. The principal relief sought by Carollo was to be declared the victor of the Mayoral election, having received a majority of the "untainted" precinct votes or, in the alternative, for a new election.

A bench trial was held and, on March 3, 1998, the trial court declared the Mayoral election void. This judgment was based on the trial court's finding of massive absentee voter fraud which affected the electoral process.

The uncontradicted statistical evidence presented by Kevin Hill, Ph.D., a political scientist and expert in research methodology and statistical analysis, indicated that the amount of fraud involved in the absentee ballots was of such consequence so as to have affected the outcome of the election. Dr. Hill analyzed the absentee ballot voting, finding that the absentee ballots cast in Commission District 3 could not be explained by any normal statistical measurement. District 3 is the area which the trial court found "was the center of a massive, well conceived and well orchestrated absentee ballot voter fraud scheme." Dr. Hill referred to the results of the absentee ballots as an "outlier" and an "aberrant case" so unlikely that it was "literally off the charts" of probability tables. The odds of this occurring by chance were 5,000 to 1.

Dr. Hill finally concluded it was "reasonable" that the absentee ballot deviation in favor of Suarez resulted only from voting fraud, ruling "out almost every other conceivable possibility to a high degree of probability."[2]

An expert documents examiner, Linda Hart, concluded that 225 illegal absentee ballots were cast, in contravention of statutory requirements. An FBI agent with 26 years of experience, Hugh Cochran, identified 113 confirmed false voter addresses. There was evidence of 14 stolen ballots, and of 140 ballots that were falsely witnessed. In addition, evidence was presented that more than 480 ballots were procured or witnessed

2. Dr. Hill estimated that the "aberrant" absentee ballots in Commission District 3 cost Mr. Carollo more than the 160 votes that he needed in order to secure outright victory in the November 4, 1997, election.

by the 29 so-called "ballot brokers" who invoked their privilege against self-incrimination instead of testifying at trial.

The trial court specifically found that the above described absentee ballot voter fraud scheme, "literally and figuratively, stole the ballot from the hands of every honest voter in the City of Miami." The trial court further found that, as a result thereof, "the integrity of the election was adversely affected." Based on our review of the record, there was certainly ample evidence of fraud to support the findings of the trial court's Final Judgment.

We are confronted with the question of whether the trial court erred in finding that the remedy for the instant absentee voting fraud was to order a new election. We hold that it did.

[In] *Bolden v. Potter* (Fla. 1984)[,] the Supreme Court of Florida expressly approve[d] the trial court's remedy, which was to invalidate all of the *absentee ballots* and, thereafter, to solely rely on the machine vote to determine the outcome of the election. Similarly, in *Boardman v. Esteva* (Fla. 1975), the Supreme Court of Florida held that "[T]he general rule is that where the number of invalid *absentee ballots* is more than enough to change the result of an election, then the election shall be determined solely upon the basis of machine vote." *Id.* (emphasis added).

We are mindful of the fact that the trial court found there was no evidence that Mr. Suarez knew of, or in any way participated in, the absentee voter fraud. However, as the Supreme Court stated in *Bolden v. Potter:*

> We also reject the district court's implication that the burden of proof, with regard to fraud or corruption, is dependent upon the status of the offender. It makes no difference whether the fraud is committed by candidates, election officials, or third parties. The evil to be avoided is the same, irrespective of the source. As long as the fraud, from whatever source, is such that the true result of the election cannot be ascertained with reasonable certainty, the ballots affected should be invalidated.

While we recognize that the above cases do not explicitly state that the exclusive remedy for massive absentee voter fraud is to determine the election solely based on machine vote, that form of remedy has, historically, been consistently approved since the 1930s. *See State ex rel. Whitley v. Rinehart* (Fla. 1939). In addition, we note a complete absence of any Florida Appellate Court decision upholding the ordering of a new election in the face of such fraudulent conduct relating to absentee ballots. Mr. Suarez contends that to eliminate all of the absentee ballots would effectively disenfranchise those absentee voters who legally voted. We first note that unlike the right to vote, which is assured every citizen by the United States Constitution, the ability to vote by absentee ballot is a privilege. In fact, the Florida Legislature created this privilege by enacting statutory provisions separate from those applicable to voting at the polls. *See Bolden v. Potter* (expressly rejecting the contention that invalidating all absentee ballots, in the face of extensive absentee vote buying, was an unjustified disenfranchisement of those voters who cast legal ballots).

Consistent with the fact that there is no legal precedent in Florida to support the action of the trial court in ordering a new election as the proper remedy upon a finding of massive absentee voter fraud is the public policy of the State of Florida to not encourage such fraud. Rather, it must be remembered that the sanctity of free and honest elections is the cornerstone of a true democracy. As the Supervisor of Elections, David Leahy, noted during his trial testimony, were we to approve a new election as the proper remedy following extensive absentee voting fraud, we would be sending out the message that the worst that would happen in the face of voter fraud would be another election.

Further, we refuse to disenfranchise the more than 40,000 voters who, on November 4, 1997, exercised their constitutionally guaranteed right to vote in the polling places of Miami. In the absence of any findings of impropriety relating to the machine vote in this election, public policy dictates that we not void those constitutionally protected votes, the majority of which were cast for Mr. Carollo. In addition, a candidate who wins an election by virtue of obtaining a majority of the votes cast is entitled to take office as a result thereof, and not be forced into a second election, whether it is a statutorily mandated run-off election or a court ordered special election, when the said second election only comes about due to absentee ballot fraud, in the first election, that favored one of his or her opponents.

As a result, the voiding of the entire election and the ordering of a new election is hereby reversed, and this cause is remanded to the trial court with directions to enter a Final Judgment, forthwith, that voids and vacates the *absentee ballots only* and, furthermore, provides that the outcome of the November 4, 1997, City of Miami Mayoral election shall be determined solely upon the machine ballots cast at the polls, resulting in the election of Joe Carollo as Mayor of the City of Miami.

HUGGINS v. SUPERIOR COURT

Supreme Court of Arizona
788 P.2d 81 (Ariz. 1990)

NOEL FIDEL, Vice Chief Judge, Court of Appeals [sitting by designation, on behalf of unanimous court]:

In a contested primary election decided by an eight-vote margin, sixteen illegal votes were cast. The loser claims that the election must be set aside because one cannot know which of the candidates received the highest number of legal votes. We have taken jurisdiction to reexamine the law that governs elections when illegal votes exceed the margin of victory.

FACTS

In the 1988 primary election for Navajo County Attorney, petitioner Bret H. Huggins narrowly lost the Democratic Party nomination to Dale K. Patton. The Secretary of State reported that Patton had won by 3,593 votes to Huggins's 3,585. This eight-vote margin, however, was exceeded by sixteen votes illegally cast. Fifteen voters registered as independents or non–partisans had been improperly permitted to vote Democratic Party ballots. The sixteenth illegal voter was a convicted felon whose electoral rights were unrestored.

Huggins contested the election, but lost [in trial court] because he was unable to prove for whom the illegal votes were cast. Though he proved that illegal votes were cast in sufficient number to change the election result, he could not prove that they changed the result in fact.

THE MORGAN-MILLET RULE

[Under prior Arizona precedent, known as *Morgan-Millet*, a candidate challenging the result of an election on the ground that the winner's margin of victory was smaller than the number of unlawful ballots cast, in addition to proving the illegality of disputed ballots, was required to prove for which candidate the disputed ballots were cast. In this respect, the *Morgan-Millet* rule was the same position as the one the trial court adopted in Washington's 2004 gubernatorial election, discussed above.]

In this case, the trial court criticized, but felt obliged to follow, the *Morgan-Millet* rule. Huggins now urges us to abandon that rule and to relieve election contestants of the burden of proving how illegal votes were cast. Huggins directs us to *Baggett v. State Election Board* (Okla. 1972), where, under circumstances similar to these, the Oklahoma Supreme Court nullified an election, stating:

> If election officials have not conducted an election according to law and knowingly permit non-registered Democrats to vote in a Democratic runoff primary election, the inexcusable conduct of the election officials should not inure to the benefit of any candidate either directly or indirectly.

The trial court described *Baggett* as having "the force of reason behind it," and Huggins urges us to make the Oklahoma approach our own.

We too see much reason in *Baggett.* Like the majority in that case, we recognize the inequity of burdening the challenger "to prove for which candidate the unlawful ballots were cast [in order] to be relieved from having the illegal ballots counted as legal ballots." *Id.* Moreover, the challenger's burden increases with the size of the unlawful vote. As Huggins argues persuasively, "it hardly seems fair that as the amount of illegal voting escalates, the likelihood of redressing the wrong diminishes."

There are additional difficulties with the *Morgan-Millet* rule, which stem from the need to prove how illegal votes were cast through the testimony of those who cast them. First, as Justice Jackson pointed out in concurrence in *Baggett,* voters who have cast unlawful ballots may choose to assert their fifth amendment privilege not to testify. Though an illegal voter might be motivated to maintain silence by a genuine fear of criminal sanctions, a supporter of the challenger's opponent might equally be motivated by the recognition that an invalid vote against the challenger would likely be cancelled only if the voter revealed how it was cast. Thus, the *Morgan-Millet* rule not only burdens a challenger onerously; it actually empowers partisans of the opposition to frustrate an election challenge and preserve illegal votes by exercising fifth amendment rights.

There is a second and related weakness to the *Morgan-Millet* rule. Voter disclosure testimony, even where offered, is highly suspect. Courts have long recognized this weakness when contemplating testimony by legal voters whose attempted votes were erroneously unrecorded. As the Utah Supreme Court stated:

> We know from common experience that those who do vote are usually unwilling that the character of their votes be made public, and that whenever there is an investigation as to the actual vote cast it is almost certain to bring about prevarication and uncertainty as to what the truth is. . . . The temptation to actual fraud and corruption on the part of the candidates and their political supporters is never so great as when it is known precisely how many votes it will take to change the result. . . .

Young v. Deming (Utah 1893); *see also Briscoe v. Between Consol. School Dist.* (Ga. 1931) ("[I]t would . . . be dangerous to receive and rely upon the subsequent statement of the voters as to their intentions, after it is ascertained precisely what effect their votes would have upon the result."). We concur in these comments and attribute comparable weakness to the testimony of illegal voters asked to disclose accomplished votes.

There is a third and especially troublesome problem associated with the *Morgan-Millet* rule: the prospect of judges compelling good faith voters who have cast invalid ballots to reveal what they supposed were private votes. The *McCavitt* opinion records the outrage of a voter so compelled: "I will not answer that question because, as far as I'm concerned, that is illegal. Nobody has the right to know who I voted for." *McCavitt v. Registrars of Voters* (Mass. 1982). Massachusetts rejects compelling voter testimony in these circumstances as "a kind of inquisitorial power unknown to the principles of our government and constitution." *Id.* This criticism strikes a responsive chord in Arizona, where our constitution explicitly assures secrecy in voting. We need not now determine whether, under any circumstances, our constitutional commitment to ballot secrecy might accommodate compelling good faith voters to disclose invalid votes. It is sufficient for present purposes to recognize the force of that commitment and to explore alternative solutions that permit us to avoid compulsion so offensive to democratic sensibilities and assumptions.

NULLIFICATION AND RESUBMISSION

The solution commended by Huggins is to nullify the contested election and to order a new election when, as here, a challenger has proven that the margin of victory is exceeded by the number of invalid votes. This solution, the one chosen in *Baggett* and *McCavitt,* permits the public a second effort to achieve a properly conducted election.

A second election, however, is not immune from illegal ballots and may prove no better than the first. Moreover, a second election is costly, and the costs are not limited to the heavy fiscal expense of running an election another time. Some votes will be lost in a second election that were properly recorded in the first; these include voters who have died, voters who have moved, and voters whose interest in the office or electoral issue is too attenuated to pull them to the polls a second time. Additionally,

> there may . . . be identifiable biases in second elections. Candidates with ready access to financing and with strong and continuing party organizations will be able to mobilize a second campaign in the short time available much more effectively than opponents who lack such advantages. Candidates with support concentrated among less active voters may be disadvantaged in a second election if such supporters do not turn out to cast ballots when only one office is at stake.

Note, *Developments in the Law: Elections,* 88 Harv. L. Rev. 1111, 1315 (1975).

These costs and biases make us hesitant to nullify first elections automatically upon proof that the winner's margin of victory was exceeded by the number of illegal votes.

THE *GROUNDS* RULE

[W]e find a better alternative in *Grounds v. Lawe* (Ariz. 1948). [There,] we considered whether the outcome would be altered by a proportionate, precinct-by-precinct extraction of the illegal votes. That is, for each district in which invalid votes were cast, we calculated a "pro rata deduction of the illegal votes according to the number of votes cast for the respective candidates in [that] election district." *Id.*[3] Because the illegal votes were insufficient, when extracted in this fashion, to change the election result, the victory of the declared winner was confirmed.

Grounds has also been cited with approval by the Supreme Court of Alaska, *Hammond v. Hickel* (Alaska 1978), and we reaffirm its application in this case.

We recognize an arbitrary element to proration. As we said in *Grounds:* "[T]he truth might be, if it could be shown, that all the illegal votes were on one side, while it is scarcely to be presumed that they would ever be divided between the candidates in exact proportion to their whole vote." [*Grounds*], quoting *McCrary on Elections,* 4th Ed., §§ 495-97. This

3. For example, consider a pair of hypothetical precincts with a mathematically convenient turnout of 100 voters in each. In the first precinct, Smith receives 60 votes, Jones receives 40, but 10 invalid votes are cast. Pro rata deduction would reduce Smith's tally by 6 votes (60% of the invalid votes) and Jones's tally by 4 (40%). In the second precinct, Jones wins 80 votes, Smith wins 20, but 5 invalid votes are cast. Here, pro rata deduction takes 4 of the invalid votes (80%) from Jones and 1 (20%) from Smith. Application of this method precinct-by-precinct is a neutral method to extract invalid ballots from the overall total.

element has led the Supreme Judicial Court of Massachusetts to reject proration in favor of nullification and resubmission to the voters "whenever the irregularity . . . of the election is such that the result . . . would be placed in doubt." *McCavitt.*

The Supreme Court of Alaska, however, has recognized that proration is a useful "analytical tool . . . for the limited purpose of determining whether . . . [there] were errors of sufficient magnitude to change the result. . . . " *Fischer v. Stout* (Alaska 1987). Alaska has not yet determined what it will do if a case arises where "the election result is put in doubt by application of the proportionate reduction rule." *Id.* Where, however, as in *Grounds,* proportionate reduction does not change the result, Alaska certifies the declared winner of the first election.

Huggins challenges the *Grounds* approach as constitutionally invalid. Article VII, § 7 of the Arizona Constitution, the source of Huggins's argument, provides: "in all elections held by the people in this state, the person, or persons, receiving the highest number of legal votes shall be declared elected." Huggins reasons from this provision that, because proration does not permit us to be certain who won the highest number of *legal* votes, it is constitutionally proscribed.

We disagree. The problem we confront is practical; the solution we choose is workable. The Arizona Constitution, in our view, permits us room to make this choice. While proration is imperfect, we lack the luxury of perfection, and proration strikes us as a sensible screening device in a multi-district case.[4] First, proration spares the body politic the offensive voter compulsion of the *Morgan-Millet* rule. Second, when limited as in *Fischer,* it permits us at least sometimes to avoid the cost and delay of a second election.

Moreover, though proration leaves some doubt that we have discovered the true winner, the other options fail to bring us nearer to that mark. The practical impact of the *Morgan-Millet* rule, with its virtually impossible burden on the challenger, is to let illegal votes count. The nullification remedy invalidates a multitude of first election legal votes, passes the choice to the inevitably different electorate that turns out for a second election, and accepts the second election biases and distortions earlier described. Proration, by comparison, has the virtue of neutrality; and in election contests, neutrality is a major constituent of fairness.

Like the Supreme Court of Alaska, we defer deciding what must be done when proration would change an election result. The law advances incrementally; we address the increment before us; the legislature may wish to consider the subject before we visit it again. For now, we reaffirm the *Grounds* approach as a limited screening device. When, as here, the margin of electoral victory is exceeded by the number of invalid votes and the invalid votes were cast in more than one precinct, the impact of those votes shall be tested

4. We observed in *Grounds* that proration can only work fairly where more than one district has undergone invalid ballots. Thus, we only announce a rule today for multi-district elections. We will deal with single district elections when the need arises.

by proportionate deduction. When, as here, proportionate reduction does not change the result, the declared victory may be confirmed.

CONCLUSION: PRORATION APPLIED

Proration in this case changes the tally in eight Navajo County precincts, taking six votes from Patton's overall tally and nine from that of Huggins. By this method Patton remains the winner with 3,587 votes to 3,576 for Huggins. Thus, we conclude that Huggins's election challenge was properly denied.

NOTE ON THE VARIATION IN STATE LAW ON BALLOT-COUNTING DISPUTES

The above cases barely scratch the surface of the existing jurisprudence among state courts on how to resolve ballot-counting disputes.* One additional case worth a brief mention here is *Bauer v. Souto*, 896 A.2d 90 (Conn. 2006), in which the Supreme Court of Connecticut ordered a new citywide election even though the problem that triggered the dispute was confined to a specific polling location. One voting machine at that polling place had malfunctioned, failing to record votes cast on that machine for one of the candidates. Had the machine worked properly, it is likely (based on a statistical analysis) that the affected candidate would have won the city council election in which he was competing, but based on the votes actually recorded by the machine this candidate was not elected. The trial court ordered a revote in the electoral district served by the polling place where the machine had malfunctioned. The Connecticut Supreme Court, however, decided that it was necessary to hold an entirely new election among all voters eligible to vote for this city council seat, which happened to be the entire city since it was an "at-large" seat. The court reasoned that only a complete do-over of the original election was "consistent with the nature of elections [and] the democratic process."

Although the Connecticut Supreme Court based its decision on state rather than federal law, insofar as its reasoning was rooted in general philosophical principles about the nature of equal voting rights among members of the electorate in a democracy, this decision raises the question of whether it could have been based on the Equal Protection Clause of the Fourteenth Amendment to the U.S. Constitution, instead of on state law. In this respect, this case raises the more general question about what role federal law plays in resolving ballot-counting disputes. This federal law question can be asked with respect to any election, even for a state or local office (because the Fourteenth Amendment binds the states), but this issue is particularly germane to election for federal offices, especially the presidency—our next topic.

* For two systematic discussions in recent law review articles on this topic, see Steven F. Huefner, *Remedying Election Wrongs*, Harv. J. Leg. 265 (2007) and Joshua A. Douglas, *Procedural Fairness in Election Contests*, 88 Ind. L. J. 1 (2013).

2. The Federal Dimension to Disputed Elections: Historical Background

The first presidential election involving a dispute over the counting of ballots occurred in 1876. (There had been a deadlocked presidential election in 1800, but that problem occurred because of the original design of the Electoral College, which caused Thomas Jefferson and his running mate Aaron Burr to receive the same number of Electoral Votes; it did not concern the counting of ballots cast by citizens to determine the presidential electors of a particular state.) The fight over the 1876 outcome primarily focused on ballots cast in three southern states: Florida, Louisiana, and South Carolina. Without any of these states, the Democratic candidate, Samuel Tilden, was just one Electoral Vote shy of the majority necessary to win the presidency. Therefore, if Tilden could prevail in any of these three states, he would be President, whereas his Republican opponent, Rutherford Hayes, needed to prevail in all three to win.

The dispute ended up being decided by a specially created Electoral Commission of 15 members. The plan had been for the Commission to have seven Democrats, seven Republicans, and one independent. But the person intended to be the independent, Justice David Davis of the U.S. Supreme Court, declined to serve, and the congressional statute creating the Commission required that his replacement be another Supreme Court justice. There was, however, no other justice who was perceived as genuinely independent, and Justice Joseph Bradley was chosen as the most moderate Republican available on the Court.

When it came time for the Commission to decide the dispute over the ballots in each of the three states, the Commission split 8-7 each time on a straight party-line vote, with Bradley siding with his fellow Republicans to give all three states to Hayes. Although Bradley professed to base his decision on principle rather than partisanship, Democrats at the time saw it otherwise and began referring to President Hayes as "His Fraudulency." From our historical vantage point, it seems less important to determine whether Bradley reached the right decision, or even whether he acted in good faith—the legal issues involved were very complicated—than it is to observe that the design of the Electoral Commission was flawed given its purpose. Since the goal had been to create the Commission with a neutral tiebreaker, the plan failed once the Commission lost its genuinely independent member.

Whether because of this experience with the 1876 election or otherwise, the U.S. Supreme Court tended to stay out of ballot-counting disputes during the twentieth century, despite the efforts of candidates to invoke the Court's jurisdiction by claiming that a state's method of counting ballots violated the Fourteenth Amendment. In 1900, at the very beginning of the century, the Court ruled in *Taylor v. Beckham*, 178 U.S. 548 (1900), that a gubernatorial candidate could not claim a Fourteenth Amendment violation even when alleging systematic ballot-counting fraud in favor of his opponent. The case involved a particularly ugly dispute over Kentucky's election for governor, during which one of the candidates was assassinated. The consequence of the Court's refusal to intervene was that the state's own handling of the ballot-counting dispute would prevail no matter how fraudulent or antidemocratic it might be. The prophetic Justice John Marshall Harlan, who came from Kentucky and was the lone dissenter in *Plessy v. Ferguson*, 163 U.S. 537 (1896) (the railroad segregation case that accepted "separate but equal" as constitutional), also dissented alone in *Taylor v. Beckham*. "[T]he overturning of the public will, as expressed at the ballot box, . . . in order to accomplish partisan ends, is a crime against free government, and deserves the execration of all lovers of liberty," Justice Harlan decried. "I cannot believe the judiciary is helpless in the presence of such a crime," he added, making it clear he would have made an honest and accurate count of ballots one of the "rights protected by the 14th Amendment of the Constitution of the United States."

At mid-century, Justice Harlan's view was again rebuffed in the infamous primary election between Lyndon Johnson and Coke Stevenson to determine the Democratic Party's nominee for U.S. Senator from Texas in 1948. Certified returns showed Johnson ahead by a mere 87 votes, and there was damning evidence that 200 entirely fabricated votes for Johnson had been added to the tally sheet for one ballot box—the notorious Ballot Box 13—from one local county under the control of a political boss loyal to Johnson. Believing he could not receive a fair hearing in state court, Coke Stevenson went to federal court claiming that the stuffing of Ballot Box 13 violated the Fourteenth Amendment. The local federal judge was willing to hear the claim and was in the process of examining the evidence when Johnson secured an order from Justice Hugo Black to halt the proceedings on the ground that the federal judiciary had no business involving itself in a state's ballot-counting dispute. Johnson's 87-vote victory thus withstood Stevenson's judicial attack, thereby giving Johnson his nickname "Landslide Lyndon" and propelling him into national politics. The principle upon which Justice Black based his order was the same one that had prevailed a half-century earlier in *Taylor v. Beckham*: The Fourteenth Amendment does not provide a basis for the federal judiciary to supervise ballot-counting by a state, no matter how egregiously flawed and undemocratic the state's ballot-counting may be.

Thus was the prevailing jurisprudence on this point at mid-century, before the Reapportionment Revolution of *Baker v. Carr* and *Reynolds v. Sims*. Those new precedents from the 1960s, along with *Harper* and *Kramer*, laid the foundation for a new voting-rights jurisprudence that ultimately would have implications for ballot-counting cases.

These implications developed slowly and did not command the U.S. Supreme Court's attention until the 2000 presidential election. In 1978, for example, the U.S. Court of Appeals for the First Circuit ruled that Rhode Island had violated the Due Process Clause of the Fourteenth Amendment when its election officials, at the secretary of state's direction, encouraged voters to use absentee ballots but the state supreme court later refused to count them on the ground that the voters were not entitled to vote absentee. *Griffin v. Burns*, 570 F.2d 1065 (1st Cir. 1978). Then, in a case stemming from Alabama's 1994 election for Chief Justice of its supreme court, the U.S. Court of Appeals for the

Eleventh Circuit found a Due Process violation when that same supreme court (other members having decided not to recuse themselves) ruled in favor of counting absentee ballots that previously would have been disqualified under Alabama law. *See Roe v. Alabama*, 43 F.3d 574 (announcing standard pretrial), 68 F.3d 404 (applying standard posttrial) (11th Cir. 1995).

Consequently, when the dispute over counting ballots in the 2000 presidential election reached the U.S. Supreme Court, there was an unresolved tension between two strands of jurisprudence. First was the longstanding principle of federal court nonintervention in these disputes, going back at least a century to *Taylor v. Beckham*. But second was the small but increasing corpus of case law among federal courts of appeals that the Fourteenth Amendment, as understood in the wake of the Warren Court's voting rights precedents from the 1960s, authorized limited federal-court intervention in state ballot-counting controversies to avoid deviations from "fundamental fairness" (in the words of both the *Burns* and *Roe* courts). The 2000 presidential election would cause the nine Justices of the U.S. Supreme Court to decide which of these two strands of jurisprudence each of them would embrace, and they would need to make this momentous decision working at what amounted to lightning speed under the glare of national spotlight as intense as it has ever been.

3. The 2000 Presidential Election: Preliminary Proceedings

The dispute over ballots in the 2000 presidential election ended with the U.S. Supreme Court's 5-4 ruling in *Bush v. Gore* on December 12 to halt any further recounting of ballots in Florida, and Al Gore's concession speech the next night. But to better understand the Court's ruling, as well as the four dissents from it, it helps to review the five weeks that occurred between the casting of ballots and the Court's decision, as well as the legal context from which the case arose. What follows is necessarily abbreviated. For those who want more, the most riveting account is Jeffery Toobin's *Too Close to Call* (2001), although it arguably tells the story from a pro-Gore perspective. Likewise, HBO's film *Recount* nicely dramatizes the events, but it too tilts in a pro-Gore direction. (A timeline summarizing key events in this chronology appears right before the opinions in *Bush v. Gore*, on page 744 below.)

As the nation watched the election returns on the night of Tuesday, November 7, it became clear that whichever candidate, George W. Bush or Al Gore, won Florida would win a majority of the Electoral College and thus the presidency. But despite the desire for a snap judgment on which candidate won Florida—the networks first called the state for Gore, then called it for Bush, and then in the early hours of the next morning left it "too close to call"—the candidates quickly realized that the outcome would depend on whether there were enough additional Gore ballots that had been cast but not yet counted to overcome Bush's miniscule lead (which stood at 327 on Friday, November 10, after ballots had been retabulated by vote-counting machines).

Figure 4-1

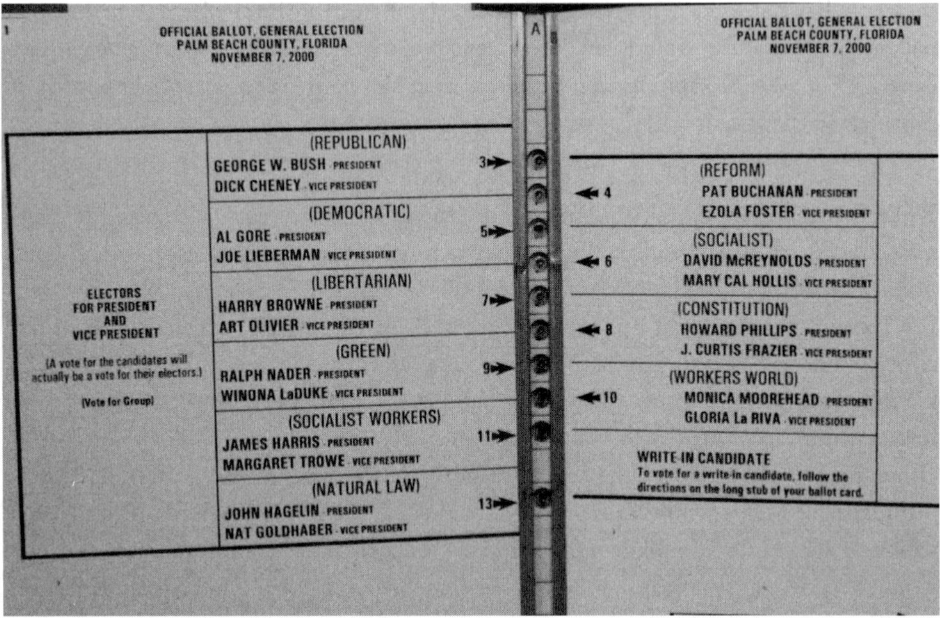

A variety of fascinating but ultimately tangential issues emerged during the five-week fight—including the controversy over the "butterfly ballot," which apparently caused thousands of elderly voters to mistakenly vote for Pat Buchanan rather than Al Gore (but for which there was no easy remedy available). See Figure 4-1 for an image of the butterfly ballot. But the dispute soon focused on the fact that the voting machines had not counted many thousands of punch-card ballots because the "chads" that the voters were supposed to punch out of the ballots to indicate their choices had not been completely dislodged and therefore the vote was not "readable" by the machine. Some of these chads had been left "hanging" (see Figure 4-2), whereas others were punctured (and thus would let light through the punch-card ballot), whereas still others were merely dimpled or "pregnant," to invoke one of the terms used at the time.

The legal question was whether any of these ballots, uncountable by machines, were still entitled to be counted in a recount conducted by hand and, if so, according to what standard. For example, should only "hanging chads" count according to a "two-corner" rule, which required a chad to be partially dislodged so that at least two corners were swinging free from the ballot itself? Or should any punctured chad count according to an examination that puts the ballot up to a light? Or should the standard even more generously permit the counting of any dimpled or "pregnant" chad, at least where the ballot contains no contrary indication that the voter did not wish to cast a vote for the candidate indicated by this indented chad?

Figure 4-2

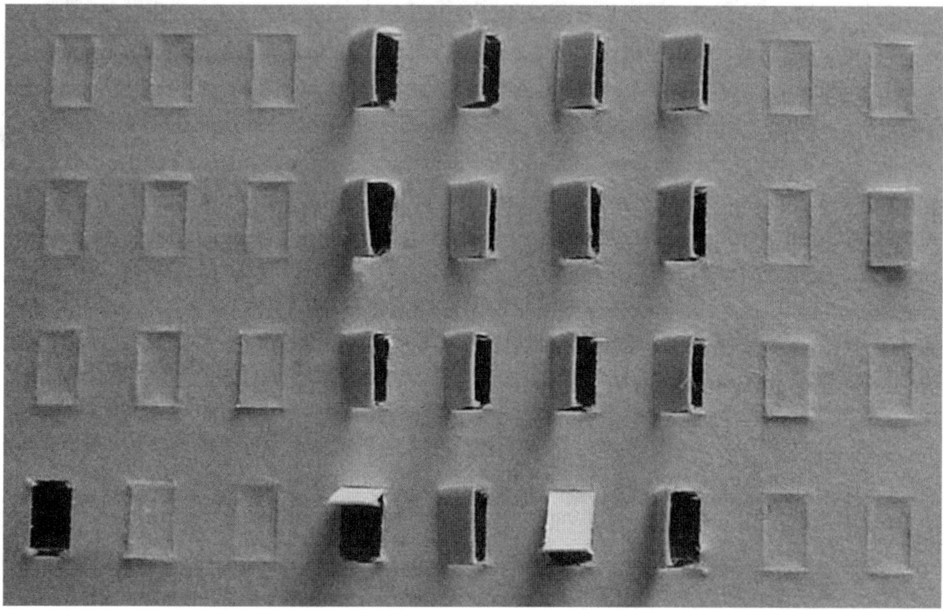

Reprinted with permission from Professor Ted Herman at the University of Iowa.

When Gore's legal team initially confronted the issue of these uncounted punch-card ballots, there seemed to be two procedural avenues available in which to pursue a possible recount. The first, called a "protest" under Florida law at the time, was an administrative proceeding by which the candidate could ask each county in the state to conduct a manual recount before certification of the election's results. The second, called a "contest" under state law, was a judicial proceeding that challenged the administrative certification on the ground that it was erroneous. On Thursday, November 9, Gore decided to go the first route, in the hope of preventing Bush from achieving a certified victory, and Gore specifically asked for a manual administrative recount of uncounted ballots in four Florida counties that voted heavily in favor of Democratic candidates.

Two problems with this strategy emerged, however, at least from the perspective of those seeking the counting of additional votes. One was the fact that Florida's statutes specified a deadline of Tuesday, November 14—one week after Election Day—by which counties were required to submit their certified returns to the Secretary of State (to be accumulated into a single statewide certified result). That one-week deadline proved to be too tight for the urban counties that Gore most wanted to conduct a manual recount. Second, in an administrative "protest," Florida's statutes did not mandate that the counties conduct a manual recount but instead gave the counties the discretion to do so. As Gore would learn, Miami/Dade County would choose to exercise its discretion against completing a manual recount.

Gore nonetheless decided to fight the deadline. On the day of the deadline, he secured a ruling from respected state judge Terry Lewis that Secretary of State Katherine Harris must at least consider a county's reasons for conducting a manual recount past the statutory deadline. But on Friday, November 17 (the final date for receipt of military and overseas absentee ballots and thus the earliest date for an official statewide certification of the election results), Judge Lewis ruled that Secretary of State Harris need not accept a county's explanation for missing the statutory deadline. Later that same day, however, the Florida Supreme Court ordered that Secretary Harris must not certify a final result of the election absent further order of that court. Then on Tuesday, November 21 (two weeks after Election Day), the seven-member Florida Supreme Court released a unanimous opinion extending the deadline for final certification to Sunday, November 26, and requiring that the state include any manual recounts conducted by that deadline in the final certification.

Bush's legal team viewed the Florida Supreme Court's decision as a partisan distortion of the relevant statutory language, by judges who were Democrats and, thus, Gore supporters. Two statutory provisions, although in tension with each other, seemed contrary to the Florida Supreme Court's decision. One, Section 102.111, using the mandatory word "shall," required Secretary Harris to "ignore" late-filed returns: "If the county returns are not received by the Department of State by 5 p.m. of the seventh day following an election, all missing counties *shall be ignored*, and the results shown by the returns on file shall be certified." (Emphasis added.) The other, Section 102.112, permitted Secretary Harris to ignore late-filed returns: "If the returns are not received by the department by the time specified, such returns *may be ignored* and the results on file at that time may be certified by the department." (Emphasis added.) Neither statutory provision, however, *prohibited* Secretary Harris from ignoring late-filed returns after a manual recount, yet that result is precisely what the Florida Supreme Court's decision achieved.

The Florida Supreme Court justified its decision by observing that the state's statutory laws contemplated the possibility of a manual recount, which can be time consuming. But Bush's lawyers saw this justification as another distortion of the statutory scheme. In their view, a manual recount was unnecessary as long as the punch-card voting machines were functioning as designed, and the machines were working properly because they could not be expected to record votes when the chads had not been completely dislodged. Moreover, because a manual recount was discretionary under the statute, the Bush team believed that the counties were obligated to exercise their discretion in a way that satisfied the explicit statutory deadline.

The Bush team, however, faced a difficulty. While their side may have had the better argument in terms of interpreting the relevant state statutes, the Florida Supreme Court was the highest judicial authority on the meaning of Florida's statutory law, and that court had ruled against them. Bush could only go to the U.S. Supreme Court on a question of federal law. Bush's lawyers then developed a federal argument based on Article II of the

U.S. Constitution, which provides: "Each State shall appoint, *in such Manner as the Legislature thereof may direct*, a Number of Electors, equal to the whole Number of Senators and Representatives to which the State may be entitled in the Congress." (Emphasis added.) Bush's argument was that because the state's *legislature* decides how to appoint the state's presidential electors, an interpretation of the legislative command by a state's supreme court that is so far off the mark as to undo the legislature's decision is a violation of Article II.

To the surprise of many observers, on Friday, November 24, the U.S. Supreme Court agreed to consider this argument. But after hearing the case on the next Friday, December 1, the nine Justices unanimously decided on the following Monday, December 4, to send the case back to the Florida Supreme Court for clarification. *Bush v. Palm Beach Canvassing Bd.*, 531 U.S. 70 (2000). The "per curiam" opinion for the Court hinted that the Justices, or at least a majority of them, were disturbed by the Florida Supreme Court's statutory interpretation: "There are expressions in the opinion of the Supreme Court of Florida that may be read to indicate that it construed the Florida Election Code without regard to the extent to which the Florida Constitution could, consistent with [Article II] circumscribe the legislative power." *Id.* at 77.

The Justices also wondered whether Florida wished to take advantage of the so-called "Safe Harbor Provision," 3 U.S.C. § 5, which purports to bind Congress to a state's resolution of a dispute over the counting of ballots cast by its citizens in a presidential election if the state's method of resolving the dispute meets certain conditions. Enacted by

Figure 4-3

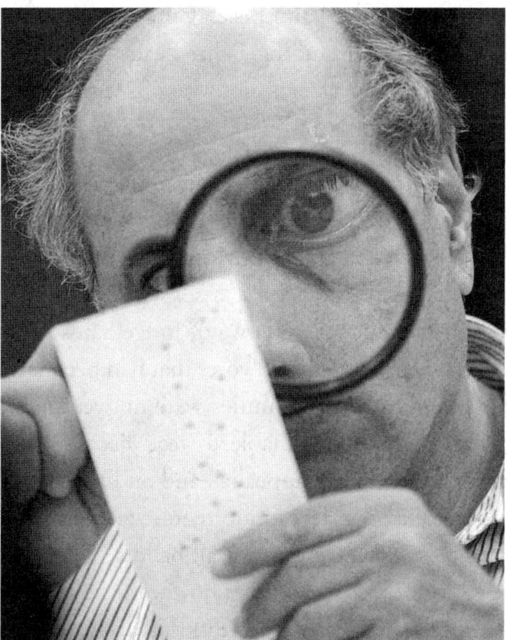

Congress as part of the Electoral Count Act of 1887 in the aftermath of the disputed Hayes-Tilden election, this Safe-Harbor Provision encourages states to resolve these disputes so that Congress can avoid the kind of unhappy ending that occurred with the Electoral Commission's partisan 8-7 decision. Specifically, if *before ballots are cast* a state's legislature establishes a procedure to handle these disputes, and if by using that procedure the state resolves a dispute *six days before the meeting of the presidential Electors*, then that resolution "shall be conclusive" when Congress meets to count and announce the Electoral votes from each state.

In 2000, the meeting of the presidential Electors was scheduled for Monday, December 18, which made Tuesday, December 12 the Safe-Harbor Deadline. Seeing that Florida was running out of time when the U.S. Supreme Court remanded the controversy on December 1, and noting that taking advantage of the Safe-Harbor Provision required following the dictates of Florida's statutory law as it stood before the casting of ballots began, the nine Justices observed: "a legislative wish to take advantage of the 'safe harbor' would counsel against any construction of the Election Code that Congress might deem to be a change in the law."

Meanwhile, back in Florida, after the Florida Supreme Court's ruling on November 21, the manual recount continued in three of the four counties where Gore had requested them (the fourth had already finished). But the very next day, Miami-Dade County decided to stop its recount after the so-called "Brooks Brother riot," in which Republican activists protested what they perceived as the unfairness of the county's recount proceedings (including the fact that the recount was occurring behind closed doors, out of public view). When the Florida Supreme Court's November 26 deadline arrived, there was no Miami-Dade recount to include, and Palm Beach County had missed the deadline by two hours. Secretary of State Harris, excluding Palm Beach County's late return, certified Bush's slate of presidential Electors as victorious by 537 citizen-cast ballots.

Gore, having hoped to avoid a post-certification judicial "contest" by prevailing in the administrative "protest," now had no choice but to file a judicial contest, which he did on Monday, November 27. The state trial judge, Sander Sauls, held a trial of the contest over the weekend of December 2 and 3. On Monday, December 4 (the same day as the U.S. Supreme Court's remand of the protest case, which had become essentially moot since the post-certification contest was underway), Judge Sauls rejected Gore's claim that the certified result wrongfully excluded valid votes that had been lawfully cast. Judge Sauls accepted the Bush team's position that counties were not required to retrieve attempted votes that their voting machines were unable to read because the voters had not fully dislodged the chads. Gore immediately appealed, and on Friday, December 8, the Florida Supreme Court issued the following decision to require all counties (not just the four that Gore wanted) to conduct a manual recount of all ballots where the voting machine had failed to record a vote for president. This time, however, the Florida Supreme Court was not unanimous, but instead split 4-3. As you read this decision, and the dissents from it, imagine how the nine Justices of the U.S. Supreme Court perceived it when this decision came before them for their review in *Bush v. Gore.*

GORE v. HARRIS

772 So. 2d 1243 (Fla. 2000)

PER CURIAM.

Although we find that the appellants are entitled to reversal in part of the trial court's order and are entitled to a manual count of the Miami-Dade County undervote, we agree with the appellees that the ultimate relief would require a counting of the legal votes contained within the undervotes in all counties where the undervote has not been subjected to a manual tabulation.

I

[Omitted.]

II. APPLICABLE LAW

This case today is controlled by the language set forth by the Legislature in section 102.168, Florida Statutes (2000). Indeed, an important part of the statutory election scheme is the State's provision for a contest process, section 102.168, which laws were enacted by the Legislature prior to the 2000 election. Although courts are, and should be, reluctant to interject themselves in essentially political controversies, the Legislature has directed in section 102.168 that an election contest shall be resolved in a judicial forum.

In carefully construing the contest statute, no single statutory provision will be construed in such a way as to render meaningless or absurd any other statutory provision. In interpreting the various statutory components of the State's election process, then, a common-sense approach is required, so that the purpose of the statute is to give effect to the legislative directions ensuring that the right to vote will not be frustrated.

Section 102.168(3) outlines the grounds for contesting an election, and includes: "Receipt of a number of illegal votes or *rejection of a number of legal votes sufficient to change or place in doubt the result of the election.*" § 102.168(3)(c) (emphasis added). Although the right to contest an election is created by statute, it has been a long-standing right since 1845 when the first election contest statute was enacted. As is well established in this State by our contest statute, "[t]he right to a correct count of the ballots in an election is a substantial right which it is the privilege of every candidate for office to insist on, in every case where there has been a failure to make a *proper count,* call, tally, or return of the votes as required by law, and this fact has been duly established as the basis for granting such relief." *State ex rel. Millinor v. Smith* (Fla. 1932) (emphasis added). The Staff Analysis of the 1999 legislative amendment expressly endorses this important principle. Similarly, the Florida

House of Representatives Committee on Election Reform 1997 Interim Project on Election Contests and Recounts expressly declared:

> Recounts are an integral part of the election process. For one's vote, when cast, to be translated into a true message, that vote must be accurately counted, and if necessary, recounted. The moment an individual's vote becomes subject to error in the vote tabulation process, the easier it is for that vote to be diluted.
>
> Furthermore, with voting statistics tracing a decline in voter turnout and in increase in public skepticism, every effort should be made to ensure the integrity of the electoral process.
>
> Integrity is particularly crucial at the tabulation stage because many elections occur in extremely competitive jurisdictions, where very close election results are always possible. In addition, voters and the media expect rapid and accurate tabulation of election returns, regardless of whether the election is close or one sided. Nonetheless, when large numbers of votes are to be counted, it can be expected that some error will occur in tabulation or in canvassing.

It is with the recognition of these legislative realities and abiding principles that we address whether the trial court made errors of law in rendering its decision.

III. ORDER ON REVIEW

Vice President Gore claims that the trial court erred in the following three ways: (1) The trial court held that an election contest proceeding was essentially an appellate proceeding where the County Canvassing Board's decision must be reviewed with an "abuse of discretion," rather than "de novo," standard of review; (2) The court held that in a contest proceeding in a statewide election a court must review all the ballots cast throughout the state, not just the contested ballots; (3) The court failed to apply the legal standard for relief expressly set forth in section 102.168(3)(c).

A. The Trial Court's Standard of Review

The Florida Election Code sets forth a two-pronged system for challenging vote returns and election procedures. The "protest" and "contest" provisions are distinct proceedings. A protest proceeding is filed with the County Canvassing Board and addresses the validity of the vote returns. The relief that may be granted includes a manual recount. A contest proceeding, on the other hand, is filed in circuit court and addresses the validity of the election itself. Relief that may be granted is varied and can be extensive. No appellate relationship exists between a "protest" and a "contest"; a protest is not a prerequisite for a contest. Moreover, the trial court in the contest action does not sit as an appellate court over the decisions of the Canvassing Board. Accordingly, while the Board's actions concerning the elections process may constitute evidence in a contest proceeding, the Board's decisions are not to be accorded the highly deferential "abuse of discretion" standard of review during a contest proceeding.

In applying the abuse of discretion standard of review to the Boards' actions, the trial court relinquished an improper degree of its own authority to the Boards. This was error.

B. Must All the Ballots be Counted Statewide?

Appellees contend that even if a count of the undervotes in Miami-Dade were appropriate, section 102.168, Florida Statutes (2000), requires a count of all votes in Miami-Dade County and the entire state [including overvotes, where a machine recorded more than one vote for a particular office on a ballot and thus voided those multiple votes] as opposed to a selected number of votes challenged. However, the plain language of section 102.168 refutes appellees' argument.

[S]ection 102.168(3)(c) explicitly contemplates contests based upon a "rejection of a number of legal votes sufficient to change the outcome of an election." Logic dictates that to bring a challenge based upon the rejection of a specific number of legal votes under section 102.168(3)(c), the contestant must establish the "number of legal votes" which the county canvassing board failed to count. This number, therefore, under the plain language of the statute, is limited to the votes identified and challenged under section 102.168(3)(c), rather than the entire county. Moreover, counting uncontested votes in a contest would be irrelevant to a determination of whether certain uncounted votes constitute legal votes that have been rejected.

We do agree, however, that it is absolutely essential in this proceeding and to any final decision, that a manual recount be conducted for all legal votes in this State, not only in Miami-Dade County, but in all Florida counties where there was an undervote and, hence, a concern that not every citizen's vote was counted. This election should be determined by a careful examination of the votes of Florida's citizens and not by strategies extraneous to the voting process. This essential principle, that the outcome of elections be determined by the will of the voters, forms the foundation of the election code enacted by the Florida Legislature and has been consistently applied by this Court in resolving elections disputes.

When an election contest is filed under section 102.168, Florida Statutes (2000), the contest statute charges the trial judge to:

> fashion such orders as he or she deems necessary to ensure that each allegation in the complaint is *investigated, examined, or checked,* to prevent or correct any alleged wrong, and to provide any relief appropriate under such circumstances.

Id. (emphasis added). Through this statute, the Legislature has granted trial courts broad authority to resolve election disputes and fashion appropriate relief. In turn, this Court, consistent with legislative policy, has pointed to the "will of the voters" as the primary guiding principle to be utilized by trial courts in resolving election contests. *Boardman v. Esteva* (Fla. 1975). For example, the Legislature has mandated that no vote shall be ignored "if there is a clear indication of the intent of the voter" on the ballot, unless it is "impossible to determine the elector's choice." § 101.5614(5)-(6) Fla. Stat. (2000). Section 102.166(7), Florida Statutes (2000), also provides that the focus of any manual examination of a ballot shall be to determine the voter's intent. The clear message from this legislative policy is that every citizen's vote be counted whenever possible, whether in an election for a local commissioner or an election for President of the United States.[11]

The demonstrated problem of not counting legal votes inures to any county utilizing a counting system which results in undervotes and "no registered vote" ballots. In a countywide election, one would not simply examine such categories of ballots from a single precinct to ensure the reliability and integrity of the countywide vote. Similarly, in this statewide election, review should not be limited to less than all counties whose tabulation has resulted in such categories of ballots. Relief would not be "appropriate under [the] circumstances" if it failed to address the "otherwise valid exercise of the right of a citizen to vote" of all those citizens of this State who, being similarly situated, have had their legal votes rejected. This is particularly important in a presidential election, which implicates both state and uniquely important national interests. The contestant here satisfied the threshold requirement by demonstrating that, upon consideration of the thousands of undervote or "no registered vote" ballots presented, the number of legal votes therein were sufficient to at least place in doubt the result of the election. However, a final decision as to the result of the statewide election should only be determined upon consideration of the legal votes contained within the undervote or "no registered vote" ballots of all Florida counties, as well as the legal votes already tabulated.

C. The Plaintiff's Burden of Proof

It is immediately apparent, in reviewing the trial court's ruling here, that the trial court failed to apply the statutory standard and instead applied an improper standard in determining the contestant's burden under the contest statute. The trial court began its analysis by stating:

> It is not enough to show a reasonable possibility that election results could have been altered by such irregularities, or inaccuracies, rather, a reasonable probability that the results of the election would have been changed must be shown.

This analysis overlooks and fails to recognize the specific and material changes to the statute which the Legislature made in 1999 that control these proceedings. While the earlier version, like the current version, provided that a contestant shall file a complaint setting forth "the grounds on which the contestant intends to establish his or her right to such office or set aside the result of the election," the prior version did not specifically

11. The Legislature has not, beyond granting to Florida's voters the right to select presidential electors, indicated in any way that it intended that a different (and unstated) set of election rules should apply to the selection of presidential electors. Of course, because the selection and participation of Florida's electors in the presidential election process is subject to a stringent calendar controlled by federal law, the Florida election law scheme must yield in the event of a conflict. [Footnote relocated. —Eds.]

enumerate the "grounds for contesting an election under this section." Those grounds, as contained in the 1999 statute, now explicitly include, in subsection (c), the "[r]eceipt of a number of illegal votes or rejection of a number of legal votes sufficient to change *or place in doubt* the result of the election." (Emphasis supplied.) Assuming that reasonableness is an implied component of such a doubt standard, the determination of whether the plaintiff has met his or her burden of proof to establish that the result of an election is in doubt is a far different standard than the "reasonable probability" standard, which was applicable to contests under the old version of the statute, and erroneously applied and articulated as a "preponderance of a reasonable probability" standard by the trial court here. A person authorized to contest an election is required to demonstrate that there have been legal votes cast in the election that have not been counted (here characterized as "undervotes" or "no vote registered" ballots) and that available data shows that a number of legal votes would be recovered from the entire pool of the subject ballots which, if cast for the unsuccessful candidate, would change or place in doubt the result of the election. Here, there has been an undisputed showing of the existence of some 9000 "undervotes" in an election contest decided by a margin measured in the hundreds. Thus, a threshold contest showing that the result of an election has been placed in doubt, warranting a manual count of all undervotes or "no vote registered" ballots, has been made.

LEGAL VOTES

Having first identified the proper standard of review, we turn now to the allegations of the complaint filed in this election contest. To test the sufficiency of those allegations and the proof, it is essential to understand what, under Florida law, may constitute a "legal vote," and what constitutes rejection of such vote.

Section 101.5614(5), Florida Statutes (2000), provides that "[n]o vote shall be declared invalid or void if there is a clear indication of the intent of the voter as determined by the canvassing board." Section 101.5614(6) provides, conversely, that any vote in which the board cannot discern the intent of the voter must be discarded. Lastly, section 102.166(7)(b) provides that, "[i]f a counting team is unable to determine a voter's intent in casting a ballot, the ballot shall be presented to the county canvassing board for it to determine the voter's intent." This legislative emphasis on discerning the voter's intent is mirrored in the case law of this State, and in that of other states.

This Court has repeatedly held, in accordance with the statutory law of this State, that so long as the voter's intent may be discerned from the ballot, the vote constitutes a "legal vote" that should be counted. *See McAlpin v. State ex rel. Avriett* (Fla. 1944); *see also State ex rel. Peacock v. Latham* (Fla. 1936) (holding that the election contest statute "affords an efficient available remedy and legal procedure by which the circuit court can investigate and determine, not only the legality of the votes cast, but can correct any inaccuracies in the count of the ballots by having them brought into the court and examining the contents of the ballot boxes if properly preserved"). As the State has moved toward electronic voting, nothing in this evolution has diminished the long-standing case law and statutory law that the intent of the voter is of paramount concern and should always be given effect *if* the intent can be determined. *Cf. Boardman v. Esteva,* (Fla. 1975) (recognizing the overarching principle that, where voters do all that statutes require them to do, they should not be disfranchised solely because of failure of election officials to follow directory statutes).

Not surprisingly, other states also have recognized this principle. *Cf. Delahunt v. Johnston,* (Mass. 1996) (holding that a vote should be counted as a legal vote if it properly indicates the voter's intent with reasonable certainty); *Duffy v. Mortenson* (S.D. 1993) (applying the rule that every marking found where a vote should be should be treated as an intended vote in the absence of clear evidence to the clear contrary); *Pullen v. Mulligan* (Ill. 1990) (holding that votes could be recounted by manual means to the extent that the voter's intent could be determined with reasonable certainty, despite the existence of a statute which provided that punch card ballots were to be recounted by automated tabulation equipment).

Accordingly, we conclude that a legal vote is one in which there is a "clear indication of the intent of the voter." We next address whether the term "rejection" used in section 102.168(3)(c) includes instances where the County Canvassing Board has not counted legal votes. Looking at the statutory scheme as a whole, it appears that the term "rejected" does encompass votes that may exist but have not been counted. As explained above, in 1999, the Legislature substantially revised the contest provision of the Election Code. One of the revisions to the contest provision included the codification of the grounds for contesting an election. The House Bill noted that one of the grounds for contesting an election at common law was the "Receipt of a number of illegal votes or rejection of a number of legal votes sufficient to change or place in doubt the result of the election." As noted above, the contest statute ultimately contained this ground for contesting the results of an election.

To further determine the meaning of the term "rejection", as used by the Legislature, we may also look to Florida case law. In *State ex rel. Clark v. Klingensmith* (Fla. 1935), an individual who lost an election brought an action for quo warranto challenging his opponent's right to hold office. The challenger challenged twenty-two ballots, which he divided into four groups. One of these groups included three ballots that the challenger claimed had not been counted. This Court concluded that "the *rejection* of votes from legal voters, not brought about by fraud, and not of such magnitude as to demonstrate that a free expression of the popular will has been suppressed," is insufficient to void an election, "at least unless it be shown that the votes rejected would have changed the result." Therefore, the Court appears to have equated a "rejection" of legal votes with the failure to count legal votes, while at the same time recognizing that a sufficient number of such votes must have been rejected to merit relief. This notion of "rejected" is also in accordance with the common understanding of rejection of votes as used in other election cases.

Here, then, it is apparent that there have been sufficient allegations made which, if analyzed pursuant to the proper standard, compel the conclusion that legal votes sufficient to place in doubt the election results have been rejected in this case.

THIS CASE

[Based on the foregoing, the Florida Supreme Court ruled that it was necessary to complete the as-yet-unfinished manual recount in Miami-Dade. The court, however, rejected Gore's contention that Palm Beach County was required to use the more lenient "dimpled" chad standard to count some 3,300 ballots that had been rejected using a more stringent standard. The court then held that those ballots that already had been manually recounted, either in Miami-Dade before the recount stopped there, or in Palm Beach's recount that was completed two hours late, needed to be added to the final certified total.]

CONCLUSION

Through no fault of appellants, a lawfully commenced manual recount in Dade County was never completed and recounts that were completed were not counted. Without examining or investigating the ballots that were not counted by the machines, the trial court concluded there was no reasonable probability of a different result. However, the proper standard required by section 102.168 was whether the results of the election were placed in doubt. On this record there can be no question that there are legal votes within the 9000 uncounted votes sufficient to place the results of this election in doubt. We know this *not* only by evidence of statistical analysis but also by the actual experience of recounts conducted. The votes for each candidate that have been counted are separated by no more than approximately 500 votes and may be separated by as little as approximately 100 votes. Thousands of uncounted votes could obviously make a difference.

Although in all elections the Legislature and the courts have recognized that the voter's intent is paramount, in close elections the necessity for counting all legal votes becomes critical. However, the need for accuracy must be weighed against the need for finality. The need for prompt resolution and finality is especially critical in presidential elections where there is an outside deadline established by federal law. Notwithstanding, consistent with the legislative mandate and our precedent, although the time constraints are limited, we must do everything required by law to ensure that legal votes that have not been counted are included in the final election results.

In addition to the relief requested by appellants to count the Miami-Dade undervote, claims have been made by the various appellees and intervenors that because this is a statewide election, statewide remedies would be called for. As we discussed in this opinion, we agree. While we recognize that time is desperately short, we cannot in good faith ignore the appellants' right to relief as to their claims concerning the uncounted votes in Miami-

Dade County, nor can we ignore the correctness of the assertions that any analysis and ultimate remedy should be made on a statewide basis.[21]

We note that the contest statutes vest broad discretion in the circuit court to "provide any relief appropriate under the circumstances." § 102.168(5). Moreover, because venue of an election contest that covers more than one county lies in Leon County, *see* § 102.1685, Fla. Stat. (2000), the circuit court has jurisdiction, as part of the relief it orders, to order the Supervisor of Elections and the Canvassing Boards, as well as the necessary public officials, in all counties that have not conducted a manual recount or tabulation of the undervotes in this election to do so forthwith, said tabulation to take place in the individual counties where the ballots are located.[22]

Accordingly, we reverse the final judgment of the trial court dated December 4, 2000, and remand this cause for the circuit court to immediately tabulate by hand the approximate 9000 Miami-Dade ballots, which the counting machine registered as non-votes, but which have never been manually reviewed, and for other relief that may thereafter appear appropriate. The circuit court is directed to enter such orders as are necessary to add any legal votes to the total statewide certifications and to enter any orders necessary to ensure the inclusion of the additional legal votes for Gore in Palm Beach County and the 168 additional legal votes from Miami-Dade County.

Because time is of the essence, the circuit court shall commence the tabulation of the Miami-Dade ballots immediately. The circuit court is authorized, in accordance with the provisions of section 102.168(8), to be assisted by the Leon County Supervisor of Elections or his sworn designees. Moreover, since time is also of the essence in any statewide relief that the circuit court must consider, any further statewide relief should also be ordered forthwith and simultaneously with the manual tabulation of the Miami-Dade undervotes.

In tabulating the ballots and in making a determination of what is a "legal" vote, the standard to be employed is that established by the Legislature in our Election Code which is that the vote shall be counted as a "legal" vote if there is "clear indication of the intent of the voter." § 101.5614(5), Fla. Stat. (2000).

21. The dissents would have us throw up our hands and say that because of looming deadlines and practical difficulties we should give up any attempt to have the election of the presidential electors rest upon the vote of Florida citizens as mandated by the Legislature. While we agree that practical difficulties may well end up controlling the outcome of the election we vigorously disagree that we should therefore abandon our responsibility to resolve this election dispute under the rule of law. We can only do the best we can to carry out our sworn responsibilities to the justice system and its role in this process. We, and our dissenting colleagues, have simply done the best we can, and remain confident that others charged with similar heavy responsibilities will also do the best they can to fulfill their duties as they see them.

22. We are mindful of the fact that due to the time constraints, the count of the undervotes places demands on the public servants throughout the State to work over this week-end. However, we are confident that with the cooperation of the officials in all the counties, the remaining undervotes in these counties can be accomplished within the required time frame. We note that public officials in many counties have worked diligently over the past thirty days in dealing with exigencies that have occurred because of this unique historical circumstance arising from the presidential election of 2000. We commend those dedicated public servants for attempting to make this election process truly reflect the vote of all Floridians.

It is so ordered. ANSTEAD, PARIENTE, LEWIS and QUINCE, JJ., concur.

HARDING, J., [with whom SHAW, J., concurs,] dissenting.*

I would affirm Judge Sauls' order because I agree with his ultimate conclusion in this case, namely that the appellants failed to carry their requisite burden of proof and thus are not entitled to relief.

I agree with Judge Sauls that the appellants have not carried their burden of showing that the number of legal votes rejected by the canvassing boards is sufficient to change or place in doubt the result of this *statewide* election. That failure of proof controls the outcome here. Moreover, as explained below, I do not believe that an adequate remedy exists under the circumstances of this case.

The basis for appellants' claim for relief under section 102.168 is that there is a "no-vote" problem, i.e., ballots which, although counted by machines at least once, allegedly have not been counted in the presidential election. The evidence showed that this no-vote problem, to the extent it exists, is a statewide problem.[33] Appellants ask that only a subset of these no-votes be counted.

The action is to determine whether the Secretary of State certified the correct winner for the entire State of Florida. Appellants failed, however, to provide any meaningful statistical evidence that the outcome of the Florida election would be different if the "no-vote" in other counties had been counted; their proof that the outcome of the vote in two counties would likely change the results of the election was insufficient. It would be improper to permit appellants to carry their burden in a statewide election by merely demonstrating that there were a sufficient number of no-votes that could have changed the returns in isolated counties. Recounting a subset of counties selected by the appellants does not answer the ultimate question of whether a sufficient number of uncounted legal votes could be recovered from the statewide "no-votes" to change the result of the statewide election. At most, such a procedure only demonstrates that the losing candidate would have had greater success in the subset of counties most favorable to that candidate.

As such, I would find that the selective recounting requested by appellant is not available under the election contest provisions of section 102.168. Such an application does not provide for a more accurate reflection of the will of the voters but, rather, allows for an unfair distortion of the statewide vote. It is patently unlawful to permit the recount of "no-votes" in a single county to determine the outcome of the November 7, 2000,

* [Editors' note: The two dissenting opinions are printed here in the opposite order from which they appear in the official reported decision. It is evident that Chief Justice Wells wrote his impassioned separate dissent after reading Justice Harding's more muted dissent.]

33. No-votes (ballots for which the no vote for presidential electors was recorded) exist throughout the state, not just in the counties selected by appellants. Of the 177,655 no-votes in the November 7, 2000, election in Florida, 28,492 occurred in Miami-Dade County and 29,366 occurred in Palm Beach County.

election for the next President of the United States. We are a nation of laws, and we have survived and prospered as a free nation because we have adhered to the rule of law. Fairness is achieved by following the rules.

Finally, even if I were to conclude that the appellants' allegations and evidence were sufficient to warrant relief, I do not believe that the rules permit an adequate remedy under the circumstances of this case. This Court, in its prior opinion, and all of the parties agree that election controversies and contests must be finally and conclusively determined by December 12, 2000. *See* 3 U.S.C. § 5. Clearly, the only remedy authorized by law would be a statewide recount of more than 170,000 "no-vote" ballots by December 12. Even if such a recount were possible, speed would come at the expense of accuracy, and it would be difficult to put any faith or credibility in a vote total achieved under such chaotic conditions. In order to undertake this unprecedented task, the majority has established standards for manual recounts—a step that this Court refused to take [in its decision during the administrative protest], presumably because there was no authority for such action and nothing in the record to guide the Court in setting such standards. The same circumstances exist in this case. All of the parties should be afforded an opportunity to be heard on this very important issue.

While this Court must be ever mindful of the Legislature's plenary power to appoint presidential electors, *see* U.S. Const. art. II, § 1, cl. 2, I am more concerned that the majority is departing from the essential requirements of the law by providing a remedy which is impossible to achieve and which will ultimately lead to chaos. In giving Judge Sauls the direction to order a statewide recount, the majority permits a remedy which was not prayed for, which is based upon a premise for which there is no evidence, and which presents Judge Sauls with directions to order entities (i.e. local canvassing boards) to conduct recounts when they have not been served, have not been named as parties, but, most importantly, have not had the opportunity to be heard. In effect, the majority is allowing the results of the statewide election to be determined by the manual recount in Miami-Dade County because a statewide recount will be impossible to accomplish. Even if by some miracle a portion of the statewide recount is completed by December 12, a partial recount is not acceptable. The uncertainty of the outcome of this election will be greater under the remedy afforded by the majority than the uncertainty that now exists.

The circumstances of this election call to mind a quote from football coaching legend Vince Lombardi: "We didn't lose the game, we just ran out of time."

WELLS, C.J., dissenting.

I want to make it clear at the outset of my separate opinion that I do not question the good faith or honorable intentions of my colleagues in the majority. However, I could not more strongly disagree with their decision to reverse the trial court and prolong this judicial process. I also believe that the majority's decision cannot withstand the scrutiny which will certainly immediately follow under the United States Constitution.

My succinct conclusion is that the majority's decision to return this case to the circuit court for a count of the under-votes from either Miami-Dade County or all counties has no foundation in the law of Florida as it existed on November 7, 2000, or at any time until the issuance of this opinion. The majority returns the case to the circuit court for this partial recount of under-votes on the basis of unknown or, at best, ambiguous standards with authority to obtain help from others, the credentials, qualifications, and objectivity of whom are totally unknown. That is but a first glance at the imponderable problems the majority creates.[26]

Importantly to me, I have a deep and abiding concern that the prolonging of judicial process in this counting contest propels this country and this state into an unprecedented and unnecessary constitutional crisis. I have to conclude that there is a real and present likelihood that this constitutional crisis will do substantial damage to our country, our state, and to this Court as an institution.

On the basis of my analysis of Florida law as it existed on November 7, 2000, I conclude that the trial court's decision can and should be affirmed.

There are two fundamental and historical principles of Florida law that this Court has recognized which are relevant here. First, at common law, there was no right to contest an election; thus, any right to contest an election must be construed to grant only those rights that are explicitly set forth by the Legislature. *See McPherson v. Flynn* (Fla. 1981). Second, this Court gives deference to decisions made by executive officials charged with implementing Florida's election laws. *See Krivanek v. Take Back Tampa Political Committee* (Fla. 1993).

These two concepts are the foundation of my analysis of the present case.

At the outset, I note that, after an evidentiary hearing, the trial court expressly found no dishonesty, gross negligence, improper influence, coercion, or fraud in the balloting and counting processes based upon the evidence presented. I conclude this finding should curtail this Court's involvement in this election through this case and is a substantial basis for affirming the trial court. Historically, this Court has only been involved in elections when there have been substantial allegations of fraud and then only upon a high threshold because of the chill that a hovering judicial involvement can put on elections. Otherwise, we run a great risk that every election will result in judicial testing. Judicial restraint in respect to elections is absolutely necessary because the health of our democracy depends on

26. Also problematic with the majority's analysis is that the majority only *requires* that the "under-votes" are to be counted. How about the "over-votes"? Section 101.5614(6) provides that a ballot should not be counted "[i]f an elector marks more names than there are persons to be elected to an office," meaning the voter voted for more than one person for president. The underlying premise of the majority's rationale is that in such a close race a manual review of ballots rejected by the machines is necessary to ensure that all legal votes cast are counted. The majority, however, ignores the over-votes. Could it be said, without reviewing the over-votes, that the machine did not err in not counting them? It seems patently erroneous to me to assume that the vote-counting machines can err when reading under-votes but not err when reading over-votes. Can the majority say, without having the over-votes looked at, that there are no legal votes among the over-votes? [Footnote relocated. —EDS.]

elections being decided by voters—not by judges. We must have the self-discipline not to become embroiled in political contests whenever a judicial majority subjectively concludes to do so because the majority perceives it is "the right thing to do." Elections involve the other branches of government. A lack of self-discipline in being involved in elections, especially by a court of last resort, always has the potential of leading to a crisis with the other branches of government and raises serious separation-of-powers concerns.

I find that the trial judge correctly concluded that plaintiffs were not entitled to a manual recount. I believe that the contest and protest statutes must logically be read together. It appears logical to me that a circuit judge in a section 102.168 contest should review a county canvassing board's determinations in a section 102.166 protest under an abuse-of-discretion standard.

The majority quotes section 101.5614(5) for the proposition of settling how a county canvassing board should count a vote. The majority states that "[n]o vote shall be declared invalid or void if there is a clear indication of the intent of the voter as determined by the canvassing board." § 101.5614(5), Fla. Stat. (2000). Section 101.5614(5), however, is a statute that authorizes the creation of a duplicate ballot where a "ballot card . . . is damaged or defective so that it cannot properly be counted by the automatic tabulating equipment." There is no basis in this record that suggests that the approximately 9000 ballots from Miami-Dade County were damaged or defective.

Laying aside this problem and assuming the majority is correct that section 101.5614(5) correctly annunciates the standard by which a county canvassing board should judge a questionable ballot, section 101.5614(5) utterly fails to provide any meaningful standard. There is no doubt that every vote should be counted where there is a "clear indication of the intent of the voter." The problem is how a county canvassing board translates that directive to these punch cards. Should a county canvassing board count or not count a "dimpled chad" where the voter is able to successfully dislodge the chad in every other contest on that ballot? Here, the county canvassing boards disagree. Apparently, some do and some do not. Continuation of this system of county-by-county decisions regarding how a dimpled chad is counted is fraught with equal protection concerns which will eventually cause the election results in Florida to be stricken by the federal courts or Congress.

Based upon this analysis, I conclude the circuit court properly looked at what the county canvassing boards had done and found that they did not abuse their discretion. Regarding Miami-Dade County, I find that the trial judge properly concluded that the Miami-Dade Canvassing Board did not abuse its discretion in deciding to discontinue the manual recount begun on November 19, 2000. I also agree with the trial judge that [Secretary of State Harris] did not abuse [her] discretion in refusing to accept either an amended return reflecting the results of a partial manual recount or a late amended return filed by the Palm Beach Board. [The majority's contrary decision] not only changes a rule after November 7, 2000, but it also changes a rule this Court made on November 26, 2000.

I conclude that this contest simply must end.

Directing the trial court to conduct a manual recount of the ballots violates article II, section 1, clause 2 of the United States Constitution, in that neither this Court nor the circuit court has the authority to create the standards by which it will count the under-voted ballots. The Legislature has given to the county canvassing boards—and only these boards—the authority to ascertain the intent of the voter. *See* § 102.166(7)(b), Fla. Stat. (2000). Clearly, in a presidential election, the Legislature has not authorized the courts of Florida to order partial recounts, either in a limited number of counties or statewide. This Court's order to do so appears to me to be in conflict with the United States Supreme Court decision [on December 4 in *Bush v. Palm Beach Canvassing Bd.*].

Laying aside the constitutional infirmities of this Court's action today, what the majority actually creates is an overflowing basket of practical problems. Assuming the majority recognizes a need to protect the votes of Florida's presidential electors, the entire contest must be completed "at least six days before" December 18, 2000, the date the presidential electors meet to vote. *See* 3 U.S.C. § 5 (1994). The safe harbor deadline day is December 12, 2000. Today is Friday, December 8, 2000. Thus, under the majority's time line, all manual recounts must be completed in five days, assuming the counting begins today.

In that time frame, all questionable ballots must be reviewed by the judicial officer appointed to discern the intent of the voter in a process open to the public. Fairness dictates that a provision be made for either party to object to how a particular ballot is counted. Additionally, this short time period must allow for judicial review. I respectfully submit this cannot be completed without taking Florida's presidential electors outside the safe harbor provision, creating the very real possibility of disenfranchising those nearly six million voters who were able to correctly cast their ballots on election day.

Another significant problem is that the majority returns this case to the circuit court for a recount with no standards. I do not, and neither will the trial judge, know whether to count or not count ballots on the criteria used by the canvassing boards, what those criteria are, or to do so on the basis of standards divined by Judge Sauls. A continuing problem with these manual recounts is their reliability. It only stands to reason that many times a reading of a ballot by a human will be subjective, and the intent gleaned from that ballot is only in the mind of the beholder. This subjective counting is only compounded where no standards exist or, as in this statewide contest, where there are no statewide standards for determining voter intent by the various canvassing boards, individual judges, or multiple unknown counters who will eventually count these ballots.

I must regrettably conclude that the majority ignores the magnitude of its decision. The Court fails to make provision for: (1) the qualifications of those who count; (2) what standards are used in the count—are they the same standards for all ballots statewide or a continuation of the county-by-county constitutionally suspect standards; (3) who is to observe the count; (4) how one objects to the count; (5) who is entitled to object to the count; (6) whether a person may object to a counter; (7) the possible lack of personnel to conduct the count; (8) the fatigue of the counters; and (9) the effect of the differing intra-county standards.

This Court's responsibility must be to balance the contest allegations against the rights of all Florida voters who are not involved in election contests to have their votes counted in the electoral college. To me, it is inescapable that there is no practical way for the contest to continue for the good of this country and state.

For a month, Floridians have been working on this problem. At this point, I am convinced of the following.

First, there have been an enormous number of citizens who have expended heroic efforts as members of canvassing boards, counters, and observers, and as legal counsel who have in almost all instances, in utmost good faith attempted to bring about a fair resolution of this election. I know that, regardless of the outcome, all of us are in their debt for their efforts on behalf of representative democracy.

Second, the local election officials, state election officials, and the courts have been attempting to resolve the issues of this election with an election code which any objective, frank analysis must conclude never contemplated this circumstance. Only to state a few of the incongruities, the time limits of sections 102.112, 102.166, and 102.168 and 3 U.S.C. §§ 1, 5, and 7 simply do not coordinate in any practical way with a presidential election in Florida in the year 2000. Therefore, section 102.168, Florida Statues, is inconsistent with the remedy being sought here because it is unclear in a presidential election as to: (1) whether the candidates or the presidential electors should be party to this election contest; (2) what the possible remedy would be; and (3) what standards to apply in counting the ballots statewide.

Third, under the United States Supreme Court's analysis in *Bush v. Palm Beach County Canvassing Board,* there is uncertainty as to whether the Florida Legislature has even given the courts of Florida any power to resolve contests or controversies in respect to presidential elections.

Fourth, there is no available remedy for the appellants on the basis of these allegations. Quite simply, courts cannot fairly continue to proceed without jeopardizing the votes and rights of other citizens through a further count of these votes.

This case has reached the point where finality must take precedence over continued judicial process. I agree with the view attributed to John Allen Paulos, a professor of mathematics at Temple University, who was quoted as saying, "The margin of error in this election is far greater than the margin of victory, no matter who wins." Further judicial process will not change this self-evident fact and will only result in confusion and disorder.

4. The Endgame of the 2000 Presidential Election

After the Florida Supreme Court issued the above 4-3 decision on Friday, December 8, two things happened immediately. First, the required statewide manual recount began under the supervision of Judge Terry Lewis, who took over the case after Judge Sauls recused himself. Second, the Bush team filed an emergency application in the U.S. Supreme Court, asking the Court to stop the recount on the ground that it violated either Article II or the Fourteenth Amendment. On Saturday, December 9, by a 5-4 vote, the Court granted the requested stay and scheduled oral argument on Monday, December 11, to consider the merits of Bush's constitutional claims. Although theoretically the Court could have lifted the stay if after oral argument it decided that these claims lacked merit, as a practical matter the Court's stay had the momentous effect of postponing any further recounting of ballots as the Safe Harbor Deadline of Tuesday, December 12, came ever closer.

Justice Stevens, joined by Justices Souter, Ginsburg, and Breyer, released a dissenting opinion to the stay order:

> To stop the counting of legal votes, the majority today departs from three venerable rules of judicial restraint that have guided the Court throughout its history. On questions of state law, we have consistently respected the opinions of the highest courts of the States. On questions whose resolution is committed at least in large measure to another branch of the Federal Government, we have construed our own jurisdiction narrowly and exercised it cautiously. On federal constitutional questions that were not fairly presented to the court whose judgment is being reviewed, we have prudently declined to express an opinion. The majority has acted unwisely.
>
> Time does not permit a full discussion of the merits. It is clear, however, that a stay should not be granted unless an applicant makes a substantial showing of a likelihood of irreparable harm. In this case, petitioners have failed to carry that heavy burden. Counting every legally cast vote cannot constitute irreparable harm. On the other hand, there is a danger that a stay may cause irreparable harm to respondents—and, more importantly, the public at large—because of the risk that the entry of the stay would be tantamount to a decision on the merits in favor of the applicants. Preventing the recount from being completed will inevitably cast a cloud on the legitimacy of the election.
>
> It is certainly not clear that the Florida decision violated federal law. The Florida Code provides elaborate procedures for ensuring that every eligible voter has a full and fair opportunity to cast a ballot and that every ballot so cast is counted. In fact, the statutory provision relating to damaged and defective ballots states that "[n]o vote shall be declared invalid or void if there is a clear indication of the intent of the voter as determined by the canvassing board." § 101.5614(5). In its opinion, the Florida Supreme Court gave weight to that legislative command. Its ruling was consistent with earlier Florida cases that have repeatedly described the interest in correctly

> ascertaining the will of the voters as paramount. Its ruling also appears to be consistent with the prevailing view in other States. As a more fundamental matter, the Florida court's ruling reflects the basic principle, inherent in our Constitution and our democracy, that every legal vote should be counted.

This dissent prompted Justice Scalia, writing solely for himself, to issue a concurrence to the Court's stay order:

> Though it is not customary for the Court to issue an opinion in connection with its grant of a stay, I believe a brief response is necessary to Justice Stevens' dissent. I will not address the merits of the case, since they will shortly be before us in the petition for certiorari that we have granted. It suffices to say that the issuance of the stay suggests that a majority of the Court, while not deciding the issues presented, believe that petitioners have a substantial probability of success.
>
> On the question of irreparable harm, however, a few words are appropriate. The issue is not, as the dissent puts it, whether "[c]ounting every legally cast vote ca[n] constitute irreparable harm." One of the principal issues in the appeal we have accepted is precisely whether the votes that have been ordered to be counted are, under a reasonable interpretation of Florida law, "legally cast vote[s]." The counting of votes that are of questionable legality does in my view threaten irreparable harm to petitioner Bush, and to the country, by casting a cloud upon what he claims to be the legitimacy of his election. Count first, and rule upon legality afterwards, is not a recipe for producing election results that have the public acceptance democratic stability requires. Another issue in the case, moreover, is the propriety, indeed the constitutionality, of letting the standard for determination of voters' intent—dimpled chads, hanging chads, etc.—vary from county to county, as the Florida Supreme Court opinion permits. If petitioners are correct that counting in this fashion is unlawful, permitting the count to proceed on that erroneous basis will prevent an accurate recount from being conducted on a proper basis later, since it is generally agreed that each manual recount produces a degradation of the ballots, which renders a subsequent recount inaccurate.
>
> For these reasons I have joined the Court's issuance of a stay, with a highly accelerated timetable for resolving this case on the merits.

The oral argument on the merits occurred as scheduled, and the next day—Tuesday, December 12, the day of the Safe-Harbor Deadline, the U.S. Supreme Court announced its decision in *Bush v. Gore*. What follows are, first, a chronology of the 2000 election dispute and, second, the text of the relevant statutory authority. We then present the Court's opinion, Chief Justice Rehnquist's concurrence (joined by Justices Scalia and Thomas), and the four dissents from Justices Stevens, Breyer, Ginsburg, and Souter.

Election 2000: Chronology

11/7 (Tue)	Election Day
11/10 (Fri)	Deadline for requesting a manual recount (requested on 11/9)
	Automatic machine recount shows Bush leading by 327 votes
11/13 (Mon)	Counties: "can't complete full manual recount by tomorrow"
11/14 (Tue)	Deadline for counties to file certified returns
	Judge Lewis: deadline mandatory; amended returns possible
11/15 (Wed)	Secretary Harris: no amended returns
11/17 (Fri)	Deadline for military and overseas absentee ballots
	Florida Supreme Court halts statewide certification
11/21 (Tue)	Florida Supreme Court's first decision: extends certification deadline
11/26 (Sun)	New deadline for certification; Bush declared winner by 537
11/27 (Mon)	Gore files "contest"
12/4 (Mon)	U.S.Supreme Court's first decision (9-0)
	Judge Sauls: "no credible evidence that recounts would change result"
12/8 (Fri)	Florida Supreme Court second decision (4-3)
12/9 (Sat)	U.S.Supreme Court stay (5-4)
12/12 (Tue)	U.S.Supreme Court's second decision (5-4)
	"Safe harbor deadline" under congressional statute
12/18 (Mon)	Electoral College vote
1/6 (Sat)	Congress meets

Presidential Election Procedures

U.S. CONSTITUTION., AMEND. 12

The Electors shall meet in their respective states . . . ; they shall name in their ballots the person voted for as President, and in distinct ballots the person voted for as Vice-President, and they shall make distinct lists of all persons voted for as President, and all persons voted for as Vice-President, and of the number of votes for each, which lists they shall sign and certify, and transmit sealed to the seat of government of the United States, directed to the president of the Senate—The President of the Senate shall, in the presence of the Senate and House of Representatives, open all the certificates and the votes shall then be counted—The person having the greatest number of votes for President shall be the President, if such number be a majority of the whole number of Electors appointed; and if no person have such majority, then the persons having the highest numbers not exceeding three on the list of those voted for as President, the House of Representatives shall choose immediately, by ballot, the President. But in choosing the President, the votes shall be taken by states, the representation from each state having one vote; a quorum for this purpose shall consist of a member of members from two–thirds of the states, and a majority of all states shall be necessary to a choice.

3 U.S.C. § 5 [SAFE HARBOR DEADLINE]

If any State shall have provided, by laws enacted prior to the day fixed for the appointment of the electors, for its final determination of any controversy or contest concerning the appointment of all or any of the electors of such State, by judicial or other methods or procedures, and such determination shall have been made at least six days before the time fixed for the meeting of the electors, such determination made pursuant to such law so existing on said day, and made at least six days prior to said time of meeting of the electors, shall be conclusive, and shall govern in the counting of the electoral votes as provided in the Constitution, and as hereinafter regulated, so far as the ascertainment of the electors appointed by such State is concerned.

3 U.S.C. § 6

It shall be the duty of the executive of each State, as soon as practicable after the conclusion of the appointment of the electors in such State by the final ascertainment, under and in pursuance of the laws of such State providing for such ascertainment, to communicate by registered mail under the seal of the State to the Archivist of the United States a certificate of such ascertainment of the electors appointed, setting forth the names of such electors and the canvass or other ascertainment under the laws of such State of the number of votes given or cast for each person for whose appointment any and all votes have been given or cast; and it shall also thereupon be the duty of the executive of each State to deliver to the electors of such State, on or before the day on which they are required by section 7 of this title to meet, six duplicate-originals of the same certificate under the seal of the State; and if there shall have been any final determination in a State in the manner provided for by law of a controversy or contest concerning the appointment of all or any of the electors of such State, it shall be the duty of the executive of such State, as soon as practicable after such determination, to communicate under the seal of the State to the Archivist of the United States a certificate of such determination in form and manner as the same shall have been made; and the certificate or certificates so received by the Archivist of the United States shall be preserved by him for one year and shall be a part of the public records of his office and shall be open to public inspection; and the Archivist of the United States at the first meeting of Congress thereafter shall transmit to the two Houses of Congress copies in full of each and every such certificate so received at the National Archives and Records Administration.

3 U.S.C. § 15

Congress shall be in session on the sixth day of January succeeding every meeting of the electors. The Senate and House of Representatives shall meet in the Hall of the House of Representatives at the hour of 1 o'clock in the afternoon on that day, and the President of the Senate shall be their presiding officer. Two tellers shall be previously appointed on the part of the Senate and two on the part of the House of Representatives, to whom shall be handed, as they are opened by the President of the Senate, all the certificates and papers purporting to be certificates of the electoral votes, which certificates and papers shall be opened, presented, and acted upon in the alphabetical order of the States, beginning with the letter A; and said tellers, having then read the same in the presence and hearing of the two Houses, shall make a list of the votes as they shall appear from the said certificates; and the votes having been ascertained and counted according to the rules in this subchapter provided, the result of the same shall be delivered to the President of the Senate, who shall thereupon announce the state of the vote, which announcement shall be deemed a sufficient declaration of the persons, if any, elected President and Vice President of the United States, and, together with a list of the votes, be entered on the Journals of the two Houses. Upon such reading of any such certificate or paper, the President of the Senate shall call for objections, if any. Every objection shall be made in writing, and shall state clearly and concisely, and without argument, the ground thereof, and shall be signed by at least one Senator and one Member of the House of Representatives before the same shall be received. When all objections so made to any vote or paper from a State shall have been received and read, the Senate shall thereupon withdraw, and such objections shall be submitted to the Senate for its decision; and the Speaker of the House of Representatives shall, in like manner, submit such objections to the House of Representatives for its decision; and no electoral vote or votes from any State which shall have been regularly given by electors whose appointment has been lawfully certified to according to section 6 of this title from which but one return has been received shall be rejected, but the two Houses concurrently may reject the vote or votes when they agree that such vote or votes have not been so regularly given by electors whose appointment has been so certified. If more than one return or paper purporting to be a return from a State shall have been received by the President of the Senate, those votes, and those only, shall be counted which shall have been regularly given by the electors who are shown by the determination mentioned in section 5 of this title to have been appointed, if the determination in said section provided for shall have been made, or by such successors or substitutes, in case of a vacancy in the board of electors so ascertained, as have been appointed to fill such vacancy in the mode provided by the laws of the State; but in case there shall arise the question which of two or more of such State authorities determining what electors have been appointed, as mentioned in section 5 of this title, is the lawful tribunal of such State, the votes regularly given of those electors, and those only, of such State shall be counted whose title as electors the two Houses, acting separately, shall concurrently decide is supported by the decision of such State so authorized by its law; and in such case of more than one return or paper purporting to be a return from a State, if there shall have been no such determination of the question in the State aforesaid, then those votes, and those only, shall be counted which the two Houses shall concurrently decide were cast by lawful electors appointed in accordance with the laws of the State, unless the two Houses, acting separately, shall concurrently decide such votes not to be the lawful votes of the legally appointed electors of such State. But if the two Houses shall disagree in respect of the counting of such votes, then, and in that case, the votes of the electors whose appointment shall have been certified by the executive of the State, under the seal thereof, shall be counted. When the two Houses have voted, they shall immediately again meet, and the presiding officer shall then announce the decision of the questions submitted. No votes or papers from any other State shall be acted upon until the objections previously made to the votes or papers from any State shall have been finally disposed of.

BUSH v. GORE

531 U.S. 98 (2000)

PER CURIAM.

I

On December 8, 2000, the Supreme Court of Florida ordered that the Circuit Court of Leon County tabulate by hand 9,000 ballots in Miami-Dade County. It also ordered the inclusion in the certified vote totals of 215 votes identified in Palm Beach County and 168 votes identified in Miami-Dade County for Vice President Albert Gore, Jr., and Senator Joseph Lieberman, Democratic candidates for President and Vice President. The State Supreme Court noted that petitioner George W. Bush asserted that the net gain for Vice President Gore in Palm Beach County was 176 votes, and directed the Circuit Court to resolve that dispute on remand. The court further held that relief would require manual recounts in all Florida counties where so-called "undervotes" had not been subject to manual tabulation. The court ordered all manual recounts to begin at once. Governor Bush and Richard Cheney, Republican candidates for President and Vice President, filed an emergency application for a stay of this mandate. On December 9, we granted the application, treated the application as a petition for a writ of certiorari, and granted certiorari.

The proceedings leading to the present controversy are discussed in some detail in our opinion in *Bush v. Palm Beach County Canvassing Bd.* (2000). On November 8, 2000, the day following the Presidential election, the Florida Division of Elections reported that petitioner Bush had received 2,909,135 votes, and respondent Gore had received 2,907,351 votes, a margin of 1,784 for Governor Bush. Because Governor Bush's margin of victory was less than "one-half of a percent . . . of the votes cast," an automatic machine recount was conducted under § 102.141(4) of the election code, the results of which showed Governor Bush still winning the race but by a diminished margin. Vice President Gore then sought manual recounts in Volusia, Palm Beach, Broward, and Miami-Dade Counties, pursuant to Florida's election protest provisions. Fla. Stat. Ann. § 102.166 (Supp. 2001). A dispute arose concerning the deadline for local county canvassing boards to submit their returns to the Secretary of State (Secretary). The Secretary declined to waive the November 14 deadline imposed by statute. §§ 102.111, 102.112. The Florida Supreme Court, however, set the deadline at November 26. We granted certiorari and vacated the Florida Supreme Court's decision, finding considerable uncertainty as to the grounds on which it was based. On December 11, the Florida Supreme Court issued a decision on remand reinstating that date. *Palm Beach County Canvassing Bd. v. Harris* (2000).

On November 26, the Florida Elections Canvassing Commission certified the results of the election and declared Governor Bush the winner of Florida's 25 electoral votes. On November 27, Vice President Gore, pursuant to Florida's contest provisions, filed a complaint in Leon County Circuit Court contesting the certification. Fla. Stat. Ann. § 102.168 (Supp. 2001). He sought relief pursuant to § 102.168(3)(c), which provides that "[r]eceipt of a number of illegal votes or rejection of a number of legal votes sufficient to change or place in doubt the result of the election" shall be grounds for a contest. The Circuit Court denied relief, stating that Vice President Gore failed to meet his burden of proof. He appealed to the First District Court of Appeal, which certified the matter to the Florida Supreme Court.

Accepting jurisdiction, the Florida Supreme Court affirmed in part and reversed in part. *Gore v. Harris* (2000). The court held that the Circuit Court had been correct to reject Vice President Gore's challenge to the results certified in Nassau County and his challenge to the Palm Beach County Canvassing Board's determination that 3,300 ballots cast in that county were not, in the statutory phrase, "legal votes."

The Supreme Court held that Vice President Gore had satisfied his burden of proof under § 102.168(3)(c) with respect to his challenge to Miami-Dade County's failure to tabulate, by manual count, 9,000 ballots on which the machines had failed to detect a vote for President ("undervotes"). Noting the closeness of the election, the court explained that "[o]n this record, there can be no question that there are legal votes within the 9,000 uncounted votes sufficient to place the results of this election in doubt." A "legal vote," as determined by the Supreme Court, is "one in which there is a 'clear indication of the intent of the voter.'". The court therefore ordered a hand recount of the 9,000 ballots in Miami-Dade County. Observing that the contest provisions vest broad discretion in the circuit judge to "provide any relief appropriate under such circumstances," § 102.168(8), the Supreme Court further held that the Circuit Court could order "the Supervisor of Elections and the Canvassing Boards, as well as the necessary public officials, in all counties that have not conducted a manual recount or tabulation of the undervotes . . . to do so forthwith, said tabulation to take place in the individual counties where the ballots are located." *Id.*

The Supreme Court also determined that both Palm Beach County and Miami-Dade County, in their earlier manual recounts, had identified a net gain of 215 and 168 legal votes for Vice President Gore. Rejecting the Circuit Court's conclusion that Palm Beach County lacked the authority to include the 215 net votes submitted past the November 26 deadline, the Supreme Court explained that the deadline was not intended to exclude votes identified after that date through ongoing manual recounts. As to Miami-Dade County, the court concluded that although the 168 votes identified were the result of a partial recount, they were "legal votes [that] could change the outcome of the election." The Supreme Court therefore directed the Circuit Court to include those totals in the certified results, subject to resolution of the actual vote total from the Miami-Dade partial recount.

The petition presents the following questions: whether the Florida Supreme Court established new standards for resolving Presidential election contests, thereby violating Art. II, § 1, cl. 2, of the United States Constitution and failing to comply with 3 U.S.C. § 5, and whether the use of standardless manual recounts violates the Equal Protection and Due Process Clauses. With respect to the equal protection question, we find a violation of the Equal Protection Clause.

II

A

The closeness of this election, and the multitude of legal challenges which have followed in its wake, have brought into sharp focus a common, if heretofore unnoticed, phenomenon. Nationwide statistics reveal that an estimated 2% of ballots cast do not register a vote for President for whatever reason, including deliberately choosing no candidate at all or some voter error, such as voting for two candidates or insufficiently marking a ballot. *See* Ho, *More Than 2M Ballots Uncounted*, AP Online (Nov. 28, 2000); Kelley, *Balloting Problems Not Rare But Only in a Very Close Election Do Mistakes and Mismarking Make a Difference*, Omaha World-Herald (Nov. 15, 2000). In certifying election results, the votes eligible for inclusion in the certification are the votes meeting the properly established legal requirements.

This case has shown that punch card balloting machines can produce an unfortunate number of ballots which are not punched in a clean, complete way by the voter. After the current counting, it is likely legislative bodies nationwide will examine ways to improve the mechanisms and machinery for voting.

B

The individual citizen has no federal constitutional right to vote for electors for the President of the United States unless and until the state legislature chooses a statewide election as the means to implement its power to appoint members of the electoral college. U.S. Const., Art. II, § 1. This is the source for the statement in *McPherson v. Blacker* (1892) that the state legislature's power to select the manner for appointing electors is plenary; it may, if it so chooses, select the electors itself, which indeed was the manner used by state legislatures in several States for many years after the framing of our Constitution. History has now favored the voter, and in each of the several States the citizens themselves vote for Presidential electors. When the state legislature vests the right to vote for President in its people, the right to vote as the legislature has prescribed is fundamental; and one source of its fundamental nature lies in the equal weight accorded to each vote and the equal dignity owed to each voter. The State, of course, after granting the franchise in the special context of Article II, can take back the power to appoint electors.

The right to vote is protected in more than the initial allocation of the franchise. Equal protection applies as well to the manner of its exercise. Having once granted the right to vote on equal terms, the State may not, by later arbitrary and disparate treatment, value one person's vote over that of another. *See, e.g., Harper v. Virginia Bd. of Elections* [(1966)]. It must be remembered that "the right of suffrage can be denied by a debasement or dilution of the weight of a citizen's vote just as effectively as by wholly prohibiting the free exercise of the franchise." *Reynolds v. Sims* (1964).

There is no difference between the two sides of the present controversy on these basic propositions. Respondents say that the very purpose of vindicating the right to vote justifies the recount procedures now at issue. The question before us, however, is whether the recount procedures the Florida Supreme Court has adopted are consistent with its obligation to avoid arbitrary and disparate treatment of the members of its electorate.

Much of the controversy seems to revolve around ballot cards designed to be perforated by a stylus but which, either through error or deliberate omission, have not been perforated with sufficient precision for a machine to register the perforations. In some cases a piece of the card—a chad—is hanging, say, by two corners. In other cases there is no separation at all, just an indentation.

The Florida Supreme Court has ordered that the intent of the voter be discerned from such ballots. For purposes of resolving the equal protection challenge, it is not necessary to decide whether the Florida Supreme Court had the authority under the legislative scheme for resolving election disputes to define what a legal vote is and to mandate a manual recount implementing that definition. The recount mechanisms implemented in response to the decisions of the Florida Supreme Court do not satisfy the minimum requirement for non-arbitrary treatment of voters necessary to secure the fundamental right. Florida's basic command for the count of legally cast votes is to consider the "intent of the voter." This is unobjectionable as an abstract proposition and a starting principle. The problem inheres in the absence of specific standards to ensure its equal application. The formulation of uniform rules to determine intent based on these recurring circumstances is practicable and, we conclude, necessary.

The law does not refrain from searching for the intent of the actor in a multitude of circumstances; and in some cases the general command to ascertain intent is not susceptible to much further refinement. In this instance, however, the question is not whether to believe a witness but how to interpret the marks or holes or scratches on an inanimate object, a piece of cardboard or paper which, it is said, might not have registered as a vote during the machine count. The factfinder confronts a thing, not a person. The search for intent can be confined by specific rules designed to ensure uniform treatment.

The want of those rules here has led to unequal evaluation of ballots in various respects. *See* [Florida Supreme Court decision] (Wells, C.J., dissenting) ("Should a county canvassing board count or not count a 'dimpled chad' where the voter is able to successfully dislodge the chad in every other contest on that ballot? Here, the county canvassing boards disagree"). As seems to have been acknowledged at oral argument, the standards for accepting or rejecting contested ballots might vary not only from county to county but indeed within a single county from one recount team to another.

The record provides some examples. A monitor in Miami-Dade County testified at trial that he observed that three members of the county canvassing board applied different standards in defining a legal vote. And testimony at trial also revealed that at least one county changed its evaluative standards during the counting process. Palm Beach County, for example, began the process with a 1990 guideline which precluded counting completely attached chads, switched to a rule that considered a vote to be legal if any light could be seen through a chad, changed back to the 1990 rule, and then abandoned any pretense of a *per se* rule, only to have a court order that the county consider dimpled chads legal. This is not a process with sufficient guarantees of equal treatment.

An early case in our one-person, one-vote jurisprudence arose when a State accorded arbitrary and disparate treatment to voters in its different counties. *Gray v. Sanders* (1963). The Court found a constitutional violation. We relied on these principles in the context of the Presidential selection process in *Moore v. Ogilvie* (1969), where we invalidated a county-based procedure that diluted the influence of citizens in larger counties in the nominating process. There we observed that "[t]he idea that one group can be granted greater voting strength than another is hostile to the one man, one vote basis of our representative government." *Id.*

The State Supreme Court ratified this uneven treatment. It mandated that the recount totals from two counties, Miami-Dade and Palm Beach, be included in the certified total. The court also appeared to hold *sub silentio* that the recount totals from Broward County, which were not completed until after the original November 14 certification by the Secretary, were to be considered part of the new certified vote totals even though the county certification was not contested by Vice President Gore. Yet each of the counties used varying standards to determine what was a legal vote. Broward County used a more forgiving standard than Palm Beach County, and uncovered almost three times as many new votes, a result markedly disproportionate to the difference in population between the counties.

In addition, the recounts in these three counties were not limited to so-called undervotes but extended to all of the ballots. The distinction has real consequences. A manual recount of all ballots identifies not only those ballots which show no vote but also those which contain more than one, the so-called overvotes. Neither category will be counted by the machine. This is not a trivial concern. At oral argument, respondents estimated there are as many as 110,000 overvotes statewide. As a result, the citizen whose ballot was not read by a machine because he failed to vote for a candidate in a way readable by a machine may still have his vote counted in a manual recount; on the other hand, the citizen who marks two candidates in a way discernible by the machine will not have the same opportunity to have his vote count, even if a manual examination of the ballot would reveal the requisite indicia of intent. Furthermore, the citizen who marks two candidates, only one of which is discernible by the machine, will have his vote counted even though it should have been read as an invalid ballot. The State Supreme Court's inclusion of vote counts based on these variant standards exemplifies concerns with the remedial processes that were under way.

That brings the analysis to yet a further equal protection problem. The votes certified by the court included a partial total from one county, Miami-Dade. The Florida Supreme Court's decision thus gives no assurance that the recounts included in a final certification must be complete. Indeed, it is respondents' submission that it would be consistent with the rules of the recount procedures to include whatever partial counts are done by the time of final certification, and we interpret the Florida Supreme Court's decision to permit this. *See* [Florida Supreme Court decision] (noting "practical difficulties" may control outcome of election, but certifying partial Miami-Dade total nonetheless). This accommodation no doubt results from the truncated contest period established by the Florida Supreme Court in *Palm Beach County Canvassing Bd. v. Harris*, at respondents' own urging. The press of time does not diminish the constitutional concern. A desire for speed is not a general excuse for ignoring equal protection guarantees.

In addition to these difficulties the actual process by which the votes were to be counted under the Florida Supreme Court's decision raises further concerns. That order did not specify who would recount the ballots. The county canvassing boards were forced to pull together ad hoc teams of judges from various Circuits who had no previous training in handling and interpreting ballots. Furthermore, while others were permitted to observe, they were prohibited from objecting during the recount.

The recount process, in its features here described, is inconsistent with the minimum procedures necessary to protect the fundamental right of each voter in the special instance of a statewide recount under the authority of a single state judicial officer. Our consideration is limited to the present circumstances, for the problem of equal protection in election processes generally presents many complexities.*

The question before the Court is not whether local entities, in the exercise of their expertise, may develop different systems for implementing elections. Instead, we are

* [Editors' note: This sentence has been particularly controversial. Many have interpreted it as an explicit admission by the Court that its decision was unprincipled and lawless, refusing to set a precedent that would apply in future cases according to the rule of law. Others have seen the sentence as innocuous, consistent with the common law heritage of adjudicating cases one at a time and not creating judicial dicta broader than necessary to decide the specific case at hand. What do you think the Court meant by this sentence? Does it matter, or instead is it now more important how future courts treat *Bush v. Gore* as a precedent? To be sure, the Court itself has not relied upon it in a subsequent case. (Justice Thomas cited it in a dissent for a rather straightforward proposition.) But, as you already have seen and will continue to see elsewhere in this casebook, lower courts have started to use *Bush v. Gore* to generate significance new Equal Protection jurisprudence applicable to the casting and counting of ballots. Thus, will the fury that this sentence sparked in some quarters upon the immediate release of the opinion continue to subside, as more time passes since 2000?]

presented with a situation where a state court with the power to assure uniformity has ordered a statewide recount with minimal procedural safeguards. When a court orders a statewide remedy, there must be at least some assurance that the rudimentary requirements of equal treatment and fundamental fairness are satisfied.

Given the Court's assessment that the recount process underway was probably being conducted in an unconstitutional manner, the Court stayed the order directing the recount so it could hear this case and render an expedited decision. The contest provision, as it was mandated by the State Supreme Court, is not well calculated to sustain the confidence that all citizens must have in the outcome of elections. The State has not shown that its procedures include the necessary safeguards. The problem, for instance, of the estimated 110,000 overvotes has not been addressed, although Chief Justice Wells called attention to the concern in his dissenting opinion.

Upon due consideration of the difficulties identified to this point, it is obvious that the recount cannot be conducted in compliance with the requirements of equal protection and due process without substantial additional work. It would require not only the adoption (after opportunity for argument) of adequate statewide standards for determining what is a legal vote, and practicable procedures to implement them, but also orderly judicial review of any disputed matters that might arise. In addition, the Secretary has advised that the recount of only a portion of the ballots requires that the vote tabulation equipment be used to screen out undervotes, a function for which the machines were not designed. If a recount of overvotes were also required, perhaps even a second screening would be necessary. Use of the equipment for this purpose, and any new software developed for it, would have to be evaluated for accuracy by the Secretary, as required by Fla. Stat. Ann. § 101.015 (Supp. 2001).

The Supreme Court of Florida has said that the legislature intended the State's electors to "participat[e] fully in the federal electoral process," as provided in 3 U.S.C. § 5. That statute, in turn, requires that any controversy or contest that is designed to lead to a conclusive selection of electors be completed by December 12. That date is upon us, and there is no recount procedure in place under the State Supreme Court's order that comports with minimal constitutional standards. Because it is evident that any recount seeking to meet the December 12 date will be unconstitutional for the reasons we have discussed, we reverse the judgment of the Supreme Court of Florida ordering a recount to proceed.

Seven Justices of the Court agree that there are constitutional problems with the recount ordered by the Florida Supreme Court that demand a remedy. See *post,* (Souter, J., dissenting); *post,* (Breyer, J., dissenting). The only disagreement is as to the remedy. Because the Florida Supreme Court has said that the Florida Legislature intended to obtain the safe-harbor benefits of 3 U.S.C. § 5, Justice Breyer's proposed remedy—remanding to the Florida Supreme Court for its ordering of a constitutionally proper contest until December 18 contemplates action in violation of the Florida Election Code, and hence could not be part of an "appropriate" order authorized by Fla. Stat. Ann. § 102.168(8) (Supp. 2001).

* * *

None are more conscious of the vital limits on judicial authority than are the Members of this Court, and none stand more in admiration of the Constitution's design to leave the selection of the President to the people, through their legislatures, and to the political sphere. When contending parties invoke the process of the courts, however, it becomes our unsought responsibility to resolve the federal and constitutional issues the judicial system has been forced to confront.

The judgment of the Supreme Court of Florida is reversed, and the case is remanded for further proceedings not inconsistent with this opinion.

Pursuant to this Court's Rule 45.2, the Clerk is directed to issue the mandate in this case forthwith.

It is so ordered.

Chief Justice REHNQUIST, with whom Justice SCALIA and Justice THOMAS join, concurring.

We join the *per curiam* opinion. We write separately because we believe there are additional grounds that require us to reverse the Florida Supreme Court's decision.

I

In most cases, comity and respect for federalism compel us to defer to the decisions of state courts on issues of state law. That practice reflects our understanding that the decisions of state courts are definitive pronouncements of the will of the States as sovereigns. Of course, in ordinary cases, the distribution of powers among the branches of a State's government raises no questions of federal constitutional law, subject to the requirement that the government be republican in character. *See* U.S. Const., Art. IV, § 4. But there are a few exceptional cases in which the Constitution imposes a duty or confers a power on a particular branch of a State's government. This is one of them. Article II, § 1, cl. 2, provides that "[e]ach State shall appoint, in such Manner as the *Legislature* thereof may direct," electors for President and Vice President. (Emphasis added.) Thus, the text of the election law itself, and not just its interpretation by the courts of the States, takes on independent significance.

Title 3 U.S.C. § 5 informs our application of Art. II, § 1, cl. 2, to the Florida statutory scheme, which, as the Florida Supreme Court acknowledged, took that statute into account. Section 5 provides that the State's selection of electors "shall be conclusive, and shall govern in the counting of the electoral votes" if the electors are chosen under laws enacted prior to election day, and if the selection process is completed six days prior to the meeting of the electoral college. As we noted in *Bush v. Palm Beach County Canvassing Bd.*:

> "Since § 5 contains a principle of federal law that would assure finality of the State's determination if made pursuant to a state law in effect before the election, a legislative wish to take advantage of the 'safe harbor' would counsel against any construction of the Election Code that Congress might deem to be a change in the law."

If we are to respect the legislature's Article II powers, therefore, we must ensure that postelection state-court actions do not frustrate the legislative desire to attain the "safe harbor" provided by § 5.

In Florida, the legislature has chosen to hold statewide elections to appoint the State's 25 electors. Importantly, the legislature has delegated the authority to run the elections and to oversee election disputes to the Secretary of State (Secretary), Fla. Stat. Ann. § 97.012(1) (Supp. 2001), and to state circuit courts, §§ 102.168(1), 102.168(8). Isolated sections of the code may well admit of more than one interpretation, but the general coherence of the legislative scheme may not be altered by judicial interpretation so as to wholly change the statutorily provided apportionment of responsibility among these various bodies.

To attach definitive weight to the pronouncement of a state court, when the very question at issue is whether the court has actually departed from the statutory meaning, would be to abdicate our responsibility to enforce the explicit requirements of Article II.

II

Acting pursuant to its constitutional grant of authority, the Florida Legislature has created a detailed, if not perfectly crafted, statutory scheme that provides for appointment of Presidential electors by direct election. Fla. Stat. Ann. § 103.011 (1992). Under the statute, "[v]otes cast for the actual candidates for President and Vice President shall be counted as votes cast for the presidential electors supporting such candidates.". The legislature has designated the Secretary as the "chief election officer," with the responsibility to "[o]btain and maintain uniformity in the application, operation, and interpretation of the election laws." Fla. Stat. Ann. § 97.012 (Supp. 2001). The state legislature has delegated to county canvassing boards the duties of administering elections. § 102.141. Those boards are responsible for providing results to the state Elections Canvassing Commission, comprising the Governor, the Secretary of State, and the Director of the Division of Elections. § 102.111.

After the election has taken place, the canvassing boards receive returns from precincts, count the votes, and in the event that a candidate was defeated by 0.5% or less, conduct a mandatory recount. Fla. Stat. § 102.141(4) (2000). The county canvassing boards must file certified election returns with the Department of State by 5 p.m. on the seventh day following the election. § 102.112(1). The Elections Canvassing Commission must then certify the results of the election. § 102.111(1).

The state legislature has also provided mechanisms both for protesting election returns and for contesting certified election results. Section 102.166 governs protests.

Any protest must be filed prior to the certification of election results by the county canvassing board. § 102.166(4)(b). Once a protest has been filed, "[t]he county canvassing board may authorize a manual recount." § 102.166(4)(c). If a sample recount conducted pursuant to § 102.166(5) "indicates an error in the vote tabulation which could affect the outcome of the election," the county canvassing board is instructed to: "(a) Correct the error and recount the remaining precincts with the vote tabulation system; (b) Request the Department of State to verify the tabulation software; or (c) Manually recount all ballots," § 102.166(5). In the event a canvassing board chooses to conduct a manual recount of all ballots, § 102.166(7) prescribes procedures for such a recount.

Contests to the certification of an election, on the other hand, are controlled by § 102.168. The grounds for contesting an election include "[r]eceipt of a number of illegal votes or rejection of a number of legal votes sufficient to change or place in doubt the result of the election." § 102.168(3)(c). Any contest must be filed in the appropriate Florida circuit court, § 102.168(1), and the canvassing board or election board is the proper party defendant, § 102.168(4). Section 102.168(8) provides that "[t]he circuit judge to whom the contest is presented may fashion such orders as he or she deems necessary to ensure that each allegation in the complaint is investigated, examined, or checked, to prevent or correct any alleged wrong, and to provide any relief appropriate under such circumstances." In Presidential elections, the contest period necessarily terminates on the date set by 3 U.S.C. § 5 for concluding the State's "final determination" of election controversies.

In its first decision, *Palm Beach Canvassing Bd. v. Harris* (2000) (*Harris I*), the Florida Supreme Court extended the 7-day statutory certification deadline established by the legislature.[2] This modification of the code, by lengthening the protest period, necessarily shortened the contest period for Presidential elections. Underlying the extension of the certification deadline and the shortchanging of the contest period was, presumably, the clear implication that certification was a matter of significance: The certified winner would enjoy presumptive validity, making a contest proceeding by the losing candidate an uphill battle. In its latest opinion, however, the court empties certification of virtually all legal consequence during the contest, and in doing so departs from the provisions enacted by the Florida Legislature.

The court determined that canvassing boards' decisions regarding whether to recount ballots past the certification deadline (even the certification deadline established by *Harris I*) are to be reviewed *de novo,* although the Election Code clearly vests discretion whether to recount in the boards, and sets strict deadlines subject to the Secretary's rejection of late tallies and monetary fines for tardiness. Moreover, the Florida court held that all late vote tallies arriving during the contest period should be automatically included in the certification regardless of the certification deadline (even the certification deadline

2. We vacated that decision and remanded that case; the Florida Supreme Court reissued the same judgment with a new opinion on December 11, 2000.

established by *Harris I*), thus virtually eliminating both the deadline and the Secretary's discretion to disregard recounts that violate it.

Moreover, the court's interpretation of "legal vote," and hence its decision to order a contest-period recount, plainly departed from the legislative scheme. Florida statutory law cannot reasonably be thought to *require* the counting of improperly marked ballots. Each Florida precinct before election day provides instructions on how properly to cast a vote, Fla. Stat. Ann. § 101.46 (1992); each polling place on election day contains a working model of the voting machine it uses, Fla. Stat. Ann. § 101.5611 (Supp. 2001); and each voting booth contains a sample ballot, § 101.46. In precincts using punchcard ballots, voters are instructed to punch out the ballot cleanly:

> "AFTER VOTING, CHECK YOUR BALLOT CARD TO BE SURE YOUR VOTING SELECTIONS ARE CLEARLY AND CLEANLY PUNCHED AND THERE ARE NO CHIPS LEFT HANGING ON THE BACK OF THE CARD.

Instructions to Voters, quoted in Brief for Respondent Harris et al. 13, n. 5.

No reasonable person would call it "an error in the vote tabulation," Fla. Stat. Ann. § 102.166(5) (Supp. 2001), or a "rejection of . . . legal votes," § 102.168(3)(c),[4] when electronic or electromechanical equipment performs precisely in the manner designed, and fails to count those ballots that are not marked in the manner that these voting instructions explicitly and prominently specify. The scheme that the Florida Supreme Court's opinion attributes to the legislature is one in which machines are *required* to be "capable of correctly counting votes," § 101.5606(4), but which nonetheless regularly produces elections in which legal votes are predictably *not* tabulated, so that in close elections manual recounts are regularly required. This is of course absurd. The Secretary, who is authorized by law to issue binding interpretations of the Election Code, §§ 97.012, 106.23, rejected this peculiar reading of the statutes. See DE 00-13 (opinion of the Division of Elections). The Florida Supreme Court, although it must defer to the Secretary's interpretations, rejected her reasonable interpretation and embraced the peculiar one. *See Palm Beach County Canvassing Bd. v. Harris* (Fla. 2000) (*Harris III*).

But as we indicated in our remand of the earlier case, in a Presidential election the clearly expressed intent of the legislature must prevail. And there is no basis for reading the Florida statutes as requiring the counting of improperly marked ballots, as an examination of the Florida Supreme Court's textual analysis shows. We will not parse that analysis here, except to note that the principal provision of the Election Code on which it relied, § 101.5614(5), was, as Chief Justice Wells pointed out in his dissent in *Gore v. Harris* (Fla. 2000) (*Harris II*), entirely irrelevant. The State's Attorney General (who was

4. It is inconceivable that what constitutes a vote that must be counted under the "error in the vote tabulation" language of the protest phase is different from what constitutes a vote that must be counted under the "legal votes" language of the contest phase.

supporting the Gore challenge) confirmed in oral argument here that never before the present election had a manual recount been conducted on the basis of the contention that "undervotes" should have been examined to determine voter intent. For the court to step away from this established practice, prescribed by the Secretary, the state official charged by the legislature with "responsibility to . . . [o]btain and maintain uniformity in the application, operation, and interpretation of the election laws," § 97.012(1), was to depart from the legislative scheme.

III

The scope and nature of the remedy ordered by the Florida Supreme Court jeopardizes the "legislative wish" to take advantage of the safe harbor provided by 3 U.S.C. § 5. December 12, 2000, is the last date for a final determination of the Florida electors that will satisfy § 5. Yet in the late afternoon of December 8th—four days before this deadline—the Supreme Court of Florida ordered recounts of tens of thousands of so-called "undervotes" spread through 64 of the State's 67 counties. This was done in a search for elusive—perhaps delusive—certainty as to the exact count of 6 million votes. But no one claims that these ballots have not previously been tabulated; they were initially read by voting machines at the time of the election, and thereafter reread by virtue of Florida's automatic recount provision. No one claims there was any fraud in the election. The Supreme Court of Florida ordered this additional recount under the provision of the Election Code giving the circuit judge the authority to provide relief that is "appropriate under such circumstances." Fla. Stat. Ann. § 102.168(8) (Supp. 2001).

Surely when the Florida Legislature empowered the courts of the State to grant "appropriate" relief, it must have meant relief that would have become final by the cutoff date of 3 U.S.C. § 5. In light of the inevitable legal challenges and ensuing appeals to the Supreme Court of Florida and petitions for certiorari to this Court, the entire recounting process could not possibly be completed by that date. Whereas the majority in the Supreme Court of Florida stated its confidence that "the remaining undervotes in these counties can be [counted] within the required time frame," it made no assertion that the seemingly inevitable appeals could be disposed of in that time. [T]he federal deadlines for the Presidential election simply do not permit even a shortened process.

As the dissent noted:

> "In [the four days remaining], all questionable ballots must be reviewed by the judicial officer appointed to discern the intent of the voter in a process open to the public. Fairness dictates that a provision be made for either party to object to how a particular ballot is counted. Additionally, this short time period must allow for judicial review. I respectfully submit this cannot be completed without taking Florida's presidential electors outside the safe harbor provision, creating the very real possibility of disenfranchising those nearly six million voters who are able to correctly cast their ballots on election day." (opinion of Wells, C.J.).

Given all these factors, and in light of the legislative intent identified by the Florida Supreme Court to bring Florida within the "safe harbor" provision of 3 U.S.C. § 5, the remedy prescribed by the Supreme Court of Florida cannot be deemed an "appropriate" one as of December 8. It significantly departed from the statutory framework in place on November 7, and authorized open-ended further proceedings which could not be completed by December 12, thereby preventing a final determination by that date.

For these reasons, in addition to those given in the *per curiam* opinion, we would reverse.

Justice STEVENS, with whom Justice GINSBURG and Justice BREYER join, dissenting.*

[ARTICLE II ISSUE]

The federal questions that ultimately emerged in this case are not substantial. Article II provides that "[e]ach *State* shall appoint, in such Manner as the Legislature *thereof* may direct, a Number of Electors." (Emphasis added.) It does not create state legislatures out of whole cloth, but rather takes them as they come—as creatures born of, and constrained by, their state constitutions. Lest there be any doubt, we stated over 100 years ago in *McPherson v. Blacker* (1892), that "[w]hat is forbidden or required to be done by a State" in the Article II context "is forbidden or required of the legislative power under state constitutions as they exist." The legislative power in Florida is subject to judicial review pursuant to Article V of the Florida Constitution, and nothing in Article II of the Federal Constitution frees the state legislature from the constraints in the State Constitution that created it. Moreover, the Florida Legislature's own decision to employ a unitary code for all elections indicates that it intended the Florida Supreme Court to play the same role in Presidential elections that it has historically played in resolving electoral disputes. The Florida Supreme Court's exercise of appellate jurisdiction therefore was wholly consistent with, and indeed contemplated by, the grant of authority in Article II.

It hardly needs stating that Congress, pursuant to 3 U.S.C. § 5, did not impose any affirmative duties upon the States that their governmental branches could "violate." Rather, § 5 provides a safe harbor for States to select electors in contested elections "by judicial or other methods" established by laws prior to the election day. Section 5, like Article II, assumes the involvement of the state judiciary in interpreting state election laws and resolving election disputes under those laws. Neither § 5 nor Article II grants federal judges any special authority to substitute their views for those of the state judiciary on matters of state law.

* [Editors' note: In the U.S. Reports, four dissenting opinions are printed in order of each author's seniority on the Court. For the sake of readability, we have ordered them in the sequence in which they appeared to have been drafted.]

[Equal Protection Issue]

Nor are petitioners correct in asserting that the failure of the Florida Supreme Court to specify in detail the precise manner in which the "intent of the voter," Fla. Stat. Ann. § 101.5614(5) (Supp. 2001), is to be determined rises to the level of a constitutional violation.[2] We found such a violation when individual votes within the same State were weighted unequally, *see, e.g., Reynolds v. Sims,* (1964), but we have never before called into question the substantive standard by which a State determines that a vote has been legally cast. And there is no reason to think that the guidance provided to the factfinders, specifically the various canvassing boards, by the "intent of the voter" standard is any less sufficient—or will lead to results any less uniform—than, for example, the "beyond a reasonable doubt" standard employed every day by ordinary citizens in courtrooms across this country.

Admittedly, the use of differing substandards for determining voter intent in different counties employing similar voting systems may raise serious concerns. Those concerns are alleviated—if not eliminated—by the fact that a single impartial magistrate will ultimately adjudicate all objections arising from the recount process. Of course, as a general matter, "[t]he interpretation of constitutional principles must not be too literal. We must remember that the machinery of government would not work if it were not allowed a little play in its joints." *Bain Peanut Co. of Tex. v. Pinson* (1931) (Holmes, J.). If it were otherwise, Florida's decision to leave to each county the determination of what balloting system to employ—despite enormous differences in accuracy[4]—might run afoul of equal protection. So, too, might the similar decisions of the vast majority of state legislatures to delegate to local authorities certain decisions with respect to voting systems and ballot design.

Even assuming that aspects of the remedial scheme might ultimately be found to violate the Equal Protection Clause, I could not subscribe to the majority's disposition of the case. As the majority explicitly holds, once a state legislature determines to select electors through a popular vote, the right to have one's vote counted is of constitutional stature. As the majority further acknowledges, Florida law holds that all ballots that reveal the intent of the voter constitute valid votes. Recognizing these principles, the majority nonetheless orders the termination of the contest proceeding before all such votes have been tabulated. Under their own reasoning, the appropriate course of action would be to remand to allow more specific procedures for implementing the legislature's uniform general standard to be established.

2. The Florida statutory standard is consistent with the practice of the majority of States, which apply either an "intent of the voter" standard or an "impossible to determine the elector's choice" standard in ballot recounts.

4. The percentage of nonvotes in this election in counties using a punchcard system was 3.92%; in contrast, the rate of error under the more modern optical-scan systems was only 1.43 Put in other terms, for every 10,000 votes cast, punchcard systems result in 250 more nonvotes than optical-scan systems. A total of 3,718,305 votes were cast under punchcard systems, and 2,353,811 votes were cast under optical-scan systems.

In the interest of finality, however, the majority effectively orders the disenfranchisement of an unknown number of voters whose ballots reveal their intent and are therefore legal votes under state law but were for some reason rejected by ballot-counting machines. It does so on the basis of the deadlines set forth in Title 3 of the United States Code. But, as I have already noted, those provisions merely provide rules of decision for Congress to follow when selecting among conflicting slates of electors. They do not prohibit a State from counting what the majority concedes to be legal votes until a bona fide winner is determined. Indeed, in 1960, Hawaii appointed two slates of electors and Congress chose to count the one appointed on January 4, 1961, well after the Title 3 deadlines. Thus, nothing prevents the majority, even if it properly found an equal protection violation, from ordering relief appropriate to remedy that violation without depriving Florida voters of their right to have their votes counted. As the majority notes, "[a] desire for speed is not a general excuse for ignoring equal protection guarantees."

[Article II Issue, Cont.]

Finally, neither in this case, nor in its earlier opinion in *Palm Beach County Canvassing Bd. v. Harris* (2000), did the Florida Supreme Court make any substantive change in Florida electoral law. Its decisions were rooted in long-established precedent and were consistent with the relevant statutory provisions, taken as a whole. It did what courts do—it decided the case before it in light of the legislature's intent to leave no legally cast vote uncounted. In so doing, it relied on the sufficiency of the general "intent of the voter" standard articulated by the state legislature, coupled with a procedure for ultimate review by an impartial judge, to resolve the concern about disparate evaluations of contested ballots. If we assume—as I do—that the members of that court and the judges who would have carried out its mandate are impartial, its decision does not even raise a colorable federal question.

What must underlie petitioners' entire federal assault on the Florida election procedures is an unstated lack of confidence in the impartiality and capacity of the state judges who would make the critical decisions if the vote count were to proceed. Otherwise, their position is wholly without merit. The endorsement of that position by the majority of this Court can only lend credence to the most cynical appraisal of the work of judges throughout the land. It is confidence in the men and women who administer the judicial system that is the true backbone of the rule of law. Time will one day heal the wound to that confidence that will be inflicted by today's decision. One thing, however, is certain. Although we may never know with complete certainty the identity of the winner of this year's Presidential election, the identity of the loser is perfectly clear. It is the Nation's confidence in the judge as an impartial guardian of the rule of law.

I respectfully dissent.

Justice Breyer, with whom Justice Stevens and Justice Ginsburg join except as to Part I-A-1, and with whom Justice Souter joins as to Part I, dissenting.

The Court was wrong to take this case. It was wrong to grant a stay. It should now vacate that stay and permit the Florida Supreme Court to decide whether the recount should resume.

I

The political implications of this case for the country are momentous. But the federal legal questions presented, with one exception, are insubstantial.

A

1

The majority raises three equal protection problems with the Florida Supreme Court's recount order: first, the failure to include overvotes in the manual recount; second, the fact that *all* ballots, rather than simply the undervotes, were recounted in some, but not all, counties; and third, the absence of a uniform, specific standard to guide the recounts. As far as the first issue is concerned, petitioners presented no evidence, to this Court or to any Florida court, that a manual recount of overvotes would identify additional legal votes. The same is true of the second, and, in addition, the majority's reasoning would seem to invalidate any state provision for a manual recount of individual counties in a statewide election.

The majority's third concern does implicate principles of fundamental fairness. The majority concludes that the Equal Protection Clause requires that a manual recount be governed not only by the uniform general standard of the "clear intent of the voter," but also by uniform subsidiary standards (for example, a uniform determination whether indented, but not perforated, "undervotes" should count). The opinion points out that the Florida Supreme Court ordered the inclusion of Broward County's undercounted "legal votes" even though those votes included ballots that were not perforated but simply "dimpled," while newly recounted ballots from other counties will likely include only votes determined to be "legal" on the basis of a stricter standard. In light of our previous remand, the Florida Supreme Court may have been reluctant to adopt a more specific standard than that provided for by the legislature for fear of exceeding its authority under Article II. However, since the use of different standards could favor one or the other of the candidates, since time was, and is, too short to permit the lower courts to iron out significant differences through ordinary judicial review, and since the relevant distinction was embodied in the order of the State's highest court, I agree that, in these very special circumstances, basic principles of fairness may well have counseled the adoption of a uniform standard to address the problem.

2

Nonetheless, there is no justification for the majority's remedy, which is simply to reverse the lower court and halt the recount entirely. An appropriate remedy would be, instead, to remand this case with instructions that, even at this late date, would permit the Florida Supreme Court to require recounting *all* undercounted votes in Florida, including those from Broward, Volusia, Palm Beach, and Miami-Dade Counties, whether or not previously recounted prior to the end of the protest period, and to do so in accordance with a single uniform standard.

The majority justifies stopping the recount entirely on the ground that there is no more time. In particular, the majority relies on the lack of time for the Secretary of State to review and approve equipment needed to separate undervotes. But the majority reaches this conclusion in the absence of *any* record evidence that the recount could not have been completed in the time allowed by the Florida Supreme Court. The majority finds facts outside of the record on matters that state courts are in a far better position to address. Of course, it is too late for any such recount to take place by December 12, the date by which election disputes must be decided if a State is to take advantage of the safe harbor provisions of 3 U.S.C. § 5. Whether there is time to conduct a recount prior to December 18, when the electors are scheduled to meet, is a matter for the state courts to determine. And whether, under Florida law, Florida could or could not take further action is obviously a matter for Florida courts, not this Court, to decide.

By halting the manual recount, and thus ensuring that the uncounted legal votes will not be counted under any standard, this Court crafts a remedy out of proportion to the asserted harm. And that remedy harms the very fairness interests the Court is attempting to protect. The manual recount would itself redress a problem of unequal treatment of ballots. [T]he ballots of voters in counties that use punchcard systems are more likely to be disqualified than those in counties using optical-scanning systems. According to recent news reports, variations in the undervote rate are even more pronounced. *See* Fessenden, *No-Vote Rates Higher in Punch Card Count*, N.Y. TIMES, Dec. 1, 2000, p. A29 (reporting that 0.3% of ballots cast in 30 Florida counties using optical-scanning systems registered no Presidential vote, in comparison to 1.53% in the 15 counties using Votomatic punchcard ballots). Thus, in a system that allows counties to use different types of voting systems, voters already arrive at the polls with an unequal chance that their votes will be counted. I do not see how the fact that this results from counties' selection of different voting machines rather than a court order makes the outcome any more fair. Nor do I understand why the Florida Supreme Court's recount order, which helps to redress this inequity, must be entirely prohibited based on a deficiency that could easily be remedied.

B

The remainder of petitioners' claims, which are the focus of The Chief Justice's concurrence, raise no significant federal questions. I cannot agree that The Chief Justice's unusual review of state law in this case is justified by reference either to Art. II, § 1, or to 3 U.S.C. § 5. Moreover, even were such review proper, the conclusion that the Florida Supreme Court's decision contravenes federal law is untenable.

The Chief Justice contends that our opinion in *Bush v. Palm Beach County Canvassing Bd.* (*per curiam*) (*Bush I*), in which we stated that "a legislative wish to take advantage of [§ 5] would counsel against" a construction of Florida law that Congress might deem to be a change in law now means that *this* Court "must ensure that post-election state-court actions do not frustrate the legislative desire to attain the 'safe harbor' provided by § 5." However, § 5 is part of the rules that govern Congress' recognition of slates of electors. Nowhere in *Bush I* did we establish that *this* Court had the authority to enforce § 5. Nor did we suggest that the permissive "counsel against" could be transformed into the mandatory "must ensure." And nowhere did we intimate, as the concurrence does here, that a state-court decision that threatens the safe harbor provision of § 5 does so in violation of Article II. The concurrence's logic turns the presumption that legislatures would wish to take advantage of § 5's "safe harbor" provision into a mandate that trumps other statutory provisions and overrides the intent that the legislature *did* express.

But, in any event, the concurrence, having conducted its review, now reaches the wrong conclusion. It says that "the Florida Supreme Court's interpretation of the Florida election laws impermissibly distorted them beyond what a fair reading required, in violation of Article II." But what precisely is the distortion? Apparently, it has three elements. First, the Florida court, in its earlier opinion, changed the election certification date from November 14 to November 26. Second, the Florida court ordered a manual recount of "undercounted" ballots that could not have been fully completed by the December 12 "safe harbor" deadline. Third, the Florida court, in the opinion now under review, failed to give adequate deference to the determinations of canvassing boards and the Secretary.

To characterize the first element as a "distortion," however, requires the concurrence to second-guess the way in which the state court resolved a plain conflict in the language of different statutes. *Compare* Fla. Stat. Ann. § 102.166 (Supp. 2001) (foreseeing manual recounts during the protest period) *with* § 102.111 (setting what is arguably too short a deadline for manual recounts to be conducted); *compare* § 102.112(1) (stating that the Secretary "may" ignore late returns) *with* § 102.111(1) (stating that the Secretary "shall" ignore late returns). In any event, that issue no longer has any practical importance and cannot justify the reversal of the different Florida court decision before us now.

To characterize the second element as a "distortion" requires the concurrence to overlook the fact that the inability of the Florida courts to conduct the recount on time is, in significant part, a problem of the Court's own making. The Florida Supreme Court thought that the recount could be completed on time, and, within hours, the Florida Circuit Court was moving in an orderly fashion to meet the deadline. This Court improvidently entered a stay. As a result, we will never know whether the recount could have been completed.

Nor can one characterize the third element as "impermissibl[e] distort[ion]" once one understands that there are two sides to the opinion's argument that the Florida Supreme Court "virtually eliminat[ed] the Secretary's discretion." The Florida statute in question was amended in 1999 to provide that the "grounds for contesting an election" include the "rejection of a number of legal votes sufficient to . . . place in doubt the result of the election." Fla. Stat. Ann. §§ 102.168(3), (3)(c) (Supp. 2001). And the parties have argued about the proper meaning of the statute's term "legal vote." The Secretary has claimed that a "legal vote" is a vote "properly executed in accordance with the instructions provided to all registered voters." On that interpretation, punchcard ballots for which the machines cannot register a vote are not "legal" votes. The Florida Supreme Court did not accept her definition. But it had a reason. Its reason was that a different provision of Florida election laws (a provision that addresses damaged or defective ballots) says that no vote shall be disregarded "if there is a clear indication of the intent of the voter as determined by the canvassing board" (adding that ballots should not be counted "if it is impossible to determine the elector's choice"). Fla. Stat. Ann. § 101.5614(5) (Supp. 2001). Given this statutory language, certain roughly analogous judicial precedent, and somewhat similar determinations by courts throughout the Nation, the Florida Supreme Court concluded that the term "legal vote" means a vote recorded on a ballot that clearly reflects what the voter intended. That conclusion differs from the conclusion of the Secretary. But nothing in Florida law requires the Florida Supreme Court to accept as determinative the Secretary's view on such a matter. Nor can one say that the court's ultimate determination is so unreasonable as to amount to a constitutionally "impermissible distort[ion]" of Florida law.

The Florida Supreme Court, applying this definition, decided, on the basis of the record, that respondents had shown that the ballots undercounted by the voting machines contained enough "legal votes" to place "the result[s]" of the election "in doubt." Since only a few hundred votes separated the candidates, and since the "undercounted" ballots numbered tens of thousands, it is difficult to see how anyone could find this conclusion unreasonable—however strict the standard used to measure the voter's "clear intent." Nor did this conclusion "strip" canvassing boards of their discretion. The boards retain their traditional discretionary authority during the protest period. And during the contest period, as the court stated, "the Canvassing Board's actions [during the protest period] may constitute evidence that a ballot does or does not qualify as a legal vote." Whether a local county canvassing board's discretionary judgment during the protest period not to conduct a manual recount will be set aside during a contest period depends upon whether a candidate provides additional evidence that the rejected votes contain enough "legal votes" to place the outcome of the race in doubt. To limit the local canvassing board's discretion in this way is not to eliminate that discretion. At the least, one could reasonably so believe.

The statute goes on to provide the Florida circuit judge with authority to "fashion such orders as he or she deems necessary to ensure that each allegation . . . is *investigated, examined, or checked,* . . . and to provide any relief appropriate." Fla. Stat. Ann. § 102.168(8) (Supp. 2001) (emphasis added). The Florida Supreme Court did just that. One might reasonably disagree with the Florida Supreme Court's interpretation of these, or other, words in the statute. But I do not see how one could call its plain language interpretation of a 1999 statutory change so misguided as no longer to qualify as judicial interpretation or as a usurpation of the authority of the state legislature. Indeed, other state courts have interpreted roughly similar state statutes in similar ways.

I repeat, where is the "impermissible" distortion?

II

Despite the reminder that this case involves "an election for the President of the United States," no preeminent legal concern, or practical concern related to legal questions, required this Court to hear this case, let alone to issue a stay that stopped Florida's recount process in its tracks. Petitioners invoke fundamental fairness, namely, the need for procedural fairness, including finality. But with the one "equal protection" exception, they rely upon law that focuses, not upon that basic need, but upon the constitutional allocation of power. Respondents invoke a competing fundamental consideration—the need to determine the voter's true intent. But they look to state law, not to federal constitutional law, to protect that interest. Neither side claims electoral fraud, dishonesty, or the like. And the more fundamental equal protection claim might have been left to the state court to resolve if and when it was discovered to have mattered. It could still be resolved through a remand conditioned upon issuance of a uniform standard; it does not require reversing the Florida Supreme Court.

Of course, the selection of the President is of fundamental national importance. But that importance is political, not legal. And this Court should resist the temptation unnecessarily to resolve tangential legal disputes, where doing so threatens to determine the outcome of the election.

The Constitution and federal statutes themselves make clear that restraint is appropriate. They set forth a road-map of how to resolve disputes about electors, even after an election as close as this one. That road-map foresees resolution of electoral disputes by *state* courts. *See* 3 U.S.C. § 5 (providing that, where a "State shall have provided, by laws enacted prior to [election day], for its final determination of any controversy or contest concerning the appointment of . . . electors . . . by *judicial* or other methods," the subsequently chosen electors enter a safe harbor free from congressional challenge). But it nowhere provides for involvement by the United States Supreme Court.

To the contrary, the Twelfth Amendment commits to Congress the authority and responsibility to count electoral votes. A federal statute, the Electoral Count Act, enacted after the close 1876 Hayes-Tilden Presidential election, specifies that, after States have tried to resolve disputes (through "judicial" or other means), Congress is the body primarily authorized to resolve remaining disputes. *See* Electoral Count Act of 1887.

The legislative history of the Act makes clear its intent to commit the power to resolve such disputes to Congress, rather than the courts:

> "The two Houses are, by the Constitution, authorized to make the count of electoral votes. They can only count legal votes, and in doing so must determine, from the best evidence to be had, what are legal votes. . . .
>
> . . . .
>
> "The power to determine rests with the two houses, and there is no other constitutional tribunal." H.R. Rep. No. 1638, 49th Cong., 1st Sess., 2 (1886).

The Act goes on to set out rules for the congressional determination of disputes about those votes. If, for example, a State submits a single slate of electors, Congress must count those votes unless both Houses agree that the votes "have not been . . . regularly given." 3 U.S.C. § 15. If, as occurred in 1876, a State submits two slates of electors, then Congress must determine whether a slate has entered the safe harbor of § 5, in which case its votes will have "conclusive" effect. If, as also occurred in 1876, there is controversy about "which of two or more of such State authorities . . . is the lawful tribunal" authorized to appoint electors, then each House shall determine separately which votes are "supported by the decision of such State so authorized by its law." If the two Houses of Congress agree, the votes they have approved will be counted. If they disagree, then "the votes of the electors whose appointment shall have been certified by the executive of the State, under the seal thereof, shall be counted."

Given this detailed, comprehensive scheme for counting electoral votes, there is no reason to believe that federal law either foresees or requires resolution of such a political issue by this Court. Nor, for that matter, is there any reason to think that the Constitution's Framers would have reached a different conclusion. Madison, at least, believed that allowing the judiciary to choose the Presidential electors "was out of the question."

The decision by both the Constitution's Framers and the 1886 Congress to minimize this Court's role in resolving close federal Presidential elections is as wise as it is clear. However awkward or difficult it may be for Congress to resolve difficult electoral disputes, Congress, being a political body, expresses the people's will far more accurately than does an unelected Court. And the people's will is what elections are about.

Moreover, Congress was fully aware of the danger that would arise should it ask judges, unarmed with appropriate legal standards, to resolve a hotly contested Presidential election contest. [Justice Breyer here recounts the history of the 1876 presidential election, which ended with the partisan 8-7 split of the Electoral Commission.]

For present purposes, the relevance of this history lies in the fact that the participation in the work of the electoral commission by five Justices, including Justice Bradley, did not lend that process legitimacy. Nor did it assure the public that the process had worked fairly, guided by the law. Rather, it simply embroiled Members of the Court in partisan conflict, thereby undermining respect for the judicial process. And the Congress that later enacted the Electoral Count Act knew it.

This history may help to explain why I think it not only legally wrong, but also most unfortunate, for the Court simply to have terminated the Florida recount. Those who caution judicial restraint in resolving political disputes have described the quintessential case for that restraint as a case marked, among other things, by the "strangeness of the issue," its "intractability to principled resolution," its "sheer momentousness, . . . which tends to unbalance judicial judgment," and "the inner vulnerability, the self-doubt of an institution which is electorally irresponsible and has no earth to draw strength from." [Alexander Bickel, THE LEAST DANGEROUS BRANCH 184 (1962).] Those characteristics mark this case.

[A]bove all, in this highly politicized matter, the appearance of a split decision runs the risk of undermining the public's confidence in the Court itself. That confidence is a public treasure. It has been built slowly over many years, some of which were marked by a Civil War and the tragedy of segregation. It is a vitally necessary ingredient of any successful effort to protect basic liberty and, indeed, the rule of law itself. We run no risk of returning to the days when a President (responding to this Court's efforts to protect the Cherokee Indians) might have said, "John Marshall has made his decision; now let him enforce it!" But we do risk a self-inflicted wound—a wound that may harm not just the Court, but the Nation.

Justice Brandeis once said of the Court, "The most important thing we do is not doing." What it does today, the Court should have left undone. I would repair the damage done as best we now can, by permitting the Florida recount to continue under uniform standards.

I respectfully dissent.

Justice GINSBURG, with whom Justice STEVENS joins, and with whom Justice SOUTER and Justice BREYER join as to Part I, dissenting.

I

The Chief Justice says that Article II, by providing that state legislatures shall direct the manner of appointing electors, authorizes federal superintendence over the relationship between state courts and state legislatures, and licenses a departure from the usual deference we give to state-court interpretations of state law. The Framers of our Constitution, however, understood that in a republican government, the judiciary would construe the legislature's enactments. Article II does not call for the scrutiny undertaken by this Court.

The extraordinary setting of this case has obscured the ordinary principle that dictates its proper resolution: Federal courts defer to a state high court's interpretations of the State's own law. This principle reflects the core of federalism, on which all agree. Were the other Members of this Court as mindful as they generally are of our system of dual sovereignty, they would affirm the judgment of the Florida Supreme Court.

II

I agree with Justice Stevens that petitioners have not presented a substantial equal protection claim. Ideally, perfection would be the appropriate standard for judging the recount. But we live in an imperfect world, one in which thousands of votes have not been counted. I cannot agree that the recount adopted by the Florida court, flawed as it may be, would yield a result any less fair or precise than the certification that preceded that recount.

Even if there were an equal protection violation, I would agree with Justice Stevens, Justice Souter, and Justice Breyer that the Court's concern about "the December 12 deadline" is misplaced. Time is short in part because of the Court's entry of a stay on December 9, several hours after an able circuit judge in Leon County had begun to superintend the recount process. More fundamentally, the Court's reluctance to let the recount go forward despite its suggestion that "[t]he search for intent can be confined by specific rules designed to ensure uniform treatment," ultimately turns on its own judgment about the practical realities of implementing a recount, not the judgment of those much closer to the process.

The Court assumes that time will not permit "orderly judicial review of any disputed matters that might arise." But no one has doubted the good faith and diligence with which Florida election officials, attorneys for all sides of this controversy, and the courts of law have performed their duties. Notably, the Florida Supreme Court has produced two substantial opinions within 29 hours of oral argument. In sum, the Court's conclusion that a constitutionally adequate recount is impractical is a prophecy the Court's own judgment will not allow to be tested. Such an untested prophecy should not decide the Presidency of the United States.

I dissent.

Justice SOUTER, with whom Justice BREYER joins, and with whom Justice STEVENS and Justice GINSBURG join as to all but Part III, dissenting.

The Court should not have reviewed either *Bush v. Palm Beach County Canvassing Bd.* (*per curiam*), or this case, and should not have stopped Florida's attempt to recount all undervote ballots by issuing a stay of the Florida Supreme Court's orders during the period of this review. If this Court had allowed the State to follow the course indicated by the opinions of its own Supreme Court, it is entirely possible that there would ultimately have been no issue requiring our review, and political tension could have worked itself out in the Congress following the procedure provided in 3 U.S.C. § 15. The case being before us, however, its resolution by the majority is another erroneous decision.

As will be clear, I am in substantial agreement with the dissenting opinions of Justice Stevens, Justice Ginsburg, and Justice Breyer. I write separately only to say how straightforward the issues before us really are.

There are three issues: whether the State Supreme Court's interpretation of the statute providing for a contest of the state election results somehow violates 3 U.S.C.

§ 5; whether that court's construction of the state statutory provisions governing contests impermissibly changes a state law from what the State's legislature has provided, in violation of Article II, § 1, cl. 2, of the National Constitution; and whether the manner of interpreting markings on disputed ballots failing to cause machines to register votes for President (the undervote ballots) violates the equal protection or due process guaranteed by the Fourteenth Amendment. None of these issues is difficult to describe or to resolve.

I

The 3 U.S.C. § 5 issue is not serious. That provision sets certain conditions for treating a State's certification of Presidential electors as conclusive in the event that a dispute over recognizing those electors must be resolved in the Congress under 3 U.S.C. § 15. Conclusiveness requires selection under a legal scheme in place before the election, with results determined at least six days before the date set for casting electoral votes. But no State is required to conform to § 5 if it cannot do that (for whatever reason); the sanction for failing to satisfy the conditions of § 5 is simply loss of what has been called its "safe harbor." And even that determination is to be made, if made anywhere, in the Congress.

II

The second matter here goes to the State Supreme Court's interpretation of certain terms in the state statute governing election "contests," Fla. Stat. Ann. § 102.168 (Supp. 2001); there is no question here about the state court's interpretation of the related provisions dealing with the antecedent process of "protesting" particular vote counts, § 102.166, which was involved in the previous case, *Bush v. Palm Beach County Canvassing Bd.* The issue is whether the judgment of the State Supreme Court has displaced the state legislature's provisions for election contests: is the law as declared by the court different from the provisions made by the legislature, to which the National Constitution commits responsibility for determining how each State's Presidential electors are chosen? Bush does not, of course, claim that any judicial act interpreting a statute of uncertain meaning is enough to displace the legislative provision and violate Article II; statutes require interpretation, which does not without more affect the legislative character of a statute within the meaning of the Constitution. What Bush does argue, as I understand the contention, is that the interpretation of § 102.168 was so unreasonable as to transcend the accepted bounds of statutory interpretation, to the point of being a nonjudicial act and producing new law untethered to the legislative Act in question.

The starting point for evaluating the claim that the Florida Supreme Court's interpretation effectively rewrote § 102.168 must be the language of the provision on which Gore relies to show his right to raise this contest: that the previously certified result in Bush's favor was produced by "rejection of a number of legal votes sufficient to change or place in doubt the result of the election." Fla. Stat. Ann. § 102.168(3)(c) (Supp. 2001). None of the state court's interpretations is unreasonable to the point of displacing the legislative enactment quoted. As I will note below, other interpretations were of course possible, and some might have been better than those adopted by the Florida court's majority; the two dissents from the majority opinion of that court and various briefs submitted to us set out alternatives. But the majority view is in each instance within the bounds of reasonable interpretation, and the law as declared is consistent with Article II.

1. The statute does not define a "legal vote," the rejection of which may affect the election. The State Supreme Court was therefore required to define it, and in doing that the court looked to another election statute, § 101.5614(5), dealing with damaged or defective ballots, which contains a provision that no vote shall be disregarded "if there is a clear indication of the intent of the voter as determined by the canvassing board." The court read that objective of looking to the voter's intent as indicating that the legislature probably meant "legal vote" to mean a vote recorded on a ballot indicating what the voter intended. It is perfectly true that the majority might have chosen a different reading. *See, e.g.*, Brief for Respondent Harris (defining "legal votes" as "votes properly executed in accordance with the instructions provided to all registered voters in advance of the election and in the polling places"). But even so, there is no constitutional violation in following the majority view; Article II is unconcerned with mere disagreements about interpretive merits.

2. The Florida court next interpreted "rejection" to determine what act in the counting process may be attacked in a contest. Again, the statute does not define the term. The court majority read the word to mean simply a failure to count. That reading is certainly within the bounds of common sense, given the objective to give effect to a voter's intent if that can be determined. A different reading, of course, is possible. The majority might have concluded that "rejection" should refer to machine malfunction, or that a ballot should not be treated as "reject[ed]" in the absence of wrongdoing by election officials, lest contests be so easy to claim that every election will end up in one. There is, however, nothing nonjudicial in the Florida majority's more hospitable reading.

3. The same is true about the court majority's understanding of the phrase "votes sufficient to change or place in doubt" the result of the election in Florida. The court held that if the uncounted ballots were so numerous that it was reasonably possible that they contained enough "legal" votes to swing the election, this contest would be authorized by the statute. While the majority might have thought (as the trial judge did) that a probability, not a possibility, should be necessary to justify a contest, that reading is not required by the statute's text, which says nothing about probability. Whatever people of good will and good sense may argue about the merits of the Florida court's reading, there is no warrant for saying that it transcends the limits of reasonable statutory interpretation to the point of supplanting the statute enacted by the "legislature" within the meaning of Article II.

III

It is only on the third issue before us that there is a meritorious argument for relief, as this Court's *per curiam* opinion recognizes. It is an issue that might well have been dealt with adequately by the Florida courts if the state proceedings had not been interrupted, and if not disposed of at the state level it could have been considered by the Congress in any electoral vote dispute. But because the course of state proceedings has been interrupted, time is short, and the issue is before us, I think it sensible for the Court to address it.

Petitioners have raised an equal protection claim (or, alternatively, a due process claim) in the charge that unjustifiably disparate standards are applied in different electoral jurisdictions to otherwise identical facts. It is true that the Equal Protection Clause does not forbid the use of a variety of voting mechanisms within a jurisdiction, even though different mechanisms will have different levels of effectiveness in recording voters' intentions; local variety can be justified by concerns about cost, the potential value of innovation, and so on. But evidence in the record here suggests that a different order of disparity obtains under rules for determining a voter's intent that have been applied (and could continue to be applied) to identical types of ballots used in identical brands of machines and exhibiting identical physical characteristics (such as "hanging" or "dimpled" chads). I can conceive of no legitimate state interest served by these differing treatments of the expressions of voters' fundamental rights. The differences appear wholly arbitrary.

In deciding what to do about this, we should take account of the fact that electoral votes are due to be cast in six days. I would therefore remand the case to the courts of Florida with instructions to establish uniform standards for evaluating the several types of ballots that have prompted differing treatments, to be applied within and among counties when passing on such identical ballots in any further recounting (or successive recounting) that the courts might order.

Unlike the majority, I see no warrant for this Court to assume that Florida could not possibly comply with this requirement before the date set for the meeting of electors, December 18. Although one of the dissenting justices of the State Supreme Court estimated that disparate standards potentially affected 170,000 votes, the number at issue is significantly smaller. The 170,000 figure apparently represents all uncounted votes, both undervotes (those for which no Presidential choice was recorded by a machine) and overvotes (those rejected because of votes for more than one candidate). But as Justice Breyer has pointed out, no showing has been made of legal overvotes uncounted, and counsel for Gore made an uncontradicted representation to the Court that the statewide total of undervotes is about 60,000. To recount these manually would be a tall order, but before this Court stayed the effort to do that the courts of Florida were ready to do their best to get that job done. There is no justification for denying the State the opportunity to try to count all disputed ballots now.

I respectfully dissent.

NOTE ON *BUSH V. GORE*

One issue that the dissenters raised is whether the Court should have involved itself at all in the case. Because the Court's certiorari jurisdiction is discretionary, the Court could have stayed out of it. Although no one can ever know for sure what would have happened if the Court had refrained from taking the case, it is probable that Gore would have lost the recount ordered by the Florida Supreme Court. A media study of the ballots afterwards determined that Gore could have won only if the statewide manual recount included an examination of overvotes as well as undervotes, but overvotes were not part of the Florida Supreme Court's order.*

Delving into the realm of speculation, if Gore somehow would have won the recount, the situation could have become even messier. The Florida legislature, which at the time was controlled by Republicans, was prepared to enact new legislation, purporting to rely on its authority under Article II of the U.S. Constitution, to award Florida's Electoral Votes directly to Bush, thereby attempting to nullify any contrary result from the recount. One could then imagine two competing certificates arriving in Congress before January 6, 2001, the date for the congressional counting of Electoral Votes. One certificate, flowing from the recount, would declare Gore the winner of Florida's Electoral Votes. The other certificate, flowing from the contrary legislation, would name Bush the winner.

What would then happen in Congress? While Gore might try to claim that his victory under the recount was entitled to Safe Harbor status (assuming the recount had been completed by December 12, absent U.S. Supreme Court intervention), there is no guarantee that the Republicans who controlled the U.S. House of Representatives at the time would have agreed. If the House voted for Bush, and the Senate voted for Gore—perhaps based on a tie-breaking vote cast by Gore himself as the incumbent Vice President (and thus President of the Senate) at the time—then according to the Electoral Count Act of 1887, the victory belonged to whichever certificate from Florida was signed by the state's "executive," presumably meaning the state's governor, who was Jeb Bush, the Republican candidate's brother.

But what if the Florida Supreme Court ordered Governor Bush to sign the certificate consistent with the result of its mandated recount, and ordered him not to sign the contrary certificate mandated by the legislature? What if the state's Attorney General, who was a Democrat, signed as "acting Governor" to comply with the Florida Supreme Court's order? What if the Democrats in the U.S. Senate refused to accept any result other than Gore's victory, based on their belief (right or wrong) that he had won more votes in Florida?

* *See* Keating & Balz, *Florida Recounts Would Have Favored Bush*, Washington Post (Nov. 12, 2001), p. A01.

Some, including Judge Richard Posner of the U.S. Court of Appeals for the Seventh Circuit, have argued that to avoid such possibilities it was better to have the Supreme Court intervene in *Bush v. Gore* even if the constitutional basis for its intervention was dubious.* That view would extend the Court's role beyond its function under *Marbury v. Madison* "to declare what the law is" to a more fuzzy power to act as it deems best in circumstances of overriding national interest. On this view, the criteria for evaluating whether the Court acted wisely in *Bush v. Gore* would be very different from assessing whether its decision was legally sound according to conventional methods of legal analysis.

5. *Ballot-Counting Disputes after* Bush v. Gore

A. THE POSSIBILITY OF ANOTHER DISPUTED PRESIDENTIAL ELECTION

After *Bush v. Gore*, many people assumed that nothing like it could ever happen again. For one thing, Congress legislated the elimination of punch-card voting machines as part of the Help America Vote Act of 2002 (HAVA). Consequently, there could be no more litigation over dimpled or hanging chads. And how likely was it that another presidential election would depend upon the outcome of a ballot-counting dispute in a single state?

Well, in 2004, the very next presidential election showed that the winner of the presidency could indeed turn on a single state, this time Ohio instead of Florida. Moreover, although President Bush's margin of victory in Ohio that year—118,601—was large enough to be immune from a ballot-counting challenge, if initial returns had showed a margin as small as Florida's in 2000, then there is no doubt that the 2004 presidential election would have become just as mired in ballot-counting litigation as the 2000 election had been.

To be sure, the fight in 2004 would not have concerned punch-card ballots. Instead, the most likely focus of a ballot-counting dispute in Ohio would have been provisional ballots, which HAVA required as a kind of safety net to protect voters from being erroneously removed from voter registration rolls and thus wrongfully denied the right to cast any ballot at all. But despite HAVA's good intentions, provisional ballots easily can become a focus of disputation in a close election, because by definition provisional ballots occupy a limbo status until election officials determine one-by-one whether each of them is entitled to be counted.

Furthermore, disputes over provisional ballots can lead to the same kind of Equal Protection and Article II issues that the Court confronted in *Bush v. Gore*. To illustrate this point, in October 2008 a consortium of academic institutions staged a mock oral

* *See* Richard A. Posner, Breaking the Deadlock: The 2000 Election, the Constitution, and the Courts (2001).

argument of a hypothetical case involving provisional ballots that would determine the outcome of the 2008 presidential election.

Obviously, the actual 2008 presidential election did not turn out that way: Barack Obama won a sweeping 365-178 Electoral College victory over John McCain, and thus no single state was decisive in the way that Florida and Ohio had been in the two previous elections. Still, the hypothetical case is useful to consider as part of analyzing what might happen the next time a presidential election does turn on a single "swing state," and the initial returns in that state show only a razor-thin margin between the two main candidates. Would the Supreme Court become involved again, as it did in *Bush v. Gore*, with the same sort of result? Would, or should, the nation be happy with that sort of repeat performance? Or, instead, is it possible to develop a better way to handle this kind of case?

The hypothetical case made Colorado the swing state for the 2008 election and imagined a snowstorm that caused polls to stay open until 9 P.M. in Denver, whereas polls closed at 7 P.M. elsewhere in the state according to the dictate of state law (Colorado Rev. Stat. 1-7-101).* As HAVA requires, the ballots cast pursuant to the two-hour extension in Denver were provisional and thus subject to dispute once it became clear (according to the hypothetical) that the outcome of the presidential election would turn on whether or not these provisional ballots would be counted. To echo the circumstances of Florida in 2000, the hypothetical envisioned that Colorado's Republican Secretary of State would oppose counting these ballots, while the Democratic majority on the state's supreme court would order that the ballots be counted notwithstanding the state statute that seemed to support the Secretary's position. (The relevant Colorado statute explicitly provided: "Any person arriving after 7 p.m. shall not be entitled to vote.") This state court ruling thus provided the basis for the McCain campaign to present to the U.S. Supreme Court both an Equal Protection and an Article II issue comparable to those presented in *Bush v. Gore.*

To stage the mock argument of this hypothetical case, the academic consortium convened a specially designed panel of three prominent former judges. The goal of the exercise was to create a panel that was evenly balanced toward both sides of the case and thus would be in a position to render as impartial a decision as humanly possible. To achieve this goal, the consortium decided to pick one judge identified as having a solid Republican background and another judge as having a solid Democratic background, and then let these two judges pick the third member of their panel. For the Republican judge, the consortium chose Thomas Phillips, the former Chief Justice of the Texas Supreme Court. For the Democratic judge, the consortium chose Patricia Wald, the former Chief Judge of the U.S. Court of Appeals for the D.C. Circuit. These two judges then chose David Levi, a former federal district judge and Dean of Duke Law School.

* This hypothetical case grew out of an exam question in an Election Law class taught by one of the authors of this casebook. As you read the details of the case, to prepare for the exam in your own class, you may wish to test your own skills by pretending that a similar case could go to the real Supreme Court in the future. If you had to write a bench memo to Justice Anthony Kennedy, the presumptive "swing vote" on the Supreme Court for this kind of case (like pretty much any other), what would you put in your memo?

Two prominent Supreme Court practitioners agreed to argue the hypothetical case before this three-judge panel. Glenn Nager, head of the appellate practice of the Jones Day law firm (and former member of the U.S. Solicitor General's office), argued McCain's side of the case. Walter Dellinger, head of the appellate practice of the O'Melveny & Myers firm (and former Acting U.S. Solicitor General) argued Obama's side of the case. After the oral argument, the three-judge panel deliberated and issued the following ruling. Although the ruling is dated "December 9, 2008" in accordance with the details of the hypothetical scenario, in reality the panel released its ruling on October 28, in advance of Election Day itself (and thus ignorant of which candidate would actually win the real election).

As you read the three-judge panel's unanimous opinion (there were no separate concurrences or dissents), compare it to *Bush v. Gore*. The three-judge panel was acting as if it were exercising the jurisdiction of the U.S. Supreme Court for the purposes of this hypothetical case, and thus it was bound by the precedent of *Bush v. Gore* to the same extent (no more and no less) than the real nine-member Supreme Court would be. Was the three-judge panel faithful to that precedent? In your view, did it rule properly? Did it do a better or worse job than the actual Court in *Bush v. Gore*, or just about the same? Does the special balanced design of the three-judge panel make any difference? Would it be a model for how future disputes of this nature should be handled?

McCAIN v. OBAMA

Mock Case No. 1 [December 9, 2008]

PER CURIAM.

I

The events leading up to the present controversy began on Election Day, November 4, 2008, when an especially severe and unusual winter storm hit the city of Denver in the mid-afternoon. The storm greatly affected driving conditions, making road travel treacherous even for drivers accustomed to winter weather. Although the storm caused minor delays in the outlying Denver suburbs, it disproportionately affected rush-hour traffic in Denver, causing extensive problems for voters trying to reach their polling places. In response, Denver Elections Director Michael Scarpello, with the approval of Denver's elected official responsible for administering elections, issued an email directive at 4:53 p.m. requiring that all polling places in Denver stay open an extra two hours, closing at 9:00 p.m. instead of the statutorily-prescribed time of 7:00 p.m. The direction provided that all ballots cast during the extended hours would be treated as provisional ballots.

At about 5:30 p.m., upon learning of the poll hour extension, Colorado's Secretary of State, Mike Coffman, filed suit in state district court seeking to enjoin the extension of polling hours beyond 7:00 p.m. The request for emergency relief was denied on the basis that the provisional ballots could be disqualified in later proceedings if the extension proved unlawful following more considered briefing and deliberation.

Secretary Coffman filed an immediate appeal to the Colorado Supreme Court. The Colorado Supreme Court issued a 5-2 ruling upholding the decision of the state district court. Secretary Coffman then sought an emergency injunction from this Court at

8:12 p.m. Our ruling, issued at 8:46 p.m. on election night, denied Coffman's application for an emergency injunction on the basis that "any such relief at this point would be moot."

During the hours of the extension, 62,729 provisional ballots were cast in Denver County. There is no dispute that 92% of registered voters cast ballots in non-Denver counties. If the provisional ballots are counted, 87% of registered voters in Denver County will have voted. If the provisional ballots are not counted, only 67% of registered voters in Denver will have voted.

With a 265-264 Electoral College vote divide, the determination of the Presidency in this election rests on Colorado's nine electoral votes. Without the provisional ballots cast in Denver pursuant to Director Scarpello's order extending polling hours, the electors for John McCain and Sarah Palin have a small but significant 13,363 vote lead over the electors for Barack Obama and Joe Biden. The provisional ballots have not been opened or counted; no one knows, therefore, whether these ballots would alter the outcome of the election in Colorado, but it is possible that they could.

On November 6, 2008, Secretary Coffman issued an administrative order that the certified results from Denver, which must be delivered to the Secretary of State by November 21, 2008, should not include any of the provisional ballots cast by persons arriving at the polls after 7:00 p.m. The following day, Director Scarpello sought a decree from the state district judge that would void Secretary Coffman's order and permit Denver election officials to process the provisional ballots and include all eligible votes in the official results submitted to the Secretary. The district judge referred the dispute to the Colorado Supreme Court for its instruction on the following question: "Under the laws of this state, and of the United States, in determining the state's presidential electors, should the certified vote totals for each presidential candidate include provisional ballots cast by individuals arriving at the polls after 7 p.m. pursuant to the directive of the Denver Elections Director, if there is no other basis for disqualifying those provisional ballots?" The district court also ordered that while the matter was pending review, Denver officials were permitted to review the provisional ballots solely to determine whether each would be eligible apart from the issue in dispute, but the eligible ballots were not to be counted. The order further prohibited the Secretary from issuing a final certification without first receiving a final order from the Colorado Supreme Court.

The Colorado Supreme Court scheduled oral argument on the question certified by the state district court. At this stage of the litigation, both the McCain and Obama campaigns intervened to protect their interests. After oral argument, the Colorado Supreme Court issued a 4-3 decision holding that "[i]t would deny Denver voters

Equal Protection not to count these provisional ballots." The Court further held that the Colorado Constitution requires this same conclusion because a citizen's equal right to vote is a "fundamental right of the first order" under the State's Constitution. Finally, the Court concluded that there is some flexibility in the statutorily-dictated 7:00 p.m. poll-closing time for "true emergencies" because the Colorado Legislature instructed its courts to construe Colorado's Election Code "liberally . . . so that eligible electors may be permitted to vote." The dissent focused exclusively on the language in section 1-7-101, which the dissent contended could not be interpreted to permit an extension of the polls beyond 7:00 p.m. The Colorado Supreme Court then remanded the case to the district court with instructions that it enter an order requiring the Secretary to accept vote totals from Denver including the provisional ballots and to include these totals in the final certification.

The petitions for certiorari filed by the campaigns and consolidated by this Court present the following questions: whether the counting of contested provisional ballots cast in Denver pursuant to extended polling hours limited to Denver voters violates the Equal Protection Clause of the Fourteenth Amendment of the United States Constitution and whether the Colorado Supreme Court's decision violates Article II's specific grant of authority to the Colorado Legislature to "direct" the "Manner" of appointing the state's presidential electors. Because we find no constitutional violation under the Equal Protection Clause and no Article II concern with the Colorado Supreme Court's interpretation of state law, we affirm.

II

A

We first address jurisdiction. Respondents contend that the issue in this case presents a nonjusticiable political question entrusted to the United States Congress for resolution—specifically, the determination of the award of Colorado's nine electoral votes. Respondents misperceive the question before us. Although our decision ultimately may affect how those votes are awarded, we do not decide today how to award Colorado's electoral votes. That decision must await action by the Colorado Secretary of State and the United States Congress. All we decide here is whether the order of the Colorado Supreme Court requiring counting of the provisional ballots is consistent with the Equal Protection Clause of the Fourteenth Amendment and Article II of the United States Constitution. Because both the Equal Protection and Article II issues presented here involve the application of judicially-manageable standards to the narrow question of whether to count the contested provisional ballots, and because no serious separation of powers concern is presented by our resolution of this question, we hold that the political question doctrine does not bar our review in these circumstances.

The political question doctrine provides that even when all other jurisdictional and justiciability requirements are met, a certain class of cases should not be adjudicated by the federal courts because these controversies have been entrusted for decision to the politically accountable branches—Congress and the President. *Baker v. Carr* (1962). The doctrine has been employed sparingly.

Determining the precise questions posed and the posture of the particular case are important preliminary components of any justiciability analysis. *See generally Baker.* The issue before us does not involve the question of who should win the presidential election or who should be on Colorado's slate of presidential electors,[3] but rather whether certain votes cast in Denver pursuant to a localized poll-hour extension can be counted in the Secretary of State's certification of results under federal law, specifically the Equal Protection Clause and Article II. *Cf. Roudebush v. Hartke* (1972) (noting that while the state was permitted to order a recount for a senatorial election even though Article I makes the Senate the "judge of the elections [for the Senate]," it cannot determine which candidate is entitled to a seat in the Senate because this presents a nonjusticiable political question).

Furthermore, the particular constitutional issues raised are similar to those that courts routinely address and for which there are judicially-manageable standards and doctrines. We have consistently found jurisdiction over Equal Protection claims raised in the election and voting contexts and have rejected application of the political question doctrine to these disputes. *See Reynolds v. Sims* (1964); *Williams v. Rhodes* (1968); *Baker v. Carr*; and *Bush v. Gore* (2000). In *Williams*, we held that the political question doctrine did not apply to prevent judicial review of possible equal protection violations in the presidential election process. These decisions alone should foreclose any further discussion of nonjusticiability. Indeed, it would be astonishing to divest this Court of jurisdiction to determine whether the counting of the ballots was permissible under the Equal Protection Clause—counsel for Respondents conceded as much at argument. With respect to the Equal Protection claim, we unquestionably have jurisdiction.

Our ability to review the Article II issue presented in these circumstances is similarly well established. *See McPherson v. Blacker* (1892) (political question doctrine did not bar resolution of a claim about the extent of the legislature's power under Article II); *Bush* (Rehnquist, C.J., concurring). The inapplicability of the political question doctrine is particularly clear when the question is the narrow one of whether Article II is compromised by the Colorado Supreme Court's decision to require the counting of the provisional ballots. As is evident from our analysis of the issue below, judicially-manageable standards are available—a deferential review to assess whether the state court's interpretation of Colorado's election law substantially complied with the Legislature's will. Such a deferential standard ensures that this Court will rarely be placed in a position where its interpretation of state law differs from state decision-makers, with the potential of drawing the Court into conflict with political departments of the state and federal governments.

3. It bears repeating that we are rendering our opinion without knowledge of whom the provisional ballots ultimately will favor in the presidential election as well as the many other election contests included on the Denver November ballot.

In short, in view of the precise questions presented under the Equal Protection Clause and Article II, we hold that the political question doctrine has no application. The Court has jurisdiction and, therefore, a duty to resolve the constitutional claims presented.

B

The central claim in Petitioners' case is that the Colorado Supreme Court's order requiring that the Secretary of State count the provisional ballots of voters who arrived at the Denver polls after 7:00 p.m. violated the Equal Protection Clause of the Fourteenth Amendment of the United States Constitution. Their equal protection claim rests solely on the premise that the extension of the voting time for Denver residents resulted in unequal treatment of and a deprivation of an important right for all eligible Colorado voters who live outside of Denver and did not vote but might have voted had they too been provided the extra time. The record contains affidavits from individual residents in neighboring suburbs who make such a claim. In no other electoral district did the local authority declare such an emergency extension of poll hours or ask the Secretary of State to do so.

We do not find Petitioners' equal justice claim to be a substantial one. In general, the residents of other electoral districts in Colorado were not "similarly situated" to those in Denver. The record states with respect to Denver that "after-work rush hour traffic [was] exceptionally gridlocked, [while] Denver's suburbs, as well as the rest of the state, largely escaped the full brunt of the freakish storm." Although "some suburban roads suffered storm-related delays, they were not significantly worse than often occurs during heavy traffic and minor in comparison to what drivers were experiencing on Denver's roads." In these circumstances we cannot conclude that the Colorado Supreme Court's sanctioning of the Denver Election Director's decision to extend poll hours for Denver residents alone constituted an "arbitrary and unjustified disparate treatment of qualified voters" in other districts not similarly affected by the storm. It was rather a reasonable response to an unanticipated and location-specific natural phenomenon. While it is certainly true, as Petitioners argue, that uniform voting rules within a state are highly desirable, and purposeful deviations without cause may in some circumstances rise to the level of a constitutional violation, the realities of holding elections in 64 districts will occasionally mean that unexpected events like severe weather, power outages, and voting machine breakdowns may require immediate adjustments to general rules of time and place to serve the overarching goals of equal access to the ballot box and facilitation of maximum voter participation. Indeed, Petitioners' counsel conceded at argument that if government-controlled conditions produced temporary inaccessibility to the polls, extension of voting hours would be permissible to make up for the time lapses, but he insisted that if similar periods of inaccessibility were caused by natural causes, the same extensions would amount to a violation of the Equal Protection Clause. This distinction makes little sense to us.

Local election officials have authority to act only for their districts. The Colorado Legislature has provided for such districts and for the election of local officials to run elections within them. These officials are required to draw up local emergency plans for dealing with unexpected events that may disrupt normal voting practices. *See* Colo. Election R. 43.10. If citizens feel they need extra time to vote due to such conditions, it is to those officials they must look initially, and if relief is not forthcoming, to the Secretary of State who has power to prescribe statewide rules. If an emergency strikes, those local officials can deal only in general responses that affect the majority of voters in their districts; they are in no position to single out those voters who, due to special individual circumstances such as location or work hours, will be especially injured by the storm. We might be faced with a different question eliciting a different response if districts equally affected by the storm responded differently in terms of granting or denying extensions, but no such differential occurred here. Like the Colorado Supreme Court, we do not view the limited response of a two-hour extension for Denver voters hit disproportionately by serious traffic congestion from a "freakish" storm as anything approaching a constitutional violation. We note that the number of provisional ballots cast after 7:00 p.m. in Denver brought its total vote count to 87% of "active" voters (as defined by the Colorado Secretary of State), in line with but below the 92% count in "non-Denver counties." Had the Denver polls closed at 7:00 p.m., some 60,000 fewer votes would have been recorded, yielding a far lower percentage (67%) of "active" voters participating in this election. These figures suggest to us that the extension succeeded merely in bringing to par the participation of Denver voters with their neighboring county residents, not in conferring a preferential impact or disadvantage on either.

Petitioners are concerned with the alleged deprivation of extra voting time to some unknown number of voters in neighboring counties. Yet, the remedy Petitioners request, were their equal protection claim recognized, is most troublesome. Petitioners ask this Court to reject over 60,000 votes cast in good faith by Denver voters after they had been told by their local official that poll hours had been extended. Would not these 60,000 plus voters then have plausible claims that they had been deprived of their right to vote by this misinformation? And the same ballots that would be rejected in the contest for Presidential electors could prove determinative in their absence from the contests for local and statewide officials which were on the same ballot. The cure, it seems to us, would be worse than the malady.

In so concluding we follow the contours of our past cases in which we have expressed reluctance to intervene in state electoral processes unless there has been a demonstrated burden placed on an identifiable group of voters, as well as reticence to supervise minutiae of elections unless there has been a significant impact on voters' accessibility to the polls. *See Crawford v. Marion County Bd. of Election* (2008) (Scalia, J., concurring) (rejecting "detailed judicial supervision of the election process, [which] would flout the Constitution's express commitment of the task to the States," stating that the Court must defer to state legislatures unless a statute "imposes a severe and unjustified burden on the right to vote, or is intended to disadvantage a particular class," and noting that "weighing the burden of a nondiscriminatory voting law upon each voter and concomitantly requiring exceptions for vulnerable voters would effectively turn back decades of equal-protection jurisprudence"); *see generally Clingman v. Beaver* (2005) ("not every electoral law that burdens associational rights is subject to strict scrutiny . . . strict scrutiny is appropriate only if the burden is severe"); *Bain Peanut Co. of Tex. v. Pinson* (1931) (as a general matter "[w]e must remember that the machinery of government would not work if it were not allowed a little play in its joints"). Here we find no undue burden or disparate impact such as to require our intervention.[4] In sum, we decline to impose our views as to how elections should be run, district by district, on the State of Colorado under these circumstances.

C

Petitioners' last point claims that the Colorado Supreme Court's judgment unconstitutionally usurps the Legislature's exclusive authority under Article II to set the time at which the state's polling places are to close. We also reject this argument.

The United States Constitution provides in relevant part: "Each State shall appoint, in such Manner as the Legislature thereof may direct, a Number of Electors. . . . " U.S. Const. art. II, § I, cl. 2. Petitioners assert that the Colorado Legislature has, as to the time during which the polls shall be open, "directed" the "Manner" of "appointing Electors" through this provision:

> All polls shall be opened continuously from 7 a.m. until 7 p.m. of each election day. . . . The polls shall remain open after 7 p.m. until every eligible voter who was at the polling place at or before 7 p.m. has been allowed to vote. Any person arriving after 7 p.m. shall not be entitled to vote.

Colo. Rev. Stat. § 1-7-101 (1). Petitioners argue that because Article II "leaves it to the legislature exclusively to define the method of effecting the object" of selecting a state's presidential electors, *McPherson,* and the Colorado Legislature has done so with respect to the hours when the polls shall be open, neither a local election judge nor any trial or appellate court member of the state judiciary may constitutionally direct a contrary closing time. Moreover, while the Colorado Secretary of State has, pursuant to authority granted by the Legislature, both promulgated rules requiring local contingency plans for certain disasters and issued a guide discussing how to deal with emergencies and disasters that may affect voting, neither mentions altering polling place hours. Thus, Petitioners say, regardless of whether extended hours were a practical, or even appropriate, response to the winter storm, and regardless of whether any voter's equal protection rights were

4. Our decision in *Bush v. Gore*, does not require a contrary result. *Bush v. Gore* governs a distinctive sub-category of election cases, and this case does not fall into that group. In that case, large numbers of local officials applied an indeterminate standard throughout the state over a period of time. Here, by contrast, one unambiguous rule was issued for one district and no further discretion was permitted. The Court in *Bush v. Gore* concluded that the recount could have been "conducted in compliance with the requirements of equal protection and due process," if the state had adopted "adequate statewide standards for determining what is a legal vote, and practical procedures to implement them," and had provided for an "orderly judicial review of any disputed matters that might arise." *Id.* Because these types of deficiencies are simply not implicated here, *Bush v. Gore* would have little precedential force in this case, even if that opinion had not explicitly been limited to its particular facts.

affected by the extension of voting hours in one county but not another, such an order would be unconstitutional unless the Legislature provided for it by statute. As to the Presidential election, therefore, no provisional ballot from Denver may be counted.

We assume, without deciding, that the "Manner" of choosing electors sweeps broadly enough to vest a state legislature with the right to exclusive constitutional authority over all details of electoral administration, including specifically the hour at which the polls must close. We further recognize that Article II "operat[es] as a limitation upon the State in any attempt to circumscribe the legislative power." *McPherson.* In modern times, the Supreme Court has unanimously recognized that Article II limits, at least to some extent, the authority of a State Constitution to "circumscribe the legislative power" over presidential elector selection. *Bush v. Palm Beach Canvassing Bd.* (2000). But even so broad a mandate does not divest the coordinate branches of the State's government of all authority, especially when the legislature expressly delegates authority to administer elections to these other branches. Here, the Colorado Legislature has conferred upon the Colorado Supreme Court "original jurisdiction for the adjudication of contests concerning presidential electors," Colo. Rev. Stat. § 1-11-204, and has delegated the responsibility of supervising the election itself to the executive branch, Colo. Rev. Stat. § 1-1-107. Similarly, in *Bush v. Gore*, the Florida Legislature had "delegated the authority to run the elections and to oversee election disputes to the Secretary of State and to state circuit courts." Chief Justice Rehnquist, concurring for three justices in that case, opined that Article II still left some interpretative role for the state judiciary in such circumstances.

Even if we accept Chief Justice Rehnquist's view of Article II and give only limited deference to the state court's interpretation of state law, we cannot conclude that the Colorado Supreme Court's construction of the relevant provisions amounts to an "impermissibl[e] distort[ion]" of the Colorado Election Code. Relying on § 1-1-103(1) of the Colorado Revised Statutes, which mandates in part that the Election Code "shall be liberally construed so that all eligible voters may be permitted to vote. . . . ," as well as its view that the literal interpretation adopted by Petitioners would bring the statute into conflict with the Equal Protection Clause of the Fourteenth Amendment of the United States Constitution and the Colorado Constitution's protection of a citizen's equal right to vote, the Colorado Supreme Court concluded that the provision in question "should not be construed to prohibit the extension of polling hours when emergencies require it." The specified 7:00 p.m. closing time was merely "a general rule," not a blanket prohibition against local initiative to protect voter access in exigent circumstances.

Whether we would interpret the Colorado Election Code in the same manner were this question left initially to us, or whether we agree with the rationale articulated by the state court to support its interpretation, are both beside the point. Under our federal system, at least some deference is due to the state judicial interpretation of state law. We cannot say that this interpretation was so novel or so strained as to fall short of constituting a "fair reading" of the state law.

For these reasons, we hold that Article II of the United States Constitution does not compel the rejection of the provisional ballots in this case.

III

The judgment of the Colorado Supreme Court is affirmed.

B. THE REALITY OF OTHER MAJOR DISPUTED ELECTIONS

While the immediately foregoing *McCain v. Obama* litigation was hypothetical, the November 2008 general election produced a real dispute in a major election between incumbent Republican Norm Coleman and challenger Democrat Al Franken for Minnesota's U.S. Senate seat. That dispute lasted eight months, until June 30, 2009, when Coleman conceded after the Minnesota Supreme Court released the following unanimous opinion.

There are many aspects of this dispute that are worthy of attention, and if you wish to learn more, here's where to begin: Jay Weiner, THIS IS NOT FLORIDA: HOW AL FRANKEN WON THE MINNESOTA SENATE RECOUNT (2010); Edward B. Foley, *The Lake Wobegone Recount*, 10 ELECTION L. J. 129 (2011). But for purposes of this introductory Election Law course, our primary interest is to compare the Equal Protection analysis of *Coleman v. Franken* with both *Bush v. Gore* and the hypothetical *McCain v. Obama* opinion.

In doing so, you should be aware that the Minnesota Supreme Court's 5-0 opinion on Equal Protection grounds affirmed a 3-0 opinion of a trial court that was designed to be evenly balanced and impartial in a way comparable to the three-judge panel in the *McCain v. Obama* exercise. For *Coleman v. Franken*, the three-judge trial court was handpicked by the Minnesota Supreme Court so that one of its judges had a Democratic background, another a Republican background, and the third an Independent background. (Minnesota has a competitive Independence Party, electing Jesse Ventura as governor in 1999. Its candidate in the 2008 U.S. Senate election captured 16 percent of the vote.) As you read the Minnesota Supreme Court's Equal Protection analysis, do you think it makes a difference that the state supreme court knew that it was reviewing the decision of its own carefully chosen trial court?

COLEMAN v. FRANKEN

767 N.W.2d 453 (Minn. S. Ct. 2009)

PER CURIAM.

Coleman filed a notice of election contest under Minn. Stat. § 209.021 (2008), challenging the State Canvassing Board's certification that Franken was entitled to receive a certificate of election as United States Senator following the November 4, 2008 general election. After a trial, the three-judge trial court we appointed to hear the election contest issued its findings of fact, conclusions of law, and order for judgment, concluding that Franken received 312 more legally cast votes than Coleman and that Franken was entitled to a certificate of election for the office of United States Senator. The question presented on appeal is whether the trial court erred in concluding that Franken received the most legally cast votes in the election for United States Senator. Because we conclude that appellants have not shown that the trial court's findings of fact are clearly erroneous or that the court committed an error of law or abused its discretion, we affirm.

More than 2.9 million Minnesotans cast ballots in the November general election, including approximately 300,000 who voted or attempted to vote by absentee ballot. On November 18, 2008, the State Canvassing Board accepted the consolidated statewide canvassing report as showing that Coleman received 1,211,565 votes and that Franken received 1,211,359 votes for the office of United States Senator, a margin of 206 votes in Coleman's favor. Because the margin separating the two candidates was less than one-half of one percent of the total number of votes counted for that office, the State Canvassing Board directed the Minnesota Secretary of State's Office to oversee a manual recount, as required by Minn. Stat. § 204C.35, subd. 1(b)(1) (2008).

The statewide manual recount was conducted between November 19, 2008, and January 5, 2009, pursuant to instructions drafted by the Secretary of State's Office and approved by the State Canvassing Board after consultation with representatives of Coleman and Franken. During the recount, local election officials and the candidates reviewed the absentee ballot return envelopes that had been rejected on or before election day and agreed that some of them had been improperly rejected. On January 3, 2009, the Secretary of State's Office opened and counted the 933 ballots identified during this process. On January 5, 2009, the State Canvassing Board certified the results of the election as 1,212,431 votes for Franken and 1,212,206 votes for Coleman, a margin of 225 votes in Franken's favor.

On January 6, 2009, Coleman filed [this] contest. Testimony in the trial commenced on January 26, 2009, and concluded on March 12, 2009. Coleman sought during trial to have additional absentee ballots counted. No claim of fraud in the election or during the recount was made by either party. At the conclusion of the trial, the court determined that 351 additional absentee ballot return envelopes satisfied the statutory requirements and ordered that these envelopes be opened and the ballots inside counted. [The result was] a margin of 312 votes in Franken's favor.

I.

[Before reaching the Equal Protection issue, the Minnesota Supreme Court rejected Coleman's argument that the trial court had violated Due Process by changing the law applicable to determining whether an absentee ballot counts. Coleman had claimed that, prior to the trial court's ruling, the law in Minnesota had been to count an absentee ballot as long as the absentee voter was eligible to participate in the election, even if the voter failed to submit required information as part of casting the ballot. The trial court, by contrast, had insisted that the voter comply with these informational requirements. Coleman's claim was based on the principle articulated in *Griffin v. Burns* and *Roe v. Alabama* (see, pp. 718, above). The Minnesota Supreme Court embraced this principle but rejected the case-specific premise of Coleman's Due Process claim, stating that Minnesota law had always been what the trial court said it was, and thus there had been no change.]

II

[The Minnesota Supreme Court's treatment of Coleman's Equal Protection claim was opposite of how it handled the Due Process claim. There was considerable evidence that different localities in the state had, in fact, treated similar absentee ballots differently. For example, one locality would count an absentee ballot even if it was missing a required witness signature, whereas another locality would reject a ballot for this same defect. The Minnesota Supreme Court thus did not question the factual premise of Coleman's Equal Protection claim, but instead rejected it in principle.]

Coleman's equal protection argument depend[s] on his assertion that differential application of the statutory requirements for absentee voting violates equal protection. But equal protection is not violated every time public officials apply facially neutral state laws differently. The United States Supreme Court has held that "an erroneous or mistaken performance of [a] statutory duty, although a violation of the statute, is not without more a denial of the equal protection of the laws." *Snowden v. Hughes* (1944). The Court then explained that the "more" that is required for a violation of equal protection is intentional or purposeful discrimination.

We conclude that the standard applied in *Snowden* is the proper standard to apply in this case. Accordingly, in order to prevail on his equal protection claim of disparate application of a facially neutral statute, Coleman was required to prove intentional discrimination. Coleman neither claims nor produced any evidence that the differing treatment of absentee ballots among jurisdictions during the election was the result of intentional or purposeful discrimination against individuals or classes. Nor does Coleman claim that the trial court's order, establishing certain categories of ballots as not legally cast, was the product of an intent to discriminate against any individual or class.

The trial court found that election jurisdictions adopted policies they deemed necessary to ensure that absentee voting procedures would be available to their residents, in accordance with statutory requirements, given the resources available to them. The court also found that differences in available resources, personnel, procedures, and technology necessarily affected the procedures used by local election officials reviewing absentee ballots. But the court found that Coleman did not prove that these differences were calculated to discriminate among absentee voters. Our review of the record convinces us that the trial court's findings are supported by the evidence and are not clearly erroneous. As a result, we conclude that Coleman did not prove his equal protection claim.[15]

Coleman makes the additional argument that the non-uniform application of the statutory standards for absentee voting nevertheless brings this case within the ambit of the United States Supreme Court's decision in *Bush v. Gore* (2000). In *Bush*, the Court held that the statewide recount of the 2000 presidential election that had been ordered by the Florida Supreme Court violated equal protection. Coleman argues that, in Minnesota's 2008 United States Senate election, different local election jurisdictions treated similarly situated absentee ballots differently and that the trial court imposed a stricter standard for compliance with absentee voting requirements than did election officials, and that those differences violate equal protection under *Bush*.

The trial court concluded that *Bush* is distinguishable in several important respects and, as a result, does not support Coleman's equal protection claim. We agree. In *Bush*, the Supreme Court specifically noted that it was not addressing the question of "whether local entities, in the exercise of their expertise, may develop different systems for implementing elections." Variations in local practices for implementing absentee voting procedures are, at least in part, the question at issue here. As previously noted, the trial court here found that the disparities in application of the statutory standards on which Coleman relies are the product of local jurisdictions' use of different methods to ensure compliance with the same statutory standards; that jurisdictions adopted policies they deemed necessary to ensure that absentee voting procedures would be available to their residents, in accordance with statutory requirements, given the resources available to them; and that differences in available resources, personnel, procedures, and technology necessarily affected the procedures used by local election officials in reviewing absentee ballots. As we noted previously, Coleman has not demonstrated that these findings are clearly erroneous.

Additionally, the essence of the equal protection problem addressed in *Bush* was that there were no established standards under Florida statutes or provided by the state supreme court for determining voter intent; as a result, in the recount process each county (indeed, each recount location within a county) was left to set its own standards for discerning voter intent. Here, there were clear statutory standards for acceptance or rejection of absentee ballots, about which all election officials received common training.

Finally, the decision to be made by Florida election officials with which the Supreme Court was concerned in *Bush* was voter intent—that is, for whom the ballot was cast—as reflected on ballots already cast in the election. In *Bush*, officials conducting the recount

15. To the extent that this case has brought to light inconsistencies in the administration of absentee voting standards, we are confident that the appropriate officials in the other branches of government understand that efforts should be made to reduce those inconsistencies, even though they were not proven to be of constitutional magnitude.

were reviewing the face of the ballot itself, creating opportunities for manipulation of the decision for political purposes. Here, the decision at issue was whether to accept or reject absentee ballot return envelopes before they were opened, meaning that the actual votes on the ballot contained in the return envelope were not known to the election officials applying the standards. In summary, we conclude that *Bush v. Gore* is not applicable and does not support Coleman's equal protection claim.

For all of these reasons, we conclude that Coleman has not proven that either election officials or the trial court violated his right to equal protection.

III

Coleman argued at trial that as a result of the trial court's order finding that certain ballots were not legally cast, there are absentee ballots included in the State Canvassing Board's certification of election results that would have been rejected if the strict compliance standard of the trial court had been applied to them. Coleman therefore argued that [to be consistent under state law] the court was required to apply a strict compliance standard to ballots already accepted and counted on election day and [thus to] reduce the parties' vote totals for any ballots that did not meet that standard.

The trial court rejected Coleman's argument and the evidence Coleman offered to support it. We conclude that the court did not abuse its discretion in excluding this evidence because the legislature has foreclosed any challenge to the legality of an absentee ballot based on the return envelope once the ballot has been deposited in the ballot box.

Minnesota Statutes § 204C.13, subd. 6 (2008), provides, in pertinent part:

> *At any time before* the ballots of any voter are deposited in the ballot boxes, the election judges or any individual who was not present at the time the voter procured the ballots, but not otherwise, may challenge the eligibility of that voter and the deposit of any received absentee ballots in the ballot boxes.

(Emphasis added.) The plain language of this statute requires challenges to absentee ballot envelopes to be made, if at all, before the ballots are deposited in the ballot box. Because the accepted absentee ballots at issue in this case were opened and deposited in the ballot boxes on election day, section 204C.13, subd. 6, bars Coleman's challenge to them during the election contest or in this appeal.

IV

[Omitted.]

V

[Omitted.]

VI

For all of the foregoing reasons, we affirm the decision of the trial court that Al Franken received the highest number of votes legally cast and is entitled under Minn.Stat. § 204C.40 (2008) to receive the certificate of election as United States Senator from the State of Minnesota.

C. LITIGATION OVER THE COUNTING OF PROVISIONAL BALLOTS

Coleman v. Franken did not involve disputed provisional ballots because Minnesota, a state with Election Day Registration (EDR), does not need provisional ballots to protect voters from erroneous purges of voter registration databases. If a previously registered Minnesota voter goes to the polls on Election Day and is not listed in the poll book, she can simply re-register on the spot and cast a regular, not provisional, ballot. Thus, the concern that led Congress in HAVA to require states to let voters cast provisional ballots does not apply to Minnesota and other EDR states.

Ohio does not have EDR. On the contrary, it has one of the highest rates of provisional ballots (as a percentage of total ballots cast in each election). Ever since 2004, when Ohio determined the outcome of the presidential election, lawyers for Democrats and Republicans have realized that the winner of a future presidential election might depend on the counting of provisional ballots in Ohio. This realization has been confirmed by the fact that other elections have turned on the counting of provisional ballots in Ohio. In 2008, a close congressional race was decided only after the provisional ballots were counted. Moreover, a 2010 local judicial election was decided only after a dispute over provisional ballots was resolved in federal court, with the Sixth Circuit weighing in at the preliminary injunction stage.

That Sixth Circuit ruling, *Hunter v. Hamilton County Board of Elections*, 635 F.3d 219 (6th Cir. 2011), invoked the "no arbitrariness" principle of *Bush v. Gore* to declare that two equivalent groups of provisional ballots must be counted the same. The first group consisted of ballots cast at the county board of election's office during early voting but which were "wrong precinct" ballots because a board employee had given the voter the wrong ballot. In its review of provisional ballots in the 2010 election, the board had decided to count these ballots because the problem was not the voter's fault but instead had been caused by the board employee's mistake. The second group of ballots had been cast by voters on Election Day in their neighborhood polling locations. With respect to this second group, a problem arose because several "precincts" shared the same polling location. The voters had gone to their correct polling location, but had received a "wrong precinct" ballot from the poll workers there because the workers had directed them to an incorrect table at the polling site. This problem occurs frequently enough to be called the "right church, wrong pew" issue among election officials. In this case, the county board of elections refused to count these "right church, wrong pew" ballots.

In a divided 2-1 decision, the Sixth Circuit affirmed a preliminary injunction that required the two groups of ballots to be treated the same. Here is the heart of the majority opinion's reasoning:

> The evidence of poll-worker error with respect to [the "right church, wrong pew"] ballots—that the ballots were cast at the correct multiple-precinct polling location—is substantially similar to the location evidence considered by the Board with respect to the ballots cast at its office. In both instances, there is no direct evidence that the poll worker erred. For the 27 ballots cast at its office, however, the Board concluded that the cause of casting the ballots in the wrong precinct must be poll-worker error because, under the Board's logic, "the voter had no choice but to walk up to just one person." The voter went to the correct location, i.e., the Board's office, and the staff at the Board's office was required to give the voter the correct ballot; thus, there is little chance that the voter erred, and the wrong-precinct ballot must be due to poll-worker error. Similarly, at the multiple-precinct polling locations, voters went to the correct location and the poll workers were required to direct voters to the correct precinct.
>
> To be sure, there may be more explanations for why the voter might have erred at the multiple-precinct polling locations than at the Board office, requiring a greater inference to conclude that the miscast ballot was a result of poll-worker error, but Defendants have not presented any persuasive rationales. Thus, we believe that the situations of voters at the Board office and at multiple-precinct polling locations are substantially similar.
>
> We think it unlikely that "a corresponding interest sufficiently weighty" for equal-protection purposes justifies the Board's decision to refuse to consider similar evidence of poll-worker error with respect to similar provisional ballots. This discriminatory disenfranchisement was applied to voters who may bear no responsibility for the rejection of their ballots, and the Board has not asserted "precise interests" that justified the unequal treatment.
>
> Furthermore, we recognize that Ohio law does not permit the consideration of poll-worker error with respect to ballots cast in the wrong precinct, but rather mandates that no ballot cast in the wrong precinct may be counted. Despite the requirements of state law, Plaintiffs have provided evidence that the Board considered evidence of poll-worker error with respect to some ballots cast in the wrong precinct but not other similarly situated ballots when it evaluated which ballots to count. In so doing, the Board exercised discretion, without a uniform standard to apply, in determining whether to count provisional ballots miscast due to poll-worker error that otherwise would be invalid under state law.
>
> The distinctions drawn by the Board at the time of its decisions were made in the midst of its review of provisional ballots, after the election. They were not the result of a broader policy determination by the State of Ohio that such distinctions would be justifiable. Therefore, they are especially vulnerable to equal-protection challenges. In light of this unguided differential treatment, Plaintiffs' allegation that the Board decided arbitrarily when to consider (in the case of the 27 votes cast at the Board's

> office), or not consider (in the case of the votes cast in multiple-precinct polling locations), similar evidence of poll-worker error raises serious equal-protection concerns.

One judge on the panel disagreed:

> I am not confident that there is a strong likelihood of success with respect to the Equal Protection claim[, which is] based on unequal treatment of two groups of ballots: 27 ballots cast in the Board's office prior to the election where the ballot was for the wrong precinct (almost certainly due to official error) and a much larger number of ballots where the voter cast a ballot at the wrong precinct table (where doing so may have been due to poll-worker error). The situations were sufficiently different that a bipartisan elections board unanimously counted the votes in the former situation, but did not count the votes in the latter situation.
>
> It is not entirely clear whether the Board acted in accordance with Ohio law in counting the 27 votes, but either way the likelihood is not particularly strong that there was an Equal Protection violation under the principle of *Bush v. Gore* (2000). The two wrong-precinct groups of ballots are sufficiently different that Ohio law could permit counting the 27 votes on the ground that the error was much more clearly and ascertainably not attributable to the voter than in the election-day polling place situations. And if Ohio law does not permit counting the 27 votes, then they were counted under a mistaken view of the law by the Board. In that circumstance, there should be a state-law challenge to the votes erroneously cast, not a counting of a much larger number of votes county-wide that were erroneously cast in a similar—but not exactly the same—way. Moreover, counting improperly cast votes county-wide, where the ballots include trans-county district and state races, raises serious Equal Protection concerns in having Hamilton County votes counted differently from those of other Ohio counties.

Hunter was a prelude to intense federal court litigation in 2012 over Ohio's rules for counting provisional ballots. As the *Hunter* judges recognized, the Ohio Supreme Court had announced a strict rule that no provisional ballot can count if cast in a way that contradicts state law, even if a government worker's mistake is the reason why it was cast in violation of state law. This strictness had caused the *Hunter* plaintiffs to raise a Due Process as well as Equal Protection claim to the rejection of the "right church, wrong pew" ballots. Regardless of the fact that the local board had counted the 27 ballots miscast at its office, the *Hunter* plaintiffs argued that it would be fundamentally unfair—and therefore a Due Process violation—to disqualify any "right church, wrong pew" ballot. The Sixth Circuit sidestepped this Due Process issue in *Hunter*, finding it sufficient to rely instead solely on Equal Protection as a reason to count the "right church, wrong pew" ballots in that case.

In advance of the 2012 election, however, voting rights advocates could not rely on the same Equal Protection issue being presented again and thus pressed forward with the Due Process claim that remained unresolved after *Hunter*. They also brought similar Due Process claims against other aspects of Ohio's provisional voting rules. In addition to claiming that

Due Process requires the counting of "right church, wrong pew" ballots, they also argued that Due Process requires the counting of "*wrong* church, wrong pew" ballots—ballots cast in the incorrect polling *location*—at least where poll-worker error was responsible for this mistake. (This might occur if a poll worker directs a voter to the wrong polling location, such as the wrong school or community center.) Likewise, they claimed that Due Process required the counting of provisional ballots where poll-worker error was responsible for a mistake in the printing or signing of the voter's name on the provisional ballot envelope.

The Sixth Circuit accepted the plaintiffs' constitutional claim with respect to the "right church, wrong pew" ballots, but rejected the two other constitutional claims. These rulings came in the following two opinions. As you will see, the Sixth Circuit analyzed what has just been described as the Due Process claim under both the Due Process and Equal Protection Clauses of the Fourteenth Amendment. But the Equal Protection analysis in these 2012 cases is not the same as in *Hunter*, which concerned the side-by-side comparison of two groups of ballots. By contrast, the Equal Protection issue here seems functionally identical to the Due Process issue, concerning only whether the state may disqualify a particular category of provisional ballots (with the baseline comparison being all of the other ballots not in this particular category, rather than a comparison to a second particular category).

NORTHEAST OHIO COALITION FOR THE HOMELESS v. HUSTED

696 F.3d 580 (6th Cir. 2012)

PER CURIAM.

At issue are Ohio's requirements that provisional ballots be cast in the correct precinct and with a completed voter affirmation, making no exception for wrong-precinct and deficient-affirmation ballots caused by poll-worker error.

I. BACKGROUND

According to the plaintiffs, Ohio's strict application of the disqualification rules to ballot deficiencies caused by poll-worker error violated, *inter alia,* the Fourteenth Amendment's Equal Protection and Due Process Clauses. The SEIU plaintiffs moved for a preliminary injunction, arguing that the relevant statutory provisions impermissibly burdened the fundamental right to vote without serving sufficient state interests. To remedy this problem, the SEIU plaintiffs proposed "remaking" wrong-precinct provisional ballots to count only "up-ballot" votes—i.e., votes in eligible races.

The district court held an evidentiary hearing on July 30, 2012, and issued its preliminary injunction on August 27, 2012.

1. Equal Protection: Wrong-Precinct Ballots Caused by Poll-Worker Error

To justify the automatic-disqualification rule, the Secretary relied on the "significant and numerous" advantages of the precinct voting system articulated in *Sandusky*

County Democratic Party v. Blackwell (6th Cir. 2004) (per curiam): (1) capping the number of voters at a polling location; (2) limiting the precinct ballot to the applicable federal, state, and local elections a citizen may vote in, which has the result of (3) making the precinct ballot less confusing; (4) simplifying election administration and oversight, so as to minimize election fraud; and (5) enabling the state to place polling locations closer to voter residences. The court deemed the first, third, and fifth *Sandusky* factors inapposite, because the automatic-disqualification rule affected voters who arrived at the right polling location and did nothing to make provisional ballots less confusing. The second *Sandusky* factor—limiting precinct ballots to eligible races—somewhat justified the disqualification of wrong-precinct ballots in the court's view, inasmuch as the State has an interest in preventing ineligible voters from casting votes in the wrong races. But because the plaintiffs sought to "remake" wrong-precinct ballots to count only "up-ballot" votes[,] the court found no likelihood of vote dilution or detrimental effect on the precinct voting system. Finally, the court rejected for lack of evidence the Secretary's purported interest in election administration, monitoring, and recordkeeping.

2. Equal Protection: Deficient-Affirmation Ballots Caused by Poll-Worker Error

Turning to the plaintiffs' claim regarding deficient-affirmation ballots, the court cited 2011 election data showing that Ohio rejected 568 provisional ballots due to such technical deficiencies as "a missing or misplaced printed name or voter signature, or the voter's signature was deemed not to match the exemplar on file with the Board." The court attributed these deficiencies to poll-worker error "because it is the poll worker's duty to ensure that provisional ballots are cast with a validly completed ballot envelope and affirmation." Still, the court conceded that the class of affected voters "is likely to be significantly smaller" than the right-place/wrong-precinct ballots, and that the burden on these voters "is arguably less severe" because "the individual voter has a greater degree of control over whether the ballot envelope contains the required elements." While it could not "quantify the precise magnitude of the burden imposed by this law's restriction on the class of affected voters," it deemed the State's interests—the same *Sandusky* factors discussed above—insufficient to support the restriction under the *Anderson/Burdick* test.

3

[Omitted.]

4. Due Process: Wrong-Precinct Ballots Caused by Poll-Worker Error

Last, the court adopted *dicta* from the post-remand judgment in the *Hunter* litigation that Ohio's strict disqualification of deficient ballots, regardless of poll-worker error, rendered the election system "fundamentally unfair," in violation of due process. *See Hunter v. Hamilton Cnty. Bd. of Elections* (S.D. Ohio 2012). Relying on the same evidence discussed in the equal protection claims, the district court found a strong likelihood that the SEIU plaintiffs would prevail on the due process claim.

5. *Injunctive Relief*

Having found a likelihood of success on the merits of these claims, the district court determined that the equitable factors favored the issuance of a preliminary injunction. Accordingly, the court granted a preliminary injunction requiring the counting of wrong-precinct and deficient-affirmation provisional ballots, unless the State could prove that the poll worker properly advised the voter to cast the ballot in the correct precinct and the voter refused.

The Secretary now appeals the deficient-affirmation aspect of the preliminary injunction, and the State intervenes to appeal the wrong-precinct remedy.

II. SCOPE OF PRELIMINARY INJUNCTION: THE WRONG-PRECINCT REMEDY

Before we may assess the propriety of the preliminary injunction, we must resolve a dispute over the scope of its relief for wrong-precinct ballots. The district court's plenary opinion and order required the Secretary to instruct Ohio's county election boards not to reject provisional ballots "cast . . . in the wrong precinct, *unless* the poll worker who processed the voter's provisional ballot" directed the voter to the correct precinct, informed the voter of the ramifications of casting a wrong-precinct vote (disqualification), and the voter nevertheless insisted on casting the ballot in the wrong precinct. The [plaintiffs] read this remedy to apply to all wrong-precinct ballots, regardless of whether the voter cast his or her ballot at the correct polling location. The State counters that the remedy applies only to provisional ballots cast at the correct polling place, citing the district court's later clarifying orders. With one small caveat, we agree with the State.

Admittedly, the plaintiffs did not confine their requested relief to right-place/wrong-precinct provisional ballots. And certain aspects of the district court's opinion appeared to follow this lead—namely, the court's summary of the SEIU plaintiffs' requested relief and the court's "order" of "Appropriate Injunctive Relief." But if any doubt remained, the district court's framing of its equal-protection analysis settles the matter: "It is the particular burden imposed by Ohio's prohibition of wrong-precinct ballots on the rights of a 'discrete class of prospective voters'—those who *arrive at the correct polling place* but are misdirected due to poll-worker error—against which the State's asserted interests must be weighed."

We do note, however, that the State's interpretation fails to account for provisional ballots cast at the county boards of election. Because Ohio law authorizes the casting of provisional ballots at the county boards, *see* O.R.C. § 3505.181(C)(2) (disqualifying certain provisional ballots where "the individual refuses to travel to the polling place for the correct jurisdiction *or to the office of the board of elections* to cast a ballot" (emphasis added)), we see no reason to distinguish these right-place/wrong-precinct provisional ballots from those cast at precinct polling locations. In both instances, the voter appears at a state-authorized polling location, but the alleged poll-worker error results in the casting of a wrong-precinct provisional ballot. Accordingly, we assume the district court's wrong-precinct remedy includes these right-place/wrong-precinct provisional ballots.

III. THE PRELIMINARY INJUNCTION

A

[Omitted.]

B. The Wrong-Precinct Ballots

1. Likelihood of Success on the Merits

The district court identified three strands of likely constitutional violations related to the wrong-precinct ballots as requiring injunctive relief: the unreasonableness and fundamental unfairness of disqualifying wrong-precinct ballots caused by poll-worker error (equal protection and due process), and the disparate treatment of deficient provisional ballots under the consent decree (equal protection). Having reviewed the record afresh, we agree on all counts.

a. Equal Protection and Disqualification Despite Poll-Worker Error

Our Constitution accords special protection for the fundamental right of voting, recognizing its essential role in the "preservati[on] of all rights," *Yick Wo v. Hopkins* (1886). Because [o]ther rights, even the most basic, are illusory if the right to vote is undermined [t]he right to vote is protected in more than the initial allocation of the franchise. Equal protection applies as well to the manner of its exercise. At the same time, the Constitution vests states with the authority to prescribe "[t]he Times, Places and Manner of holding Elections for Senators and Representatives." U.S. Const. Art. I, § 4, cl. 1. "[W]hen a state election law provision imposes only 'reasonable, nondiscriminatory restrictions' upon the First and Fourteenth Amendment rights of voters, the State's important regulatory interests are generally sufficient to justify the restrictions." *Burdick* (quoting *Anderson*). When equal protection challenges ask us to resolve these competing interests, we calibrate the equal protection standard to "[t]he precise character of the state's action and the nature of the burden on voters." *Obama for America* [*v. Husted* (6th Cir. 2012)].

While a rational basis standard applies to state regulations that do not burden the fundamental right to vote, strict scrutiny applies when a state's restriction imposes "severe" burdens. For the majority of cases falling between these extremes, we apply the "flexible" *Anderson/Burdick* balancing test.

The State defendant, intervening as appellant, resists this standard, arguing that Ohio's automatic-disqualification rule for wrong-precinct ballots treats all voters equally and therefore does not "involve any classification that could violate the equal protection standard." But the State overlooks the fact that a clear majority of the Supreme Court in *Crawford* applied some form of *Burdick*'s burden-measuring equal protection standard to Indiana's facially neutral voter-identification requirement. Because the plaintiffs "demonstrated that their right to vote is . . . burdened by" Ohio's law that rejects wrong-precinct ballots regardless of poll-worker error, "[t]he *Anderson-Burdick* standard . . . applies." *Obama for America* (rejecting Ohio's attempt to limit the *Anderson/Burdick* test to First Amendment free association claims and Fourteenth Amendment due process claims).

i. The Burden on Provisional Voters

Here, the district court identified a substantial burden on provisional voters. The court's factual findings detail Ohio's "systemic" disqualification of thousands of wrong-precinct provisional ballots and a strong likelihood that the majority of these miscast votes result from poll-worker error. Ohio tossed out more than 14,000 wrong-precinct ballots in 2008 and 11,000 more in 2010, with such rejections occurring across the state. [T]he State intervening as appellant does not contest the accuracy of this data, but emphasizes that wrong-precinct ballots make up a small percentage of the total votes cast. (State Br. (explaining that wrong-precinct ballots made up 0.248% of the ballots cast in the 2008 election, with right-place/wrong-precinct ballots comprising an even smaller share).)

Though the district court did not make specific factual findings regarding the incidence of poll-worker error, it found such error evident in poll workers' statutory duty to direct voters to the correct polling place. As the State acknowledges, Ohio law requires poll workers to "determine whether an individual is eligible to vote in a specific precinct, and direct them to the precinct in which 'the individual appears to be eligible to vote.'" (State Br. (quoting O.R.C. § 3505.181(C)(1)).) *See also Hunter* ("Ohio has created a system in which state actors (poll workers) are given the ultimate responsibility of directing voters to the right location to vote."). The court also cited the proliferation of multi-precinct polling locations in Ohio's counties as increasing the likelihood of poll-worker error causing right-place/wrong-precinct ballots.

In addition to these findings, the plaintiffs presented voluminous evidence that poll workers give voters wrong-precinct ballots for a number of reasons, ranging from misunderstanding counties' precinct location guides to failing to understand the vote-disqualifying ramifications of handing out wrong-precinct ballots. [A] sample of Franklin County's precinct location guide, which shows how different house numbers on the same street end up in different precincts, almost at random, demonstrates how easily poll workers can make mistakes under the pressures of election day. The Secretary failed to present evidence to the district court that other factors besides poll-worker error caused wrong-precinct ballots, and the State offers none now. Given this record and the clear legal duty imposed on poll workers by Ohio law, the district court deduced:

> As a matter of law, if a person casts a provisional ballot in the wrong precinct, it is *always* going to be due to poll-worker error unless the poll worker has instructed the individual

> where the correct polling location is and that individual "refuses to travel to the polling place for the correct [precinct] or to the office of the board of elections to cast a ballot."

Ohio Rev. Code §§ 3505.181(C)(2), 181(E)(1). Such an act would be an irrational and futile exercise by the voter, because, as required by Ohio Rev. Code § 3505.181(C)(1), the poll worker must first inform him that if he insists on voting in the wrong precinct, his ballot will not be counted.

Because the State offers no evidence of alternative causes, we find no clear error with the district court's factual conclusion that most right-place/wrong-precinct ballots result, and will continue to result, from poll-worker error.

The application of Ohio [statutory law] to right-place/wrong-precinct ballots caused by poll-worker error effectively requires voters to have a greater knowledge of their precinct, precinct ballot, and polling place than poll workers. Absent such omniscience, the State will permanently reject their ballots without an opportunity to cure the situation. The mere fact that these voters cast provisional ballots does not justify this additional burden; as the district court explained, Ohio law now requires thirteen different categories of voters to cast provisional ballots, ranging from individuals who do not have an acceptable form of identification to those who requested an absentee ballot or whose signature was deemed by the precinct official not to match the name on the registration forms.

ii. The State's Interests: Sandusky *Factors*

Faced with this burden on voters, the State falls back on the same *Sandusky* factors rejected by the district court. First, the State objects to the district court's conclusion that the first *Sandusky* factor—capping the number of voters at a polling place—does not support disqualifying right-place/wrong-precinct ballots. We find no error here. By definition, right-place/wrong-precinct ballots *are* cast at the right polling location, demonstrating that these voters attempted to comply with the State's precinct requirement. Of course, if a recalcitrant voter insists on casting a wrong-precinct ballot after making the effort to arrive at the correct polling place, the State would have a strong interest in rejecting that non-compliant vote. But the State offers no evidence or logical support for this phenomenon, while the plaintiffs provided substantial evidence of poll-worker error.

As for the second and third *Sandusky* factors, the State argues that it has a strong interest in limiting precinct ballots to eligible races, which facilitates the administration of elections and simplifies the ballot for voters. No disagreement there, but these interests do not justify the precise restriction challenged here: the exclusion of wrong-precinct ballots caused by poll-worker error. Additionally, the State asserts "an interest in avoiding a circumstance in which voters are in effect given the option of surrendering their right to vote in 'down ballot,' precinct-specific races in exchange for the ability to cast 'up ballot' votes in a (perhaps less busy) precinct other than their own." Again, the State offers no evidence for this speculation. We have no reason to think that voters, who will be correctly advised by poll workers about their assigned precinct will opt to roll the dice in a less busy precinct on pain of having their votes disqualified. The State offers no reason to think that the district court's limited relief for the narrow class of right-place/wrong-precinct ballots caused by poll-worker error—which has no effect on the design of precinct ballots—will undermine Ohio's precinct system or make ballots more confusing.

Turning to the fourth *Sandusky* factor, the State claims that the district court's remedy makes it more difficult to monitor the voting process and prevent election fraud. According to the State,

> moving toward a system in which (absent new and affirmative evidentiary "verification" actions by the boards) the total potential number of provisional ballots that must be counted is not capped by reference to the number of registered voters assigned to a given precinct, or capable of estimation at any time until after the polls have closed would, almost by definition, make it more difficult for elections officials to monitor and keep up with the voting process.

Not only will the injunction make it more difficult to administer the election on election day, the State argues, but it will make it more difficult for the State to comply with the federal safe harbor deadline for Presidential electors, December 11, 2012. *See* 3 U.S.C. § 5; O.R.C. § 3515.041. Beyond these administrative burdens, [an amicus brief argues] that the district court's remedy opens the door to more poll-worker error, which will result in the dilution of proper votes via the counting of ineligible votes. We find neither argument persuasive.

First, the record does not support the State's fear that the district court's limited remedy will increase the number of voters attempting to cast votes at the wrong polling location or facilitating voter fraud. Barring substantial numbers of recalcitrant voters insisting on casting wrong-precinct votes—again, a phenomenon not supported by the record or logic—the district court's limited remedy should not burden poll workers with longer lines or tax county boards with an unmanageable number of ballot verifications after election day. Second, neither the State nor amici present evidence that county boards err in remaking wrong-precinct ballots to count only votes in "up-ballot" races. The State's chief election official apparently believes that poll workers and county boards can both implement the district court's injunctive relief and perform their other election duties within the time allotted.

iii. Conclusion

In sum, while the *Sandusky* factors reflect a state's legitimate interests in maintaining a precinct-based election system, the State does not show how these interests support the specific restriction challenged here: the summary rejection of poll-worker-induced right-place/wrong-precinct ballots. Because the State fails to identify precise interests justifying this substantial burden, we agree with the district court that the plaintiffs have shown a likely equal protection violation.

b. Due Process & Disqualification Despite Poll-Worker Error

The voter burden identified by the plaintiffs likewise supports the district court's finding of a probable due process violation. The Due Process Clause protects against extraordinary voting restrictions that render the voting system fundamentally unfair. [G]arden variety election irregularities do not rise to that level, but substantial changes to state election procedures and/or the implementation of non-uniform standards run afoul of due process if they result in significant disenfranchisement and vote dilution. So too do state actions that induce voters to miscast their votes.

Although this issue was not ripe at the time, *Hunter* expressed "substantial constitutional concerns regarding the invalidation of votes cast in the wrong precinct due solely to poll-worker error."

Ohio has created a system in which state actors (poll workers) are given the ultimate responsibility of directing voters to the right location to vote. Yet, the state law penalizes the voter when a poll worker directs the voter to the wrong precinct, and the penalty, disenfranchisement, is a harsh one indeed. To disenfranchise citizens whose only error was relying on poll-worker instructions appears to us to be fundamentally unfair.

The plaintiffs have shown, and the State does not deny, that poll-worker error causes thousands of qualified voters to cast wrong-precinct ballots from the correct polling locations.

Even so, the State argues that a due process violation requires intentional conduct. It appears we have not opined on the scienter necessary for a voting restriction to violate due process. Yet, accepting the State's premise, we find sufficient indicia of purposeful conduct in the State's intent to enforce its strict disqualification rules without exception, despite the systemic poll-worker error identified in this litigation and others. *Hunter* shed light on this problem last year, but the State persisted in its position. In light of the well-documented problem of wrong-precinct provisional ballots caused by poll-worker error, resulting in the rejection of thousands of provisional ballots each year, we have no basis on which to disagree with the district court's finding of a likely due process violation.

2. Irreparable Injury, Substantial Harm to Others, Public Interest

Turning to the equitable considerations, the State does not contest the district court's core findings of irreparable harm to the voter and absence of harm to others. Rather, it offers only vague public-interest concerns, speculating that the injunction will spawn additional poll-worker error, vote dilution, and post-election litigation. The State has not shown that the district court abused its discretion in weighing the equitable considerations.

Nor has the State shown abuse in the district court's fashioning of injunctive relief tailored to the identified harm. The State would disqualify thousands of right-place/wrong-precinct provisional ballots, where the voter's only mistake was relying on the poll-worker's precinct guidance. That path unjustifiably burdens these voters' fundamental right to vote. Recognizing that a prospective remedy could not undo all of the harm occasioned by poll-worker error, the district court crafted a narrow remedy that preserves as much of a miscast ballot as possible. The Secretary has now adopted regulations implementing the district court's limited remedy for right-place/wrong-precinct provisional ballots. These regulations enable the State to identify and document recalcitrant voters that disregard poll-workers' precinct instructions, so that these provisional ballots can be excluded. Because the State offers no persuasive reason to disturb the district court's remedy, as implemented by the Secretary, we affirm the wrong-precinct aspect of the preliminary injunction.

C. The Deficient-Affirmation Ballots

The district court identified only one probable constitutional violation as supporting the injunction's deficient-affirmation remedy: the unreasonableness of disqualifying deficient-affirmation ballots caused by poll-worker error, in derogation of equal protection. Because the spotty record and Ohio law do not support the district court's presumption of poll-worker error, we find no likely constitutional violation and reverse this aspect of the preliminary injunction.

In our view, the difficulty in measuring the voter burden imposed by the ballot-affirmation requirement stems from the fact that all of the identified deficiencies arise from voters' failure to follow the form's rather simple instructions: (1) print name, (2) provide identification, and (3) sign the affirmation appearing at the bottom. Even the last step is optional, because Ohio law permits voters to cast a provisional ballot without signing the affirmation upon notifying a poll worker. Contrary to the district court's suggestion, Ohio law does not task poll-workers with quality control of ballot affirmations.

During oral argument, the [plaintiffs] conceded that Ohio's ballot-affirmation requirement imposes a lesser burden on voters than Ohio's precinct requirement. In light of Ohio's similar signature requirements for casting regular ballots with proper identification, absentee ballots, and issue petitions, we agree. Ohio's legitimate interests in election oversight and fraud prevention easily justify the minimal, unspecified burden asserted by the plaintiffs. Because the plaintiffs have not shown a likelihood of success on the merits, we reverse the preliminary injunction's deficient-affirmation remedy.

CONCLUSION

For the above reasons, we affirm in part and reverse in part the district court's preliminary injunction. Specifically, the preliminary injunction's wrong-precinct remedy is affirmed, and the deficient-affirmation remedy is reversed.

SERVICE EMPLOYEES INTERNATIONAL UNION LOCAL 1 v. HUSTED

698 F.3d 341 (6th Cir. 2012)

PER CURIAM.

The State of Ohio and Jon Husted, Ohio's Secretary of State ("Secretary"), move for a stay pending appeal of the district court's October 26, 2012 order granting the plaintiffs' renewed motion for a preliminary injunction. The order requires Ohio and the Secretary to count provisional ballots cast in the wrong polling place due to poll-worker error—so-called wrong-place/wrong-precinct ballots—in the November 6, 2012 election. We grant the motion.

We recently affirmed a preliminary injunction entered by the district court on August 27, 2012, directing Ohio and the Secretary to count right-place/wrong-precinct provisional ballots caused by poll-worker error in the upcoming election. *See Ne. Ohio Coal. for the Homeless v. Husted* (6th Cir. 2012) [hereinafter *NEOCH*]. In that opinion, we noted that the August 27 order did not require the counting of wrong-place/wrong-precinct ballots. But we expressed no view on whether the refusal to count such ballots imposed an unconstitutional burden on voters, leaving the question open for possible future litigation. On October 17, the plaintiffs filed a renewed motion for a preliminary injunction in the district court that would mandate the counting of wrong-place/wrong-precinct ballots, reiterating a request made in their original June 22, 2012 motion for a preliminary injunction but not included in the August 27 order. The district court granted the renewed motion after a hearing. Ohio and the Secretary unsuccessfully moved for a stay of the preliminary injunction during the hearing, prompting this emergency appeal.

We begin by considering the likelihood that the district court's preliminary injunction order will be upheld on appeal. This involves examination of the four factors the district court considered when assessing the plaintiffs' motion for a preliminary injunction—likelihood of success on the merits, irreparable harm to the moving party, harm to other parties, and the public interest. While a grant or denial of a preliminary injunction is reviewed for an abuse of discretion, we are mindful that a preliminary injunction is an extraordinary form of relief and that the moving party in the district court has the burden of proving that the circumstances clearly demand it.

Ohio and the Secretary are quite likely to demonstrate on appeal that plaintiffs failed to show a strong likelihood of success on the merits of their constitutional claims with respect to wrong-place/wrong-precinct ballots. The salient feature of the right-place/wrong-precinct problem addressed in *NEOCH* is the disenfranchisement of voters who arrive at the correct polling place (and are otherwise eligible to vote) solely as a consequence of poll-worker error, a situation caused by Ohio's system of multi-precinct polling places. Yet, the district court's expanded preliminary injunction glosses over this distinguishing feature—that the voter arrived at the correct polling place—by finding that Ohio law imposes an "identical" burden on voters who cast wrong-place/wrong-precinct ballots.

In other words, because poll workers make the same errors, the voter burden must be the same. This conclusion absolves voters of all responsibility for voting in the correct precinct or correct polling place by assessing voter burden solely on the basis of the outcome—i.e., the state's ballot validity determination. While poll-worker error may contribute to the occurrence of wrong-place/wrong-precinct ballots, the burden on these *voters* certainly differs from the burden on right-place/wrong-precinct voters—and likely decreases—because the wrong-place/wrong-precinct voter took affirmative steps to arrive at the wrong polling location. The district court abused its discretion by failing to distinguish these burdens.

Though voters must rely heavily on poll workers to direct them to the proper precinct in a multi-precinct voting place, they are not as dependent on poll workers to identify their correct polling place. Ohio law requires election officials to provide notice to voters of where they are eligible to vote after they register or if their precinct changes. *See* Ohio Rev. Code § 3503.16(E) (change in address of voter); *id.* § 3503.17 (change in precinct boundaries); *id.* § 3503.19(C)(1) (new voters). Furthermore, information about where to vote is easily accessible by calling county boards of elections or accessing the Secretary's webpage. In our view, a voter who fails to utilize these tools and arrives at the wrong polling location cannot be said to be blameless in the same way as a right-place/wrong-precinct voter. And the district court's findings of thousands of rejected wrong-precinct ballots overstates the sparse evidence of poll workers sending voters to the wrong polling location.

Even assuming that Ohio law imposes an "identical" burden on wrong-place/wrong-precinct voters, the state's interest in enforcing a particular rule varies according to the impact of non-enforcement on its legitimate interests. We suggested in the *NEOCH* opinion that shifting all responsibility for determining the proper polling place to poll workers would have far-reaching implications for Ohio's precinct-based voting system that go well beyond the issues created by multi-precinct polling places.

Moreover, the district court's injunction, in disregarding the importance of voting place, has a significant effect on the State's legitimate interest in maintaining its precinct-based voting system. Unlike the prior injunction, the expanded injunction opens the door for steering last-second voters to convenient (though incorrect) polling places, in the hopes that some of the votes will count. This perverse incentive did not exist with right-place/wrong-precinct voters; voters who make the effort to arrive at the correct polling place would have no reason to miscast their vote at the wrong table or in the wrong line. And even if shorter precinct lines presented such an incentive for a handful of those voters, the district court's August 27 preliminary injunction requires poll-workers to inform voters that a miscast vote would not count. These considerations lead us to conclude that Ohio and the Secretary will more than likely demonstrate on appeal that the plaintiffs failed to "show more than a mere possibility of success" on the merits of their constitutional claim.

Turning to the plaintiffs' assertions of irreparable harm, the obstacles the plaintiffs will face in defending the wrong-place/wrong-precinct injunction on appeal become manifest. [P]laintiffs' original appellate briefing tacitly acknowledged the district court's failure to grant broader relief for wrong-place/wrong-precinct ballots by arguing that the record—not the district court's opinion—justified such relief. Accordingly, it is fair to say that, following our decision in *NEOCH*, the plaintiffs *renewed* their request for broader injunctive relief by repeating arguments with no new facts or law to support them.

As a general rule, last-minute injunctions changing election procedures are strongly disfavored. *Purcell v. Gonzalez* (2006) ("Court orders affecting elections . . . can themselves result in voter confusion. . . . As an election draws closer, that risk will increase."); *Ne. Coal. for the Homeless v. Blackwell* (6th Cir. 2006) ("[T]here is a strong public interest in smooth and effective administration of the voting laws that militates against changing the rules in the middle of submission of absentee ballots."). The application of that principle is particularly appropriate when a party does not seek to clarify or expand the scope of relief after having an opportunity to do so, in the district court and on appeal, in the months before an election, and then asks for reconsideration of that relief days before an election. The plaintiffs' failure to act earlier in pursuing these claims significantly undermines their assertions of irreparable harm in the absence of the injunction.

Meanwhile, the harm to Ohio, the Secretary, and the general public caused by issuance of this injunction easily outweighs any potential harm to the plaintiffs if their view of the law is eventually determined to be correct. The injunction, it should be noted, *both* requires the expedited issuance of new instructions to poll workers less than two weeks before the election *and* refuses enforcement of a presumptively constitutional policy regarding voter eligibility. *Blackwell* ("There is . . . a strong public interest in permitting legitimate statutory processes to operate to preclude voting by those who are not entitled to vote."). Moreover, the inevitable result of the injunction's dramatic changes to Ohio's precinct voting system will be interference with orderly election administration and greater confusion among poll workers and voters. Early voting is already underway in Ohio. Changing election rules in this manner while voting is occurring disrupts the electoral process and threatens its fairness. These harms to the public and its elected government are significant ones. We therefore find that Ohio and the Secretary have demonstrated a high likelihood of success on their appeal of the October 27 preliminary injunction.

For these reasons, we grant Ohio and the Secretary's emergency motion to stay the district court's October 26, 2012 order.

F. The Limits of Litigation as a Tool of Election Law Reform

Building on *Hunter*, the *NEOCH* decision concerning "right church, wrong pew" ballots was a big victory for the use of the Fourteenth Amendment as a constraint on the wrongful disenfranchisement of voters by state law. Together with the Obama campaign's victory over Ohio's rollback of early voting (in *Obama for America v. Husted*, page 673), *NEOCH* demonstrated that it is possible for voting rights advocates to employ federal court litigation as a tactic for reforming a state's voting laws.

Still, it is important not to overstate these victories. Both *NEOCH* and the early voting case are situations in which the federal judges saw state law as flunking the "no arbitrariness" principle of *Bush v. Gore*, and it is rare that judges will view a state's election law as arbitrary. Indeed, the Sixth Circuit's decisions to uphold Ohio's disqualification of ballots in both the "*wrong* church, wrong pew" and the erroneous ballot-affirmation situations, neither of which the court considered arbitrary, illustrate the limits of the "no arbitrariness" test.

Moreover, there will be many aspects of election law that are untouchable by the federal judiciary, no matter how much voting rights advocates might wish for reform in these areas. For example, reformers would like to eliminate using the Electoral College as the mechanism for presidential elections on the ground that it unequally gives residents of small states like Wyoming a disproportionate share of Electoral Votes compared to large states like California. Nonetheless, despite the doctrine of one person, one vote articulated in *Reynolds v. Sims* and reaffirmed in *Bush v. Gore*, this doctrine cannot be used to invalidate the Electoral College since it is specifically mandated by other provisions of the U.S. Constitution. In other words, no matter how activist the federal judiciary might become in enforcing the principle of one-person, one-vote, purportedly part of the Fourteenth Amendment, the judiciary will not use it to void other explicit provisions of the U.S. Constitution. On this point, see *New v. Ashcroft*, 293 F. Supp. 2d 256 (E.D.N.Y. 2003) (internal quotations omitted):

> The Court is not empowered to strike the document's text on the basis that it is offensive to itself or is in some way internally inconsistent. In other words, the Electoral College cannot be questioned constitutionally because it is established by the Constitution.

We close, therefore, with two cases that further demonstrate the limits on using federal constitutional law to invalidate a state's choice of voting practices: one involving the use of electronic voting machines and the other about San Francisco's unique electoral system under which voters rank the candidates in order of preference. Both cases demonstrate how states still have wide leeway in administering their elections.

ANDRADE v. NAACP OF AUSTIN

345 S.W.3d 1 (Tex. 2011)

Chief Justice JEFFERSON delivered the opinion of the Court.

Technology is changing the way we vote. It has not eliminated controversy about the way votes are recorded and verified. We must decide whether voters have standing to pursue complaints about an electronic voting machine that does not produce a contemporaneous paper record of each vote. Because we conclude that most of the voters' allegations involve generalized grievances about the lawfulness of government acts, and because their remaining claims fail on their merits, we reverse the court of appeals' judgment and render judgment dismissing the case.

I. BACKGROUND

Voters in different parts of the state utilize a number of different voting systems, all of which must first be certified by the Secretary of State. To obtain certification, voting system manufacturers must submit an application to a board of examiners appointed by the Secretary and the Attorney General. After the board prepares a report, the Secretary conducts a public hearing to provide interested persons an opportunity to express their views about a particular system. The Secretary reviews the report, considers public input, and determines whether the system has satisfied the applicable approval requirements. If so, she certifies the system for use in elections. For each application, she submits a report explaining whether the system was approved. Once a system is certified, local political subdivisions may adopt it for use in elections.

Following certification and adoption, additional testing is required for direct recording electronic machines (DREs). DREs are designed to allow a direct vote on the machine by the manual touch of a screen, monitor, or other device. DREs store individual votes and vote totals electronically, usually in several places within the unit. Immediately after receiving a DRE from a vendor, the election records custodian must perform a hardware diagnostic test and a "public test of logic and accuracy." The latter involves creating a testing board that will then cast votes, verifying that each contest can be voted and is accurately counted. The test must evaluate, to the extent possible, undervotes, overvotes, straight-party votes, and crossover votes. It must also account for write-in and provisional votes. Notice of the test must be published at least forty-eight hours in advance, and the test is open to the public. The test is successful only if the actual results are identical to the expected results. Travis County conducts these tests before each early voting period and election day. The Secretary of State may prescribe additional testing. DREs must also satisfy, to the extent possible, requirements applicable to other electronic voting systems.

In countywide polling place programs, the Secretary requires an audit of each DRE before, after, and, if feasible, during each election. The general custodian of election records must secure access control keys or passwords to DREs, and use of such keys and passwords must be witnessed and documented. The DRE may not be connected to any external communications network, including the Internet, nor are wireless communications permitted (except under certain limited circumstances). The general custodian of election records must create a contingency plan in case of DRE failure.

Copies of the program codes, operator manuals, and copies or units of all other software and any other information, specifications, or documentation required by the

Secretary must be kept on file with the Secretary. The Secretary also requires that DREs meet or exceed the minimum requirements established by the Federal Election Commission. Although DREs must provide contemporaneous printouts of "significant election events," there is no explicit statutory requirement that DREs provide a contemporaneous paper record of each vote cast. Repeated efforts to pass such legislation have failed, both at the federal and state levels.

The eSlate, a paperless DRE manufactured by Hart Intercivic, is one of a handful of DREs the Secretary has certified. Voters arriving at the polls in counties using the eSlate are given a unique access code. The voter enters the code into the eSlate, which then displays the ballot. Voters turn a dial to highlight their ballot choice and then press "enter" to make a selection. After a voter completes his selections, the eSlate displays a ballot summary page. If the voter's choices are correctly displayed, the voter presses the "cast ballot" button, and the vote is recorded. Travis County purchased the eSlate system in 2001 and has used it since 2003.

The NAACP of Austin, Sonia Santana (a Travis County voter), and David Van Os (a candidate for attorney general) (collectively, the voters), sued Esperanza Andrade, the Secretary of State, arguing that her certification of the eSlate violated the Election Code and our constitution. The voters assert that the Secretary's failure to require a contemporaneous paper record of an electronic vote violates their statutory right to a recount and an audit, as well as Texas constitutional guarantees of equal protection, the purity of the ballot box, and the right of suffrage. The voters sought a declaration that the Secretary acted illegally and an injunction prohibiting the use of paperless election systems without an independent paper ballot mechanism.*

II. THE VOTERS HAVE STANDING TO ASSERT AN EQUAL PROTECTION CLAIM

The Secretary urges a blanket rule that would ensure no voter ever has standing to challenge a voting system. We think the Secretary overreaches in that respect. The voters assert a denial of equal protection—a claim voters often have standing to bring. *See Baker v. Carr* (1962) (noting that voters have standing to bring equal protection challenges to complain of vote dilution). For example, the Supreme Court has permitted Virginia residents to sue for a declaration that Virginia's poll tax was unconstitutional. *Harper v. Va. State Bd. of Elections* (1966). It has allowed a Hawaii voter to challenge as unconstitutional the state's ban on write-in candidates. *Burdick v. Takushi* (1992). While equal protections claims involving the use of DREs have been largely unsuccessful, none has been dismissed for lack of standing.

* Editors' note: Although this case is decided in state court under state law, imagine whether the analysis or result would be any different if the same plaintiffs had sought relief in federal court under federal law based on the same underlying factual allegations.

III. THE STATE'S REGULATORY INTEREST JUSTIFIES THIS REASONABLE, NONDISCRIMINATORY RESTRICTION ON THE RIGHT TO VOTE

We turn then to the merits of the voters' equal protection challenge, cognizant that the Secretary retains immunity from suit unless the voters have pleaded a viable claim.

The voters assert two equal protections claims. Broadly, they complain that voters who cast paper ballots have a greater level of protection against fraud or system malfunction than DRE voters do. The voters do not allege that DREs are less accurate—that they suffer from higher error rates or lead to more invalid ballots—than other voting systems. Instead, they complain that DREs' vulnerabilities make it more likely that votes will be manipulated or lost. More narrowly, the voters make a recount-related claim. Recounts of "regular paper ballots" are conducted manually, by a counting team composed of three individuals. One person reads the ballots; the other two tally the votes. Votes from DREs are recounted differently. A person requesting a recount of electronic voting system ballots has three choices: (1) an electronic recount using the same program as the original count; (2) if the program is defective, an electronic recount using the corrected program; or (3) a manual recount. The voters assert that the paperless computerized voting systems only allow for a retabulation of the votes cast and recorded, which creates a disparity in the manual recount methodology. Voters not required to use the DRE (absentee, military, or those living in a Texas county that does not use the eSlate) are granted the right to a hand recount of votes, and the voters allege that this recount disparity violates constitutional equal protection guarantees.

The right to vote is fundamental, as it preserves all other rights. *Yick Wo v. Hopkins* (1886); *see also Bush* [*v. Gore*]. But that does not mean states cannot regulate the franchise. Instead, the Supreme Court has explained that laws impacting the right to vote must be evaluated on a sliding scale: when the law severely restricts the right to vote, the regulation must be narrowly drawn to advance a compelling state interest. *Burdick.* But when a state election law provision imposes "'reasonable, nondiscriminatory restrictions'" upon voters' constitutional rights, "'the State's important regulatory interests are generally sufficient to justify' the restrictions." *Id.*

So our initial determination depends on the severity of the burden on the right to vote. The United States Court of Appeals for the Ninth Circuit, one of three federal circuit courts to reject equal protection challenges to DREs, has held that the use of paperless, touchscreen voting systems does not severely restrict the right to vote. *Weber v. Shelley* (9th Cir. 2003). As that court noted, DREs "bring[ ] about numerous positive changes (increasing voter turnout, having greater accuracy than traditional systems, being user-friendly, decreasing the number of mismarked ballots, saving money, etc.)." *Id.* That court held that, under *Burdick,* the use of DREs was not subject to greater scrutiny simply because the system may make the possibility of some kinds of fraud more difficult to detect.

We cannot say that use of paperless, touchscreen voting systems severely restricts the right to vote. No balloting system is perfect. Traditional paper ballots, as became evident during the 2000 presidential election, are prone to overvotes, undervotes, "hanging chads," and other mechanical and human errors that may thwart voter intent. *See generally Bush v. Gore.* Meanwhile, touchscreen voting systems remedy a number of these problems, albeit at the hypothetical price of vulnerability to programming "worms." The [DRE] does not leave Riverside voters without any protection from fraud, or any means of verifying votes, or any way to audit or recount. The unfortunate reality is that the possibility of electoral fraud can never be *completely* eliminated, no matter which type of ballot is used. Weber points out that none of the advantages of touch-screen systems over traditional methods would be sacrificed if voter-verified paper ballots were added to touchscreen systems. However, it is the job of democratically-elected representatives to weigh the pros and cons of various balloting systems. So long as their choice is reasonable and neutral, it is free from judicial second-guessing. In this instance, California made a reasonable, politically neutral and non-discriminatory choice to certify touchscreen systems as an alternative to paper ballots. Likewise, Riverside County in deciding to use such a system. Nothing in the Constitution forbids this choice.

The Eleventh Circuit came to a similar conclusion. *See Wexler v. Anderson* (11th Cir. 2006). Specifically, in considering whether differing recount mechanisms for DRE votes deprived DRE voters of equal protection, the court noted that "the differences [in] procedures [were] necessary given the differences in the technologies themselves and the types of errors voters are likely to make in utilizing those technologies." *Id.* DRE voters were less likely to cast ambiguous votes than were voters using, say, optical scan ballots, on which a voter might leave a stray pencil mark or circle a candidate's name rather than filling in the appropriate bubble. Moreover, the court noted that DREs had certain benefits, making voting more accessible to disabled voters and preventing some voter errors that were common with optical scan machines. Thus, Florida's regulatory interests justified the manual recount procedures and, "therefore, they do not violate equal protection." *Wexler.*

Adopting the reasoning of *Weber* and *Wexler,* the Georgia Supreme Court has also rejected an equal protection challenge to that state's DRE system, as has the Superior Court of New Jersey. We agree with the conclusions reached by those courts. DREs are not perfect. No voting system is. We cannot say that DREs impose severe restrictions on voters, particularly in light of the significant benefits such machines offer. As the *Wexler* court noted, different recount methodologies are necessary for DREs because ambiguous votes—often scrutinized during recounts—are virtually eliminated. A DRE with a voter-verified paper audit trail may provide more security; it may not. But the equal protection clause does not require infallibility. The Secretary made a reasonable, nondiscriminatory choice to certify the eSlate, a decision justified by the State's important regulatory interests. "[N]othing in the constitution forbids that choice." *Weber.*

CONCLUSION

The voters raise legitimate concerns about system integrity and vulnerability. But these are policy disputes more appropriately resolved in the give-and-take of politics. Perhaps the Secretary will decide, as California has, to de-certify certain DREs. Perhaps the Legislature will require a contemporaneous paper record of votes cast, or perhaps Texas will curtail or abandon DRE use altogether. But we cannot say the Secretary's decision to certify this device violated the voters' equal protection rights. We reverse the court of appeals' judgment and render judgment dismissing the case.

DUDUM v. ARNTZ

640 F.3d 1098 (9th Cir. 2011)

BERZON, Circuit Judge:

In 1873, Charles Lutwidge Dodgson, better known by his pen name, Lewis Carroll, spotted what he took to be an "extraordinary injustice": using simple plurality voting to determine the winners of elections. Dodgson, celebrated for his whimsical classics *Alice's Adventures in Wonderland* and *Through the Looking Glass,* was also a mathematician who developed election systems—meaning, simply, methods for translating preferences, or votes, into winners of elections. Dodgson disliked simple plurality voting because, in fields with several candidates, it can elect a candidate who receives the most first-place votes but is strongly *disfavored* by a majority of the electorate. Dodgson's innovative election systems were designed to remedy that limitation, and are still praised today because they tend to elect candidates with widespread electoral support.

While Dodgson preferred his systems to simple plurality voting, he recognized that his innovations were themselves imperfect. In a letter accompanying one of his pamphlets, Dodgson lamented: "A really scientific method for arriving at the result which is, on the whole, most satisfactory to a body of electors, seems to be still a desideratum."

Over a century later, Dodgson's wish remains unfulfilled. No perfect election system has been devised. Nonetheless, some governmental entities continue to experiment with innovative methods for electing candidates. At issue here is one such system, used by San Francisco for the election of certain city officials.

FACTUAL AND PROCEDURAL HISTORY

In March 2002, San Francisco voters approved a ballot measure, Proposition A, amending the City Charter to adopt a new electoral system for certain municipal elections. Before adoption of Proposition A, most city officials were selected in a two-round election: The city first held a general election. Then, unless one candidate won an outright majority in the first-round election, the two candidates who had garnered the most votes faced each other in a runoff election. Proposition A implemented instant runoff voting ("IRV") to replace the two-round runoff election system for the following city offices: Mayor, Sheriff,

District Attorney, City Attorney, Treasurer, Assessor-Recorder, Public Defender, and members of the Board of Supervisors.

IRV allows voters to rank, in order of preference, candidates for a single office. The Department of Elections (the "Department") then tabulates the voters' preferences as follows: First, all first-choice rankings indicated on the ballots are counted. If a candidate wins a majority of these first-choice votes, he wins the election. If not, the candidate who received the fewest first-choice votes is "eliminated," meaning that that candidate cannot win the election. The second-choice votes on the ballots that had selected the eliminated candidate are then distributed to those voters' second-choice candidates. Some candidates' vote totals, as a result, now reflect a combination of first- and second-choice votes. If all candidates ranked by a voter are eliminated, that voters' ballot is "exhausted," meaning that it is not recounted as the tabulation continues. As long as no candidate receives a majority of the votes from the "continuing" ballots—that is, the nonexhausted ballots—the process of eliminating candidates, transferring preferences, and "exhausting" ballots repeats. A candidate is declared elected when he receives a majority of the operative votes on the "continuing" ballots.

San Francisco's Charter provides that IRV ballots are to allow voters to rank a number of candidates equal to the total number of candidates running in an election. For instance, if ten candidates are running for mayor, then voters are to be able to rank all ten of them. But the Charter also provides that if the voting system or equipment used by the Department cannot "feasibly accommodate" ranking that many choices, the Director of Elections can limit the number of candidates voters may rank to no fewer than three. We refer to this variant as "restricted IRV."

As it has turned out, in all of the City's IRV elections since Proposition A passed, the Department has restricted the number of rankings on each ballot to three. San Francisco maintains, and the plaintiffs, several San Francisco voters (collectively "Dudum"), do not dispute, that this choice is one of necessity: The voting machines currently in use are not equipped to tabulate unlimited rankings; cost and logistical concerns make accommodating the unlimited option untenable; and providing a ballot on which voters may rank every candidate in a large field could result in confusion, voter error, and inaccuracies in vote calculation.

The Department makes publicly available on its website tables showing the election results for the City's past IRV elections. These tables tally the total ballots cast in each election; provide synopses of vote distribution during the tabulation process and of the final votes attributed to each candidate; and show the numbers of ballots "exhausted" as the tabulations proceeded. These tables provide helpful illustrations of how restricted IRV has worked in practice.

Dudum filed suit in federal court seeking injunctive relief against San Francisco and its election officials. Principally, Dudum maintains that when more than four candidates run for a particular office, the restricted IRV system precludes some groups of voters from participating to the same extent as others. That argument is premised on an analogy: It would be unconstitutional, Dudum asserts, to prevent qualified voters from casting ballots in a runoff election; "exhausting" the ballot of a voter who would have ranked more than three candidates if allowed to do so, Dudum contends, is no different. Dudum also points out that the City's Charter declares that "exhausted" ballots are "*not counted* in further stages of the tabulation," and argues that not including the votes of certain voters in the later tabulation stages once all three of their chosen candidates have been eliminated is similar to disenfranchisement of those voters, and so unconstitutional. In support of those arguments, Dudum points to several recent elections in which significant numbers of ballots were "exhausted" before tabulation was completed, sometimes in numbers greater than the final margin of victory. Dudum maintains that as a result of the mandatory "exhaustion" feature and its impact, the restricted IRV system violates the First Amendment, the Equal Protection and Due Process clauses of the Fourteenth Amendment, and the Civil Rights Act, 42 U.S.C. § 1983. He requests declaratory and injunctive relief prohibiting the City from using the system in future elections.

Agreeing that material facts are not in dispute, the parties filed cross-motions for summary judgment. The district court granted summary judgment for the City on all claims. Dudum appealed.

DISCUSSION

A. Overview

As a way of "structuring elections," San Francisco's IRV system is fairly innovative in the context of American elections, yet has a historied pedigree. First developed in the 1870s by W.R. Ware, a professor at the Massachusetts Institute of Technology, instant runoff systems have been used in the United States and elsewhere at various times since then. Australia, Ireland, and London use IRV for certain elections, and several U.S. cities use versions of the restricted IRV system at issue here, including Oakland and Berkeley, California, and Minneapolis, Minnesota, among others.

Like all electoral systems, including widely-used systems such as plurality voting and two-round runoff elections, IRV offers a package of potential advantages and disadvantages. Dodgson's disappointed "desideratum" observation, made in 1877, remains true. For instance, in the familiar simple plurality system, sometimes called "first-past-the-post" elections, voters chose one candidate, and the winner is the candidate with the most votes. Plurality voting is widely used in the United States for single-office elections, including races for mayors and governors. Plurality voting has the benefit of simplicity: It is easy for voters to use, and also easy for voters to understand how their votes are tabulated and the winning candidate determined. Plurality voting also avoids the expense and burden of holding a runoff election.

But the system has less auspicious features as well. In contests with several candidates, it privileges candidates with a robust and organized core of support, even if they are strongly disapproved of by most of the electorate. Likewise, plurality voting allows a candidate to win with a small minority of the total votes cast when many candidates are on the ballot.

A two-round runoff system, sometimes called a "double-ballot" election, similarly has both significant strengths and troublesome weaknesses. In such a system, long used in many local elections and in some state races, voters select a single candidate in the first round of voting, much like plurality voting. If no candidate receives a majority of the vote, a second round of voting is held, in which voters choose between the two candidates who received the highest number of votes in the first round. Two-round runoff systems result in the election of candidates with majority support of those voters who turn out for the second election.

That majority support, however, is misleading in some respects. When the second- and third-place candidates, or second-, third-, and fourth-place candidates, are relatively close in a first-round election, a runoff scheme can arbitrarily eliminate a candidate who might otherwise have won the election at the runoff stage. Also, an elected candidate will likely receive support from voters who strongly preferred candidates eliminated in the first-round election, as voters may choose between the two candidates left standing on a "lesser of two evils" basis. And, of course, the system requires the expense and burden of holding two separate elections, and results in two different, albeit overlapping, electorate pools, the relative sizes of which can be affected by the choice of dates for the runoff round.

Unrestricted and restricted IRV systems eliminate the need for a separate runoff and ordinarily will result in the election of a candidate with more widespread support than would simple plurality voting. IRV systems also tend to produce fewer votes cast only for losing candidates—in academic parlance, "wasted votes"—than does straight plurality voting, because votes that would otherwise be cast for losing candidates can be redistributed to candidates with a chance of winning. Likewise, IRV systems allow the voters more say over who they want to represent them: if it is not to be their first choice, then they can choose a second.

Under restricted or unrestricted IRV, a candidate who did not receive the most number of first-choice votes can be elected. Whether that feature is a disadvantage or an advantage is, of course, debatable. Where, for instance, there is no candidate with a majority, and the vote spread between the top plurality candidates is small, the more nuanced IRV systems can be seen as better tests of the depth of voter support for each candidate than a simple first-past-the-post plurality system. Additionally, while both IRV systems allow voters to rank their preferences, neither system allows voters to *reconsider* their choices after seeing which candidates have a chance of winning. In other words, voters must submit their preferences before polls close, and, even though they might have chosen differently with more specific information about other voters' selections, they are not provided an opportunity to revise their choices. A two-round runoff system, in contrast, provides voters that opportunity through a new round of balloting in a runoff election. Finally, both IRV systems are unfamiliar to many voters, and so some voters might not entirely understand how their votes will affect the election.

Moreover, all voting systems in elections with more than two candidates can be manipulated through strategic voting. In a plurality voting scheme, a voter might choose a candidate who is not his first-choice preference, but who he believes has a realistic chance of winning. In a two-round runoff system, a voter might cast a vote in the first-stage election for a weak candidate, so that his actual first-choice candidate will face that weak candidate in the runoff. The risk of strategic voting exists in IRV but is less severe than in plurality voting or the first stage of a runoff election: Voters are more free to vote their true preferences, because they face less of a threat of having their votes entirely "wasted" on unsuccessful candidates.

In sum, restricted IRV, like every election system, offers a menu of benefits and limitations. But that observation does not mean it is a constitutionally acceptable system, so we now turn to Dudum's constitutional objections to the City's restricted IRV system.

B. The Burden on Voters

Dudum concentrates on challenging the three-rank restriction aspect of San Francisco's system. We consider below the characteristics of restricted IRV Dudum does challenge, to determine the degree to which those features burden voters' constitutional rights, if at all, and if so, whether the burdens are so severe as to trigger strict scrutiny.

1

Dudum first contends that the treatment accorded "exhausted" ballots as the vote tabulation proceeds under the City's restricted IRV scheme is akin to prohibiting certain voters from voting in an election, and so imposes a severe, or at least a serious, burden on voters' constitutional rights. To support that characterization, Dudum points out that IRV replaced a two-round runoff system, and that explanations of how IRV works often analogize the successive vote calculation steps to a series of elections. For instance, the supervisors who supported adoption of Proposition A stated in their official ballot argument that "[t]he 'instant' runoff works much like December's 'delayed' runoff."

But the analogy is just that—an analogy. Upon examination, the analogy is off the mark in describing the real impacts of restricted IRV on voters' opportunities to cast ballots.

In actuality, all voters participating in a restricted IRV election are afforded a single and equal opportunity to express their preferences for three candidates; voters can use all three preferences, or fewer if they choose. Most notably, once the polls close and calculations begin, no new *votes* are cast. To determine the winner of the election based on that single set of votes cast, restricted IRV uses an algorithm. The ballots, each representing three or fewer preferences, are the initial inputs; the sequence of calculations mandated by restricted IRV is used to arrive at a single output—one winning candidate. The series of calculations required by the algorithm to produce the winning candidate are simply steps of a single tabulation, not separate rounds of voting.

In contrast, a two-round runoff system involves at least two rounds of voting, or *inputs,* explaining why it is sometimes referred to as a "double-ballot" election. For instance, in a two-round runoff system, even if a voter's chosen candidate in the first round successfully proceeds to the runoff election, that voter is still afforded an opportunity in the runoff election to select a different candidate, or not to vote at all. In a restricted IRV system, in contrast, if that voter chooses a successful candidate in one round, he is *not* afforded the opportunity to switch his vote to a different candidate as the tabulation progresses. That is so because restricted IRV considers only one round of inputs, i.e., votes.

Restricted IRV, of course, can be used *in place of* a two-round runoff election, which is what occurred in San Francisco and explains why the city supervisors compared the two. But restricted IRV does not *replicate* a two-round runoff system because, as we just explained, in two-round runoffs, voters cast ballots twice—that is, make and record their choices twice—whereas IRV allows only one chance to vote.

Dudum's contention that restricted IRV threatens to exclude some voters from *voting* is therefore incorrect. The contention sidesteps the basic fact that there is only one round of voting in restricted IRV.

2

Dudum tries a second tack: He maintains that the tabulation scheme under San Francisco's system burdens voters' constitutional rights to vote by effectively discarding, rather than counting, the votes from "exhausted" ballots.

In support of this characterization, Dudum points to the text of two provisions in the San Francisco Charter: First, according to the Charter, voters whose ballots are "exhausted" do not have their ballots "counted in further stages of the tabulation." Second, a candidate wins the election when he receives "a majority of the votes from the continuing ballots," meaning the nonexhausted ballots. *Id.* § 13.102(c) & (d) (emphasis added). Dudum reads this text as meaning that "exhausted" ballots are discarded, and so not counted, in determining the election's ultimate outcome.

An examination of how restricted IRV works, however, indicates that the supposed inequity Dudum has identified is one of surface appearances and semantics, not substance. The algorithm used to determine the winner in an election conducted pursuant to the City's IRV system can be elaborated so that the outcome is mathematically identical, yet the features forming the basis of Dudum's characterization of the system as not counting some votes disappear. In essence, a more complete explication of the tabulation process demonstrates that "exhausted" ballots *are* counted in the election, they are simply counted as votes for losing candidates, just as if a voter had selected a losing candidate in a plurality or runoff election.

In other words, even though last-place candidates could no longer mathematically win the election, and could not obtain further votes, one could clutter the tabulation process by showing their votes on the tabulation tables even after they had been proven incapable of prevailing. The winner could then be defined as the candidate who receives a plurality of the *total votes cast* (including votes cast for candidates mathematically eliminated in prior stages), as long as he also receives a majority of the votes cast for candidates who were not mathematically eliminated previously. This "show your work" alternative—to quote many high school teachers—is more cumbersome than San Francisco's actual tabulation regime, but it accomplishes precisely the same result. As pertinent to Dudum's challenge, the rephrasing makes explicit what is implicit in the current scheme: "Exhausted" ballots *are* counted in the election, they are just counted for losing candidates in the tally of total votes. In the terms used by election experts, these are "wasted" votes, not because they aren't counted, but because they were cast for candidates not ultimately elected.

3

Dudum's final contention regarding the voting burden imposed by the restricted IRV system is that San Francisco's restricted IRV system is nonetheless unconstitutional because it results in the *dilution* of certain votes. Specifically, Dudum maintains that "some voters—those who vote for continuing candidates—only have one vote counted in 'the election'; other voters, however, have votes counted for three different candidates." Therefore, the argument goes, the City's IRV system violates the equal protection guarantee of "one person, one vote." At its core, Dudum's argument is that some voters are literally allowed more than one vote (i.e., they may cast votes for their first-, second-, and third-choice candidates), while others are not.

Once again, Dudum's contention mischaracterizes the actual operation of San Francisco's restricted IRV system and so cannot prevail. In fact, the option to rank multiple *preferences* is not the same as providing additional *votes,* or more heavily-weighted votes, relative to other votes cast. Each ballot is counted as no more than one vote at each tabulation step, whether representing the voters' first-choice candidate or the voters' second- or third-choice candidate, and each vote attributed to a candidate, whether a first-, second- or third-rank choice, is afforded the same mathematical weight in the election. The ability to rank multiple candidates simply provides a chance to have several preferences recorded and counted *sequentially,* not at once.

Dudum's vote dilution argument fails, because the ability to rank preferences sequentially does not affect the ultimate weight accorded any vote cast in the election.

Therefore, *if* the characteristics of the City's system Dudum has identified impose any burdens on the right to vote, they are minimal at best. For the sake of completeness, we shall assume *some* burden is imposed, however limited, and so consider whether the restricted IRV system serves governmental interests sufficient to justify that minimal at best burden under the flexible balancing analysis. *See, e.g.*, *Burdick*.

C. The Governmental Interests

Because restricted IRV does not impose severe burdens on voting rights, we do not apply strict scrutiny. And here, the City's "important regulatory interests" are more than substantial enough to justify the minimal at best burdens imposed by the City's chosen system.

1

Dudum challenges only the three-candidate limitation, not IRV generally. In light of that limited challenge, one would expect Dudum to argue that the interests advanced by the City *in favor of the three-candidate restriction* are inadequate. But Dudum does not contest those specific justifications. Instead, he argues that the interests advanced in favor of IRV *generally* can be served just as well by either a plurality system or a two-round runoff scheme. Dudum's logic seems to be that if the three-candidate limit imposes a burden on voting rights, and if the City maintains that it cannot eliminate that restriction, then restricted IRV should be compared to election systems whose constitutionality is not in question.

In the end, then, Dudum is effectively asking the court to choose between electoral systems (i.e., between restricted IRV, plurality voting, or two-round runoff elections). As explained, however, electoral systems serve diverse interests with various degrees of success. That is why, absent a truly serious burden on voting rights, it is the job of democratically-elected representatives to weigh the pros and cons of various [election] systems.

2

The City advances several interests justifying the minimal at best burdens of which Dudum complains. Some of those interests concern the three-candidate restriction, and some support IRV as compared to the two-round runoff system it replaced.

First, the City adduces evidence that (1) the current voting machines cannot process ballots allowing unlimited ranking, and (2) permitting voters to rank more than three candidates might exceed the memory capacity of the machines now in use. The City maintains that the state certification necessary for new voting software or hardware or for redesigned ballots could take months or years, so allowing unlimited choices would disrupt the City's preparation for upcoming elections. Moreover, contends the City, (1) because some elections include many candidates, allowing unlimited rankings would require either extremely large, confusing ballots or multiple ballots for each voter; (2) multiple ballots could lead to calculation errors; and (3) in testing, voters regarded ballots offering four choices as confusing. Notably, Dudum introduced no evidence suggesting that San Francisco *could* conduct unrestricted elections without running into the problems identified, and does not now argue that the City's interests are inadequate to justify the three-candidate restriction.

Assuming for the moment the constitutional validity of IRV systems generally, then, the three-candidate restriction furthers important interests in maintaining the orderly administration of San Francisco's elections and in avoiding voter confusion.

We could stop there, as Dudum purports to challenge only the three-rank restriction, not IRV generally. But even if we expand the comparative inquiry to other election systems, as Dudum would have us do, his challenge fares no better.

The City points to evidence that restricted IRV will save money compared to a two-round runoff system (the election system in place prior to IRV), as each runoff election costs the City between $1.5 million and $3 million. The interest in alleviating the costs and administrative burdens of conducting additional elections can be "a legitimate state objective" that also justifies the use of IRV, given the minimal at best burdens the system imposes on voters' constitutional rights to vote.

Further, restricted IRV advances the City's legitimate interests in providing voters an opportunity to express nuanced voting preferences and electing candidates with strong plurality support. Unlike a two-round runoff election, restricted IRV will not always produce a candidate with majority support. But restricted IRV also does not limit voters' choices to only two candidates, and so it allows voters to express a wider range of preferences. Moreover, in practice, the ability to express more nuanced preferences means that candidates with *greater* plurality support (although not necessarily majority support) tend to be elected, as compared to a traditional plurality system.

In sum, we have no difficulty holding that these important governmental interests are more than sufficient to outweigh the extremely limited burdens—if any—that the restricted IRV features Dudum challenges impose upon San Francisco's voters.

CONCLUSION

If the aspects of the City's restricted IRV scheme Dudum challenges impose any burdens on voters' constitutional rights to vote, they are minimal at best. Moreover, the City has advanced valid, sufficiently-important interests to justify using its system. We, of course, express no views on the wisdom of using IRV, restricted IRV, or any other electoral method. There is no perfect election system, and our search for one would prove no more successful than a hunt for the mythical snark. Happily, we are not required to engage in any such endeavor. We hold only that Dudum has not established that the City's chosen system is unconstitutional. Affirmed.

SUMMARY OF THE LAW OF VOTING

Of the four areas of election law that this book has covered, the Law of Voting is the one that has been most in turmoil since 2000 and is likely to undergo considerable additional changes in the future.

The basic rules of voter eligibility are fairly stable. Since the Warren Court revolution of the 1960s, the Equal Protection Clause of the U.S. Constitution essentially has required equal voting rights for all adult citizens. Apart from the extremely narrow category of individuals not mentally competent to exercise the franchise, the only exception to this constitutional requirement of equal eligibility to the franchise for all adult citizens is the explicit permission in the Fourteenth Amendment for felon disenfranchisement. And the federal courts of appeals have refused to apply and interpret the Voting Rights Act to invalidate felon disenfranchisement on the theory that it causes a racially discriminatory impact on African-American voters.

But even though the basic rules of voter eligibility have been stable during the last decade, the laws governing the operation of the voting process have been very much in flux. Some of the changes are statutory, with the enactment of the Help America Vote Act of 2002 and a myriad of new voting laws adopted by state legislatures. But a more fundamental jurisprudential shift has occurred because of the new applicability of the Equal Protection Clause to the rules for administering the casting and counting of ballots.

Bush v. Gore ushered in this shift, but it did not end there. Cases like *Crawford* (over new voter ID laws), *Obama for America v. Husted* (over rollbacks in early voting), and *Hunter v. Hamilton County* (over provisional ballots) illustrate the novel uses to which the Equal Protection Clause has been put in the aftermath of *Bush v. Gore*. By no means were all these new Equal Protection claims successful (*Crawford* was not), but some of them (like *Obama for America* and *Hunter*) were. Moreover, the sheer indeterminacy of the Equal Protection principle from *Bush v. Gore* and these subsequent cases invites even more litigation in the future.

Indeed, the last decade has been especially striking for just how voluminous the litigation over the voting process has been. The rules for absentee voting, the maintenance of voter registration databases, or polling place challenges—no aspect of the voting process has been immune from a lawsuit if a candidate, party, or interest group thinks that a judicial victory can help produce an electoral victory. The funds for this litigation (or the donation of attorney time) has been forthcoming to fuel the filing of all these new lawsuits. No end to this era of electoral litigiousness is in sight, at least not until the U.S. Supreme Court is able to provide much greater clarity to the meaning of Equal Protection in this context.

All of these new judicial decisions over the rules of the voting process, including *Bush v. Gore* itself, have prompted an additional observation: Is the judiciary up to the task of adjudicating these cases fairly and impartially? Some of the evidence—like the 2008 appellate-level cases over voter registration—seems disconcerting on this point. But in 2012 the judiciary, both state and federal, appeared to acquit itself quite well, acting as an appropriate check against inappropriate disenfranchisement imposed by apparently partisan legislatures.

What developments in the Law of Voting will occur in 2016 and 2020, the dates of our next two presidential elections? The judiciary's role in these elections may prove as unpredictable as the last four presidential election seasons (2000, 2004, 2008, and 2012). But of this, we can be confident: State legislatures will continue to enact changes in the voting process, often for apparent partisan advantage; lawsuits will be filed challenging these new rules, as well as implementing regulations adopted by secretaries of state and other election administrators; some elections will be close enough that ballot-by-ballot litigation over the outcome will be worthwhile; and problems that occurred in an inevitably imperfect administrative process will be examined under a judicial microscope. The Law of Voting will not lack excitement for the foreseeable future.

A CONCLUDING OBSERVATION

As you reflect on your examination of election law, is there any overarching way to tie together all four units that we have studied? Scholars in the field have searched for the "holy grail" of a unified theory of all election law. But much like physicists who seek a Grand Unified Theory that would tie together all four forces in nature (gravity, electromagnetism, and the strong and weak nuclear interactions), election law scholars so far have been unsuccessful in this quest. Or, to be precise, some such "general theories of election law" have been offered, but none have commanded a prevailing consensus in the field.

To be sure, there are some overarching themes. The cases in all four Parts of this casebook raise questions about the meaning of the constitutional right to vote and the proper constitutional test for election regulations. The decisions force us to question whether the judiciary is competent to create fair, impartial, and manageable standards. Are judges a valid check on entrenchment, or the concern that incumbents will enact laws to favor their own reelection (or to keep their political party in power)? Should courts enter the "political thicket"? Is broad access to the ballot inconsistent with maintaining integrity of the electoral system, and if so, how do we reconcile these competing concerns? Thus, broad themes emerge, but we are still searching for a common overarching theory to harmonize the case law.

What is the best explanation for why there is no successful unified theory of election law? Is it perhaps the fault of the U.S. Supreme Court? After all, how can scholars be expected to make sense of the Court's jurisprudence in this area when the Justices themselves seem so confused and bewildered? Consider Justice Kennedy's ambivalence over the topic of political gerrymandering: If he cannot decide what to do, can scholars find the underlying truth lying behind his tentativeness? Or consider *Crawford*, where the Court was split 3-3-3, and the plurality's test was exceptionally vague and indeterminate: If the fundamental principle of constitutional law applicable to election cases—so-called *Anderson-Burdick-Crawford* balancing—is entirely "ad hoc" and fact-specific, what measure of predictability or insight could scholars be expected to bring to the field?

But maybe the Justices are not to blame. Maybe the difficulty lies inherently within the field itself. As you review the issues that the Justices have confronted—from partisan gerrymandering, to the regulation of party primaries, to the validity of various versions of voter identification laws—do you not appreciate that answers cannot be plucked easily from the air? Is it really possible for the Court to develop a more precise standard than *Anderson-Burdick-Crawford* balancing, which essentially condemns any electoral rule that imposes burdens that are excessive, or disproportionate, in relation to its justifiable benefits?

Moreover, even if we could come to understand three of the four areas of election law as governed by an overarching, and serviceable, "disproportionality" standard of the kind that *Anderson-Burdick-Crawford* balancing is striving for—these three areas being the Law of Districting, the Law of Nominating Candidates, and the Law of Voting—it is hard to see campaign finance (or the regulation of campaign practices more generally) as being governed by such a general "disproportionality" standard. Whether because it involves threats to Free Speech rights or otherwise, the specific area of campaign finance seems inevitably to remain governed by a different standard than other types of electoral regulation. In this respect, campaign finance seems to be analogous to gravity. Physicists have managed to unify three of the four basic forces of nature—but not gravity, which remains stubbornly immune to their efforts. Likewise, campaign finance presents theoretical problems for election law scholars that are distinct from other areas of election law. These theoretical obstacles, furthermore, seem deeper than simply the question whether the Court was right or wrong in *Citizens United* or any other particular case. Even proponents of robust campaign finance regulation, who oppose the current deregulatory trend in this area, acknowledge that the First Amendment imposes limits on how far legislatures can go: Traditional media enterprises, like the *New York Times*, are entitled to spend freely on their editorializing in favor of candidates. And once this proposition is accepted, it becomes difficult to fold the regulation of campaign finance into a single overarching principle of electoral regulation.

If the intrinsic nature of election law means that it is not susceptible to a single Grand Unified Theory, should that bother us? Can't we just go on living our collective life as a democratic society as we have done for over 200 years, since the Founding of the Republic? Who needs theoretical neatness if we can make our way pragmatically in the world?

But if we remain uneasy about just muddling through in the area of election law (without a clear theoretical compass to guide us), is this unease because we have an intuitive sense that this field—above all others—should be comprehensible? Election law, after all, is about democracy, and our democracy belongs to all of us. We all should be able to understand it. Unlike theoretical physics, it should not remain inherently impenetrable. Therefore, if at its core democracy is intrinsically incomprehensible—we cannot make sense of what, even in principle, it should entail—something seems wrong with that conclusion. In other words, we want to think that at least in theory there should be right answers to the questions of how to do legislative districting, and the nomination of candidates, and the administration of the voting process, and so forth. Even if partisanship (or other frailties of the human spirit) sometimes impedes the implementation of these right answers in practice, we want a yardstick that can show us where and by how much we fall short. But if there are no answers to these questions of how to conduct democracy even in principle, where does that leave us—and our desire to govern ourselves according to the fundamental ideal of popular sovereignty?

At the end of this book, we are going to leave you without a definitive answer to this most basic question. You must decide for yourself, based on your own study of this topic, whether the uncertainties and perplexities that currently exist in the field of election law are caused by the inadequacies of our existing system, including the Justices of the Supreme Court, or instead are intrinsic to the topic. You must decide for yourself, too, what you think the future of election law is capable of being.

But whatever you decide intellectually about the nature of election law and its potential trajectory, remember this: Ultimately, it is your democracy, whatever its limitations or capacities might be. Whether or not you will have a professional career that focuses on election law, you share in the responsibility for democracy as a citizen. Therefore, as the authors of this book, we hope that you will put it to use in making your own contributions to the future of democracy, as you think most appropriate.

Table of Cases

Principal cases appear in italics.

Index